MAZDA
323/626/929/GLC/MX-6/RX-7
1978-89 REPAIR MANUAL

CHILTON'S

CHILTON'S

President, Chilton Enterprises	David S. Loewith
Senior Vice President	Ronald A. Hoxter
Publisher & Editor-In-Chief	Kerry A. Freeman, S.A.E.
Executive Editors	Dean F. Morgantini, S.A.E., W. Calvin Settle, Jr., S.A.E.
Managing Editor	Nick D'Andrea
Special Products Managers	Eric O. Cole, Ken Grabowski, A.S.E., S.A.E.
Senior Editors	Debra Gaffney, Michael L. Grady
	Kevin M. G. Maher, Richard J. Rivele, S.A.E.
	Richard T. Smith, Jim Taylor
	Ron Webb
Project Managers	Martin J. Gunther, Richard Schwartz
Production Manager	Andrea Steiger
Product Systems Manager	Robert Maxey
Director of Manufacturing	Mike D'Imperio
Editor	Richard Schwartz

CHILTON BOOK COMPANY

ONE OF THE **DIVERSIFIED PUBLISHING COMPANIES,**
A PART OF **CAPITAL CITIES/ABC,INC.**

Manufactured in USA
© 1995 Chilton Book Company
Chilton Way, Radnor, PA 19089
ISBN 0-8019-8581-1
Library of Congress Catalog Card No. 94-071952
1234567890 4321098765

Contents

Contents

DRIVE TRAIN **7**

SUSPENSION AND STEERING **8**

BRAKES **9**

BODY **10**

GLOSSARY

MASTER INDEX

SAFETY NOTICE

Proper service and repair procedures are vital to the safe, reliable operation of all motor vehicles, as well as the personal safety of those performing repairs. This manual outlines procedures for servicing and repairing vehicles using safe, effective methods. The procedures contain many NOTES, CAUTIONS, and WARNINGS which should be followed along with standard procedures to eliminate the possibility of personal injury or improper service which could damage the vehicle or compromise its safety.

It is important to note that the repair procedures and techniques, tools and parts for servicing motor vehicles, as well as the skill and experience of the individual performing the work vary widely. It is not possible to anticipate all of the conceivable ways or conditions under which vehicles may be serviced, or to provide cautions as to all of the possible hazards that may result. Standard and accepted safety precautions and equipment should be used when handling toxic or flammable fluids, and safety goggles or other protection should be used during cutting, grinding, chiseling, prying,or any other process that can cause material removal or projectiles.

Some procedures require the use of tools specially designed for a specific purpose. Before substituting another tool or procedure, you must be completely satisfied that neither your personal safety, nor the performance of the vehicle will be endangered.

Although information in this manual is based on industry sources and is complete as possible at the time of publication, the possibility exists that some car manufacturers made later changes which could not be included here. While striving for total accuracy, Chilton Book Company cannot assume responsibility for any errors, changes or omissions that may occur in the compilation of this data.

PART NUMBERS

Part numbers listed in this reference are not recommendation by Chilton for any product by brand name. They are references that can be used with interchange manuals and aftermarket supplier catalogs to locate each brand supplier's discrete part number.

SPECIAL TOOLS

Special tools are recommended by the vehicle manufacturer to perform their specific job. Use has been kept to a minimum, but where absolutely necessary, they are referred to in the text by the part number of the tool manufacturer. These tools can be purchased, under the appropriate part number, from your local dealer or regional distributor, or an equivalent tool can be purchased locally from a tool supplier or parts outlet. Before substituting any tool for the one recommended, read the SAFETY NOTICE at the top of this page.

ACKNOWLEDGMENTS

The Chilton Book Company expresses appreciation to Mazda Corp. for their generous assistance.

1

GENERAL INFORMATION & MAINTENANCE

HOW TO USE THIS BOOK

Chilton's Total Car Care manual is intended to help you learn more about the inner workings of your Mazda and save you money on its upkeep and operation. It is designed to aid owners of both piston engine and rotary engine powered Mazdas to perform service operations on their vehicles.

The first two sections will be the most used, since they contain maintenance and tune-up information and procedures. Studies have shown that a properly tuned and maintained car can get at least 10% better gas mileage than an out-of-tune car. The other sections deal with the more complex systems of your vehicle. Operating systems from engine through brakes are covered to the extent that the average do-it-yourselfer becomes mechanically involved. This manual will not explain such items as rebuilding an automatic transmission or transaxle for the simple reason the the expertise required and the investment in special tools make this task impractical. It will give you detailed instructions to help you change your own brake pads and shoes, replace points (where applicable) and plugs, and do many more jobs that will save you money, give you personal satisfaction, and help you avoid expensive problems.

A secondary purpose of this book is as a reference for owners who want to better understand their car and/or what their mechanic has to say. In this case, no tools at all are required.

Before starting disassembly, read through the entire procedure. This will give you the overall view of what tools and supplies will be required. There is nothing more frustrating than having to walk to the bus stop on Monday morning because you were short one bolt on Sunday afternoon. There is nothing more embarrassing than to have to call the local gas station to tow your car from the driveway because you can't get something to go back together the way it came apart. So read ahead and plan ahead. Take or draw a picture of the component if you have to. Each operation should be approached logically and all procedures thoroughly understood before attempting any work.

All sections contain adjustments, maintenance, removal and installation procedures, and repair or overhaul procedures. When repair is not considered practical, we tell you how to remove the part and then how to install the new or rebuilt replacement. In this way, you at least save the labor costs. Backyard repair of such components as the alternator is just not practical.

Two basic mechanic's rules should be mentioned here. First, whenever the LEFT side of the car or engine is referred to, it is meant to specify the DRIVER'S side of the car. Conversely, the RIGHT side of the car means the PASSENGER'S side. Secondly, most screws and bolts are removed by turning COUNTERCLOCKWISE, and installed by turning CLOCKWISE.

Safety is always the most important rule. Constantly be aware of the dangers involved in working on an automobile and take the proper precautions. (See "SERVICING YOUR VEHICLE SAFELY" in this section and the SAFETY NOTICE on the acknowledgment page.)

Pay attention to the instructions provided. There are 3 common mistakes in mechanical work:

1. Incorrect order of assembly, disassembly or adjustment. When taking something apart or putting it together, doing things in the wrong order usually just costs you extra time; however, it CAN break something. Read the entire procedure before beginning disassembly. Do everything in the order in which the instructions say you should do it, even if you can't immediately see a reason for it. When you're taking apart something that is very intricate (for example, a carburetor), you might want to draw a picture of how it looks when assembled at one point in order to make sure you get everything back in its proper position. (We will supply exploded views whenever possible.) When making adjustments, especially tune-up adjustments, do them in order; often, one adjustment affects another, and you cannot expect even satisfactory results unless each adjustment is made only when it cannot be changed by any other.

2. Overtorquing (or undertorquing). While it is more common for overtorquing to cause damage, undertorquing can cause a fastener to vibrate loose, resulting in serious damage. Especially when dealing with aluminum parts, pay attention to torque specifications and utilize a torque wrench in assembly. If a torque figure is not available, remember that if you are using the right tool to do the job, you will probably not have to strain yourself to get a fastener tight enough. The pitch of most threads is so slight that the tension you put on the wrench will be multiplied many, many times in actual force on what you are tightening. A good example of how critical torque is can be seen in the case of spark plug installation, especially where you are putting the plug into an aluminum cylinder head. Too little torque can fail to crush the gasket, causing leakage of combustion gases and consequent overheating of the plug and engine parts. Too much torque can damage the threads, or distort the plug, which changes the spark gap.

➡️**There are many commercial products available for ensuring that fasteners won't come loose, even if they are not torqued just right (a common brand is Loctite®). If you are concerned about getting something together tight enough to hold, but loose enough to avoid mechanical damage during assembly, one of these products might offer substantial insurance. Read the label on the package and make sure the product is compatible with the materials, fluids, etc. involved before choosing one.**

3. Crossthreading. This occurs when a part such as a bolt is screwed into a nut or casting at the wrong angle and forced. Cross threading is more likely to occur if access is difficult. It helps to clean and lubricate fasteners and to start threading with the part to be installed going straight in. Then, start the bolt, spark plug, etc. with your fingers. If you encounter resistance, unscrew the part and start over again at a different angle until it can be inserted and turned several times without much effort. Keep in mind that many parts, especially spark plugs, use tapered threads so that gentle turning will automatically bring the part you're threading to the proper angle, if you don't force it or resist a change in angle. Don't put a wrench on the part until it's been tightened a couple of turns by hand. If you suddenly encounter resistance, and the part has not seated fully, don't force it. Pull it back out and make sure it's clean and threading properly. Crossthreading a spark plug can transform a simple maintenance task into a major expense.

Always take your time and be patient; once you have some experience, working on your car will become an enjoyable hobby.

TOOLS AND EQUIPMENT

▶ **See Figures 1, 2, 3, 4, 5, 6, 7, 8, 9, 10, 11, 12, 13 and 14**

Naturally, without the proper tools and equipment it is impossible to properly service your vehicle. It would be impossible to catalog each tool that you would need to perform each or any operation in this book. It would also be unwise for the amateur to rush out and buy an expensive set of tools on the theory that he may need one or more of them at some time.

The best approach is to proceed slowly, gathering together a good quality set of those tools that are used most frequently. Don't be misled by the low cost of bargain tools. It is far better to spend a little more for better quality. Forged wrenches, 6 or 12-point sockets and fine tooth ratchets are by far preferable to their less expensive counterparts. As any good mechanic can tell you, there are few worse experiences than trying to work on a car or truck with bad tools. Your monetary savings will be far outweighed by frustration and mangled knuckles.

You will find that virtually every nut and bolt on your Mazda is metric. Therefore, despite a few close size similarities, standard inch-size tools will not fit and must not be used. You will need a set of metric wrenches as your most basic tool kit, ranging from about 6mm to 17mm in size. High quality forged wrenches are available in three styles: open end, box end, and combination open/box end. The combination tools are generally most desirable as a starter set; the wrenches shown in the photograph are of the combination type.

The other set of tools inevitably required is a ratchet handle and socket set. This set should have the same size range as your wrench set. The ratchet, extension, and flex drives for the sockets are available in many sizes; it is advisable to choose a ⅜ in. drive set initially. One break in the inch/metric sizing dilemma is that metric-sized sockets sold in the U.S. have inch-sized drives (¼, ⅜, ½, etc.). Thus, if you already have an inch-size socket set, you need only buy new metric sockets in the sizes needed. Sockets are available in 6 and 12-point versions; 6-point types are stronger and are a good choice for a first set. The choice of a drive handle for the sockets should be made with some care. If this is your first set, take the plunge and invest in a flex-head ratchet; it will get into many places otherwise accessible only through a long chain of universal joints, extensions, and adapters. An alternative is a flex handle, which lacks the ratcheting feature, but has a head which pivots 180 degrees. In addition to the range of sockets mentioned, a rubber-lined spark plug socket should be purchased. As a final note, you will probably find a torque wrench necessary for all but the most basic work. Beam type models are perfectly adequate; although click (breakaway) type models are more precise, they require periodic calibration.

Begin accumulating those tools that are used most frequently: those associated with routine maintenance and tune-up.

In addition to the normal assortment of screwdrivers and pliers, you should have the following tools for routine maintenance:

- Metric or SAE/Metric wrenches and sockets, and combination open end/box end wrenches in sizes from 3mm to 19mm. If possible, buy various length socket drive extensions.
- Jack and jackstands for support
- Oil filter wrench
- Oil filler funnel for pouring fluids
- Grease gun for chassis lubrication
- Hydrometer for checking the battery
- A container for draining oil
- Many rags for wiping up the inevitable mess

In addition to the above items there are several others that are not absolutely necessary, but handy to have around. These include an oil absorber, a transmission funnel and the usual supply of lubricants, antifreeze and fluids, although these can be purchased as needed. This is a basic list for routine maintenance, but only your personal needs and desires can accurately determine your list of tools.

The second list of tools is for tune-ups. While the tools involved here are slightly more sophisticated, they need not be outrageously expensive. There are several inexpensive tach/dwell meters on the market that are every bit as good for the average mechanic as an expensive professional model. A tachometer which can be used on 4, 6 or 8-cylinder engines may be useful if you intend to work on other vehicles; all of the vehicles covered by this manual, however, require either a 4 or 6-cylinder setting. Just be sure that the tachometer scale goes to at least 1,200-1,500 rpm.

➡**Although it contains no cylinders, rotary engines require a tachometer suitable for 4-cylinder engines.**

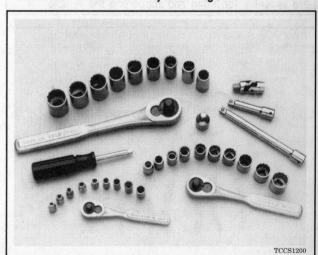

TCCS1200

Fig. 1 All but the most basic procedure will require an assortment of ratchets and sockets

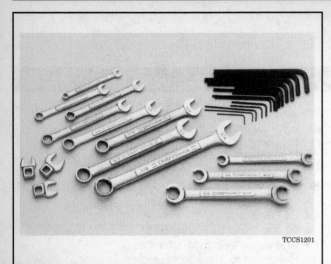

TCCS1201

Fig. 2 In addition to ratchets, a good set of wrenches and hex keys will be necessary

TCCS1202

Fig. 3 A hydraulic floor jack and a set of jackstands are essential for lifting and supporting the vehicle

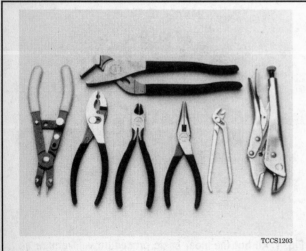

TCCS1203

Fig. 4 An assortment of pliers will be handy, especially for old rusted parts and stripped bolt heads

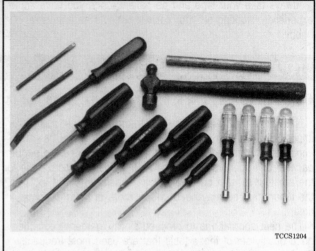

TCCS1204

Fig. 5 Various screwdrivers, a hammer, chisels and prybars are handy to keep in your toolbox

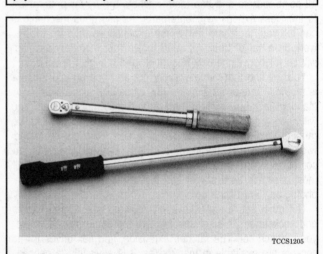

TCCS1205

Fig. 6 Many repairs will require the use of a torque wrench to ensure that components are properly fastened

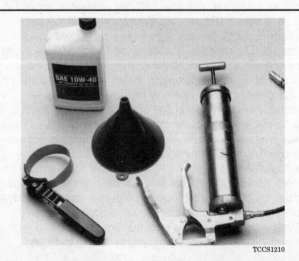

TCCS1210

Fig. 7 A few inexpensive lubrication tools will make regular service easier

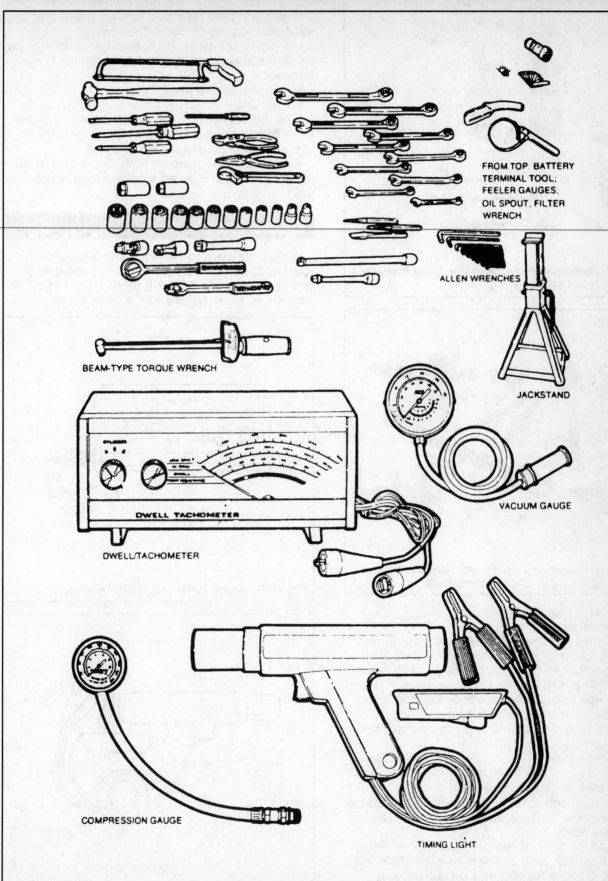

FROM TOP: BATTERY
TERMINAL TOOL;
FEELER GAUGES;
OIL SPOUT; FILTER
WRENCH

ALLEN WRENCHES

BEAM-TYPE TORQUE WRENCH

JACKSTAND

DWELL TACHOMETER

DWELL/TACHOMETER

VACUUM GAUGE

COMPRESSION GAUGE

TIMING LIGHT

TCCS1004

Fig. 8 A good set of tools need not be outrageously expensive

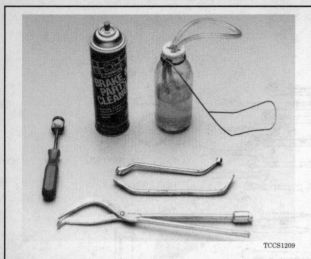

Fig. 9 Although not always necessary, using specialized brake tools will save time

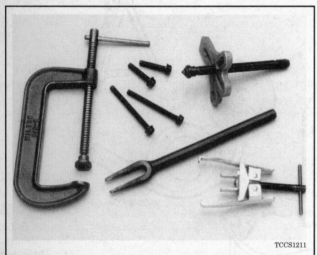

Fig. 10 Various pullers, clamps and separator tools are needed for the repair of many components

A basic list of tune-up equipment could include:
- Tach/dwell meter
- Timing light. The choice of a timing light should be made carefully. A light which works on DC voltage supplied by the car battery is the best choice; it should have a xenon tube for brightness. Since most late model cars have electronic ignition, and since nearly all cars will have it in the future, the light should have an inductive pickup which clamps around the number one spark plug cable (the timing light illustrated has one of these pickups).
- Spark plug socket ($^{13}/_{16}$ in. or $^{5}/_{8}$ in., depending on plug type)
- Wire spark plug gauge/adjusting tools
- Set of feeler blades. You will need both wire-type and flat-type feeler gauges, the former for the spark plugs and the latter for the valves.

Here again, be guided by your own needs. A feeler blade will set the points as easily as a dwell meter, but slightly less accurately. And since you will need a tachometer anyway... well, make your own decision.

In addition to these basic tools, there are several other tools and gauges you may find useful. These include:
- A compression gauge. The screw-in type is slower to use, but eliminates the possibility of a faulty reading due to escaping pressure.
- A manifold vacuum gauge
- A test light
- An induction meter. This is used for determining whether or not there is current in the wire. It is especially handy if a wire is broken somewhere in a wiring harness.
- A simple, hand-held vacuum pump. This is used for finding vacuum leaks or inspecting and testing many emission control systems.

Special Tools

Normally, the use of special factory tools is avoided for repair procedures, since these are not readily available for the do-it-yourself mechanic. When it is possible to perform the job with more commonly available tools, it will be pointed out.

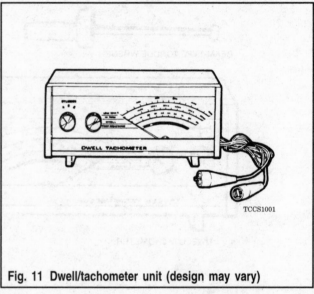

Fig. 11 Dwell/tachometer unit (design may vary)

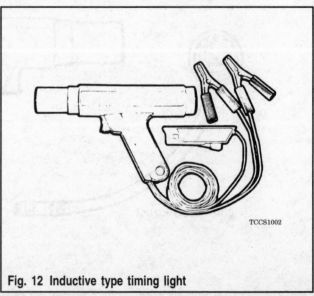

Fig. 12 Inductive type timing light

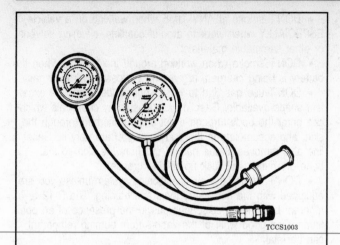

Fig. 13 Compression gauge and a combination vacuum/fuel pressure test gauge

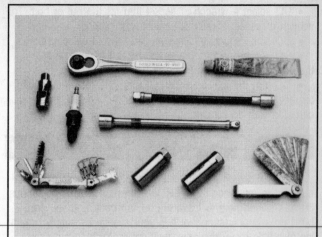

Fig. 14 A variety of tools and gauges is needed for spark plug service

Occasionally, however, a special tool was designed to perform a specific function and should be used. Before substituting another tool, you should be convinced that neither your safety nor the performance of the vehicle will be compromised.

An example of this is using a piston engine compression gauge to measure cylinder compression in a rotary engine. Conventional piston engine compression gauges will not render the degree of accuracy that is required for rotary engines. With these engines, a special digital compression tester is required to measure the pressure of the three combustion chambers.

Some special tools are available commercially from major tool manufacturers. Others can be purchased from your car dealer. In most cases where a tool is designed for a particular job on a particular car model, and therefore made available through the dealer network. You can usually purchase a similar tool at an automotive parts store or elsewhere. You might want to give the factory part number to not only your dealer, but to other sources, and shop competitively for the item you need.

➡**Special tools are occasionally necessary to perform a specific job or are recommended to make a job easier. Their use has been kept to a minimum. When a special tool is indicated, it will be referred to by the manufacturer's part number and, where possible, an illustration of the tool will be provided so that an equivalent tool may be used.**

SERVICING YOUR VEHICLE SAFELY

It is virtually impossible to anticipate all of the hazards involved with automotive maintenance and service, but care and common sense will prevent most accidents.

The rules of safety for mechanics range from "don't smoke at ANY TIME when working on a vehicle" to "do use the proper tool for the job". The trick to avoiding injuries is to develop safe work habits and take every possible precaution.

Do's

• DO keep a fire extinguisher and first aid kit within easy reach.

• DO wear safety glasses or goggles when cutting, drilling, grinding or prying, even if you have 20/20 vision. If you wear glasses for the sake of vision, and the lenses are made of impact resistant plastic, these may serve as safety glasses; however, safety goggles are recommended in any event, because of their contouring design.

• DO shield your eyes whenever you work around the battery. Batteries contain sulfuric acid; in case of contact with the eyes or skin, flush the area with water or a mixture of water and baking soda and get medical attention immediately.

• DO use safety stands for any undercar service. Jacks are for raising vehicles; safety stands are for making sure the vehicle stays raised until you want it to come down. Whenever the vehicle is raised, block the wheels remaining on the ground and set the parking brake.

• DO use adequate ventilation when working with any chemicals. Like carbon monoxide, the asbestos dust resulting from brake lining wear can be poisonous in sufficient quantities.

• DO disconnect the negative battery cable when working on the electrical system. The secondary ignition system can contain EXTREMELY HIGH VOLTAGE. In some systems, it may even exceed 50,000 volts.

• DO follow manufacturer's directions whenever working with potentially hazardous materials. Both brake fluid and antifreeze are poisonous if taken internally.

• DO properly maintain your tools. Loose hammerheads, mushroomed punches and chisels, frayed or poorly grounded electrical cords, excessively worn screwdrivers, spread wrenches (open end), cracked sockets, slipping ratchets, or faulty droplight sockets can cause accidents.

• DO use the proper size and type of tool for the job being done.

• DO pull on a wrench handle rather than push on it, when possible, and adjust your stance to prevent a fall.

• DO be sure that adjustable wrenches are tightly adjusted on the nut or bolt and pulled so that the face is on the side of the fixed jaw.

• DO select a wrench or socket that fits the nut or bolt. The wrench or socket should sit straight, not cocked.

• DO strike squarely with a hammer; avoid glancing blows.

• DO set the parking brake and block the drive wheels if the work requires that the engine be running.

• DO turn the ignition switch **OFF** on late model cars with an electric cooling fan. With the ignition turned **ON**, the fan can start with no warning!

Don'ts

• DON'T run an engine in a garage or anywhere else without proper ventilation — EVER! Carbon monoxide is poisonous; it takes a long time to leave the human body and you can build up a deadly supply of it in your system by simply breathing in a little every day. You may not realize you are slowly poisoning yourself. Always use power vents, windows, fans or open the garage door(s).

• DON'T work around moving parts while wearing a necktie or other loose clothing. Short sleeves are much safer than long, loose sleeves, and hard-toed shoes with neoprene soles protect your toes and give a better grip on slippery surfaces. Jewelry such as watches, fancy belt buckles, beads or body adornment of any kind is not safe when working around a car. Long hair should be hidden under a hat or cap.

• DON'T use pockets for toolboxes. A fall or bump can drive a screwdriver deep into your body. Even a wiping cloth hanging from the back pocket can wrap around a spinning shaft or fan.

• DON'T smoke at ANY TIME when working on a vehicle, ESPECIALLY when working around gasoline, cleaning solvent or other flammable materials.

• DON'T smoke when working around the battery. When the battery is being charged, it gives off explosive hydrogen gas.

• DON'T use gasoline to wash your hands; there are excellent soaps available. Gasoline contains many chemicals which can enter the body through a cut or be absorbed through the skin, and accumulate in the body until you are very ill. Gasoline also removes all the natural oils from the skin so that bone dry hands will suck up oil and grease.

• DON'T service the air conditioning system unless you are equipped with the necessary tools and training. The R-12 refrigerant becomes a poisonous gas in the presence of an open flame. One good whiff of the vapors from burning refrigerant can be fatal.

• DON'T hurry. This means avoid getting yourself into a time trap because you didn't allow enough time to do the job or because you're working outside and the weather is changing. Working at a sensible pace, you're more likely to anticipate safety problems by thinking ahead and by using tools more effectively.

• DON'T lose track of your tools or parts. Wrenches left on fan shrouds and in the area of drive belts become potential missile hazards. Items like these often suddenly find their way to an eye, face, limb or the engine. Scan the engine compartment for any loose tools or any parts that may have been replaced. It's great to be able to fix your car, save money and get satisfaction, but it's not worth the price of personal injury!

SERIAL NUMBER IDENTIFICATION

▶ See Figures 15, 16, 17 and 18

Vehicle

EXCEPT RX-7

The serial number (otherwise known as a Vehicle Identification Number or VIN) is stamped on a plate located on the driver's side windshield pillar, and is visible through the glass.

A plate, bearing the Vehicle Identification Number and other data, is attached to the cowl at the rear of the engine compartment.

RX-7

The Vehicle Identification Number (VIN) is located on a plate attached to the upper left hand corner of the instrument panel, and is visible through the windshield.

The model plate and the chassis number are located on the right and left sides of the underhood firewall, respectively, on the 1979 model. On the 1980-89 RX-7, both the model plate and the chassis number are located on the right side of the underhood firewall.

The motor vehicle safety certification label indicates that the vehicle has passed all safety requirements in force at the time of manufacture and is located on the driver's side door jamb.

85811001

Fig. 15 The vehicle identification number (VIN) is visible through the windshield

Engine

EXCEPT RX-7

On piston engines through 1981, the serial number and engine type code are located on a plate mounted at the right

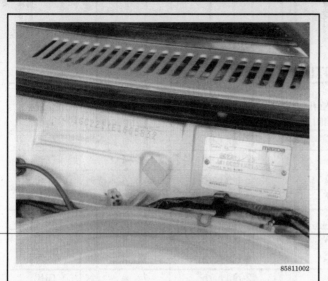

Fig. 16 Underhood serial number identification plates

RX-7

The engine identification number is stamped on the front of the engine between the distributor (or crank angle sensor on later engines) and the alternator.

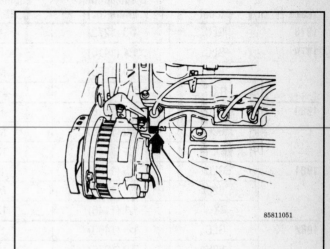

Fig. 17 Location of the engine series code and serial number — 1982-89 piston engines

front, top of the block, except for the GLC type TC engine, which has the plate on the front of the cylinder head. On 1982-89 models, the engine number is located on a machined pad extending from the cylinder block, just below the No. 1 spark plug (between the distributor and the alternator).

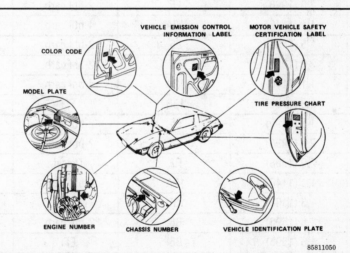

Fig. 18 RX-7 vehicle and component identification/information stickers. (On 1980-89 models, the chassis number is located beside the model number.)

ENGINE IDENTIFICATION

Year	Model	Engine Displacement Liters (cc)	Engine Series (ID/VIN)	Fuel System	No. of Cylinders	Engine Type
1978	GLC	1.3 (1272)	TC	2-bbl carb.	4	OHC
1979	GLC	1.4 (1416)	E5	2-bbl carb.	4	OHC
	626	2.0 (1970)	MA	2-bbl carb.	4	OHC
	RX-7	1.1 (1146)	12A	4-bbl carb.	2 rotors	Rotary
1980	GLC	1.4 (1416)	E5	2-bbl carb.	4	OHC
	626	2.0 (1970)	MA	2-bbl carb.	4	OHC
	RX-7	1.1 (1146)	12A	4-bbl carb.	2 rotors	Rotary
1981	GLC	1.5 (1490)	E5	2-bbl carb.	4	OHC
	626	2.0 (1970)	MA	2-bbl carb.	4	OHC
	RX-7	1.1 (1146)	12A	4-bbl carb.	2 rotors	Rotary
1982	GLC	1.5 (1490)	E5	2-bbl carb.	4	OHC
	626	2.0 (1970)	MA	2-bbl carb.	4	OHC
	RX-7	1.1 (1146)	12A	4-bbl carb.	2 rotors	Rotary
1983	GLC	1.5 (1490)	E5	2-bbl carb.	4	OHC
	626	2.0 (1998)	FE	2-bbl carb.	4	OHC
	RX-7	1.1 (1146)	12A	4-bbl carb.	2 rotors	Rotary
1984	GLC	1.5 (1490)	E5	2-bbl carb.	4	OHC
	626	2.0 (1998)	FE	2-bbl carb.	4	OHC
	RX-7	1.1 (1146)	12A	4-bbl carb.	2 rotors	Rotary
	RX-7	1.3 (1308)	13B	EFI	2 rotors	Rotary
1985	GLC	1.5 (1490)	E5	2-bbl carb.	4	OHC
	626	2.0 (1998)	FE	2-bbl carb.	4	OHC
	626	2.0 (1998)	RF	Diesel	4	OHC
	RX-7	1.1 (1146)	12A	4-bbl carb.	2 rotors	Rotary
	RX-7	1.3 (1308)	13B	EFI	2 rotors	Rotary
1986	323	1.6 (1596)	B6	2-bbl carb.	4	OHC
	323	1.6 (1596)	B6	EFI	4	OHC
	626	2.0 (1998)	FE	EFI	4	OHC
	626	2.0 (1998)	FE	EFI	4	OHC/Turbo
	RX-7	1.3 (1308)	RE 13B	EFI	2 rotors	Rotary
	RX-7	1.3 (1308)	RE 13B	EFI	2 rotors	Rotary/Turbo
1987	323	1.6 (1596)	B6	2-bbl carb.	4	OHC
	323	1.6 (1596)	B6	EFI	4	OHC
	626	2.0 (1998)	FE	EFI	4	OHC
	626	2.0 (1998)	FE	EFI	4	OHC/Turbo
	RX-7	1.3 (1308)	RE 13B	EFI	2 rotors	Rotary
	RX-7	1.3 (1308)	RE 13B	EFI	2 rotors	Rotary/Turbo

858110C1

ENGINE IDENTIFICATION

Year	Model	Engine Displacement Liters (cc)	Engine Series (ID/VIN)	Fuel System	No. of Cylinders	Engine Type
1988	323	1.6 (1596)	B6	EFI	4	OHC
	323	1.6 (1596)	B6	EFI	4	DOHC/Turbo
	626	2.2 (2184)	F2	EFI	4	OHC
	626	2.2 (2184)	F2	EFI	4	OHC/Turbo
	MX-6	2.2 (2184)	F2	EFI	4	OHC
	MX-6	2.2 (2184)	F2	EFI	4	OHC/Turbo
	929	3.0 (2954)	JE	EFI	6	OHC
	RX-7	1.3 (1308)	RE 13B	EFI	2 rotors	Rotary
	RX-7	1.3 (1308)	RE 13B	EFI	2 rotors	Rotary/Turbo
1989	323	1.6 (1596)	B6	EFI	4	OHC
	323	1.6 (1596)	B6	EFI	4	DOHC/Turbo
	626	2.2 (2184)	F2	EFI	4	OHC
	626	2.2 (2184)	F2	EFI	4	OHC/Turbo
	MX-6	2.2 (2184)	F2	EFI	4	OHC
	MX-6	2.2 (2184)	F2	EFI	4	OHC/Turbo
	929	3.0 (2954)	JE	EFI	6	OHC
	RX-7	1.3 (1308)	RE 13B	EFI	2 rotors	Rotary
	RX-7	1.3 (1308)	RE 13B	EFI	2 rotors	Rotary/Turbo

858110C3

Transmission

The transmission identification label can be found on the side of the transmission housing next to the shift mechanism.

Transaxle

The transaxle identification label can be found either on the top of the transaxle or on the right side.

ROUTINE MAINTENANCE

Air Cleaner

The air cleaner uses a disposable paper element on carbureted, diesel and fuel injected engines. The air filter should be replaced at least every two years or 24,000-30,000 miles (38,647-48,309 km). If the car is driven in a dry and dusty climate, clean or replace the air filter twice as often. Inspect the air cleaner element for accumulations of dirt and oil and wipe the air cleaner housing with a clean, lint-free rag. Replace the element as necessary.

If the engine is equipped with a carburetor, the air filter may be cleaned by blowing low pressure air through the filter, outward from the center.

➡️On fuel injected engines, do not attempt to clean the air filter with low pressure air.

REMOVAL & INSTALLATION

Filter Element
▶ See Figures 19, 20, 21, 22, 23 and 24

Replacing the air cleaner element is a simple, routine maintenance operation. You should be careful, however, to keep dust and dirt out of the air cleaner housing, as they accelerate engine wear. If the outside of the air cleaner housing is dusty, wipe it with a clean, lint-free rag before beginning work.

On carburetor equipped engines, you typically have to remove only the top cover of the air cleaner. Remove the wingnut at the center of the housing and unfasten the three clips situated around the sides. Then, pull the top cover off and remove the air cleaner element. When installing the new element, make sure it seats squarely around the bulge in the center of the lower air cleaner housing. Install the housing top, turning it until the wingnut mounting stud lines up with the hole in the top (it's usually off center). Note that the top cover should seat tightly all around. Install the wingnut and fasten the clips.

On fuel injected models, loosen the clamp on the air intake hose and pull the hose off the housing. Then, disconnect the airflow sensor electrical connector. Finally, unbolt and remove the housing. Note the direction in which the element is positioned and install the new element in the same way (it may be marked **TOP**). Install the top of the housing in reverse order.

Air Cleaner Housing
▶ See Figures 25, 26, 27, 28, 29 and 30

In order to access the carburetor/throttle body or other component(s) beneath the air cleaner assembly, it may be necessary to remove the entire air cleaner assembly. Disconnect all hoses and vacuum lines leading to the air cleaner assembly (it may be helpful to tag these lines for easier installation), and remove the necessary fasteners. Installation is the reverse of removal.

Fig. 20 Unlatch the clips around the perimeter of the air cleaner assembly

Fig. 21 Remove the cover to expose the air cleaner element

Fig. 19 On vehicles equipped with a carbureted engine, remove the nut on top of the air cleaner housing

Fig. 22 Lift out the used air cleaner element

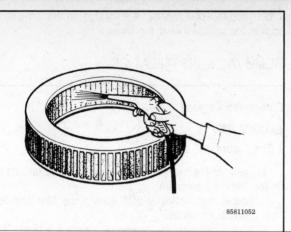

Fig. 23 The air cleaner element of carburetor equipped vehicles may be cleaned with compressed air

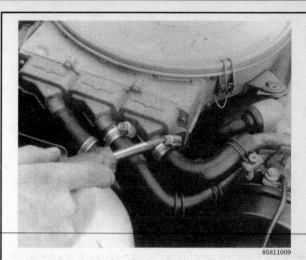

Fig. 26 Disconnect the hoses at the reed valve assembly

Fig. 24 A disposable breather element may also be found inside the air cleaner assembly

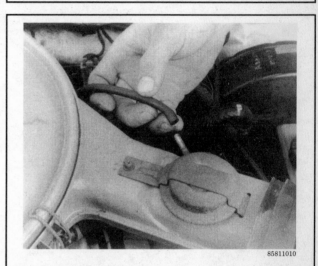

Fig. 27 Disconnect the vacuum line at the air cleaner's vacuum diaphragm

Fig. 25 Disconnect the hose at the rocker arm cover

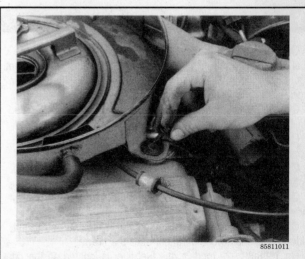

Fig. 28 Remove the exterior bolts securing the air cleaner assembly

Fig. 29 Remove any fasteners securing the assembly to the carburetor air horn, but be VERY CAREFUL not to drop them into the carburetor

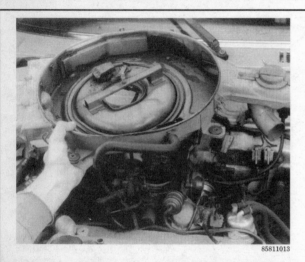

Fig. 30 After disconnecting/removing all hoses and fasteners, lift the air cleaner assembly from the engine

Fuel Filter

On GLC sedans, hatchbacks and early model wagons, the fuel filter is located on the left side of the engine compartment.

On later model GLC wagons, it is located under the floor in front of the fuel tank.

On 1986-87 carbureted 323 models, the fuel filter is located on the left side of the frame.

On 1986-89 fuel injected 323 models, it is mounted to the upper center of the firewall.

On 1979-82 626 models, the fuel filter is located under the floor in front of the fuel tank.

On 1983-85 626 models, the fuel filter is located on the left side of the engine compartment.

On 1986-89 626 and MX-6 models, it is located on the left side of the engine compartment near the firewall.

On 1988-89 929 models, the fuel filter is located on the right fender well, near the fuel pulsation damper.

On 1979-85 RX-7 models, the fuel filter is located beneath the car, just in front of the fuel tank.

On 1986-89 RX-7 models, it is located on the left side of the engine compartment near the firewall.

REMOVAL & INSTALLATION

Carbureted Engines

EXCEPT RX-7

▶ See Figures 31 and 32

1. Remove the trim panel, if so equipped, by unfastening its two securing screws.
2. Loosen the clamps at both ends of the filter and detach both hoses from the filter.
3. Note which way the directional arrows are facing, then unfasten the filter from its mounting bracket.
   To install:
4. Install the new filter in its mounting bracket. Make sure that the arrows are properly positioned.

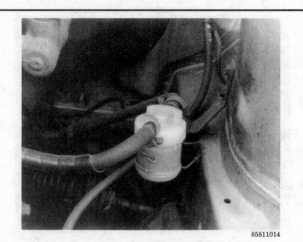

Fig. 31 A disposable, cartridge type fuel filter is commonly mounted in the fuel line between the fuel tank and the fuel pump

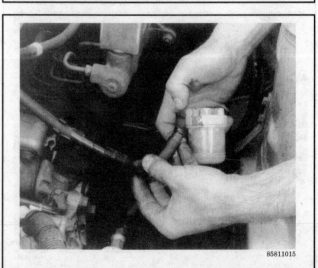

Fig. 32 Inlet and outlet hoses are fastened to the fuel filter's connectors

5. Connect the inlet and outlet hoses to the filter and secure with the hose clamps.

➡If the fuel lines are connected to the filter with spring tension clamps, it is advisable to replace them with new clamps when the filter is changed.

6. Start the engine and check the filter connections for leaks by running the tip of your finger around the circumference of each hose.

7. Install the trim panel, if so equipped.

RX-7

▶ **See Figure 33**

1. Raise the rear of the car and safely support it on jackstands. Locate the filter; use the illustration as a guide to its shape and location.

2. Loosen the clamps at both ends of the filter and place a collection pan beneath it to catch any of the fuel that is in the lines.

3. Disconnect the fuel filter lines and remove the filter from its retainer.

To install:

4. Install the new filter, paying close attention to the direction of the filter in relation to the direction of fuel flow. See the illustration for correct positioning.

5. Connect the inlet and outlet hoses to the filter and secure with the hose clamps.

➡If the fuel lines are connected to the filter with spring tension clamps, it is advisable to replace them with new clamps when the filter is changed.

6. Start the engine and check the fuel filter connections for leaks.

Fuel Injected Engines

✳✳CAUTION

On fuel injected engines, there is considerable residual pressure inside the fuel lines even when the engine is not running. To avoid the possibility of fire or personal injury, fuel pressure must first be relieved from the system as described in this section.

EXCEPT RX-7

▶ **See Figure 34**

1. Relieve the pressure from the fuel system, as described later in this section.

2. Disconnect the negative battery cable.

3. Slide the fuel line clamps back off the connections on the filter. Then, slowly pull one connection off just until fuel begins to seep out. Place a small plastic container or stuff a couple of rags under the filter to absorb any excess fuel.

4. Pull both fuel hoses off the connectors or loosen the union bolts on the "banjo" fittings. Remove the filter from the clamp. On some models, it will be necessary to unbolt the fuel filter from the mounting bracket.

➡If the fuel filter is equipped with "banjo" type fittings, discard the copper crush gaskets and replace them with new ones.

To install:

5. Place the new filter in the clamp or attach it to the bracket, if so equipped.

6. On "banjo" type fittings, install new copper washers and torque the union bolts to 25 ft. lbs. (34 Nm).

7. Attach the hoses to the filter connectors. Make sure the hoses are pushed all the way over the raised portion of the connectors, then secure with hose clamps.

➡If the fuel lines are connected to the filter with spring tension clamps, it is advisable to replace them with new clamps when the filter is changed.

8. Connect the negative battery cable.

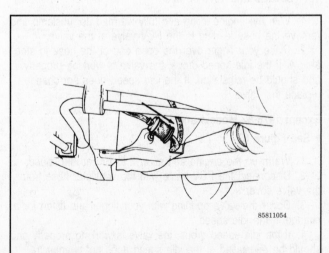

Fig. 33 1979-85 RX-7 fuel filter location. The arrow shows the direction of fuel flow.

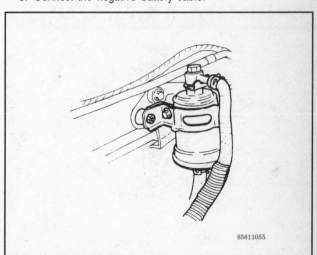

Fig. 34 On some applications, a "banjo" fitting connects the fuel line and fuel filter

9. Start the engine and check the fuel filter connections for leaks.

RX-7

1. Relieve the pressure from the fuel system, as described later in this section.
2. Disconnect the negative battery cable.
3. On 1984-85 models, raise the rear of the vehicle and support it safely. On 1986-89 models, raise the front of the vehicle and support it safely.
4. Loosen the clamps on both hoses and disconnect the hoses from the filter.
5. Loosen the clamp bolts and remove the filter from the bracket.

To install:

6. Install the new filter in the bracket and tighten the clamp bolts.
7. Push the inlet and outlet hoses all the way onto the fittings and secure them with hose clamps.

➡**If the fuel lines are connected to the filter with spring tension clamps, it is advisable to replace them with new clamps when the filter is changed.**

8. Lower the vehicle and connect the negative battery cable.

Diesel Engines
▸ **See Figure 35**

The fuel filter is located between the sedimenter and the injection pump. The filter element is the replaceable cartridge type.

1. Using an oil filter wrench, unscrew the fuel filter from its mounting bracket on the cowl and remove it. Make sure the O-ring comes off with the filter.

To install:

2. Thoroughly coat the O-ring on the new filter with clean fuel. Install the new filter and tighten it by hand only. Make sure that your hands and the outside of the filter are dry and clean.

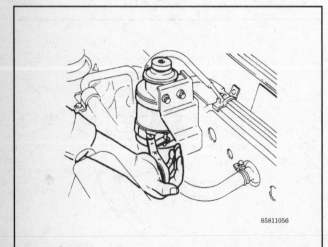

85811056

Fig. 35 Remove the diesel engine fuel filter with an oil filter wrench

3. Bleed the system by repeatedly depressing the bleeder handle on top of the filter mounting bracket until it can no longer be readily depressed.

RELIEVING FUEL SYSTEM PRESSURE

All Fuel Injected Engines

Any time the fuel system is opened for maintenance, the fuel system pressure must be relieved first. On fuel injected engines, there is pressure in the fuel lines even when the engine is not running.

1. Start the engine.
2. While the engine is running, disconnect the fuel pump or circuit opening relay connector(s).
3. Allow the engine to run until it stalls.
4. Reconnect the fuel pump or circuit opening relay connector(s).
5. Proceed with the fuel system repair or service. Whenever a connection is loosened, use rags to prevent fuel leakage. If a line or connection is to be left open for an extended period of time, plug or cover it.

PCV Valve

▸ **See Figure 36**

The PCV valve is an emission control device operated by intake manifold vacuum to prevent crankcase blow-by gases from escaping into the atmosphere. When the engine is running at idle, the valve opens slightly to allow a small amount of blow-by gas to be drawn into the intake manifold/dynamic chamber where it mixes with intake air for combustion in the cylinders. As engine speed increases, the valve opens to allow more of the blow-by gases into the chamber.

TESTING

1978-82 GLC and 1979-82 626

1. With the engine idling and fully warmed up, unclamp and remove the hose leading to the PCV valve at the valve.
2. Place your finger over the open end of the hose to stop airflow. If the idle speed drops, the valve is working properly and should be reinstalled. If the idle speed does not change, replace the valve.

Except 1978-82 Models and RX-7
▸ **See Figure 37**

1. Warm up the engine and allow it to run at idle speed.
2. Disconnect the PCV valve with the ventilator hose from the valve cover.
3. Cover the valve opening with your finger and listen for a change in the idle speed.
4. If the idle speed drops, the valve is working properly and should be reinstalled. If the idle speed does not change, replace the valve.

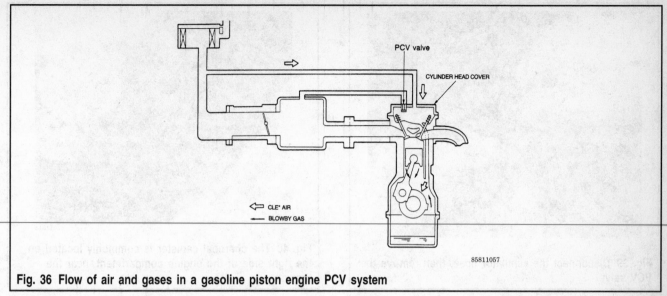

Fig. 36 Flow of air and gases in a gasoline piston engine PCV system

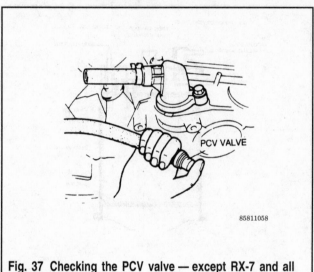

Fig. 37 Checking the PCV valve — except RX-7 and all 1978-82 models

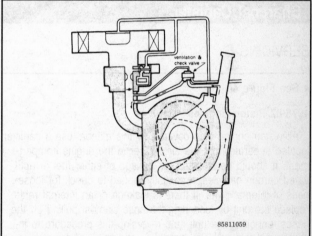

Fig. 38 Location of the ventilation and check valve on 1979-80 RX-7 models. Arrows indicate the flow of blow-by gases while the engine is running.

RX-7

▶ See Figure 38

Since rotary engines are not equipped with a PCV system, there is no inspection or replacement procedure for a PCV valve. Instead, blow-by gases in the crankcase are kept from being released into the atmosphere by a ventilation and check valve on 1979-80 models, or by a check and cut valve on later models. (Testing and replacement information on these valves appears in Section 4.)

REMOVAL & INSTALLATION

Except RX-7

▶ See Figure 39

1. Remove the air cleaner assembly on carburetor equipped models.

2. If so equipped, remove the clip fastening the hose to the outer end of the PCV valve, then pull the hose off the valve.

➡Although 1983 and newer models typically use a PCV valve which mounts in a valve cover grommet, most models prior to 1983 use a threaded PCV valve which screws into the intake manifold. Such PCV valves have a hex head section which permits the use of an ordinary open end wrench, deep well socket, or factory tool 49-1011-120 to remove or install the valve.

3. Rotate and pull the PCV valve from the valve cover grommet or unscrew the valve from the intake manifold, as applicable. Be careful to retain the washer used on some GLCs, if so equipped.

4. Installation is the reverse of removal. Make sure that both ends of the valve are properly seated, and replace any of the ventilator hoses if they are cracked.

Fig. 39 Disconnect the ventilator hose, then remove the PCV valve

Fig. 40 The charcoal canister is commonly located on the right side of the engine compartment, near the firewall

Charcoal Canister

SERVICING

▶ **See Figure 40**

1978-82 Piston Engines

All piston engine cars covered by this manual use a canister located separate from the air cleaner in the engine compartment. It should be checked for leakage of either fuel or activated carbon particles, and lightly tapped to check for looseness of internal parts. If there is leakage or an internal rattle, replace the unit by loosening the hose clamps, pulling off the hoses, unbolting the unit, and reversing this procedure to install a replacement. The inspection should be performed every 25,000 miles (40,258 km)/24 months.

1983-85 GLC

▶ **See Figure 41**

1. Check the canister for signs of leaking charcoal. Tap it lightly with your finger for a rattle, indicating loose charcoal inside. If either type of inspection reveals trouble, replace the unit.

2. Reroute the hoses to port **A** so manifold vacuum is directly applied. Idle the engine. Then, disconnect the hose going to port **B** and blow through it. Air should pass through freely. Otherwise, replace the canister. Reconnect the hoses if the canister is okay.

1983-85 626

▶ **See Figure 42**

1. Remove the air cleaner assembly. Plug the hoses going to the idle compensator, thermosensor, and reed valves. Disconnect the air vent hose coming from the carburetor and plug it.

2. Run the engine until it is warm and leave it idling. Cover the bottom of the canister with your hand in order to feel air

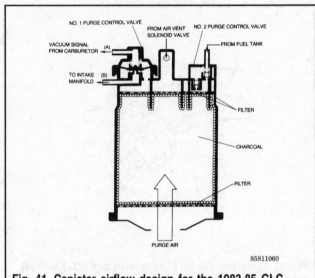

Fig. 41 Canister airflow design for the 1983-85 GLC

being drawn in from underneath. Increase the engine speed slightly. Air should be drawn in. If so, the No. 1 purge valve (and water thermovalve) are working.

3. Should there be no suction at the bottom of the canister, remove the vacuum line going to the No. 1 purge valve and make sure there is vacuum at the end of the hose under all the same conditions. If so, replace the canister; if not, check for and repair a vacuum hose problem of the water thermovalve.

4. Disconnect the vacuum sensing tube at the pipe coming from the engine. There should be slight resistance to both blowing and suction. If not, or if you cannot make air pass in either direction, replace the canister.

1986-89 323, 626, MX-6 and 929

These models do not require checking of the canister or related hardware on a routine basis. If your car exhibits fuel leaks, fuel odor, or idling problems, inspect and test these systems as described in Section 4.

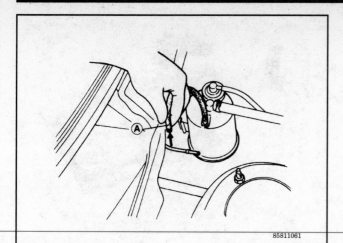

85811061

Fig. 42 Disconnect vacuum sensing tube (A) at pipe coming from the engine on 1983-85 626 models

RX-7

1979-80 VEHICLES
▶ **See Figure 43**

The charcoal canister is located in the top cover of the air cleaner assembly. When the engine is not running, the canister absorbs fuel vapor from the carburetor float bowl and gases trapped in the crankcase. Every time the air filter element is inspected, check the charcoal canister for oil or gasoline saturation and signs that the absorbent carbon material is leaking.

For the following test of the charcoal canister you will need a vacuum gauge.

1. Disconnect, plug and tie off the two hoses as shown in the illustration.

2. Start the engine. You should get a vacuum of 2.36 in. Hg (7.97 kPa) to 0 at 2,500 rpm. If the reading is not within

this limit, the canister is probably blocked and should be replaced.

➡ **The canister cannot be removed from the top cover of the air cleaner. If the canister is defective, replace the entire canister/top cover assembly.**

3. Remove the vacuum gauge, then untie and reconnect the hoses.

1981-89 VEHICLES

1981-89 RX-7 models are equipped with a standard charcoal canister mounted near the carburetor or intake manifold, on the passenger side fender well. Visually inspect the canister for any activated carbon staining or leakage. Tap the canister with your finger; if this produces a rattle, replace the canister.

Battery

GENERAL MAINTENANCE

▶ **See Figures 44, 45, 46, 47 and 48**

Loose, dirty, or corroded battery cable terminals are a major cause of no-start. Every 3 months or so, disconnect the battery cables and clean them, giving them a light coating of petroleum jelly when you are finished. This will help to retard corrosion. After cleaning, make sure that the vinyl or rubber protector on the positive terminal covers the terminal completely.

Check the battery cables for signs of wear or chafing and replace any cable or clamp that looks marginal. Battery terminals can be easily cleaned and inexpensive terminal cleaning tools are an excellent investment that will pay for themselves many times over. They can usually be purchased from any well equipped auto store or parts department. Side terminal batteries require a different tool to clean the threads in the battery case. The accumulated white powder and corrosion can

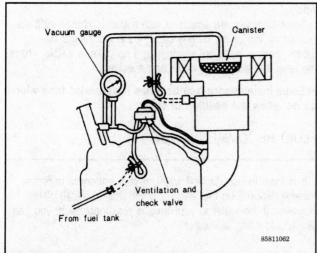

85811062

Fig. 43 Checking the air cleaner-mounted charcoal canister — 1979-80 RX-7

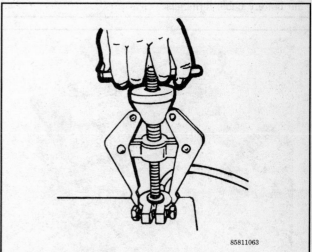

85811063

Fig. 44 Stubborn battery cable terminals may be separated from the battery by using a puller

Fig. 45 Battery maintenance may be accomplished with household items (such as baking soda to neutralize spilled acid), or with special tools such as this post and terminal cleaner

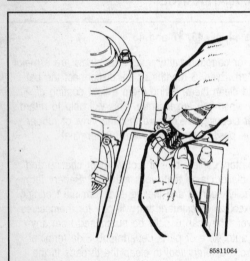

Fig. 46 To insure good conductivity, clean the inside of the battery cable terminals

Fig. 47 The underside of this special battery tool has a wire brush to clean post terminals

Fig. 48 Place the tool over the terminals and twist to clean the post

be cleaned from the top of the battery with an old toothbrush and a solution of baking soda and water.

✳✳CAUTION

Avoid contact with battery acid. In addition to damaging your clothing, it can harm your eyes and skin. Also, the effects of battery acid are not always immediately noticed.

Check the condition of the battery tray and any hold-down hardware. The battery is supposed to be held in a stationary position; loose, rusted or missing hold-down hardware will result in battery movement which could damage the battery, its cables and/or clamps.

Unless you have a sealed, maintenance-free battery, check the electrolyte level and test its specific gravity at each battery cell. Be sure that the vent holes in each cell cap are not blocked by grease or dirt. The vent holes allow hydrogen gas, formed by the chemical reaction in the battery, to escape safely.

Some batteries are equipped with a built-in charge indicator, located on top of the battery case. If the indicator is blue or green, there is sufficient electrolyte; if no color is visible, check the level and add clean water as necessary.

➡**Some maintenance-free batteries have sealed tops which do not allow the addition of water.**

FLUID RECOMMENDATION

It is ideal to use distilled water in your battery to minimize mineral deposits on the lead (or other type of metal) plates. However, if the water in your area is reasonably soft, you can simply add clean tap water.

FLUID LEVEL

▶ **See Figures 49 and 50**

Check the fluid level in the battery at least once a month and more frequently in cold weather. Check the battery first, if the vehicle's ammeter indicates an abnormality.

The electrolyte level should be 0.4-0.8 in. (10-20mm) above the plates in each cell. Add distilled or clean, reasonably soft tap water, if necessary. Do not overfill. If the temperature is below 32°F (0°C), run the engine for five minutes after adding water so the charging action will mix newly added water with the battery acid and prevent freezing.

☀☀CAUTION

Do not smoke around the battery while the caps are removed. Escaping fumes could cause an explosion.

CABLES AND CLAMPS

When battery removal or other circumstances require the cables to be disconnected from the battery, begin with the negative cable. Use the correct size open end wrench to loosen the nut on the cable clamp (top post batteries) or the bolt on the cable end (side terminal batteries). If you encounter corrosion, use a little penetrating oil to avoid rounding off the edges of the fasteners. After loosening the appropriate fastener, lift the cable clamp or cable end from the battery terminal. If you encounter resistance with top post batteries, try gently turning the clamp as you lift it, but be careful not to damage the battery terminal. Clean the battery posts and cable clamps or ends, as necessary.

➡**On top post batteries, the positive cable clamp may be covered by a protective hood, which must be moved aside for terminal access.**

Check the cables at the same time that the terminals are cleaned. If the cable insulation is cracked or broken, or if the ends are frayed, the cable should be replaced with a new cable of the same length and gauge.

Before connecting the cables, loosen the battery hold-down clamp or strap, remove the battery and check the battery tray. Clear it of any debris, and check it for soundness. Rust should be wire brushed away, and the metal given a coat of anti-rust paint. Replace the battery and tighten the hold-down clamp or strap securely. Be careful not to overtighten, however, as you might crack the battery case.

When it is time to connect the cables to the battery, attach the positive cable first and the negative cable last. On top post batteries, do not hammer on the clamps to install. Tighten the clamps securely, but do not distort them. If the battery cable is OK, but its clamp is worn or damaged, you may want to install a replacement clamp. Give the clamps and terminals a thin external coat of grease after installation, to retard corrosion. On top post batteries, cover the positive terminal and cable clamp with the cable's vinyl or rubber protective hood, if so equipped.

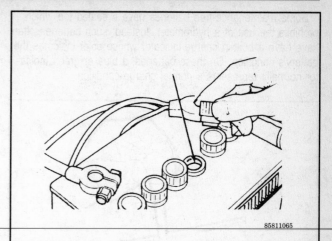

Fig. 49 On non-sealed batteries, remove vent caps to check the fluid level or test the specific gravity

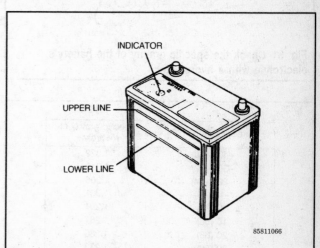

Fig. 50 Electrolyte should be maintained 0.4-0.8 in. (10-20mm) above the plates in each cell, or between the upper and lower lines on the battery case

TESTING

▶ **See Figures 51 and 52**

Specific gravity is a good indication of the battery's state of charge. Check the specific gravity of each cell's electrolyte with a hydrometer. To use a hydrometer, remove a vent cap and insert the tip of the hydrometer into the electrolyte. Squeeze the bulb on the hydrometer so that a sufficient amount of fluid is drawn into the tester. Note the specific gravity of the electrolyte, as indicated by the hydrometer. (One common, inexpensive type of hydrometer uses a series of floating balls, another type uses a float, and a third type uses a pivoting pointer. Follow the instructions for your particular type.) After noting the reading, return the fluid to the cell from which it came, and repeat this procedure for the remaining cells. If all readings do not fall within the specified range for the given temperature, recharge or replace the battery as necessary. Be sure to check all of the individual cells. Often when a battery fails, only one of its cells has an abnormal reading.

Some maintenance-free batteries have a sealed top which prohibits the use of a hydrometer. Instead, such batteries often have have a built-in charge indicator whose color indicates the battery's condition. On these batteries, a blue or green indicator normally represents a normal charge condition.

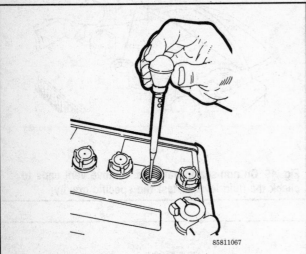

Fig. 51 Check the specific gravity of the battery's electrolyte with a hydrometer

Temperature [°C (°F)]	Specific gravity of electrolyte
−40 (−40)	1.322
−30 (−22)	1.315
−20 (− 4)	1.308
−10 (14)	1.301
0 (32)	1.294
10 (50)	1.287
20 (68)	1.280
30 (86)	1.273
40 (104)	1.266
50 (122)	1.259
60 (140)	1.252
Charged rate ; 100%	

85811068

Fig. 52 Specific gravity readings for a fully charged battery. Note that they vary with ambient temperature.

REPLACEMENT

The cold cranking amps (CCA) of a battery indicates available starting power at a given temperature (generally 32°F/0°C). Although there is a rough correlation between engine size and battery power requirements, the actual needs will depend, in part, on the extent of power accessories, the local climate and one's driving habits. As a general rule of thumb, the CCAs of a replacement battery should match or exceed those of the original battery. However, since electrical wiring develops increased resistance with age, it may be advisable to select a replacement battery with CCAs at least 10 % higher than the original.

The reserve capacity of a battery indicates the number of minutes that power could be supplied in the event of a charging system failure, or a sizable current drain with the engine **OFF**. While there may be no guidelines regarding a minimum reserve capacity, the higher the capacity, the greater the "cushion".

Belts

INSPECTION

All Models

Belt tension is very important, as a belt that is too tight will put too much stress on the bearings of the components it drives, causing them to wear out prematurely. A belt that is too loose will slip, causing (1) the belt to wear out quickly due to friction heat, and (2) inefficient alternator, air pump, cooling fan or air conditioner operation because much of the turning power supplied by the main drive pulley is lost.

The belts should be inspected and/or adjusted at 2,000 miles (3,221 km) and then every 4,000 miles (6,441 km). First, make sure that the belt is properly positioned in the pulley. Check the pulleys for damage. Inspect the belts for cracks and signs of fraying. These usually develop on the inner surface and extend into the backing or outer surface of the belt. Check also for glazing, a completely smooth appearance which indicates slippage. A belt that is in good shape will have a slightly grainy appearance like cloth. Replace belts that show cracks or glazing.

Check belt tension. Apply pressure with your thumb at the mid-point between two pulleys, and the belt should stretch or deflect about 1/4-1/2 in. (6-13mm). If the belt is too tight or too loose, adjust/replace as necessary.

ADJUSTING

Except RX-7
▶ See Figures 53, 54 and 55

To adjust belts, first locate the mounting bolt on the air pump or alternator (each has its own belt and adjusts to permit that belt to be tensioned correctly). This bolt attaches the unit to the engine and has a nut on the end. Put a wrench on either end and loosen the bolt until there is practically no tension on it. Then, loosen the adjusting bolt, which is located on the opposite side of the unit and which passes through a slot. Pull the alternator or air pump away from the engine and tighten the adjusting bolt just enough to hold the unit while you check tension. Repeat the adjustment procedure until the belt deflects the proper amount, then fully tighten the adjusting and mounting bolts. Avoid too much belt tension or overtightening of bolts. A new belt should be tensioned just slightly more (about 0.4 in. or 10mm deflection) and checked after several hundred miles of operation to make sure that tension is still adequate. (Tension is lost very rapidly until a new belt is broken in.)

Late model GLCs, 323s, 626s, MX-6s and 929s may use an adjusting bolt on either the idler pulley (a pulley which is not

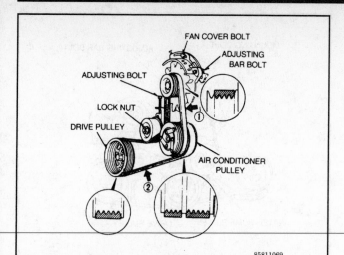

Fig. 53 Some engines utilize an idler pulley with a locknut at its center

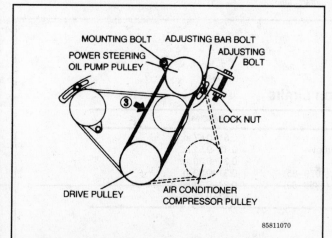

Fig. 54 After loosening the idler adjuster locknut, turn the adjusting bolt clockwise to increase belt tension or counterclockwise to decrease it

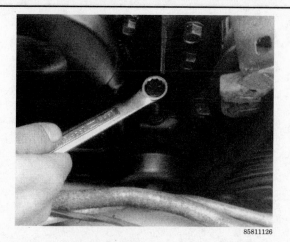

Fig. 55 On some GLC engines equipped with power steering, the pump pulley uses a slotted adjusting bar, adjusting bolt and locknut to adjust belt tension

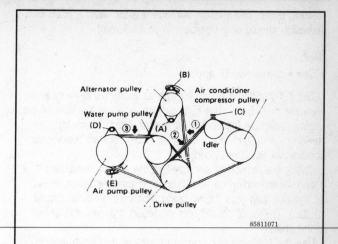

Fig. 56 Checking belt tension on 1979-85 RX-7

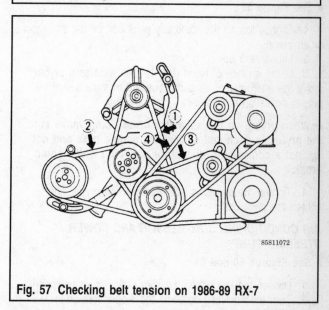

Fig. 57 Checking belt tension on 1986-89 RX-7

directly associated with any of the accessories) or on the power steering pump itself. This bolt makes adjustment much easier because you don't have to hold the accessory under a great deal of tension while tightening the mounting bolts.

On models where the idler pulley has a locknut at its center, simply loosen the locknut, then turn the adjusting bolt clockwise to increase belt tension or counterclockwise to decrease it or remove the belt. Do not forget to retighten the locknut when tension is correct, or vibration may cause it to fall off. Recheck the tension with the locknut tightened and readjust if necessary.

To adjust the power steering pump pulley on the GLC, loosen the slotted adjusting bar bolt, the mounting bolt across from it, and the locknut at the bottom of the adjusting bolt. Turn the adjusting bolt counterclockwise to remove the belt or reduce tension, and clockwise to increase it. When tension is correct, tighten the adjusting bolt locknut, adjusting bar bolt, and pump mounting bolt.

On 626, MX-6 and 929 models with a 4-ridge or 5-ridge ribbed type V-belt driving both the air conditioner and power steering pump, belt tension is much greater. With a used belt, deflection should only be about ¼ in. (6.35mm).

RX-7

▶ See Figures 56, 57 and 58

The RX-7 may be equipped with as many as three or four separate drive belts. The belts are arranged at the front of the engine and drive the cooling fan/water pump, alternator, power steering pump, emission control air pump and air conditioner compressor (if so equipped).

Check the tension of each belt at the arrows numbered 1, 2, 3 and 4 (depending on year) shown in the illustration. Press on the belt with your thumb using moderate pressure (about 22 lbs.). The belts should give or deflect the amounts shown in the chart.

Use the following appropriate procedure and illustration to make drive belt adjustment(s).

ALTERNATOR AND AIR PUMP

▶ See Figure 59

1. Slightly loosen the stationary pivot bolt on the alternator or air pump.
2. Loosen the adjusting bolt.
3. Using a piece of wood (tool handle, etc.) as a prybar, move the alternator or air pump outward or inward until the proper deflection is obtained.

➡ When prying on the alternator or air pump, make sure the prybar is anchored against the engine case and not against a component (distributor cap, etc.) which could break.

4. Tighten the adjusting bolt. Remove the prybar and tighten the pivot bolt.

AIR CONDITIONING COMPRESSOR AND POWER STEERING PUMP

▶ See Figures 60 and 61

1. Loosen the locknut on the idler pulley, if so equipped.
2. Turn the adjusting bolt until the proper tension is reached.

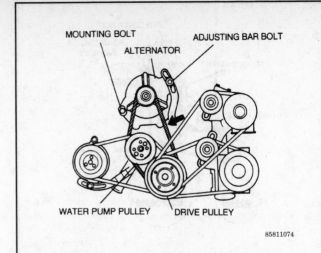

Fig. 59 Adjusting alternator drive belt tension on 1986-89 RX-7

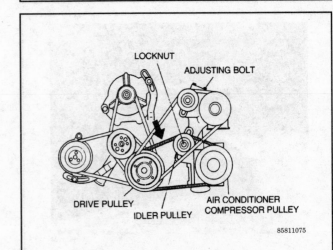

Fig. 60 Adjusting air conditioning compressor drive belt tension on 1986-89 RX-7

Belt Deflection Limits

Arrow Position	Belt	Deflection
1	Alternator	0.51–0.67 in.
2	Air Pump (non-turbo)	0.43–0.51 in.
	(turbo)	0.31–0.39 in.
3	A/C Compressor (1979–85)	0.31–0.39 in.
	(1986–89)	0.24–0.31 in.
4	P/S Pump	0.43–0.51 in.

85811073

Fig. 58 RX-7 belt deflection limits

3. Tighten the locknut and recheck the belt tension.

REMOVAL & INSTALLATION

All Models

1. Loosen the accessory being driven and move it on its pivot point to free the belt.

2. Remove the belt. If an idler pulley is used, it is often only necessary to loosen the idler pulley to provide enough slack to remove the belt.

To install:

3. After the new belt is in place and properly tensioned, start the engine and allow it to run for about five minutes to seat the new belt.

4. Stop the engine and recheck the belt tension. Adjust as necessary.

➡On engines with many driven accessories, other belts may have to be removed to access the one being replaced.

Timing Belts

INSPECTION

Piston Engines

Timing belt replacement on 1983-85 2.0L gasoline and all 1986-89 engines is recommended AT LEAST every 60,000 miles (96,000 km). On diesel engines, replacement of both front and rear timing belts is recommended AT LEAST every 100,000 miles. Because of the inconvenience and possible

damage a snapped belt may cause, it is wise to replace the belt well before the interval has been reached.

➡Please refer to Section 3 of this manual for timing belt removal and installation procedures.

✳✳WARNING

Some of the engines covered by this manual are of the "interference" type, meaning that the valves and pistons could strike each other if either the camshaft or the crankshaft is rotated without the other. Failure to replace the timing belt(s) by the recommended intervals could result in damage to interference engines should the belt snap in service. We recommend that belt replacement as a maintenance item be strictly adhered to for all timing belts.

Hoses

REMOVAL & INSTALLATION

▶ See Figures 62 and 63

Except RX-7

1. Remove the radiator cap.

2. Drain the coolant from the radiator by opening the radiator petcock, if so equipped, or by disconnecting the lower radiator hose. If your car is equipped with a petcock, it might be a good idea to squirt a little penetrating oil on it first.

✳✳CAUTION

When draining coolant, keep in mind that cats and dogs are attracted by ethylene glycol antifreeze, and are quite likely to drink any that is left in an uncovered container or in puddles on the ground. This will prove fatal in sufficient quantity. Always drain the coolant into a sealable container. Coolant should be reused unless it is contaminated or several years old.

3. To replace the bottom hose, drain all the coolant from the radiator. If only the top hose is to be replaced, drain just enough fluid to bring the level down below the level of the top hose.

➡If the fluid is more than two years old, this might be a good time to drain and refill the cooling system.

4. Loosen and slide the hose clamps in toward the center of the hose(s) being removed, then disconnect the hose(s). If a hose is tight, try using a twisting motion to break it free.

To install:

5. If the old clamps are badly rusted or damaged in any way, replace them with new ones.

6. When installing the new hose, slide the clamps over each end of the hose, approximately 2 inches (51mm) from each end. Slide each end of the hose over the bead and onto its fitting as far as it can go.

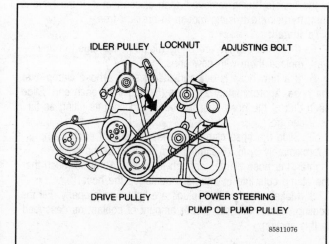

IDLER PULLEY   LOCKNUT   ADJUSTING BOLT

DRIVE PULLEY   POWER STEERING PUMP OIL PUMP PULLEY

85811076

Fig. 61 Adjusting power steering pump drive belt tension on 1986-89 RX-7

7. Position each clamp about ¼ in. (6.35mm) from the end of the hose and tighten.

✳✳CAUTION

Do not overtighten at the radiator connections as it is very easy to crush the metal.

8. Close the radiator petcock, if applicable, and refill with the old coolant or with a new mixture of 50/50 coolant/water. (To determine cooling system capacity, please refer to the chart at the end of this section.) Run the engine for a few minutes and check for leaks. Top up the radiator with coolant if necessary.

➡If those old hoses do not leak, you might want to stick them in a plastic bag and store them in the vehicle. In an emergency, an old hose makes a good short term repair should a hose fail when you are "in the middle of nowhere".

RX-7

The coolant in the RX-7 circulates in a similar manner to that of a conventional piston engine. The water pump sucks cool liquid out from the bottom of the radiator and pushes hot liquid back in at the top of the radiator. Hoses connect the top and bottom of the radiator to the engine. Check the condition of these hoses and the two smaller hoses which pass through the firewall and into the heater assembly often, and especially before long trips.

➡The radiator must be drained somewhat to remove the upper hose, and must be drained completely to remove the lower hose. Allow the engine to cool before draining.

1. On 1979-85 vehicles, raise the front of the vehicle and support it safely.

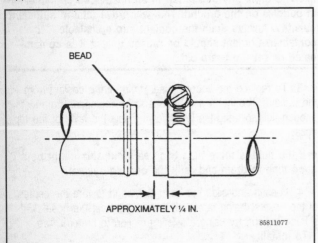

BEAD

APPROXIMATELY ¼ IN.

85811077

Fig. 62 Position the clamp so the end of the clamp is approximately ¼ in. (6.35mm) from the hose edge

85811017

Fig. 63 Drain the radiator and loosen the hose clamp before removing the lower radiator hose

2. Remove the radiator cap and drain the cooling system as described later in this section.

✳✳CAUTION

When draining coolant, keep in mind that cats and dogs are attracted by ethylene glycol antifreeze, and are quite likely to drink any that is left in an uncovered container or in puddles on the ground. This will prove fatal in sufficient quantity. Always drain the coolant into a sealable container. Coolant should be reused unless it is contaminated or several years old. Never remove the radiator cap when the engine is hot. Wrap a thick cloth around the cap and slowly remove it.

3. If the lower hose is being removed, remove the splash panel from under the front of the engine.
4. Loosen and slide the hose clamps in toward the center of the hose(s) being removed, then disconnect it. If the hose is tight, try using a twisting motion to break it free.
To install:
5. If the old clamps are badly rusted or damaged in any way, replace them with new ones.
6. If a new hose is being installed, slide a hose clamp over the hose, approximately 2 inches (51mm) from each end. Slide each end of the hose over the bead and onto its fitting as far as it can go.
7. Slide the hose clamps so that the end of each clamp is approximately ¼ in. (6.35mm) from the end of the hose. Tighten the hose clamps enough to seal, but not so much that the clamp cuts into or internally damages the hose.
8. Make sure the drain plugs are tightened properly. Fill the cooling system with the proper amount of coolant as described in this section.

9. Refit the splash panel and/or lower the car, if applicable. Run the engine for a few minutes and check for leaks. Top up the radiator with coolant if necessary.

➡️**If those old hoses do not leak, you might want to stick them in a plastic bag and store them in the vehicle. In an emergency, an old hose makes a good short term repair should a hose fail when you are "in the middle of nowhere".**

CV-Boots (Driveshaft Boots)

INSPECTION

The CV-boots found on FWD halfshafts perform the extremely important function of keeping your CV-joints (and their lubricant) sealed and protected from corrosion/damage. They should be quickly checked for damage EVERY time you have occasion to crawl underneath your car. In addition, thoroughly examine driveshaft dust boots for cracks, tears, leakage of grease or looseness of band(s) at the proper time or mileage intervals, whichever come first:

- 1981-85 vehicles with front wheel drive: every 7½ months or 7,500 miles (12,077 km)
- All 1986 vehicles: every 15 months or 15,000 miles (24,155 km)
- 1987 vehicles except RX-7: every 30 months or 30,000 miles (48,309 km)
- 1987 RX-7: every 15 months or 15,000 miles (24,155 km)
- All 1988-89 vehicles: every 30 months or 30,000 miles (48,309 km)

❋❋WARNING

Failure to replace a damaged driveshaft boot can result in contamination that causes joint failure.

➡️**For information on CV-boot replacement, please refer to Section 7 of this manual.**

Air Conditioning System

GENERAL INFORMATION

◀ **See Figures 64, 65, 66 and 67**

The purpose of the air conditioning system is to maintain a comfortable environment inside the passenger compartment by controlling air temperature, circulation, humidity and purity. The air conditioning system is designed to cycle a compressor on and off to maintain the desired cooling within the passenger compartment. Passenger compartment comfort is maintained by the temperature lever or switch located on the control head. The system is also designed to prevent the evaporator from freezing.

When an air conditioning mode is selected, electrical current is sent to the compressor clutch coil. The clutch plate and the hub assembly is then drawn rearward, which then engages the pulley. The clutch plate and pulley are then locked together and act as one unit. This, in turn, drives the compressor shaft, which compresses low pressure refrigerant vapor from the evaporator into high pressure. The compressor also circulates refrigerant oil and refrigerant through the air conditioner system. On certain models, the compressor is equipped with a cut-off solenoid which will shut the compressor off momentarily under certain conditions such as wide-open throttle and low idle speed.

The most important aspect of air conditioning service is the maintenance of a pure and adequate charge of refrigerant in the system. A refrigerant leak may occur because of a loose fitting or cracked line, caused by the vibrations commonly present on an engine during operation. A refrigeration system cannot function properly if a significant percentage of the charge is lost.

The problem can be understood by considering what happens to the system as it is operated with a continuous leak. Because the expansion valve regulates the flow of refrigerant to the evaporator, the level of refrigerant there is fairly constant. The receiver/drier stores any excess of refrigerant, so a loss will first appear there as a reduction in the level of liquid. As this level nears the bottom of the vessel, some refrigerant vapor bubbles will begin to appear in the stream of liquid supplied to the expansion valve. This vapor decreases the capacity of the expansion valve very little as the valve opens to compensate for its presence. As the quantity of liquid in the condenser decreases, the operating pressure will drop there and throughout the high side of the system. As the Refrigerant 12 (R-12) continues to be expelled, the pressure available to force the liquid through the expansion valve will continue to decrease and, eventually, the valve's orifice will prove to be too much of a restriction for adequate flow even with the needle fully withdrawn.

At this point, low side pressure will start to drop, and severe reduction in cooling capacity, marked by freeze-up of the evaporator coil, will result. Eventually, the operating pressure of the evaporator will be lower than the pressure of the atmosphere surrounding it, and air will be drawn into the system wherever there are leaks in the low side.

Because all atmospheric air contains at least some moisture, water will enter the system and mix with the R-12 and the oil. Trace amounts of moisture will cause sludging of the oil, and corrosion of the system. Saturation and clogging of the filter-drier, and freezing of the expansion valve orifice will eventually result. As air fills the system to a greater and greater extent, it will interfere more and more with the normal flows of refrigerant and heat.

From the preceding description, it should be obvious that much of a repairman's time will be spent detecting leaks, repairing them, and restoring the purity and quantity of the refrigerant charge.

SAFETY WARNINGS

When working with air conditioning systems and R-12 refrigerant, be EXTREMELY careful to observe the following safety precautions:

1. Avoid contact with a charged refrigeration system, even when working on another part of the air conditioning system or vehicle. If a heavy tool comes into contact with a section of

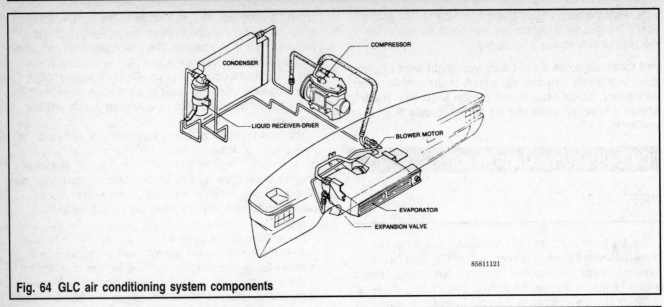

Fig. 64 GLC air conditioning system components

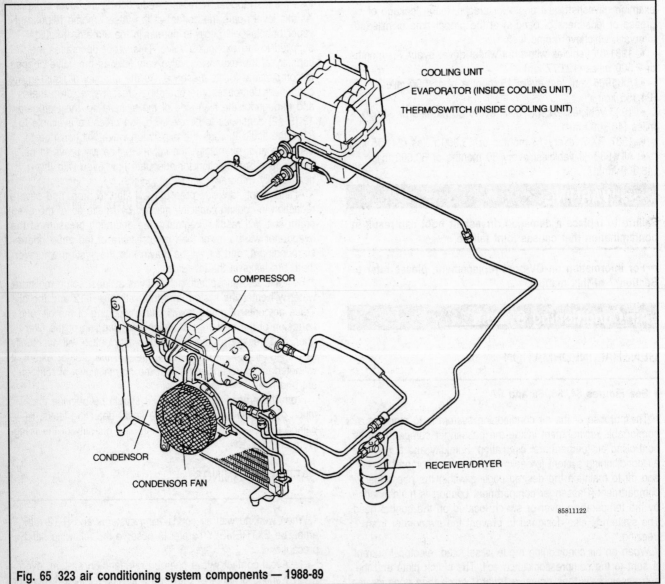

Fig. 65 323 air conditioning system components — 1988-89

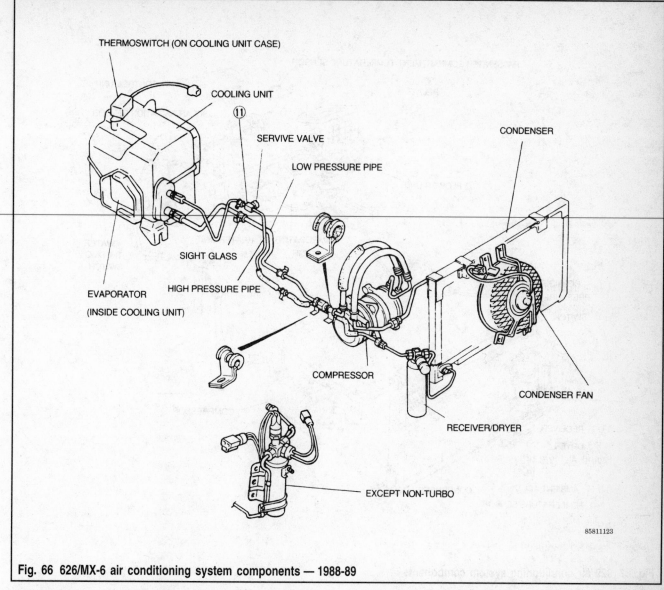

THERMOSWITCH (ON COOLING UNIT CASE)

COOLING UNIT

⑪

SERVIVE VALVE

LOW PRESSURE PIPE

CONDENSER

SIGHT GLASS

EVAPORATOR
(INSIDE COOLING UNIT)

HIGH PRESSURE PIPE

COMPRESSOR

CONDENSER FAN

RECEIVER/DRYER

EXCEPT NON-TURBO

85811123

Fig. 66 626/MX-6 air conditioning system components — 1988-89

copper tubing or a heat exchanger, it can easily cause the relatively soft material to rupture.

2. When it is necessary to apply force to a fitting which contains refrigerant, as when checking that all system couplings are securely tightened, use a wrench on both parts of the fitting involved, if possible. This will avoid putting excessive torsional stress on refrigerant tubing. (It is advisable, when possible, to use tube or line wrenches when tightening these flare nut fittings).

3. Do not attempt to discharge the system by merely loosening a fitting, or removing the service valve caps and cracking these valves. Discharging an A/C system without an approved R-12 recovery/recycling station may be illegal in your area, and precise control is possibly only when using the service gauges. Wear protective gloves when connecting or disconnecting service gauge hoses. Escaping refrigerant will immediately freeze any part of the body that it comes in contact with (frostbite). If frostbite does occur, consult a physician immediately.

4. Discharge the system only in a well ventilated area, as high concentrations of the gas can exclude oxygen and act as

an anesthesia. When leak testing or soldering, this is particularly important, as toxic phosgene gas is formed when R-12 contacts any flame. Phosgene gas is fatal to both humans and animals. Never smoke near R-12 or allow it to discharge into an open flame.

5. Never start a system without first verifying that both service valves (if so equipped) are backseated, and that all fittings throughout the system are snugly connected.

6. Avoid applying heat to any refrigerant line or storage vessel. Charging may be aided by using water heated to less than +125°F (+51°C) to warm the refrigerant container. Never allow a refrigerant storage container to sit out in the sun, or near any other source of heat, such as a radiator.

7. Always wear goggles when working on a system to protect the eyes. If refrigerant contacts the eye, see a physician as soon as possible. Goggles are an inexpensive insurance policy that could save your sight.

8. Always keep refrigerant can fittings capped when not in use. Avoid sudden shock to the can which might occur from dropping it, or from banging a heavy tool against it. NEVER carry a can in the passenger compartment of a car.

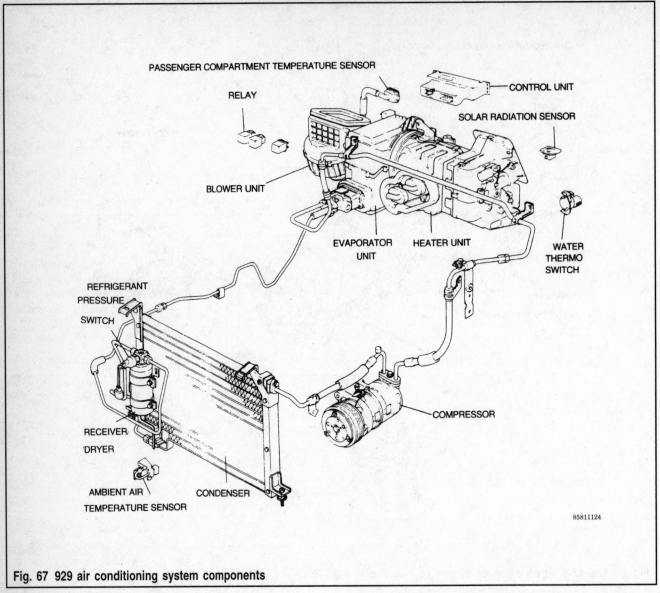

PASSENGER COMPARTMENT TEMPERATURE SENSOR

RELAY

CONTROL UNIT

SOLAR RADIATION SENSOR

BLOWER UNIT

EVAPORATOR UNIT

HEATER UNIT

WATER THERMO SWITCH

REFRIGERANT PRESSURE SWITCH

RECEIVER/DRYER

AMBIENT AIR TEMPERATURE SENSOR

CONDENSER

COMPRESSOR

85811124

Fig. 67 929 air conditioning system components

9. Always completely discharge the system before painting the vehicle (if the paint is to be baked on), or before welding anywhere near the refrigerant lines.

GENERAL SERVICING PROCEDURES

In addition to the preceding safety precautions, the following list of general procedures should be observed while servicing an air conditioning system:

1. Keep all tools as clean and dry as possible.
2. Thoroughly purge the service gauges and hoses of air and moisture before connecting them to the system. Keep them capped when not in use.
3. Plan any operation that requires opening the system beforehand, in order to minimize the length of time it will be exposed to open air. Cap or seal the open ends to minimize the entrance of foreign material.
4. Thoroughly clean any refrigerant fitting before disconnecting it, in order to minimize the entrance of dirt into the system.

5. Use a wrench on both halves of a fitting that is to be disconnected, so as to avoid placing torque on any of the refrigerant lines.
6. When adding oil, pour it through an extremely clean and dry tube or funnel. Keep the oil capped whenever possible. Do not use oil that has not been kept tightly sealed.
7. Use only R-12 refrigerant.

➡**Although you are unlikely to find R-12 for sale to the general public, DO NOT use old containers of impure R-12 which were intended to power air horns or other devices.**

8. Completely evacuate any system that has been opened to replace a component, other than when isolating the compressor, or that has leaked sufficiently to draw in moisture and air. This requires evacuating air and moisture with a good vacuum pump for at least one hour.

➡**If a system has been open for a considerable length of time, it may be advisable to evacuate the system for up to 12 hours (overnight).**

SYSTEM INSPECTION

➡**R-12 refrigerant is a chlorofluorocarbon which, when released into the atmosphere, can contribute to the depletion of the ozone layer in the upper atmosphere. Ozone filters out harmful radiation from the sun.**

The easiest and often the most important check of an air conditioning system is a visual inspection of the system's components. Periodically inspect the air conditioning system for refrigerant leaks, damaged compressor clutch, unsatisfactory compressor drive belt tension/condition, plugged evaporator drain tube, blocked condenser fins, disconnected or broken wires, blown fuses, corroded connections and poor insulation.

A refrigerant leak will usually appear as an oily residue at the leakage point in the system. The oily residue soon picks up dust or dirt particles from the surrounding air and appears greasy. Through time, this will build up and appear to be a heavy dirt-impregnated grease. Most leaks are caused by damaged or missing O-ring seals at the component connections, damaged charging valve cores or missing service gauge port caps.

For a thorough visual and operational inspection:

1. Check the surface of the radiator and condenser for dirt, leaves or other material which might block air flow.

2. Check for kinks in hoses and lines. Check the system for leaks.

3. Make sure the drive belt is under the proper tension. When the compressor is operating, make sure the drive belt is free of noise or slippage.

4. Make sure the blower motor operates at all appropriate positions, then check for air distribution from all outlets with the blower on **HIGH**.

➡**Keep in mind that under conditions of high humidity, air discharged from the A/C vents may not feel as cold as expected, even if the system is working properly. This is because the vaporized moisture in humid air retains heat more effectively than does dry air, making the humid air more difficult to cool.**

5. Make sure the air passage selection lever or switch is operating correctly. Start the engine and warm it to normal operating temperature, then make sure the hot/cold selector is operating correctly.

Compressor

1. Connect the manifold gauge set to the high and low pressure fittings, as described later in this section.

2. Run the engine at fast idle (about 1,500 rpm) and turn the air conditioner onto its maximum setting.

3. Check the compressor for the following:

   a. Normal high and low pressure

   b. Metallic sound from the compressor (replace the compressor)

   c. Oil leaks. Refrigerant leaks show up as oily areas on the various components because the compressor oil is transported around the entire system along with the refrigerant. Look for oily spots on all the hoses and lines, and especially on the hose and tubing connections. If there are oily depos-

its, the system may have a leak, and you should have it checked by a qualified repairman.

4. Repair or replace the compressor as necessary.

5. Check the magnetic clutch for the following:

   a. Oil leaks from the pressure plate and pulley

   b. Noise or leakage from the clutch bearings

6. Turn the air conditioner off and stop the engine.

7. Make sure that the high and low pressure readings on the gauges are the same immediately after the unit is shut off. If they are not the same, this suggests that the gasket or the valve inside the compressor is damaged.

8. Using an ohmmeter, check the resistance of the stator coil between the clutch lead wire and ground. The standard resistance at 68°F (20°C) is 2.7-3.1 ohms. If the resistance is not within specification, replace the magnetic coil.

Condenser

1. Periodically inspect the front of the condenser for bent fins or foreign material (dirt, bugs, leaves, etc.) If any cooling fins are bent, straighten them carefully with needlenose pliers. You can remove any debris with a stiff bristle brush or hose.

2. Check the condenser fittings for leakage, and tighten them as necessary.

➡**Bug screens are regarded as obstructions and should be avoided, if possible.**

Condenser Fan

Connect terminal **B** of the fan motor to ground to make sure that the motor operates.

Receiver/Drier

1. Using a leak detector, inspect the sight glass, fuse plugs and refrigerant fittings for leakage.

2. Check the receiver/drier for clogging as follows:

   a. Run the engine at fast idle with the air conditioner on.

   b. Feel the inlet and outlet piping with your hand. If there is a great difference in temperature, replace the receiver/drier.

Expansion Valve

1. Connect the manifold gauge set to the high and low pressure fittings as described in this section.

2. Run the engine at fast idle (about 1500 rpm) and turn the air conditioner on and set it to MAX COOLING.

3. Check the high and low pressures. The high pressure should be between 210-260 psi (1,448-1,793 kPa). The low pressure should be between 28-43 psi (193-296 kPa).

4. If the low pressure is below the limit, replace the expansion valve. If the low pressure is too high, tighten the sensing bulb well located on the evaporator case. If that does not correct the problem, replace the expansion valve.

Refrigerant Lines

1. Using a leak detector, check all the fittings for leaks. Replace O-rings or the line as necessary.

2. Check all the hose and pipe clamps for looseness and tighten as necessary.

Additional Preventive Maintenance Checks

ANTIFREEZE

In order to prevent heater core freeze-up during A/C operation, it is necessary to maintain permanent type antifreeze protection of +15°F, or lower. A reading of -15°F is ideal since this protection also supplies sufficient corrosion inhibitors for the protection of the engine cooling system.

➡**The same antifreeze should not be used longer than the manufacturer specifies.**

RADIATOR CAP

For efficient operation of an air conditioned car's cooling system, the radiator cap should have a holding pressure which meets manufacturer's specifications. A cap which fails to hold these pressures should be replaced.

CONDENSATION DRAIN TUBE

This single molded drain tube expels the condensation, which accumulates on the bottom of the evaporator housing, into the engine compartment. If this tube is obstructed, the air conditioning performance can be restricted and condensation buildup can spill over onto the vehicle's floor.

PREVENTIVE MAINTENANCE

Many air conditioning problems can be avoided by simply running the air conditioner periodically, regardless of the season. Simply let the system run for a few minutes every week or so, even in the winter. This will help keep internal parts, such as the compressor seals and O-rings, lubricated, as well as prevent hoses from hardening.

REFRIGERANT LEVEL CHECK

The appropriate way to check refrigerant level depends on the design of your vehicle's air conditioning system. Generally, when a system is equipped with a sight glass, the sight glass is used to evaluate charge condition. On vehicles not so equipped, the charge condition can be determined by comparing temperatures of various system lines.

With Sight Glass
▶ **See Figures 68, 69 and 70**

You can safely make a few simple checks to determine if your air conditioning system needs service. The tests work best if the temperature is warm (about 70°F (21.1°C)).

➡**If your vehicle is equipped with an aftermarket air conditioner, the following system check may not apply. You should contact the manufacturer of the unit for instructions on system checks.**

The first order of business when checking the sight glass is to locate it. It will either be in the head of the receiver/drier, or in one of the metal lines leading from the top of the re-

ceiver/drier. Once you've located the sight glass, wipe it clean and proceed as follows:

1. Place the automatic transmission in Park or the manual transmission in Neutral. Set the parking brake.
2. Run the engine at a fast idle (about 1,500 rpm), either with the help of a friend or by temporarily readjusting the idle speed screw.
3. Set the controls for maximum cold with the blower on High.
4. Observe the sight glass:
   a. If you see bubbles, the system is low on refrigerant and must be recharged. Very likely there is a leak at some point.
   b. Oil streaks in the sight glass are an indication of trouble. Most of the time, if you see oil in the sight glass, it will appear as a series of streaks, although occasionally it may be a solid stream of oil. In either case, it means that part of the charge has been lost.
   c. If there are no bubbles, there is either no refrigerant at all or the system is fully charged. Feel the two hoses going

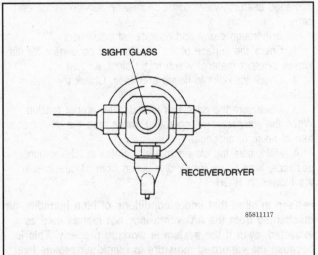

85811117

Fig. 68 The air conditioning sight glass is commonly located on top of the receiver/drier

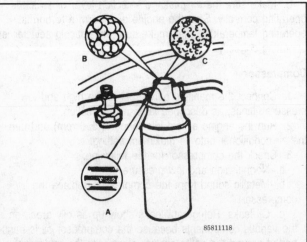

85811118

Fig. 69 Oil streaks (A), constant bubbles (B), or foam (C) in the sight glass indicate an undercharged condition

to the belt-driven compressor. If they are both at the same temperature, the system is empty and must be recharged.

❊❊WARNING

If it is determined that the system has a leak, it should be corrected as soon as possible. Leaks may allow moisture to enter and cause a very expensive rust problem.

5. If one hose (high pressure) is warm and the other (low pressure) is cold, the system may be all right. However, you are probably making these tests because you think there is something wrong, so proceed to the next step.

6. Have an assistant in the car turn the fan control on and off to operate the compressor clutch. Watch the sight glass.

7. If bubbles appear when the clutch is disengaged and disappear when it is engaged, the system is properly charged.

8. If the refrigerant takes more than 45 seconds to bubble when the clutch is disengaged, the system is overcharged. This usually causes poor cooling at low speeds.

Without Sight Glass

On vehicles without a sight glass, the receiver/drier is known as a receiver-drier/accumulator and is connected to the system differently. On a standard system containing a sight glass, the drier is in a high pressure line running from the bottom of the condenser (in front of the radiator) to the expansion valve (a small part shaped somewhat like a mushroom and mounted on or near the evaporator). On vehicles without a sight glass, however, the accumulator is located in a low pressure, large diameter line running from the evaporator to the suction side of the compressor.

Run the air conditioning unit with the vehicle windows open and the fan on high. Feel the temperature of the line going into the evaporator right at the evaporator unit itself, after the orifice tube fitting (where the line should go from warm to cold). Also feel the temperature of the line leaving the evaporator at the top and going into the accumulator. Feel the lower surface of the accumulator.

If the system has enough refrigerant, all these pipes should be at the same temperature. If it is low on refrigerant, the lower accumulator surface and line coming out of the evaporator will be warmer than the line going to the evaporator. If the line to the accumulator is cold but the accumulator surface is much warmer, the system may be just slightly undercharged.

If the line leading out of the accumulator and to the compressor is just as cold as the line going in, the system has excessive refrigerant in it. In case of either too little or too much refrigerant, have a professional refrigeration mechanic add or remove refrigerant as necessary.

MANIFOLD GAUGE SET

▶ See Figure 71

Most of the service work performed in air conditioning requires the use of a set of two gauges, one for the high (head) pressure side of the system, the other for the low (suction) side.

The low side gauge records both pressure and vacuum. Vacuum readings are calibrated from 0 to 30 inches Hg and the pressure graduations read from 0 to no less than 60 psi.

The high side gauge measures pressure from 0 to at least 600 psi.

Both gauges are threaded into a manifold that contains two hand shut-off valves. Proper manipulation of these valves and the use of an approved R-12 recovery/recycling station allow the user to perform the following services:
- Test high and low side pressures
- Remove air, moisture and/or contaminated refrigerant
- Purge the system of refrigerant
- Charge the system with refrigerant

The manifold valves are designed so that they have no direct effect on gauge readings, but serve only to provide for, or cut off, the flow of refrigerant through the manifold. During all testing and hook-up operations, the valves are kept in a closed position to avoid disturbing the refrigeration system. The valves are opened only to discharge, evacuate and charge the system.

➡**The high and low pressure service valves are located on the high and low pressure refrigerant pipes.**

Item	Symptom	Amount of refrigerant	Remedy
1	Bubbles present in sight glass.	Insufficient refrigerant.	Check for leakage with a gas leak tester.
2	No bubbles present in sight glass.	No (or insufficient) refrigerant.	Refer to items 3 and 4.
3	No temperature difference between compressor inlet and outlet.	System is empty or nearly empty.	Evacuate and charge the system. Then check for leakage with a gas leak tester.
4	Temperature between compressor inlet and outlet is noticeably different.	Proper amount of (or too much) refrigerant.	Refer to items 5 and 6.
5	Immediately after the air conditioner is turned off, refrigerant in sight glass stays clear.	Too much refrigerant.	Discharge the excess refrigerant (to the specified amount).
6	When the air conditioner is turned off, refrigerant foams and then stays clear.	Proper amount of refrigerant.	Refrigerant amount is normal.

85811119

Fig. 70 Refrigerant level diagnosis

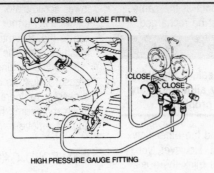

LOW PRESSURE GAUGE FITTING

CLOSE CLOSE CLOSE

HIGH PRESSURE GAUGE FITTING

THE HIGH AND LOW PRESSURE REFRIGERANT SERVICE
FITTINGS ARE LOCATED ON THE HIGH AND LOW PRES-
SURE PIPES

85811120

Fig. 71 Connecting the manifold gauge set to the high and low pressure service fittings

1. Close both valves of the manifold gauge set and connect the charging hoses to the manifold.

2. Wipe the dirt and grease from the service fitting caps, then remove them.

3. Connect the low pressure hose to the low pressure line fitting.

4. Connect the high pressure hose to the high pressure line fitting.

➡**Tighten the hose fittings by hand only.**

5. Suspend the manifold set from the hood latch or other convenient location.

LEAK TESTING

Leak test the air conditioning system whenever the system is suspected of losing its charge, after component replacement or after any refrigerant lines have been disconnected. There are two generally accepted methods of checking the air conditioning system for leaks. One is with the use of a Halide torch and the other is with an electronic leak detector. Both are designed to detect small amounts of halogen when placed near a fitting or connection suspected of leaking. The electronic leak detector provides a greater degree of sensitivity and is the most preferred (and expensive) method. When using this equipment, make sure that you follow the manufacturer's instructions carefully.

➡**Some leak tests can be performed with a soapy water solution, but there must be at least a ½ lb. charge in the system for a leak to be detected.**

To leak test with soapy water, apply a water and soap solution to the air conditioning system fittings in the engine compartment and check for bubbles. The presence of bubbles indicates a leak.

Refrigerant leaks can sometimes appear as oily areas on various components, due to the compressor oil that is transported along with refrigerant, throughout the air conditioning system. During your visual inspection of system components, look for oily spots on all air conditioning hoses and lines,

especially in areas of hose and tube connections and crimpings. If oily deposits are present, you may have a refrigerant leak at that point.

➡**A slight amount of oil in front of the compressor may be normal. Unless the compressor or other system component is replaced, it is generally unnecessary to add refrigerant oil.**

If a leak is found, have the system professionally repaired, or proceed as follows:

1. Check the tightness of the suspect fitting or connection, and if necessary re-tighten it. Recheck for leaks with a leak detector.

2. If leakage persists after re-tightening the fitting, discharge the refrigerant from the system and disconnect the fitting. Visually inspect the fitting seating surfaces for damage and replace as necessary. Even minor damage will require replacement of the fitting. If you disconnect a fitting for any reason, always replace the 0-ring.

3. Partially charge the system and perform another leak test. If no leaks are found, discharge, evacuate and recharge the system.

DISCHARGING THE SYSTEM

➡**R-12 refrigerant is a chlorofluorocarbon which, when released into the atmosphere, can contribute to the depletion of the ozone layer in the upper atmosphere. Ozone filters out harmful radiation from the sun. An approved R-12 recovery/recycling station that meets SAE standards should be used when discharging the system. Follow the operating instructions provided with the equipment exactly to properly discharge the system.**

1. Remove the caps from the high and low pressure charging valves in the high and low pressure lines.

2. Connect an approved R-12 recovery/recycling station to the valves and follow the instructions provided with the unit.

3. Open the low pressure gauge valve slightly and allow the system pressure to bleed off.

4. When the system is just about empty, open the high pressure valve very slowly to avoid losing an excessive amount of refrigerant oil. Do not allow any refrigerant to escape.

EVACUATING THE SYSTEM

➡**This procedure requires the use of a vacuum pump.**

Before charging the air conditioning system, it is necessary to remove any trapped air and moisture with a vacuum pump. Failure to do so may result in poor operation of the system and possible component failure.

When evacuating an R-12 filled air conditioning system, an approved R-12 recovery/recycling station that meets SAE standards should be employed. Follow the operating instructions provided with the equipment exactly to properly discharge the system.

1. Connect the manifold gauge set, as described earlier in this section.
2. Discharge the system, as described earlier in this section.
3. Connect the center service hose to the inlet fitting of the vacuum pump.
4. Turn both gauge set valves to the wide open position.
5. Start the pump and note the low side gauge reading.
6. Operate the pump until the low pressure gauge reads 25-30 in. Hg. Continue running the vacuum pump for 10 minutes more. If you have replaced some component in the system, run the pump for an additional 20-30 minutes.
7. Leak test the system. Close both gauge set valves. Turn off the pump. The needle should remain stationary at the point at which the pump was turned off. If the needle drops to zero rapidly, there is a leak in the system which must be repaired.

CHARGING THE SYSTEM

✳✳CAUTION

Never open the high pressure side with a refrigerant container connected to the system! Opening the high pressure side will overpressurize the canister, causing it to explode! Always wear safety goggles when working on a system to protect the eyes. If refrigerant contacts the eye, it is advisable in all cases to see a physician as soon as possible.

1. Connect an approved R-12 recovery/recycling station to the valves and follow the instructions provided with the unit.
2. Open the R-12 source valve and allow liquid R-12 to flow into the system through the low side fitting.
3. Turn on the A/C system and allow the compressor operation to draw in the remainder of the preset amount of R-12 into the system. The sight glass should be free of bubbles.
4. Turn off the source valve and run the engine for 30 seconds to clear the lines and gauges.
5. Quickly unscrew the adaptors and recap the fittings.

6. Leak check the system and check for proper performance.
7. When the charging process has been completed, close all valves. Run the system for at least five minutes to allow it to normalize.

Windshield Wipers

Intense heat from the sun, as well as snow and ice, road oils and the chemicals used in windshield washer solvents combine to deteriorate rubber wiper refills. The refills should be replaced about twice a year or whenever the blades begin to streak or chatter.

WIPER REFILL REPLACEMENT

▸ **See Figure 72**

Normally, if the wipers are not cleaning the windshield properly, only the refill has to be replaced. The blade and arm usually require replacement only in the event of damage. It is not necessary (except on new Tridon® refills) to remove the arm or the blade to replace the refill (rubber part), though you may have to position the arm higher on the glass. You can do this by turning the ignition switch **ON** and operating the wipers. When the wipers are positioned in an accessible location, turn the ignition switch **OFF**.

There are several types of refills and your vehicle could have any of them, since aftermarket blades and arms may not use exactly the same type refill as the original equipment. Therefore, it is important to first identify the present brand and type.

Most Trico® styles use a release button that is pushed down to allow the refill to slide out of the yoke jaws. The new refill slides in and locks in place. Some Trico® refills are removed by locating where the metal backing strip or the refill is wider. Insert a small screwdriver blade between the frame and metal backing strip. Press down to release the refill from the retaining tab.

The Anco® style is unlocked at one end by squeezing 2 metal tabs, and the refill slides out of the frame jaws. When the new refill is installed, the tabs will click into place, locking the refill.

The polycarbonate type is held in place by a locking lever that is pushed downward and out of the groove in the arm to free the refill. When the new refill is installed, it will lock in place automatically.

The Tridon® refill has a plastic backing strip with a notch about 1 in. (25.4mm) from the end. Hold the blade (frame) on a hard surface so that the frame is tightly bowed. Grip the tip of the backing strip and pull up while twisting counterclockwise. The backing strip will snap out of the retaining tab. Do this for the remaining tabs until the refill is free of the arm. The length of these refills is molded into the end and they should be replaced with identical types.

No matter which type of refill you use, be sure that all of the frame claws engage the refill. Before operating the wipers, be sure that no part of the metal frame is contacting the windshield.

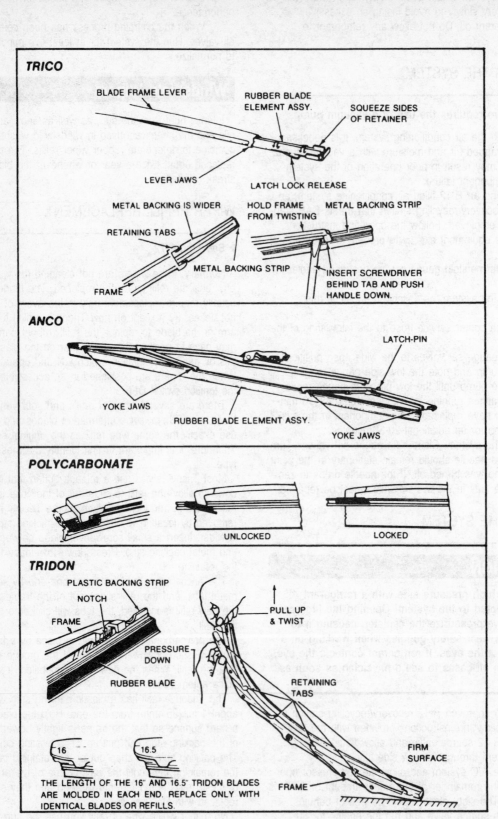

TRICO

BLADE FRAME LEVER

RUBBER BLADE ELEMENT ASSY.

SQUEEZE SIDES OF RETAINER

LEVER JAWS

LATCH LOCK RELEASE

METAL BACKING IS WIDER

HOLD FRAME FROM TWISTING

METAL BACKING STRIP

RETAINING TABS

METAL BACKING STRIP

FRAME

INSERT SCREWDRIVER BEHIND TAB AND PUSH HANDLE DOWN.

ANCO

LATCH-PIN

YOKE JAWS

RUBBER BLADE ELEMENT ASSY.

YOKE JAWS

POLYCARBONATE

UNLOCKED

LOCKED

TRIDON

PLASTIC BACKING STRIP

NOTCH

FRAME

PULL UP & TWIST

PRESSURE DOWN

RUBBER BLADE

RETAINING TABS

16

16.5

FIRM SURFACE

FRAME

THE LENGTH OF THE 16" AND 16.5" TRIDON BLADES ARE MOLDED IN EACH END. REPLACE ONLY WITH IDENTICAL BLADES OR REFILLS.

85811078

Fig. 72 Wiper refill replacement

Tires and Wheels

TIRE ROTATION

▶ **See Figure 73**

Tire wear can be equalized by switching the position of the tires about every 4,000-7,500 miles (6,441-12,077 km). Including a conventional spare in the rotation pattern can give up to 20% more tire life.

✳✳CAUTION

Do not include a Spacesaver® or temporary spare tire in the rotation pattern.

Due to their design, radial tires tend to wear faster in the shoulder area, particularly in the front positions. Radial tires in non-drive locations, may develop an irregular wear pattern that can generate tire noise. It was originally thought the radial tires should not be cross-switched (from one side of the vehicle to the other); because of their wear patterns and because they would last longer if their direction of rotation is not changed. The manufacturer's tire rotation recommendations for most late model vehicles covered by this manual now allows for, and even suggests, cross-switching radial tires to allow for more uniform tire wear.

➡**Some specialty tires may be directional (certain snow or performance tires), meaning they may only be mounted to rotate in one direction. Some special performance tires/wheels will fall into this category and will be marked with directional rotation arrows on the tire sidewalls. NEVER switch the direction of rotation on tires so marked or poor performance/tire damage could occur. This should be taken into consideration in choosing a rotation pattern for directional tires.**

If you have any doubt as to the correct rotation pattern for the tires which are currently mounted on your vehicle, consult the tire manufacturer or one of their facilities for recommendations.

TIRE DESIGN

Tires are of two basic designs: bias ply (or bias-belted) and radial ply. It is important to understand that there are radical differences between the bias and radial designs.

Radials were designed to substantially enhance the tire's ability to keep the tread uniformly in contact with the road. This means that radials have a substantially better ability to maintain their grip on the road in tight cornering situations. Since handling stability depends greatly upon maintaining similar adhesion for both the front and rear of the car, IT IS EXTREMELY DANGEROUS TO MIX RADIALS WITH EITHER BIAS OR BIAS-BELTED TIRES. Make sure all four tires are either radials, bias or bias-belted tires; the consequences of mixing the two basic types can be extremely dangerous!

TREAD DEPTH

▶ **See Figures 74, 75 and 76**

All tires made since 1968, have 8 built-in tread wear indicator bars that show up as ½ in. (12.7mm) wide smooth bands across the tire when ¹⁄₁₆ in. (1.59mm) of tread remains. The appearance of tread wear indicators means that a tire should be replaced. In fact, many states have laws prohibiting the use of tires with less than ¹⁄₁₆ in. (1.59mm) tread.

You can check your own tread depth with an inexpensive gauge or by using a Lincoln head penny. Slip the Lincoln penny into several tread grooves. If you can see the top of Lincoln's head in 2 adjacent grooves, the tire has less than ¹⁄₁₆ in. (1.59mm) tread remaining and should be replaced. You can measure snow tires in the same manner by using the tail side of the Lincoln penny. If you can see the top of the Lincoln Memorial, it's time to replace the snow tires.

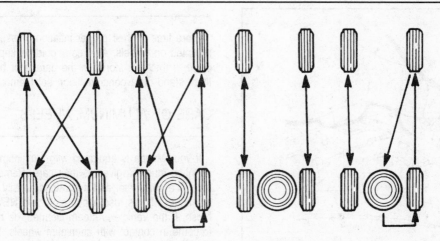

85811079

Fig. 73 Tire rotation patterns

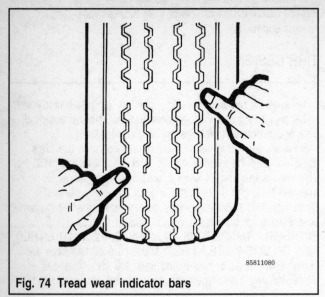

Fig. 74 Tread wear indicator bars

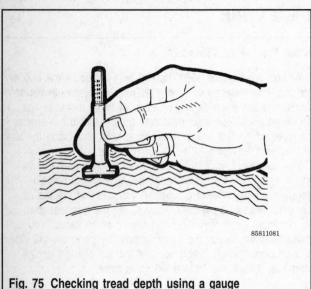

Fig. 75 Checking tread depth using a gauge

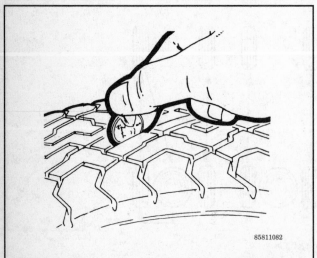

Fig. 76 Checking tread depth using a Lincoln head penny

TIRE INFLATION

Tire inflation is the most ignored item of auto maintenance. Gasoline mileage can drop as much as 0.8 percent for every 1 pound per square inch (psi) of underinflation. Since kicking the tires won't tell you a thing (and will only hurt your foot), it is important to regularly check inflation pressure with a tire pressure gauge.

Service station air hose gauges are often broken or missing, and are notoriously inaccurate. Therefore, a pocket type tire pressure gauge should be a permanent fixture in every glove compartment. Check the tire air pressure (including the spare) at least once a month.

The tire pressures recommended for your car are usually found on the glove box door, the left side door jamb or in the owner's manual. Ideally, inflation pressure should be checked when the tires are cool. When the air becomes heated, it expands and the pressure increases. Every 10°F (5.56°C) rise or drop in temperature means a difference of 1 psi (6.89 kPa), which also explains why the tires appear to lose air on a very cold night. When it is impossible to check the tires cold, allow for pressure buildup due to heat. If the hot pressure exceeds the cold pressure by more than 15 psi (103.42 kPa), reduce your speed, load or both. Otherwise, internal heat is created in the tire. When the heat approaches the temperature at which the tire was cured during manufacture, the tread can separate from the body.

✳✳CAUTION

Never counteract excessive pressure buildup by bleeding off air pressure (letting some air out). This will only further raise the tire operating temperature.

Before starting a long trip with lots of luggage, you can add about 2-4 psi (14-28 kPa) of air to the tires to make them run cooler, but never exceed the maximum inflation pressure on the side of the tire.

TIRE STORAGE

Store tires at their proper inflation pressure if they are mounted on wheels. All tires should be kept in a cool, dry place. If they are stored in the garage or basement, do not let them stand on a concrete floor; set them on strips of wood.

CARE OF ALUMINUM WHEELS

If your Mazda is equipped with aluminum wheels, special attention must be given to their care. Remember that aluminum is a soft metal and it scratches easily. When washing aluminum wheels, use a soft cloth and NEVER use a wire brush. If the vehicle is steam cleaned, do not allow the steam to come in contact with aluminum wheels. If alkaline compounds (such as road salts or salt water) build up on the wheels, wash them as soon as possible to prevent corrosion and damage. Finally, if replacements are required, do not use wheels other than what is recommended by the manufacturer.

FLUIDS AND LUBRICANTS

Fluid Disposal

Used fluids such as engine oil, transmission fluid, coolant (antifreeze) and brake fluid are hazardous wastes and must be disposed of properly. Before draining any fluids, consult with the local authorities; in many areas, waste oil, coolant, etc. is being accepted as part of a recycling program. A number of service stations and auto parts stores are also accepting waste fluids for recycling.

Be sure of the recycling center's policies before draining any fluids, as many will not accept different fluids that have been mixed together, such as engine oil and coolant.

Fuel and Engine Oil Recommendations

▶ **See Figure 77**

The American Petroleum Institute (API) designation indicates the classification of engine oil for use under given operating conditions. While modern lubrication technology has led to updated classifications such as "Service SE", "Service SF" and "Service SG", most 1978-88 vehicles covered by this manual only require oil with a "Service SD" designation. Exceptions include the 1986-88 RX-7 and 1988 323 (DOHC engine only), for which Mazda recommended a fuel efficient SF grade. Mazda also recommended against the use of synthetic oil in 1986-88 RX-7 models. 1989 vehicles covered by this manual require oil with a "Service SF" designation. In any case, it is OK to use oil with a newer classification (such as "Service SG"), that has superceded earlier grades. Oil of these types perform a variety of functions inside the engine in addition to the basic function as a lubricant. Through a balanced system of metallic detergents and polymeric dispersants, the oil prevents formation of high and low temperature deposits, and also keeps sludge and dirt particles in suspension. Acids, particularly sulfuric acid, as well as other by-products of combustion, are neutralized.

The Society of Automotive Engineers (SAE) grade number indicates the viscosity of the engine oil, and thus, its ability to lubricate at a given temperature. The lower the SAE grade number (or viscosity), the lighter the oil; the higher the SAE grade number (or viscosity), the heavier the oil. Since lighter oil has a reduced resistance to flow, it is easier to crank an engine filled with low viscosity oil in cold weather. Warm weather, on the other hand, requires heavier (higher viscosity) oil for adequate protection.

Multi-viscosity oils offer the important advantage of being adaptable to temperature extremes. They allow easy starting at low temperatures, yet give good protection at high speeds and engine temperatures. This is a decided advantage in changeable climates or in long distance touring. Oil viscosities should be chosen from those oils recommended for the lowest anticipated temperatures during the oil change interval.

➡**Both the SAE grade number and the API designation can be found on the label of the oil container.**

Non-detergent or straight mineral oils must never be used. Also, do not use oil that is unlabeled or which has been reprocessed. Oil viscosity should be chosen on the basis of

the range of temperatures you expect during the time the oil will be in the crankcase. You need not change oil because of a short period of unusual temperatures. Temperature ranges and related viscosities for most 1978-85 vehicles are as follows:

- 0 to 85°F (-18° to +29°C): SAE 10W-30
- 0° to 100°F (-18° to +38°C): SAE 10W-40
- 0° to 120°F (-18° to 49°C): SAE 10W-50
- 10° to 100°F (-12° to +38°C): SAE 20W-40
- 10° to 120°F (-12° to 49°C): SAE 20W-50
- Below 25°F (-4°C): SAE 5W-30
- Below 0°F (-18°C): SAE 5W-20

➡**For 1986-89 models, the viscosity limits have been slightly modified. See the accompanying illustration.**

All engines with catalytic converters require the use of unleaded fuel exclusively, as leaded fuel will almost immediately destroy the effectiveness of the catalytic converter. Unleaded fuel minimizes the accumulation of carbon deposits and corrosion in the engine and exhaust system, thus offering further benefit.

Engine

OIL LEVEL CHECK

▶ **See Figures 78 and 79**

Check the oil level, on all models, with the engine cold or as the last procedure at a fuel stop, to allow the oil time to drain back into the sump (about 10 minutes). The engine is equipped with an oil level sensor which signals, through a light on the instrument panel, when oil level is low. If the light comes on while driving, stop the engine and check the oil level immediately.

1. Remove the dipstick and wipe the oil off of the end using a clean, lint-free rag.
2. Insert the dipstick all the way into its tube.
3. Remove the dipstick and hold it level, so that the oil won't run up or down the stick and give a false reading. Note the oil level. It should be between the **L** and **F** marks. If not, fill the engine with clean oil until it is level with or near the **F** mark. Do not overfill the engine.

➡**By nature, the rotary engine uses oil. In fact, there is a small pump on the engine which mixes a small amount of oil with the fuel to lubricate the gas seals in the engine. Normally, the rotary engine consumes about one quart of oil every thousand miles, although one quart every five hundred miles is not unheard of.**

OIL AND FILTER CHANGE

▶ **See Figures 80, 81, 82, 83, 84 and 85**

You will need a large capacity drain pan, which you can purchase at an automotive store. Another necessity is containers for the used oil. You will find that plastic bottles such as

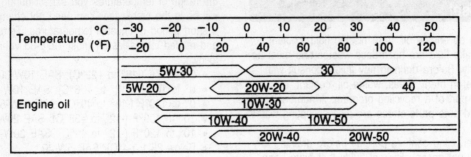

Temperature	°C (°F)	−30 / −20	−20 / 0	−10 / 20	0 / 40	10 / 60	20 / 80	30 / 100	40 / 120	50
Engine oil			5W-30				30			
		5W-20			20W-20					40
					10W-30					
				10W-40			10W-50			
					20W-40			20W-50		

85811083

Fig. 77 Engine oil viscosity chart for 1986-89 vehicles

85811018

Fig. 78 With the engine OFF, withdraw the dipstick to check the oil level

85811020

Fig. 80 Using the proper size wrench or socket, remove the oil pan drain plug

85811019

Fig. 79 With the dipstick held level, the oil reading should be between the L and F marks

those used for bleach or fabric softener, make excellent storage jugs. One ecologically desirable solution to the used oil disposal problem is to find a cooperative gas station owner who will allow you to dump your used oil into his tank.

Change the oil and filter at least every 6,000 miles. The car should be driven about 10 miles in order to get the oil hot immediately before draining it.

There is considerable debate in the auto industry about how frequently the oil filter should be changed. Note that the recommendation of both Mazda Motor Corporation and Chilton is that the filter be changed at every oil change. This not only ensures adequate filtration even if the car is driven short distances in cold weather, but removes dirty oil from the filter and oil galleries, permitting more effective removal of acids and abrasive materials.

1. Park the car on a level surface. Set the parking brake and block the wheels.

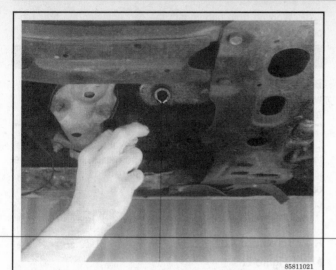

Fig. 81 Allow the oil to drain into a suitable container

2. Working from underneath the car, remove the oil pan drain plug. Have a large, flat container of sufficient capacity ready to catch the oil.

✳✳CAUTION

Be careful not to come into contact with any components of the exhaust system. A serious burn could result!

3. Allow all of the oil to drain into the container.

✳✳CAUTION

The EPA warns that prolonged contact with used engine oil may cause a number of skin disorders, including cancer! You should make every effort to minimize your exposure to used engine oil. Protective gloves should be worn when changing the oil. Wash your hands and any other exposed skin areas as soon as possible after exposure to used engine oil. Soap and water, or waterless hand cleaner should be used.

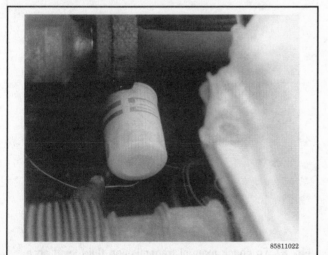

Fig. 82 It is advisable to change the oil filter at each oil change

Fig. 83 Before installing a new oil filter, coat the rubber gasket with clean oil

On rotary engine cars, the oil filter is easily accessible; it is located on top of the engine, next to the oil filler tube. On cars with piston engines, it is located on the right side or rear of the engine.

4. Use a band wrench to remove the oil filter. Note that on the diesel, there are two oil filters: a standard, full-flow oil filter and a bypass oil filter. The bypass filter is replaced at the same interval and in the same way as the standard filter.

➡**Place a container underneath the filter as it will leak oil.**

5. Clean the oil filter mounting flange with a cloth.
6. Lubricate the oil filter O-ring and the mounting surface of the filter with engine oil.
7. Install the filter, being careful not to damage the O-ring.
8. Tighten the filter by hand, approximately ³⁄₄ turn after the gasket contacts the sealing surface. Do not use the band-wrench to tighten it. On diesel engines, tighten the bypass oil filter ²⁄₃ turn after the gasket contacts the sealing surface, using a band wrench only if necessary.
9. Wipe off and then install the drain plug, using care not to damage its threads.

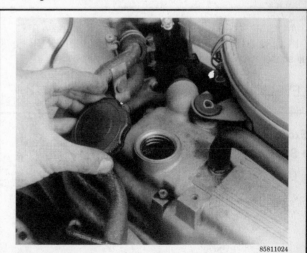

Fig. 84 The engine oil filler cap is commonly located on the rocker arm cover

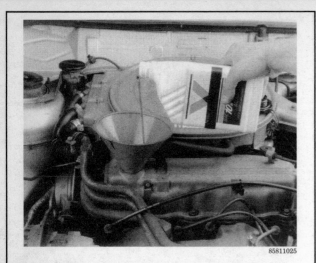

Fig. 85 Add the proper amount of clean engine oil using a clean, dry funnel

10. Working from above the engine, remove the oil filler cap and add the specified amount of proper viscosity oil through the filler opening. (If the filter is being replaced in conjunction with an oil change, be sure the crankcase is refilled with the specified total oil capacity, as indicated in the Capacities chart.)

11. Start the engine without applying throttle and idle it until a few seconds after the oil light goes out. Stop the engine and allow it to sit for five minutes or so until all oil has drained back into the crankcase. Then, check the oil level with the dipstick and replenish as necessary. Check for leaks around the drain plug and the filter sealing surfaces.

Manual Transmission

➡Only rear wheel drive vehicles are equipped with a manual transmission; front wheel drive and 4-wheel drive vehicles are equipped with a transaxle.

FLUID RECOMMENDATIONS

Add SAE 90 EP gear oil if the temperature is above 0°F (-18°C) or SAE 80 EP gear oil if it is below 0°F (-18°C). For all-season type driving, use SAE 80W-90 gear oil.

LEVEL CHECK

Except RX-7 Turbo and 929
▸ **See Figures 86 and 87**

Check the transmission oil every 7,500 miles (12,077 km).
1. Park the car on a level surface and block the wheels.

2. Working from underneath the car, unfasten the filler (upper) plug.

❋❋CAUTION

Be careful if you are working under the car when it is warm; the exhaust system (which is protected by wire mesh) gets extremely hot.

3. Use your finger to check the oil level; it should be up to the bottom of the oil fill hole. Add oil as necessary through the fill hole and install the plug. If possible, use the proper size open end wrench to tighten the plug; avoid the use of a crescent wrench.
4. Unblock the wheels.

RX-7 Turbo and 929
▸ **See Figure 88**

Check the transmission oil every 7,500 miles (12,077 km).
1. Park the car on a level surface and block the wheels.

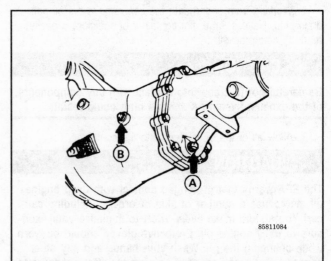

Fig. 86 Manual transmission drain plug "A" and filler plug "B"

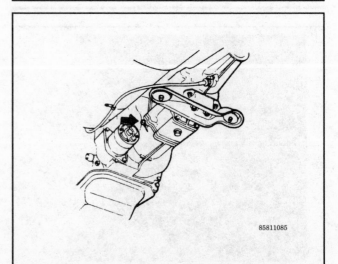

Fig. 87 To check manual transmission fluid level on a non-turbo RX-7, remove plug indicated by the arrow

2. Working from underneath the car, remove check plug "D" in the illustration.

✳✳CAUTION

Be careful if you are working under the car when it is warm; the exhaust system (which is protected by wire mesh) gets extremely hot.

3. Use your finger to check the oil level; it should be up to the bottom of the check plug port. If the oil level is low, remove plug "C" and add oil through fill hole "C" until it reaches the bottom of check port "D".

4. Coat the threads of the check and fill plugs with sealant and install them. If possible, use the proper size open end wrench to tighten the plugs; avoid the use of a crescent wrench.

5. Unblock the wheels.

DRAIN AND REFILL

Except RX-7 Turbo and 929

▶ See Figure 86

Under "normal" operating conditions, manual transmission oil should be changed at 7,500 miles (12,077 km), then at 30,000 mile (48,309 km) intervals. Proceed in the following manner:

1. Warm up the engine and park on a level surface. Shut off the engine, set the parking brake and block the wheels.

2. Position a large, flat drain pan beneath the transmission. Using the proper size open end wrench, remove the drain (lower) plug from underneath the car. (Apply upward pressure

on the drain plug until you can remove it.) Allow the fluid to completely drain into the pan.

✳✳CAUTION

Be careful not to come in contact with any components of the exhaust system. Severe burns could result.

3. Wipe the magnetic drain plug clean and reinstall it, using the proper size open end wrench.

✳✳CAUTION

The EPA warns that prolonged contact with used engine oil may cause a number of skin disorders, including cancer! You should make every effort to minimize your exposure to used engine oil. Protective gloves should be worn when changing the oil. Wash your hands and any other exposed skin areas as soon as possible after exposure to used engine oil. Soap and water, or waterless hand cleaner should be used.

4. Remove the filler plug using the proper size open end wrench.

➡The gear oil must be pumped into the transmission. There are a number of inexpensive pumps (hand operated or drill driven) on the market to do this. Some gear oil containers have their own pumps. The best way to add transmission oil, if you do not have a regular pump, is to fill a bulb siphon (turkey baster) with oil, insert it into the filler plug hole and squeeze it until oil just starts to drip out of the filler hole.

5. Fill the transmission with the recommended fluid (based on the expected temperature during operation) until the oil level reaches the bottom of the fill hole. (Please refer to the Capacities chart in this section.)

6. Reinstall the filler plug with the proper size open end wrench.

7. Remove the drain pan and unblock the wheels.

RX-7 Turbo and 929

▶ See Figure 88

Under "normal" operating conditions, manual transmission oil should be changed at 60,000 mile (96,000 km) intervals, or every 60 months, whichever comes first. Proceed in the following manner:

1. Warm up the engine and park on a level surface. Shut off the engine, set the parking brake and block the wheels.

2. Position a large, flat drain pan beneath the transmission. Using the proper size open end wrench, remove the plugs labeled "A", "B" , "C" and "D" in the illustration. (Apply upward pressure on drain plugs "A" and "B" until you can remove them.) Allow the fluid to completely drain into the pan.

✳✳CAUTION

Be careful not to come in contact with any components of the exhaust system. Severe burns could result.

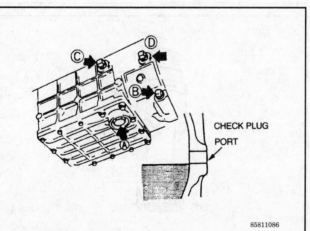

CHECK PLUG PORT

85811086

Fig. 88 To check manual transmission fluid level on an RX-7 Turbo or 929, remove plug "D" from the check plug port

3. Wipe the magnetic drain plugs clean.

✳✳CAUTION

The EPA warns that prolonged contact with used engine oil may cause a number of skin disorders, including cancer! You should make every effort to minimize your exposure to used engine oil. Protective gloves should be worn when changing the oil. Wash your hands and any other exposed skin areas as soon as possible after exposure to used engine oil. Soap and water, or waterless hand cleaner should be used.

4. Coat the drain plug threads with sealant and install them with the proper size open end wrench. Tighten plug "A" to 29-43 ft. lbs. (39-58 Nm) and plug "B" to 18-29 ft. lbs. (24-39 Nm).

5. Add the recommended lubricant (based on the temperature) through hole "C," until the oil level reaches the bottom of hole "D." Please refer to the Capacities chart in this section for approximate fluid requirements.

➡**The gear oil must be pumped into the transmission. There are a number of inexpensive pumps (hand operated or drill driven) on the market to do this. Some gear oil containers have their own pumps. The best way to add transmission oil, if you do not have a regular pump, is to fill a bulb siphon (turkey baster) with oil, insert it into the filler plug hole and squeeze it until oil just starts to drip out of check plug port.**

6. Coat the inspection plug threads with sealant and install them with the proper size open end wrench. Tighten plugs "C" and "D" to 18-29 ft. lbs. (24-39 Nm).

7. Remove the drain pan and unblock the wheels.

Manual Transaxle

➡**Only front wheel drive and 4-wheel drive vehicles are equipped with a manual transaxle; rear wheel drive vehicles are equipped with a transmission.**

FLUID RECOMMENDATIONS

Add SAE 90 EP gear oil if the temperature is above 0°F (-18°C); add SAE 80 EP gear oil or ATF (M2C33 or Dexron®II) if the temperature is below 0°F (-18°C).

LEVEL CHECK

▶ See Figures 89, 90 and 91

➡**Checking and replenishing the manual transaxle fluid is accomplished by removing the speedometer driven gear from the top of the transaxle case. Checking the transaxle oil is not required as routine maintenance (it is changed at 30,000 mile or 48,309 km intervals). However, if you suspect leakage, you might want to check fluid level as a precaution.**

1. Park the vehicle on level ground and block the wheels.

2. Remove the speedometer cable from the gear assembly by unscrewing the knurled fitting.

3. Unbolt and remove the speedometer driven gear. Pull the gear case upward to remove it from the housing, or use a flat-tipped screwdriver to pry it loose.

4. The oil level should cover the gear and gear shoulder. On 1988-89 626s and MX-6s with turbocharged engines, use the level marks located on the upper portion of the speedometer driven gear (please refer to the illustration).

5. Add gear oil, if necessary, through the speedometer gear mounting hole.

6. Reinstall the speedometer driven gear. Reconnect the speedometer cable.

7. Unblock the wheels.

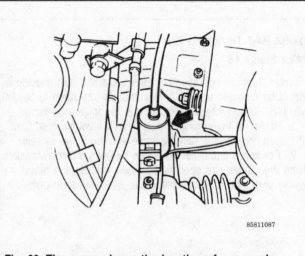

Fig. 89 The arrow shows the location of a manual transaxle's speedometer cable/driven gear unit

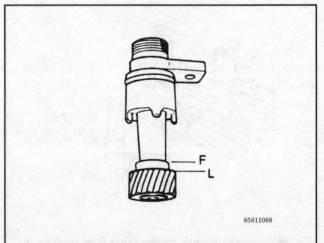

Fig. 90 Checking the manual transaxle fluid level with the speedometer driven gear — except 1988-89 626 and MX-6

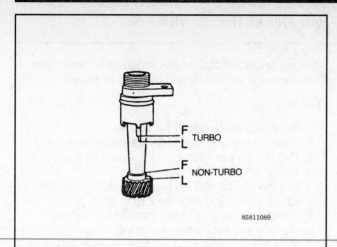

Fig. 91 Checking the manual transaxle fluid level with the speedometer driven gear — 1988-89 626 and MX-6

DRAIN AND REFILL

♦ **See Figures 89, 90 and 91**

Under "normal" operating conditions, manual transaxle fluid is to be changed at 30,000 mile (48,309 km) intervals. Proceed in the following manner:

1. Park the vehicle on level ground and block the wheels.
2. Unscrew and remove the speedometer cable/driven gear assembly from the top of the transaxle.
3. Place a large, flat container of sufficient capacity under the transaxle drain plug. Remove the plug from underneath the car.
4. After the oil has completely drained, install the drain plug and tighten it.
5. Add fluid meeting API specifications GL-4 or GL-5. See the Capacities chart for the amount. Check the level by reinserting the speedometer driven gear. The level is correct when the gear is entirely covered with lube oil, but the level does not exceed the level of the ridge slightly above the top of the gear. On 1988-89 turbocharged 626s and MX-6s, use the level marks on the upper portion of the speedometer drive gear to determine the proper oil level (please refer to the illustration).
6. Add further fluid if necessary and reinstall the cable/gear unit into the case.
7. Remove the drain pan and unblock the wheels.

Automatic Transmission

➡**Only rear wheel drive vehicles are equipped with an automatic transmission; front wheel drive vehicles are equipped with a transaxle.**

FLUID RECOMMENDATIONS

Mazda automatic transmissions prior to 1987 use Type F fluid only. Do not use Type A fluid, as the fluid characteristics affect shifting and may cause damage to the transmission clutches. On 1987-89 vehicles, only Dexron®II or M-III fluids should be used in automatic transmissions.

LEVEL CHECK

♦ **See Figures 92 and 93**

The automatic transmission dipstick is located behind the engine, next to the hood latch. Check the fluid level every 4,000-7,500 miles (6,441-12,077 km) on vehicles through 1982. On later models, check the fluid level at 7,500 miles (12,077 km), and then again at 30,000 miles (48,309 km), 60,000 miles (96,618 km) and so on.

There are two ranges indicated on the dipstick of some models. One is labeled COLD and the other HOT.

To check the fluid level when the transmission is cold (when the car has been sitting overnight), proceed as follows:

1. Start the engine and allow it to warm up for at least two minutes. Firmly set the parking brake and block the wheels. Move the selector lever through all gear positions, then put it in Park.
2. Remove the dipstick and wipe it with a clean cloth.
3. Reinsert the dipstick.

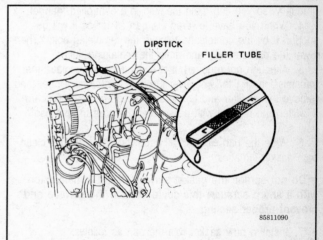

Fig. 92 Withdraw the dipstick and add fluid through the filler tube. The fluid level should be between the L and F marks.

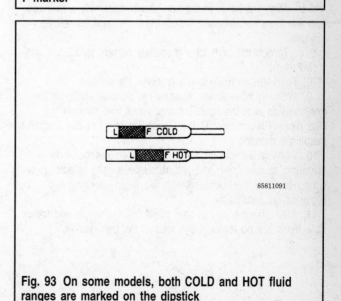

Fig. 93 On some models, both COLD and HOT fluid ranges are marked on the dipstick

4. Withdraw the dipstick again and note the level. (On dual range dipsticks, be sure to read it on the COLD side.) Add fluid as necessary. The difference between **L** and **F** is about **1 pint**.

➡The procedure for checking the fluid level when the transmission is hot is the same as above, except that the reading should be taken on the HOT range side of the dipstick.

DRAIN AND REFILL

▶ **See Figures 92 and 93**

1. Raise the car and support it securely on jackstands. Place a large drain pan under the transmission oil pan.
2. Loosen the bolts along the forward edge of the pan (including the ones in the corners at the front), as far as they will go without coming out of the housing. Then, remove all the other pan bolts.
3. Carefully and slowly pull the rear edge of the pan downward to break the seal with the gasket. Tilt the pan downward gradually, so you can drain the fluid in a controlled manner.
4. When you have lowered the pan as far as it will go, support it by the center and remove the remaining bolts. Then, lower the pan carefully and drain the remaining fluid.
5. Although not required, it is a good idea to replace the transmission oil filter whenever the fluid is drained. Unbolt and remove the oil filter and O-ring seal, if so equipped. Discard the filter and replace with a new one. Be sure to also use a new seal.
6. Wipe the pan clean of all deposits, then carefully clean both gasket surfaces.

➡Do not scrape the gasket surface of the transmission with a sharp scraper; this could scratch the surface and prevent proper sealing.

7. Install a new gasket with the pan as follows:
   a. Coat both sides of the gasket with sealer and align the gasket holes with those in the pan. (The sealer will help keep the gasket in place on the pan.)
   b. Align the holes in the pan/gasket assembly with those in the transmission case, install the bolts, and tighten very gently.
   c. Torque the bolts in a crisscross pattern to 3.5-5 ft. lbs. (5-7 Nm).
8. Remove the drain pan and lower the vehicle.
9. Working from above, remove the dipstick and refill the transmission with the specified amount of fluid through the oil filler pipe. (Please refer to the Capacities chart in this section.) Install the dipstick.
10. Run the vehicle until the transmission reaches normal operating temperature, and shift through all gear selector positions. Recheck the fluid level with the engine running and replenish as necessary.
11. After about a day of use, crawl under the car and make sure there are no leaks in the area of the pan gasket.

PAN AND FILTER SERVICE

Oil pan gasket and filter service should be performed when the transmission fluid is changed. Proceed as follows:

Fluid Pan

1. Raise and safely support the vehicle.
2. Place a large drain pan under the transmission pan.
3. Remove the pan attaching bolts, except for those at the front. Loosen the front bolts slightly.
4. Pull the rear edge of the pan downward to break the seal with the gasket and allow the fluid to drain.
5. Remove the front pan bolts, then remove the pan.
6. Remove and discard the pan gasket.
7. Wipe the pan clean of all deposits, then carefully clean both gasket surfaces.

➡Do not scrape the gasket surface of the transmission with a sharp scraper; this could scratch the surface and prevent proper sealing.

8. Install a new gasket with the pan as follows:
   a. Coat both sides of the gasket with sealer and align the gasket holes with those in the pan. (The sealer will help keep the gasket in place on the pan.)
   b. Align the holes in the pan/gasket assembly with those in the transmission case, install the bolts, and tighten very gently.
   c. Torque the bolts in a crisscross pattern to 3.5-5 ft. lbs. (5-7 Nm).
9. Remove the drain pan and lower the vehicle. Fill the transmission with the specified amount of fluid through the oil filler pipe. (Please refer to the Capacities chart in this section.) Install the dipstick and check the transmission operation.

Filter

1. Remove the transmission oil pan, as previously described.
2. Remove the attaching bolts and the filter assembly. Some models use an O-ring seal with the filter. This seal should also be replaced.
3. Install the filter and torque the bolts alternately (diagonally) is several stages to 4-5 ft. lbs. (5.5-7 Nm).

Automatic Transaxle

➡Only front wheel drive vehicles are equipped with an automatic transaxle; rear wheel drive vehicles are equipped with a transmission.

FLUID RECOMMENDATIONS

Mazda automatic transaxles prior to 1987 use Type F fluid only. Do not use Type A fluid, as the fluid characteristics affect shifting and may cause damage to the transaxle clutches. On 1987-89 vehicles, only Dexron®II or M-III fluids should be used in automatic transaxles.

LEVEL CHECK

▶ **See Figures 94 and 95**

The automatic transaxle dipstick is located on the left front side of the engine. Check the fluid level every 4,000-7,500 miles (6,441-12,077 km) on vehicles through 1982. On later models, check the fluid level at 7,500 miles (12,077 km), and then again at 30,000 miles (48,309 km), 60,000 miles (96,618 km) and so on.

There are two ranges indicated on the dipstick of some models. One is labeled COLD and the other HOT.

To check the fluid level when the transaxle is cold (when the car has been sitting overnight), proceed as follows:

1. Start the engine and allow it to warm up for at least two minutes. Firmly set the parking brake and block the wheels. Move the selector lever through all gear positions, then put it in Park.
2. Remove the dipstick and wipe it with a clean cloth.
3. Reinsert the dipstick.

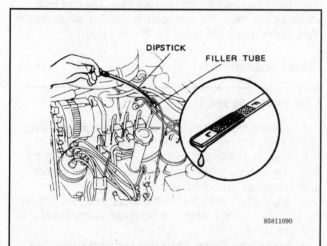

Fig. 94 Withdraw the dipstick and add fluid through the filler tube. The fluid level should be between the L and F marks.

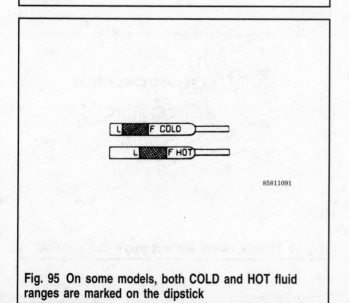

Fig. 95 On some models, both COLD and HOT fluid ranges are marked on the dipstick

4. Withdraw the dipstick again and note the level. (On dual range dipsticks, be sure to read it on the COLD side.) Add fluid as necessary. The difference between **L** and **F** is about 1 pint.

➡**The procedure for checking the fluid level when the transmission is hot is the same as above, except that the reading should be taken on the HOT range side of the dipstick.**

DRAIN AND REFILL

▶ **See Figures 94 and 95**

1. Raise the car and support it securely on jackstands. Place a large drain pan under the drain plug on the lower part of the differential.
2. Using the correct size socket or open end wrench, remove the drain plug. (Apply upward pressure on the drain plug until you can remove it.)
3. Once the fluid stops draining, reinstall the drain plug.

➡**The entire fluid capacity cannot be drained through the differential drain port. To completely drain the transaxle, remove the oil pan after draining the differential.**

4. Position a large drain pan under the transaxle's oil pan. Loosen the bolts along the forward edge of the pan (including the ones in the corners at the front) as far as they will go without coming out of the housing. Then, remove all the other pan bolts.
5. Carefully and slowly pull the rear edge of the pan downward to break the seal with the gasket. Tilt the pan downward gradually, so you can drain the fluid in a controlled manner.
6. When you have lowered the pan as far as it will go, support it by the center and remove the remaining bolts. Then, lower the pan carefully and drain the remaining fluid.
7. Although not required, it is a good idea to replace the transaxle oil strainer (filter) whenever the fluid is drained. Unbolt and remove the oil strainer and O-ring seal, if so equipped. Discard the strainer and replace with a new one. Be sure to also use a new seal.
8. Wipe the pan clean of all deposits, then carefully clean both gasket surfaces.

➡**Do not scrape the gasket surface of the transaxle with a sharp scraper; this could scratch the surface and prevent proper sealing.**

9. Install a new gasket with the pan as follows:
   a. Coat both sides of the gasket with sealer and align the gasket holes with those in the pan. (The sealer will help keep the gasket in place on the pan.)
   b. Align the holes in the pan/gasket assembly with those in the transaxle case, install the bolts, and tighten very gently.
   c. Torque the bolts in a crisscross pattern to 3.5-5 ft. lbs. (5-7 Nm).
10. Remove the drain pan and lower the vehicle.
11. Working from above, remove the dipstick and refill the transaxle with the specified amount of fluid through the oil filler pipe. (Please refer to the Capacities chart in this section.) Install the dipstick.

12. Run the vehicle until the transaxle reaches normal operating temperature, and shift through all gear selector positions. Recheck the fluid level with the engine running and replenish as necessary.

13. After about a day of use, crawl under the car and make sure there are no leaks in the area of the pan gasket or drain plug.

PAN AND FILTER SERVICE

Oil pan gasket and filter service should be performed when the transaxle fluid is changed. Proceed as follows:

Fluid Pan

1. Raise and safely support the vehicle.
2. Place a large drain pan under the transaxle's oil pan.
3. Remove the pan attaching bolts, except for those at the front. Loosen the front bolts slightly.
4. Pull the rear edge of the pan downward to break the seal with the gasket and allow the fluid to drain.
5. Remove the front pan bolts, then remove the pan.
6. Remove and discard the pan gasket.
7. Wipe the pan clean of all deposits, then carefully clean both gasket surfaces.

➡**Do not scrape the gasket surface of the transaxle with a sharp scraper; this could scratch the surface and prevent proper sealing.**

8. Install a new gasket with the pan as follows:
   a. Coat both sides of the gasket with sealer and align the gasket holes with those in the pan. (The sealer will help keep the gasket in place on the pan.)
   b. Align the holes in the pan/gasket assembly with those in the transaxle case, install the bolts, and tighten very gently.
   c. Torque the bolts in a crisscross pattern to 3.5-5 ft. lbs. (5-7 Nm).
9. Remove the drain pan and lower the vehicle.
10. Working from above, remove the dipstick and refill the transaxle with the specified amount of fluid through the oil filler pipe. (Please refer to the Capacities chart in this section.) Install the dipstick.
11. Run the vehicle until the transaxle reaches normal operating temperature, and shift through all gear selector positions. Recheck the fluid level with the engine running and replenish as necessary.

Filter

1. Remove the transmission oil pan, as previously described.
2. Remove the four attaching bolts and the filter assembly. Some models use an O-ring seal with the filter. This seal should also be replaced.
3. Install the filter and torque the bolts alternately (diagonally) is several stages to 4-5 ft. lbs. (5.5-7 Nm).

Transfer Carrier

Only 323s with 4-wheel drive (4WD) are equipped with transfer carriers. Under "normal" operating conditions, the oil in the transfer carrier should be replaced every 60,000 miles (96,618 km).

FLUID RECOMMENDATIONS

Use API GL-5 oils: SAE 90 above 0°F (-18°C) and SAE 80W below 0°F (-18°C).

LEVEL CHECK

▶ **See Figure 96**

Check the fluid level in the transfer carrier a least once a year. To check the oil level, make sure the vehicle is on level ground and then remove the fill/check plug. The fluid level should be just below the plug opening. Add the proper amount of oil as necessary and install the fill/check plug.

DRAIN AND REFILL

▶ **See Figures 96 and 97**

1. Remove the fill/check plug on the side of the transfer carrier, using a proper size socket or open end wrench.
2. Position a drain pan under the carrier and remove the drain plug, using a proper size socket or open end wrench. Drain the carrier, then reinstall the drain plug.
3. Add 0.53 qt. (0.50 liter) of the appropriate fluid through the fill/check opening, using a turkey baster or equivalent syringe type pump.
4. Reinstall the fill/check plug and remove the drain pan.

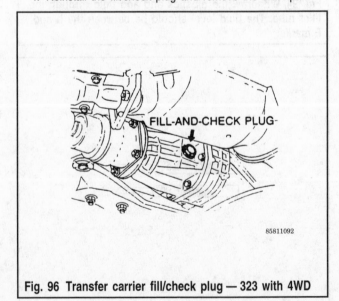

FILL-AND-CHECK PLUG

85811092

Fig. 96 Transfer carrier fill/check plug — 323 with 4WD

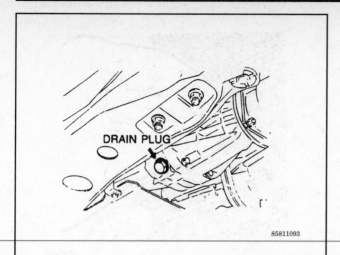

Fig. 97 Transfer carrier drain plug — 323 with 4WD

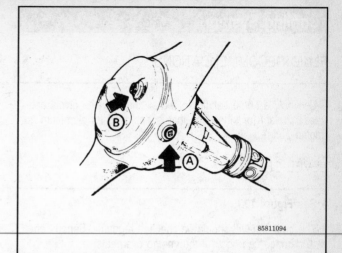

Fig. 98 Common rear axle housing showing drain plug "A" and filler plug "B"

Rear Axle/Differential

FLUID RECOMMENDATIONS

Rear axles and differentials use API GL-5 oils: SAE 90 above 0°F (-18°C) and SAE 80W below 0°F (-18°C). On models with limited slip differentials, use API GL-5 special SAE 90 lubricant.

LEVEL CHECK

▶ See Figures 98 and 99

Periodic checking of the lubricant level is required at 6,000-7,500 mile (9,662-12,077 km) intervals. However, if you notice oil seepage from the rear axle, or a change in the sound of the axle, it is a good idea to check the oil level and replenish it if necessary. Any significant leaks should be repaired as soon as possible.

1. Park the car on a level surface, set the parking brake and block the wheels.
2. Remove the filler (upper) plug from the differential, using the proper size socket or ratchet and extension.
3. Check the oil level; it should be up to the bottom of the filler hole. Add lubricant, as necessary.
4. Clean the threads and reinstall the filler plug.
5. Unblock the wheels.

DRAIN AND REFILL

▶ See Figures 98 and 99

The oil should be changed at 7,500 miles (12,077 km), then at 30,000 mile (48,309 km) intervals. Proceed as described below:

1. Park the car on a level surface. Set the parking brake and block the wheels.

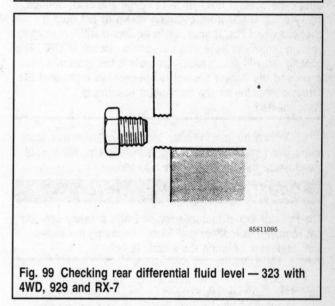

Fig. 99 Checking rear differential fluid level — 323 with 4WD, 929 and RX-7

2. Position a drain pan beneath the rear axle/differential and remove the drain (lower) plug, using the proper size socket or ratchet and extension. Allow the oil to empty into the container.
3. Clean and reinstall the drain plug.
4. Unscrew the filler (upper) plug, using the proper size socket or ratchet and extension, then add the appropriate grade of lubricant, depending upon ambient temperature.
5. Fill to capacity, until the level reaches the bottom of the filler hole. See the Capacities chart at the end of this section.
6. Clean and reinstall the filler plug.
7. Remove the drain pan and unblock the wheels.

Cooling System

FLUID RECOMMENDATIONS

Use only a 50/50 solution of water and ethylene glycol anti-freeze/coolant (or other type that is approved for aluminum engine parts).

LEVEL CHECK

▶ See Figure 100

The coolant level should be checked regularly. Serious engine damage can occur if the engine overheats.

✳✳CAUTION

Check the coolant level when the engine is cold; serious injury could result from escaping steam or hot fluid if checked when hot. If your car is equipped with an electric cooling fan, make sure that the ignition switch is OFF. The cooling fan will automatically operate if the ignition switch is on and the engine coolant temperature is high, or if the wiring connector on the thermostat housing is disconnected.

1. Depress the button on the thermal expansion tank (coolant recovery reservoir) safety cap, if there is one. Allow all of the pressure trapped in the system to escape.

✳✳CAUTION

The radiator is not factory-equipped with a safety cap. Do not remove the radiator cap before removing the expansion tank cap, or when the engine is hot.

2. Remove the expansion tank cap. The expansion tank should be ⅓ full, unless Full and Low marks are provided. The level should be well above the bottom of the tank when the engine is cold.
3. If it is not, carefully remove the cap from the radiator. The radiator should be full.
4. Add a 50/50 solution of ethylene glycol (or other suitable coolant) and clean water. If there was no coolant in the expansion tank, fill the radiator until the level is near the inlet port and install the radiator cap. Then, fill the expansion tank to the specified level, and secure the expansion tank cap.

When checking the coolant level, the pressure cap should be examined for signs of age or deterioration. Check it for a worn or cracked gasket. If the cap doesn't seal properly, fluid will be lost and the engine will overheat. A worn cap should be replaced with a new one. The fan belt and other drive belts should be inspected and adjusted to the proper tension. (Please refer to the belt inspection and adjusting procedures, earlier in this section.)

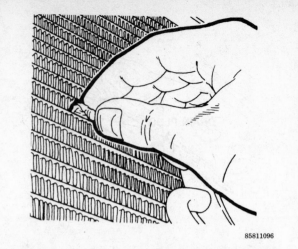

85811096

Fig. 100 Remove insects and debris from the radiator fins

Remove the radiator cap and run the tip of your finger around the inside of the filler neck. Check for excessive deposits of rust or scale around the filler neck lip and the filler port. Make sure the coolant is free of oil. Replace the coolant as necessary.

Hose clamps should be tightened, and soft or cracked hoses replaced. Damp spots, or accumulations of rust or dye near hoses, the water pump or other areas indicate possible leakage, which must be corrected before filling the system with fresh coolant.

Periodically clean any debris, leaves, paper, insects, etc. from the radiator fins. Pick the large pieces off by hand. The smaller pieces can be washed away with water pressure from a hose.

Carefully straighten any bent radiator fins with a pair of needle nose pliers. Be careful as the fins are very soft. Don't wiggle the fins back and forth too much. Straighten them once and try not to move them again.

DRAIN AND REFILL

▶ See Figures 101, 102, 103, 104, 105 and 106

The engine coolant should be drained and the system flushed periodically. (Please refer to the recommended maintenance interval charts in this section.) New coolant mixed with the proper amount of clean water should be used, since antifreeze eventually becomes corrosive. While draining and refilling may only be required every 30 months/30,000 miles (48,309 km), the coolant should be inspected at 15 months/15,000 miles (24,155 km) and replaced if it shows signs of rust or corrosion. Good coolant appears in its original color, while coolant that is permitting corrosion will appear cloudy and darker than its original color.

Complete draining and refilling of the cooling system will remove accumulated rust, scale and other deposits. To make the job easier, park your car close to a faucet or other source of water and run a garden hose to the radiator.

1. With the engine cold, remove the radiator cap and air bleeder plug. (Air bleeder plugs are only installed on the RX-7.)

❋❋CAUTION

When draining coolant, keep in mind that cats and dogs are attracted by ethylene glycol antifreeze, and are quite likely to drink any that is left in an uncovered container or in puddles on the ground. This will prove fatal in sufficient quantity. Always drain the coolant into a sealable container. Coolant should be reused unless it is contaminated or several years old.

2. Drain the existing antifreeze/coolant into a suitable drain pan by opening the radiator and engine drain petcocks, or by disconnecting the bottom radiator hose at the radiator outlet.

Before opening the radiator petcock, spray it with some penetrating lubricant, if necessary.

➡On 1979-85 RX-7s, coolant is drained by removing the drain plug in the intermediate engine housing and by disconnecting the lower radiator hose. On 1986-89 RX-7s, coolant is drained by removing the intermediate housing drain plug and opening the radiator drain cock.

3. Detach the hose at the base of the expansion tank (coolant recovery reservoir), and drain the old coolant into a suitable drain pan. Rinse the inside of this tank with clean water, if necessary, and reattach the hose.

➡In order to drain the expansion tank, it may be helpful to temporarily remove it from the vehicle.

4. Set the heater control to the MAXIMUM heat position.
5. Flush the cooling system with clean water. (Directions for flushing and cleaning the system follow.)
6. Close the drain cocks or reinstall the drain plugs.

Fig. 101 With the engine cold, remove the radiator cap

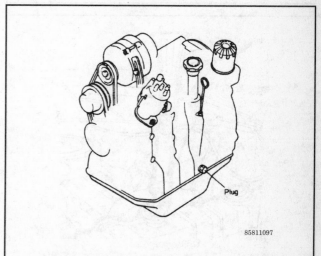

Fig. 103 On RX-7 models, remove the drain plug from the intermediate engine housing

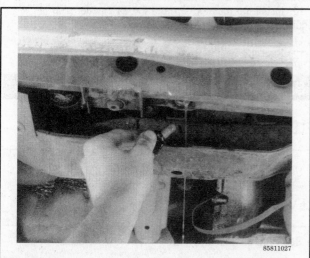

Fig. 102 With a suitable container in position, turn and open the radiator petcock

Fig. 104 After flushing the system and closing the drain plug(s), properly refill the system using a proper mixture of antifreeze/coolant and water

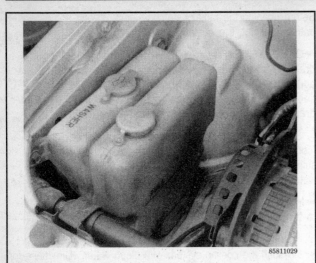

Fig. 105 Drain and refill the coolant in the expansion tank

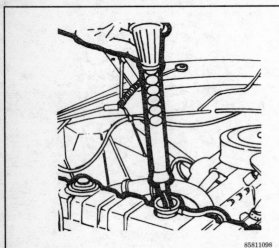

Fig. 106 Use an antifreeze tester, such as this syringe type, to test the level of protection

7. Fill the cooling system with the proper amount and mixture of ethylene glycol or other aluminum-compatible coolant and water. Be sure to also add a fresh coolant mixture to the expansion tank. (The expansion tank and windshield washer fluid reservoir may be part of a dual reservoir; if so, be careful not to mix these two different types of fluid.)

✳✳CAUTION

Do not use alcohol or methanol-based coolants!

8. Run the engine at idle with the radiator cap removed to allow all the air to bleed out of the system. Add coolant as necessary to attain the proper level.
9. Install the radiator cap and the air bleeder plug (if equipped).
10. Check the level of protection with an antifreeze tester.
11. Start the engine and inspect for leaks.

FLUSHING AND CLEANING THE SYSTEM

➡**Commercial flushing agents may only be used if they are not harmful to aluminum components.**

1. Drain the cooling system and leave the drain cock or engine drain plugs open.

✳✳CAUTION

When draining coolant, keep in mind that cats and dogs are attracted by ethylene glycol antifreeze, and are quite likely to drink any that is left in an uncovered container or in puddles on the ground. This will prove fatal in sufficient quantity. Always drain the coolant into a sealable container. Coolant should be reused unless it is contaminated or several years old.

2. Set the heater controls to the MAXIMUM heat position.
3. Place a garden hose into the radiator filler opening.
4. Turn on the water supply and regulate the water so that the level in the radiator remains constant.
5. Start the engine and flush the system until the water leaving the radiator or engine is clear. This may take four or five minutes depending on the condition of the cooling system.
6. Stop the engine and allow the cooling system to drain completely.
7. Close the radiator drain cock and install the drain plugs (if equipped).
8. Fill the cooling system with the proper amount and mixture of ethylene glycol or other aluminum-compatible coolant and water.

✳✳CAUTION

Do not use alcohol or methanol based coolants!

9. Run the engine at idle with the radiator cap removed to allow all the air to bleed out of the system. Add coolant as necessary to attain the proper level.
10. Install the radiator cap and the air bleeder plug (if equipped).
11. Check the level of protection with an antifreeze tester.
12. Start the engine and inspect for leaks.

Brake/Clutch Master Cylinder

FLUID RECOMMENDATIONS

Use only brake fluids labeled DOT-3 or DOT-4.

LEVEL CHECK

◆ **See Figures 107 and 108**

Check the level in the brake and clutch master cylinder reservoirs regularly, at least every 4,000-7,500 miles (6,441-12,077 km). On plastic, translucent reservoirs, the fluid level can be seen without removing the cap. If the level is below or near the **MIN** mark, clean any dirt away from the top, then remove the cap from the reservoir and add brake fluid to the **MAX** mark. Always add fluid slowly, so that bubbles do not form in the hydraulic lines. Reinstall the cap.

✳✳CAUTION

Be careful not to spill brake fluid on painted surfaces, as it is an all-too-effective paint remover.

Bleed the brake system if bubbles are apparent. See Section 9.

➡**If the brake warning light comes on when the brake pedal is depressed and the parking brake is off, stop the vehicle immediately and check the fluid level in the brake master cylinder reservoir.**

Power Steering Pump

On 1978-83 vehicles with power steering, check the fluid level every 7,500 miles (12,077 km) and fill as necessary. On

Fig. 107 Brake fluid level in the master cylinder should be maintained between the MIN and MAX marks

Fig. 108 Unscrew the cap from the reservoir to add fluid

1984-89 vehicles, check the fluid level every 15,000 miles (24,155 km) and fill as necessary.

FLUID RECOMMENDATIONS

Power steering systems use Dexron®II, M2C33 or equivalent ATF.

LEVEL CHECK

➡**Check the power steering pump level while the fluid is cold.**

If there are level indicator markings on the level gauge, make sure that they are facing the front of the vehicle while checking the fluid level. Some level gauges will just have two raised bulges on the gauge.

Remove the level gauge from the power steering pump, and check that the fluid level is within the range of the **H** and **L** marks. Wipe the gauge clean and check it again. If not, add fluid until the level is at the (upper) **H** mark. On 1988-89 626 and MX-6 models, the fluid level should be between the **MIN** and **MAX** marks on the translucent reservoir.

Steering Gear

FLUID RECOMMENDATIONS

Use API GL-4 for manual steering boxes. Use Dexron®II or MIII ATF for the rear steering gear of 1988-89 626s and MX-6s equipped with four wheel steering.

LEVEL CHECK

Manual Steering Except Rack and Pinion

Check the lubricant in the steering gear every 15,000 miles (24,155 km).
1. Remove the filler plug.
2. The oil level should be up to the bottom of the fill hole.
3. Add SAE 90 EP gear lubricant, as required.
4. Replace the filler plug.

1988-89 626 and MX-6 With Four Wheel Steering (4WS)
⬧ **See Figure 109**

On 626 and MX-6 vehicles equipped with four wheel steering, check the rear steering gear fluid level every 30,000 miles (48,310 km).
1. Remove the bleeder valve on the rear steering gear housing.
2. Insert a small piece of wire into the bleeder valve opening and check the level. The fluid level (as indicated by the length of the double-arrow line in the accompanying illustration) should be 1.6-1.8 in. (41-46mm). The total capacity of the unit is 0.9-1.1 qt. (0.8-1.0 liter). Add fluid as required.
3. Install the bleeder valve.

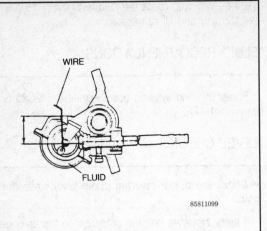

Fig. 109 Check the rear steering gear oil level with a piece of wire — 1988-89 626 and MX-6 with 4WS

Sub-Zero Starter Assist (RX-7 Only)

▶ See Figure 110

On RX-7 models, except those sold in California, a sub-zero starting assist fluid reservoir is located to the right of the engine near the firewall. When the outside temperature is below 0°F (-18°C), a thermoswitch operates a small electric pump in the reservoir which injects a pre-measured squirt of 90% aluminum-compatible antifreeze and 10% water into the carburetor throttle bore or intake manifold while the starter is being cranked. This keeps the fuel from icing and promotes better starting.

FLUID RECOMMENDATIONS

Use only ethylene glycol (or other aluminum-compatible antifreeze) and water.

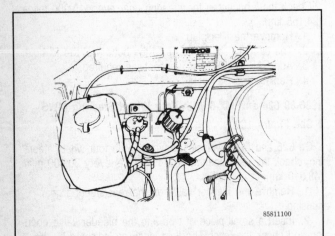

Fig. 110 On most RX-7s, a sub-zero starter assist reservoir is located near the windshield washer reservoir

LEVEL CHECK

Check the fluid level in the sub-zero starter assist reservoir every two weeks in cold weather. If necessary, unscrew the reservoir cap and refill the reservoir with a 90/10% mixture of ethylene glycol or other suitable antifreeze and water.

Body Lubrication and Maintenance

Door and hood hinges, as well as door holders, should be lubricated each time the engine oil is changed. For long-lasting results, use white lithium grease. It is also a good idea, in very cold weather, to squirt a small amount of lock antifreeze into the door locks. Small "acid brushes" make ideal applicators for those hard-to-reach places.

Front Wheel Bearings

→**Maintenance in this section covers the front wheel bearings on rear wheel drive cars. These are the only wheel bearings which require periodic lubrication on the rear wheel drive vehicles covered by this manual. (Mazda also recommends periodic lubrication of the front wheel bearings on front wheel drive GLCs.) For drive axle bearing information, please refer to Section 7 for rear wheel drive models or Section 8 for front wheel drive models.**

Applicable front wheel bearings should be repacked with lithium grease (NGLI No. 1) every 30,000 miles (48,309 km) or 30 months, whichever comes first.

LOOSENESS TEST

Except 929

▶ See Figure 111

1. Raise the front of the car and safely support it with jackstands.
2. Grasp the wheel at the 1 o'clock and 7 o'clock positions and shake it sideways.
3. Rotate the tire and make sure that it turns smoothly and that the bearings are not noisy.
4. If considerable play or any abnormal noise is noticed, the bearings are either worn or loose.
5. Repeat the procedure for the other front wheel.
6. Lower the vehicle.

929

▶ See Figures 112 and 113

1. Raise the front of the vehicle and safely support it with jackstands.
2. Grasp the wheel at the 1 o'clock and 7 o'clock positions and shake it sideways.
3. Rotate the tire and make sure that it turns smoothly and that the bearings are not noisy.
4. Remove the front wheel.
5. Remove the caliper assembly with the brake hose attached, and suspend it with wire or twine from the strut as-

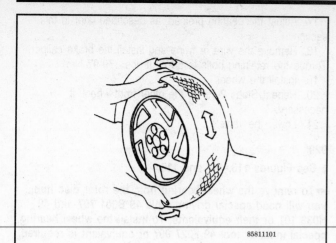

Fig. 111 Checking front wheel bearing looseness on rear wheel drive vehicles

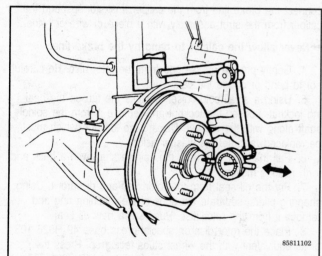

Fig. 112 Checking front wheel bearing axial play using a dial indicator — 1988 929

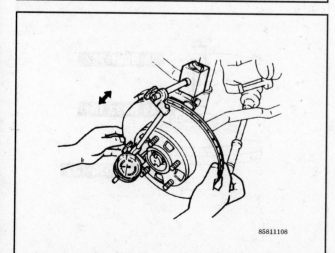

Fig. 113 Checking front wheel bearing axial play using a dial indicator — 1989 929

sembly. (See Section 9 for caliper removal and installation procedures.)

6. Mount a dial indicator so that the stylus is positioned on the face of the grease cap (1988 929) or on the hub collar (1989 929). Zero the indicator.

7. Grasp the rotor disc by hand and try to move it in the axial direction (in and out). Check the end-play on the dial indicator. The maximum allowable end-play is 0.002 in. (0.05mm). If the end-play exceeds that amount, replace the wheel bearing.

8. Remove the dial indicator.

9. Remove the wire or twine and install the brake caliper assembly. Torque the caliper retaining bolts to 58-86 ft. lbs. (79-116 Nm).

10. Install the wheel and torque the wheel lug nuts to 65-87 ft. lbs. (88-118 Nm).

11. Repeat the procedure for the other front wheel.

12. Lower the vehicle.

REMOVAL, PACKING AND INSTALLATION

➡ **For all brake caliper/disc removal and installation procedures, please refer to Section 9 of this manual.**

Rear Wheel Drive GLC and 626

▶ **See Figures 114 and 115**

1. Raise the front end and safely support it on jackstands.

2. Remove the front wheel.

3. Remove the disc brake caliper with the brake hose attached and secure it to the coil spring with wire or twine.

4. Remove the grease cap from the wheel hub. This can usually be done by prying between it and the wheel hub with a flat blade screwdriver. Be careful not to bend or gouge the cap.

5. Wipe some of the grease away and remove the cotter pin in the end of the spindle.

6. Remove the nut lock and adjusting nut, the thrust washer, and the outer wheel bearing. If the washer and bearing will not readily come out, try tilting the hub a little to one side.

7. Remove the brake disc/hub assembly from the spindle.

8. Remove the inner grease seal. This can usually be done using a screwdriver and prying from the inside of the seal. Do not try to force the screwdriver between the seal and the hub, as you may scratch the hub. Remove the inner bearing.

9. If necessary, drive out the bearing outer race with a brass drift applied to the slots provided for this purpose.

➡ **Never remove the outer races unless you are replacing them.**

10. Clean the inner and outer bearings completely and dry them with compressed air.

✴✴WARNING

Do not use compressed air to spin the bearings dry.

11. Clean the spindle and the hub cavity with solvent.

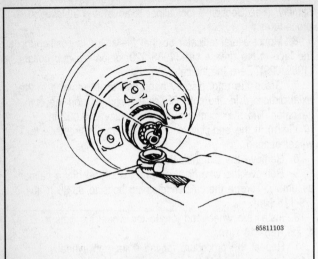

Fig. 114 Remove the grease cap, cotter pin and lock nut to access the wheel bearing adjusting nut

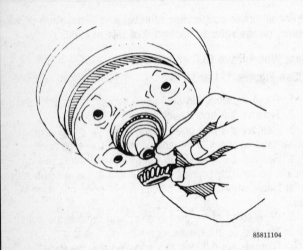

Fig. 115 Pack the front wheel bearings with lithium base grease before installing them

12. Repack the bearings and the hub cavity with lithium grease. Do not overpack them.

13. If the bearing outer race was removed, install a new race into the hub, using either a tool made for that purpose, or a socket of large enough diameter to press on the outside rim of the race only.

✳✳WARNING

Use care not to cock the bearing race in the hub. If it is not fully seated, the bearings cannot be adjusted properly.

14. Install the inner bearing into its race, then press a new grease seal over it.

15. Position the brake disc/hub assembly on the spindle. Install the outer bearing in the hub.

16. Apply a thin coat of grease to the washer and the threaded portion of the spindle, then loosely install the thrust washer and adjusting nut.

17. Adjust the bearing preload, as described later in this section.

18. Remove the wire or twine and install the brake caliper. Torque the retaining bolts to 58-72 ft. lbs. (79-97 Nm)

19. Install the wheel.

20. Repeat Steps 2-19 for the other front wheel, if necessary.

21. Lower the vehicle.

929

▶ See Figures 116, 117 and 118

➡To remove the wheel bearing from the rotor disc hub, you will need special driving tools 49 B001 797 and 49 H033 101 or their equivalents. To install the wheel bearing, special installer tool 49 F027 007 or equivalent is required.

1. Raise the front of the car and safely support it on jackstands.

2. Remove the front wheel.

3. Remove the brake caliper and its bracket. Do not disconnect the brake line from the caliper. Instead, suspend the caliper from the strut assembly with a piece of wire or twine.

➡Never allow the caliper to hang by the brake line.

4. Gently pry the grease cap from the rotor disc. Be careful not to bend or gouge the cap.

5. Using a small cold chisel, unstake the tab on the bearing locknut. Loosen the locknut and remove it from the spindle shaft along with the washer. Discard the locknut (which must be replaced) and set the washer aside.

6. Pull the rotor disc from the spindle shaft with a back and forth rocking motion.

7. Pry the oil seal from the rotor disc and discard it. Using snapring pliers, separate the ends of the retaining ring and remove it from the rotor disc. Purchase a new oil seal.

8. Place the rotor disc on special press base 49 H026 103 or its equivalent with the wheel studs facing up. Press the bearing from the rotor disc using special tools 49 B001 797

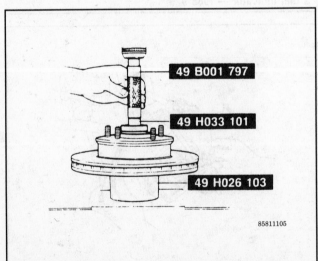

Fig. 116 Pressing the front wheel bearing from the rotor disc — 929

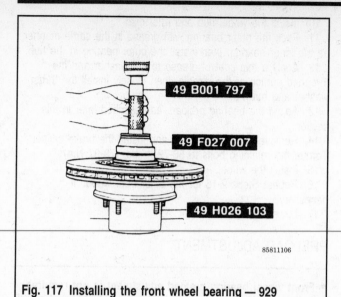

Fig. 117 Installing the front wheel bearing — 929

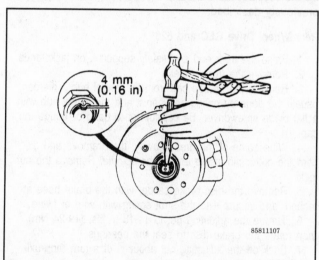

4 mm
(0.16 in)

Fig. 118 To properly stake the locknut, leave a 0.16 in. (4.06mm) clearance between the nut and spindle groove

and 49 H033 101 or their equivalents. Discard the bearing and purchase a new one. DO NOT reuse it.

➡️**On vehicles equipped with Anti-Lock Brake Systems (ABS), take care not to damage the teeth of the sensor rotor, located in the center of the rotor disc, when pressing the bearing out.**

9. Invert the rotor disc on the base so that the wheel studs are now facing down.

10. Install the new bearing and press it into the rotor disc using special tool 49 F027 007 or its equivalent.

11. Install the retaining ring.

12. Drive the new oil seal into the rotor disc using the proper tool. Coat the lip of the oil seal with lithium based NGLI No. 2 wheel bearing grease.

13. Install the disc plate with the washer and new locknut. Torque the locknut to 72-130 ft. lbs. (98-176 Nm). Once the specified torque is reached, check that the tab on the locknut

is aligned with the groove in the spindle shaft. If not, use the torque wrench to tighten the locknut until the tab is properly aligned, but do not exceed 130 ft. lbs. (176 Nm).

14. Check the bearing end-play, as described previously in this section. Maximum end-play is 0.002 in. (0.05mm).

15. Stake the locknut tab with a small cold chisel. The tab should have a 0.16 in. (4.06mm) clearance from the shaft groove (see the illustration).

16. Install the caliper assembly and torque the retaining bolts to 65-87 ft. lbs. (88-118 Nm).

17. Install the wheel and torque the lug nuts to 65-87 ft. lbs. (88-118 Nm).

18. Repeat Steps 2-17 for the other front wheel, if necessary.

19. Lower the vehicle.

1979-85 RX-7

▶ See Figures 114 and 115

➡️**The disc brake rotor and caliper must be removed to inspect the inner wheel bearing.**

1. Raise the front of the car and safely support it on jackstands.

2. Remove the front wheel.

3. Remove the brake caliper and its bracket. Do not disconnect the brake line from the caliper. Instead, suspend the caliper from the strut assembly with a piece of wire or twine.

➡️**Never allow the caliper to hang by the brake line.**

4. Remove the grease cap from the wheel hub. This can usually be done by prying between it and the wheel hub with a flat blade screwdriver. Be careful not to bend or gouge the cap.

5. Wipe some of the grease away and remove the cotter pin in the end of the spindle.

6. Remove the nut lock and adjusting nut, the thrust washer, and the outer wheel bearing. If the washer and bearing will not readily come out, try tilting the hub a little to one side.

7. Carefully pull the hub off the spindle.

➡️**The inner bearing is held in place by a grease seal. If you plan to inspect the inner bearing, you should have a new grease seal on hand, since replacement is recommended whenever the old one is removed.**

8. Remove the inner grease seal. This can usually be done using a screwdriver and prying from the inside of the seal. Do not try to force the screwdriver between the seal and the hub, as you may scratch the hub. Remove the inner bearing.

9. Clean both bearings in clean, unused solvent and inspect the bearings for wear. Clean all of the grease out of the hub with clean solvent and check the bearing outer race for wear. The outer race can be removed by driving it out using a suitable drift in the slots provided for that purpose.

➡️**Never remove the outer races unless you are replacing them.**

10. If the outer race was removed, install a new race into the hub, using either a tool made for that purpose, or a socket

of large enough diameter to press on the outside rim of the race only.

✳✳WARNING

Use care not to cock the bearing race in the hub. If it is not fully seated, the bearings cannot be adjusted properly.

11. Pack the inside area of the hub and cups with grease. Pack the inside of the grease cap, but do not yet install the cap into the hub.

12. Completely pack the inner bearing with grease, by placing a large glob of grease in your palm, then repeatedly sliding the bearing through the grease. The grease must be forced through the side of the bearing and in between each roller. Continue until the grease begins to ooze out the other side through the gaps between the rollers. Install the inner bearing into its race in the hub, then press a new grease seal over it.

13. Install the hub and rotor onto the spindle. Pack the outer bearing with grease in the same manner as the inner bearing, then install the outer bearing in the hub.

14. Apply a thin coat of grease to the washer and the threaded portion of the spindle, then loosely install the washer and adjusting nut.

15. Perform the bearing preload adjustment, as described later in this section.

16. Remove the wire or twine and install the brake caliper.

17. Install the wheel.

18. Repeat Steps 2-17 for the other front wheel, if necessary.

19. Lower the vehicle.

1986-89 RX-7

1. Raise the front of the car and safely support it on jackstands.

2. Remove the front wheel.

3. Remove the brake caliper and its bracket. Do not disconnect the brake line from the caliper. Instead, suspend the caliper from the strut assembly with a piece of wire or twine.

➡**Never allow the caliper to hang by the brake line.**

4. Remove the grease cap, cotter pin, set cover (nut lock) and hub nut.

5. Carefully remove the wheel hub and rotor disc from the wheel spindle, along with the thrust washer and outer wheel bearing.

6. Place the rotor disc on two wood blocks. Pry the oil seal from the wheel hub and remove the bearing. Discard the used oil seal.

7. Clean the inner and outer bearings in clean, unused solvent and inspect the bearings for wear. Clean all of the grease out of the hub with clean solvent and check the bearing outer races for wear.

➡**If the hub is worn, the inner and outer bearings and the hub must be replaced as an assembly.**

8. Pack the inner and outer bearing cones with lithium based, NLGI No. 2 wheel bearing grease.

9. Insert the inner bearing into the hub. Mount the hub on wood blocks and drive the new oil seal into the hub with a suitable press. The lip of the seal must be flush with the surface of the hub.

10. Install the wheel hub and rotor disc.

11. Pack the outer bearing with grease in the same manner as the inner bearing, then install the outer bearing in the hub.

12. Apply a thin coat of grease to the washer and the threaded portion of the spindle, then loosely install the thrust washer and hub nut.

13. Adjust the bearing preload, as described later in this section.

14. Remove the wire or twine and install the brake caliper. Torque the retaining bolts to 58-72 ft. lbs. (79-97 Nm)

15. Install the wheel.

16. Repeat Steps 2-15 for the other front wheel, if necessary.

17. Lower the vehicle.

PRELOAD ADJUSTMENT

➡**Front wheel bearing preload adjustment is not required on the 929, but make sure that you check the end-play, as previously described.**

Rear Wheel Drive GLC and 626

1. Raise the front end and safely support it on jackstands.

2. Remove the front wheel.

3. Remove the grease cap from the wheel hub. This can usually be done by prying between it and the wheel hub with a flat blade screwdriver. Be careful not to bend or gouge the cap.

4. Wipe some of the grease away, then remove and discard the cotter pin in the end of the spindle. Remove the nut lock.

5. Remove the disc brake caliper with the brake hose attached, and secure it to the strut spring with wire or twine.

6. Torque the adjusting nut to 14-18 ft. lbs. (19-24 Nm), then rotate the brake disc to seat the bearings.

7. Back off the adjusting nut about $1/6$ of a turn (approximately 60 degrees).

8. Install one hub bolt into the wheel hub to serve as an anchor for the spring scale.

9. Hook a spring scale onto the hub bolt.

10. Pull the scale squarely, until the hub just begins to rotate, and note the reading. The reading should be 0.33-1.32 lbs. (0.15-0.60 kg) for the GLC, or 0.77-1.92 lbs. (0.035-0.87 kg) for the 626. Tighten the adjusting nut until the proper reading is obtained. Remove the scale and hub bolt.

11. Place the castellated nut lock over the adjusting nut. Align one of the slots in the nut lock with the hole in the spindle. (If the holes do not align, tighten the adjusting nut only until the holes align.) Then, insert a new cotter pin and bend the ends to secure it in place.

➡**Always tighten the adjusting nut to its next castellation to align cotter pin holes of the nut lock and spindle shaft. NEVER loosen it.**

12. Repack the grease cap with fresh grease and install on the hub.

13. Remove the wire or twine and install the brake caliper assembly.

14. Install the wheel.

15. Repeat Steps 2-14 for the other front wheel, if necessary.

16. Lower the vehicle.

1979-85 RX-7

1. Raise the front end and safely support it on jackstands.

2. Remove the front wheel.

3. Remove the disc brake caliper with the brake hose attached, and secure it to the strut spring with wire or twine.

4. Remove the grease cap from the wheel hub. This can usually be done by prying between it and the wheel hub with a flat blade screwdriver. Be careful not to bend or gouge the cap.

5. Wipe some of the grease away, then remove and discard the cotter pin in the end of the spindle. Remove the nut lock.

6. Install one hub bolt into the wheel hub to serve as an anchor for the spring scale.

7. Tighten the adjusting nut to 18-22 ft. lbs. (24-30 Nm) to lock the wheel hub, then back off the nut until the wheel hub turns smoothly.

8. Rotate the hub back and forth three or four times to seat the bearings, then hook a spring scale onto the hub bolt.

9. Pull the scale at a 90 degree angle and note the reading when the hub starts to turn. The reading should be 0.99-1.43 lbs. (0.5-0.65 kg).

10. Either loosen or tighten the adjusting nut until the scale reads within the above range, then remove the scale and hub bolt.

11. Install the nut lock and insert a new cotter pin through the nut lock and spindle. (If the holes do not align, tighten the adjusting nut only until the holes align.)

➡Always tighten the adjusting nut to its next castellation to align cotter pin holes of the nut lock and spindle shaft. NEVER loosen it.

12. Bend up the ends of the cotter pin to secure it in place.

13. Repack the grease cap with fresh grease and install on the hub.

14. Remove the wire or twine and install the brake caliper assembly.

15. Install the wheel.

16. Repeat Steps 2-15 for the other front wheel, if necessary.

17. Lower the vehicle.

1986-89 RX-7

▶ **See Figure 119**

1. Raise the front end and safely support it on jackstands.

2. Remove the front wheel.

3. Remove the disc brake caliper assembly and secure it to the strut spring with wire or twine.

4. Remove the grease cap, cotter pin and set cover (nut lock). Discard the cotter pin.

5. Loosen the hub nut.

6. Using a torque wrench, tighten the hub nut to 14-22 ft. lbs. (19-30 Nm). Turn the wheel hub two or three times to seat the bearing.

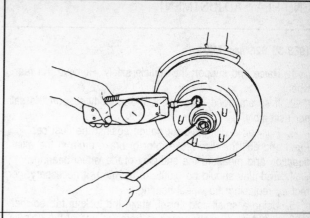

Fig. 119 Adjusting front wheel bearing preload using a spring scale

7. Loosen the hub nut again until it is finger-tight.

8. Connect a spring scale to one of the lug bolts. Pull on the spring scale at a 90 degree angle and measure the frictional force that is required to turn the wheel. The force (preload) should be 0.9-0.22 lbs. (0.4-1.0 kg).

9. Tighten the hub nut in small amounts until the reading on the scale is within the range, then remove the scale.

10. Position the set cover and secure it with a new cotter pin. (If the holes do not align, tighten the hub nut only until the holes align.)

➡Always tighten the adjusting nut to its next castellation to align cotter pin holes of the nut lock and spindle shaft. NEVER loosen it.

11. Repack the grease cap with fresh grease and install on the hub.

12. Remove the wire or twine and install the brake caliper assembly.

13. Install the wheel.

14. Repeat Steps 2-13 for the other front wheel, if necessary.

15. Lower the vehicle.

Rear Wheel Bearings

➡**Maintenance in this section covers the rear wheel bearings on front wheel drive cars. These are the only wheel bearings which require periodic lubrication on most front wheel drive vehicles covered by this manual. (Mazda does not require periodic lubrication of the rear wheel bearings on rear wheel drive vehicles covered by this manual.) For drive axle bearing information, please refer to Section 7 for rear wheel drive models or Section 8 for front wheel drive models.**

Applicable rear wheel bearings should be repacked with lithium grease (NGLI No. 1) every 30,000 miles (48,309 km) or 30 months, whichever comes first.

END-PLAY ADJUSTMENT

1983-89 626 and MX-6

1. Raise and support the vehicle safely. Remove the rear wheel.

2. If so equipped, disconnect and properly support the caliper assembly.

3. Position a dial indicator gauge against the dust cap. Push and pull the disc brake rotor or brake drum in the axial direction and measure the end-play of the wheel bearing.

4. End-play should be 0.008 in. (0.2mm). If necessary, correct by replacing the wheel bearing.

5. Using a small cold chisel, stake the locknut tab so that 0.08 in. (2mm) or more protrudes from the end of the spindle groove.

➡**Do not use a pointed tool for staking.**

6. If applicable, install the caliper assembly.

7. Install the wheel.

8. If necessary, remove the other rear wheel and repeat Steps 2-7 for that side.

9. Lower the vehicle.

PRELOAD ADJUSTMENT

323

1. Raise and support the vehicle safely. Remove the rear wheel.

2. Remove the dust cap and torque the locknut to 18-21 ft. lbs. (24-29 Nm).

3. Turn the wheel assembly to seat the bearing properly. Loosen the locknut slightly until it can be turned by hand.

4. Hook a spring seal to a wheel lug stud in order to measure the oil seal drag. Pull the spring scale squarely.

5. Note the oil seal drag value (when the wheel hub starts to turn) and record this measurement.

6. Add the oil seal drag value to the specified value of 0.6-1.9 lb. (2.6-8.5 N). This sum should represent the standard bearing preload of 1.30-4.34 inch lbs. (0.15-0.49 Nm). Turn the locknut slowly until the standard bearing preload is obtained while pulling the scale.

7. Using a small cold chisel, stake the locknut tab so that 0.08 in. (2mm) or more protrudes from the end of the spindle groove.

➡**Do not use a pointed tool for staking.**

8. Insert the dust cap, then install the wheel.

9. If necessary, remove the other rear wheel and repeat Steps 2-8 for that side.

10. Lower the vehicle.

REMOVAL & INSTALLATION

1. Raise and support the vehicle safely.

2. Remove the rear wheel and the grease cap.

3. Using a cape chisel and a hammer, raise the staked portion of the hub nut.

4. Remove and discard the hub nut.

5. Remove the brake drum or disc brake rotor assembly from the spindle. Please refer to Section 9 of this manual.

6. Using a small prybar, pry the grease seal from the brake drum or rotor and discard it.

7. Remove the snapring. Using a shop press, press the wheel bearing from the brake drum or rotor.

To install:

8. Using a shop press, press the new wheel bearing into the brake drum or rotor until it seats and install the snapring.

9. Lubricate the new seal lip with grease and install the seal, using a suitable installation tool.

10. Position the brake drum or rotor onto the wheel spindle.

11. Install a new locknut and tighten to specifications.

12. Check the wheel bearing end-play as follows:

   a. Rotate the drum or rotor to make sure there is no brake drag.

   b. Install a suitable dial indicator and check the wheel bearing end-play. End-play should not exceed 0.008 in. (0.2mm).

13. Using a dull cold chisel, stake the locknut, then install the grease cap.

➡**If the nut splits or cracks after staking, it must be replaced with a new nut.**

14. Install the wheel and tighten the lug nuts to 65-87 ft. lbs. (88-118 Nm).

15. If necessary, for the other rear wheel and repeat Steps 2-14 for that side.

16. Lower the vehicle.

TRAILER TOWING

General Recommendations

Your vehicle was primarily designed to carry passengers and cargo. It is important to remember that towing a trailer will place additional loads on your vehicle's engine, drive train, steering, braking and other systems. However, if you find it necessary to tow a trailer, using the proper equipment is a must.

Local laws may require specific equipment such as trailer brakes or fender mounted mirrors. Check your local laws.

Trailer Weight

The weight of the trailer is the most important factor. A good weight-to-horsepower ratio is about 35:1, which is 35 lbs. of GCW (Gross Combined Weight) for every horsepower your engine develops. Multiply the engine's rated horsepower by 35 and subtract the weight of the car passengers and luggage. The result is the approximate ideal maximum weight you should tow, although a numerically higher axle ratio can help compensate for heavier weight.

Hitch (Tongue) Weight

▶ **See Figure 120**

Figure the hitch weight to select a proper hitch. Hitch weight is usually 9-11% of the trailer gross weight and should be measured with the trailer loaded. Hitches fall into various categories: Those that mount on the frame and rear bumper, and the bolt-on/weld-on distribution type used for larger trailers are acceptable. However, axle mounted or clamp-on bumper hitches should never be used.

Check the gross weight rating of your trailer. Tongue weight is usually figured as 10% of gross trailer weight. Therefore, a trailer with a maximum gross weight of 2,000 lbs. will have a maximum tongue weight of 200 lbs. Class I trailers fall into this category. Class II trailers are those with a gross weight rating of 2,000-3,000 lbs., while Class III trailers fall into the 3,500-6,000 lbs. category. Class IV trailers are those over 6,000 lbs. and are for use with fifth wheel trucks only.

When you've determined the hitch that you'll need, follow the manufacturer's installation instructions exactly, especially when it comes to fastener torques. The hitch will be subjected to a lot of stress and good hitches come with hardened bolts. **Never** substitute an inferior bolt for a hardened bolt.

Cooling

ENGINE

One of the most common, if not THE most common, problems associated with trailer towing is engine overheating. If you have a standard cooling system, without an expansion tank, you'll definitely need to get an aftermarket expansion tank kit, preferably one with at least a 2 quart (1.89 liter) capacity. These kits are easily installed on the radiator's overflow hose, and come with a pressure cap designed for expansion tanks.

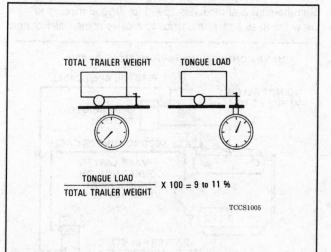

TONGUE LOAD / **TOTAL TRAILER WEIGHT** × 100 = 9 to 11 %

TCCS1005

Fig. 120 Calculating proper tongue weight for your trailer

Another helpful accessory for vehicles using a belt-driven radiator fan is a flex fan. These fans are large diameter units which are designed to provide more airflow at low speeds, with blades that have deeply cupped surfaces. The blades then flex, or flatten out, at high speeds, when less cooling air is needed. These fans are far lighter in weight than stock fans, requiring less horsepower to drive them. Also, they are far quieter than stock fans. If you do decide to replace your stock fan with a flex fan, note that if your car has a fan clutch, a spacer will be needed between the flex fan and water pump hub.

Aftermarket engine oil coolers are helpful for prolonging engine oil life and reducing overall engine temperatures. Both of these factors increase engine life. While not absolutely necessary in towing Class I and some Class II trailers, they are recommended for heavier Class II and all Class III towing. Engine oil cooler systems consists of an adapter, screwed on in place of the oil filter, a remote filter mounting and a multi-tube, finned heat exchanger, which is mounted in front of the radiator or air conditioning condenser.

TRANSMISSION

An automatic transmission is usually recommended for trailer towing. Modern automatics have proven reliable and, of course, easy to operate, in trailer towing. The increased load of a trailer, however, causes an increase in the temperature of the automatic transmission fluid. Heat is the worst enemy of an automatic transmission. As the temperature of the fluid increases, the life of the fluid decreases.

It is essential, therefore, that you install an automatic transmission oil cooler. The oil cooler, which consists of a multi-tube, finned heat exchanger, is usually installed in front of the radiator or air conditioning condenser, and is connected inline with the transmission's radiator cooling tank inlet line. Follow the cooler manufacturer's installation instructions.

Select an oil cooler of sufficient capacity, based upon the combined gross weights of the towing vehicle and trailer.

Cooler manufacturers recommend that you use an aftermarket cooler in addition to, and not instead of, the present cooling tank in your radiator. If you do want to use it in place of the radiator cooling tank, get a cooler at least two sizes larger than normally necessary.

➡**A transmission oil cooler can, sometimes, cause slow or harsh shifting in the transmission during cold weather, until the fluid has a chance to warm up to normal operating temperature. Some coolers can be purchased with, or retrofitted with, a temperature bypass valve which will allow fluid flow through the cooler only when the fluid has reached a designated operating temperature.**

Handling A Trailer

Towing a trailer with ease and safety requires a certain amount of experience. It's a good idea to learn the feel of a trailer by practicing turning, stopping and backing in an open area such as an empty parking lot.

JUMP STARTING A DEAD BATTERY

Whenever a vehicle must be jump started, precautions must be followed in order to prevent the possibility of personal injury. Remember that batteries contain a small amount of explosive hydrogen gas which is a byproduct of battery charging. Sparks should always be avoided when working around batteries, especially when attaching jumper cables. To minimize the possibility of accidental sparks, follow the procedure carefully.

✳✳WARNING

NEVER hook the batteries up in a series circuit or the entire electrical system will go up in smoke, especially the starter!

Cars equipped with a diesel engine utilize two 12-volt batteries, one on either side of the engine compartment. The batteries are connected in a parallel circuit (positive terminal to positive terminal, negative terminal to negative terminal). Hooking the batteries up in a parallel circuit increases battery cranking power, without increasing total battery voltage output. Output remains at 12 volts. On the other hand, hooking two 12-volt batteries up in a series circuit (positive terminal to negative terminal, positive terminal to negative terminal) increases total battery output to 24 volts (12 volts plus 12 volts).

Jump Starting Precautions

1. Be sure that both batteries are of the same voltage. All vehicles covered by this manual and most vehicles on the road today utilize a 12 volt charging system.
2. Be sure that both batteries are of the same polarity (have the same terminal grounded; in most cases NEGATIVE).
3. Be sure that the vehicles are not touching or a short circuit could occur.
4. On serviceable batteries, be sure the vent cap holes are not obstructed.
5. Do not smoke or allow sparks anywhere near the batteries.
6. In cold weather, make sure the battery electrolyte is not frozen. This can occur more readily in a battery that has been in a state of discharge.
7. Do not allow electrolyte to contact your skin or clothing.

Jump Starting Procedure

◆ See Figure 121

1. Make sure that the voltages of the 2 batteries are the same. Most batteries and charging systems are of the 12 volt variety.
2. Pull the jumping vehicle (with the good battery) into a position so the jumper cables can reach the dead battery and that vehicle's engine. Make sure that the vehicles do NOT touch.

3. Place the transmissions of both vehicles in **NEUTRAL** or **PARK**, as applicable, then firmly set their parking brakes.

➡**If necessary for safety reasons, both vehicle's hazard lights may be operated throughout the entire procedure without significantly increasing the difficulty of jump starting the dead battery.**

4. Turn all lights and accessories off on both vehicles. Make sure the ignition switches on both vehicles are turned to the **OFF** position.
5. Cover the battery cell caps with a rag, but do not cover the terminals.
6. Make sure the terminals on both batteries are clean and free of corrosion or proper electrical connection will be impeded. If necessary, clean the battery terminals before proceeding.
7. Identify the positive (+) and negative (-) terminals on both batteries
8. Connect the first jumper cable to the positive (+) terminal of the dead battery, then connect the other end of that cable to the positive (+) terminal of the booster (good) battery.
9. Connect one end of the other jumper cable to the negative (-) terminal of the booster battery and the other cable clamp to an engine bolt head, alternator bracket or other solid, metallic point on the dead battery's engine. Try to pick a ground on the engine that is positioned away from the battery, in order to minimize the possibility of the 2 clamps touching should one loosen during the procedure. DO NOT connect this clamp to the negative (-) terminal of the bad battery.

✳✳CAUTION

Be very careful to keep the jumper cables away from moving parts (cooling fan, belts, etc.) on both engines.

10. Check to make sure that the cables are routed away from any moving parts, then start the donor vehicle's engine. Run the engine at moderate speed for several minutes to allow the dead battery a chance to receive some initial charge.

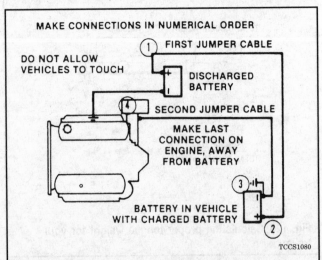

Fig. 121 Connect jumper cables to the batteries and engine ground in the order shown

TCCS1080

11. With the donor vehicle's engine still running slightly above idle, try to start the vehicle with the dead battery. Crank the engine for no more than 10 seconds at a time and let the starter cool for at least 20 seconds between tries. If the vehicle does not start within 3 tries, it is likely that something else is also wrong or that the battery needs additional time to charge.

12. Once the vehicle is started, allow it to run at idle for a few seconds to make sure that it is properly operating.

13. Turn on the headlights, heater blower and, if equipped, the rear defroster of both vehicles in order to reduce the severity of voltage spikes and subsequent risk of damage to the vehicles' electrical systems when the cables are disconnected.

14. Carefully disconnect the cables in the reverse order of connection. Start with the negative cable that is attached to the engine ground, then the negative cable on the donor battery. Disconnect the positive cable from the donor battery, then disconnect the positive cable from the formerly dead battery. Be careful when disconnecting the cables from the positive terminals not to allow the alligator clips to touch any metal on either vehicle or a short circuit and sparks will occur.

TOWING THE VEHICLE

Proper towing equipment is necessary to prevent damage to the vehicle during any towing operation. Laws and regulations applicable to vehicles in tow should always be observed, and the recommended procedures must be used.

Before towing the vehicle, release the parking brake, place the shift lever in Neutral, and set the ignition key in the "ACC" position. As a rule, vehicles should be towed with their drive wheels off the ground. If excessive vehicle damage or other conditions prevent towing a vehicle with its drive wheels up, use wheel dollies. With all four wheels on the ground, the vehicle should only be towed forward. (Mazda does not recommend towing the 1989 626/MX-6 in either direction with all four wheels on the ground.) When towing a vehicle with four wheels on the ground, do not exceed 35 mph (56 Km/h) or travel more than 50 miles (80 Km); otherwise, you risk damaging the transmission/transaxle.

✳✳WARNING

If the towing speed must exceed 35 mph (56 km/h), or the towing distance must exceed 50 miles (80 km), be sure to take the appropriate precautions.

Rear Wheel Drive Models

➡**The front or rear towing hook(s) should only be used in an emergency situation, such as pulling the vehicle from a ditch, snowbank or mud.**

WITH MANUAL TRANSMISSION

If the transmission, rear axle and steering system are not damaged, the vehicle may be towed on all four wheels. If any of these components are damaged, use a towing dolly.

WITH AUTOMATIC TRANSMISSION

If excessive vehicle damage or other conditions prevent towing a vehicle with its rear (drive) wheels up, use wheel dollies. With all four wheels on the ground, the vehicle should only be towed forward. In this case, the vehicle cannot be towed at a speed exceeding 35 mph (56 Km/h) for more than 50 miles (80 Km) without danger of damaging the transmission.

✳✳WARNING

If the towing speed must exceed 35 mph (56 km/h), or the towing distance must exceed 50 miles (80 km), be sure to either place the rear wheels on a dolly, raise the rear wheels off the ground, or disconnect the propeller shaft.

➡**If the transmission or rear axle is inoperative, tow the vehicle with its rear wheels off the ground or have the propeller shaft disconnected.**

Front Wheel Drive Models

➡**The rear towing hook should only be used in an emergency situation, such as pulling the vehicle from a ditch, snowbank or mud.**

➡**On 1988-89 626 and MX-6 models, do not use the hook loops under the front and rear of the vehicle for towing purposes. These hooks are designed ONLY for transport tie-down. If tie-down hook loops are used for towing, the front/rear skirt and bumper will be damaged.**

If excessive vehicle damage or other conditions prevent towing a vehicle with its front (drive) wheels up, use wheel dollies. With all four wheels on the ground, the vehicle should **only** be towed **forward**. In this case, the vehicle cannot be towed at a speed exceeding 35 mph (56 Km/h) for more than 50 miles (80 Km) without danger of damaging the transaxle.

➡**Mazda does not recommend towing the 1989 626/MX-6 with all four wheels on the ground.**

✳✳WARNING

Do not tow the vehicle backward with the front wheels on the ground, as this could damage the transaxle's internal parts. Do not start or run the engine while the vehicle is being towed. If the towing speed must exceed 35 mph (56 km/h), or the towing distance must exceed 50 miles (80 km), be sure to either place the front wheels on a dolly or raise them off the ground.

➡**On vehicles equipped with 4-wheel steering, be sure that the rear wheels are in the straight-ahead position when towing with the front wheels raised.**

323 With Four Wheel Drive

➡The rear towing hook should only be used in an emergency situation, such as pulling the vehicle from a ditch, snowbank or mud.

❋❋WARNING

The center differential must NEVER be in the "Lock" position when the vehicle is being towed.

If excessive vehicle damage or other conditions prevent towing the vehicle with its drive wheels up, use wheel dollies.

JACKING

▶ **See Figures 122, 123, 124, 125 and 126**

Vehicles covered by this manual were factory-equipped with a scissors jack. This jack is used by positioning it under a jacking point on the side sill, then turning the screw to raise/lower the vehicle. Specific instructions for the use of this jack, including the jacking points, are found in the owner's manual (and often on stickers attached to the jack or in the luggage compartment). Although this type of jack is suitable for tire changing, you might need a better jack for maintenance.

If you plan to use a jack for more than the occasional tire change, consider a floor jack. Unlike the scissors jack, a floor jack relies on hydraulics to lift its load. After the floor jack is rolled under a lifting member, you simply pump the handle for easy lifting. This will not only save some time, but could also save your back! Generally, when lifting the front of a vehicle, the floor jack should be positioned under the center of the crossmember. When lifting the rear of a vehicle, the floor jack should usually be placed under the center of the crossmember

With all four wheels on the ground, the vehicle should **only** be towed **forward**. In this case, the vehicle cannot be towed at a speed exceeding 35 mph (56 Km/h) for more than 50 miles (80 Km) without danger of damaging the transaxle.

❋❋WARNING

Do not tow the vehicle backward with the front wheels on the ground, as this could damage the transaxle's internal parts. Do not start or run the engine while the vehicle is being towed. If the towing speed must exceed 35 mph (56 km/h), or the towing distance must exceed 50 miles (80 km), be sure to either place the front wheels on a dolly or raise them off the ground.

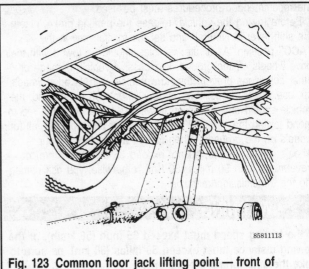

Fig. 123 Common floor jack lifting point — front of vehicle

or differential. For specific information on floor jack use, please refer to the jack manufacturer's instructions.

➡Since not all vehicles utilize the same lifting points, it is imperative to verify correct placement before raising the vehicle. Failure to observe the manufacturer's recommended lifting points and/or procedures can jeopardize you as well as the vehicle.

Although the specifics vary with the jack being used, there are some general precautions to observe when jacking:
• NEVER climb underneath a vehicle supported only by a jack. ALWAYS use jackstands as **additional** means of support.
• NEVER use cinder blocks or wood to support a vehicle. They could crumble, causing personal injury or death.
• ALWAYS keep the car on level ground when jacking it. Otherwise, the car may roll or fall off the jack.
• When raising the FRONT of the car, set the parking brake and block the rear wheels. When raising the REAR of the car, block the front wheels instead.

➡Never support the vehicle using a suspension member or underbody panel; since damage and/or injury could occur.

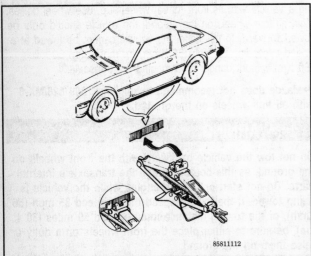

Fig. 122 The scissor jack's saddle engages a jacking point on the side sill — all models

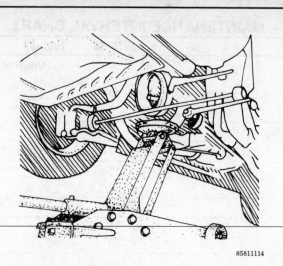

Fig. 124 Common floor jack lifting point — rear of vehicle

Fig. 125 Common jackstand position — front of vehicle

Fig. 126 Common jackstand position — rear of vehicle

MAINTENANCE INTERVAL CHART

Operation	1978–80	1981–82	1983–84	1985–86	1987–89
ENGINE		(Number of months or miles in thousands—whichever comes first)			
Air cleaner element—Replace	30	30	30	30	30
Clean	2	2	—	—	—
Charcoal canister filter—Check or replace	25	25	—	—	—
Fuel filter—Replace	12	12	30	30	60
Drive belts—Inspect	15	15	30	30	30
Replace	②	②	②	②	②
Battery check	7.5	7.5	⑨	⑨	⑨
Cooling system—Check	7.5	7.5	15	15	30
Drain and refill	30	30	30	30	30
Engine oil—Level check	①	①	①	①	①
Change oil	7.5	7.5	7.5	7.5	④
Change filter	7.5	7.5	7.5	7.5	④
Change bypass filter ⑮	—	—	—	15	—
Spark plug replacement	30㉔	30	30⑩	60	30
Ignition points and condenser	10	—	—	—	—
Timing adjustment	30	30	30	30	30
PCV valve replacement	30	30	—	—	—
Valve clearance adjustment	15	15	15	15	15
Intake, exhaust and cylinder head bolts adjustment	③	③	15⑪	—	—
Timing belt replacement (miles only)	—	—	60	60⑯	60
CHASSIS					
Manual transmission fluid level—Check	7.5	7.5	—	—	—
Replace	⑤	⑤	⑫	⑰	㉑
Automatic transmission fluid level check	7.5	7.5	⑤	⑱	⑱
Front wheel bearings—Lubricate	30	30	30⑬	30⑬	30⑬
Rear axle lubricant check	⑤	⑤	—	—	—
Steering gear lubricant check	⑥	⑥	15	⑲	15
Tire pressures	⑦	⑦	⑦	⑦	⑦
Tire rotation	7.5	7.5	4	7.5	7.5
Ball joint lubrication	—	—	⑭	⑲	⑭
Front steering linkage inspection	30	30	15	15	30
Master cylinder fluid	⑧	⑧	⑧	⑳	⑳
Brake system inspection (lining)	7.5	7.5	15	㉒	㉓

① Each fuel stop
② Replace as necessary
③ 1st 15,000 miles, then every 30,000 miles
④ 7.5—Non-Turbo; 5.0—Turbo
⑤ 1st 7,500 miles, then every 30,000 miles
⑥ 1st 2,000 miles, then every 15,000 miles
⑦ Once every month
⑧ Check level at least every 4,000 miles.
  It is recommended by the manufacturer that the fluid be changed every 30,000 miles.
⑨ Check indicator if so equipped
⑩ Clean and inspect at 15,000 mile intervals
⑪ Torque head bolts only
⑫ Checking not required—replace every 30,000 miles
⑬ Rear wheel bearings also require repacking on 4WD vehicles

⑭ Inspect at 30,000 mile/30 month intervals—no lubrication required
⑮ Diesel only
⑯ Diesel—Replace both timing belts at 100,000 miles
⑰ Replace at 30,000 miles/30 months
⑱ First 3,000 miles, then every 30,000 miles/30 months
⑲ Inspect at 30,000 mile/30 month intervals; no lubrication required.
  Diesel intervals for inspection only—15,000 miles/15 months.
⑳ Inspect fluid level at 15,000 mile intervals, replace at 30,000 mile intervals
㉑ Replace at 60,000 miles/60 months
㉒ Inspect drum brakes at 15, disc brakes at 7.5
㉓ 1987–88: Inspect drum brakes at 30, disc brakes at 15
  1989: Inspect drum brakes at 30, disc brakes at 30
㉔ 10,000 miles/10 months for vehicles with a conventional (breaker point) ignition system

858110C4

CAPACITIES

Year	Model	Engine ID/VIN	Engine Displacement Liters (cc)	Engine Crankcase with Filter (qts.)	Transmission (pts.)			Drive Axle (pts.)	Fuel Tank (gal.)	Cooling System (qts.)
					4-Spd	5-Spd	Auto.			
1978	GLC	TC	1.3 (1272)	①	2.8	3.6	12.0	1.6	10.6	5.8
1979	GLC	E5	1.4 (1415)	①	2.8	3.6	12.0	2.2	10.6	5.8
	626	MA	2.0 (1970)	4.1	3.0	3.6	13.2	2.6	14.5	7.9
	RX-7	12A	1.1 (1146)	5.5	3.6	3.6	13.2	2.6	14.5	10.0
1980	GLC	E5	1.4 (1415)	①	2.8	3.6	12.0	2.2	10.6	5.8
	626	MA	2.0 (1970)	4.1	3.0	3.6	13.2	2.6	14.5	7.9
	RX-7	12A	1.1 (1146)	5.5	3.6	3.6	13.2	2.6	14.5	10.0
1981	GLC	E5	1.5 (1490)	②	6.8	6.8	12.0	—	11.1	5.8
	GLC Wagon	E5	1.5 (1490)	②	2.8	3.6	12.0	1.6	11.9	5.8
	626	MA	2.0 (1970)	4.1	—	3.6	13.2	2.6	14.5	7.9
	RX-7	12A	1.1 (1146)	5.5	—	3.6	13.2	2.6	16.4	10.0
1982	GLC	E5	1.5 (1490)	②	6.8	6.8	12.0	—	11.1	5.8
	GLC Wagon	E5	1.5 (1490)	②	2.8	3.6	12.0	1.6	11.9	5.8
	626	MA	2.0 (1970)	3.8	—	3.6	13.2	2.6	14.5	7.9
	RX-7	12A	1.1 (1146)	5.5	—	4.2	13.2	2.6	16.4	10.0
1983	GLC	E5	1.5 (1490)	3.9	6.8	6.8	12.0	—	11.1	5.8
	GLC Wagon	E5	1.5 (1490)	3.9	2.8	3.6	12.0	1.6	11.9	5.8
	626	FE	2.0 (1998)	4.8	—	7.2	12.0	—	15.6	7.4
	RX-7	12A	1.1 (1146)	5.2	—	4.2	13.2	2.6	16.6	10.0
1984	GLC	E5	1.5 (1490)	3.9	6.8	6.8	12.0	—	11.1	5.8
	626	FE	2.0 (1998)	4.8	—	7.2	12.0	—	15.6	7.4
	RX-7 (Carbureted)	12A	1.1 (1146)	4.9	—	4.2	15.8	2.6③	16.4	10.0
	RX-7 (Fuel Injected)	13B	1.3 (1308)	6.1	—	4.2	15.8	2.6③	16.4	10.0
1985	GLC	E5	1.5 (1490)	3.9	6.8	6.8	12.0	—	11.1	5.8
	626 (Gasoline)	FE	2.0 (1998)	4.8	—	7.2	12.0	—	15.6	7.4
	626 (Diesel)	RF	2.0 (1998)	6.8	—	7.2	12.0	—	15.6	9.5
	RX-7 (Carbureted)	12A	1.1 (1146)	4.9	—	4.2	15.8	2.6③	16.4	10.0
	RX-7 (Fuel Injected)	13B	1.3 (1308)	6.1	—	4.2	15.8	2.6③	16.4	10.0
1986	323	B6	1.6 (1597)	3.6	6.8	6.8	12.0	—	11.9	5.3④
	626	FE	2.0 (1998)	4.5	—	7.2	12.0	—	15.9	7.4
	626 Turbo	FE	2.0 (1998)	4.5	—	7.2	12.0	—	15.9	7.4
	RX-7	13B	1.3 (1308)	6.1	—	4.2	15.8	2.8	16.6	7.7
	RX-7 Turbo	13B	1.3 (1308)	6.1	—	4.2	—	2.8	16.6	9.2

858110C6

CAPACITIES

Year	Model	Engine ID/VIN	Engine Displacement Liters (cc)	Engine Crankcase with Filter (qts.)	Transmission (pts.) 4-Spd	5-Spd	Auto.	Drive Axle (pts.)	Fuel Tank (gal.)	Cooling System (qts.)
1987	323	B6	1.6 (1597)	3.6	—	6.8	12.0	—	11.7	5.3④
	626	FE	2.0 (1998)	4.5	—	7.2	12.6	—	15.9	7.4
	626 Turbo	FE	2.0 (1998)	4.5	—	7.2	12.6	—	15.9	7.4
	RX-7	13B	1.3 (1308)	6.1	—	5.2	15.8	2.8	16.6	7.7
	RX-7 Turbo	13B	1.3 (1308)	6.1	—	5.2	15.8	2.8	16.6	9.2
1988	323	B6	1.6 (1597)	3.6	—	6.8	13.4⑦	—	12.7	5.3④
	323 Turbo	B6	1.6 (1597)	3.8	—	7.2⑥	13.4	—	13.2	6.3
	626	F2	2.2 (2184)	4.9	—	7.0	14.4	—	15.9	7.9
	626 Turbo	F2	2.2 (2184)	4.9	—	7.8	14.4	—	15.9⑨	7.9
	MX-6	F2	2.2 (2184)	4.9	—	7.0	14.4	—	15.9	7.9
	MX-6 Turbo	F2	2.2 (2184)	4.9	—	7.8	14.4	—	15.9	7.9
	929	JE	3.0 (2954)	5.7	—	5.2	15.4	2.8	18.5	9.9
	RX-7	13B	1.3 (1308)	6.1	—	4.2	15.8	2.8	16.6	7.7
	RX-7 Turbo	13B	1.3 (1308)	6.1	—	5.2	15.8	2.8	16.6	9.2
1989	323	B6	1.6 (1597)	3.6	—	6.8	13.4⑦	—	12.7	5.3④
	323 Turbo	B6	1.6 (1597)	3.8	—	7.1⑥	13.4	—	12.7⑧	6.3
	626	F2	2.2 (2184)	4.9	—	7.0	14.4	—	15.9	7.9
	626 Turbo	F2	2.2 (2184)	4.9	—	7.8	14.4	—	15.9	7.9
	MX-6	F2	2.2 (2184)	4.9	—	7.0	14.4	—	15.9⑨	7.9
	MX-6 Turbo	F2	2.2 (2184)	4.9	—	7.8	14.4	—	15.9⑨	7.9
	929	JE	3.0 (2954)	5.7	—	5.2	15.4	2.8	18.5	9.9⑤
	RX-7	13B	1.3 (1308)	6.1	—	4.2	15.8	2.8	16.6	7.7
	RX-7 Turbo	13B	1.3 (1308)	6.1	—	5.2	15.8	2.8	16.6	9.2

① Add 3.2 qts., run engine, shut off and check level; add to FULL mark on stick
② Add 3.9 qts., run engine, shut off and check level; add to FULL mark on stick
③ Applies to standard differential; limited slip differential: 3.4 pts.
④ Applies to manual transaxle; automatic: 6.3
⑤ Applies to manual transmission; automatic: 9.5
⑥ With 4WD: transaxle capacity—7.6 pts.
    transfer carrier capacity—1 pt.
⑦ Station Wagon: 12.0 pts.
⑧ Applies to 2WD; 4WD: 13.2 gallons
⑨ With 4 wheel steering: 15.0 gallons

858110C7

2

ENGINE PERFORMANCE AND TUNE-UP

TUNE-UP PROCEDURES

The tune-up is a routine maintenance operation which is essential for the efficient and economical operation, as well as for the long life of your car's engine. The interval between tune-ups is a variable factor which depends upon the way you drive your car, the conditions under which you drive it (weather, road type, etc.), and the type of engine installed in your car. It is generally correct to say that no car should be driven more than 30,000 miles (48,309 km) between tune-ups, especially in this era of emission controls. If you plan to drive your car extremely hard or under severe weather conditions, the tune-ups should be performed at closer intervals. High performance engines require more frequent tuning than other engines, regardless of weather or driving conditions. Maintenance intervals will be provided whenever possible, but for a complete and comprehensive breakdown, please refer to the Maintenance Interval Charts in Section 1 of this manual.

A small note book or log is recommended for recording the completion of all regular maintenance activities, as well as their dates and intervals.

Spark Plugs

A typical spark plug consists of a metal shell surrounding a ceramic insulator. A metal electrode extends downward through the center of the insulator and protrudes a small distance. Located at the end of the plug and attached to the side of the outer metal shell is the side electrode. The side electrode bends in at a 90 degree angle so that its tip is even with, and parallel to, the tip of the center electrode. The distance between these two electrodes (measured in thousandths of an inch or millimeters) is called the spark plug gap. The spark plug in no way produces a spark but merely provides a gap across which the current can arc. The coil produces between 20,000 and 40,000 volts. This high voltage travels to the distributor where it is routed through the spark plug wires to the spark plugs. The current passes along the center electrode and jumps the gap to the side electrode; in so doing, it ignites the air/fuel mixture in the combustion chamber.

For the rotary engine used in the RX-7, each of the two rotors in the engine is equipped with both a leading and a trailing spark plug. The leading spark plug fires first, igniting the fuel/air mixture as in conventional engines; the trailing plug fires a moment later, igniting any unburned mixture. This aids in more complete combustion and helps to reduce exhaust emissions.

➡On 1986-89 models, the leading and trailing side spark plugs are different and must be installed in the proper position. Trailing side spark plugs are identified by blue lines on the top of the porcelain section of the plug.

The 1979-80 RX-7 uses a special three electrode spark plug for better ignition characteristics. The 1981-85 model uses a four electrode spark plug which, due to rotor housing modification, is the only type spark plug which can be used. On 1986-89 models, the spark plug incorporates a design that deletes the side electrodes and only uses the center electrode to produce a spark. Spark plug gap on these models is not adjustable. Use only the appropriate special type of spark plug for any RX-7 model.

HEAT RANGE

◗ **See Figure 1**

Spark plug heat range is the ability of the plug to dissipate heat. The longer the insulator (or the farther it extends into the engine), the hotter the plug will operate; the shorter the insulator the cooler it will operate. A plug that absorbs little heat and remains too cold will quickly accumulate deposits of oil and carbon since it is not hot enough to burn them off. This leads to plug fouling and consequently to misfiring. A plug that absorbs too much heat will have no deposits, but, due to the excessive heat, the electrodes will burn away quickly and in some instances, pre-ignition may result. Pre-ignition takes place when plug tips get so hot that they glow sufficiently to ignite the fuel/air mixture before the actual spark occurs. This early ignition will usually cause a pinging during low speeds and heavy loads.

The general rule of thumb for choosing the correct heat range when picking a spark plug is: if most of your driving is long distance, high speed travel, use a colder plug; if most of your driving is stop and go, use a hotter plug. Original equipment plugs are compromise plugs, and most people never have reason to change their plugs from the factory recommended heat range.

➡Some of the spark plugs listed in this chapter are especially designed and built for use in the Mazda rotary engine. Use only these plugs; do NOT substitute a different type of plug.

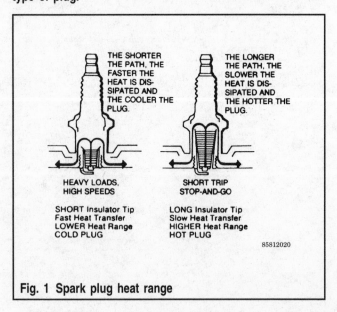

Fig. 1 Spark plug heat range

REMOVAL & INSTALLATION

A set of spark plugs usually requires replacement after about 10,000 miles (16,103 km) on cars with conventional ignition systems and after about 20,000-30,000 miles (32,206-48,309 km) on cars with electronic ignition, depending on your style of driving. In normal operation, plug gap increases about 0.001 in. (0.025mm) for every 1,000-2,500 miles (1,610-4,026 km). As the gap increases, the plug's voltage requirement also increases. It requires a greater voltage to jump the wider gap and about two-to-three times as much voltage to fire a plug at high speeds than at idle.

➡ **Special platinum tipped spark plugs may be available for some of the vehicles covered by this manual. These plugs wear at a greatly reduced rate when compared with conventional plugs. Refer to the plug manufacturers recommendations for service intervals, though keep in mind that periodic inspection is always a good idea.**

On the RX-7, all of the ignition components for the leading spark plugs have darker colored caps on their wires than the trailing spark plug components. Even so, when replacing the spark plugs, it would be wise to remove and replace one plug at a time and reconnect its cable before moving on to the next plug. The spark plug holes can be identified by the letter and number codes adjacent to them. **T1** means trailing spark plug, first rotor, **L1** means leading spark plug, first rotor, etc.

Regardless of your type of vehicle and its ignition system, it is advisable to only work on one spark plug at a time. Don't start by removing the plug wires all at once, because unless you number them, they may become mixed up. Take a minute before you begin and number the wires with tape. The best location for numbering is near where the wires come out of the cap.

Except RX-7

▶ **See Figures 2, 3, 4, 5, 6, 7, 8 and 9**

1. Grasp the spark plug wire by its boot and twist to remove the boot and wire from the plug. Do not pull on the wire itself, as this will ruin the wire.

2. Remove the spark plug using the proper size deep-well socket. Turn the socket counterclockwise to remove the plug. Be sure the socket goes all the way onto the plug to avoid breaking the plug, or rounding off its hexagonal wrenching surface. If the spark plug is equipped with a crushable gasket, make sure that this gasket is removed with the plug.

3. Once the plug is out, inspect it for abnormal wear and note any problems. Check the plug against the accompanying chart to determine engine condition. This is crucial since plug readings are vital signs of engine condition.

4. Replace any plug that shows excessive wear or damage.

➡ **Unless any underlying problem is corrected, a replacement spark plug may also fail prematurely.**

5. Use a round wire feeler gauge to check the plug gap. The correct size gauge should pass through the electrode gap with a slight drag. If you're in doubt, try one size smaller and one larger. The smaller gauge should go through easily while the larger one shouldn't go through at all. If the gap is incorrect, use the electrode bending tool on the end of the gauge

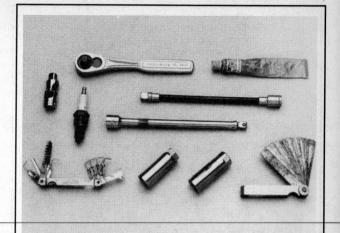

TCCS1212

Fig. 2 A variety of tools and gauges is needed for spark plug service

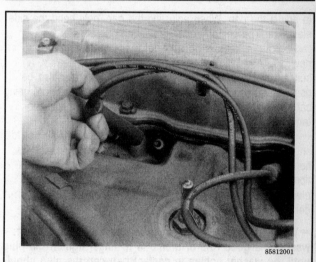

85812001

Fig. 3 Grasp and pull the spark plug wire by the boot only

85812002

Fig. 4 Use the correct size deep-well socket and an extension to remove spark plugs

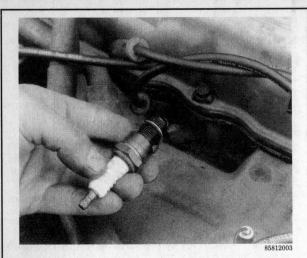

Fig. 5 Be sure to remove the crushable gasket with the plug

to adjust the gap. When adjusting the gap, only bend the side electrode. The center electrode is non-adjustable.

6. Squirt a drop of penetrating oil on the threads of the new plug and install it. Don't oil the threads too heavily. A suitable high temperature anti-seize compound may also be used. Turn the plug in clockwise by hand until it is snug, being careful not to cross-thread the plug. If you encounter resistance, remove the plug and try again.

7. When the plug is finger-tight, use a deep-well socket to snug it. If the plug manufacturer provided a torque specification, use a torque wrench to tighten the plug. If no specification is available, tighten the plug carefully. An overtightened plug may distort the gap, or worse, may snap off in the cylinder head.

➡When tightening plugs which are equipped with crush washers, a good rule of thumb is to finger-tighten the plug until the washer comes in contact between the plug shoulder and the cylinder head. Then tighten the plug ¼ turn to flatten the crush washer.

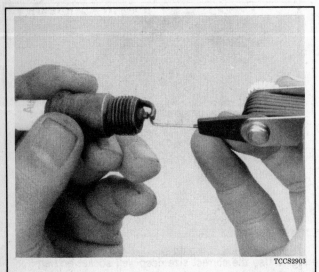

Fig. 6 Checking the spark plug gap with a feeler gauge

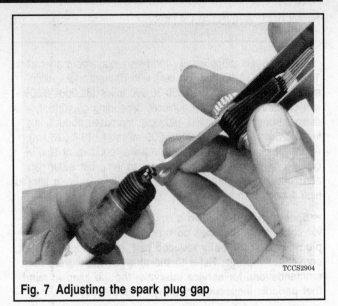

Fig. 7 Adjusting the spark plug gap

8. Install the plug boot over the plug, so that the terminal inside the boot firmly engages the end of the plug. Proceed to the next spark plug.

RX-7
▶ See Figures 3, 4, 10, 11 and 12

1. Remove the spark plug cable. Do not yank on the cable to remove it; firmly grasp the spark plug boot at the elbow and pull it straight off.

2. Use a brush or rag to clean the area around the spark plug. Make sure that all the dirt is removed so that none will enter the cylinder after the plug is removed.

➡If compressed air is available, use it to blow any dirt or debris away from the spark plug hole. Be sure to wear safety goggles when using compressed air.

3. Using a deep-well socket wrench, remove the spark plug from the engine. If the spark plug is equipped with a crushable gasket, make sure that this gasket is removed with the plug.

4. For 1979-85 models, clean the spark plugs with a wire brush or a spark plug cleaning machine and replace if any of the electrodes are burned away or badly eroded.

➡On 1986-89 RX-7 models, do not use a spark plug cleaning machine because sand particles may become trapped in the tip of the plug and damage the plug.

5. Measure the electrode gap of each plug using a wire gauge (do not use a flat feeler gauge). On 1979-80 models, the gap for each of the three electrodes should be 0.037-0.041 in. (0.95-1.05mm). On 1981-85 models, the gap for each of the four electrodes should be 0.053-0.057 in. (1.35-1.45mm). If not, replace the plug. Do not attempt to adjust the electrode gap; you may crack and/or break the insulator or the electrodes. On 1986-89 models, measure the gap from the outer beveled edge of the plug to the edge of the center electrode. If the gap is not 0.08 in. (2.0mm), replace the plug.

6. Apply a thread lubricant to the spark plug threads in order to prevent the plug from seizing in the rotor case.

7. Position and start turning the spark plug by hand, being careful not to cross-thread the plug. If you encounter resistance, remove the plug and try again.

GAP BRIDGED

IDENTIFIED BY DEPOSIT BUILD—UP CLOSING GAP BETWEEN ELECTRODES.

CAUSED BY OIL OR CARBON FOULING. REPLACE PLUG, OR, IF DEPOSITS ARE NOT EXCESSIVE THE PLUG CAN BE CLEANED.

OIL FOULED

IDENTIFIED BY WET BLACK DEPOSITS ON THE INSULATOR SHELL BORE ELECTRODES.

CAUSED BY EXCESSIVE OIL ENTERING COMBUSTION CHAMBER THROUGH WORN RINGS AND PISTONS, EXCESSIVE CLEARANCE BETWEEN VALVE GUIDES AND STEMS, OR WORN OR LOOSE BEARINGS. CORRECT OIL PROBLEM. REPLACE THE PLUG.

CARBON FOULED

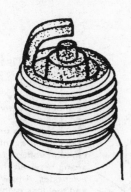

IDENTIFIED BY BLACK, DRY FLUFFY CARBON DEPOSITS ON INSULATOR TIPS, EXPOSED SHELL SURFACES AND ELECTRODES.

CAUSED BY TOO COLD A PLUG, WEAK IGNITION, DIRTY AIR CLEANER, DEFECTIVE FUEL PUMP, TOO RICH A FUEL MIXTURE, IMPROPERLY OPERATING HEAT RISER OR EXCESSIVE IDLING. CAN BE CLEANED.

NORMAL

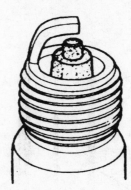

IDENTIFIED BY LIGHT TAN OR GRAY DEPOSITS ON THE FIRING TIP

PRE-IGNITION

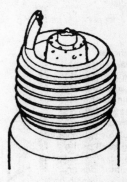

IDENTIFIED BY MELTED ELECTRODES AND POSSIBLY BLISTERED INSULATOR. METALIC DEPOSITS ON INSULATOR INDICATE ENGINE DAMAGE.

CAUSED BY WRONG TYPE OF FUEL, INCORRECT IGNITION TIMING OR ADVANCE, TOO HOT A PLUG, BURNT VALVES OR ENGINE OVERHEATING. REPLACE THE PLUG.

OVERHEATING

IDENTIFIED BY A WHITE OR LIGHT GRAY INSULATOR WITH SMALL BLACK OR GRAY BROWN SPOTS AND WITH BLUISH-BURNT APPEARANCE OF ELECTRODES.

CAUSED BY ENGINE OVER-HEATING, WRONG TYPE OF FUEL, LOOSE SPARK PLUGS, TOO HOT A PLUG, LOW FUEL PUMP PRESSURE OR INCORRECT IGNITION TIMING. REPLACE THE PLUG.

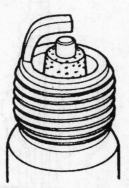

FUSED SPOT DEPOSIT

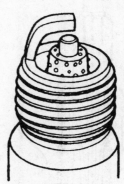

IDENTIFIED BY MELTED OR SPOTTY DEPOSITS RESEMBLING BUBBLES OR BLISTERS.

CAUSED BY SUDDEN ACCELERATION. CAN BE CLEANED IF NOT EXCESSIVE, OTHERWISE REPLACE PLUG.

TCCS2002

Fig. 8 Inspect the spark plug to determine engine running conditions

Tracking Arc
High voltage arcs between a fouling deposit on the insulator tip and spark plug shell. This ignites the fuel/air mixture at some point along the insulator tip, retarding the ignition timing which causes a power and fuel loss.

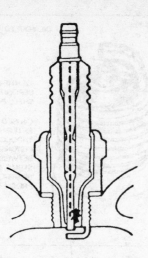

Wide Gap
Spark plug electrodes are worn so that the high voltage charge cannot arc across the electrodes. Improper gapping of electrodes on new or "cleaned" spark plugs could cause a similar condition. Fuel remains unburned and a power loss results.

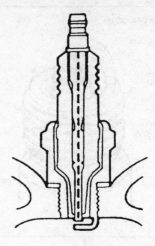

Flashover
A damaged spark plug boot, along with dirt and moisture, could permit the high voltage charge to short over the insulator to the spark plug shell or the engine. A buttress insulator design helps prevent high voltage flashover.

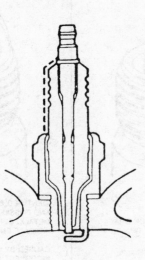

Fouled Spark Plug
Deposits that have formed on the insulator tip may become conductive and provide a "shunt" path to the shell. This prevents the high voltage from arcing between the electrodes. A power and fuel loss is the result.

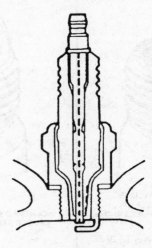

Bridged Electrodes
Fouling deposits between the electrodes "ground out" the high voltage needed to fire the spark plug. The arc between the electrodes does not occur and the fuel air mixture is not ignited. This causes a power loss and exhausting of raw fuel.

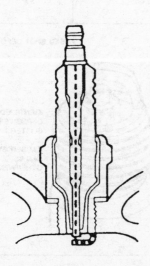

Cracked Insulator
A crack in the spark plug insulator could cause the high voltage charge to "ground out." Here, the spark does not jump the electrode gap and the fuel air mixture is not ignited. This causes a power loss and raw fuel is exhausted.

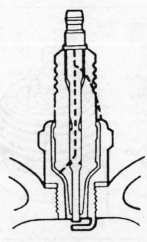

TCCS201A

Fig. 9 Used spark plugs which are damaged may indicate fuel, electrical or engine mechanical problems

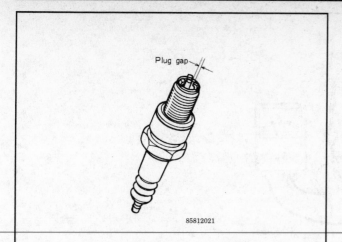

Fig. 10 Measure the gap between the center electrode and all three side electrodes — 1979-80 RX-7

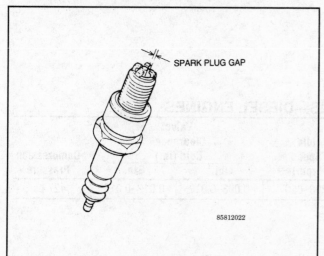

Fig. 11 Measure the gap between the center electrode and all four side electrodes — 1981-85 RX-7

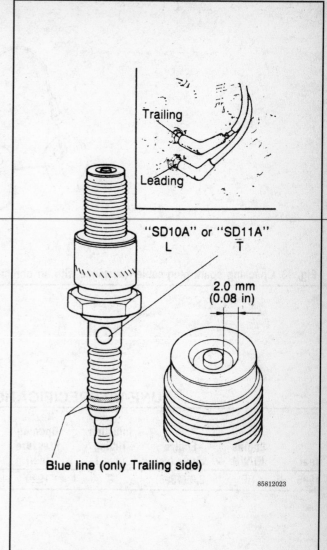

Fig. 12 Spark plug used on 1986-89 RX-7. Although it can be measured, the plug gap is non-adjustable.

8. When the plug is finger-tight, use a deep-well socket and tighten it to 9-13 ft. lbs. (12-17 Nm).

9. Install the boot over the plug, so that the terminal inside the boot firmly engages the end of the plug. Proceed to the next spark plug.

Spark Plug Wires

TESTING

▶ See Figure 13

Visually inspect the spark plug cables for burns, cuts, or breaks in the insulation. Check the spark plug boots and the nipples on the distributor cap and coil. Replace any damaged wiring. If no physical damage is obvious, the wires can be checked with an ohmmeter for excessive resistance. Remove the first wire from the spark plug and the distributor cap, and connect one of the leads from the ohmmeter to each end of the wire. Factory recommendations are that resistance should not exceed 22,400 ohms per 39.37 in. (1 meter) of cable. The factory preferred resistance per 39.37 in. (1 meter) is 16,000 ohms.

REMOVAL & INSTALLATION

When installing a new set of spark plug cables, replace the cables one at a time so there will be no mix-up. Start by replacing the longest cable first. Install the boot firmly over the spark plug. Route the wire exactly as the original was routed. Insert the nipple firmly into the tower on the distributor cap. Repeat the process for each cable, including the one which runs from the center of the distributor cap to the ignition coil. (On the RX-7, there are two ignition coil cables running to the distributor cap.)

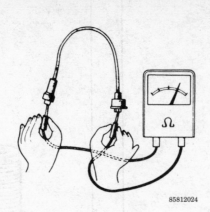

Fig. 13 Checking spark plug cable resistance with an ohmmeter

85812024

TUNE-UP SPECIFICATIONS—DIESEL ENGINES

Year	Engine ID/VIN	Engine Liters (cc)	Injection Timing (deg.)	Nozzle Opening Pressure (psi)	Idle Speed (rpm)	Valve Clearance Cold (in.) Int.	Valve Clearance Cold (in.) Exh.	Compression Pressure
1985	RF	2.0 (1998)	0	1920	800–850	0.008–0.012	0.012–0.016	427 psi

858120C2

TUNE-UP SPECIFICATIONS—ROTARY ENGINES

Year	Engine ID/VIN	Engine Displacement Liters (cc)	Spark Plugs	Gap	Distributor Point Gap	Dwell	Ignition Timing (deg.)		Idle Speed Man.	Idle Speed Auto.
1979	12A	1.1 (1146)	BR6ET	0.040	0.018	58	0	20A	750	750
1980	12A	1.1 (1146)	BR7ET	0.040	Electronic		0	20A	750	750
1981	12A	1.1 (1146)	BR7ET	0.040	Electronic		0	20A	750	750
1982	12A	1.1 (1146)	BR7ET	0.040	Electronic		0	20A	750	750
1983	12A	1.1 (1146)	BR7ET	0.053	Electronic		0	20A	750	750
1984	12A	1.1 (1146)	BR7ET	0.053	Electronic		0	20A	750	750
	13B	1.3 (1308)	BR7EQ14	0.053	Electronic		5A	20A	800	800
1985	12A	1.1 (1146)	BR7ET	0.053	Electronic		0	20A	750	750
	13B	1.3 (1308)	BR7EQ14	0.053	Electronic		5A	20A	800	800
1986	13B	1.3 (1308)	①	0.080	Electronic		5A	20A	750	750
1987	13B	1.3 (1308)	①	0.080	Electronic		5A	20A	750	750
1988	13B	1.3 (1308)	②	0.080	Electronic		5A	20A	750	750
1989	13B	1.3 (1308)	②	0.080	Electronic		5A	20A	750	750

① Leading: S-29A
Trailing: S-31
② Leading: SD10A
Trailing: SD11A

858120C3

TUNE-UP SPECIFICATIONS—PISTON ENGINES

Year	Engine ID/VIN Year	Engine Displacement Liters (cc)	Spark Plugs Type	Spark Plugs Gap (in.)	Distributor Point Gap (in.)	Distributor Dwell (deg.)	Ignition Timing (deg.) Man. Trans.	Ignition Timing (deg.) Auto. Trans.	Idle Speed Man. Trans.	Idle Speed Auto. Trans.	Valve Clearance In.	Valve Clearance Exh.
1978	TC	1.3 (1272)	BP-6ES	0.031	0.020	49–55	7B①	11B	725	625	0.010	0.012
1979	E5	1.4 (1415)	BP-5ES	0.031	0.020	49–55	7B②	7B③	④	⑤	0.010	0.012
	MA	2.0 (1970)	BP-5ES	0.031	Electronic		8B	8B	675	625	0.012	0.012
1980	E5	1.4 (1415)	BP-5ES	0.031	Electronic		5B	5B	725	625	0.010	0.012
	MA	2.0 (1970)	BPR-5ES	0.031	Electronic		5B③	5B③	675	675	0.012	0.012
1981	E5	1.5 (1490)	BPR-5ES	0.031	Electronic		8B	8B	825	750	0.010	0.012
	MA	2.0 (1970)	BPR-5ES	0.031	Electronic		5B⑥	5B⑥	675	650	0.012	0.012
1982	E5	1.5 (1490)	BPR-5ES	0.031	Electronic		8B	8B	825	750	0.010	0.012
	MA	2.0 (1970)	BPR-5ES	0.031	Electronic		8B	8B	675	650	0.012	0.012
1983	E5	1.5 (1490)	BPR-5ES	0.031	Electronic		6B	6B	850	750	0.007	0.009
	FE	2.0 (1998)	BPR-5ES	0.031	Electronic		6B	6B	750	700	0.012	0.012
1984	E5	1.5 (1490)	BPR-5ES	0.031	Electronic		6B	6B	850	750	0.007	0.009
	FE	2.0 (1998)	BPR-5ES	0.031	Electronic		6B	6B	750	700	0.012	0.012
1985	E5	1.5 (1490)	BPR-5ES	0.031	Electronic		6B	6B	850	700	0.010	0.012
	FE	2.0 (1998)	BPR-5ES	0.031	Electronic		6B	6B	750	700	0.012	0.012
1986	B6	1.6 (1597)	BPR-5ES11	0.041	Electronic		7B	7B	850	1100	0.012	0.012
	FE	2.0 (1998)	BPR-5ES11	0.031	Electronic		6B	6B	775	925	0.012	0.012
	FE	2.0 (1998) Turbo	BPR-6ES11	0.031	Electronic		6B	6B	775	925	0.012	0.012
1987	B6	1.6 (1597)	BPR-5ES11	0.041	Electronic		2B⑦	2B⑦	850	975	0.012	0.012
	FE	2.0 (1998)	BPR-5ES	0.031	Electronic		6B	6B	825	925	0.012	0.012
	FE	2.0 (1998) Turbo	BPR-6ES	0.031	Electronic		6B	6B	825	925	0.012	0.012
1988	B6	1.6 (1597)	BPR-5ES11	0.041	Electronic		2B	2B	850	850	Hyd.	Hyd.
	B6	1.6 (1597) Turbo	BCPR-6E11	0.041	Electronic		12B	12B	850	850	Hyd.	Hyd.
	F2	2.2 (2184)	ZFR5A-11	0.041	Electronic		6B	6B	750	750	Hyd.	Hyd.
	F2	2.2 (2184) Turbo	ZFR5A-11	0.041	Electronic		9B	9B	750	750	Hyd.	Hyd.
	JE	3.0 (2954)	ZFR5A-11	0.041	Electronic		15B	15B	650	650	Hyd.	Hyd.
1989	B6	1.6 (1597)	BPR-5ES11	0.041	Electronic		2B	2B	850	850	Hyd.	Hyd.
	B6	1.6 (1597) Turbo	BCPR-5E11	0.041	Electronic		12B	12B	850	850	Hyd.	Hyd.
	F2	2.2 (2184)	ZFR5A-11	0.041	Electronic		6B	6B	750	750	Hyd.	Hyd.
	F2	2.2 (2184) Turbo	ZFR5A-11	0.041	Electronic		9B	9B	750	750	Hyd.	Hyd.
	JE	3.0 (2954)	ZFR5A-11	0.041	Electronic		⑧	⑧	⑨	⑨	Hyd.	Hyd.

B: Before top dead center
A: After top dead center
Hyd.: Hydraulic lash adjusters; no adjustment is necessary
① California—8B
② California—5B
   Canada—8A
③ Canada—8B
④ Canada: 825
   USA: 725
⑤ Canada: 725
   USA: 625
⑥ USA—5B
   Canada—8B

⑦ 7B with vacuum hose disconnected on models equipped with EFI
⑧ 929: 15B w/Test connector grounded
⑨ 929: 650 w/Test connector grounded

858120C1

FIRING ORDERS

▶ See Figures 14, 15, 16, 17, 18 and 19

➡ To avoid confusion, remove and tag the wires one at a time, for replacement.

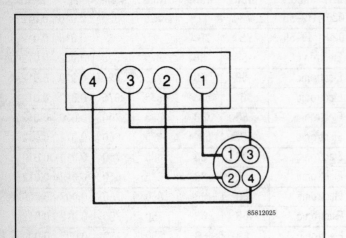

Fig. 14 4-Cylinder Engines — Except FWD GLC
Engine Firing Order: 1-3-4-2
Distributor Rotation: Clockwise

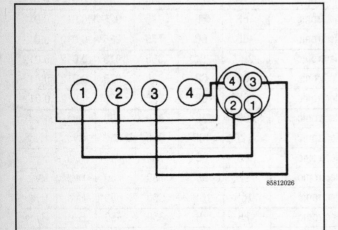

Fig. 15 Front Wheel Drive GLC Models
Engine Firing Order: 1-3-4-2
Distributor Rotation: Counterclockwise

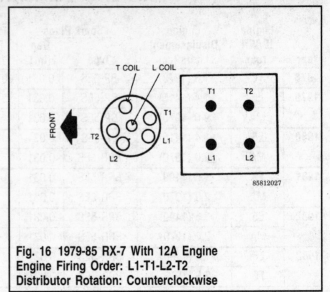

Fig. 16 1979-85 RX-7 With 12A Engine
Engine Firing Order: L1-T1-L2-T2
Distributor Rotation: Counterclockwise

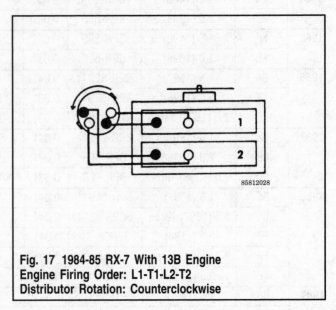

Fig. 17 1984-85 RX-7 With 13B Engine
Engine Firing Order: L1-T1-L2-T2
Distributor Rotation: Counterclockwise

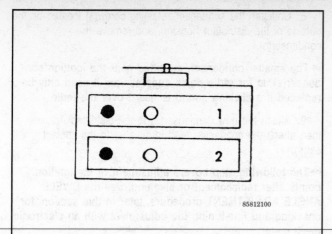

**Fig. 18 1986-89 RX-7 With 13B Engine
Engine Firing Order: L1-T1-L2-T2
Distributorless Ignition**

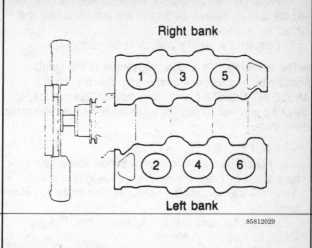

**Fig. 19 3.0L Engine
Engine Firing Order: 1-2-3-4-5-6**

POINT TYPE IGNITION

Breaker Points and Condenser

Many piston engines are equipped with breaker point distributors through 1979. Although most GLC models used a breakerless distributor as of 1977, the 1977-78 models built for California and Canada, as well as 1979 Canadian models, did utilize breaker point systems. All other 1979 and later models are equipped with a breakerless ignition. On the breakerless distributors, there are no points or condenser to replace.

The 1979 RX-7 is the only RX-7 model equipped with breaker points and condensers. 1980-89 RX-7 models have electronic ignitions in which no breaker points are needed. The 1979 model has a single distributor which contains two sets of points (leading and trailing). Be sure to check both sets when performing a tune-up.

CHECKING BREAKER ARM SPRING TENSION

▶ **See Figure 20**

Remove the distributor cap and hook a spring scale to the contact arm as shown in the illustration. Make sure the spring scale is as close as possible to the moveable breaker point and measure how much pressure it takes to separate the points. The points should start to separate at between 1.1-1.4 lbs. (0.50-0.65 kg). If not, the contact arm spring is too weak and the breaker points should be replaced.

REMOVAL & INSTALLATION

Although lightly pitted points may be cleaned with a point file, a new set of points and new condenser should be installed every 12 months or 10,000 miles (16,100 km).

➡ **The condenser capacity is 0.27 mfd (micro-Farads).**

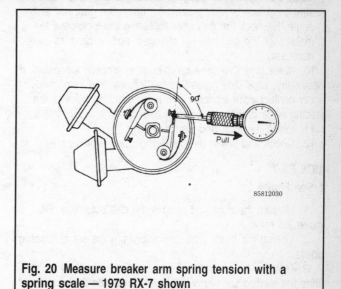

Fig. 20 Measure breaker arm spring tension with a spring scale — 1979 RX-7 shown

Except 1979 RX-7

1. Unfasten the clips and remove the distributor cap. Leave the ignition cables attached to the cap.
2. Remove the rotor from the distributor.
3. Unplug the blade type electrical connector from the contact set (breaker points).
4. Remove the two mounting screws, noting the location of any condenser lead. Unfasten the condenser lead terminal and remove the contact set.
5. Unfasten the condenser retaining screw located on the outside of the distributor housing, and remove the condenser.

➡ **The smaller condenser, mounted next to the ignition condenser, is for radio noise suppression. It need only be replaced if a clicking sound is heard over the radio.**

To install:
6. Attach the new condenser to the distributor housing.

7. Install the new contact set, the condenser lead terminal, and the screws. Tighten the screws just enough to hold the contact set in place.

8. Reattach the blade connector to the contact set.

➡The following step covers adjustment of the ignition points after replacement or cleaning. See the DWELL ANGLE ADJUSTMENT procedure, later in this section, for checking and fine-tuning the adjustment with an electronic dwell meter.

9. Adjust the point gap as follows:

a. Rotate the engine by using a remote starter switch, or have someone inside the car operate the ignition key to "bump the starter" until the rubbing block is at the top of the cam.

b. Check the point gap with a feeler gauge. The gap should be 0.020 in. (0.50mm).

c. Adjust the gap with a screwdriver. Loosen the lockscrew just enough to permit the stationary contact to be moved, using the screwdriver as a lever in the slot provided. The lockscrew must be tight enough, however, to hold the stationary contact in one place while you adjust it. Use a clean, flat type feeler gauge to check the gap, and make sure the blade is sliding straight through the gap, not at an angle. Recheck the gap after tightening the lockscrew to make sure the gap has not changed, and readjust as necessary.

10. Make sure that the cam follower is properly lubricated. If necessary, wipe dirty grease off the follower and cam, then apply contact point lubricant with a high melting point to the leading edge of the cam follower and cam.

11. Install the rotor and distributor cap.

12. Check and adjust the dwell angle, as necessary.

1979 RX-7

▶ **See Figure 21**

1. Unsnap the clips and remove the distributor cap. Remove the rotor.

2. Unplug the blade type connector from the set of **leading** points.

3. Remove the mounting screw (or "set screw") which retains the leading set of breaker points and note the position of any condenser wire. Unfasten the condenser lead terminal, if applicable, and remove the point set.

4. Install a new leading set of breaker points, making sure the points fit over any mounting dowels. Install the mounting screw with its wire and tighten.

5. Unplug the blade type connector from the set of **trailing** points.

6. Remove the mounting screw (or "set screw") which retains the trailing set of breaker points and note the position of any condenser wire. Unfasten the condenser lead terminal, if applicable, and remove the point set.

7. Install a new trailing set of breaker points, making sure the points fit over any mounting dowels. Install the mounting screw with its wire and tighten.

8. Unfasten the condenser retaining screw(s) located on the outside of the distributor housing, and remove the condenser(s).

➡The smaller condenser, mounted near the ignition condenser(s), is for radio noise suppression. It need only be replaced if a clicking sound is heard over the radio.

9. Attach the new condenser(s) to the distributor housing, then attach the condenser lead terminal(s) to the contact set(s).

➡The following step covers adjustment of the ignition points after replacement or cleaning. See the DWELL ANGLE ADJUSTMENT procedure, later in this section, for checking and fine-tuning the adjustment with an electronic dwell meter.

10. Adjust the point gap of **each** contact set as follows:

a. Rotate the engine using a remote starter switch, or have someone inside the car operate the ignition key to "bump the starter" until the rubbing block on the leading set of points is at the top of the cam.

b. Check the point gap with a feeler gauge. The gap should be 0.016-0.020 in. (0.40-0.50mm).

c. Adjust the point gap with a screwdriver. Loosen the set screw just enough to permit the stationary contact to be moved, then use the screwdriver as a lever. The set screw must be tight enough, however, to hold the stationary contact in one place while you adjust it. Use a clean flat bladed feeler gauge to check the gap, and make sure the blade slides straight through the gap, not at an angle. Recheck the gap after tightening the set screw to make sure the gap didn't change. A good idea is to use a second screwdriver to tighten the set screw while keeping the first screwdriver on the stationary contact to prevent the gap from changing.

11. Make sure that the rubbing block cam is properly lubricated. If necessary, wipe dirty grease off the cam and rubbing block, then apply contact point lubricant with a high melting point to the contact surfaces of these components.

12. Install the rotor and distributor cap.

13. Check and adjust the dwell angle, as necessary.

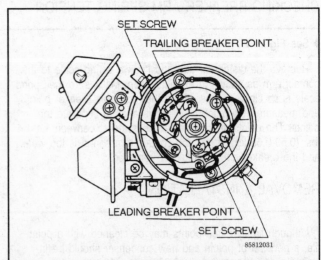

SET SCREW

TRAILING BREAKER POINT

LEADING BREAKER POINT

SET SCREW

85812031

Fig. 21 The 1979 RX-7 distributor contains leading and trailing breaker point sets

DWELL ANGLE ADJUSTMENT

The dwell angle or cam angle is the number of degrees that the distributor cam rotates while the points are closed. There is an inverse relationship between dwell angle and point gap. Increasing the point gap will decrease the dwell angle and vice versa. Checking the dwell angle with a meter is a far more accurate method of measuring point opening than the feeler gauge method.

Except 1979 RX-7

1. Start the engine and run it at idle speed, until it reaches normal operating temperature.

✳✳CAUTION

NEVER run the engine in an unventilated area such as a closed garage. Make sure the doors are open and there is adequate airflow. If possible use fans to provide additional air.

2. Connect a dwell meter to the ignition coil as described in the tool manufacturer's instructions. Read the dwell and compare the reading to the figure shown in the Tune-Up Specifications charts in this section.
3. If dwell is incorrect, stop the engine, remove the distributor cap and rotor, then adjust the point gap as previously described. If the dwell reading is too high, open the point gap slightly; if the dwell reading is too low, close the point gap slightly.
4. After contact point adjustment, replace the cap and rotor, start the engine, then read the dwell again. Readjust as necessary.

1979 RX-7

▶ See Figures 22 and 23

➡The method of dwell angle adjustment described here requires that some of the high tension wiring be re-routed to permit the engine to run with the distributor cap and rotor off. While this re-routing process requires some extra time, the dwell adjustment may be made with the engine running, which will save considerable time and make it possible for the dwell to be brought to specification on the first adjustment.

1. Start and run the engine until hot, then turn the engine **OFF**.
2. Note their locations, then disconnect the high tension leads at the leading and trailing ignition coils.
3. Note its location in the distributor cap, then disconnect the leading spark plug wire for the front rotor (L1) at the cap. Connect it to the tower of the leading ignition coil.
4. Note its location in the distributor cap, then disconnect the leading spark plug wire for the rear rotor (L2) at the cap. Connect it to the tower of the trailing ignition coil.

5. Remove the distributor cap and rotor.
6. The plug wires for the top two plugs may still be connected to the distributor cap, but the bottom two plugs must be wired directly to the ignition coils as shown.
7. Connect the dwell angle tester to the trailing ignition coil. Then, start the engine and read the dwell. If incorrect, loosen the set screw for the trailing contact set only slightly (or the engine will stop). Then, very gradually move the stationary contact back and forth until dwell is within the specified range (55-61 degrees).
8. When dwell is correct, tighten the set screw and recheck dwell. Readjust it as necessary.
9. Connect the dwell meter to the leading ignition coil and repeat steps 7 and 8 for the leading contact set.
10. Reconnect all wiring, then reinstall the cap and rotor.

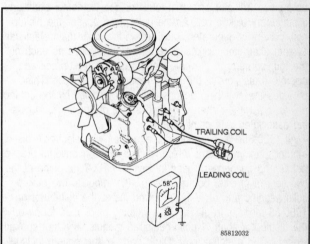

Fig. 22 Temporarily re-route the high tension (secondary) wiring to adjust dwell with the engine running — 1979 RX-7

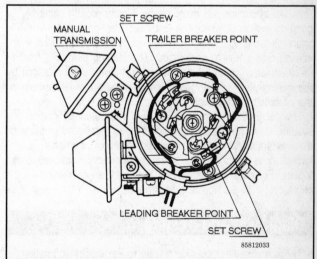

Fig. 23 Adjust dwell by slightly loosening the set screw and moving the stationary contact

ELECTRONIC IGNITION

Description and Operation

Most of the vehicles covered by this manual use an electronic ignition system in place of the old breaker point system. The electronic systems used on vehicles covered by this manual come in two basic forms: with and without distributor. Although, just like the breaker point systems, the distributors used on rotary engines is significantly different from those found on piston engines.

The electronic distributor systems replace the contact points (used in traditional breaker point systems) with an electromagnetic generator. The generator consists, in part, of a rotating pole piece (reluctor or signal rotor) on the distributor shaft and a stationary pickup coil. As the pole piece passes the pickup coil, current is generated, much as in the car's main electrical system alternator. Spikes of current are produced as each of the four corners on the pole piece pass the pickup coil and operate transistors in the igniter mounted on the coil. This provides the switching actions ordinarily handled by the contact points, but without the arcing and stress of opening and closing associated with point operation.

All 1980-85 RX-7 models are equipped with electronic distributor ignition systems which replace the conventional breaker points and condensers used in the 1979 RX-7. In place of the two sets of breaker points used in 1979 models, two pickup coils (leading and trailing) are found inside the distributor on 1980-85 models. In place of the rubbing block cam found on the distributor shaft of point-equipped models, is a four-spoked wheel called a signal rotor. Other parts of the system include the igniter, the two ignition coils and all attaching wires. When each of the spokes on the signal rotor passes in front of one of the pickup coils, it creates a signal. The pickup coil then sends this signal to the igniter and the appropriate ignition coil. This signal causes the magnetic field in the coil to collapse, creating the spark which the distributor cap passes on to the spark plug. As with the 1979 breaker point system, there is a leading and a trailing spark plug. The leading plug fires first, followed (after about 10 degrees of distributor shaft rotation) by the trailing plug, which ignites any remaining air/fuel mixture in the combustion chamber.

The 1986-89 RX-7 models utilize a distributorless ignition system, in which the distributor has been eliminated in favor of a crank angle sensor (for crankshaft position information) and ignition coils which fire the spark plugs directly from their own towers. For more information on the crank angle sensor, please refer to Section 3 of this manual.

Diagnosis and Testing

There are several checks, unique to the electronic ignition system, which can be made to locate or repair trouble. The gap between the pole piece and pickup coil can be checked and adjusted, and the electrical resistance of the pickup coil can be checked on most vehicles built through 1982. Although it can be checked, the gap is non-adjustable on the RX-7. The resistance of the ignition coil(s) can be checked on all electronic ignition equipped vehicles.

PICKUP COIL RESISTANCE

1978-82 Vehicles

Unplug the primary ignition wire connector, then insert an ohmmeter between the two prongs of the connector on the distributor side. The resistance of the pickup coil should be 670-790 ohms (GLC) or 720-1,050 ohms (626), as measured at room temperature. If resistance is out of range, replace the pickup coil.

IGNITION COIL RESISTANCE

For ignition coil resistance test procedures, please refer to Section 3 of this manual.

SECONDARY IGNITION CHECK (SPARK TEST)

▶ **See Figure 24**

1. Disconnect the high tension lead from the ignition coil at the distributor cap.
2. Wrap a protective cloth around the cable and hold its electrical connector 0.020-0.040 in. (0.50-1.00mm) from a good ground. Have someone crank the engine. The ignition system should produce a plainly visible, bluish/white spark.

✳✳CAUTION

A properly operating secondary ignition system can produce enough voltage to give you a nasty shock. Be sure to wrap an insulating cloth around any high tension leads, before grasping them with the engine running or cranking. Better yet, carefully hold the wire using a rubber insulated tool.

3. Reconnect the high tension lead.

85812004

Fig. 24 Disconnect the high tension lead from the ignition coil at the distributor cap

4. If there is doubt about the adequacy of the spark, run the engine until it is hot, then shut the engine **OFF** and make checks of the coil primary and secondary resistance, as described in Section 3 of this manual.

If no spark or an inadequate one is produced, and the coil tests out okay, the igniter and pickup coil may require replacement. However, you should make sure before doing this work that there are no basic maintenance problems in the secondary circuit of the system, since it is often impossible to return electrical parts. We suggest that before you replace the igniter and pickup coil, you carefully inspect the cap and rotor for carbon tracks or cracks, and also check the condition of the high tension wires. Check for cracks in the insulation and measure the resistance of the spark plug wires with an ohmmeter, as described earlier in this section. Resistance should be 16,000 ohms per 3.28 feet (1 meter). Replace secondary parts as inspection/testing deems necessary before replacing the igniter and pickup coil.

Adjustments

AIR GAP

The air gap (between the signal rotor and pickup coil when one of the rotor spokes is lined up with the pickup coil) can be measured with a feeler gauge.

1979-82 Except RX-7

▶ See Figures 25, 26 and 27

1. Remove the distributor cap and rotor. Turn the engine over (using the starter or by using a socket wrench on the crankshaft pulley bolt) until one of the four high points on the pole piece lines up directly with the metallic portion of the pickup coil.

2. Using a non-magnetic (i.e. brass or paper) feeler gauge, check the gap. If it is not 0.010-0.018 in. (0.25-0.45mm) for the GLC, or more than 0.008 in. (0.2mm) wide for the 626, loosen the two adjusting screws and slide the pickup in or out until the dimension is correct. Tighten the screws and recheck the gap. Readjust if necessary.

1980-85 RX-7

Air gap is checked in the same manner as for the other Mazda engines described earlier, but is not adjustable. If the air gap is not within 0.020-0.035 in. (0.5-0.9mm), the only way to correct it is to replace the entire pickup coil base/bearing assembly or the distributor driveshaft. Checking the air gap should not be considered a routine tune-up procedure.

Fig. 25 Unfasten the retaining screws and remove the distributor cap

Fig. 26 Unfasten and remove the rotor

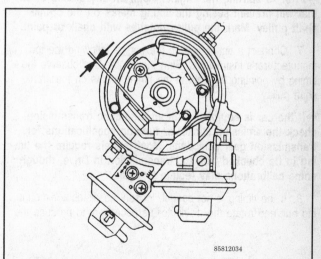

Fig. 27 Measuring the air gap on 1979-82 electronic ignition systems

IGNITION TIMING

Timing

INSPECTION AND ADJUSTMENT

Piston Engines

EXCEPT 1988-89 626, MX-6 AND 929

▶ See Figures 28, 29, 30, 31, 32, 33 and 34

➡Most 1978 and later models require that the ignition timing be adjusted with the vacuum line connected to the distributor. Refer to the emission sticker (under the hood) to determine if the vacuum line is to be connected or disconnected and plugged. If the sticker is missing, see a dealer about obtaining a replacement with the proper calibrations for your vehicle.

1. If required, disconnect and plug the distributor vacuum line. Though this is not required on most late model cars, it is needed on the 1986-87 626. On that model, be sure to disconnect BOTH vacuum lines and plug them.

➡A small pencil or old golf tee works well for this purpose.

2. Set the parking brake and block the front wheels. Put automatic transmission cars in Neutral.
3. Turn off all electrical loads on all models (don't forget the heater fan). If the car has an electric fan, unplug the electrical connector.
4. On the 1986-89 323 with electronic fuel injection, disconnect the black connector at the distributor.
5. Start and run the engine until it reaches the normal operating temperature. Shut the engine **OFF** and connect a tachometer.
6. Restart then engine, then check the engine idle speed and adjust if necessary. Shut the engine **OFF**..

➡Prior to starting the engine, clean off any grease or oil that will prevent seeing the timing marks on the crankshaft pulley. Mark the pulley notches with chalk or paint.

7. Connect a timing light to the engine following the tool manufacturer's instructions. Start the engine and observe the timing by pointing the light at the timing marks on the crankshaft pulley.

➡If the car is equipped with an automatic transmission, check the emission sticker or tune-up specifications for transmission gear selections. Most models require the timing to be checked with the transmission in Drive, though some calibrations may require Neutral.

8. If the timing is not correct, loosen the distributor mounting bolt and rotate the distributor as necessary to produce the

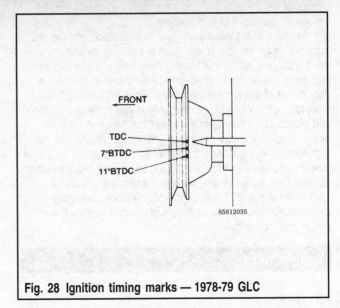

Fig. 28 Ignition timing marks — 1978-79 GLC

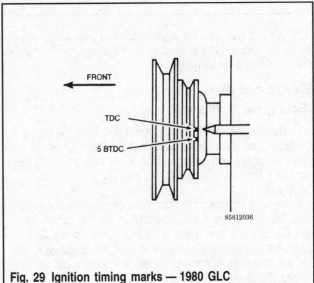

Fig. 29 Ignition timing marks — 1980 GLC

correct timing mark alignment. Recheck the timing after tightening the lock bolt and readjust if necessary. Check the idle speed.

➡Some Canadian models require that the bullet connectors at the water temperature wiring be disconnected before timing the ignition; check the emission sticker for requirements.

9. Reconnect the vacuum line(s) or bullet connectors, if applicable. Recheck the idle speed and readjust, if necessary.

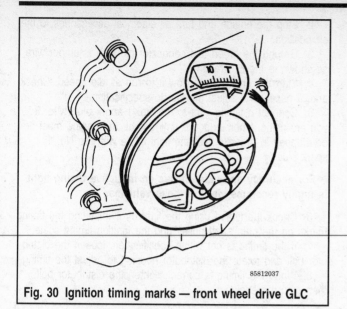

Fig. 30 Ignition timing marks — front wheel drive GLC

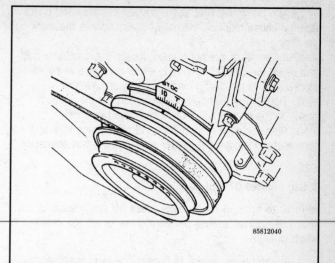

Fig. 33 Ignition timing marks — 1986-87 626

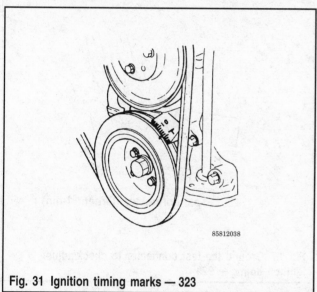

Fig. 31 Ignition timing marks — 323

Fig. 34 While aiming the timing light, rotate the distributor as necessary to align the designated timing marks

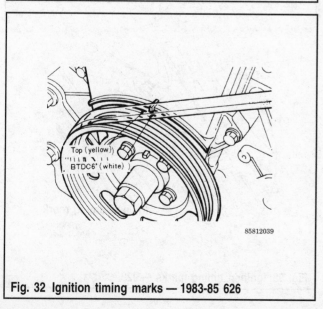

Fig. 32 Ignition timing marks — 1983-85 626

1988-89 626 AND MX-6

▶ See Figures 35 and 36

➡Prior to starting the engine, clean off any grease or oil that will prevent seeing the timing marks on the crankshaft pulley.

1. Warm up the engine to normal operating temperature.
2. Stop the engine and turn all electrical accessories to the off position.
3. Connect a tachometer and timing light to the engine in accordance with the tool manufacturer's instructions.
4. Connect a jumper wire from the test connector to a suitable ground.
5. Start the engine and allow it to run at idle speed. Check and adjust the idle to specification, if necessary.
6. On non-turbocharged engines, disconnect the two vacuum hoses from the vacuum control unit and plug them. Leave the test connector grounded.

7. Aim the timing light at the crankshaft pulley and check that the yellow mark on the pulley is aligned with the mark on the timing belt cover.

8. If the marks are not aligned, loosen the distributor bolt and move the distributor housing either clockwise or counterclockwise until the timing marks are properly aligned.

9. Tighten the distributor bolt and connect the vacuum hoses to the control unit (non-turbocharged engines).

10. Stop the engine, then disconnect the timing light and tachometer. Remove the jumper wire from the test connector.

929

▶ **See Figures 37 and 38**

➡**Prior to starting the engine, clean off any grease or oil that will prevent seeing the timing marks on the crankshaft pulley.**

1. Warm up the engine to normal operating temperature. Check the idle speed and adjust as necessary.

2. Stop the engine and turn all electrical accessories to the off position.

3. Ground the green test connector pin with a jumper wire, as shown in the illustration.

4. Start the engine and allow it to run at idle speed. Check and, if necessary, adjust the idle to specification.

5. Connect a timing light to the No. 1 spark plug wire. If you are using a non-inductive timing light, the engine must first be stopped in order to wire the light inline with the No. 1 spark plug.

➡**For accuracy and ease of use an inductive timing light is highly recommended on these vehicles.**

6. Check the timing using the light by illuminating the timing marks on the crankshaft pulley and the ignition timing scale.

7. If the timing is not within specification, loosen the distributor bolt and rotate the distributor housing to adjust the timing.

8. When the timing is correct, tighten the distributor bolt, then stop the engine.

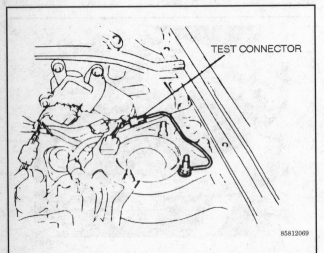

Fig. 35 Ground the test connector to check/adjust ignition timing — 626 and MX-6

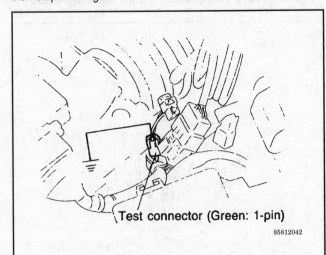

Fig. 37 Ground the test connector to check/adjust ignition timing — 929

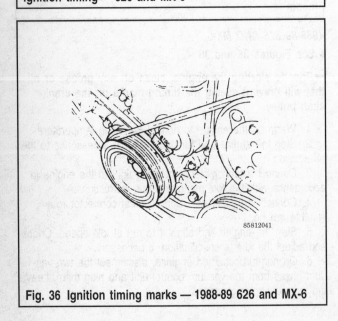

Fig. 36 Ignition timing marks — 1988-89 626 and MX-6

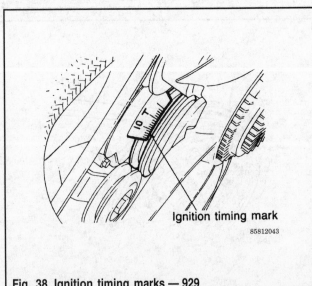

Fig. 38 Ignition timing marks — 929

9. Disconnect the timing light and remove the jumper wire from the test connector.

Rotary Engines

1979 RX-7

▶ See Figures 39 and 40

➡This timing procedure applies to all 1979 RX-7s *EXCEPT* those after chassis No. 522504 that are equipped with an automatic transmission. For 1979 RX-7s after chassis No. 522504 with an automatic transmission, see the procedure which immediately follows.

1. Warm the engine up until it reaches operating temperature, then shut the engine **OFF** and connect a tachometer.

2. On automatic transmission equipped vehicles, securely apply the handbrake, block the wheels, and put the car in Drive.

3. Read the tachometer as for a conventional four cylinder engine to verify that the engine is running at its normal idle speed. If not, adjust idle speed to specification.

85812046

Fig. 39 Timing marks on 1979-85 RX-7s — the arrow points to the LEADING mark, while the TRAILING mark is beside it

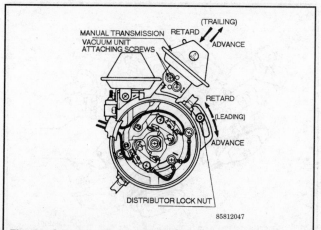

85812047

Fig. 40 On early model 1979 RX-7s (and late models with MT), adjust the leading timing by rotating the distributor, then adjust the trailing timing by moving the vacuum unit (MT) or adjusting lever (AT) in or out

4. Stop the engine and connect a timing light to the leading (lower) spark plug of the front rotor. Then, restart the engine. Aim the timing light at the pin on the front housing cover and observe the timing.

5. If the timing pointer does not line up with the first (yellow) notch on the pulley, loosen the distributor locknut and rotate the distributor either way until timing is correct. Tighten the locknut and check that timing is still correct.

6. Stop the engine and connect the timing light to the trailing (upper) spark plug of the front rotor. Start the engine (put automatic transmission equipped cars in Drive), and check the trailing timing. The timing pointer should line up with the second (red) notch in the pulley.

7. If the trailing timing is not correct, loosen the vacuum unit attaching screws (manual transmission) or the adjusting lever attaching screws (automatic transmission), and move the vacuum unit (manual transmission) or adjusting lever (automatic transmission) in or out until the timing pointer lines up with the second mark on the pulley. Then, tighten the screws and recheck the timing.

1979 RX-7 WITH AUTOMATIC TRANSMISSION AFTER CHASSIS NO. 522504

▶ See Figures 39 and 41

1. Warm the engine up until it reaches operating temperature, then shut the engine **OFF** and connect a tachometer.

2. On automatic transmission equipped vehicles, securely apply the handbrake, block the wheels, and put the car in Drive.

3. Read the tachometer as for a conventional four cylinder engine to verify that the engine is running at its normal idle speed. If not, adjust idle speed to specification.

4. Stop the engine and connect a timing light to the leading (lower) spark plug of the front rotor. Then, restart the engine. Aim the timing light at the pin on the front housing cover and observe the timing.

5. If the timing pointer does not line up with the first (yellow) notch on the pulley, loosen the distributor locknut and rotate the distributor either way until timing is correct. Tighten the locknut and check that timing is still correct.

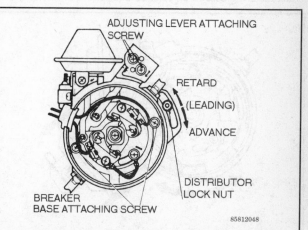

85812048

Fig. 41 On late model 1979 RX-7s (with AT), adjust the trailing timing by loosening the breaker base attaching screws, then loosen the external lever attaching screws and move the lever in or out

6. Stop the engine and connect the timing light to the trailing (upper) spark plug of the front rotor. Start the engine (put automatic transmission equipped cars in Drive), and check the trailing timing. The timing pointer should line up with the second (red) notch in the pulley.

7. To adjust the trailing timing, stop the engine and remove the distributor cap and rotor.

8. Slightly loosen the breaker base attaching screws, then reinstall the rotor and distributor cap.

9. Start the engine. Set the transmission selector lever in Drive and run the engine at idle speed. Move the external adjusting lever in or out until the timing pointer lines up with the second (red) mark on the pulley, then tighten the adjusting lever attaching screws.

10. Stop the engine, remove the distributor cap and rotor, and tighten the two breaker base attaching screws.

11. Install the rotor and cap, then recheck the trailing timing.

1980-85 RX-7

▶ **See Figures 39 and 42**

1. Warm up the engine to normal operating temperature.

2. Stop the engine and connect a tachometer.

3. Connect a timing light to the wire of the leading (lower) spark plug on the front rotor.

4. To check/adjust the **leading** timing:

a. Start the engine and run it at the specified idle speed. Verify that the engine is running at its normal idle speed. If not, adjust idle speed to specification.

b. Aim the light at the front cocver timing indicator pin.

c. If the timing pointer does not line up with the first (yellow) notch on the pulley, loosen the locknut and rotate the distributor until the timing is correct. Tighten the locknut and check that the timing is still correct.

5. To check/adjust the **trailing** timing:

a. Stop the engine and connect the timing light to the trailing (upper) spark plug on the front rotor. Start the engine, position the detent lever in Drive (AT vehicles), and check the trailing timing. The pointer should line up with the second (red) notch in the pulley.

b. If the trailing timing is not correct, loosen the vacuum unit attaching screws on vehicles equipped with manual

transmission or the adjusting lever attaching screws on vehicles equipped with automatic transmission. Move the vacuum unit or adjusting lever in or out until the timing pointer lines up with the second mark on the pulley, then tighten the screws and recheck the trailing timing.

1986-89 RX-7

▶ **See Figures 43 and 44**

1986-89 models do not use a distributor. Instead, ignition timing is adjusted by means of a crank angle sensor. The sensor is mounted in the front rotor housing and extends down towards the eccentric shaft. The sensor detects the angle of the eccentric shaft and feeds this information to the control unit in the form a reference signal. This, along with other input signals, allows the control unit to monitor the various engine operating conditions which it uses to calculate ignition timing.

1. Warm up the engine to normal operating temperature.

2. Stop the engine, connect a tachometer and turn off all accessories.

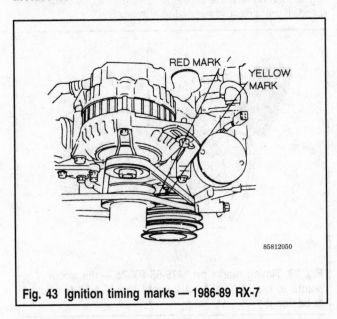

Fig. 43 Ignition timing marks — 1986-89 RX-7

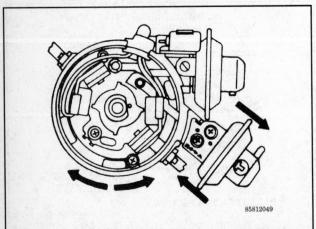

Fig. 42 For all 1980-85 RX-7s, adjust the leading timing by rotating the distributor, then adjust the trailing timing by moving the vacuum unit (MT) or adjusting lever (AT) in or out

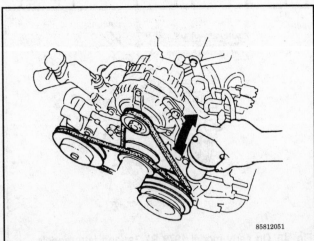

Fig. 44 On 1986-89 RX-7s, ignition timing is adjusted by rotating the crank angle sensor

3. Start the engine and verify that the engine is running at its normal idle speed. If not, adjust idle speed to specification.

4. To Check/Adjust the **leading** timing:

a. Connect a timing light to the lower spark plug wire from the front rotor.

b. Aim the light at the pulley and verify the yellow plulley timing mark is aligned with the indicator pin.

c. If the marks are not aligned, remove the rubber cap that covers the crank angle sensor adjusting bolt.

d. Loosen the bolt and move the crank angle sensor to adjust the leading timing.

5. To Check/Adjust the **trailing** timing:

a. Connect the timing light to the upper spark plug wire from the front rotor.

b. Check that the red pulley mark aligns with the indicator pin.

c. If not, loosen the adjusting bolt and rotate the crank angle sensor to align the marks.

d. Tighten the crank angle sensor adjusting bolt and install the rubber cap. Recheck the timing.

VALVE LASH

Gasoline Engines

1978-87 Vehicles

▶ See Figures 45, 46 and 47

Valve lash adjustment is recommended on 1978 models at 2,000 miles (3,221 km), and then at 12,500 miles (20,129 km), 25,000 miles (40,258 km), 37,500 miles (60,386 km), etc. On 1979 and later models, no 2,000 mile (3,221 km) adjustment is required; adjustments are recommended only at 15,000 mile (24,155 km) intervals. This adjustment is performed to correct for wear in the valve train and changes in dimensions of various engine parts that occur during normal engine operation and, at a faster rate, during the break-in process. Failure to keep valves properly adjusted can result in excessive wear or burning of valves or valve train parts, poor performance, and/or noisy valve train operation. To perform a gasoline engine valve adjustment, proceed as follows:

1. Operate the engine until several miles after the temperature gauge indicates operating temperature has been reached. Then, stop the engine and remove the valve cover.

2. Rotate the engine forward only with a wrench on the crankshaft pulley bolt or with the starter until the mark on the crankshaft pulley indicates it has reached Top Dead Center (TDC), and the valves for Number 1 cylinder (at front) are both fully closed (are not moving as the crankshaft is turned). If the engine is at TDC and these valves are still open, rotate the crankshaft one full revolution until it is again at Top Dead Center.

3. Refer to the valve clearance columns of the Tune-Up Specifications chart found in this section. Insert a flat feeler gauge of the proper dimension between the exhaust valve and the exhaust valve rocker lever for the No. 1 cylinder. (The exhaust valve is in line with the front exhaust manifold passage.) The gauge should slide between these two parts with a slight pull. If the gauge will not slide readily, or there is no resistance when pulling it through, loosen the locknut and use a screwdriver to rotate the adjusting screw clockwise to tighten the adjustment, or counterclockwise to loosen it. When a slight pull is obtained, hold the adjusting screw in place with a screwdriver and use a box or open end wrench to tighten the locknut. If the adjustment has tightened up, change the setting of the adjusting screw. If a great deal of effort is required to pull the gauge (adjustment too tight), burned valves may result.

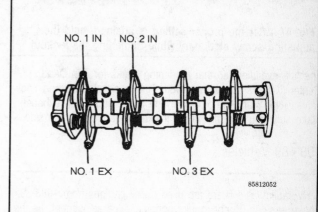

Fig. 45 Adjust the valves shown with the No. 1 cylinder at TDC firing position

Fig. 46 Use a flat feeler gauge to check clearance between each valve and valve rocker lever. Turn the adjusting screw to attain the appropriate setting.

4. Select the gauge for the adjusting dimension of the intake valves (see the Tune-Up Specifications chart). Repeat Step 3 for the front intake valve (lined up with the front intake manifold passage).

5. Adjust the remaining valves shown in the illustration (No. 2 Intake and No. 3 Exhaust). Then, rotate the engine exactly

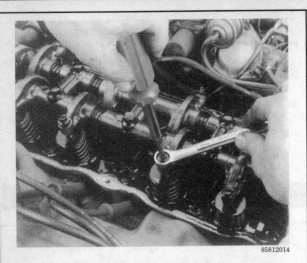

Fig. 47 After the proper setting is attained, hold the adjusting screw stationary while tightening the locknut

one full revolution, so that the timing marks for Top Dead Center (TDC) are again lined up. Finally, adjust the remaining valves (No. 3 and No. 4 intake and No. 2 and No. 4 exhaust). Make sure you use the proper thickness gauge on each side.

1988-89 Vehicles

Hydraulic valve lifters are used on all engines from 1988-89. These engines do not require periodic valve adjustment, as the hydraulic valve lifter automatically compensates for any small changes in valve train wear.

Diesel Engine

♦ See Figures 48 and 49

➡Adjusting the valves on the Mazda diesel engine involves replacing discs that rest in a recess in the top of each tappet. To do this, a special tool (MAZDA tappet holder 49 S120 220 or equivalent) is required, along with a selection of discs of different dimensions. The tool depresses the valve tappet, opening the valve slightly, for access to the replaceable disc.

1. Remove the valve cover, as described in Section 3 of this manual. Rotate the engine by the crankshaft pulley bolt until the valve cams of the No. 1 cylinder are both pointing upward (not contacting the shims), and the timing marks indicate that No. 1 cylinder is at Top Dead Center (TDC) on the firing stroke.

2. Measure the clearance between the top surface of the tappet and the cam's lower surface, as shown in the illustration. Check the intake valves of cylinders No. 1 and No. 2, and the exhaust valves of cylinders No. 1 and No. 3. The proper clearances are — Intake: 0.008-0.012 in. (0.2-0.3mm); Exhaust: 0.012-0.016 in. (0.3-0.4mm).

3. If the clearance is outside the specified range, determine the thickness of the required new disc. Discs are marked to indicate their thickness in millimeters. Thicknesses range from 3.70mm to 4.30mm in intervals of 0.050mm. For example, 3825 means 3.825mm. Calculate the required thickness of the new disc using the following, simple formula:

The new shim which is required in order to achieve the specified clearance is equal to the thickness of the original disc PLUS the measured clearance, then MINUS the required clearance specification. Think of this another way, if you added the measured clearance and the thickness of the original shim, then selected a shim based on that number, you would have zero clearance. But zero clearance is not what you what. Since a certain clearance is necessary, subtracting the specification from the total thickness just calculated (current shim

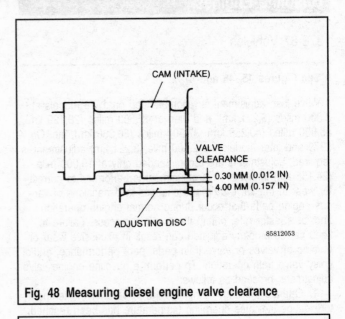

Fig. 48 Measuring diesel engine valve clearance

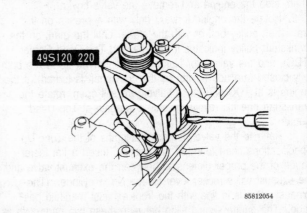

Fig. 49 During valve adjustment on the diesel engine, tappet holder 49 S120 220, or equivalent, must be used to depress the valve tappets

plus current clearance) tells you what size shim will leave the specified clearance between the new shim and the cam lobe.

✳✳WARNING

The engine must be positioned so that the intake cam lobe for the cylinder you are working on is facing directly upward before installing the special tool. Attempting to depress the valve without properly positioning the engine may cause damage to the valve train.

4. If the valves you have checked require adjustment, turn each of the tappets around so one of the notches is facing toward the left side of the car for access to the discs. Before working on each valve, rotate the engine by the crankshaft pulley bolt so that the intake cam lobe for that cylinder is pointing straight upward. Then, install the tool in the position shown (right between the cams). Tighten the bolt to force the tool halves together and depress the tappets. Then, pry the disc out with a small prytool and replace it with one of the proper thickness (as determined by your calculation).

5. Rotate the crankshaft one full revolution (360 degrees). Repeat the inspection procedure for the intake valves of cylinders No. 3 and No. 4, and the exhaust valves of cylinders No. 2 and No. 4. Then, adjust those valves, as necessary. When you are finished, install the valve cover as described in Section 3 of this manual.

IDLE SPEED AND MIXTURE ADJUSTMENTS

Idle Speed Adjustment

PISTON ENGINES

1978-87 Models

EXCEPT 626 DIESEL

▶ **See Figures 50, 51 and 52**

Idle speed adjustments are easily accomplished, but you must be careful to perform them under the proper conditions. The engine must be fully warmed up. The best procedure is to drive the vehicle for several miles after the temperature gauge indicates that the coolant has reached operating temperature. All normal operating conditions should be maintained. For example, the air cleaner and all vacuum hoses should be installed or connected, the choke should be wide open, and all accessories should be off. This includes the engine cooling fan if it is electrical. If necessary, unplug it. Also, avoid extremes of outside temperature, and replace a thermostat that makes the engine operate too hot or too cold before proceeding.

On the 1978-79 GLC and 1979 626 models, disconnect the canister purge hose between the canister and the air cleaner.

On the 1986-87 626 and MX-6, run the engine at 2,500-3,000 rpm in Neutral for three minutes before proceeding.

1. Warm up the engine to normal operating temperature and turn off all accessories.

2. Connect a reliable tachometer according to tool manufacturer's instructions (usually between the coil negative (-) terminal and ground).

3. On 1987 626s only, disconnect the air bypass solenoid connector at altitudes of less than 3,280 feet or 1,000 meters (sea level).

4. Note the idle speed. Compare this reading to the appropriate range in the Tune-Up Specifications chart located in this section.

➡**Read the tachometer's 4-cylinder scale, for both rotary and piston engines. If the tachometer has only a 6-cylinder scale and an 8-cylinder scale, read the 8-cylinder scale and multiply all readings by two to get the correct rpm. For example, if the specified rpm is 700, set the idle speed at 350 rpm, as indicated on the 8-cylinder scale.**

5. If the idle speed does not fall within the designated range, locate and turn the appropriate idle speed adjusting screw until the desired reading is attained:

a. On carburetor-equipped engines, the throttle adjusting screw is usually located on the lower portion of the carburetor near the throttle valve shaft. The screw acts directly on a flange which is integral with the throttle shaft; it does not actuate any cams or levers.

b. On models equipped with electronic fuel injection, the air adjusting screw is located on top of the throttle body.

6. On 1986-87 323s, after adjusting the idle speed, the dashpot must be adjusted as follows:

a. Start the engine and warm it up to normal operating temperature.

b. With the tachometer still connected, increase the engine speed to 3,000 rpm, then slowly reduce the engine speed and make sure the dashpot rod contacts the lever at 2,400-2,600 rpm.

c. If it does not operate as described, loosen the locknut and adjust the rod by turning the dashpot.

7. On 1987 626s, fasten the air bypass solenoid connector, if applicable.

8. Disconnect and remove the tachometer.

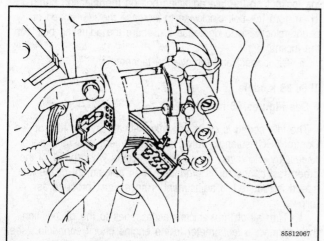

85812067

Fig. 50 Disconnect the air bypass solenoid connector when checking idle speed on a 1987 626 below sea level

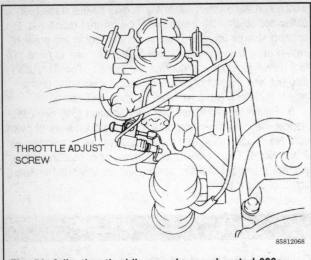

Fig. 51 Adjusting the idle speed on carbureted 323s — Carbureted GLC and 626 models similar

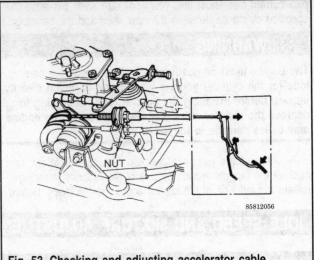

Fig. 53 Checking and adjusting accelerator cable deflection on the 626 diesel

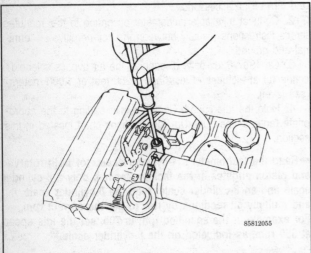

Fig. 52 Adjusting the idle speed on fuel injected 323 models — 626 fuel injected models similar

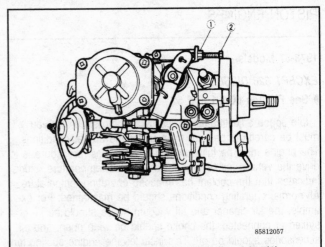

Fig. 54 Adjust idle speed on the 626 diesel by (1) loosening the locknut, then (2) turning the adjusting bolt

626 DIESEL ENGINE

▶ See Figures 53 and 54

➡Adjusting the idle speed on the diesel requires you to have a special tachometer which measures idle speed from a special sensor on the injection pump.

1. Turn all of the vehicle's accessories to the off position, then connect a diesel tachometer, according to the tool manufacturer's instructions.

2. Place a ruler near the accelerator pedal and then depress the pedal to determine the play in the cable. It should be 0.04-0.12 in. (1-3mm). If necessary, lengthen the cable (to increase play) by loosening the nut on the firewall side of the cable bracket and then tightening the nut on the other side. You would shorten the cable, in order to decrease play, by reversing the order in which the nuts are loosened.

3. Drive the car until several miles after the temperature gauge indicates normal operating temperature, to warm up the engine. Measure the engine rpm with the tachometer.

4. If the rpm is outside the range of 800-850 rpm, loosen the locknut on the idle adjusting bolt on the injection pump. Then, turn the bolt clockwise to increase the idle speed or counterclockwise to decrease it. Secure the adjusting bolt with the locknut.

5. Disconnect and remove the tachometer.

1988-89 Models

▶ See Figures 55 and 56

The idle speed is controlled automatically by the Idle Speed Control (ISC) solenoid valve, and adjustment is usually not necessary. However, if rough idling occurs when pin 1 of the green test connector is grounded, then adjustment of the idle speed is required. If adjustment is necessary, proceed as follows:

1. Turn all of the vehicle's accessories to the off position, then connect a tachometer to the engine check connector (see illustration).

2. Warm up the engine to normal operating temperature.

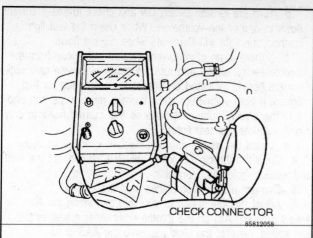

Fig. 55 Tachometer hooked up to the underhood check connector — 929 shown

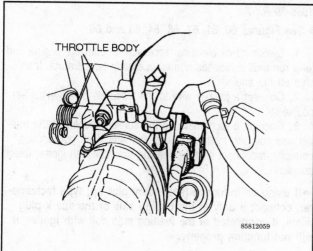

Fig. 56 Idle speed adjustment for the 929 — other models similar

3. Ground pin 1 of the green test connector with a jumper wire. (An illustration of this step is shown in the ignition timing portion of this section.)

4. With the test connector grounded, check the idle speed. Compare this reading to the Tune-Up Specifications chart located in this section. If it is not within the specified range, remove the rubber cap from the air adjusting screw on the throttle body and turn the screw to adjust the idle speed.

5. Once the idle speed is within specification, install the cap and disconnect the jumper wire from the test connector.

6. On 1988 323s, after adjusting the idle speed, the dashpot must be adjusted as follows:

   a. Start the engine and warm it up to normal operating temperature.

   b. With the tachometer still connected, increase the engine speed to 3,000 rpm, then slowly reduce the engine speed and make sure the dashpot rod contacts the lever at 2,400-2,600 rpm.

   c. If it does not operate as described, loosen the locknut and adjust the rod by turning the dashpot.

7. Disconnect and remove the tachometer.

ROTARY ENGINES

Carbureted Vehicles

➡All 1979-83 RX-7s were equipped with a carburetor. 1984-85 RX-7s were equipped with either a carburetor (12A engine) or fuel injection (13B engine).

1. If possible, set up an extra cooling fan to blow additional air into the engine compartment.

2. Set the parking brake and block the wheels.

3. Switch all accessories to the off position.

4. Remove the fuel tank filler cap.

5. On 1979-83 models, disconnect and plug the hose at the idle compensator in the air cleaner. On 1984-85 vehicles with a manual transmission, disconnect the richer solenoid connector.

➡On 1981-83 models, make sure the throttle opener (if equipped with air conditioning) and dashpot do not prevent the idle lever from returning to the idle stop.

6. Connect a tachometer to the engine.

7. Start the engine and allow it to reach normal operating temperature. On vehicles equipped with an automatic transmission, shift the selector lever to the D (Drive) position.

8. Check the idle speed with the tachometer. (Read the tachometer as if testing a conventional 4-cylinder engine.) If the idle speed is not correct, adjust it by turning the throttle adjusting screw on the carburetor.

➡Read the tachometer's 4-cylinder scale, for both rotary and piston engines. If the tachometer has only a 6-cylinder scale and an 8-cylinder scale, read the 8-cylinder scale and multiply all readings by two to get the correct rpm. For example, if the specified rpm is 700, set the idle speed at 350 rpm, as indicated on the 8-cylinder scale.

9. Unplug and reconnect the hose at the idle compensator on the air cleaner, or secure the richer solenoid connector, if applicable. Install the fuel tank filler cap.

➡After adjusting idle speed, the throttle sensor on the carburetor should also be adjusted. For information on that procedure, please refer to Section 5 of this manual.

10. Disconnect the tachometer and unblock the wheels.

Fuel Injected Vehicles

1984-85 RX-7

▶ See Figures 57, 58 and 59

1. Switch all electrical accessories to the off position and remove the fuel filler cap.

2. Start the engine and let it run until it reaches normal operating temperature.

3. Check/adjust the throttle sensor by performing the following:

   a. With the engine **OFF**, connect a pair of voltmeters to the green check connector as shown in the illustration. If voltmeters are not available, a dual set of test lights may be used instead.

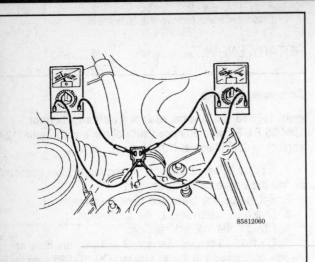

Fig. 57 Use a pair of voltmeters or test lights to check the throttle sensor setting — 1984-85 fuel injected RX-7

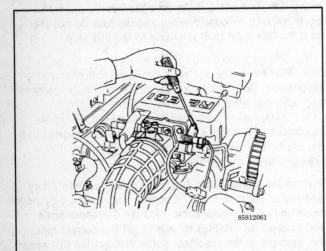

Fig. 58 If necessary, turn the throttle sensor adjusting screw — 1984-85 fuel injected RX-7

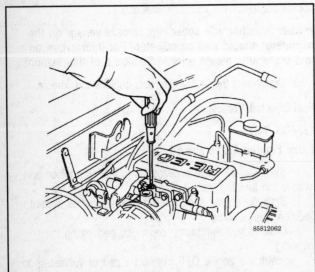

Fig. 59 Adjust idle speed by turning the AAS

b. Turn the ignition switch **ON** and check to see if current flows to one of the voltmeters. When using the test light method, the light will illuminate when current flows.

c. If there is no current, remove the rubber cap from the throttle sensor screw and turn the screw clockwise only until current flow is indicated on one of the voltmeters (or test lights). If both voltmeters show current, remove the cap and turn the screw counterclockwise so that current flows to only one voltmeter (or test light).

d. Install the rubber cap and disconnect the voltmeters.

4. Once the throttle sensor is adjusted, disconnect the vent and vacuum solenoid connector.

5. Connect a tachometer, then start the engine.

6. Adjust the idle speed to 800 rpm by turning the Air Adjust Screw (AAS) on the throttle body. After adjusting the idle speed, reinstall the blind cap onto the AAS, if so equipped.

7. Shut off the engine, then attach the vent and vacuum solenoid connector. Disconnect and remove the tachometer, then install the fuel tank filler cap.

1986-89 RX-7

▶ **See Figures 60, 61, 62, 63, 64, 65 and 66**

1. Switch off all electrical accessories. Start the engine and let it run until it reaches normal operating temperature, then shut off the engine.

2. Connect a jumper wire to the terminals of the initial set coupler.

3. Connect a tachometer to the service coupler at the trailing side coil with igniter. If the tachometer does not function correctly, reconnect it at the leading side coil with igniter (black coupler).

➡ **If using an inductive (secondary pick-up) type tachometer, connect it only at the trailing side of the spark plug wires. If connected at the leading side coil with igniter, it will not function properly.**

4. Check/adjust the throttle sensor by performing the following:

a. With the engine **OFF**, connect dual checker lamps 49 F018 001 or equivalent to the green check connector.

b. Turn the ignition switch to the **ON** position and check that one of the lamps illuminates.

c. If both lamps illuminate or neither one does, turn the throttle sensor adjusting screw until only one of the lamps illuminates. If both of the lamps illuminate, remove the rubber cap and turn the screw counterclockwise. If neither lamp illuminates, turn the screw clockwise. Do not use excessive pressure on the screw.

d. Remove the checker lamps and reinstall the rubber cap.

5. On 1986-89 non-turbo models, remove the blind cap from the throttle body and adjust the idle speed by turning the Air Adjust Screw (AAS). On 1987-89 turbocharged models, remove the blind cap from the Bypass Air Control (BAC) valve and adjust the idle speed by turning the AAS.

6. When adjustment is complete, shut the engine **OFF**, then disconnect and remove the tachometer.

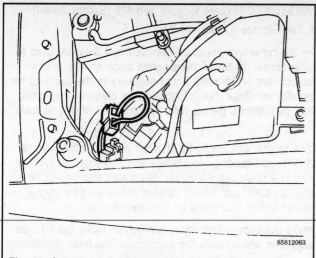

Fig. 60 Connect a jumper wire to the terminals of the initial set coupler — 1986-89 RX-7

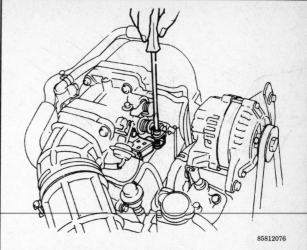

Fig. 63 If necessary, turn the throttle sensor adjusting screw — 1986-89 non-turbo RX-7

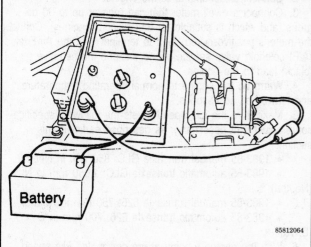

Fig. 61 Connect a tachometer to the service coupler at the trailing side coil with igniter — 1986-89 RX-7

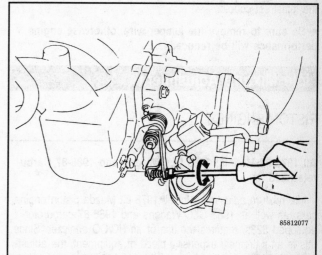

Fig. 64 If necessary, turn the throttle sensor adjusting screw — 1986-89 turbocharged RX-7

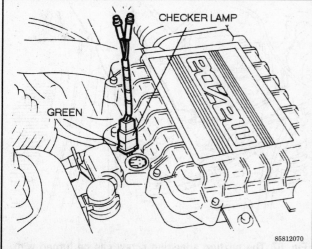

Fig. 62 Use dual checker lamps to verify the throttle sensor setting — 1986-89 RX-7

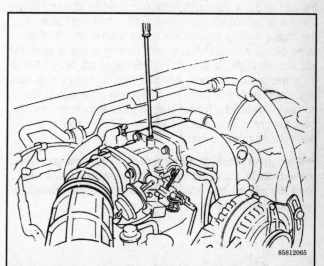

Fig. 65 Adjust the idle speed by turning the AAS on the throttle body — 1986-89 non-turbo RX-7

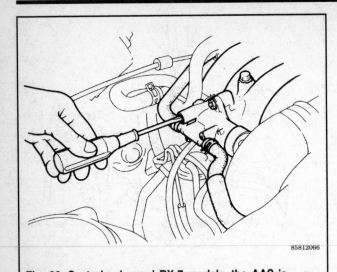

Fig. 66 On turbocharged RX-7 models, the AAS is located on the BAC valve

7. Install the blind cap and disconnect the jumper wire from the initial set coupler.

➡Be sure to remove the jumper wire, otherwise engine performance will be reduced.

Idle Mixture Adjustment

PISTON ENGINES

All 1978-82 Models; 1983 GLC Wagon and 1986-87 Carbureted 323

Idle mixture adjustment for all 1978-82 Mazda piston engine cars, as well as 1983 GLC Wagons and 1986-87 carburetor-equipped 323s, requires the use of an HC/CO analyzer. Since this is an extremely expensive piece of equipment, the adjustment procedure is complex, and this adjustment is not required as a part of ordinary maintenance, no procedures are included here. This adjustment can, however, be checked at a reasonable cost at many diagnostic centers, or may be checked during mandatory vehicle emission inspections, where applicable. If the engine exhibits a rough idle and/or smoke, combined (in some cases) with hesitation or poor running at low speeds, the idle mixture might be at fault. First, check all the basic tune-up adjustments such as dwell, ignition timing, and spark plug condition, and verify that there are no vacuum leaks due to disconnected or leaking hoses. Then, if these symptoms persist, have the idle mixture checked with an HC/CO meter at a dealer or diagnostic center.

➡If incorrect readings are detected, we suggest you take the vehicle to a shop or dealer familiar with Mazdas and have the idle mixture adjusted according to the procedure specified by the factory.

1983-85 GLC (Except Wagon) and 626 (Except Diesel)

◗ See Figures 67, 68 and 69

➡The carburetor must be removed and disassembled to gain access to the mixture screw since an idle mixture adjustment is normally only necessary in the event of carburetor overhaul. For information on carburetor removal and installation, please refer to Section 5 of this manual.

The air/fuel mixture for most 1983-85 carbureted piston engine models can readily be checked with a dwell/tachometer. An incorrect reading can indicate either an improper idle mixture or a faulty oxygen sensor. Make sure that the engine is properly tuned and that all vacuum hoses are properly connected before suspecting an improper idle mixture.

➡Do not secure the spring pin (which locks the mixture adjusting screw) until the adjustment has been performed.

To check/adjust the idle mixture:

1. On 1984 626s only, disconnect and plug the idle compensator, thermosensor, and reed valve hoses.
2. Connect a tachometer to the engine.
3. Connect a dwell meter that can register up to 90 degrees (and which is suitable for four-cylinder engines). Connect the meter's positive (+/red) lead to terminal Y of the Air/Fuel (A/F) solenoid valve service connector, and the negative (-/black) lead to the engine.
4. Warm up the engine to normal operating temperature and turn off all accessories.
5. Make sure the idle speed meets the following specifications; adjust it (if necessary), as described earlier in this section:

- 1983-85 manual transaxle GLC: 850 rpm in Neutral
- 1983-85 automatic transaxle GLC: 1,050 rpm in N (Neutral)
- 1983-85 manual transaxle 626: 750 rpm in Neutral
- 1983-85 automatic transaxle 626: 700 rpm in D (Drive)

6. With the engine running at the designated idle speed, note the reading on the dwell meter; the reading should be 32-40 degrees.

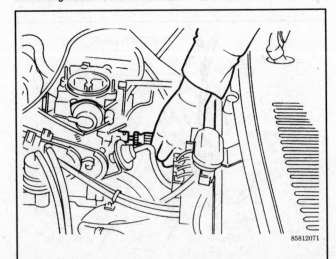

Fig. 67 The mixture adjusting screw can be turned with a screwdriver

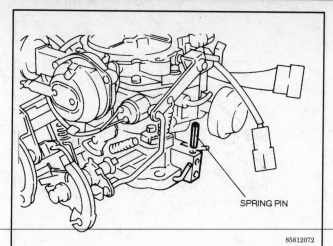

85812072

Fig. 68 A spring pin is used to lock the mixture adjusting screw in place

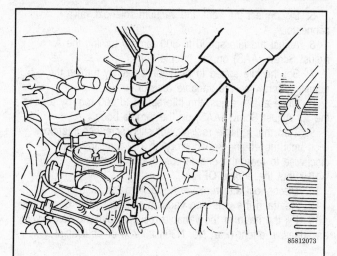

85812073

Fig. 69 Gently tap the spring pin into position after adjusting the idle mixture

7. If the dwell reading is not within the appropriate range, adjust the idle mixture by turning the mixture adjusting screw, located near the base of the carburetor.

8. Make sure that the idle speed still meets specifications.

➡**Idle speed of the GLC with automatic transaxle should now be checked with the gear selector in D (Drive), but MAKE SURE the parking brake is set and the drive wheels are blocked. The correct reading is 750 rpm.**

9. After the mixture is properly set, press in the spring pin to lock the adjusting screw.

10. On 1984 626s only, unplug and reconnect the idle compensator, thermosensor, and reed valve hoses.

11. Disconnect the dwell meter and tachometer. Re-attach the A/F solenoid valve connector.

1986-89 Fuel Injected Models

On all 1986-89 fuel injected piston engine vehicles covered by this manual, idle mixture is automatically maintained by the electronic engine control unit, and thus, cannot be manually adjusted.

ROTARY ENGINES

Carbureted Vehicles

Most 1979-85 RX-7s were equipped with a carburetor.

➡**Idle mixture adjustment is normally only necessary in the event of carburetor overhaul. For information on carburetor removal and installation, please refer to Section 5 of this manual.**

1. Remove the throttle body, then cut out the idle limiter cap with a hacksaw.

2. Assemble and install the carburetor. Be sure to install a new mixture adjusting screw. Tighten it lightly until it seats, then turn it counterclockwise three revolutions to attain the preliminary setting.

3. Connect a tachometer to the engine, then start the engine.

4. With the gear selector set to Neutral (or N), turn the throttle adjusting screw to adjust the idle speed to 770 rpm (manual transmission) or 870 rpm (automatic transmission). Read the tachometer as if testing a conventional 4-cylinder engine.

5. Set the idle speed to its highest rpm by turning the mixture adjusting screw, located at the base of the carburetor.

6. With the gear selector still set to Neutral (or N), again turn the throttle adjusting screw to adjust the idle speed to 770 rpm (manual transmission) or 870 rpm (automatic transmission).

7. Turn the mixture adjusting screw clockwise to lower the idle speed to 750 rpm (manual transmission) or 840 rpm (automatic transmission).

❊❊CAUTION

When making adjustments with the engine running, especially with the automatic transmission in drive, ALWAYS make sure the parking brake is firmly set and the drive wheels are blocked in position.

8. On vehicles equipped with an automatic transmission, shift the selector lever to the D position and adjust the idle speed to 750 rpm by turning the throttle adjusting screw.

9. Shut the engine OFF.

10. Install a new idle limiter cap onto the mixture adjustment screw.

➡**After adjusting idle speed, the throttle sensor on the carburetor should also be adjusted. For information on that procedure, please refer to Section 5 of this manual.**

11. Disconnect and remove the tachometer.

Fuel Injected Vehicles

1984-85 RX-7

♦ See Figures 70, 71, 72, 73 and 74

➡Idle mixture adjustment is normally only necessary when the variable resistor is replaced. The variable resistor should be replaced when it lacks continuity between terminals A and C or B and C, or whenever the engine is replaced.

1. Switch all electrical accessories to the off position and remove the fuel filler cap.
2. Connect a tachometer to the engine.
3. Start the engine and let it run until it reaches normal operating temperature.
4. Check/adjust the throttle sensor, as described in the idle speed adjustment procedure.

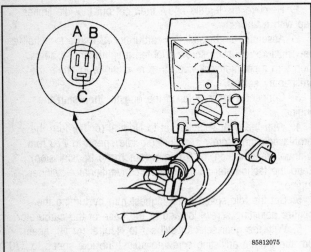

Fig. 70 Check the variable resistor for continuity between terminals A and C or B and C

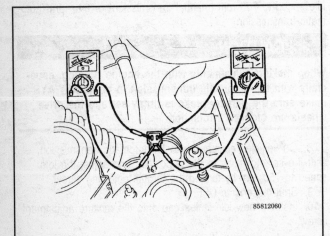

Fig. 71 Use a pair of voltmeters or test lights to check the throttle sensor setting — 1984-85 RX-7 with fuel injection

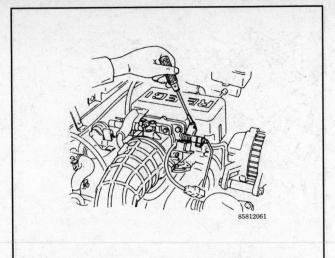

Fig. 72 If necessary, turn the throttle sensor adjusting screw — 1984-85 RX-7 with fuel injection

5. Disconnect the vent and vacuum solenoid valve connector.
6. Adjust the idle speed to 800 rpm by turning the Air Adjust Screw (AAS) on the throttle body.
7. Set the idle speed to its highest rpm by turning the adjusting screw on the variable resistor.
8. Once again, adjust the idle speed to 800 rpm by turning the Air Adjust Screw (AAS) on the throttle body.
9. Turn the variable resistor adjusting screw counterclockwise until the engine speed drops to 780 rpm, then turn it clockwise to reset the engine speed to 800 rpm.
10. Shut the engine **OFF**.
11. Disconnect and remove the tachometer.
12. Reattach the vent and vacuum solenoid valve connector.
13. Fill the head of the variable resistor adjusting screw with an adhesive agent (Part No. N304 23 795 or equivalent).

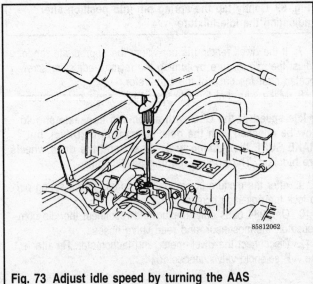

Fig. 73 Adjust idle speed by turning the AAS

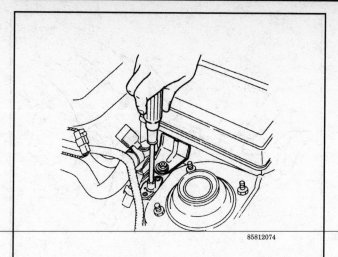

Fig. 74 Adjust the variable resistor with a screwdriver

1986-89 RX-7

▶ See Figures 75, 76, 77, 78, 79, 80, 81, 82 and 83

➡Idle mixture adjustment is normally only necessary when the variable resistor is replaced. The variable resistor should be replaced if it lacks continuity between terminals A and C or B and C, or whenever the engine is replaced.

1. Switch all electrical accessories to the off position.
2. Start the engine and let it run until it reaches normal operating temperature, then shut off the engine.
3. Connect a jumper wire to the terminals of the initial set coupler.
4. Connect a tachometer to the service coupler at the trailing side coil with igniter. If the tachometer does not function correctly, reconnect it at the leading side coil with igniter (black coupler).

➡If using an inductive (secondary pick-up) type tachometer, connect it only at the trailing side of the spark plug wires. If connected at the leading side coil with igniter, it will not function properly.

5. Check/adjust the throttle sensor, as described in the idle speed adjustment procedure.
6. Remove the blind cap and adjust the idle speed to 750 rpm by turning the Air Adjust Screw (AAS) on the throttle body.
7. Set the idle speed to its highest rpm by turning the adjusting screw on the variable resistor.
8. Once again, adjust the idle speed to 750 rpm by turning the Air Adjust Screw (AAS) on the throttle body.
9. Turn the variable resistor adjusting screw counterclockwise until the engine speed drops to 730 rpm, then turn it clockwise to reset the engine speed to 750 rpm.
10. Shut off the engine and disconnect the tachometer.
11. Install the blind cap and disconnect the jumper wire.

➡Be sure to remove the jumper wire, otherwise engine performance will be reduced.

12. Fill the head of the variable resistor adjusting screw with an adhesive agent (Part No. N304 23 795 or equivalent).

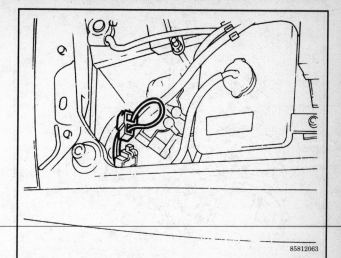

Fig. 75 Connect a jumper wire to the terminals of the initial set coupler — 1986-89 RX-7

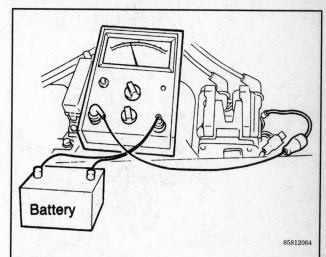

Fig. 76 Connect a tachometer to the service coupler at the trailing side coil with igniter — 1986-89 RX-7

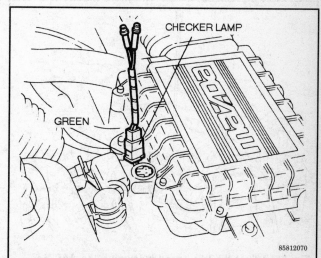

Fig. 77 Use dual checker lamps to verify the throttle sensor setting — 1986-89 RX-7

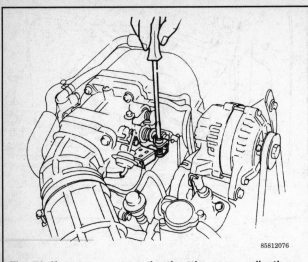

Fig. 78 If necessary, turn the throttle sensor adjusting screw — 1986-89 non-turbo RX-7

85812076

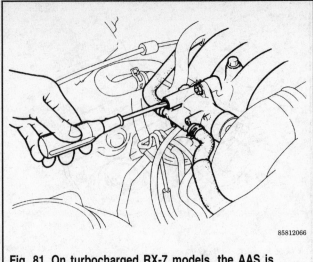

Fig. 81 On turbocharged RX-7 models, the AAS is located on the BAC valve

85812066

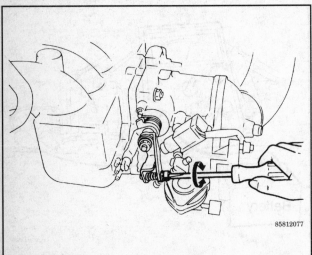

Fig. 79 If necessary, turn the throttle sensor adjusting screw — 1986-89 turbocharged RX-7

85812077

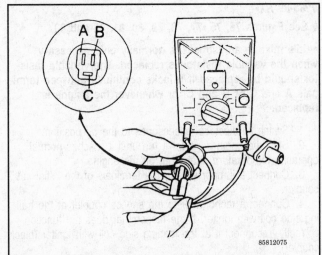

Fig. 82 Check the variable resistor for continuity between terminals A and C or B and C

85812075

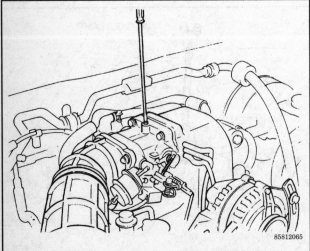

Fig. 80 Adjust the idle speed by turning the AAS on the throttle body — 1986-89 non-turbo RX-7

85812065

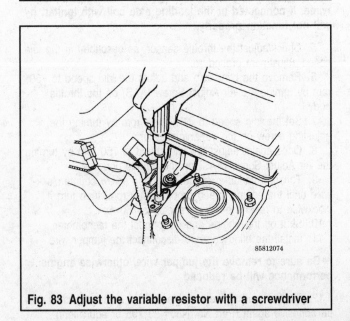

Fig. 83 Adjust the variable resistor with a screwdriver

85812074

3

ENGINE AND ENGINE OVERHAUL

ENGINE ELECTRICAL

Ignition Coil

CHECKING IGNITION COIL RESISTANCE

Except RX-7

1978-81 VEHICLES

▶ See Figures 1 and 2

1. Run the engine until it reaches operating temperature (coil must be hot). Disconnect the high tension lead from the coil tower.

2. Measure primary resistance with an ohmmeter, connecting between the coil's negative (-) and positive (+) primary terminals. Resistance should be 1.15-1.28 ohms (GLC) or 0.9-1.15 ohms (626).

3. Measure secondary resistance, connecting the ohmmeter between the coil tower and the positive (+) primary terminal. Resistance should be 13,500 ohms (GLC) or 7,000 ohms (626).

4. Replace the coil if either resistance is incorrect by more than 10%.

1982-89 VEHICLES

▶ See Figures 3, 4 and 5

1. Connect an ohmmeter, set to the x 1 scale, to the positive (+) and negative (-) primary terminals of the coil. The coil should have good continuity; resistance should be approximately 1.0-1.3 ohms on all models except the 1988-89 626/MX-6 turbo and 929. Resistance on the 1988-89 626/MX-6 turbo and 929 should be 0.72-0.88 ohms.

2. Disconnect the high tension wire from the coil. Connect the ohmmeter to the positive (+) coil terminal and the metallic connector inside the coil tower. Set the ohmmeter to the x

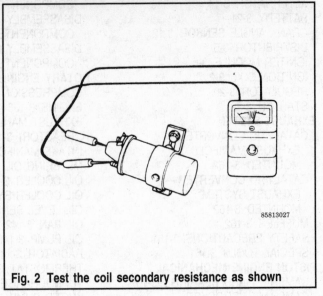

Fig. 2 Test the coil secondary resistance as shown

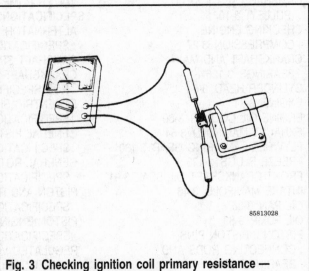

Fig. 3 Checking ignition coil primary resistance — 1986-89 323, 626/MX-6 and 929

1000 scale. Resistance must be 10,000-30,000 ohms, except on the following:

- 1986-89 323: 6,000-30,000 ohms
- 1988-89 626/MX-6 (non-turbo): 7,000-9,700 ohms
- 1988-89 626/MX-6 (turbo): 10,300-13,900 ohms

3. You can also check for bad coil insulation by measuring the resistance between the coil negative (-) primary connection and the metal body (housing) of the coil. If resistance is less than 10,000 ohms, replace the coil.

➡This test may not be entirely satisfactory unless you have a tester that produces 500 volts. If the tests below do not reveal the problem and, especially, if operating the engine at night produces some bluish sparks around the coil, you may want to remove the coil and have it tested at a diagnostic center.

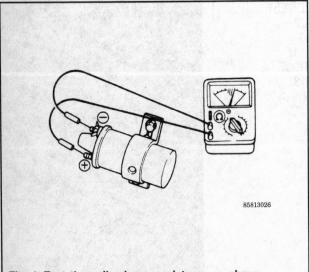

Fig. 1 Test the coil primary resistance as shown

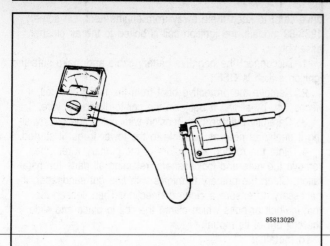

**Fig. 4 Checking ignition coil secondary resistance —
1986-89 323, 626/MX-6 and 929**

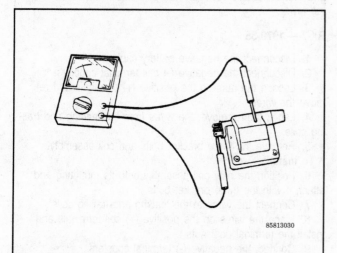

**Fig. 5 Checking ignition coil insulation — 1986-89 323,
626/MX-6 and 929**

4. If the coil resistances are not as specified, replace the
coil.

5. If the coil tests OK, replace the igniter and pickup coil.
However, you should make sure before doing this work that
there are no basic maintenance problems in the secondary
circuit of the system, since it is often impossible to return
electrical parts. We suggest that before you replace the igniter
and pickup coil, you carefully inspect the cap and rotor for
carbon tracks or cracks. Also, disconnect the wires and measure their resistance with an ohmmeter. Resistance should be
16,000 ohms per length of 3.28 feet (1 meter). Also, check for
cracks in the insulation. Replace secondary parts as inspec-
tion/testing deems necessary before replacing the igniter and
pickup coil.

RX-7

1979-85 VEHICLES

➡The coil(s) must be at normal operating temperature to
perform this test, so either start the engine or turn the
ignition ON until the coils heat up. If one or both coils
won't get hot, check your wiring or try to substitute
coil(s).

1. Check the leading ignition first. Remove the high tension
cable from its center tower and connect the leads of an ohmmeter to the two side terminals. Resistance should be
1.22-1.48 ohms.

2. Test the trailing coil in the same manner. It should also
give a reading of 1.22-1.48 ohms.

3. If either reading is out of specification, replace the
coil(s).

1986-89 VEHICLES

◗ See Figures 6 and 7

➡This testing procedure covers both the leading and trailing side ignition coils; however, the coils differ in appearance and design. On the trailing side coil, there are two
sets of terminals that require resistance checks, whereas
the leading side has only one set. When checking the coil
resistance, be sure to distinguish between the two coils.

1. Disconnect the negative battery cable.

2. Set your ohmmeter to the x 1 scale, then connect the
ohmmeter probes to the positive (+) and negative (-) coil terminals. On the trailing side, test both sets of terminals.

3. If the resistance is above 1 ohm, replace the coil.

CHECKING EXTERNAL RESISTOR

1979 RX-7 Only

◗ See Figure 8

The external resistor block is located inside the engine compartment on the driver's side strut pod. The external resistor
modifies the current going into the positive primary terminal of

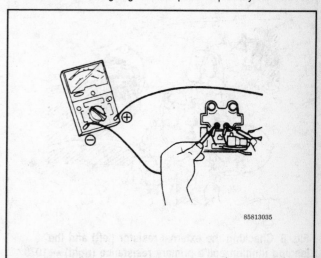

**Fig. 6 Checking the leading ignition coil resistance —
1986-89 RX-7**

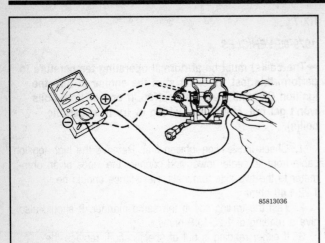

Fig. 7 Checking the trailing ignition coil resistance — 1986-89 RX-7. Note the two sets of terminals to be checked

the ignition coil. This allows the coil to be constructed so that a strong spark is generated at high engine speeds.

➡**All of the electrical terminals for the trailing ignition coil have light colored protective caps, while all leading coil terminals have dark colored caps.**

Connect the leads of an ohmmeter to the trailing coil side of the resistor (the side with the light colored caps). Resistance should be 1.26-1.54 ohms. Repeat the test on the leading side of the resistor (the side with dark caps). The reading should be the same as for the trailing side. If the reading is not within or close to this range, replace the resistor.

REMOVAL & INSTALLATION

Except RX-7

Most Mazda coils are located on the fender well (rear wheel drive cars) or the front engine compartment panel (front wheel

Fig. 8 Checking the external resistor (left) and the leading ignition coil's primary resistance (right) — 1979 RX-7

drive cars) to keep them away from engine heat. On some 1986-89 models, the ignition coil is bolted to the air cleaner assembly.

1. Disconnect the negative battery cable and make sure the ignition switch is **OFF**.
2. Remove the protective boot from the top of the coil, if necessary, by sliding it back on the coil-to-distributor wire.
3. Carefully pull the high tension wire out of the coil, twisting it gently as near as possible to the tower to get it started.
4. Note the routing and colors of the primary wires, then remove the nuts and lockwashers, retaining all parts for installation. Clean the primary terminals with fine grit sandpaper, if necessary, to ensure a clean connection. Then, loosen the through-bolt or bolts which clamp the coil in place and slide the coil out of its mount.
   To install:
5. Install the new coil in exact reverse order, making sure the primary (+ and -) connections are clean and tight. Ensure also that the coil-to-distributor wire is fully seated in the tower and that the protective boot is fully installed on the outside of the tower.

RX-7 — 1979-85

1. Disconnect the negative battery cable.
2. Disconnect the negative (-) coil terminal couplers.
3. Loosen the nuts on the positive (+) terminals and remove the wires.
4. Label, then remove, the wires from the leading and trailing coils.
5. Remove the three bracket bolts and coil assembly.
   To install:
6. Position the new coil assembly onto its mounting and attach it with the three bracket bolts.
7. Connect the wires to the leading and trailing coils.
8. Place the wires on the positive (+) coil terminals and install the terminal post nuts.
9. Connect the negative (-) terminal couplers.
10. Connect the negative battery cable.

RX-7 — 1986-89

➡**The 1986-89 RX-7 leading and trailing ignition coils each have a built-in igniter.**

LEADING SIDE

1. Disconnect the negative battery cable.
2. Label the wires for identification.
3. Loosen the nuts and disconnect the primary wires from the coil/igniter.
4. Disconnect the 2-prong connector.
5. Remove the bracket bolts and coil/igniter assembly.
6. Installation is the reverse of removal.

TRAILING SIDE

1. Disconnect the negative battery cable.
2. Label the wires for identification.
3. Loosen the nuts and disconnect the (B) and (L) primary wires from the coil/igniter.
4. Disconnect the 2 and 4-prong connectors.
5. Remove the bracket bolts and coil assembly.
6. Installation is the reverse of removal.

Igniter Module

➡**On the 929, the igniter module is a separate, replaceable component.**

REMOVAL & INSTALLATION

929

▶ **See Figure 9**

The igniter module is located next to the ignition coil on the driver's side of the engine compartment.

1. Disengage the harness connector from the top of the igniter.
2. Remove the two attaching screws and remove the ignitor.
3. Install the new igniter and secure it with the two attaching screws.
4. Engage the harness connector.

Distributor

REMOVAL & INSTALLATION

Piston Engines

1978-85 ALL MODELS

▶ **See Figures 10, 11, 12, 13, 14 and 15**

1. Unfasten the clips or remove the screws which hold the distributor cap to the top of the distributor, then remove the cap. Note the location of the wire going to the No. 1 cylinder (the front cylinder on rear drive cars, or the cylinder on the left side of the car on front drive cars) where it enters the cap.

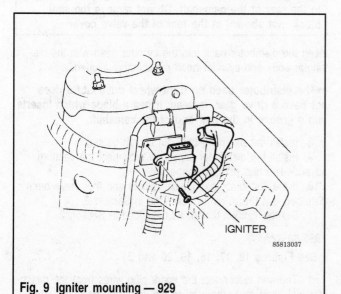

Fig. 9 Igniter mounting — 929

2. Rotate the engine with the starter, or by using a socket wrench on the bolt retaining the crankshaft pulley (turning in the normal direction of rotation), until the timing mark on the pulley is aligned with the pin on the front cover. Check to see if the contact on the rotor is pointing toward the No. 1 spark plug wire's cap location (tower). If the rotor is half a turn away from the No. 1 plug wire, turn the crankshaft ahead one full rotation until the timing mark is again aligned with the pin.

3. Disconnect the vacuum advance or advance/retard line(s) at the advance unit, and disconnect the primary wire or wires at the connector near the distributor.

4. Matchmark the distributor body and rotor with the cylinder head or retaining bracket.

5. Remove the retaining/adjusting bolt, then pull the distributor out of the engine. If so equipped, remove the O-ring.

➡**For easier installation, avoid rotating the engine with the distributor removed.**

Fig. 10 Matchmark the distributor body and rotor with the cylinder head or retaining bracket

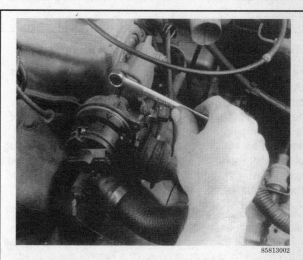

Fig. 11 Use the correct size box wrench to remove the retaining/adjusting bolt

Fig. 12 Withdraw the distributor assembly from the engine

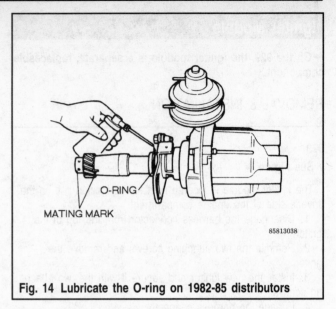

Fig. 14 Lubricate the O-ring on 1982-85 distributors

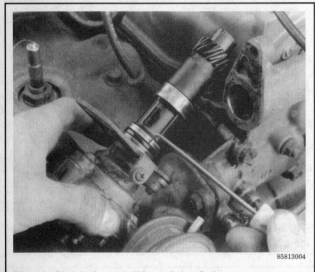

Fig. 13 Check the condition of the O-ring

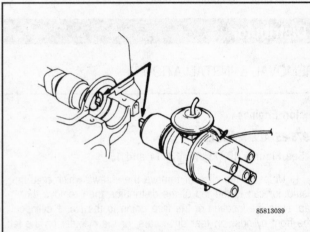

Fig. 15 On FWD GLC, the distributor engages a notch in the rear of the camshaft. Do not remove the seal block (not shown) at the rear of the valve cover

To install:

➡️If the engine has been rotated while the distributor was out, it will be necessary to turn the crankshaft until the point where the No. 1 cylinder is about to fire. This is known as Top Dead Center (TDC). To do this, remove the No. 1 spark plug and rotate the engine until you can feel compression building (with your finger over the spark plug hole). Then, rotate the engine until the timing mark on the front pulley is aligned with the pin on the front cover, and proceed with Step 6.

6. Lightly oil and install a new O-ring near the top of the distributor shaft on applicable 1981-85 models.

7. Lightly oil the distributor drive gear, then align the dimple on the gear with the mark cast into the base of the distributor body by rotating the shaft. Being careful not to rotate the shaft,

insert the distributor back into the cylinder head with the distributor body and cylinder head matchmarks aligned.

➡️The distributor used on front wheel drive GLCs does not have a drive gear. Instead, it has a blade which inserts into a groove in the rear end of the camshaft.

8. Install the mounting bolt, but do not tighten it.

9. Install the distributor cap, then reconnect the vacuum advance line and primary connector.

10. If the distributor has ignition points and they have been disturbed, set the dwell as described in Section 2.

11. Set the ignition timing, as described in Section 2.

1986-89 323

▶ See Figures 16, 17, 18, 19, 20 and 21

1. Tag and disconnect the spark plug wires from the distributor cap, then route them off to the side and out of the way.

➡️If the same distributor cap is to be reinstalled, remove the cap with the wires attached.

2. Disconnect the vacuum hose(s) and the electrical connector from the distributor.

3. Rotate the engine so that the No. 1 piston is at Top Dead Center (TDC) as follows:

a. Engage the starter motor, or turn a socket wrench (in the direction of normal engine rotation) on the bolt retaining the crankshaft pulley, until the timing mark on the pulley is aligned with the pin on the front cover.

b. Check to see if the contact on the rotor is pointing toward the No. 1 spark plug wire's cap location (tower). If the rotor is half a turn away from the No. 1 plug wire, turn the crankshaft ahead one full rotation until the timing mark is again aligned with the pin.

4. Remove the distributor hold-down bolt(s) and withdraw the distributor from the cylinder head.

5. Remove the O-ring seal and discard it.

➡ For easier installation, avoid rotating the engine with the distributor removed.

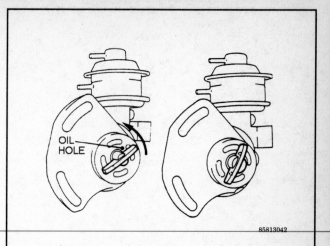

Fig. 18 Distributor blade and rotor alignment — 1986-89 323 non-turbo

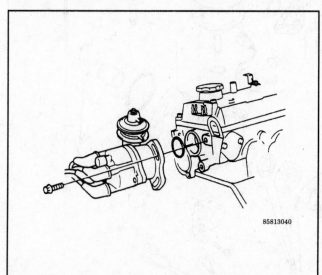

Fig. 16 Distributor mounting — 1986-89 323 non-turbo

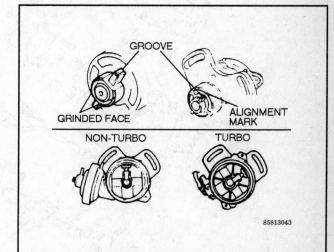

Fig. 19 On 1988-89 turbocharged 323s, align the distributor blade with the groove in the housing

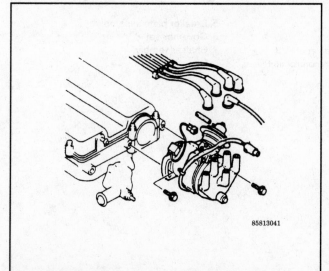

Fig. 17 Distributor mounting — 1988-89 323 turbo

To install:

➡ If the engine has been rotated while the distributor was out, it will be necessary to turn the crankshaft until the point where the No. 1 cylinder is at TDC. To do this, remove the No. 1 spark plug and rotate the engine until you can feel compression building (with your finger over the spark plug hole). Then, rotate the engine until the timing mark on the front pulley is aligned with the pin on the front cover, and proceed with Step 6.

6. Coat the new O-ring seal with a light film of clean engine oil and install it into the cylinder head opening.

➡ Make sure that the number one piston is at top dead center before installing the distributor.

7. On non-turbocharged engines, turn the distributor blade so that it aligns with the small oil holes in the bottom of the distributor. On turbocharged engines, align the distributor blade with the grooved matchmark on the body.

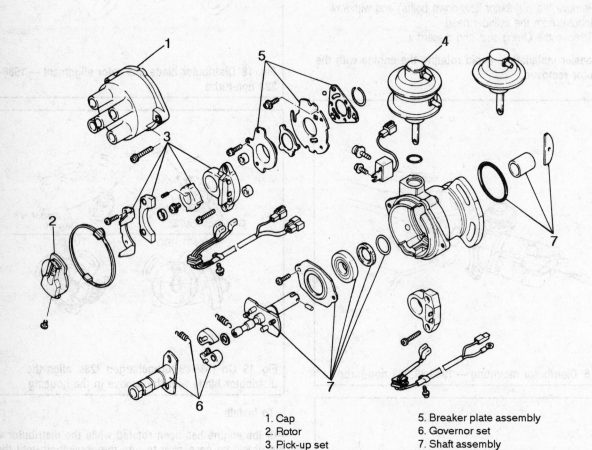

1. Cap
2. Rotor
3. Pick-up set
4. Vacuum control unit
5. Breaker plate assembly
6. Governor set
7. Shaft assembly

85813044

Fig. 20 Distributor components — 1986-89 323 non-turbo

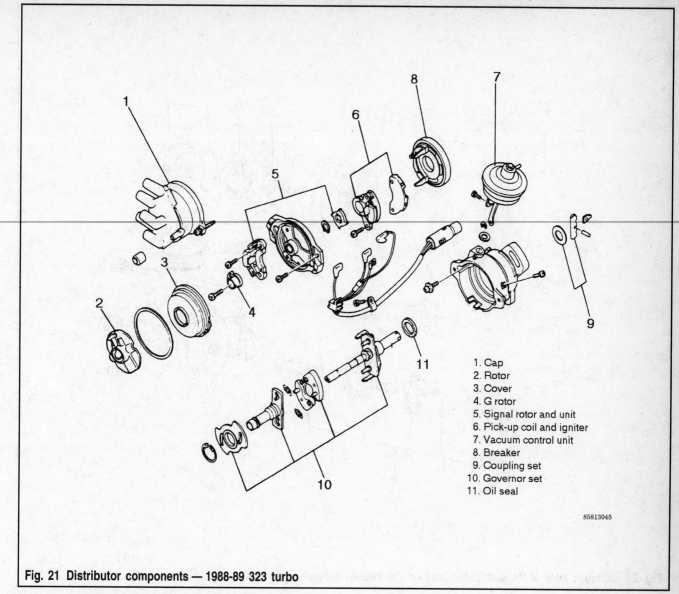

Fig. 21 Distributor components — 1988-89 323 turbo

1. Cap
2. Rotor
3. Cover
4. G rotor
5. Signal rotor and unit
6. Pick-up coil and igniter
7. Vacuum control unit
8. Breaker
9. Coupling set
10. Governor set
11. Oil seal

85813045

8. Install the distributor, then engage the wiring connector, vacuum hose(s) and spark plug wires.

9. Set the ignition timing, as described in Section 2.

1986-89 626 AND MX-6

▶ **See Figures 22 and 23**

1. Tag and disconnect the spark plug wires from the distributor cap, then route them off to the side and out of the way.

➡**If the same distributor cap is to be reinstalled, remove the cap with the wires attached.**

2. On non-turbocharged engines, disconnect the vacuum hoses and wiring. On turbocharged engines, disconnect the electrical coupler.

3. Rotate the engine so that the No. 1 piston is at Top Dead Center (TDC) as follows:

a. Engage the starter motor, or turn a socket wrench on the bolt retaining the crankshaft pulley (in the normal direction of engine rotation), until the timing mark on the pulley is aligned with the pin on the front cover.

b. Check to see if the contact on the rotor is pointing toward the No. 1 spark plug wire's cap location (tower). If the rotor is half a turn away from the No. 1 plug wire, turn the crankshaft ahead one full rotation until the timing mark is again aligned with the pin.

4. Loosen the lockbolt(s) and remove the distributor.

5. Remove and discard the O-ring from the coupling shaft.

✳✳WARNING

For easier installation, do not rotate the engine with the distributor removed, unless necessary.

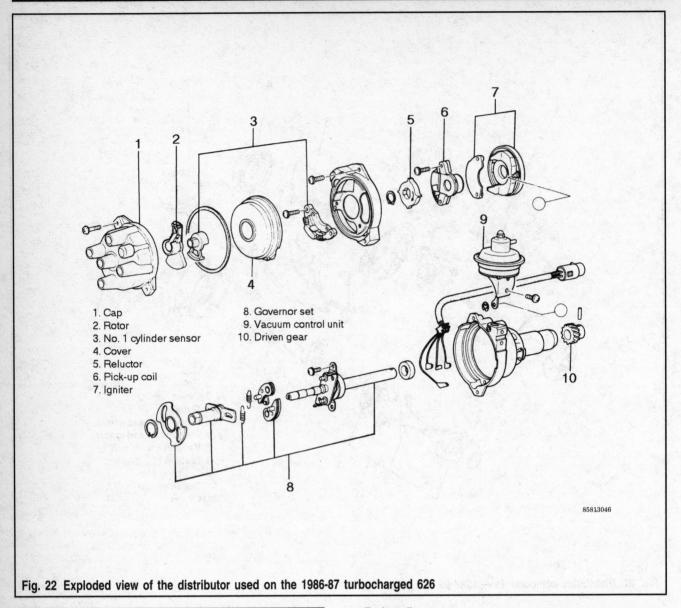

1. Cap
2. Rotor
3. No. 1 cylinder sensor
4. Cover
5. Reluctor
6. Pick-up coil
7. Igniter
8. Governor set
9. Vacuum control unit
10. Driven gear

85813046

Fig. 22 Exploded view of the distributor used on the 1986-87 turbocharged 626

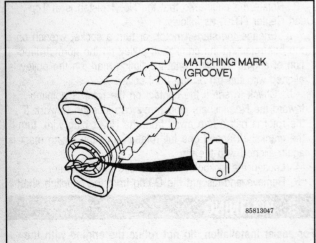

MATCHING MARK
(GROOVE)

85813047

Fig. 23 Distributor blade and rotor alignment — 1988-89 626/MX-6

To install:

➡If the engine has been rotated while the distributor was out, it will be necessary to turn the crankshaft until the point where the No. 1 cylinder is at TDC. To do this, remove the No. 1 spark plug and rotate the engine until you can feel compression building (with your finger over the spark plug hole). Then, rotate the engine until the timing mark on the front pulley is aligned with the pin on the front cover, and proceed with Step 6.

6. Install a new O-ring onto the coupling shaft, then apply a coat of clean engine oil to the O-ring and to the driven gear.

7. On 1986-87 models, first align the dimple on the distributor drive gear with the mark cast into the base of the distributor body by rotating the shaft.

8. On 1988-89 models, align the shaft coupling blade with the alignment marks on the distributor body, then turn the distributor over and check that the rotor is aligned as shown in the illustration.

9. Install the distributor and engage the wiring connector, vacuum hose(s) ad spark plug wires.

10. Set the ignition timing, as described in Section 2.

929

▶ **See Figures 24 and 25**

1. Tag and disconnect the spark plug wires from the distributor cap, then route them off to the side and out of the way.

➡ **If the same distributor cap is to be reinstalled, remove the cap with the wires attached.**

2. Disengage the distributor electrical connector.
3. Rotate the engine so that the No. 1 piston is at Top Dead Center (TDC) as follows:

a. Engage the starter motor, or turn a socket wrench on the bolt retaining the crankshaft pulley (in the normal direction of engine rotation), until the yellow mark on the pulley is aligned with the "T" mark on the timing scale.

b. Check to see if the contact on the rotor is pointing toward the No. 1 spark plug wire's cap location (tower). If the rotor is half a turn away from the No. 1 plug wire, turn

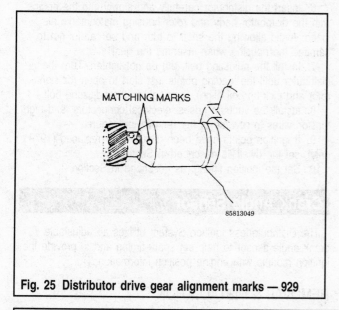

Fig. 25 Distributor drive gear alignment marks — 929

MATCHING MARKS

85813049

the crankshaft ahead one full turn until the marks are again aligned.

4. Loosen the lockbolt and remove the distributor. Remove and discard the O-ring from the distributor shaft.

✳✳WARNING

For easier installation, do not rotate the engine with the distributor removed, unless necessary.

To install:

➡ **If the engine has been rotated while the distributor was out, it will be necessary to turn the crankshaft until the point where the No. 1 cylinder is at TDC. To do this, remove the No. 1 spark plug and rotate the engine until you can feel compression building (with your finger over the spark plug hole). Then, rotate the engine until the timing mark on the front pulley is aligned with the "T" mark on the timing scale, and proceed with Step 5.**

5. Install the new O-ring onto the distributor shaft and lightly oil both the O-ring and the driven gear. Be sure to use only clean engine oil.
6. Align the matchmarks on the distributor housing with the driven gear.
7. Install the distributor, then engage the electrical connector and the spark plug wires.
8. Set the ignition timing, as described in Section 2. Torque the lockbolt to 14-18 ft. lbs. (19-24 Nm) once the timing is set.

Rotary Engines

1979-85 RX-7

▶ **See Figures 26 and 27**

1. Rotate the engine in its normal direction of rotation until the first (TDC or "Leading") timing mark aligns with the pin on the front cover. Matchmark the body of the distributor and the engine rotor housing.
2. The easiest method to move the high tension wires out of the way it to simply remove the cap and set it aside with the wires still attached. However, if you wish to keep the cap

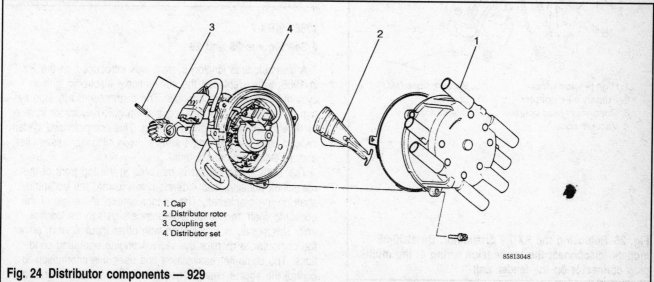

1. Cap
2. Distributor rotor
3. Coupling set
4. Distributor set

85813048

Fig. 24 Distributor components — 929

with the distributor, tag the wires for identification, then remove them from the cap.

3. Disconnect the vacuum advance and, if equipped, vacuum retard hoses. Disengage the primary electrical connector (1979) or the pick-up coil and condenser lead wiring (1980-85).

4. Remove the distributor adjusting bolt. Pull the distributor vertically out of the engine.

✳✳WARNING

For easier installation, do not rotate the engine with the distributor removed, unless necessary.

To install:

5. Make sure the engine has not been disturbed. If it has been rotated, again turn the crankshaft until the first timing mark lines up with the pin on the front cover. Then, align the dimple in the distributor gear with the dot or line cast into the body of the distributor (see illustrations).

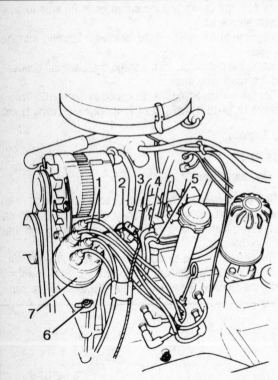

1. High tension wires
2. Primary wire coupler
3. Condenser lead coupler
4. Vacuum hose
5. Vacuum hose (M/T)
6. Lock nut
7. Distributor

85813050

Fig. 26 Removing the RX-7's distributor. On 1980-85 models, disconnect the low tension wiring at the multi-plug connector on the fender wall

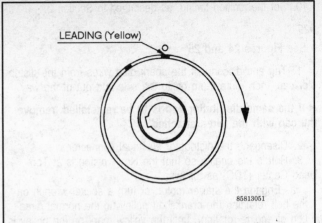

LEADING (Yellow)

85813051

Fig. 27 When removing and installing the distributor, make sure that the leading (yellow) timing mark on the front pulley and the pointer on the engine case are aligned

6. Insert the distributor carefully and slowly into the engine with the distributor body and rotor housing matchmarks aligned. Avoid allowing the shaft to turn and be careful not to damage the housing when inserting the gear.

7. Install the adjusting bolt, but do not tighten. Turn the distributor until the leading points just start to open (or signal rotor and pick-up coil align), then tighten the adjusting bolt.

8. Install the vacuum hoses, electrical connectors, and high tension wires in reverse of the removal procedure.

9. If ignition points have been disturbed or replaced (1979 only), set the dwell as described in Section 2.

10. Set the ignition timing, as described in Section 2.

Crank Angle Sensor

The Distributorless Ignition System utilizes an adjustable crank angle sensor to help set spark timing and to provide the ignition module with engine position information.

REMOVAL & INSTALLATION

1986-89 RX-7
▶ See Figures 28 and 29

A distributorless ignition system was introduced on the RX-7 in 1986, which replaced the conventional electronic ignition system used on earlier models. The distributorless ignition system does not use a distributor, pick-up coil, reluctor or ignition module to control the ignition timing. This computerized system instead uses a crank angle sensor, two coil/igniter assemblies, and an electronic control unit.

The crank angle sensor is mounted in the top front of the crankshaft housing, and extends down toward the eccentric shaft on the crankshaft. The sensor detects the angle of the eccentric shaft and sends a reference signal to the control unit. This signal, in conjunction with other input signals, allows the computer to monitor the various engine operating conditions. The computer assimilates and uses this information to control the engine timing. The control unit varies the ignition timing by controlling the interruption of the current flow in the primary windings of the coil igniter units.

1. Rotate the engine so that the leading (yellow) timing mark on the pulley is aligned with the timing indicator pin.

2. Matchmark the crank angle sensor with the front rotor housing using a piece of chalk or white crayon. These matchmarks must be neatly and accurately placed.

3. Unplug the connector from the crank angle sensor.

4. Loosen the locknut and pull the sensor straight out of the rotor housing. Cover the opening with masking tape to prevent anything from falling into the engine.

5. Remove and discard the O-ring from the sensor.

To install:

6. Coat a new O-ring with a light film of clean engine oil and install it on the crank angle sensor.

7. Insert the crank angle sensor into the front rotor housing opening and align the matchmarks, then install the locknut.

8. Reattach the sensor's connector.

9. Set the ignition timing, as described in Section 2 of this manual. Tighten the locknut to 70-96 inch lbs. (8-11 Nm).

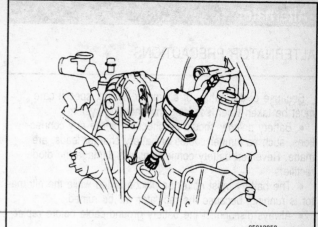

85813053

Fig. 29 Crank angle sensor mounting — 1986-89 RX-7

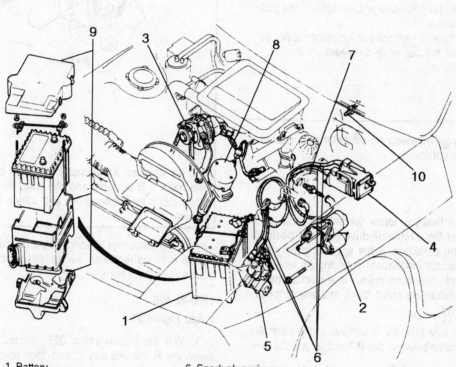

1. Battery
2. Starter motor
3. Alternator
4. Coil with igniter (Trailing side)
5. Coil with igniter (Leading side)
6. Spark plug wires
7. Spark plugs
8. Crank angle sensor
9. Battery cover
10. Interlock switch

85813052

Fig. 28 Components of the distributorless ignition system — 1986-89 RX-7

Alternator

ALTERNATOR PRECAUTIONS

Because of the nature of alternator design, special care must be taken when servicing the charging system:
• Battery polarity should be checked before any connections, such as jumper cables or battery charger leads, are made. Reversed battery connections will damage the diode rectifiers.
• The battery must never be disconnected while the alternator is running, because the regulator will be ruined.
• Always disconnect the battery ground cable before replacing the alternator.
• Do not attempt to polarize an alternator.
• Do not short across or ground any alternator terminals.
• Always disconnect the battery ground cable before removing the alternator output cable, whether the engine is running or not.
• If electric arc welding equipment is to be used on the car, first disconnect the battery and alternator cables. Never start the engine with the electric arc welding equipment attached.
• If the battery is to be quick-charged, disconnect the positive cable from the battery.
• Do not use any type of high voltage resistance tester in the electrical circuits of the car, while the alternator is connected.

TESTING

➡For these tests, you will need an ammeter and, except for the 1980 GLC, a voltmeter.

1980 GLC

▶ See Figure 30

➡This test assumes that you know the battery is undercharged, and that the alternator drive belt and basic wiring are in working condition. If the specific gravity of the battery cells indicate inadequate charging (is less than 1.260) and the vehicle has been driven in a normal manner (without too many extremely short trips), the alternator is not charging properly.

1. Disconnect the wire from the **B** terminal of the alternator, and connect an ammeter between the **B** terminal and the wire.

➡Refer to the accompanying illustration, as necessary, for terminal designations.

2. Disconnect the alternator's multi-connector and attach jumper wires, as shown.
3. Start the engine and run it at 2,000 rpm (you can use a dwell/tachometer to measure rpm). Read the ammeter, and note the reading. Then, pull the wire off the female **F** terminal and connect it to the female **A** terminal just long enough to get a current reading. Shut off the engine.

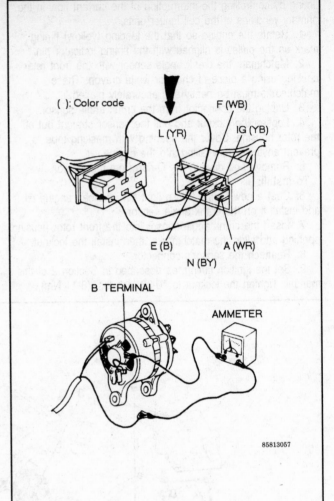

( ): Color code

F (WB)
L (YR)
IG (YB)
E (B)
A (WR)
N (BY)

B TERMINAL

AMMETER

85813057

Fig. 30 Connect an ammeter in series between the alternator's B terminal and the wire, then unplug the alternator's multi-connector and attach jumper wires, as shown

4. If the amperage reading increases significantly, the trouble is in the regulator; if it remains exactly the same, the trouble is in the alternator.

1980-82 626

▶ See Figure 31

1. With the ignition switch **OFF**, connect the voltmeter between the **R** terminal and ground, then read the voltage. Do the same for the **L** terminal. If there is voltage at either terminal, the alternator is defective.
2. With the voltmeter still connected to the **L** terminal, turn the ignition switch **ON** and read the voltmeter. Note the reading, then check the voltage across the battery terminals. **L** terminal voltage should be 1-3 volts DC. If there is no voltage, the alternator or associated wiring is bad. If the voltage is close to the battery's voltage, connect a jumper wire between the **F** terminal and ground. If the voltage at the **L** terminal

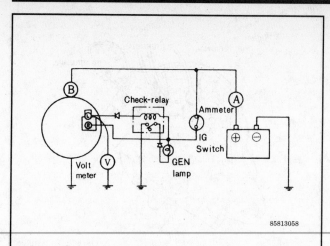

Fig. 31 Connect the voltmeter and ammeter as shown to test alternator output — 1981-85 GLC and 1980-85 626 (except diesel)

drops lower than the battery voltage, this indicates that the IC regulator may be faulty.

➡The F terminal is neither exposed on the surface of the alternator rear bracket, nor marked for its location. It is located at a depth of 0.79 in. (20mm) in a hole near the mark of B terminal.

✳✳WARNING

Do not start the engine with the connector for the L and R terminals unplugged, and do not ground the L terminal while the engine is running.

3. Start the engine and turn on the headlights. Gradually increase the engine speed as you read the output voltage and current. If output voltage is higher than battery voltage, and there is output current, the alternator is operating satisfactorily.

➡**On 1982 models, you can go a step further and check the no-load adjustment voltage as follows:**

4. With the battery fully charged, connect a voltmeter between the battery's positive terminal and ground. Connect a voltmeter between the L terminal on the rear of the alternator and ground. Connect an ammeter between the alternator's B terminal and the battery's positive terminal. Jumper the ammeter with a heavy-gauge wire (as illustrated by the dotted line) while starting the engine, then remove the jumper. Run the engine at 2,000-2,500 rpm (check rpm with a dwell/tach). This will turn the alternator 5,000 rpm. The ammeter should read less than 5 amps, and the voltmeter 14.1-14.7 volts DC. Now, turn on the lights. If the alternator responds by putting out increased amperage, and the voltage is higher than the battery voltage, it is functioning properly.

1981-85 GLC and 1983-85 626

EXCEPT DIESEL

▶ See Figures 31, 32, 33 and 34

1. With the ignition switch **OFF**, connect the voltmeter between the L terminal and ground, then read the voltage. If there is any voltage, the alternator is defective.

2. With the voltmeter still connected to the L terminal, turn the ignition switch **ON** and read the voltmeter. If the reading is 0 volts, there is probably a malfunction in the alternator, but check the wiring first. If the voltage is close to the battery's voltage, connect a jumper wire between the F terminal and ground. If the voltage at the L terminal drops lower than the battery voltage, this indicates a malfunction of the IC regulator.

✳✳WARNING

Do not start the engine with the connector for the L and R terminals unplugged, and do not ground the L terminal while the engine is running.

3. Start the engine and turn on the headlights. Gradually increase the engine speed as you read the output voltage and current. If output voltage is higher than battery voltage, and there is output current, the alternator is operating satisfactorily.

4. Check the no-load adjustment voltage after installing a shunt to protect the ammeter during start-up, as illustrated. With the battery fully charged, connect a voltmeter between

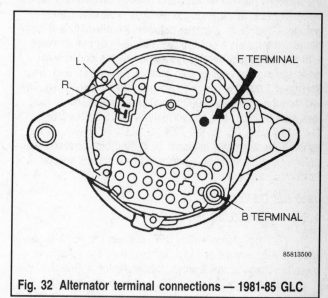

Fig. 32 Alternator terminal connections — 1981-85 GLC

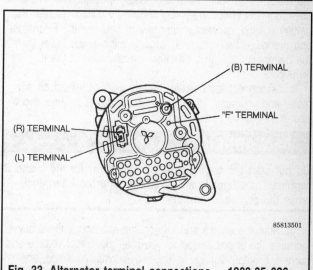

Fig. 33 Alternator terminal connections — 1983-85 626 (except diesel)

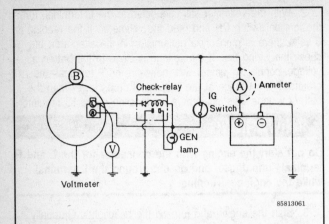

Fig. 34 Before checking the no-load adjustment voltage, temporarily install a shunt (as indicated by the dotted line) to short circuit the ammeter during engine start-up — 1983-85 626

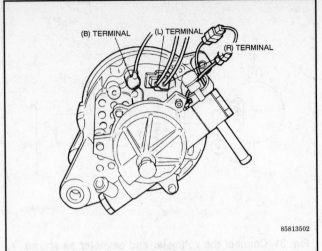

Fig. 35 Alternator terminal connections — 1985 626 diesel

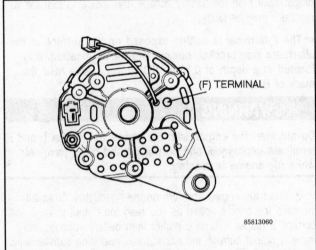

Fig. 36 Location of the F terminal on the 626 diesel alternator

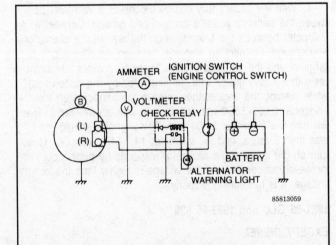

Fig. 37 Connect the voltmeter and ammeter as shown to test alternator output — 1985 626 diesel

the battery's positive terminal and ground. Connect a voltmeter between the **L** terminal on the rear of the alternator and ground. Connect an ammeter between the alternator's **B** terminal and the battery's positive terminal. Jumper the ammeter with a heavy-gauge wire (as illustrated by the dotted line) while starting the engine, then remove the jumper. Run the engine at 2,000-2,500 rpm (check rpm with a dwell/tach). This will turn the alternator 5,000 rpm. The ammeter should read less than 5 amps, and the voltmeter 14.4-15.0 volts DC (14.1-14.7 volts DC for the 1981-83 GLC). Now, turn on the lights. If the alternator responds by putting out increased amperage, and the voltage is higher than the battery voltage, it is functioning properly.

1985 626 DIESEL

▶ See Figures 35, 36 and 37

1. With the ignition switch **OFF**, connect the voltmeter between the **L** terminal and ground, then read the voltage. If there is voltage at the terminal, the alternator is defective.

2. Turn the ignition switch **ON** and read the voltmeter. If the reading is 0 volts, there is probably a malfunction in the alternator, but check the wiring first. If the voltage is near the battery voltage, connect a jumper wire between the **F** terminal and ground. If the voltage at the **L** terminal drops lower than the battery voltage, this indicates a malfunction of the IC regulator.

3. Disconnect the negative battery cable. Connect an ammeter and voltmeter, as shown in the illustration. Then, reconnect the negative battery cable.

✳✳WARNING

Do not start the engine with the connector for the L and R terminals unplugged, and do not ground the L terminal while the engine is running.

4. Start the engine and turn on the headlights. Gradually increase the engine speed as you read the output voltage and current. If output voltage is higher than battery voltage, and there is output current, the alternator is operating satisfactorily.

1986-87 323 and 1986 626

♦ See Figures 38 and 39

➡Steps 1-8 should be followed if the battery constantly discharges. If the battery overcharges, proceed to Step 9.

1. Start the engine and allow it to idle. Disconnect the alternator **B** terminal wire and connect an ammeter with a capacity of 60 amps or more between the wire and the terminal.

✳✳CAUTION

Make connections carefully to avoid grounding the B terminal, which would burn out the alternator.

2. Turn headlights and all accessories on.
3. Speed the engine up until it is turning 2,500-3,000 rpm. Read the output on the ammeter. Compare the reading with the nominal output shown on the Alternator and Regulator Specifications chart. On the 323s, if the output is 90% or more of the nominal indicated output, the alternator is okay. On the 1986 626, a minimum output of 51 amps is normal. If the current reading meets or exceeds the appropriate minimum level, turn off the headlights and accessories, and shut off the engine, then remove the ammeter and reconnect the alternator wire to terminal **B**. However, if the current reading does not meet the applicable minimum level, proceed with the following steps.

4. Turn off all lights and electrical accessories. Charge the battery until the charging rate is less than 5 amps at idle or replace the battery with one that is fully charged, if available. Then, read the ammeter at 2,500 rpm. If the reading is now more than 5 amps, there is a short (ground) somewhere in the vehicle wiring. If the indication is still less than 5 amps, proceed with the next step.

5. This step should be performed with the car at a normal room temperature of about 68°F (20°C). Disconnect the ammeter and reconnect the alternator wire to terminal **B**. Pull the **R-L** connector out just slightly, so you can get the probe of a voltmeter in to read the voltage while the connection is maintained. Connect a voltmeter to the **L** terminal of the alternator

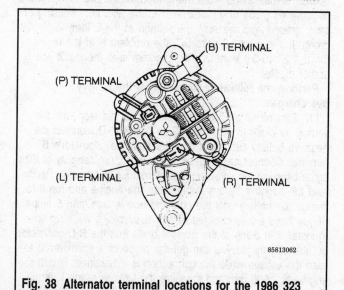

Fig. 38 Alternator terminal locations for the 1986 323

(B) TERMINAL ... (R) TERMINAL

(L) TERMINAL

(F) TERMINAL (IN THE HOUSING)

85813063

Fig. 39 Alternator terminal locations for the 1986 626

and to the alternator housing (ground). Accelerate the engine to 2,500 rpm and read the voltage. If the reading is 14.4-15.0 volts DC, the problem is in the alternator's stator coil and/or diodes. If it is less than 14.4 volts DC, proceed with the next step.

6. Unplug the **R-L** connector from the alternator terminals. Connect a voltmeter between the female **R** terminal (coming from the wiring harness) and the alternator housing or other ground. Then, turn the ignition switch **ON** and measure the voltage. If it is equal to the battery's voltage, proceed to the next step. If the measured voltage is lower, correct the problem in the wiring harness.

7. Turn the ignition switch **OFF**. Disconnect the wire from the **B** terminal of the alternator. Measure the resistance between the **L** and **F** terminals with an ohmmeter. The resistance should be 3-6 ohms. If resistance is not within this range, the problem is in the field coil (rotor) or slip ring, and the alternator must be replaced, or disassembled and repaired. If resistance is 3-6 ohms, proceed with the following steps.

8. Reconnect the **B** terminal connector to the alternator. Turn the ignition switch **ON**. Pull the **R-L** connector out just slightly, so you can get the probe of a voltmeter in to read the voltage while the connection is maintained. Measure the voltage at the **L** terminal prong. If it is over 3.0 volts DC, the problem is in the regulator. If it is 1.0-3.0 volts DC, the problem is in the stator coil and/or diodes.

Perform the following steps only if the battery overcharges:

9. Turn off all electrical loads. Run the test with the vehicle as close to 68°F (20°C) as possible. Disengage the wiring connector from the alternator's **B** terminal. Connect an ammeter with a minimum capacity of 60 amps between the wire and the alternator's **B** terminal. Start the engine and run it to charge the battery until the charging rate is less than 5 amps. (If you have a fully charged battery available, it will save time to install it in place of the present one.) Pull the **R-L** connector out just slightly, so you can get the probe of a voltmeter in to read the voltage while the connection is maintained. Run the engine at 2,500 rpm and measure the voltage at the **L** terminal prong. If the voltage is 14.4-15.0 volts DC, the alternator is

okay. If it is over 15.0 volts DC, proceed with the next step. Turn the engine **OFF**.

10. Disengage the **R** connector at the alternator. Connect a voltmeter between the **R** connector and a good ground. Turn the ignition switch **ON** and measure the voltage at the connector. If the voltage is less than battery voltage, repair the wiring harness. If the voltage is equal to battery voltage, proceed with the next step.

11. Turn the ignition switch **OFF**, then disconnect the wire from the alternator's **B** terminal. Connect an ohmmeter and measure the resistance between the **L** and **F** terminals. If resistance is 3-6 ohms, the problem lies in the voltage regulator. If resistance is outside that range, the problem is in the field coil or slip ring.

1987 626

▶ **See Figure 40**

➡**Steps 1-10 should be followed if the battery constantly discharges. If the battery overcharges, proceed to Step 11.**

1. Disconnect the negative battery cable.
2. Disconnect the alternator **B** terminal wire and connect an ammeter with a capacity of 60 amps or more between the wire and the terminal.

✳✳CAUTION

Make connections carefully to avoid grounding the B terminal, which would burn out the alternator.

3. Reconnect the negative battery cable.
4. Turn the headlights and all accessories on, then depress (and hold) the brake pedal.
5. Start the engine and idle it at 2,500-3,000 rpm. Read the output on the ammeter; it should be a minimum of 55 amps. (If the current reading meets or exceeds this level, the alternator is functioning normally. If the current reading does not meet this level, proceed with the following steps.)
6. Turn off all lights and accessories, and release the brake pedal. Charge the battery until the charging rate is less than 5 amps at idle or replace the battery with one that is fully charged, if available. Then, read the ammeter at 2,500 rpm. If the reading is now more than 5 amps, there is a short (ground) somewhere in the vehicle wiring. If the indication is still less than 5 amps, proceed with the next step.
7. This step should be done with the car at a normal room temperature of about 68°F (20°C). Shut off the engine and disconnect the negative battery cable. Disconnect the ammeter and reconnect the alternator wire to terminal **B**. Reconnect the negative battery cable and restart the engine. Pull the **R-L** connector out just slightly, so you can get the probe of a voltmeter in to read the voltage while the connection is maintained. Connect a voltmeter to the **L** terminal of the alternator and to the alternator housing (ground). Accelerate the engine to 2,500 rpm and read the voltage. If the reading is less than 14.2 volts DC or more than 15.2 volts DC, there may be a problem in the alternator's field coil or diodes. (However, such a voltage reading could also stem from a poor connection between the **B** terminal and the positive battery cable, or from a poor connection of the negative battery cable. It could also result from a poor connection between the 2-pin **R-L** connector

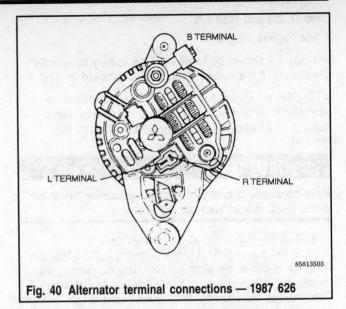

Fig. 40 Alternator terminal connections — 1987 626

and the positive battery cable.) If the voltage reading is 14.2-15.2 volts DC, proceed with the next step.

8. Turn the ignition switch **OFF** and unplug the **R-L** connector from the alternator terminals. Connect a voltmeter between the female **R** terminal (coming from the wiring harness) and the alternator housing or other ground. Then, turn the ignition switch **ON** and measure the voltage. If it is equal to the battery's voltage, proceed to the next step. If the measured voltage is lower, correct the problem in the wiring harness.

9. Turn the ignition switch **OFF**, then disconnect the negative battery cable. Disconnect the wire from the **B** terminal of the alternator, as well as the **R-L** connector. Measure the resistance between the **L** and **F** terminals with an ohmmeter. The resistance should be 3-6 ohms. If resistance is not within this range, the problem is in the rotor coil or brush(es), and the alternator must be replaced or disassembled and repaired. If resistance is 3-6 ohms, proceed with the following steps.

10. Reconnect the wire to the alternator's **B** terminal. Loosely attach the **R-L** connector, so you can get the positive (+) probe of a voltmeter in to read the voltage while the connection is maintained. Turn the ignition switch **ON**. Connect the negative (-) probe of the voltmeter to the alternator housing or other ground, and measure the voltage at the **L** terminal prong. If it is over 3.0 volts DC, the problem is in the regulator. If it is 1.0-3.0 volts DC, the problem is in the stator coil and/or diodes.

Perform the following steps only if the battery overcharges:

11. Turn off all electrical loads. Perform this step with the vehicle as close to 68°F (20°C) as possible. Disconnect the negative battery cable and the wire from the alternator's **B** terminal. Connect an ammeter with a minimum capacity of 60 amps between the wire and the alternator's **B** terminal. Reconnect the negative battery cable. Start the engine and run it to charge the battery until the charging rate is less than 5 amps. (If you have a fully charged battery available, it will save time to install it in place of the present one.) Pull the **R-L** connector out just slightly, so you can get the probe of a voltmeter in to read the voltage while the connection is maintained. Run the engine at 2,500 rpm and measure the voltage at the **L** terminal prong. If the voltage is 14.2-15.2 volts DC, the alternator is

okay. If it is over 15.2 volts DC, there is a problem in the alternator; proceed with the next step.

12. Turn the ignition switch **OFF**. Disconnect the **L-R** connector at the alternator. Connect a voltmeter between the female **R** terminal (coming from the wiring harness) and the alternator housing or other ground. Turn the ignition switch **ON** and measure the voltage at the connector. If the voltage is less than battery voltage, repair the wiring harness. If the voltage is equal to battery voltage, proceed with the next step.

13. Turn the ignition switch **OFF**, then disconnect the negative battery cable and the wire from the alternator's **B** terminal. Connect an ohmmeter and measure the resistance between the **L** and **F** terminals on the alternator. If resistance is 3-6 ohms, the problem lies in the voltage regulator. If resistance is outside that range, the problem is in the rotor coil or brush(es).

REMOVAL & INSTALLATION

▶ **See Figures 41, 42, 43, 44 and 45**

1. Disconnect the battery ground cable at the negative (-) terminal.

2. Remove the air cleaner as required. Remove the nut, and disconnect the alternator **B** terminal. Unplug the connector from the rear of the alternator.

3. Remove the alternator adjusting link bolt(s). Do not remove the adjusting link. Remove the alternator drive belt. On the 626 diesel, this first requires loosening the air conditioner idler pulley, then removing the two alternator belts and the single air conditioning drive belt.

4. Remove the alternator securing nuts and bolts. Pull the drive belt(s) off the pulley and remove the alternator.

To install:

5. Position the alternator onto its mounting and install the attaching hardware.

6. Install the drive belt(s).

7. Plug the connector into the rear of the alternator. Clean the **B** wire terminal and install the wire with the nut.

8. Install the air cleaner, if removed, and connect the negative battery cable.

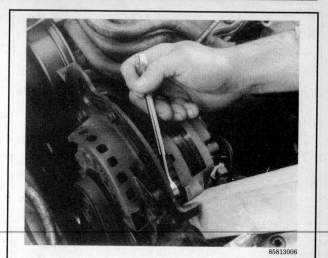

Fig. 42 Remove the bolt which secures the alternator to the adjusting link

Fig. 43 Loosen the alternator pivot bolt, and relax the drive belt tension, before removing the drive belt(s)

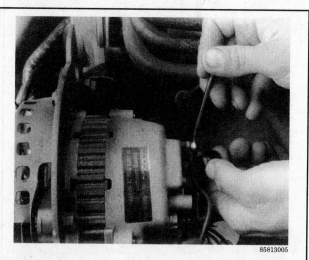

Fig. 41 Remove the nut, and disconnect the alternator B terminal

Fig. 44 Remove the alternator drive belt(s) and then the alternator

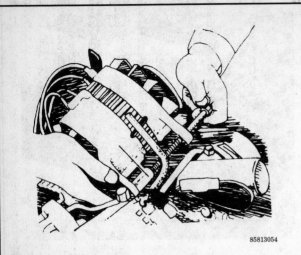

Fig. 45 On 1979-82 RX-7s, alternator mounting clearance is adjusted with shims

9. Adjust the drive belt tension as described in Section 1.

➡On 1979-82 RX-7s, when installing the alternator, check the clearance between the alternator and bracket. If the clearance is greater than 0.006 in. (0.15mm), reduce it with shims.

Regulator

➡All 1978-80 models, except the 626, are equipped with separate voltage regulators that can be adjusted. While all 1981-89 models have IC (integrated circuit) voltage regulators located inside the alternator housing. These are not adjustable, and can only be replaced. All service on IC regulators should be referred to a qualified technician.

REMOVAL & INSTALLATION

1978-79 GLC and RX-7

1. Disconnect the battery ground cable at the negative (-) battery terminal.
2. Disconnect the wiring from the regulator.
3. Remove the regulator mounting screws.
4. Remove the regulator.
To install:
5. Install the new regulator and attach with the mounting screws.
6. Connect the regulator wiring.
7. Connect the negative battery cable.

VOLTAGE ADJUSTMENTS

1978-79 GLC and RX-7
▶ See Figures 46 and 47

1. Remove the cover from the regulator.
2. Check the air gap, point gap and back gap with a feeler gauge (see illustration).

3. If they do not fall within the specifications given in the Alternator and Regulator Specifications chart, adjust the gap(s) by bending the stationary contact bracket.
4. Connect a voltmeter between the **A** and **E** terminals of the regulator, on the RX-7. On the GLC, connect a voltmeter between the top terminal of the alternator and the coil mounting bolt.

➡Be sure that the car's battery is fully charged before proceeding with this test. The ammeter must read 5 amps or less.

5. Start the engine and run it at the rpm specified in the accompanying chart. The voltage reading should as specified in the same chart.
6. Stop the engine.
7. Bend the upper plate down to decrease the voltage setting, or up to increase the setting, as required.
8. If the regulator cannot be brought within specifications, replace it.
9. When the test is completed, disconnect the voltmeter and replace the regulator cover.

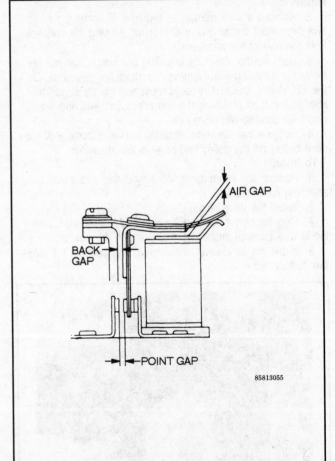

Fig. 46 The air gap, point gap and back gap are adjustable on 1978-79 GLC and RX-7 voltage regulators

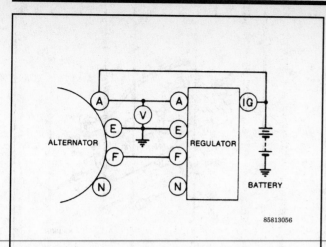

85813056

Fig. 47 On the 1979 RX-7, connect a voltmeter between the A and E terminals of the voltage regulator

Battery

REMOVAL & INSTALLATION

1. If so equipped, remove the protective battery shield.
2. Using the correct size wrench, loosen the nut which secures the negative (-) cable clamp, then remove the negative (-) battery cable from its top terminal post. If the battery has side terminals, simply loosen the retaining bolt and disconnect the cable.

3. Using the correct size wrench, loosen the nut which secures the positive (+) cable clamp, then remove the positive (+) battery cable from its top terminal post. Again, if the battery has side terminals, simply loosen the retaining bolt and disconnect the cable.
4. Remove the battery hold-down clamp or other hardware, then carefully remove the battery from the vehicle.

To install:
5. Inspect the battery carrier and the fender panels for damage caused by loss of battery acid.
6. If the battery is to be reinstalled, clean its top with a solution of clean, warm water and baking soda. Scrub heavily deposited areas with a stiff, bristly brush, being careful not to scatter corrosion residue.
7. Rinse off the top of the battery with clean, warm water.

➡**Keep the cleaning solution and water out of the battery cells.**

8. Examine the battery case and cover for cracks.
9. Gently clean the battery posts and cable connectors (clamps) with a wire brush. Replace damaged or worn cables.
10. Install the battery in the car. Tighten the hold-down clamp nuts or associated hardware.
11. Connect the positive (+) cable to its corresponding battery terminal and tighten the clamp nut or retaining bolt.
12. Connect the negative (-) cable to its corresponding battery terminal and tighten the clamp nut or retaining bolt.
13. After securing the cables, coat the battery/cable connections with petroleum jelly to prevent corrosion.
14. If the battery has filler caps and the electrolyte level is low, fill the battery to the recommended level with distilled water.
15. If so equipped, install the protective battery shield.

ALTERNATOR AND REGULATOR SPECIFICATIONS

| Year | Model | Alternator | | Regulator | | | Regulator | | | |
| | | Field Current @ 14V | Output (amps) | Air Gap (in.) | Point Gap (in.) | Back Gap (in.) | Field Relay | | | |
							Air Gap (in.)	Point Gap (in.)	Back Gap (in.)	Volts @ 75°
1978–80	GLC	—	30	0.039–0.059	0.020–0.035	0.028–0.059	0.028–0.051	0.012–0.018	0.028–0.059	14–15
1981–85	GLC	—	50	← Not Adjustable →						
1981–85	626	—	60	← Not Adjustable →						
1986–89	323	—	53①	← Not Adjustable →						
1986–89	All	—	65	← Not Adjustable →						

① 60 amps with Electronic Fuel Injection

85813C11

REGULATED VOLTAGE TEST SPECIFICATIONS

Model/Year	Alternator rpm	Engine rpm	Regulated Voltage
1978–82 GLC①	—	2000	14–15
1981–83 GLC②	5000	2000	14.1–14.7
1982 626	5000	2000	14.1–14.7
1983–89 626, MX-6, 929	5000	2500	14.4–15.0
1984–85 GLC	5000	2500	14.4–15.0
1986–89 626, MX-6	5000	2500	14.4–15.0

① without internal regulator
② with internal regulator

85813C12

Starter

REMOVAL & INSTALLATION

Except RX-7 and 1988-89 626/MX-6

▶ See Figures 48 and 49

There are two possible locations for the starter motor; one is the lower right-hand side of the engine and the other is on the upper right-hand side.

1. Remove the ground cable from the negative (-) battery terminal.

2. If the car is equipped with the lower mounted starter, remove the gravel shield from underneath the engine. On vehicles equipped with automatic transmission, remove the two bolts attaching the starter bracket to the transmission. On 1989 323 with 4WD, remove the differential lock assembly from the transaxle, as described in Section 7.

3. Remove the battery cable from the starter terminal.

4. Label and disconnect the leads from the solenoid or magnetic switch terminals.

5. Remove the starter securing bolts and withdraw the starter assembly.

To install:

6. Position the starter onto the flywheel housing and install the attaching bolts. On 1986-89 323, 1986-87 626 and 1988-89 929, torque the starter mounting bolts to 23-34 ft. lbs. (31-46 Nm).

7. Connect the leads to the appropriate terminals on the solenoid or magnetic switch.

8. Connect the battery cable to the starter terminal.

9. On 1989 323 with 4WD, install the center differential lock assembly onto the transaxle, as described in Section 7.

10. Install the starter bracket (automatic transmissions) or the gravel shield, if removed.

11. Connect the negative battery cable.

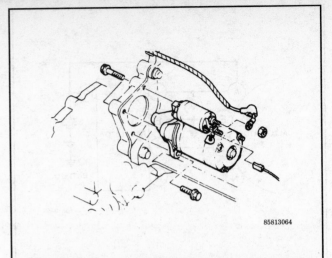

Fig. 48 Common starter mounting — except RX-7 and 1988-89 626/MX-6

Fig. 49 The solenoid is mounted on top of the starter

1988-89 626/MX-6

▶ See Figure 50

1. Disconnect the negative battery cable.

2. Disconnect the starter wiring.

3. Raise the front of the vehicle and support it safely.

4. Unbolt and remove the intake manifold bracket.

5. Remove the upper starter bolts and loosen, but do not yet remove the lower bolt.

6. Remove the lower bolt and withdraw the starter from the lower side of the vehicle.

To install:

7. Position the starter onto the flywheel housing and install the lower bolt for support. Install the remaining bolts and torque all bolts to 27-38 ft. lbs. (37-51 Nm).

8. Install the intake manifold bracket. Torque the bracket bolt to 27-38 ft. lbs. (37-51 Nm) and the nut to 14-19 ft. lbs. (19-26 Nm).

9. Lower the vehicle.

10. Connect the starter wiring.

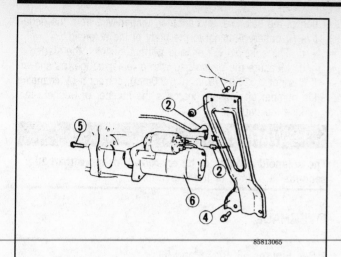

Fig. 50 Starter mounting — 1988-89 626/MX-6

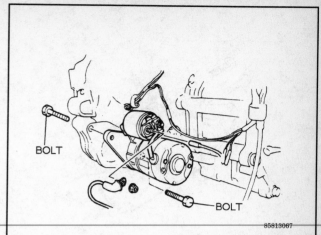

Fig. 52 Starter mounting — 1986-89 RX-7

11. Connect the negative battery cable.

RX-7

▶ **See Figures 51 and 52**

➡**The starter is mounted on the driver's side bottom of the engine.**

1. Disconnect the negative battery cable.
2. Raise the vehicle and support it safely with jackstands.
3. Disconnect the heavy battery cable from the terminal marked **B** on the starter solenoid (or magnetic switch on later models).
4. Disconnect the thinner ignition switch wire from the terminal marked **S** on the solenoid/magnetic switch.
5. On vehicles with automatic transmissions, remove the front starter motor bracket bolts and the bracket. Remove the two starter attaching bolts and remove the starter.
   To install:
6. Support the starter by and hand and position it onto the flywheel housing. Install the two mounting bolts. On 1986-89

RX-7s, torque the bolts to 24-33 ft. lbs. (33-45 Nm). Install the front starter bracket, if removed.

7. Connect the starter wiring to the appropriate solenoid or switch terminals. On 1986-89 models, torque the **B** terminal (battery cable) nut to 8 ft. lbs. (11 Nm).
8. Lower the vehicle.
9. Connect the negative battery cable.

SOLENOID REPLACEMENT

▶ **See Figures 53, 54 and 55**

➡**Perform solenoid replacement with the starter motor removed from the car. On later model starters, the solenoid is referred to as a magnetic switch; these terms are interchangeable.**

1. Disconnect the negative battery cable.

✳✳CAUTION

This is necessary as the wiring coming from the battery could ground and cause a fire or other damage!

2. Detach the field strap, the "hot wire" from the battery, and the ignition wiring connector from the solenoid terminals.
3. Remove the solenoid securing bolts.
4. Withdraw the solenoid, washers, spring and plunger, lifting the assembly to disconnect the plunger where it engages with the fork.
5. Assemble the plunger, spring, washers and solenoid assembly and engage the plunger with the fork.
6. Hold the plunger assembly in place and install the attaching screws.
7. Reconnect the starter-to-solenoid wiring.
8. Assemble the solenoid, then check the pinion gap as follows:
   a. Leave the connection between solenoid terminal **M** and the starter motor disconnected.
   b. Energize the solenoid by running one jumper wire from the battery's positive (+) terminal to the **S** terminal connec-

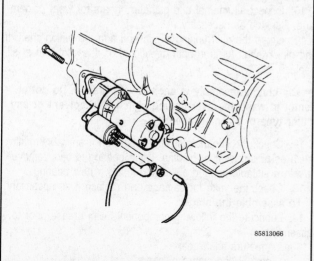

Fig. 51 Starter mounting — 1979-85 RX-7

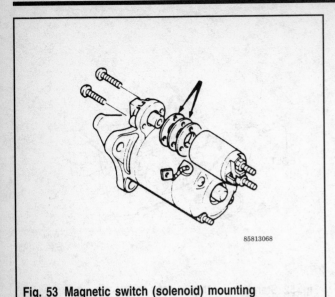

Fig. 53 Magnetic switch (solenoid) mounting

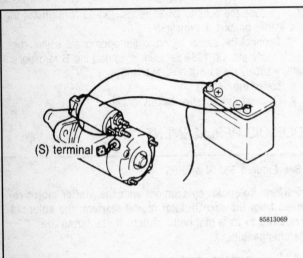

(S) terminal

Fig. 54 To check pinion gap, energize the solenoid with jumper wires . . .

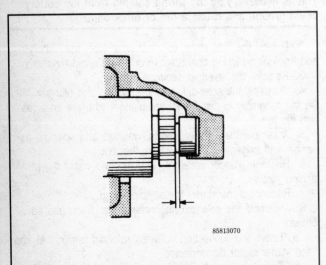

Fig. 55 . . . and insert a feeler gauge between the front of the pinion gear and the starter body

tion of the solenoid, and another jumper wire from the negative (-) battery terminal to the body of the solenoid.

c. The solenoid will engage without spinning the starter.

d. Measure the pinion gap with a feeler gauge, as shown. If it is not 0.020-0.079 in. (0.5-2.0mm), correct it by changing the number of washers (increase the number of washers to reduce the gap).

✳✳WARNING

The solenoid should not be energized for more than 20 seconds at a time, or it will overheat.

OVERHAUL

▶ **See Figures 56, 57, 58 and 59**

1. On cars with automatic transmissions, remove the bracket from the rear of the starter.

2. Disconnect the field strap from the terminal on the solenoid, remove the solenoid attaching screws, and remove the solenoid, spring and washers.

3. Detach the plunger at the drive lever, and remove it.

4. Remove the starter through-bolts and the brush holder attaching screws. Matchmark the rear bracket/cover with the yoke housing. Remove the rear cover.

5. Remove the insulator and washers from the rear end of the armature shaft. Remove the brush holder and the wave washer (later models).

6. Matchmark the yoke and front housing. Pull the yoke off the drive housing. Remove the rubber packing, spring and spring seat.

7. Pull the armature, drive lever and overrunning clutch assembly from the drive housing. Note the direction of the drive lever before removing it. Do not lose the ball (later models).

8. Position the armature with the front end upward in a soft jawed vise. Drive the pinion stop collar rearward until the stop ring can be removed. Then, remove the stop ring, stop collar and overrunning clutch.

9. Disconnect the brush from the brush holder using a suitable prying tool, and remove it from the rear housing.

10. Inspect all internal and planetary gears for wear or damage. Replace as necessary.

11. Grasp the overrunning clutch and turn the pinion shaft. If the pinion shaft turns in both directions, or does not turn at all, replace it.

➡**The clutch assembly is packed with grease. Do not attempt to wash the overrunning clutch with solvent or any other type of cleaning agent.**

12. Check the commutator shaft bearing for any abnormality such as noise, wear or binding. If the bearing is bad, remove it with a suitable bearing puller and install a new bearing.

13. Check the yoke for damage and replace it as necessary.

To assemble the starter:

14. Lubricate the following components with grease prior to assembly:

    a. Armature shaft gear

    b. Internal and planetary gears

    c. Plunger circumference

    d. Lever

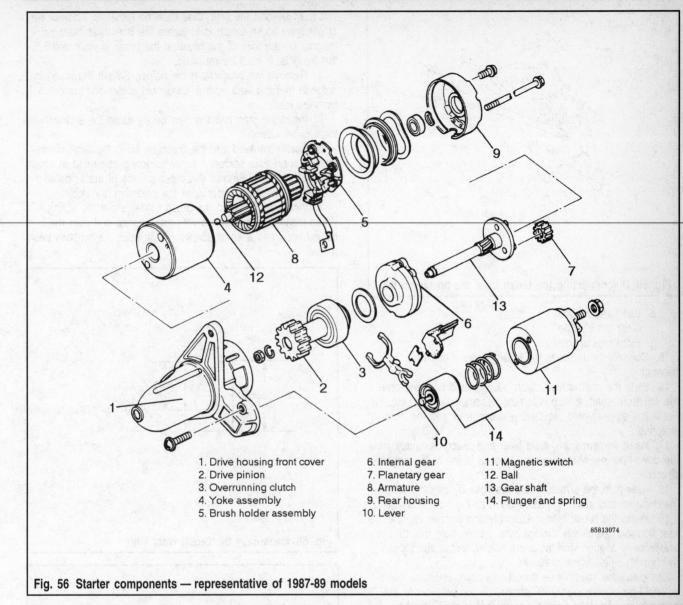

1. Drive housing front cover
2. Drive pinion
3. Overrunning clutch
4. Yoke assembly
5. Brush holder assembly
6. Internal gear
7. Planetary gear
8. Armature
9. Rear housing
10. Lever
11. Magnetic switch
12. Ball
13. Gear shaft
14. Plunger and spring

85813074

Fig. 56 Starter components — representative of 1987-89 models

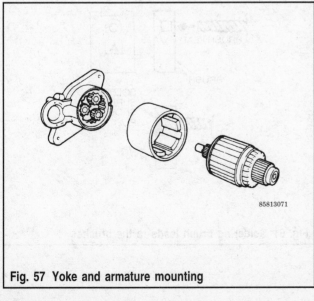

85813071

Fig. 57 Yoke and armature mounting

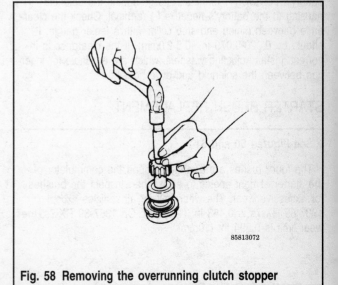

85813072

Fig. 58 Removing the overrunning clutch stopper

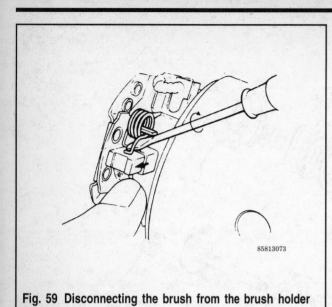

85813073

Fig. 59 Disconnecting the brush from the brush holder

   e. Ball (later models)
   f. Gear shaft spline
   g. Front bracket bushing
  15. Connect the brush to the brush holder in the rear housing.
  16. Slide the overrunning clutch, stopper and snapring onto the armature shaft, then position the assembly on a press. Press the stopper onto the shaft and secure it with the snapring.
  17. Insert the armature, drive lever and clutch assembly into the drive housing. Make sure the lever is facing in the original direction.
  18. Assemble the armature and the yoke by aligning the matchmarks and install the assembly onto the front housing.
  19. Install the brush holder assembly and washer into the rear housing. Install the through-bolts making sure that they are properly aligned with the brush holder. Install and tighten the brush holder retaining screws.
  20. Install the solenoid as described above. Energize the solenoid by connecting the **S** terminal on the solenoid to the battery's positive (+) terminal, and grounding the solenoid housing to the battery's negative (-) terminal. Check the clearance between pinion and stop collar with a feeler gauge. It should be 0.020–0.079 in. (0.5–2.0mm). If the clearance is incorrect, install adjusting washers, which are available for insertion between the solenoid and drive housing.

STARTER BRUSH REPLACEMENT

▶ **See Figures 60 and 61**

The four brushes are arranged around the commutator of the starter at right angles to each other. Inspect the brushes for excessive wear. The wear limit for all vehicles except 1987-89 RX-7s is 0.453 in. (11.5mm). On 1987-89 RX-7s, the wear limit is 0.394 in. (10mm).

If worn beyond the limit, they must be replaced. Another way of checking brush length is to locate the little three diamond insignia on the side of the brush; if the brush is worn down to this insignia, it must be replaced.
  1. Remove the brush from the holder. Smash the brush in order to free the lead from it. Clean old solder and corrosion from the lead.
  2. Insert the lead into the new brush, using the end with the smaller chamfer.
  3. Solder the lead into the brush by filling the large chamfer with rosin core solder. A small soldering iron rated at about 150 watts is best. Smooth the outer surface of the soldered connection with sandpaper after the soldering is complete.
  4. Install the brush in the brush holder under the spring. When fitting the brush plate with the brushes in it over the commutator, use a small screwdriver to push the brushes back a little.

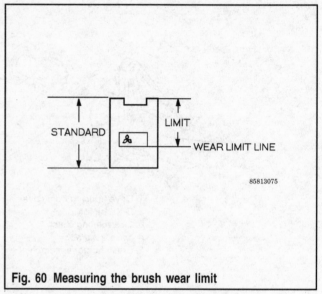

85813075

Fig. 60 Measuring the brush wear limit

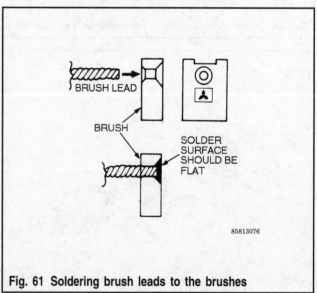

85813076

Fig. 61 Soldering brush leads to the brushes

PISTON ENGINE MECHANICAL

➡The Piston Engine Mechanical portion of Section 3 covers both gasoline and diesel engines. Rotary engine service is covered separately, later in this section.

Checking Engine Compression

A noticeable lack of engine power, excessive oil consumption and/or poor fuel mileage measured over an extended period are all indicators of internal engine wear. Worn piston rings, scored or worn cylinder bores, blown head gaskets, sticking or burnt valves and worn valve seats are all possible culprits here. A check of each cylinder's compression will help you locate the problems.

As mentioned in the Tools and Equipment section of Section 1, a screw-in type compression gauge is more accurate than the type you simply hold against the spark plug hole. Although the screw-in type takes slightly longer to use, it's worth it to obtain a more accurate reading.

GASOLINE ENGINES

▶ **See Figures 62 and 63**

1. Before checking the engine compression, make sure that the battery is fully charged.
2. Warm up the engine to its normal operating temperature.
3. Shut off the engine, then remove all spark plugs.
4. Disconnect the high tension lead from the ignition coil.
5. Fully open the throttle either by operating the carburetor throttle linkage by hand, or by having an assistant floor the accelerator pedal.
6. Screw the compression gauge into the No. 1 spark plug hole until the fitting is snug.

➡**Be careful not to crossthread the plug hole. Use extra care on aluminum cylinder heads, as the threads in these heads are easily ruined.**

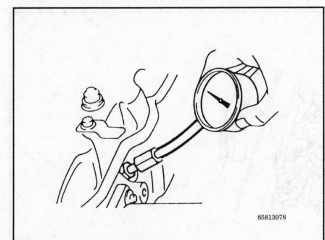

85813078

Fig. 62 A screw-in type compression gauge is preferable

7. Ask an assistant to depress and hold the accelerator pedal fully (on both carbureted and fuel injected vehicles). Then, while you read the compression gauge, ask the assistant to crank the engine two or three times in short bursts using the ignition switch.
8. Read the compression gauge at the end of each series of cranks, and record the highest of these readings. Repeat this procedure for each of the engine's cylinders. Compare the highest reading of each cylinder to the readings of the other cylinders. The readings should be similar throughout the engine.

➡**A cylinder's compression pressure is usually acceptable if it is not less than 80% of the highest reading. For example, if the highest reading is 150 psi, the lowest should be no lower than 120 psi. Also, no cylinder should be less than 100 psi.**

9. If a cylinder is unusually low, pour a tablespoon of clean engine oil into the cylinder through the spark plug hole and repeat the compression test. If the compression comes up after adding the oil, it appears that the cylinder's piston rings or bore are damaged or worn. If the pressure remains low, the valves may not be seating properly (a valve job is needed), or the head gasket may be blown near that cylinder. If compression in any two adjacent cylinders is low, and if the addition of oil doesn't help the compression, there is probably leakage past the head gasket. Oil and coolant water in the combustion chamber can result from this problem. There may be evidence of water droplets on the engine dipstick when a head gasket has blown.

DIESEL ENGINES

▶ **See Figure 64**

Checking cylinder compression on diesel engines is basically the same procedure as on gasoline engines, except for the following:

➡**Before checking the engine compression, make sure that the battery is fully charged.**

1. A special compression gauge adaptor suitable for diesel engines must be used (since these engines have much greater compression pressures).
2. Remove the fuel lines and gaskets, and then remove the injectors from each cylinder. See Section 5.

➡**Don't forget to remove the washer and gasket underneath each injector; otherwise, it may get lost when the engine is cranked.**

3. When fitting the compression gauge adaptor to the cylinder head, make sure the gauge bleeder (if equipped) is closed.
4. When reinstalling the injector assemblies, install new washers underneath each injector. See Section 5.

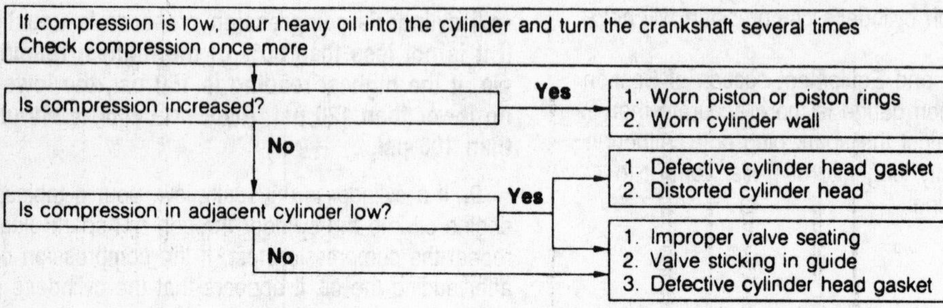

If compression is low, pour heavy oil into the cylinder and turn the crankshaft several times Check compression once more

Is compression increased? —— **Yes** →
1. Worn piston or piston rings
2. Worn cylinder wall

—— **No**

Is compression in adjacent cylinder low? —— **Yes** →
1. Defective cylinder head gasket
2. Distorted cylinder head

—— **No** →
1. Improper valve seating
2. Valve sticking in guide
3. Defective cylinder head gasket

85813079

Fig. 63 Engine compression diagnosis

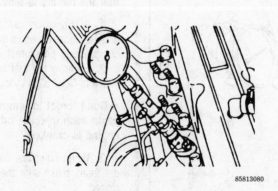

85813080

Fig. 64 Diesel engines require a special compression gauge and adapter

GENERAL ENGINE SPECIFICATIONS
Piston Engines

Engine	Years	Fuel System Type	SAE Net Horsepower @ rpm	SAE Net Torque ft. lbs. @ rpm	Bore x Stroke (in.)	Comp. Ratio	Oil Pressure (psi) @ 2000 rpm
1.3L	1978	2-bbl	67 @ 4300	89 @ 2400	2.87 x 2.99	9.2:1	57
1.4L	1979–80	2-bbl	77 @ 4300	109 @ 2400	3.03 x 2.99	9.0:1	57
1.5L	1981–85	2-bbl	78 @ 5000	82 @ 3000	3.03 x 3.15	9.0:1	57
1.6L	1986–87	2-bbl	82 @ 5000	92 @ 2500	3.07 x 3.29	9.3:1	50
	1987–89	EFI	91 @ 5000	101 @ 2000	3.07 x 3.29	9.3:1	50
	1988–89 Turbo	EFI	120 @ 5000	115 @ 3000	3.07 x 3.29	7.8:1	55
2.0L (Code MA)	1979–82	2-bbl	75 @ 4000	105 @ 2500	3.15 x 3.86	8.6:1	55
2.0L (Code FE)	1984–85	2-bbl	83 @ 4800	110 @ 2500	3.39 x 3.39	8.6:1	55
(Code RF)	1985	Diesel	72 @ 4650	100 @ 2750	3.39 x 3.39	22.7:1	65
(Code FE)	1986–87	EFI	93 @ 5000	115 @ 2500	3.39 x 3.39	8.6:1	55
(Code FE)	1986–87 Turbo	EFI	120 @ 5000	115 @ 3000	3.39 x 3.39	7.8:1	55
2.2L	1988–89	EFI	97 @ 5000	120 @ 2500	3.39 x 3.70	8.6:1	55
	1988–89 Turbo	EFI	125 @ 5000	155 @ 3500	3.39 x 3.70	7.8:1	55
3.0L	1988–89	EFI	150 @ 5000	165 @ 4000	3.54 x 3.85	8.5:1	60

858130C1

VALVE SPECIFICATIONS

Engine	Seat Angle (deg.)	Face Angle (deg.)	Spring Test Pressure (lbs. @ in.)	Spring Free Length (in.)	Stem-to-Guide Clearance (in.)		Stem Diameter (in.)	
					Intake	Exhaust	Intake	Exhaust
1.3L	45	45	①	②	0.0007–0.0021	0.0007–0.0023	0.3150	0.3150
1.4L	45	45	①	②	0.0007–0.0021	0.0007–0.0023	0.3150	0.3150
1.5L	45	45	③	④	0.0007–0.0021	0.0007–0.0023	⑤	⑤
1.6L	45	45	157 @ 1.565	1.575	⑥	⑥	⑦	⑦
2.0L (Code MA)	45	45	①	②	0.0007–0.0021	0.0007–0.0023	0.3150	0.3150
2.0L Gasoline (Code FE)	45	45	⑧	⑨	0.0010–0.0024	0.0010–0.0024	0.3161–0.3167	0.3159–0.3165
2.0L Diesel (Code RF)	45	45	211 @ 1.000	⑩	0.0016–0.0031	0.0020–0.0031	0.3138–0.3144	0.3136–0.3142
2.2L	45	45	⑪	⑫	0.0016–0.0018	0.0018–0.0020	0.3161–0.3167	0.3159–0.3165
3.0L	45	45	⑬	⑭	0.0010–0.0024	0.0012–0.0026	0.2744–0.2750	0.3159–0.3165

① Outer: 43.7 @ 1.319
 Inner: 20.9 @ 1.230
② Outer: 1.339
 Inner: 1.260
③ 1981–83: 63.3 @ 1.319
 1984–85: 164 @ 1.00
④ 1981–83: 1.339
 1984–85: 1.555
⑤ 1981–82: 0.3150
 1983–85: 0.3164
⑥ 1986–87
   Intake: 0.0018–0.0051
   Exhaust: 0.0019–0.0053
 1988–89
   Intake: 0.0010–0.0024
   Exhaust: 0.0011–0.0026
⑦ Non-turbo: 0.2750
 Turbo
   Intake: 0.2350–0.2356
   Exhaust: 0.2348–0.2350
⑧ 1983–84
   Outer: 50.5 @ 1.563
   Inner: 50.5 @ 1.300
 1985–87
   Outer: 101 @ 1.00
   Inner: 90 @ 0.890
⑨ Outer: 1.150
 Inner: 1.000
⑩ Measure valve seat sink. Sink is the distance from the spring seat to the top of the valve. Sink should be 0.030–0.041. If sink exceeds 0.100, replace the head.
⑪ Measure valve seat sink. Sink is the distance from the spring seat to the top of the valve. Sink should be 1.831–1.850. If sink is 1.850–1.890, the spring can be shimmed. If sink exceeds 1.890, replace the head.
⑫ Inner: 1.681
 Outer: 1.984
⑬ Measure valve seat sink. Sink is the distance from the spring seat to the top of the valve. Sink should be 1.988 for intakes; 1.949 for exhausts. If sink is 1.988–2.047 for intakes or 1.949–2.008 for exhausts, the spring can be shimmed. If sink exceeds 2.047 for intakes or 2.008 for exhausts, replace the head.
⑭ Intake inner: 1.835
 Intake outer: 2.000
 Exhaust inner: 2.126
 Exhaust outer: 2.386

CAMSHAFT SPECIFICATIONS
(All specifications in inches)

Engine	Journal Diameter					Bearing Clearance	Elevation		End-Play
	1	2	3	4	5		Int.	Exh.	
1.3L	1.6516	1.6516	1.6516	1.6516	1.6516	①	1.729	1.729	0.004
1.4L	1.6536	1.6536	1.6536	1.6536	1.6536	①	1.737	1.737	0.004
1.5L	⑤	⑤	⑤	⑤	⑤	①	1.737	1.737	0.004
1.6L	1.7105	1.7095	1.7095	1.7095	1.7105	①	1.441	1.441	0.004
1.6L Turbo	1.0215	1.0215	1.0215	1.0215	1.0215	0.0023	1.610	1.610	0.004
2.0L (Code MA)	1.7716	1.7716	1.7716	—	—	②	1.772	1.772	0.004
2.0L Gasoline (Code FE)	1.2579	1.2567	1.2567	1.2567	1.2579	③	1.504	1.504	0.004
2.0L Diesel (Code RF)	1.2585	1.2585	1.2585	1.2585	1.2585	0.0018	1.744	1.783	0.007
2.2L	1.2579	1.2567	1.2567	1.2567	1.2579	③	1.504	1.504	0.004
3.0L	1.9272	1.9264	1.9264	1.9272	—	④	1.618	1.626	0

① Nos. 1, 2, 4 and 5: 0.0014–0.0030
   No. 3: 0.0026–0.0043
② Nos. 1, 2, 4 and 5: 0.0017
   No. 3: 0.0021
③ Nos. 1 and 5: 0.0014–0.0035
   Nos. 2, 3, 4: 0.0026–0.0045
④ Nos. 1 and 4: 0.0024–0.0035
   Nos. 2 and 3: 0.0035–0.0045
⑤ 1981: 1.6536
   1982–85
     Nos. 1 and 5: 1.6519
     Nos. 2, 3, 4: 1.6507

858130C3

CRANKSHAFT AND CONNECTING ROD SPECIFICATIONS
(All specifications in inches)

| Engine | Crankshaft | | | | Connecting Rod | | |
	Main Bearing Journal Dia.	Main Bearing Oil Clearance	Shaft End Play	Thrust on No.	Journal Dia.	Oil Clearance	Side Clearance
1.3L	2.4804	0.0012–0.0024	0.003–0.009	5	1.7717	0.0011–0.0029	0.004–0.008
1.4L	1.9685	0.0009–0.0017	0.004–0.006	5	1.5748	0.0009–0.0019	0.004–0.008
1.5L	1.9668	0.0009–0.0017	0.004–0.006	5	1.5734	0.0009–0.0019	0.004–0.010
1.6L	1.9975	0.0009–0.0017	0.003–0.011	4	①	0.0011–0.0027	0.004–0.010
2.0L (Code MA)	2.4783	0.0012–0.0024	0.003–0.009	3	2.0846	0.0011–0.0030	0.004–0.008
2.0L Gasoline (Code FE)	2.3618	0.0012–0.0019	0.003–0.007	3	2.0079	0.0010–0.0026	0.004–0.010
2.0L Diesel (Code RF)	2.3610	0.0012–0.0019	0.002–0.011	3	2.0063	0.0012–0.0024	0.004–0.010
2.2L	2.3602	0.0012–0.0019	0.003–0.007	3	2.0059	0.0011–0.0026	0.004–0.010
3.0L	2.4390	0.0010–0.0015	0.003–0.011	3	2.0748	0.0009–0.0010	0.007–0.013

① 1986–88: 1.7696
  1989: 1.8901

858130C4

PISTON AND RING SPECIFICATIONS
(All specifications in inches)

Engine	Ring Gap			Ring Side Clearance			Piston-to-Bore Clearance
	#1 Compr.	#2 Compr.	Oil Control	#1 Compr.	#2 Compr.	Oil Control	
1.3L	0.0079–0.0157	0.0079–0.0157	0.0079–0.0157	0.0014–0.0028	0.0012–0.0025	0.0079–0.0157	0.0021–0.0026
1.4L	0.0079–0.0157	0.0079–0.0157	0.0118–0.0354	0.0012–0.0025	0.0012–0.0025	0.0079–0.0157	0.0021–0.0026
1.5L	0.0079–0.0157	0.0079–0.0157	0.0118–0.0354	0.0012–0.0028	0.0012–0.0028	0.0079–0.0157	0.0010–0.0026
1.6L	0.0079–0.0157	0.0059–0.0157	0.0118–0.0354	0.0012–0.0035	0.0010–0.0030	0.0010–0.0030	0.0015–0.0020
2.0L (Code MA)	0.0079–0.0157	0.0079–0.0157	0.0118–0.0354	0.0014–0.0028	0.0012–0.0025	snug	①
2.0L Gasoline (Code FE)	0.0078–0.0118	0.0059–0.0118	0.0118–0.0354	0.0014–0.0028	0.0014–0.0028	snug	0.0014–0.0030
2.0L Diesel (Code RF)	0.0079–0.0157	0.0079–0.0157	0.0079–0.0157	0.0020–0.0035	0.0016–0.0031	snug	0.0012–0.0020
2.2L	0.0078–0.0138	0.0059–0.0118	0.0118–0.0354	②	0.0012–0.0028	0.0059 max.	0.0014–0.0030
3.0L	0.0078–0.0138	0.0059–0.0138	0.0079–0.0276	0.0012–0.0028	0.0012–0.0028	0.0059 max.	0.0019–0.0026

① 1979–81: 0.036–0.076
 1982: 0.048–0.063
② Non-turbo: 0.0012–0.0028
 Turbo: 0.0012–0.0035

858130C5

TORQUE SPECIFICATIONS
Piston Engines
(All specifications in ft. lbs.)

Engine	Cyl. Head	Conn. Rod	Main Bearing	Crankshaft Damper	Camshaft Sprocket	Flywheel	Manifold Intake	Manifold Exhaust
1.3L	47–51	29–33	43–47	80–87	51–58	60–65	14–19	12–17
1.4L	47–51	22–25	43–47	80–87	51–58	60–65	14–19	12–17
1.5L	56–59	22–25	48–51	80–87	51–58	①	14–19	14–17
1.6L	56–60	⑥	40–43	36–45	51–58	71–76	14–19	⑩
2.0L (Code MA)	②	⑤	61–65	④	51–58	③	14–19	16–21
2.0L Gasoline (Code FE)	59–64	37–41	61–65	9–12	35–48	71–76	14–19	16–21
2.0L Diesel (Code RF)	⑪	51–54	61–65	116–123	35–48	130–137	14–19	16–20
2.2L	59–64	48–51	61–65	9–12	35–48	71–76	14–19	16–21
3.0L	⑦	⑧	⑨	116–123	52–59	76–81	14–19	16–21

① 1981–84
   Man. Trans.: 60–65
   Auto. Trans.: 51–61
   1985 all: 80–87
② 1979–81: 59–64 Cold
         69–72 Normal Operating Temperature
   1982–84: 65–69 Cold
         69–72 Normal Operating Temperature
③ 1979–81: 112–118
   1982–84: 108–118
④ 1979–82: 101–108
   1983–84: 116–123
⑤ 1979–81: 30–33
   1982–84: 36–40
⑥ Single overhead cam engine: 37–41
   Dual overhead cam engine: 48–51

⑦ Tighten in 3 steps:
   1. 14 ft. lbs.
   2. plus a 90 degree turn
   3. plus another 90 degree turn
⑧ Tighten in 2 steps:
   1. 22 ft. lbs.
   2. plus a 90 degree turn
⑨ Tighten in 3 steps:
   1. 14 ft. lbs.
   2. plus a 90 degree turn
   3. plus a 45 degree turn
⑩ Single overhead cam engine: 12–17
   Dual overhead cam engine: 29–42
⑪ See text

858130C6

Engine

REMOVAL & INSTALLATION

Rear Wheel Drive GLC

EXCEPT WAGON

1. Mark the outline of the hood hinges for reinstallation alignment. Unfasten the bolts and remove the hood.
2. Disconnect the negative battery cable.
3. Drain the cooling system by opening the radiator drain cock.
4. Disconnect upper and lower water hoses.
5. Remove radiator.
6. Remove air cleaner.
7. Disconnect the ECS hoses, heater hose, accelerator and choke cables, fuel lines and vacuum hoses.
8. Disconnect the wiring from the distributor, starter, temperature sending unit, thermostatic switch, and alternator.
9. Disconnect the exhaust pipe at the exhaust manifold.
10. Remove the starter.
11. Safely support the car on axle stands and support the transmission with a jack.
12. Connect a suitable lifting sling to the engine hanger brackets and to a hoist, then take up the slack. Remove the engine mount bolts.
13. Remove transmission mounting bracket from the left side, and transmission-to-engine bolts from the right side.
14. Pull the engine forward until it clears the transmission input shaft, then remove it from the vehicle.
15. Installation is the reverse of the removal procedure.

GLC WAGON

1. Mark its location on the hinges, then unfasten the bolts and remove the hood.
2. Disconnect the negative battery cable.
3. Allow the engine to cool and drain the coolant.

4. Disconnect the upper and lower radiator hoses. On vehicles with automatic transmissions, disconnect the transmission cooler lines at the radiator, being careful to collect the transmission fluid that drains out.

5. Remove the radiator and cooling fan. Remove the air cleaner assembly (first disconnect the air hoses). Disconnect the accelerator cable. Cover the carburetor inlet to keep dirt out.

6. Disconnect the necessary wiring:
- Distributor primary leads
- Coil-to-distributor high tension wire
- Oil pressure gauge line
- Water temperature gauge line
- Accelerator switch wire
- Slow fuel cut solenoid wire
- Automatic choke wire
- Engine ground strap
- Starter motor wiring

7. Remove the right side engine mount through-bolt.

8. Disconnect the wire from the alternator **B** terminal and the alternator wiring connector.

9. Disconnect the air control valve and air vent hoses, all vacuum hoses, and the fuel lines.

10. Disconnect the accelerator cable, power brake vacuum hose, and heater hoses. Remove the hot air hose leading to the air cleaner.

11. Remove the left side engine mount through-bolt.

12. Raise the vehicle and safely support it on axle stands or a lift. Working underneath, disconnect the exhaust pipe and clutch cable. Remove the clutch cable bracket, and the lower clutch cover.

13. Support the transmission securely from underneath. On automatic transmission equipped vehicles, remove the bolts fastening the torque converter to the drive plate. Then, remove the transmission support bolts and nuts (automatic or manual transmission).

14. Remove the starter motor. Remove the forward catalytic converter.

15. Attach a lifting sling to the engine lifting brackets, and support the engine with the sling and a hoist. Slide the engine forward until it clears the clutch shaft (manual transmission) or torque converter (automatic transmission), and lift it out of the vehicle.

16. Install the engine in reverse order, torquing the clutch cover to 13-20 ft. lbs. (18-27 Nm), or the drive plate-to-torque converter bolts to 25-36 ft. lbs. (34-49 Nm) and converter housing-to-engine bolts to 23-34 ft. lbs. (31-46 Nm).

Front Wheel Drive GLC

▶ See Figures 65 and 66

➡**The manufacturer recommends that the engine and transaxle be removed from the car as a unit.**

1. Mark the outline of the hood hinges for reinstallation alignment. Unfasten the bolts and remove the hood.

2. Disconnect the battery cables from the battery, negative cable first. Remove the battery.

3. Loosen the front wheel lugs. Jack up the car and safely support it on jackstands.

4. Remove the two front wheels. Remove the bottom and side splash shields.

Fig. 65 Engine mount through-bolt — 1981-82 front wheel drive GLC

85813081

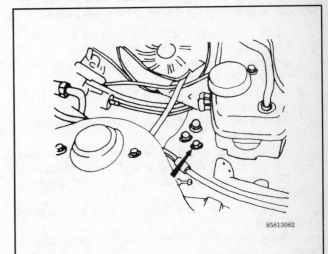

Fig. 66 Engine mount through-bolt — 1983-85 front wheel drive GLC

85813082

5. Drain the coolant, engine oil and transaxle fluid.

6. Remove the air cleaner assembly. Remove the radiator hoses and the radiator shroud and electric fan assembly.

7. Connect an engine lifting sling to the engine lifting brackets. Connect a chain hoist or portable engine crane to the lifting sling, then apply slight upward pressure to the engine and transaxle assembly.

8. Remove the mounting bolts from the engine crossmember. Remove the crossmember.

9. Disconnect the lower ball joints, the steering knuckles and drive axles. For details, please refer to Section 8.

10. For cars equipped with a manual transaxle, disconnect the shifting rod and extension bar.

11. For cars equipped with an automatic transaxle, disconnect the selector rod and counter rod.

12. Remove the front and rear transaxle mounting bushings. Disconnect the exhaust pipe from the converter. Remove the transaxle crossmember.

13. Label, then disconnect all wires and hoses below the engine and transaxle.

14. Label, then disconnect all wires, heater hoses and vacuum hoses from the upper side of the engine and transaxle.

15. Disconnect the accelerator cable, speedometer cable, clutch cable, power brake booster line and fuel lines.

16. Check to be sure all remaining hoses and wiring are disconnected. Remove the evaporative canister. Remove the right side upper engine mount through-bolt.

17. Lift the engine/transaxle assembly from the car. Take care not to allow the assembly to swing forward into the radiator.

18. If the car must be moved from underneath the engine, remount the steering knuckles, secure the drive axles so that they can still turn, mount the front wheels and lower the car from the jackstands.

19. Installation is in the reverse order of removal. When installing the battery, connect the positive cable first.

323 — Except 1988-89 Turbo

➡On 1987 vehicles and on all 1988-89 vehicles equipped with fuel injection, release the pressure from the fuel system before beginning the engine removal procedure.

1. Scribe matchmarks on the hood where the hinges attach, then unfasten the bolts and remove the hood.

2. Disconnect both battery cables, negative first. Remove the battery and the battery carrier.

3. Drain the engine oil, transaxle fluid and coolant.

4. Remove the air cleaner assembly.

5. Remove the oil level dipstick and tube. Remove the cooling fan and the radiator assembly.

6. Remove the accelerator cable and, if so equipped, the cruise control cable. Disconnect the speedometer cable.

7. Disconnect the fuel hoses, draining them into a suitable container.

8. Disconnect and remove the heater hoses and the brake vacuum hose.

9. Disconnect and remove the three-way solenoid valve hoses and canister hoses.

10. Disconnect the engine harness connectors. Disconnect the engine ground strap.

11. Disconnect and remove the upper and lower radiator hoses. On vehicles with automatic transmissions, remove the secondary air pipe from the exhaust manifold.

12. Disconnect and lower the exhaust pipe, supporting it in a safe manner.

13. Unbolt and dismount the air conditioner compressor without attempting to disconnect the lines. Tie the compressor in a convenient spot so that the refrigerant lines will not be under tension.

14. Unbolt and dismount the power steering pump without attempting to disconnect the lines. Tie the pump in a convenient spot so that the lines will not be under tension.

15. Disconnect the driveshafts at the transaxle on either side, as described in Section 7.

16. Disconnect and remove the clutch control cable and shift control rod on manual transmission cars, or the shift control cable on automatic transmission cars.

17. Remove the splash shields from under the engine and on both sides.

18. Unbolt the engine mounts at the body and remove them. Attach a lifting sling to the engine's lifting brackets and, using a hoist, remove the engine/transaxle assembly from above.

To install:

19. Carefully align the engine/transaxle assembly with its original position in the engine compartment. Then, work it slowly into position so as to avoid damaging anything. Install each item below in reverse order of the removal procedure.

   a. Engine mount-to-body bolts (see illustration for torque specifications).

   b. Splash shields.

   c. Shift control rod and clutch cable (manual transmission) or automatic transmission shift control cable.

   d. Driveshafts (see Section 7).

   e. Power steering pump (avoiding putting stress on the lines).

   f. Air Conditioner compressor (avoiding putting stress on the lines).

   g. Exhaust pipe and, on cars with automatic transmissions, the secondary air lines.

   h. Upper and lower radiator hoses.

   i. Engine ground strap.

   j. Engine electrical connectors.

   k. Emission canister hoses.

   l. Three-way solenoid valve hoses.

   m. Brake vacuum hose.

   n. Heater hoses.

   o. Fuel hoses.

   p. Speedometer cable.

   q. Accelerator and cruise control cable (if applicable).

   r. Cooling fan and radiator (connect the hoses and electrical connectors).

   s. Oil dipstick tube and dipstick.

   t. Air cleaner assembly.

   u. Battery tray and battery (positive cable first).

   v. Hood, aligning the hinges as they were, using the matchmarks.

20. Check all fluid levels and replenish as necessary, using approved antifreeze/water mixture, power steering fluid, and engine oil.

1988-89 323 Turbo

1. Release the pressure from the fuel system as described in Section 5.

2. Scribe matchmarks on the hood where the hinges align, then unfasten the bolts and remove the hood.

3. Disconnect both battery cables, negative first.

4. Raise the front of the vehicle, support it safely with jackstands and block the rear wheels. Remove the front wheels.

5. Drain the engine oil, transaxle fluid and coolant into suitable containers.

6. Remove the battery and the battery carrier. Remove the air cleaner assembly.

7. If equipped, loosen the air conditioning unit from its mounting and slip the drive belt from the pulley. DO NOT disconnect the refrigerant hoses. Tie the unit off to the side of the vehicle or to the radiator support bracket, so that it will not interfere with the removal of the engine. Do the same for the power steering pump, if so equipped.

8. Remove the clutch release cylinder and disconnect the body-to-transmission ground cable and the back-up light switch connector.

9. Unfasten the engine harness connectors. Disconnect the shift control and speedometer cables from their respective linkages.

10. Loosen the hose clamps and remove the two heater hoses.

11. Disconnect the coolant temperature and cooling fan switch connectors.

12. Unbolt and remove the radiator.

13. Disconnect and remove the fuel and evaporator canister hoses. Plug the fuel hoses to prevent leakage and the entry of foreign matter. Have a small plastic container on hand to collect the excess fuel. Label and disconnect any vacuum hoses. Disconnect the accelerator cable from its linkage.

14. Loosen the hose clamps and remove the intercooler. Be careful not to damage the fins of the intercooler during removal. Cover the air pipe and hose openings with masking tape to prevent the entry of foreign matter.

15. Working from underneath the vehicle, unbolt and remove the side and under covers.

16. Label and disconnect the electrical leads and connectors from the starter, oil pressure switch and alternator.

17. Disconnect the driveshafts from either side. For details, please refer to Section 7.

18. Unbolt and remove the exhaust pipe. On 4WD models, disconnect the propeller shaft (see Section 7). Remove the engine mount crossmember. Disengage the harness connector from the control unit and remove it. Store the control unit in a safe place.

19. Connect a lifting sling to the engine lifting brackets and attach a suitable hoist to the sling. Tension the hoist. Support the bottom of the transaxle with a jack.

20. Remove the No. 3 and No. 2 engine mounts (all models) and the No. 4 mount (4WD models only).

21. Lift the engine/transaxle assembly from the car and mount it on a stand or suitable holding fixture.

To install:

22. Carefully align the engine/transaxle assembly with its original position in the engine compartment. Then, work it slowly into position so as to avoid damaging anything. Install each item below in reverse order of the removal procedure:

   a. No. 3, No. 2 and No. 4 (4WD models only) engine-to-body mounts.

   b. Control unit and harness connector.

   c. Engine mount crossmember.

   d. Propeller shaft (4WD models only).

   e. Exhaust pipe and driveshafts.

   f. Alternator, oil pressure switch and starter motor connectors.

   g. Undercover and side covers.

   h. Intercooler.

   i. Accelerator cable, vacuum, canister and fuel hoses.

   j. Radiator, cooling fan and thermoswitch connectors.

   k. Speedometer and shift control cables, heater hoses and engine harness connectors.

   l. Back-up light switch connector, body-to-transmission ground cable and clutch release cylinder.

   m. Battery carrier, battery and cables (positive cable first).

   n. Air cleaner assembly and front wheels.

   o. Air conditioning compressor and power steering pump.

   p. Hood, aligning the hinges as they were, using the matchmarks.

23. Check all fluid levels and replenish as necessary, using approved antifreeze/water mixture, power steering fluid, and engine oil.

1979-82 626

1. Scribe matchmarks on the hood where the hinges align, then unfasten the bolts and remove the hood.

2. Disconnect the negative battery cable.

3. Drain the cooling system.

4. Remove the upper and lower radiator hoses.

5. On cars equipped with an automatic transmission, disconnect the cooler lines at the radiator.

6. Remove the radiator cowling and fan.

7. Remove the radiator.

8. Remove the intake hoses from the air cleaner, then remove the air cleaner.

9. Disconnect the wiring from the distributor (primary), ignition coil, oil pressure gauge unit and the alternator **B** terminal. Disconnect the alternator wiring coupler, and remove the right side engine mounting nut.

10. Disconnect the wiring from the water temperature gauge unit, fuel cut solenoid, automatic choke, and starter motor.

11. Disconnect the air hoses (reed valve), vacuum hoses (three way solenoid valve), fuel hoses, acceleration wire, master vacuum hose, and the left side engine mounting nut.

12. Raise the front of the vehicle and safely support with jackstands.

13. Remove the under cover.

14. Disconnect the exhaust pipe.

15. Remove the clutch under cover plate and stays.

16. On cars equipped with automatic transmission, remove the torque converter and driving plate support bolts.

17. Support the transmission with a suitable jack, then remove the transmission supporting bolts and nuts.

18. Remove the starter motor and the clutch release cylinder.

19. Connect a suitable lifting sling to the engine hanger brackets and to a hoist, then remove the slack.

20. Pull the engine forward until it clears the clutch shaft, then lift the engine from the vehicle.

21. To install, reverse the removal procedure.

1983-87 626

EXCEPT DIESEL

▶ See Figures 67, 68 and 69

➡ To perform this procedure, you will need a special tool, a differential side gear holder, Mazda part number 49 G030 455 or equivalent. For details, see the Driveshaft Removal and Installation procedure in Section 7. You will also have to support the vehicle with the front wheels removed as you lift the engine from above.

1. Scribe matchmarks on the hood where the hinges align, then unfasten the bolts and remove the hood.

2. On 1986-87 vehicles, release the fuel system pressure as described in Section 5, before proceeding with the engine removal.

3. Disconnect both battery cables, negative first. Remove the air cleaner assembly.

4. Disconnect the fuel supply hose and, on 1983-85 models, the return hose. Disconnect the accelerator cable at the carburetor or injection system throttle body.

5. Disconnect the clutch cable (1983-85 models) or remove the clutch slave (release) cylinder (1986-87 models) from the transaxle. On automatic transaxle equipped models, disconnect the control cable.

6. Disconnect the engine ground strap. On 1986 models, disconnect the related connector at the same time. Disconnect the power brake unit vacuum hose. Remove the three-way valve vacuum switch and its mounting bracket from the firewall.

7. Drain the cooling system through both the radiator drain cock and the block drain plug. Then, disconnect and remove both heater hoses.

8. On 1983-85 models, disconnect the duty solenoid valve and vacuum sensor.

9. On all models, label and then disconnect all wiring to the engine and transaxle.

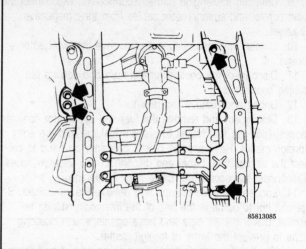

Fig. 69 Remove the engine mount bolts from the locations shown — 1983-87 626

10. Disconnect both the air vent and vacuum hoses from the storage canister.

11. Remove the electric fan and radiator (refer to the procedures later in this section).

12. On air conditioned models, remove the windshield washer tanks and the alternator. (Refer to the alternator removal procedure earlier in this section.) For non-air conditioned models, proceed to Step 14.

13. On air conditioned models, remove the A/C compressor from its mounts without attempting to disconnect any refrigeration lines. Securely tie the compressor to the front cowl in such a way that the refrigerant lines are not under stress.

14. Raise the car and support it safely on jackstands. Remove the front wheels and splash shields.

15. On cars with manual steering, go on to Step 16. On cars with power steering, loosen the power steering pump pulley bolt. Then, remove the pump drive belt. Remove the power steering pump pulley and pump installation bolts, holding the pump so the hoses will not be stressed. Support the pump above the crossmember so that the hoses can remain connected without any stress.

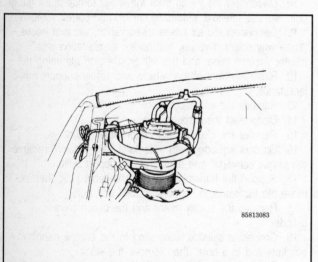

Fig. 67 Tie the air conditioner compressor as shown while removing the engine — 1983-87 626

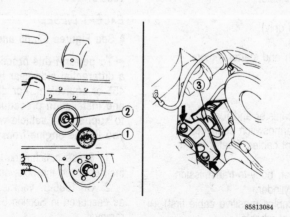

Fig. 68 Remove the rubber cap (1) from the right wheelhouse and the bolt (2) shown in the illustration. Then, unfasten the arrowed bolts from inside the engine compartment and remove the torque stopper (3) — 1983-87 626

16. Remove the driveshafts as described in Section 7. Make sure to use a holder to prevent misalignment of the differential side gear splines and to keep the gears in position.

17. On cars with a manual transaxle, remove the shift rod and torque rod along with the related joints and nuts. Then, install a lifting sling and support the engine securely by the lifting brackets.

18. Remove the rubber cap from the right wheelhouse, and the bolt shown in the illustration. Remove the arrowed bolts from inside the engine compartment, then remove the torque stopper.

19. Disconnect the exhaust pipe.

20. Remove the mounting bolts (arrowed in the illustration) from the engine mounts. Then, carefully lift the engine/transaxle assembly out of the engine compartment. Take extra care not to damage air conditioner or power steering parts.

To install:

21. Carefully align the engine/transaxle assembly with its original position in the engine compartment. Then, work it slowly into position so as to avoid damaging anything.

22. Connect the exhaust pipe. Install the torque rods and bolts, and then the cap. Install the engine mount bolts.

23. Install each of the following items in the reverse order of removal:

    a. Shift rod and torque rod and related parts.

    b. Driveshafts (refer to Section 7).

    c. Power steering pump.

    d. Splash shields and front wheels.

24. Lower the car. Then, continue installing parts as listed:.

    a. Air conditioner compressor.

    b. Alternator (if applicable).

    c. Electric fan and radiator.

    d. Air vent and vacuum hoses.

    e. Wiring.

    f. Heater hoses.

    g. Three-way valve vacuum switch and bracket and the power brake unit vacuum hoses (make sure connections are secure).

    h. Engine ground strap and connector.

    i. Clutch release cylinder/cable or automatic transaxle control cable.

    j. Speedometer and accelerator cables.

    k. Fuel hose(s) and the air cleaner.

    l. Battery cables (positive cable first).

    m. Hood, aligning the hinges as they were, using the matchmarks.

25. Check all fluid levels and replenish as necessary, using approved antifreeze/water mixture, power steering fluid, and engine oil.

626 DIESEL

▶ See Figures 68, 69 and 70

➡To perform this procedure, you will need a differential side gear holder, Mazda part number 49 G030 455 or equivalent. For details, see the Driveshaft Removal and Installation procedure in Section 7. You will also have to support the vehicle with the front wheels off as you remove the engine from above.

1. Scribe matchmarks on the hood where the hinges align, then unfasten the bolts and remove the hood.

2. Disconnect both battery cables, negative first.

3. Remove the oil filler and radiator caps. Then raise the vehicle and safely support the front end on jackstands.

4. Drain the engine oil and coolant. Drain the transaxle fluid. Remove both front wheels.

5. Disconnect the starter motor cable and ignition switch wire at the starter. Disconnect the oil pressure switch connection nearby.

6. Disconnect the lower radiator hose from the water inlet pipe on the block.

7. Disconnect the two rubber hoops which support the exhaust pipe at the crossmember. Then, unbolt the exhaust pipe at its support bracket and at the flange adjacent to the exhaust manifold.

8. Disconnect the shift control rod and torque rod at the transaxle.

9. Remove the tie rod clinch bolts and nuts, and then pry the lower control arms on both sides downward to separate the knuckle and lower ball joint.

10. Pry the right driveshaft out of the transaxle. See Section 7 of this manual.

11. Remove the engine mount attaching nuts. Then, lower the vehicle to the ground.

12. Remove the Quick Start and Afterglow relays from the air cleaner bracket. Then, unbolt and remove the air cleaner assembly and bracket.

13. Unbolt and remove the clutch release (slave) cylinder from the transaxle housing. Disconnect the speedometer cable from the transaxle housing, as well.

14. Remove the engine wiring harness bracket. Disconnect the ground strap or cable from the transaxle case. Disconnect the speedometer cable at the case, as well.

15. Disconnect the left side driveshaft from the transaxle (see Section 7). Make sure to install the required holder to prevent misalignment of the differential side gear splines and to keep the gears in position.

16. Disconnect the electric fan motor and back-up lamp switch connectors.

17. Disconnect the fuel supply and return hoses at the injection pump, draining the fuel into a suitable container. Cap the open ends to keep the connections clean.

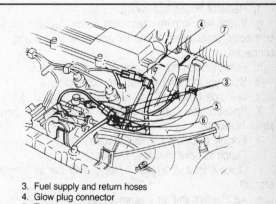

3. Fuel supply and return hoses
4. Glow plug connector
5. Tachometer electrical connector
6. Engine stop valve connector
7. Water temperature sensor connector

85813086

Fig. 70 Disconnect the fuel supply and return hoses, as well as the indicated electrical connectors

18. Unfasten the glow plug connector, tachometer sensor connector and engine stop valve connector.

19. Unfasten the water temperature sensor connector (at the thermostat housing)

20. Disconnect the upper radiator hose at the thermostat housing. Disconnect the water lever sensor connector, water temperature switch connector and ground wire. Disconnect the lower radiator hose, then remove the radiator and its rubber mounts.

21. Disconnect the accelerator cable at the injection pump. Disconnect the cold start device cable at the injection pump. Then, disconnect the plug and terminal type connector from the alternator.

22. Disconnect the power brake vacuum hose at the pipe leading from the vacuum pump. Disconnect the two coolant hoses and two oil hoses from the oil cooler, draining them into a convenient container to avoid spillage.

23. On cars with a manual transaxle, remove the shift rod and torque rod and related joints and nuts.

24. Remove the rubber cap from the right wheelhouse, and the bolt shown in the illustration. Remove the arrowed bolts from inside the engine compartment, then remove the torque stopper.

25. Install a lifting sling and support the engine securely by the two lifting brackets.

26. Disconnect the engine ground strap at the body.

27. Remove the mounting bolts (arrowed in the illustration) from the engine mounts. Then, carefully lift the engine and transaxle assembly out of the engine compartment. Take extra care not to damage air conditioner or power steering parts.

To install:

28. Carefully align the engine with its original position in the engine compartment. Then, work it slowly into position so as to avoid damaging anything.

29. Install the engine mount bolts.

30. Install/reconnect each of the items below in reverse of its removal:

  a. Engine torque stopper.
  b. Oil cooler hoses and brake vacuum hose.
  c. Alternator wiring.
  d. Cold start and accelerator cables to the injection pump.
  e. Radiator and mounts.
  f. Radiator hoses and wiring.
  g. Water temperature sensor connector, fuel cut valve connector, tachometer connector and glow plug wiring connector.
  h. Fuel injection pump supply and return hoses.
  i. Back-up light and electric fan connectors.
  j. Left side driveshaft (as described in Section 7).
  k. Speedometer cable and engine ground (at the transaxle housing).
  l. Engine electrical harness bracket.
  m. Clutch release hydraulic cylinder.
  n. Quick start and afterglow relays onto the air cleaner bracket.
  o. Air cleaner and air cleaner bracket.
  p. Right side driveshaft (as described in Section 7).
  q. Tie rod ends.
  r. Exhaust pipe and rubber supports.
  s. Oil pressure sending unit, radiator lower hose (at the inlet pipe on the block), and the starter wiring.

31. Replenish all fluids, reinstall the wheels and lower the vehicle to the ground.

32. Install the filler caps and reconnect the battery (positive cable first).

33. Reinstall the hood, aligning the hinges as they were, using the matchmarks.

1988-89 626/MX-6

1. Release the pressure from the fuel system as described in Section 5.

2. Drain the engine oil and the cooling system.

3. Scribe matchmarks on the hood where the hinges align, then unfasten the bolts and remove the hood.

4. Disconnect the battery cables, negative first, then remove the battery and battery carrier.

5. Remove the fuse box and air cleaner assembly.

6. Tag and disconnect the spark plug wires from the distributor cap. Disconnect the accelerator cable from the throttle body. On automatic transaxle equipped vehicles, disconnect the throttle cable.

7. Disconnect the fuel hoses from the fuel injector rail. Plug the fuel hose openings to prevent leakage.

8. Loosen the hose clamps and remove the two radiator hoses. On manual transaxle equipped vehicles, disconnect the transaxle fluid cooler lines from the bottom of the radiator. Plug the openings to prevent leakage.

9. Unfasten the connector from the bottom of the radiator.

10. On turbocharged engines, disconnect the turbocharger pipe and hose. Cover the opening of the turbocharger with masking tape to prevent anything from falling into the turbine casing.

11. Unfasten the water thermoswitch connector.

12. Disconnect the fuel injection harness and label all the individual connectors. Do the same for the engine harness.

13. Disconnect the vacuum hose and the three-way solenoid assembly. On turbocharged engines, disconnect the EGR solenoid assembly.

14. Disconnect the heater hoses and the evaporative canister hoses.

15. Remove the harness from the transaxle. Disconnect the speedometer cable and the clutch release cylinder (manual transaxle, with the pipe still connected) or control cable (automatic transaxle).

16. Remove the drive belts. If equipped, disconnect the air conditioning compressor and bracket from its mounting, and securely tie the unit off to the side of the vehicle with the lines still connected.

17. Position the power steering pump and pulley in the same manner as the air conditioner.

18. Working from underneath the vehicle, remove the engine side covers.

19. Raise the vehicle and safely support with jackstands. Block the rear wheels, then remove the front wheels.

20. Remove the tie rod ends, stabilizer control rod and lower arm control bushing (see Section 8).

21. Pry the driveshafts from the transaxle as described in Section 7. Make sure to use a holder to prevent misalignment of the differential side gear splines and to keep the gears in position.

22. On cars with a manual transaxle, remove the change rod and shift bar, along with the related joints and nuts. Remove the exhaust pipe.

23. Install a lifting sling and support the engine securely by the lifting brackets. Remove the engine mounts.

24. Lift the engine/transaxle from the engine and position the assembly on a stand or suitable holding fixture. Separate the transaxle from the engine.

To install:

25. Attach the transaxle to the engine.

26. Carefully line the engine up with its original position in the engine compartment. Then, work it slowly into position so as to avoid damaging anything.

27. Install the engine mount bolts.

28. Install each of the items below in reverse order of removal:

    a. Exhaust pipe. Torque the converter nuts to 47-66 ft. lbs. (64-89 Nm), manifold nuts to 23-34 ft. lbs. (31-46 Nm) and bracket bolt to 14-19 ft. lbs. (19-26 Nm).

    b. Extension bar and change rod (manual transmissions). Torque the bar-to-transaxle bolt to 23-34 ft. lbs. (31-46 Nm).

    c. Driveshafts. Grease the driveshaft splines and use new retaining clips. After installation, pull out on the drive hub to verify that the driveshaft is held properly by the clip.

    d. Lower arm. Torque the locknut to 32-40 ft. lbs. (43-54 Nm).

    e. Stabilizer control rod. Adjust the front stabilizer control rods so that there is 0.79 in. (20mm) from the top of the rod bolt to the bottom of the adjusting locknut. Once this dimension is obtained, torque the locknut to 12-17 ft. lbs. (16-23 Nm).

    f. Tie rod ends. Connect the tie rod end to the steering knuckle and torque the castellated nut to 22-33 ft. lbs. (30-45 Nm). Install a new cotter pin and spread the ends.

    g. Front wheels

29. Lower the vehicle and install the following:

    a. Engine side covers.

    b. Power steering pump and air conditioning compressor with pulleys and brackets. Torque the power steering pump mounting bolts to 23-34 ft. lbs. (31-46 Nm) and the pulley locknut to 29-43 ft. lbs. (39-58 Nm). Connect the air conditioning compressor strap to the power steering pump and torque the mounting bolt to 14-19 ft. lbs. (19-26 Nm). Torque the air conditioning compressor mounting bracket bolts to 27-46 ft. lbs. (37-62 Nm) and the mounting bolts with locknuts to 27-38 ft. lbs. (37-51 Nm).

    c. Drive belts (adjust the deflection).

    d. Control cable (on vehicles with an automatic transaxle). Adjust the shift selector position (see Section 7).

    e. Clutch release cylinder (on vehicles with a manual transaxle). Torque the pipe bracket mounting bolts to 69-95 inch lbs. (8-11 Nm) and the cylinder mounting bolts to 14-19 ft. lbs. (19-26 Nm).

    f. Speedometer cable.

    g. Transaxle harness.

    h. Heater and canister hoses.

    i. EGR solenoid assembly (turbo). Torque the mounting nuts to 69-95 inch lbs. (8-11 Nm).

    j. Three-way solenoid assembly. Torque the mounting nuts to 69-95 inch lbs. (8-11 Nm).

    k. Brake vacuum hose.

    l. Engine and fuel injection harnesses.

    m. Water thermoswitch and heat gauge connectors.

    n. Turbocharger pipe and hose (turbo). Torque the outer mounting nut to 47-66 ft. lbs. (64-89 Nm) and the inner mounting nut to 69-95 inch lbs. (8-11 Nm).

    o. Radiator and cooling fan. Torque the mounting bolts to 69-95 inch lbs. (8-11 Nm).

    p. Radiator harness.

    q. Transaxle fluid hoses to radiator (automatic transaxle).

    r. Fuel hoses.

    s. Throttle cable (automatic transaxle).

    t. Accelerator cable.

    u. Spark plug wires.

    v. Air cleaner assembly.

    w. Battery tray, fuse box and battery (positive cable first).

    x. Hood, aligning the hinges as they were, using the matchmarks.

30. Check all fluid levels and replenish as necessary, using approved antifreeze/water mixture, power steering fluid, and engine oil. Adjust all drive belts, cables and linkages. Adjust the ignition timing and idle speed, as described in Section 2.

929

1. Relieve the fuel system pressure as described in Section 5.

2. Disconnect the negative battery cable.

3. Drain the engine oil and the cooling system.

4. Scribe matchmarks on the hood where the hinges align, then unfasten the bolts and remove the hood.

5. Disconnect and remove the fresh air duct and the air cleaner assembly.

6. Disconnect the accelerator cable from the throttle body.

7. Remove the cooling fan pulley bolts, then remove the cooling fan and the radiator cowling.

8. Remove the drive belts, spark plug wires and spark plugs.

9. Disconnect the evaporative canister and brake hoses.

10. Disconnect the fuel hoses from the connections on the fuel rail ends. Plug the hoses to prevent leakage and the entry of foreign matter.

11. Remove the heater hoses and disconnect the engine wiring harness.

12. Working from underneath the vehicle, remove the engine undercover.

13. Loosen the hose clamps, then remove the upper and lower radiator hoses.

14. On models equipped with an automatic transmission, disconnect the automatic transmission fluid cooler lines from the radiator bottom. Plug the openings to prevent leakage.

15. Disconnect the radiator harness and remove the radiator.

16. Unbolt and remove the alternator and the alternator strap.

17. If equipped, disconnect the air conditioning compressor and bracket from its mounting and tie the unit off to the side of the vehicle with its lines intact and connected. Position the power steering pump in the same manner as the air conditioner.

18. Unbolt and remove the section of exhaust pipe that runs from the catalytic converter to the exhaust manifold.

19. Connect a lifting strap to the engine lifting brackets, then attach a hoist to the sling and tension the hoist. Support and remove the transmission. See Section 7.

20. Remove the engine mounting nuts and lift the engine out of the vehicle.

21. Mount the engine on a stand or suitable holding fixture.

To install:

22. Position the engine into the vehicle. Using the hoist, guide the engine over the mount studs and install the engine mount nuts. Torque the mount nuts to 35-36 ft. lbs. (47-49 Nm).

23. Install the transmission by reversing the removal procedure.

24. Connect the exhaust pipe to the manifold and the converter. Torque the exhaust pipe nuts to 23-34 ft. lbs. (31-46 Nm).

25. Position and install the power steering pump onto its mounting. Torque the mounting bolts to 23-34 ft. lbs. (31-46 Nm).

26. Install the air conditioning compressor and torque the mounting bolts to 22-29 ft. lbs. (30-39 Nm).

27. Install the alternator and mounting strap. Torque the alternator mounting bolts to 27-38 ft. lbs. (37-51 Nm).

28. Install the radiator and torque the mounting bolts to 16-22 ft. lbs. (22-30 Nm). Connect the radiator harness and, if equipped with an automatic transmission, install the transmission fluid lines.

29. Connect the upper and lower radiator hoses. Make sure the clamps are positioned properly on the hose.

30. Connect heater, fuel, brake vacuum and evaporative canister hoses.

31. Coat the spark plug threads with a suitable anti-seize compound and torque the plugs to 11-17 ft. lbs. (15-23 Nm).

32. Install the cooling fan, alternator, power steering pump (if equipped), crankshaft pulley and air conditioning compressor drive belts. Adjust the drive belt tensions.

33. Install the radiator fan with the cowling. Install the cooling fan/pulley bolts and torque to 69-95 inch lbs. (8-11 Nm). Also torque the cowling bolts to 69-95 inch lbs. (8-11 Nm).

34. Working from underneath the vehicle, install the engine under cover and torque the mounting screws to 69-95 inch lbs. (8-11 Nm).

35. Connect the spark plug wires and the negative battery cable.

36. Connect the accelerator cable and check the cable deflection by pressing lightly on the cable. Cable deflection should be 0.04-0.12 in. (1-3mm).

37. Install the air cleaner assembly and the fresh air duct.

38. Replenish the engine and cooling system fluid levels, using approved antifreeze/water mixture, power steering fluid, and engine oil. Adjust all drive belts, cables and linkages. Set the ignition timing and idle speed, as described in Section 2.

Rocker Arm (Valve) Cover

➡**Mazda often refers to this component as a "cylinder head cover."**

REMOVAL & INSTALLATION

▶ **See Figures 71, 72, 73, 74, 75, 76 and 77**

1. On carbureted engines, remove the air cleaner. On fuel injected engines, loosen the clamps and remove the air intake crossover. On turbocharged engines, loosen the clamps at either end and disconnect the turbocharger outlet line.

2. Disconnect/remove the PCV valve at the rocker arm cover or PCV line (diesel).

➡**On 3.0L engines, PCV valve removal is only necessary when servicing the right side rocker arm cover.**

3. If so equipped, unfasten the choke cable and the air bypass valve cable.

4. Unfasten the retaining bolts, then remove the rocker arm cover.

5. Using a suitable scraper, carefully remove all traces of old gasket material and/or sealant from the rocker arm cover and cylinder head mating surface. Be careful not to dislodge any material into the exposed cylinder head.

To install:

6. Position a new gasket on the rocker arm cover. On the 1.6L engine (turbo and non-turbo), apply a suitable RTV sealant to the groove in the cover prior to installing the new gasket. On the 2.2L engine (turbo and non-turbo), apply seal-

Fig. 71 Unfasten any cable brackets which are attached to the cylinder head cover

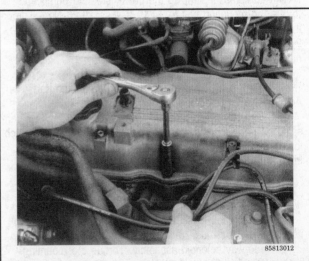

Fig. 72 Unfasten the cylinder head cover retaining bolts with the correct size socket

Fig. 73 Lift the cover from the cylinder head

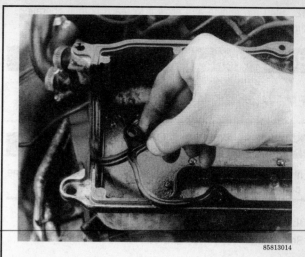

Fig. 74 Remove the used gasket from the cylinder head cover

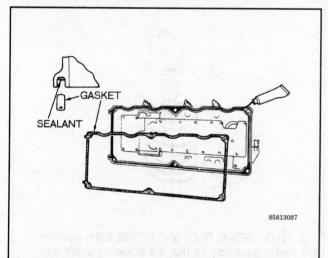

Fig. 75 Apply RTV sealant to the cylinder head cover prior to installing the gasket — 1.6L engine

Fig. 77 Install new seal washers with the bolts on 2.0L and 3.0L engines (3.0L right side cylinder head cover shown)

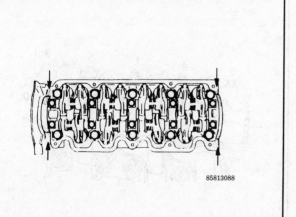

Fig. 76 On the 2.2L engine, be sure to apply sealant to the arrowed areas of the cylinder head

ant to the corners of the cylinder head, as indicated by the arrows in the accompanying illustration, before installing the cover.

7. On the 2.0L (turbo and non-turbo) and 3.0L engines, install new seal washers with the bolts.

8. Tighten the bolts in several stages, going back and forth across the cover. You can use the following torque figures for most 1983-89 engines, but the important point is to tighten the bolts evenly and just until they are slightly snug. The recommended torque values are:

- 1.6L Engine: 3.6-6.5 ft. lbs. (5-9 Nm)
- 2.0L Engine: 2.2-2.9 ft. lbs. (3-4 Nm)
- 2.2L Engine: 4.3-5.7 ft. lbs. (6-8 Nm)
- 3.0L Engine: 2.5-3.3 ft. lbs. (3.4-4.5 Nm)

9. If applicable, fasten the choke cable and the air bypass valve cable.

10. On turbocharged engines, connect the turbocharger outlet line.

11. Install/connect the PCV valve and the air cleaner or air intake crossover.

12. Start the engine and allow it to reach normal operating temperature. Check for oil leaks.

Rocker Shafts

REMOVAL & INSTALLATION

❊❊WARNING

This operation should only be performed when the engine is cold!

1.3L, 1.4L, 1.5L and 1979-82 2.0L Engines
▶ See Figures 78, 79, 80 and 81

1. Remove the rocker arm cover, as previously described.
2. Loosen the cylinder head retaining bolts using several stages using of the sequence indicated by the illustration.

➡Although the cylinder head need not be removed, the same bolts which retain the cylinder head to the block also secure the rocker shaft assembly.

3. Remove the rocker shaft and bolts as an assembly. Stuff a rag in the drain hole to prevent the valve keepers from falling into the oil pan.
   To install:
4. Remove the rag. Align the dowels and place the rocker shaft assembly on the cylinder head.
5. Make sure that all the spherical valve operators at the outer ends of the rocker levers are positioned so that the flat surface is against the top of the valve stem.
6. Position the rocker assembly so that the exhaust valve rocker arms are offset 0.039 in. (1mm) from the centers of the valve stems (see illustration).
7. Torque the cylinder head retaining bolts using several stages of the appropriate sequence, as illustrated. For all but the 2.0L engine, tighten the bolts to 56-59 ft. lbs. (78-82 Nm). On the 1981 2.0L engine, tighten the bolts to 59-64 ft. lbs.

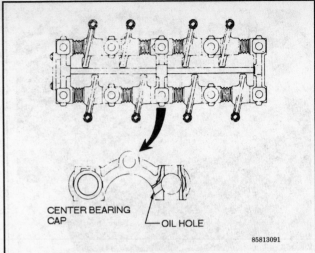

Fig. 79 Position the rocker assembly on 1979-82 2.0L engines so that the oil passages align as shown

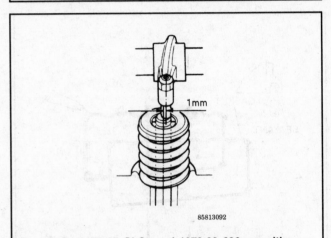

Fig. 80 On 1978-85 GLCs and 1979-82 626s, position the rocker assembly so that the adjusting studs are offset 0.039 in. (1mm) from the centers of the exhaust valve stems

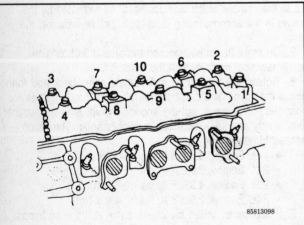

Fig. 78 Cylinder head bolt loosening sequence — 1.3L, 1.4L, 1.5L and 1979-82 2.0L engines

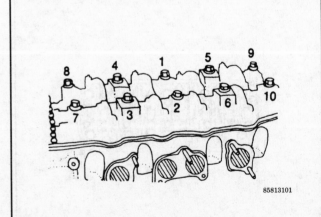

Fig. 81 Cylinder head bolt tightening sequence — 1.3L, 1.4L, 1.5L and 1979-82 2.0L engines

(80-87 Nm); on the 1982 2.0L engine, tighten the bolts to 65-69 ft. lbs. (88-93.5 Nm).

8. Adjust the valve clearances, as described later in this section.

9. Install the rocker arm cover, as previously described.

1.6L, 1983-87 2.0L, and 2.2L Engines

♦ See Figures 82, 83, 84, 85, 86, 87, 88, 89 and 90

1. Remove the cylinder head cover, as previously described.

2. Loosen the rocker shaft bolts, a little at a time, in the sequence indicated by the illustration.

➡**Do not remove the rocker shaft bolts.**

3. On the 2.0L engine, the rear housing and gasket may have to be removed before the rocker shaft assembly can be separated (if a stud extends from the assembly's end cap through the rear housing). If applicable, unfasten the appropriate nuts and bolts, then remove the rear housing and gasket.

Fig. 84 If applicable, unfasten the retaining nuts and bolts . . .

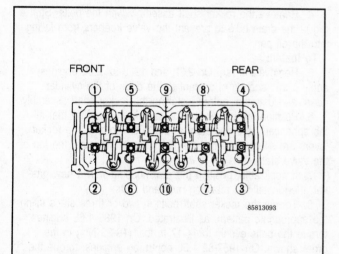

Fig. 82 Rocker shaft bolt loosening sequence — 1.6L engine

Fig. 85 . . . then remove the rear housing and gasket

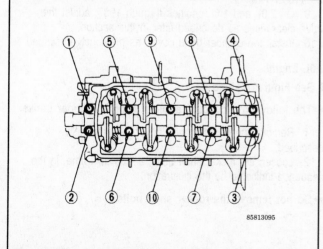

Fig. 83 Rocker shaft bolt loosening sequence — 2.2L and 1983-87 2.0L engines

Fig. 86 Loosen (but do not withdraw) the rocker shaft bolts, then lift the shaft assembly from the head

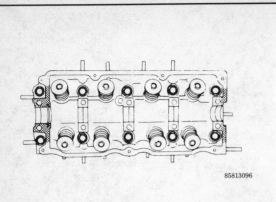

Fig. 87 On 2.2L and 1983-87 2.0L engines, coat each end of the cylinder head with sealer (as indicated by the shaded areas), before installing the rocker shaft assembly

Fig. 88 After positioning the rocker shaft assembly, tighten the bolts to specification

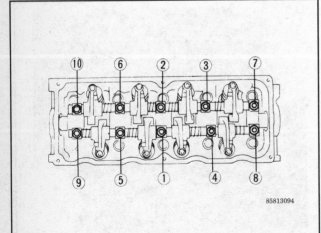

Fig. 89 Rocker shaft bolt tightening sequence — 1.6L engine

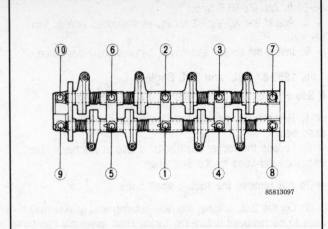

Fig. 90 Rocker shaft bolt tightening sequence — 2.2L and 1983-87 2.0L engines

4. Remove the rocker shaft assembly with the bolts. Stuff a rag in the drain hole to prevent the valve keepers from falling into the oil pan.

To install:

5. Remove the rag. On 2.2L and 1983-87 2.0L engines, apply a thin coating of sealant to the ends of the cylinder head, as illustrated, before installing the rocker shaft assembly.

6. Position the rocker shaft assembly. Make sure that all the spherical valve operators at the outer ends of the rocker levers are situated so that the flat surface is against the top of the valve stem.

7. If applicable, position the rear housing with a new gasket, then install the retaining nuts and bolts.

8. Torque the rocker shaft bolts in two or three steps using the appropriate pattern, as illustrated. On 1986 1.6L engines, torque the bolts evenly to 14-17 ft. lbs. (19-23 Nm) in the order shown. On 1987-89 1.6L non-turbo engines, torque the bolts evenly to 16-21 ft. lbs. (22-28 Nm), using the same torque pattern as for 1986. On 2.2L and 1983-87 2.0L engines, torque the bolts evenly in the order shown to 13-20 ft. lbs. (18-27 Nm).

9. On 2.0L and 1.6L engines through 1987, adjust the valve clearances as described later in this section.

10. Install the cylinder head cover, as previously described.

3.0L Engine

▶ See Figures 91 and 92

➡The following procedure applies to both cylinder banks.

1. Remove the cylinder head cover, as previously described.

2. Loosen the rocker shaft bolts, a little at a time, in the sequence indicated by the illustration.

➡**Do not remove the rocker shaft bolts.**

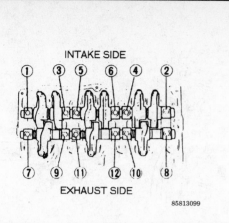

INTAKE SIDE

EXHAUST SIDE

85813099

Fig. 91 Rocker arm shaft loosening sequence — 3.0L engine

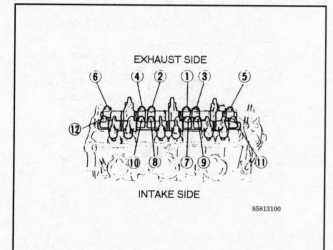

EXHAUST SIDE

INTAKE SIDE

85813100

Fig. 92 Rocker arm shaft tightening sequence — 3.0L engine

3. Remove the rocker shaft assembly and bolts as an assembly. Stuff a rag in the drain hole to prevent the valve keepers from falling into the oil pan.

To install:

4. Remove the rag and position the rocker shaft assembly. Make sure all the spherical valve operators at the outer ends of the rocker levers are positioned so the flat surface is against the top of the valve stem.

5. Torque the rocker shaft bolts, in two or three steps using the illustrated sequence, to 14-19 ft. lbs. (19-26 Nm). Be careful not to catch the rocker arm shaft spring between the shaft and the mounting boss during installation.

6. Install the cylinder head cover, as previously described.

Thermostat

REMOVAL & INSTALLATION

▶ **See Figures 93, 94, 95, 96, 97 and 98**

1. Position a drain pan below the radiator, then drain a gallon or so of coolant, so that the coolant level is below the thermostat.

2. Disconnect the radiator hose from the thermostat housing. If so equipped, disengage the electrical connector going to the coolant temperature sensor in the housing.

3. Remove the thermostat housing mounting nuts/bolts, housing, gasket and thermostat.

4. Clean all gasket surfaces thoroughly.

To install:

5. Install the new thermostat with the temperature sensing pellet downward or inside the block, or with the "jiggle pin" at the top. On the 2.0L gasoline and diesel engines, install the thermostat gasket with the printed side of the gasket facing the cylinder head. Also, on all models, make sure the thermostat is positioned in the head or manifold before the gasket is installed.

6. Use a new mounting gasket and install the housing with the housing bolts. On the 929, install the thermostat cover so that the mark is facing the front of the engine. Torque the housing bolts to 14-22 ft. lbs. (19-30 Nm).

7. On models so equipped, connect the thermosensor switch to the housing.

8. Connect the radiator hose to the housing and install the hose clamp.

9. Refill the cooling system to the proper level.

10. Start the engine and run it for a couple of minutes. Inspect for coolant leaks around the thermostat housing gasket sealing surface.

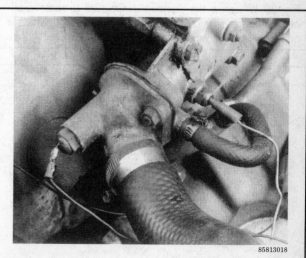

85813018

Fig. 93 Some models have a wire attached to a coolant temperature sensor in the tip of the housing

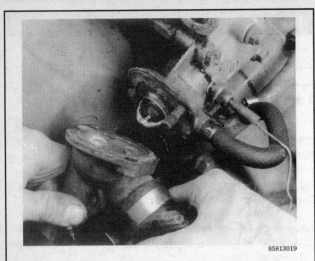

Fig. 94 Unfasten the thermostat housing nuts/bolts, then remove the housing

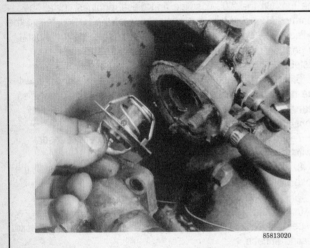

Fig. 95 Withdraw the thermostat. Be sure to remove all old gasket material and to install a new gasket (whether or not a new thermostat is installed)

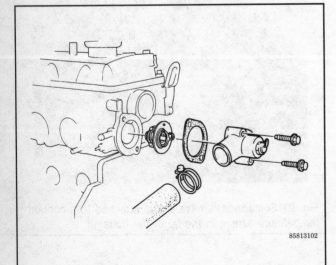

Fig. 96 Thermostat mounting — 323

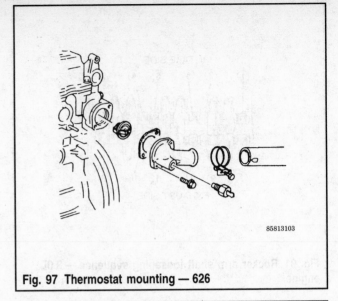

Fig. 97 Thermostat mounting — 626

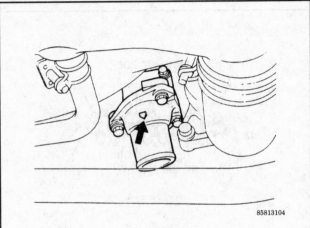

Fig. 98 On a 929, install the thermostat cover with its mark facing the front of the engine

Intake Manifold

REMOVAL & INSTALLATION

Carbureted and Diesel Engines
▶ **See Figures 99, 100 and 101**

1. Drain the cooling system and remove the air cleaner assembly. Remove the oil dipstick.
2. Disconnect the following:
   - Throttle and choke linkage
   - Fuel line(s)
   - PCV valve hose
   - Fuel and fuel pump hoses
   - Heater hoses
   - Distributor vacuum line
   - Ventilation valve hose (at the manifold)
   - Air pump hose at the anti-afterburn valve

- Brake vacuum hose
- Canister hoses
- Engine harness connectors
- Spark plug wires

3. Remove the following components as required to gain access to the intake manifold:
- Distributor
- Spark plugs
- Carburetor secondary air pipe manifold assembly
- Front engine hanger and ground wire
- Upper radiator hose and coolant bypass hose with mounting bracket

4. Unfasten manifold attaching bolts and remove the manifold and gasket from the cylinder head (on the diesel, an engine lifting hook will come off with the manifold).

5. Cover the ports on the cylinder block to prevent any foreign objects from falling into the engine.

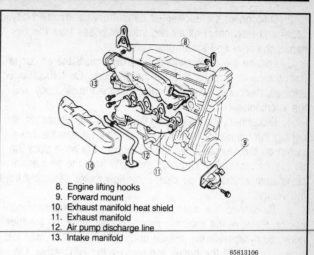

8. Engine lifting hooks
9. Forward mount
10. Exhaust manifold heat shield
11. Exhaust manifold
12. Air pump discharge line
13. Intake manifold

85813106

Fig. 101 Diesel intake and exhaust manifolds — exploded view

To install:

6. Replace the gaskets, making sure all surfaces are clean and smooth. Check manifold for warpage as described in the cylinder head overhaul procedures. Repair if necessary.

7. Install the manifold and, working from the center outward, tighten the bolts gradually and in several stages, to specifications.

8. Install the following components in the reverse order of removal as required:
- Coolant bypass hose and bracket
- Upper radiator hose
- Front engine hanger and ground wire
- Secondary air pipe manifold
- Spark plugs
- Distributor (see the beginning of this section for installation procedures)

9. Connect the following components:
- Spark plug wires
- Engine harness connectors
- Canister hoses
- Vacuum hoses (including brake)
- Heater hoses
- Fuel pump and fuel hoses
- Accelerator and cruise control cables
- PCV valve hose

10. Install the oil dipstick and refill the cooling system. Adjust all the linkages and cables. Set the ignition timing and the idle speed, as described in Section 2.

Fuel Injected Engines

323 MODELS

▶ See Figures 102 and 103

✳✳CAUTION

Before removing the intake manifold, release the fuel system pressure. (See Section 5 for details.)

1. Disconnect the negative battery cable and drain the cooling system.

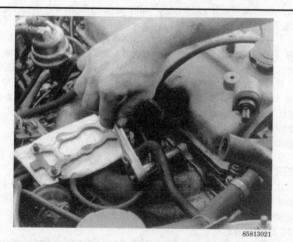

85813021

Fig. 99 Remove the bolts securing the intake manifold to the cylinder head (note that the carburetor may be left installed on most models)

85813022

Fig. 100 Withdraw the intake manifold from the cylinder head

2. Disconnect the accelerator cable from the throttle body. Label and disconnect all air and vacuum hoses from the dynamic chamber and the throttle body.

3. Loosen the hose clamps, then disconnect the air funnel from the air flow meter and the throttle body. On turbocharged engines, disconnect the air funnel from the throttle body and the intercooler.

4. Disconnect the spark plug wires from the distributor and unplug the connector from the ignition coil. Loosen the hose clamp on the flexible hose and disconnect the hose from the air cleaner assembly. Unfasten the bolts from the air cleaner cover and remove the air cleaner/air flow meter assembly from the vehicle.

5. Disconnect the water hoses and the throttle sensor connector. Remove the retaining nuts and bolts from the throttle body, then separate the throttle body from the intake manifold.

6. Disconnect the hoses and remove the BAC valve. On turbocharged engines, disconnect the water hose for the oil cooler and plug the opening to prevent leakage.

7. On turbocharged engines, unbolt the intake manifold and dynamic chamber assembly from the cylinder block, then lift it out of the vehicle.

8. On non turbocharged engines, unbolt the dynamic chamber from the intake manifold and remove it along with the gasket, then remove the intake manifold.

9. Remove the intake manifold gasket from the cylinder block. Cover or plug the intake ports to prevent anything from falling into the engine.

10. Thoroughly clean the intake manifold and cylinder block gasket mating surfaces. Visually inspect the intake manifold and dynamic chamber for cracks.

To install:

11. Place a new gasket on the cylinder block and lower the intake manifold onto the gasket. On turbocharged engines, attach the dynamic chamber to the intake manifold with a new gasket. Install the retaining nuts and bolts and torque them to 14-19 ft. lbs. (19-26 Nm).

12. Install the remaining components in the reverse order of removal:
- Oil cooler water hose (turbocharged engines)
- BAC valve and hoses
- Throttle body (with new gasket) and throttle sensor connector
- Water and vacuum hoses
- Air cleaner/air flow meter assembly, spark plug wires and distributor connector
- Air funnel
- Accelerator cable

13. Refill the cooling system to the proper level and connect the negative battery cable. Check the accelerator cable deflection.

626/MX-6 MODELS

▶ See Figure 104

✳✳CAUTION

Before removing the intake manifold, release the fuel system pressure. (See Section 5 for details.)

1. Disconnect the negative battery cable and drain the cooling system.

2. Unplug the air flow meter connector. Disconnect the air cleaner duct (1987 only), secondary air hoses and air control vacuum hoses, then remove the air cleaner. On 1988-89 models, disconnect and remove the air duct along with the No. 1 resonance chamber.

3. Remove the air flow meter and attendant air hoses. On 1988-89 non-turbocharged engines, the No. 2 resonance chamber is connected to the bottom of the flexible air hose by a small hose with a hose clamp, and is retained by one attaching screw. Disconnect and remove the No. 2 resonance chamber.

4. On 1988-89 turbocharged engines, trace the upper hose on the intercooler to the air bypass valve. (There are three hoses connected to the valve.) Loosen the hose clamps and disconnect the hoses. Unbolt and remove the air bypass valve from its mounting bracket, then remove the intercooler.

5. Unfasten the electrical connectors from the throttle body. Disconnect the water and vacuum hoses, then plug the openings.

6. Disconnect the accelerator cable from the throttle body and remove the throttle body (with gasket) from the dynamic chamber.

7. Disconnect the PCV hose and the vacuum pipe assembly. Remove the nuts and bolts that attach the dynamic chamber to the intake manifold and remove it along with the gasket.

8. Unfasten connectors from the fuel injectors, then route the wiring harness off to the side and out of the way. Disconnect the fuel hose from the injector rail and remove the rail assembly with the injectors attached. Plug all the fuel openings.

9. Disconnect the remaining vacuum hoses and remove the EGR pipe.

10. Remove the intake manifold bracket, followed by the intake manifold and gasket. Cover or plug the intake ports with clean rags or masking tape to prevent anything from falling into the engine.

11. Thoroughly clean the intake manifold and cylinder block gasket mating surfaces with a gasket scraper and solvent. Visually inspect the intake manifold and dynamic chamber for cracks.

To install:

12. Place a new gasket on the cylinder block and lower the intake manifold onto the gasket. Install the retaining nuts and torque them to 14-22 ft. lbs. (19-30 Nm).

13. Install the remaining components in the reverse order of removal:
- Intake manifold bracket
- EGR pipe and vacuum hoses
- Fuel rail and injector harness assembly
- Dynamic chamber with new gasket
- Vacuum pipe assembly and PCV hose
- Throttle body with new gasket
- Accelerator cable
- Vacuum and water hoses
- Throttle body connectors
- Intercooler
- Air bypass valve with hoses
- No. 2 resonance chamber (1988-89 non-turbocharged models only)
- Airflow meter
- No. 1 resonance chamber
- Air duct, air cleaner and air flow meter connector

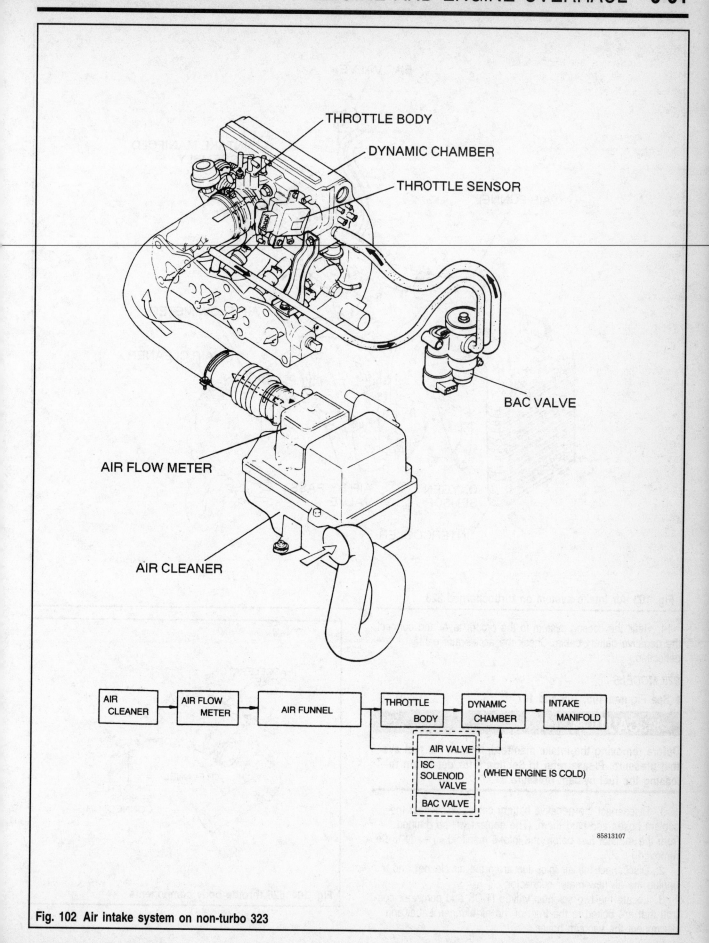

THROTTLE BODY

DYNAMIC CHAMBER

THROTTLE SENSOR

BAC VALVE

AIR FLOW METER

AIR CLEANER

| AIR CLEANER | AIR FLOW METER | AIR FUNNEL | THROTTLE BODY | DYNAMIC CHAMBER | INTAKE MANIFOLD |

AIR VALVE
ISC SOLENOID VALVE (WHEN ENGINE IS COLD)
BAC VALVE

85813107

Fig. 102 Air intake system on non-turbo 323

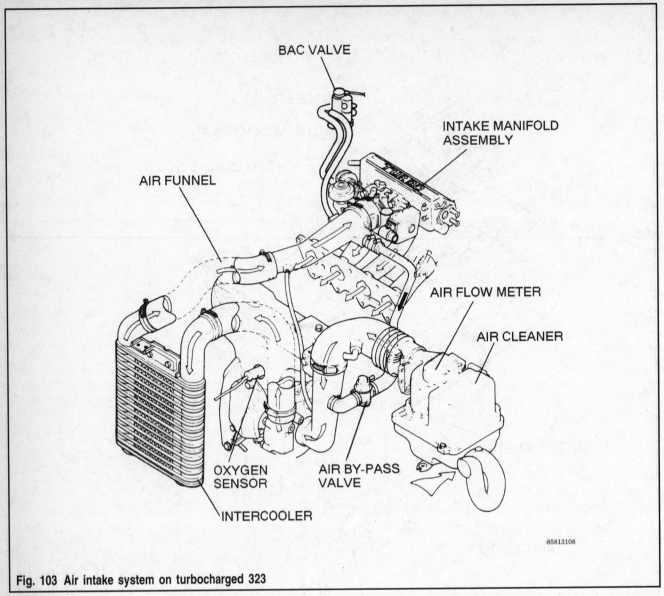

Fig. 103 Air intake system on turbocharged 323

14. Refill the cooling system to the proper level and connect the negative battery cable. Check the accelerator cable deflection.

929 MODELS

▶ See Figures 105, 106 and 107

✳✳CAUTION

Before removing the intake manifold, release the fuel system pressure. Please refer to Section 5 for details on releasing the fuel system pressure.

1. Disconnect the negative battery cable. Disconnect the coolant hoses and plug them. (The coolant will be drained from the radiator just before the intake manifold is ready to be removed.)
2. Disconnect the air inlet duct from the air cleaner and unplug the air flow meter connector.
3. Locate the two solenoid valves (TICS and purge air control) that are bolted to the front of the air cleaner. Label and disconnect the vacuum hoses.

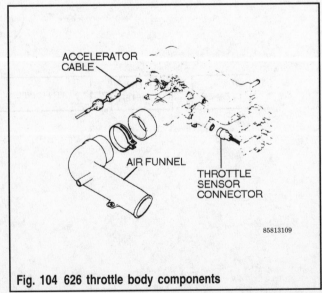

Fig. 104 626 throttle body components

4. Remove the air cleaner assembly, air flow meter and air funnel.

5. Disconnect the Bypass Air Control (BAC) valve connector and coolant hoses, then remove the valve.

6. Disconnect the throttle sensor connector and the accelerator cable. Remove the throttle body and gasket.

7. Disconnect all vacuum hoses, EGR pipe, EGR position sensor connector, coolant hose and ground wire.

8. Remove the wiring harness bracket.

9. Disconnect the air intake pipe from the dynamic chamber with the gasket.

10. Mark the extension manifolds RIGHT and LEFT for assembly reference, as they are not interchangeable. Remove the six extension manifolds with their gaskets from the dynamic chamber.

11. Disconnect the intake air thermosensor connector, vacuum hoses and ground connectors.

12. Remove the attaching nuts and lift the dynamic chamber straight up from the intake manifold studs. Drain the radiator at

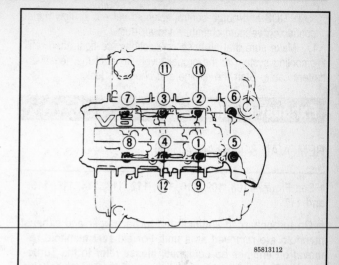

Fig. 107 Intake manifold tightening sequence — 929

this time and disconnect all remaining connectors, fuel hoses, and coolant hoses.

13. Using the sequence shown in the illustration, loosen the intake manifold nuts in two stages. Lift the intake manifold from the engine and remove the two intake manifold gaskets. Insert clean rags into the intake ports or cover them with masking tape to prevent anything from falling into the engine.

14. Immerse the intake manifold in a suitable solvent and blow it dry with compressed air. Visually inspect the intake manifold for cracks, warpage or any other type of damage and replace as necessary. Remove all gasket material from the seating surface on the manifold and the engine. Forward of one of the studs that secures the dynamic chamber is an O-ring that seals the manifold to the dynamic chamber. Remove this O-ring and replace it with a new one.

To install:

15. Place the new intake manifold gaskets onto the cylinder block and lower the manifold over the gaskets. Install the intake manifold washers with the white paint marks facing up. Install the retaining nuts and torque them in two stages to 14-18 ft. lbs. (19-24 Nm) using the sequence shown in the illustration.

16. Install the remaining components in the reverse of the removal procedure:

   a. Connectors, fuel hoses, coolant hoses and vacuum hoses.

   b. Dynamic chamber. Torque the retaining nuts to 14-18 ft. lbs. (19-24 Nm)..

   c. Intake air thermosensor ground connectors and vacuum hoses.

   d. Extension manifolds with new gaskets and O-rings.

   e. Intake air pipe with new gaskets and wiring bracket.

   f. Ground wire, coolant hose, EGR position connector, EGR pipe and vacuum hoses.

   g. Throttle body with new gasket, accelerator cable and throttle sensor connector. Check the deflection of the accelerator cable. If not within 0.04-0.12 in. (1-3mm), adjust with the nuts on the cable bracket.

   h. BAC valve, coolant hoses and connector.

   i. Air funnel, air hoses, air flow meter, and air cleaner assembly.

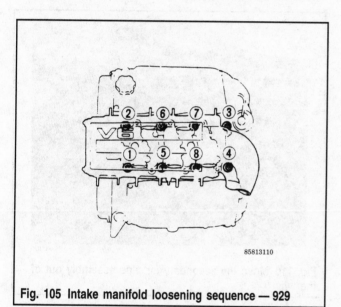

Fig. 105 Intake manifold loosening sequence — 929

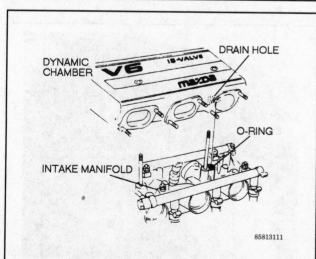

Fig. 106 Always replace the O-ring before installing the intake manifold — 929

j. TICS and purge control solenoid valves, air flow meter connector, vacuum chamber and air duct.

17. Make sure that all hose connections are tight, then refill the cooling system to the proper level. Connect the negative battery cable. Start the engine and check for leaks.

Exhaust Manifold

REMOVAL & INSTALLATION

▶ **See Figures 108, 109, 110, 111, 112, 113, 114, 115, 116 and 117**

➡**On turbocharged engines, the turbocharger and exhaust manifold are removed as a unit. For exhaust manifold removal on engines so equipped, please refer to the Turbocharger Removal and Installation procedure which follows later in this section.**

1. On carbureted engines, disconnect the hot air duct from the exhaust manifold insulator assembly (heat stove).
2. Disconnect the secondary air pipe assembly at the exhaust manifold, and position the pipes out of the way.
3. Disconnect the oxygen sensor's electrical lead. Unscrew and remove the sensor, if necessary.

➡**If both the manifold and sensor are to be re-used, the oxygen sensor need not be removed.**

4. Remove the insulator assembly from the exhaust manifold.
5. Remove the exhaust pipe or front catalytic converter attaching nuts, then disconnect the exhaust pipe or converter.
6. Unfasten the exhaust manifold attaching nuts, then remove the manifold and gaskets.
7. Check the manifold for distortion with a metal straight edge and a feeler gauge as described under Cylinder Head Overhaul. Repair or replace as necessary.

To install:

8. Position new gasket(s) and the manifold over the mounting studs. Torque the nuts to specification in several stages, working from the center outwards.

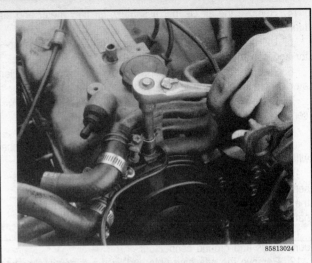

Fig. 109 Remove the bolt which fastens the secondary air pipes to the rocker arm cover

Fig. 110 Move the secondary air pipe assembly out of the way

Fig. 108 Disconnect the secondary air pipe at the exhaust manifold

Fig. 111 Remove the bolt which fastens the insulator assembly to the exhaust manifold

Fig. 112 Unscrew the secondary air pipe fitting from the exhaust manifold

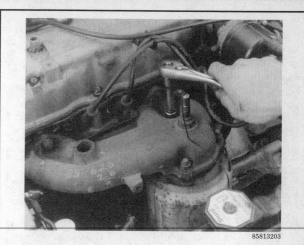

Fig. 114 Remove the nuts which secure the front catalytic converter or exhaust pipe to the exhaust manifold

Fig. 113 Lift off the insulator

Fig. 115 Remove the nuts which fasten the exhaust manifold to the cylinder head

9. Connect and fasten the exhaust pipe/front catalytic converter to the manifold, using a new gasket.

10. Position and fasten the insulator assembly over the manifold. Install the fitting for the secondary air pipe assembly.

11. Coat the threads with anti-seize compound and install the oxygen sensor, if applicable. Reconnect the electrical lead.

12. Position the secondary air pipe assembly and connect it to the manifold fitting. Fasten any retaining brackets or clamps.

13. On carbureted engines, connect the hot air duct to the insulator assembly.

Fig. 116 Withdraw the exhaust manifold from its mounting studs

Fig. 117 Remove the exhaust manifold gasket

Turbocharger

REMOVAL & INSTALLATION

1988-89 323

▶ See Figure 118

➥When replacing the turbocharger, always check the oil level and condition, along with the turbo oil inlet and outlet lines. If the oil is dirty or the lines are damaged, replace them.

1. Disconnect the negative battery cable.
2. Drain the cooling system.
3. From underneath the vehicle, remove the engine undercover.
4. Disconnect the two air hoses that are attached to the throttle body inlet hose and remove the air pipe.
5. Remove the exhaust manifold insulator covers.
6. Remove the water hoses.
7. Remove the oil pipe and the oil return hose.
8. Support the turbocharger by hand, then remove the nuts and bolts from the exhaust manifold. Remove the turbocharger and the exhaust manifold as an assembly. Remove the mounting gasket.
9. Remove the nuts and lift the turbocharger from the exhaust manifold studs. Cover the exhaust manifold ports with a clean rag or masking tape to prevent the entry of foreign matter. If the gasket is bent or cracked, replace it with a new one. If the turbocharger mounting nuts are damaged, install only Mazda genuine replacement nuts.

✳✳CAUTION

Be careful to avoid dropping the turbocharger or handling it roughly. Be careful not to bend the wastegate actuator mounting or rod.

To install:

10. Attach the turbocharger to the exhaust manifold with the mounting gasket, and torque the nuts to 20-25 ft. lbs. (27-34 Nm).
11. Place the assembly onto the engine with a new gasket and torque the manifold nuts to specification.
12. Connect the oil return hose and oil pipe.
13. Connect the water hoses.
14. Install the manifold insulator covers.
15. Install the air pipe and air hoses.
16. Install the engine under cover.
17. Refill the cooling system.
18. Connect the negative battery cable.
19. Start the engine and inspect for leaks.

1986-87 626

➥When replacing the turbocharger, always check the oil level and condition, along with the turbo oil inlet and outlet lines. If the oil is dirty or the lines are damaged, replace them.

✳✳CAUTION

This work should be performed with the engine cold.

1. Drain the cooling system. Rotate the engine until the No. 1 piston is at TDC. (Use the front timing marks as a reference, and remove the distributor cap to check the position of the rotor.) Tag and disconnect the high tension wires. Unfasten the distributor mounting bolt, then remove the distributor, as described earlier in this section.
2. Loosen the clamps and remove the hose leading from the air cleaner to the turbo compressor intake. Do the same for the duct leading from the compressor discharge to the intake manifold.
3. Remove the thin secondary air injection pipe from the exhaust manifold. Remove the lower insulator cover from around the turbocharger turbine (the exhaust side of the unit).
4. Remove the thicker secondary air injection pipe from the exhaust manifold. Remove the oil supply line from the turbocharger. Disconnect the oil drain line.
5. Remove the upper insulator cover from the exhaust manifold. Remove the EGR pipe.
6. Disconnect and remove the turbo's cooling water hoses. Disconnect and remove the oxygen sensor.
7. Disconnect and support the front exhaust pipe at the catalytic converter. Remove the bolts attaching the turbo mounting bracket to the turbocharger.
8. Support the manifold and remove the manifold mounting bolts, then remove the manifold, turbocharger, and catalytic converter as an assembly. Remove the attaching nuts, then separate the converter from the turbocharger, and the turbocharger from the manifold. Cover all openings in the turbocharger.

✳✳CAUTION

Be careful to avoid dropping the turbocharger or handling it roughly. Be careful not to bend the wastegate actuator mounting or rod.

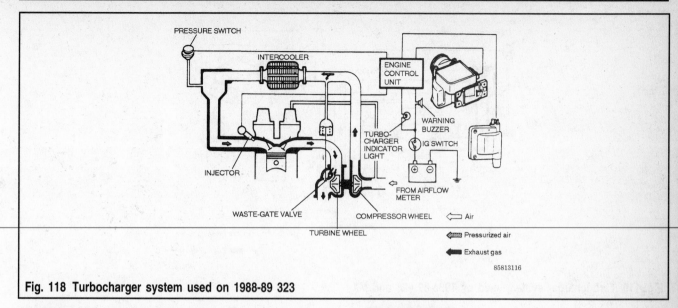

Fig. 118 Turbocharger system used on 1988-89 323

To install:

9. Carefully clean all gasket surfaces. Pour 1.5 cu. in. (25cc) of clean engine oil into the opening for the turbo oil line.

10. Install the turbocharger onto the exhaust manifold, replacing the gasket if it is bent or cracked. Torque the attaching nuts to 23-32 ft. lbs. (31-43 Nm). Connect the catalytic converter to the turbocharger with a new gasket and tighten the mounting nuts.

11. Install the exhaust manifold/turbocharger/catalytic converter assembly onto the cylinder head with new gaskets and torque the nuts to 16-21 ft. lbs. (22-28 Nm). Secure the turbocharger to the turbo mounting bracket.

12. Connect the front exhaust pipe to the catalytic converter, using a new gasket.

13. Install and connect the oxygen sensor and the cooling water hoses.

14. Install the EGR pipe and the upper insulator cover.

15. Connect the turbocharger's oil supply and oil drain lines.

16. Connect the secondary air injection pipes to the exhaust manifold.

17. Install the lower insulator cover.

18. Connect the hose leading from the air cleaner to the turbo compressor intake. Do the same for the duct leading from the compressor discharge to the intake manifold.

19. Install the distributor and connect the high tension wires, as described earlier in this section.

20. Refill the cooling system.

21. Before starting the engine, disconnect the negative (-) primary wire at the coil. Then, crank the engine for 20 seconds to build up oil pressure. Reconnect the coil wire, then start the engine without applying throttle; idle it for 30 seconds to purge air from the turbo oil lines before the throttle is applied. Check all parts for leaks and correct as necessary.

22. Check the ignition timing and adjust as necessary. For further information on this procedure, refer to Section 2.

1988-89 626/MX-6

▶ See Figure 119

➡When replacing the turbocharger, always check the oil level and condition, along with the turbo oil inlet and outlet lines. If the oil is dirty or the lines are damaged, replace them.

1. Disconnect the negative battery cable and drain the cooling system.

2. Remove the air hoses and air bypass hose.

3. Remove the exhaust manifold insulators.

4. Disconnect the oil inlet and return pipes from the turbocharger, then plug the ends.

5. Disconnect the water hoses from the water pipe and plug the ends.

6. Disconnect the EGR pipe from the exhaust manifold.

7. Remove the oxygen sensor.

8. Disconnect the front exhaust pipe from the turbocharger and set the gasket aside. Remove the bolt from the turbocharger joint pipe.

9. Support the turbocharger by hand and remove the exhaust manifold retaining nuts. Remove the turbocharger and manifold as an assembly. Cover the exhaust manifold ports with a clean rag or masking tape to prevent the entry of foreign matter.

❋❋CAUTION

Do not drop the turbocharger or carry it around by the actuating handle. When laying the unit down, do so with the turbine shaft in the horizontal position. Be careful not to bend the actuator mounting or rod.

To install:

10. Remove all the sealant and gasket material from the turbocharger and exhaust manifold mating surfaces.

11. Pour 1.5 cu. in. (25cc) of clean engine oil into the opening for the turbo oil line.

12. Attach the turbocharger to the exhaust manifold and torque the nuts to 20-29 ft. lbs. (27-39 Nm). Attach the assembly to the engine using new gaskets and torque the nuts to speci-

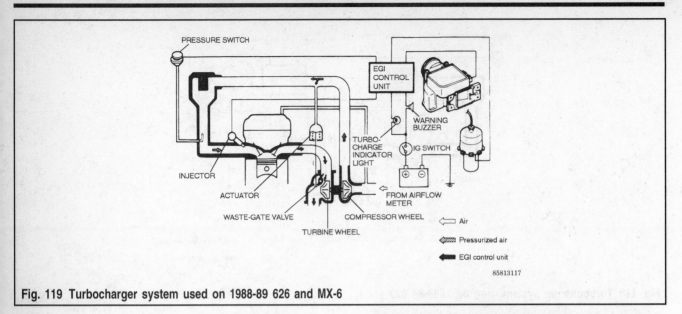

Fig. 119 Turbocharger system used on 1988-89 626 and MX-6

fication. Torque the turbocharger joint pipe bolt to 27-46 ft. lbs. (37-62 Nm) and the turbocharger bracket bolts to 23-30 ft. lbs. (31-41 Nm).

13. Connect the front exhaust pipe.

14. Install the oxygen sensor.

15. Connect the EGR pipe to the exhaust manifold and the water hose to the inlet pipe.

16. Connect the oil inlet and return pipes to the turbocharger. Install the exhaust manifold insulators.

17. Install the air bypass valve and air hoses.

18. Refill the cooling system and connect the negative battery cable.

19. Unfasten the connector from the ignitor and crank the engine for 20 seconds. Reattach the connector, then start the engine and run it at idle for 20 seconds. Stop the engine and disconnect the negative battery cable. Depress and hold the brake pedal for 5 seconds to clear the malfunction code. Reconnect the negative battery cable.

Radiator

REMOVAL & INSTALLATION

▶ See Figures 120, 121, 122, 123, 124, 125 and 126

✳✳CAUTION

Many vehicles are equipped with an electric fan motor, which operates in response to temperature and may run even when the ignition is OFF. Be sure to disconnect the wiring harness or negative battery cable before proceeding.

1. Drain the coolant from the radiator.

2. Disconnect the coolant reservoir hose at the radiator. On 929s, disconnect the vacuum hoses from the fresh air duct and remove the duct. If so equipped, detach the water temperature switch electrical connector at the bottom of the radiator.

3. Remove the fan shroud and fan blade assembly. On models equipped with an electric fan motor, disconnect the

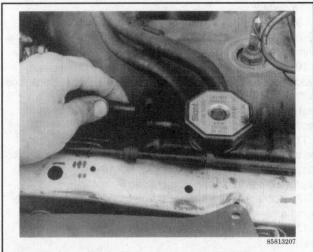

Fig. 120 Disconnect the coolant reservoir hose at the radiator

Fig. 121 A water temperature switch electrical connector may be located near the lower radiator hose

Fig. 122 If equipped with an electric fan, disconnect the wiring harness before removing the fan and cowling

Fig. 123 Loosen the clamps, then remove the upper (shown) and lower radiator hoses

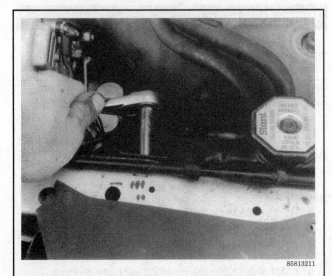

Fig. 124 Remove the radiator mounting bolts

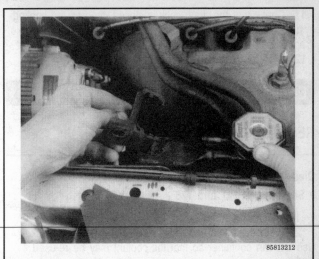

Fig. 125 After removing the bolts, the mounting brackets can be separated from the radiator

Fig. 126 Lift the radiator up and out of the vehicle

wiring harness (if not already done), then remove the fan and cowling mount.

4. Remove the upper and lower radiator hoses. Disconnect the automatic transmission/transaxle cooler lines, if equipped. Plug the openings to prevent leakage.

5. Remove the radiator mounting bolts and brackets, then remove the radiator.

6. Inspect the radiator for cracks, damage and leakage. Remove all road debris from the cooling fins.

To install:

7. Lower the radiator into the vehicle and onto its mounting. Install the attaching hardware.

8. Connect the automatic transmission/transaxle cooler lines, if equipped. Connect the upper and lower hoses.

9. Install the fan blade assembly and shroud or fan/cowling mount assembly. On electric models, fasten the harness connector.

10. If applicable, connect the water temperature switch electrical lead. On the 929, install the fresh air duct and connect the vacuum hoses.

11. Check that the drain cock is closed, then fill the cooling system to the proper level. Connect the negative battery cable, if applicable.

12. Start the engine and check for leaks.

Engine Oil Cooler

REMOVAL & INSTALLATION

Diesel Engine

▶ **See Figures 127 and 128**

1. Disconnect the negative battery cable.
2. Drain the engine coolant from the radiator and block. Use a clean container so that the coolant may be re-used if desired.
3. Unclamp and disconnect the heater (water) hose attached to the oil cooler.
4. Remove the oil filter.
5. Remove the bolts and then disconnect the water inlet pipe. Unclamp and disconnect the oil bypass return hose.
6. Remove the bolts mounting the oil return pipe to the block. Remove the through-bolts and then disconnect the oil return pipe and the oil bypass inlet hose at the cooler.
7. Remove the two mounting bolts and two nuts, then remove the cooler from the block. Make sure to remove the O-rings from the recesses where the cooler fits against the block.
8. Inspect the water and oil hoses, and replace any that are bulging or cracked.

To install:

9. Apply clean engine oil to the area represented by the shaded portion of the illustration. Then, position the O-rings and position the cooler. Install the bolts and nuts, torquing them to 23-34 ft. lbs. (31-46 Nm).
10. Fasten the oil return pipe and oil bypass inlet hose to the cooler with through-bolts. Fasten the oil return pipe to the block.
11. Connect the oil bypass return hose to the oil return pipe. Connect the water inlet pipe and gasket to the cooler.
12. Install a new oil filter.

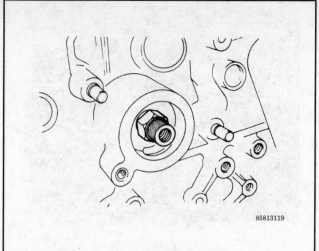

Fig. 128 Apply clean engine oil to the shaded area before installing the diesel oil cooler

13. Connect the heater hose to the oil cooler.
14. Close the drain cock(s), then refill the cooling system.
15. Connect the negative battery cable.
16. Start the engine and check for leaks.

Turbocharged 323 and 626/MX-6

1. Drain the engine oil.
2. On 323 models, remove the engine under cover.
3. Remove the oil filter and disconnect the cooling hoses from the oil cooler. Plug the ends to prevent leakage.
4. Loosen the nut that holds the cooler to the oil filter post and remove the unit. Wipe all the cooler mating surfaces with a clean rag.

To install:

5. Install the oil cooler and torque the retaining nut to 22-29 ft. lbs. (30-39 Nm). Install a new oil filter and connect the water hoses. Install the under cover on the 323.
6. Fill the crankcase with clean oil to the proper level. Start the engine and check for leaks.

Water Pump

REMOVAL & INSTALLATION

Rear Wheel Drive GLC

1. Drain the engine coolant into a suitable container.
2. Remove the retaining bolt and cooling fan from the water pump.
3. Remove the drive belt(s) and the water pump pulley.
4. Remove the nuts and washers which retain the water pump.
5. Remove the water pump and gasket.

To install:

6. Thoroughly clean all gasket surfaces.
7. Position the water pump with a new gasket.
8. Install and tighten the mounting nuts and washers.
9. Attach the water pump pulley.
10. Install and tension the drive belt(s).
11. Attach the cooling fan to the water pump.

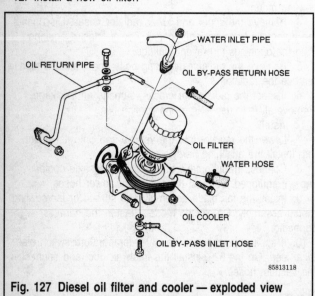

WATER INLET PIPE
OIL RETURN PIPE
OIL BY-PASS RETURN HOSE
OIL FILTER
WATER HOSE
OIL COOLER
OIL BY-PASS INLET HOSE

85813118

Fig. 127 Diesel oil filter and cooler — exploded view

12. Refill the system with coolant. Start the engine and check for leaks.

Front Wheel Drive GLC

1. Drain the engine coolant into a suitable container.
2. Jack up the front of the car and safely support it on jackstands.
3. Remove the under cover and the drive belt.
4. Disconnect the lower hose and bypass pipe with O-ring.
5. Unbolt and remove the water pump.

To install:

6. Thoroughly clean all gasket surfaces.
7. Position the water pump with a new gasket.
8. Install and tighten the mounting bolts.
9. Apply vegetable oil to the O-ring on the bypass hose. Connect the bypass hose and the lower hose to the water pump.
10. Install and tension the drive belt.
11. Attach the under cover.
12. Remove the jackstands and carefully lower the car.
13. Refill the system with coolant. Start the engine and check for leaks.

1979-82 626

1. Drain the engine coolant into a suitable container.
2. Remove the cooling fan and fan drive assembly.
3. Remove the radiator cowling.
4. Remove the air pump drive belt, if so equipped.
5. Remove the alternator drive belt.
6. Disconnect the lower hose and the bypass hose.
7. If so equipped, disconnect the heater hose.
8. Unbolt and remove the water pump.

To install:

9. Thoroughly clean all gasket surfaces.
10. Position the water pump with a new gasket.
11. Install and tighten the mounting bolts.
12. If applicable, connect the heater hose.
13. Connect the bypass hose and the lower hose.
14. Install and tension the alternator drive belt.
15. If applicable, install and tension the air pump drive belt.
16. Install the radiator cowling.
17. Install the cooling fan and fan drive assembly.
18. Refill the system with coolant. Start the engine and check for leaks.

1983-87 626

▶ **See Figures 129, 130, 131, 132 and 133**

1. Turn the crankshaft so that the No. 1 cylinder is at TDC.
2. Drain the engine coolant into a suitable container.
3. Remove the alternator drive belt.
4. Remove the upper timing belt cover.
5. Remove the engine side cover (splash shield).
6. Remove the crankshaft pulley.
7. Remove the lower timing belt cover.
8. Unfasten its mounting bolt and remove the timing belt tensioner and spring.
9. Remove the timing belt.
10. Disconnect the inlet pipe from the water pump.
11. Unbolt and remove the water pump.

To install:

12. Thoroughly clean all gasket surfaces.

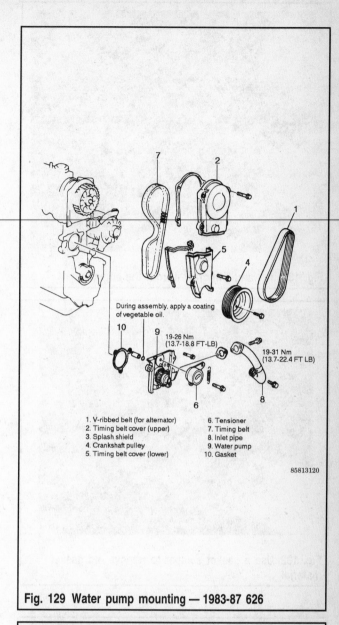

During assembly, apply a coating of vegetable oil.

19-26 Nm (13.7-18.8 FT-LB)

19-31 Nm (13.7-22.4 FT LB)

1. V-ribbed belt (for alternator)
2. Timing belt cover (upper)
3. Splash shield
4. Crankshaft pulley
5. Timing belt cover (lower)
6. Tensioner
7. Timing belt
8. Inlet pipe
9. Water pump
10. Gasket

85813120

Fig. 129 Water pump mounting — 1983-87 626

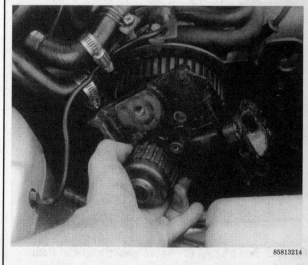

85813214

Fig. 130 Grasp the water pump by its pulley . . .

Fig. 131 . . . and withdraw it from the engine

Fig. 132 Use a gasket scraper to remove old gasket material

Fig. 133 Don't forget to remove gasket material from the inlet pipe mating surface

13. Position the water pump with a new gasket.
14. Install and tighten the mounting bolts.
15. Connect the inlet pipe with a new gasket.
16. Install the timing belt tensioner and spring, as described later in this section.
17. Install the timing belt, as described later in this section.
18. Install the lower timing belt cover.
19. Attach the crankshaft pulley.
20. Install the engine side cover.
21. Install the upper timing belt cover.
22. Install and tension the alternator drive belt.
23. Refill the system with coolant. Start the engine and check for leaks.

1986-87 323

1. Turn the crankshaft so that the No. 1 cylinder is at TDC.
2. Drain the engine coolant into a suitable container.
3. Remove the alternator drive belt.
4. Remove the water pump pulley.
5. Remove the oil pump (crankshaft) pulley.
6. Remove the timing belt cover.
7. Unfasten its mounting bolt and remove the timing belt tensioner and spring.
8. Remove the timing belt.
9. Disconnect the cooling inlet pipe from the water pump.
10. Unbolt and remove the water pump.

To install:

11. Thoroughly clean all gasket surfaces.
12. Position the water pump with a new gasket.
13. Install and tighten the mounting bolts.
14. Connect the cooling inlet pipe with a new gasket.
15. Install the timing belt tensioner and spring, as described later in this section.
16. Install the timing belt, as described later in this section.
17. Install the timing belt cover.
18. Attach the oil pump pulley.
19. Install the water pump pulley.
20. Install and tension the alternator drive belt.
21. Refill the system with coolant. Start the engine and check for leaks.

1988-89 626/MX-6

▶ See Figure 134

1. Disconnect the negative battery cable.
2. Turn the crankshaft so that the No. 1 piston is at TDC.
3. Drain the engine coolant into a suitable container.
4. Remove the crankshaft pulley.
5. Remove the upper timing belt cover.
6. Remove the lower timing belt cover.
7. Remove the baffle plate.
8. Unbolt and remove the timing belt tensioner and spring.
9. Unbolt and remove the idler pulley from the water pump housing.
10. Remove the timing belt.
11. Unfasten the water pump retaining bolts and remove the water pump with the O-ring seal and three rubber seals. Discard the seals and O-ring.

To install:

12. Remove all the old gasket fragments, oil and grease from the water pump housing and the cylinder block. Install the three rubber seals, as shown in the illustration.

13. Install the new O-ring in the water pump sealing groove. To avoid dropping the O-ring when positioning the water pump, coat the inside of the seal groove with silicone sealant to hold the O-ring in place. Do not apply sealant to the contact surfaces.

14. Position the water pump with a new gasket onto the block and align all bolt holes. Install the retaining bolts and torque them to 14-19 ft. lbs. (19-26 Nm).

15. Install the idler pulley and torque the pulley bolt to 27-38 ft. lbs. (37-51 Nm).

16. Install the timing belt tensioner and spring.

17. Install the timing belt.

18. Install the baffle plate, along with the lower and upper timing belt covers.

19. Install the crankshaft pulley.

20. Refill the cooling system to the proper level and connect the negative battery.

21. Start the engine and check for leaks.

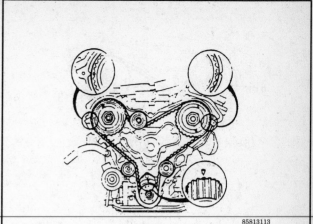

Fig. 135 Timing mark alignment on 3.0L engine — 929

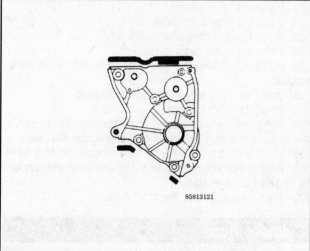

Fig. 134 Water pump seal installation on 1988-89 626/MX-6

929

➡This procedure requires removal of the automatic timing belt tensioner. Before the tensioner is re-installed, it must be reset using an arbor press or vice.

▶ **See Figures 135, 136, 137 and 138**

1. Disconnect the negative battery cable.

2. Tag and disconnect the high tension leads, then remove the spark plugs.

3. Turn the crankshaft so that the No. 1 piston is at TDC.

4. Drain the engine coolant into a suitable container.

5. Disconnect and remove the fresh air duct at the air cleaner assembly.

6. Remove the cooling fan and radiator cowling.

7. Remove any accessory drive belts which engage the crankshaft pulley.

8. Remove the water pump pulley.

9. Remove the A/C compressor idler pulley.

10. Remove the crankshaft pulley and baffle plate.

11. Disconnect the coolant bypass hose.

12. Disconnect the upper radiator hose.

13. Remove the left timing belt cover and gasket.

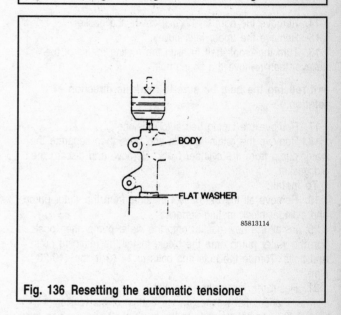

Fig. 136 Resetting the automatic tensioner

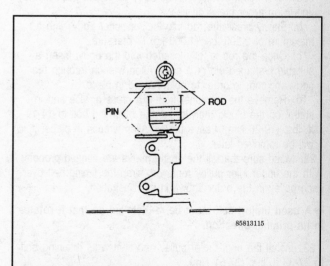

Fig. 137 Once the tensioner is reset, use a pin or Allen wrench to hold the rod in place

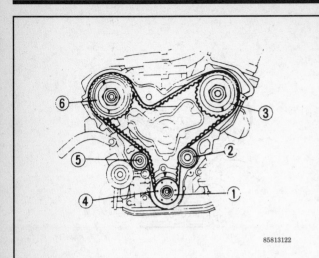

85813122

Fig. 138 Wrap the timing belt around each pulley in the order shown

14. Remove the right timing belt cover and gasket.
15. Remove the upper idler pulley.
16. Turn the crankshaft to align the mating marks of the pulleys, then remove the timing belt.

➡**If reusing the belt, be sure to mark its direction of rotation.**

17. Remove the timing belt auto tensioner.
18. Remove the retaining bolts and nuts, then separate the water pump from the cylinder block. Remove and discard the old gasket.

To install:

19. Remove all the old gasket material from the water pump and cylinder block mating surfaces.
20. Install the new gasket onto the water pump, then position the water pump onto the block. Install the retaining nuts and bolts. Torque the nuts and bolts to 14-19 ft. lbs. (19-26 Nm).
21. Reset the tensioner as follows:
  a. Place a flat washer on the bottom of the tensioner body (to prevent damage to the body plug) and position the unit in an arbor press or vice.
  b. Slowly press the rod into the tensioner body, with a maximum of 2,200 lbs. (1,000 kg) of pressure.
  c. Once the rod is fully inserted into the body, insert a suitable L-shaped pin or a small Allen wrench through the body and rod, in order to hold the rod in place.
  d. Remove the tensioner from the press or vice and install it on the block, then torque the mounting bolt to 14-19 ft. lbs. (19-26 Nm). Leave the pin/Allen wrench in place; it will be removed later.
22. Make sure that all the timing marks are aligned properly. With the upper idler pulley removed, wrap the timing belt over each pulley in the order shown in the illustration.

➡**A used timing belt must be re-installed so that it rotates in its original direction.**

23. Install the upper idler pulley and tighten its retaining bolt to 27-38 ft. lbs. (37-51 Nm).

24. Rotate the crankshaft twice in the normal direction of rotation and align all the timing marks.

➡**If the matching marks do not align, remove the upper idler pulley, then repeat Steps 22-24.**

25. Remove the pin/Allen wrench from the tensioner. Again turn the crankshaft twice in the normal direction of rotation and make sure that all the timing marks are aligned properly.
26. Check the timing belt deflection by applying 22 lbs. (10 kg) of force. If the deflection is not 0.20-0.28 in. (5-7mm), repeat the resetting procedure.

➡**Excessive belt deflection is caused by auto tensioner failure or an excessively stretched timing belt. If correct tension cannot be obtained, the belt and/or tensioner must be replaced.**

27. Install the timing belt gaskets and covers.
28. Connect the upper radiator hose.
29. Connect the coolant bypass hose.
30. Install the baffle plate.
31. Install the crankshaft pulley.
32. Install the A/C compressor idler pulley.
33. Install the water pump pulley.
34. Install and tension the accessory drive belts which were removed.
35. Install the cooling fan and radiator cowling.
36. Install the fresh air duct.
37. Apply anti-seize compound or molybdenum-based lubricant to the spark plug threads. Install and tighten the spark plugs to 11-17 ft. lbs. (15-23 Nm), then connect the plug wires.
38. Refill the cooling system to the proper level and connect the negative battery cable.
39. Start the engine and check for leaks.

Cylinder Head

REMOVAL & INSTALLATION

Gasoline Engines

GLC AND 1979-82 626

▶ **See Figures 139, 140, 141 and 142**

➡**Be sure that the cylinder head is cold before removal, as this will help prevent warpage.**

1. Disconnect the negative battery cable.
2. Rotate the crankshaft so that the No. 1 cylinder is at TDC.
3. Drain the cooling system.
4. Remove the air cleaner assembly.
5. On rear wheel drive models, remove the water pump.
6. Remove the distributor, as described earlier in this section.
7. Disconnect the front catalytic converter from the exhaust manifold, then unfasten and remove the exhaust manifold from the cylinder head.
8. Disconnect all applicable electrical wires and leads.
9. If necessary, remove the alternator drive belt, alternator and adjusting strap.
10. Remove the thermostat housing and thermostat.

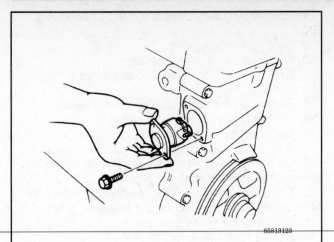

Fig. 139 Removing the tensioner — GLC front wheel drive models

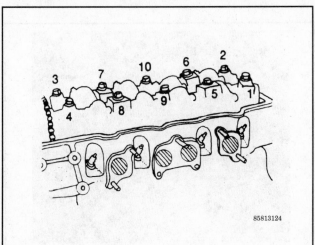

Fig. 140 Cylinder head bolt loosening sequence for GLC and 1979-82 626 (1981-85 GLC shown)

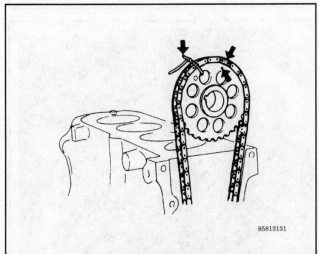

Fig. 141 Wire the camshaft sprocket and timing chain together to maintain their proper relationship

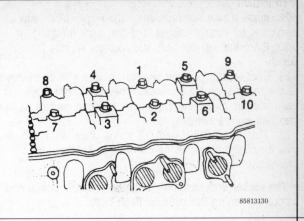

Fig. 142 Cylinder head bolt tightening sequence for GLC and 1979-82 626 (1981-85 GLC shown)

11. Disconnect the accelerator linkage.

12. Remove the intake manifold and carburetor assembly.

13. Remove the rocker arm cover and gasket, along with the semi-circular oil seal(s). Clean the mating surface of the rocker arm cover.

14. On front wheel drive GLC models, remove the tensioner (chain adjuster) from the timing chain cover.

15. Remove the locknut, washer and, on the 626 and GLC wagon only, the distributor drive gear and spacer from the camshaft.

16. If so equipped, remove the cylinder head-to-cylinder block bolt.

➡️**Although 1.3L and 1.4L engines have their camshaft sprocket at the opposite end, they utilize the same loosening sequence (in reference to the front of the vehicle).**

17. Loosen the cylinder head bolts in several stages of the illustrated sequence. (In order to avoid cylinder head distortion, only loosen the bolts a few turns at a time.)

➡️**The cylinder head bolts also retain the rocker arm assembly and camshaft.**

18. Remove the rocker arm assembly.

19. Separate the camshaft sprocket and chain from the camshaft. Be sure to support the timing chain so the tensioner will not come apart. On the front wheel drive GLC, even though the tensioner has been removed, you still must support the camshaft sprocket so the timing relationship between the chain links and upper/lower sprockets will not be lost.

➡️**Do not remove the camshaft sprocket from the chain. Maintain the relationship between the timing chain and sprocket by temporarily wiring them together.**

20. Remove the camshaft.

21. Lift off the cylinder head and remove the gasket. Thoroughly clean off all old gasket material from the mating surfaces and inspect the components for wear or damage, as described later in this section. Repair or replace parts, as necessary.

To install:

22. Install a new head gasket on the engine block with all oil passages, water passages, and bolt holes matching up.

23. Place the cylinder head into position, aligning the dowels.

24. Coat all the camshaft bearing surfaces with clean engine oil before installing the camshaft. (These include the cylinder head and cap or bearing insert inner surfaces, as well as the camshaft journal surfaces).

25. Slide the sprocket (with the timing chain still attached) onto the camshaft. Install the camshaft and rocker arm assembly.

➡️**The rocker arm assembly must be properly positioned before tightening the cylinder head bolts.**

26. Slide the rocker arm assembly to one side until the adjusting studs are offset 0.04 in. (1mm) from the centers of the valve stems. (This is necessary for proper valve rotation.) Then, torque the bolts using several stages of the indicated sequence.

➡️**Although 1.3L and 1.4L engines have their camshaft sprocket at the opposite end, they utilize the same tightening sequence (in reference to the front of the vehicle).**

27. Check the valve clearance using a feeler gauge and adjust, if necessary, as described in Section 2.

28. If applicable, install the cylinder head-to-cylinder block bolt.

29. On the 626 and GLC wagon, align the key groove with the pin, then install the spacer and distributor drive gear on the camshaft.

30. Install the washer and sprocket locknut on the camshaft. Tighten the locknut to 51-58 ft. lbs. (70-80 Nm).

31. Check the camshaft end-play (clearance between the sprocket and thrust plate) with a feeler gauge. If the clearance exceeds 0.008 in. (0.20mm), replace the thrust plate.

32. On front wheel drive GLC models, reset the chain adjuster by pushing the sleeve completely into the body, then securing it with the built-in latch and pin. Install this device on the timing chain cover.

➡️**After the adjuster is installed, the pin is automatically released by the timing chain when the engine is cranked.**

33. Apply RTV or rubber sealer to the semi-circular oil seal(s) and install on the cylinder head with the "OUT" mark facing away from the engine.

34. Position a new gasket on the cylinder head, then install the rocker arm cover. Tighten the retaining nuts to 1.1-1.4 ft. lbs. (1.5-1.9 Nm), or the bolts to 1.4-2.5 ft. lbs. (1.9-3.4 Nm).

35. Complete the installation of the remaining components in reverse of the removal procedure. Be sure to use new gaskets and O-rings, and to properly tension the drive belt, if necessary.

36. Refill the cooling system to the proper level and connect the negative battery cable. Start the engine and check for leaks.

1983-85 626

▶ **See Figures 143, 144, 145, 146, 147, 148, 149 and 150**

➡️**Be sure that the cylinder head is cold before removal, as this will help prevent warpage.**

1. Rotate the crankshaft so that the No. 1 cylinder is at TDC.

2. Drain the cooling system.

3. Remove the air cleaner assembly.

4. Remove the distributor, as described earlier in this section.

5. Remove the thermostat housing and thermostat.

6. Remove the fuel pump.

7. Disconnect the accelerator cable.

8. Remove the intake manifold and carburetor assembly.

9. On vehicles equipped with air conditioning, remove the alternator and alternator strap.

10. On vehicles equipped with air conditioning, remove the A/C compressor and alternator bracket installation bolts.

11. Disconnect the engine ground wire.

12. Remove the upper timing belt cover.

13. Remove the timing belt, as described later in this section.

14. Disconnect the secondary air pipes.

15. Unfasten the oxygen sensor connector.

85813218

Fig. 143 With the bolts removed, use a prytool to carefully separate the cylinder head from the engine block

85813219

Fig. 144 Lift the cylinder head from the engine block

Fig. 145 Remove the cylinder head gasket from the engine block

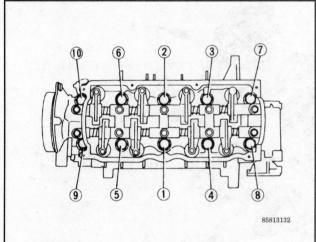

Fig. 146 Cylinder head bolt tightening sequence — 1983-87 626

16. Remove the exhaust manifold insulator assembly.

17. Remove the three nuts and gasket which retain the front catalytic converter to the exhaust manifold.

18. Remove the cylinder head's rear housing and gasket.

19. Remove the rocker arm cover and gasket.

20. Remove the cylinder head bolts and washers in the appropriate sequence, as illustrated.

➡**In order to avoid cylinder head distortion, loosen and remove the cylinder head bolts only a few turns at a time.**

21. Remove the cylinder head and exhaust manifold as an assembly. If necessary, first unfasten and remove the exhaust manifold from the cylinder head.

➡**Exhaust manifold removal is normally unnecessary in order to remove the cylinder head.**

22. Remove the cylinder head gasket. Thoroughly clean off all old gasket material from the mating surfaces and inspect the components for wear or damage, as described later in this section. Repair or replace parts, as necessary.

To install:

23. If applicable, re-attach the exhaust manifold to the cylinder head, using a new gasket. (If preferred, this step may be performed after the cylinder head is installed.)

24. Install a new head gasket on the engine block with all oil passages, water passages, and bolt holes matching up.

25. Place the cylinder head into position, then insert the cylinder head washers and bolts. Torque the bolts to 59-65 ft. lbs. (82-88 Nm) in several stages, following the proper sequence.

26. Position a new gasket on the rocker arm cover. Apply a coating of sealant to the portions of the rocker shaft assembly which are shaded in the illustration, then position the gasket and cover on the cylinder head. Insert the retaining bolts with their seal washers and tighten to 2.2-2.9 ft. lbs. (3-4 Nm).

27. Complete the installation of the remaining components in reverse of the removal procedure. Be sure to use new gaskets and O-rings, and to properly tension the drive belt(s). For information on timing belt installation and adjustment, refer to the procedure later in this section.

28. Refill the cooling system to the proper level. Start the engine and check for leaks.

1986-87 626

▶ **See Figures 146, 148, 150 and 151**

1. Disconnect all applicable electrical wires and leads.

2. Disconnect the drive belt(s), then remove the alternator.

3. Remove the cylinder head's rear housing and gasket.

➡**Be sure that the cylinder head is cold before removal, as this will help prevent warpage.**

4. Disconnect the negative battery cable.

5. Drain the cooling system.

6. Disconnect the accelerator cable.

7. On turbocharged models, disconnect the secondary air pipe from the exhaust manifold.

8. Remove the distributor.

9. Remove the rear housing and gasket.

10. Disconnect the intake air hose.

11. On turbo models, disconnect the secondary air pipes from the front catalytic converter. Then, disconnect the oil pipe from the turbocharger.

12. Remove the exhaust manifold insulator. On turbo models, also remove the two smaller insulators near the front catalytic converter.

13. On turbo models, remove the bracket connecting the turbocharger to the front catalytic converter. Disconnect the front catalytic converter and the oil return hose from the turbocharger. Then, disconnect the water inlet and outlet hoses, and the EGR pipe.

14. On non-tubo models, disconnect the exhaust pipe from the manifold.

15. Remove the exhaust manifold (or manifold/turbocharger assembly) and gasket.

16. Remove the intake manifold assembly and gasket.

17. Remove the upper timing belt cover.

18. Remove the timing belt, as described later in this section.

19. Remove the rocker arm cover.

20. In order to avoid cylinder head distortion, loosen and remove the cylinder head bolts only a few turns at a time. The

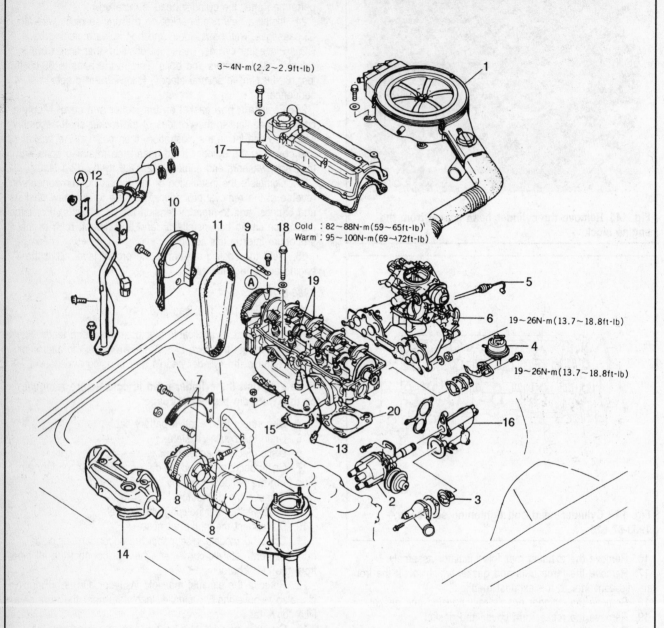

3~4N·m(2.2~2.9ft-lb)

Cold : 82~88N·m(59~65ft-lb)
Warm : 95~100N·m(69~72ft-lb)

19~26N·m(13.7~18.8ft-lb)

19~26N·m(13.7~18.8ft-lb)

1 Air cleaner
2 Distributor
3 Thermostat
4 Fuel pump
5 Accelerator cable
6 Intake manifold & carburetor
7 Alternator & alternator strap
  (vehicles with an air conditioner)

8 Cooler compressor &
  alternator bracket installation
  bolts (vehicles with an
  air conditioner)
9 Engine ground wire
10 Timing belt cover (upper)
11 Timing belt
12 Secondary air pipes

13 O$_2$ sensor connector (disconnect)
14 Insulator assembly
15 Nuts (3) & gasket
16 Rear housing & gasket
17 Cylinder head cover & gasket
18 Cylinder head bolts
19 Cylinder head & exhaust manifold
20 Cylinder head gasket

85813158

Fig. 147 Exploded view of the cylinder head and upper engine components — 1983-85 626

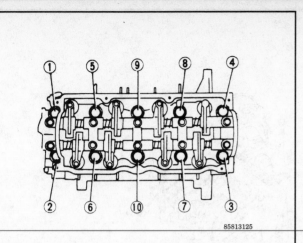

**Fig. 148 Cylinder head bolt loosening sequence —
1983-87 626**

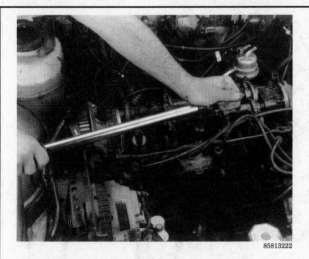

**Fig. 149 Torque the cylinder head bolts in several
stages, beginning with the front center bolt**

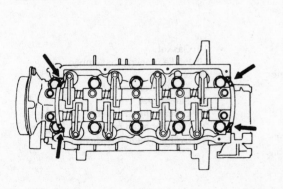

**Fig. 150 Apply sealant to the shaded areas (indicated
by the arrows) before installing the rocker arm cover —
1983-87 626**

bolts should be removed in the appropriate sequence, as illustrated.

21. Lift off the cylinder head and remove the gasket. Thoroughly clean off all old gasket material from the mating surfaces and inspect the components for wear or damage, as described later in this section. Repair or replace parts, as necessary.

To install:

22. Install a new head gasket on the engine block with all oil passages, water passages, and bolt holes matching up.

23. Place the cylinder head into position, then insert the cylinder head washers and bolts. Torque the bolts to 59-65 ft. lbs. (82-88 Nm) in several stages, following the proper sequence.

24. Position a new gasket on the rocker arm cover. Apply a coating of sealant to the portions of the rocker shaft assembly which are shaded in the illustration, then position the gasket and cover on the cylinder head. Insert the retaining bolts with their seal washers and tighten to 2.2-2.9 ft. lbs. (3-4 Nm).

25. Complete the installation of the remaining components in reverse of the removal procedure. Be sure to use new gaskets and O-rings, and to properly tension the drive belt(s). For information on timing belt installation and adjustment, refer to the procedure later in this section.

26. Refill the cooling system to the proper level. Start the engine and check for leaks.

1986-89 323 NON-TURBO

▶ See Figures 152, 153, 154 and 155

1. Disconnect the negative battery cable and drain the cooling system.

2. Remove or disconnect the following parts:
   - Air cleaner
   - Oil dipstick
   - Accelerator cable and (if so equipped) cruise control cable
   - Fuel hoses (drain fuel into a suitable container, then plug them)
   - Fuel pump (carbureted engines only)
   - Heater hoses
   - Power brake vacuum hose
   - Emissions canister hoses
   - Engine electrical harness connectors
   - High tension wires (label them first)
   - Distributor
   - Spark plugs
   - Secondary air pipe assembly (carbureted engines only)
   - Front engine hanger and the nearby ground wire
   - Upper radiator hose (at the thermostat housing)
   - Water bypass hose and bracket
   - Intake and exhaust manifolds
   - Engine side cover
   - Alternator and drive belt(s)
   - Water pump pulley
   - Crankshaft pulley and baffle plate

3. Remove the timing belt covers, as described later in this section. Rotate the crankshaft until the matchmarks on the camshaft and timing belt pulleys are aligned with the corresponding marks on the cylinder block. Then, remove the timing belt, also as described later in this section.

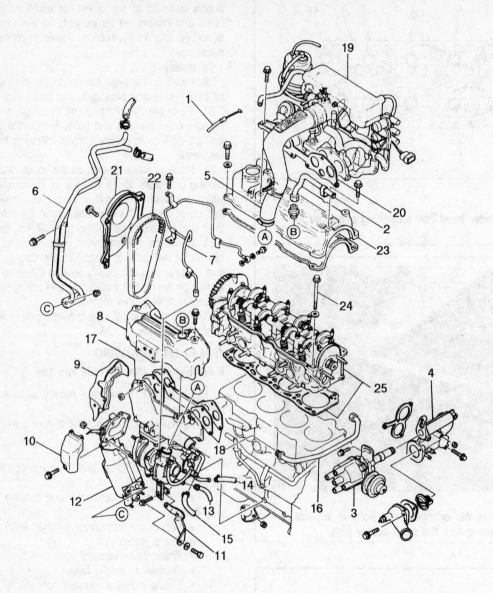

1 Accelerator cable
2 Secondary air pipe
3 Distributor
4 Rear housing
5 Air hose
6 Secondary air pipe
7 Oil pipe
8 Insulator No.1
9 Insulator No.2
10 Insulator No.3
11 Bracket
12 Front catalitic converter
13 Oil return hose
14 Water inlet hose
15 Water outlet hose
16 EGR pipe
17 Exhaust manifold and
      turbocharger assembly
18 Gasket
19 Intake manifold assembly
20 Gasket
21 Timing belt cover
22 Timing belt
23 Cylinder head cover
24 Cylinder head bolt
25 Cylinder head and gasket

85813159

Fig. 151 Exploded view of the cylinder head and upper engine components — 1986-87 626 turbo

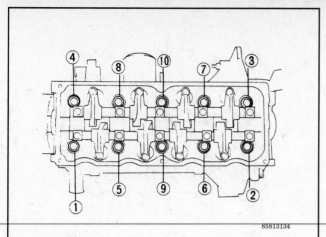

Fig. 152 Cylinder head bolt loosening sequence — 1986-87 323 non-turbo

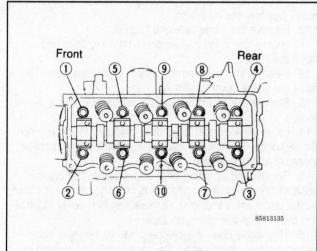

Fig. 153 Cylinder head bolt loosening sequence — 1988-89 323 non-turbo

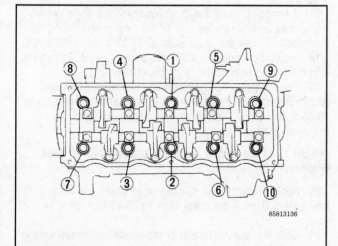

Fig. 154 Cylinder head bolt torque sequence — 1986-87 323 non-turbo

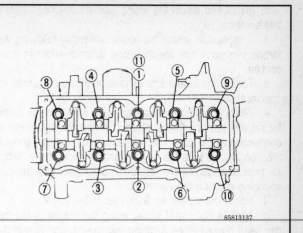

Fig. 155 Cylinder head bolt torque sequence — 1988-89 323 non-turbo

4. If you will be removing the camshaft or performing other major work on the cylinder head itself, remove the camshaft pulley. To remove the pulley, insert a small prytool in one of the slots on the face of the pulley to hold it in place while loosening the bolt with a wrench. After removing the bolt, withdraw the pulley from the camshaft.

5. If you will be removing the camshaft or performing other major work on the cylinder head itself, also remove the rocker assembly, as described earlier in this section.

6. Remove the rear engine hanger from the cylinder head.

7. Loosen the cylinder head cover retaining bolts and remove the cover.

8. Loosen the cylinder head bolts using several stages of the the sequence shown. Remove the head bolts, then lift off the cylinder head and head gasket. If necessary, remove the thermostat cover and thermostat.

9. Thoroughly clean both mating surfaces and inspect the components for warping or other damage, as described later in this section. Repair or replace parts, as necessary.

To install:

10. If removed, install the thermostat with the jiggle pin facing upward and the printed side of the new gasket facing the thermostat. Torque the cover bolts to 14-19 ft. lbs. (19-26 Nm).

11. Install a new head gasket on the engine block with all oil passages, water passages, and bolt holes matching up.

12. Place the cylinder head into position and install the head bolts finger-tight. Then, torque the cylinder head bolts to 63-67 ft. lbs. (85-91 Nm) in three stages, using the appropriate sequence.

➡**Step 11 of the torque sequence only applies to 1988 engines.**

13. Install the camshaft pulley onto the end of the camshaft with the dowel pin and keyway in proper positions and the matchmark straight up. Install the retaining bolt and torque it to 36-45 ft. lbs. (49-61 Nm).

14. Perform the remaining installation steps in reverse of the removal procedure. Note the following points:

   a. Replace all gaskets which were removed with new ones.

b. Install and adjust the timing belt, as described later in this section.

c. If applicable, install the rocker assembly following the torque sequence and specifications outlined earlier in this section.

d. Torque the intake and exhaust manifold bolts/nuts to specification.

e. When installing the distributor, be sure that the distributor rotor is pointing in the direction of the No. 1 cylinder wire connection at the cap. The distributor's drive blade should then be aligned with the oil hole on the base of the distributor prior to engaging the distributor drive gear with the corresponding gear on the camshaft.

f. Adjust the valves as described in Section 2.

g. Apply a coating of sealer along the groove in the cylinder head cover before installing the gasket, and torque the bolts to 43-78 inch lbs. (5-9 Nm).

h. Refill the cooling system and connect the negative battery cable.

i. Start the engine and check for leaks.

1988-89 323 TURBO

▶ **See Figures 156 and 157**

1. Properly relieve the fuel system pressure. Disconnect the negative battery cable. Drain the cooling system.

2. Remove the air cleaner assembly.

3. Remove the distributor, distributor wires and spark plugs.

4. Remove the air intake pipe, air pipe, air bypass valve and hoses.

5. Remove the radiator.

6. Remove the engine side cover and the engine under cover.

7. Disconnect the exhaust pipe at the exhaust manifold. Remove the turbocharger mounting bracket, along with the the exhaust manifold and turbocharger insulators. Unfasten the exhaust manifold retaining bolts, then remove the exhaust manifold and turbocharger assembly from the engine.

8. Remove the radiator hose and coolant bypass pipe. Disconnect the accelerator cable.

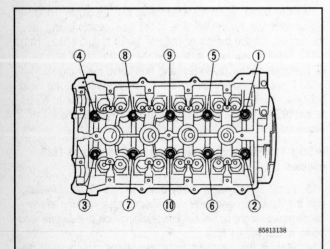

Fig. 156 Cylinder head bolt loosening sequence — 323 turbo

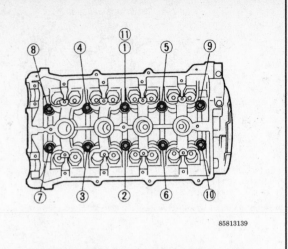

85813139

Fig. 157 Cylinder head bolt torque sequence — 323 turbo

9. Disconnect all required electrical connections, vacuum hoses and fuel line couplings.

10. Remove the surge tank and bracket.

11. Loosen the cylinder head cover retaining bolts and remove the cover.

12. Remove the timing cover assembly retaining bolts. Remove the timing cover assembly.

13. Remove the timing belt, as described later in this section.

14. Loosen the cylinder head bolts gradually in the appropriate sequence. Remove the cylinder head and intake manifold assembly from the engine.

15. Remove the attaching bolts and separate the intake manifold from the cylinder head. If necessary, remove the thermostat cover and thermostat. Remove any old gasket material and clean all gasket mounting surfaces.

16. Thoroughly clean the cylinder head and engine block mating surfaces, then inspect the components for warping or other damage, as described later in this section. Repair or replace parts, as necessary.

To install:

17. If removed, install the thermostat with the jiggle pin facing upward and the printed side of the new gasket facing the thermostat. Torque the cover bolts to 14-19 ft. lbs. (19-26 Nm).

18. Install the intake manifold with a new gasket. Torque the intake manifold bolts to 14-19 ft. lbs. (19-26 Nm).

19. Place a new head gasket onto the engine block and position the cylinder head. Install the bolts and torque them to 56-60 ft. lbs. (76-81 Nm) in several stages, following the proper sequence.

➡ **Step 11 of the torque sequence only applies to 1988 engines.**

20. Apply sealant to the cylinder head cover and install a new gasket. Torque the cover bolts to 26-35 inch lbs. (3-4 Nm).

21. Complete the installation of the remaining components in reverse of the removal procedure.

22. Refill the cooling system to the proper level and connect the negative battery cable.

23. Start the engine and check for leaks. Perform any necessary tune-up adjustments.

1988-89 626/MX-6

▶ **See Figures 158, 159 and 160**

1. Disconnect the negative battery cable and drain the cooling system.

2. Disconnect the spark plug wires and remove the spark plugs.

3. Disconnect the accelerator cable. If equipped with an automatic transaxle, disconnect the throttle cable and route it off to the side.

4. Remove the air intake pipe.

5. Remove the air intake pipe and fuel hose. Cover the fuel hose to prevent leakage.

6. Remove the upper radiator hose, water bypass hose, heater hose, oil cooler hose (turbo only) and brake vacuum hose.

7. Remove the 3-way and EGR solenoid valve assemblies.

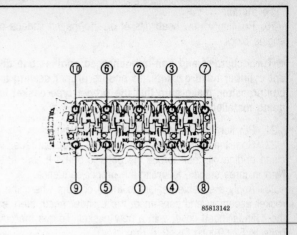

85813142

Fig. 160 Cylinder head bolt torque sequence — 1988-89 626 and MX-6

8. Disconnect the engine harness connector and ground wire.

9. Remove the vacuum chamber and exhaust manifold insulator.

10. Remove the EGR pipe, turbo oil pipes (if so equipped) and exhaust pipe.

11. Remove the exhaust manifold and the turbocharger, if so equipped.

12. Remove the intake manifold bracket and the intake manifold.

13. Remove the distributor, as described earlier in this section.

14. Loosen the air conditioning compressor and bracket assembly; position and tie it off to the side and out of the way.

➡**Do not disconnect the refrigerant lines.**

15. Remove the upper timing belt cover and the timing belt tensioner spring.

16. To remove the timing belt, perform the following:

   a. Rotate the crankshaft so that the **1** on the camshaft pulley is aligned with the timing mark on the front housing (see illustration).

   b. When the timing marks are aligned, loosen the timing belt tensioner lockbolt. Pull the tensioner as far out as it will go, then temporarily tighten the lockbolt to hold it there.

   c. Lift the timing belt from the camshaft pulley and position it out of the way.

17. Loosen the retaining bolts, then remove the cylinder head cover and gasket.

18. Loosen the cylinder head bolts in the proper sequence, then remove the cylinder head and head gasket.

19. Thoroughly clean the cylinder head and engine block mating surfaces, then inspect the components for warping or other damage as described later in this section. Repair or replace parts as necessary.

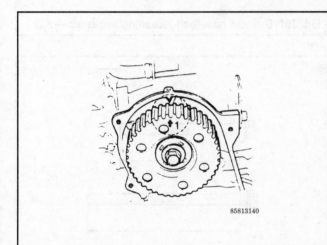

85813140

Fig. 158 Camshaft pulley and front housing alignment marks — 1988-89 626 and MX-6

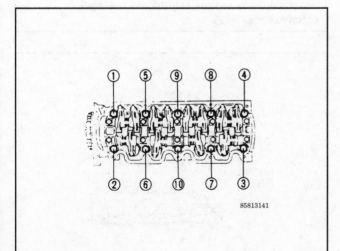

85813141

Fig. 159 Cylinder head bolt loosening sequence — 1988-89 626 and MX-6

To install:

20. Position a new head gasket on the mating surface of the engine block.

➡**Turbocharged and non-turbocharged engines use different cylinder head gaskets. To ensure proper sealing and compression, make sure that the proper type gasket is being installed.**

21. Position the cylinder head on the gasket.

22. Coat the cylinder head bolt threads and seat faces with clean engine oil, then torque the bolts to 59-64 ft. lbs. (80-87 Nm) in three stages, following the proper sequence.

23. Apply a suitable sealant to the 4 corners where the rocker assembly end caps meet the cylinder head, then install the cylinder head cover with a new gasket. Torque the cover bolts to 52-69 inch lbs. (6-8 Nm).

24. Make sure that the camshaft pulley and front housing timing marks are still aligned, then install the timing belt, as described later in this section.

25. Complete the remainder of the installation procedures in reverse of their removal. Be sure to replace all gaskets which were removed with new ones.

26. Refill the cooling system to the proper level and connect the negative battery cable.

27. Start the engine and check for leaks. Check and adjust the ignition timing and idle speed, as described in Section 2.

929

▶ **See Figures 161, 162, 163, 164 and 165**

➡**The following procedure applies to removal of either side cylinder head.**

1. Properly relieve the fuel system pressure. Disconnect the negative battery cable.

2. Drain the coolant and remove the air cleaner assembly.

3. Rotate the crankshaft so that the No. 1 cylinder is at TDC. (All the pulley matchmarks should be aligned.)

4. Remove the timing cover assembly. Mark the timing belt's direction of rotation (if it will be re-used), then remove the belt.

5. Disconnect and plug the canister, brake vacuum and fuel hoses. If equipped with an automatic transmission, disconnect the automatic transmission vacuum hose.

6. Remove the 3-way solenoid valve assembly and disconnect all engine harness connectors and grounds.

7. If equipped with an automatic transmission, remove the dipstick. Disconnect the required vacuum hoses. Disconnect the accelerator linkage.

8. Remove the distributor, as described earlier in this section, and the EGR pipe.

9. Remove the six extension manifolds. Remove and discard the O-rings from the extension manifolds (new ones must be used). Remove the intake manifold by loosening the retaining bolts in the proper sequence.

10. Remove the cylinder head cover, gasket and seal washers.

11. Remove the insulator and center exhaust pipe pipe. Disconnect the exhaust manifold retaining bolts. Remove the exhaust manifold with insulator.

12. Remove the seal plate.

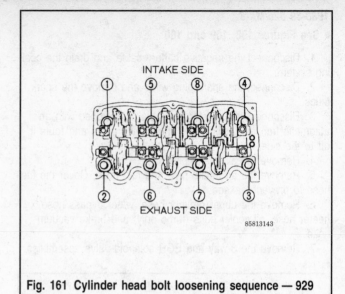

Fig. 161 Cylinder head bolt loosening sequence — 929

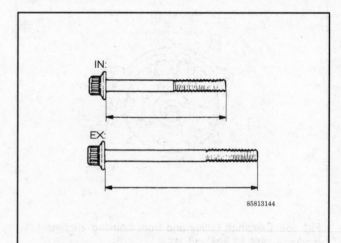

Fig. 162 Measure the length of each head bolt before installation, and replace any that do not meet specifications — 929

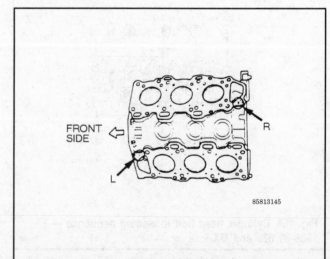

Fig. 163 Be sure to properly position the cylinder head gaskets with the marks facing up — 929

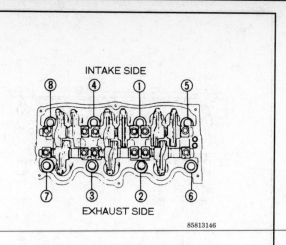

INTAKE SIDE

⑧ ④ ① ⑤

⑦ ③ ② ⑥

EXHAUST SIDE

85813146

Fig. 164 Cylinder head bolt torque sequence — 929

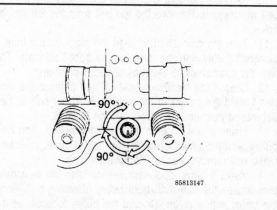

90°

90°

85813147

Fig. 165 After tightening the head bolts to specification, paint a reference mark on each bolt head and use the angular torque method to achieve proper final torque — 929

13. Remove the cylinder head retaining bolts in the proper sequence, in 2 or 3 stages. Remove the cylinder head from the vehicle.

14. Thoroughly clean the cylinder head and engine block mating surfaces, then inspect the components for warping or other damage, as described later in this section. Repair or replace parts, as necessary.

To install:

15. After they have been cleaned, measure the length of each cylinder head bolt. Replace any out-of-specifications bolts as required.

Length:
- Intake — 4.25-4.29 in. (108-109mm)
- Exhaust — 5.43-5.47 in. (138-139mm)

16. Check the oil control plug projection at the cylinder block. The projection should be 0.0209-0.0224 in. (0.53-0.57mm). If correct, apply clean engine oil to a new O-ring and position it on the control plug.

17. Position the new correct side cylinder head gasket on the engine block.

➡ **A left bank gasket should be positioned with the L mark facing up, and a right bank gasket should be positioned with the R mark facing up.**

18. Install the cylinder head onto the block. Tighten the head bolts in the following manner:
    a. Coat the threads and the seating faces of the head bolts with clean engine oil.
    b. Torque the bolts in the proper sequence to 14 ft. lbs. (19 Nm).
    c. Paint a mark on the head of each bolt.
    d. Using this mark as a reference, tighten the bolts in the proper sequence an additional 90 degrees.
    e. Repeat Step d.

19. Complete the installation of the remaining components in reverse of their removal. Be sure to replace all gaskets which were removed with new ones. For timing belt installation and adjustment, refer to the procedure later in this section.

20. Refill the cooling system to the proper level and connect the negative battery cable.

21. Start the engine and check for leaks. Perform any required tune-up adjustments.

Diesel Engines

▶ **See Figures 166, 167, 168 and 169**

➡ **To perform this procedure, you will need two size M8 x 1.25 x 45mm bolts, a wheel puller for a selection of bolts with metric threads, and plastic caps (or another appropriate means to seal off fuel injection line openings).**

1. Disconnect the negative battery cable. Disconnect the air cleaner hose at the intake manifold.

2. Position a suitable pan, then drain the coolant by opening the radiator drain plug.

3. Disconnect the following hoses/electrical connectors at the cylinder head:
- Heater outlet hose at the oil cooler
- Upper radiator hose at both ends
- Fuel supply and return hoses at the injection pump (and plug or cap the hoses and pump openings, once disconnected)
- Temperature gauge sending unit electrical connector
- Glow plug electrical connector
- Engine ground strap

4. Disconnect the exhaust pipe at the exhaust manifold. Then, remove the right side splash shield.

5. Remove the drive belts. Remove the attaching bolts, then remove the cam cover and gasket.

6. Remove the rear timing belt. For details, refer to the timing belt procedure later in this section.

7. Put an open-end wrench on the flats of the camshaft to keep it from turning and loosen the camshaft rear pulley mounting bolt. Then, remove the pulley with a puller.

8. Screw two M8 x 1.25 x 45mm bolts into the rear seal plate so they pass through the two holes in the injection pump drive pulley. Remove the pulley lockbolt, then remove the affixing bolts, pulley and Woodruff key.

9. Remove the tensioner, spring and lockbolt from the rear timing belt mechanism. Then, remove the rear seal plate.

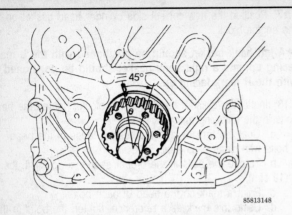

Fig. 166 Turn the crankshaft (on the injection pump end of the engine) clockwise until the timing marks align, then turn it an additional 45 degrees. In this position, the work can be performed on the diesel engine without risking piston or valve damage

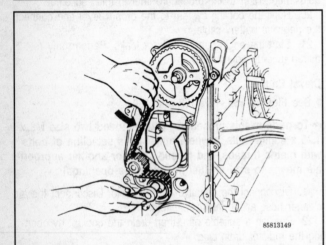

Fig. 167 Loosen the timing belt tensioner lockbolt, depress the belt as shown, then retighten the lockbolt — diesel engine

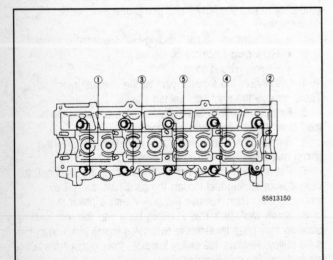

Fig. 168 Cylinder head bolt loosening sequence — diesel engine

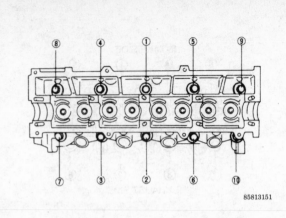

Fig. 169 Cylinder head bolt torque sequence — diesel engine

10. Remove the right timing belt cover from the front timing belt mechanism. Remove the top bolt from the left timing belt cover.

11. Turn the crankshaft to align the mark on the front camshaft pulley with the mark on the front seal plate. Then, turn the crankshaft 45 degrees ahead, as shown.

12. Loosen the tensioner lockbolt, and depress the timing belt toward the center of the engine. Hold the belt in the depressed position, then retighten the lockbolt.

13. Install a wrench onto the camshaft pulley, then turn the pulley gently counterclockwise and hold it there, in order to make belt removal easier. Remove the belt.

14. Install a large, open-end wrench onto the camshaft flats, then loosen the camshaft front pulley mounting bolt. Remove the pulley with a puller. Discard the pulley lockbolt, as it must be replaced with a new one when the pulley is reinstalled.

➡**Do not attempt to hammer the pulley or camshaft to remove the pulley.**

15. Remove the front seal lockplate bolts, then remove the lockplate and seals. For details on seal removal, refer to the camshaft procedure later in this section.

16. If you will probably be working on the valves or prechambers, remove the camshaft cap bolts and the camshaft at this time (see the appropriate procedure, later in this section). Otherwise, remove the cylinder head mounting bolts in several stages, turning them a little at a time in the indicated order. Remove the cylinder head.

17. Thoroughly clean the cylinder head and engine block mating surfaces, then inspect the components for warping or other damage, as described later in this section. If distortion of the head surface which mates with the block exceeds the limit, *replace* the head. If distortion of either manifold contact surface exceeds the limit, grind or replace the head. Repair or replace other parts, such as cylinder head bolts, as necessary.

To install:

18. Position a new head gasket onto the block. Make sure the crankshaft is still positioned as described in Step 10. Then, position the cylinder head onto the block.

19. Measure the length of every head bolt from the lower surface of the cap to the lower end of the bolt. If the length

exceeds 4.5079 in. (114.5mm), replace the bolt. Lubricate the threads on all the bolts you are going to use with engine oil.

20. Install the bolts finger-tight.

21. Torque the head bolts to 22 ft. lbs. (29 Nm) in the numbered sequence. Paint or punch a mark on the outer surface of the bolt head. Then, in the same sequence, turn each bolt 90-105 degrees. When this is completed, turn each bolt in the same sequence another 90-105 degrees.

➡**The double tightening of each cylinder head bolt by 90-105 degrees is to secure the uniform force load on the head gasket. If not done properly, air-tightness of the cylinders may be insufficient.**

22. If applicable, install the camshaft. Install the front and rear camshaft oil seals by first oiling the lips of the seals with clean engine oil, then install them by pressing on either side with your thumbs. Note that the rear seal is just slightly larger.

23. Install the front camshaft pulley with its Woodruff key onto the camshaft. Hold the camshaft in position, using a wrench on the flats, then install a new pulley lockbolt, torquing it to 41-48 ft. lbs. (56-65 Nm). Turn the camshaft to align the mark on the pulley with the mark on the front seal plate (at about 2 o'clock).

24. Remove the cover for the inspection hole from the clutch housing. Then, turn the crankshaft back to Top Dead Center (TDC), as marked on the flywheel.

25. Install and adjust the timing belt. For details, refer to the timing belt procedure found later in this section. Install the top bolt for the left side belt cover (removed in Step 9). Install the right side timing belt cover.

26. Install the rear seal plate. Install the fuel injection pump pulley with its Woodruff key. Then, rotate the pulley until the mark on the pulley aligns with the mark on the rear seal plate. Install the two bolts used in removal, then install the pulley bolt and torque it to 43-51 ft. lbs. (58-69 Nm). Leave the affixing bolts in place until the rear timing belt has been installed.

27. Install the rear camshaft pulley and Woodruff key onto the camshaft. Hold the camshaft in place, using a wrench on the flats, and install the lockbolt, torquing to 41-48 ft. lbs. (56-65 Nm).

28. Install the tensioner, spring and lockbolt in the fully loosened position. Rotate the tensioner clockwise as far as it will go, then temporarily tighten it.

29. Install and tension the rear timing belt as described under Rear Timing Belt Removal and Installation, later in this section.

30. Remove the affixing bolts from the fuel injection pump pulley.

31. Check the valve clearance and adjust as necessary, using the appropriate procedure in Section 2.

32. Perform the remaining steps in reverse of the removal procedure.

33. Start the engine and check for leaks. Perform any necessary adjustments.

CLEANING AND INSPECTION

➡ **See Figures 170, 171, 172, 173, 174, 175, 176, 177, 178, 179 and 180**

1. Thoroughly clean the cylinder head and cylinder block contact surfaces to remove any dirt, oil or old gasket material.

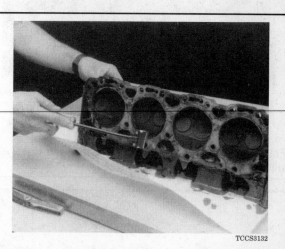

TCCS3132

Fig. 170 Use a gasket scraper to remove the bulk of the old head gasket from the cylinder head's mating surface

2. Check the cylinder head for distortion in six planes, as shown, by placing a straightedge horizontally and diagonally across the cylinder head, and across each end, while attempting to insert a feeler gauge between the head surface and the straightedge. The permissible limit is 0.006 in. (0.15mm) for 4-cylinder gasoline engines or 0.004 in. (0.10mm) for 6-cylinder and diesel engines.

➡**If distortion exceeds the limit, measure the cylinder head height. If the height is within specifications, based on the following figures, resurface (grind) the cylinder head surface (except diesel engines) or replace it. If a diesel engine cylinder head's distortion exceeds the limit, replace the head.**

- 1978-85 GLC: 3.551-3.560 in. (90.3-90.5mm)
- 1986-89 323: 4.228-4.236 in. (107.40-107.60mm)
- 1979-82 626: 4.289-4.293 in. (108.95-109.05mm)
- 1983-89 626/MX-6: 3.620-3.624 in. (91.95-92.05mm)
- 1988-89 929: 4.931-4.935 in. (125.25-125.35mm)

➡**As long as the specified minimum height is maintained, a cylinder head may be ground up to the appropriate maximum amount, as follows:**

- 1978-85 GLC: 0.008 in. (0.20mm)
- 1986-89 323: 0.008 in. (0.20mm)
- 1979-82 626: 0.008 in. (0.20mm)
- 1983-89 626/MX-6 (except diesel): 0.008 in. (0.20mm)
- 1988-89 929: 0.006 in. (0.15mm)

3. On 1979-82 engines, also check the intake and exhaust manifold mating surfaces for distortion by placing a straightedge horizontally across the manifold, while attempting to insert a feeler gauge between the manifold surface and the

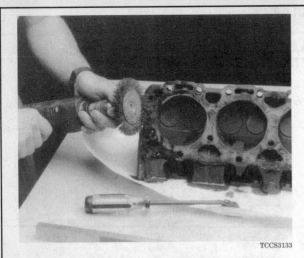

Fig. 171 An electric drill equipped with a wire wheel will expedite complete gasket removal

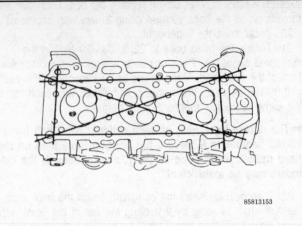

Fig. 173 The cylinder heads on 6-cylinder gasoline engines should also be checked for warpage across 6 planes

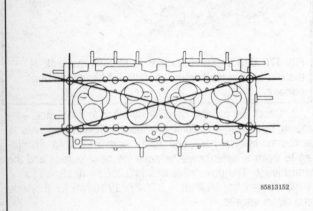

Fig. 172 Check the cylinder head for distortion by using a straightedge and feeler gauge along six planes of the block mating surface (as indicated by the straight lines) — 4-cylinder gasoline engine

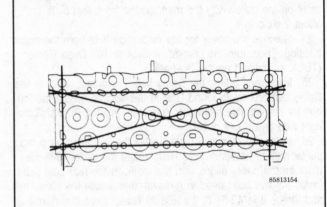

Fig. 174 Check the diesel cylinder head for distortion in the same manner as for gasoline engines

straightedge. The permissible limit is 0.006 in. (0.15mm). If excessive distortion is detected, grind or replace the manifold.

4. On diesel engines and 1988-89 gasoline engines, also check the cylinder head's intake and exhaust manifold contact surfaces for distortion in three planes each, as shown. Do this by placing a straightedge across the contact surface, while attempting to insert a feeler gauge between the surface and the straightedge. Repeat for the opposite side. The limit is 0.006 in. (0.15mm) for 4-cylinder gasoline engines, 0.004 in. (0.10mm) for 6-cylinder engines, or 0.008 in. (0.20mm) for diesel engines.

➡If distortion exceeds the limit, grind (resurface) the cylinder head contact surface or replace it.

5. Inspect the cylinder head's water passages to make sure they are fully open. If necessary, hot tank the head in a solution that is compatible with aluminum to clean the passages.

Fig. 175 When checking for warpage be sure to use a precision straightedge and a feeler gauge

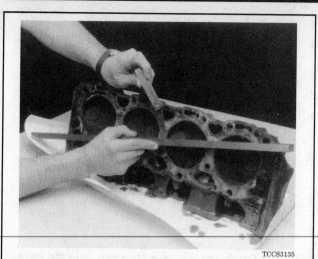

TCCS3135

Fig. 176 Check for warpage at all angles, not just one or two of them

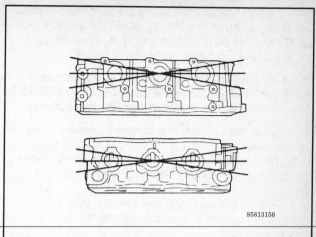

85813156

Fig. 178 Again, the cylinder heads on 1988-89 6-cylinder engines should be checked along 3 planes for each of the manifold mating surfaces

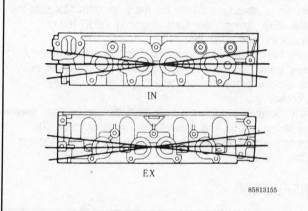

IN

EX

85813155

Fig. 177 Check the cylinder head's intake and exhaust manifold contact surfaces for distortion in three planes each — 1988-89 4-cylinder engine

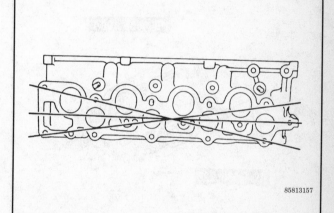

85813157

Fig. 179 Check the diesel engine cylinder head's manifold contact surfaces in the same manner as for gasoline engines

6. Inspect the cylinder head bolts for damaged threads and make sure they are free from grease and dirt. Repair or replace any damaged threads or broken studs.

RESURFACING

Due to the special equipment and required precision, it is recommended that cylinder head regrinding only be performed by an experienced and reputable machine shop.

Valves

REMOVAL & INSTALLATION

▶ **See Figures 181, 182 and 183**

1. Remove the cylinder head from the engine, as previously described. Position the cylinder head on a suitable workstand.

85813221

Fig. 180 Before installing the cylinder head, be sure to also remove old gasket material from the engine block

2. Attach a special Valve Spring Lifter and Pivot combination (such as Mazda Part Nos. 49 0636 100A and either 49 G030 222 or 49 BO12 006, depending on engine model) to the valve head and spring cap (retainer).

➡️ If such a tool is not available, you may substitute a Valve Spring Lifter (such as Mazda Part No. 49 0223 105B or equivalent), which is applied from the top side only.

3. Screw down or otherwise compress the valve spring until the two valve keys (keepers) can be removed from the groove in the valve head. Remove the keepers, then slowly release the spring tension. Remove the spring retainer and valve spring.
4. Remove the valve stem seal from the valve guide.
5. Invert the cylinder head and withdraw the valve from the cylinder head bore.
6. Inspect and repair or replace components, as necessary.

To install:

7. Insert the valve through the cylinder head bore.

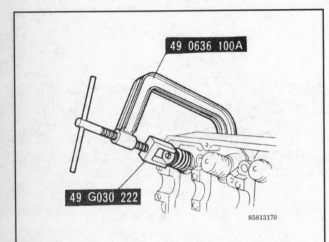

Fig. 181 A suitable valve spring lifter and pivot combination may be used to remove and install valves in the cylinder head

Fig. 182 Invert the cylinder head and withdraw the valve from the cylinder head bore

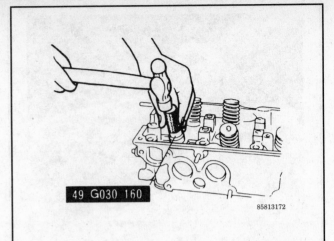

Fig. 183 Gently tap the valve stem seal onto the valve guide, using a suitable driver (such as an appropriately sized socket)

8. Apply a coating of engine oil to the inner surface of the new valve stem seal. Gently tap the valve stem seal onto the valve guide, using Valve Seat Pusher 49 G030 160 or equivalent, and a hammer.
9. Position the valve spring and spring retainer over the valve stem. Compress the spring (using the same tool as in the removal procedure) until the keeper groove is fully exposed.
10. Securely position the keepers in the groove, then release the spring tension, and remove the compressor tool. The spring pressure against the retainer should lock the keepers firmly in place.

INSPECTION

▶ **See Figures 184, 185, 186 and 187**

Remove all carbon from the valves and inspect for warpage, cracks, or excessive burning. (On the diesel, inspect the valves for stem wear, bending of the stem in relation to the head, mechanical damage, or dents of any kind.) Replace valves that cannot be cleaned up and refaced without removal of an excessive amount of metal. Measure the stem diameter at three places using a micrometer, and note the smallest figure. Then, determine the inner diameter of the corresponding valve guide, using a dial indicator at two positions. (First, take one reading at an arbitrary point, then rotate the indicator 90 degrees to obtain the second reading.) Note the larger figure. You can then calculate the stem-to-guide clearance by subtracting the stem diameter from the valve guide's inner diameter.

It may not be necessary to replace both the valve and valve guide if the stem-to-guide clearance is excessive; replacing either a worn valve guide, or a valve whose stem diameter is below specification, may bring the clearance within specifications. However, it is important to take accurate measurements. Excessive wear in a valve guide or valve stem is often accompanied by a worn mating part, necessitating replacement of both the valve guide and valve stem.

Before installing new or re-usable valves, be sure to remove any carbon deposits from the combustion chambers.

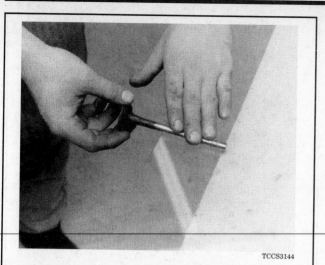

Fig. 184 Valve stems may be rolled on a flat surface to check for bends

Fig. 187 With the valves removed, use a wire wheel to clean the carbon deposits from combustion chambers

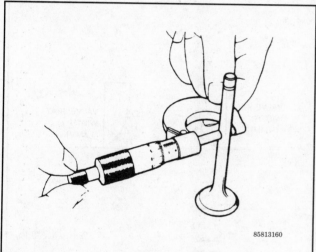

Fig. 185 Measuring valve stem diameter with a micrometer

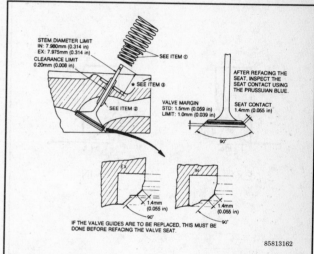

Fig. 188 Valve seat/face angles, and dimensions — 1.3L and 1.4L engines

REFACING

▶ See Figures 188, 189, 190, 191, 192, 193, 194 and 195

➡Because of the tools and skill involved, valve refacing should only be performed by a machine shop. Great care must be taken not to remove excessive metal or the valve will be damaged.

Valve faces and seats should be refaced with a special refacing tool, following the tool manufacturer's instructions. (Refer to the illustrations for dimensions and angles.) The technician should remove just enough metal to clean up the valve faces and seats. If, during the refacing process, the valve margin becomes less than 0.039 in. (1mm), the valve must be replaced, with the following exceptions: On 2.0L, 1988-89 1.6L and 2.2L engines, the minimum exhaust valve margin is 0.039 in. (1mm), but the minimum intake valve margin is only 0.020 in. (0.5mm). On 1986-87 1.6L engines, the minimum thickness is 0.039 in. (1mm) for intake valves and 0.051 in. (1.3mm) for exhaust valves. On 1988-89 1.6L turbocharged engines, the

Fig. 186 Measuring valve guide inner diameter with a dial gauge

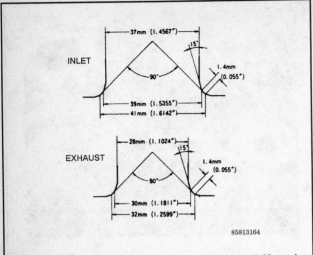

Fig. 190 Valve seat angles and dimensions — 1.6L and 2.0L (Code MA) engines

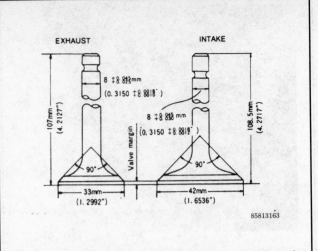

Fig. 189 Valve face angles and dimensions — 1.6L and 2.0L (Code MA) engines

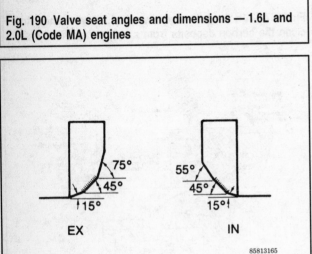

Fig. 191 Valve seat grinding angles and dimensions — 1986-87 1.6L engine

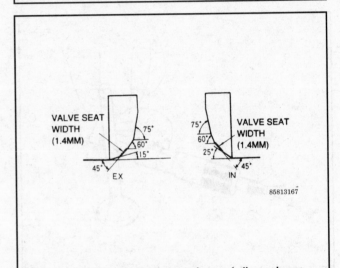

Fig. 193 Valve seat grinding angles and dimensions — 2.0L (code FE) and 2.2L engines

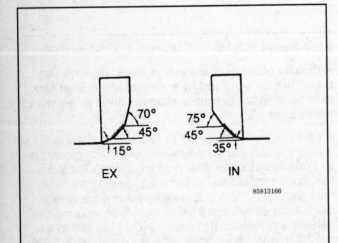

Fig. 192 Valve seat grinding angles — 1988-89 1.6L turbo and non-turbo engines

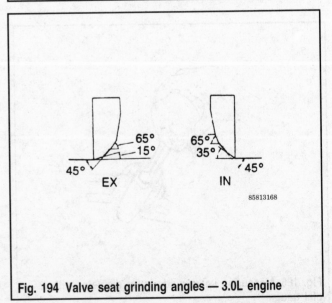

Fig. 194 Valve seat grinding angles — 3.0L engine

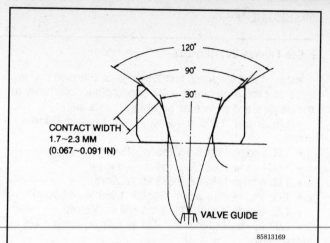

Fig. 195 Valve seat grinding angles and dimensions — 2.0L diesel (code RF) engine

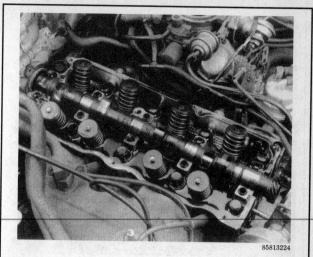

Fig. 196 The valves and springs are held in position by retainers and keepers

limit is 0.020 in. (0.5mm) for both intake and exhaust valves. On 3.0L engines, the margin thickness must be 0.030-0.049 in. (0.75-1.25mm) for intake valves and 0.047-0.071 in. (1.2-1.8mm) for exhaust valves.

On the diesel engine, there is no margin limit, provided contact width can be brought to specification, which is 0.067-0.091 in. (1.7-2.3mm). To check margin width, apply a thin coating of red lead to the valve seat, then press the valve firmly against the seat without rotating it. Measure the width of the mark.

Valve Springs

REMOVAL & INSTALLATION

▶ See Figures 196, 197, 198, 199 and 200

➡Although valve springs are normally serviced along with the valves after the cylinder head has been removed from the engine, the springs may also be removed with the cylinder head still installed if an air compressor and adapter is available. The compressed air is introduced to the combustion chamber through the spark plug fitting and is then used to hold the valves up in the cylinder head. Be careful when performing this procedure, should air pressure be lost with the valve retainers off, the valve will drop into the cylinder bore requiring cylinder head removal to retrieve it.

1. If the valve springs are to be removed with the cylinder head off the engine, remove the head assembly as described earlier in this section.

2. If the valve springs are to be removed with the cylinder head still on the engine, remove the cylinder head (rocker arm) cover and rocker assembly, as described earlier in this section. Position the crankshaft so the cylinder on which you are about to work is at TDC (the valves must be closed in order to hold air pressure), then install the fitting and pressurize the cylinder. Follow the fitting manufacturer's instructions, but a significant amount of the pressure is necessary.

3. Using an appropriate tool, compress the valve spring until the two valve keys (keepers) can be removed from the

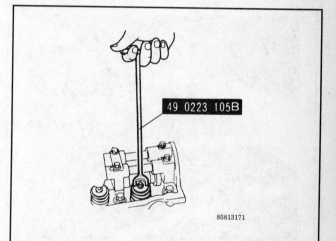

Fig. 197 Use a valve spring lifter, such as Mazda Part No. 49 0223 105B or equivalent, if the cylinder head is still on the engine

Fig. 198 With the valve spring compressed, the valve keys (keepers) can be removed with a magnet

Fig. 199 Be careful not to lose the valve keepers

Fig. 200 After the keepers have been removed, lift the compressed spring and retainer from the valve stem

groove in the valve head. Remove the keepers, then slowly release the spring tension. Remove the spring retainer and valve spring.

➡For additional piece of mind when performing this on a cylinder head which is still installed, you can tie a piece of string to the top of the valve while the spring and keepers are removed. Should air pressure be lost, the string should keep the valve from falling completely into the combustion chamber (thus preventing the need for cylinder head removal to retrieve the valve).

To install:

4. Position the valve spring and spring retainer over the valve stem. Compress the spring (using the same tool as in the removal procedure) until the keeper groove is fully exposed.

5. Securely position the keepers in the groove, then release the spring tension, and remove the compressor tool. The spring pressure against the retainer should lock the keepers firmly in place.

INSPECTION

▶ **See Figures 201 and 202**

Inspect the valve springs for breakage or corrosion and replace as necessary. Measure the free length for conformity to specification and replace as necessary. Limits are:

- 1.3L engine: 1.406 in. (36mm) inner; 1.539 in. (39mm) outer
- 1.5L engine 1981-82: 1.705 in. (43mm)
- 1.5L engine 1983-85: 1.654 in. (42mm)
- 1.6L engine 1986-87: 1.673 in. (42.5mm)
- 1.6L engine (non-turbo) 1988-89: 1.665 in. (42.3mm)
- 1.6L engine (turbo) 1988-89: 1.803 in. (46mm)
- 2.0L (Code MA) engine: 1.449 in. (37mm) inner; 1.469 in. (37mm) outer
- 2.0L (Code FE) engine 1983-85: 1.984 in. (50mm) outer; 1.744 in. (44mm) inner
- 2.0L (Code FE) engine 1986-87: 2.000 in. (50mm) outer; 1.681 in. (43mm) inner
- 2.0L diesel engine: 1.764 in. (45mm)
- 2.2L engine: 1.902 in. (48mm) intake and 1.937 in. (49mm) exhaust
- 3.0L engine: 1.819 in. (46mm) intake inner and 1.988 (50.5mm) intake outer; 2.063 (52.5mm) exhaust inner and 2.264 (57.5mm) exhaust outer.

On some engines, the valve springs should also be checked for straightness. Sit them flat next to a perpendicular surface and rotate each spring until there is a maximum gap between the top of the spring and the perpendicular surface. Then, measure that distance. The limits are:

- 1.6L engine 1986-87: 0.055 in. (1.4mm)
- 1.6L engine 1988-89: 0.059 in. (1.5mm)
- 2.0L (Code FE) engine: 0.066 in. (1.67mm)
- 2.0L diesel engine: 0.062 in. (1.57mm)
- 2.2L engine: 0.067 in. (1.7mm)
- 3.0L engine: 0.064 (1.63mm) intake inner and 0.070 (1.77mm) intake outer; 0.074 (1.89mm) exhaust inner and 0.083 (2.11mm) exhaust outer

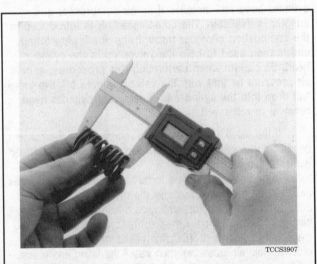

Fig. 201 Use a caliper gauge to check the valve spring's free length

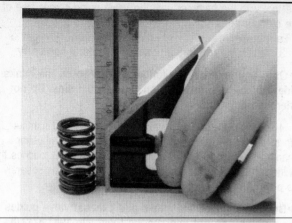

Fig. 202 A carpenter's square can be used to check the valve spring for squareness. The spring should be straight up and down when placed like this

TCCS3908

Valve Seats

REMOVAL & INSTALLATION

While some Mazda engines use pressed-in seats, none are replaceable. If the seats cannot be machined to restore proper dimensions, the cylinder head must be replaced.

REFACING

➡**Because of the tools and skill involved, valve refacing should only be performed by a machine shop. Great care must be taken not to remove excessive metal or the valve seat will be damaged.**

If any valve seats have cracks, burrs, or ridges, or the angles and dimensions are incorrect, remove the minimum amount of metal that will correct them with a valve seat grinder. See the appropriate illustration for dimensions. Note that seat grinding must be done after valve guide replacement, where it is required. Contact of valve and seat must be checked by applying Prussian Blue dye to the seat and seating valve, then repeatedly reseating the valve while rotating it. If the dye marking on the valve is uneven, the valve must be lapped in.

When valve/seat machining has been performed, it is necessary to check the distance between the valve spring seat on the cylinder head and the top of the valve stem so that adequate spring tension is assured. Check the dimension using Vernier calipers. Standard dimensions are:
- 1.3L and 1.5L engines: 1.555 in. (39.5mm)
- 2.0L (Code MA) engine: intake 1.59 in. (40.4mm), exhaust 1.48 in. (37.6mm)
- 2.0L (Code FE) engine: 1.831 in. (46.5mm)

If this dimension is exceeded by more than 0.020 in. (0.5mm), shims must be inserted on the spring seat to bring the dimension to within specifications. If the dimension is greater than 0.069 in. (1.8mm), replace the valve.

On the 1.6L non-turbo engine, the head can be used if the dimension is 1.555-1.575 in. (39.5-40mm). If the dimension is 1.575-1.614 in. (40-41mm), shim the spring so that the total dimension is 1.555-1.575 in. (39.5-40mm). If the dimension is beyond 1.614 in. (41mm), replace the head.

On the 1.6L turbo engine, the head can be used if the dimension is 1.713-1.732 in. (43.5-44.0mm). If the dimension is 1.732-1.772 in. (43.5-44.0mm), shim the spring so that the total dimension is 1.713-1.732 in. (43.5-44.0mm). If the dimension is beyond 1.772 in. (45mm), replace the head.

On the 2.2L engine, the head can be used if the dimension is 1.976-2.008 in. (50.2-51.0mm). If the dimension is 2.008-2.035 in. (51.0-51.7mm), shim the spring so that the total dimension is 1.976-2.008 in. (50.2-51.0mm). If the dimension is beyond 2.035 in. (51.7mm), replace the head.

On the 3.0L engine, the head can be used if the dimension is 1.969-2.008 in. (50.0-51.0mm) for intake and 1.929-1.969 (49.0-51.0mm) for exhaust. If the dimension is 2.008-2.047 in. (51.0-52.0mm) for intake and 1.969-2.008 (50.0-51.0mm) for exhaust, shim the spring so that the total dimension is as specified in the re-use specification above. If the dimension is beyond 2.047 in. (52.0mm) for intake and 2.008 in. (51.0mm) for exhaust, replace the head.

On the diesel engine, valve recession below the height of the cylinder head deck is measured with the valve in its installed position. Place a straightedge across the center of the valve head diameter, then attempt to slide a flat feeler gauge of appropriate thickness under the straightedge. If the gauge fits without a great deal of pressure, valve recession is excessive. Valve recession may also be measured with a dial indicator installed in a sled gauge adapter, if such equipment is available. Make sure that the bottom surface of the head is clean and flat. Zero the indicator stylus on the cylinder head next to the valve. Slide the gauge across the valve and record the reading. The limits are 0.030-0.041 in. (0.762-1.041mm) for both intake and exhaust valves. If a dial indicator is used, a minus reading will result. Positive readings are not acceptable. If the recession dimension is 0.061-0.100 in. (1.55-2.54mm), you may re-use the cylinder head, but a washer of a thickness sufficient to compensate for the recession must be used under the valve spring. For example, if the recession were 0.090 in. (2.3mm), you would use a washer equal to 0.090 in. (2.3mm) minus the 0.035 in. (0.889mm) average for a thickness of 0.055 in. (1.4mm). If recession exceeds 0.100 in. (2.54mm), the cylinder head must be replaced.

Valve Guides

REMOVAL & INSTALLATION

▶ **See Figures 203, 204 and 205**

➡**Press-out valve guide replacement requires the use of a valve guide installer (Mazda Part No. 49 0221 251A or equivalent) and hammer from the side opposite the combustion chamber.**

1. If not already done, remove the valve spring, valve stem seal and valve, as previously outlined.
2. Invert the cylinder head and position the special removal/installation tool against the valve guide. Carefully strike

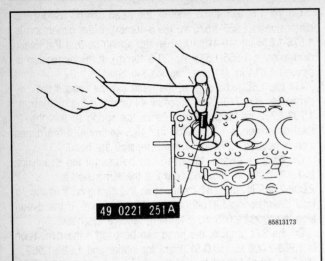

Fig. 203 Invert the cylinder head and tap out the valve guide using a hammer and valve guide tool

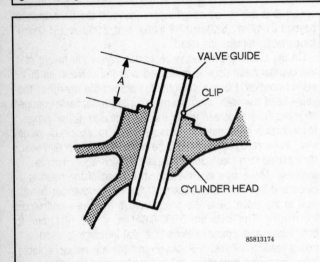

Fig. 204 After the valve guide is installed, check that dimension "A" falls within the designated range

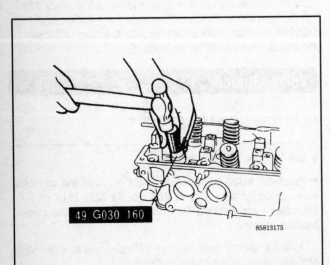

Fig. 205 Use a suitable driver to gently seat the valve stem seal

the tool with the hammer until the valve guide comes free of the cylinder head.
To install:
3. Attach the clip to the new valve guide, if necessary.

➡**On diesel engines, the longer guides go on the intake side, and the shorter ones on the exhaust side. Do not interchange them.**

4. Using the same removal/installation tool and hammer, tap in a new guide from the side opposite the combustion chamber, stopping when the clip on the guide just touches the cylinder head. Be sure to hit the end of the tool as squarely as possible.

➡**On 1.5L engines, the intake and exhaust valve guides are different; do not interchange them. On 1983-87 2.0L (Code FE) and 3.0L engines, although the intake and exhaust valve guides originally used were different shapes, exhaust type guides should be used for replacement on both sides.**

5. Check for the proper valve guide extension. Dimension "A" (from the valve spring seating surface to the top of the guide) should be 0.752-0.772 in. (19.0-19.5mm) for 2.0L (Code FE and RF) engines. On the 1.6L non-turbo engines, this dimension must be 0.520-0.543 in. (13.2-13.8mm). On 1.6L turbo engines, the dimension should be 0.661-0.685 in. (16.8-17.4mm). On 2.2L engines, the dimension should be 0.780-0.799 in. (19.8-20.3mm). On 3.0L engines, the dimension should be 0.520-0.543 in. (13.2-13.8mm) intake and 0.772-0.795 in. (19.6-20.2mm) exhaust.

6. Install a new valve stem seal, using Valve Seat Pusher 49 G030 160 or equivalent. Be sure that the seal is properly seated; otherwise, oil could work its way down the valve stem.

Oil Pan

REMOVAL & INSTALLATION

Except 626 Diesel, 323, 1988-89 626/MX-6 and 929
▶ **See Figures 206, 207, 208 and 209**

1. Disconnect the negative battery cable.
2. Raise the front of the car and safely support it on jackstands.
3. Remove the under cover, if applicable, and drain the engine oil. Remove the engine splash shield or skid plate.
4. Remove the clutch slave cylinder, if so equipped. Do not disconnect the hydraulic line; let the cylinder hang or support it with rope or wire.
5. Remove the engine rear brace attaching bolts and loosen the bolts on the left side, if present.
6. Disconnect the emission line from the oil pan, if so equipped.
7. Loosen the front motor mounts, raise the front of the engine and support with a wooden block to gain clearance, if necessary (except on front wheel drive GLCs and 626s).
8. On front wheel drive cars, loosen the bolts attaching the exhaust pipe to the manifold and lower the pipe; also, disconnect the engine torque brace. On the 626, disconnect the No. 3 engine mount, located near the driver's side of the pan.

Fig. 206 Lower the oil pan after removing the retaining bolts and any obstructions

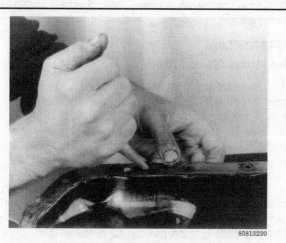

Fig. 207 Carefully examine the flange of the oil pan and clean off all traces of old gasket or sealer. Clean the engine block's mating surface, too

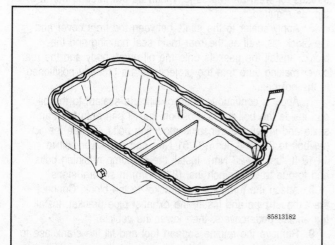

Fig. 208 Apply a continuous bead of sealant to the flange of a gasketless oil pan

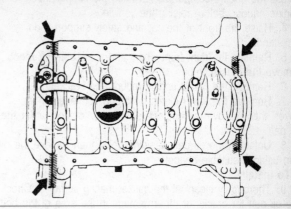

Fig. 209 When installing with a gasket, apply sealant to the joints where the front cover and rear main seal mate with the block

9. Unfasten the oil pan retaining bolts, then remove the oil pan and allow it to rest on the crossmember. Remove the oil pump pickup tube, if necessary, to remove the oil pan.

To install:

10. Thoroughly clean all the gasket mating surfaces. Check the oil pan for cracks or other damage in the area of the bolt holes. Remove the oil pan drain plug and check the pan threads for wear and damage. Clean up the threads with a tap, as required.

11. Install the oil pump pickup tube, if previously removed.

12. On 1983-87 2.0L engines, there is no gasket. Apply a gasket forming sealant as shown in the illustration before installing the pan. Be sure to install the pan and torque the retaining bolts within 30 minutes.

13. On engines using a pan gasket, apply sealer to the joints between the front cover and block, as well as the rear main seal housing and block, before installing the gasket. Install the oil pan and torque the retaining bolts.

14. On front wheel drive cars, fasten the engine torque brace and the No. 3 engine mount, if applicable. Connect the exhaust pipe to the manifold.

15. On rear wheel drive cars, remove the wooden support block, if applicable, then lower the front of the engine and fasten the motor mounts.

16. If so equipped, connect the emission line to the oil pan.

17. Tighten the bolts on the left side of the engine, then install the rear brace attaching bolts, if applicable.

18. Install the clutch slave cylinder, if applicable.

19. Install the engine splash shield or skid plate.

20. Lower the vehicle and fill the crankcase to the proper level.

21. Connect the negative battery cable. Start the engine and inspect for leaks.

626 Diesel

♦ See Figures 208 and 209

1. Disconnect the negative battery cable. Drain the engine oil and coolant.

2. Remove the No. 3 engine mount nuts, under the vehicle.

3. Reposition the engine hanger and attach engine support apparatus (Nos. 49 G030 025 and 49 E301 027, or equivalent)

across the engine compartment. Attach the support hook to the engine hanger, before raising the vehicle.

4. Raise the front of the car and safely support it on jackstands.

5. Remove the right front wheel and splash shield, then remove the crossmember.

6. Remove the No. 3 engine mount and bracket.

7. Remove the lower clutch or torque converter under cover, then remove the coolant return pipe, located under the oil pan.

8. Unfasten the oil pan retaining bolts, then remove the oil pan using a suitable prytool.

To install:

9. Thoroughly clean all the gasket mating surfaces. Check the oil pan for cracks or other damage in the area of the bolt holes. Remove the oil pan drain plug and check the pan threads for wear and damage. Clean up the threads with a tap, as required.

10. Apply a gasket forming sealant to the pan's mating surface before installing the pan. Be sure to install the pan and torque the retaining bolts within 30 minutes. If using a gasket, apply sealer to the joints between the front cover and block, as well as the rear main seal housing and block, before installing the gasket. Install the oil pan and torque the retaining bolts.

11. Connect the coolant return pipe and the under cover.

12. Install the No. 3 engine mount and bracket.

13. Install the crossmember, the splash shield, and the right front wheel.

14. Lower the vehicle and remove the engine support apparatus.

15. Fill the crankcase with oil to the proper level.

16. Fill the cooling system to the proper level.

17. Connect the negative battery cable. Start the engine and inspect for leaks.

1986-89 323 Non-Turbo

▶ See Figures 209 and 210

1. Disconnect the negative battery cable. Raise and safely support the front of the vehicle. Drain the engine oil.

2. Remove the engine splash shields. Disconnect and lower the exhaust pipe. Reposition the components, as required, in order to gain access to the oil pan retaining bolts.

3. Remove the oil pan retaining bolts and the stiffening strips that go under the bolts, then lower the oil pan.

To install:

4. Thoroughly clean all the gasket mating surfaces. Check the oil pan for cracks or other damage in the area of the bolt holes. Remove the oil pan drain plug and check the pan threads for wear and damage. Clean up the threads with a tap, as required.

5. Apply sealer to the joints between the front cover and block, as well as the rear main seal housing and block. Also apply sealer to the concave portion of the flange at each end of the oil pan, as illustrated. Place a new gasket on the pan, then install the pan and stiffener onto the block. Torque the pan retaining bolts to 52-78 inch lbs. (6-9 Nm).

6. Connect the exhaust pipe and install the splash shields. Lower the vehicle and fill the crankcase to the proper level.

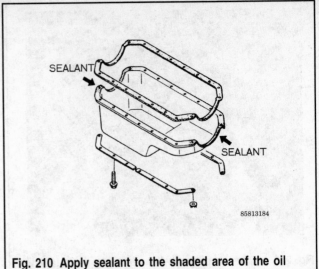

Fig. 210 Apply sealant to the shaded area of the oil pan flange before attaching the gasket

7. Connect the negative battery cable. Start the engine and inspect for leaks.

1988-89 323 Turbo

▶ See Figures 208 and 209

1. Disconnect the negative battery cable. Mount engine support tool 49 B017 5A0, or equivalent, and suspend the engine. Raise and safely support the front of the vehicle.

2. Drain the engine oil. Remove the engine under cover assembly.

3. Remove the exhaust pipe bracket and disconnect the exhaust pipe. Remove the turbocharger bracket.

4. Unfasten the oil pan retaining bolts. Remove the oil pan from the engine by prying gently on the area where the pan mates with the transaxle and nowhere else. Loosen the mounting member bolts until the pan can be removed.

To install:

5. Clean all the gasket contact surfaces thoroughly. Check the oil pan for cracks or other damage in the area of the bolt holes. Remove the oil pan drain plug and check the pan threads for wear and damage. Clean up the threads with a tap, as required.

6. Apply sealer to the joints between the front cover and the block, as well as the rear main seal housing and the block. Install the gaskets onto the oil pump body and the rear cover making sure that the projections are properly positioned in the notches.

7. Apply a continuous bead of silicone sealant to the oil pan inside the bolt holes. Position the oil pan onto the transaxle and install the transaxle mounting bolts. Torque the upper bolt to 27-38 ft. lbs. (37-51 Nm) and the lower bolt to 14-19 ft. lbs. (19-26 Nm). Install the oil pump retaining bolts and torque to 69-95 inch lbs. (8-11 Nm) in several steps.

8. Attach the turbocharger bracket to the block. Connect the exhaust pipe and install the exhaust pipe bracket. Install the engine undercovers, then lower the vehicle.

9. Remove the engine support tool and fill the crankcase to the proper level.

10. Connect the negative battery cable. Start the engine and inspect for leaks.

1988-89 626/MX-6

▶ See Figure 208

➡These vehicles use a gasketless oil pan.

To install:

1. Disconnect the negative battery cable.

2. Raise and safely support the front of the vehicle. Drain the engine oil.

3. Unbolt and remove the exhaust pipe and gusset plate. Remove the clutch housing under cover.

4. Remove the right-hand subframe.

5. Remove the oil pan retaining bolts and lower the oil pan. Wedge a scraper or small prying tool between the pan and the stiffener to achieve separation. Remove the oil stainer and stiffener. Discard the strainer gasket and purchase a new one.

➡Be careful not to bend the oil pan when separating it from the block.

To install:

6. Check the oil pan for cracks or other damage in the area of the bolt holes. Remove the oil pan drain plug and check the pan threads for wear and damage. Clean up the threads with a tap, as required.

7. Thoroughly clean all contact surfaces and apply a continuous bead of silicone sealant to the stiffener around the inside of the bolt holes. Raise the stiffener up onto the bottom of the block and install the retaining bolts. Torque the retaining bolts to 61-104 inch lbs. (7-12 Nm). Install a new strainer and gasket, then torque the bolts to 69-104 inch lbs. (8-12 Nm).

8. Apply silicone sealant to the oil pan contact surface in the same manner as the stiffener. Raise the oil pan up and against the stiffener, then install its retaining bolts. Torque the retaining bolts to 61-104 inch lbs. (7-12 Nm).

9. Lower the vehicle and fill the crankcase to the proper level.

10. Connect the negative battery cable. Start the engine and check for oil leaks.

1988-89 929

▶ See Figures 208 and 209

➡Some of these vehicles use a gasketless oil pan.

1. Disconnect the negative battery cable.

2. Raise and safely support the front of the vehicle.

3. Drain the engine oil. Remove the engine under cover.

4. Remove the oil pan retaining bolts. With a scraper or suitable prying tool, separate the oil pan from the block and remove it.

➡Be careful not to bend the oil pan when separating it from the block.

To install:

5. Thoroughly clean all the gasket mating or contact surfaces. Check the oil pan for cracks or other damage in the area of the bolt holes. Remove the oil pan drain plug and check the pan threads for wear and damage. Clean up the threads with a tap, as required.

6. On oil pans with a gasket, apply sealer to the joints between the front cover and block, as well as the rear main seal housing and block. On gasketless oil pans, apply a continuous bead of sealant to the oil pan flange around the inside of the bolt holes and overlap the ends.

7. Raise the oil pan onto the block and install the retaining bolts. Torque the bolts to 69-95 inch lbs. (8-11 Nm).

8. Install the engine undercover and lower the vehicle. Fill the crankcase to the proper level.

9. Connect the negative battery cable. Start the engine and check for leaks.

Oil Pump

REMOVAL & INSTALLATION

1978-80 GLC and 1979-82 626

1. Drain the crankcase and remove the oil pan, as previously described in this section.

2. Remove the nut and lockwasher, then disengage the oil pump sprocket and chain.

3. Unfasten the bolts attaching the oil pump to the block and remove the pump assembly.

To install:

4. Fit the O-ring to the outlet hole on the oil pump and align the dowel pins. Attach the oil pump to the engine block.

5. Wrap the oil pump drive chain around the sprocket, then slide the sprocket onto the shaft. Be sure to align the key on the oil pump shaft with the keyway of the pump sprocket.

6. Tighten the nut and lockwasher to secure the sprocket.

7. Install the oil pan, as previously described in this section.

8. Fill the crankcase to the proper level. Start the engine and check for leaks.

Front Wheel Drive GLC

1. Drain the crankcase and remove the oil pan, as previously described in this section.

2. Remove the oil pump mounting bolts, disengage the drive chain, and remove the pump.

➡If the sprocket must be separated after the pump has been removed, it will have to be pressed off the pump shaft using a suitable support and a press that can develop as much as 3,000 lbs. pressure. Reinstall the sprocket using 1,540-2,860 lbs. of pressure until the sprocket's outer edge is flush with the outer end of the shaft.

To install:

3. Wrap the oil pump drive chain around the sprocket, then position the oil pump to the engine block. Fasten the oil pump mounting bolts.

4. Install the oil pan, as previously described in this section.

5. Fill the crankcase to the proper level. Start the engine and check for leaks.

GLC Wagon

1. Position a suitable drain pan beneath the engine's front cover.

2. Remove the crankshaft pulley, front cover and oil slinger, as described later in this section.

3. Remove the oil pump drive sprocket retaining nut and lockwasher. Slide both oil pump drive chain sprockets and the

chain off the crankshaft and oil pump shaft. Be careful not to lose the sprocket keys.

4. Remove the oil pump cover, then withdraw the pump shaft and rotor assembly.

To install:

5. Position the oil pump shaft and rotor assembly in the engine block.

6. Attach the oil pump cover, then insert the key into the oil pump shaft.

7. Wrap the oil pump drive chain around both sprockets, then align and slide the sprockets onto the crankshaft and oil pump shaft.

8. Hand-start the oil pump drive sprocket lockwasher and retaining nut, then torque the nut to 22-25 ft. lbs. (30-34 Nm).

9. Position the oil slinger, so that its keyway is aligned with those of the crankshaft sprockets, then insert the key.

10. Install the front cover with new gaskets. (Don't forget to remove the drain pan.)

11. Install the crankshaft pulley.

1983-87 626

1. Rotate the engine so that the No. 1 cylinder is at TDC. Remove the timing belt cover and timing belt, as described later in this section.

2. Remove the retaining bolt and, using a puller, remove the lower timing belt sprocket.

3. Raise and safely support the front of the vehicle.

4. Drain the crankcase and remove the oil pan, as described earlier in this section.

5. Unfasten the bolts which secure the oil strainer's pickup tube and brace, then remove the oil strainer.

6. Remove the pump mounting bolts and pump body from the front of the engine.

➡ **The inner and outer gears may be removed and inspected after unfastening the pump cover plate.**

To install:

7. If disassembled after removal, coat a new oil seal lip with engine oil, then install the seal, taking care not to damage the lip.

8. Coat the O-ring with grease and install it over the oil hole at the top right of the pump, viewed from the rear. Coat all sealing surfaces that contact the front of the block with sealer. Keep sealant out of the oil passages.

9. Position the pump body and torque the mounting bolts to 14-19 ft. lbs. (19-26 Nm).

10. Position and fasten the oil strainer, using a new gasket.

11. Install the oil pan, as described earlier in this section.

12. Lower the vehicle, then install the timing belt sprocket.

13. Install the timing belt and timing belt cover, as described later in this section.

14. Fill the crankcase to the proper level. Start the engine and check for leaks.

323 and 1988-89 626/MX-6

1. Remove the front cover and timing belt, as described later in this section.

2. Remove the bolt at the center of the lower timing belt sprocket, then remove the sprocket and key.

3. Drain the crankcase and remove the oil pan, as described earlier in this section.

4. Unbolt and remove the oil strainer and its gasket.

5. Unfasten the bolts from the oil pump housing (lower front of the block), then remove the pump.

To install:

6. Position the oil pump and install the retaining bolts. On 323s, torque the bolts to 14-19 ft. lbs. (19-26 Nm). On 1988-89 626/MX-6s, torque the M8 (smaller) bolts to 14-19 ft. lbs. (19-26 Nm) and the M10 (larger) bolts to 27-38 ft. lbs. (37-51 Nm).

7. Position and fasten the oil strainer, using a new gasket.

8. Install the oil pan, as described earlier in this section. On 323s, torque the retaining bolts to 6-7 ft. lbs. (8-9 Nm). On 1988-89 626/MX-6s, torque the retaining bolts to 5-9 ft. lbs. (7-12 Nm).

9. Align the timing belt sprocket and keyway, then install the timing belt sprocket and key.

10. Install the timing belt and front belt cover, as described later in this section.

11. Fill the crankcase to the proper level. Start the engine and check for leaks.

1988-89 929 With Positive Displacement Gear Pump

▶ **See Figure 211**

➡ **Models which have a positive displacement gear-type oil pump are identifiable by the absence of a pressure regulator cover in front of the automatic timing belt tensioner. Please refer to the accompanying illustration.**

1. Disconnect the negative battery cable.

2. Raise and safely support the front of the vehicle.

3. Drain the engine oil. Remove the engine under cover.

4. Unfasten the oil pan retaining bolts, then remove the oil pan, as described earlier in this section.

5. Remove the oil pump and strainer assembly retaining bolts. Remove the oil pump assembly from its mounting.

6. Remove the oil pump driveshaft and O-ring.

To install:

7. Install a new O-ring on the oil pump body.

8. Insert the pump driveshaft into the engine, and manually rotate to check for smooth operation.

9. Insert the other end of the driveshaft into the oil pump, then mount the pump/strainer assembly to the engine block. Torque the oil pump retaining bolts to 6-8 ft. lbs. (8-11 Nm).

10. Install the oil pan, as described earlier in this section. Be sure to use new gaskets or RTV sealant, as required.

11. Install the engine under cover, then lower the vehicle.

12. Fill the crankcase to the proper level.

13. Connect the negative battery cable. Start the engine and check for leaks.

1989 929 With Trochoid Gear Pump

▶ **See Figure 211**

➡ **The trochoid gear-type oil pump is not used on 1988 models. All 1989 models which are equipped with this type of pump are identifiable by a pressure regulator cover in front of the automatic timing belt tensioner. Please refer to the accompanying illustration.**

1. Disconnect the negative battery cable.

2. Raise and safely support the vehicle.

3. Drain the engine oil and the cooling system.

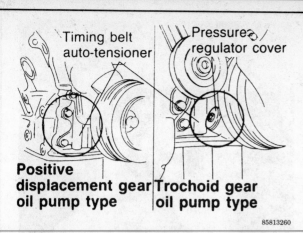

85813260

Fig. 211 The trochoid gear oil pump is identifiable by a pressure regulator cover in front of the automatic timing belt tensioner; the positive displacement gear oil pump has no such cover

4. Remove the associated pulleys and the timing belt, as described later in this section.

5. Remove the thermostat and gasket.

6. Remove the oil pan, as described earlier in this section. Remove the oil strainer and O-ring.

7. Unbolt and remove the oil pump and gasket.

To install:

8. Position the oil pump with a new gasket. Install and torque the oil pump retaining bolts to 14-19 ft. lbs. (19-26 Nm).

9. Install the oil strainer, using a new O-ring.

10. Install the oil pan, as described earlier in this section.

11. Install the thermostat with a new gasket.

12. Install the timing belt and associated pulleys, as described later in this section.

13. Lower the vehicle. Fill the crankcase and cooling systems to their proper levels.

14. Connect the negative battery cable. Start the engine and check for leaks.

Timing Chain Cover Oil Seal

REMOVAL & INSTALLATION

➡This procedure applies to engines with timing chains, on which the oil seal is located in the front cover, rather than in the oil pump.

GLC and 1979-82 626

➡The front cover oil seal can be replaced, in most cases, without removing the front cover.

1. If necessary, drain the cooling system and remove the radiator, to provide sufficient clearance. This step should not be necessary on front wheel drive GLC models.

2. Remove the drive belts.

3. Unfasten and remove the crankshaft pulley.

4. With a small prytool, carefully pry the seal out of the timing chain cover.

5. Clean the seal bore out thoroughly. No dirt or grease should be allowed to remain inside the bore, since such foreign matter will cause premature failure of the new oil seal.

To install:

6. Coat the lip of the new seal with engine oil. Using a piece of pipe or a socket slightly smaller than the bore of the oil pump (and about the diameter of the seal itself), tap a new seal into place. Position the seal so its front edge is aligned with the front edge of the timing chain cover.

7. Apply sealant to the pulley side of the bolt, then position and install the crankshaft pulley. Torque the crankshaft pulley bolt to 80-87 ft. lbs. (110-120 Nm) for the GLC, or 101-108 ft. lbs. (140-150 Nm) for the 626.

8. Install and properly tension the drive belts.

9. If applicable, install the radiator and fill the cooling system to the proper level.

Front Crankshaft Oil Seal

REMOVAL & INSTALLATION

➡This procedure applies to engines with timing belts, on which the seal is located at the front of the oil pump body instead of in the engine front (timing belt) cover.

Except GLC and 1979-82 626

▶ **See Figures 212, 213, 214, 215 and 216**

1. Remove the timing belt covers, timing belt, and timing belt crankshaft pulley, as described later in this section.

2. With a small prytool, carefully pry the seal out of the front cover. Be careful not to damage the bore of the oil pump housing with the screwdriver blade.

3. Clean the seal bore out thoroughly. No dirt or grease should be allowed to remain inside the bore, since such foreign matter will cause premature failure of the new oil seal.

To install:

4. Coat the lip of the new seal with engine oil. Using a piece of pipe or a socket slightly smaller than the bore of the oil pump (and about the diameter of the seal itself), tap a new

85813241

Fig. 212 Unfasten and remove the timing belt crankshaft pulley lockbolt

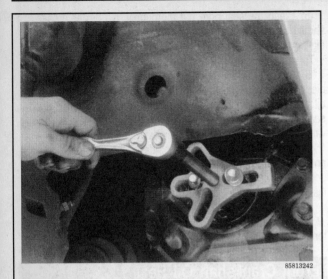

Fig. 213 If necessary, attach a puller and . . .

Fig. 214 . . . remove the timing belt crankshaft pulley

Fig. 215 Carefully pry out the oil pump body oil seal

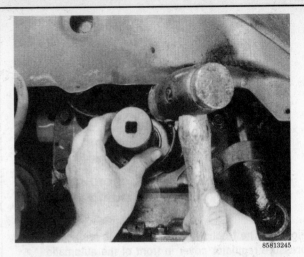

Fig. 216 After coating the lip of the new seal with oil, gently tap it into place

seal into place. Position the seal so its front edge is aligned with the front edge of the oil pump body.

5. Install the timing belt crankshaft pulley, timing belt and timing belt covers in reverse order of their removal.

Timing Chain and Cover

REMOVAL & INSTALLATION

GLC and 1979-82 626
▶ See Figures 217, 218 and 219

➡On front wheel drive GLC models, the manufacturer recommends engine removal before removing the timing chain. However, you *might* be able to remove/install the timing chain *without removing the engine*. Before performing this procedure without removing the engine, be certain that sufficient clearance exists, and be careful not to damage any components. If the engine must be removed, follow the engine removal procedure earlier in this section, then proceed to Step 9 of the following procedure.

1. Rotate the engine so that the No. 1 piston is at TDC.
2. Drain the crankcase and the cooling system.
3. Remove the radiator hoses, thermostat housing, thermostat, fan, water pump and radiator.
4. Remove all lower and side splash/skid shields. Remove the crankshaft pulley and any driven units (alternator, air pump, etc.) that will interfere with timing chain cover removal.
5. On rear wheel drive models, remove the blind cover (a small plate retained by two or three bolts that covers the chain adjuster), then install a chain adjuster guide (Part No. 49 3953 260) or equivalent clamping tool, to prevent the chain adjuster's slipper head from popping out.
6. Remove the oil pan, as described earlier in this section.
7. Remove the rocker arm cover. Unfasten the cylinder head bolts, in the proper sequence, as described earlier in this section. Remove the rocker assembly.

8. Temporarily wire the timing chain to the camshaft sprocket, as illustrated, to maintain their relationship. Then, remove the camshaft sprocket and chain from the camshaft.

➡**Do not remove the timing chain from the camshaft sprocket; if they do become separated, their reference marks will need to be aligned before installation.**

9. On GLC front wheel drive models, remove the chain tensioner (located on the upper left side of the timing chain cover).

10. Unfasten and remove the timing chain front cover.

11. If so equipped, remove the oil slinger from the crankshaft.

12. Remove the timing chain and sprocket from the crankshaft. If necessary, loosen the timing chain guide strip and remove the chain adjuster.

➡**On some engines, you must first remove an oil pump sprocket and drive chain.**

To install:

13. Inspect the slipper head of the chain adjuster, the chain guide strip and the vibration damper for wear or damage. Check the adjuster spring for loss of tension. Replace parts as necessary.

14. Install the timing chain onto the crankshaft sprocket, being careful to match the shiny link (or pair of links) on the timing chain with the timing mark on the sprocket (see the appropriate illustration). Then, align and slide the sprocket onto the crankshaft. If applicable, also attach the oil pump sprocket and drive chain, and the oil slinger. Be sure to install the shaft key.

➡**When installing the oil pump sprocket, check the chain for excessive slack and replace it, if necessary. On 1979-82 626 models, the slack should be 0.015 in. (0.38mm). Adjusting shims (between the oil pump and mounting) are available in thicknesses of 0.006 in. (0.15mm).**

15. If applicable, install the timing chain adjuster with the adjuster guide attached (except front wheel drive GLC). Make sure the adjuster spring is fully compressed.

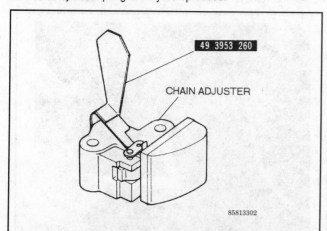

Fig. 217 Install a chain adjuster guide (Part No. 49 3953 260) or equivalent clamping tool, before removing or installing the chain adjuster — rear wheel drive GLC and 1979-82 626

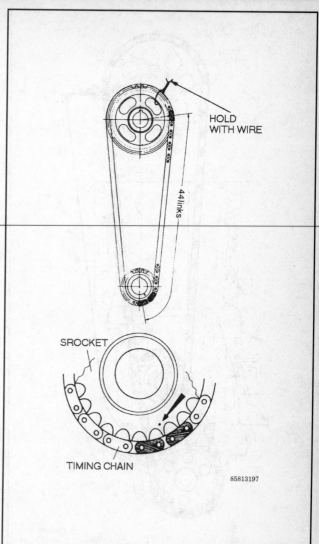

Fig. 218 Wire the camshaft sprocket and timing chain together to maintain their proper relationship — 626 shown (GLC wagon similar)

16. If previously removed, position the cylinder head on the engine block with a new gasket.

17. Install the wired sprocket and timing chain on the camshaft, being careful to install/align the shaft key. Then, remove the wire.

✳✳WARNING

If the chain comes off the sprocket, be sure to rematch the shiny mark on the timing chain with the timing mark on the sprocket. Failure to maintain this alignment can result in incorrect timing, as well as engine damage.

18. Install the rocker assembly, then torque the cylinder head bolts in sequence, as described earlier in this section.

19. Position a new timing chain cover gasket, then install the cover.

20. Adjust the timing chain tension on all but front wheel drive GLCs as follows:

a. Rotate the crankshaft slightly in its normal direction.

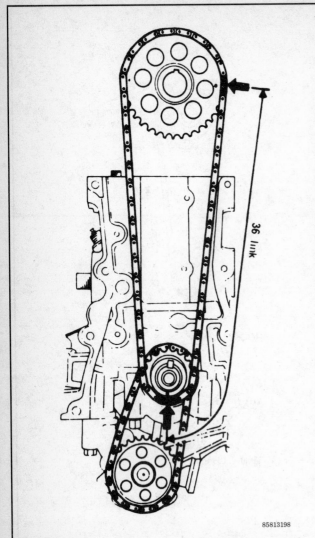

Fig. 219 Timing chain and sprocket alignment — 1.5L front wheel drive GLC. (The smaller chain and sprocket at the bottom drive the oil pump.)

b. Remove the blind plugs and aluminum washers from the two holes in the timing chain cover.

c. If necessary, loosen the guide strip attaching screws.

d. Press the top of the chain guide strip through the opening in the top right side of the timing chain cover (626s) or through the opening of the cylinder head (GLCs). Insert a screwdriver through the two holes in the timing chain cover, and tighten the guide strip attaching screws.

e. Remove the clamping tool from the tensioner. (Let the spring-loaded slipper head take up the slack in the chain).

➡The timing chain should now have the proper tension; therefore no further manual adjustment is required.

f. Install the blind plugs and aluminum washers in the two holes of the timing chain cover.

g. Install the blind cover and gasket on the chain cover.

21. On GLC front wheel drive models, reset and install the chain tensioner on the upper left side of the timing chain cover.

22. Install the rocker arm cover with a new gasket.

23. Install the oil pan with a new gasket, as described earlier in this section.

24. Complete installation in the reverse of removal.

➡If applicable, refer to the GLC's engine installation procedure, earlier in this section.

25. Fill the crankcase and cooling system to their proper levels.

Timing Belt and Covers

REMOVAL & INSTALLATION

1983-87 626 — Except Diesel

▶ See Figures 220, 221, 222, 223, 224, 225, 226, 227, 228, 229, 230 and 231

➡For access, safely support the car, then remove the right front wheel and splash shield.

1. Loosen the alternator mounting bolts and relieve belt tension, then remove the alternator belt.

2. Unfasten the attaching bolts, then remove the upper timing belt cover and gasket.

3. Unfasten the four mounting bolts and remove the front pulley from the hub on the crankshaft. Then, remove the attaching bolts and the lower timing belt cover and gasket.

4. Now, rotate the engine in its normal direction (clockwise when viewed from the passenger's side) until the camshaft pulley mark (A) aligns with the V-notch at the top of the front housing. At this point, the notch in the crankshaft pulley will align with the arrow on the front housing. Note that if the belt has jumped time, these marks will not align simultaneously. If that is true, your first step after belt removal should be align the crankshaft marks.

5. Loosen the tensioner lockbolt until it can be turned by hand. Then, remove the tensioner spring (brake pliers may be helpful).

6. Mark the direction of rotation on the belt if it may be reused and remove it. Inspect the belt and replace if it is oil

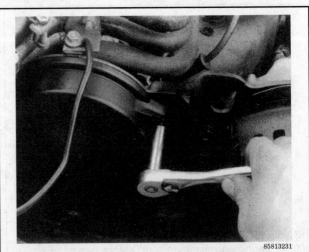

Fig. 220 Remove the bolts which fasten the upper timing belt cover . . .

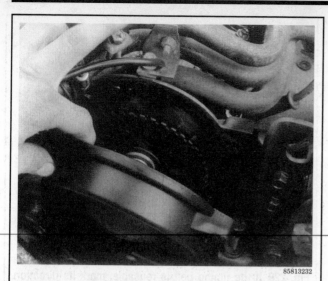

Fig. 221 . . . and remove the cover

Fig. 224 If necessary, pull outward slightly on the fender skirt to provide clearance for crankshaft pulley removal

Fig. 222 Unfasten the four mounting bolts which retain the crankshaft pulley . . .

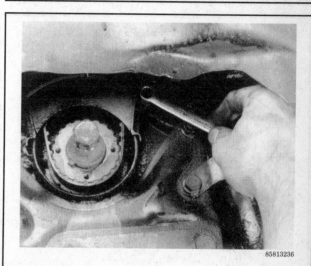

Fig. 225 Unfasten and remove the lower timing belt cover

Fig. 223 . . . and remove the pulley

Fig. 226 Align the camshaft pulley mark (A) with the V-notch at the top of the front housing

soaked, or shows excessive wear, peeling, cracking, or hardening. Inspect the tensioner for free and smooth rotation; replace if it does not turn smoothly.

To install:

7. Position the tensioner all the way toward the intake valve side.

8. Install a new belt or reinstall the old one with the arrow indicating the proper direction of rotation (that is, the arrow should point clockwise around the top pulley when viewed from the passenger side of the car). Make sure the belt teeth engage the water pump pulley and the camshaft/crankshaft pulleys, with the belt running straight from top to bottom on the right side. Then, route the belt around the tensioner pulley.

9. Install the spring to the tensioner. With a wrench on the crankshaft pulley, turn the engine in its normal direction of rotation until the crankshaft has rotated two turns and verify that the camshaft pulley returns to its former position. Torque the tensioner lockbolt to 28-38 ft. lbs. (38-51 Nm). If the belt is a used one, check deflection. Under 22 lbs. (10 kg) pressure, the belt should deflect 0.47-0.55 in. (12-14mm). You can re-

Fig. 229 If the timing belt is reusable, mark its direction of rotation before removal

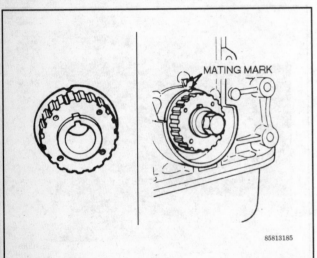

Fig. 227 Align the notch in the crankshaft pulley with the arrow on the front housing

Fig. 230 Slip the timing belt off the crankshaft pulley and remove from above

Fig. 228 Use a wrench to loosen the tensioner lockbolt

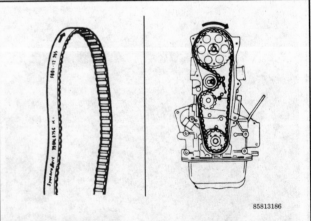

Fig. 231 Install the timing belt around the camshaft, crankshaft, and water pump pulleys, then inside the tensioner pulley. If present, be sure the directional arrow on the belt points in the proper direction

peat this step to reseat and retension the belt, then recheck deflection. If a used belt won't pass the test, replace it.

10. Install the lower timing belt cover, using a new gasket if necessary. Torque the bolts to 5-7 ft. lbs. (7-9 Nm). Do the same with the upper cover.

11. Install the front pulley and alternator belt. Be sure to properly tension the belt.

12. Install the splash shield and right front wheel, then lower the car.

626 Diesel

FRONT TIMING BELT

▶ **See Figures 232 and 233**

This procedure includes camshaft pulley (sprocket) removal and timing belt crankshaft pulley (sprocket) removal, even though belt removal/installation is possible without those steps. If you choose not to remove the camshaft pulley and timing belt crankshaft pulley, omit Steps 9-13.

➡**To perform this procedure, you will need a 6mm hexagonal (Allen type) socket wrench. If you choose to remove the camshaft pulley, you will also need a puller with bolts that screw into the threaded holes in the pulley.**

1. Disconnect the negative battery cable.
2. Remove the drive belts and right side splash shield. Remove the cylinder head cover.
3. Using a 6mm hex (Allen type) wrench, unfasten the bolts and remove the crankshaft pulley.
4. Remove the right and left timing belt covers along with their gaskets.
5. Turn the crankshaft via the bolt at its center until the timing marks on the camshaft pulley and front seal plate align.
6. Loosen the lockbolt on the belt tensioner, push the tensioner to the left (so as to tighten the spring and loosen the belt), then hold it there as you retighten the lockbolt. Now, unbolt and remove the torque stop from in front of the timing belt.
7. If you plan on reusing the belt, mark the direction of rotation, then remove the belt.

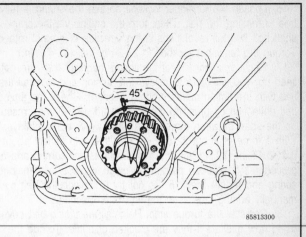

Fig. 233 After removing the timing belt, rotate the crankshaft 45° clockwise to guard against piston or valve damage

8. Turn the crankshaft 45 degrees to the right of the timing mark on the front of the oil pump housing, as shown. (This will prevent damaging the pistons and valves.)

9. Hold the camshaft with an open-end wrench installed on the flats located just behind the center bearing. Loosen the pulley lockbolt, but do not remove it. Then, install a puller by screwing its two outer bolts into the threaded holes in the pulley. When these two bolts are threaded in all the way, tighten the bolt at the center of the puller, so that its inner end rests against the lockbolt. Continue tightening the center bolt until it frees the pulley from the camshaft. Be sure to retain the key and examine it; if the key is worn or scored, dress it with a fine jeweler's file or a piece of emery cloth. If worn to excess, replace the key.

10. If the timing belt crankshaft pulley must be removed, use a tire iron or suitable flywheel locking device to hold the flywheel in place as you remove the lockbolt. The pulley slides right off the crankshaft. Be sure to retain both the washer and key. Inspect the key as described above.

11. Inspect all parts. Check the belt for peeling and cracks or for excessively worn/broken teeth. Check the tensioner for rough rotation. Replace worn or damaged parts, as necessary.

To install:

12. Install the timing belt crankshaft pulley with its key, the spacer, and the bolt. Restrain the flywheel and torque the bolt to 116-123 ft. lbs. (157-167 Nm).

13. Install the camshaft pulley and lockbolt. Hold the camshaft by the flats with an open-end wrench as you torque the bolt to 41-48 ft. lbs. (56-65 Nm).

14. Realign the camshaft pulley and front seal plate timing marks (located at about 2 o'clock). Turn the crankshaft backward (counterclockwise) until the timing mark on the oil pump housing and the notch on the rear of the timing belt crankshaft pulley again align.

15. Install the timing belt (in the same direction of rotation, if it is being reused). The teeth should engage, the right side should be straight (without play), and the timing marks should align for both the camshaft and crankshaft pulleys. Make sure to route the belt over the tensioner and around the water pump pulley.

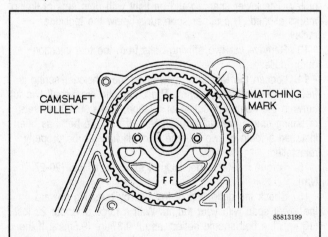

Fig. 232 Align the mark on the camshaft pulley with the mark on the front seal plate

16. Loosen the tensioner lockbolt so that the spring is fully free to tension the belt. Then, turn the engine via the crankshaft bolt two full revolutions in the direction of normal rotation. Torque the tensioner lockbolt to 23-34 ft. lbs. (31-46 Nm).

17. Recheck alignment of the timing marks (if they are not lined up, you will have to relieve the tension and reinstall the belt with the timing marks properly aligned). Check the timing belt deflection by pressing the belt inward with thumb pressure on the span between the camshaft and water pump pulleys. With a force of about 22 lbs. (10 kg), it should deflect about 0.41-0.47 in. (10.5-12mm). If the tension is not correct and all procedures have been properly followed, replace the tensioner spring and repeat Step 16. Do not try to tension the belt by manually adding tension to the tensioner mechanism!

18. Reinstall the torque stop. Reinstall the timing belt covers, using new gaskets if they are cracked or brittle. Torque the cover bolts to 5-7 ft. lbs. (7-9 Nm).

19. Install the crankshaft pulley, being careful to align its dowel pin. Using a hexagonal socket, torque the bolts to 17-24 ft. lbs. (23-33 Nm).

20. Install the cylinder head cover and right side splash shield.

21. Install and properly tension the drive belts. Connect the negative battery cable.

REAR TIMING BELT

▶ See Figure 234

This procedure includes camshaft pulley (sprocket) removal and fuel injection pump pulley (sprocket) removal, even though belt removal/installation is possible without those steps. If you choose not to remove the camshaft pulley and fuel injection pump pulley, omit Steps 7-11.

➡️**If you choose to remove the camshaft pulley and the fuel injection pump pulley, you will also need a puller and two bolts M8 x 32mm x 45mm.**

1. Disconnect the negative battery cable.
2. Remove the rear timing belt cover.
3. Remove the cylinder head cover and gasket.
4. Turn the crankshaft until the rear camshaft pulley and rear seal plate timing marks align.

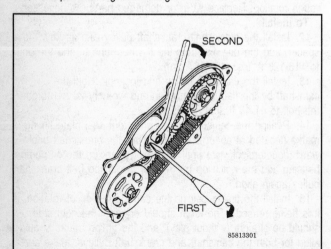

SECOND

FIRST

85813301

Fig. 234 To remove tension from the rear timing belt, use a small prytool to lift the tensioner away from the belt, then tighten the locknut

5. Loosen the locknut for the belt tensioner. Using a small prytool as shown in the illustration, turn the tensioner to remove all tension from the belt. Tighten the tensioner locknut while holding the tensioner in the fully released position.

6. If you plan on reusing the belt, be sure to mark it for reinstallation in the same position. Then, remove the belt.

7. Hold the camshaft with an open-end wrench installed on the flats located just behind the center bearing. Loosen the pulley lockbolt, but do not remove it. Then, install a puller by screwing its two outer bolts into the threaded holes in the pulley. When these two bolts are threaded in all the way, tighten the bolt at the center of the puller, so that its inner end rests against the lockbolt. Continue tightening the center bolt until it frees the pulley from the camshaft. Be sure to retain the key and examine it; if the key is worn or scored, dress it with a fine jeweler's file or a piece of emery cloth. If worn to excess, replace the key.

8. Install the two M8 x 32mm x 45mm bolts through the two holes in the injection pump drive pulley and into the rear seal plate. (These will keep the pulley from turning.) Unfasten the pulley locknut, then use a puller to remove the pulley from the injection pump driveshaft.

9. Inspect all parts. Check the belt for peeling and cracks or for excessively worn/broken teeth. Check the tensioner for rough rotation. Replace worn or damaged parts, as necessary.

   To install:

10. Install the fuel injection pump pulley onto the pump shaft with the key. If necessary, rotate the pulley slightly to align the timing marks. Install the bolts which prevent it from rotating. Leave these bolts in position as you complete the procedure. Then install the washer and locknut and torque it to 43-51 ft. lbs. (58-69 Nm).

11. Install the camshaft pulley and lockbolt. Hold the camshaft by the flats with an open-end wrench as you torque the bolt to 41-48 ft. lbs. (56-65 Nm). Then, make sure the mark on the camshaft pulley is still aligned with the mark on the rear seal plate.

12. Install the timing belt (in the proper direction of rotation, if it is being reused). Engage it with the teeth of the injection pump pulley first, and then with the teeth of the camshaft pulley. The lower span should be tight with both sets of timing marks aligned. The upper span runs below the tensioner pulley.

13. Remove the two affixing bolts from the fuel injection pump pulley.

14. Loosen the tensioner locknut so the tensioner spring is free to position the tensioner. Then, turn the crankshaft two full turns in the normal direction of rotation. Make sure both sets of timing marks are still in alignment. If not, the belt has been installed a tooth or two off-time and will have to be properly reinstalled.

15. Torque the tensioner locknut to 15-20 ft. lbs. (20-27 Nm).

16. Check the deflection of the belt by pressing upward on the lower span with your thumb. With a force of about 22 lbs. (10 kg), the belt should deflect about 0.37 in. (9.5mm). If the tension is not correct and all procedures have been properly followed, replace the tensioner spring and repeat Step 14. Do not try to tension the belt by manually adding tension to the tensioner mechanism!

17. Install the rear timing belt cover and the cylinder head cover with a new gasket.

18. Reconnect the negative battery cable.

1988-89 626/MX-6

▶ **See Figures 235, 236, 237 and 238**

1. Disconnect the negative battery cable.
2. Tag and disconnect the spark plug wires, then remove the spark plugs (for easier crankshaft rotation).
3. Remove the engine side cover and the accessory drive belts.
4. Unbolt the crankshaft pulley, then remove the upper and lower timing belt covers along with their gaskets. Remove the crankshaft pulley baffle plate and note how it is installed. The curved side should be facing out.
5. Engage the timing belt pulley's lockbolt with an appropriate size metric socket and breaker bar, then turn the crankshaft in its normal direction of rotation until the "arrowed" 1 mark on the camshaft is aligned with the mark on top of the front housing (see illustration). Unbolt and remove the tensioner, then disconnect the tensioner spring from its mount.

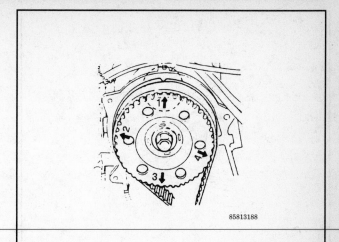

85813188

Fig. 236 Camshaft pulley and front housing timing mark alignment — 1988-89 626 and MX-6

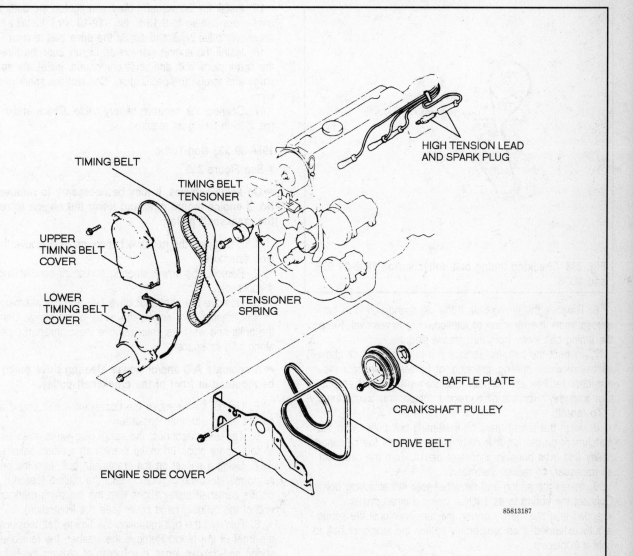

TIMING BELT

TIMING BELT TENSIONER

UPPER TIMING BELT COVER

LOWER TIMING BELT COVER

TENSIONER SPRING

HIGH TENSION LEAD AND SPARK PLUG

BAFFLE PLATE

CRANKSHAFT PULLEY

DRIVE BELT

ENGINE SIDE COVER

85813187

Fig. 235 Timing belt components — 1988-89 626 and MX-6

Fig. 237 Timing belt pulley and front housing timing mark alignment — 1988-89 626 and MX-6

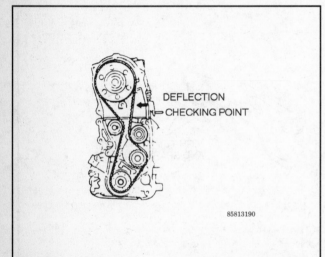

Fig. 238 Checking timing belt deflection on 1988-89 626 and MX-6

6. Remove the timing belt. If the old timing belt is to be reused, mark the direction of rotation, prior to removal. Keep the timing belt away from dirt, grease and oil.

7. Inspect the belt and replace if it is oil soaked, or shows excessive wear, peeling, cracking, or hardening. Inspect the tensioner for free and smooth rotation; replace if it does not turn smoothly. Replace all damaged components as necessary.

To install:

8. Align the timing mark on the timing belt pulley with the matchmark on the lower front housing. Recheck the camshaft pulley and front housing alignment marks. Turn the camshaft as necessary to realign the marks.

9. Install the spring and tensioner with the attaching bolt. Connect the spring to its anchor. Using a small prybar wrapped in a rag, gently pry on the tensioner until the spring is fully extended, then temporarily tighten the tensioner bolt to hold it in place.

10. Install the timing belt. (A used belt should be installed in the original direction of rotation as indicated by the rotational arrow marked on the belt prior to removal.) Make sure that

there is no looseness on the water pump pulley and idler pulley side of the belt.

11. Loosen the tensioner lockbolt and turn the crankshaft twice in the direction of engine rotation to align the timing marks on the camshaft and crankshaft pulleys.

12. Make sure that all timing marks are aligned correctly. If not, remove the timing belt tensioner and timing belt, then repeat Steps 8-11 until all the timing marks are correctly aligned.

13. Torque the tensioner lockbolt to 27-38 ft. lbs. (37-51 Nm). Apply 22 lbs. (10 kg) of pressure to the belt and check the timing belt deflection. Deflection should be 0.35-0.39 in. (9-10mm) for a used belt, or 0.30-0.33 in. (8-9mm) for a new belt . If the deflection is not correct, loosen the tensioner lockbolt and adjust the tension. Repeat Steps 11-13 to adjust the tension. If it still cannot be brought to specification, replace the tensioner spring.

14. Install the baffle plate so that the curved side faces outward. Install the upper and lower timing belt covers, using new gaskets if necessary.

15. Install the crankshaft pulley and tighten the bolts in a criss-cross pattern to 9-13 ft. lbs. (12-18 Nm). Install all the accessory drive belts and adjust the drive belt tension.

16. Install the engine side cover. Lightly coat the threads of the spark plugs with anti-seize compound. Install the spark plugs and torque to specification. Connect the spark plug wires.

17. Connect the negative battery cable. Check and/or adjust the ignition timing as required.

1986-89 323 Non-Turbo

▶ **See Figure 239**

➡**On some vehicles, it may be necessary to remove the No. 3 engine mount nuts and lower the engine to remove the crankshaft pulley.**

1. Disconnect the negative battery cable. Remove the engine side cover.

2. Remove the power steering and/or air conditioning belt, if applicable.

3. Remove the alternator drive belt and the alternator.

4. Unfasten and remove the water pump pulley. Unfasten the bolts and washers, then remove the crankshaft pulley along with its spacer.

➡**A separate A/C and/or power steering drive pulley may be mounted in front of the crankshaft pulley.**

5. Unbolt, then remove the upper and lower timing belt covers along with their gaskets.

6. Tag and disconnect the spark plug wires, then remove all four spark plugs (to make crankshaft rotation easier).

7. Using a socket on the crankshaft bolt, turn the engine in its normal direction of rotation until the trailing (second) mark on the camshaft pulley aligns with the matching mark on the end of the cylinder head cover (see the illustration).

8. Remove the bolt mounting the timing belt tensioner to the front of the block. Remove the washer, the tensioner spring and the tensioner. If you plan of reusing the belt, be sure to mark the direction of rotation, then remove the timing belt.

9. Inspect the belt and replace if it is oil soaked, or if it shows excessive wear, peeling, cracking, or hardening. Inspect

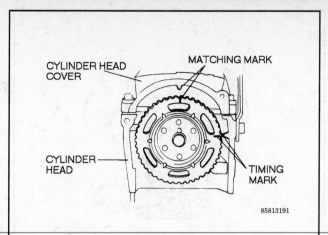

Fig. 239 Align the marks as shown before removing/installing the timing belt — 1986-89 323 nonturbo

the tensioner for free and smooth rotation; replace if it does not turn smoothly. Replace all damaged components as necessary.

To install:

10. Position the tensioner on the block, then install the bolt and washer, just starting the threads. Connect the spring, then slide the tensioner as far as it will go to the left (away from tensioning the belt), so that spring tension is maximized. Tighten the bolt enough to hold the tensioner in this position.

11. Check to make sure that the marks on the camshaft pulley and cylinder head cover are still aligned. Also, check that the marks on the front of the block and the timing belt pulley are still aligned; realign the marks, if necessary.

12. Install the timing belt. (If the belt is being reused, make sure that the directional arrow is facing in the normal direction of rotation.) The belt should be installed so that the pulleys and teeth mesh, the right side is slightly tight, and the timing marks remain aligned.

13. Loosen the tensioner lockbolt. Turn the crankshaft two full revolutions in the normal direction of engine rotation (clockwise), so that the timing marks again align. If the marks align, proceed to Step 14. If they do not align, reshift the tensioner away from tensioning the belt and lock it there with the bolt. Remesh the teeth on the belt so the timing marks align and the right side of the belt is straight, then repeat this step.

14. Torque the tensioner lockbolt to 14-19 ft. lbs. (19-26 Nm). Place a ruler near the right side of the belt at the center of the span. Depress the belt with a thumb and measure the deflection while applying 22 lbs. (10 kg) pressure. The belt should deflect 0.35-0.39 in. (9-10mm) on 1986 models, 0.35-0.51 in. (9-13mm) on 1987 models, or 0.47-0.51 in. (12-13mm) on 1988-89 models. If the tension is correct, proceed to Step 15. If the tension is incorrect, do not try to adjust the belt by hand. Instead, fix any binding in the mechanism, if present; otherwise, replace the tensioning spring and repeat Steps 12-14.

15. Install the timing belt covers, using new gaskets if necessary. Torque the retaining bolts to 69-95 inch lbs. (8-11 Nm).

16. Install the spark plugs, torquing to 11-17 ft. lbs. (15-23 Nm), and reconnect the plug wires.

17. Install the baffle plate along with the crankshaft pulley and spacer. (Be sure to also install the A/C and/or power steering drive pulley, if applicable.) Torque the pulley bolts to 9-13 ft. lbs. (12-18 Nm).

➡**Be sure to raise the engine and fasten the No. 3 engine mount bracket, if previously moved.**

18. Install and tension the drive belts, then install the engine side cover.

19. Connect the negative battery cable.

1988-89 323 Turbo

▶ **See Figure 240**

1. Disconnect the negative battery cable. Remove the engine side cover.

2. Remove the required accessory drive belts, then remove the water pump pulley and crankshaft pulley. (An A/C and/or power steering drive pulley may also be attached to the crankshaft pulley.)

➡**Support the engine with a suitable hoist and remove the No. 3 engine mount installation bolts, then lower the engine in order to remove the air conditioning and/or power steering drive pulley and the crankshaft pulley.**

3. Tag and disconnect the spark plug wires, then remove all four spark plugs (to make crankshaft rotation easier).

4. Rotate the crankshaft so that the No. 1 piston is at TDC.

5. Remove the timing cover assembly retaining bolts. Remove the upper, middle and lower timing covers and gaskets from their mountings.

6. Remove the baffle plate. Remove the timing belt tensioner and spring, then remove the timing belt. (If the old belt is being reused, first mark its direction of rotation.)

7. Inspect all parts. Check the belt for peeling and cracks or for excessively worn/broken teeth. Check the tensioner for rough rotation.

To install:

8. Be sure that the timing mark on the timing belt pulley is aligned with the mark on the engine. Also, be sure that the camshaft pulleys are properly aligned as shown in the timing mark illustration. (Note that the **I** mark on the intake side

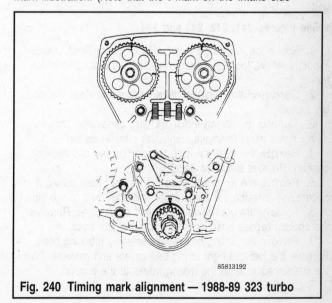

Fig. 240 Timing mark alignment — 1988-89 323 turbo

camshaft pulley should be at the top. The **E** mark on the exhaust side camshaft pulley should also be at the top.)

9. Install the spring and tensioner with the attaching bolt. Move the tensioner to the left until the spring is fully extended, then temporarily tighten the tensioner bolt to hold it in place.

10. Install the timing belt by keeping as much tension on the right side of the belt as possible. Used belts must be installed in their original direction of rotation.

11. Turn the crankshaft twice in the normal direction of rotation and make sure that all the timing marks are aligned (see illustration). Loosen the tensioner lockbolt and apply tension to the belt.

12. Torque the tensioner lockbolt to 27-38 ft. lbs. (37-51 Nm), then turn the crankshaft twice in the normal direction of rotation to ensure that all the timing marks are still correctly aligned.

13. Measure the belt tension by applying 22 lbs. (10 kg) of pressure between the camshaft pulleys. The deflection should be 0.33-0.45 in. (8.5-11.5mm) between the pulleys for both new and used timing belts.

14. If the timing belt tension is not within specifications, repeat Steps 11-13 or replace the tensioner spring.

15. Install the lower, middle and upper timing belt covers, using new gaskets if necessary.

16. Lightly coat the threads of the spark plugs with a suitable anti-seize compound and torque the plugs to 11-17 ft. lbs. (15-23 Nm). Reconnect the plug wires.

17. Position the baffle plate, making sure that the curved surface faces outward, then install the crankshaft pulley. (Be sure to also install the A/C and/or power steering drive pulley, if applicable.) Torque the pulley bolts to 9-13 ft. lbs. (12-17 Nm).

18. Install the water pump pulley and torque its mounting bolts to 6-8 ft. lbs. (8-11 Nm).

19. Raise the vehicle and install the No. 3 engine mount bracket. Torque the bolts to 44-63 ft. lbs. (60-85 Nm). Remove the lifting equipment, then install and properly tension the drive belts.

20. Install the engine side cover and connect the negative battery cable. Check and/or adjust the ignition timing, as required.

929

▶ See Figures 241, 242, 243 and 244

1. Rotate the engine so that the No. 1 piston is at TDC. Properly relieve the fuel system pressure, as described in Section 5.

2. Disconnect the negative battery cable and drain the cooling system.

3. Tag and disconnect the spark plug wires, then remove all six spark plugs (to make crankshaft rotation easier).

4. Remove the fresh air duct, the cooling fan and radiator cowling. Remove the drive belts.

5. Remove the air conditioning compressor idler pulley. If necessary, unfasten the compressor and position it to the side.

6. Remove the crankshaft pulley and baffle plate. Remove the coolant bypass hose and the upper radiator hose.

7. Remove the timing belt cover assembly retaining bolts. Remove the left and right timing belt covers and gaskets. Turn the crankshaft to align the mating marks of the pulleys.

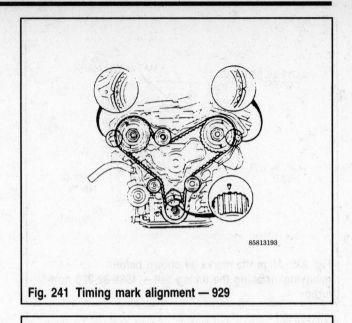

Fig. 241 Timing mark alignment — 929

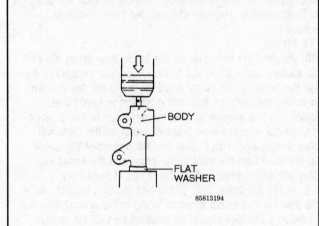

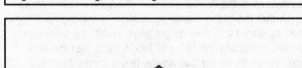

Fig. 242 Loading the timing belt auto tensioner — 929

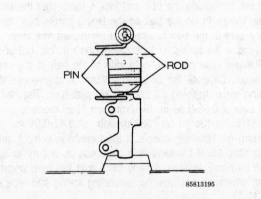

Fig. 243 Once the tensioner is loaded, use an "L" shaped pin or a small Allen wrench to hold it in place

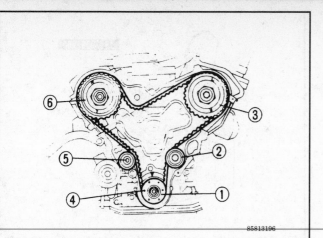

Fig. 244 Install the timing belt onto the pulleys in the order shown

8. Remove the upper idler pulley. Remove the timing belt. If reusing the belt, be sure to mark the direction of rotation. Remove the timing belt auto tensioner.

To install:

9. Reload the timing belt tensioner as follows:

a. Place a flat washer on the bottom of the tensioner body to prevent damage to the body and position the unit on an arbor press.

b. Press the rod into the tensioner body. Do not use more than 2,000 lbs of pressure.

c. Once the rod is fully inserted into the body, insert a suitable "L" shaped pin or a small Allen wrench through the body and the rod to hold the rod in place.

d. Remove the unit from the press.

10. Install the tensioner onto the block and torque the mounting bolt to 14-19 ft. lbs. (19-26 Nm).

➡**Leave the pin in place, it will be removed later.**

11. Make sure that all the timing marks are aligned properly. With the upper idler pulley removed, wrap the timing belt around each pulley in the order shown in the illustration. Install the upper idler pulley and torque the mounting bolt to 27-38 ft. lbs. (37-51 Nm). Rotate the crankshaft twice in the normal direction of rotation to align all the timing marks.

12. Make sure all the marks are aligned correctly. If not, repeat Step 11.

13. Remove the pin or wrench from the tensioner. Again turn the crankshaft twice in the normal direction of rotation, and make sure that all the timing marks are aligned properly.

14. Check the timing belt deflection by applying 22 lbs. (10 kg) of force midway between the right-side camshaft pulley and the lower idler pulley. If the deflection is not 0.20-0.28 in. (5-7mm), repeat the adjustment procedure.

➡**Excessive belt deflection is caused by auto tensioner failure or an excessively stretched timing belt.**

15. Install the left and right timing belt covers, using new gaskets if necessary.

16. Connect the coolant bypass hose and the upper radiator hose to their respective fittings.

17. Install the crankshaft pulley and baffle plate. Torque the retaining bolts to 7-11 ft. lbs. (10-15 Nm).

18. Reposition and fasten the air conditioner compressor, if necessary. Install the air conditioning compressor idler pulley.

19. Install and properly tension the drive belts.

20. Install the cooling fan, radiator cowling and fresh air duct.

21. Lightly coat the threads of the spark plugs with a suitable anti-seize compound and torque the plugs to 11-17 ft. lbs. (15-23 Nm). Reconnect the plug wires.

22. Fill the cooling system to the proper level.

23. Connect the negative battery cable. Check and adjust the ignition timing, if necessary.

Camshaft Sprocket (Pulley)

REMOVAL & INSTALLATION

323 Non-Turbo and 1983-87 626 — Except Diesel

▶ **See Figure 245**

1. Remove the timing belt, as previously described.

2. On the 1.6L engine, remove the cylinder head cover.

3. In order to hold the camshaft and pulley stationary while the lockbolt is turned, on the 1.6L engine, install an open-end wrench on the flats of the camshaft directly in front of the front bearing. On the 2.0L engine, insert a socket wrench with an extension through one of the holes in the camshaft sprocket and onto the top bolt for the front seal plate. (Do not turn this bolt; the wrench is simply to provide resistance which prevents the pulley from turning.)

4. Unfasten the lockbolt, then remove the pulley.

To install:

5. Properly position the pulley on the end of the camshaft. On the 1.6L engine, align the dowel pin and keyway, so that the pulley's matching mark points straight up; the timing marks on the camshaft pulley and cylinder head should also align. On the 2.0L engine, mark "A" on the camshaft pulley should be at the top, aligned with the mating mark on the front housing.

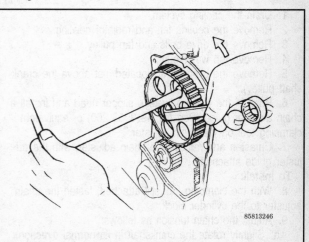

Fig. 245 Hold a socket wrench and extension against the front housing bolt to keep the camshaft pulley from turning — 1983-87 626 (except diesel)

6. Torque the lockbolt to 36-45 ft. lbs. (49-61 Nm) on the 1.6L engine, or 35-48 ft. lbs. (47-65 Nm) on the 2.0L engine.

7. On the 1.6L engine, install the cylinder head cover with a new gasket.

8. Install the timing belt, as previously described.

1988-89 323 Turbo

▶ See Figure 240

1. Remove the timing belt covers and timing belt, as previously described.

2. Remove the cylinder head cover.

3. Engage the camshaft journal that is closest to the seal plate with an adjustable wrench to hold it stationary. Using a box wrench, loosen the camshaft pulley bolt. Remove the bolt and washer, then slide the camshaft pulley from the camshaft. (The other camshaft pulley is removed in exactly the same manner.)

To install:

4. Properly position the camshaft pulley on the end of the camshaft. Install the exhaust side camshaft pulley so that the **E** mark stamped on its face is aligned with the timing mark at the top of the seal plate. Similarly, install the intake side camshaft pulley so that the **I** mark stamped on its face is aligned with the timing mark at the top of the seal plate.

5. Insert and hand-start the pulley bolts and washers.

6. Hold the camshaft stationary, as described in Step 3, while torquing the bolt to 36-45 ft. lbs. (49-61 Nm). Repeat the torquing procedure for the other camshaft pulley.

7. Install the cylinder head cover with new gaskets and bolt seals.

8. Install the timing belt and timing belt covers, as previously described.

Timing Chain Tensioner (Adjuster)

REMOVAL, INSTALLATION AND ADJUSTMENT

Rear Wheel Drive GLC and 1979-82 626

▶ See Figure 246

1. Drain the cooling system.

2. Remove the cooling fan and radiator cowling.

3. Remove the drive belts and fan pulley.

4. Remove the water pump.

5. Remove the blind cover (located just above the crankshaft pulley).

6. Push in the chain adjuster's slipper head and install a chain adjuster guide (Part No. 49 3953 260) or equivalent clamping tool on the chain adjuster.

7. Unfasten and remove the chain adjuster, with the adjuster guide attached.

To install:

8. With the clamping tool still attached, fasten the chain adjuster to the cylinder block.

9. Adjust the chain tension as follows:

   a. Slightly rotate the crankshaft in its normal direction.

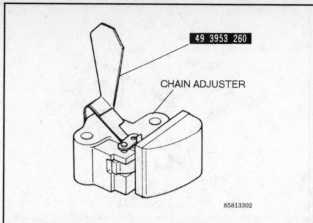

49 3953 260

CHAIN ADJUSTER

85813302

Fig. 246 Install a chain adjuster guide (Part No. 49 3953 260) or equivalent clamping tool, before removing or installing the chain adjuster — rear wheel drive GLC and 1979-82 626

   b. Remove the two blind plugs and aluminum washers from the timing chain cover.

   c. Loosen the guide strip attaching screws.

   d. Press the top of the chain guide strip through the opening in the top right side of the timing chain cover (626s) or through the opening of the cylinder head (GLCs). Insert a screwdriver through the two holes in the timing chain cover, and tighten the guide strip attaching screws.

➡ **On GLCs, you must first remove the cylinder head cover to access the top of the chain guide strip.**

   e. Remove the clamping tool from the tensioner. (Let the spring-loaded slipper head take up the slack in the chain).

   f. Install the blind plugs and aluminum washers.

   g. Install the blind cover and gasket.

   h. If applicable, install the cylinder head cover with a new gasket.

10. Install the water pump with a new gasket.

11. Install the fan pulley and drive belts. Properly tension the belts.

12. Install the cooling fan and radiator cowling.

13. Fill the cooling system to the proper level.

Front Wheel Drive GLC

▶ See Figure 247

The chain tensioner is located on the left upper side of the timing chain cover; it is operated by a spring and hydraulic pressure. The tensioner has a one-way locking system and an automatic release device. After assembly, it will automatically adjust when the engine is rotated one or two times. No disassembly of the tensioner is required.

1. The tensioner is retained by two bolts. Remove the bolts and the tensioner.

2. Check the number of teeth showing on the sleeve of the tensioner. If thirteen or more notches are showing, the timing chain is stretched and must be replaced.

To install:

3. Push the sleeve back into the body and lock it with the swivel catch on the tensioner body.

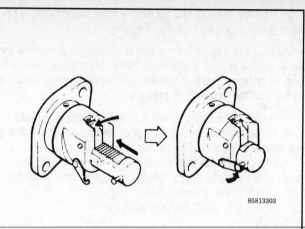

Fig. 247 Resetting the timing chain tensioner — front wheel drive GLC

4. Position and fasten the tensioner onto the timing chain cover.

➡ **After installation, the catch is released by the action of the timing chain when the engine is rotated one-to-two revolutions. The sleeve projects automatically, providing proper chain adjustment.**

Timing Belt Tensioner

REMOVAL & INSTALLATION

1983-87 626

▶ **See Figure 248**

1. Loosen the alternator mounting bolts, release the belt tension and remove the alternator belt.

2. Unfasten the attaching bolts, then remove the upper timing belt cover and gasket. Rotate the engine in the normal direction of rotation until the camshaft pulley mark aligns with the V-notch at the top of the front housing. The notch in the crankshaft pulley will now be aligned with the arrow on the front housing, unless the belt has jumped time.

3. With brake pliers or another suitable tool, unhook the tensioning spring. Now, unfasten the bolt and remove the tensioner.

4. Inspect the tensioner for bearing wear. It should rotate freely and smoothly. If not, replace it.

To install:

5. Make sure the belt remains engaged at all three pulleys and that the crankshaft and camshaft pulleys are properly timed. Locate the tensioner on its swivel pin with the slot (through which the mounting bolt passes) centered over the bolt hole. Install the bolt, but do not tighten it.

6. Connect the tensioner spring. With a wrench on the crankshaft pulley, turn the engine in the normal direction of rotation (clockwise) exactly two full turns until the timing marks are again aligned. Torque the lockbolt to 28-38 ft. lbs. (38-51 Nm).

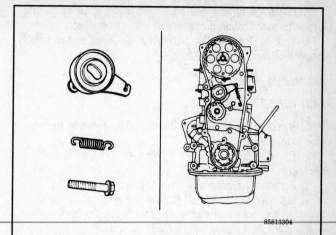

Fig. 248 The timing belt tensioner, tensioner spring and bolt are shown disassembled at the left, and in their installed position at the right

7. Install the timing belt cover, using a new gasket if necessary.

8. Install and properly tension the alternator belt.

1988-89 626/MX-6

1. Disconnect the negative battery cable.

2. Tag and disconnect the spark plug wires, then remove the spark plugs.

3. Remove the engine side cover and the accessory drive belts.

4. Unfasten the crankshaft pulley, then remove the upper and lower timing belt covers and gaskets. Remove the crankshaft pulley baffle plate and make a note of how it is installed. The curved side should be facing out.

5. Engage the crankshaft pulley bolt with the appropriate size metric socket and a breaker bar, then turn the crankshaft in the normal direction of rotation until the "arrowed" **1** mark on the camshaft pulley is aligned with the mark on top of the front housing.

6. Unbolt and remove the tensioner, then disconnect the tensioner spring from its mount.

7. Inspect the tensioner for free and smooth rotation; replace if it does not turn smoothly.

To install:

8. Connect the spring to the tensioner, then install the spring and tensioner with the attaching bolt. Connect the spring to its anchor. Using a small prybar wrapped in a rag, gently pry on the tensioner until the spring is fully extended, then temporarily tighten the tensioner bolt to hold it in place.

9. Torque the tensioner lockbolt to 27-38 ft. lbs. (37-51 Nm). Apply 22 lbs. (10 kg) of pressure to the belt and check the timing belt deflection. Deflection for a used belt is 0.35-0.39 in. (9-10mm) and for a new belt is 0.31-0.35 in. (8-9mm). If the deflection is not correct, loosen the tensioner lockbolt and adjust the tension as required.

10. Install the baffle plate so that the curved side faces outward. Install the upper and lower timing belt covers, using new gaskets if necessary.

11. Install the crankshaft pulley and tighten the pulley screws in a criss-cross pattern to 9-13 ft. lbs. (12-18 Nm). Install all the accessory drive belts and adjust the drive belt tension.

12. Install the engine side cover. Install the spark plugs and torque to specification. Connect the spark plug wires.

13. Connect the negative battery cable. Check and/or adjust the ignition timing as required.

323 Models

NON-TURBO

1. Disconnect the negative battery cable. Remove the engine side cover.

2. Remove the power steering and air conditioning belts, if applicable.

3. Remove the alternator drive belt and the alternator.

4. Unfasten the bolts and remove the water pump pulley. Unfasten the bolts and washers, then remove the front portion of the crankshaft pulley together with its spacer.

5. Tag and disconnect the spark plug wires, then remove all four spark plugs (to make crankshaft rotation easier).

6. Unfasten and remove both the upper and lower timing belt covers along with their gaskets.

7. Remove the bolt mounting the timing belt tensioner to the front of the block. Remove the washer, the tensioner spring and the tensioner. If you plan on reusing the belt, be sure to mark the direction of rotation before removal.

8. Inspect all parts. Check the tensioner for rough rotation. Check the condition of the tensioner spring and replace as necessary.

To install:

9. Position the tensioner on the block, then install the bolt and washer, just starting the threads. Connect the spring and slide the tensioner as far as it will go to the left (away from tensioning the belt), so that spring tension is maximized. Tighten the bolt enough to hold the tensioner in this position.

10. Torque the tensioner lockbolt to 14-19 ft. lbs. (19-26 Nm). Place a ruler near the right side of the belt at the center of the span. Depress the belt with a thumb (to produce approximately 22 lbs. or 10 kg pressure) and measure deflection. The belt should deflect 0.35-0.39 in. (9-10mm) on 1986 models, 0.35-0.51 in. (9-13mm) on 1987 models, or 0.47-0.51 in. (12-13mm) on 1988-89 models. If tension is incorrect, do not try to tension the belt by hand. Instead, fix any binding in the mechanism, if necessary; otherwise, replace the tensioning spring.

11. Install the timing belt covers, using new gaskets if necessary. Torque the bolts to 69-95 inch lbs. (8-11 Nm).

12. Install the spark plugs, torquing to 11-17 ft. lbs. (15-23 Nm), then connect the plug wires.

13. Install the baffle plate along with the crankshaft pulley and washer, torquing the pulley bolts to 11-13 ft. lbs. (15-18 Nm). Install and properly tension the drive belts.

14. Install the engine side cover. Connect the negative battery cable.

TURBO

1. Disconnect the negative battery cable. Remove the engine side cover.

2. Remove the required accessory drive belts. Remove the water pump pulley and crankshaft pulley.

➡Support the engine with a suitable hoist and remove the No. 3 engine mount installation bolts, then lower the engine in order to remove the air conditioning/power steering pulley and the crankshaft pulley.

3. Rotate the engine so that the No. 1 piston is at TDC.

4. Unfasten and remove the upper, middle and lower timing belt covers along with gaskets from the mountings.

5. Remove the baffle plate. Remove the timing belt tensioner and spring by disconnecting the spring from its anchor, then loosening the tensioner bolt.

6. Check the tensioner for rough rotation.

To install:

7. Connect the spring to the tensioner, then install the spring and tensioner with the attaching bolt. Move the tensioner to the left until the spring is fully extended and temporarily tighten the tensioner bolt to hold it in place. Torque the tensioner lockbolt to 27-38 ft. lbs. (37-52 Nm).

8. Measure the belt tension by applying 22 lbs. (10 kg) of pressure between the camshaft pulleys. The deflection should be 0.33-0.45 in. (8.5-11.5mm) between the two pulleys. Loosen and tighten the tensioner, as required, to adjust the tension.

9. Install the lower and upper timing belt covers, using new gaskets if necessary. Install the spark plugs and connect the plug wires.

10. Install the baffle plate, with the curved surface facing outward. Install the crankshaft pulley and, where applicable, the air conditioning/power steering pump pulley. Torque the pulley bolts to 9-13 ft. lbs. (12-18 Nm).

11. Raise the vehicle and install the No. 3 engine mount bracket. Torque the bolts to 44-63 ft. lbs. (60-85 Nm), then remove the lifting equipment.

12. Install and properly tension the drive belts. Install the engine side cover.

13. Connect the negative battery cable. Check and/or adjust the ignition timing as required.

929

These vehicles are equipped with an automatic spring-loaded tensioner. Prior to installation, the automatic tensioner must be loaded. For this operation, a press that is capable of producing 2,000 lbs. of force will be required. For illustrations of the loading procedure, refer to the Timing Belt Removal and Installation procedure, earlier in this section.

1. Rotate the engine so that the No. 1 piston is at TDC. Properly relieve the fuel system pressure, then disconnect the negative battery cable.

2. Drain the cooling system. Tag and disconnect the spark plug wires, then remove all six spark plugs (to make crankshaft rotation easier).

3. Remove the fresh air duct assembly, the cooling fan and radiator cowling. Remove the drive belts.

4. Remove the air conditioning compressor idler pulley. If necessary, disconnect the compressor and position it to the side.

5. Remove the crankshaft pulley and baffle plate. Remove the coolant bypass hose and the upper radiator hose.

6. Unfasten and remove the right timing belt cover and gasket. Unbolt and remove the timing belt automatic tensioner.

➡️**If necessary for access, also remove the left timing belt cover and gasket.**

To install:

7. Place a flat washer on the bottom of the tensioner body to prevent damage to the body. Press the rod into the tensioner body using an arbor press. DO NOT use more than 2,000 lbs of pressure. Once the rod is fully inserted into the body, insert an "L" shaped pin or small Allen wrench through the body to hold the rod in place. Remove the unit from the press and install it onto the engine block. Torque the mounting bolt to 14-19 ft. lbs. (19-26 Nm).

8. Remove the pin from the auto tensioner. Turn the crankshaft twice in the normal direction of rotation and check that all the timing marks are aligned properly.

9. Check the timing belt deflection by applying 22 lbs. (10 kg) of force midway between the right-side camshaft pulley and the lower idler pulley. If the deflection is not 0.20-0.28 in. (5-7mm), repeat the adjustment procedure.

➡️**Excessive belt deflection is caused by tensioner failure or an excessively stretched timing belt.**

10. Install the timing belt cover(s), using new gasket(s) if necessary.

11. Connect the coolant bypass hose and the upper radiator hose to their respective fittings.

12. Install the crankshaft pulley and baffle plate. Torque the retaining bolts to 7-11 ft. lbs. (10-15 Nm).

13. Reposition and fasten the air conditioner compressor, if necessary. Install the air conditioning compressor idler pulley.

14. Install and properly tension the drive belts.

15. Install the cooling fan, radiator cowling and fresh air duct.

16. Lightly coat the threads of the spark plugs with a suitable anti-seize compound and torque the plugs to 11-17 ft. lbs. (15-23 Nm). Reconnect the plug wires.

17. Fill the cooling system to the proper level.

18. Connect the negative battery cable. Check and adjust the ignition timing, if necessary.

Camshaft and Bearings

REMOVAL & INSTALLATION

GLC and 1979-82 626

➡️**Perform this operation on a cold engine only.**

✳️**WARNING**

Do not remove the camshaft sprocket from the timing chain. Be sure that the sprocket and chain relationship is not disturbed. Wire the timing chain and sprocket together, so that they will not fall into the front cover. Maintain tension on the chain to avoid loss of timing at the crankshaft sprocket.

1. Remove the water pump (except GLC front wheel drive).

2. Rotate the crankshaft so that the No. 1 cylinder is at TDC.

3. Remove the distributor, as described earlier in this section.

4. Remove the rocker arm cover.

5. Release the tension on the timing chain by using an appropriate clamping tool (rear wheel drive models) or by removing the tensioner (front wheel drive GLC). Refer to the procedures earlier in this section.

6. Remove the cylinder head bolts using several passes in the reverse of the torque sequence (refer to the Cylinder Head Removal & Installation procedure, earlier in this section).

7. Remove the rocker arm assembly.

8. If so equipped, remove the nut, washer and distributor drive gear from the camshaft.

9. Remove the nut and washer securing the camshaft sprocket.

10. Remove the camshaft and inspect for wear, as described later in this section.

To install:

11. Position the camshaft in the cylinder head, and fasten the timing chain sprocket. Coat the bearing surfaces with engine oil.

12. If applicable, install the distributor drive gear, washer and nut on the camshaft.

13. Re-tension the timing chain, as described earlier in this section.

14. Check that the camshaft end-play is within specifications, and correct if necessary.

15. Install the rocker arm assembly, then tighten the cylinder head bolts in several stages, using the appropriate torquing sequence. Check and adjust the valves, as described in Section 2.

16. Install the rocker arm cover with a new gasket.

17. Install the distributor, as described earlier in this section.

18. If applicable, install the water pump.

1983-87 626 — Except Diesel

1. Loosen the alternator mounting bolts, release belt tension, and remove the alternator belt.

2. Remove the cylinder head cover and gasket, then remove the upper timing belt cover and gasket.

3. Using a wrench on the crankshaft pulley bolt, turn the engine in its normal direction of rotation until the camshaft pulley "A" mark aligns with the V-notch at the top of the front housing.

4. Loosen the tensioner lockbolt until it can be turned by hand.

5. Block the camshaft pulley from turning by putting a socket and extension (or prybar of some sort) through one of the holes in the pulley. Secure this "wedge" against one of the front housing bolts, while loosening the pulley's lockbolt.

6. Remove the pulley from the camshaft, being careful to maintain tension on the timing belt so it won't slip off the timing belt crankshaft pulley below.

➡️**If the belt does not maintain sufficient contact with the timing belt pulley, you will have to remove the crankshaft pulley and realign the timing marks.**

7. Loosen the rocker assembly mounting bolts in several stages, following the proper sequence (refer to the Rocker

Shafts Removal & Installation procedure, earlier in this section). Remove the rocker assembly (with the bolts intact), then remove the camshaft.

To install:

8. Before replacing or reinstalling the camshaft and related parts, check the bearing clearance, end-play, along with the cam and journal dimensions, as described later in this section.

9. Lubricate all parts thoroughly with clean engine oil and position the camshaft on the cylinder head with the pin in the front positioned at the top.

10. Lubricate the bearing surfaces and position the rocker assembly on the cylinder head. Torque the bolts in several stages to 13-19 ft. lbs. (18-26 Nm), following the appropriate sequence.

11. Raise the camshaft pulley into position at the front of the camshaft without losing the timing. To do this, maintain upward tension on the pulley while carefully levering the tensioner upward against spring tension. When the pulley is high enough, position it on the front of the camshaft so that the lockpin engages the hole in the pulley. Install and tighten the pulley lockbolt to 35-48 ft. lbs. (47-65 Nm), while keeping the pulley from turning, as described above.

12. Using a wrench on the crankshaft pulley bolt, turn the engine two revolutions in its normal direction. You can check that belt timing is correct by aligning the crankshaft pulley and oil pump body timing marks, then checking that the marks on the camshaft pulley and timing cover are still aligned. Torque the tensioner bolt to 28-38 ft. lbs. (38-51 Nm).

13. Check and adjust the valves, as described in Section 2.

14. Install the timing belt cover, with a new gasket if necessary, and torque the bolts to 5-7 ft. lbs. (7-9 Nm).

15. Reinstall the cylinder head cover with a new gasket.

16. Install and properly tension the alternator belt.

626 Diesel

▶ See Figures 249, 250 and 251

➡To perform this procedure, you will need a 6mm hexagonal (Allen type) socket and a puller with bolts that screw into the threaded holes of the camshaft's front and rear pulleys. You will also need two M8 x 32mm x 45mm bolts to remove the rear pulley.

1. Disconnect the negative battery cable. Remove the drive belts and right side splash shield.

2. Remove the cylinder head cover and gasket. Using a 6mm hexagonal socket, unfasten and remove the front portion of the crankshaft pulley.

3. Remove the rear timing belt cover. Turn the crankshaft until the rear camshaft pulley and rear seal plate timing marks align.

4. Loosen the lockbolt for the belt tensioner. Use a screwdriver to turn the tensioner and remove all tension from the belt. Hold the tensioner all the way in the released position, then tighten the tensioner lockbolt to hold it in this position.

5. Mark the timing belt for reinstallation in the same direction, then remove the belt.

6. Hold the camshaft with an open-end wrench installed on the flats located just behind the center bearing. Loosen the rear pulley lockbolt, but do not remove it. Install a puller by screwing its two outer bolts into the threaded holes of the pulley. When they are threaded in all the way, tighten the bolt

at the center of the puller so that its inner end rests against the lockbolt. Continue turning the center bolt until the pulley comes free of the camshaft. Remove the puller and pulley, along with the key. Be sure to retain the key.

7. Install the two bolts described in the note above through the two holes in the injection pump drive pulley and into the rear seal plate. Then, unscrew the pulley lockbolt. After the lockbolt is removed, use a puller to remove the pulley from the injection pump driveshaft.

8. Remove both front timing belt covers and their gaskets.

9. Turn the crankshaft via the bolt at its center so the timing marks on the camshaft pulley and front seal plate align.

10. Loosen the lockbolt on the belt tensioner, push the tensioner to the left (so as to tighten the spring and loosen the belt), then hold it there as you retighten the lockbolt. Unbolt and remove the torque stop from in front of the timing belt.

11. Mark the timing belt for its direction of rotation, then remove the belt.

12. Turn the crankshaft 45 degrees clockwise from the timing mark on the front of the oil pump housing, as shown.

➡Do not attempt to hammer the pulley or camshaft to remove the pulley.

13. Hold the camshaft with an open-end wrench installed on the flats located just behind the center bearing. Loosen the front pulley lockbolt, but do not remove it. Then, install a puller by screwing its two outer bolts into the threaded holes in the pulley. When they are threaded in all the way, tighten the bolt at the center of the puller so its inner end rests against the lockbolt. Continue turning the center bolt until the pulley comes free of the camshaft. Remove the puller and pulley, along with the key. Be sure to retain the key.

14. To remove the timing belt crankshaft pulley, use a tire iron to hold the flywheel in place as you remove the lockbolt. The pulley should slide straight off the crankshaft. Make sure to retain both the washer and key.

15. Loosen the camshaft bearing cap nuts a little at a time, using several stages of the numbered order. Then, remove the camshaft front and rear bearing caps. Next, remove both the front and rear camshaft oil seals.

16. Use a small prytool and carefully pry the oil pump (front crankshaft) oil seal out of the oil pump.

17. Remove the tensioner lockbolts, springs, and tensioners from both the front and rear of the engine. Remove the lockbolts and remove both the front and rear seal plates.

18. Remove the attaching nuts and remaining camshaft bearing caps, then remove the camshaft.

To install:

19. Inspect the camshaft bearing surfaces and bearing clearances, then check the camshaft dimensions as described later in this section. Replace any worn parts. Thoroughly lubricate all bearing surfaces (saddles, caps, and cam journals), then carefully position the camshaft in the block.

✳✳CAUTION

Install the camshaft so that the groove for the front pulley's key faces straight upward. Otherwise, the valve and pistons may be damaged when the caps are torqued!

20. Install front and rear seal plates and their lockbolts. Coat the entire surfaces on which both the front and rear camshaft

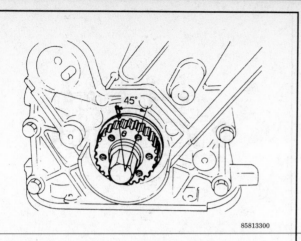

Fig. 249 After removing the timing belt, rotate the crankshaft 45° clockwise to guard against piston or valve damage

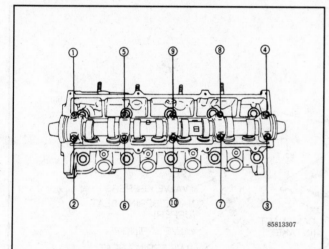

Fig. 250 Diesel engine camshaft caps must be loosened in the order shown

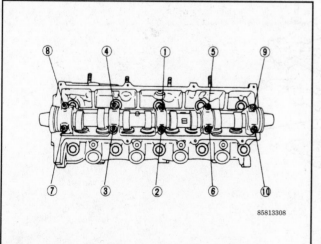

Fig. 251 Diesel engine camshaft caps must be tightened in the order shown

caps rest with a sealer. Then, install the camshaft caps and nuts. Tighten the nuts very slightly.

21. Install front and rear camshaft seals by hand. Note that the rear seal is slightly larger. Make sure you coat the seal lips with oil first.

22. Tighten the caps in three stages of the numbered order to 15-21 ft. lbs. (20-28 Nm). Oil its lips, then install a new oil pump oil seal around the crankshaft. Use a hammer and a 1.4 in. (35.5mm) diameter pipe to gently tap the oil pump seal into position. The oil pump seal's front edge should be aligned with the front edge of the oil pump body.

23. Use a 1.3 in. (33mm) or slightly smaller pipe to tap the front and rear camshaft seals into position. The front edge of the front seal should be aligned with the front edge of the cylinder head; the front edge of the rear seal should be aligned with the rear edge of the cylinder head.

24. The remaining steps of the installation procedure are the reverse of the removal procedure. Refer to timing belt removal and installation procedures to install and adjust the belts. If the camshaft has been replaced, adjust the valves before running the engine.

323 Models

NON-TURBO

1. Remove the cylinder head cover, as described previously in this section.

2. Remove the camshaft pulley after inserting a small prytool in one of the slots on the face of the pulley to hold it in place while loosening the bolt with a wrench. After removing the bolt, withdraw the pulley from the camshaft.

3. Remove the rocker shaft assembly, as described earlier in this section.

4. Unfasten the attaching bolt, then remove the camshaft thrust plate from the front bearing. Carefully pry the camshaft oil seal out of the front cylinder head bore with a small prytool. Be careful not to damage the bore or camshaft! Slide the camshaft out of the bearing bores in the head.

5. Inspect the camshaft bearing surfaces and bearing clearances, then check the camshaft dimensions as described later in this section. Replace any worn parts.

To install:

6. Thoroughly lubricate all bearing surfaces (bores and cam journals), then carefully slide the camshaft into position in the block.

7. Install the camshaft thrust plate and attaching bolt. Torque the thrust plate attaching bolt to 6-8 ft. lbs. (8-11 Nm).

8. Coat the outer bore of a new camshaft oil seal and the inner bore of the cylinder head with a thin coat of engine oil. With a piece of pipe approximately the diameter of the oil seal (but not larger), gently tap the seal straight into position around the front of the camshaft.

9. Install the camshaft pulley onto the dowel pin with the pin groove facing straight upward, then torque the camshaft pulley bolt to 36-45 ft. lbs. (49-61 Nm).

10. Install the rocker shaft assembly, as described previously in this section. Check and adjust the valve clearances.

11. Install the cylinder head cover with a new gasket, as described previously in this section.

TURBO

▶ **See Figures 252 and 253**

1. Remove the cylinder head cover, as described previously in this section.

2. Engage the camshaft journal that is closest to the seal plate with an adjustable wrench to hold it stationary. Using a box wrench, loosen the camshaft pulley bolt. Remove the bolt and washer, then slide the camshaft pulley from the camshaft. The remaining camshaft pulley is removed in exactly the same manner.

3. Unbolt and remove the seal plate from the cylinder head. Gently insert the end of a suitable prying tool between the cylinder head and the camshaft oil seal, then remove the seal. Be careful not to damage the seal bore during removal. Remove the remaining oil seal in the same manner.

4. Remove the camshaft cap retaining bolts in reverse of the tightening sequence and remove the caps. (Although the caps are numbered, it might be advisable to record fore and aft orientation for easier reference.)

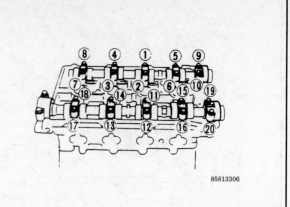

85813306

Fig. 253 Camshaft cap bolt tightening sequence — 323 turbo

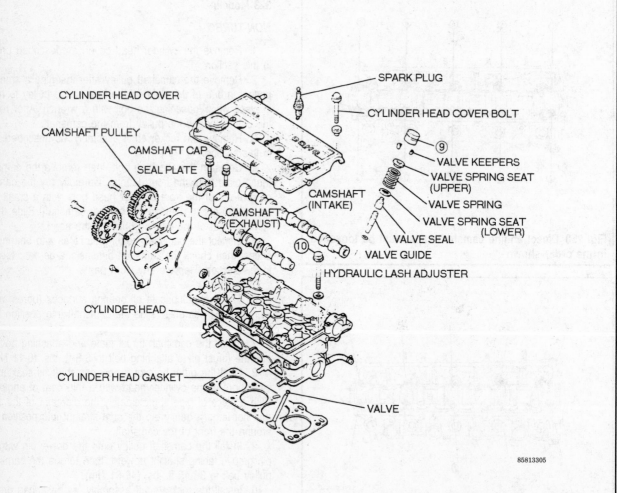

85813305

Fig. 252 Cylinder head components — 323 turbo

5. Lift the intake and exhaust camshafts from the bearing saddles in the cylinder head. Clean the camshafts thoroughly with a lint-free rag and set the camshaft on V-blocks. Proceed to the inspection procedures, as described later in this section.

To install:

6. Coat the bearing, journal and lobe surfaces of the camshaft with clean engine oil. Gently place the camshafts into the cylinder head.

7. Apply a thin coat of oil to the camshaft oil seal bores and the lip of the new seals. Install the seals into the cylinder head using a hammer and socket or a length of pipe that closely approximates the diameter of the seal. Tap the seals evenly into the seal bores.

8. Wipe each cap with a clean rag. Locate the front camshaft cap and apply a thin coat of non-hardening sealant to the cap surface. Do not apply sealant to the bearing surface!

9. Install the camshaft caps in their original locations. Gradually torque the camshaft cap bolts in the proper sequence to 8-11 ft. lbs. (11-15 Nm).

10. Install the exhaust side camshaft pulley so that the **E** mark stamped on its face is aligned with the upper timing mark on the front housing. Similarly, install the intake side camshaft pulley so that the **I** mark is aligned with the upper timing mark on the front housing. Install the pulley bolts and washers. Hold the camshaft stationary as described earlier and torque the bolts to 36-45 ft. lbs. (49-61 Nm).

11. Install the cylinder head cover with a new gasket and seal washers, as described previously in this section.

1988-89 626/MX-6

1. Disconnect the negative battery cable.

2. Tag and disconnect the spark plug wires, then remove the spark plugs (for easier crankshaft rotation).

3. Remove the engine side cover and the accessory drive belts.

4. Unbolt the crankshaft pulley, then remove the upper and lower timing belt covers and gaskets. Remove the crankshaft pulley baffle plate and note how it is installed. The curved side should be facing out.

5. Engage the timing belt pulley's lockbolt with an appropriate size metric socket and breaker bar, then turn the crankshaft in its normal direction of rotation until the "arrowed" **1** mark on the camshaft is aligned with the mark on top of the front housing (see illustration). Unbolt and remove the tensioner, then disconnect the tensioner spring from its mount.

6. Remove the timing belt. If the old timing belt is to be reused, mark the direction of rotation, prior to removal.

7. Block the camshaft pulley from turning by putting a socket and extension (or prybar of some sort) through one of the holes in the pulley. Secure this "wedge" against one of the front housing bolts, while loosening the pulley's lockbolt and washer.

8. Remove the pulley from the camshaft.

9. Remove the cylinder head cover, as described earlier in this section.

10. Unfasten and remove the front and rear cylinder head housings, along with their gaskets.

11. Wipe all the camshaft journals with a clean lint-free rag. Before removing the rocker arm shafts, refer to the inspection procedures, later in this section, then check the camshaft end-

play and journal oil clearances. These measurements will help you determine if the camshaft is acceptable for reinstallation or whether it should be replaced.

12. Loosen the rocker arm shaft bolts following the appropriate sequence, as described earlier in this section. Loosen each bolt gradually, in several stages, and remove along with the spacers. Mark the shafts based on which side of the head they are installed (intake or exhaust), and keep the components of each shaft in a separate plastic bag. Look at the amount of holes in both shafts to determine on what side they are installed. The intake shaft has twice the amount of holes as the exhaust side. The stepped ends of both shafts go toward the rear of the head.

➡**Do not remove the hydraulic lash adjusters, unless it is absolutely necessary to do so. The lash adjusters are sealed in the rocker arms by an O-ring. If this O-ring is disturbed or damaged, the lash adjusters may leak. If they are removed, make sure that new O-ring are installed and that the oil reservoirs in the rocker arms are filled with clean engine oil.**

13. The camshaft caps are marked with arrows that show the installation position. Note the direction of the arrows, so that they will be installed in the original positions. Remove the camshaft caps and lift the camshaft from the bearing saddles in the cylinder head. There are five camshaft caps, with No. 3 at the center. The No. 3 cap has a drilled oil passage from which it receives oil from the cylinder head. It must be reinstalled in its original position. Clean the shaft thoroughly and set the camshaft on V-blocks. Proceed to the inspection section.

To install:

14. Liberally coat all the camshaft bearing, journal and lobe surfaces with clean engine oil. Gently place the camshaft into the cylinder head. Rotate the camshaft until the dowel pin on the end of the shaft is facing straight up.

15. Install the camshaft caps so that the arrows are facing in the original direction. Make sure that the No. 3 cap is installed correctly.

16. Install the rocker arm shafts so that the stepped ends are facing the rear of the head. Install the rocker arm shaft retaining bolts and spacers. Torque the bolts gradually in the proper sequence to 13-20 ft. lbs. (18-27 Nm). When tightening the bolts, prevent the rocker arm and spacers from being pinched between the shaft and the camshaft cap.

17. Apply engine oil to a new oil seal and to the front housing bore, then press the seal in place.

18. Apply engine oil to the oil seal lip, then install the cylinder head front housing with a new gasket.

19. Install the cylinder head rear housing with a new gasket.

20. Attach the cylinder head cover with sealant and bolts, as described earlier in this section.

21. Install the timing belt tensioner and timing belt, as described earlier in this section. Install the crankshaft pulley baffle plate.

22. Install the timing belt covers, using new gaskets if necessary.

23. Position the crankshaft pulley, and torque the botls to 9-13 ft. lbs. (12-17 Nm).

24. Install and properly tension the accessory drive belts. Install the engine side cover.

25. Install the spark plugs and connect the plug wires.

26. Connect the negative battery cable.

929

➤The following procedure applies to the camshaft in either cylinder bank.

1. Rotate the engine so that the No. 1 piston is at TDC. Properly relieve the fuel system pressure, as described in Section 5.

2. Disconnect the negative battery cable and drain the cooling system.

3. Tag and disconnect the spark plug wires, then remove all six spark plugs (to make crankshaft rotation easier).

4. Remove the fresh air duct, the cooling fan and radiator cowling. Remove the drive belts.

5. Remove the air conditioning compressor idler pulley. If necessary, unfasten the compressor and position it to the side.

6. Remove the crankshaft pulley and baffle plate. Remove the coolant bypass hose and the upper radiator hose.

7. Remove the timing belt cover assembly retaining bolts. Remove the left and right timing belt covers and gaskets. Turn the crankshaft to align the mating marks of the pulleys.

8. Remove the upper idler pulley. Remove the timing belt. If reusing the belt, be sure to mark the direction of rotation. Remove the timing belt auto tensioner.

9. Remove the cylinder head cover and gasket. If necessary, first remove/reposition any components which interfere.

10. Engage the camshaft pulley with a suitable spanner wrench type holding tool and loosen the retaining bolt. Remove the pulley from the end of the camshaft.

11. Loosen the rocker arm shaft retaining bolts in the sequence shown in Rocker Arm/Shaft Removal and Installation section described earlier in this section. Loosen the bolts gradually and in several stages. Remove the rocker arm and shaft assemblies.

➤Do not remove the hydraulic lash adjusters, unless it is absolutely necessary to do so. The lash adjusters are sealed in the rocker arms by an O-ring. If this O-ring is disturbed or damaged, the lash adjusters may leak. If they are removed, make sure that new O-rings are installed and that the oil reservoirs in the rocker arms are filled with clean engine oil.

12. Insert the blade of a small prytool between the camshaft oil seal and gently pry the seal from the cylinder head bore. Be careful not to damage the seal bore. Discard the seal and purchase a new one.

13. Before removing the camshaft thrust plate, proceed to the inspection section to measure the camshaft end-play. This will determine if the thrust plate or the camshaft have to be replaced.

14. Remove the thrust plate, then slowly and carefully withdraw the camshaft from the cylinder head. Clean off the lobe and journal surfaces, then proceed to the inspection section, which follows.

➤The camshaft in the left cylinder bank fits into a distributor/oil pump drive gear. Since this drive gear engages both the distributor shaft and the oil pump driveshaft gear, you must also remove the necessary parts to disengage the gears, before the left camshaft can be removed.

To install:

15. If applicable, apply sealant to the end of the distributor/oil pump drive gear which mates with the left camshaft, then fully seat the gear.

16. Apply a liberal coating of clean engine oil to the surfaces of the cam lobes, bearing and journal surfaces. Slowly and carefully insert the camshaft into the cylinder head. Install the camshaft thrust plate and torque the retaining bolt to 6-8 ft. lbs. (8-11 Nm).

17. Wipe down the surface of the seal bore with a clean rag and coat the lip of the new oil seal with clean engine oil. Install the seal into the cylinder head using a socket or a length of pipe (that closely approximates the diameter of the seal) as an installation tool. Tap the seal evenly into the seal bore.

18. Coat the surfaces of the rocker arm and the rocker arm shafts with clean engine oil. Install the rocker shafts in their original positions. The intake side shaft has twice as many oil holes as the exhaust side. Torque the rocker shaft bolts to 14-19 ft. lbs. (19-26 Nm) in several stages of the proper sequence. When tightening the rocker shaft bolts, makes sure the rocker arm shaft spring does not get pinched between the shaft and the mounting boss.

19. Align the camshaft so that its key points upward, then install the camshaft pulley. On the left cylinder bank, the **L** mark on the face of the pulley should be at the top, while on the right cylinder bank, the **R** mark should be at the top. Tighten the retaining bolt to 52-59 ft. lbs. (71-80 Nm).

20. Install the cylinder head cover with a new gasket and new seal washers.

21. If applicable, install the oil pump drive gear and gear cover, as well as the distributor spacer and distributor on the left cylinder head. Be sure to replace the O-rings with new ones and to lubricate the drive gears and O-rings with engine oil.

22. The remainder of the installation is the reverse of the removal procedure. Be sure to reload the timing belt tensioner and install the timing belt, as described earlier in this section.

23. Fill the cooling system to the proper level and reconnect the negative battery cable.

INSPECTION

◆ **See Figures 254, 255, 256, 257 and 258**

1. Inspect the camshaft cam faces and bearing journals for roughness or obvious excessive wear. Measure the cam height with a micrometer, taking measurements at the outer edge of the cam on both sides. The surface of the cam must be clean to ensure accurate readings.

Replace the camshaft if it is obviously worn/damaged, or if the cam height is worn beyond limits as listed in the "Camshaft Specifications Chart" in this section.

2. Measure the camshaft bearing journals with a micrometer. The cam journals should also be measured at 90 degree angles to determine elliptical wear. Subtract the smaller reading from the larger. The limit is 0.002 in. (0.05mm) for all

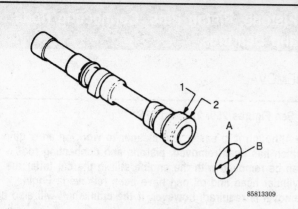

Fig. 254 Use a micrometer to measure camshaft journal diameter at the outer edge of each cam (as indicated by the numbers 1 and 2). Also take measurements 90 degrees apart to determine elliptical wear (as indicated by letters A and B)

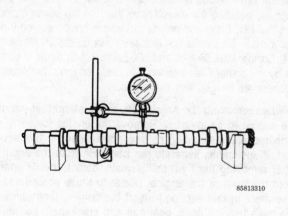

Fig. 255 Checking camshaft run-out with a dial indicator

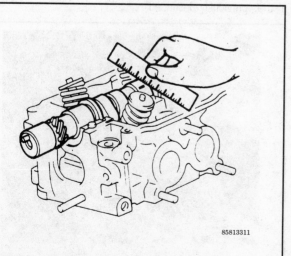

Fig. 256 Checking camshaft journal bearing oil clearances using Plastigage® inserts

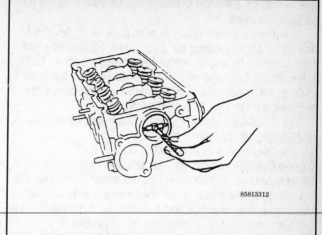

Fig. 257 Measuring camshaft bore diameter to determine the camshaft journal oil clearance — 1.6L non-turbo and 3.0L engines

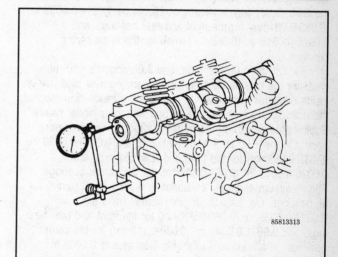

Fig. 258 Checking camshaft end-play with a dial indicator

engines except the 3.0L. On the 3.0L engine, maximum out-of-round is 0.0012 in. (0.03mm).

➡On 1.3L, 1.5L, 1.6L and 2.0L (Codes FE and RF) engines, the camshaft must be replaced if worn beyond limits. On 2.0L (Code MA) engines, the journals may be ground and undersize bearings may be installed.

3. Mount the camshaft on metal V-blocks and check camshaft runout with a dial indicator, taking the measurement at the center bearing. The limit is 0.0012 in. (0.03mm).

4. Check the camshaft bearing clearances. This is done by installing Plastigage® or equivalent inserts, which will flatten out according to the bearing clearance when the camshaft bearing caps are torqued to specification. You can determine the clearance after removing the rocker assembly and inserts,

then measuring the insert's dimensions. Be sure to follow the package directions.

• Torque rocker assembly bolts to 56-60 ft. lbs. (76-81 Nm) on all engines except the 2.0L (Codes FE and RF) and 2.2L. On the 2.0L engine, torque the assembly bolts to 13-19 ft. lbs. (18-26 Nm), and on the 2.2L engine, torque the bolts to 13-20 ft. lbs. (18-27 Nm). On 1.6L turbo engines, torque the camshaft caps to 8-11 ft. lbs. (11-15 Nm).

• Torque the diesel engine camshaft bearing caps to 15-20 ft. lbs. (20-27 Nm).

• Clearance should be 0.0007-0.0027 in. (0.018-0.069mm) for front and rear bearings, and 0.0011-0.0031 in. (0.03-0.08mm) for the center bearing on the 2.0L (Code MA) engines, which use bearing inserts. On the 1.5L engine, the clearance limit is 0.0059 in. (0.15mm). On the 1.6L turbo engine, the oil clearance for all journals is 0.0014-0.0032 in. (0.035-0.080mm). On the 2.0L gasoline and 2.2L engines, clearance should be 0.0014-0.0033 in. (0.035-0.084mm) on bearings 1 and 5 (at either end), and 0.0026-0.0045 in. (0.066-0.114mm) on bearings 2 and 4. On the 2.0L diesel engine, clearance should be 0.0014-0.0033 in. (0.035-0.084mm) for the front and rear bearings, and 0.0026-0.0045 in. (0.066-0.114mm) for the three center bearings.

• On the 1.6L non-turbo and 3.0L engines, you must measure the outside diameter of the cam journals, and use an inside diameter micrometer to measure the inside diameters of the bearing bores (these are integral with the cylinder head). Subtract the smaller figure from the larger to get the clearance. On the 1.6L engine, normal limits are 0.0014-0.0033 in. (0.035-0.085mm) for the front and rear bearings, and 0.0026-0.0045 in. (0.065-0.115mm) for the center bearings. The maximum allowable clearance is 0.0059 in. (0.15mm) for all bearings. On the 3.0L engine, normal limits are 0.0024-0.0035 in. (0.060-0.090mm) for the front and rear bearings, and 0.0031-0.0045 in. (0.080-0.115mm) for the center bearings. The maximum allowable clearance is 0.0059 in. (0.15mm) for all bearings.

• Except on the 2.0L (Code MA) engines (which have replaceable bearings), the cylinder head assembly and rocker assembly must be replaced if the camshaft is within limits, but the clearance is still excessive.

5. With the camshaft installed in the cylinder head, measure camshaft end-play by inserting a feeler gauge between the camshaft pulley surface and the surface of the thrust plate, or by mounting a dial indicator against the cylinder head, and pushing the camshaft along its axis. Although their standard ranges may vary slightly, the camshaft end-play wear limit is 0.008 in. (0.20mm) for all piston engines covered by this manual. If clearance is excessive, replace the thrust plate.

Pistons, Piston Pins, Connecting Rods and Bearings

REMOVAL

▶ See Figures 259, 274 and 275

➡Although it is easier and cleaner to work on an engine which has been removed, pistons and connecting rods can be removed with the engine still in the car (after the cylinder head and oil pan have been removed). Engine removal is required, however, if the crankshaft will also be removed.

All parts must be retained in order — including the bearings and caps. Mark the caps for installation in the same position in both directions, if they are not already marked. Note that on all engines except those used in the 1983-89 626/MX-6 and the 1986-89 323, thrust bearings are at the rear main. This main bearing cap must be removed with a puller. The 1983-87 2.0L engines, including the diesel, have them on the center main, and the 1.6L turbo and non-turbo engines have them on the No. 4 main. Be careful not to lose or mix up the thrust washers. On the 1988-89 626 and MX-6, crankshaft thrust is taken up by the center main bearing. On these engines, the thrust washers are integral with the bearing.

➡When removing the crankshaft, use a stand that permits the engine to be inverted. Remove the engine (or engine/transaxle assembly) as described earlier in this section. If applicable, separate the transaxle from the engine. After removing the flywheel/flexplate, detach the oil pump from the front of the engine. (Refer to these procedures elsewhere in this section.) Invert the engine, then remove the main bearing caps, bearings and crankshaft, as described later in this section.

1. If applicable, remove the engine from the vehicle, as previously described in this section, and mount it on a suitable workstand. Otherwise, remove the cylinder head(s) and oil pan, also as previously described.

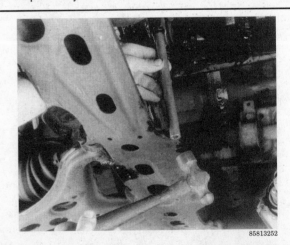

85813252

Fig. 259 Loosen the connecting rod nuts until flush with the bolt ends, then gently tap them until the cap is free

2. Note the position of each piston, connecting rod and connecting rod cap before removal, to ensure reinstallation in the same location. Check the tops of the pistons and the sides of the connecting rods for identifying marks. If no identifying numbers or marks are present, use a number punch set and stamp in the numbers yourself.

3. Rotate the crankshaft until the piston to be removed is at the bottom of the cylinder. Inspect the upper area of the cylinder wall for a ridge above the top piston ring. If cylinder wall wear has created a noticeable ridge, it should be removed with a ridge reamer, to prevent damage to the rings during piston removal. For further information on ridge removal, refer to the procedure later in this section.

✳✳WARNING

Be very careful if you are unfamiliar with operating a ridge reamer. It is very easy to remove more cylinder bore material than intended, possibly requiring a cylinder overbore and piston replacement that could have been avoided.

4. Loosen the connecting rod nuts until they are flush with the ends of the rod bolts. Use a hammer and brass drift or piece of wood to lightly tap on the nuts/bolts until the connecting rod cap comes free of the connecting rod. Remove the nuts, rod cap and lower bearing insert.

5. Slip a length of snug fitting rubber hose over each rod bolt, to prevent the bolt threads from damaging the crankshaft during removal.

6. Using a hammer handle or piece of wood or plastic, tap the rod and piston upward in the bore until the piston rings clear the cylinder block. Remove the piston and connecting rod assembly from the top of the cylinder bore.

7. If applicable, repeat Steps 3-6 for the other pistons.

CLEANING AND INSPECTION

▶ See Figures 260, 261, 262, 263, 264, 265, 266, 267, 268, 269, 270, 271, 272 and 273

1. Check the top deck of the block for distortion by running a straightedge along both sides, both ends, and diagonally. Check for distortion exceeding 0.006 in. (0.15mm), (0.004 in./0.10mm on the diesel) by attempting to insert an appropriate size flat feeler gauge between the block deck and the lower edge of the straightedge all along its length, in every direction shown. If distortion exceeds the limit, have the block top deck ground by a competent machine shop or, if distortion is excessive, replace the block.

➡**Do not attempt to save a diesel cylinder block through grinding! If the distortion exceeds the limit, the block must be replaced. Otherwise, the pistons will hit the valves!**

2. Also inspect the block for cracks or wetness, indicating coolant has leaked through the cracks. If you have any doubt about such problems, you should have the block inspected by the Zyglo®, Magnaflux® or similar process, to ensure it can

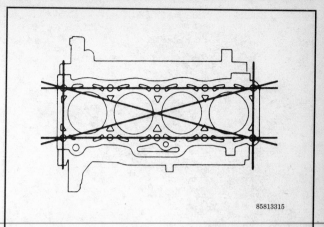

Fig. 260 After removing all head gasket material, check the cylinder block deck for distortion by placing a straightedge along both sides, both ends, and diagonally

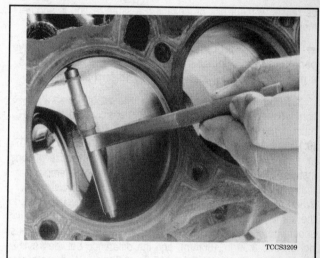

Fig. 261 A telescoping gauge or inside micrometer may be used to measure the cylinder diameter bore

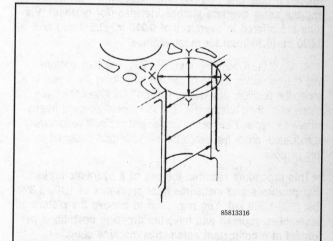

Fig. 262 Measure the diameter of each cylinder at three different depths; also, take three additional readings, perpendicular to the first ones

Fig. 263 Measure the piston's outside diameter using a micrometer

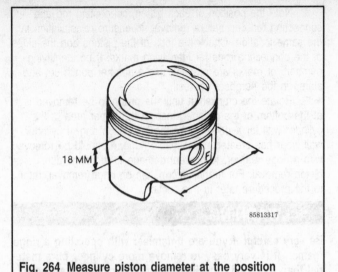

Fig. 264 Measure piston diameter at the position shown — gasoline engines

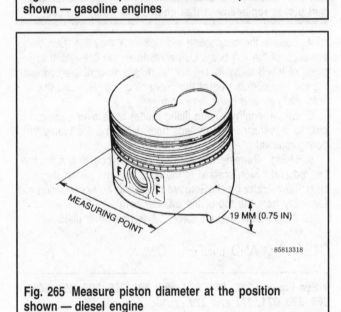

Fig. 265 Measure piston diameter at the position shown — diesel engine

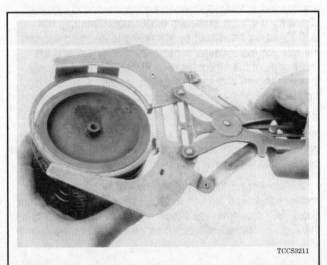

Fig. 266 Use a ring expander tool to remove the piston rings

be reused without risk of leakage. Pressure testing is another means by which the block may be tested for cracks.

➡ The Zyglo® process coats parts with a fluorescent dye penetrant that is suitable for any material. Magnaflux® is a magnetic process applicable only to ferrous materials.

3. Measure the diameter of each cylinder at the six locations shown. Subtract the minimum dimension from the maximum dimension. If this difference exceeds 0.0059 in. (0.15mm), or the difference between cylinders exceeds 0.0007 in. (0.01778mm), cylinders must be bored and oversize pistons installed. If boring is required, you should base the amount that you remove on the dimensions of an oversize piston. When one cylinder is bored, all other cylinders must be bored the same amount. Any time this type of machining is done, it should be documented. On the diesel, maximum diameter must not exceed 3.39 in. (86mm), and the difference between cylinder bores must not exceed 0.009 in. (0.23mm). Wall scoring or signs of piston seizure also mean cylinders must be rebored.

➡ Even if only one cylinder is damaged, all must be bored and the same oversize pistons installed (for balance). Pistons are offered in oversizes of 0.010 in. (0.254mm) and 0.020 in. (0.508mm) for most engines.

4. On 2.0L (Codes FE and RF), 2.2L and 3.0L engines, test the oscillation torque of the rod by holding the piston in a horizontal position, and raising the rod until it touches the piston skirt, then releasing it. The rod should descend freely; otherwise, replace the piston and/or piston pin. If replacement is indicated, press the piston pin out with tools designed for this purpose.

➡ This procedure requires the use of a hydraulic press that produces and measures total pressures of 1,100-3,300 lbs. (500-1,500 kg). You may wish to remove the piston/rod assemblies yourself and have the pressing operations performed at a competent automotive machine shop.

5. On gasoline engines, other than the 1.3L engine, if the pressure required to press the pin from the piston is less than 1,100 lbs. (500 kg), replace the piston pin or the connecting rod.

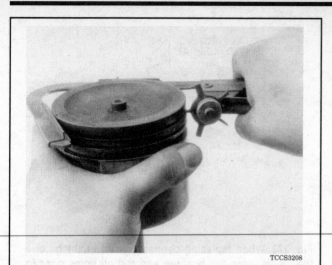

Fig. 267 Clean the piston grooves using a ring groove cleaner . . .

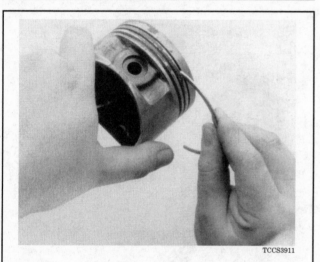

Fig. 268 . . . or part of a broken piston ring. Be careful, since the ring is sharp

6. Measure piston diameter in the thrust direction, below the bottom of the oil ring groove and 90 degrees from the piston pin, as shown in the illustration. On the diesel, measure it 0.75 in. (19mm) above the bottom edge of the piston skirt. This dimension must compare with cylinder diameter so as to produce piston-to-cylinder clearance that is within specifications. If clearance exceeds the maximum wear specification, all cylinders must be bored and appropriate oversize pistons must be installed. If the clearance is within specification, only light finish honing is required.

7. Using a ring expander tool, as illustrated, remove the piston rings. The various rings on each piston are not identical. Be careful not to mix them up, in case they may be reused.

➡️If the piston is to be replaced, also install new piston rings.

8. Clean the pistons thoroughly with a suitable solvent or in a dip tank. All the ring lands must be free and clear of any carbon deposits. Use a ring groove cleaning tool or a broken

piston ring, which allows you to reach the innermost part of the land. DO NOT use a file or wire brush to clean the piston. Inspect the rings for damage or cracks and measure side clearance, as shown, using a **new** piston ring. Also measure end-gap, as shown, with the rings near the bottom of the cylinder — below the area of ring wear. This should be done even for new rings.

9. Install the connecting rods in a jig designed to test straightness and check that the bend or twist does not exceed 0.0016 in. (0.04mm) per 3.94 in. (100mm) of length on all 1978-88 gasoline engines. On 1989 1.6L engines, the bend or twist should not exceed 0.0078 in. (0.20mm) per 3.94 in. (100mm), and on 1989 2.2L and 3.0L engines, the limit is 0.0024 in. (0.06mm). On the 1985 2.0L diesel engine, bend or twist should not exceed 0.006 in. (0.15mm) per 3.94 in. (100mm) of length.

10. Measure the piston pin diameter and the piston pin hole diameter each in eight places, as illustrated. Compare the readings and replace any out-of-round components. Also, if pin-to-hole clearance is beyond the specified limit, replace the piston and/or piston pin.

11. On diesel engines, the upper ends of the connecting rods are bushed. Measure the outside diameter of the piston pin with a micrometer; use an inside micrometer to measure the inside diameter of the bushing. Then, subtract the smaller figure from the larger. The standard inner diameter of the bushing is 0.9846-0.9854 in. (25.01-25.03mm), and the clearance limit between the two is 0.002 in. (0.05mm). If the clearance exceeds this figure, press the bushing out of the rod and replace it as follows:

a. Press the bushing out by supporting the upper rod end on a block with a suitable hole in it (for passage of the bushing downward). Place a pipe of 1.06-1.08 in. (27.0-27.4mm) diameter under the press, squarely aligned with the end of the pin (NOT touching the rod). Press the bushing out.

b. Thoroughly coat the outer bore of the new bushing and the inner bore of the rod with clean engine oil. Precisely align the oil holes of the bushing and rod bore. Then, press in the new bushing until its edges are aligned with the sides of the rod and the oil holes are precisely lined up.

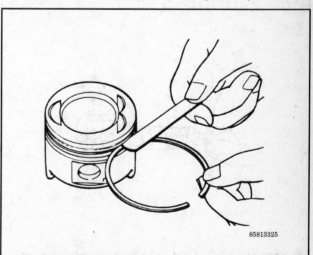

Fig. 269 Check the piston ring side clearance using a new ring and a feeler gauge

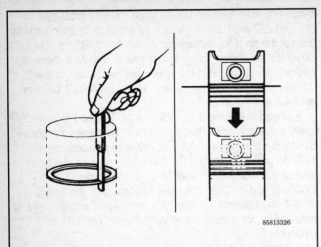

Fig. 270 Measure ring end-gap by placing the ring inside the cylinder, in the area of ring-induced wear. Use an inverted piston to keep the ring from cocking

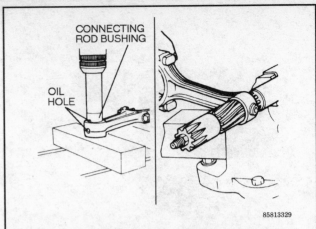

Fig. 273 When replacing connecting rod bushings on the diesel, align the bushing and rod oil holes prior to pressing in the bushing. If necessary, ream the new bushing to provide the proper clearance

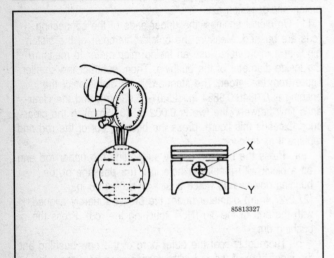

Fig. 271 Use an inside caliper to measure the piston pin hole diameter in eight places

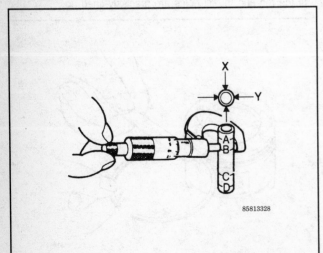

Fig. 272 Use a micrometer to take eight measurements of a piston pin

Fig. 274 Before extracting the pistons, remove any ridges from the upper portions of the cylinder walls

c. Add the minimum required piston pin-to-rod clearance to the actual pin diameter. Then, using a spiral expansion reamer, repeatedly enlarge and measure the inside diameter of the bushing until clearance is within specification.

RIDGE REMOVAL AND HONING

▶ **See Figures 274, 275, 276 and 277**

1. Before the piston is removed from the cylinder, check for a ridge at the top of the cylinder bore. This ridge occurs because the piston ring does not travel all the way to the top of the bore, thereby leaving an unused portion of cylinder bore.

2. In order to see the extent of the ridge more clearly, clean away any carbon buildup at the top of the cylinder with sandpaper. If the ridge is slight, it will be safe to remove the pistons without damaging the rings or piston ring lands. If the ridge is severe, and easily catches your fingernail, it will have to be removed using a ridge reamer.

➡**A severe ridge is an indication of excessive bore wear. Before removing the piston, check the cylinder bore diameter with a bore gauge, as explained in the piston and connecting rod cleaning and inspection procedure. Compare your measurement with specification. If the bore is excessively worn, all cylinders will have to bored (to maintain balance), then oversize pistons and rings must be installed.**

3. Before reaming the ridge, cover the piston top with a rag to minimize the amount of metal which enters the cylinder. Install the ridge removal tool in the top of the cylinder bore, then carefully follow the manufacturer's operating instructions. Only take off the amount of material necessary to remove the

TCCS3913

Fig. 276 Using a ball-type cylinder hone is an easy way to finish the cylinder bore

TCCS3216

Fig. 277 A properly cross-hatched cylinder bore

ridge. Clean up all metal shavings before attempting to remove the piston/rod assembly.

✳✳WARNING

Be very careful if you are unfamiliar with operating a ridge reamer. It is very easy to remove more cylinder bore material than you want, possibly requiring a cylinder over-bore and piston replacement that may not have been necessary.

4. After the piston and connecting rod assembly have been removed, check the clearances as explained in the piston and connecting rod cleaning and inspection procedure, to determine whether boring and honing or just light honing are required. If boring is necessary, consult an automotive machine shop. If light honing is all that is necessary, proceed to Step 5.

5. Honing is best done with the crankshaft removed, to prevent damage to the crankshaft and to make post-honing cleaning easier, since the honing process will scatter metal particles. However, if you do not want to remove the crank-

TCCS3916

Fig. 275 Removing the ridge from a cylinder bore with a ridge reamer

shaft, position the connecting rod journal for the cylinder being honed as far away from the bottom of the cylinder bore as possible, and wrap a shop cloth around the journal.

6. Honing can be done either with a flexible glaze breaker-type hone or with a rigid hone that has honing stones and guide shoes. The flexible hone removes the least amount of metal, and is especially recommended if your piston-to-cylinder bore clearance is on the loose side. The flexible hone is useful to provide a finish on which the new piston rings will seat. A rigid hone will remove more material than the flexible hone and requires more operator skill.

7. Regardless of which type of hone you use, carefully follow the manufacturer's instructions for operation.

8. The hone should be moved up and down the bore at sufficient speed to obtain a uniform finish. A rigid hone will provide a definite cross-hatch finish; operate the rigid hone at a speed to obtain a 45-65° included angle in the cross-hatch. The finish marks should be clean, but not sharp, and free from embedded particles and torn or folded metal.

9. Periodically during the honing procedure, thoroughly clean the cylinder bore and check the piston-to-bore clearance with the piston for that cylinder.

10. After honing is completed, thoroughly wash the cylinder bores and the rest of the engine with hot water and detergent. Scrub the bores well with a stiff bristle brush and rinse thoroughly with hot water. Thorough cleaning is essential, for if any abrasive material is left in the cylinder bore, it will rapidly wear the new rings and the cylinder bore. If any abrasive material is left in the rest of the engine, it will be picked up by the oil and carried throughout the engine, damaging bearings and other parts.

11. After the bores are cleaned, wipe them down with a clean cloth coated with light engine oil, to keep them from rusting.

PISTON ASSEMBLY

▶ See Figures 278, 279, 280, 281, 282, 283 and 284

1. If applicable, pistons and rods must be assembled (piston pins installed) with rods facing in the proper direction. With the **F** mark on the piston facing you, turn the connecting rod so the oil hole which lubricates the cylinder is on the left. (This also applies to the diesel.) On 1979-82 626 engines, the rod is assembled with the connecting rod bolt heads pointing to the right, as shown. The piston pin (and other related parts) must be thoroughly lubricated with clean engine oil and pressed in from the **F** mark side. On the 1.3L engine, heat the piston slightly if the pin is a tight fit, press it into the piston, and install new circlips. On the diesel, heat the piston to 122°-168°F (50°C-76°C). Then, install the connecting rod in the proper direction into the piston, slide the pin into position, and lock the pin with circlips.

➡**On gasoline engines, other than the 1.3L engine, this job requires special tools and a press that can apply and measure 1,100-3,300 lbs. (500-1,500 kg) of force. If it requires less than 1,100 lbs. (500 kg) to insert the pin, the pin or connecting rod must be replaced.**

2. On the 2.0L (Codes FE and RF), 2.2L and 3.0L engines, the completed assembly must pass the connecting rod oscilla-

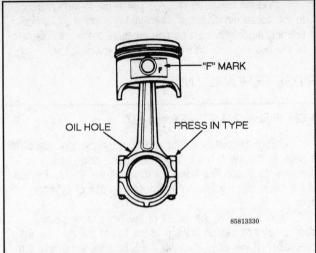

Fig. 278 Piston and connecting rod assembly — except 1979-82 2.0L (Code MA) engine

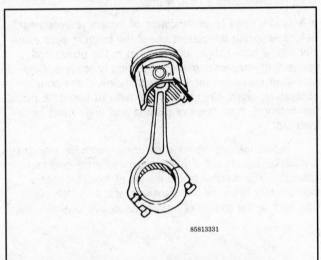

Fig. 279 On 1979-82 2.0L (Code MA) engines, the connecting rod bolt heads angle to the right

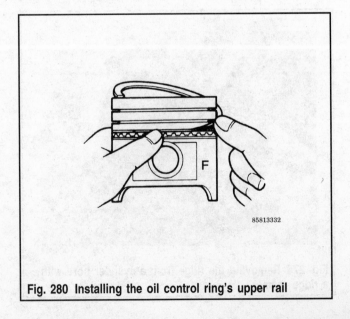

Fig. 280 Installing the oil control ring's upper rail

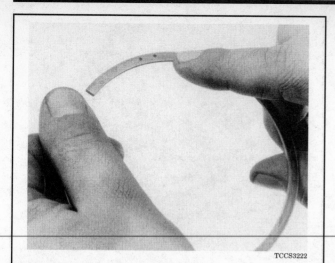

Fig. 281 Most rings are marked to show which side faces upward

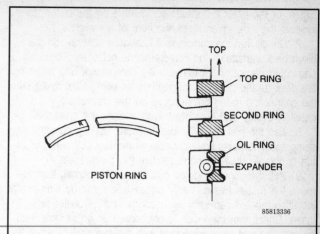

Fig. 284 Install rings for the 2.0L diesel engine as shown. Make sure that the "R" or "RN" marks face upward

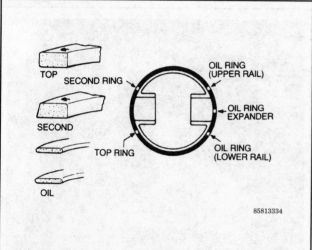

Fig. 282 Stagger the positions of the ring gaps around the piston as shown

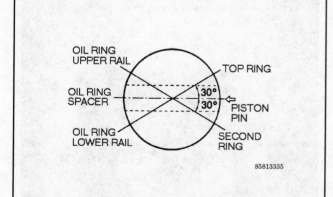

Fig. 283 Using the piston pin as a baseline, upper and lower compression ring openings should each be offset 30° in opposite directions. The oil control ring's upper and lower rails should also be offset

tion torque test previously described. If the rod does not descend freely, replace the piston and/or piston pin.

3. Install the three-piece oil control ring with its rails and grooves thoroughly lubricated. Start with the oil control ring spacer (expander). Next, install the oil control upper rail by inserting one edge between the groove and spacer, and holding it in place with your thumb. Then, run your other thumb along the edge of the rail to work it into the groove. Install the lower rail similarly. Check that both rails are expanded by the spacer tangs, so that they turn smoothly in both directions.

➡On many engines, the upper and lower rails are identical, and can be installed with either face upward.

4. Install the lower (second) compression ring, followed by the upper ring, with **R** or **RN** markings facing upward. Use a ring expander, but open the rings as little as possible. When the rings are installed, oil them and stagger their gaps as shown in the illustrations, to prevent excessive oil consumption and loss of compression.

INSTALLATION

◆ See Figures 285, 286, 287, 288, 289 and 290

1. Make sure the cylinder bore and shaft journal are clean.
2. Position the crankshaft journal at its furthest position away from the bottom of the cylinder bore.
3. Coat the cylinder bore with light engine oil.
4. Make sure the rod bearing shells are correctly installed. Slip a length of snug rubber hose over each rod bolt, to prevent the threads from damaging the shaft during installation.
5. Check that the piston rings are installed with the end-gaps properly positioned. Install a ring compressor over the piston and rings, then compress the rings into their grooves. (Follow the ring compressor manufacturer's instructions.)
6. Place the piston and connecting rod assembly into the cylinder bore. (If more than one piston was removed, make sure the assembly is in the proper bore.) Also, make sure that the piston and connecting rod are facing in the correct direction. Most pistons have an arrow or notch on the top of the

piston, or the letter **F** appears somewhere on the piston, to indicate the side which faces the front of the engine.

7. Check that the compressor is seated squarely on the block deck surface. If the compressor is not seated squarely, a ring could pop out from beneath the compressor and catch on the deck as the piston is tapped into its bore. Also, make sure the connecting rod is not hung up on the crankshaft counterweights, and is in position to engage the crankshaft.

8. Tap the piston slowly into the bore, making sure the ring compressor remains squarely against the block. When the piston is completely in its bore, remove the compressor.

9. Pull the connecting rod onto the crank journal, then remove the rubber hoses. Verify proper bearing fit by temporarily installing the rod cap with dry bearings and a Plastigage® insert. Check that the insert is not seated on an oil hole, and be sure the cap mark is aligned with the rod mark. Torque the connecting rod nuts to specification. Unfasten the connecting rod nuts, then remove the cap and the Plastigage®. Compare the insert's dimensions with specifications.

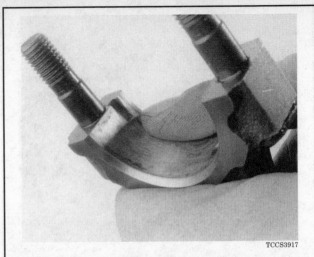

Fig. 287 The notch on the side of the connecting rod matches the groove on the bearing insert

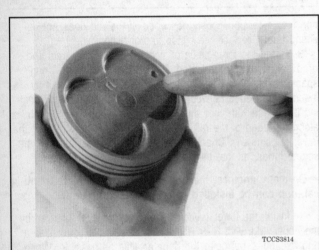

Fig. 285 Most pistons are marked to indicate positioning in the engine. Usually, a mark indicates the side facing front

Fig. 286 Installing a piston into the block using a ring compressor and hammer handle

Fig. 288 Apply a strip of gauging material to the bearing journal, before installing the cap

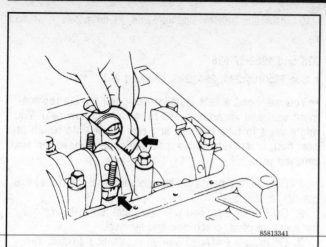

Fig. 289 Install the connecting rod cap with matchmarks on the cap and rod aligned

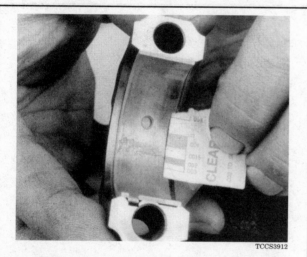

Fig. 290 After removing the cap, compare the gauging material dimensions with clearance specifications

➡**Even when the crankpin journal diameter surpasses minimum specifications, it is possible that bearing clearance is excessive. If the crankpin bearing oil clearance exceeds the maximum limit of 0.0039 in. (0.10mm) for gasoline engines, or 0.0031 in. (0.08mm) on the diesel, the journals must be machined and undersize bearings installed. If this work is necessary, it should be coordinated with a check of the crankshaft main bearings and journals, as well as end-play, as described later in this section.**

10. After verifying proper bearing fit, coat the crankshaft journal and connecting rod bearings with engine assembly lube or clean engine oil. Attach the connecting rod cap, then lightly oil the bolt threads and torque the nuts. Make sure the crankshaft rotates freely after each rod cap in torqued.

11. Measure the clearance between the sides of the connecting rod itself (not the cap) and the crankshaft, with a feeler gauge. If the clearance is below minimum specifications, the connecting rod will have to be removed and machined. If the clearance is excessive, substitute an unworn rod and recheck.

If clearance is still excessive, the crankshaft must be welded and reground, or replaced.

12. If applicable, repeat Steps 1–11 for the other pistons.

Freeze Plugs

REMOVAL AND INSTALLATION

▶ **See Figures 291 and 292**

1. Raise and safely support the vehicle, as required.
2. Drain the cooling system. Depending on the freeze plug's location, it may also be advisable to remove the drain plug from the side of the block; this will permit more thorough drainage of the coolant.
3. Drill a ½ in. (13mm) hole in the center of the freeze plug, then remove it with a slide hammer or prybar. Be careful to stop drilling as soon as the bit breaks through the plug to prevent damaging the engine.

➡**If drilling is not practical, you may instead remove the plug with a hammer and punch.**

4. Clean all dirt and corrosion from the freeze plug bore. Check the freeze plug bore for damage that would interfere with sealing. If the bore is damaged, it will have to be machined for an oversize plug.

To install:

5. Coat the plug bore and the freeze plug sealing surface with waterproof sealer.
6. Install cup-type freeze plugs with the flanged edge outward. The plug must be driven in with a tool that does not contact the flange of the plug. If an improper tool is used, the plug sealing edge will be damaged and leakage will result.
7. Expansion-type freeze plugs are installed with the flanged edge inward. The plug must be driven in with a tool that does not contact the crowned portion of the plug. If an improper tool is used, the plug and/or plug bore will be damaged.
8. Replace any drain plugs that were removed and lower the vehicle.

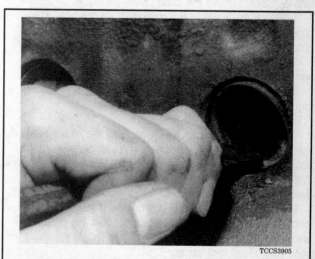

Fig. 291 The freeze plug can be loosened using a hammer and punch

Fig. 292 Once the freeze plug has been loosened, it can be removed from the block

9. Fill the cooling system to the proper level, then start the engine and check for leaks.

Rear Main Oil Seal

REMOVAL & INSTALLATION

GLC and 1979-82 626

If the rear main oil seal is being replaced independently of any other parts, it can be done with the engine in place. If the rear main oil seal and the rear main bearing are being replaced together, the engine must be removed.

1. Remove the transmission/transaxle, as described in Section 7 of this manual.
2. On models equipped with a manual transmission/transaxle, remove the pressure plate, clutch disc and flywheel.
3. On models equipped with an automatic transmission/transaxle, remove the driving plate (flexplate).
4. Punch two holes in the crankshaft rear oil seal. They should be punched on opposite sides of the crankshaft, just above the bearing cap-to-cylinder block split line.
5. Install a sheet metal screw in each hole. Pry against both screws at the same time to remove the oil seal.
6. Clean the oil recess in the cylinder block and bearing cap. Clean the oil seal surface on the crankshaft.

To install:

7. Coat the seal surfaces with oil. Coat the oil surface and the steel surface on the crankshaft with Lubriplate® or equivalent white grease. Install the new oil seal and make sure that it is not cocked. Be sure that the seal surface was not damaged.
8. On models equipped with a manual transmission/transaxle, install the flywheel, clutch disc and pressure plate. Be sure to coat the threads of the flywheel attaching bolts with oil-resistant sealer.
9. On models equipped with an automatic transmission/transaxle, install the driving plate (flexplate).

10. Install the transmission/transaxle, as described in Section 7.

323 and 1983-87 626

▶ See Figures 293, 294, 295, 296 and 297

➡ You will need a seal installer designed for the replacement seal and an arbor press to install the new seal. You might want to take the seal and rear cover (into which the seal fits), to an automotive machine shop to have the seal pressed in.

1. Remove the transaxle, as described in Section 7 of this manual.
2. On models equipped with a manual transaxle, remove the pressure plate, clutch disc and flywheel.
3. On models equipped with an automatic transaxle, remove the driving plate (flexplate).
4. Using a rag as a pivot point, pry the seal out with a flat tipped screwdriver.
5. Unbolt and remove the rear cover.

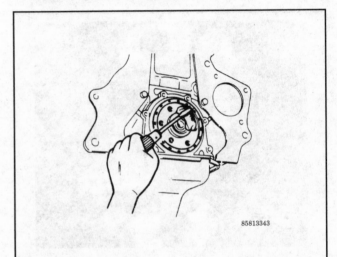

Fig. 293 Removing the rear main oil seal from a 1983-87 2.0L engine

Fig. 294 Unfasten the rear cover retaining bolts . . .

Fig. 295 . . . and separate the cover from the engine block

Fig. 296 Remove the rear cover assembly (2.0L engine shown; 1.6L similar)

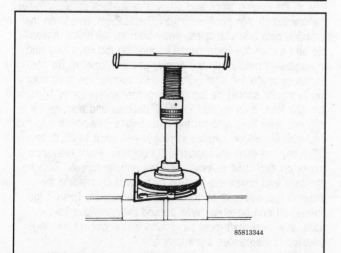

Fig. 297 Pressing in a new rear main oil seal for a 2.0L engine

To install:

6. Apply a coating of oil to the lip of the new seal. Start the seal into the rear cover by hand, then press it in using a seal installer (which fits precisely into the inner seal bore) and an arbor press. It must be straight and the front edge of the seal must align with the front edge of the cover.

7. Install the rear cover onto the engine, torquing the bolts to 6-9 ft. lbs. (8-12 Nm) on the 2.0L engine and 69-95 inch lbs. (8-11 Nm) on the 1.6L engine.

8. On models equipped with a manual transaxle, install the flywheel, clutch disc and pressure plate. Be sure to coat the threads of the flywheel attaching bolts with oil-resistant sealer.

9. On models equipped with an automatic transaxle, install the driving plate (flexplate).

10. Install the transaxle, as described in Section 7.

1988-89 626/MX6

1. Disconnect the negative battery cable. Raise and support the vehicle safely.

2. Remove the transaxle, as described in section 7.

3. If equipped with a manual transaxle, remove the pressure plate, the clutch disc and the flywheel. If equipped with an automatic transaxle, remove the drive plate from the crankshaft.

4. Remove the rear oil pan-to-seal housing bolts.

5. Remove the rear main seal housing bolts and the housing from the engine.

6. Remove the oil seal from the rear main housing.

7. Clean the gasket mounting surfaces.

To install:

8. Coat the new seal and housing with oil. Press the seal into the housing, using an arbor press.

9. Complete installation in reverse of the removal procedure. Be sure to use new gaskets and apply sealant to the oil pan mounting surface. Torque the rear seal housing bolts to 6-8 ft. lbs. (8-11 Nm).

929

1. Raise and support the vehicle safely.

2. Remove the transmission from the vehicle, as described in Section 7.

3. If equipped with a manual transmission, remove the clutch pressure plate and flywheel.

4. If equipped with automatic transmission, remove the flywheel assembly.

5. Drain the engine oil, then remove the oil pan.

6. Unfasten the rear main seal cover retaining bolts and remove the cover. Remove the seal from the cover.

To install:

7. Installation is the reverse of the removal procedure. Be sure to apply clean engine oil to the seal before pressing it into the cover. Torque the cover retaining bolts to 5-8 ft. lbs. (7-11 Nm).

8. After installing the rear cover, cut away the portion of the gasket that projects out toward the oil pan side.

Crankshaft and Main Bearings

REMOVAL & INSTALLATION

▶ See Figures 298, 299, 300, 301, 302, 303, 304 and 305

1. Remove the engine from the car, as described earlier in this section.
2. Remove the front crankshaft pulley and the flywheel. (The flywheel removal procedure is found later in this section.)
3. Invert the engine on a suitable workstand, then remove the oil pan and rear main oil seal. If so equipped, also remove the rear cover.
4. Remove the front cover, timing chain/belt, and oil pump.
5. Mark all main and connecting rod bearing caps for location.

Fig. 298 Unfasten the main bearing cap bolts . . .

Fig. 299 . . . then remove each cap and bearing

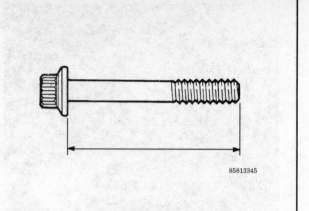

Fig. 300 Measure the length of each main bearing bolt before installation, and replace any that are out-of-range — 3.0L engine

➡You might want to check crankshaft end-play and main bearing oil clearances (as described under the installation procedure) at this time, before removing the bearing caps and crankshaft. In any event, be sure to check them when the crankshaft is reinstalled or replaced.

6. Unfasten the cap bolts, then remove the caps and bearings. (On engines in which the rear bearing cap also retains oil seals, you'll have to use a puller.) Keep all bearings and caps in position (and in order).
7. If the engine uses a manual transmission and has reached the normal time for overhaul, remove the pilot bearing (which supports the transmission input shaft) from the rear of the crankshaft with an appropriate puller.
8. Carefully lift the crankshaft from the cylinder block.
9. Clean and inspect the crankshaft for wear and run-out, and the bearings for wear, as described below. Repair or re-place parts as necessary.

To install:

10. Make sure all parts are clean and dry. Position the bearings in the engine block and bearing caps, then carefully lower the crankshaft into position. Install Plastigage® inserts on the main journals and crankpins, away from the oil holes. Assemble and torque the bearing and connecting rod caps (dry and in numbered order) with the arrows pointing forward. Be careful not to rotate the shaft. On the 3.0L engine, the main bearing cap bolts should be torqued in proper sequence to 14 ft. lbs. (20 Nm), then an additional 90 degrees and another 45 degrees after that. Also on the 3.0L engine, the connecting rod cap nuts should be torqued in proper sequence to 22 ft. lbs. (29 Nm), and then an additional 90 degrees. Paint reference marks on each bolt to assist with the angular torque. Remove the caps and check the bearing clearances by reading the width of the mark left by the insert in each case. Even if the crankshaft and bearings have passed their previous inspections, the crankshaft must be ground and undersize bearings installed, if clearances are improper.
11. Once the measured bearing clearances are correct, clean the insert marks off, thoroughly lubricate all wear surfaces with engine oil (bearing insert backs must remain dry), then reassemble and retorque all caps and cap bolts. On all GLC and 1979-82 2.0L engines, insert new side seals in the

rear main cap grooves with their holes facing forward and backward, not side-to-side. On the 3.0L engine, measure the length of each main bearing bolt prior to final installation. The bolts are acceptable only if they are 3.35-3.37 in. (85.0-85.5mm). If any bolt length differs from this specification, replace that bolt.

12. Mount a dial indicator on the block with the pin resting against the end of the crankshaft. Push the shaft as far as it will go away from the indicator, then zero the indicator. Now, pull the crankshaft all the way toward the indicator and read the end-play. If excessive, adjust it with oversize thrust bearings (washers) or, in the case of 2.2L and 1983-87 2.0L engines, a standard undersize center bearing, including appropriate grinding of the center journal. The end-play check should be done in conjunction with a check of connecting rod side clearance, as previously described. Thrust bearings must be installed with the groove outward (toward the crankshaft thrust surface).

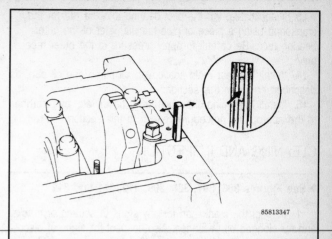

Fig. 303 Insert new side seals in the rear main cap grooves with their holes facing forward and backward — GLC and 1979-82 626 engines

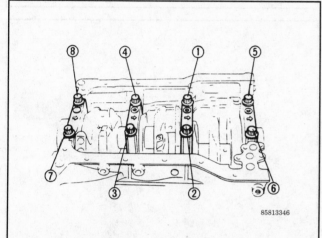

Fig. 301 Main bearing cap bolt torque sequence — 3.0L engine

Fig. 304 Mount a dial gauge against the end of the crankshaft to measure end-play

Fig. 302 Use a torque wrench to properly torque the cap bolts

Fig. 305 Carefully pry the shaft back and forth while reading the dial gauge

13. If applicable, tap the pilot bearing into the rear of the crankshaft using a piece of pipe the diameter of the outer bearing race. Be careful to apply pressure to the outer race only.

14. Install the rear main seal/cover, oil pump and oil pan, as described earlier in this section.

15. Install the timing chain/belt, front cover, etc. by referring to the appropriate procedures earlier in this section.

CLEANING AND INSPECTION

▶ See Figures 306, 307, 308, 309, 310, 311 and 312

1. Inspect the crankshaft for any signs of scoring or cracks and for clogged oil passages. Also, inspect for signs of discoloration which indicate overheating has occurred. Clogged oil passages must be cleaned in a solvent tank or with solvent and brushes (steam cleaning is not a suitable alternative). After the crankshaft is removed from the solvent, it must be flushed with fresh water, dried completely and coated with a generous film of clean engine oil. Inspect the crankshaft for scoring and minor scratching. This type of surface damage means that the crankshaft should be machined and undersize bearings installed; cracks may indicate the shaft must be replaced. Consult a competent machine shop in the case of the latter two problems. If work on the crankshaft is suspended for any length of time, fabricate a set of wood V-blocks to support the crankshaft.

2. Support the crankshaft in metal V-blocks, mount a dial indicator on the center journal, and zero it. Now, rotate the crankshaft 360 degrees to check for runout. The reading of the indicator should not exceed 0.0012 in. (0.03mm) on the 1.5L, 1.6L and 2.2L engines, or 0.0016 in. (0.04mm) on the 3.0L engine. If it does, the crankshaft must be replaced.

➡If V-blocks are not available, the crankshaft run-out may instead be checked with the shaft installed in the engine block.

3. Using a caliper, check the diameters of all main journals and crankpins, in four places, as shown. If they are worn past the limit, they must be ground and undersize bearings in-

Fig. 307 If you prefer, run-out can instead be checked with the crankshaft mounted in the engine block

Fig. 308 Position the dial indicator against the crankshaft's center main bearing journal

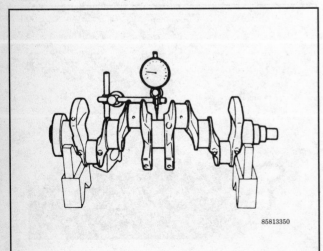

Fig. 306 With the crankshaft mounted in V-blocks, run-out can be checked using a dial gauge

stalled. In addition, on 1981-89 engines, determine the elliptical measurement for each bearing journal by subtracting the smallest reading from the largest. This elliptical limit for both the main and rod journals is 0.0020 in. (0.05mm). If the wear is elliptical beyond the limit, the crankshaft must be machined and undersize bearings installed, regardless of the total wear.

➡If the crankshaft is machined, the rolled fillet area must not be removed. Make sure the machinist is aware of the fillet "R" dimension of 0.12 in. (3mm) for gasoline engine crankshafts, or 0.102-0.118 in. (2.6-3.0mm) for diesels.

In addition, on 1983-87 2.0L engines, you must measure the front and rear oil seal sliding surface diameters. The rear seal surface must measure 3.5412-3.5434 in. (89.9-90.0mm). The front oil pump body assembly seal surface must measure 1.3371-1.3386 in. (33.96-34.00mm). Both must also be within the elliptical limit described above.

4. Inspect the bearings for scoring, flaking, grooving, bluish color (due to heat), partial elimination of the overlay (appear-

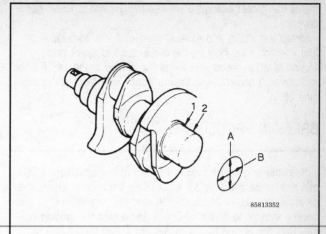

Fig. 311 Each wear surface should be measured at four places, including two perpendicular readings

Fig. 309 Turn the crankshaft slowly by hand while checking the dial gauge for run-out

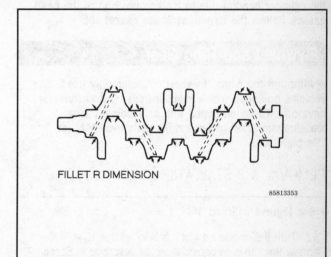

FILLET R DIMENSION

Fig. 312 If the crankshaft must be machined, do not disturb the rolled fillet areas

ance of a different color in certain areas), or a polished appearance. Replace if any such indications appear.

COMPLETING THE REBUILDING PROCESS

Fill the oil pump with oil, to prevent cavitating (sucking air) on initial engine start up. Install the oil pump and the pickup tube on the engine. Seal the oil pan gasket as appropriate, then install the gasket and pan. Mount the flywheel and the crankshaft vibration damper or pulley on the crankshaft.

➡Always use new bolts when installing the flywheel. Inspect the clutch shaft pilot bushing in the crankshaft. If the bushing is excessively worn, remove it with an expanding puller and a slide hammer, then tap a new bushing into place.

Position the engine, cylinder head side up. Lubricate the valve lifters, and install them into their bores. Install the cylinder head assembly (or assemblies), and torque as specified.

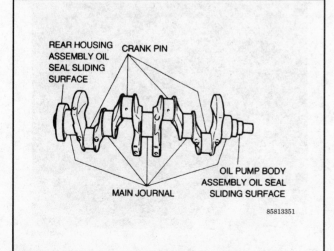

REAR HOUSING ASSEMBLY OIL SEAL SLIDING SURFACE

CRANK PIN

MAIN JOURNAL

OIL PUMP BODY ASSEMBLY OIL SEAL SLIDING SURFACE

Fig. 310 Measure all the crankshaft wear surface diameters

Install the rocker assembly (or assemblies) and cylinder head cover(s).

Install the intake and exhaust manifolds, the carburetor or fuel injection components, the distributor and spark plugs. Mount all accessories and install the engine in the car. Fill the radiator with coolant, and the crankcase with high quality engine oil.

BREAK-IN PROCEDURE

Start the engine, and allow it to run at low speed for a few minutes, while checking for leaks. Stop the engine, check the oil level, and fill as necessary. Restart the engine, and fill the cooling system to capacity. Check and adjust the ignition timing. Run the engine at low-to-medium speed (800-2,500 rpm) for approximately ½ hour, then retorque the cylinder head bolts. Road test the car, and check again for leaks.

➡**Some gasket manufacturers recommend not retorquing the cylinder head(s) due to the composition of the head gasket. Follow the directions in the gasket set.**

Flywheel and Ring Gear

➡**Although the word "flywheel" is commonly used, only vehicles equipped with a manual transaxle/transmission have one. Those equipped with an automatic transaxle/transmission utilize a drive plate assembly (or "flexplate").**

REMOVAL & INSTALLATION

▶ **See Figures 313 and 314**

1. Turn the engine so that the No. 1 piston is at TDC. Remove the transaxle/transmission, as described in Section 7.

2. Install a device to lock the flywheel/flexplate, such as Mazda Part No. 49 E301 060 or equivalent. (On the 2.0L engine, use Mazda Part No. 49 V101 060 or equivalent). Such devices typically bolt to the rear engine plate. Install the device in the direction which will keep the flywheel/flexplate from turning as the mounting bolts are turned.

➡**If such a locking device is unavailable, thread a bolt partway into the engine block (to serve as a fulcrum), then carefully wedge a screwdriver or similar tool between the ring gear teeth and the bolt.**

3. If equipped with a manual transaxle/transmission, remove the clutch as described in Section 7.

4. Support the flywheel/flexplate in a secure manner. Unfasten the bolts, then remove the assembly. Run the appropriate size metric tap through each bolt hole to ensure proper thread contact. Wire brush the bolts to remove any dirt or grease from the threads.

To install:

5. On the 323, 626, MX-6 and 929, coat the bolt threads with a sealant, such as Mazda part No. 8530 77 743 or equivalent. Position the flywheel/flexplate, then install the bolts loosely.

Fig. 314 Unfasten the retaining bolts, then carefully lower the flywheel

6. Turn the locking device around so the bolts may be torqued without turning the flywheel/flexplate. Torque the bolts to specification.

7. If applicable, install the clutch as described in Section 7.

8. Install the transaxle/transmission as described in Section 7.

RING GEAR REPLACEMENT

➡**The ring gear can only be replaced separately on those vehicles with a flywheel. On vehicles with a flexplate, the ring gear is integral.**

▶ **See Figure 315**

1. Remove the flywheel as previously described. Use a torch, confining the flame carefully to the ring gear itself, to heat and expand the ring gear. Then, support the flywheel at its center and tap the ring gear all around to remove it.

Fig. 313 Use a spray solvent to clean the flywheel and retaining bolts

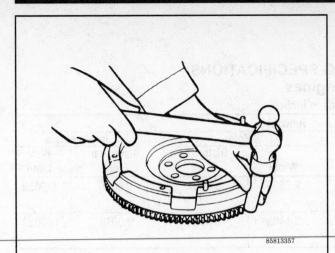

85813357

Fig. 315 Removing the flywheel ring gear

2. Put the new ring gear in an oven and heat it to 480°-570°F (249°-299°C). Give the ring gear plenty of time to rise to the oven temperature (at least 20 minutes).

❊❊CAUTION

Handle the ring gear with insulated gloves only!

3. Position the ring gear with the beveled side facing the engine side of the flywheel. Then, work it evenly onto the flywheel using a short piece of 2 x 4 lumber and a hammer. Install the flywheel as previously described.

ROTARY ENGINE SERVICE

Compression Test

The conventional compression gauges that are used for gasoline and diesel engines are not suitable for use on a rotary engine, as they only measure the highest pressure of the three combustion chambers in the rotor housing. To accurately determine compression pressure on rotary engines, a special electronic compression tester (49-F018-9A0) is required. This piece of test equipment reads the compression of all three combustion chambers.

GENERAL ENGINE SPECIFICATIONS
Rotary Engines

Engine	Years	Fuel System Type	SAE Net Horsepower @ rpm	SAE Net Torque ft. lbs. @ rpm	Comp. Ratio	Oil Pressure (psi) @ 2000 rpm
1.1L Rotary (Code 12A)	1979–85	4-bbl	101 @ 6000	105 @ 4000	9.4:1	70
1.3L Rotary (Code 13B)	1981–89	EFI	146 @ 6500	138 @ 3800	9.4:1	70
	1986–89 Turbo	EFI	182 @ 6500	183 @ 3500	8.5:1	70

858130C7

ROTOR AND HOUSING SPECIFICATIONS
Rotary Engines
(All specifications in inches)

| Engine Type | Rotor Clearance to Side Housing | Housings | | | | | | |
| | | Front & Rear | | Rotor | | Intermediate | |
		Distortion Limit	Wear Limit	Width	Distortion Limit	Distortion Limit	Wear Limit
1.1L (Code 12A)	0.0047–0.0075	0.0016	0.0039	2.7559	0.0024	0.0016	0.0039
1.3L (Code 13B)	0.0047–0.0083	0.0016	0.0039	3.1493	0.0024	0.0016	0.0039

858130C8

ECCENTRIC SHAFT SPECIFICATIONS
Rotary Engines
(All specifications in inches)

| Engine Type | Journal Diameter | | Oil Clearance | | Shaft End Play | Maximum Shaft Run-out |
	Main Bearing	Rotor Bearing	Main Bearing	Rotor Bearing		
1.1L (Code 12A)	1.6929	2.9194	0.0016–0.0028	0.0016–0.0031	0.0016–0.0028	0.0024
1.3L (Code 13B)	1.6921	2.9125	0.0016–0.0031	0.0016–0.0031	0.0016–0.0028	0.0047

858130C9

TORQUE SPECIFICATIONS
Rotary Engines
(All specifications in ft. lbs.)

| Engine Type | Tension Bolts | Eccentric Shaft Pulley | Flywheel | Manifolds | | Oil Pan | Front Cover | Bearing Housing | Rear Stationary Gear |
				Intake	Exhaust				
1.1L (Code 12A)	23–27	72–87	290–360	14–19	23–34	6–8	15	15	15
1.3L (Code 13B)	23–29	80–98	290–360	14–19	23–34	6–8	15	15	15

85813C10

Engine

REMOVAL & INSTALLATION

➡**Be sure that the engine has completely cooled before attempting to remove it.**

1979-85 Carbureted RX-7

1. Disconnect the negative battery cable. Scribe matchmarks on the hood and hinges, then remove the hood.
2. Working from underneath the vehicle, remove the gravel shield, then drain the cooling system and engine oil into separate containers.
3. Disconnect the high tension wires from the center towers of the ignition coils.

➡**A good rule of thumb when disconnecting the engine wiring and vacuum hoses, is to first mark each pair of wires/hoses with a numbered piece of masking tape. Use the same number on both sides of a connection, but be sure to number each set of connections differently. When reconnecting the wires/hoses, simply match the pieces of tape.**

4. Disconnect the distributor wiring, the oil level sensor lead, the water temperature lead and, on all except California vehicles, the coupler from the oil thermosensor.
5. On all California vehicles and on vehicles equipped with an automatic transmission, disconnect the vacuum sensing tube from the vacuum switch. Disconnect the evaporative hose.
6. Disconnect the hoses from the oil cooler, located beneath the radiator. Disconnect the radiator coolant level sensor lead from the top of the radiator, and disconnect the coolant reservoir hose.
7. Unfasten the bolts, then remove the drive pulley from the cooling fan and drive unit. Remove the air cleaner assembly.

➡**On vehicles equipped with air conditioning, it will be necessary to remove the compressor and the condenser from their mounts. Do not unfasten the refrigerant lines. Tie the units off to a convenient place on the body or engine compartment.**

8. On all vehicles, except California and Canada, detach the connectors from the No. 2 water temperature sensor, located on the radiator next to the radiator cap.
9. Disconnect the lower and upper radiator hoses. If equipped, disconnect the automatic transmission fluid lines at the radiator.
10. Remove the cooling fan/drive unit, along with the radiator and fan shroud assembly.
11. Disconnect the vacuum hose for the brake booster. Disconnect the heat exchanger pipe from the rear of the intake manifold.
12. Disconnect the coupler from the power valve solenoid, on all except Canadian vehicles equipped with a manual transmission.
13. Disconnect the coasting enrichment connector on vehicles equipped with a manual transmission. Disconnect the leads from the choke heater and the anti-afterburn solenoid. Disconnect the idle switch coupler on manual transmission

equipped vehicles. Disconnect the throttle sensor, the MAB solenoid valve, the idle richer solenoid, and the port air solenoid valve.
14. On all vehicles, except California and Canada, disconnect the lead from the choke return solenoid valve.
15. If equipped, remove the rear cover from the exhaust manifold.
16. Disconnect the accelerator, choke and hot start assist cables.
17. Disconnect the fuel lines from the carburetor and plug the fuel intake line to prevent leakage. Disconnect the cruise control cable, if equipped.
18. Disengage the wiring connector and the "B" terminal from the alternator. On all vehicles, except California, disconnect the sub-zero start assist hose.
19. Disconnect the wiring from the No. 1 water temperature vacuum switch, the 3-way valve, the engine strap and the air vent solenoid. Disconnect the heater hoses from the engine.
20. From underneath the vehicle, disconnect and remove the starter. Remove the engine to transmission bolts.
21. On automatic transmission vehicles, remove the converter housing lower cover, matchmark the drive plate in relation to the torque converter, then remove the torque converter-to-drive plate bolts.
22. Disconnect all interfering exhaust system components.
23. Support the front of the transmission with a floor jack, then remove the left and right side engine mount bolts.
24. Attach a suitable sling to the engine hanger brackets, then raise the engine with a hoist slightly.
25. Pull the engine forward until it clears the clutch shaft or torque converter, then lift it out of the vehicle.
26. Mount the engine on a suitable engine stand. Remove the valve and piping assemblies from the engine.

➡**A special three-part workstand, designed for the rotary engine, is available from Mazda.**

To install:
27. Install the engine valve and piping assemblies. Reconnect the sling to the lifting brackets and connect a suitable lifting hoist to the sling.
28. Lower and guide the engine into the vehicle until it engages the clutch shaft or torque converter. Once the engine is in place, tension the hoist slightly to hold it there. Install the right and left engine mount bolts. Remove the jack from underneath the transmission.
29. Connect all exhaust components that were disconnected for engine removal clearance.
30. On automatic transmission equipped vehicles, attach the drive plate to the torque converter using the previously made alignment marks. Install the retaining bolts, after rotating the engine as necessary. Install the torque converter housing lower cover.
31. Install and tighten the lower engine-to-transmission bolts. Install the starter.
32. Connect the heater hose to the left side of the engine. Connect the electrical wiring to the air solenoid and water temperature switch.
33. Connect the alternator wiring. Connect the sub-zero start assist hose, if applicable.
34. Unplug and connect the fuel lines to the carburetor.
35. Connect the hot start assist, choke and accelerator cables. If equipped, install the exhaust manifold rear cover.

36. Install the two upper engine-to-transmission bolts.

37. On 1980 and later models, except California and Canada, connect the electrical lead to the choke return solenoid valve.

38. On manual transmission equipped vehicles, connect the idle switch coupler and coasting enrichment connector. Connect the leads to the choke heater and the anti-afterburn solenoid.

39. On all 1980 models, 1979 models equipped with automatic transmission, and California manual transmission equipped models, connect the power solenoid valve coupler.

40. Connect the heat exchanger pipe to the rear of the intake manifold. Connect the brake booster vacuum hose.

41. Install the radiator and fan shroud assembly.

42. On automatic transmission equipped vehicles, connect the transmission fluid cooler lines to the radiator.

43. On all 1980 and later models (except California and Canada), fasten the connectors for the No. 2 water temperature sensor, located next to the radiator cap. If equipped, install the air conditioning compressor and condenser onto their mounts.

44. Install the air cleaner assembly and associated brackets. Attach the cooling fan and drive unit to the drive pulley, then install the retaining bolts.

45. Attach the coolant reservoir hose, then connect the radiator coolant temperature sensor lead at the top portion of the radiator. Working from the bottom of the radiator, connect the oil cooler hoses.

46. Connect the evaporative hose. On all California models, and on all 1980 and later models equipped with an automatic transmission, connect the vacuum sensing tube to the vacuum switch.

47. On all models with the exception of California, connect the oil thermosensor coupler. Connect the water temperature and oxygen sensor leads. Connect the distributor wires.

48. Connect the wires to the center towers of the ignition coils. Connect the negative battery cable.

49. Fill the crankcase and the cooling system to their proper levels (see the Capacities chart in Section 1). Install the gravel shield from underneath the car.

50. Position and install the hood onto its hinges using the alignment marks made previously.

51. Adjust all cables, drive belts and linkages. Perform a complete tune-up.

1984-89 Fuel Injected RX-7

NON-TURBO

♦ See Figure 316

1. Properly relieve the fuel system pressure, as described in Section 5. Disconnect the negative battery cable.

2. Scribe matchmarks on the hood and hinges, then remove the hood.

3. Remove the engine under cover. Drain the coolant and engine oil into separate containers.

✳✳WARNING

Be sure to consult the laws in your area before servicing the air conditioning system. In most areas, it is illegal to service a refrigerant system without a certified recovery/recycling station. R-12 refrigerant is a chlorofluoro-carbon which, when released into the atmosphere, can contribute to depletion of the ozone layer in the upper atmosphere.

4. As required, properly discharge and recover refrigerant from the air conditioning system, using a proper recycling/recovery station.

➡ **A good rule of thumb when disconnecting the engine wiring and vacuum hoses, is to first mark each pair of wires/hoses with a numbered piece of masking tape. Use the same number on both sides of a connection, but be sure to number each set of connections differently. When reconnecting the wires/hoses, simply match the pieces of tape.**

5. Disconnect the spark plug wires at the plugs. If so equipped, remove the distributor cap and spark plug wires, along with the rotor. (On 1986-89 models, disconnect the crank angle sensor.) Disconnect the oil pressure gauge and oil temperature gauge wiring harnesses. Disconnect the accelerator cable, fuel lines and evaporator lines. Plug the lines to prevent leakage and contamination.

6. From the left side of the engine compartment, disconnect the air conditioner compressor drive belt and remove the compressor. Remove the power steering pump and mounting brackets. Disconnect the rear oil hose (or oil cooler pipe) and drain the engine oil into a container. Remove the starter cable harness bracket. Disconnect the heater hoses and water temperature gauge unit wiring.

7. From the right side of the engine compartment, remove or disconnect the air pump hose, the air funnel, air flow meter connector and the air cleaner assembly. Disconnect the radiator hoses and heater hose from the radiator.

8. Disconnect the fan wiring harness, then remove the cooling fan and cover (shroud). Disconnect the coolant level sensor, then remove the radiator. Disconnect the oil cooler hoses.

9. Disconnect the cruise control cable and the oil pump metering rod connector. Disconnect the water hoses, brake booster hose and air pump hoses.

10. Detach the intake air temperature sensor connector, the air supply valve connector and the throttle sensor connector. Remove the mounting nut and disconnect the terminal cover wire at the dynamic chamber.

11. If the engine will be disassembled, disconnect the eight vacuum sensor tubes from the dynamic chamber, then unfasten and remove the dynamic chamber from the engine.

12. Unfasten the following wiring connectors: oxygen sensor, fuel injectors, water temperature sensor, vacuum control solenoid valve, pressure regulator control solenoid, vent solenoid, vacuum valve solenoid, engine ground and alternator wiring harness.

13. Raise and safely support the vehicle. Remove the exhaust pipe front cover and catalytic converter cover. Disconnect the No. 1 Pre-monolith converter from the exhaust manifold. Disconnect the starter motor wiring harness, then remove the starter motor.

14. Remove the transmission-to-engine attaching bolts and the engine mount nuts.

15. Lower the vehicle. Attach a suitable lifting sling to the engine's lifting brackets and to a hoist. Carefully remove the engine after pulling it forward slightly to disengage the transmission.

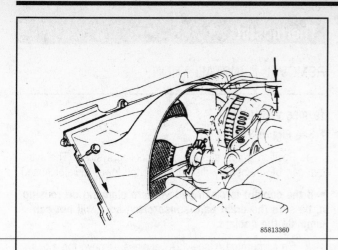

85813360

Fig. 316 Checking cooling fan clearance on fuel injected non-turbo RX-7

16. Mount the engine on a stand or suitable holding fixture and remove the sling from the lifting brackets.

➡**A special three-part workstand, designed for the rotary engine, is available from Mazda.**

To install:

17. Reconnect the sling to the lifting brackets and connect a hoist to the sling.

18. Lower and guide the engine into the vehicle until it engages the clutch or torque converter input shaft. Once the engine is in place, tension the hoist slightly to hold it there. Install the right and left engine mount bolts, along with the transmission-to-engine bolts.

19. Install the starter motor and connect its wiring harness. Connect the No. 1 pre-monolith converter to the exhaust manifold. Install the catalytic converter cover and exhaust pipe front cover.

20. Connect the alternator wiring harness, engine ground, vacuum valve solenoid, vent solenoid, pressure regulator control solenoid and vacuum control solenoid. Attach the water temperature sensor, fuel injector connectors and oxygen sensor wiring.

21. If applicable, install the dynamic chamber and connect the eight vacuum sensor tubes.

22. Connect the terminal cover wire with the attaching nut. Attach the throttle sensor, air supply valve and intake air temperature sensor wiring connectors.

23. Connect the air pump, brake booster and water hoses. Connect the oil pump metering rod connector and the cruise control cable.

24. Connect the oil cooler hoses. Install the radiator and connect the coolant level sensor.

25. Install the cooling fan and cover, then connect the fan wiring harness. Adjust the cover so that there is 0.63-0.94 in. (16-24mm) clearance from the tip of the fan blade to the edge of the cover.

26. Install the radiator and heater hoses. From the right side of the engine, connect/install the air cleaner assembly and brackets, air flow meter connector, air funnel and air pump hose.

27. Connect the heater hoses and temperature gauge unit wiring at the engine. Install the starter wiring harness bracket. Connect the rear oil hose. Install the power steering pump mounting bracket and the power steering pump. Install the air conditioning compressor with the drive belt.

28. Connect the evaporator and fuel lines, then connect the accelerator cable. Connect the wiring harnesses to the oil temperature and pressure gauges.

29. From the left side of the engine, install the rotor and distributor cap (or connect the crank angle sensor). Connect the spark plug wires.

✳✳WARNING

Be sure to consult the laws in your area before charging the air conditioning system. In most areas it is illegal to service a system without a certified recovery/recycling station. R-12 refrigerant is a chlorofluorocarbon which, when released into the atmosphere, can contribute to depletion of the ozone layer in the upper atmosphere.

30. Charge the air conditioning system, using the proper equipment.

31. Connect the negative battery cable.

32. Fill the crankcase and the cooling system to their proper levels (see the Capacities chart in Section 1).

33. Position and install the hood onto its hinges, using the alignment marks made previously.

34. Adjust all cables and linkages. Perform a complete tune-up.

TURBO

1. Properly relieve the fuel system pressure, as described in Section 5. Disconnect the negative battery cable.

2. Drain the engine oil and coolant into separate containers.

3. Starting from the front and right side of the engine, remove the following components:

  a. Air intake pipe and air cleaner assembly.

  b. Battery and battery box.

  c. Cooling fan and upper and lower radiator hoses.

  d. Heater return hose, coolant level sensor connector and radiator switch connector. Remove the automatic transmission fluid hose (1987-89 vehicles only).

  e. Radiator, cowling and intercooler.

  f. Accelerator cable and, if equipped, cruise control cable. Brake vacuum hose, pressure sensor vacuum hose, relief silencer hose and spilt air pipe.

  g. Oxygen sensor connector, insulator covers, front converter upper nut and engine harness connector.

4. Working from the left side of the engine, remove/disconnect the following components:

  a. Power steering pump and drive belt. Leave the hoses connected to the power steering pump and secure it out of the way.

  b. Air conditioning compressor and drive belt. Leave the hoses connected to the compressor and secure it out of the way.

  c. Spark plug wires, crank angle sensor connector and alternator connector.

  d. Canister hose. Remove and plug the fuel hose.

e. Oil pressure connector, heater hose, clutch release cylinder, engine ground and oil cooler pipe and bracket.

5. Raise and safely support the vehicle. Remove the under cover and catalytic converter insulator. Disconnect the split air pipe, exhaust pipe bracket and catalytic converter. Remove the exhaust pipe and front converter, starter, transmission attaching bolts and engine mounting nuts.

6. Lower the vehicle, then attach a suitable lifting sling and hoist to the engine lifting brackets and a hoist. Carefully remove the engine after pulling it forward slightly to disengage the transmission.

7. Mount the engine on a stand or suitable holding fixture. Disconnect the sling from the lifting brackets.

➡A special three-part workstand, designed for the rotary engine, is available from Mazda.

To install:

8. Reconnect the sling to the lifting brackets, then connect a hoist to the sling and carefully raise the engine.

9. Lower and guide the engine into the vehicle until it engages the clutch or torque converter input shaft. Once the engine is in place, tension the hoist slightly to hold it there. Install the right and left engine mount bolts, along with the transmission-to-engine bolts.

10. Install the catalytic converter, exhaust pipe bracket, split air pipe, catalytic converter insulator and the under cover. Lower the vehicle.

11. Working from the left side of the vehicle, install/connect the following components:

a. Oil cooler pipe and bracket, engine ground, clutch release cylinder, heater hose and the oil pressure switch connector

b. Fuel and canister hoses.

c. Alternator and crank angle sensor connectors. Connect the spark plug wires.

d. Position the air conditioning compressor onto its mounting, slip the drive belt over the pulley and adjust it. Install the power steering pump in the same manner.

12. Working from the right and the front sides of the engine, install/connect the following components:

a. Engine harness connector, front converter upper nut, insulator covers and oxygen sensor connector.

b. Split air pipe, relief silencer hose, pressure sensor vacuum hose, brake vacuum hose, cruise control and accelerator cables.

c. Intercooler, radiator and radiator cowling.

d. Battery box and battery.

e. Air cleaner assembly and air intake pipe.

13. Connect the negative battery cable.

14. Fill the crankcase and the cooling system to their proper levels (see the Capacities chart in Section 1).

15. Position and install the hood onto its hinges, using the alignment marks made previously.

16. Adjust all cables and linkages. Perform a complete tune-up.

Thermostat

REMOVAL & INSTALLATION

1979-85 Vehicles

▶ **See Figure 317**

1. Position a pan and drain the cooling system. (The system can be drained by disconnecting the lower radiator hose.)

➡If the coolant is clean and you are planning on reusing it, be sure the drain pan is also clean so it will not contaminate the coolant.

2. On carbureted (Code 12A) engines, remove the air cleaner assembly.

3. Disconnect the upper radiator hose from the engine, then remove the two nuts or bolts attaching the thermostat housing cover.

4. Remove the cover, then lift out the thermostat and gasket.

5. Carefully scrape any old gasket material from the mating surfaces.

To install:

6. Position a new gasket, and install the thermostat with the jiggle pin facing up.

7. Attach the thermostat cover and tighten the retaining nuts or bolts.

8. Connect the upper radiator hose and tighten the hose clamp.

9. Install the air cleaner assembly (Code 12A engines only).

10. Connect the lower radiator hose and tighten the hose clamp.

11. Fill the radiator to the proper level with a suitable coolant mixture.

12. Start the engine and inspect for coolant leaks.

1986-89 Vehicles

▶ **See Figure 318**

1. Position a pan under the radiator drain plug. Open the plug and drain the cooling system.

➡If the coolant is clean and you are planning on reusing it, be sure the drain pan is also clean so it will not contaminate the coolant.

2. Loosen the hose clamp and disconnect the upper radiator hose.

3. Disconnect the water thermoswitch terminal at the thermostat cover.

4. Remove the two bolts and separate the cover from the engine.

5. Remove the thermostat and gasket from the housing.

6. Carefully scrape any old gasket material from the mating surfaces.

To install:

7. Position a new gasket onto the housing. Install the thermostat into the housing so that the jiggle pin is facing up.

8. Install the cover and tighten the retaining bolts.

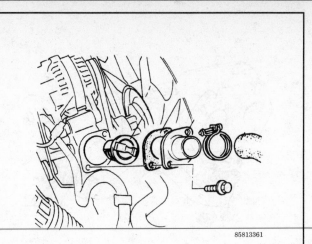

Fig. 317 Thermostat assembly — 1979-85 RX-7

Fig. 318 Thermostat assembly — 1986-89 RX-7

9. Attach the water thermoswitch connector to the terminal on the cover.

10. Using a moderate twisting motion, connect the upper radiator hose by aligning the marks on the hose with those on the cover. Tighten the hose clamp.

11. Check that the drain plug is closed, then fill the radiator to the proper level with a suitable coolant mixture.

12. Start the engine and inspect for coolant leaks.

Intake Manifold

REMOVAL & INSTALLATION

Carbureted Engine

1. Remove the air cleaner assembly. Disconnect the carburetor linkage. Drain the radiator.

2. Tag and disconnect all vacuum hoses and fuel lines from the carburetor (plug the fuel lines to prevent leakage).

3. Tag and disconnect all carburetor wiring.

4. Disconnect and remove the air pump.

5. Disconnect the metering oil pump connecting rod and hoses.

6. Remove the air outlet pipe from the end of the manifold. Disconnect the vacuum sensing tube.

7. Remove the exhaust manifold cover, then unbolt and remove the inlet manifold, complete with the carburetor.

8. Remove the gasket and O-rings. Thoroughly clean the mating surfaces.

To install:

9. Position a new gasket and O-rings.

10. Position the inlet manifold and install its retaining bolts. Torque the bolts to 14-19 ft. lbs. (19-26 Nm).

11. Install the exhaust manifold cover.

12. Connect the air outlet pipe and the vacuum sensing tube.

13. Attach the metering oil pump connecting rod and hoses.

14. Install the air pump.

15. Connect the carbureter wiring.

16. Connect the fuel lines and applicable vacuum hoses.

17. Fasten the carbureter linkage, then install the air cleaner assembly.

18. Fill the cooling system to the proper level with a suitable coolant mixture.

Fuel Injected Engine

NON-TURBO

1. Properly relieve the fuel system pressure, then disconnect the negative battery cable.

2. Remove the air funnel and disconnect the accelerator cable.

3. Disconnect the cruise control cable, if equipped.

4. Disconnect the throttle sensor connector.

5. Disconnect the metering pump oil rod.

6. Label then remove the water, fuel and vacuum hoses. Plug the fuel hose openings.

7. If so equipped, disconnect the air supply valve (1985) or bypass air control valve (1986-89).

8. Unfasten the air intake temperature sensor connector.

9. Remove the nuts and bolts, then lift the dynamic chamber from the engine. Remove the gasket and cover the intake ports with a clean rag to prevent anything from falling into the engine. Thoroughly clean all gasket mating surfaces and inspect the chamber for cracks or any other type of damage.

To install:

10. Place a new gasket onto the lower chamber flange, then install the chamber and attaching hardware.

11. Connect the intake air temperature sensor.

12. If applicable, connect the bypass air control valve or air supply valve.

13. Connect the vacuum, fuel and water hoses.

14. Connect the metering oil pump rod.

15. Fasten the throttle sensor connector.

16. Connect the cruise control (if so equipped) and accelerator cables.

17. Install the air funnel and connect the negative battery cable.

TURBO

1. Disconnect the negative battery cable and drain the cooling system.

2. Disconnect the inlet and outlet hoses, then remove the intercooler.

3. Unbolt and remove the oil filler pipe with the gasket. *Immediately* cover the oil filler opening to prevent anything from falling into the engine.

4. Disconnect the accelerator cable from the throttle body.

5. Disconnect the cruise control cable, if so equipped.

6. Disconnect the metering pump oil rod.

7. Tag and disconnect all electrical connectors from the throttle body.

8. Disconnect the vacuum tubes and water hoses.

9. Remove the nuts and bolts, then lift the dynamic chamber from the engine. Remove the gasket and cover the intake ports with a clean rag to prevent anything from falling into the engine. Thoroughly clean all gasket mating surfaces and inspect the chamber for cracks or any other type of damage.

To install:

10. Place a new gasket onto the lower chamber flange studs, then install the chamber with the nuts and bolts.

11. Connect the water hoses and vacuum tubes.

12. Connect the throttle body electrical connectors.

13. Connect the metering pump oil rod.

14. Connect the cruise control cable, if so equipped.

15. Connect the accelerator cable.

16. Inspect the oil filler pipe flange gasket for rips or tears. If in good condition, reuse it. Install the oil filler pipe with its attaching bolts.

17. Install the intercooler, then connect the inlet and outlet hoses.

18. Fill the cooling system to the proper level with a suitable coolant mixture.

19. Connect the negative battery cable. Start the engine and inspect for leaks.

Exhaust Manifold (Thermal Reactor)

REMOVAL & INSTALLATION

Carbureted Engine

▶ **See Figure 319**

➡**1979-80 RX-7 models use a thermal reactor, instead of a traditional or reactive exhaust manifold.**

1. Remove the air cleaner assembly and hot air duct hose. Remove the air injection pump.

2. If so equipped, disconnect the thermal reactor-to-air control valve air pipe.

3. Remove the intake manifold/thermal reactor upper side nuts. Mazda makes a special angled T-bar wrench for this job (tool number 49-8501-125 or equivalent).

4. Raise the vehicle and safely support it on jackstands. Disconnect the air pipe, running between the inlet manifold and the heat exchanger, from the inlet manifold.

5. If applicable, remove the air pipe running between the thermal reactor and the air duct.

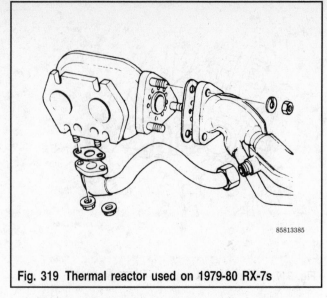

85813385

Fig. 319 Thermal reactor used on 1979-80 RX-7s

6. If applicable, unfasten the air duct hanger bracket from the transmission housing, and disconnect the air duct from the thermal reactor.

7. Remove the intake manifold/thermal reactor lower side nuts.

8. Remove the intake manifold/thermal reactor and gasket. Thoroughly clean the gasket mating surfaces.

To install:

9. Position a new gasket and install the intake manifold/thermal reactor. Attach the lower side mounting nuts and tighten them in several stages to 33-40 ft. lbs. (45-54 Nm).

10. If applicable, connect the air duct, then fasten its hanger bracket to the transmission housing.

11. If applicable, install the air pipe between the thermal reactor and the air duct.

12. Connect the air pipe from the heat exchanger at the inlet manifold.

13. Lower the vehicle.

14. Attach the upper side mounting nuts and tighten them in several stages to 33-40 ft. lbs. (45-54 Nm).

15. If applicable, connect the air pipe between the thermal reactor and air control valve.

16. Install the air injection pump.

17. Install the air cleaner assembly. Be sure to connect the hot air duct hose.

Fuel Injected Engine

NON-TURBO

▶ **See Figure 320**

1. Disconnect the negative battery cable.

2. Remove the air intake manifold (throttle and dynamic chamber), as described earlier in this section.

3. Unfasten the screws and nuts that attach the exhaust absorber plate to the exhaust manifold insulator, then remove the plate.

4. Detach the oxygen sensor connector, then route the wiring so that it can be readily removed with the exhaust manifold.

5. Raise and safely support the front end on jackstands. Remove the exhaust pipe front cover, catalytic converter cover

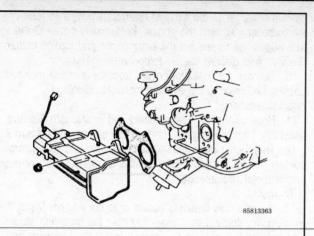

Fig. 320 Exhaust manifold assembly — fuel injected non-turbo engine

and exhaust pipe bracket. Disconnect the exhaust pipe from the exhaust manifold.

6. Loosen and remove the exhaust manifold retaining nuts and lockwashers.

7. Separate the manifold and insulator from the engine, then pull the manifold from the engine mounting studs. Remove the gasket and discard it.

8. Thoroughly clean the exhaust manifold contact surfaces, then check the exhaust manifold for warpage using a metal straightedge.

To install:

9. Position a new manifold gasket on the engine. Install the exhaust manifold assembly over the mounting studs, flush with the gasket. Install the lockwashers and mounting nuts, then torque to 23-34 ft. lbs. (31-46 Nm).

10. Connect all the exhaust manifold components, using new gaskets as required.

11. Attach the oxygen sensor connector. Install the exhaust absorber plate, and torque the retaining screws to 6-8 ft. lbs. (8-11 Nm).

12. Install the air intake manifold, as described earlier in this section.

13. Connect the negative battery cable.

14. Start the engine and allow it to reach normal operating temperature, then check for exhaust leaks.

TURBO

1. Disconnect the negative battery cable. Drain the cooling system.

2. Disconnect the hoses from the air pump, then remove the air pump from the engine.

3. Loosen the hose clamps, then disconnect the funnel and air hose from the air cleaner and turbocharger. Remove the air funnel and air hose from the engine.

4. Detach the connector from the air control valve and remove the valve from the engine.

5. Disconnect the split air pipe from the engine and remove the pipe, along with the gasket.

6. Disconnect and remove the water hose and water pipe from the engine.

7. Disconnect the supply and return oil pipes from the turbocharger. (There may be some oil left in the lines, so be prepared to collect any residual oil with a small plastic container. Be sure to cover the openings to protect the system.)

8. Remove the front catalytic converter insulator covers, then disconnect the front converter from the turbocharger. Remove and discard the old gasket.

9. Unstake the retainer tabs from the retainer plate with a small prying tool. Remove the nuts and washers that secure the turbocharger to the exhaust manifold studs, then remove the turbocharger from the engine. Immediately cover all the turbo openings to prevent the entry of dirt and foreign matter. Remove the turbocharger gasket and purchase a new one.

10. Remove the insulator covers from the exhaust manifold. Loosen and remove the exhaust manifold retaining nuts/lockwashers.

11. Remove the exhaust manifold and waste gate actuator assembly from the engine. Remove the gasket and discard it.

12. Thoroughly clean the exhaust manifold and turbocharger contact surfaces, then check the exhaust manifold for warpage with a metal straightedge.

To install:

13. Place a new manifold gasket on the engine. Install the exhaust manifold/actuator assembly over the mounting studs and position it flush with the gasket. Install the lockwashers and mounting nuts, then torque them to 23-34 ft. lbs. (31-46 Nm).

14. Install a new turbocharger gasket onto the exhaust manifold, then carefully guide the turbo assembly over the mounting studs and onto the gasket. Install the lockwashers and mounting nuts, and torque them to 33-40 ft. lbs. (45-54 Nm). Once the nuts are torqued, crimp the tabs on the nut retaining plate to prevent the nuts from loosening. Remove the protective covers from the turbo openings.

15. Connect the front converter to the turbocharger with a new gasket. Torque the nuts to 33-40 ft. lbs. (45-54 Nm).

16. Install the remaining components in reverse of their removal procedure. Install a new gasket for any part requiring one:

- Insulator covers
- Oil pipes
- Water pipe and water hose
- Split air pipe
- Air control valve
- Air funnel and air hose
- Air pump and air hoses

17. Fill the cooling system to the proper level with a suitable coolant mixture and connect the negative battery cable.

18. Start the engine and check for leaks. Make all necessary adjustments.

Turbocharger

▶ See Figure 321

REMOVAL & INSTALLATION

1. Disconnect the negative battery cable. Drain the cooling system.

2. Disconnect the hoses from the air pump and remove the air pump from the engine.

3. Loosen the hose clamps, then disconnect the funnel and air hose from the air cleaner and the turbocharger. Remove the air funnel and air hose from the engine.

4. Disengage the connector from the air control valve and remove the valve from the engine.

5. Disconnect the split air pipe from the engine and remove the pipe, along with the gasket.

6. Disconnect and remove the water hose and water pipe from the engine.

7. Disconnect the supply and return oil pipes from the turbocharger. (There may be some oil left in the lines, so be prepared to collect any residual oil with a small plastic container. Be sure to cover the openings to protect the system.)

8. Remove the front converter insulator covers and disconnect the front converter from the turbocharger. Remove and discard the old gasket.

9. Unstake the retainer tabs from the retainer plate with a small prying tool. Remove the nuts and washers that secure the turbocharger to the exhaust manifold studs, then remove the turbocharger from the engine. Immediately cover all the turbo openings to prevent the entry of dirt and foreign matter. Remove and discard the old turbocharger gasket.

10. Remove the insulator covers from the exhaust manifold. Loosen and remove the exhaust manifold retaining nuts/lockwashers.

11. Remove the exhaust manifold and waste gate actuator assembly from the engine. Remove the gasket and discard it.

12. Thoroughly clean the exhaust manifold and turbocharger contact surfaces, then check the exhaust manifold for warpage with a metal straightedge.

To install:

13. Place a new manifold gasket onto the engine. Install the exhaust manifold/actuator assembly over the mounting studs and position it flush with the gasket. Install the lockwashers and mounting nuts, then torque them to 23-34 ft. lbs. (31-46 Nm).

14. Install a new turbocharger gasket onto the exhaust manifold, then carefully guide the turbo over the mounting studs and onto the gasket. Install the mounting nuts/lockwashers.

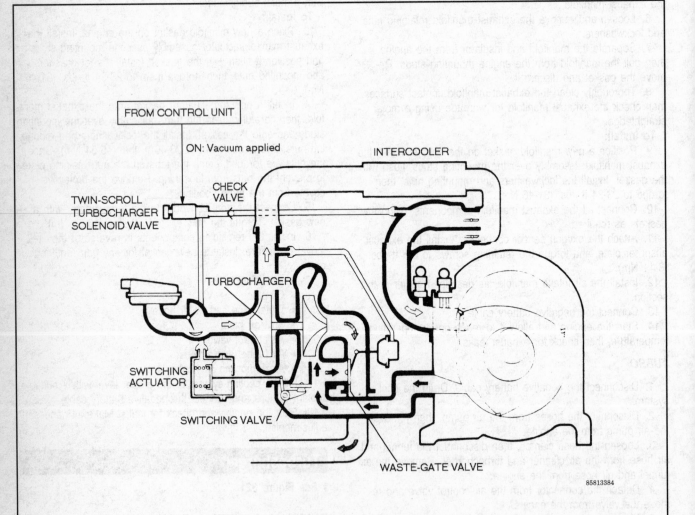

Fig. 321 Twin-scroll turbocharger system used on the 1986-89 RX-7

Torque the mounting nuts to 33-40 ft. lbs. (45-54 Nm). Once the nuts are torqued, crimp the tabs on the nut retaining plate to prevent the nuts from loosening. Remove the protective covers from the turbo openings.

15. Connect the front converter to the turbocharger with a new gasket. Torque the nuts to 33-40 ft. lbs. (45-54 Nm).

16. Install the remaining components in reverse of the removal procedure. Install a new gasket for any part requiring one:

- Insulator covers
- Oil pipes
- Water pipe and water hose
- Split air pipe
- Air control valve
- Air funnel and air hose
- Air pump and air hoses

17. Fill the cooling system to the proper level with a suitable coolant mixture and connect the negative battery cable.

18. Start the engine and check for leaks. Make all necessary adjustments.

Radiator

REMOVAL & INSTALLATION

1979-85 Vehicles

1. Disconnect all sensor wiring from the radiator. Detach the coolant reservoir hose.

2. Unbolt and remove the cooling fan and drive assembly.

3. From beneath the car, remove the gravel shield. Place a suitable container beneath the lower radiator hose, then remove the hose and allow the coolant to drain.

4. Disconnect the heater hose at the bottom of the radiator, and disconnect the upper radiator hose.

5. On automatic transmission equipped models, disconnect the automatic transmission fluid cooling hoses at the lower left side of the radiator. (Do not confuse them with the engine oil cooling hoses.)

6. Remove the radiator shroud, mounting bolts and brackets, then remove the radiator.

To install:

7. Position the radiator, then install the brackets, mounting hardware and shroud.

8. If equipped, connect the automatic transmission cooling lines.

9. Connect the upper radiator, heater and lower hoses. Install the gravel shield.

10. Install the cooling fan and drive assembly.

11. Connect the coolant reservoir hose, then engage all sensor and electrical wiring. Fill the cooling system to the proper level with a suitable coolant mixture. Start the engine and check for coolant leaks.

1986-89 Vehicles

1. Position a suitable drain pan under the radiator, then loosen the drain plug and empty the radiator.

2. Remove the cooling fan from the water pump pulley.

3. Remove the air inlet pipe.

4. Disconnect both cables from the battery, then unfasten and remove the battery and bracket.

5. Disconnect the heater hose and upper hose from the radiator.

6. Disconnect the coolant level sensor and the radiator switch connectors.

7. If equipped with an automatic transmission, disconnect the transmission fluid cooling hoses from the bottom of the radiator, and plug the ends to prevent leakage.

8. Remove the radiator and the radiator cowling.

To install:

9. Install the radiator cowling and the radiator. Leave the cowling bolts snug.

10. Connect the transmission cooling hoses, if equipped.

11. Connect the radiator switch and coolant level sensor connectors.

12. Connect the upper radiator and heater hoses to the radiator.

13. Install the battery bracket and battery. Connect the battery cables.

14. Install and connect the air inlet pipe.

15. Install the cooling fan onto the water pump pulley, and tighten the mounting bolts. Check the clearance between the blades of the cooling fan and the fan shroud. If the clearance is not sufficient to allow the blades to turn without contacting the cowling, adjust the cowling as required, then properly tighten the retaining bolts.

16. Fill the cooling system to the proper level with a suitable coolant mixture. Start the engine and check for coolant leaks.

Water Pump

REMOVAL & INSTALLATION

▶ **See Figures 322 and 323**

1. Disconnect the negative battery cable.

2. On carbureted engines, remove the air cleaner assembly and disconnect the wiring from the water temperature switch.

3. On fuel injected engines, turn the eccentric shaft so that the top mark of the pulley is aligned with the indicator pin.

4. Remove the air conditioner compressor, air pump, power steering, and alternator drive belts. Remove the alternator and the air pump.

5. Remove the cooling fan and drive assembly.

6. Remove the drive pulley for the air conditioner compressor, in front of the alternator/air pump drive pulleys. (It is the pulley on the eccentric shaft, not the one on the front of the compressor.)

7. Place a pan under the lower radiator hose, then disconnect the hose (or remove the drain plug, if so equipped) and allow the coolant to drain from the system.

8. Disconnect the upper radiator hose and coolant bypass hose.

9. On fuel injected engines equipped with an automatic transmission, disconnect the water thermosensor connector and the water thermo switch connector.

10. Unfasten the attaching bolts and remove the water pump, along with the cooling fan pulley. Retrieve the spacers

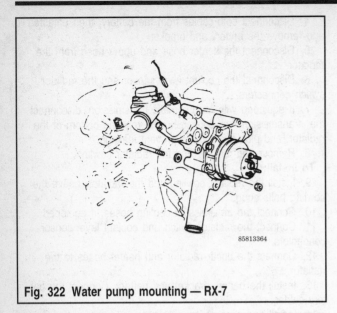

Fig. 322 Water pump mounting — RX-7

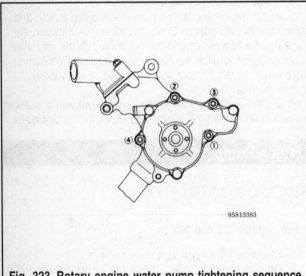

Fig. 323 Rotary engine water pump tightening sequence

or shims from the two studs where the gasket does not mount. Thoroughly clean old gasket material from the mating surfaces.

To install:

11. Position and install a new gasket with sealer.

12. Install the water pump with spacers or shims, as required, and torque the attaching bolts in the indicated sequence to 13-20 ft. lbs. (18-27 Nm).

13. On fuel injected engines equipped with an automatic transmission, attach the water thermosensor and water thermo switch connectors.

14. Connect the coolant bypass and upper radiator hoses to the water pump.

15. Connect the lower radiator hose at the radiator (or close the drain plug).

16. Install the air conditioner compressor drive pulley.

17. Install the cooling fan and drive assembly. Check the clearance between the tip of the cooling fan blades and the cowling. Adjust the cowling until there is 0.63-0.94 in. (16-24mm) clearance.

18. Install the alternator and air pump.

19. Install and properly tension all drive belts.

20. On carbureted engines, install the air cleaner assembly and connect the water temperature switch wiring.

21. Connect the negative battery cable. Fill the cooling system to the proper level with a suitable coolant mixture.

22. Start the engine and check for coolant leaks.

Oil Pan

REMOVAL & INSTALLATION

Carbureted Engine

▶ See Figures 324 and 325

➡ **The only components that can be serviced by removing the oil pan are the oil strainer and the oil pressure control valve.**

1. Drain the engine oil.

2. Disconnect the oil level sensor and the oil thermo unit (non-California vehicles).

3. Remove the pan bolts, then lower the pan.

4. Thoroughly clean the old gasket material off the pan and engine mating surfaces.

To install:

5. Apply a continuous bead of sealer (Mazda Part No. 8527 77 739 or equivalent) to the pan surface. The bead should be 0.16-0.24 in. (4-6mm) wide and should overlap at the end. Apply the sealer as shown in the illustration.

6. Fit the gasket on the pan, then apply an identical bead of sealer on top of the gasket.

7. Position the pan and torque the bolts to 6-8 ft. lbs. (8-11 Nm).

8. Connect the oil level sensor and, if applicable, the oil thermo unit.

9. Fill the crankcase with engine oil (see Section 1 for details).

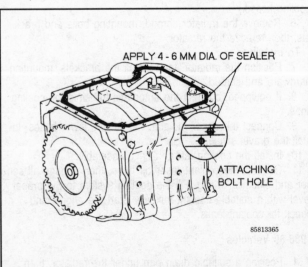

APPLY 4 - 6 MM DIA. OF SEALER

ATTACHING BOLT HOLE

Fig. 324 Apply sealant before installing the oil pan

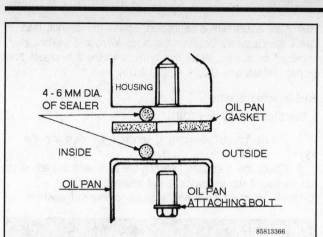

Fig. 325 Apply sealant to both the top and bottom of the oil pan gasket. Be sure that it loops around the bolt holes toward the inside

Fuel Injected Engine

▶ See Figures 324, 325 and 326

1. Disconnect the negative battery cable. Drain the engine oil.

2. Raise and safely support the vehicle, then remove the engine under cover.

3. Disconnect the oil level sensor and, if so equipped, the oil thermo unit.

4. Support the engine from above with a suitable hoist and engine sling, then remove the right-side engine mount nut and lift the engine about 2-3 in. (51-76mm) to gain working clearance.

5. Remove the pan bolts. Separate the pan from the housing using an appropriate prying tool, then lower the pan from the engine.

6. Thoroughly clean the old gasket material off the pan and engine mating surfaces.

To install:

7. Apply a continuous bead of sealer, (Mazda Part No. 8527 77 739 or equivalent) to the pan surface. The bead

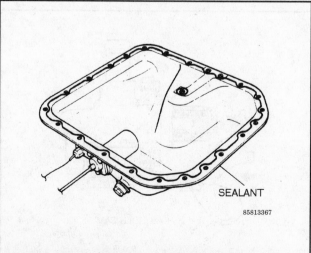

Fig. 326 Apply sealant to a gasketless oil pan in a similar manner — 1986-89 RX-7

should be from 0.16-0.24 in. (4-6mm) wide and should overlap at the end. Make sure the bolt holes are properly encircled by the sealant bead.

8. Install the gasket on the pan, then apply an identical bead of sealer on top of the gasket. Install the gasket and torque the bolts to 6-8 ft. lbs. (8-11 Nm). The oil pan must be installed no more than 30 minutes after the sealant is applied.

➡**Some engines are not equipped with an oil pan gasket. On these engines, apply the sealant in the same manner described above, but only apply the sealant to the pan surface.**

9. Carefully lower the engine to its normal position, then fasten the engine mount nut.

10. Connect the oil level sensor and, if applicable, the oil thermo unit.

11. Install the engine under cover, then lower the vehicle.

12. Fill the crankcase with oil and connect the negative battery cable.

Oil Pump

REMOVAL & INSTALLATION

Oil pump removal and installation is contained in the Engine Overhaul section at the end of this section. Perform only the steps needed in order to remove the oil pump.

Metering Oil Pump

OPERATION

A metering oil pump, mounted at the front side of the engine, is used to provide additional lubrication to the engine when it is operating under a load. The metering pump is a plunger type, and is controlled by throttle opening.

On carbureted engines, the pump provides oil to the carburetor, where it is mixed in the float chamber with fuel to be burned. The pump uses a cam arrangement, connected to the carburetor throttle lever, to operate a plunger. This plunger, in turn, acts on a differential plunger, whose stroke determines the amount of oil flow. When the throttle opening is small, the amount of the plunger stroke is small; as the throttle opening increases, so does the amount of the plunger stroke.

On fuel injected engines, the pump is part of a parallel system, in which oil fed by the pump and air from the throttle chamber are directly supplied to the intake manifold, the apex seal and the rotor housing trochoid surfaces.

TESTING

Carbureted Engine

▶ See Figure 327

1. Disconnect the oil lines which run from the metering oil pump to the carburetor, at the carburetor.

2. Use a container which has a scale calibrated in cubic centimeters (cc) to catch the pump discharge from the oil lines.

➡Such a container is available from a scientific equipment supply house.

3. Run the engine at 2,000 rpm for six minutes.

4. At the end of this time, 2.0-2.4cc of oil should be collected in the container on 1979-83 vehicles, or 1.8-2.2cc on 1984-85 vehicles. If not, adjust the pump as explained later in this section.

➡While the measurement is being taken, a proper amount of clean engine oil should be added into the carburetor (to compensate for oil lost during the test).

Fuel Injected Engine

1. Start the engine and allow it to reach normal operating temperature. Shut off the engine.

2. Connect a tachometer to the engine according to the manufacturer's instructions.

3. Disconnect the two housing oil hoses from the metering oil pump. (Only disconnect two hoses at one time.)

4. Fabricate and connect suitable hoses to the metering oil pump for measurement.

5. Pull the metering pump rod up to its maximum stop. Make sure to lift the rod fully while the engine is running.

6. Start and run the engine at 2,000 rpm for five minutes and measure the oil discharge; it should be 4.2-5.6cc for non-turbocharged engines and 5.2-6.6cc for turbocharged engines.

7. Install the housing hoses and measure the manifold metering oil discharge in the same manner.

ADJUSTMENTS

Carbureted Engine

▶ See Figure 328

Rotate the adjusting screw on the metering oil pump to obtain the proper oil flow. Clockwise rotation of the screw increases the flow; counterclockwise rotation decreases the oil flow. After adjustment is completed, tighten the locknut, then check the clearance between the pump lever and washer as shown; if necessary, install one or more washers to create the proper clearance of 0-0.04 in. (0-1.0mm).

Fuel Injected Engine

▶ See Figures 329 and 330

1. Rotate the fast idle cam to separate the cam and the roller.

2. Check the clearance between the lever and the adjusting rod washer. If the clearance is not between 0-0.04 in. (0-1mm), adjust it by adding the proper amount of washers.

Oil Cooler

On all but 1984-85 carbureted engines, the oil cooler is mounted below the radiator. It is equipped with a bypass valve, which does not allow oil to circulate through the oil cooler until the oil temperature reaches 149-158°F (65-70°C).

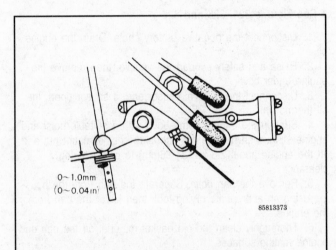

Fig. 328 Metering oil pump adjusting screw (large arrow). Once the adjustment is complete, check/adjust clearance between the washer(s) and pump lever

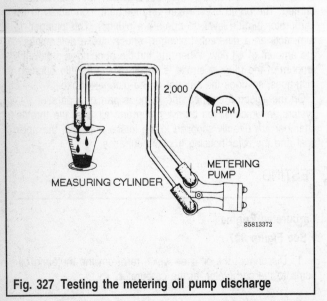

Fig. 327 Testing the metering oil pump discharge

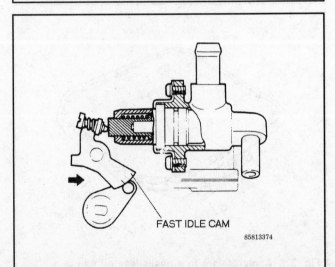

Fig. 329 Rotate the fast idle cam to separate the cam from the roller — fuel injected engine

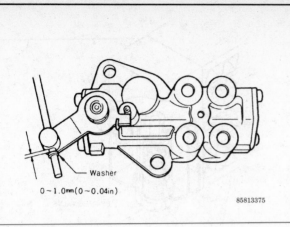

Fig. 330 Check/adjust the clearance between the metering pump's oil rod retaining washer and lever

If necessary, the bypass valve may be removed for inspection and/or replacement.

REMOVAL & INSTALLATION

Except 1984-85 Carbureted Engine

▶ See Figures 331 and 332

1. Drain the crankcase and cooling system into separate containers.
2. Raise the front of the vehicle and safely support it. Block the rear wheels.
3. Remove the under cover and the radiator grill upper cover.
4. Disconnect the oil inlet and oil outlet hoses from the oil cooler. Drain the lines completely and plug the ends.

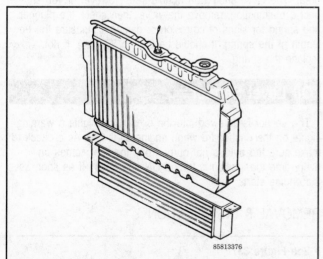

Fig. 331 The oil cooler is mounted below the radiator — except 1984-85 carbureted engines

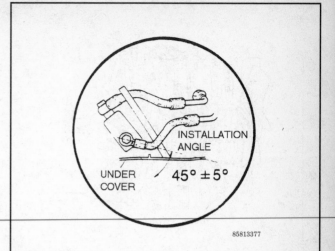

Fig. 332 Oil cooler positioning on rotary engines

5. Unfasten the retaining nuts, then remove the oil cooler assembly. If necessary, remove/install the bypass valve as described later in this section.
   To install:
6. Position the oil cooler assembly, and fasten the mounting nuts.
7. Unplug and connect the oil outlet hose to the top of the cooler.
8. Unplug and connect the oil inlet hose, using new sealing washers.
9. Install the radiator grill upper cover and the under cover. The oil cooler should be at a 40-50 degree angle with the under cover to ensure proper air flow across the cooling fins.
10. Lower the vehicle and unblock the wheels.
11. Refill the crankcase and the cooling system to their proper levels.
12. Start the engine and check for leaks.

1984-85 Carbureted Engine

▶ See Figures 333 and 334

1. Drain the crankcase and cooling system into separate containers.
2. Disconnect the inlet and outlet coolant lines from the oil cooler. Drain the lines completely and plug the ends.
3. Disconnect the oil pipe and remove the sealing washer.
4. Unbolt and remove the oil cooler and filter assembly as a unit. Remove and discard the O-rings and filter cartridge.
   To install:
5. Assemble the oil cooler with a new filter cartridge and O-rings.
6. Position a new sealing washer, then connect the oil pipe.
7. Unplug and fasten the inlet and outlet cooling lines to the oil cooler.
8. Refill the crankcase and the cooling system to their proper levels.

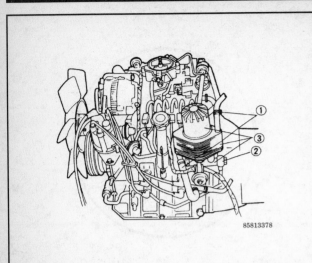

Fig. 333 On 1984-85 carbureted RX-7s, the oil cooler is at the base of the oil filter

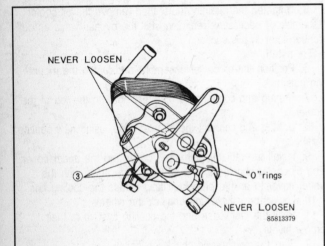

Fig. 334 Be careful to only turn the appropriate fasteners when removing the oil cooler

Oil Cooler Bypass Valve

REMOVAL & INSTALLATION

▶ See Figure 335

1. Raise the car and safely support it on jackstands.
2. Remove the under cover from beneath the engine.
3. Drain the engine oil.
4. Remove the cap nut and pull out the bypass valve. If necessary, test the valve as described later in this section.
   To install:
5. Position the bypass valve in its chamber, then install the cap nut.
6. Install the under cover beneath the engine, then lower the car.
7. Fill the crankcase with engine oil. Start the engine and check the bypass valve cap nut for leaks.

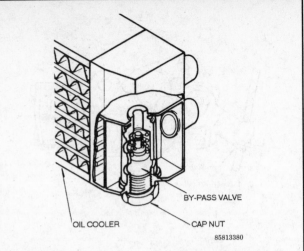

Fig. 335 The oil cooler bypass valve is retained by a cap nut

TESTING

Remove the valve from the oil cooler and place it in a pan of cool oil, then gradually heat the oil until it reaches 149-158°F (65-70°C). Use a thermometer to verify the temperature. When the above temperature is reached, measure the protrusion of the valve end. The end of the valve should protrude through the valve housing at least 0.2 in. (5mm). If not, replace the valve.

Oil Pressure Control Valve

▶ See Figure 336

The oil pressure control valve is located at the bottom of the front engine cover and is accessible by removing the oil pan. The valve prevents engine oil pressure from becoming too great. The valve should be trouble-free. However, if you suspect a malfunction, remove the valve, then check the plunger and spring for signs of corrosion or damage. Measure the free length of the spring. It should be 2.87 in. (73mm). If not, replace the spring.

Oil Level Sensor

The sensor is screwed into the oil pan and lights a warning signal on the dashboard when engine oil is low. As a check to make sure the bulb is not burned out, the light comes on every time the ignition is turned **ON** and goes off as soon as the engine starts.

REMOVAL & INSTALLATION

▶ See Figure 337

➡Do not confuse the oil level sensor with the oil thermal unit (mounted below it) on some models.

1. Drain the engine oil.
2. Disconnect the sensor wiring.
3. Remove the attaching nut or bolts and remove the sensor.

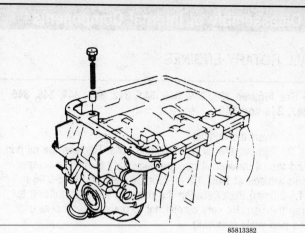

Fig. 336 Oil pressure control valve assembly

4. Check the oil holes in the sensor and clean with solvent if clogged.

To install:

5. Fit the gasket onto the sensor, then install the sensor with the **L** mark (1979-80 only) on its body pointing downward.

6. Tighten the nut to 18-22 ft. lbs. (24-30 Nm) and connect the wiring.

7. Fill the crankcase with oil to the proper level, then check the sensor for oil leaks with the engine running.

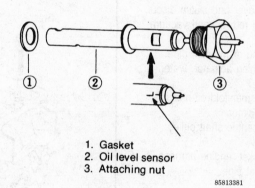

1. Gasket
2. Oil level sensor
3. Attaching nut

Fig. 337 Oil level sensor. On 1979-80 models, install with the L mark facing down

ROTARY ENGINE OVERHAUL

Disassembly of External Components

➡Because of the design of the rotary engine, it is not practical to attempt component removal and installation. It is best to disassemble and assemble the entire engine, or go as far with the disassembly and assembly procedure as needed.

CARBURETED ENGINE

1. Remove the engine from the vehicle and mount on a suitable stand or holding fixture.

➡To simplify reassembly, mark or label all components before disassembly.

2. Remove the oil hose support bracket from the front housing.

3. Disconnect the vacuum hoses and air hoses, then remove the decel valve.

4. Remove the air pump and drive belt. Remove the air pump adjusting bar.

5. Remove the alternator and drive belt.

6. Disconnect the metering oil pump connecting rod, oil tubes and vacuum sensing tube from the carburetor.

7. Remove the exhaust manifold cover, if equipped. Remove the carburetor and intake manifold as an assembly.

8. Remove the gasket and two rubber O-rings.

9. Remove the thermal reactor/exhaust manifold and gaskets. Remove the engine mount.

10. Remove the distributor.

11. On 1984-85 models, disconnect and remove the oil cooler assembly, as described earlier in this section. Do not

remove the oil filter from the cooler housing unless replacement is desired.

12. Unbolt the A/C compressor pulley and remove the water pump.

FUEL INJECTED ENGINE

Non-Turbo

1. Remove the engine from the vehicle and mount on a suitable stand or holding fixture.

➡ **To simplify reassembly, mark or label all components before disassembly.**

2. Remove the air conditioning compressor and the power steering pump bracket.
3. Remove the left engine mount, spark plugs, oil level dipstick, oil filler pipe, oil filter and filter body.
4. Remove the oil pressure gauge and distributor/crank angle sensor.
5. Remove the air pump, drive belt, and air pump bracket.
6. Remove the alternator and drive belt.
7. If so equipped, remove the clutch cover and clutch disc.
8. Remove the metering oil connecting rod, second vacuum piping, and throttle/dynamic chamber.
9. Remove the primary fuel injector and distribution pipe.
10. Remove the air control valve, switching actuator, water pipe and air hose.
11. Remove the housing oil nozzle and manifold oil nozzle, intake manifold, exhaust manifold and insulator.
12. Remove the metering oil pump, eccentric shaft pulley, and water pump.
13. Remove the dynamic chamber bracket, engine harness and vacuum piping, and finally, the oil inlet pipe.

Turbo

1. Remove the engine from the vehicle and mount on a suitable stand or holding fixture.

➡ **To simplify reassembly, mark or label all components before disassembly.**

2. Remove the air conditioning compressor and the power steering pump bracket.
3. Remove the left engine mount, spark plugs, oil level dipstick, oil filler pipe, oil filter and filter body.
4. Remove the oil pressure gauge and crank angle sensor.
5. Remove the air pump, drive belt, and air pump bracket. Remove the alternator and drive belt.
6. If so equipped, remove the clutch cover and clutch disc.
7. Remove the metering oil pump connecting rod, secondary vacuum piping, and throttle/dynamic chamber.
8. Remove the primary fuel injector and distribution pipe. Remove the air control valve, switching actuator, water pipe, turbocharger with insulator, and the air hose. Cover the intake and exhaust port openings of the turbocharger with masking tape to prevent the entry of dirt and foreign matter.
9. Remove the housing oil nozzle and manifold oil nozzle, intake manifold, exhaust manifold and insulator.
10. Remove the metering oil pump, eccentric shaft pulley, water pump, dynamic chamber bracket, engine harness and vacuum piping, and finally, the oil inlet pipe.

Disassembly of Internal Components

ALL ROTARY ENGINES

▶ **See Figures 338, 339, 340, 341, 342, 343, 344, 345, 346, 347, 348 and 349**

1. Invert the engine.
2. Remove the oil pan retaining bolts. Remove the oil pan and the oil strainer. It may be necessary to drive a scraper with a blade at least 1.2 in. (30mm) wide and 0.06-0.08 in. (1.5-2.0mm) thick between the pan and the rear housing to free the pan. Be very careful not to damage the housing or the pan while removing.
3. Remove the oil strainer and gasket.
4. It will be necessary to lock the flywheel/flexplate to remove the pulley from the front of the eccentric shaft. For manual transmissions, Mazda offers a brake device (tool number 49-1881-060 or equivalent for earlier models, and tool

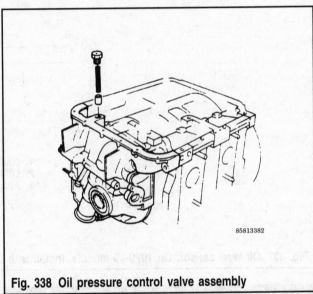

Fig. 338 Oil pressure control valve assembly

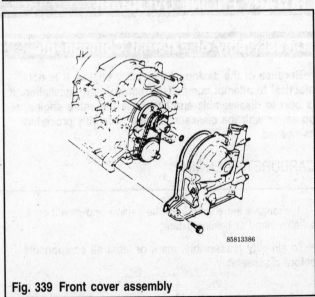

Fig. 339 Front cover assembly

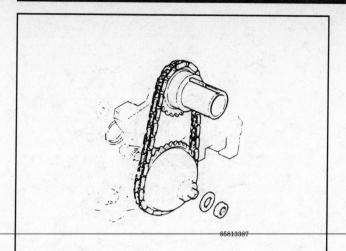

Fig. 340 Oil pump drive assembly

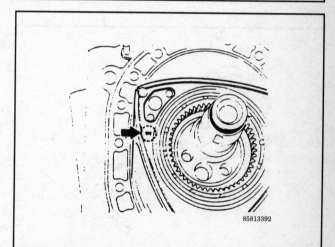

Fig. 343 Rotary engine tension bolt loosening sequence

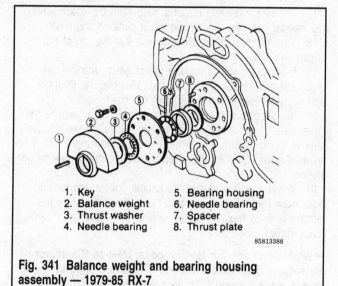

1. Key
2. Balance weight
3. Thrust washer
4. Needle bearing
5. Bearing housing
6. Needle bearing
7. Spacer
8. Thrust plate

Fig. 341 Balance weight and bearing housing assembly — 1979-85 RX-7

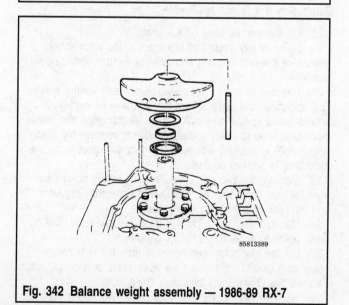

Fig. 342 Balance weight assembly — 1986-89 RX-7

Fig. 344 Rotor, apex and side seals are identified by a number which corresponds to the number on each rotor face seal groove

number 49-FO11-101 or equivalent for later models). For automatic transmissions, Mazda offers a stopper which fits on the counterweight (tool number 49-1881-055 or equivalent). With the flywheel/flexplate locked, remove the bolt from the eccentric shaft pulley and remove the pulley.

5. Identify the front and rear rotor housings with a felt tip pen. These are look-alike parts and must be identified to be assembled in their respective locations.

6. Turn the engine on the stand so that the top of the engine is up.

7. Remove the engine mounting bracket from the front cover.

8. Remove the eccentric shaft pulley. On 1986-89 models, remove the eccentric shaft bypass valve and spring. On 1985-89 models, remove the O-ring from the eccentric shaft lockbolt and discard it. Remove the eccentric shaft pulley boss (1986-89). Turn the engine on a stand so that the front end of the engine is up.

9. On 1986-89 models, unscrew and withdraw the oil pressure control valve and actuating spring from the bore in the

front cover. Unbolt and remove the front cover with the gasket. Slide the distributor drive gear from the eccentric shaft. The gear is retained with a key. Remove the key from the keyway and tape it to the gear.

10. Remove the O-ring from the oil passage on the front housing.

11. Remove the oil slinger and distributor drive gear from the shaft.

12. Unbolt and remove the chain adjuster.

13. Remove the locknut and washer from the oil pump driven sprocket.

14. Slide the oil pump drive sprocket and driven sprocket, together with the drive chain, off the eccentric shaft and oil pump, simultaneously.

15. Detach the baffle plate from the oil pump (turbocharged engines only). Remove the keys from the eccentric and oil pump shafts. Remove the oil pump.

16. Slide the balance weight, thrust washer and needle bearing from the shaft.

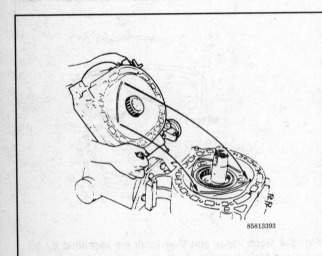

Fig. 345 If a seal sticks to the housing during removal, put it back on the rotor

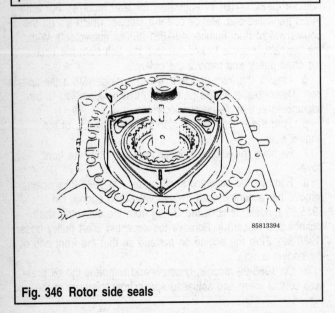

Fig. 346 Rotor side seals

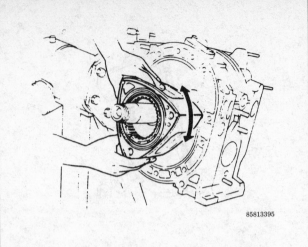

Fig. 347 Removing the rotor from the intermediate housing

17. Unbolt the bearing housing, then slide the bearing housing, needle bearing, spacer and thrust plate off the shaft.

18. Turn the engine on the stand so that the top of the engine is up.

19. If equipped with a manual transmission, remove the clutch pressure plate and clutch disc. Remove the flywheel with a puller. Remove the key from the shaft.

20. If equipped with an automatic transmission, remove the drive plate. Remove the counterweight. Block the weight and remove the mounting nut. Remove the counterweight with a suitable puller. On 1986-89 engines, remove the counterweight stopper.

21. Working at the rear of the engine, loosen the tension bolts evenly in small stages to prevent distortion. Mark the tension bolts to replace in their original holes during reassembly.

➡When removing the tension bolts, refer to the appropriate removal illustration. 1984-85 carbureted engines do not have a No. 6 tension bolt, so delete that bolt from the illustration if it is not applicable.

22. Lift the rear housing off the shaft.

23. Remove any seals that are stuck to the rotor sliding surface of the rear housing and reinstall them in their original locations.

24. Remove all the corner seals, corner seal spring, side seal and side seal springs from the rear side of the rotor. Mazda has a special tray which holds all the seals and keeps them separated to prevent mistakes during reassembly. Each seal groove is marked with numbers near the grooves on the rotor face to prevent confusion.

25. Remove the two rubber seals, two O-rings or oil seal from the rear rotor housing. Remove the pressure regulator and the rear rotor housing side pieces.

26. Remove the tubular dowels from the rear rotor housing using puller tool 49-0813-215A or equivalent.

27. Lift the rear rotor housing away from the rear rotor, being very careful not to drop the apex seals on the rear rotor. Remove the O-ring from the upper dowel hole.

28. Remove each apex seal, side piece and spring from the rear rotor and separate them accordingly.

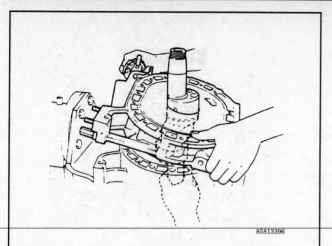

Fig. 348 Remove the intermediate housing while applying upward pressure to the eccentric shaft

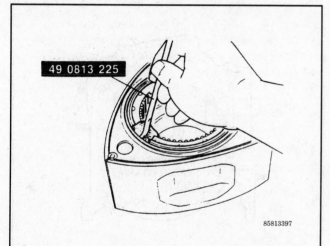

49 0813 225

Fig. 349 Use a special tool to remove the rotor outer oil seal

29. Remove the rear rotor from the eccentric shaft and place it upside down on a clean rag. Do not place the rotor on a hard surface.

30. Remove each seal and spring from the other side of the rotor and separate them.

31. If some of the seals fall off the rotor, reinstall being careful not to change the original position of each seal.

32. Identify the bottom of each apex seal with a felt tip pen.

33. Remove the oil seals and the spring. The outer oil seal is removed with the use of special tool 49-0813-225 or equivalent. Do not exert heavy pressure at only one place on the seal, since it could be deformed. Replace the O-rings in the oil seal when the engine is overhauled.

34. Hold the intermediate housing down and remove the dowels from it using an appropriate pulling tool.

35. Lift off the intermediate housing, being careful not to damage the eccentric shaft. Slide the intermediate housing beyond the rear rotor journal on the eccentric shaft, while pushing the eccentric shaft up. Lift out the eccentric shaft.

36. Repeat to remove the front rotor housing and front rotor.

CLEANING

Front, Rear and Intermediate Housings

Remove carbon from the housings with extra fine emery paper. If you use a carbon scraper, be very careful not to damage the finished surfaces of the housing. Remove the sealant remnants with a cloth or brush soaked in a solution of ketone or thinner.

Rotor Housing

▶ See Figure 350

Remove carbon from the inner surface of the rotor housing by wiping it off with a cloth. Soak the cloth in a solution of ketone or thinner, if the carbon is difficult to remove. Rust deposits should be carefully removed from the cooling water passages on the housing. Remove sealant remnants with a cloth or brush soaked in ketone or thinner. Be careful not to remove the felt tip pen marks made while disassembling the engine.

Rotor

Remove carbon with a carbon remover or extra fine emery paper. Clean the rotor in a standard cleaning solution and blow dry with compressed air.

✳✳WARNING

Do not use emery paper on the apex or side seal grooves. The side surfaces are coated with a very soft material. Do not use excessive pressure on these surfaces while cleaning. Lightly polish them.

Seals and Springs

Gas seals can be cleaned in a standard cleaning solution. Never attempt to clean seals with emery paper or you will ruin them. Be careful not to damage the seals or springs while handling them. Do not mix up the seals and springs when cleaning.

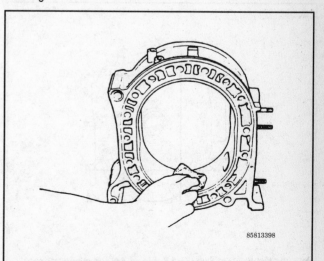

Fig. 350 Clean the rotor housing using a clean cloth which has been soaked in solvent

Eccentric Shaft

Immerse the shaft in cleaning solution and blow the oil passages dry with compressed air. Apply a light film of clean engine oil to the shaft to prevent rusting.

INSPECTION AND COMPONENT REPLACEMENT

Front, Intermediate and Rear Housings

▶ **See Figures 351, 352, 353, 354 and 355**

1. Check the housing for signs of gas or water leakage.
2. Remove the sealing compound from the housing surface with a cloth or brush soaked in solvent or thinner.
3. Remove the carbon deposits from the front housing with extra fine emery cloth. When using a carbon scraper, take extra care not to damage the surface of the housing.
4. Check for distortion by placing a straightedge on the surface of the housing. Measure the clearance between the straightedge and the housing with a feeler gauge. If the clearance is greater than 0.0016 in. (0.04mm) at any point, replace the housing.
5. Use a dial indicator with a sled attachment (gauge body) to check for wear on the rotor contact surfaces of the housing. Mazda offers such an attachment under part number 49-0727-570 or equivalent. To check for stepped wear on the rotor housing sliding surfaces, mount the dial indicator on the sliding surface of the housing. To measure stepped wear caused by the side seal at the sides of the housing, move the dial indicator gauge feeler to and fro as shown in the illustration. The wear limit is 0.0039 in. (0.10mm). Check the side seal stepped wear across the middle of the housing with the dial indicator, moving it as shown in the illustration. The wear limit inside the oil seal tracing marks is 0.0004 in. (0.01mm), and the wear limit outside the oil seal tracing marks is 0.0039 in. (0.10mm). Check for stepped wear by the oil seal with the dial gauge. The wear limit is 0.0008 in. (0.02mm).
6. If the front, intermediate and/or rear side housings are beyond the above wear limits, they can be ground if the re-

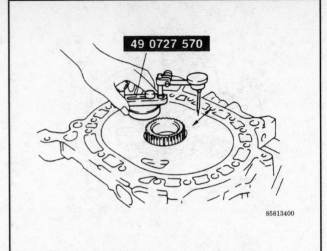

Fig. 352 Checking for housing wear with a dial indicator and gauge body

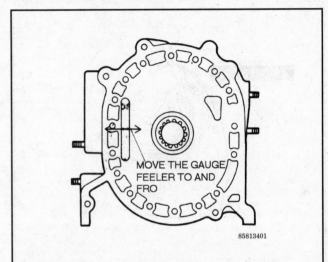

Fig. 353 Measuring stepped wear at the sides of the housing

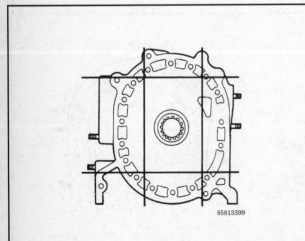

Fig. 351 Check the rotor housings for warpage along these lines

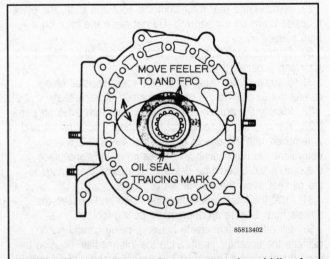

Fig. 354 Measuring stepped wear across the middle of the housing

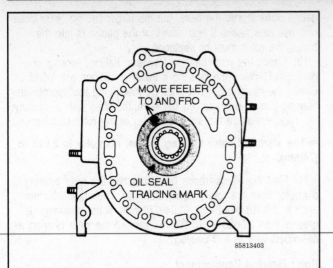

Fig. 355 Measuring stepped wear caused by the oil seal

quired finish can be maintained. If the wear is greater than the values provided above, replace the housing.

➡**The wear at either end of the minor axis is greater than at any other point on the housing. However, this is normal and should not be cause for concern.**

Front Stationary Gear and Main Bearing

1. Examine the teeth of the stationary gear for wear or damage.
2. Be sure that the main bearing shows no signs of excessive wear, scoring, or flaking.
3. Check the main bearing-to-eccentric journal clearance by measuring the journal with a vernier caliper and the bearing with a pair of inside calipers. The standard clearance is 0.0016-0.0031 in. (0.04-0.08mm). If the clearance exceeds the limit, replace the front main bearing as described later in this section.

Front Main Bearing Replacement

1. Unfasten the securing bolts, if used. Remove the stationary gear and main bearing assembly from the housing, using puller tool 49-0813-235 or equivalent.
2. Press the main bearing out of the stationary gear.
3. Press a new main bearing into the stationary gear, so that it is in the same position as the old one.
4. Align the slot in the stationary gear flange with the dowel pin in the housing, then press the gear into place. On later engines, align the bearing lug with the slot in the gear. Install the securing bolts, if applicable.

Rear Stationary Gear and Main Bearing

Inspect the rear stationary gear and main bearing in a similar manner to the front. In addition, examine the O-ring, which is located in the stationary gear, for signs of wear or damage. Replace the O-ring, if necessary. If the stationary gear must be replaced, follow the rear main bearing replacement procedure.

Rear Main Bearing Replacement

1. Remove the rear stationary gear securing bolts.
2. Drive the stationary gear out of the rear housing with a brass drift.
3. Apply a light coating of grease to a new O-ring and fit it into the groove on the stationary gear.
4. Apply sealer to the flange of the stationary gear.
5. Install the stationary gear on the housing so that the slot on its flange aligns with the pin on the rear housing. On later engines, align the bearing lug with the housing slot. Use care not to damage the O-ring during installation.
6. Tighten the stationary gear bolts evenly, in several stages, to 12-17 ft. lbs. (16-23 Nm).

Rotor Housings

▶ See Figure 356

1. Examine the inner margin of both housings for signs of gas or water leakage.
2. Wipe the inner surface of each housing with a clean cloth to remove the carbon deposits.
3. Clean all of the rust deposits out of the cooling passages of each rotor housing.
4. Remove the old sealer using the proper removal solvent.
5. Examine the chromium-plated inner surfaces for scoring, flaking, or other signs of damage. If any are present, the housing must be replaced.
6. Check the rotor housings for distortion by placing a straightedge on the axes.
7. If distortion exceeds 0.002 in. (0.05mm), replace the rotor housing.
8. Check the widths of both rotor housings, at points A, B, C, and D near the trochoid surfaces of each housing, using a vernier caliper, as illustrated. Compare the difference between the value obtained at point A and the minimum value of points B, C and D. If the difference between the values obtained is greater than 0.0024 in. (0.06mm), replace the housing. A rotor housing in this condition will be prone to gas and coolant leakage.

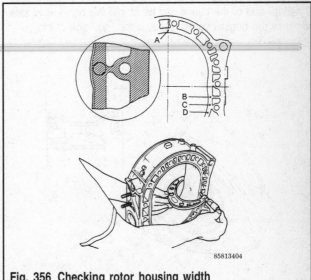

Fig. 356 Checking rotor housing width

Rotors

▶ **See Figure 357**

1. Check the rotor for signs of blow-by around the side and corner seal areas.

2. The color of the carbon deposits on the rotor should be brown, just as in a piston engine. Usually, the carbon deposits on the leading side of the rotor are brown, while those on the trailing side tend toward black (as viewed from the direction of rotation).

3. Remove the carbon on the rotor with a scraper or extra fine emery paper. Use the scraper carefully when cleaning the seal grooves to avoid any damage.

4. Wash the rotor in solvent and blow it dry with compressed air.

5. Examine the internal gear for cracks or damaged teeth. If the internal gear is damaged, the rotor and gear must be replaced as a single assembly.

6. With the oil seal removed, check the land protrusions by placing a straightedge over the lands. Measure the gap between the rotor surface and the straightedge with a feeler gauge.

7. Check the clearance between the housings and the rotor on both of its sides:

   a. Measure the rotor width with a vernier caliper at the points indicated in the corresponding illustration.

   b. Compare the rotor width against the width of the previously measured rotor housing.

   c. Replace the rotor, if the difference between the two measurements is not 0.0047-0.0074 in. (0.12-0.19mm) for the 1979-85 carbureted engine or 0.0047-0.0083 in. (0.12-0.21mm) for the 1984-90 fuel injected engine.

8. If the clearance *exceeds* the specified values, replace the rotor. If the clearance is *less* than specification, it means that the internal gear must be removed. To dislodge the gear from the rotor bore, smack it lightly with a plastic-faced hammer, being careful not to damage the rotor. With the gear removed, recheck the side housing-to-rotor clearance again.

9. The corner seal bores can be checked with a gauge (tool number 49 0839 15 or equivalent), available from Mazda. If neither end of the gauge can be fit into the bores, it is safe to reuse the original corner seals. If the "go" side of the gauge does fit into the bore, but the larger "no go" side does not, use new seals. If both sides of the gauge fit into the bores, the rotor must be replaced.

10. Check the rotor bearing for wear, flaking, scoring or damage. Replace the bearing if these conditions are found. Check the bearing oil clearance by measuring the appropriate bearing journal diameter on the eccentric shaft with a micrometer. Next, measure the inner diameter of the rotor bearing.

➡**The standard rotor bearing journal diameter is 2.913 in. (74mm).**

11. Find the oil clearance by subtracting the rotor bearing diameter from the rotor journal diameter. The standard clearance is 0.0016-0.0031 in. (0.04-0.08mm). If the clearance is greater than 0.0039 in. (0.10mm), replace the rotor bearing as described later in this section.

Rotor Bearing Replacement

1. Check the clearance between the rotor bearing and the rotor journal on the eccentric shaft. Measure the inner diameter of the rotor bearing and the outer diameter of the journal. The wear limit is 0.0039 in. (0.1mm); replace the bearing if it exceeds specification.

2. Place the rotor on the support so that the internal gear is facing downward. Using puller tool 49-0813-240 (or equivalent) without its adaptor ring, press the bearing out of the rotor. Being careful not to damage the internal gear.

3. Place the rotor on the support with the internal gear facing upward. Place the new rotor bearing on the rotor so that the bearing lug is in line with the slot of the rotor bore.

4. Remove the screws which attach the adaptor ring to the special tool. Using the special tool and adaptor ring, press fit the new bearing until the bearing is flush with the rotor boss.

Oil Seal Inspection

▶ **See Figures 358 and 359**

1. Examine the oil seal while it is mounted in the rotor.

2. If the width of the oil seal lip is greater than 0.020 in. (0.5mm), replace the oil seal.

3. If the protrusion of the oil seal is greater than 0.020 in. (0.5mm), replace the seal.

Oil Seal Replacement

1. Pry the seal out by inserting a small prybar into the slots on the rotor. Be careful not to deform the lip of the oil seal if it is to be reinstalled.

2. Fit both the oil seal springs into their respective grooves, so that their ends are facing upward and their gaps are opposite each other on the rotor.

3. Insert a new O-ring into each of the oil seals. Before installing the O-rings into the oil seals, fit each of the seals into its proper groove on the rotor. Check to see that all of the seals move smoothly and freely.

4. Coat the oil seal groove and the oil seal with clean engine oil.

5. Gently press the oil seal into the groove with your fingers. Be careful not to distort the seal. Be sure that the white mark is on the bottom side of each seal when it is installed.

6. Repeat the installation procedure for the oil seals on both sides of each rotor.

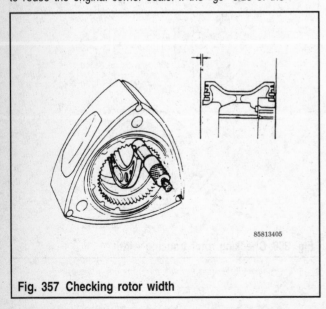

85813405

Fig. 357 Checking rotor width

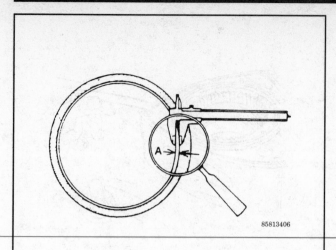

Fig. 358 Checking rotor oil seal width

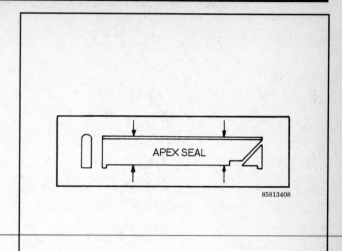

Fig. 360 Apex seal height

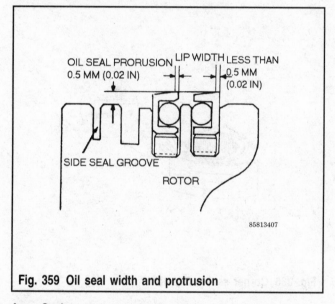

Fig. 359 Oil seal width and protrusion

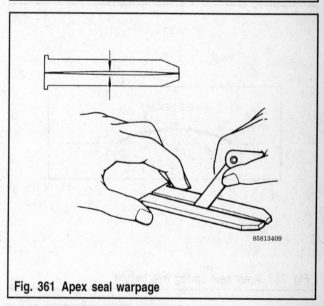

Fig. 361 Apex seal warpage

Apex Seals

▶ See Figures 360, 361, 362 and 363

1. Remove the carbon deposits from the apex seals and their springs. Do not use emery cloth on the seals, as it will damage their finish.
2. Wash the seals and the springs in cleaning solution.
3. Check the apex seals for cracks.
4. Test the seal springs for weakness.
5. Use a micrometer to check the seal height.
6. With a feeler gauge, check the side clearance between the apex seal and the groove in the rotor. Insert the gauge until its tip contacts the bottom of the groove. If the gap is greater than 0.0035 in. (0.09mm) for the 1983-85 12A engine, or 0.0059 in. (0.15mm) for the 1984-90 13B engine, replace the seal. The standard range for non-turbo engines is 0.0024-0.0040 in. (0.06-0.10mm) and 0.0020-0.0040 in. (0.05-0.10mm) for turbo engines.
7. Check the gap between the apex seals and the side housing by using a vernier caliper to measure the length of

each apex seal. Compare this measurement to the minimum figure obtained for the rotor housing width.
8. Check the apex seal spring for wear and measure its free height. If less than 0.2165 in. (5.5mm), replace the spring.
9. If the seal is too long, sand the ends of the seal with emery cloth until the proper length is reached. Do not use the emery cloth on the faces of the seal.

Side Seals

▶ See Figures 364 and 365

1. Check the side seal free movement in the rotor groove. You should be able to press down along its length with your finger.
2. Measure the side seal protrusion from the rotor surface. If the protrusion is less than 0.02 in (0.5mm), replace the side seal spring.
3. Measure the clearance between the side seal and its groove in the rotor with a feeler gauge. (The standard clearance is given in the specification chart, earlier in this section.)

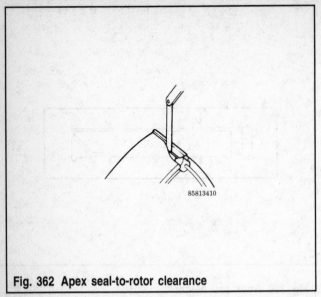

Fig. 362 Apex seal-to-rotor clearance

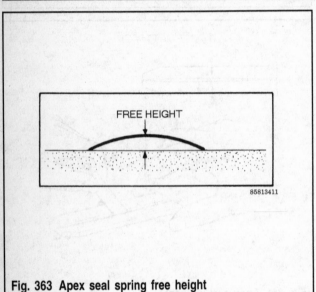

FREE HEIGHT

Fig. 363 Apex seal spring free height

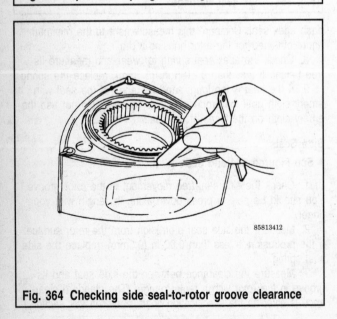

Fig. 364 Checking side seal-to-rotor groove clearance

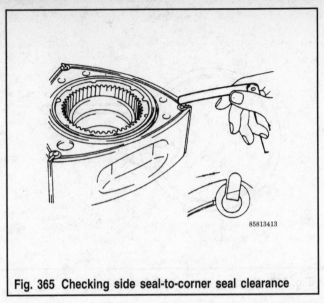

Fig. 365 Checking side seal-to-corner seal clearance

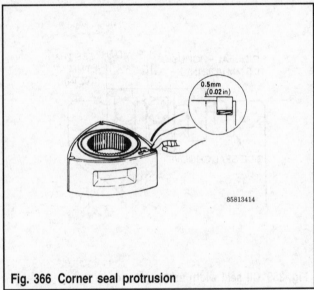

0.5mm
(0.02 in)

Fig. 366 Corner seal protrusion

If the clearance is greater than 0.0039 in. (0.10mm), replace the side seal.

4. Using a feeler gauge, check the clearance between the side seal and the corner seal when the seals are installed on the rotor. If the clearance is greater than 0.0157 in. (0.4mm), replace the side seal. When installing a new side seal, correct the clearance between the side and corner seals by grinding the end of the side seal and the rounded corner seal with a fine file. The clearance should be 0.0020-0.0059 in. (0.05-0.15mm). If it exceeds this, the performance of the seals will deteriorate.

➡️**There are 4 different types of side seals, depending upon location. Do not mix up the seals and be sure to use the proper type of seal for replacement.**

Corner Seals
◆ **See Figure 366**

1. Inspect the corner seal and spring for wear, cracks, or damage and replace, if necessary.

2. Make sure the corner seal has free movement by pressing on it with your finger.

3. Measure the corner seal protrusion from the rotor surface. It should protrude at least 0.02 in (0.5mm). If not, replace the corner seal spring.

4. Inspect the corner seal spring for wear.

Seal Springs

Check the seal springs for damage or weakness. Be especially careful when checking the spring areas which contact either the rotor or the seal.

Eccentric Shaft

◆ See Figures 367 and 368

1. Wash the eccentric shaft in solvent and blow the oil passages dry with compressed air.

2. Check the shaft for wear, cracks, or other signs of damage. Make sure that none of the oil passages are clogged.

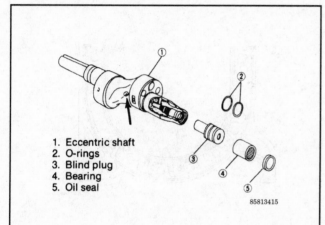

1. Eccentric shaft
2. O-rings
3. Blind plug
4. Bearing
5. Oil seal

85813415

Fig. 367 Exploded view of eccentric shaft. Remove the oil jet plug (indicated by the arrow) to check the spring and steel ball

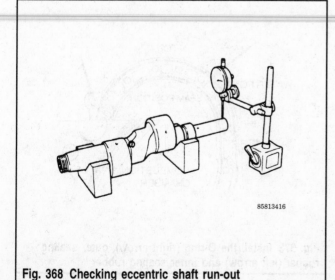

85813416

Fig. 368 Checking eccentric shaft run-out

3. Measure the shaft journals. Replace the shaft if any of its journals show excessive wear.

4. Check eccentric shaft run-out. Rotate the shaft slowly and note the dial indicator reading. Run-out should not exceed 0.0047 in. (0.12mm) as measured from the end of the shaft. If run-out is greater than specification, replace the eccentric shaft.

5. Check the blind plug at the end of the shaft. If it is loose or leaking, remove it with an Allen wrench and replace the O-ring.

6. Check the operation of the needle roller bearing for smoothness by inserting a mainshaft into the bearing and rotating it. Examine the bearing for signs of wear or damage. Check the oil jet for spring weakness, sticking or ball damage.

7. Replace the bearings, if necessary, with special bearing replacer tools 49-0823-073 and 49-0823-072, or equivalent.

Needle Bearing and Thrust Plate

1. Inspect the needle bearing for wear and damage.

2. Inspect the bearing housing and the thrust plate for wear and damage.

Oil Pump Drive Chain and Sprocket

1. Lay the chain on a flat surface and check the entire length for broken links.

2. Check the oil pump drive and driven sprockets for missing and broken teeth.

3. Replace parts as necessary.

Assembly of Internal Components

◆ See Figures 369, 370, 371, 372, 373, 374, 375, 376 and 377

1. Replace all O-rings, rubber seals and gaskets with new parts. Place the rotor on a rubber pad or cloth. Coat all the engine sliding surfaces with clean engine oil.

2. Install the oil seal rings in their respective grooves in the rotors with the edge of the spring in the stopper hole. The oil seal springs are painted cream or blue in color. The cream colored springs must be installed on the front faces of both rotors. The blue colored springs must be installed on the rear faces of both rotors. When installing each oil seal spring, the painted, square side of the spring must face upward toward the oil seal.

3. Coat the new O-ring with clean engine oil and install in each seal groove. Place each oil seal in the groove so that the square edge of the spring fits in the stopper hole of the oil seal. Push on the head of the oil seal slowly with your fingers, being careful that the seal is not deformed. Be sure that the oil seal moves smoothly in the groove **before** installing the O-ring. An old seal can be used as an installation tool.

4. Lubricate each oil seal and groove with engine oil. Check the movement of the seal. It should move freely when the head of the seal is pressed.

5. Check the oil seal protrusion and install the seals on the other side of each rotor. Oil seal protrusion must not exceed 0.016 in. (0.4mm).

6. Install the apex seals (without springs and side pieces) into their respective grooves, so that each side piece will be positioned to the rear side of the rotor.

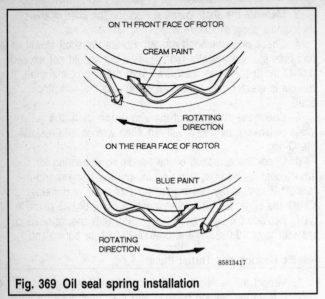

Fig. 369 Oil seal spring installation

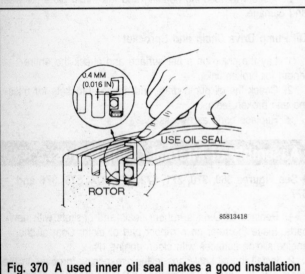

Fig. 370 A used inner oil seal makes a good installation tool for pressing in the new seal

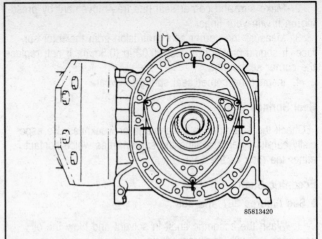

Fig. 371 When meshing the internal and stationary gears, make sure at least one of the rotor apexes is positioned as shown

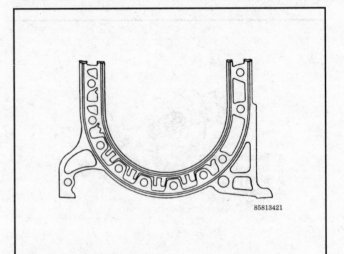

Fig. 372 Apply sealant to the front side of the front rotor housing

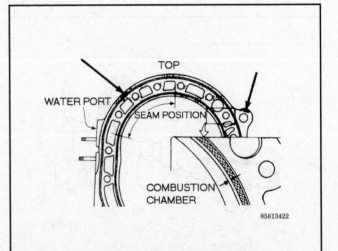

Fig. 373 Install the O-ring (right arrow), outer sealing rubber (left arrow) and inner sealing rubber

7. Install the corner seal springs and corner seals into their respective grooves.

8. Install the side seal springs and side seals into their respective grooves.

9. Confirm the smooth movement of each seal by pressing its head.

10. Mount the front housing on a workstand so that the top of the housing is up. Install the thrust plate so that the chamfered edge faces the front of the housing. Torque the thrust plate bolts to 12-17 ft. lbs. (16-23 Nm).

11. Lubricate the internal gear of the rotor with engine oil.

12. Hold the apex seals with a rubber band around the rotor's perimeter to keep the seals attached. Place the rotor on the front housing, being careful not to drop the seals. Turn the front housing so that the sliding surface faces upward.

13. Mesh the internal and stationary gears so that one of the rotor apexes is at any one of the four places shown, then remove the rubber band which is holding the apex seals in position.

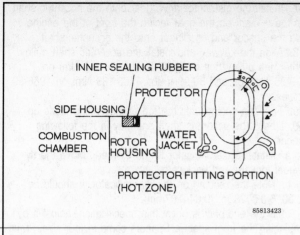

Fig. 374 Install the seal protector behind the inner sealing rubber

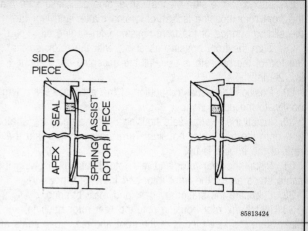

**Fig. 376 Install the side piece as shown under "O."
(The spring must butt against the apex seal lip.)**

14. Lubricate the front rotor journal of the eccentric shaft and the eccentric shaft main journal with engine oil.

15. Insert the eccentric shaft. Be careful that you do not damage the rotor bearing and main bearing.

16. Apply sealing agent to the front side of the front rotor housing.

17. Apply a light coat of petroleum jelly (not grease) onto new O-rings and rubber seals, then install the O-rings and seals on the front side of the rotor housing. If the engine is being overhauled, install the seal protector behind the inner sealing rubber to improve durability.

➡**The inner rubber seal is of the square type. The wider white line of the rubber seal should face the combustion chamber and the seam of the rubber seal should be positioned as illustrated. Do not stretch the rubber seal.**

18. Invert the front rotor housing, being careful not to let the rubber seals and O-rings fall from their grooves, and mount it on the front housing.

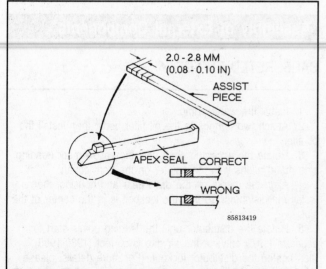

Fig. 375 Fitting an assist piece on the apex seal

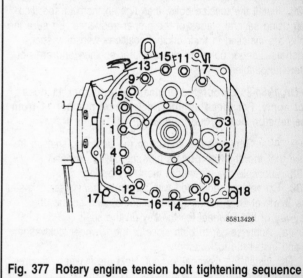

Fig. 377 Rotary engine tension bolt tightening sequence

19. Lubricate the tubular dowels with engine oil, then insert them through the front rotor housing holes and into the front housing.

20. Insert each apex seal spring so that both ends of the spring may support the back side of the seal.

21. Install the corner seal springs and corner seals into their respective grooves.

22. Install the side seal springs and side seals into their respective grooves.

23. Fit an assist piece between the spring and seal, then install each side piece in its original position. Be sure that the spring seats properly on the side piece, as shown.

24. Confirm the smooth movement of each seal by pressing its head.

25. Apply sealer to the rear side of the front rotor housing.

26. Install new O-rings, rubber seals and seal protector on the rear side of the front rotor housing, in the same manner as on the front side.

27. Lubricate the side pieces with engine oil. Make sure that the front rotor housing is free of foreign matter and lubricate the sliding surface of the front housing with engine oil.

28. Turn the front housing assembly with the rotor, so that the top of the housing is up. Pull the eccentric shaft about 1 in. (25mm).

29. Position the eccentric portion of the eccentric shaft diagonally, to the upper right.

30. Install the intermediate housing over the eccentric shaft and onto the front rotor housing. Turn the engine so that the rear of the engine is up.

31. Install the rear rotor and rear rotor housing, following the same steps as for the front rotor and front rotor housing.

32. Lubricate the stationary gear and main bearing.

33. Install the rear housing onto the rear rotor housing. Make sure the side pieces of the front and rear apex seals are not pinched between the rotor and side housings.

34. If necessary, turn the rear rotor slightly to mesh the rear housing stationary gear with the rear rotor internal gear.

35. Install a new washer on each tension bolt, and lubricate each bolt with engine oil.

36. Install the tension bolts, then tighten them to specification using several stages of the proper sequence. Be sure the bolts are installed in their original positions with new seal washers. Longer bolts are used in later engines and are not interchangeable.

➡ On 1984-85 carbureted engines, bolt number 11 does not apply. For those engines, delete bolt number 11 from the tension bolt torque sequence.

37. After tightening the bolts, turn the eccentric shaft to be sure that the shaft and rotors turn smoothly and easily.

38. Lubricate the oil seal in the rear housing.

39. On vehicles equipped with a manual transmission, install the flywheel on the rear of the eccentric shaft so that the keyway of the flywheel fits the key on the shaft.

    a. Apply sealer to both sides of the flywheel lockwasher and install the lockwasher.

    b. Install the flywheel locknut. Hold the flywheel securely and tighten the nut to 350 ft. lbs. (475 Nm).

40. On vehicles with an automatic transmission, install the key, counterweight, lockwasher and nut. Tighten the nut to 350 ft. lbs. (475 Nm). Install the driveplate on the counterweight and tighten the attaching nuts.

41. Turn the engine so that the front faces up.

42. Install the thrust plate with the tapered face down, and install the needle bearing on the eccentric shaft. Lubricate with engine oil.

43. Install the bearing housing on the front housing. Tighten the bolts and bend up the lockwasher tabs. The spacer should be installed so that the center of the needle bearing comes to the center of the eccentric shaft, and the spacer should be seated on the thrust plate.

44. Install the needle bearing on the shaft and lubricate it with engine oil.

45. Install the balancer and thrust washer on the eccentric shaft.

46. Install the oil pump drive chain over both of the sprockets. Install the sprocket and chain assembly over the eccentric shaft and oil pump shaft simultaneously. Install the key on the eccentric shaft. Be sure that both of the sprockets are engaged with the chain before installing them over the shafts.

47. Install the distributor drive gear onto the eccentric shaft with the **F** mark on the gear facing the front of the engine. Slide the spacer and oil slinger onto the eccentric shaft.

48. Align the keyway and install the eccentric shaft pulley. Tighten the pulley bolt to 72-87 ft. lbs. (98-118 Nm) on 1979-85 engines and 80-98 ft. lbs. (108-133 Nm) on 1986-89 engines.

49. Turn the engine until the top of the engine faces up.

50. Check the eccentric shaft end-play in the following manner:

    a. Attach a dial indicator to the flywheel. Move the flywheel forward and backward.

    b. Note the reading on the dial indicator, it should be 0.0016-0.0028 in. (0.04-0.07mm).

    c. If the end-play is not within specification, adjust it by replacing the front spacer. Spacers come in four sizes, ranging from 0.3150-0.3181 in. (8.00-8.08mm). If necessary, a spacer can be ground on a surface plate with emery paper.

    d. Check the end-play again and, if it is now within specification, proceed with the next Step.

51. Remove the pulley from the front of the eccentric shaft. Tighten the oil pump drive sprocket nut and bend the locktabs on the lockwasher.

52. Fit a new O-ring over the front cover oil passage.

53. Install the chain tensioner, if equipped, and tighten its securing bolts.

54. Position the front cover gasket and the front cover on the front housing, then secure the front cover with its attachment bolts.

55. Install the eccentric shaft pulley again. Tighten its bolt to the required torque value.

56. Turn the engine so that the bottom faces up.

57. Cut off the excess gasket on the front cover along the mounting surface of the oil pan.

58. Install the oil strainer gasket and strainer on the front housing, then tighten the attaching bolts.

59. Apply sealer to the joint surfaces of each housing.

60. Install the oil pan.

61. Turn the engine so that the top is up, then complete assembly of the external components.

Assembly of External Components

CARBURETED ENGINES

1. Install the water pump.

2. Attach two O-rings to the oil filter body, then install the oil filter.

3. Rotate the eccentric shaft until the yellow mark (leading side mark) aligns with the pointer on the front cover.

4. Align the marks on the drive gear and housing, then install the distributor so that the lockbolt is in the center of the slot.

5. Rotate the distributor until the leading points start to separate (1979 only) or the air gap is correct (1980-1985), then tighten the distributor locknut. (For more details, please refer to Section 2.)

6. Install the gaskets and thermal reactor/exhaust manifold.

7. Install the hot air duct.

8. Install the carburetor (if applicable) and intake manifold assembly.

9. Connect the oil tubes, vacuum tube and metering oil pump connecting rod to the carburetor.

10. Install the decel valve, then connect the vacuum lines, air hoses and wires.

11. Install the alternator bracket, alternator and retaining bolt, then check the clearance. If the clearance is more than 0.006 in. (0.15mm), adjust the clearance using a shim. Shims are available in three sizes: 0.0059 in. (0.15mm), 0.012 in. (0.30mm), and 0.02 in. (0.50mm).

12. Install and properly tension the alternator and accessory drive belts.

13. Remove the engine from the stand and install it in the vehicle.

FUEL INJECTED ENGINES

1. Install the water pump and tighten the nuts in a criss-cross sequence. Tighten to 13-20 ft. lbs. (18-27 Nm). Be sure to use shims on the side housing contact surfaces.

➡**If shims are not used, the coolant will leak.**

2. Apply engine oil to the new O-ring, then install the metering oil pump to the front housing.

3. Place the exhaust manifold gasket in position and install the exhaust manifold. Tighten to 23-34 ft. lbs. (31-46 Nm).

4. Install the hot air duct and absorber plate.

5. Install the intake manifold auxiliary ports. Installation should be made so that the bigger sides of the auxiliary port valve shaft align with the matching mark on the gasket, as illustrated.

6. Install the O-rings and the intake manifold and gasket.

7. Connect the metering oil pump pipes, and tighten to 14-19 ft. lbs. (19-26 Nm).

8. Install the fuel injection nozzles.

9. Install the delivery pipe assembly, the throttle/dynamic chamber, and the emission device assembly as one piece. Tighten the delivery pipe body to 14-19 ft. lbs. (19-26 Nm), and the emission device assembly to 14-19 ft. lbs. (19-26 Nm).

10. Install the vacuum sensing tube, the air pump, and the engine hanger bracket.

11. Align the leading timing mark (painted yellow) on the eccentric shaft pulley with the indicator pin on the front cover.

12. On models equipped with a distributor, align the tally marks on the distributor housing and driven gear. Install the distributor and locknut. Turn the distributor housing until the projection of the signal rotor aligns with the core of the leading side pick-up coil. Tighten the locknut. Install the distributor rotor and cap.

13. On models equipped with a crank angle sensor, apply engine oil to a new O-ring and install it on the crank angle sensor. Apply engine oil to the drive gear, then match the mating mark and install the crank angle sensor on the front housing.

14. Attach two O-rings to the oil filter body, then install the oil filter.

15. Install and properly tension the alternator and accessory drive belts.

16. Remove the engine from the stand and install it in the vehicle.

EXHAUST SYSTEM

▶ **See Figures 378, 379, 380, 381, 382 and 383**

➡**The exhaust system components and configurations described herein are based on Mazda's original designs. Since many aftermarket parts deviate somewhat from original factory parts, your exhaust system may vary.**

Safety Precautions

For a number of different reasons, exhaust system work can be among the most dangerous types of work you can do on your car. **Always** observe the following precautions:

• Support the car extra securely. Not only will you often be working directly under it, but you'll frequently be using a lot of force--such as heavy hammer blows, to dislodge rusted parts. This can cause a car that's improperly supported to shift and possibly fall.

• Wear goggles. Exhaust system parts are always rusty. Metal chips can be dislodged, even when you're only turning rusted bolts. Attempting to pry pipes apart with a chisel makes chips fly even more frequently.

• If you're using a cutting torch, keep it at a great distance from both the fuel tank and fuel lines. Stop what you're doing and feel the temperature of fuel bearing pipes and the tank frequently. Even slight heat can expand or vaporize the fuel, resulting in accumulated vapor or even a liquid leak near your torch.

• Watch where your hammer blows fall. You could easily tap a brake or fuel line when you hit an exhaust system part with a glancing blow. Inspect all lines and hoses in the area where you've been working before driving the car.

Special Tools

A number of special exhaust system tools can be rented from auto supply houses or local stores that rent special equipment. A common one is a tail pipe expander, designed to enable you to join pipes of identical diameter.

It may also be quite helpful to use solvents designed to loosen rusted bolts or flanges. Soaking rusted parts the night before you do the job can speed the work of freeing rusted parts considerably. Remember that these solvents are often flammable. Apply them only after the parts are cool.

Catalytic Converter — Exhaust Manifold Mounted

REMOVAL & INSTALLATION

GLC

1. Remove the clamp supporting the pipe running from the exhaust mounted converter to the front of the rear converter. Remove the nuts and the springs which fasten the rear of this pipe to the front of the rear converter.
2. Remove the three nuts and washers fastening this pipe to the bottom of the exhaust manifold mounted converter. Disconnect the secondary air line where it passes into the top of this pipe.
3. Pull the pipe down and off the exhaust manifold mounted converter, then forward and off the rear converter. Remove both gaskets.
4. Remove the nuts from the upper side of the flange on the exhaust manifold. Then, pull the converter downward and off the exhaust manifold. Remove the gasket.
5. Clean all flanges, then install a new exhaust manifold mounted converter in reverse order, using new gaskets. Work the pipe connecting the two converters onto the studs of the rear converter before connecting it with the exhaust manifold mounted studs.

Catalytic Converter — Exhaust System Mounted

REMOVAL & INSTALLATION

GLC and 323

1. Remove the attaching nuts and washers/springs from the exhaust manifold or exhaust manifold mounted converter studs. Disconnect the secondary air line from the pipe connecting the two converters on the GLC. Remove the nuts and washers from the studs or bolts on the front of the rear converter. On the 323, remove the bolts from the front of the front converter.
2. Pull the pipe downward and off the manifold mounted converter or manifold. Then, pull it off the exhaust system converter. Remove all gaskets.
3. On the GLC, disconnect the secondary air line where it runs into the converter. On both models, remove the studs and nuts connecting the main exhaust system mounted converter to the front of the exhaust pipe. Pull the unit forward and off the studs. Unbolt and remove the upper and lower heat shields on the GLC. Remove the gasket.
4. Clean all flanges and install in reverse order, using new gaskets.

626/MX-6

1. The catalytic converter is integral with a pipe and the resonator, as well as the pipe linking the resonator to the exhaust pipe and muffler. First, support this assembly in front of the resonator.

2. Remove the nuts and springs holding the studs in the forward end of the catalytic converter to the front pipe flange. Then, remove the nuts from the forward ends of the bolts attaching the assembly to the center pipe and muffler. Pull the bolts out to the rear.
3. Remove the rubber support donuts at the forward hangers and at the resonator. Then, lower the assembly at the rear and, when the rear is clear of the flange behind, slide the converter studs out of the flange in the front pipe. Remove the gaskets at both ends, as well as the ring type seal located in the rear of the front pipe.
4. Clean all flanges and install in reverse order, using new gaskets and seals.

Muffler

REMOVAL & INSTALLATION

GLC

The GLC muffler assembly is attached at the front via a flange, and at the rear via a clamped pipe connection.
1. Raise and safely support the front end on jackstands.
2. Unbolt the clamp at the rear, then slide it forward and away from the connection.
3. Remove the nuts from the rear side of the flange at the front.
4. Support the assembly, then pull the bolts forward and out of the flange at the front.
5. Remove the donut type hangers at the front and pull the rear hangers off the support prongs.
6. Turn the assembly back and forth, then pull the rear pipe out of the connector for the rear pipe and remove it.
7. Unbolt the halves of the heat shield from the front pipe and install it onto the new assembly.
8. Remove the gasket from the flange at the front and replace it during reassembly.
9. Installation is the reverse of removal. Make sure that all parts have sufficient clearance from underbody members, **before** tightening the clamps.

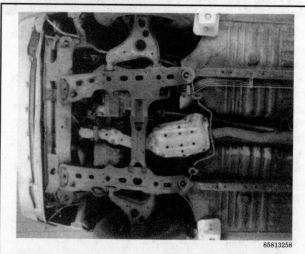

Fig. 378 On some vehicles, the catalytic converter is covered by a heat shield — 1984 626 shown

Fig. 379 The muffler (or main silencer) is located at the rear of the exhaust system — 1984 626 shown

323

1. Raise and safely support the front end on jackstands.
2. Remove the nuts from the flange connecting the resonator rear pipe and muffler inlet pipe.
3. Pull the bolts out at the front.
4. Disconnect the hangers from the prongs at the front and rear of the muffler, and at the rear of the tail pipe, then remove the assembly. On the Hatchback only, unclamp and remove the tail pipe, and install it on the new assembly.
5. Installation is the reverse of removal. Make sure that all parts have sufficient clearance from underbody members, **before** tightening the clamps.

626/MX-6 and 929

The muffler or main silencer assembly is flanged at the front. The muffler configuration is the same for both 626/MX-6 turbo and non-turbo models.

1. Raise and safely support the rear end on jackstands.
2. Remove the nuts and bolts connecting the muffler at the flange. Then, on gasoline engine vehicles, unhook the hangers at the prongs and remove the assembly. On diesel-equipped vehicles, unhook the donut type rubber connectors at the front and outboard on the rear support.
3. Installation is the reverse of removal. If the rubber hangers are broken or worn, replace them. Make sure that all parts have sufficient clearance from underbody members, **before** tightening the clamps.

RX-7

1979-85 models are equipped with only one muffler, as opposed to the dual muffler system used on 1986-89 RX-7s (with turbo and non-turbo engines).

1. Raise and safely support the rear end on jackstands.
2. Remove the lower protective cover from the pre-monolith converter and the rear of the exhaust pipes.
3. Remove the main converter cover.
4. Disconnect the split air pipe from the muffler by removing the flange nuts.
5. Unhook and remove the muffler bracket rubber pieces.
6. Lower the muffler from the vehicle.
7. On dual muffler systems, remove the remaining muffler in the same manner.
8. Installation is the reverse of removal. Use new gaskets during installation. Make sure that all parts have sufficient clearance from underbody members, **before** tightening the clamps.

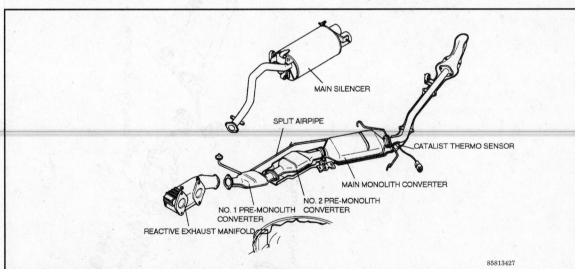

Fig. 380 Exploded view of the 1979-85 RX-7 exhaust system

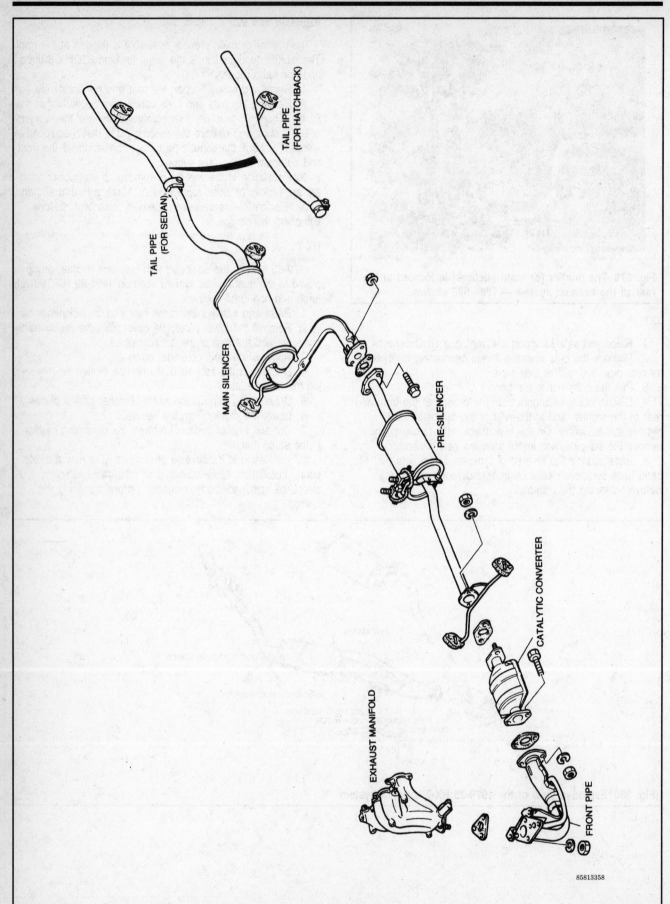

TAIL PIPE (FOR HATCHBACK)

TAIL PIPE (FOR SEDAN)

MAIN SILENCER

PRE-SILENCER

CATALYTIC CONVERTER

EXHAUST MANIFOLD

FRONT PIPE

85813358

Fig. 381 Exploded view of the 323 exhaust system (non-turbo shown)

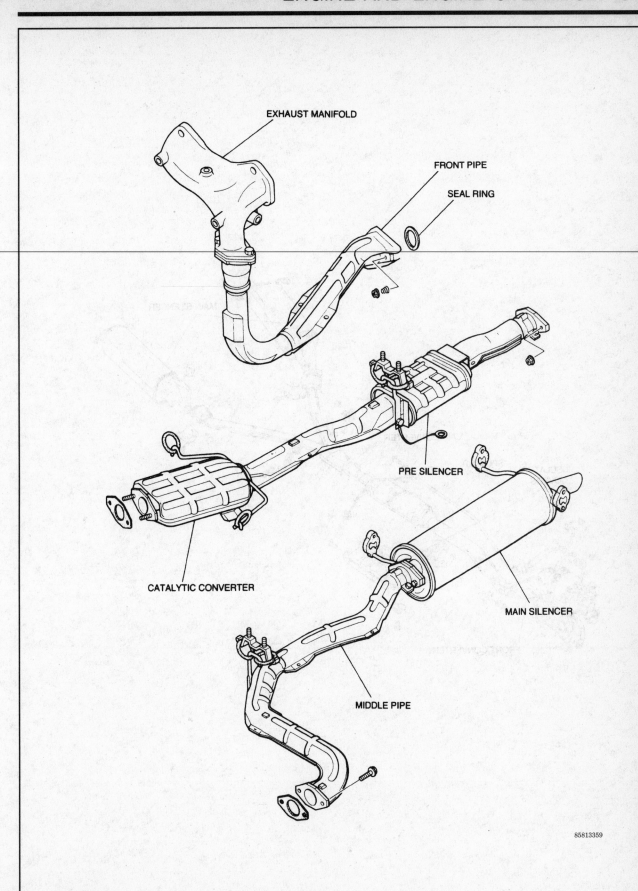

EXHAUST MANIFOLD

FRONT PIPE

SEAL RING

PRE SILENCER

CATALYTIC CONVERTER

MAIN SILENCER

MIDDLE PIPE

85813359

Fig. 382 Exploded view of the 1983-89 626 exhaust system (non-turbo shown)

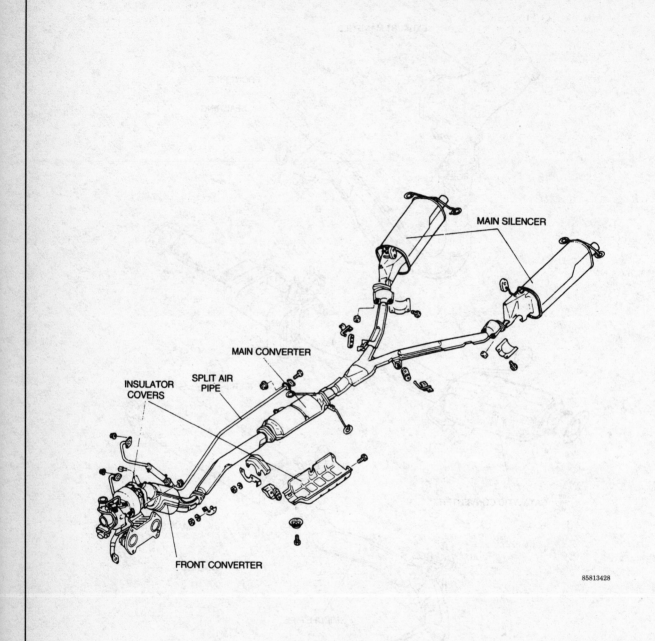

MAIN SILENCER

MAIN CONVERTER

INSULATOR
COVERS

SPLIT AIR
PIPE

FRONT CONVERTER

85813428

Fig. 383 Dual muffler exhaust system for the 1986-89 RX-7 (turbo shown; non-tubo similar)

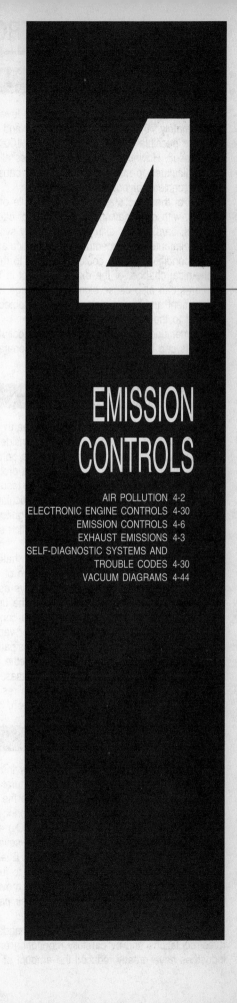

4

EMISSION CONTROLS

AIR POLLUTION

The earth's atmosphere, at or near sea level, consists of approximately 78% nitrogen, 21% oxygen and 1% other gases. If it were possible to remain in this state, 100% clean air would result. However, many varied causes allow other gases and particulates to mix with the clean air, causing the air to become unclean or polluted.

Some of these pollutants are visible while others are invisible, with each having the capability of causing distress to the eyes, ears, throat, skin and respiratory system. Should these pollutants be concentrated in a particular area under certain conditions, death could result due to the displacement, or chemical change, of the oxygen content in the air. These pollutants can also cause significant damage to the environment and to the many man-made objects that are exposed to the elements.

To better understand the causes of air pollution, the pollutants can be categorized into three separate types: natural, industrial and automotive.

Natural Pollutants

Natural pollution has been present on earth since before man appeared. It is still a factor to be considered when discussing air pollution, although it causes only a small percentage of the present overall pollution problem existing in our country. Natural pollution is the direct result of decaying organic matter, wind born smoke and particulates from such natural events as plains and forest fires (ignited by heat or lightning), volcanic ash, sand and dust which spreads over a large area of the countryside.

Such a phenomenon of natural pollution has included recent volcanic eruptions, with the resulting plume of smoke, steam and volcanic ash blotting out the sun's rays as it spreads and rises higher into the atmosphere. There, the upper air currents catch and carry the smoke and ash, while condensing the steam back into water vapor. As the water vapor, smoke and ash travel on their journey, the smoke dissipates into the atmosphere while the ash and moisture settle back to earth in a trail hundreds of miles long. In many cases, lives are lost and millions of dollars of property damage result. Ironically, man can only stand by and watch it happen.

Industrial Pollutants

Industrial pollution is caused primarily by industrial processes, the burning of coal, oil and natural gas, which in turn produces smoke and fumes. Because the burning fuels contain significant amounts of sulfur, the principal ingredients of smoke and fumes are sulfur dioxide (SO_2) and particulate matter. This type of pollution occurs most severely during still, damp and cool weather, such as at night. Even in its less severe form, this pollutant is not confined to just cities. Because of air movements, the pollutants move for miles over the surrounding countryside, leaving in their path a barren and unhealthy environment for all living things.

Working with Federal, State and local mandated rules/regulations and by carefully monitoring emissions, industries have greatly reduced the amount of pollution which they emit, while striving to obtain an acceptable level. Because of the mandated industrial emission clean-up, many land areas and streams in and around the cities that were formerly barren of vegetation and life, have now begun to move back in the direction of nature's intended balance.

Automotive Pollutants

The third major source of air pollution is automotive emissions. Years ago, emissions from the internal combustion engine were not an appreciable problem because of the small number of registered vehicles and the nation's small highway system. However, during the early 1950's, the trend of the American people was to move from the cities to the surrounding suburbs. This caused an immediate problem in the transportation area, since most suburbs were not afforded mass transit convenience. This lack of transportation created an attractive market for the automobile manufacturers, which resulted in a dramatic increase in the number of vehicles produced and sold, along with a marked increase in highway construction between cities and the suburbs. Multi-vehicle families emerged with much emphasis placed on an individual vehicle per family member. As vehicle ownership and usage increased, so did the pollutant levels in and around the cities. This was due, in large part, to the suburbanites' daily driving to their employment in the city, then returning at the end of the day to their homes in the suburbs.

It was noted that a fog and smoke type haze was formed and, at times, remained in suspension over the cities without quickly dissipating. At first this "smog," derived from the words "smoke" and "fog," was thought to result from industrial pollution, but it was determined that the automobile emissions were largely to blame. It was discovered that as normal automobile emissions were exposed to sunlight for a period of time, complex chemical reactions would take place.

It was found that smog is a photo-chemical layer which develops when certain oxides of nitrogen (NOx) and unburned hydrocarbons (HC) from the automobile emissions are exposed to sunlight. The problem intensifies when the smog remains stagnant over an area in which a warm layer of air settles above a cooler air mass at ground level. This results in the trapping and holding of automobile emissions, instead of the emissions being dispersed and diluted through normal air flow. This type of air stagnation was given the name "Temperature Inversion."

Temperature Inversion

In normal weather situations, the surface air is warmed by the heat radiating from the earth's surface and the sun's rays. It then rises upward, into the atmosphere, to be cooled through a convection-type heat that expands with the cooler upper air. As the warm air rises, the surface pollutants are carried upward and dissipated into the atmosphere.

When a temperature inversion occurs, we find the higher air is no longer cooler but, rather, is warmer than the surface air, causing the cooler surface air to become trapped and unable to move. This warm air blanket can extend from above ground level to a few hundred or even a few thousand feet high. As the surface air is trapped, so are the pollutants, causing a severe smog condition. Should this stagnant air mass extend to a few thousand feet high, enough air movement with the inversion takes place to allow the smog layer to rise above ground level, but the pollutants still cannot dissipate. This inversion can remain for days over an area, with only the smog level rising or lowering from ground level to a few hundred feet high. Meanwhile, the pollutant levels increase, causing eye irritation, respiratory problems, reduced visibility, plant damage and in some cases, cancer-like diseases.

This inversion phenomenon was first noted in the Los Angeles, California area. The city lies in a basin-type of terrain and during certain weather conditions, a cold air mass is held in the basin while a warmer air mass covers it like a lid.

Because this type of condition was first documented as prevalent in the Los Angeles area, this type of smog was named Los Angeles Smog, although it occurs in other areas where a large concentration of automobiles can be found and the air remains stagnant for any length of time.

Internal Combustion Engine Pollutants

Consider the internal combustion engine as a machine in which raw materials must be placed so that a finished product emerges. As in any machine operation, a certain amount of wasted material is formed. When we relate this to the internal combustion engine, we find that by putting in air and fuel, we obtain power (during the combustion process) to drive the vehicle. The by-product or waste of this power is heat and the exhaust gases (with which we must concern ourselves).

EXHAUST EMISSIONS

Composition Of The Exhaust Gases

The exhaust gases emitted into the atmosphere are a combination of burned and unburned fuel. To understand exhaust emission and its composition, review some basic chemistry.

When the air/fuel mixture is introduced into the engine, we are mixing air, composed of nitrogen (78%), oxygen (21%) and other gases (1%) with the fuel, which is 100% hydrocarbons (HC), in a semi-controlled ratio. As the combustion process is accomplished, power is produced to move the vehicle while the heat of combustion is transferred to the cooling system. The exhaust gases are then composed of nitrogen, a diatomic gas (N_2), the same as was introduced in the engine, carbon dioxide (CO_2), the same gas that is used in beverage carbonation, and water vapor (H_2O). The nitrogen (N_2), for the most part, passes through the engine unchanged, while the oxygen (O_2) reacts (burns) with the hydrocarbons (HC) and produces the carbon dioxide (CO_2) and water vapor (H_2O). If this chemical process would be the only process to take place, the exhaust emissions would be harmless. However, during the combustion process, other pollutants are formed and are considered dangerous. These pollutants are carbon monoxide (CO), hydrocarbons (HC), oxides of nitrogen (NOx), oxides of sulfur (SOx) and engine particulates.

Heat Transfer

The heat from the combustion process can rise to over 4000°F (2204°C). The dissipation of this heat is controlled by a ram air effect, the use of cooling fans to cause air flow, and having a liquid coolant solution which surrounds the combustion area and transfers the heat of combustion through the cylinder walls and into the coolant. The coolant is then directed to a thin-finned, multi-tubed radiator, from which the excess heat is transferred to the outside air by one or more of the three heat transfer methods: conduction, convection or radiation.

The cooling of the combustion area is an important part in the control of exhaust emissions. To understand the behavior of the combustion and transfer of its heat, consider the air/fuel charge. It is ignited and the flame front burns progressively across the combustion chamber until the burning charge reaches the cylinder walls. Some of the fuel in contact with the walls is not hot enough to burn, thereby snuffing out or "quenching" the combustion process. This leaves unburned fuel in the combustion chamber. This unburned fuel is then forced out of the cylinder, along with the exhaust gases, into the exhaust system.

Many attempts have been made to minimize the amount of unburned fuel in the combustion chambers due to the snuffing out or quenching, by increasing the coolant temperature and lessening the contact area of the coolant around the combustion chamber. Design limitations within the combustion chambers prevent the complete burning of the air/fuel charge, so a certain amount of the unburned fuel is still expelled into the exhaust system, regardless of these modifications.

Lead (Pb), is considered one of the particulates and is present in the exhaust gases whenever leaded fuels are used. Lead (Pb) does not dissipate easily. Levels can be high along roadways when it is emitted from vehicles and can pose a health threat. However, with the use of unleaded gasoline and the phase out of leaded gasoline for fuel, this pollutant has all but disappeared.

HYDROCARBONS

Hydrocarbons (HC) are essentially unburned fuel that has not been successfully burned during the combustion process or has escaped into the atmosphere through fuel evaporation. The main sources of incomplete combustion are rich air/fuel mixtures, low engine temperatures and improper spark timing. The main sources of hydrocarbon emission through fuel evaporation come from the vehicle's fuel tank and carburetor bowl.

To reduce combustion hydrocarbon emissions, engine modifications were made to minimize dead space and surface area in the combustion chamber. In addition, the air/fuel mixture was made more lean through improved carburetion and fuel injection. External controls were also added to further the combustion of hydrocarbons outside the engine. Two such methods were the addition of an air injection system, to inject fresh air into the exhaust manifolds and the installation of a catalytic converter, a unit that is able to burn traces of hydrocarbons without significantly affecting the internal combustion process or fuel economy.

To control hydrocarbon emissions through fuel evaporation, modifications were made to the fuel tank and carburetor bowl (if equipped) to allow storage of the fuel vapors during periods of engine shut-down. During specific engine operating conditions, these modifications will purge and burn the vapors by blending them with the air/fuel mixture.

CARBON MONOXIDE

Carbon monoxide is formed when not enough oxygen is present during the combustion process to convert carbon (C) to carbon dioxide (CO_2). An increase in the carbon monoxide (CO) emission is normally accompanied by an increase in the hydrocarbon (HC) emission because of the lack of oxygen to completely burn all of the fuel mixture.

Carbon monoxide (CO) also increases the rate at which the photo-chemical smog is formed by speeding up the conversion of nitric oxide (NO) to nitrogen dioxide (NO_2). The carbon monoxide (CO) combines with oxygen (O_2) and nitric oxide (NO) to produce carbon dioxide (CO_2) and nitrogen dioxide (NO_2). ($CO + O_2 + NO = CO_2 + NO_2$).

The dangers of carbon monoxide, which is an odorless, colorless and toxic gas, are many. When carbon monoxide is inhaled into the lungs and passed into the blood stream, oxygen is replaced by the carbon monoxide in the red blood cells, causing a reduction in the amount of oxygen supplied to the many parts of the body. This lack of oxygen causes headaches, lack of coordination, reduced mental alertness and, should the carbon monoxide concentration be high enough, death could result.

NITROGEN

Normally, nitrogen is an inert gas. When heated to approximately 2500°F (1371°C) through the combustion process, this gas becomes active and causes an increase in the nitric oxide (NOx) emission.

Oxides of nitrogen (NOx) are composed of approximately 97-98% nitric oxide (NO). Nitric oxide is a colorless gas but when it is passed into the atmosphere, it combines with oxygen and forms nitrogen dioxide (NO_2). The nitrogen dioxide then combines with chemically active hydrocarbons (HC) and, when in the presence of sunlight, causes the formation of photo-chemical smog.

OZONE

To further complicate matters, some of the nitrogen dioxide (NO_2) is broken apart by the sunlight to form nitric oxide and oxygen. (NO_2 + sunlight = NO + O). This single atom of oxygen then combines with diatomic (meaning 2 atoms) oxygen (O_2) to form ozone (O_3). Ozone is one of the smells associated with smog. It has a pungent and offensive odor, irritates the eyes and lung tissues, affects the growth of plant life and causes rapid deterioration of rubber products. Ozone can be formed by sunlight as well as electrical discharge into the air.

The most common discharge area on the automobile engine is the secondary ignition electrical system, especially when inferior quality spark plug cables are used. As the surge of high voltage is routed through a secondary cable, the circuit builds up an electrical field around the wire, and acts upon the oxygen in the surrounding air to form the ozone. The faint glow along the cable with the engine running that may be visible on a dark night, is called the "corona discharge." The combination of corona and ozone has been a major cause of cable deterioration. Recently, different types and better quality insulating materials have lengthened the life of the electrical cables.

Although ozone at ground level can be harmful, ozone is beneficial to the earth's inhabitants. By having a concentrated ozone layer called the "ozonosphere," between 10-20 miles (16-32km) up in the atmosphere, much of the ultraviolet radiation from the sun's rays is absorbed and screened. If this ozone layer was not present, much of the earth's surface would be burned, dried and unfit for human life.

There is much discussion concerning the ozone layer and its density. A feeling exists that this protective layer of ozone is slowly diminishing and corrective action must be directed to this problem. Much experimenting is presently being conducted to determine if a problem exists and, if so, the short and long-term effects of the problem and how it can be remedied.

OXIDES OF SULFUR

Oxides of sulfur (SOx) were initially ignored in the exhaust system emissions, since the sulfur content of gasoline as a fuel is less than $1/10$ of 1%. Because of this small amount, it was felt that it contributed very little to the overall pollution problem. However, because of the difficulty in solving the sulfur emissions in industrial pollution, as well as the introduction of catalytic converters to automobile exhaust systems, a change was mandated. The automobile exhaust system, when equipped with a catalytic converter, changes the sulfur dioxide (SO_2) into sulfur trioxide (SO_3).

When sulfur trioxide (SO_3) combines with water vapor (H_2O), a sulfuric acid mist (H_2SO_4) is formed. This sulfuric acid mist is a very difficult pollutant to handle and is extremely corrosive. It is the same mist that rises from the vents of an automobile storage battery when an active chemical reaction takes place within the battery cells.

When a large concentration of vehicles equipped with catalytic converters are operating in an area, this acid mist will rise and be distributed over a large ground area causing land, plant, crop, paint and building damage.

PARTICULATE MATTER

A certain amount of particulate matter is present in the burning of any fuel, with carbon constituting the largest percentage of the particulates. In gasoline, the remaining percentage of particulates is the burned remains of various other compounds used in its manufacture. When a gasoline engine is in good internal condition, the particulate emissions are low but as the engine wears internally, the particulate emissions increase. By visually inspecting the tailpipe emissions, a determination can be made as to where an engine defect may exist. An engine with light gray smoke emitting from the tail pipe normally indicates an increase in the oil consumption through burning due to internal engine wear. Black smoke would indicate a defective fuel delivery system, causing the engine to operate in a rich mode. Regardless of the color of the smoke, the internal part of the engine or the fuel delivery system should be repaired to a "like new" condition to prevent excessive particulate emissions.

Diesel and turbine engines emit a darkened plume of smoke from the exhaust system because of the type of fuel used. Emission control regulations are mandated for this type of emission and more stringent measures are being used to prevent excessive emission of the particulate matter. Electronic components are being introduced to control the injection of the fuel at precisely the proper time of piston travel, to achieve the optimum in fuel ignition and fuel usage. Other particulate after-burning components are being tested to achieve lower particulate emissions.

Good grades of engine lubricating oils should be used, meeting the vehicle manufacturer's specification. "Cut-rate" oils can contribute to the particulate emission problem because of their low "flash" or ignition temperature point. Such oils burn prematurely during the combustion process causing emissions of particulate matter.

The cooling system is an important factor in the reduction of particulate matter. With the cooling system operating at a temperature specified by the manufacturer, optimal combustion will occur. The cooling system must be maintained in the same manner as the engine oiling system, since each system must perform properly in order for the engine to operate efficiently for a long time.

Other Automobile Emission Sources

Before emission controls were mandated on internal combustion engines, other sources of engine pollutants were discovered in addition to exhaust emissions. It was determined that engine combustion exhaust produced only 60% of the total emission pollutants. Fuel evaporation from the fuel tank and carburetor vents produced 20%, and the other 20% was produced through the crankcase as a by-product of the combustion process.

CRANKCASE EMISSIONS

Crankcase emissions are made up of water, acids, unburned fuel, oil fumes and particulates. The emissions are classified as hydrocarbons (HC) and are formed by the small amount of unburned, compressed air/fuel mixture which enters the crankcase from the combustion area. This infiltration occurs during the compression and power strokes, by passing between the cylinder walls and piston rings.

Since the first engines, crankcase emissions were allowed to go into the air through a road draft tube, mounted on the lower side of the engine block. Fresh air came in through an open oil filler cap or breather. The air passed through the

crankcase mixing with blow-by gases. The motion of the vehicle and the air blowing past the open end of the road draft tube caused a low pressure area at the end of the tube. Crankcase emissions were simply drawn out of the road draft tube into the air.

To control the crankcase emission, the road draft tube was deleted. A hose and/or tubing was routed from the crankcase to the intake manifold so the blow-by emission could be burned with the air/fuel mixture. However, it was found that intake manifold vacuum, used to draw the crankcase emissions into the manifold, would vary in strength at the wrong time and not allow the proper emission flow. A regulating type valve was needed to control the flow of air through the crankcase.

Testing showed that removal of the blow-by gases from the crankcase, as quickly as possible, was most important to the longevity of the engine. Should large accumulations of blow-by gases remain and condense, dilution of the engine oil would occur to form water, soots, resins, acids and lead salts, resulting in the formation of sludge and varnish. This condensation of blow-by gases occurs more frequently on vehicles used in numerous starting and stopping conditions, excessive idling and when the engine is not allowed to attain normal operating temperature due to short runs. The crankcase purge control or PCV system was designed to combat this problem, and will be described in detail later in this section.

FUEL EVAPORATIVE EMISSIONS

Gasoline fuel is a major source of pollution, before and after it is burned in the automobile engine. From the time the fuel is refined, stored, pumped and transported, and again stored until it is pumped into the fuel tank of the vehicle, the gasoline gives off unburned hydrocarbons (HC) into the atmosphere. Through redesigning of the storage areas and venting systems, the pollution factor has been diminished but not eliminated, from the refinery standpoint. However, the automobile still remains the primary source of vaporized, unburned hydrocarbon (HC) emissions.

Fuel pumped from an underground storage tank is cool, but when exposed to a warmer ambient temperature will expand. Before controls were mandated, an owner would fill the fuel tank with fuel from an underground storage tank and park the vehicle for some time in a warm area, such as a parking lot. As the fuel would warm, it would expand and should no provisions or area be provided for the expansion, the fuel would spill out the filler neck and onto the ground, causing hydrocarbon (HC) pollution and creating a severe fire hazard. To correct this condition, the vehicle manufacturers added overflow plumbing and/or gasoline tanks with built-in expansion areas or domes.

However, this did not control the fuel vapor emissions from the fuel tank and the carburetor bowl. It was determined that most of the fuel evaporation occurred when the vehicle was stationary and the engine not operating. Most vehicles carry 5-25 gallons (19-95 liters) of gasoline. Should a large concentration of vehicles be parked in one area, such as a large parking lot, excessive fuel vapor emissions would take place, increasing as the temperature rises.

To prevent the vapor emissions from escaping into the atmosphere, the fuel system is designed to trap the vapors while the vehicle is stationary, by sealing the fuel system from the atmosphere. A storage system is used to collect and hold the fuel vapors from the fuel tank and the carburetor or air cleaner assembly when the engine is not operating. When the engine is started, the storage system is then purged of the fuel

vapors, which are drawn into the engine and burned with the air/fuel mixture.

The components of this fuel evaporative system will be described in detail later in this section.

EMISSION CONTROLS

There are three types of automotive pollutants: crankcase fumes, exhaust gases and gasoline evaporation. The pollutants formed from these substances fall into three categories: unburned hydrocarbons (HC), carbon monoxide (CO), and oxides of nitrogen (NOx). The devices used to limit the release of these pollutants into the atmosphere are commonly referred to as emission control equipment.

Positive Crankcase Ventilation (PCV) System

OPERATION

Gasoline and Diesel Engines
▶ See Figures 1 and 2

The positive crankcase ventilation (PCV) valve is located on the intake manifold below the carburetor (if so equipped), or inline with (or on) the cylinder head cover. Routine periodic maintenance of this system basically involves inspection of the breather hose and replacement of the PCV valve.

The diesel uses a very simple system designed to operate under the extremely low manifold vacuum conditions that exist in an engine which has no throttle valve. A breather hose connects the cylinder head cover with a fitting in the intake manifold. The system does not require routine periodic replacement of any part. You should inspect the breather hose occasionally and replace it if it deteriorates. At 30,000 mile (48,309 km) intervals, or whenever removing the cylinder head cover, you should clean the breather hose and nipples in both the cylinder head cover and manifold in case to prevent oil or carbon clogging.

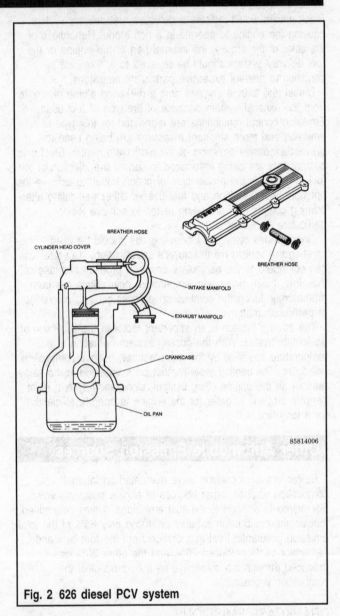

Fig. 2 626 diesel PCV system

Rotary Engines
▶ See Figure 3

When the engine is running, small amounts of combustion gases leak by the rotor seals and enter the rotor housings and oil pan. Since these gases are under pressure, they tend to escape into the atmosphere. If these gases were allowed to remain for any length of time, pressure would build up and possibly blow out an oil seal. They would also contaminate the engine oil and cause sludge to build up. If the gases were allowed to escape into the atmosphere, they would pollute the air, as they contain hydrocarbons. The crankcase emission control equipment recycles these gases back into the engine combustion chambers where they are reburned.

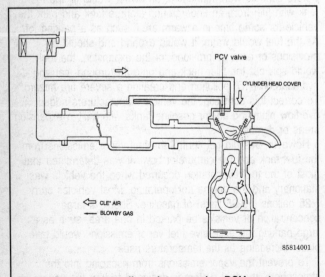

Fig. 1 Common gasoline piston engine PCV system

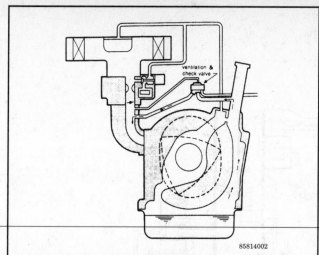

85814002

Fig. 3 Arrows indicate the flow of blow-by gases through a rotary engine — 1979-80 RX-7

In the case of the rotary engine, the word crankcase is not quite correct, however, since the Mazda rotary engine has no crankcase in the usual sense of the term. As a result, rotary engines do not employ a conventional PCV valve. Instead, the "crankcase" emission control equipment for 1979-80 models consists of a ventilation and check valve and its related hoses, which meter the flow of fuel and air vapors through the rotor housings and oil pan. When the engine is running, vacuum from the intake manifold opens the ventilation and check valve. This allows blow-by gases to flow out of the rotor housings and oil pan, and into the intake manifold where they mix with the air/fuel mixture to be burned in the combustion chambers. When the engine is not running, the ventilation valve is closed and blow-by gases are trapped inside the housings until the engine is started again. The ventilation and check valve also controls evaporative emissions, as explained later in this section.

➡1981-89 models do not contain a ventilation and check valve. In its place, a check and cut valve is used.

TESTING AND REPLACEMENT

The procedures for PCV valve testing and replacement may be found under Routine Maintenance, in Section 1.

Evaporative Emission Control System

OPERATION

Gasoline Engines
▶ See Figure 4

The evaporative emission control system is designed to control the emission of gasoline vapors into the atmosphere.

On GLC and carbureted 323 models, the system consists of a charcoal canister, a check and cut valve, a liquid separator (wagon only), and purge control valves. On 626 models prior to 1988, the system consists of a charcoal canister, a check

and cut valve (or three-way check valve), purge control valves, and on some early models, an evaporator shutter valve in the air cleaner.

On fuel injected 323s, as well as the 1988-89 626, MX-6 and 929, the system takes fuel vapor that is generated in the fuel tank and stores it in the charcoal canister when the engine is not running. This fuel vapor remains in the canister until the engine is started, at which time the fuel vapor is drawn into the intake manifold and burned. The system on these models is made up of the charcoal canister, purge control solenoid valves, a three-way check valve, a vacuum switch control valve and an electronic control unit.

Rotary Engines
▶ See Figures 5 and 6

When raw fuel evaporates, the vapors contain hydrocarbons. To prevent these vapors from escaping into the atmosphere, the fuel evaporative emission control system was developed. The 1979-80 RX-7 models use a ventilation and check valve and a charcoal canister located in the air cleaner. The 1981-85 RX-7 with carbureted engine is equipped with a conventional charcoal canister located beside the carburetor. On these models, the flow of vapor is controlled by a purge control valve located on top of the charcoal canister. On the 1984-89 RX-7 with fuel injection, evaporative fumes from the gas tank along with those from the canister are regulated by the purge control valve, which introduces them to the intake manifold. The purge control valve is located on the side of the oil filler pipe.

On 1979-80 RX-7 models, a ventilation and check valve prevents fuel vapors from reaching the atmosphere in the following manner: When the engine is off, the fuel vapor from the gasoline in the fuel tank is trapped in the fuel tank and evaporative line until it reaches a certain pressure. When that pressure is reached, the ventilation and check valve opens, allowing fuel vapors to pass into the rotor housings and oil pan, and mix with the blow-by gases trapped there. The trapped gases are then fed into the charcoal canister, along with vapors from the fuel in the carburetor float bowl. The fuel vapors remain in the canister until the engine is started, when manifold vacuum opens the check valve, allowing all of the vapors and blow-by gases in the rotor housings/oil pan and charcoal canister to flow into the intake manifold. There, the vapors and blow-by gases mix with the air/fuel mixture to be burned in the combustion chambers.

On 1981-89 RX-7 models, a check and cut valve prevents fuel vapors from reaching the atmosphere by performing the following functions: (1) When vapor pressure in the fuel tank becomes too great, the valve releases the pressure into the charcoal canister and rotor housings to prevent the tank from bursting; (2) When vacuum pressure in the tank becomes too high, the valve allows air into the tank to prevent it from collapsing and to insure that sufficient fuel is pumped to the carburetor or throttle body and not drawn back by the vacuum in the fuel tank; (3) When the vehicle is overturned, the valve prevents fuel from flowing out of the tank. On later models, when the engine is not running, vapors from the fuel tank are fed into the charcoal canister where they are trapped by the purge valve. When the engine is running with the throttle open, manifold vacuum opens the purge valve and the vapors trapped in the canister are allowed to flow out into the throttle and dynamic chamber. There, these vapors combine with the

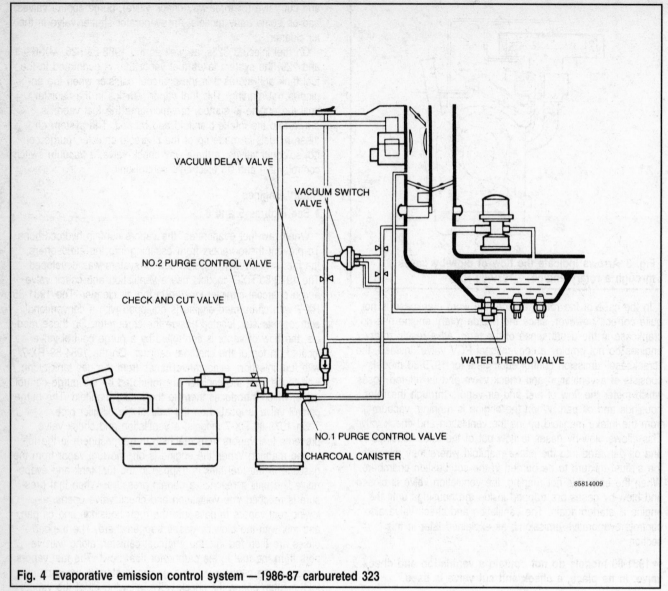

VACUUM DELAY VALVE

VACUUM SWITCH VALVE

NO.2 PURGE CONTROL VALVE

CHECK AND CUT VALVE

WATER THERMO VALVE

NO.1 PURGE CONTROL VALVE

CHARCOAL CANISTER

85814009

Fig. 4 Evaporative emission control system — 1986-87 carbureted 323

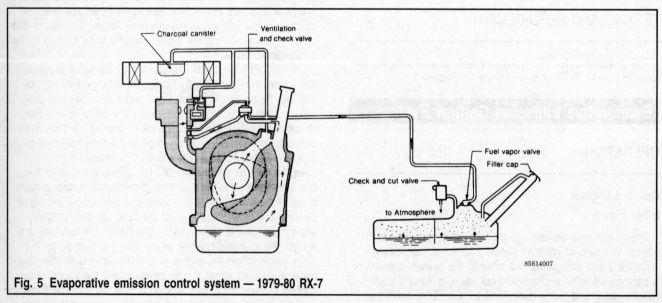

Charcoal canister

Ventilation and check valve

Fuel vapor valve

Filler cap

Check and cut valve

to Atmosphere

85814007

Fig. 5 Evaporative emission control system — 1979-80 RX-7

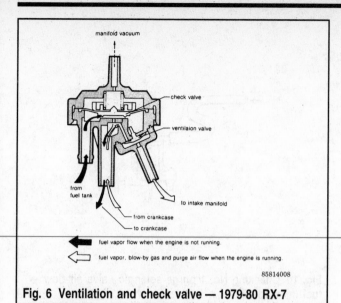

Fig. 6 Ventilation and check valve — 1979-80 RX-7

air/fuel mixture and pass through the intake manifold to be burned in the combustion chambers. The bottom of the canister contains an air filter on most models.

SYSTEM TESTING

There are several things to check if a malfunction of the evaporative emission control system is suspected.

Piston Engines

EXCEPT 323 AND 1986-89 626/MX-6

1. Leaks may be traced by using an infrared hydrocarbon tester. Run the test probe along the lines and connections. The meter will indicate the presence of a leak by a high hydrocarbon (HC) reading. This method is much more accurate than a visual inspection, which would indicate only the presence of a leak large enough to pass liquid.

2. Leaks may be caused by any of the following, so always check these areas when looking for them:
   a. Defective or worn lines
   b. Disconnected or pinched lines
   c. Improperly routed lines
   d. A defective check valve

➡**If it becomes necessary to replace any of the lines used in the evaporative emission control system, use only those hoses which are fuel resistant or are marked EVAP.**

3. If the fuel tank has collapsed, it may be the fault of clogged or pinched vent lines, a defective vapor separator, or a plugged or incorrect check valve.

CARBURETED 323

▶ **See Figure 7**

➡**This test requires the use of a precisely calibrated pressure gauge and a source of compressed air. If you do not have these items on hand, it may be advisable to go to a professional for testing.**

1. Start out by testing the No. 1 and No. 2 purge control valves, as described in Steps 6 and 7 of the procedure for the 626/MX-6, which follows.

2. Remove the air cleaner. Place a finger on top of the air vent solenoid valve, located on top of the carburetor. Have someone turn the ignition switch **ON** and **OFF** as you feel for operation of the solenoid. If the solenoid does not click audibly or operate so that you can feel it, replace the valve.

3. Test the water temperature valve, as described in Step 3 of the 626/MX-6 procedure. Replace the valve if it fails the test.

4. Remove the check and cut valve, noting that the horizontal connection goes to the fuel tank and the vertical connection is vented to the air. Tee a pressure gauge into the horizontal passage (normally connected to the tank). Hold the valve horizontally for proper internal air flow. Gradually admit air into the valve while watching the pressure. Air should start to flow through the valve at 0.14-0.71 psi (0.98-4.9 kpa). Connect the gauge to the vertical (vented) connection. Again, gradually admit air into the valve while watching the pressure. It should open at 0.78-1.00 psi (5.39-6.87 kpa). Replace the valve if it fails either test.

5. Test the vacuum switching valve, as described in Step 8 of the 626/MX-6 procedure.

6. Disconnect the vacuum delay valve. Connect the vacuum pump to the end of the valve away from the arrow with a length of hose 40 in. (1 meter) long. Draw a vacuum of 24 in. Hg. Then, watch as the vacuum decreases from 19.7 in. Hg to 3.9 in. Hg, timing how long it takes. It should take 0.2-1.2 seconds. If the valve fails the test, replace it.

FUEL INJECTED 323

▶ **See Figures 8, 9 and 10**

1. Warm up the engine and allow it to run at idle speed.

2. Connect a voltmeter to the **Y** terminal of the No. 1 purge control solenoid valve, located at the top of the canister. You should read approximately 12V on the meter.

3. Disconnect the vacuum hose from the No. 1 purge control valve and place a finger over the opening of the hose.

4. Increase the engine speed to 2,000 rpm and make sure that no air is being sucked into the hose.

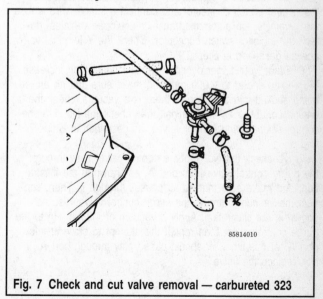

Fig. 7 Check and cut valve removal — carbureted 323

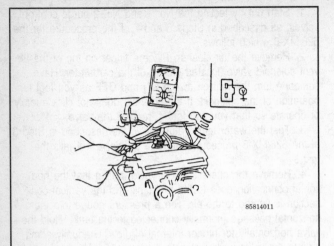

Fig. 8 Checking No. 1 purge solenoid "Y" terminal voltage — fuel injected 323

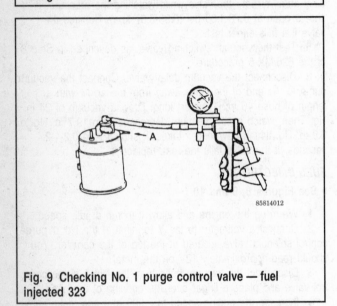

Fig. 9 Checking No. 1 purge control valve — fuel injected 323

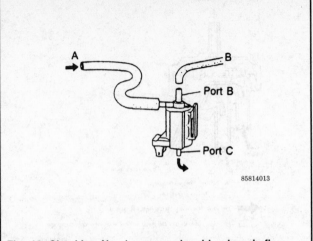

Fig. 10 Checking No. 1 purge solenoid valve air flow — fuel injected 323

5. On vehicles equipped with a manual transaxle, detach the neutral switch connector and connect a jumper wire across the terminals. On automatic transaxle-equipped vehicles, detach the inhibitor switch connector. Check the **Y** terminal voltage as described in Step 2.

6. Place your finger over the vacuum hose, then increase the engine speed to 2,000 rpm and make sure that no air is being sucked into the hose. If there is a vacuum, check the engine control unit's 2P terminal, then check the No. 1 purge control solenoid and control valves, as described in Steps 7 and 8.

7. To check the No. 1 purge control valve, blow through the purge control valve from port **A**, as shown in the illustration, and make sure that no air passes through it. Then, connect the vacuum pump to the purge control valve, also as shown in the illustration. Apply a vacuum of 4.33 in. Hg to the purge control valve, then repeat the attempt to blow air into port **A**. At this time, air should pass freely through port **A**. If not, replace the valve.

8. To check the No. 1 purge solenoid valve, disconnect the vacuum lines from ports **A** and **B** on the solenoid. Detach the electrical connector from the bottom of the solenoid. Blow into port **A** and verify that air comes out of port **C**. Apply battery voltage to the solenoid with a jumper wire, then blow into port **A** and verify that air passes freely from port **B**. If the valve does not function as described, replace. Proceed with the remainder of the procedure to finish the emission control system inspection.

9. Fasten the neutral or inhibitor switch connector, depending on the type of transaxle.

10. Disconnect the vacuum hose leading directly to the canister (not passing through the purge valve). Disconnect the rubber hose at the canister, then connect a vacuum source to the open end of the hose, so that air will be drawn out of the steel pipe mounted to the car body. Operate the vacuum pump. Air should be drawn into the pump freely. If the system holds vacuum, inspect the pipe or the three-way check valve (located near the fuel tank) for clogging.

1986-89 626 AND MX-6

▶ See Figures 11, 12 and 13

1. Warm up the engine, then let it idle. Disconnect the vacuum hose leading to the purge control valve on top of the canister. Connect a vacuum gauge or special tester 49-9200-750A, or equivalent, to the open end of the hose. Connect a tachometer to the ignition system.

2. Increase the engine rpm to 2,500 and read the vacuum gauge. Vacuum must be a minimum of 5.9 in. Hg. If the vacuum is okay, go to Step 4. Otherwise, test the water temperature valve as described in Step 3.

3. Drain some coolant out of the system, then unscrew the water temperature valve from the intake manifold. Connect two short lengths of vacuum hose to the valve's connection points. Immerse the lower portion of the valve in a container of water with the vacuum hoses above the liquid level. Immerse a suitable thermometer in the water, then heat the water to more than 130°F (54°C) and attempt to blow air through the valve. If air passes, the valve is okay; otherwise, replace it. Reconnect the vacuum hose.

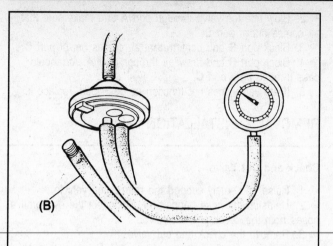

Fig. 11 Disconnect vacuum hose "B" from the No. 3 purge control valve and plug it — 1986-89 626 and MX-6

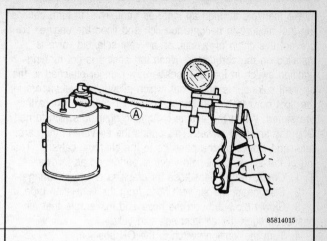

Fig. 12 Blow into port "A" to begin inspection of the No. 1 purge control valve — 1986-89 626 and MX-6

4. Disconnect the vacuum hose labeled **B** from the No. 3 purge control valve and plug it. Then, with another length of hose, connect a vacuum gauge to the open port in the purge control valve, as shown. Run the engine to more than 1,500 rpm and check for vacuum. If there is no vacuum, inspect the three-way solenoid valve, the No. 3 purge control valve and the EGR control unit's 2P terminal. Disconnect the vacuum gauge and reconnect the vacuum hose.

5. Disconnect the vacuum hose leading directly into the canister (not passing through the purge valve). Disconnect the hose at the canister, then connect a vacuum source to the open end of the rubber hose, so that air will be drawn out of the steel pipe mounted to the car body. Operate the vacuum pump. Air should be drawn into the pump freely. If the system holds vacuum, inspect the pipe or the three-way check valve (located near the fuel tank) for clogging.

6. Attempt to blow air into the port labeled **A**. No air should pass into it. Connect the vacuum pump to the purge control valve, as shown in the illustration. Apply a vacuum of 4.33 in. Hg to the purge control valve. Then, repeat the attempt to blow air into **A**. This time, air should flow. Otherwise, replace the purge control valve.

7. Disconnect the hose referred to in Step 5 at the metal pipe, but this time, blow into the hose with it still connected to the canister. Air should flow freely. Otherwise, replace the No. 2 purge valve.

8. First, label the connecting hoses, then remove the No. 3 purge control valve. Blow into the center port on the flat side of the valve and check for air flow leaving the outboard port on the flat side. There should be no air flow without vacuum being applied to the valve. Apply vacuum of 2.95 in. Hg to the single port located on the convex side of the valve. Then, blow through the center port again, as you did at the beginning of this step. Air should now flow out of the outboard port. Install a new valve, if necessary, or reinstall the old one with all hoses properly connected, according to your labeling.

9. Remove the three-way check valve located on the gas tank vent line near where the filler pipe connects with the fuel tank. Blow through Port **A** and make sure air comes out Port **B**. Seal off Port **B** and blow again from Port **A**. Air should flow out of Port **C**. Now, block Port **B** and blow through port **C**. Air

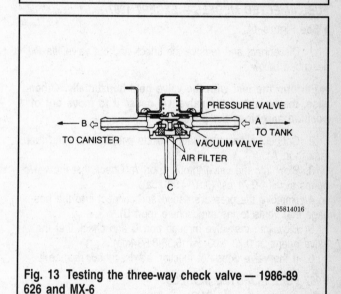

Fig. 13 Testing the three-way check valve — 1986-89 626 and MX-6

should come out of Port **A**. If the valve fails any of these tests, replace it.

10. The three-way solenoid valve is located at the right of the three valves mounted on the fender well. Label, then disconnect the two hoses at the bottom of the valve. Connect a short length of hose to the port leading into the side of the valve near the bottom, leaving the vertical port (which discharges out in a downward direction) open. First, blow through the hose and check for discharge of air through the filter at the top. Then, energize the valve by applying battery voltage to the electrical connector at the top with a jumper wire. Now, when you blow through the hose, air should be discharged through the port at the bottom of the valve. If the valve fails either test, replace it.

Rotary Engines

CARBURETED MODELS

When the car is parked after operation for some distance, the fuel in the float chamber tends to evaporate and enter the intake manifold through an inner air vent. This, in turn, causes the fuel mixture to become too rich and flood the engine. To prevent this chain of events, an air vent solenoid valve is installed on the carburetor. When the engine is not running (ignition switch in the **OFF** position), a plunger attached to the air vent solenoid is pulled out, which allows the fuel vapors in the float bowl to be fed into the charcoal canister, where they are stored. When the engine is running (ignition switch turned **ON**), the solenoid closes. This opens the air vent in the carburetor and closes off the passage to the charcoal canister. Testing of the air vent solenoid valve is performed as follows:

1. Check the air vent hose for cracking or other damage.
2. Disconnect the air vent hose from the ventilation pipe.
3. Slowly blow through the hose and make sure that air passes through the air vent solenoid valve.
4. Turn the ignition switch to the **ON** position.
5. Slowly blow through the hose; air should not pass through the air vent solenoid. If it does, check the solenoid wiring or replace the solenoid.

FUEL INJECTED MODELS — EXCEPT 1987

▶ **See Figure 14**

1. Disconnect and remove the check and cut valve, as described below.

➡**Perform the test with the valve held horizontally. Otherwise, the weight of the valve will cause it to move out of position and close the passage.**

2. Connect a pressure gauge to the passage from the fuel tank (port **A**).
3. Blow into the valve through port **A**. Check that the valve opens at 0.14-0.71 psi (0.97-4.90 kpa).
4. Remove the pressure gauge and connect it to the passage that vents to the atmosphere (port **B**).
5. Blow into the valve through port **B** and check that the valve opens at 0.78-1.00 psi (5.38-6.89 kpa).
6. If the valve does not function as described, replace it.

1987 FUEL INJECTED MODELS

1. Disconnect and remove the check and cut valve.

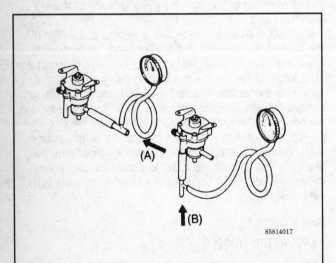

85814017

Fig. 14 Testing the check and cut valve — fuel injected RX-7

2. Blow into the valve through port **A** and make sure that air comes out of port **B**.
3. Block port **B** and confirm that air comes out of port **C**.
4. Block port **B** and draw air through port **A**. Air should pass through from port **C**.
5. If the valve does not function as described, replace it.

REMOVAL & INSTALLATION

Check and Cut Valve

1. Raise and safely support the rear of the vehicle.
2. Unfasten the hose bands and disconnect the evaporative hoses from the check and cut valve.
3. Remove the check and cut valve.
4. Installation is the reverse of removal. Be sure to route the hoses properly.

Exhaust Gas Recirculation System — Gasoline Engines

OPERATION

This system is used to meter a small amount of exhaust gas back into the intake manifold to slow the combustion process, and slightly reduce the maximum temperatures in the combustion chambers, thereby reducing nitrogen oxides. A water temperature switch or three-way solenoid valve may stop exhaust gas recirculation when the engine is cold. On most models, the EGR Control Valve must be serviced periodically, and on some models, a maintenance warning system reset. The EGR valve is by far the most sensitive part of the system, as it can become carbon clogged.

➡**Fuel injected 323s do not utilize an EGR system.**

EGR CONTROL VALVE TESTING

▶ **See Figure 15**

If the EGR system gets clogged or the valve stem seizes due to carbon clogging, the engine may ping even when the proper fuel is used and ignition timing is correct. One way to check the system is to run the engine at idle speed while placing your finger on the EGR valve diaphragm, by reaching in under the housing at the top of the valve. Have an assistant increase the throttle opening. The valve should open and its position should modulate as the throttle is open and closed, adjusting for each engine operating speed and throttle opening variation.

If you doubt that the system is performing properly, the best procedure is to test the EGR valve with the engine at idle and full manifold vacuum applied to the valve diaphragm, as follows:

Except 1988-89 626/MX-6 and 929

1. Remove the air cleaner assembly.
2. Run the engine at idle.

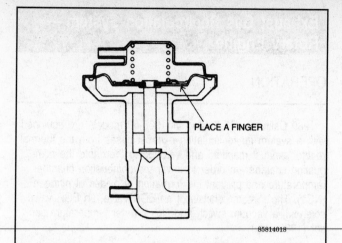

Fig. 15 Place the tip of your finger as shown to check for EGR valve function

Fig. 16 Hook up an ohmmeter to the EGR valve position sensor connector as shown — 1985 626

3. On 1983-84 626 models, plug the hoses of the idle compensator, thermosensor, and reed valves. (Consult the underhood sticker showing vacuum hose routing to identify these).

4. Disconnect the vacuum sensing tube from the EGR control valve, and make connections directly to an intake manifold tap (not to the carburetor) with a vacuum hose.

5. Connect this vacuum tube to the EGR control valve. The engine should suddenly run very roughly or stall. If it does not, clean or replace the EGR control valve.

1988-89 626/MX-6 and 929

1. Grasp the rod of the EGR control valve or apply pressure to the spring diaphragm, to make sure that it moves freely up and down and that there is resistance from the actuating spring.

2. Disconnect the vacuum hose from the EGR control valve and connect a vacuum pump to the valve.

3. Start the engine and run it at idle speed. Apply vacuum to the valve. Check that the engine runs roughly or stalls when 1.6-2.4 in. Hg (40-60mm Hg) of vacuum is applied to the valve.

4. If the engine does not behave as described with the specified amount of vacuum applied, replace the EGR control valve.

EGR VALVE POSITION SENSOR TESTING

1985 626
▶ See Figure 16

Disconnect the position sensor connector, which leads to the bottom of the EGR valve. Connect an ohmmeter as shown. If there is an open circuit, the position sensor is defective and the EGR valve should be replaced. If there is resistance, the sensor may be presumed to be okay.

EGR MODULATOR VALVE TESTING

➡ **You will need a source of vacuum such as a vacuum pump and a vacuum gauge to make these tests. You may be able to disconnect and plug off the hoses leading to this valve, then operate the engine and use engine vacuum to make the tests. In this case, you can tee a vacuum gauge into the line which will apply vacuum.**

1986-87 323

1. Note the routing of all hoses leading to the modulator valve, especially the hose which is connected to the exhaust side of the EGR valve. Remove the EGR Modulator valve. Plug the No. 1 port, then attach a source of vacuum to the No. 3 port.

2. Attach a clean hose to the exhaust gas port. Blow into the end of the hose and maintain pressure. Apply vacuum to the No. 3 port, then seal off the source of vacuum. Vacuum should be maintained as long as air pressure is applied.

3. Stop applying air pressure. The vacuum should be released. If the valve fails to respond properly in either Step 2 or 3, replace it.

1986-87 626

1. Note the routing of all hoses leading to the modulator valve, especially the hose which is connected to the exhaust side of the EGR valve. Remove the valve. Plug the ports numbered **2** and **3**. Attach a source of vacuum to the No. 1 port.

2. Attach a clean hose to the exhaust gas port. Blow into the end of the hose and maintain pressure. Apply vacuum to the No. 1 port, then seal off the source of vacuum. Vacuum should be maintained as long as air pressure is applied.

3. Stop applying air pressure. The vacuum should be released. If the valve fails to respond properly in either Step 2 or 3, replace it.

VACUUM DELAY VALVE TESTING

1985 626

➡You will need a source of vacuum such as a vacuum pump and a vacuum gauge to make these tests. You may be able to disconnect and plug the hoses leading to this valve, then operate the engine to produce vacuum for testing. In this case, you can tee a vacuum gauge into the line which will apply vacuum. You will also need about four feet of vacuum line, the diameter of that used to connect this valve into the system.

1. Remove the vacuum delay valve. Cut a vacuum hose of the size used to connect this valve into the system to 40 in. (1 meter) in length. Connect the hose to the inlet end of this valve (the arrow on the valve should point away from the hose connection), then attach a source of vacuum and the vacuum gauge to the other end of the hose.

2. Hold your thumb tightly against the open end of the valve. Apply a vacuum of over 20 in. Hg (508mm Hg). Then, seal off the source of vacuum. Release your thumb and watch the gauge as vacuum decreases to 4 in. Hg (102mm Hg). This should take 1.3-2.3 seconds. If the time elapsed during the pressure drop is outside this range, replace the valve.

REMOVAL & INSTALLATION

EGR Control Valve

1. On carburetor-equipped vehicles, remove the air cleaner assembly.

2. Disconnect the vacuum sensing tube from the EGR control valve.

3. Disconnect the EGR control valve-to-exhaust manifold pipe. Disconnect all vacuum hoses.

4. Disconnect the pipe between the EGR control valve and the intake manifold. On the 929, disconnect the two water hoses that are routed in front of the valve and detach the electrical connector.

5. Unbolt and remove the EGR control valve.

6. If the old valve is to be reused, it should be cleaned with a wire brush before installation.

To install:

7. Install the EGR valve with a new gasket. On the 929, fasten the electrical connector and the two water hoses. Connect the EGR valve-to-intake manifold pipe with a new gasket.

8. Connect all vacuum hoses. Connect the exhaust manifold-to-EGR valve pipe.

9. If applicable, install the air cleaner assembly.

10. Start the engine and inspect for exhaust gas leaks. On the 929, check for water leaks also.

Exhaust Gas Recirculation System — Rotary Engine

OPERATION

1980 California RX-7s and all 1986-89 models are equipped with a system for recirculating exhaust gases from the thermal reactor/exhaust manifold and introducing them into the combustion chamber, in order to lower the combustion chamber temperature and prevent the formation of oxides of nitrogen (NOx). The system consists of an EGR valve, an EGR valve solenoid, a vacuum switch and No. 1 water temperature sensor (1980 only).

EGR SYSTEM TESTING

1980 RX-7

▶ See Figure 17

1. Run the engine until it reaches normal operating temperature, and connect a tachometer to the engine.

2. Connect a voltmeter to the brown and yellow wire in the electrical connector of the EGR solenoid valve.

3. Start the engine and quickly rev it to 2,500 rpm. Current should flow to the terminal for a few seconds and then stop.

4. Disconnect the electrical coupler of the vacuum switch and connect a jumper wire to both terminals in the coupler. Increase engine speed with the throttle. Current flow to the solenoid valve should stop when the engine speed is 2,700-3,300 rpm for manual transmission models, or 3,000-3,600 rpm for automatic transmission models.

5. Increase the engine speed to 2,000 rpm with the throttle. Slowly decrease the engine speed and record the engine speed at which the current stops flowing to the terminal. Engine speed should be around 1,050-1,250 rpm.

6. Slowly increase the engine speed from idle and check the engine speed at which the current begins to flow. Compare

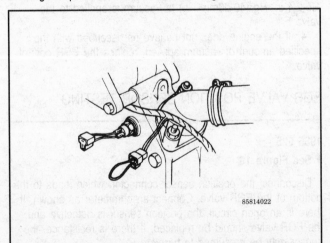

85814022

Fig. 17 Detach the connector from the No. 1 water temperature switch, and connect a jumper wire — 1980 RX-7

this figure with that recorded in Step 5. The difference in engine speed between the two should be about 90-220 rpm.

7. On vehicles equipped with a manual transmission, increase the engine speed to 2,000 rpm with the throttle. Current flow to the terminal should stop when the idle switch lever is fully pushed up to the idle position.

8. Disconnect the coupler of the No.1 water temperature switch, then connect a jumper wire to both terminals on the wiring harness, as illustrated. No current should flow to the solenoid valve at any rpm.

9. Stop the engine, then start the engine with the choke knob pulled fully out, and set the engine speed at 2,000 rpm with the choke knob. Current should flow to the solenoid after 104-156 seconds from the time the engine was started with the choke valve pulled out.

10. On vehicles with a manual transmission, set the engine speed to 2,000 rpm using the throttle, then depress the clutch pedal and shift the transmission into 4th and 5th gears. Current to the solenoid should stop when the gears are engaged.

11. If the results of all tests are as described above, the EGR signal system is working properly.

EGR VALVE TESTING

The EGR valve is located between the air cleaner and the bank of solenoid valves on the engine.

1. Run the engine to operating temperature, then shut it off.

2. Disconnect the vacuum sensing tube from the EGR valve, and connect a vacuum pump to the valve.

3. Start the engine and run it at idle. The engine should operate smoothly.

4. Apply a vacuum of 15.7 in. Hg (399mm Hg) for 1980 models, or 3.9 in. Hg (99mm Hg) for 1986-89 models to the EGR valve. The engine should stall or experience a sharp drop in speed if the valve is working properly.

EGR SOLENOID VALVE TESTING

1980 RX-7 (California Only)

The EGR solenoid valve is located in the bank of solenoids on the engine and can be identified by the gray dab of paint on its body.

1. Disconnect the vacuum sensing tubes from the solenoid valve and the vacuum pipe.

2. Blow through the solenoid valve from tube **B**. Air should come out of air filter **A** on the valve.

3. Detach the electrical connection from the EGR solenoid valve, then activate the valve using jumper cables from the battery.

4. Blow through vacuum tube **B**. Air should come out of port **C**.

5. If the solenoid does not operate as indicated above, replace it.

1986-89 RX-7 (All Models)
▶ See Figures 18 and 19

The EGR solenoid valve is located in the bank of solenoids on the engine. It supplies intake manifold vacuum to the EGR valve.

1. Locate the EGR valve in the engine solenoid valve bank, and disconnect the vacuum hose from the valve (see illustration).

2. Blow into the solenoid valve through port **B** and place your hand under the air filter. Air should pass freely through the valve and exit from the air filter.

3. Detach the connector from the solenoid valve, then connect a 12-volt power source and a ground to the solenoid terminals. Blow through port **B** of the valve and place your hand over the opening of port **A**. Air should pass freely through the valve and exit through port **A**.

4. If the air flow is not as described above, replace the solenoid valve.

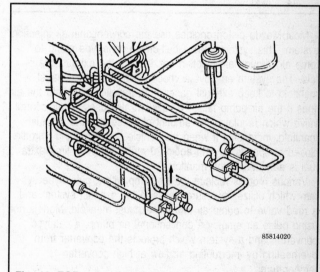
85814020

Fig. 18 EGR solenoid valve location on 1986-89 RX-7

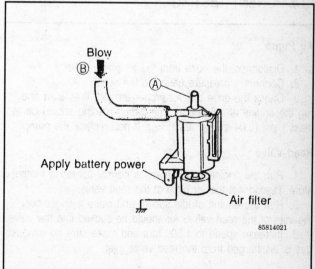

Blow
Ⓑ
Ⓐ
Apply battery power
Air filter
85814021

Fig. 19 Checking EGR solenoid valve on 1986-89 RX-7

EGR Maintenance Warning System

➡ This system is used only on rotary engine cars.

RESETTING

After the passages of the EGR valve have been cleaned with solvent and the outlet of the valve has been wire brushed, reset the maintenance warning system as follows:

1. Detach the connector, located under the left side of the dashboard.
2. Turn one side 180 degrees, then reconnect it.

Piston Engine Air Injection System

OPERATION

Most Mazda piston engines use the conventional air injection system. This system uses a belt-driven vane-type pump to force air through air injection nozzles into the exhaust manifold. The system employs a check valve near the exhaust manifold to keep exhaust gases from traveling back into the air lines if the air pump fails. The system also uses an air control valve which regulates the amount of air sent to the exhaust manifold, increasing it when the vehicle is overrunning (throttle closed at speeds beyond about 20 mph), at which time extra fuel is admitted to the manifold.

Various models replace the air pump with a pulse-type system which utilizes pressure waves in the exhaust system and a reed valve to pump air into the exhaust manifold. Models not using pulse air employ a conventional air pump, a catalytic converter, and a system which protects the converter from overheating by interrupting air flow at high converter temperatures.

COMPONENT TESTING

Air Pump

1. Disconnect the hose from the air pump outlet.
2. Connect a pressure gauge to the outlet.
3. Check the drive belt for proper tension, then start and run the engine at 1,500 rpm. The gauge reading should be at least 1 psi (2.04 in. Hg/52mm Hg). If not, replace the pump.

Reed Valve

1. Run the engine until it reaches normal operating temperature. Disconnect the air hose at the reed valve.
2. Run the engine at idle speed, and place a finger over the inlet of the reed valve. Air should be sucked into the valve.
3. Increase speed to 1,500 rpm and make sure no exhaust gas is discharged from the reed valve inlet.

Relief Valve

1. Run the engine at idle.
2. At idle, no air should be felt at the relief valve. If air flow is felt, replace the valve.

3. Increase the idle to 2,000 rpm on the 1.6L engine, or 4,000 rpm on other engines. If air flow is felt, the valve is working properly.

Check Valve

1. Run the engine until it reaches normal operating temperature. Disconnect the air hose at the check valve on the exhaust manifold.
2. Gradually increase the engine speed to 1,500 rpm, while carefully checking for exhaust (hot) gas leakage from the check valve. Replace the valve if exhaust gases are present.

Air Control Valve

1. Start the engine and run it at idle.
2. Hold a finger over the relief valve port of the air control valve. Discharge air should be felt.
3. Disconnect the vacuum sensing tube from the air control valve and plug the tube. No air should be felt at the relief port.

Air Control Valve Check Valve

1. Disconnect the vacuum sensing tube from the air control valve solenoid.
2. Blow through the vacuum tube; air should pass through the valve. Suck on the tube; no air should pass through the valve.

COMPONENT REPLACEMENT

Air Pump

1. Disconnect the inlet and outlet hoses at the pump.
2. Unfasten the adjusting bolt and remove the drive belt.
3. Support the pump and remove the mounting bolts. Lift out the pump.

To install:

4. Lower the pump onto its mounting and install the retaining bolts.
5. Install the drive belt onto the pulley, then insert the adjusting bolt. Adjust the drive belt to specification.
6. Connect the inlet and outlet hoses to the pump.

Air Control Valve

1. Disconnect the vacuum lines from the valve.
2. Disconnect the wiring from the valve.
3. Disconnect the air hoses from the valve.
4. Unbolt and remove the valve.

To install:

5. Place the valve into position and bolt it in place.
6. Connect the air hoses, wiring and vacuum lines to the valve.

Check Valve/Reed Valve

1978-82 MODELS

1. Disconnect the inlet air hose.
2. Unscrew the valve from the exhaust manifold.

To install:

3. Screw the valve into the exhaust manifold.
4. Connect the inlet air hose.

Pulse Air Injection System

REED VALVE INSPECTION/REPLACEMENT

This system is usually trouble-free. One symptom of improper operation would be a high hydrocarbon emissions reading, assuming the basic engine functions, including idle mixture adjustment, are okay. To check the reed valves for proper function, proceed as follows:

1983-85 Models

▶ **See Figures 20 and 21**

1. Run the engine until it is fully warmed up. Shut off the engine and remove the air cleaner cover and element. Get a small piece of ordinary paper.
2. Place the paper against the inlet port for the air injection system. Have someone start the engine and let it idle. Air flowing into the system should draw the paper against the air inlet.
3. Accelerate the engine until it reaches 1,500 rpm, and check that the exhaust pressure does not force the paper away from the air inlet.
4. If either test is failed, replace the reed valves.

1986-87 Models

1. The air control valve (ACV) must be checked before the reed valves. It is located on the side of the air cleaner. Disconnect the vacuum hose, remove the screws and the mounting bracket, then remove the air control valve. Connect a vacuum source to the valve, and tee in a vacuum gauge. (You can use engine vacuum to do this, if you pinch off the vacuum line before having someone start the engine. Be careful to gradually unpinch the line when releasing vacuum to the gauge and valve.)
2. Apply vacuum gradually while watching the stem of the air control valve and the vacuum gauge. The valve stem must start to move at 7.1-11.0 in. Hg (180-279mm Hg). If the valve does not pass this test, replace it. If it does pass, install the

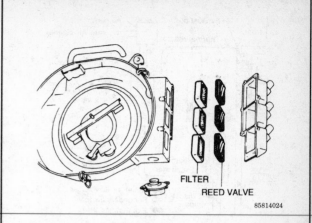

Fig. 21 Exploded view of common pulse air injection system reed valves

ACV back onto the air cleaner, leaving the gauge and vacuum source connected to it.

3. Apply a source of vacuum to the air control valve. Vacuum must be 20 in. Hg. (508mm Hg). If necessary, start the engine. Now, lift off the top of the air cleaner. Check to make sure there is air flow into the ACV intake, accessible from the inside of the air cleaner. Have someone accelerate the engine to 2,550 rpm, then check the ACV intake again to make sure exhaust gas is not being expelled. If either test is failed, replace the reed valve.

Rotary Engine Air Injection System

OPERATION

▶ **See Figures 22, 23 and 24**

The air injection system used on the Mazda rotary engine differs from the type used on a conventional piston engine in two respects:

1. Air is not only supplied to burn the gases in the exhaust ports, but is also used to cool the thermal reactor/exhaust manifold.
2. A three-way air control valve is used in place of the conventional anti-backfire and diverter valves. It contains an air cutout valve, a relief valve, and a safety valve.

Air is supplied to the system by a normal vane-type air pump. The air flows from the pump to the air control valve, where it is routed to the air injection nozzles to cool the thermal reactor/exhaust manifold or, in the case of a system malfunction, to the air cleaner. A check valve, located beneath the air control valve seat, prevents the back-flow of hot exhaust gases into the air injection system, in the event of air pressure loss.

Air injection nozzles are used to feed air into the exhaust ports, just as in a conventional piston engine.

On 1979-80 RX-7s, an air pump feeds fresh air into the hot exhaust gas as the gas leaves the exhaust ports. This burns the HC and CO in the exhaust gas. The system works as follows: The air pump draws in fresh air from the air cleaner

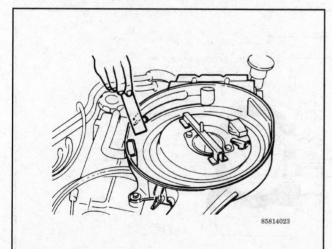

Fig. 20 Checking pulse air injection system — 1983-84 626

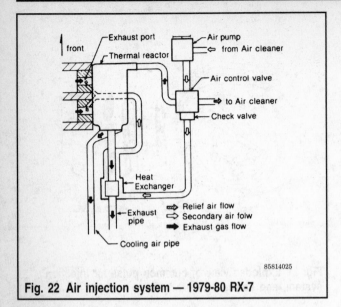

Fig. 22 Air injection system — 1979-80 RX-7

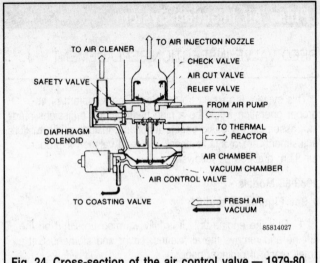

Fig. 24 Cross-section of the air control valve — 1979-80 RX-7

and sends it to the air control valve, which routes it through the heat exchanger and into the exhaust ports. Not all of the air from the pump follows this path, however; some of the air is, at times, sent through the outer shell of the thermal reactor to keep the reactor from reaching destructively high temperatures. At other times, excess air from the pump is fed back into the air cleaner by the air control valve.

When the air from the air pump passes through the heat exchanger, it is pre-heated so that cold air is not pumped into the exhaust ports, which would lower the basic temperature in the exhaust system and affect the thermal reactor's ability to consume noxious gases. The fresh air injected into the exhaust ports adds oxygen to the exhaust gases, and they begin to burn as they pass into the thermal reactor. By the time the gases pass out of the thermal reactor, the previously unburned hydrocarbons and the carbon monoxide have been brought down to legal emission levels.

On 1981-89 RX-7s, the system used on these models replaces the thermal reactor with two catalytic converters (No.1 monolith and No. 2 monolith) and a reactive exhaust manifold. The system retains the air pump and the air control valve.

Air is pulled in from the air cleaner by the air pump and sent to the air control valve, where, according to engine operating conditions, the air is either sent into the exhaust ports or directed down to the dual bed-type catalyst. Excess air is sent back to the air cleaner. The air-burned hydrocarbons and carbon monoxide ignite these unused gases in much the same way the thermal reactor does on 1979-80 RX-7s. The air control valve sends air to the exhaust ports, mainly during deceleration and low engine speeds when HC and CO tend to be produced in large amounts. During this phase, the catalysts act as backup units to insure that fewer noxious gases are produced.

At the middle engine speeds, the air control valve routes air down to the two-bed catalyst. Air is injected through a nozzle between the two pellet beds of the rear catalyst. When the exhaust port air is stopped, the front bed of the rear catalyst processes oxides of nitrogen (NOx), while the rear bed, with the help of the injected fresh air, oxidizes hydrocarbons and carbon monoxide. The monolithic catalyst, located in front of the two-bed catalyst, acts as a backup system for the two-bed unit.

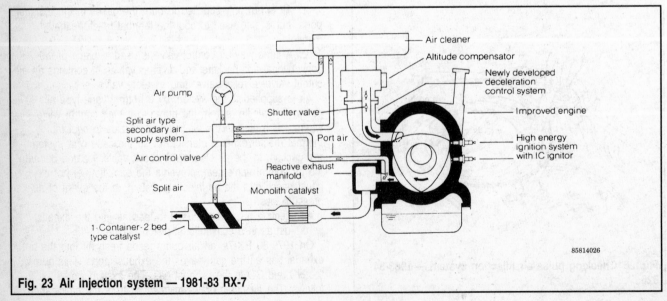

Fig. 23 Air injection system — 1981-83 RX-7

COMPONENT TESTING

Air Pump

▶ **See Figures 25 and 26**

1. Check the air pump drive belt tension by applying 22 lbs. (10 kg) of pressure halfway between the water pump and air pump pulleys. The belt should deflect 0.28-0.35 in. (7-9mm). Adjust the belt if necessary, or replace if it is cracked or worn.

2. Remove the belt and turn the pump by hand. If it has seized, the pump will be very difficult or impossible to turn.

➡**Disregard any chirping, squealing or rolling sounds coming from inside the pump; these are normal when it is being turned by hand.**

3. Check the hoses and connections for leaks. Soapy water, applied around the area is question, is a good method of detecting leaks.

4. Connect a pressure gauge between the air pump and the air control valve with a T-fitting.

5. Plug the other hose connections (outlets) on the air control valve, as illustrated. A gauge set which is similar to the illustrated rig (Mazda Part No. 49-2113-010B or equivalent) is available to test the air pump.

✳✳CAUTION

Be careful not to touch the thermal reactor/exhaust manifold; severe burns will result.

6. Connect a tachometer to the engine and check the idle speed. If the idle speed is not within specifications, adjust as necessary. With the engine at 800 rpm, the pressure gauge should read 1.64 psi (3.34 in. Hg). Replace the air pump if it is less than this.

7. If the air pump is not defective, leave the pressure gauge connected, but unfasten the connections at the air control valve and plug or cap the T-fitting, as shown, before proceeding with the next test.

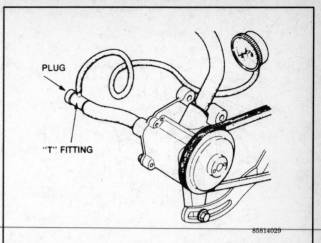

Fig. 26 After confirming the air pump's operation, disconnect the pressure gauge from the air control valve and seal off the T-fitting — RX-7

Air Control Valve

1979-80 RX-7

▶ **See Figures 27, 28 and 29**

The air control valve on 1979-80 models consists of three valves: No. 1 relief valve, No. 2 relief valve, and an anti-afterburn valve. The No. 1 relief valve controls the flow of cooling air to the thermal reactor and is controlled by air pump air pressure. The No. 2 relief valve controls fresh air flow into the exhaust ports when closed, and re-routes excess fresh air back into the air cleaner when open. The anti-afterburn valve allows additional air into the intake manifold to prevent afterburn when the ignition is turned **OFF**.

Testing of the air control valve is performed as follows:

1. Check all hoses and vacuum sensing tubes for loose connections and damage. Make sure the air pump drive belt is properly adjusted.

2. Check that the air control valve is attached to the carburetor tightly.

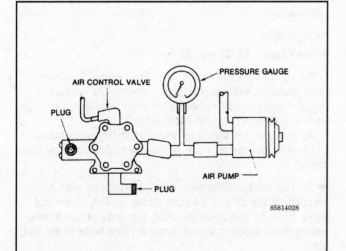

Fig. 25 Test connections for the RX-7's air pump

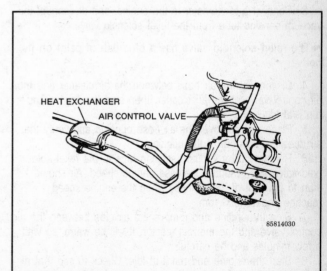

Fig. 27 Location of the air control valve — 1979-80 RX-7

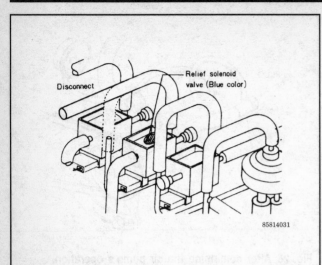

85814031

Fig. 28 Disconnect the vacuum sensing tube from the relief solenoid valve — RX-7

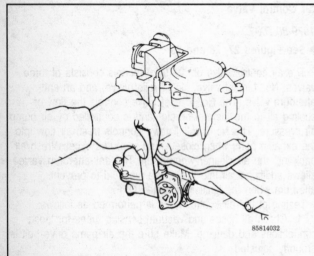

85814032

Fig. 29 Check the air control valve by placing a piece of paper in front of it — 1979-80 RX-7

3. Connect a tachometer to the engine, and disconnect the vacuum sensing tube from the relief solenoid valve.

➡**The relief solenoid valve has a blue dab of paint on its body.**

4. Disconnect the air hose between the air cleaner and the air control valve at the air cleaner, then start the engine and run it at idle.

5. Place a finger over the air hose opening and verify that air does not flow out of the opening.

6. Reconnect the vacuum sensing tube to the relief solenoid valve and gradually increase engine speed. Air should start to flow out of the air hose when the engine speed reaches about 1,300 rpm.

7. Stop the engine and remove the air pipe between the air control valve and the thermal reactor. It will be warm, so wait a few minutes and be careful.

8. Start the engine and run it at idle. Check to see that air does not flow out from the air control valve by placing a piece of paper in front of the valve, as shown in the illustration.

9. Increase engine speed to 4,500 rpm; air should flow out of the air control valve.

If the results for any of these tests differ from the information given here, the air control valve is not working properly and should probably be replaced.

1981-83 RX-7

▶ **See Figure 28**

The air control valve consists of an air relief valve, an air switching valve and a No. 1 anti-afterburn valve. The air relief valve controls fresh air flow into the exhaust ports when closed, and re-routes excess fresh air back into the air cleaner when open. The air switching valve switches the flow of fresh air back and forth between the exhaust ports and the two-bed catalyst according to engine demand. The anti-afterburn valve allows additional air into the intake manifold to prevent afterburn when the ignition is turned **OFF**.

1. Check that all solenoid valve connections are tight and that the air pump drive belt is adjusted properly.

2. Make sure the air control valve is firmly attached to the engine.

3. Connect a tachometer to the engine. Disconnect the relief solenoid valve vacuum sensing tube and connect the tube to a suitable vacuum source.

➡**The relief solenoid valve has a blue dab of paint on its body.**

4. Disconnect the hose running from the air control valve to the air cleaner at the air cleaner.

5. Start the engine and run it at idle; no air should be flowing through the hose when the choke is off and the engine is warm.

6. Slowly raise the engine rpm. Air should now begin to flow through the hose when the vacuum is removed from the sensing tube.

7. Reconnect the vacuum source to the relief solenoid valve vacuum sensing tube.

8. Set the engine speed to 2,500 rpm with the throttle, and disconnect the vacuum sensing tube from the switching solenoid valve (gray painted valve); air should flow through the air hose. Air should stop flowing when this vacuum tube is reconnected.

1984-89 RX-7

▶ **See Figures 30, 31 and 32**

The air control valve functions to direct intake air to one of three locations: exhaust port, main converter, or relief air silencer. The air control valve system consists of the relief valve, switching valve and anti-afterburn valve.

1. Warm up the engine to normal operating temperature. Connect a tachometer to the engine and check/adjust the idle speed.

➡**On 1987-89 turbocharged vehicles equipped with ABS, disconnect the air and vacuum hoses on the air control valve from the turbocharger. Plug the ends of the hoses before disconnecting the air control valve hose in the next step.**

2. Disconnect the hose that runs from the air silencer to the air control valve at the valve.

3. Place a finger over the air control outlet port.

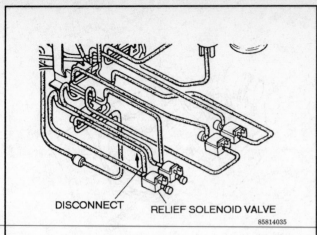

Fig. 30 Relief solenoid valve location — 1986-89 non-turbo RX-7

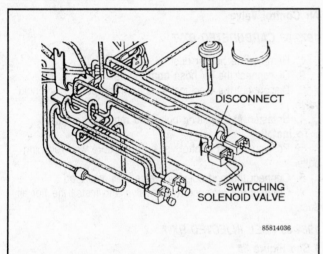

Fig. 31 Switching solenoid valve location — 1986-89 non-turbo RX-7

4. Have an assistant gradually increase the engine speed to 1,500-2,500 rpm for 1984-89 non-turbo vehicles, or 3,750-3,850 rpm for 1986-89 turbocharged vehicles.

5. Run the engine at idle speed.

6. On 1984-89 non-turbocharged models, locate the vacuum hose that runs between the relief solenoid valve and the air control valve. Disconnect the hose from the relief solenoid valve. On 1986-89 turbocharged vehicles, unfasten the relief solenoid valve connector.

➡The relief solenoid valve is identified by a blue tab or blue dab of paint on some models.

7. Make sure air flows from the relief solenoid valve at 1,200 rpm or greater. Reattach the vacuum hose or the electrical connector.

8. Locate the split air hose that runs from the intake manifold to the check valve. Disconnect the hose from the check valve and place a finger over the port. Disconnect the vacuum hose from the switching solenoid valve.

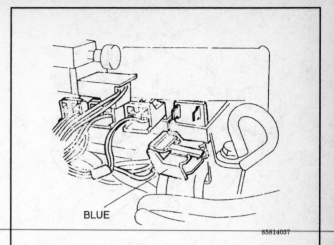

Fig. 32 Relief solenoid valve connector — 1986-89 RX-7 turbo

9. Make sure air flows from the switching solenoid valve port.

10. If air flow is not as described, replace the air control valve.

Check Valve

◗ **See Figures 33 and 34**

The check valve prevents exhaust gases from traveling backwards into the air pump and damaging it. There are two check valves used in the secondary air injection system. One is installed in the intake manifold, and the other is located inline between the intake manifold and catalytic converter. Both check valves are tested the same way and perform the same protective function.

1. Warm the engine to normal operating temperature, and connect a tachometer to the engine.

2. Disconnect the hose between the air pump and the air control valve at the air control valve. Disconnect the switching solenoid valve coupler (1981 models). If testing the catalytic converter check valve, locate the hose that runs from the in-

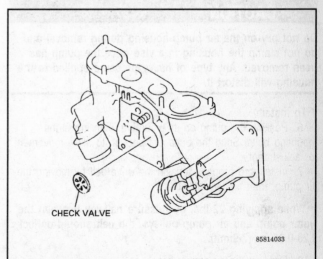

Fig. 33 Intake manifold-mounted check valve — 1985-87 fuel injected RX-7

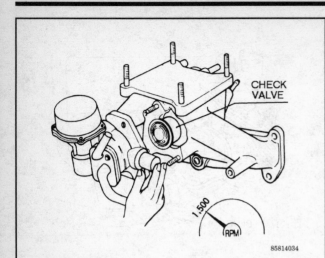

85814034

Fig. 34 Exhaust gas leakage at the air control valve's air inlet indicates a defective check valve

take manifold to the converter at the rear of the intake manifold, and disconnect it.

3. Slowly increase the engine speed to 1,500 rpm and watch for exhaust gas leakage at the air inlet fitting on the air control valve. If exhaust gas is coming out of the inlet, replace the check valve.

REMOVAL & INSTALLATION

Air Pump

▶ **See Figure 35**

1. If applicable, remove the air cleaner assembly from the carburetor.
2. Disconnect the air supply hoses from the pump.
3. Loosen and remove the air pump strap bolt.
4. Push the pump toward the engine to slacken belt tension, then remove the drive belt from the pulley.
5. Unfasten the pump securing bolts and remove the pump.

✳✳CAUTION

Do not pry on the air pump housing during removal and do not clamp the housing in a vise once the pump has been removed. Any type of heavy pressure applied to the housing will distort it.

To install:

6. Position the pump on its mounting, then install the mounting bolts. Snug the bolts just enough to allow movement for adjustment.
7. Install and properly tension the drive belt by moving the air pump, then tighten the bolts.

➡**While applying 22 lbs. of pressure halfway between the water pump and air pump pulleys, the belt should deflect 0.28-0.35 in. (7-9mm).**

8. Connect the air supply hoses.
9. If applicable, install the air cleaner assembly.

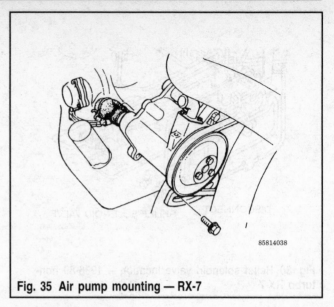

85814038

Fig. 35 Air pump mounting — RX-7

Air Control Valve

1979-85 CARBURETED RX-7

1. Remove the hot air duct.
2. Disconnect the air hose from the valve.
3. Disconnect the electrical lead from the port air solenoid valve.
4. Unfasten the retaining bolts and remove the valve.

To install:

5. Position the air control valve and secure with retaining bolts.
6. Connect the port solenoid valve electrical lead.
7. Connect the air hose to the valve and install the hot air duct.

1984-89 FUEL INJECTED RX-7

▶ **See Figure 36**

1. On 1984-85 models, remove the throttle chamber funnel.
2. Detach all solenoid valve connectors. (The number of connectors will vary depending on the year.)
3. Unfasten and remove the valve.

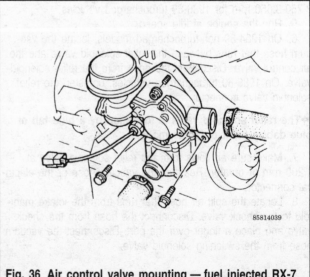

85814039

Fig. 36 Air control valve mounting — fuel injected RX-7

To install:

4. Position the air control valve and secure with retaining bolts.

5. Fasten all the wiring connectors.

6. On 1984-85 models, install the throttle chamber funnel.

Check Valve

1. Remove the air control valve, as described earlier in this section.

2. Unscrew and remove the check valve and gasket from the manifold.

To install:

3. Screw the check valve into the manifold, using a new gasket.

4. Install the air control valve, as described above.

Air Injection Nozzle

1. Remove the gravel shield from underneath the car.

2. Remove the oil pan removal procedure, as detailed in Section 3 of this manual.

3. Unbolt the air injection nozzles from both ends of the rotor housing.

To install:

4. Attach and fasten the air injection nozzles to both ends of the rotor housing.

5. Install the oil pan, as detailed in Section 3.

6. Fasten the gravel shield to the bottom of the car.

Thermal Reactor (Rotary Engine)

▶ **See Figure 37**

A thermal reactor is used in place of the conventional exhaust manifold on 1979-80 RX-7 models. It is used to oxidize unburned hydrocarbons and carbon monoxide before they can be released into the atmosphere.

If the engine speed exceeds 4,000 rpm, or if the car is decelerating, the air control valve diverts air into passages in the thermal reactor housing in order to cool the reactor. (On later models equipped with catalytic converters, air flow into the reaction chamber is cut off under these conditions.)

A one-way valve prevents hot exhaust gases from flowing back into the air injection system. The valve is located at the reactor air intake.

INSPECTION

▶ **See Figure 38**

✳✳CAUTION

Perform thermal reactor inspection only after the reactor has cooled sufficiently to eliminate the danger of being severely burned.

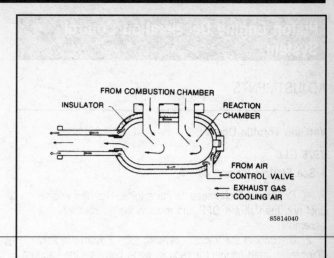

Fig. 37 Thermal reactor cooling unit

1. Examine the reactor housing for cracks or other signs of damage.

2. Remove the air supply hose from the one-way valve. Insert a screwdriver into the valve and test the butterfly for smooth operation. Replace the valve if necessary.

3. If the valve is functioning properly, reconnect the hose to it.

➡**Remember to check the components of the air injection system which are related to the thermal reactor.**

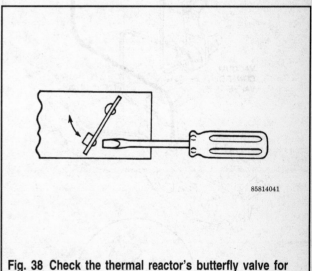

Fig. 38 Check the thermal reactor's butterfly valve for smooth operation

REMOVAL & INSTALLATION

Thermal reactor removal and installation procedures are given in Section 3 of this manual.

Piston Engine Deceleration Control System

ADJUSTMENTS

Vacuum Throttle Opener

1978 GLC

▶ **See Figures 39 and 40**

1. Connect a tachometer to the engine. Run the engine until hot, then shut it **OFF** and remove the air cleaner assembly.

2. Disconnect the vacuum sensing tube **F** from the servo diaphragm, then connect a vacuum hose between the vacuum tap on the intake manifold and the diaphragm.

3. Disconnect the vacuum line that runs from the carburetor to the distributor at the distributor, and plug the open end.

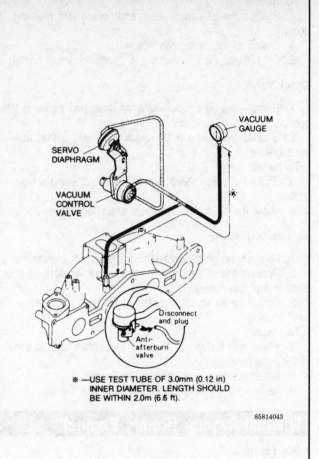

※ —USE TEST TUBE OF 3.0mm (0.12 in) INNER DIAMETER. LENGTH SHOULD BE WITHIN 2.0m (6.6 ft).

85814043

Fig. 40 Disconnect/plug the anti-afterburn valve vacuum line, then tee a gauge between the intake manifold and vacuum control valve — 1978 GLC

4. Start the engine and read the tachometer. Engine speed should be 1,300-1,500 rpm. If the speed is not to specification, turn the throttle opener adjusting screw to bring engine speed within the range.

5. Reconnect the distributor and servo diaphragm vacuum lines, then disconnect and plug the vacuum line going to the anti-afterburn valve. Disconnect the vacuum line going from the intake manifold to the vacuum control valve, and tee in a vacuum gauge as shown.

6. Start the engine and accelerate to 3,000 rpm. Watch the vacuum gauge and release the throttle. After a rapid rise in vacuum, the gauge reading should stabilize at 22.0-22.8 in. Hg (559-579mm Hg) for a few seconds while the system gradually closes the throttle, then drop off.

7. If vacuum does not stabilize in the right range, loosen the locknut and turn the adjusting screw in the end of the vacuum control valve until vacuum is in the specified range. Turn the screw clockwise to increase the vacuum reading, and counterclockwise to decrease it.

8. Tighten the locknut, then restore all vacuum connections. Install the air cleaner assembly and remove the tachometer.

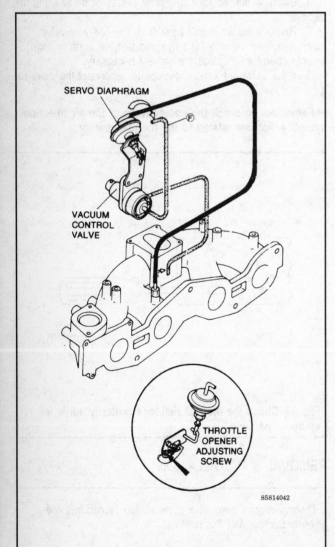

85814042

Fig. 39 Adjusting the vacuum throttle opener system — 1978 GLC

Servo Diaphragm

1. Connect a tachometer to the engine.
2. Run the engine at idle to normal operating temperature.
3. Stop the engine and remove the air cleaner assembly.
4. Disconnect the vacuum sensing tube at the servo diaphragm.
5. Connect the inlet manifold and the servo diaphragm with a suitable tube, so that the inlet manifold vacuum can be led directly to the servo diaphragm.
6. Disconnect the vacuum sensing tube (which runs from the carburetor to the distributor) at the distributor, then plug the tube.
7. Start the engine and check to see that the engine speed increases to 1,100-1,300 rpm (GLC) or 1,000-1,200 rpm (626).
8. Turn the throttle positioner adjuster screw in or out, as required, to adjust to specifications.

COMPONENT TESTING

Three-Way Solenoid Valve
▶ See Figures 41 and 42

1. Disconnect the vacuum sensing tube **A** from the servo diaphragm.
2. Disconnect the vacuum sensing tube **B** from the three-way solenoid valve.
3. Detach the connector (blue/black wire) from the engine speed switch and ground the three-way solenoid valve using a jumper wire.
4. Turn the ignition switch **ON**.
5. Blow into the three-way solenoid valve through tube **A** and make sure air comes out of the valve's filter.
6. Turn the ignition switch **OFF**.
7. Blow into the valve through tube **A** and make sure air comes out of port **A**.
8. Replace the three-way solenoid valve if it does not operate properly.

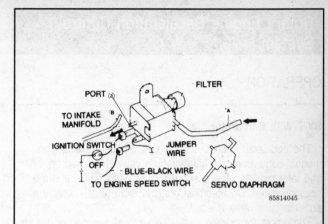

Fig. 42 Three-way solenoid valve check with the ignition switch OFF

Engine Speed Switch
▶ See Figure 43

1. Detach the engine speed switch connector.
2. Attach a voltmeter to the connector.
3. Increase the engine speed to 2,000 rpm, then slowly decrease the engine speed.
4. Record the engine speed at which the current flows to the circuit. The engine speed should be 1,600-1,800 rpm (California AT) and 1,400-1,600 rpm (Canada MT).
5. Slowly increase the engine speed again and record the engine speed at which the current does not flow to the circuit. The difference between the engine speed recorded in steps 4 and 5 should be 150-250 rpm.
6. Replace the engine speed switch if the rpm specifications are not met.

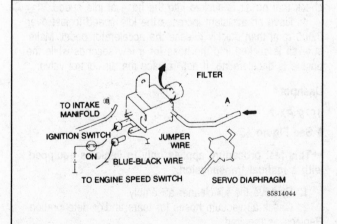

Fig. 41 Three-way solenoid valve check with the ignition switch ON

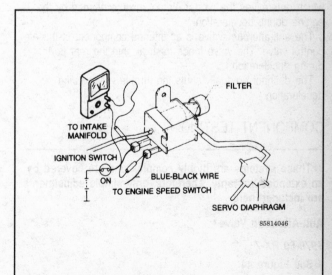

Fig. 43 Engine speed switch check

Rotary Engine Deceleration Control System

OPERATION

RX-7 With Carburetor

The deceleration control system on manual transmission models consists of the anti-afterburn valve (two used on 1981 and later models), the dashpot and its delay valve, and the coasting valve. On automatic transmission models, only the anti-afterburn valve is used.

The single (or primary) anti-afterburn valve is part of the air control valve. Please refer to the preceding Air Injection System coverage for additional information.

On 1981 and later models, the second anti-afterburn valve is located to the rear of the carburetor. It controls air intake to the rear rotor, while the anti-afterburn valve (in the air control valve) controls air intake to the front rotor.

The dashpot acts to slow down the closing speed of the throttle valve in the carburetor when the accelerator pedal is released. This helps prevent engine misfire. The dashpot also acts as an emission control device.

The coasting valve allows additional air into the intake manifold to prevent engine misfire during deceleration at engine speeds over 1,150 rpm. It is regulated by the control unit and the idle switch on the carburetor.

RX-7 With Fuel Injection

The deceleration control system on fuel injected RX-7s consists of a fuel cut-off circuit, throttle sensor, anti-afterburn valve and dashpot.

The fuel cut-off circuit stops flow to the fuel injectors while decelerating during certain engine speed ranges.

The throttle sensor measures the opening angle of the primary throttle valve; it sends this information to the control unit, which determines the proper air/fuel mixture needed by the engine during deceleration.

The anti-afterburn valve is an integral component of the air control valve. The valve feeds fresh air into the rear port during deceleration.

The dashpot gradually shuts the throttle valve during deceleration.

COMPONENT TESTING

➡️These systems are highly complex and are covered by an extended warranty. Therefore, only simple adjustments are included here.

Anti-Afterburn Valve

1979-80 RX-7

◗ See Figure 44

1. Check all hoses and vacuum sensing tubes for improper connections and signs of wear; replace as necessary.
2. Disconnect the hose which runs from the air control valve to the air cleaner at the air cleaner assembly.

3. Disconnect the vacuum sensing tube from the relief solenoid valve, which can be identified by the blue spot of paint on its body.
4. Start the engine and run it at idle. Place your finger over the disconnected hose to the air cleaner; no vacuum should be present.
5. Detach the electrical connection of the anti-afterburn solenoid valve; vacuum should now be present in the hose. If not, the anti-afterburn valve, its solenoid valve or its vacuum lines are defective and must be replaced.

1981-85 RX-7 WITH CARBURETOR

Test the No. 1 anti-afterburn valve as follows:
1. Warm up the engine and run it at idle speed.
2. Locate the hose that runs between the air control valve and the air pump. Disconnect the hose at the air pump.
3. Place a finger over the opening of the air hose and check that no air is sucked into the hose at idle speed.
4. Have an assistant increase the idle speed to just over 3,000 rpm, then quickly release the accelerator pedal. Make sure air is sucked into the hose for a few seconds while the engine is decelerating. If not, replace the air control valve.

Test the No. 2 anti-afterburn valve as follows:
5. Warm up the engine and run it at idle speed.
6. Locate the hose that runs between the air cleaner and the No. 2 anti-afterburn valve. Disconnect the hose at the air cleaner.
7. Place a finger over the opening of the air hose and check that no air is sucked into the hose at idle speed.
8. Have an assistant increase the idle speed to just over 3,000 rpm, then quickly release the accelerator pedal. Make sure air is sucked into the hose for a few seconds while the engine is decelerating. If not, replace the air control valve.

1984-89 RX-7 WITH FUEL INJECTION

1. Warm up the engine and run it at idle speed.
2. Locate the hose that runs between the air control valve and the air pump. Disconnect the hose at the air pump.
3. Place a finger over the opening of the air hose and check that no air is sucked into the hose at idle speed.
4. Have an assistant increase the idle speed to just over 3,000 rpm, then quickly release the accelerator pedal. Make sure air is sucked into the hose for a few seconds while the engine is decelerating. If not, replace the air control valve.

Dashpot

1979 RX-7

◗ See Figure 45

➡️This test procedure applies only to vehicles equipped with a manual transmission.

1. Remove the air cleaner assembly.
2. Check all vacuum hoses for tears and/or deterioration. Replace as required.
3. Make sure the dashpot plunger rod does not keep the throttle lever from returning to its idle stop when closed.
4. Quickly operate the throttle lever; the dashpot plunger rod should quickly extend.
5. Release the throttle lever; the plunger rod on the dashpot should slow its return to the idle position.
6. Connect a tachometer to the engine.

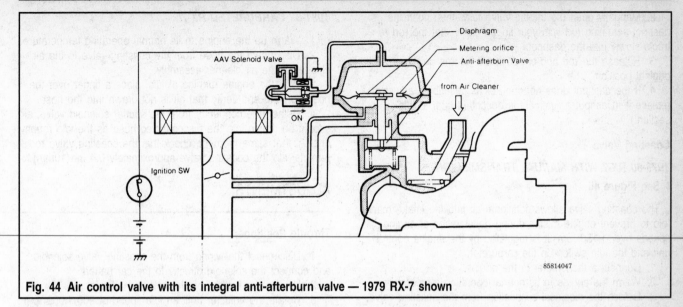

Fig. 44 Air control valve with its integral anti-afterburn valve — 1979 RX-7 shown

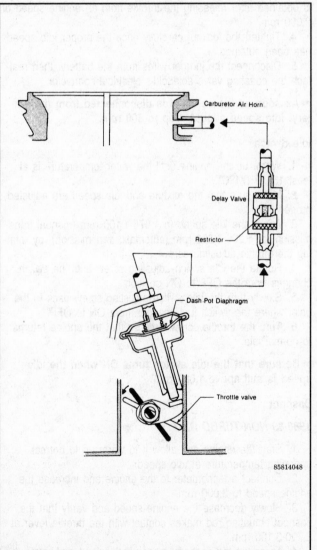

Fig. 45 A dashpot affects closing of the throttle valve on some RX-7s

7. Start and run the engine until it reaches normal operating temperature. Make sure the idle speed is within specifications; adjust as necessary.

8. Disconnect the vacuum sensing tube from the top of the dashpot and move the throttle lever away from the dashpot plunger rod. Close the vacuum inlet at the top of the dashpot with your finger.

9. Release the throttle lever and check the engine speed at which the dashpot stops moving after it has been pushed in by the throttle lever. This speed should be 1,650-1,850 rpm. If not, loosen the locknut on the dashpot and adjust by turning the dashpot body. Repeat Step 9 to verify the adjustment.

1980-85 RX-7

➡On 1980-82 models, this test procedure applies only to vehicles equipped with a manual transmission.

1. Remove the air cleaner assembly (carbureted models only).

2. Check to see that the dashpot does not keep the throttle lever from returning to the idle stop.

3. Quickly operate the throttle lever fully; when the throttle lever is open, the dashpot plunger rod should quickly extend.

4. Release the throttle lever. The lever should quickly snap closed until it hits the dashpot plunger rod, then slowly close until it reaches its stop.

5. Connect a tachometer to the engine. Run the engine until it reaches normal operating temperature, then make sure the idle speed is correct.

6. Move the throttle lever until it is away from the dashpot plunger rod.

7. Slowly close the throttle lever and note the engine speed when the throttle lever just touches the dashpot plunger rod. If engine speed is not 3,500-3,900 rpm for 1980 models, 3,800-4,200 rpm for 1981-85 carbureted models, or 2,350-2,650 rpm for fuel injected models, loosen the locknut and adjust the dashpot by turning it until its plunger rod is in the correct position.

1986-89 RX-7

1. On turbocharged models, drain the cooling system and remove the intercooler.

2. Manually open the throttle valve fully, then push the dashpot actuating rod with your finger; verify that the rod retracts slowly into the dashpot.

3. Release the rod and check that it returns quickly to its original position.

4. If the dashpot does not operate as described, adjust or replace it. (Dashpot adjustment is described later in this section.)

Coasting Valve

1979-80 RX-7 WITH MANUAL TRANSMISSION

▶ See Figure 46

The coasting valve allows additional air into the intake manifold to prevent engine misfire during deceleration at engine speeds over 1,150 rpm. It is regulated by the engine control unit and the idle switch on the carburetor.

1. Connect a tachometer to the engine.

2. Warm the engine to its normal operating temperature.

3. Detach the electrical connection from the coasting valve, then attach a voltmeter to the harness side of the connection. Disconnect the vacuum sensing tube from the dashpot diaphragm on 1979 models.

4. Start the engine and increase the engine speed to 3,000 rpm, using the throttle. Quickly release the throttle lever; current flow should stop when the engine speed falls below 1,050-1,250 rpm (1,000-1,200 rpm on Canadian models). Shut off the engine.

5. Disconnect the voltmeter, then detach the air hose (running from the coasting valve to the air cleaner) at the air cleaner assembly.

➡ Do not yet reconnect the coasting valve electrical connection.

6. Start the engine. There should be no vacuum at the air hose. Activate the coasting valve by attaching jumper wires to its electrical connection from the battery; when the engine is running, vacuum should be present in the air hose.

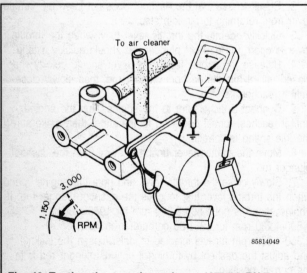

Fig. 46 Testing the coasting valve — 1979-80 RX-7

1981-85 CARBURETED RX-7

1. Warm up the engine to its normal operating temperature.

2. Disconnect the hose from the coasting valve to the air cleaner at the air cleaner assembly.

3. With the engine running at idle, place a finger over the hose opening and verify that air is not drawn into the hose.

4. Detach the connector from the shutter solenoid valve; air should be drawn into the disconnected hose as the idle roughens. At that same moment, check that the coasting valve rod retracts into the coasting valve approximately 0.4 in. (10mm).

ADJUSTMENTS

Throttle Positioner

1. Disconnect the wiring from the coasting valve solenoid, and connect the solenoid directly to the car battery.

2. Loosen the locknut on the solenoid adjuster.

3. Rotate the adjuster until an idle speed of 900-1,000 rpm is obtained after releasing the throttle from an engine speed of 2,000 rpm.

4. Tighten the locknut carefully once the proper idle speed has been obtained.

5. Disconnect the jumper wires from the battery, then reattach the coasting valve solenoid's electrical connector.

➡ As soon as the solenoid is disconnected from the battery, idle speed should drop to 800 rpm.

Idle Switch

1. Warm up the engine until the water temperature is at least 159°F (71°C).

2. Make sure that the mixture and idle speed are adjusted properly.

3. Adjust the idle speed to 1,075-1,100 rpm (manual transmission) or 1,200-1,300 rpm (automatic transmission), by rotating the throttle adjusting screw.

4. Rotate the idle switch adjusting screw until the switch changes from the OFF to ON position.

5. Slowly turn the idle switch adjusting screw back to the point where the switch just changes from ON to OFF.

6. Turn the throttle screw back so that the engine returns to normal idle.

➡ Be sure that the idle switch turns ON when the idle speed is still above 1,000 rpm.

Dashpot

1986-89 NON-TURBO RX-7

1. Start the engine and allow it to warm up to normal operating temperature at idle speed.

2. Connect a tachometer to the engine and increase the engine speed to 3,000 rpm.

3. Slowly decrease the engine speed and verify that the dashpot actuating rod makes contact with the throttle lever at 2,700-3,100 rpm.

4. To adjust the dashpot, loosen the locknut and rotate the dashpot body clockwise or counterclockwise until the rod makes contact with the lever at the specified rpm.

1986-89 RX-7 TURBO

▶ **See Figure 47**

1. Drain the cooling system and remove the intercooler.
2. Detach the throttle sensor connector.
3. Attach an ohmmeter to terminals **A** and **B** of the throttle sensor connector, as shown in the illustration. Set the meter to the 1000x scale.
4. Manually separate the dashpot actuating rod from the throttle lever and observe the reading on the meter. As the rod and lever separate, the resistance should be 1.8-3.8 kilohms. If the reading is not as specified, adjust by loosening the locknut on top of the dashpot and rotating the dashpot body either clockwise or counterclockwise, until the proper resistance is obtained. Once the adjustment is complete, tighten the locknut.

Oxygen Sensor

As part of the vehicle's closed loop (or feedback control) system, the oxygen sensor monitors the density of oxygen in the exhaust gas. The sensor consists of a closed-end tube made of ceramic zirconia and other components. Porous platinum electrodes cover the tube's inner and outer surfaces. The tube's outer surface is exposed to the exhaust gases in the exhaust manifold (or, if so equipped, just beyond the turbocharger). After detecting the amount of oxygen in the exhaust gas, the oxygen sensor outputs an electrical signal to the engine control unit.

REMOVAL & INSTALLATION

Gasoline Engines

▶ **See Figures 48 and 49**

The oxygen sensor is installed in the exhaust manifold (or the front catalytic converter on turbocharged vehicles), and is removed in similar manner to a spark plug. (Unlike spark plug removal, use an open-end wrench to avoid interference with the electrical lead.)

1. Disconnect the negative battery cable.

2. Unfasten the sensor's electrical connector.
3. Using the correct size wrench, loosen and unscrew the oxygen sensor. If so equipped, be sure to also remove the crush ring gasket with the sensor.

➡ **Exercise care when handling the sensor; do not drop or handle it roughly. The electrical connector and louvered end must be kept free of grease and dirt.**

4. Clean the threads of the sensor and its mounting location.

To install:

5. If applicable, make sure that the crush ring gasket is threaded onto the sensor.
6. Coat the threads of the sensor with an anti-sieze compound. Be careful to coat only the threads of the sensor; do not get compound on the sensor itself.
7. Screw the sensor and gasket into its mounting location and torque to specification.
8. Attach the sensor's electrical connector.
9. Connect the negative battery cable.

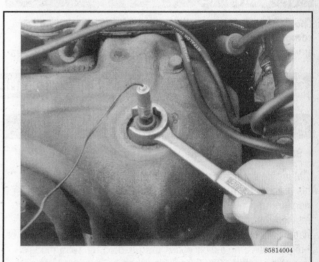

Fig. 48 Use an open-end wrench to remove and install the oxygen sensor

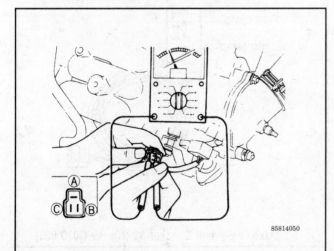

Fig. 47 Checking dashpot resistance — 1986-89 RX-7 turbo

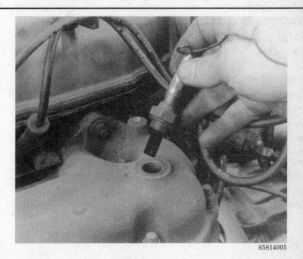

Fig. 49 Handle the oxygen sensor very carefully, be sure not to damage the insulator

ELECTRONIC ENGINE CONTROLS

Engine Control Unit (ECU)

OPERATION

As the electronic brain of a closed loop system, the engine control unit receives data from a number of vehicle-mounted sensors. Such data pertains to (but is not limited to) engine speed, coolant temperature, exhaust gas oxygen content, manifold vacuum and throttle valve position. In response to these ongoing inputs, the ECU continually controls the operation of a series of solenoid valves in order to maintain optimal operating conditions. As an example of its many functions, the ECU determines the operating period of the Air/Fuel (A/F) solenoid and controls the air/fuel ratio.

✳✳WARNING

The ECU is a very sensitive and EXPENSIVE electronic component. NEVER disconnect power from the ECU (or any computer module) with the ignition key turned ON, as this could destroy the module. This warning includes disconnecting the battery cables. If the cables are removed with the key turned ON, this will remove power from the ECU and quite possibly destroy it.

REMOVAL & INSTALLATION

1. Disconnect the negative battery cable.
2. Remove the passenger and driver side cover walls from the center console unit.
3. Detach the ECU electrical connectors.
4. Unfasten the mounting bolts/nuts and remove the ECU.
To install:
5. Position the ECU and fasten its mounting hardware.
6. Attach the electrical connectors.
7. Install the passenger and driver side cover walls on the center console unit.
8. Connect the negative battery cable.

SELF-DIAGNOSTIC SYSTEMS AND TROUBLE CODES

General Information

▶ **See Figures 50 and 51**

Many carbureted and all fuel injected vehicles covered by this manual have self-diagnostic capabilities. The ECU monitors all input and output functions within the electronic engine control system. If a malfunction is detected, the information will be stored in the ECU memory in the form of a 1 or 2-digit code. Single-digit codes (as used on all 1985 models, as well as many 1986-87 vehicles) can be accessed through the use of Mazda's System Checker 83 (No. 49 G030 920) or equivalent, which uses a red lamp and buzzer to indicate sensor or related wiring faults. Two-digit codes (as applicable to most 1986-89 vehicles) can be accessed through the use of Mazda's Digital Code Checker (No. 49 G018 9A0 or equivalent) or Mazda's Self-Diagnosis Checker (No. 49 H018 9A1 or equivalent). When using one of these testers, the codes will be output and displayed as numbers, such as 09. Regardless of which type of tester is used, the tester's wire connector must be attached to the vehicle's control unit check connector. Follow the tester's instructions for specific hook-up and testing procedures.

➡If such a tester is not available, the codes may instead be read using an analog voltmeter. When using a voltmeter, the code's digits will be represented by needle sweeps.

Clearing Codes

Codes stored within the ECU memory must be erased when repairs are completed. Erasing codes during diagnosis can help you to separate hard (consistent) faults from intermittent malfunctions. To erase stored codes, disconnect the negative battery cable, then depress the brake pedal for at least 10 seconds. After reconnecting the battery cable, check the system for any remaining or newly set codes.

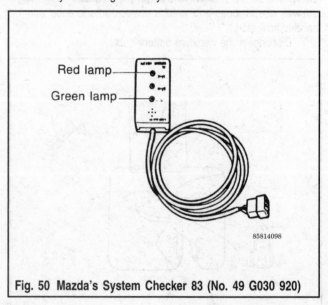

Red lamp
Green lamp

85814098

Fig. 50 Mazda's System Checker 83 (No. 49 G030 920)

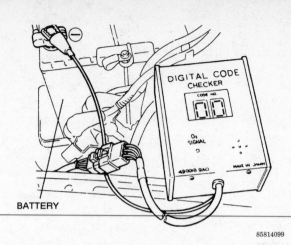

BATTERY

85814099

Fig. 51 Mazda's Digital Code Checker (No. 49 G018 9A0)

	Code No.	Checking item	Indicated pattern (Lamp ON: −, OFF: · · · ·)
S T E P 1 (R E D)	1	Engine speed (rpm signal)	ON: 0.4 sec. OFF: 2.0 sec. ← 1 CYCLE →
	2	Water thermo sensor	0.4 0.4 0.4 / 0.4 0.4 0.4 2.0 ← 1 CYCLE →
	*3	Feed back system	2.0 / 2.0 ← 1 CYCLE →

*3 If the troubles have been found, do not turn off the ignition switch.
If it is turned off, feed back system can not be checked with the system checker.

85814101

Fig. 52 Diagnostic codes — 1985 GLC

① Red lamp and buzzer

Code no.	Location of problem	Indication
1	Engine speed	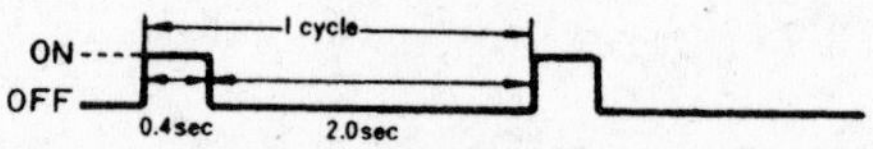
2	Water thermo-sensor	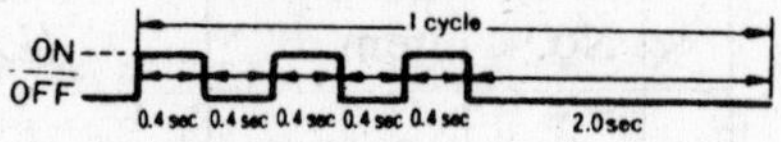
3	Feed back system	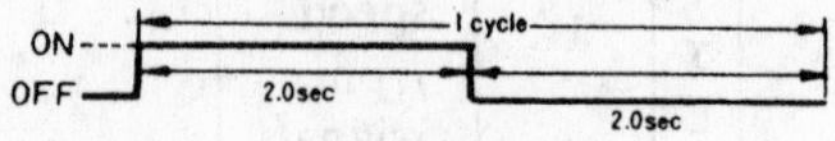
4	Vacuum sensor	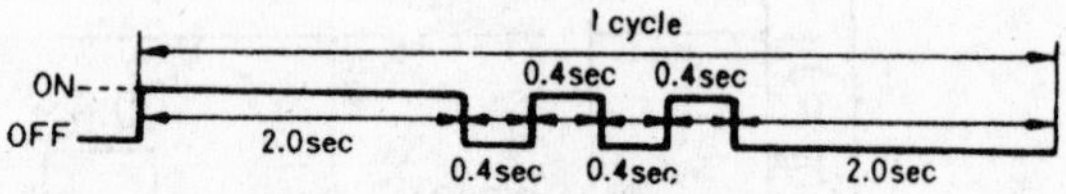
5	EGR position sensor	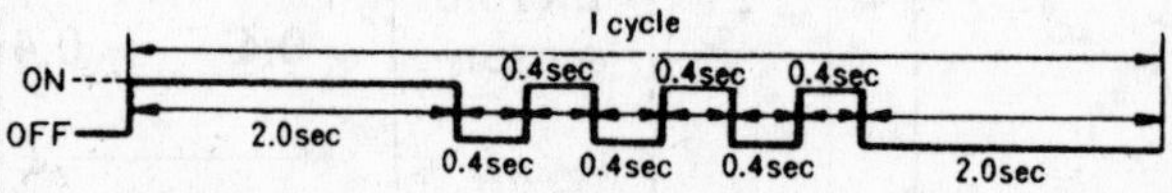

85814102

Fig. 53 Diagnostic codes — 1985 626 (gasoline engine)

1. RED LAMP AND BUZZER

Code No.	Location of problem	Indication	Checking procedure
1	Engine speed	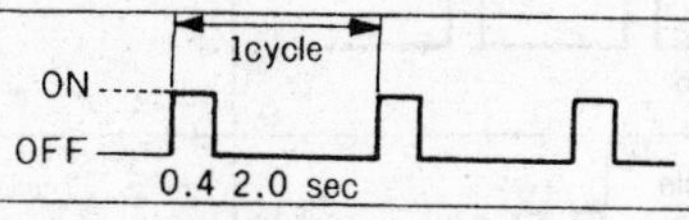 ON ---- OFF ---- 1cycle 0.4 2.0 sec	Disconnect the trailing coil – terminal crank engine at least 1.5 seconds, with IG "ON" code should be heard.
2	Air flow meter	 ON ---- OFF ---- 0.40.40.4 2.0 sec.	Disconnect air flow meter connector, turn IG "ON" code should be heard.
3	Water thermo sensor	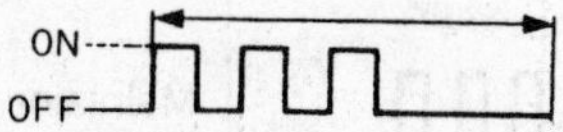 ON ---- OFF ----	Disconnect the water thermo sensor connector, turn IG "ON" code should be heard.
4	Oxygen (O_2) sensor	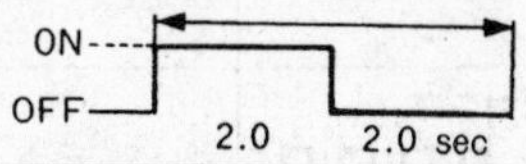 ON ---- OFF ---- 2.0 2.0 sec	Refer to page 4B–72.
5	Throttle sensor	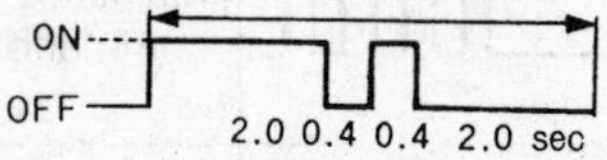 ON ---- OFF ---- 2.0 0.4 0.4 2.0 sec	Disconnect throttle sensor connector, turn IG "ON" code should be heard.
6	Atmospheric pressure sensor	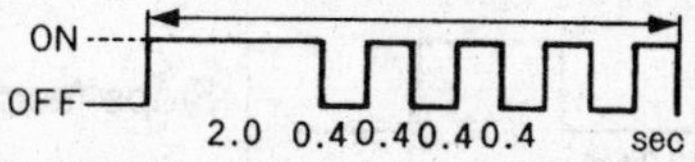 ON ---- OFF ---- 2.0 0.40.40.40.4 sec	Disconnect the atmospheric pressure sensor, turn IG "ON" code should be heard.

Note
1) If there is trouble in 2 or more places, the indication will be for the smaller code number first.
2) Even if the problem is corrected during indication, 1 cycle will be indicated.

85814103

Fig. 54 Diagnostic codes — 1985 fuel injected RX-7

RED LIGHT AND BUZZER

Code No.	Location of problem	Indication	Fail-safe function
1	IG Pulse	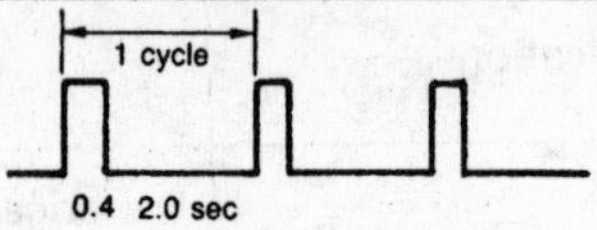 ON / OFF — 1 cycle — 0.4 2.0 sec	—
2	Air Flow Meter	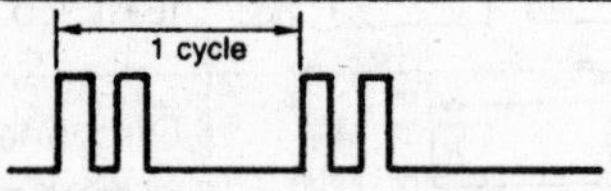 ON / OFF — 1 cycle	Maintains the basic signal at a preset value
3	Water Thermo Sensor	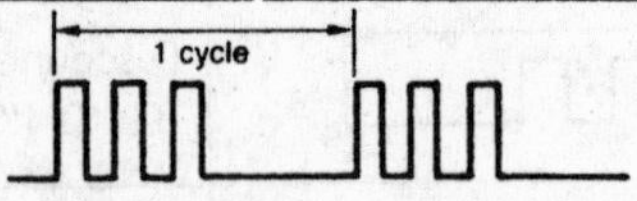 ON / OFF — 1 cycle	Maintains a constant 20°C (68°F) command
4	Temperature Sensor	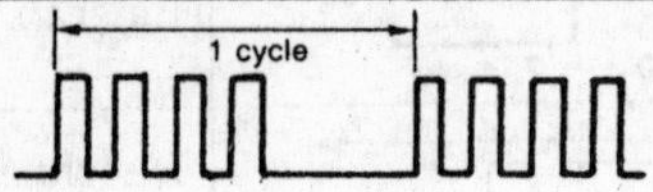 ON / OFF — 1 cycle	Maintains a constant 20°C (68°F) command
5	Feed Back System	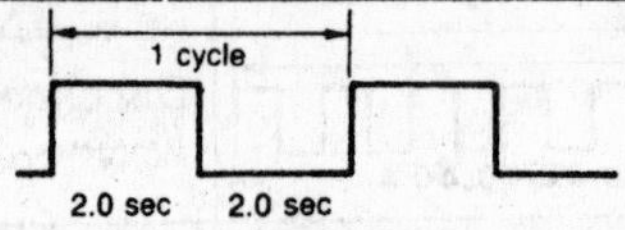 ON / OFF — 1 cycle — 2.0 sec 2.0 sec	Stops feed back correction
6	Atmospheric Pressure Sensor	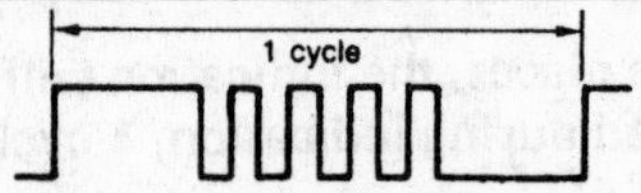 ON / OFF — 1 cycle	Maintains a constant command of the sea-level pressure

85814084

Fig. 55 Diagnostic codes — 1986-87 fuel injected 323

Code Number and Buzzer

Code Number	Location of problem	Buzzer	Fail-safe function
1	IG Pulse	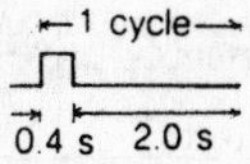 ←1 cycle→ 0.4 s 2.0 s	—
2	Air Flow Meter	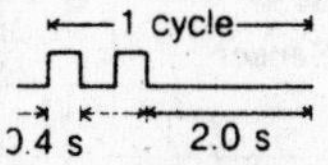 ←1 cycle→ 0.4 s 2.0 s	Maintains the basic signal at a preset value.
3	Water Thermo Sensor	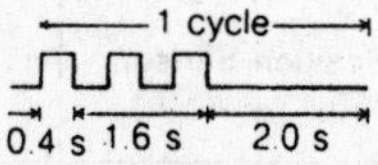 ←1 cycle→ 0.4 s 1.6 s 2.0 s	Maintains a constant 35°C(95°F) command.
4	Intake Air Temperature Sensor	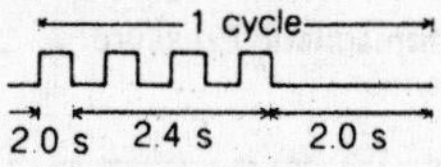 ←1 cycle→ 2.0 s 2.4 s 2.0 s	Maintains a constant 20°C(68°F) command.
5	Feedback System	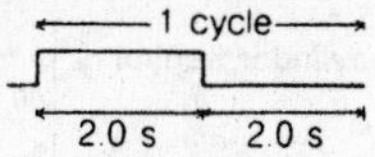 ←1 cycle→ 2.0 s 2.0 s	Dose not take in the feed-back.
6	Throttle Sensor	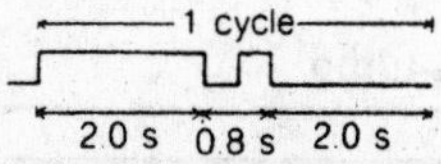 ←1 cycle→ 2.0 s 0.8 s 2.0 s	Maintains a constant command opened the throttle valve fully
9	Atomspheric Pressure Sensor	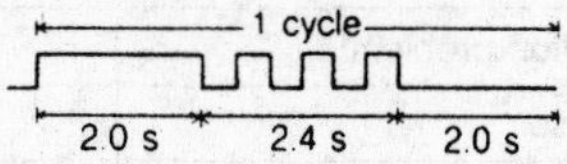 ←1 cycle→ 2.0 s 2.4 s 2.0 s	Maintains a constant command of the sea level pressure

85814085

Fig. 56 Diagnostic codes — 1986-87 626 non-turbo

Code Number

Code No.	Location of problem	Buzzer	Fail-safe function
1	IG Pulse	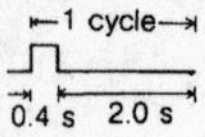 1 cycle 0.4 s 2.0 s	—
2	Air Flow Meter	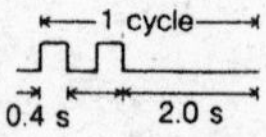 1 cycle 0.4 s 2.0 s	Maintains the basic signal at a preset value.
3	Water Thermo Sensor	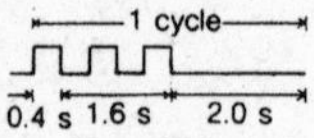 1 cycle 0.4 s 1.6 s 2.0 s	Maintains a constant 35°C(95°F) command.
4	Intake Air Temperature Sensor	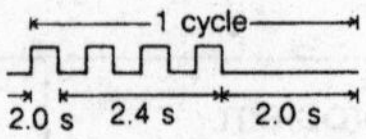 1 cycle 2.0 s 2.4 s 2.0 s	Maintains a constant 20°C(68°F) command.
5	Feedback system	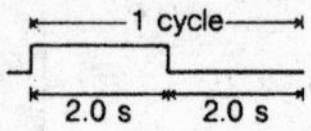 1 cycle 2.0 s 2.0 s	Does not take in the feed-back correction
6	Throttle Sensor	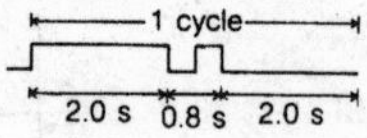 1 cycle 2.0 s 0.8 s 2.0 s	Maintains a constant command opened the throttle valve fully
8	EGR Position Sensor	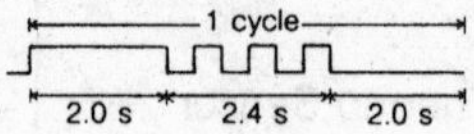 1 cycle 2.0 s 2.4 s 2.0 s	Cuts off EGR
9	Atomspheric Pressure Sensor	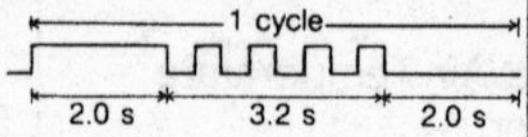 1 cycle 2.0 s 3.2 s 2.0 s	Maintains a constant command of the sea level pressure
22	No.1 cylinder sensor	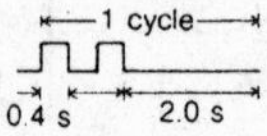 1 cycle 0.4 s 2.0 s	Injects fuel at the same time (1 time/2 revolutions)

85814086

Fig. 57 Diagnostic codes — 1986-87 626 turbo

Code No.	Location problem	Fail safe function
01	Crank angle sensor	—
02	Air flow meter	Maintains the basic signal at a preset value.
03	Water thermo sensor	Maintains a constant 80°C (176°F) command.
04	Intake air temperature sensor (Air flow meter)	Maintains a constant 20°C (68°F) command.
05	Oxygen (O2) sensor	Stop the feedback correction
06	Throttle sensor	Maintains a constant 100% (approx.18°) command.
07	Boost sensor	Maintains a constant −96 mmHg (3.78 inHg) command.
09	Atmospheric pressure sensor	Maintains a constant command of the sea-level pressure.
12	Coil with igniter (Trailing side)	Stop the operation of ignition system (only trailing side)
15	Intake air temperature sensor (Dynamic chamber)	Maintains a constant 20°C (68°F) command.

85814087

Fig. 58 Diagnostic codes — 1986-87 RX-7 non-turbo

Code No.	Location problem	Fail safe function
01	Crank angle sensor	–
02	Air flow meter	Maintains the basic signal at a preset value.
03	Water thermo sensor	Maintains a constant 80°C (176°F) command.
04	Intake air temperature sensor (air flow meter)	Maintains a constant 20°C (68°F) command.
05	Oxygen (O2) sensor	Stops feedback correction
06	Throttle sensor	Maintains a constant 100% (approx.18°) command.
07	Pressure sensor	Maintains a constant 958 mmHg (37.7 inHg) command.
09	Atmospheric pressure sensor	Maintains a constant command of sea-level pressure.
12	Coil with igniter (trailing side)	Stops operation of ignition system (only trailing side)
15	Intake air temperature sensor (intake air pipe)	Maintains a constant 20°C (68°F) command.

85814088

Fig. 59 Diagnostic codes — 1986-87 RX-7 turbo

Code No.	Sensor or subsystem	Malfunction	Fail-safe function	Pattern of output signals (Self-Diagnosis Checker or MIL)
01	Ignition pulse	No ignition signal	–	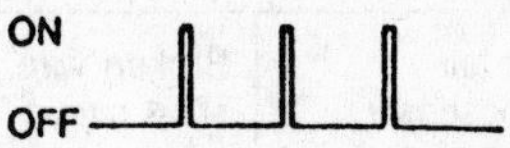 ON / OFF
08	Airflow meter	Broken wire, short circuit	Basic fuel injection amount fixed as for 2 driving modes 1) Idle switch: ON 2) Idle switch: OFF	 ON / OFF
09	Water thermosensor	Broken wire, short circuit	Coolant temp. input fixed at 80°C (176°F)..for ISC, at 20°C (68°F)... for fuel injection	 ON / OFF
10	Intake air thermosensor (airflow meter)	Broken wire, short circuit	Intake air temp. input fixed at 20°C (68°F)	 ON / OFF
14	Atmospheric pressure sensor	Broken wire, short circuit	Atmospheric pressure input fixed at 760 mmHg (29.9 inHg)	 ON / OFF
15	Oxygen sensor	Sensor output continues less than 0.55V 120 sec after engine at above 1,500 rpm	Feedback system operation canceled	 ON / OFF
17	Feedback system	Oxygen sensor output not changed 30 sec after engine exceeds 1,500 rpm	Feedback system operation canceled	 ON / OFF
26	Solenoid valve (No.1 purge control)	Broken wire, short circuit	–	 ON / OFF
27	Solenoid valve (No.2 purge control)	Broken wire, short circuit	–	 ON / OFF
34	Solenoid valve (idle-speed control)	Broken wire, short circuit	–	 ON / OFF

85814089

Fig. 60 Diagnostic codes — 1988-89 323 non-turbo

Code No.	Sensor or subsystem	Malfunction	Fail-safe function	Pattern of output signals (Self-Diagnosis Checker or MIL)
01	Ignition pulse	No ignition signal	—	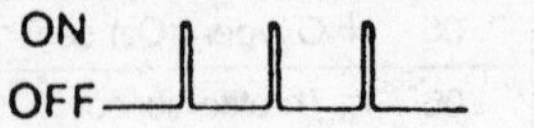 ON / OFF
03	Distributor (G signal)	No G signal	—	 ON / OFF
08	Airflow meter	Broken wire, short circuit	Basic fuel injection amount fixed as for 2 driving modes 1) Idle switch: ON 2) Idle switch: OFF	 ON / OFF
09	Water thermosensor	Broken wire, short circuit	Coolant temp. input fixed at 80°C (176°F) ...for ISC, at 60°C (140°F) ...for fuel injection	 ON / OFF
10	Intake air thermosensor (airflow meter)	Broken wire, short circuit	Intake air temp. input fixed at 20°C (68°F)	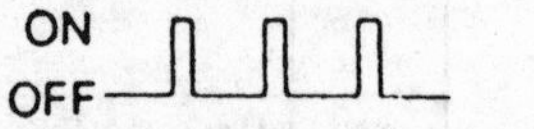 ON / OFF
12	Throttle sensor	Broken wire, short circuit	Throttle valve opening angle signal input fixed at full open	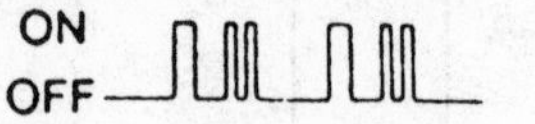 ON / OFF
14	Atmospheric pressure sensor	Broken wire, short circuit	Atmospheric pressure input fixed at 760 mmHg (29.9 inHg)	 ON / OFF
15	Oxygen sensor	Sensor output continues less than 0.55V 120 sec after engine at above 1,500 rpm	Feedback system operation canceled	 ON / OFF
17	Feedback system	Oxygen sensor output not changed 30 sec after engine exceeds 1,500 rpm	Feedback system operation canceled	 ON / OFF
25	Solenoid valve (pressure regulator control)	Broken wire, short circuit	—	 ON / OFF
26	Solenoid valve (No.1 purge control)	Broken wire, short circuit	—	 ON / OFF
27	Solenoid valve (No.2 purge control)	Broken wire, short circuit	—	 ON / OFF
34	Solenoid valve (idle-speed control)	Broken wire, short circuit	—	 ON / OFF

85814090

Fig. 61 Diagnostic codes — 1988-89 323 turbo

Malfunction display		Sensor or subsystem	Self-diagnosis	Fail-safe
Code No.	MIL output signal pattern			
01	ON / OFF 	Ignition pulse	No ignition signal	—
08	ON / OFF 	Air flow meter	Open or short circuit	Maintains basic signal at preset value
09	ON / OFF 	Water thermo sensor	Open or short circuit	Maintains constant command • 35°C (95°F) for EGI • 50°C (122°F) for ISC control use
10	ON / OFF 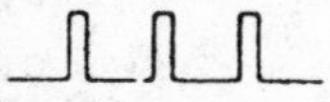	Intake air thermo sensor (air flow meter)	Open or short circuit	Maintains constant 20°C (68°F) command
12	ON / OFF 	Throttle sensor	Open or short circuit	Maintains constant command of throttle valve fully open
14	ON / OFF 	Atmospheric pressure sensor	Open or short circuit	Maintains constant command of sea level pressure
15	ON / OFF 	Oxygen sensor	Sensor output continues less than 0.55V 120 sec. after engine starts (1,500 rpm)	Cancels EGI feedback operation
17	ON / OFF 	Feedback system	Sensor output not changed 20 sec. after engine exceeds 1,500 rpm	Cancels EGI feedback operation
25	ON / OFF 	Solenoid valve (pressure regulator)	Open or short circuit	—
26	ON / OFF 	Solenoid valve (purge control)		—
28	ON / OFF 	Solenoid valve (EGR)		—
34	ON / OFF 	Solenoid valve (Idle speed control)		—

85814091

Fig. 62 Diagnostic codes — 1988-89 626/MX-6 non-turbo

Malfunction display		Sensor or subsystem	Self-diagnosis	Fail-safe
Malfunction code no.	MIL output signal pattern			
01	 ON / OFF pattern	Ignition pulse	No ignition signal	—
02	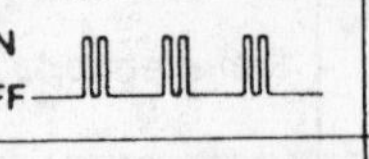 ON / OFF pattern	Ne signal	No Ne signal from crank angle sensor	—
03	 ON / OFF pattern	G1 signal	No G1 signal	Neither G1 nor G2 signal: Engine stopped
04	 ON / OFF pattern	G2 signal	No G2 signal	
05	 ON / OFF pattern	Knock sensor and knock control unit	Open or short circuit	• Retards ignition timing 6° in heavy-load condition • Waste gate opens earlier
08	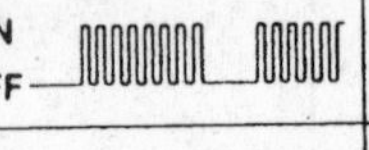 ON / OFF pattern	Air flow meter	Open or short circuit	Maintains basic signal at preset value
09	 ON / OFF pattern	Water thermo sensor	Open or short circuit	Maintains constant command • 35°C (95°F) for EGI • 50°C (122°F) for ISC control use
10	 ON / OFF pattern	Intake air thermo sensor (air flow meter)	Open or short circuit	Maintains constant 20°C (68°F) command
12	 ON / OFF pattern	Throttle sensor	Open or short circuit	Maintains constant command of throttle valve fully open
14	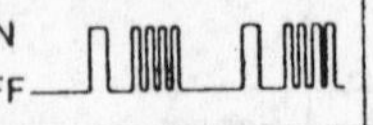 ON / OFF pattern	Atmospheric pressure sensor	Open or short circuit	Maintains constant command of sea level pressure
15	 ON / OFF pattern	Oxygen sensor	Sensor output continues less than 0.55V 120 sec. after engine starts (1,500 rpm)	Cancels EGI feedback operation
16	 ON / OFF pattern	EGR position sensor	Open or short circuit / Sensor output does not match target value (incorrect output)	Cuts off EGR / —
17	 ON / OFF pattern	Feedback system	Sensor output not changed 20 sec. after engine exceeds 1,500 rpm	Cancels EGI feedback operation
25	 ON / OFF pattern	Solenoid valve (pressure regulator)		—
26	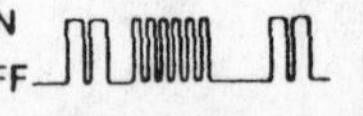 ON / OFF pattern	Solenoid valve (purge control)		—
28	 ON / OFF pattern	Solenoid valve (EGR-vacuum)	Open or short circuit	—
29	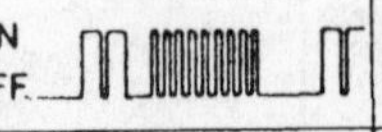 ON / OFF pattern	Solenoid valve (EGR-vent)		—
34	 ON / OFF pattern	Solenoid valve (Idle speed control)		—
42	 ON / OFF pattern	Solenoid valve (waste gate)		—

85814092

Fig. 63 Diagnostic codes — 1988-89 626/MX-6 turbo

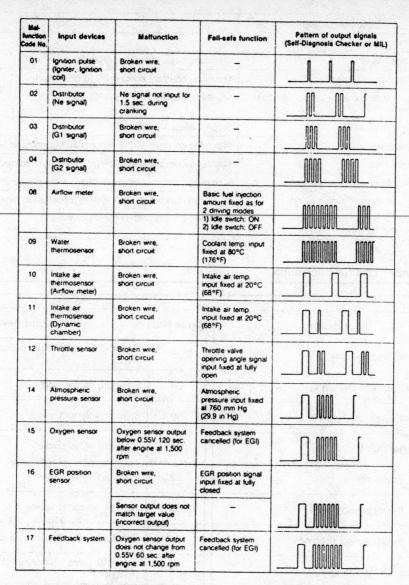

Malfunction Code No.	Input devices	Malfunction	Fail-safe function	Pattern of output signals (Self-Diagnosis Checker or MIL)
01	Ignition pulse (Igniter, Ignition coil)	Broken wire, short circuit	—	
02	Distributor (Ne signal)	Ne signal not input for 1.5 sec. during cranking	—	
03	Distributor (G1 signal)	Broken wire, short circuit	—	
04	Distributor (G2 signal)	Broken wire, short circuit	—	
08	Airflow meter	Broken wire, short circuit	Basic fuel injection amount fixed as for 2 driving modes 1) Idle switch: ON 2) Idle switch: OFF	
09	Water thermosensor	Broken wire, short circuit	Coolant temp. input fixed at 80°C (176°F)	
10	Intake air thermosensor (Airflow meter)	Broken wire, short circuit	Intake air temp. input fixed at 20°C (68°F)	
11	Intake air thermosensor (Dynamic chamber)	Broken wire, short circuit	Intake air temp. input fixed at 20°C (68°F)	
12	Throttle sensor	Broken wire, short circuit	Throttle valve opening angle signal input fixed at fully open	
14	Atmospheric pressure sensor	Broken wire, short circuit	Atmospheric pressure input fixed at 760 mm Hg (29.9 in Hg)	
15	Oxygen sensor	Oxygen sensor output below 0.55V 120 sec. after engine at 1,500 rpm	Feedback system cancelled (for EGI)	
16	EGR position sensor	Broken wire, short circuit	EGR position signal input fixed at fully closed	
		Sensor output does not match target value (incorrect output)	—	
17	Feedback system	Oxygen sensor output does not change from 0.55V 60 sec. after engine at 1,500 rpm	Feedback system cancelled (for EGI)	

Malfunction code	Output devices	Pattern of output signals (Self-Diagnosis Checker or MIL)
25	Solenoid valve (Pressure regulator control)	
26	Solenoid valve (No. 2 purge control)	
27	Solenoid valve (No. 1 purge control)	
28	Solenoid valve (EGR, vacuum side)	
29	Solenoid valve (EGR, vent side)	
34	Idle speed control valve (ISC valve)	
40	Solenoid valve (Triple induction control system) and oxygen sensor relay	
41	Solenoid valve (Variable resonance induction system)	

85814093

Fig. 64 Diagnostic codes — 929

Code No.	Location problem	Fail safe function
01	Crank angle sensor	—
02	Air flow meter	Maintains basic signal at preset value
03	Water thermo sensor	Maintains constant 80°C (176°F) command
04	Intake air temperature sensor (Air flow meter)	Maintains constant 20°C (68°F) command
05	Oxygen (O_2) sensor	Stops feedback correction
06	Throttle sensor	Maintains constant 100% (approx.18°) command
07	Boost sensor	Maintains constant −96 mmHg (3.78 inHg) command
09	Atmospheric pressure sensor	Maintains constant command of sea-level pressure
12	Coil with igniter (Trailing side)	Stops operation of ignition system (only trailing side)
15	Intake air temperature sensor (Dynamic chamber)	Maintains constant 20°C (68°F) command

85814094

Fig. 65 Diagnostic codes — 1988 RX-7 non-turbo

Code No.	Input device	Code No.	Output device
01	Ignition coil (Trailing side)	25	Solenoid valve (Pressure regulator control (PRC))
02	Crank angle sensor (Ne-signal)	26	Stepping motor (Metering oil pump)
03	Crank angle sensor (G-signal)	30	Split air solenoid valve
08	Airflow meter (AFM)	31	Solenoid valve (Relief)
09	Water thermosensor	32	Solenoid valve (Switch)
10	Intake air thermosensor (AFM)	33	Port air solenoid valve
11	Intake air thermosensor (Engine)	34	Solenoid valve (Bypass air control (BAC))
12	Throttle sensor (Full range)	38	Solenoid valve (Accelerated warm-up system (AWS))
13	Pressure sensor	40	Auxiliary port valve
14	Atmospheric pressure sensor (Built in ECU)	41	Solenoid valve (Variable dynamic effect intake (VDI) control)
15	Oxygen sensor	51	Fuel pump resistor relay
17	Feedback system	71	Injector (Front secondary)
18	Throttle sensor (Narrow range)	73	Injector (Rear secondary)
20	Metering oil pump position sensor		
27	Metering oil pump		
37	Metering oil pump		

85814096

Fig. 66 Diagnostic codes — 1989 RX-7 non-turbo

Code No.	Location problem	Fail safe function
01	Crank angle sensor	—
02	Air flow meter	Maintains basic signal at preset value
03	Water thermo sensor	Maintains constant 80°C (176°F) command
04	Intake air temperature sensor (air flow meter)	Maintains constant 20°C (68°F) command
05	Oxygen (O₂) sensor	Stops feedback correction
06	Throttle sensor	Maintains constant 100% (approx.18°) command
07	Pressure sensor	Maintains constant 26.3 kPa (0.27 kg/cm², 3.82 psi) command
09	Atmospheric pressure sensor	Maintains constant command of sea-level pressure
12	Coil with igniter (trailing side)	Stops operation of ignition system (only trailing side)
15	Intake air temperature sensor (intake air pipe)	Maintains constant 20°C (68°F) command

85814095

Fig. 67 Diagnostic codes — 1988 RX-7 turbo

Code No.	Input device	Code No.	Output device
01	Ignition coil (Trailing side)	25	Solenoid valve (Pressure regulator control (PRC))
02	Crank angle sensor (Ne-signal)	26	Step motor (Metering oil pump)
03	Crank angle sensor (G-signal)	30	Split air solenoid valve
05	Knock sensor	31	Solenoid valve (Relief)
08	Airflow meter (AFM)	32	Solenoid valve (Switching)
09	Water thermosensor	33	Port air solenoid valve
10	Intake air thermosensor (AFM)	34	Solenoid valve (Bypass air control (BAC))
11	Intake air thermosensor (Engine)	38	Solenoid valve (Accelerated warm-up system (AWS) and Air supply valve (ASV))
12	Throttle sensor (Full range)	42	Solenoid valve (Waste gate control)
13	Pressure sensor	51	Fuel pump resistor relay
14	Atmospheric pressure sensor (Built in ECU)	71	Injector (Front secondary)
15	Oxygen sensor	73	Injector (Rear secondary)
17	Feedback system		
18	Throttle sensor (Narrow range)		
20	Metering oil pump position sensor		
27	Metering oil pump		
37	Metering oil pump		

85814097

Fig. 68 Diagnostic codes — 1989 RX-7 turbo

VACUUM DIAGRAMS

Following is a compilation of vacuum diagrams for most of the engine and emissions package combinations covered by this manual. Because vacuum circuits will vary based on various engine and vehicle options, always refer first to the vehicle emission control information label, if present. Should the label be missing, or should the vehicle be equipped with a different engine than the car's original equipment, refer to the following diagrams for the same or similar configuration.

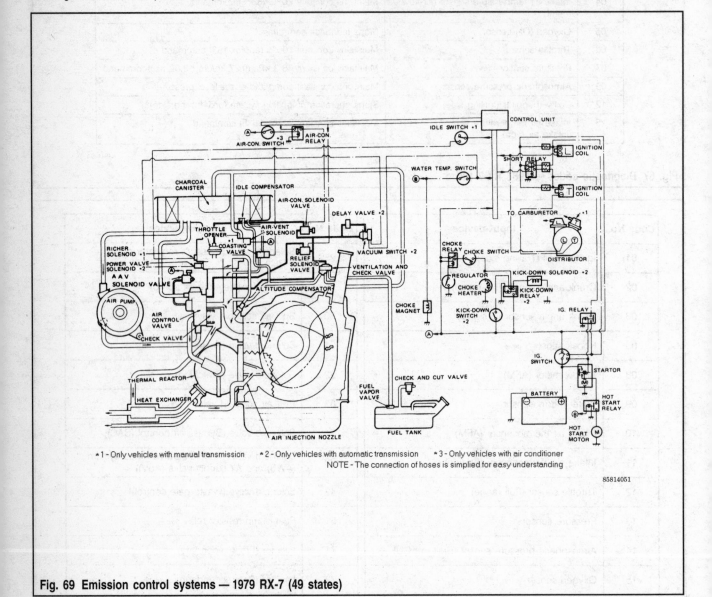

* 1 - Only vehicles with manual transmission   * 2 - Only vehicles with automatic transmission   * 3 - Only vehicles with air conditioner
NOTE - The connection of hoses is simpled for easy understanding

85814051

Fig. 69 Emission control systems — 1979 RX-7 (49 states)

If you wish to obtain a replacement emissions label, most manufacturers offer them for purchase. These labels can usually be ordered from a local dealer, though you will need to provide them with various serial number or calibration information.

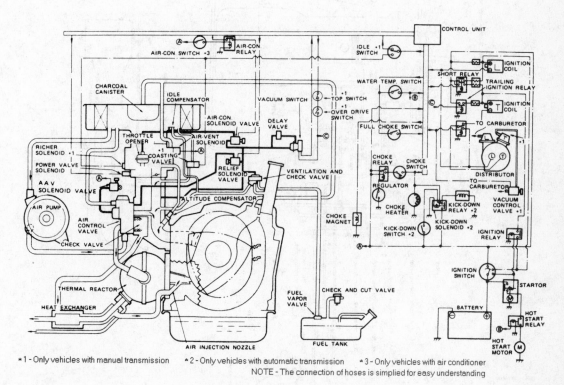

*1 - Only vehicles with manual transmission   *2 - Only vehicles with automatic transmission   *3 - Only vehicles with air conditioner
NOTE - The connection of hoses is simplified for easy understanding

85814052

Fig. 70 Emission control systems — 1979 RX-7 (California)

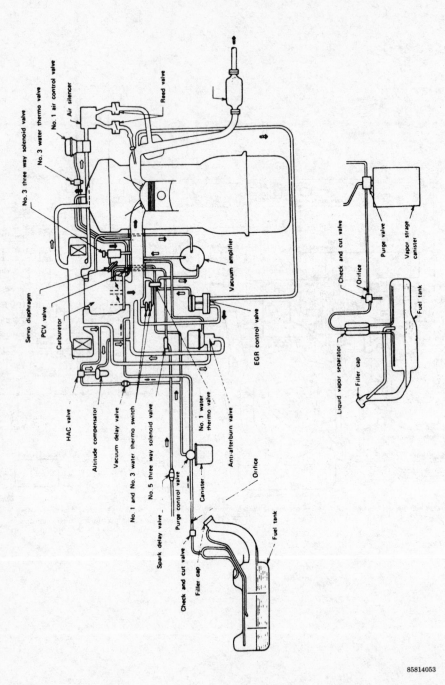

Fig. 71 Emission control systems — 1980 GLC (USA)

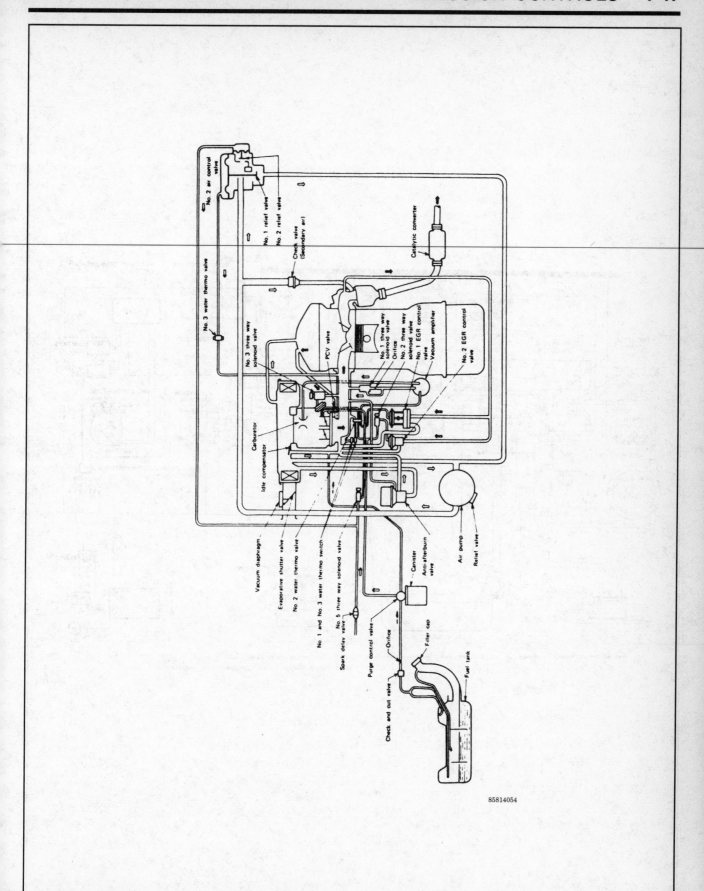

Fig. 72 Emission control systems — 1980 GLC (Canada)

85814054

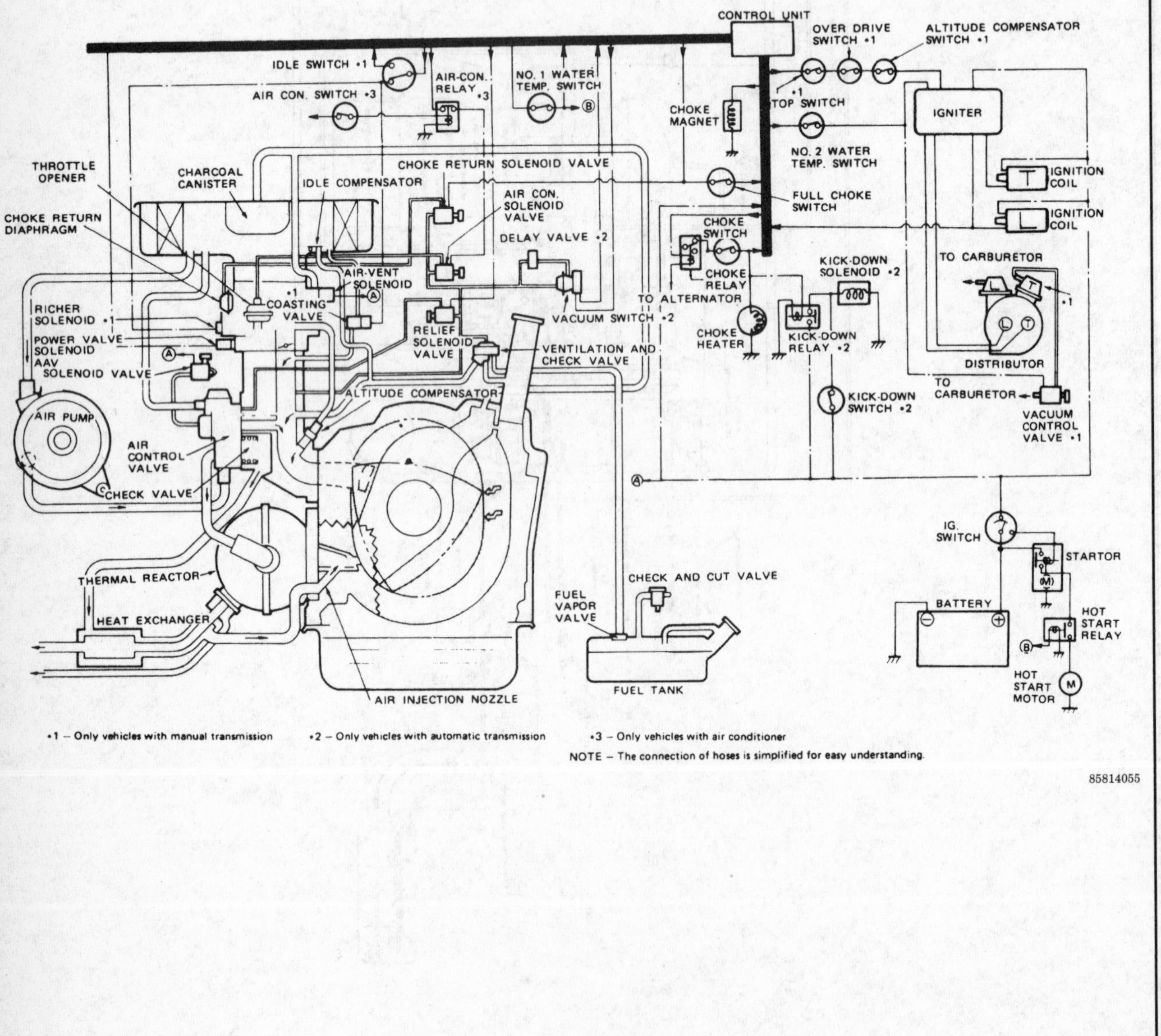

IDLE SWITCH •1
AIR CON. SWITCH •3
AIR-CON. RELAY •3
NO. 1 WATER TEMP. SWITCH
CONTROL UNIT
OVER DRIVE SWITCH •1
ALTITUDE COMPENSATOR SWITCH •1
CHOKE MAGNET
TOP SWITCH
NO. 2 WATER TEMP. SWITCH
IGNITER
IGNITION COIL
IGNITION COIL
THROTTLE OPENER
CHARCOAL CANISTER
IDLE COMPENSATOR
CHOKE RETURN SOLENOID VALVE
AIR CON. SOLENOID VALVE
DELAY VALVE •2
FULL CHOKE SWITCH
CHOKE RETURN DIAPHRAGM
AIR-VENT SOLENOID
COASTING VALVE
RELIEF SOLENOID VALVE
VACUUM SWITCH •2
TO ALTERNATOR
CHOKE SWITCH
CHOKE RELAY
KICK-DOWN SOLENOID •2
TO CARBURETOR
RICHER SOLENOID •1
POWER VALVE SOLENOID
AAV SOLENOID VALVE
VENTILATION AND CHECK VALVE
ALTITUDE COMPENSATOR
CHOKE HEATER
KICK-DOWN RELAY •2
DISTRIBUTOR
TO CARBURETOR
AIR PUMP
AIR CONTROL VALVE
KICK-DOWN SWITCH •2
VACUUM CONTROL VALVE •1
CHECK VALVE
THERMAL REACTOR
HEAT EXCHANGER
CHECK AND CUT VALVE
IG. SWITCH
STARTOR
AIR INJECTION NOZZLE
FUEL VAPOR VALVE
BATTERY
HOT START RELAY
FUEL TANK
HOT START MOTOR

•1 — Only vehicles with manual transmission   •2 — Only vehicles with automatic transmission   •3 — Only vehicles with air conditioner
NOTE — The connection of hoses is simplified for easy understanding.

85814055

Fig. 73 Emission control systems — 1980 RX-7 (49 states)

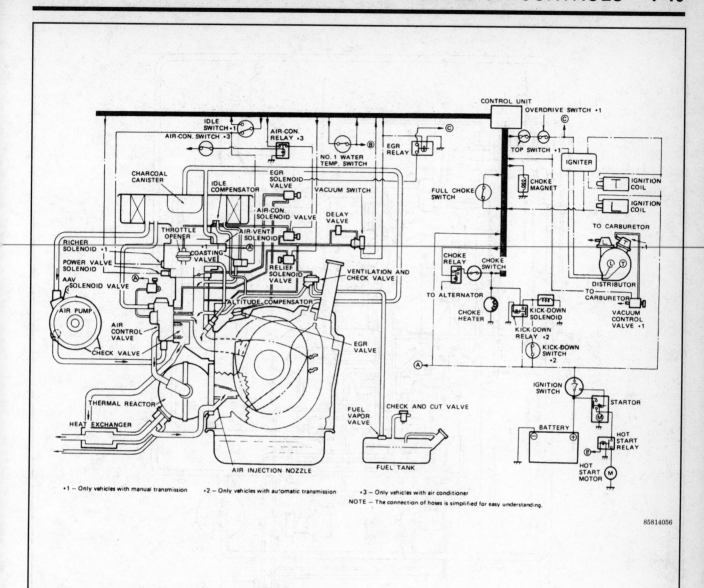

Fig. 74 Emission control systems — 1980 RX-7 (California)

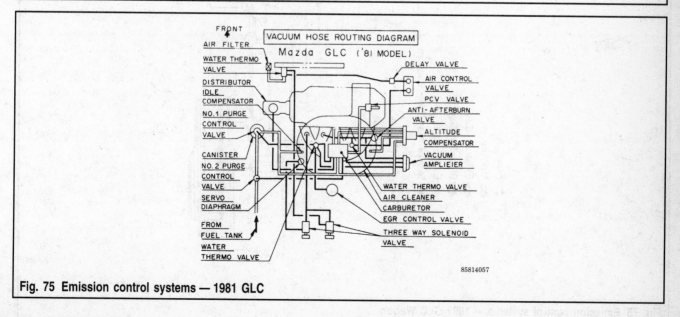

Fig. 75 Emission control systems — 1981 GLC

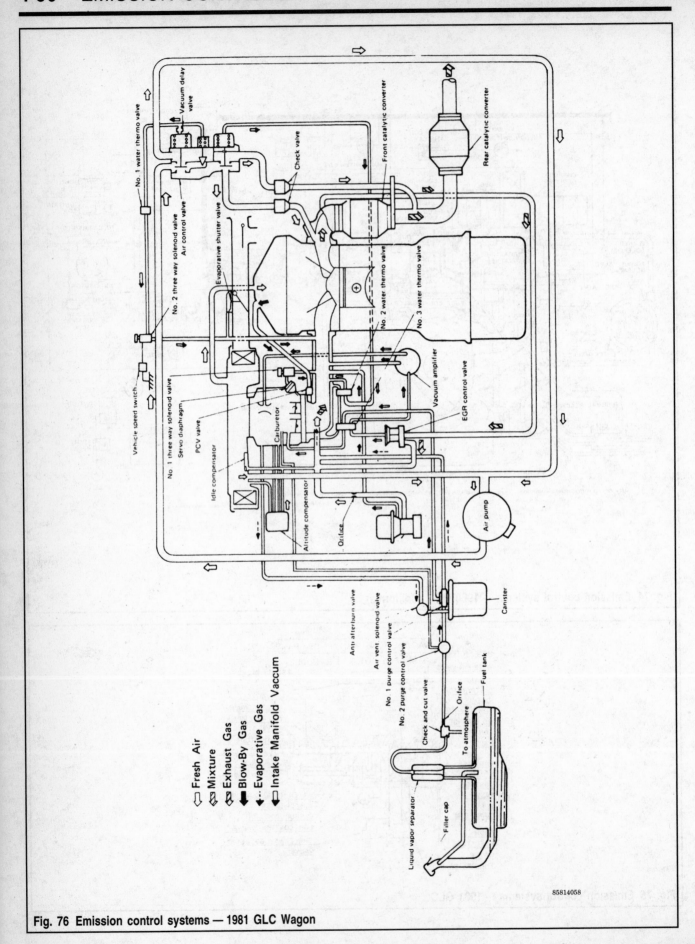

Fig. 76 Emission control systems — 1981 GLC Wagon

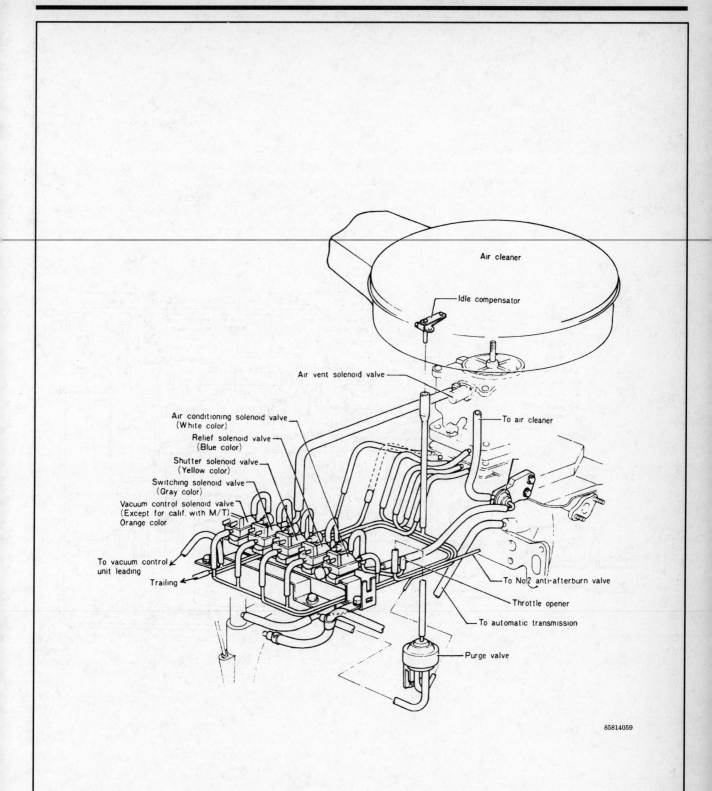

Air cleaner

Idle compensator

Air vent solenoid valve

Air conditioning solenoid valve
(White color)

Relief solenoid valve
(Blue color)

Shutter solenoid valve
(Yellow color)

Switching solenoid valve
(Gray color)

Vacuum control solenoid valve
(Except for calif. with M/T)
Orange color

To air cleaner

To vacuum control
unit leading

Trailing

To No.2 anti-afterburn valve

Throttle opener

To automatic transmission

Purge valve

85814059

Fig. 77 Emission control systems — 1981-82 RX-7

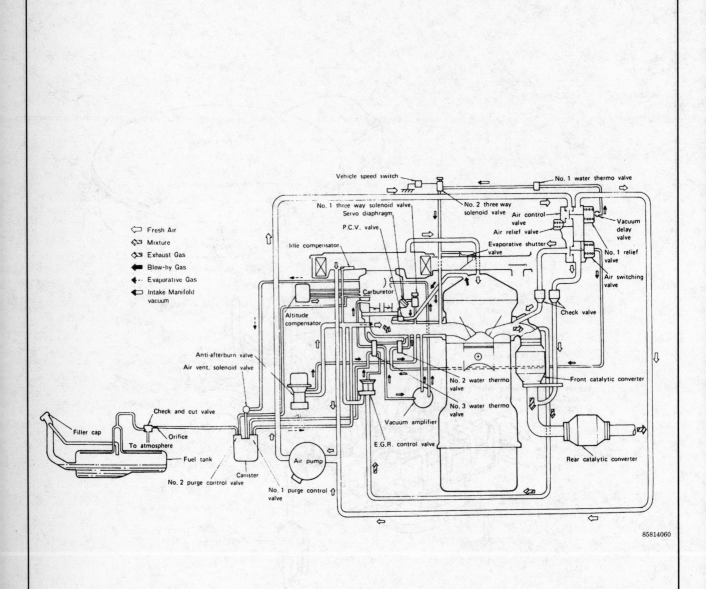

Fresh Air
Mixture
Exhaust Gas
Blow-by Gas
Evaporative Gas
Intake Manifold vacuum

Vehicle speed switch

No. 1 water thermo valve

No. 1 three way solenoid valve
Servo diaphragm

No. 2 three way solenoid valve

Air control valve

Vacuum delay valve

P.C.V. valve

Air relief valve

No. 1 relief valve

Idle compensator

Evaporative shutter valve

Air switching valve

Carburetor

Check valve

Altitude compensator

Anti-afterburn valve
Air vent. solenoid valve

No. 2 water thermo valve

Front catalytic converter

Check and cut valve

No. 3 water thermo valve

Filler cap

Orifice

To atmosphere

Fuel tank

Canister

Vacuum amplifier

E.G.R. control valve

Rear catalytic converter

No. 2 purge control valve

No. 1 purge control valve

Air pump

85814060

Fig. 78 Emission control systems — 1982 GLC and GLC Wagon

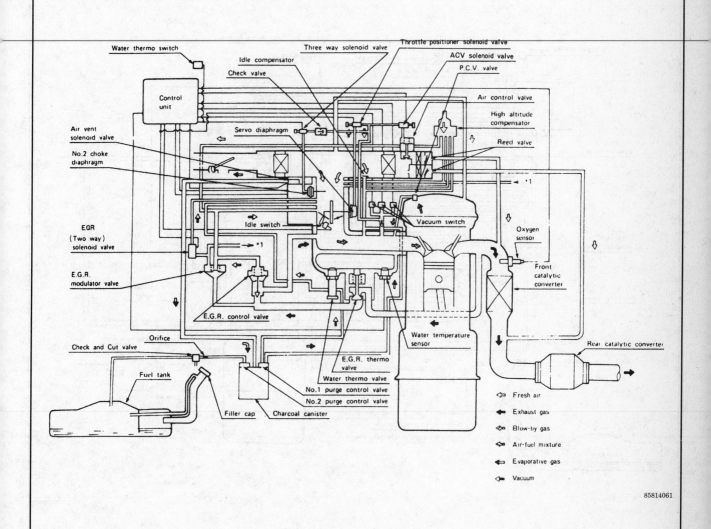

Fig. 79 Emission control systems — 1983 GLC and GLC Wagon (49 states)

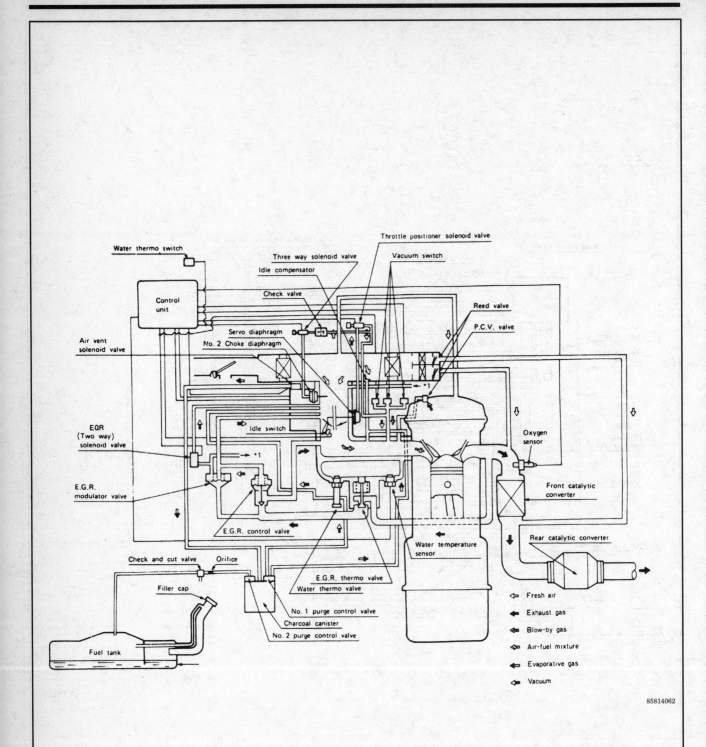

Fig. 80 Emission control systems — 1983 GLC and GLC Wagon (California)

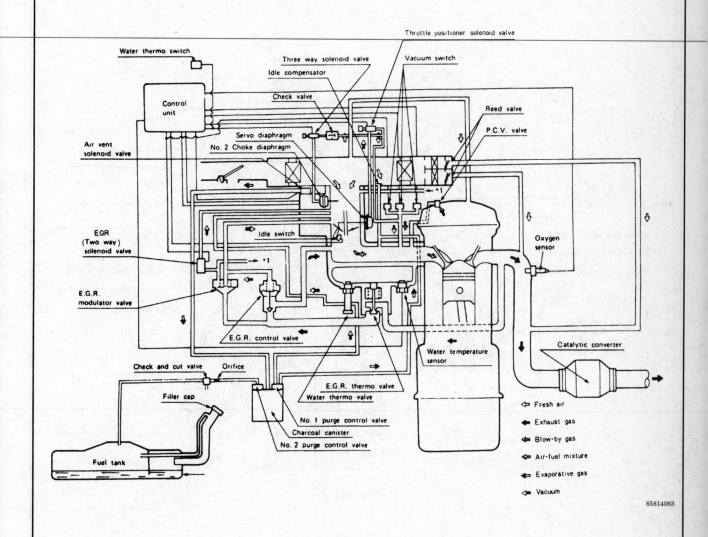

Throttle positioner solenoid valve

Water thermo switch

Three way solenoid valve

Idle compensator

Vacuum switch

Check valve

Control unit

Reed valve

P.C.V. valve

Air vent solenoid valve

Servo diaphragm

No. 2 Choke diaphragm

EGR (Two way) solenoid valve

Idle switch

Oxygen sensor

E.G.R. modulator valve

E.G.R. control valve

Catalytic converter

Check and cut valve   Orifice

Water temperature sensor

Filler cap

E.G.R. thermo valve

Water thermo valve

No. 1 purge control valve

Charcoal canister

No. 2 purge control valve

Fuel tank

⟨▭ Fresh air

◀ Exhaust gas

◀ Blow-by gas

◀ Air-fuel mixture

◀ Evaporative gas

◀ Vacuum

85814063

Fig. 81 Emission control systems — 1983 GLC and GLC Wagon (Canada)

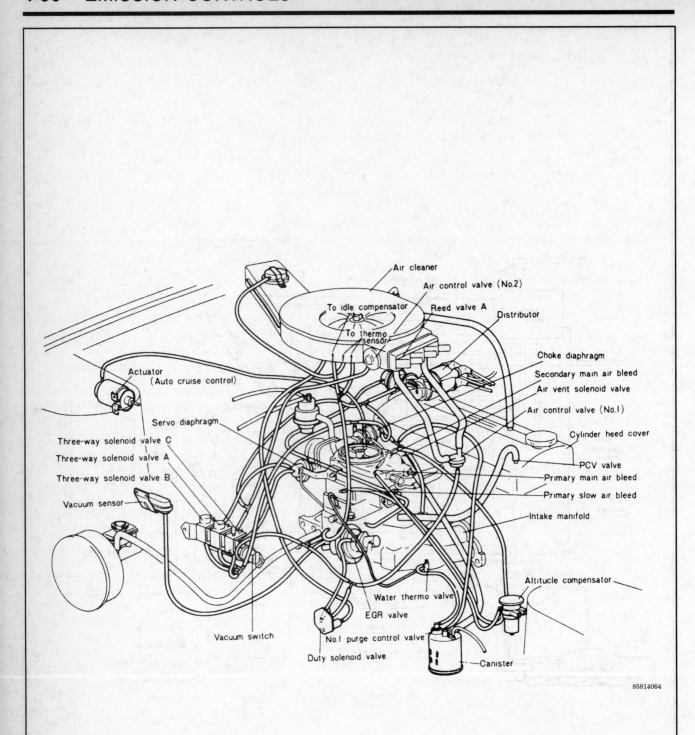

Air cleaner

Air control valve (No.2)

To idle compensator

Reed valve A

Distributor

To thermo sensor

Choke diaphragm

Secondary main air bleed

Actuator
(Auto cruise control)

Air vent solenoid valve

Air control valve (No.1)

Servo diaphragm

Cylinder heed cover

Three-way solenoid valve C

Three-way solenoid valve A

PCV valve

Three-way solenoid valve B

Primary main air bleed

Primary slow air bleed

Vacuum sensor

Intake manifold

Altitucle compensator

Water thermo valve

Vacuum switch

EGR valve

No.1 purge control valve

Duty solenoid valve

Canister

85814064

Fig. 82   Emission control systems — 1983 626 (49 states)

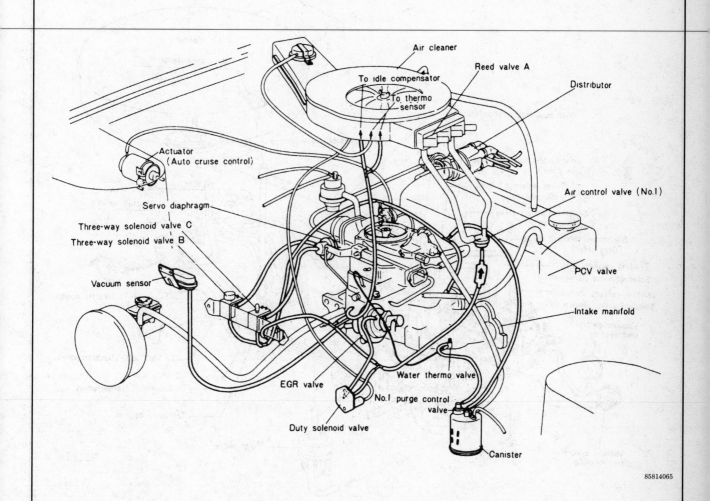

Fig. 83 Emission control systems — 1983 626 (California and Canada)

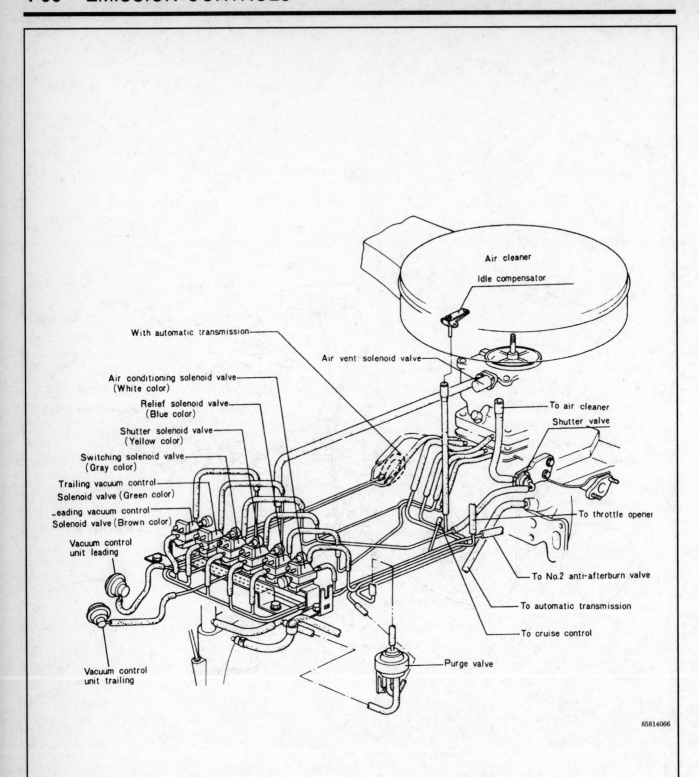

Fig. 84 Emission control systems — 1983 RX-7

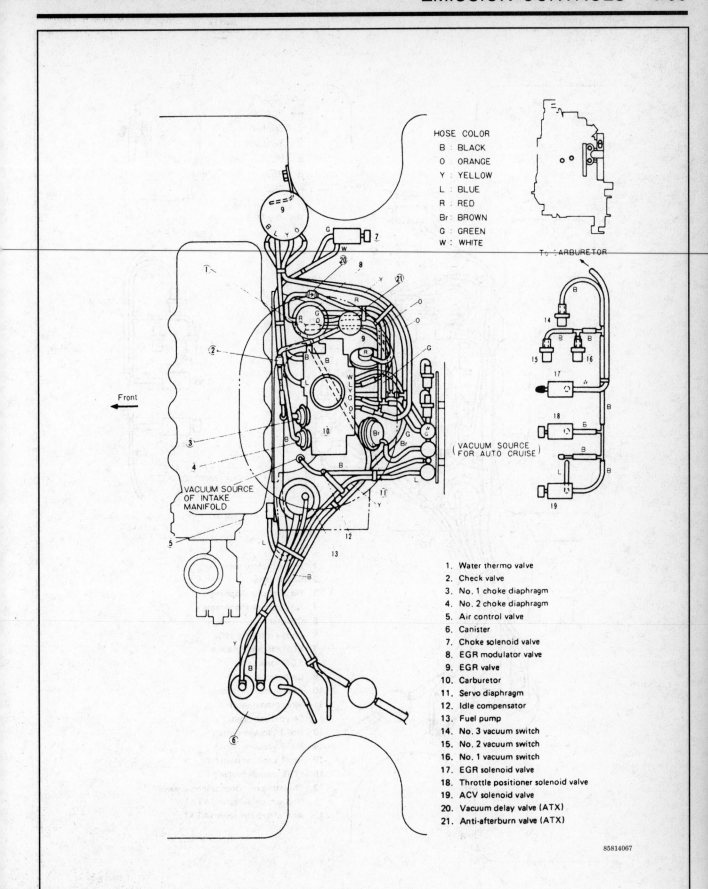

Fig. 85 Emission control systems — 1984-85 GLC (49 states)

HOSE COLOR
B : BLACK
O : ORANGE
Y : YELLOW
L : BLUE
R : RED
Br : BROWN
G : GREEN
W : WHITE

To CARBURETOR

VACUUM SOURCE
(FOR AUTO CRUISE)

VACUUM SOURCE
OF INTAKE
MANIFOLD

Front

1. Water thermo valve
2. Check valve
3. No. 1 choke diaphragm
4. No. 2 choke diaphragm
5. Air control valve
6. Canister
7. Choke solenoid valve
8. EGR modulator valve
9. EGR valve
10. Carburetor
11. Servo diaphragm
12. Idle compensator
13. Fuel pump
14. No. 3 vacuum switch
15. No. 2 vacuum switch
16. No. 1 vacuum switch
17. EGR solenoid valve
18. Throttle positioner solenoid valve
19. ACV solenoid valve
20. Vacuum delay valve (ATX)
21. Anti-afterburn valve (ATX)

85814067

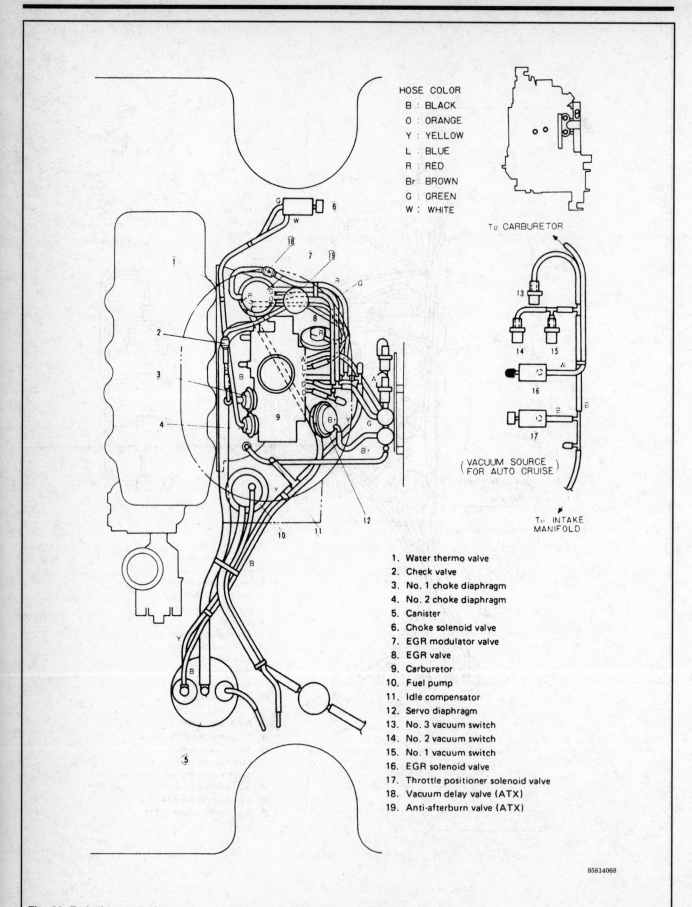

HOSE COLOR
B : BLACK
O : ORANGE
Y : YELLOW
L : BLUE
R : RED
Br : BROWN
G : GREEN
W : WHITE

To CARBURETOR

(VACUUM SOURCE)
FOR AUTO CRUISE

To INTAKE
MANIFOLD

1. Water thermo valve
2. Check valve
3. No. 1 choke diaphragm
4. No. 2 choke diaphragm
5. Canister
6. Choke solenoid valve
7. EGR modulator valve
8. EGR valve
9. Carburetor
10. Fuel pump
11. Idle compensator
12. Servo diaphragm
13. No. 3 vacuum switch
14. No. 2 vacuum switch
15. No. 1 vacuum switch
16. EGR solenoid valve
17. Throttle positioner solenoid valve
18. Vacuum delay valve (ATX)
19. Anti-afterburn valve (ATX)

85814068

Fig. 86 Emission control systems — 1984-85 GLC (California and Canada)

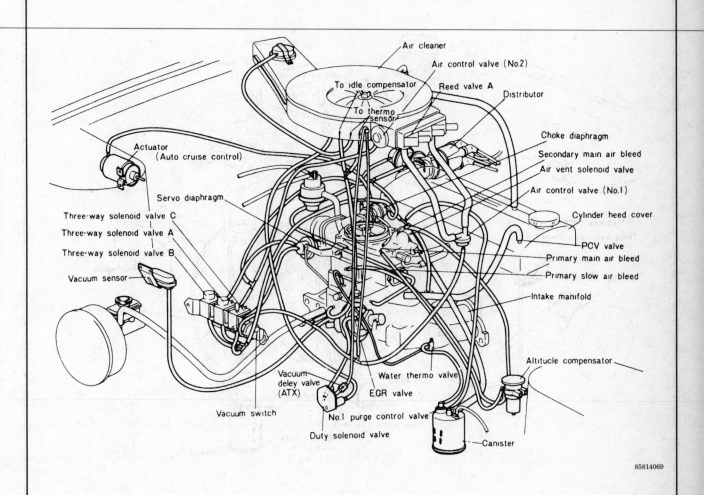

Air cleaner
Air control valve (No.2)
To idle compensator
Reed valve A
Distributor
To thermo sensor
Choke diaphragm
Secondary main air bleed
Air vent solenoid valve
Air control valve (No.1)
Actuator (Auto cruise control)
Servo diaphragm
Cylinder heed cover
Three-way solenoid valve C
Three-way solenoid valve A
Three-way solenoid valve B
PCV valve
Primary main air bleed
Primary slow air bleed
Vacuum sensor
Intake manifold
Altitucle compensator
Vacuum deley valve (ATX)
Water thermo valve
EGR valve
Vacuum switch
No.1 purge control valve
Duty solenoid valve
Canister

85814069

Fig. 87 Emission control systems — 1984-85 626 (49 states)

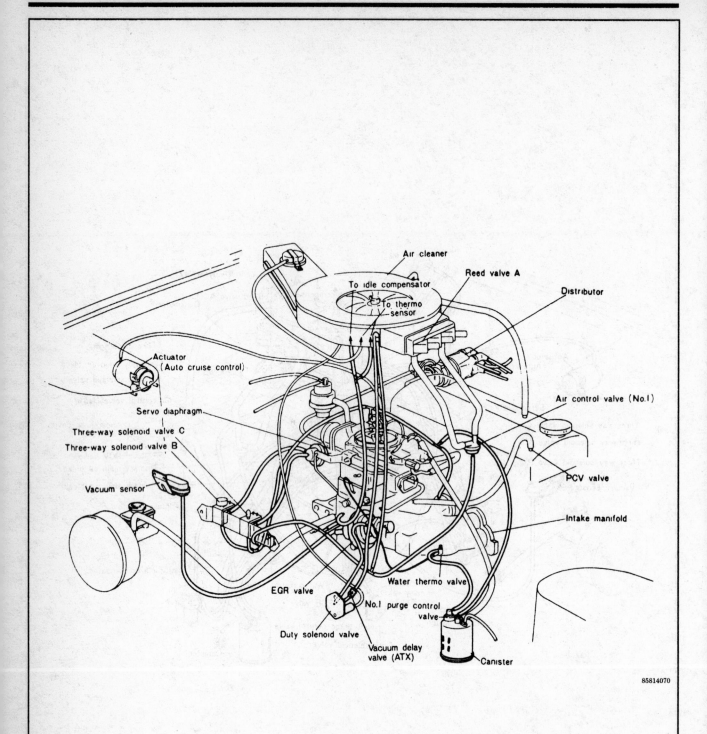

Air cleaner

Reed valve A

Distributor

To idle compensator

To thermo sensor

Actuator (Auto cruise control)

Air control valve (No.1)

Servo diaphragm

PCV valve

Three-way solenoid valve C

Three-way solenoid valve B

Vacuum sensor

Intake manifold

EGR valve

Water thermo valve

No.1 purge control valve

Duty solenoid valve

Vacuum delay valve (ATX)

Canister

85814070

Fig. 88 Emission control systems — 1984-85 626 (California and Canada)

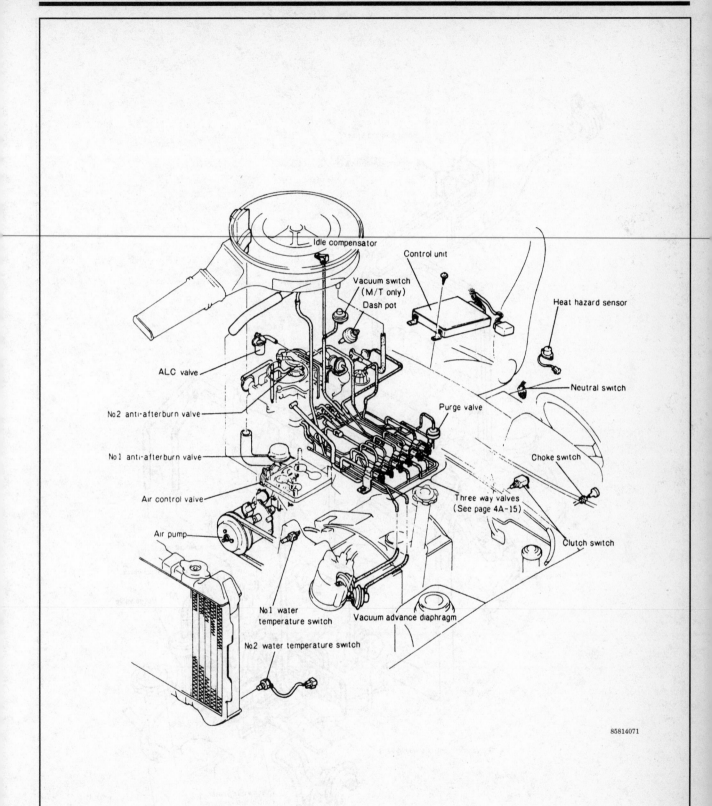

Fig. 89 Emission control systems — 1984-85 carbureted RX-7

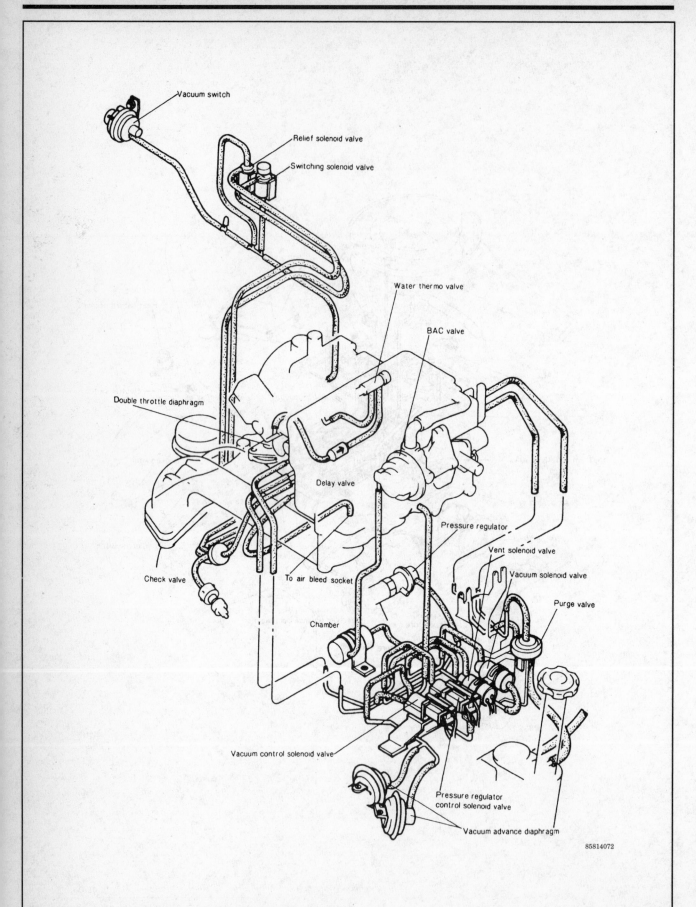

Fig. 90 Emission control systems — 1984-85 fuel injected RX-7

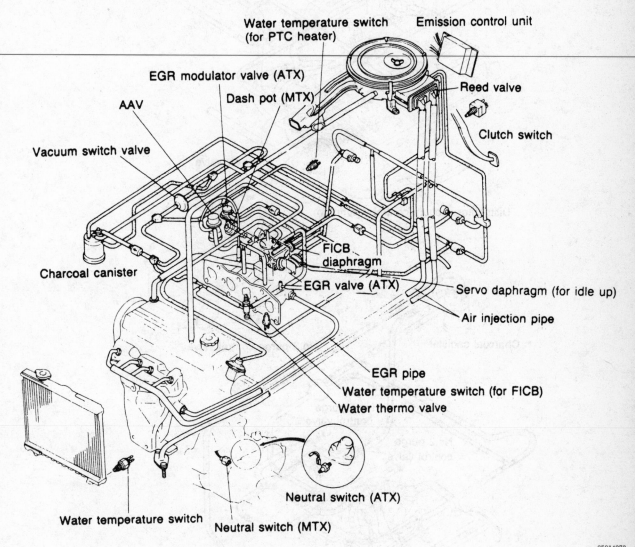

Water temperature switch
(for PTC heater)

Emission control unit

EGR modulator valve (ATX)

Dash pot (MTX)

Reed valve

Clutch switch

AAV

Vacuum switch valve

FICB
diaphragm

Charcoal canister

EGR valve (ATX)

Servo daphragm (for idle up)

Air injection pipe

EGR pipe

Water temperature switch (for FICB)

Water thermo valve

Neutral switch (ATX)

Water temperature switch

Neutral switch (MTX)

85814073

Fig. 91 Emission control systems — 1986-87 carbureted 323

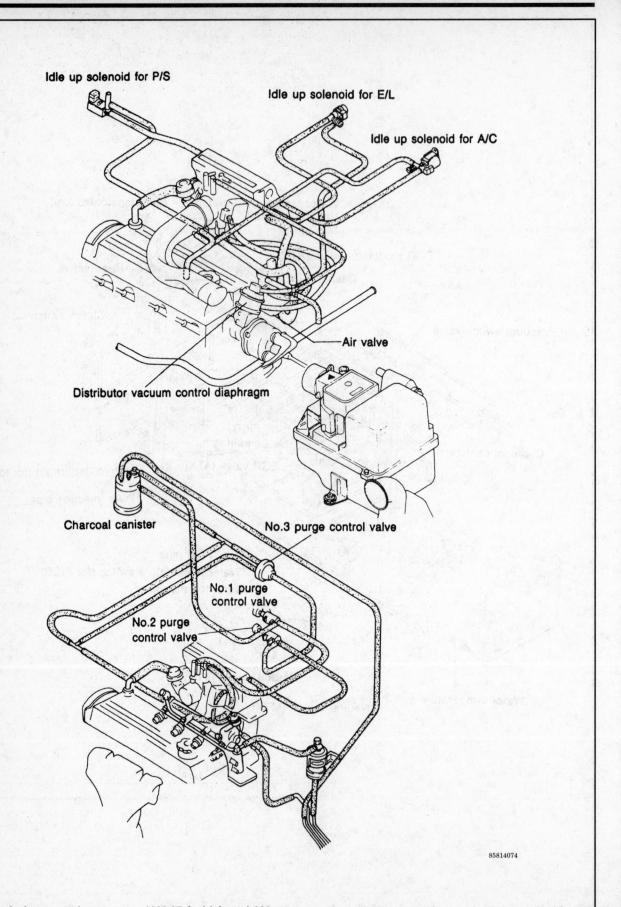

Idle up solenoid for P/S

Idle up solenoid for E/L

Idle up solenoid for A/C

Air valve

Distributor vacuum control diaphragm

Charcoal canister

No.3 purge control valve

No.1 purge control valve

No.2 purge control valve

85814074

Fig. 92 Emission control systems — 1986-87 fuel injected 323

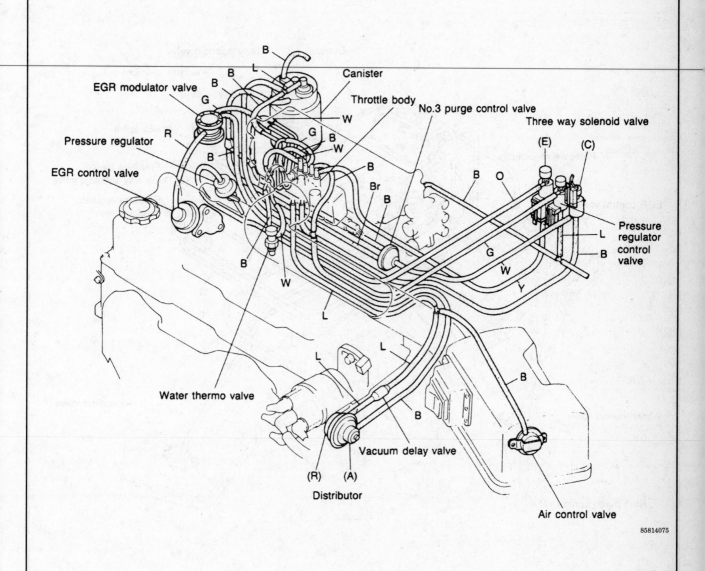

EGR modulator valve

B

B

L

B

Canister

Throttle body

No.3 purge control valve

Three way solenoid valve

G

W

(E)

(C)

Pressure regulator

R

G

B

B

W

B

O

EGR control valve

B

Br

B

Pressure regulator control valve

G

L

B

W

Y

L

B

Water thermo valve

L

L

W

L

B

B

L

B

(R)   (A)

Vacuum delay valve

Distributor

Air control valve

85814075

Fig. 93 Emission control systems — 1986-87 non-turbo 626

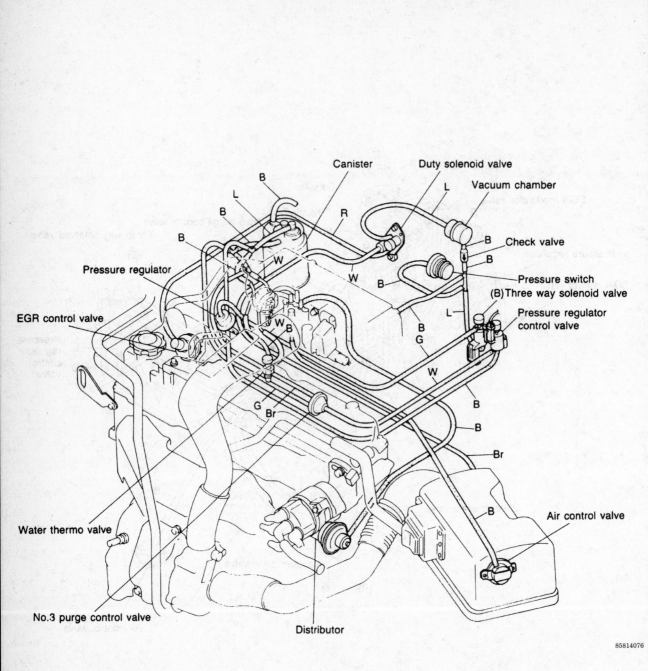

Canister
Duty solenoid valve
Vacuum chamber
Check valve
Pressure switch
(B) Three way solenoid valve
Pressure regulator control valve
Pressure regulator
EGR control valve
Air control valve
Water thermo valve
No.3 purge control valve
Distributor

85814076

Fig. 94 Emission control systems — 1986-87 626 turbo

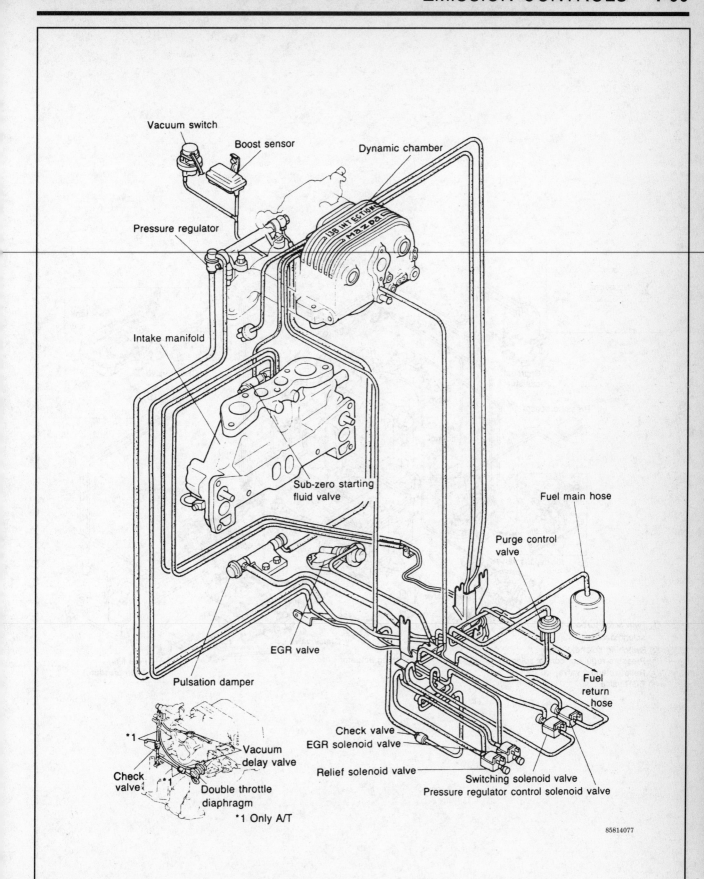

Vacuum switch

Boost sensor

Dynamic chamber

Pressure regulator

Intake manifold

Sub-zero starting fluid valve

Fuel main hose

Purge control valve

EGR valve

Pulsation damper

Fuel return hose

*1

Check valve

Vacuum delay valve

*1

Double throttle diaphragm

*1 Only A/T

Check valve
EGR solenoid valve

Relief solenoid valve

Switching solenoid valve
Pressure regulator control solenoid valve

85814077

Fig. 95 Emission control systems — 1986-89 non-turbo RX-7

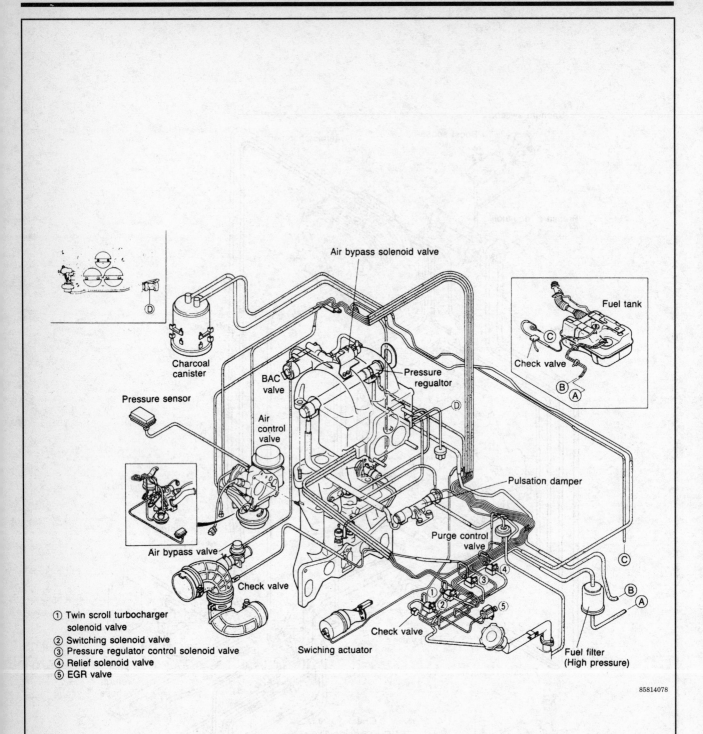

Air bypass solenoid valve

Charcoal canister

Pressure sensor

BAC valve

Air control valve

Pressure regualtor

Fuel tank

Check valve

Pulsation damper

Purge control valve

Air bypass valve

Check valve

Check valve

Swiching actuator

Fuel filter (High pressure)

① Twin scroll turbocharger solenoid valve
② Switching solenoid valve
③ Pressure regulator control solenoid valve
④ Relief solenoid valve
⑤ EGR valve

85814078

Fig. 96 Emission control systems — 1986-89 RX-7 turbo

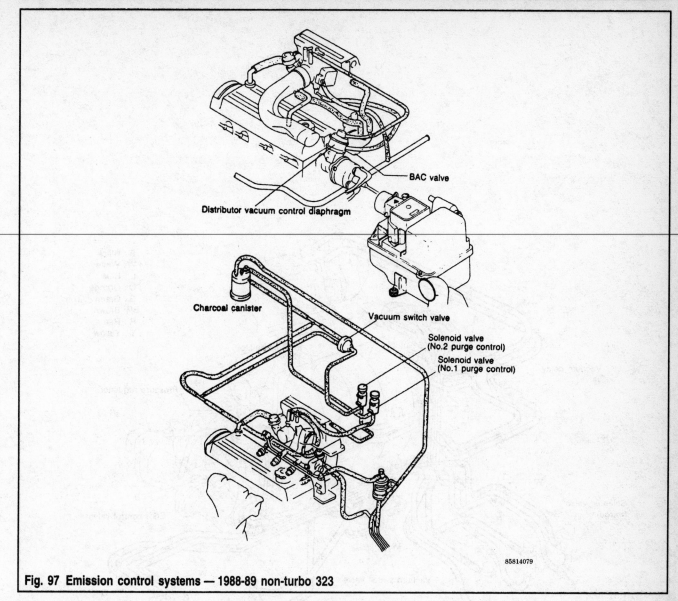

Fig. 97 Emission control systems — 1988-89 non-turbo 323

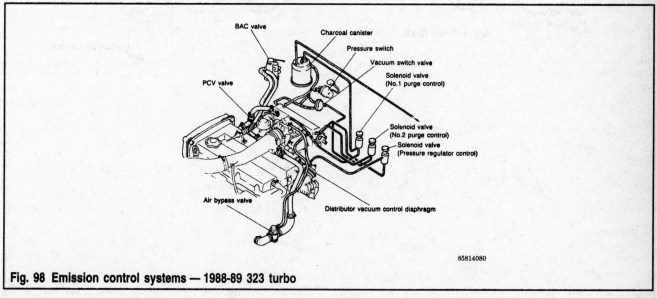

Fig. 98 Emission control systems — 1988-89 323 turbo

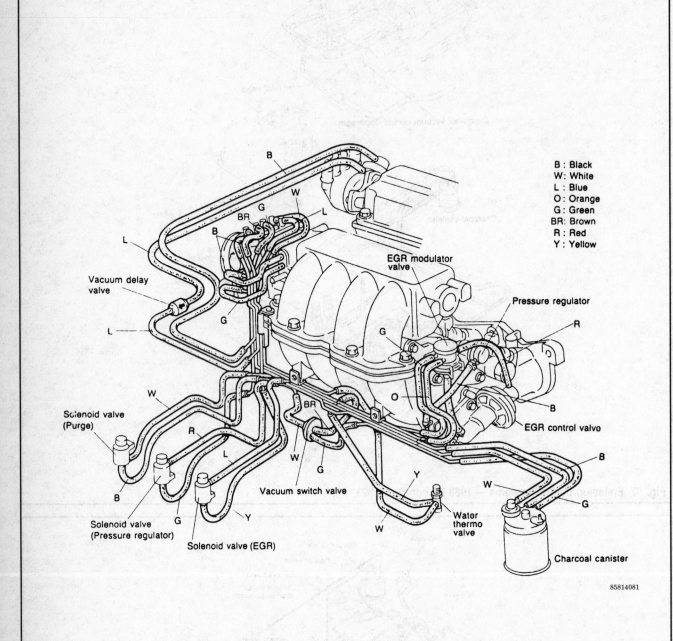

B : Black
W : White
L : Blue
O : Orange
G : Green
BR : Brown
R : Red
Y : Yellow

Vacuum delay valve

EGR modulator valve

Pressure regulator

Solenoid valve (Purge)

Solenoid valve (Pressure regulator)

Solenoid valve (EGR)

Vacuum switch valve

Water thermo valve

EGR control valve

Charcoal canister

85814081

Fig. 99 Emission control systems — 1988-89 non-turbo 626 and MX-6

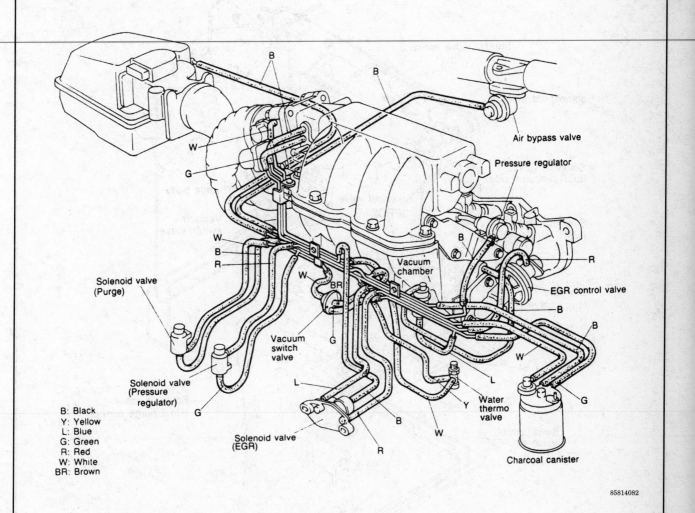

B: Black
Y: Yellow
L: Blue
G: Green
R: Red
W: White
BR: Brown

Solenoid valve
(Purge)

Solenoid valve
(Pressure
regulator)

Vacuum
switch
valve

Solenoid valve
(EGR)

Air bypass valve

Pressure regulator

Vacuum
chamber

EGR control valve

Water
thermo
valve

Charcoal canister

85814082

Fig. 100 Emission control systems — 1988-89 626 and MX-6 turbo

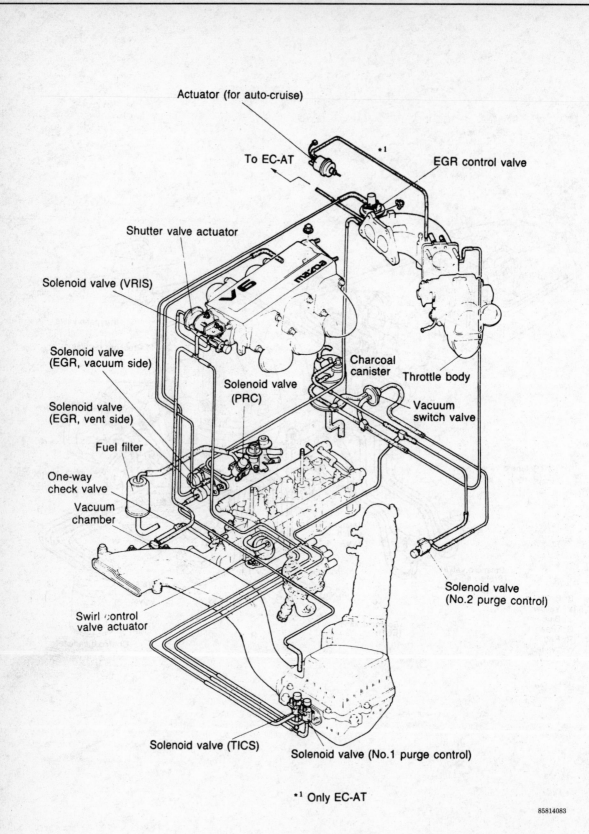

Actuator (for auto-cruise)

To EC-AT

*1

EGR control valve

Shutter valve actuator

Solenoid valve (VRIS)

Solenoid valve (EGR, vacuum side)

Solenoid valve (PRC)

Charcoal canister

Throttle body

Solenoid valve (EGR, vent side)

Vacuum switch valve

Fuel filter

One-way check valve

Vacuum chamber

Solenoid valve (No.2 purge control)

Swirl control valve actuator

Solenoid valve (TICS)

Solenoid valve (No.1 purge control)

*1 Only EC-AT

85814083

Fig. 101 Emission control systems — 1988-89 929

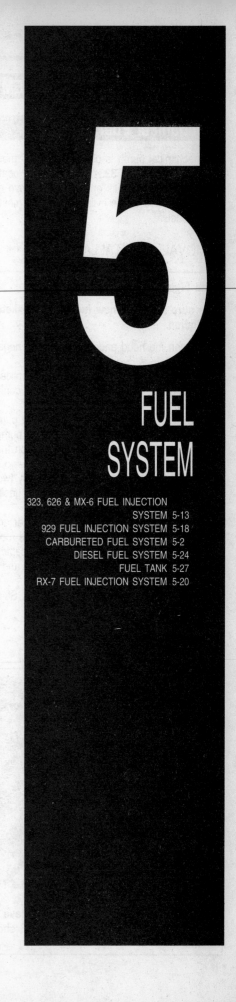

5

FUEL
SYSTEM

CARBURETED FUEL SYSTEM

Mechanical Fuel Pump

A mechanical pump is used on all GLC models, 1983-85 626s, and carbureted 323s. The pump is located on the right side of the engine block on rear wheel drive models and on the left rear side of the cylinder head on most front wheel drive models.

REMOVAL & INSTALLATION

▶ **See Figures 1, 2, 3, 4, 5, 6, 7 and 8**

➡**Be sure to obtain new fuel pump gaskets before installation.**

1. Open the hood and disconnect the negative battery cable.
2. Mark the fuel inlet, outlet and (if applicable) return lines near the fuel pump connections, to avoid confusion during installation.
3. Slide the fuel line clips back off the pump connectors. Then, twist and pull the fuel lines off the pump. Note that the 323 and 626 have inlet and return lines on the top of the pump and an outlet on the side.
4. Unfasten the mounting bolts (usually two) from the block or cylinder head, then remove the pump, gaskets, and spacer.

To install:

5. Position new gaskets with the spacer and fuel pump on the block or cylinder head, then install the mounting bolts.
6. Attach the inlet, outlet and (if applicable) return lines to the appropriate connections on the pump and secure them with the line clips.
7. Connect the negative battery cable. Start the engine and check for fuel leaks.

Fig. 1 Most mechanical fuel pumps have inlet and return lines attached at the top — 626 shown; 323 similar

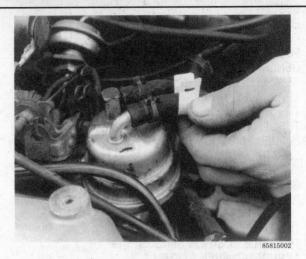

Fig. 2 Before disconnecting any lines, label them for easier installation

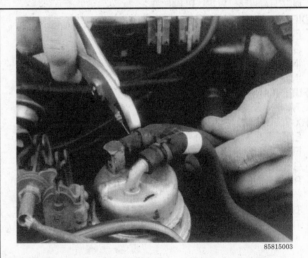

Fig. 3 Squeeze the spring-type fuel line clips with a pliers in order to slide them back at free the line

TESTING

1. Disconnect the fuel inlet line going to the carburetor. Install a calibrated pressure gauge into the line coming from the pump. Be careful not to spill any fuel, but if you do, remove all spillage before starting the engine.
2. Start the engine and run it at idle using the fuel still in the carburetor float bowl. Allow the engine to run until the pressure gauge reaches a maximum reading. Note the pressure reading. Normal specifications are 2.84-3.84 psi (20-26 kPa), except for the 323, whose specifications are 3.98-4.98 psi (27.4-34.3 kPa) for the Sedan or 3.91-4.93 psi (27-34 kPa) for the Wagon.
3. Stop the engine. Remove the pressure gauge, reinstall the fuel line into the carburetor, and run the engine until the carburetor float bowl is full of fuel.

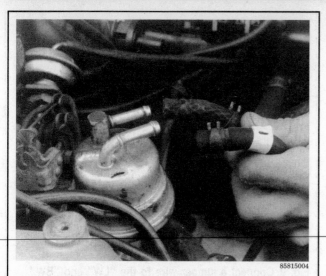

Fig. 4 Twist and pull the fuel lines from the pump

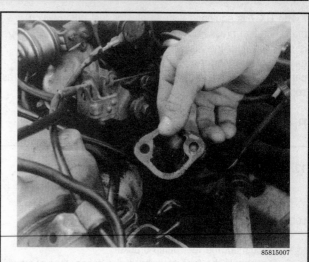

Fig. 7 Be sure to also remove the old gaskets and spacer

Fig. 5 Unfasten the fuel pump's retaining bolts

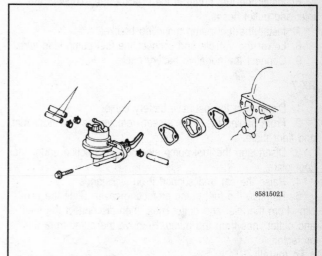

Fig. 8 Exploded view of mechanical fuel pump components — 323 shown

4. To test the volume of fuel discharged by the pump, the engine must be run at idle for one minute. Position a durable container (preferably metal) with a capacity of at least 1½ qts. near the carburetor fuel inlet line. Disconnect the fuel line at the carburetor, and put the open end into the container. Idle the engine until it stops (or for one minute) and time how long it has run. Then, reconnect the fuel line to the carburetor and run the starter or idle the engine until the float bowl is full. Repeat the fuel discharge and timing operation until the engine has run for a total of one full minute at idle speed and all the fuel discharged by the pump has been collected. The pump must discharge at least 1.1 qts. per minute.

5. The pump should be replaced if it fails either the pressure or volume test.

Electric Fuel Pump

The 1979-82 and 1986-89 626 models are equipped with an electric fuel pump. The pump is located under the floor of the car in front of the fuel tank.

Fig. 6 Disengage the fuel pump's actuating lever, then remove the pump

The RX-7 is equipped with an electric fuel pump which maintains fuel pressure at 3.7-4.7 psi (26-32 kPa). The pump is mounted near the fuel tank and access to the pump is gained by removing the rear floor mat and the storage compartment behind the driver's seat. The fuel pump comes on as soon as the ignition switch is turned to the **ON** position.

REMOVAL & INSTALLATION

1979-82 and 1986-89 626

1. Disconnect the negative battery cable.
2. Disconnect the fuel pump lead wire in the luggage compartment.
3. Raise the vehicle and support with jackstands.
4. Disconnect the fuel pump bracket.
5. Disconnect the fuel inlet and outlet hoses, then remove the fuel pump from the bracket.

To install:

6. Install the fuel pump in the bracket, then connect the inlet and outlet hoses.
7. Install the fuel pump mounting bracket.
8. Lower the vehicle and connect the fuel pump lead wire.
9. Connect the negative battery cable.

RX-7

1. Disconnect the negative battery cable.
2. From behind the driver's seat, remove the rear floor mat and floor plate.
3. Disengage the fuel pump electrical connection under the floor plate.
4. Raise the car and support it on jackstands.
5. Remove the fuel pump protecting cover. Slide the two clips from the inlet and outlet lines, then disconnect the inlet and outlet lines from the pump. Remove the pump from the protector.

To install:

6. Insert the fuel pump into the protector. Connect the fuel lines to the pump by firmly pushing the end of each line onto the pump connection using a twisting motion. Secure the lines with the clips.
7. Lock the cover onto the protector and lower the vehicle.
8. Engage the fuel pump connector, then replace the floor plate and floor mat.
9. Connect the negative battery cable.

TESTING

▸ **See Figure 9**

➡**Make sure the fuel filter is not clogged before testing the fuel pump.**

1. Remove the air cleaner assembly. Position an approved fuel container with a capacity of at least 1½ qts. near the carburetor fuel inlet line.
2. Disconnect the carburetor fuel inlet line. Turn the ignition switch **ON** and allow air to be purged from the system with the line pointed into the container.

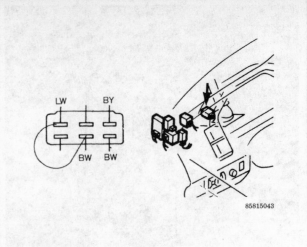

Fig. 9 Connect a jumper wire to the "LW" and "BW" (center) terminals — 1984-85 RX-7

3. Turn the ignition **OFF**. Install a pressure gauge, restrictor and length of fuel-resistant flexible hose into the line.
4. On 1984-85 RX-7s, unfasten the connector from the fuel pump cut relay and connect a jumper wire as shown.
5. Turn the ignition **ON**. When the pressure has stabilized, note the reading, then turn the ignition **OFF**. On 626s, the pressure should be 5.4 psi (37 kPa). On RX-7s, the pressure should be 3.7-4.7 psi (26-32 kPa) for 1979-82 models, or 2.84-3.55 psi (20-24 kPa) for 1983-85 models.
6. Detach the pressure gauge from the fuel line and position the line so fuel will be discharged into the container. Turn the ignition switch **ON** for one minute. The volume should be 0.9 qts. for 1983-85 RX-7, or 1.22 qts. for all other cars, including 1979-82 RX-7s.
7. If the pump fails one or both tests, replace it.

Carburetor

ADJUSTMENTS

Fast Idle

1978 GLC

➡**This adjustment can be performed only with the carburetor removed from the engine.**

1. Close the choke valve fully, and measure the clearance between the lower edge of the throttle and the throttle bore with a wire feeler gauge. The dimension is 0.05-0.06 in. (1.2-1.5mm).
2. If necessary adjust by bending the rod which connects the choke shaft and fast idle cam.

1979-85 GLC AND 1979-82 626

▸ **See Figures 10 and 11**

1. On the 1.4L GLC engine, remove the bimetal cover.
2. Using your finger close the choke valve fully.
3. Make sure the fast idle cam is on the 1st position (3rd position for the 1.5L GLC engine).

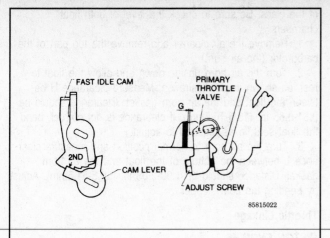

Fig. 10 Fast idle cam adjustment — 1.4L engine

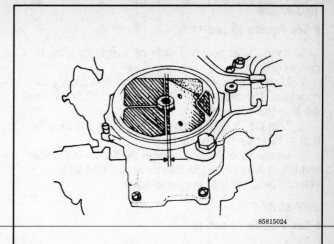

Fig. 12 Fast idle adjustment — RX-7

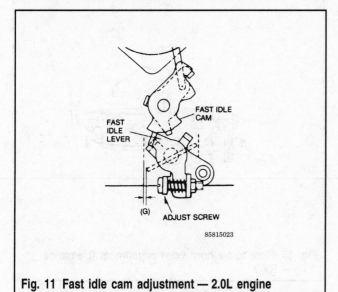

Fig. 11 Fast idle cam adjustment — 2.0L engine

4. The throttle valve opening (clearance G) should be:
- 1.4L engine: 0.06 in. (1.4mm) in 1979; 0.04 in. (1.04mm) in 1980
- 1.5L engine: 0.03 in. (0.66mm)
- 2.0L engine: 0.04 in. (1.04mm) in 1979; 0.02 in. (0.61mm) for 1980-82

5. Adjust by turning the adjustment screw.

➠Turn the adjustment screw clockwise to increase the clearance.

RX-7

◗ See Figure 12

➠To adjust the fast idle, it is necessary for the carburetor to be removed from the car.

1. Remove the carburetor from the vehicle.

2. Fully close the check valve.

3. Measure the clearance between the primary throttle valve and the wall of the throttle bore. Clearances are as follows:
- 1979 (California) and 1980 — 0.05-0.06 in. (1.30-1.50mm)
- 1979 (49 states, Canada) and 1981 — 0.035-0.043 in. (0.90-1.10mm)
- 1982 (All models) — 0.03-0.04 in. (0.8-1.0mm)
- 1983-85 (All models) — 0.04-0.05 in. (1.0-1.2mm)

4. If clearance is not correct, bend the fast idle rod until proper clearance is obtained.

Float and Fuel Level

GLC

1. Invert the air horn and lower the float slowly until the seat lip just touches the needle valve. Measure the clearance between the float and air horn gasket surface (remove the gasket). It should be 0.43 in. (11mm). Bend the float seat lip as necessary to correct the dimension.

2. With air horn still inverted, lift the float upward until the float stop contacts the air horn. Measure the clearance between the top of the needle valve and the float seat lip. It should be 0.05-0.07 in. (1.3-1.7mm). If not, bend the float stop until the clearance is correct.

1979-82 626

1. Invert the air horn and allow the float to lower by its own weight.

2. Measure the clearance between the float and the air horn bowl. The clearance should be 0.43 in. (11mm). Bend the float seat lip to adjust.

3. Turn the air horn to the normal position and allow the float to lower by its own weight.

4. Measure the distance between the bottom of the float and the air horn bowl. The distance should be 1.8 in. (46mm). Bend the float stopper to adjust.

1983-87 626

▶ **See Figures 13 and 14**

1. Invert the air horn and allow the float to lower by its own weight.

2. Measure the clearance between the float and the air horn bowl. The clearance should be 0.53 in. (13.5mm). Bend the float seat lip to adjust.

3. Turn the air horn to the normal position and allow the float to lower by its own weight.

4. Measure the distance between the bottom of the float and the air horn bowl. The distance should be 1.93 in. (49mm). Bend the float stopper to adjust.

1979-85 RX-7

▶ **See Figures 15 and 16**

The float bowl fuel level can be checked through the sight glass in the carburetor body. Fuel level should be in the center of the glass. Be sure to check the level of both float chambers.

1. Remove the air cleaner and remove the top part of the carburetor (the air horn).

2. Turn the air horn upside down and allow the float to rest, as shown in the illustration. Measure clearance **H** between the float and the air horn gasket. Clearance should be 0.61-0.65 in. (15.5-16.5mm). If clearance is not correct, bend the float seat lip as required to adjust.

3. Turn the air horn to normal position and measure clearance **L** between the bottom of the float and the air horn gasket. Distance should be 1.99-2.03 in. (50.5-51.5mm). Adjust by bending the float stopper.

Throttle Linkage

PISTON ENGINES

1. Check the accelerator pedal position; it should be lower than the brake pedal.

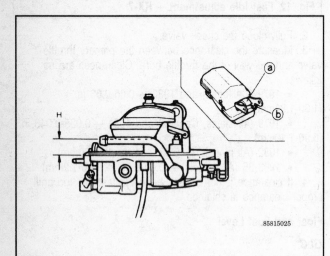

Fig. 13 Float to air horn bowl adjustment (clearance "H") — 1983-87 626

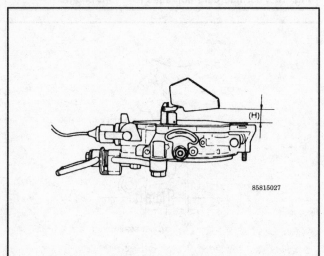

Fig. 15 Float to air horn bowl adjustment (clearance "H") — RX-7

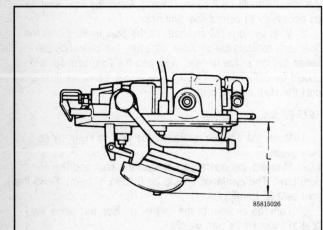

Fig. 14 Float bottom to air horn bowl adjustment (clearance "L") — 1983-87 626

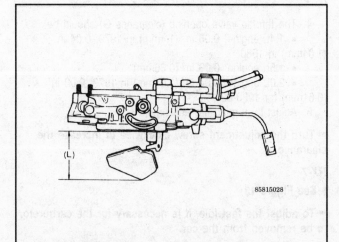

Fig. 16 Float bottom to air horn bowl adjustment (clearance "L") — RX-7

2. If necessary, adjust the nut on the linkage above the pedal to obtain the proper height.

3. Check the free-play of the cable at the carburetor. It should be 0.04-0.12 in. (1-3mm). If not, adjust by turning the clevis nut.

4. The accelerator pedal distance below the brake pedal should be 1.78-2.17 in. (45-55mm) for the 1983-85 GLC.

5. On vehicles other than 1983-85 GLCs, depress the accelerator pedal to the floor and confirm that the throttle valve is fully open. Adjust as necessary, by using the adjusting bolt or nut on the linkage above the accelerator pedal.

ROTARY ENGINES

▶ See Figure 17

To check the adjustment of the throttle linkage, remove the air cleaner and observe the position of the two primary throttle valves when the accelerator is fully depressed. The valves should be in a vertical (wide open) position. When checking the throttle linkage, also make sure that the accelerator cable does not bind or stick in its outer cable.

1. Measure accelerator pedal height. It should be 1.46-1.85 in. (37-47mm) lower than the brake pedal. If not, adjust it using nut **A** in the illustration.

2. Check the free-play of the cable at the carburetor by applying light finger pressure to the middle of the cable. It should be between 0.04-0.12 in. (1-3mm). If not, adjust it using nut **B** in the illustration.

3. Fully depress the accelerator pedal and check to see that the primary throttle valves are wide open. If not, adjust stopper bolt **C** in the illustration.

Semi-Automatic Choke

1979-80 RX-7

▶ See Figures 18, 19 and 20

You will need a vacuum source of more than 19.7 in. Hg. (500 mm Hg) to make this adjustment.

1. Disconnect the vacuum sensing tube from the vacuum diaphragm.

2. Pull the choke lever link out fully and hold it in this position.

3. Apply vacuum to the vacuum diaphragm.

4. Check the clearance between the top of the choke valve and the throttle bore body, with a wire gauge.

5. Measure the temperature of the bimetal spring, then compare it and the clearance with the specifications given in the accompanying charts.

6. If clearance is not within specifications, adjust it by turning the adjusting nut.

Primary Throttle Valve Initial Opening Angle

1979-80 RX-7

▶ See Figure 21

This adjustment should be performed when the throttle body, throttle lock lever and/or adjusting screw have been tampered with or changed.

1. Remove the carburetor from the engine.

2. Loosen the locknut and turn the adjusting screw to the left (counterclockwise).

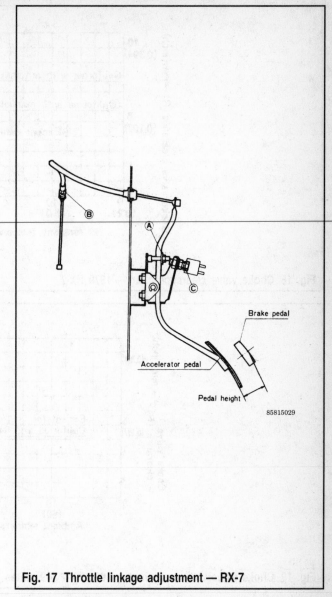

Fig. 17 Throttle linkage adjustment — RX-7

3. Close the throttle valve completely and gradually tighten the adjusting screw until it just touches the throttle lock lever. Tighten the screw an additional ⅛-⅜ of a turn, then tighten the locknut.

4. Measure the clearance and the angle of opening for the primary throttle valve when closed. Clearance should be 0.002 in. (0.05mm) and the angle of opening should be 1 degree. If not, reset the throttle opening with the adjusting screw.

Automatic Choke

GLC AND 626

▶ See Figure 22

1. Fully depress the accelerator pedal to make sure the choke valve closes properly.

2. Check for binding in the choke valve by pushing it with your finger.

3. Make sure that the bimetal cover index mark is set to the center choke housing index mark; adjust if necessary.

4. Check the automatic choke heater source wiring for proper connection.

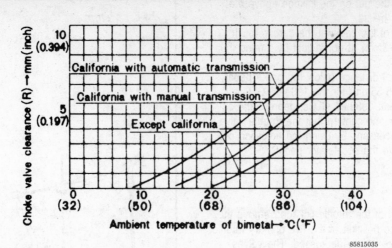

Fig. 18 Choke valve clearance chart — 1979 RX-7

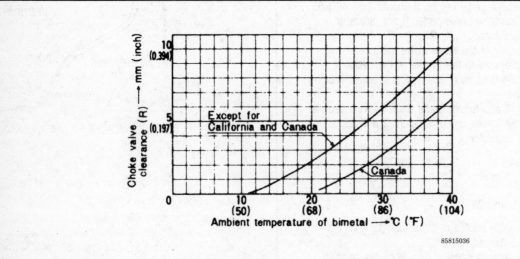

Fig. 19 Choke valve clearance chart — 1980 RX-7 (49 states and Canada)

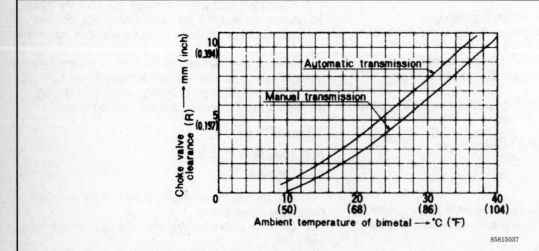

Fig. 20 Choke valve clearance chart — 1980 RX-7 (California)

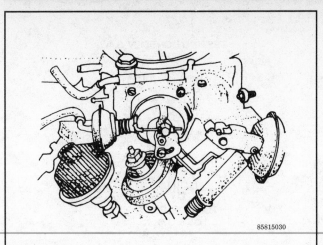

Fig. 21 Primary throttle valve adjustment — 1979-80 RX-7

5. Start the engine and let it idle.

6. After the engine warms up, check that the choke valve is fully opened.

7. If the valve does not open fully, and the automatic choke heater source wiring is normal, replace the bimetal cover.

RX-7

Perform this check with the engine "overnight" cold.

1. With a cold engine and the ignition switch in the **OFF** position, pull the choke knob out fully and make sure the knob returns automatically.

2. Connect a tachometer to the engine.

3. Start the engine and use the choke knob to set the idle speed to 2,000 rpm. Allow the engine to run at this speed and observe the temperature gauge. The choke knob should return back to its original position when the pointer on the gauge rises to just about the low mid-range portion of the scale.

Choke Unloader

GLC AND 626

1. Close the choke valve fully, then open the primary throttle valve fully.

2. Measure the choke valve clearance. The clearance should be 0.08-0.09 in. (2.00-2.40mm) for the GLC and 0.10-0.14 in. (2.65-3.45mm) for the 626.

3. Bend the tab to adjust.

Secondary Throttle Valve

GLC and 626

▶ See Figure 23

1. The secondary throttle valve starts to open when the primary throttle valve is open 49-51 degrees, and opens completely at the same time that the primary throttle valve is fully open.

2. Check the clearance between the primary throttle valve and the wall of the throttle bore when the secondary throttle valve starts to open.

3. The clearance should be:
  • Rear wheel drive GLC hatchback: 0.21-0.26 in. (5.40-6.60mm)
  • Rear wheel drive GLC wagon: 0.29-0.32 in. (7.30-8.25mm)
  • Front wheel drive GLC — except 1982: 0.21-0.26 in. (5.40-6.60mm); 1982: 0.29-0.33 in. (7.30-8.50mm)
  • 626: 0.24-0.28 in. (6.20-7.20mm)

4. To adjust the clearance, bend the connecting rod.

Throttle Sensor

RX-7

▶ See Figures 24, 25, 26 and 27

The throttle sensor should be checked, and adjusted as necessary, whenever the idle speed has been adjusted.

1. Warm up the engine to its normal operating temperature.

2. Connect a suitable tachometer to the engine.

3. Detach the brown connector, as illustrated.

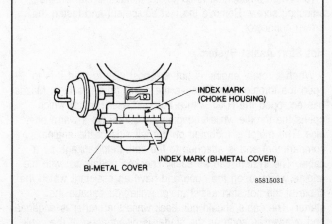

Fig. 22 The bimetal cover index mark should be set to the center mark on the choke housing — GLC and 626

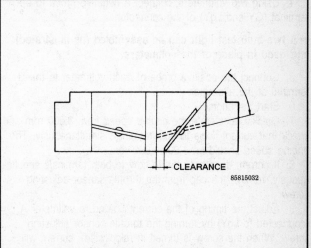

Fig. 23 Secondary throttle valve adjustment — GLC and 626

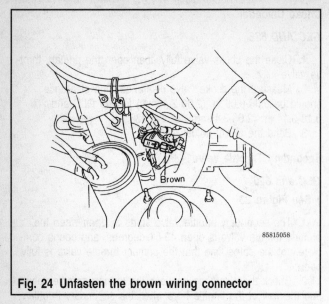

Fig. 24 Unfasten the brown wiring connector

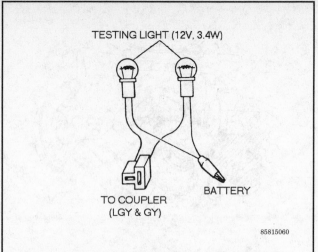

Fig. 26 A two-bulb test light can be assembled and used instead of the voltmeters

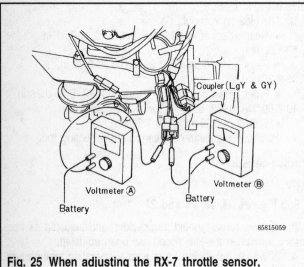

Fig. 25 When adjusting the RX-7 throttle sensor, connect a pair of voltmeters as illustrated

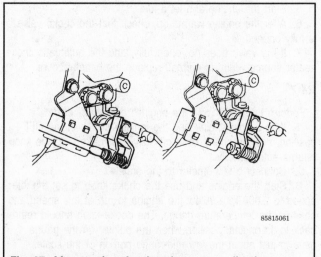

Fig. 27 After turning the throttle sensor adjusting screw, reposition its protective cap

4. Using two voltmeters, connect a negative probe to each terminal (GY and LgY) of the connector.

➡**A two-bulb test light can be assembled (as illustrated) and used in place of the voltmeters.**

5. Connect the positive probe of each voltmeter to the **B** terminal of the alternator.

6. Start the engine.

7. Quickly decelerate the engine speed from 3,000 rpm and check that current flows to both terminals simultaneously. The engine speed should be 1,000-1,200 rpm.

8. If current does not start to flow to both terminals simultaneously, remove the cap from the throttle sensor adjusting screw.

9. Adjust the timing of the current flowing to voltmeter A (connected to LgY) by turning the throttle sensor adjusting screw. When the screw is turned in (clockwise), current will begin to flow earlier; when the screw is turned out (counterclockwise), current will begin to flow later.

10. When adjustment is complete, install the cap on the adjusting screw. Remove the test equipment and fasten the brown connector.

Hot Start Assist System

When a rotary engine is hot, the best way to start it is to open the throttle fully. To save the driver from this task, Mazda has equipped the RX-7 with a hot start assist motor which opens the throttle while engaging the starter on a warm engine. The motor is mounted on the left side of the engine compartment and is attached to the carburetor linkage by a cable. The system can be easily checked as follows: with the engine warm, open the hood and have an assistant watch the cable at the hot start assist motor while you engage the starter. The cable should pull back while the starter is engaged and release as soon as the starter is disengaged. If the cable requires adjustment, proceed as follows:

1979-83 RX-7

▶ See Figure 28

1. Remove the lock spring on the cable bracket.
2. Slowly pull the outer cable until the hot start lever just touches the stopper lever. Check the clearance between the cable bracket and the locknut of the cable. Clearance should be 0.05 in. (1.25mm). Adjust the clearance by turning the locknut.
3. Install the lock spring.

1984-85 RX-7

▶ See Figure 29

1. Pull the start assist motor inner cable until the stopper lever makes contact with the start lever and check the free-play; it should be 0.04-0.08 in. (1-2mm).
2. If the free-play is not as specified, loosen the screw and adjust it.

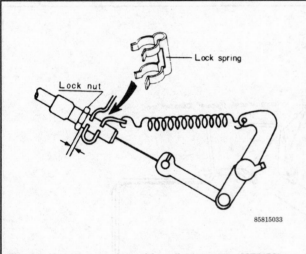

Fig. 28 Hot start assist cable adjustment — 1979-83 RX-7

REMOVAL & INSTALLATION

Piston Engines

1. Disconnect the negative battery cable.
2. Remove the air cleaner assembly.
3. Disconnect the accelerator cable. If equipped, disconnect the cruise control cable.
4. Disengage all wire connections, vacuum sensing tubes and fuel hoses.
5. Unfasten and remove the carburetor. Cover the opening to keep dirt out of the intake manifold.
6. Installation is the reverse of removal. Be sure to use a new carburetor gasket. Adjust the throttle linkage as previously described.

Rotary Engines

▶ See Figure 30

The RX-7 is equipped with a 4-barrel carburetor which is similar in design to the carburetors used on piston engines. Two primary barrels feed a constant mixture of air and fuel to the rotors. The primary barrels are supplemented by two vacuum operated secondary barrels during acceleration and high speed driving.

1. Disconnect the negative battery cable.
2. Remove the air cleaner assembly.
3. Label and unfasten all electrical connections from the carburetor and necessary surrounding components.
4. Label and disconnect all necessary vacuum hoses.
5. Disconnect the oil metering pump linkage at the carburetor.
6. Disconnect the hot start assist cable, along with the choke and accelerator cables, from the carburetor. Route the cables off to the side and out of the way.
7. Disconnect the air vent hose. On all except California vehicles, disconnect the sub-zero start assist fluid hose.
8. Disconnect the fuel return and the main fuel hoses. Plug the main fuel line to prevent leakage.
9. Disconnect the metering oil pump lines from the carburetor. Disconnect the air vent solenoid valve coupler.

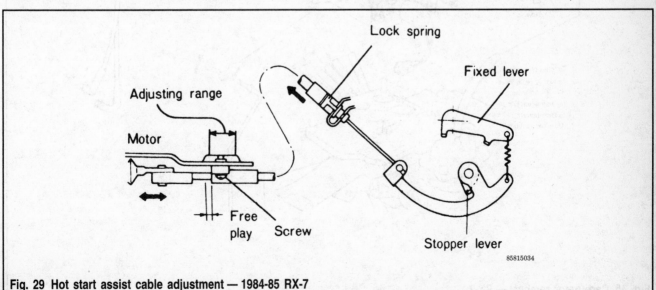

Fig. 29 Hot start assist cable adjustment — 1984-85 RX-7

10. Remove the carburetor attaching nuts and remove the carburetor. Cover the intake manifold with masking tape to prevent dirt and debris from entering the engine. Discard the old gasket; a new one should be used during assembly to assure proper vacuum seal.

To install:

11. Place the new gasket onto the intake manifold, then install the carburetor over the mounting studs and onto the gasket.

12. Install and tighten the attaching nuts.

13. Complete the remainder of the installation in reverse of the removal procedure. Adjust the throttle linkage as previously described.

14. Connect the negative battery cable.

OVERHAUL

Carburetor rebuilding kits usually include specific procedures and exploded views for order of assembly and disassembly, therefore, only general applicable rebuilding suggestions are provided here. Efficient carburetion depends greatly on careful cleaning and inspection during overhaul since dirt, gum, water, or varnish in or on the carburetor parts are often responsible for poor performance.

Overhaul your carburetor in a clean, dust-free area. Carefully disassemble the carburetor, referring often to the exploded views. Be sure to keep all similar/look-alike parts segregated during disassembly and cleaning to avoid accidental interchange during assembly. Make a note of all jet sizes.

When the carburetor is disassembled, wash all parts (except diaphragms, electric choke units, pump plunger, and any other plastic, leather, fiber, or rubber parts) in clean carburetor solvent. Do not leave parts in the solvent any longer than is necessary to sufficiently loosen the deposits. Excessive cleaning may remove the special finish from the float bowl and choke valve bodies, leaving these parts unfit for service. Rinse all parts in clean solvent and blow them dry with compressed air or allow them to air dry. Wipe clean all cork, plastic, leather, and fiber parts with a clean, lint-free cloth.

Blow out all passages and jets with compressed air; be sure that there are not restrictions or blockages. Never use wire or

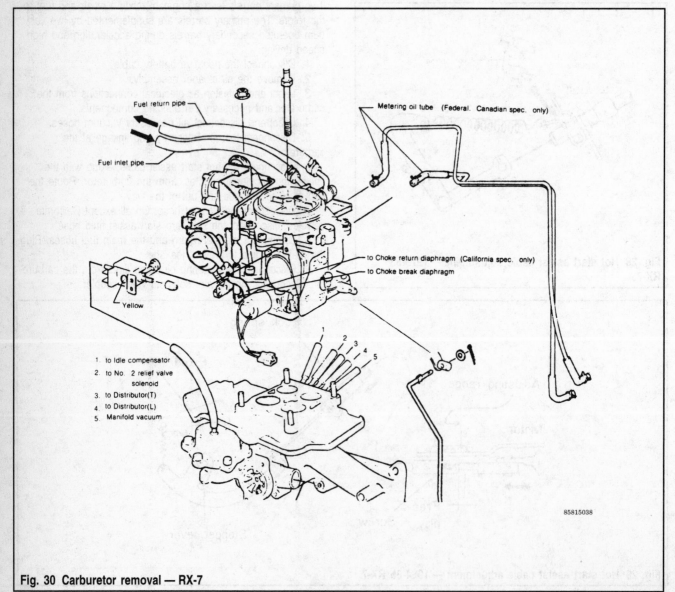

Fig. 30 Carburetor removal — RX-7

similar tools to clean jets and valves. Also, be sure to clean all jets and valves separately to avoid accidental interchange.

Check all parts for wear or damage; replace all defective parts. During inspection, pay careful attention to the following:

1. Check the float needle and seat for wear. If wear is found, replace the complete assembly.

2. Check the float hinge pin for wear and check the float(s) for dents or distortion. Replace the float if fuel has leaked into it.

3. Check the throttle and choke shaft bores for wear or an out-of-round condition. Damage or wear to the throttle arm, shaft, or shaft bore will often require replacement of the throttle body. These parts require a close tolerance of fit; wear may allow air leakage, which could affect starting and idling.

➡**Throttle shafts and bushings are not usually included in overhaul kits, but they can often be purchased separately.**

4. Inspect the idle mixture adjusting needles for burrs or grooves. Any such condition requires replacement of the needle, since you will not be able to obtain a satisfactory idle.

5. Test the accelerator pump check valves. They should pass air one way but not the other. Test for proper seating by blowing and sucking on the valve. Replace the valve if necessary. If the valve is satisfactory, wash the valve again to remove breath moisture.

6. Check the bowl cover for warped surfaces with a straightedge.

7. Closely inspect the valves and seats for wear and damage, replacing as necessary.

8. After the carburetor is assembled, check the choke valve for freedom of operation.

Carburetor overhaul kits are recommended for each overhaul. These kits contain all gaskets and new parts to replace those that deteriorate most rapidly. Failure to replace all parts supplied with the kit (especially gaskets) can result in poor performance later.

Some carburetor manufacturers supply overhaul kits of three basic types: minor repair; major repair; and gasket kits. Basically, they contain the following:

Minor Repair Kits:
- All gaskets
- Float needle valve
- Volume control screw
- All diaphragms
- Spring for the pump diaphragm

Major Repair Kits:
- All jets and gaskets
- All diaphragms
- Float needle valve
- Volume control screw
- Pump ball valve
- Main jet carrier
- Float
- Complete intermediate rod
- Intermediate pump lever
- Complete injector tube
- Some cover hold-down screws and washers

Gasket Kits
- All gaskets

After cleaning and checking all components, reassemble the carburetor, using new parts and referring to the exploded view. When reassembling, make sure that all screws and jets are tight in their seats, but do not overtighten, as the tips could be distorted. Tighten all screws gradually, in rotation. Do not tighten needle valves into their seats; uneven jetting will result. Always use new gaskets. Be sure to adjust the float level when reassembling.

323, 626 & MX-6 FUEL INJECTION SYSTEM

General Information

The injection system supplies fuel required for combustion at constant pressure to the injectors. Fuel is metered and injected into the intake manifold according to signals from the Engine Control Unit (ECU). In general, the system consists of the fuel pump, fuel filters, delivery pipe, pulsation damper, pressure regulator, fuel injectors, fuel pump switch and circuit opening relay. On the 1988-89 turbocharged 323 (with 4WD) and MX-6 (with 4WS), there is also a fuel transfer pump built into the system.

The fuel pump is mounted inside the fuel tank to reduce the operating noise that is characteristic of electric fuel pumps. The fuel injectors are supplied with direct battery voltage by the main relay, while the ECU varies ground for operation. Fuel injector connectors on these systems are color coded to distinguish turbocharged from non-turbocharged injectors.

Relieving Fuel System Pressure

The fuel system contains high pressure fuel, even when the engine is not running. Before disconnecting any fuel lines, release the fuel pressure to reduce the risk of injury or fire. Relieve the fuel pressure as follows:

1. Locate the fuel pump electrical connector. For more information, please refer to the fuel pump procedures located in this section.

2. Start the engine.

3. For vehicles other than 1988-89 626/MX-6s, disengage the fuel pump connector with the engine running. On 1988-89 626/MX-6s, disconnect the circuit opening relay (to the left of the clutch or brake pedal) with the engine running.

4. After the engine stalls from lack of fuel, turn the ignition switch OFF.

5. Use a shop rag to cover the fuel lines when disconnecting, and plug all fuel lines after they have been separated.

➡**Be sure to engage the fuel pump connector or circuit opening relay after testing and/or removal/installation procedures are completed.**

Electric Fuel Pump

→Before starting this procedure, purchase a new connecting hose which runs between the pump outlet and the top of the pump/gauge assembly. This would also be an ideal time to replace the in-tank filter.

REMOVAL & INSTALLATION

▶ See Figure 31

✳✳CAUTION

Before removing the fuel pump, release the fuel system pressure to prevent personal injury or fire hazard!

1. Remove the rear seat cushion.
2. Relieve the fuel system pressure, then disconnect the negative battery cable.
3. Unfasten the attaching screws and remove the service hole cover.
4. Note the hookup locations of the fuel hoses. Disconnect the fuel supply and return hoses, then plug them to prevent system contamination. Unfasten the attaching screws and remove the pump/gauge unit assembly and gasket. If the gasket appears worn, replace it.
5. Unscrew and detach the electrical connector(s) for the pump from the assembly.
6. Loosen the screw at the clamp which holds the pump in position. Loosen the clamps and remove the hose connecting the outlet of the pump to the assembly. Remove the pump from the vehicle.

To install:

7. Install the pump into its mounting bracket and connect the fuel outlet hose to the pump. Secure the outlet hose with the clamps.
8. Support the pump by hand and install the retaining screw that holds the pump in place in the bracket. Attach the electrical connector(s) to the pump. Install the pump/gauge assembly and secure with the attaching screws.
9. Connect the fuel inlet and outlet lines to their respective connections. Physically check the fuel lines and the pump wiring to make sure that they are tight and in place. Use tie straps as required to secure the fuel hoses and the wiring.
10. Install the fuel pump cover and attach the connector to it. Install the rear seat cushion.
11. Connect the negative battery cable.

TESTING

1. Disconnect the negative battery cable.

✳✳CAUTION

Make sure the engine is cold. Otherwise, escaping fuel could start a fire!

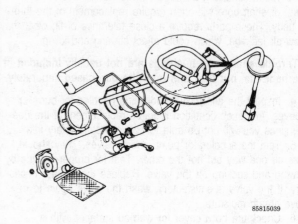

85815039

Fig. 31 Exploded view of fuel pump assembly — 323, 626 and MX-6

2. Cover the connection with a rag because the fuel is under pressure, then disconnect the fuel line at the discharge side of the pump. Connect a gauge directly to the discharge port.
3. Reconnect the battery.
4. On the 626, detach the fuel pump check connector, which is located on the firewall, and jumper the terminals. On 1988-89 626s and MX-6s, the connector is yellow and is located on the firewall near the washer/wiper motor.
5. On the 323, turn the ignition **ON**, then jumper the GW and B terminals of the fuel pump check connector. On 323s, the fuel pump check connector is located between the battery and the washer wiper pump.
6. Observe the reading on the pressure gauge. It should be 64-85 psi (441-586 kPa). If the wiring to the pump and its relay are good, replace the fuel pump.

Fuel Transfer Pump

REMOVAL & INSTALLATION

1988-89 323 Turbo w/4WD; 1988-89 626 and MX-6 w/4WS

The transfer pump is an impeller type pump. On 626s and MX-6s, the pump is mounted in the fuel tank next to the main fuel pump. On 323s, the pump is mounted on a bracket on the underside of the fuel tank. The transfer pump generates an output pressure of 0.4-5.7 psi (3-39 kPa).

1. Disconnect the negative battery cable.
2. On 323s, work from underneath the vehicle and separate the transfer pump from the mounting bracket.
3. On 626s and MX-6s, remove the fuel tank from the vehicle, then remove the cover plate attaching screws and withdraw the pump from the fuel tank.
4. Detach the fuel hoses and electrical connector from the pump.

To install:

5. Attach the hoses and connectors to the pump.
6. On 323s, connect the pump to the mounting bracket.
7. On 626s and MX-6s, position the transfer pump in the fuel tank. Use a new cover plate gasket and install the cover plate attaching screws. Properly install the fuel tank.
8. Connect the negative battery cable.

Throttle Body

REMOVAL & INSTALLATION

The throttle body is part of the vehicle's air intake system. It is used to control the amount of air supplied to the engine for combustion.

The throttle body is calibrated at the factory. If there are problems with the setting of the throttle adjusting screw or with the action, air tightness, or operation of the throttle, replace the assembly or refer the repair to a qualified shop.

323 Models

1. Disconnect the negative battery cable.
2. Disconnect the accelerator cable from the throttle linkage.
3. Unclamp and disconnect the air intake tube from the throttle body.
4. Label, then disconnect the vacuum hoses at the throttle body.
5. Disconnect the PCV and evaporative control system hoses.
6. Detach the throttle position sensor connector.
7. Unfasten the nuts from the mounting studs for the throttle body, and remove it from the air intake surge tank or

dynamic chamber (1988-89). Make sure to remove the gasket(s) and spacer.

To install:

8. Using new gasket(s), install the throttle body onto the surge tank or dynamic chamber. Install and tighten the mounting nuts.
9. Attach the throttle sensor connector.
10. Connect the PCV and evaporative hoses to the throttle body.
11. Connect the air hose and tighten the clamps.
12. Connect the accelerator cable and check the cable deflection. Cable deflection should be 0.04-0.10 in. (1.0-2.5mm). Adjust the throttle sensor as described later in this section.
13. Connect the negative battery cable.

1986-87 626

▶ **See Figure 32**

1. Disconnect the negative battery cable.
2. Drain engine coolant out of the bottom of the radiator (about 2.5 qts.).
3. On 1986-87 turbocharged models, unfasten the clamp on the side of the air funnel, then remove the spark plug wire bracket and position it off to the side.
4. Unclamp and remove the air intake hose or funnel.
5. Disconnect the accelerator cable at the actuating cam on the throttle body. Detach the throttle sensor connector by pulling downward on the locking tab located underneath.
6. On 1986-87 turbocharged models, unfasten the connector from the No. 3 injector.
7. Label, then disconnect the vacuum hoses from the upper ports in the throttle body. Note the connections, then detach the water hoses and air bypass hose.
8. Remove the four attaching nuts from the studs and pull the throttle body off the air surge tank or dynamic chamber (1988-89). On 1986-87 turbocharged models, disconnect the vacuum hose from the lower port of the throttle body to free the throttle body. Cover the surge tank or dynamic chamber opening with masking tape to prevent anything from falling into the engine.

To install:

9. Install the throttle body onto the air surge tank with the attaching nuts and a new gasket. On turbo models, connect the vacuum hose to the lower port first. Tighten the attaching nuts in a crisscross pattern.
10. Connect the air bypass, water and vacuum hoses to their respective upper port connections on the throttle body. On 1986-87 turbocharged models, fasten the No. 3 injector connector.
11. Fasten the throttle sensor connector and the accelerator cable. Connect the air intake hose or air funnel to the throttle body and tighten the hose clamps. On turbo models, install the spark plug wire bracket and hose clamp to the side of the air funnel.
12. Connect the negative battery cable and refill the cooling system.
13. Adjust the throttle position sensor as described later in this section and check/adjust the idle speed.

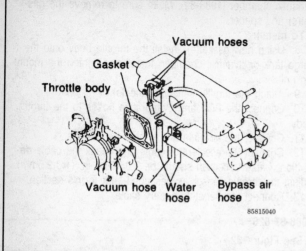

Fig. 32 Throttle body removal and installation — 1986-87 626

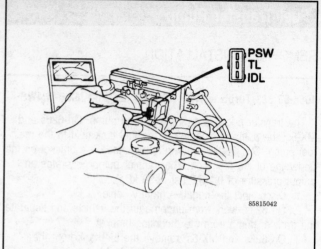

Fig. 33 Connect an ohmmeter between terminals "TL" and "IDL" to adjust the throttle position sensor — 323

Throttle Position Sensor

ADJUSTMENT

323 Models
▶ **See Figure 33**

1. Install a 0.02 in. (0.5mm) thick gauge between the throttle lever and adjusting screw. Connect an ohmmeter between the **IDL** and **TL** terminals of the connector. There should be continuity.

2. Replace the 0.02 in. (0.5mm) gauge with a 0.03 in. (0.7mm) gauge. Recheck between the same terminals with the ohmmeter. There should not be continuity.

3. If continuity does not disappear with the installation of the thicker gauge or is not there with the thinner gauge installed, adjust the throttle adjusting screw so that the throttle sensor passes the test. Reattach the throttle sensor electrical connector.

1986-87 626
▶ **See Figure 34**

1. Install a 0.015 in. (0.4mm) thick gauge between the throttle lever and adjusting screw. Connect an ohmmeter between the **B** and **D** terminals of the connector. There should be continuity.

2. Replace the 0.015 in. (0.4mm) gauge with a 0.022 in. (0.55mm) gauge. Recheck between the same terminals with the ohmmeter. There should not be continuity.

3. If continuity does not disappear with the installation of the thicker gauge, or is not present with the thinner gauge installed, turn the throttle adjusting screw so that the throttle sensor passes the test. Reattach the throttle sensor electrical connector.

1988-89 626 and MX-6

Throttle sensor adjustment on the 1988-89 626 and MX-6 requires the use of a special test harness. Adjustment of the

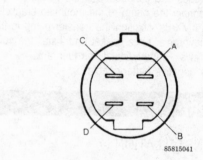

Fig. 34 Connect an ohmmeter between terminals "B" and "D" to adjust the throttle position sensor — 1986-87 626

throttle sensor on these models should be performed by a qualified technician.

Fuel Injectors

REMOVAL & INSTALLATION

323 Models

1. Properly relieve the fuel system pressure, then allow the engine to cool and disconnect the negative battery cable.

2. Disconnect the accelerator cable from the throttle linkage.

3. Unclamp and disconnect the air intake tube from the throttle body.

4. Label, then disconnect the vacuum hoses at the throttle body.

5. Disconnect the PCV and evaporative control system hoses.

6. Detach the throttle position sensor connector.

7. In order to obtain the necessary clearance on vehicles through 1987, remove the attaching nuts from the underside of the air intake surge tank (upper portion of the intake manifold), then remove it and the gasket.

8. For 1988-89 models, unfasten the nuts from the mounting studs for the throttle body, and remove it from the dynamic chamber. Make sure to remove the gasket(s) and spacer.

9. Detach the injector electrical connectors and cover the high pressure fuel connections with a rag. Unfasten the banjo connector from the top of the fuel distribution pipe, and the high pressure fuel line from the bottom of the fuel pressure regulator.

10. Remove the two mounting bolts from the underside of the fuel distribution pipe. Gently pull the assembly away from the intake manifold so the injectors and seals slide out of their recesses in the manifold. Pull the injectors and seals out of the distribution pipe.

11. Installation is the reverse of the removal procedure. Be sure to coat the injector O-rings with clean engine oil prior to installation. When inserting the injectors into the distribution pipe, make sure that they are installed straight and not cocked, or fuel leakage will result. Torque the delivery pipe bolts to 14-19 ft. lbs. (19-26 Nm). Reattach all connectors securely. Jumper the fuel pump connector, as described under the fuel pump removal and installation procedure, then check for injector leaks. Make repairs as necessary, before operating the engine.

1986-87 626

1. Properly relieve the fuel system pressure, then allow the engine to cool and disconnect the negative battery cable.

2. Cover the high pressure fuel connections with a rag. Detach the outlet connection from the end of the distribution pipe, and the inlet connection from the bottom of the pressure regulator. Disconnect the vacuum line from the top of the pressure regulator.

3. Unfasten the injector electrical connectors and route them off to the side.

4. Remove the two bolts that fasten the fuel distribution pipe to the intake manifold. Gently pull the assembly away from the intake manifold so the injectors and seals slide out of their recesses in the manifold. Pull the injectors and seals out of the distribution pipe.

5. Installation is the reverse of removal. Use new injector seals at both ends. Reattach all connectors securely. Jumper the fuel pump connector, as described under the fuel pump removal and installation procedure, and check for injector leaks. Make repairs as necessary, before operating the engine.

1988-89 626 and MX-6

1. Properly relieve the fuel system pressure and disconnect the negative battery cable.

2. Unbolt and remove the injector wiring harness bracket.

3. On non-turbo models, unbolt and remove the EGR modulator valve bracket.

4. Remove the vacuum pipe mounting bolts and disconnect the vacuum pipe from the side of the rocker arm cover.

5. Loosen the hose clamp and disconnect the flexible air hose from the throttle body.

6. Unfasten the four bolts that attach the engine hanger bracket to the block and remove the bracket.

7. Unfasten the dynamic chamber mounting bolts and nuts, then raise the unit off the block and remove it from the engine. Cover the opening with a clean rag or masking tape to prevent anything from falling into the engine.

8. Remove the two mounting clamps that secure the fuel return pipe to the intake manifold. Detach the injector connectors. Gently pull the delivery pipe with pressure regulator and pulsation damper away from the intake manifold so the injectors and seals slide out of their recesses in the manifold. Pull the injectors, grommets and insulators out of the distribution pipe.

9. Installation is essentially the reverse of removal. Use new injector seals at both ends. Coat the injector seals with clean engine oil prior to installation. When inserting the injectors into the distribution pipe, make sure that they are installed straight and not cocked or fuel leakage will result. Torque the delivery pipe, dynamic chamber and engine hanger bolts to 14-19 ft. lbs. (19-26 Nm). Reattach all connectors securely. Jumper the fuel pump connector, as described under the fuel pump removal and installation procedure, and check for injector leaks. Make repairs as necessary, before operating the engine.

TESTING

Injector Continuity

You can test injectors electrically either on or off the car. Unfasten the electrical connector and attach an ohmmeter between the two prongs of the electrical connector. The injectors used in the 323 should have a resistance of 1.5-3 ohms; those used in the 626 and MX-6 should have a resistance of 12-16 ohms.

Injector Fuel Leak

1. Relieve the fuel pressure from the fuel system.

2. Remove the delivery pipe and fuel injectors. Affix the injectors to the distribution pipe with some wire. On 323, connect the delivery pipe and injector assembly between the fuel filter and the return pipe and secure with wire as previously mentioned.

➡ **Affix the injectors firmly to the distribution pipe so no movement of the injectors is possible.**

3. Turn the ignition switch to the **ON** position. Use a jumper wire and connect the terminals of the fuel pump check connector. Make sure that the fuel does not leak from the injector nozzles.

4. After approximately five minutes, a very small (slight) amount of fuel leakage from the injectors is acceptable. If this leakage exceeds more than a few drops, replace the injector.

5. If the injector leaks fuel at a fast rate, replace the injector. If the injectors do not leak, remove all test equipment and install the components in the reverse order of their removal.

929 FUEL INJECTION SYSTEM

General Information

The injection system supplies fuel required for combustion at constant pressure to the injectors. Fuel is metered and injected into the intake manifold according to signals from the Engine Control Unit (ECU). In general, the system consists of the fuel pump, fuel filters, delivery pipe, pulsation damper, pressure regulator, fuel injectors, fuel pump switch and circuit opening relay.

The fuel pump is mounted inside the fuel tank to reduce the operating noise that is characteristic of electric fuel pumps. The fuel injectors are supplied with direct battery voltage by the main relay, while the ECU varies ground for operation. The fuel injector connectors are color coded to distinguish turbocharged from non-turbocharged injectors.

Relieving Fuel System Pressure

The fuel in the fuel system remains under high pressure even when the engine is not running. Before disconnecting any fuel lines, release the fuel pressure to reduce the risk of injury or fire. Relieve the fuel pressure as follows:

1. Start the engine.
2. Disengage the wiring connector from the circuit opening relay (beneath the instrument panel) with the engine running.
3. After the engine stalls from lack of fuel, turn the ignition switch **OFF**.
4. Reconnect the circuit opening relay.
5. Position a shop rag to cover the fuel lines before loosening the fittings. Be sure to plug all fuel lines after they have been disconnected.

Electric Fuel Pump

➡Purchase a new connecting hose which runs between the pump outlet and the top of the pump/gauge assembly. This would also be an ideal time to replace the in-tank filter.

REMOVAL & INSTALLATION

❈❈CAUTION

Before removing the fuel pump, release the fuel system pressure to prevent personal injury or fire hazard!

1. Properly relieve the fuel system pressure, then disconnect the negative battery cable.
2. Lift up the rear floor mat. Unfasten the attaching screws and remove the fuel pump cover.
3. Disconnect the fuel pump switch connector.
4. Note the hookup locations of the fuel hoses. Disconnect the fuel supply and return hoses and plug them.
5. Unfasten the attaching screws, then remove the pump/gauge unit assembly and gasket. If the gasket appears worn, replace it.

6. Loosen the screw at the clamp which holds the pump in position. Loosen the clamps and remove the hose connecting the outlet of the pump to the assembly. Remove the pump.
   To install:
7. Install the pump into its mounting bracket and connect the fuel outlet hose to the pump. Secure the outlet hose with the clamps.
8. Support the pump by hand and install the retaining screw that holds the pump in place in the bracket.
9. Install the pump/gauge assembly and secure with the attaching screws.
10. Attach the fuel inlet and outlet lines to their respective connections. Physically check the fuel lines and the pump wiring to make sure that they are tight and in place. Use tie straps as required to secure the fuel hoses and the wiring.
11. Attach the fuel pump switch electrical connector.
12. Install the fuel pump cover, then position the rear floor mat.
13. Connect the negative battery cable.

TESTING

Operation Test
▶ See Figure 35

1. Connect a jumper wire to the yellow test connector, as illustrated.
2. Loosen the fuel filler cap.
3. Turn the ignition switch **ON**.
4. Listen for the operational sound of the fuel pump.
5. Tighten the fuel filler cap.
6. If no sound is heard, check the voltage at the fuel pump connector (LO) wire and a ground. Normal voltage is approximately 12 volts DC (battery voltage).
7. If the voltage is normal and the pump will not operate, it should be replaced.
8. Disconnect the jumper wire, and turn the ignition switch **OFF**.

Volume Test
▶ See Figure 35

1. Relieve the fuel system pressure, as described earlier in this section.
2. Disconnect the fuel return hose from the fuel return pipe. Position an approved gasoline container with a capacity of at least 1½ pts. near the return hose.
3. Connect a jumper wire to the yellow test connector, as illustrated.
4. Direct the fuel hose into the container, then turn the ignition switch **ON** for 10 seconds.
5. Check the quantity of the collected fuel; the normal feeding capacity is approximately 190-200cc in 10 seconds.
6. If the collected quantity is not within specifications, check the fuel filter and fuel line.
7. Disconnect the jumper wire, and turn the ignition switch **OFF**.

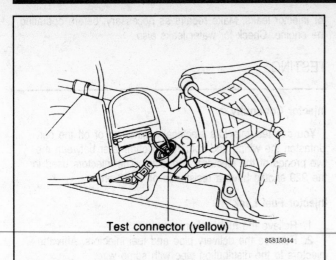

Fig. 35 Fuel pump test connector — 929

Throttle Body

REMOVAL & INSTALLATION

The throttle body is part of the vehicle's air intake system. It regulates the amount of air supplied to the engine for combustion.

The throttle body is calibrated at the factory. If there are problems with the adjustment of the throttle adjusting screw or with the action, air tightness, or operation of the throttle, replace the assembly or refer the repair to a qualified shop.

1. Disconnect the negative battery cable.
2. Disconnect the accelerator cable from the throttle linkage.
3. Unclamp and disconnect the air intake tube from the throttle body.
4. Label, then disconnect the vacuum hoses at the throttle body. Disconnect the PCV and evaporative control system hoses.
5. Unfasten the connector and water hoses from the Bypass Air Control (BAC) which is located on the side of the throttle body. Unbolt and remove the valve.
6. Detach the throttle position sensor connector. Then, unfasten the nuts from the mounting studs for the throttle body, and remove it from the air intake surge tank or dynamic chamber. Make sure to remove the gasket(s) and spacer.

To install:

7. Using new gasket(s), install the throttle body onto the surge tank or dynamic chamber. Install and tighten the mounting nuts. Fasten the throttle sensor connector.
8. Attach the BAC valve to the throttle body, then fasten the water hoses and electrical connector.
9. Connect the PCV and evaporative hoses to the throttle body.
10. Connect the air hose and tighten the clamps.

11. Connect the accelerator cable and check the cable deflection; it should be 0.04-0.10 in. (1.0-2.5mm). Adjust the throttle sensor as described later in this section.
12. Connect the negative battery cable, then check for water leaks in the area of the BAC valve water hoses.

Throttle Position Sensor

ADJUSTMENT

▶ **See Figure 36**

1. Unfasten the throttle sensor connector, then connect an ohmmeter across the **A** and **D** terminals. The resistance should read 3.5-6.5 ohms.
2. Connect the ohmmeter across the **B** and **D** terminals. Gradually open and close the throttle valve by hand while measuring the resistance. When fully closed, the resistance should be approximately 1k ohms. When fully open the resistance should read 3.5-6.5k ohms.
3. If the resistance readings are not as specified, check the throttle sensor idle switch adjustment.

➡**To adjust the throttle sensor idle switch, you will need a set of flat blade feeler gauges.**

4. Connect an ohmmeter across the **C** and **D** terminals, then check for continuity across the terminals with a feeler gauge inserted between the throttle stopper screw and throttle valve lever. With a 0.02 in. (0.5mm) feeler gauge inserted, there should be continuity. With a 0.03 in. (0.7mm) feeler gauge, there should be no continuity.
5. If the switch is not adjusted properly, loosen the throttle sensor retaining screws and move the sensor as required until the continuity readings are as specified. After the adjustment, seal the screws with white paint to retain the setting.

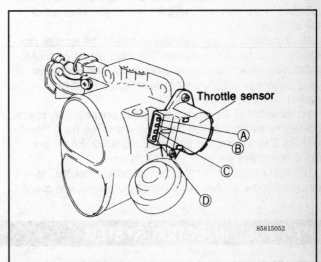

Fig. 36 Throttle position sensor terminal locations — 929

Fuel Injectors

REMOVAL & INSTALLATION

▶ See Figure 37

1. Release the fuel system pressure and disconnect the negative battery cable.

2. Disconnect the air, vacuum and water hoses from the throttle body and air funnel. Plug the water hoses to prevent leakage.

3. Loosen the hose clamps and remove the air funnel.

4. Disconnect the Bypass Air Control (BAC) valve connector and water hoses, then remove the valve.

5. Detach the throttle sensor connector and the accelerator cable. Remove the throttle body and gasket. Disconnect all vacuum hoses, EGR pipe, EGR position sensor connector, water hose and ground wire.

6. Remove the wiring harness bracket. Disconnect the air intake pipe from the dynamic chamber with the gasket. Mark the extension manifolds RIGHT and LEFT for assembly reference, as they are not interchangeable. Remove the six extension manifolds with their gaskets from the dynamic chamber.

7. Disconnect the intake air thermo sensor connector, vacuum hoses and ground connectors. Remove the attaching nuts and lift the dynamic chamber straight up from the intake manifold studs.

8. Detach the injector electrical connectors and the fuel hoses from the pressure regulator, then cover the high pressure fuel connections with a rag. Unfasten the banjo connector from the top of the fuel distribution pipe, and the high pressure fuel line from the bottom of the fuel pressure regulator. Repeat this procedure for the fuel rail on the other side.

9. Remove the two mounting bolts from the underside of the fuel distribution pipe. Gently pull the assembly away from the intake manifold so the injectors and seals slide out of their recesses in the manifold. Pull the injectors and seals out of the distribution pipe.

10. Installation is essentially the reverse of the removal procedure. Coat the injector O-rings with clean engine oil prior to installation. When inserting the injectors into the distribution pipe, make sure that they are installed straight and not cocked, or fuel leakage will result.

11. Reattach all the injector connectors securely. The injector connectors are color coded black and white. The No. 1, No. 3 and No. 5 connectors are black, and the No. 2, No. 4. and No. 6 connectors are white (see illustration).

12. After installation, jumper the fuel pump connector, as described under the fuel pump testing procedures, and check for injector leaks. Make repairs as necessary, before operating the engine. Check for water leaks also.

TESTING

Injector Continuity

You can test injectors electrically either on or off the car. Unfasten the wiring and connect an ohmmeter between the two prongs of the electrical connector. The injectors used in the 929 should have a resistance of 12-16 ohms.

Injector Fuel Leak

1. Relieve the fuel system pressure.

2. Remove the delivery pipe and fuel injectors. Affix the injectors to the distribution pipe with some wire.

➡ Affix the injectors firmly to the distribution pipe so no movement of the injectors is possible.

3. Turn the ignition switch to the ON position. Use a jumper wire and connect the terminals of the fuel pump check connector. Make sure that the fuel does not leak from the injector nozzles.

4. After approximately five minutes, a very small (slight) amount of fuel leakage from the injectors is acceptable. If this leakage exceeds more than a few drops, replace the injector. After one minute, a drop of leakage is acceptable.

5. If the injector leaks fuel at a fast rate, replace the injector. If the injectors do not leak, remove all test equipment and install the components in the reverse order of their removal.

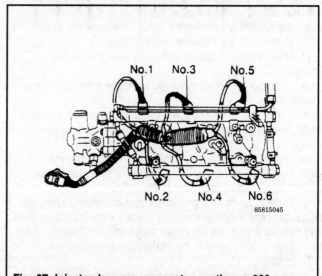

Fig. 37 Injector harness connector routing — 929

RX-7 FUEL INJECTION SYSTEM

General Information

The Mazda Electronic Gasoline Injection (EGI) system is a computer controlled, port-type fuel injection system used on 1984-89 RX-7 models equipped with the 13B rotary engine. Fuel is metered to the engine by two solenoid-type injectors that open and close in response to signals from the Electronic Control Unit (ECU). By varying the amount of time the injectors remain open, the ECU precisely controls the fuel mixture according to data on engine operating conditions provided by various engine sensors.

The EGI fuel supply system consists of the fuel tank and lines, fuel filter, electric fuel pump, pulsation damper, fuel pressure regulator, fuel delivery manifold and two solenoid-type fuel injectors. A check and cut valve releases excessive pressure or vacuum in the fuel tank to the atmosphere and prevents the loss of fuel if the vehicle overturns. The fuel system is constantly under pressure, which is regulated to 37 psi (255 kPa).

The fuel pump provides more fuel than the injection system needs for normal operation, with excess fuel being returned to the tank via the fuel return line. The fuel pump is a roller cell type, which is capable of providing 49-71 psi (338-490 kPa) of pressure as measured at the pump outlet.

On 1984-85 models, the pump is located near the fuel tank, under a protective shield on the underbody of the vehicle. The pump connector is located under the storage compartment located behind the driver's seat. On 1986-89 models, the pump is mounted inside the fuel tank.

The pressure regulator and pulsation damper are mounted on the fuel delivery manifold, located under the dynamic chamber just above the injectors. The operation of the fuel delivery system is controlled through the main relay mounted in the engine compartment next to the master cylinder, with power feeding through a fusible link located near the battery.

Relieving Fuel System Pressure

The fuel system remains under high pressure even when the engine is not running. Before disconnecting any fuel lines, release the fuel pressure to reduce the risk of injury or fire. Relieve the fuel pressure as follows:

1. Locate the fuel pump connector. For more information, refer to the fuel pump removal procedures found later in this section.
2. Start the engine.
3. Disengage the fuel pump connector with the engine running.
4. After the engine stalls from lack of fuel, turn the ignition switch **OFF**.
5. Use a shop rag to cover the fuel lines when disconnecting, and plug all fuel lines after they have been disconnected.

Electric Fuel Pump

REMOVAL & INSTALLATION

❋❋CAUTION

The fuel system is under pressure even when the fuel pump is not in operation. Always relieve the fuel system pressure before servicing the system. Also, wrap a clean cloth around the fuel connection when loosening to catch any fuel spray from residual pressure and take precautions to avoid the risk of fire.

1984-85 RX-7

1. Remove the storage compartment located behind the driver's seat and detach the fuel pump connector. Properly relieve the fuel system pressure.
2. Raise the vehicle and support it safely.
3. Remove the pump bracket clamp bolt.

4. Disconnect the inlet and outlet hoses from the fuel pump and plug the lines. Make a note of where each hose connects.
5. Remove the fuel pump from its bracket.

To install:

6. Position the fuel pump in its bracket. Unplug, then connect the fuel lines to their proper fittings.
7. Install the pump bracket clamp bolt, then lower the vehicle.
8. Attach the fuel pump connector and install the storage compartment.

1986-89 RX-7

▶ See Figure 38

1. Lift up the rear mat.
2. Unfasten and remove the fuel pump cover.
3. Relieve the fuel system pressure by running the engine and disengaging the fuel pump electrical connector.
4. Disconnect and plug the main fuel and fuel return hoses. Make a note of where each hose connects.
5. Unfasten the retaining screws and remove the fuel pump from the tank.

To install:

6. Install the fuel pump into the fuel tank and fasten the retaining screws.
7. Connect the main fuel hose (labeled **A** in the illustration) to the **A** fitting on the pump. Do the same for the **B** hose. Secure the hoses with the hose clips and make sure they are tight.
8. Attach the pump's electrical connector.
9. Install the fuel pump cover and reposition the rear mat.

TESTING

▶ See Figure 39

1. Relieve the fuel system pressure, as previously described.
2. Disconnect the negative battery cable.
3. Disconnect the main fuel hose from the main fuel line.
4. Connect a suitable fuel pressure gauge.

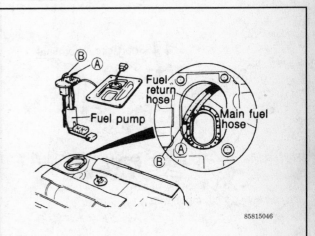

85815046

Fig. 38 The fuel pump is mounted inside the fuel tank, beneath a cover plate — 1986-89 RX-7

5. Connect the negative battery cable.

6. Connect the terminals of the yellow check connector with a jumper wire (see illustration). Turn the ignition switch **ON** to operate the fuel pump.

7. Check that the fuel pressure is within the following specifications:

Fuel Pump Pressure:
- 1984-85 — 49.8-71.1 psi (343-490 kPa)
- 1986-89 except Turbo — 64-85.3 psi (441-588 kPa)
- 1986-89 Turbo — 49.8-71.1 psi (343-490 kPa)

Throttle Body

REMOVAL & INSTALLATION

The throttle body is part of the vehicle's air intake system. It regulates the amount of air supplied to the engine for combustion.

The throttle body is calibrated at the factory. If there are problems with the adjustment of the throttle adjusting screw or with the action, air tightness, or operation of the throttle, replace the assembly or refer the repair to a qualified shop.

Non-Turbo

1. Disconnect the negative battery cable.

2. Detach the accelerator cable from the throttle linkage. Disconnect the cruise control cable (if so equipped).

3. Disconnect the air funnel. Disconnect the hoses and tubes from the throttle body.

4. Detach the throttle position sensor connector. Disconnect the metering oil pump connecting rod from the throttle actuating lever.

5. Unfasten the throttle body retaining screws and remove the throttle body assembly from the dynamic chamber.

To install:

6. Position the throttle body on the dynamic chamber with a new gasket. Install and tighten the attaching screws.

7. Connect the metering oil pump connecting rod to the throttle actuating lever. Connect the throttle position sensor.

8. Connect the air and vacuum hoses. Connect the air funnel and tighten the hose clamps.

9. Connect the cruise control (if applicable) and accelerator cables. Check and adjust the accelerator cable deflection.

10. Connect the negative battery cable.

Turbo

In order to remove the throttle body, the dynamic chamber assembly must be removed. Removal of the dynamic chamber is described in Section 3.

Throttle Position Sensor

INSPECTION

▶ **See Figure 40**

1. Unfasten the throttle sensor connector. Connect a suitable ohmmeter to the sensor as shown in the illustration.

2. Open the throttle valve and observe the resistance readings. Normal readings are as follows:

Throttle opening A to B:
- Idle position: approximately 1k ohms
- Full open position: approximately 4-6k ohms

Throttle opening A to C:
- Idle position: approximately 4-6k ohms
- Full open position: approximately 4-6k ohms

3. Reattach the connector. If the resistance readings are not as specified, adjust the throttle sensor.

ADJUSTMENT

▶ **See Figures 41 and 42**

1. Warm up the engine to operating temperature, then shut it **OFF**. Unfasten the connector from the throttle position sensor. Connect the throttle position sensor tester (Part No. 49-F018-001 or equivalent) to the green check connector. Turn

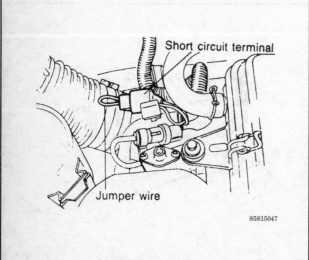

Fig. 39 Fuel pump test connector location on RX-7

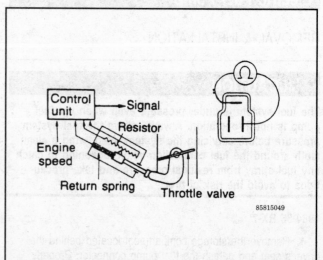

Fig. 40 Checking the RX-7's throttle sensor resistance with an ohmmeter

the ignition switch **ON** and check whether one of the tester lamps illuminates.

➡**If such a tester is not available, you can substitute two voltmeters as illustrated. Instead of illumination, look for needle sweeps.**

2. If both lamps illuminate or if neither one does, turn the throttle sensor adjusting screw until only one of them lights. Turn the adjusting screw counterclockwise if both lamps illuminate or clockwise if both lamps DO NOT illuminate.

3. Reinstall the cap on the screw after adjustment is completed.

➡**Do not apply excessive pressure on the adjusting screw, as it may cause incorrect adjustment.**

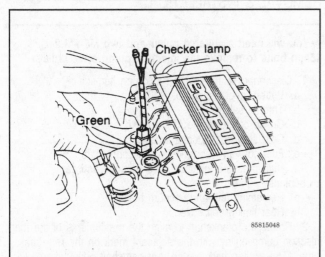

Fig. 41 The RX-7's throttle sensor can be checked with a special test lamp (Part No. 49-F018-001 or equivalent)

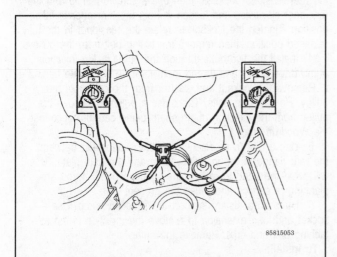

Fig. 42 Checking current flow to the RX-7's throttle sensor with a pair of voltmeters

Fuel Injectors

REMOVAL & INSTALLATION

1. Properly relieve the fuel system pressure, then disconnect the negative battery cable.

2. Remove the throttle body (dynamic chamber) as described earlier in this section.

3. Disconnect the fuel hose and pipe.

4. Unfasten the injector connectors.

5. Remove the pressure regulator and distribution pipe.

6. Remove the injectors.

7. Installation is the reverse of removal. Be sure to install new O-rings.

8. After installation, check for leaks with the fuel pressure applied.

TESTING

Injector Continuity

You can test injectors electrically either on or off the car. Detach the electrical wiring and use an ohmmeter between the two prongs of the electrical connector. The injectors used in the RX-7 should have a resistance of 1.5-3 ohms.

Injector Fuel Leak

1. Properly relieve the fuel system pressure.

2. Remove the delivery pipe and fuel injectors. Affix the injectors to the distribution pipe with some wire.

➡**Affix the injectors firmly to the distribution pipe so no movement of the injectors is possible.**

3. Turn the ignition switch to the **ON** position. Use a jumper wire and connect the terminals of the fuel pump check connector. Make sure that the fuel does not leak from the injector nozzles.

4. After approximately five minutes, a very small (slight) amount of fuel leakage from the injectors is acceptable. If this leakage exceeds more than a few drops, replace the injector.

5. If the injector leaks fuel at a fast rate, replace the injector. If the injectors do not leak, remove all test equipment and install the components in the reverse order of their removal.

DIESEL FUEL SYSTEM

Injection Lines

REMOVAL & INSTALLATION

High Pressure Lines

✳✳CAUTION

You should not remove the high pressure injection lines from the pump and nozzles unless you have a suitable means (plastic caps) to seal off the openings, so dirt cannot enter the delicate diesel fuel system.

The four injection pipes are clamped together as an assembly to dampen vibration.

1. Unscrew the four caps on the pump ends and the four caps on the nozzle ends.
2. Remove the assembly. Be sure to plug all openings with suitable plastic caps if the assembly is to be removed for more than a few minutes.
3. During installation, make sure that all lines are positioned squarely in their openings at both ends to prevent crossthreading of the caps and nozzles or pump connections. Torque the caps to 23-34 ft. lbs. (31-46 Nm).

Fuel Return Lines

1. Remove the high pressure injection lines, as described earlier.
2. Disconnect the flexible drain line from the return line assembly, then plug the openings.
3. Remove the four nozzle nuts which retain the return line assembly to the injection nozzles, then lift the assembly squarely off the nozzles. Remove the washers underneath and supply new ones. If the assembly will be removed for a any length of time, cover the open ends of the nozzles with a clean rag.
4. Installation is the reverse of removal.

Injection Nozzles

REMOVAL & INSTALLATION

➡**It is recommended that you not attempt to work on the injection nozzles of your Mazda, as this service requires special tools and highly specialized training. However, if you keep all parts clean and seal off openings, you may want to remove the nozzles and take them to a qualified professional for service.**

1. Remove the high pressure and return injection lines.
2. Unscrew the nozzles to be removed with a wrench located on the larger flats of the nozzle holder. Make sure to remove the ring-type washer and the corrugated gasket underneath each nozzle. During installation, you will have to provide new replacements for these parts.

To install:

3. Position a new washer on the bottom of each nozzle, then install a new, corrugated gasket on the underside of the nozzle with the red painted side facing upward.
4. Carefully screw the nozzles into the cylinder head. Torque them by the large flats of the nozzle holders to 43-51 ft. lbs. (58-69 Nm). Install the injection lines in reverse of their removal procedure.

Fuel Injection Pump

REMOVAL & INSTALLATION

➡**You will need a suitable puller and two M8 x 1.2 x 45mm bolts to remove the injection pump drive pulley.**

1. Disconnect or remove the following items:
   a. Battery negative cable.
   b. Throttle cable.
   c. Cruise control cable (if the car has cruise control).
   d. Cold start device control cable.
   e. Fuel cut valve and pickup coil connectors.
   f. High pressure injection lines (remove and cap openings).
   g. Remaining fuel and vacuum hoses.
   h. Rear timing belt cover.
2. Rotate the crankshaft to align the matchmarks of the fuel injection pump pulley with the adjacent mark on the rear seal plate. (The similar mark on the rear camshaft pulley should also align with the nearby mark on the rear seal plate.)
3. Mark the rear timing belt for direction of rotation. Loosen the rear tensioner lockbolt, then use a screwdriver to turn the tensioner clockwise and loosen it; hold the tensioner in this position. Tighten the lockbolt to retain the tensioner in the fully released position, then remove the timing belt from the pulleys.
4. Install the two bolts through the holes in the injection pump drive pulley and thread them into the seal plate behind it. Remove the locknut and washer from the center of the pulley. Remove the bolts. Then, use a puller to remove the pulley from the injection pump shaft, being careful not to lose the Woodruff key.
5. Use a drift to precisely mark the relationship between the rear flange of the injection pump and the seal plate. This will avoid the need to re-time the injection pump if you are planning to service and reuse the present unit.
6. Have an assistant support the injection pump. Use a socket and long extension to remove the injection pump attaching bolt and nuts. Remove the pump.

To install:

7. Position the pump on the mounting flange, then install the attaching bolt and nuts just until they touch the rear of the pump flange. Turn the pump carefully to precisely align the matchmarks made earlier. When these marks are precisely aligned, torque the nuts to 14-18 ft. lbs. (19-24 Nm). and the bolt to 24-34 ft. lbs. (33-46 Nm).
8. Install the Woodruff key onto the pump driveshaft, and lightly tap it with a lightweight hammer to make sure it is fully

seated in the groove. Then, slide the pulley over it and onto the shaft.

9. Align the matchmarks on the pulley and seal plate, then install the two bolts used to keep the pulley from turning during removal. Install the locknut and torque it to 44-50 ft. lbs. (60-68 Nm).

❋❋WARNING

Once the locknut is properly tightened, be sure to remove the bolts which were used to lock the pulley in position.

10. Install and adjust the timing belt as described in Section 3. Unless a new belt is being installed, make sure the belt will be turning in the same direction.

11. Install the items which were disconnected or removed in Step 1, in reverse order of disassembly.

12. Operate the pump on top of the fuel filter by repeatedly depressing the large knob until it can no longer be readily moved. This will bleed the system.

13. If you installed a new injection pump, properly set the pump injection timing.

INJECTION TIMING

▶ **See Figures 43, 44, 45 and 46**

➡**To perform this procedure, you must have a special dial indicator and mounting jig designed for this particular job. The Mazda part number is 49-9140-074; you may want to shop around to get the equivalent tool from the least expensive source.**

1. Run the engine until it reaches normal operating temperature. Remove the high pressure injection lines as described earlier, leaving the pump fittings uncapped.

2. Remove the service hole cover from the top of the flywheel housing, then rotate the engine to align the TDC (thicker) mark on the flywheel with the indicator pin inside the hole.

3. Remove the delivery valve assembly from the top injection pump fitting, as shown in the illustration. The valve is

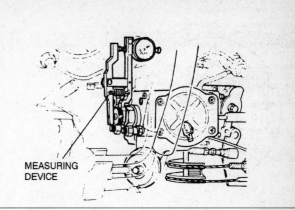

MEASURING DEVICE

85815055

Fig. 44 Mount the measuring jig into the plug hole on the hydraulic head of the pump

removed by placing a socket wrench on the flats (the injection line cap screws onto the outer valve). Make sure you keep all valve parts together, in order, and in a clean environment. Supply a new gasket and discard the old one. Remove the hydraulic head plug from the front surface of the injection pump.

4. Mount the measuring jig and dial indicator into the plug hole on the hydraulic head of the pump. The tip of the dial gauge should contact the plunger end of the pump, with the gauge indicating approximately 0.08 in. (2.0mm).

5. Turn the flywheel counterclockwise (in reverse of normal rotation) until the crankshaft pulley timing mark moves from TDC to about 30-50° BTDC and the dial indicator stops moving. Then, zero the indicator. Turn the crankshaft slightly to the right and left to make sure its motion does not affect the indicator. If it does, the timing must be advanced further before zeroing the indicator.

6. Now, turn the flywheel clockwise to set the timing mark to TDC. Read the dial indicator. The reading should be 0.0392-0.0408 in. (0.98-1.02mm). If not, loosen the pump nuts/bolt and turn the pump until the figure is correct. Turn the pump clockwise if the figure is too high (timing is advanced), or counterclockwise if it is too low (retarded). Retorque the nuts to 14-18 ft. lbs. (19-24 Nm) and the bolt to 24-34 ft. lbs. (33-46 Nm). Remove the timing device, then install the delivery valve with a new gasket and torque it to 36 ft. lbs. (49 Nm)

7. Connect the injection lines, then bleed the system by repeatedly depressing the large knob on top of the fuel filter until it can no longer be readily moved.

BLEEDING THE SYSTEM

▶ **See Figure 47**

If the engine runs out of fuel during operation and air enters the injection system, or whenever the injection pump is removed, the system must be air-bled in the following manner:

1. Bleed air from the fuel filter's vent plug.

2. Pump the head of the fuel filter repeatedly until it becomes hard (about 15 times).

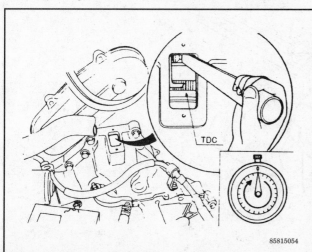

TDC

85815054

Fig. 43 Turn the crankshaft to align the TDC timing mark on the flywheel with the indicator pin

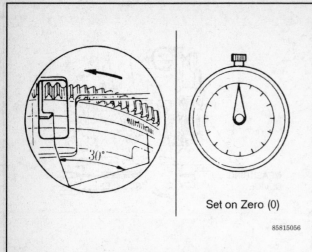

Fig. 45 Turn the flywheel 30-50 degrees counterclockwise before zeroing the dial gauge

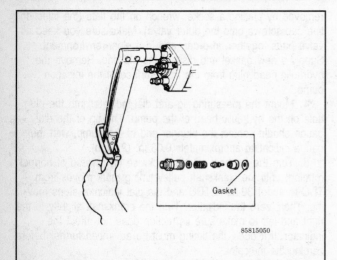

Fig. 46 After setting the timing, install and torque the delivery valve to specifications

Glow Plugs

DIAGNOSIS & TESTING

Glow Plug Inspection

1. Disconnect the wiring from the glow plug.
2. Using an ohmmeter, check the continuity between each glow plug terminal and the cylinder head.
3. If continuity does not exist, remove and replace the glow plug.

Glow Plug Relay Inspection

1. Unfasten the glow plug relay connector. Using a suitable jumper, attach the wire to the battery and the relay connector. Also, connect a suitable ohmmeter to the relay connector.
2. If the ohmmeter shows continuity when the battery is connected, the relay is good.
3. If the ohmmeter shows no continuity when the battery is connected, the relay is not good and should be replaced.

REMOVAL & INSTALLATION

1. Disconnect the negative battery cable.
2. Remove the glow plug connector nut, lockwasher and flatwasher, then remove the glow plug connector wire from its terminal.
3. Using a suitable tool, remove the glow plug from the engine.
4. Installation is the reverse order of the removal procedure.

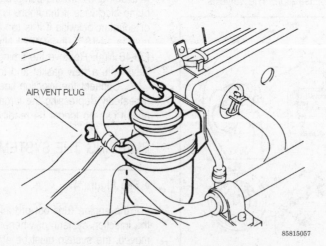

Fig. 47 Bleed air by repeatedly depressing the large knob on top of the fuel filter

FUEL TANK

Tank Assembly

REMOVAL & INSTALLATION

GLC with Rear Wheel Drive, 1979-87 626 and 1986-87 323

▶ **See Figure 48**

On sedans and coupes, the fuel tank is located behind the partition board in the trunk. On wagons, it is under the rear of the car.

1. On sedans and coupes, open the trunk and remove the partition board. For fuel injected vehicles, be sure to properly relieve fuel system pressure.

2. On the 626, push the access hole cover inward toward the tank. On the 626 diesel, remove the lower cushion for the rear seat.

3. Raise and safely support wagon models on axle stands.

4. Disconnect the inlet line from the fuel filter on 1978-85 carbureted vehicles. Remove the tank filler hose clamp, and disconnect the hose at the tank. On fuel injected vehicles, there will be two hoses to disconnect at the top of the tank.

5. Raise and safely support the vehicle on axle stands (all models).

6. Disconnect the condensing tank hoses.

7. Unfasten the mounting bolts and remove the tank.

8. Installation is the reverse of removal. Where clamps are used, make sure that the clamp is firmly positioned on the hose, so that there is one clamp width of bare hose at the end. On the 626, install the large filler hose so that it is at least 1.42 in. (36mm) onto the tank fitting and filler tube at each end.

GLC with Front Wheel Drive

The fuel tank is located under the rear of the car.

1. Remove the rear seat.

2. Remove the fuel tank gauge unit and drain the gas tank. Siphon if necessary.

3. Raise the rear of the car and safely support it on jackstands.

4. Disconnect all hoses at the tank.

5. Remove the mountings, then lower the fuel tank from the car.

6. Installation is the reverse of removal.

1988-89 323, 626 and MX-6

EXCEPT TURBO WITH 4WD OR 4WS

1. Relieve the fuel system pressure. Disconnect the negative battery cable.

2. Remove the rear seat cushion from the 323. Detach the connector from the fuel tank gauge unit, then remove the cover plate and gasket.

3. Disconnect the fuel main and return the hoses. Plug the ends of the hoses to prevent leakage.

4. Raise the vehicle and support it safely on jackstands. Position a suitable waste container under the fuel tank and remove the fuel filler cap. Remove the drain plug and drain all the fuel from the tank into the waste container. Disconnect all the remaining fuel, evaporative, filler or breather hoses and label them for assembly reference.

5. Support the fuel tank and disconnect it from its mounting by removing the retaining straps. Carefully lower the fuel tank to the ground and slide it out from under the vehicle. Send the fuel tank to a repair shop where it can be steam cleaned to remove all the explosive gases from the tank. Check the tank for cracks. If the tank is not to be reinstalled for an extended period of time, store it outside in a cool and shady area.

To install:

6. Raise the fuel tank onto its mounting and secure it with the retaining straps. Connect the fuel hoses that were disconnected in Step 4. Push the hose ends at least 0.98 in. (25mm) onto the end of each connection. On the section of hose that connects the filler neck to the fuel tank, push the hose at least

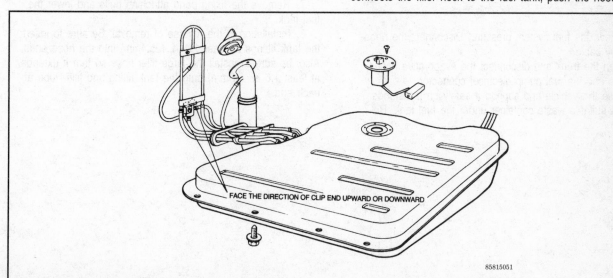

FACE THE DIRECTION OF CLIP END UPWARD OR DOWNWARD

85815051

Fig. 48 Hose routing on the GLC Wagon fuel tank

1.5 in. (38mm) over the connections. Install and tighten the drain plug, then lower the vehicle.

7. Connect the main and return fuel hoses. Install the fuel tank cover plate with a new gasket. Fasten the electrical connector to the gauge unit.

8. Fill the fuel tank and install the filler cap, then start the engine and conduct a thorough inspection of all fuel line connections to be sure that there are no leaks. Run the tip of your finger around the edge of the drain plug and check for leaks. When the integrity of the fuel system is verified, install the rear seat cushion on the 323.

323 TURBO WITH 4WD

1. Relieve the fuel system pressure. Disconnect the negative battery cable.

2. Remove the rear seat cushion. Unfasten the connector from the fuel tank gauge unit, then remove the cover plate and gasket.

3. Disconnect the fuel main and return hoses. Plug the ends of the hoses to prevent leakage.

4. Disconnect the section of exhaust pipe that runs between the catalytic converter and muffler.

5. Disconnect and remove the propeller shaft. For details, please refer to Section 7.

6. Detach the transfer pump connector. Loosen the transfer pump retaining screws and remove the transfer pump from the fuel tank. Refer to the previous procedure for 323 non-4WD models for the remainder of the removal and installation procedure.

626 AND MX-6 TURBO WITH 4WS

1. Relieve the fuel system pressure. Disconnect the negative battery cable.

2. Detach the electrical connectors from the main and transfer fuel pumps.

3. Remove the cover plates and disconnect the steering angle transfer shaft. Remove the cross member. Refer to the previous procedure for 626 non-4WS models for the remainder of the removal and installation procedure. Torque the retaining strap bolts to 32-45 ft. lbs. (43-61 Nm).

929

1. Relieve the fuel system pressure. Disconnect the negative battery cable.

2. Open the trunk and disconnect the evaporative hoses, fuel hoses and the fuel pump electrical connector.

3. Raise the vehicle and support it safely on jackstands. Position a suitable waste container under the fuel tank. Remove the filler cap, then unfasten the drain plug and drain all the fuel from the tank into the waste container. Disconnect all the remaining fuel, evaporative, filler or vent hoses and label them for assembly reference.

4. Support the fuel tank and disconnect it from its mounting by removing the two retaining straps. Carefully lower the fuel tank to the ground and slide it out from under the vehicle. Send the fuel tank to a repair shop where it can be steam cleaned to remove all the explosive gases from the tank. Check the tank for cracks. If the tank is not to be reinstalled for an extended period of time, store it outside in a cool and shady area.

To install:

5. Raise the fuel tank onto its mounting and secure it with the retaining straps. Working from underneath the vehicle, connect the fuel hoses that were disconnected in Step 3. Push the hose ends at least 0.98 in. (25mm) onto the end of each connection. On the section of hose that connects the filler neck to the fuel tank, push the hose at least 1.5 in. (38mm) over the connections. Install and tighten the drain plug, then lower the vehicle.

6. Working from inside the trunk, attach the fuel pump connector, the fuel (main and return) lines, and the evaporative hoses. Make sure that all connections are tight.

7. Fill the fuel tank and install the filler cap. Start the engine and conduct a thorough inspection of all fuel line connections to be sure that there are no leaks. Run the tip of your finger around the edge of the drain plug and check for leaks.

RX-7

1. On fuel injected models, relieve the fuel system pressure, then disconnect the negative battery cable.

2. On 1986-89 models, remove the fuel pump as described previously in this section.

3. Disconnect the fuel filler hose from the tank.

4. Raise the rear of the vehicle and safely support it with jackstands.

5. Remove the front and side tank protectors.

6. Disconnect the fuel main hose, fuel return hose and evaporation hoses from the fuel tank.

7. Remove the fixing band attaching bolts and lower the fuel tank.

8. Installation is the reverse of removal. Be sure to insert the tank fittings at least 1.0 in. (25.4mm) into the hose ends. Also, be sure to install the large filler hose so that it extends at least 1.6 in. (40mm) onto the tank fitting and filler tube at each end.

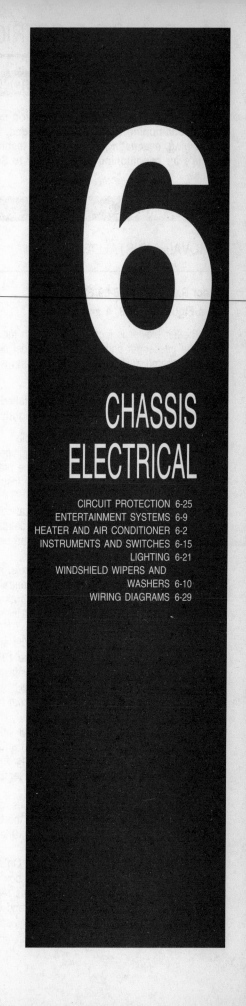

6

CHASSIS ELECTRICAL

HEATER AND AIR CONDITIONER

➡ Some of the procedures in this section may require that the air conditioning system be discharged. For discharging, evacuating, charging and testing of the vehicle's air conditioning system, refer to Section 1 of this manual.

Blower Motor

REMOVAL & INSTALLATION

Except RX-7 and 1988-89 626/MX-6

♦ See Figures 1, 2, 3, 4 and 5

The heater blower is located underneath the dash panel, inside the passenger compartment. On most models, the blower is located next to the heater box and is connected to it by a duct.

➡ On models equipped with dealer installed air conditioning, blower access may be slightly more difficult.

1. Disconnect the negative battery cable.
2. Remove the dash under cover if equipped. On the 1986-87 323, remove the glovebox and the brace that locates the rear of the glovebox, then remove the instrument panel bracket.
3. Unfasten the blower motor's electrical connector(s).
4. If necessary, remove the right-side defroster hose for clearance. On the 1986-87 323, remove the blower unit-to-heater unit duct.
5. If equipped with sliding heater controls, move the control to the HOT position and disconnect the control wire if it is in the way. On the 323, set the FRESH-REC air selector control to REC, then disconnect the FRESH-REC air selector control wire.
6. Unfasten the mounting screws or nuts and remove the blower motor. On the 1986-87 626 and the 1986-89 323, remove the blower case assembly, then unfasten the clips, separate the case halves, and remove the blower motor and wheel. If necessary, separate the wheel from the blower motor.

To install:

7. If applicable, attach the blower motor wheel to the blower motor shaft, then install the locknut and washer. Position the blower motor onto its mounting and install the retaining screws. On the 323 and 626, assemble the case halves and secure with the clips.
8. Connect all the selector control cables to their respective control levers. On 1986-89 323s, connect the blower unit-to-heater unit duct. On other models, connect the right-side defroster hose if it was removed.
9. Fasten the blower motor connector. On 1986-87 323s, install the instrument panel bracket, glove box and support brace. Install the dash under cover if it was removed.
10. Connect the negative battery cable and test the blower to make sure that it operates properly at all speeds.

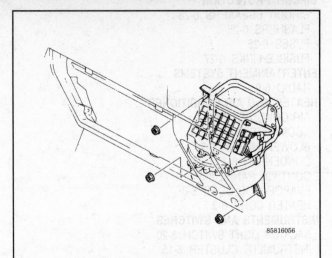

Fig. 1 Unfasten the retaining nuts to remove the 323's blower case assembly

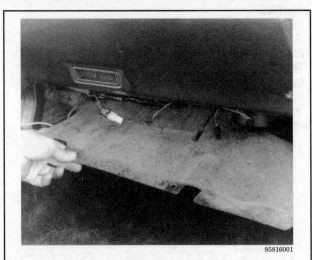

Fig. 2 Remove the dash under cover to access the blower assembly — 626 shown

1988-89 626 and MX-6

The blower motor is located under the glove box.

1. Disconnect the negative battery cable.
2. Remove the glove box under cover. Unfasten the five retaining screws and remove the glove box.
3. Detach the blower motor connector and remove the blower motor retaining screws. Lower the blower motor from its mounting.

To install:

4. Raise the blower motor up onto its mounting and install the retaining screws.
5. Fasten the blower motor connector.
6. Install the glove box and under cover. Connect the negative battery cable.
7. Test the blower motor to make sure that it operates properly.

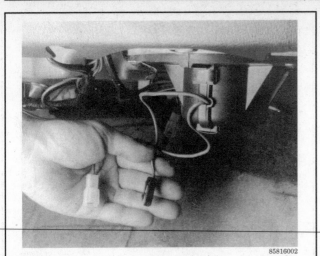

Fig. 3 Disconnect the electrical leads from the blower motor

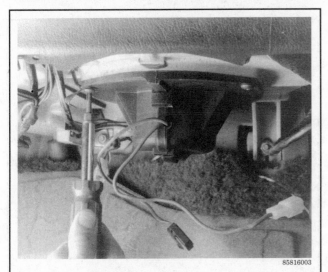

Fig. 4 Unfasten the retaining screws . . .

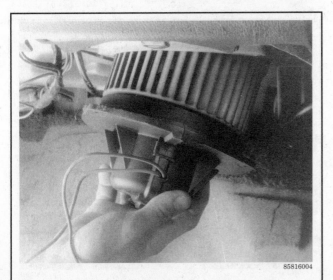

Fig. 5 . . . and remove the blower motor assembly

RX-7 Models

The heater blower is located on the passenger side of the car under the dashboard. It is a turbine-type fan coupled to a variable speed electrical motor. The fan also acts as the air conditioner blower on cars so equipped.

1. Disconnect the negative battery cable.
2. Remove the three Phillips-head screws holding the plastic cover over the bottom of the fan motor.
3. Unfasten the drain funnel from the cover, then detach the blower motor electrical multi-connector.
4. Pull down slightly on the motor to clear the screw mounts, then push the motor toward the right side of the car to remove the fan.

To install:

5. Installation is the reverse of removal. Be sure to install both gaskets in their original positions. Test the blower for proper operation at all speeds.

Heater Core

REMOVAL & INSTALLATION

▶ See Figures 6, 7, 8, 9, 10 and 11

➡On models equipped with air conditioning, access to the heater core will be more difficult.

1. Disconnect the negative battery cable. Drain the coolant from the radiator.
2. Disconnect the heater hoses at the engine firewall. Note how the hose clamps are installed so that they may be reinstalled the same way.
3. Disconnect the duct which runs between the heater box and the blower motor or, depending on the model, remove the crush pad and instrument panel pad from the dash. This will be required on the 323, 626 and MX-6. (Refer to Section 10 for pad and panel removal.) On 1986-87 323s, disconnect the center duct, located in front of the heater box. On 1988-89 323s, remove the floor cover under the heater unit.
4. If necessary, disconnect the defroster duct(s), then set the controls to the DEF and HOT positions and disconnect the control cables if they are in the way. Unfasten all electrical connectors which are in the way.
5. Unfasten the retaining screws or clips that secure the halves of the heater box together, or remove the entire heater unit and separate the heater box for access to the heater core.

➡When removing the heater unit, take care not to drain the coolant from the heater hoses. Plug the hoses first.

6. Remove the heater core. Check the core for cracked or bent fins, distorted or bent inlet/outlet connections, and signs of leakage. The heater core may be leak tested by pressurizing the unit with water.

To install:

7. Install the heater core and secure with the mounting clips. Assemble the heater box with the screws or clips, then install the heater unit.
8. Attach all disconnected control cables to their respective control levers. Connect the defroster duct(s), if removed. On 1988-89 323s, install the floor cover under the heater unit. On

1986-87 323s, connect the center duct to the heater box. Fasten all electrical connectors.

9. Install the instrument panel or crash pad (as described in Section 10). Connect the heater hoses to the heater unit. Make sure that the hose clamps are installed in their original positions.

10. Fill the cooling system to the proper level. Connect the negative battery cable, then start the engine and check the heating system for proper operation.

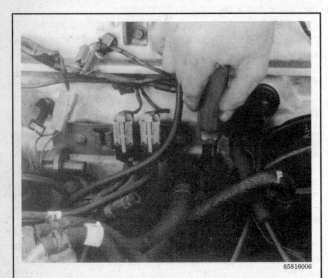

Fig. 6 Unfasten the hose clamp . . .

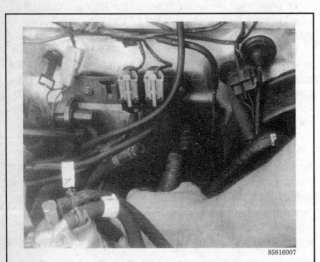

Fig. 7 . . . and disconnect the heater hose at the firewall

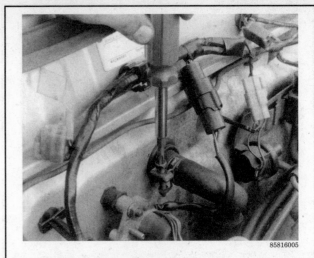

Fig. 8 Disconnect the other heater hose, too. Note that the two hoses may not be adjacent

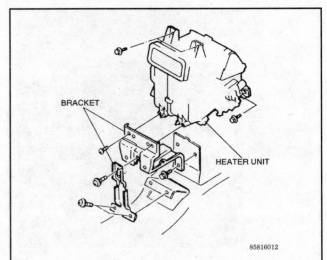

Fig. 9 If applicable, disconnect the heater unit from the bracket assembly (323 shown)

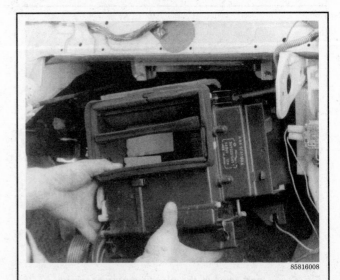

Fig. 10 Remove the heater unit from the vehicle

Fig. 11 Open the heater unit and withdraw the heater core

Control Panel

REMOVAL & INSTALLATION

323 Models

1. Remove the screws from the center panel. Do so gently to avoid damaging the panel finish.

2. Detach the cigarette lighter connector and remove the lamp.

3. Pull the control panel from the opening in the dash. Note how the control cables are routed. Two cables connect to the heater unit and the third runs to the blower unit. Disconnect the cables from the control panel.

To install:

4. Attach the control cables to the control panel.

5. Adjust the MODE control cable as follows:

  a. Set the mode control knob to the DEF position.

  b. Pull the cable wire downward to its extreme stop. Install the loop of the wire onto the lever.

  c. Pull the connecting rod downward to its extreme stop, then install the connecting rod fastener.

  d. Use the retaining clip to clamp the rod into position.

  e. Position the fan speed at detent number 4 to insure proper air circulation.

  f. Proceed to Step 6 to perform the AIR-MIX door control cable adjustment.

6. Adjust the AIR-MIX door control cable as follows:

  a. Set the temperature lever to the MAX COLD detent.

  b. Pull the cable lever downward to its extreme stop. Position the cable onto the lever.

  c. Pull the connecting rod lever upward to its extreme stop, then attach the connecting rod to its mounting.

  d. Use the retaining clip to hold the rod in place.

  e. Check for proper operation of the temperature control.

  f. Proceed to Step 7 to perform the REC-FRESH selector cable adjustment.

7. Adjust the REC-FRESH selector cable as follows:

  a. Position the selector lever in the fresh air intake position.

  b. Push the lever forward to the extreme stop, then attach the cable to the lever.

  c. Check for proper operation of the air selector control.

8. Install the lamp and fasten the cigarette lighter connector. Gently push the panel into the dash opening and install the retaining screws. Check all the panel control functions for proper operation.

626 and MX-6 With Logic Control

▶ See Figure 12

1. Disconnect the negative battery cable.

2. Remove the ashtray and radio box from the center console.

3. Remove the four center panel retaining screws and gently pull the panel outward and away from the dash. Reach in behind the panel and detach the cigarette lighter connector. Remove the center panel.

4. Remove the two control panel retaining screws and pull the panel out from the console. Unfasten the electrical connectors from the rear of the unit and remove the control panel from the console.

To install:

5. Fasten the electrical connectors at the rear of the unit. Push the panel gently into the opening, then install and tighten the retaining screws.

6. Attach the cigarette lighter connector and hold the center panel against the console. Install and tighten the center panel retaining screws.

7. Install the radio box and the ashtray.

8. Connect the negative battery cable.

626 and MX-6 With Wire Control

▶ See Figures 13, 14, 15, 16, 17 and 18

1. Remove the under cover and the glove box.

2. Disconnect the TEMPERATURE BLEND control cable from the heater unit.

3. Disconnect the REC-FRESH control cable from the blower case.

4. On the driver's side, remove the air duct and the under cover.

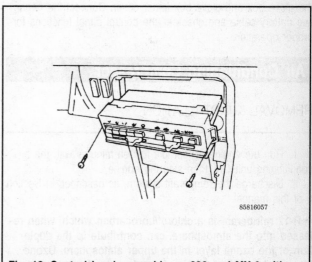

Fig. 12 Control head assembly on 626 and MX-6 with Logic Control

5. Disconnect the AIRFLOW MODE cable from the actuating cam on the heater unit.

6. On 1988-89 models, remove the ashtray and radio box from the center console.

7. On 1988-89 models, unfasten the stereo cover or center panel retaining screws. Detach the cigarette lighter connector, then remove the cover or panel.

8. On 1983-87 models, remove the center louver assembly (which frames the control panel).

9. Remove the two control panel retaining screws and pull the panel out from the instrument panel or console.

To install:

10. Push the control panel gently into the instrument panel/console and install the retaining screws.

11. If applicable, install the center louver assembly.

12. If applicable, fasten the cigarette lighter connector, then install the stereo cover or center panel.

13. If applicable, install the radio box and the ashtray.

14. Adjust the AIRFLOW MODE cable as follows:

a. Position the mode control cable to the DEF detent.

b. Connect and clamp the control cable with the shutter lever on the heater unit to the closest point. Move the temperature control lever to be sure that the cable is attached. Be sure it can move from stop to stop without difficulty.

c. Proceed to Step 15 to perform the TEMPERATURE BLEND cable adjustment.

15. Adjust the TEMPERATURE BLEND cable as follows:

a. Position the temperature lever control to the MAX-COLD detent.

b. Connect the clamp of the control cable to the shutter lever on the right side of the heater unit. Move the temperature control lever to be sure that the cable is attached. Be sure it can move from stop-to-stop without difficulty.

c. Proceed to Step 16 to perform the REC-FRESH cable adjustment.

16. Adjust the REC-FRESH cable as follows:

a. Position the selector lever in the REC detent.

b. Connect the clamp of the control cable to the shutter lever on the blower unit at its closest point. Move the temperature control lever to be sure that the cable is attached. Be sure it can move from stop-to-stop without difficulty.

17. Install the driver's side air duct and under cover. Install the glove box and glove box under cover. Connect the negative battery cable and check all the control panel functions for proper operation.

Air Conditioning Compressor

REMOVAL & INSTALLATION

1. Run the engine at fast idle for ten minutes with the air conditioning unit **ON**, then stop the engine.

2. Discharge the refrigerant system, as described in Section 1 of this manual.

➡**R-12 refrigerant is a chlorofluorocarbon which, when released into the atmosphere, can contribute to the depletion of the ozone layer in the upper atmosphere. Ozone filters out harmful radiation from the sun. An approved R-12 recovery/recycling station that meets SAE standards**

Fig. 13 Remove the glove box to access the blower unit and cable

Fig. 14 Remove the center louver assembly on 1983-87 626 models

Fig. 15 Unfasten the screws which retain the control panel

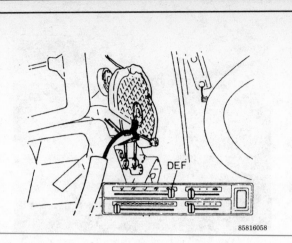

Fig. 16 AIRFLOW MODE cable adjustment — 626 and MX-6

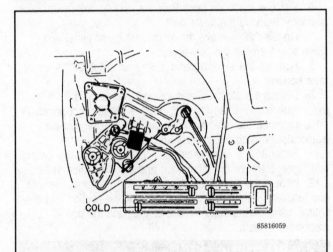

Fig. 17 TEMPERATURE BLEND cable adjustment — 626 and MX-6

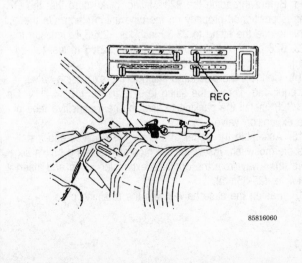

Fig. 18 REC-FRESH cable adjustment — 626 and MX-6

should be used when discharging the system. Follow the operating instructions provided with the equipment exactly to properly discharge the system.

3. Disconnect the negative battery cable and the wire from the magnetic clutch.

4. Disconnect the suction and discharge hoses from the compressor and plug the ends of the hoses to prevent the entry of moisture and contamination.

5. Loosen the compressor mounting bolts and slip the drive belt from the pulley.

6. Unfasten the mounting bolts and remove the compressor from the vehicle.

To install:

7. Position the compressor onto its mounting and install the mounting bolts. Place the drive belt onto the pulley.

8. Connect the suction and discharge hoses to the compressor and adjust the drive belt tension.

9. Connect the magnetic clutch wire and the negative battery cable.

10. Evacuate and charge the system using approved equipment, as described in Section 1.

Condenser

REMOVAL & INSTALLATION

➡R-12 refrigerant is a chlorofluorocarbon which, when released into the atmosphere, can contribute to the depletion of the ozone layer in the upper atmosphere. Ozone filters out harmful radiation from the sun. An approved R-12 recovery/recycling station that meets SAE standards should be used when discharging the system. Follow the operating instructions provided with the equipment exactly to properly discharge the system.

1. Discharge the refrigerant system, as described in Section 1 of this manual.

2. Disconnect the negative battery cable.

3. If necessary, remove the air cleaner assembly.

4. As required, remove the front grille, air seal cover and side lamps. Remove the clamps and the hood lock brace, if installed.

5. Disconnect and plug the condenser inlet, outlet and liquid lines to prevent the entry of moisture and dirt.

6. Remove the necessary components (such as the cooling fan on 323 models) in order to gain access to the condenser mounting bolts.

7. Unfasten the condenser mounting bolts and remove the condenser from the vehicle.

To install:

8. Lower the condenser into the vehicle and secure it with the mounting bolts. Reinstall all interference items.

9. Connect the suction, discharge and liquid lines to the condenser.

10. Install the hood lock brace and the clamps, if removed. Install the air seal and the front grille and side lamps.

➡If a new condenser was installed, add approximately 30cc of clean compressor oil to the unit.

11. If applicable, install the air cleaner assembly.

12. Connect the negative battery cable.

13. Evacuate, charge and test the system as described in Section 1.

Evaporator Core

REMOVAL & INSTALLATION

▶ See Figures 19 and 20

➡R-12 refrigerant is a chlorofluorocarbon which, when released into the atmosphere, can contribute to the depletion of the ozone layer in the upper atmosphere. Ozone filters out harmful radiation from the sun. An approved R-12 recovery/recycling station that meets SAE standards should be used when discharging the system. Follow the operating instructions provided with the equipment exactly to properly discharge the system.

1. Discharge the refrigerant system, as described in Section 1 of this manual.

2. Disconnect the negative battery cable.

3. On the 626 and MX-6, remove the under cover and glove box at this time.

4. Disconnect and plug the evaporator suction and discharge lines from their respective fittings. Plug the fittings immediately to prevent the entry of dirt and moisture into the system.

5. On the 929, remove the grommets from the expansion valve. On the 323 and 626, remove the grommets from the suction and discharge lines. On the 323, remove the glove box at this time.

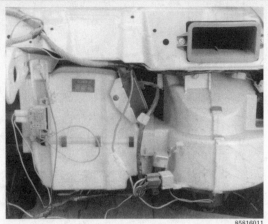

Fig. 20 The core is located inside an evaporator housing (on the left in this photo), and the blower unit is on the right

6. Remove the drain hose from the cooling unit (evaporator housing). Remove the lower duct.

7. On the 929, remove the instrument lower panel and glove box. Remove the blower duct.

8. Remove the sealing plates from both sides of the evaporator housing.

9. Detach the electrical and vacuum connections from the evaporator housing. On the 323, remove the air duct bands.

10. Unfasten the retaining bolts or nuts and remove the evaporator housing assembly from the vehicle.

11. Separate the evaporator housing and remove the evaporator core. Remove the thermostat and the expansion valve.

12. Inspect the fins of the evaporator for blockage. Remove any blockage with compressed air. Check the suction and discharge fitting connections for cracks. Replace the core if cracks are evident.

✳✳WARNING

Never clean the evaporator core with water!

To assemble:

13. Connect the expansion valve to the evaporator inlet fitting. Before threading the 929's fitting, make sure that the O-ring is positioned properly on the pipe union fitting. On the 929, torque the fitting to 23-30 inch lbs. (2.6-3.4 Nm). On the 323, 626 and MX-6, torque the fitting to 22-25 ft. lbs. (30-34 Nm).

14. Connect the discharge fitting to the expansion valve, if so equipped. Torque the fitting to 9-10 ft. lbs. (12-14 Nm). On the 323, install the packing to seal the heat sensitive tube of the expansion valve.

15. Assemble the upper and lower case halves and install the thermoswitch. Install the thermoswitch sensing bulb's six core fins away from the opposite expansion valve and insert it 1-1½ in. (25-38mm).

16. Fasten the case halves with the retaining clips.

Fig. 19 Remove the glove box to access the evaporator housing

To install:

17. Installation of the cooling unit is essentially the reverse of the removal procedure with the following exceptions:

a. Adjust the position of the cooling unit so that its connections are aligned with those on the heater and blower units.

b. On the 323, torque the discharge tube fitting to 9-10 ft. lbs. (12-14 Nm) and the suction tube fitting to 22-25 ft. lbs.

(30-34 Nm). On the 626, MX-6 and 929, torque both tube fittings to 11-18 ft. lbs. (15-24 Nm).

c. If the evaporator core was replaced, add approximately 50cc of new compressor oil to the compressor.

d. Evacuate, charge and leak test the system as described in Section 1. Check the system for proper operation.

ENTERTAINMENT SYSTEMS

Radio

REMOVAL & INSTALLATION

✳✳WARNING

Never operate the radio with the speaker disconnected or with the speaker leads shorted together, since damage to the output transistors could result. When replacing the speaker, be sure to use one with the same impedance (ohms).

1978-82 GLC

1. Disconnect the negative battery cable.
2. Remove the crash pad, meter hood, and wood grain center panel, as outlined in the instrument cluster removal procedure, later in this section.
3. Remove the attaching screws from either side of the dash panel. Detach the antenna wiring, power connector, and speaker connector, then pull the radio out of the dash.
4. Install in the reverse order.

1983-85 GLC

1. Disconnect the negative battery cable. Pull off the switch knobs.
2. Remove the mounting bolts and slide the radio out of the dashboard.
3. Disconnect the antenna feeder and wiring connector, then remove the radio.
4. Install in the reverse order.

1979-87 626

1. Disconnect the negative battery cable.
2. Remove the ashtray, radio knobs, heater control lever knob, and the fan control switch knob.
3. Remove the center panel attaching screws and pull the center panel rearward.
4. Remove the radio attaching screws and disconnect the antenna.
5. Installation is the reverse of removal.

1988-89 626/MX-6

1. Disconnect the negative battery cable.
2. Remove the ashtray. On vehicles equipped with a compact disc player, gently pry the ornamental plate from the center panel with a protected tool. On conventional sound sys-

tems, withdraw the box from the center panel. Unfasten the lower center panel attaching screws and remove the panel by releasing the upper retaining clips.

3. Remove the audio unit bracket retaining screws and carefully slide the unit out from the dash until the electrical connections are visible and accessible.
4. Detach all the electrical connections and antenna leads from the rear of the unit and pull it out of the dash.

To install:

5. Rest the audio unit on the dash and fasten all the electrical connections. Slide the unit into the dash until the mounting holes align with the bracket holes. Install and tighten the bracket retaining screws.
6. Position the lower center panel and engage the retaining clips. Install and tighten the retaining screws.
7. On conventional sound systems, push the box into the center panel. On compact disc equipped systems, gently push the ornamental plate into the center panel.
8. Install the ashtray and connect the negative battery cable.

323 Models

1. Pull the ashtray out, depress the tang in back, and remove it from its slot in the dash.
2. On models with 4WD, remove the side panels from the shift console to gain access to the radio brackets and retaining screws.
3. On non-4WD models, remove the two fastening screws from the area of the panel fascia behind the ashtray, and remove the panel, disconnecting the cigarette lighter when you can reach in and unplug it.
4. Remove the two screws from atop of the two mounting brackets and slide the radio out. Detach the antenna's wiring lead and the electrical connector plug, then remove the radio.

To install:

5. Installation is the reverse of removal. If the unit is being replaced, transfer the mounting brackets to the new radio.

929 Models

➥**On vehicles equipped with an automatic transmission, apply the parking brake and move the lever to the "L" position to gain sufficient removal and installation clearance. Protect the console and trim surfaces with soft cloth and do not attempt to pry the trim from the face of the audio system.**

1. Disconnect the negative battery cable.
2. Remove the three plastic Phillips head screws from the duct panel under cover located on the passenger's side. Lo-

cate and remove the single large plastic hex nut that holds the duct panel under cover in place.

3. Reach in behind the audio unit and remove the two attaching nuts. Push on the mounting studs and pull the unit from the dash until the electrical connections are visible and accessible. Detach the electrical connections and antenna leads from the rear of the unit, then pull the radio from the dash.

To install:

4. Installation is the reverse of the removal procedure. Make sure that the duct panel under cover on the passenger's side is aligned properly with the ductwork under the dash.

RX-7 Models

1. Disconnect the negative battery cable.
2. Remove the center panel as described previously in this section.
3. Disconnect the radio wiring and the antenna cable.

4. Unfasten the attaching screws and remove the radio.

To install:

5. Position the radio in the console opening and install the attaching screws.
6. Connect the radio and antenna wiring.
7. Install the center panel.
8. Connect the negative battery cable.

➡**If a new antenna was installed with the radio, use the following adjustment procedure to obtain optimum radio and antenna reception sensitivity. If the antenna is a telescoping type, extend it fully. Turn the ignition switch to the ACC position. Turn on the radio and set it to the AM range. Select a weak station in the 1,400 khz range. If no station exists in that range, use static to make the adjustment. Turn the antenna trim adjustment screw to the left and right to find the maximum sensitivity. If the sensitivity does not change, there is either a problem with the antenna, a broken wire, or the signal is too strong.**

WINDSHIELD WIPERS AND WASHERS

Windshield Wiper Blade

▶ **See Figure 21**

1. Cycle the arm and blade assembly to a position on the windshield where removal of the blade can be performed without difficulty. Turn the ignition **OFF** at the desired position.
2. If so equipped, depress the locking tab near the center of the blade, while sliding the blade off the pin of the arm.

➡**Some vehicles' wiper blades may utilize a different type of release method. In most cases, however, the blade can be removed from the arm after tension on the pin is released.**

To install:

3. Push the blade assembly onto the pin so that the locking tab (or other device, if applicable) engages the pin. Be sure that the blade is securely attached to the wiper arm.
4. Turn the ignition **ON** and check the wipers for normal operation.

Windshield Wiper Arm

REMOVAL & INSTALLATION

▶ **See Figures 22 and 23**

The wiper arm is held in place either with a screw which threads directly into the wiper arm drive shaft or a nut which screws onto the end of the shaft.

➡**Note the angle of the wiper arm, so that it can be installed in the same position on the linkage assembly's output shaft.**

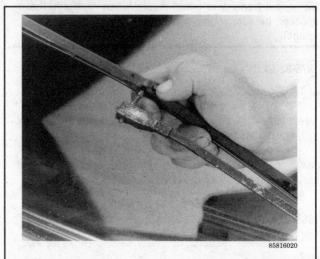

Fig. 21 Depress the locking tab and disengage the wiper blade from the arm

1. Unfasten the screw or nut, then pull the wiper arm off the linkage assembly's output shaft.

To install:

2. Properly position the wiper arm over the splines of the linkage assembly's output shaft, then fasten the screw or nut. The wiper arm/blade assemblies on the 1988-89 626/MX-6 and the 1986-89 RX-7 are identified by letters on the portion of the arm that connects to the wiper linkage. The driver's side arm is marked **DL** and the passenger's side is marked **PL**. Make sure that they are installed in their original positions. The wiper arms are not interchangeable.

➡**For more information on windshield wiper service, refer to Section 1 of this manual.**

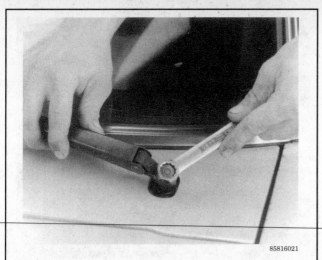

Fig. 22 Unfasten the retaining nut at the base of the wiper arm . . .

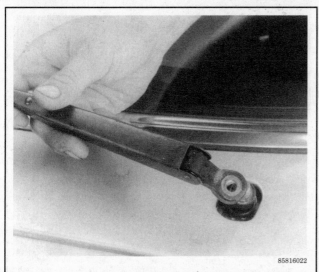

Fig. 23 . . . and lift the arm from the linkage assembly

Windshield Wiper Motor

REMOVAL & INSTALLATION

1978-82 Models — Except RX-7

1. Disconnect the negative battery cable.
2. Unfasten the attaching screws or nuts and remove the wiper arms.
3. Raise the hood and remove the screws from the front of the cowl plate or from the service hole panel on the firewall. Raise the front of the plate and disconnect the windshield washer hose at the nozzle, then remove the plate.
4. Disconnect the motor wiring. Unfasten the motor and transmission attaching bolts, then remove the motor and transmission.

To install:
5. Position the transmission and motor onto its mounting and install the attaching bolts. Connect the wiring to the motor.
6. Install the cowl plate and raise it enough to connect the washer hose to the nozzle. Lower the cowl plate and fasten it with the retaining screws.
7. Install the wiper arms.
8. Connect the negative battery cable. Check the system for proper operation.

1983 GLC Wagon

1. Disconnect the negative battery cable.
2. Unfasten the attaching nuts and remove the two wiper arms.
3. Unfasten the screws from the front of the cowl grille and remove it.
4. Mark the relationship between the linkage and motor shaft, then disconnect the linkage at the shaft.
5. Detach the motor's electrical connector.
6. Unfasten the three motor mounting bolts (two from the firewall and one from the bracket located directly in front of the windshield) and remove the motor.

To install:
7. Installation is the reverse of removal. Make sure the wiper arms are installed so they part in the proper position.

1983-85 GLC Sedan

1. Disconnect the negative battery cable.
2. Remove the wiper arms.
3. Open the hood and remove the driver's side service hole cover from the cowl.
4. Detach the wiring connector, then unfasten and remove the motor and linkage, as an assembly. If it is necessary to disconnect the crank arm and linkage at the motor, mark their relationship first. This will permit installation in the same position (which is necessary for proper parking).

To install:
5. Installation is the reverse of removal.

323 Models

1. Disconnect the negative battery cable.
2. Unfasten and remove the access cover from the cowl, adjacent to the wiper motor.
3. Detach the motor's electrical connector. Remove the three mounting bolts and pull the motor away from the cowl.

➡ **Do not disconnect the motor arm unless it absolutely necessary. The relationship of the motor arm to the motor shaft determines the position of the automatic stop angle. If this relationship is disturbed, wiper arm positioning will be affected.**

4. Mark the angle of the linkage drive lever on the motor. Remove the nut and washer, then pry the linkage lever off the motor shaft. Remove the motor.

To install:
5. Install the motor in reverse order, with the linkage lever at the same angle. Check the system for proper operation.

1983-87 626

▶ **See Figures 24, 25, 26, 27, 28 and 29**

1. Disconnect the negative battery cable.

2. Unfasten the attaching nuts and remove the wiper arms.

3. Pry out the attaching clips from the front of the cowl cover, then remove the cowl cover. Use a screwdriver to release the clips at the rear of the service hole covers.

4. Remove the two linkage mounting bolts from the cowl area.

5. Unfasten the motor's electrical connector.

6. Unfasten the mounting bolts, then remove the motor and linkage assembly.

7. If the motor and linkage must be separated to replace either, first mark the relationship between the crank arm and linkage, then remove the nut. Use a large screwdriver to pry the linkage off the crank arm.

To install:

8. If the linkage and crank arm were separated, press the linkage onto the arm, making sure to observe the original relationship described in Step 7.

9. Position the motor and linkage onto its mounting, then install the mounting bolts.

10. Fasten the electrical connector.

11. Install the two linkage bolts in the cowl.

12. Install the service hole covers and the cowl cover.

13. Install the wiper arms and properly tighten the attaching nuts.

14. Connect the negative battery cable and check the system for proper operation.

1988-89 626 and MX-6

1. Disconnect the negative battery cable.

2. Remove the wiper blade and arm assemblies.

3. Unfasten the attaching screws and remove the lower molding.

4. Unfasten and remove the two lower cover pieces from the left and right sides of the vehicle.

5. Disconnect the wiper linkage from the wiper motor shaft. DO NOT disconnect the motor arm unless it is absolutely necessary. The relationship of the motor arm to the motor shaft

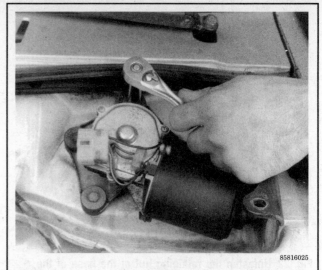

Fig. 25 Use a wrench to unfasten . . .

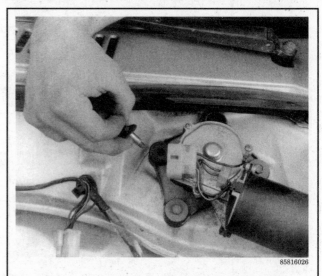

Fig. 26 . . . and remove the motor's mounting bolts

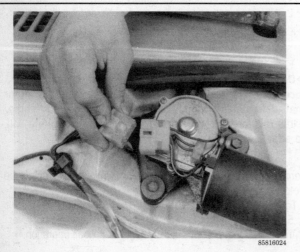

Fig. 24 Unfasten the electrical connector from the wiper motor

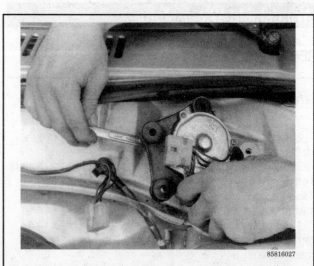

Fig. 27 If necessary, remove the nut which retains the linkage to the wiper motor . . .

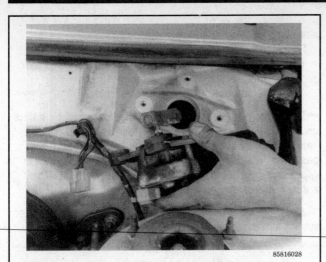

Fig. 28 . . . then remove the wiper motor from the vehicle

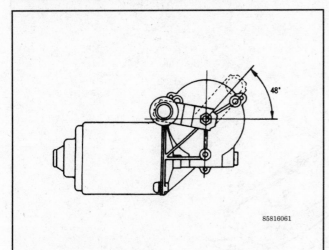

Fig. 29 **Proper installation angle for wiper linkage on the 1983-87 626**

determines the position of the automatic stop angle. If this relationship is disturbed, wiper arm positioning will be affected.

6. Detach the wiper motor connector. Unfasten the attaching bolts and remove the wiper motor.

To install:

7. Position the motor onto its mounting and install the attaching bolts. Connect the wiring to the motor.

8. Connect the wiper linkage to the motor shaft and tighten the nut.

9. Attach the left and right lower covers, then install the lower molding.

10. Install the wiper arm/blade assemblies.

➡The wiper arm/blade assemblies are identified by letters on the portion of the blade that connects to the wiper linkage. The driver's side arm is marked "DL" and the passenger's side is marked "PL". Make sure that the wiper arms are installed in their original positions, as they are not interchangeable.

11. Connect the negative battery cable. Check the wiper system for proper operation.

929 Models

▶ **See Figure 30**

1. Disconnect the negative battery cable.

2. Remove the wiper arms.

3. Unfasten the attaching screws and remove the lower front window molding.

4. Detach the wiper motor electrical connector, then unfasten and separate the linkage assembly from the wiper motor.

5. Unfasten the mounting bolts and remove the wiper motor from the vehicle.

To install:

6. Align the tang in the motor shaft with the slot in the linkage. When properly aligned, engage the motor shaft and linkage, then install the wiper motor attaching bolts.

7. Fasten the wiper motor electrical connector and install the lower front window molding.

8. Install the wiper arms by placing the blade on top of the wiper stopper and tightening the locknut to 7-11 ft. lbs. (9.5-15 Nm). After the nuts are tightened, move the wiper blades down to the stop position.

9. Connect the negative battery cable and check the wiper system for proper operation.

1979-85 RX-7

1. Turn the ignition switch **ON**. Activate and stop the windshield wipers, so that the wiper blades are positioned at the center of the windshield, by disconnecting the negative battery cable.

2. Remove the wiper arms.

3. Remove the seal caps, then unfasten the nuts on the wiper linkage shafts.

4. Remove the cup washers and outer bushings.

5. Unfasten the cowl plate attaching screws and remove the cowl plate.

6. Disconnect the washer hose at the washer nozzle.

7. Detach the wiper motor electrical connections and unfasten the mounting bolts.

8. Remove the wiper motor and linkage assembly as a unit.

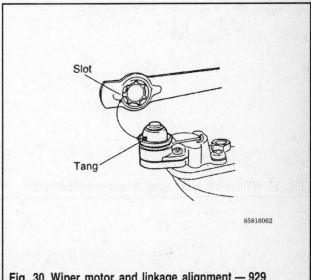

Fig. 30 **Wiper motor and linkage alignment — 929**

9. Installation is the reverse of the removal procedure.

1986-89 RX-7

▶ See Figure 31

1. Disconnect the negative battery cable.
2. Disengage the wiper arms from the linkage shafts.
3. Unfasten the attaching screws and remove the cowl grille.
4. Disconnect the wiper link from the motor arm. DO NOT disconnect the motor arm unless it is absolutely necessary. The relationship of the motor arm to the motor shaft determines the position of the automatic stop angle. If this relationship is disturbed, wiper arm positioning will be affected.

5. Detach the wiper motor connector. Unfasten the motor attaching bolts and remove the wiper motor.

To install:

6. Position the wiper motor onto its mounting, then install and tighten the bolts. Attach the wiper motor connector.
7. Install the cowl grille and the wiper arms.

➡The wiper arm/blade assemblies are identified by letters on the portion of the blade that connects to the wiper linkage. The driver's side arm is marked "DL" and the passenger's side is marked "PL". Make sure that the wiper arms are installed in their original positions. They are not interchangeable.

8. Connect the negative battery cable and check the wiper system for proper operation.

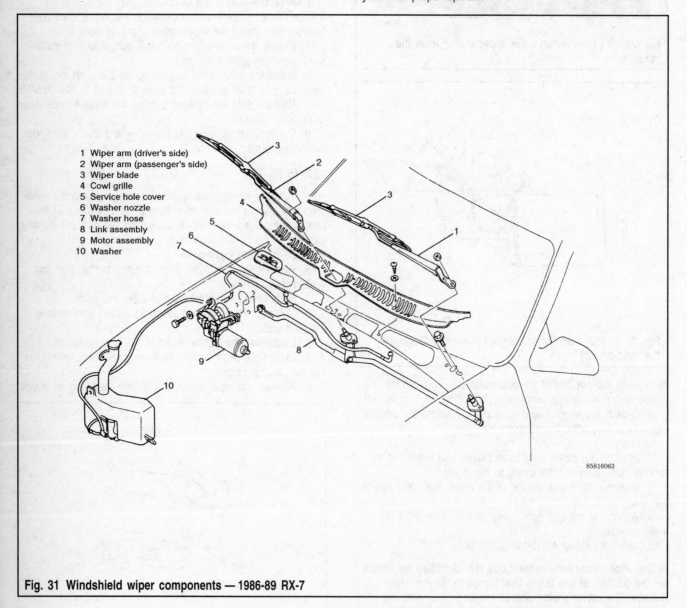

1 Wiper arm (driver's side)
2 Wiper arm (passenger's side)
3 Wiper blade
4 Cowl grille
5 Service hole cover
6 Washer nozzle
7 Washer hose
8 Link assembly
9 Motor assembly
10 Washer

85816063

Fig. 31 Windshield wiper components — 1986-89 RX-7

Rear Window Wiper Motor

REMOVAL & INSTALLATION

323 Models

1. Disconnect the negative battery cable.
2. Note the installation angle of the wiper arm, then unfasten the attaching nut from the end of the shaft and remove the arm.
3. The rear wiper motor on the 323 may be located either behind a panel in the rear hatch (hatchback) or behind the rear seat (sedan). Remove the door panel or rear seat back, depending on the model.
4. Detach the electrical connector. Remove the mounting bolts, then carefully withdraw the motor. Slide the shaft straight through the rubber seal to avoid damaging the seal.
   To install:
5. Installation is the reverse of removal. Replace the rubber seal if it is damaged or worn.

1979-87 626

1. Disconnect the negative battery cable.
2. Note the installation angle of the wiper arm, then unfasten the attaching nut from the end of the shaft and remove the arm.
3. Remove the panel from the inside of the rear hatch.
4. Detach the electrical connector. Remove the mounting bolts for the motor mounting bracket from the door. Remove the motor and bracket by carefully pulling the motor toward you. Slide the shaft straight through the rubber seal to avoid damaging the seal.
5. Remove the attaching screws and transfer the mounting bracket to the new motor.
   To install:
6. Installation is the reverse of removal. Replace the rubber shaft seal if it has been damaged.

1988-89 626 and MX-6

1. Disconnect the negative battery cable.
2. Remove the rear wiper arm.
3. Raise the rear hatch. Remove the rear hatch upper, lower and rear side trim to expose the wiper motor assembly.
4. Remove the rear hatch screen carefully so that it may be reused.
5. Detach the rear wiper motor connector. Unfasten the attaching bolts and remove the motor.
   To install:
6. Position the motor onto its mounting and install the attaching bolts. Connect the motor wiring.
7. Install the rear hatch screen. If the screen was damaged during removal, replace it. Install the rear hatch trim and close the hatch.
8. Install the rear wiper arm.
9. Connect the negative battery cable. Test the wiper system for proper operation.

RX-7 With Rear Glass Hatch

The wiper motor is located under the hatch.
1. Disconnect the negative battery cable.
2. Remove the nut and separate the rear wiper arm from the motor shaft. Remove the bushings, nuts and shaft seal from the wiper motor shaft.
3. Raise the rear hatch and detach the wiper motor connector.
4. Remove the attaching screws and lower the wiper motor unit from the mounting plate.
   To install:
5. Position the motor onto the mounting plate and install the attaching screws. Connect the motor wiring and close the hatch.
6. If the shaft seal is worn or damaged, replace it. Install the motor shaft seal, bushing and locknuts.
7. Install the rear wiper arm and tighten the retaining nut.
8. Connect the negative battery cable and check the system for proper operation.

INSTRUMENTS AND SWITCHES

Instrument Cluster

REMOVAL & INSTALLATION

GLC and GLC Wagon With Standard Dash

1. Disconnect the negative battery cable.

➡**Place masking tape on the instrument panel pad directly below the instrument cluster to prevent damage to the pad during the procedure.**

2. Remove the meter hood by removing the screw above either dial, and pulling the hood off the dash.
3. Remove the wood grain center panel cover by removing the screw from the left side and unclipping the panel on the right.
4. Unfasten the three screws located under the front edge of the crash pad, and remove the pad.
5. Reach behind the speedometer and disconnect the cable by pressing on the flat surface of the connector.
6. Remove the three screws from the instrument cluster, and pull the cluster out of the dash.
7. Detach the multiple connectors from the rear of the unit and remove the cluster from the vehicle.
8. Installation is the reverse of the removal procedure.

GLC With Sport Dash
▶ **See Figure 32**

1. Disconnect the negative battery cable.
2. Put masking tape along the panel just below where the cluster will come out to protect it.
3. Unfasten the tripmeter knob (1), screws (2), and clips (3), then remove the meter hood (4), as referenced in the illustration.

4. Remove the wood grain center panel cover by unfastening the screw from the left side and unclipping the panel on the right.

5. Unfasten the three screws located under the front edge of the instrument panel pad, then remove the pad.

6. Remove the three screws from the top of the combination instrument cluster, and pull the cluster outward.

7. Disconnect the speedometer cable by pressing on the flat surface of the plastic connector. Detach the wiring connectors and remove the cluster.

8. Installation is the reverse of the removal procedure.

1979-84 626

▶ See Figures 33, 34, 35 and 36

1. Disconnect the negative battery cable.
2. Remove the steering wheel.
3. Remove the column cover.
4. Disconnect the speedometer cable.
5. Unfasten and remove the meter hood.
6. Remove the meter assembly attaching screws, then detach the wire connections and remove the combination meter assembly.
7. Installation is the reverse of the removal procedure.

1985 626

1. Disconnect the negative battery cable. Tilt the steering wheel downward.

2. Remove the cover from the top of the meter hood. Remove the two screws from the top of the meter assembly.

3. Remove the two attaching screws from the underside of the meter hood. Then, remove the four screws from the underside of the assembly.

4. Remove the four screws attaching the meter assembly to the hood. Pull the assembly out slightly, then depress the retaining clip and disconnect the plugs.

5. Disconnect the speedometer cable and remove the light. Pull the assembly out.

6. Installation is the reverse of the removal procedure.

Fig. 33 Unfasten all of the upper and lower retaining screws . . .

Fig. 34 . . . and remove the meter hood

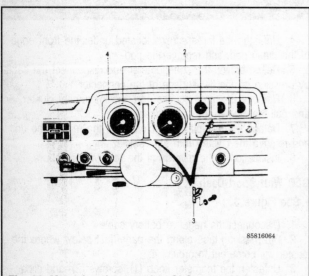

Fig. 32 Meter hood removal — GLC sport dash

Fig. 35 Remove the screws retaining the meter assembly

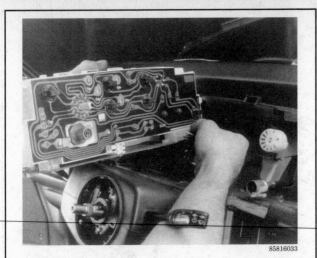

85816033

Fig. 36 Unfasten the electrical connectors from the rear of the meter assembly

1986-87 626

1. Disconnect the negative battery cable.
2. Tilt the steering wheel downward. Disconnect the speedometer cable from the rear of the cluster by reaching up behind the cluster and unscrewing the collar.
3. Remove the four screws from the underside of the instrument cluster assembly where it attaches to the underside of the dash and the three screws from the underside of the hood.
4. Remove the two screws attaching the cluster to the hood at the top. Then, pull the assembly slightly outward and detach the wiring connectors. In order to disconnect the plugs, you must depress the retaining clips.
5. Remove the cluster assembly.
6. Installation is the reverse of the removal procedure.

1988-89 626 and MX-6

1. Disconnect the negative battery cable.
2. Remove the shift lever knob. On vehicles equipped with an automatic transaxle, first remove the two attaching screws that hold the shift knob to the shaft.
3. Remove the rear console mounting screws, then pull the console rearward to remove it.
4. Remove the front console mounting screws.
5. Pry the ornament from the steering wheel pad, then remove the steering wheel mounting nut.
6. Remove the horn cap. Attach a suitable puller and remove the steering wheel.
7. Remove the attaching screws and separate the upper and lower column covers. Unfasten the under cover attaching screws and remove the under cover. Reach behind the hood release and remove the nut and hood release knob.
8. Remove the meter hood attaching screws and pull the meter hood out until the electrical connectors are visible and accessible. Disconnect the speedometer cable at the speedometer. Detach all the connectors from the rear of the meter hood and remove it.
9. Remove the attaching screws and pull the meter assembly outward. Detach the speedometer cable and meter connectors, then remove the meter assembly.

To install:

10. Rest the meter assembly on top of the combination switch and connect the wiring to the rear of the unit. Fasten the speedometer cable to the speedometer cable connection.
11. Gently push the meter into the dash and secure with the attaching screws.
12. Attach the meter hood electrical connectors and push the meter hood into place. Fasten the meter hood with the attaching screws.
13. Install the hood release knob and the under cover.
14. Assemble the upper and lower column cover with the attaching screws.
15. Install the steering wheel, cap, mounting nut and ornament.
16. Install the front console retaining screws. Push the rear console into place and secure with the attaching screws.
17. Install the shift lever knob.
18. Connect the negative battery cable and check all the meter functions for proper operation.

1986-87 323

▶ See Figure 37

1. Disconnect the negative battery cable.
2. Remove the three screws from under the top edge of the instrument hood.
3. Pull the hood out for access, unplug the electrical connectors to the cluster switches on either side, and remove it.
4. Unfasten the screw located near the bottom of the cluster on either side. Remove the cluster from the dash, unplugging the connectors when you can reach them.

To install:

5. Rest the cluster on the dash and plug in all the connectors. Push the cluster into the dash and install the side attaching screws.
6. Plug in the meter hood connectors and install the meter hood into the dash. Install the top instrument hood retaining screws.
7. Connect the negative battery cable. Check the meter functions for proper operation.

1988-89 323

1. Remove the steering wheel, upper and lower column covers and the combination switch assembly.
2. Unfasten the attaching screws and remove the meter hood.
3. Remove the meter attaching screws and pull the meter out until the electrical connectors are visible. Disconnect the speedometer cable at the speedometer. Detach all the connectors from the rear of the meter and remove it.

To install:

4. Rest the meter on the dash and plug all the electrical connectors into the rear of the unit. Connect the speedometer cable to the speedometer. Push the meter into the dash and install the attaching screws.
5. Install the meter hood.
6. Install the combination switch, upper and lower steering wheel column covers and steering wheel.
7. Check the meter functions for proper operation.

929 Models

1. Disconnect the negative battery cable.

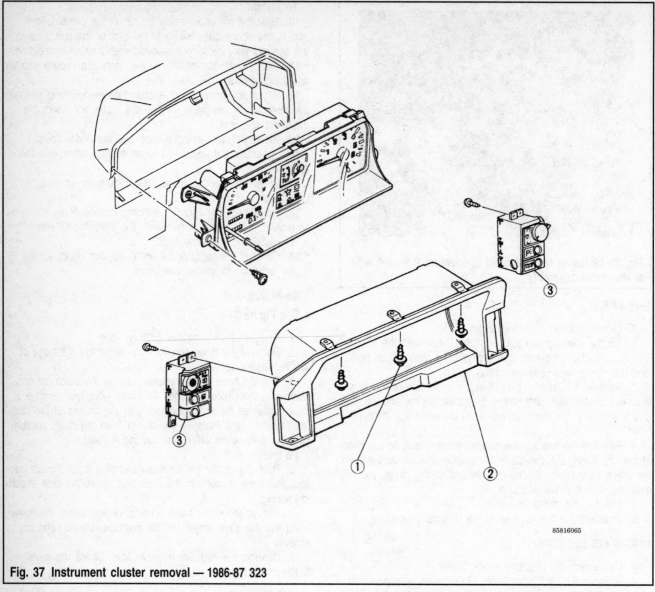

Fig. 37 Instrument cluster removal — 1986-87 323

2. Disconnect the speedometer cable at the transmission.

3. Remove the ashtray and detach the cigarette lighter connector.

4. Gently pry the horn cap loose, then remove the steering wheel nut and the horn pad. Remove the steering wheel using a suitable steering wheel puller. DO NOT strike the steering wheel with a hammer, as its collapsibility might be severely impaired.

5. Remove the steering wheel upper and lower cover assemblies.

6. Unscrew and pull the switch panel out and away from the dash. Detach the electrical connectors and remove the switch panel.

7. Remove the meter hood attaching screws and pull the meter hood out until the electrical connectors are visible. Disconnect the speedometer cable at the speedometer. Detach all the connectors from the rear of the meter cluster and remove it.

To install:

8. Rest the meter assembly on the dash and connect the speedometer cable to the speedometer. Plug in all the electri-

cal connections to the rear of the meter assembly. Gently push the meter into the dash opening and install the attaching screws.

9. Plug in the switch panel connectors and push the panel into the dash. Install the attaching screws.

10. Assemble the upper and lower steering wheel covers and install the attaching screws.

11. Install the steering wheel, horn pad, steering wheel nut and horn cap.

12. Attach the cigarette lighter connector and install the ashtray.

13. Connect the speedometer cable to the transmission.

14. Connect the negative battery cable and check all the meter functions for proper operation.

1979-85 RX-7

▶ **See Figure 38**

1. Disconnect the negative battery cable.

2. Unscrew the speedometer cable from the back of the instrument cluster.

3. Pull off the steering wheel center cap.

4. Remove the steering wheel as described in Section 8 of this manual.

5. On 1979-83 models, pull the light switch knob off the shaft.

6. Remove the upper and lower steering column covers. On 1984-85 models, remove the combination switch and detach the cluster switches (left side: hazard and headlight retractor switches; right side: rear wiper, rear washer and rear defroster switches) from the sides of the cluster. The switches are retained by screws.

7. On 1979-83 models, remove the instrument cluster cover by unfastening the two upper screws. On 1984-85 models, gently pry the meter hood from the face of the cluster assembly.

8. Remove the instrument cluster attaching screws, draw out the instrument cluster and unfasten the multiple connectors from the back of the cluster. Remove the instrument cluster.

To install:

9. Rest the cluster on the dash and plug in all the connectors. Gently push the cluster into the dash and install the attaching screws.

10. On 1984-85 models, push the meter hood onto the face of the cluster until it locks in place. On 1979-83 models, install the cover with the attaching screws.

11. On 1984-85 models, connect the switch assemblies to the cluster and install the combination switch. On 1979-83 models, push the light switch knob onto the shaft. Install the upper and lower steering wheel covers.

12. Install the steering wheel and horn cap.

13. Connect the speedometer cable and the negative battery cable. Check all the meter functions for proper operation.

1986-89 RX-7

The instrument cluster front bezel contains switches for headlamps and other lighting, cruise control, turn signals and headlamp high beams, and windshield wipers.

1. Unfasten the seven screws which secure the bezel and switch assembly.

2. Pull the cluster gently and disconnect the instrument cluster wiring harness from the switch assemblies.

3. Remove the bezel, then withdraw the switch assemblies from the rear of the unit.

4. Unfasten the mounting screws, then disconnect the speedometer cable and wiring connectors.

5. Installation is the reverse of the removal procedure.

Speedometer Cable

REMOVAL & INSTALLATION

▶ **See Figure 39**

Speedometer cable removal and installation requires reaching behind the instrument cluster and disconnecting the cable from the rear of the speedometer. On some vehicles, the cluster must be removed to gain access to the speedometer.

➡**If the cable housing is intact, the cable core may be removed separately.**

1. Reach behind the instrument cluster and disconnect the speedometer cable by depressing the flat portion of the connector, while pulling the connector off.

2. Pull the cable core out of the cable housing. (If the entire cable core does not come out due to breakage, it will be necessary to unscrew the speedometer cable housing at the transmission/transaxle, and pull the lower end of the cable out.)

3. If necessary, disconnect the cable housing from the transmission/transaxle. Some cables are protected by a dust boot where the cable connects to the transmission/transaxle. Raise the vehicle and support it safely, as required. If there is a dust boot installed, pull it up a couple of inches to uncover the cable connector. If the dust boot is worn, replace it.

To install:

4. If applicable, reconnect the lower end of the cable housing to the transmission/transaxle. Make sure the cable connector on the transmission/transaxle is tightened properly.

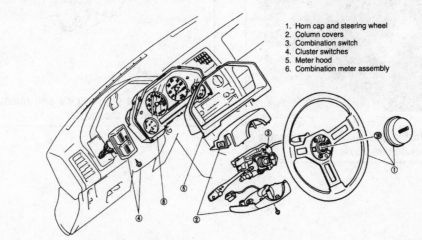

1. Horn cap and steering wheel
2. Column covers
3. Combination switch
4. Cluster switches
5. Meter hood
6. Combination meter assembly

85816066

Fig. 38 Instrument cluster and steering wheel components — 1979-85 RX-7

5. If installing a new cable core, lubricate it with speedometer cable lubricant (powdered graphite), and insert it into the instrument cluster end of the cable housing.

➡**Take care not to force any radical bends, as these will cause the cable core to bind and wear out quickly.**

6. Work the cable core through the housing until it bottoms against the drive gear in the transmission/transaxle. Then, simultaneously push the core inward while rotating it until the square end of the core engages and seats against the driven gear.

7. Reconnect the cable housing to the back of the speedometer. When attaching the cable to the instrument cluster, make sure the square end of the core fits into the drive yoke in the cable connection.

Instrument Cluster Mounted Switches

REMOVAL & INSTALLATION

▶ **See Figures 40 and 41**

On late model Mazdas, these switches are mounted in a cluster on either side of the instrument cluster.

1. Remove the instrument cluster as described earlier in this section.
2. Working from the rear, unfasten the attaching screws at the top and bottom, then remove the switch cluster.
3. Carefully pry the switch knob off the front of the cluster. Release the lockpins at the rear, then pull the switch out the back of the cluster.

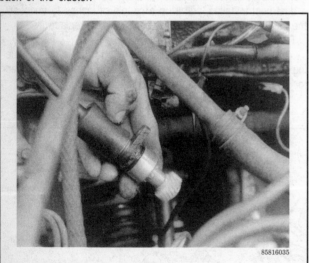

85816035

Fig. 39 If necessary, unfasten and disconnect the cable housing from the transmission/transaxle

4. Install in the reverse order, making sure the plugs are securely connected.

Back-up Light Switch

The back-up light switch is mounted on the transmission/transaxle. For back-up light switch service, refer to Section 7 of this manual.

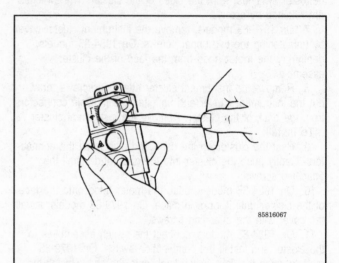

85816067

Fig. 40 Prying a switch knob off a cluster of switches (common on later model)

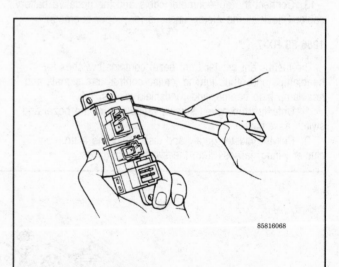

85816068

Fig. 41 Release the lockpins and remove the switch from the rear of the cluster

LIGHTING

Headlights

REMOVAL & INSTALLATION

Except RX-7

♦ See Figures 42, 43, 44, 45 and 46

➡On some 323, 626, MX-6 and 929 models, you must remove the radiator grille to gain access to the headlights.

1. If the grille blocks removal of the headlamp assembly or adjacent bezel, remove the attaching screws or disconnect the clips (usually 5 or 6 of them), then remove the grille.

2. Unfasten the attaching screws, then remove the bezel (or half bezel) that runs around the outside of the headlight.

3. Identify the two adjusting screws for the headlight. There are either (A) two at the top or (B) one on the side and one at the top or bottom. These long screws are tensioned by a spring. The spring either works in opposition to the screw at the opposite side of the headlight, or it surrounds the screw.

✴✴WARNING

Do not tamper with the headlight beam adjusting screws, or you may need to have the headlights readjusted by a professional shop, since aiming requires the use of special equipment.

4. Remove the 2, 3 or 4 short screws which fasten the headlight in place. On many models with round or rectangular headlights, these screws retain a thin metal ring which actually holds the light in place. If a round ring has elongated slots, instead of round holes, loosen (but do not remove) the screws, then rotate the ring until the rounded parts of the slots line up with the screw heads.

5. If so equipped, remove the ring, then pull the headlight out until you can unplug it. Remove the headlight.

➡Be careful not to mix up the inner and outer lights if both must be replaced at the same time. The inner lights have only one filament, while the outer lights have two.

To install:

6. Securely fasten the wiring connector to the new headlight.

7. Position a rectangular light so the glass lugs seat securely against the mounting plate; turn a round light until the glass lug on the light locks into the notch in the mounting plate. Then, install the retaining screws or the ring and its retaining screws.

8. Install the bezel (or half bezel) and, if necessary, the grille.

➡Headlight aiming is normally not required if the adjusting screws have not been turned. When necessary, however, have the headlights checked and/or adjusted by a professional using special aiming equipment.

Fig. 42 Unfasten and remove the headlamp bezel

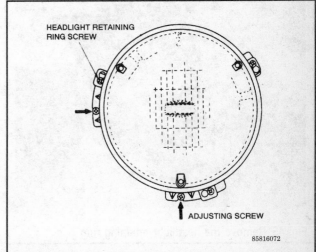

Fig. 43 Do not turn the adjusting screws (indicated by arrows)

RX-7 Models

♦ See Figures 47, 48 and 49

The RX-7 is equipped with retractable headlights. In the event that the headlights do not open when activated, they can be opened using the manual control knobs located at the top of the retractor motors. The knobs are underneath plastic covers and are accessible through the engine compartment. To perform the manual adjustment, disconnect the negative battery cable and turn the manual control knob on the retractor motor shaft until the headlight is raised to the fully open position.

Fig. 44 Unfasten the screws which secure the retaining ring

Fig. 45 Remove the headlight retaining ring

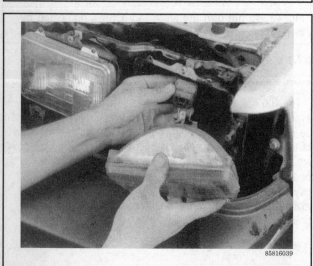

Fig. 46 Unplug the electrical connector and remove the headlight

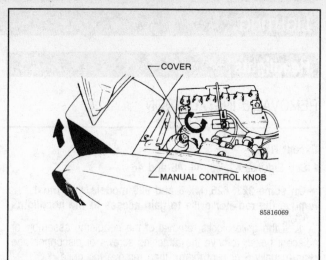

Fig. 47 RX-7 headlights can be opened by turning the manual control knob

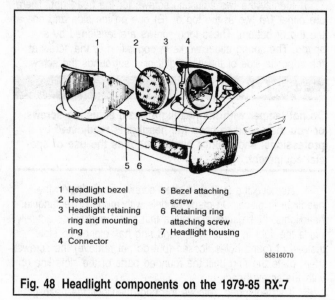

1 Headlight bezel
2 Headlight
3 Headlight retaining ring and mounting ring
4 Connector
5 Bezel attaching screw
6 Retaining ring attaching screw
7 Headlight housing

Fig. 48 Headlight components on the 1979-85 RX-7

Removal and installation of the headlights is performed as follows:

1. Turn on the headlight retractor switch to raise the headlights.

➡ **If the headlights will not open when the retractor switch is operated, manually open them as described above.**

2. If not already done, disconnect the negative battery cable.

➡ **1986-89 RX-7 headlights have a two-piece bezel.**

3. Unfasten and remove the headlight bezel(s).

✱✱WARNING

Do not tamper with the headlight beam adjusting screws, or you may need to have the headlights readjusted by a professional shop, since aiming requires the use of special equipment.

4. On models with round headlights, loosen (but do not remove) the retaining ring attaching screws. Rotate the headlight ring counterclockwise and remove it while holding the headlight.

5. On models with rectangular headlights, unfasten and remove the screws and retaining ring.

6. Remove the headlight and detach the electrical connector.

To install:

7. Attach the electrical connector to the new headlight.

8. Hold the headlight stationary, then position and install the retaining ring. If equipped with round headlights, turn the ring clockwise, then tighten the retaining screws.

9. Install the bezel(s).

10. Connect the negative battery cable. Raise and lower the headlights several times to make sure they operate properly.

➡**Headlight aiming is normally not required if the adjusting screws have not been turned. When necessary, however, have the headlights checked and/or adjusted by a professional using special aiming equipment.**

ADJUSTING THE HEADLIGHT LIDS

1979-85 RX-7

▶ **See Figure 50**

1. Raise the headlights and open the hood.

2. Disconnect the link from the headlight hinge assembly. The link should pull off fairly easily. DO NOT bend it. Lower the headlights.

3. Loosen the locknut on the adjusting screw and turn the adjusting screw in or out until the headlights are positioned properly. Tighten the locknut.

4. Turn the manual control knob until the motor link reaches its lowest position.

5. Loosen the retractor motor mounting bolts and nuts.

6. Connect the link to the hinge assembly.

➡**Connect the link to its ball socket using your finger. Do not use pliers. You should hear a click when the link is attached.**

7. Move the motor back and forth until the headlight lid is in the desired position, then tighten the motor mounting bolts and nuts.

Signal and Marker Lights

REMOVAL & INSTALLATION

▶ **See Figures 51, 52, 53, 54, 55, 56, 57 and 58**

Some instrument, marker and other bulbs are accessible without removing the lens. To service these bulbs, grasp and twist the socket from the rear, then withdraw the socket and bulb assembly. Simply pull out the bulb and push in a replacement, then reposition and twist the socket in place.

➡**The access to some rear light bulbs is often hidden behind carpeting or other interior trim.**

1. If necessary, unfasten the attaching screw(s) from the lens, then remove the lens and gasket.

2. Depress and twist the lamp to the left (counterclockwise) to remove it.

3. Inspect the socket for corrosion and clean or replace, if necessary.

To install:

4. Align the retaining pins on the side of the bulb with the socket channels, then push and twist the bulb to the right (clockwise) until it locks in position.

5. If the socket was removed from the light housing, reposition and gently twist the socket to lock it in place. Otherwise, position the lens and gasket, then fasten the retaining screw(s).

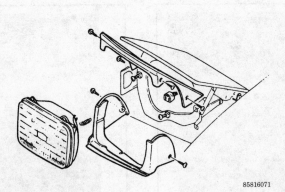

85816071

Fig. 49 Headlight components on the 1986-89 RX-7

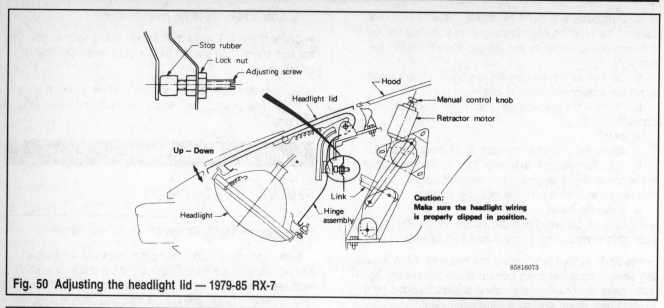

Fig. 50 Adjusting the headlight lid — 1979-85 RX-7

Fig. 51 Some bulbs are easily removed after twisting and removing the socket . . .

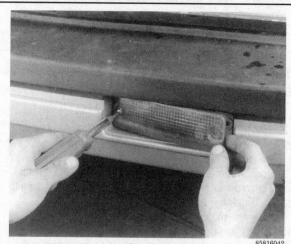

Fig. 53 On some applications, the lens must be removed in order to access the bulb

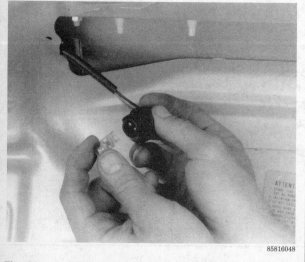

Fig. 52 . . . then pulling the bulb straight out

Fig. 54 Signal light bulbs often have locking pins on their bases. These bulbs must be depressed, then twisted slightly, before they can be removed

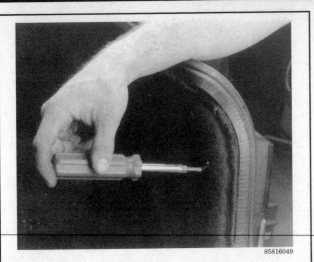

Fig. 55 In order to reach some rear light bulbs, you must unfasten . . .

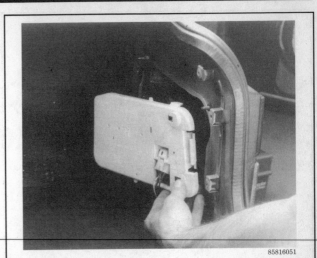

Fig. 57 If applicable, disengage the locking tangs which secure the rear light cluster

Fig. 56 . . . and remove a carpeted trim panel

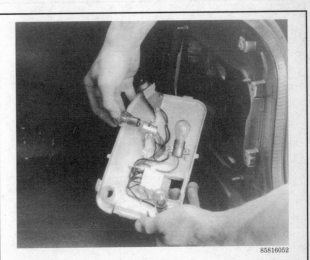

Fig. 58 Once the cluster is removed, its bulbs can be easily serviced

CIRCUIT PROTECTION

Fuses

REPLACEMENT

▶ See Figures 59 and 60

✳✳WARNING

When replacing a fuse, always install a new fuse that has the same amperage capacity as the one that was removed. Make sure the ignition switch is in the OFF position when making a replacement.

All fuses up to 60 amps are the blade type; these are replaced by simply pulling out the old fuse and pushing in a new one. Always use a proper fuse pulling tool (preferably the one in the fuse box, if so equipped). Fuse box locations are given below.

➡**If a fuse blows repeatedly, there is probably a short circuit that will require investigation and repair.**

If an 80 amp (main) fuse is to be replaced, the main fuse box must be removed from the engine compartment.

✳✳CAUTION

When a main fuse is replaced, always disconnect the negative battery cable first.

Remove the fuse box cover, then unscrew the wire terminal from the main fuse and remove the fuse. Push the new fuse in and connect the wire with the attaching screw. Position the cover and reinstall the fuse box in the engine compartment. Reconnect the negative battery cable.

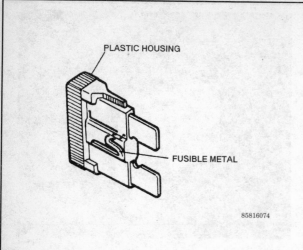

Fig. 59 Common blade-type fuse. The amperage rating is printed on top of the fuse

Fig. 61 The fuse box is commonly located underneath the dashboard on the driver's side kick panel

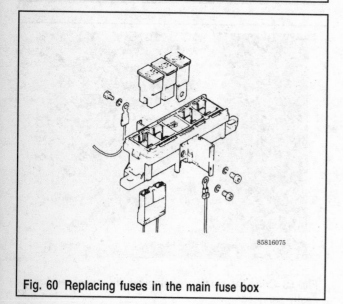

Fig. 60 Replacing fuses in the main fuse box

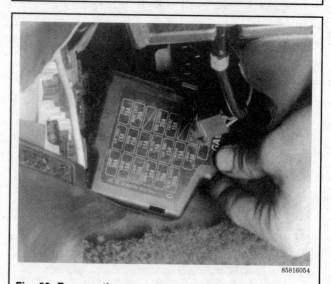

Fig. 62 Remove the cover to expose the fuses

LOCATION

▶ See Figures 61 and 62

On the GLC and 1979-87 626, the fuse box (or joint box) is located underneath the left side of the dash panel or on the left-side kick panel. Box covers list the location, amperage, and circuit protected by each individual fuse. On the 1986-89 626 and MX-6, the main fuse block is between the battery and the distributor cap on the driver's side of the engine compartment.

On the 323, the joint box (which contains fuses, one or more circuit breakers, harnesses and harness connectors) is located under the dash, in front of the driver. The main fuse block is located in the engine compartment in front of the driver's side strut, next to the battery. On 1986 models, use the special fuse puller provided in the fuse box cover to pull a fuse.

On the 929, the main fuse block is located on the right side of the engine compartment between the battery and the window washer reservoir. The fuse panel is located on the driver's side of the passenger compartment, just above the brake pedal.

On the RX-7, the fuse block is located under the dash on the driver's side. Remove the plastic cover to gain access to the fuses. On 1986-89 models only, there is also a main fuse box located in the engine compartment on the driver's side.

Fusible Links

Fusible links are designed to melt when an overload strikes the protected circuit, thereby opening the circuit before damage to the wiring or circuit components can occur.

REPLACEMENT

▶ **See Figures 63, 64 and 65**

On 1978-82 GLCs, there is a connector block on the radiator panel, located on the right side of the radiator (inside the engine compartment). On 1983 and later models, the connector block is on the left inner fender panel, behind the battery. Two links connected there are color coded red and green. On the GLC wagon, the fusible link is located between the connector plugs near the battery.

On 1979-85 626s, three fusible links are visible in a box of links and relays mounted on the inner fender panel behind the battery.

The fusible links used on the RX-7 are of the plug-in type and are found only on 1979-85 models. The main bank of fusible links is located inside the engine compartment on the left-side fender near the front suspension tower. There are also two fusible links located near the steering column under the dashboard.

On 1986-89 models, fusible links are replaced by main fuses located in the engine compartment. Their location is described above.

➡**Always correct the short in the circuit or the overload *before* replacing the link, or it will probably melt again.**

1. Disconnect the negative battery cable.
2. Unfasten the damaged fusible link.
3. Install a new fusible link.
4. Connect the negative battery cable.

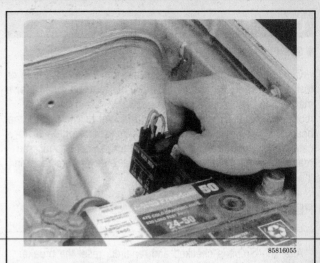

Fig. 63 On some vehicles, fusible links are of the plug-in type — 1984 626 shown

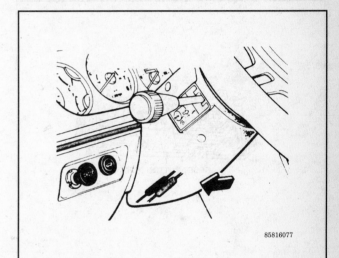

Fig. 64 Steering column fusible link location — 1979-85 RX-7

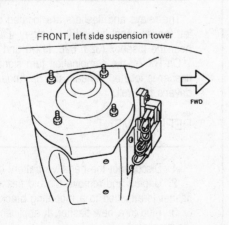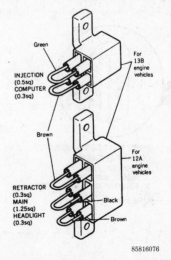

Fig. 65 Engine compartment fusible link location — 1979-85 RX-7

Circuit Breakers

▶ **See Figures 66, 67 and 68**

Circuit breakers operate in much the same way as a fuse or fusible link, except that they have the ability to be reset after a malfunction has occurred. On the 323, MX-6 and later 626 models, a circuit breaker is used in the joint box to protect the heater blower circuit. On 1986-89 RX-7s, a circuit breaker located in the fuse box protects the heater, air conditioner and rear window defroster circuits. All circuit breakers are reset in the manner described below.

RESETTING

After the circuit is checked and repaired, reset the breaker by depressing the button on the breaker with a small pointed instrument. The tip of a pen will do the job nicely.

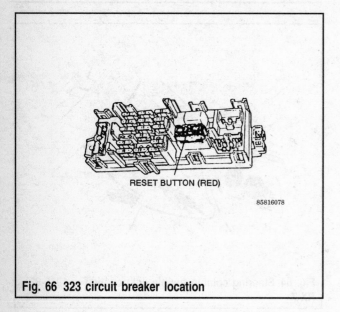

Fig. 66 323 circuit breaker location

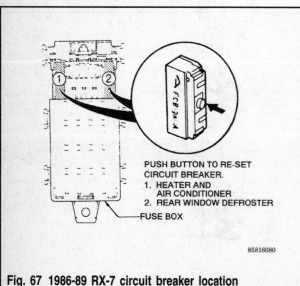

Fig. 67 1986-89 RX-7 circuit breaker location

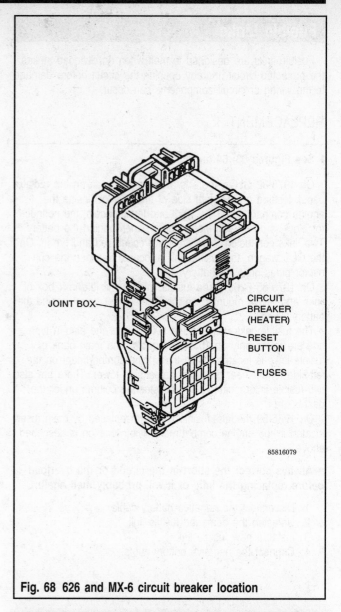

Fig. 68 626 and MX-6 circuit breaker location

Flashers

The relays and flashers are located either in a box on the left fender panel behind the battery (GLC) or under the dash, near the fusebox (323, 626, MX-6 and 929).

On RX-7s, the combination turn signal and emergency flasher is located beneath the dashboard on the left side of the driver's footwell.

REPLACEMENT

1. Disconnect the negative battery cable.
2. Unplug and remove the old flasher. (If the side of the flasher is attached to a mounting bracket, be sure to unclip it.)
3. Plug in a new flasher. If applicable, engage the mounting bracket.
4. Connect the negative battery cable.

WIRING DIAGRAMS

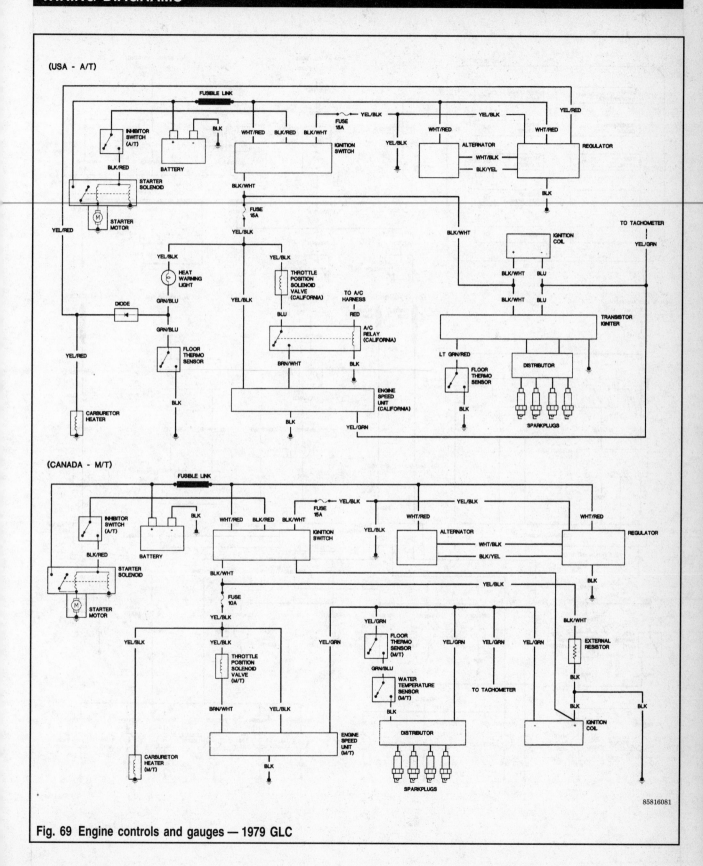

Fig. 69 Engine controls and gauges — 1979 GLC

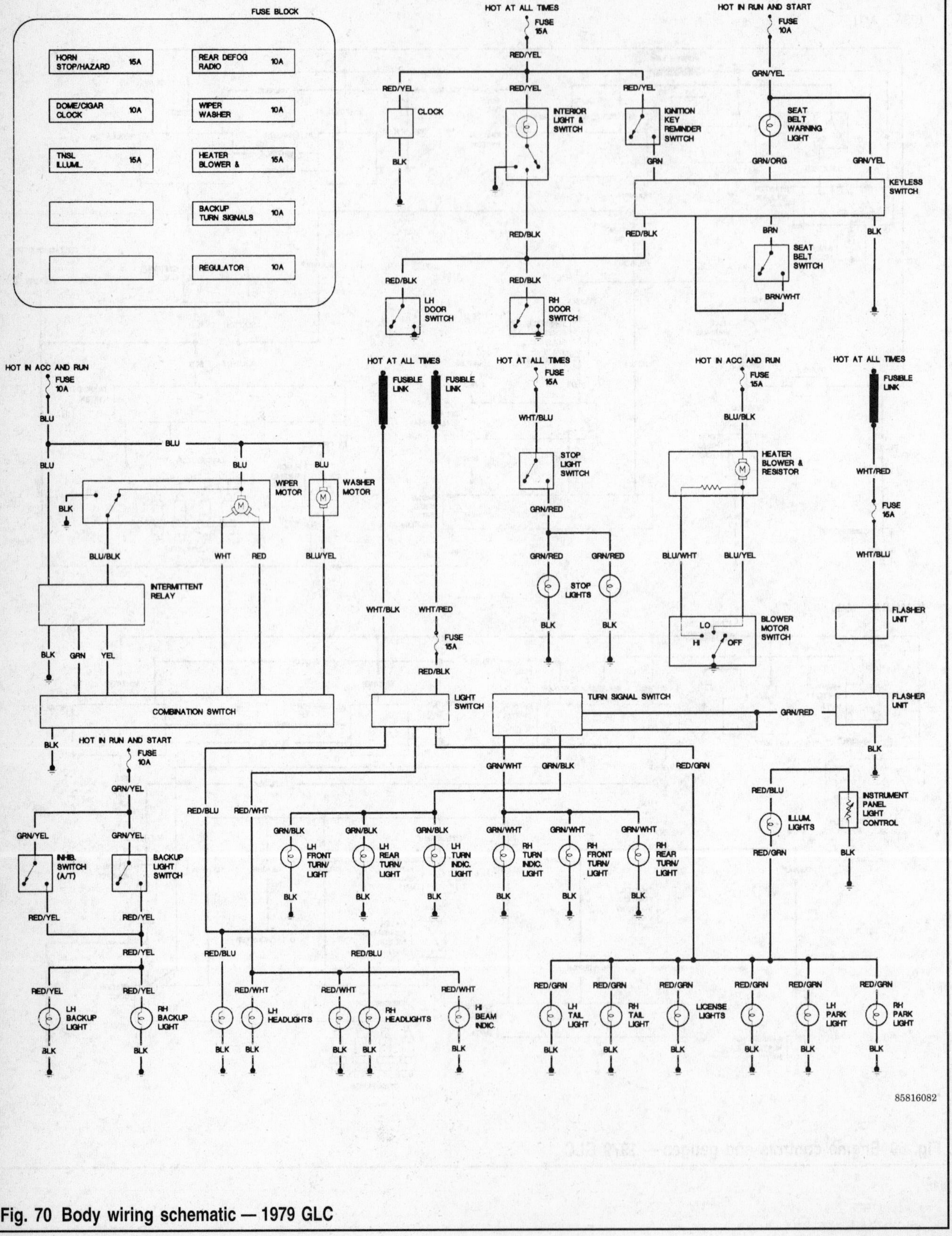

Fig. 70 Body wiring schematic — 1979 GLC

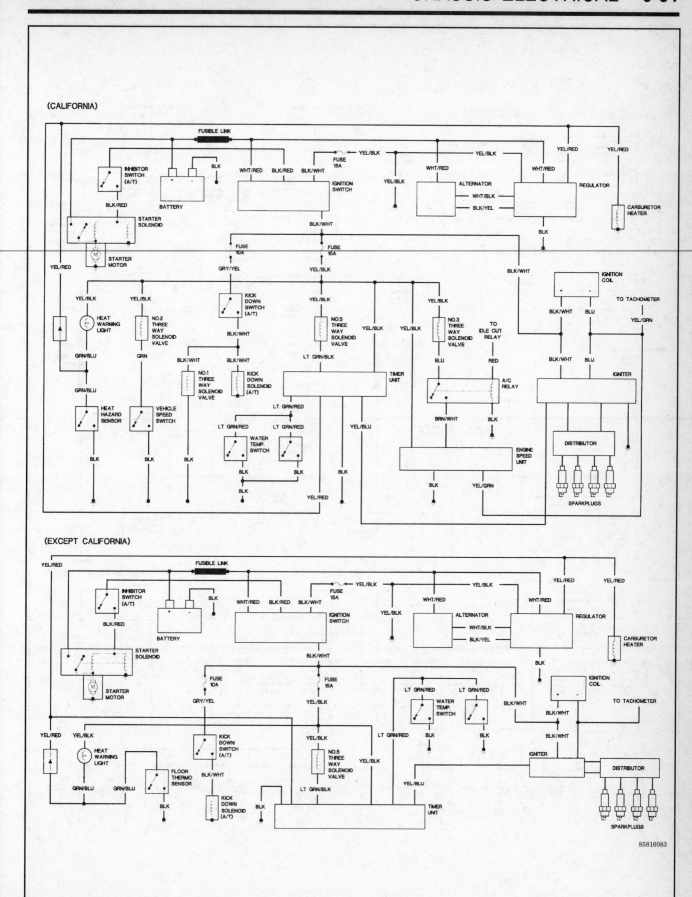

Fig. 71 Engine controls and gauges — 1980 GLC

85816083

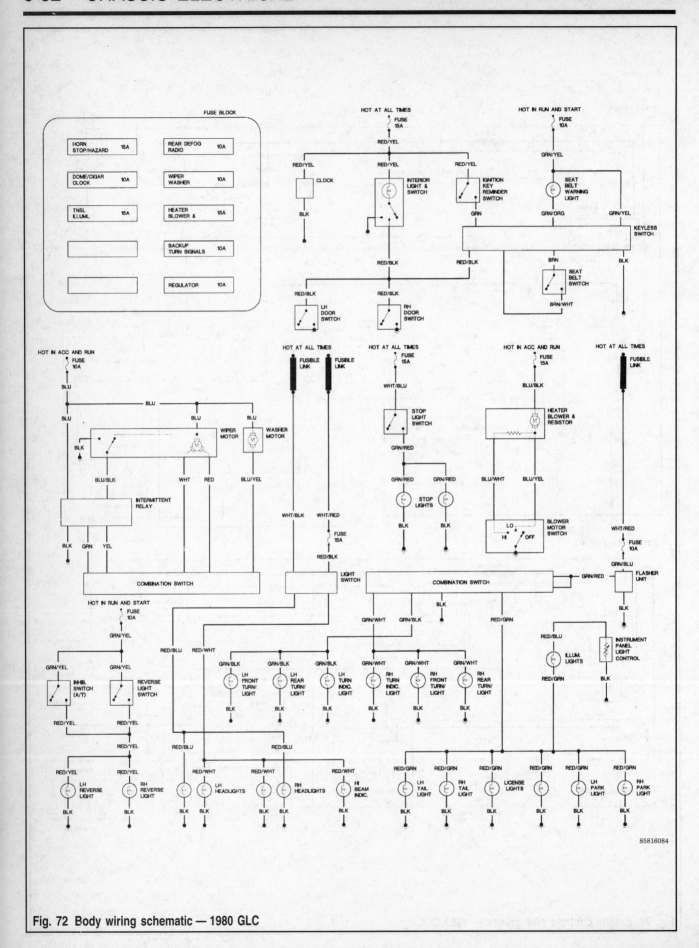

Fig. 72 Body wiring schematic — 1980 GLC

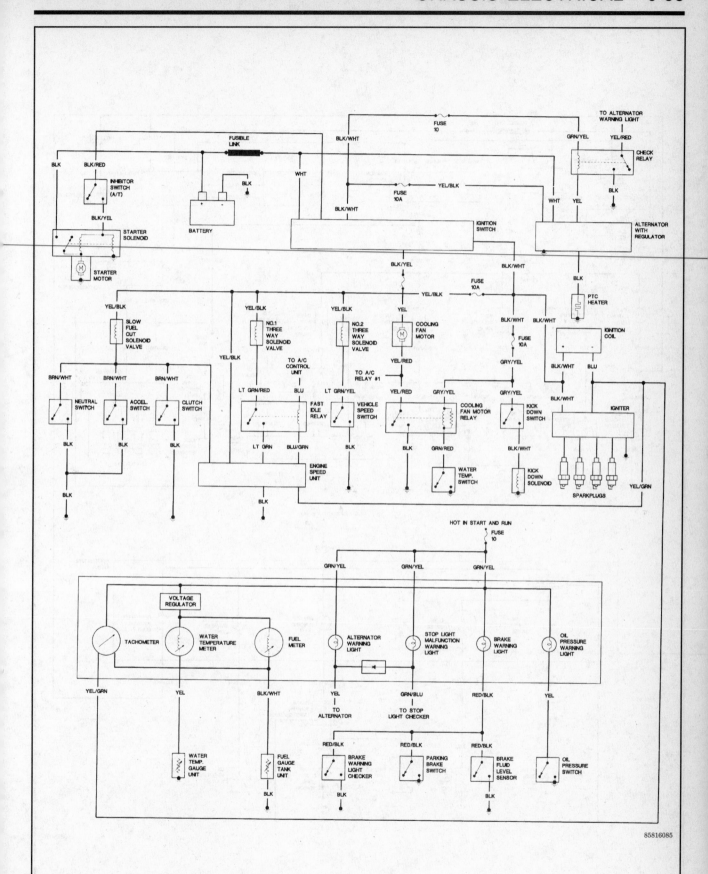

Fig. 73 Engine controls and gauges — 1981 GLC (front wheel drive)

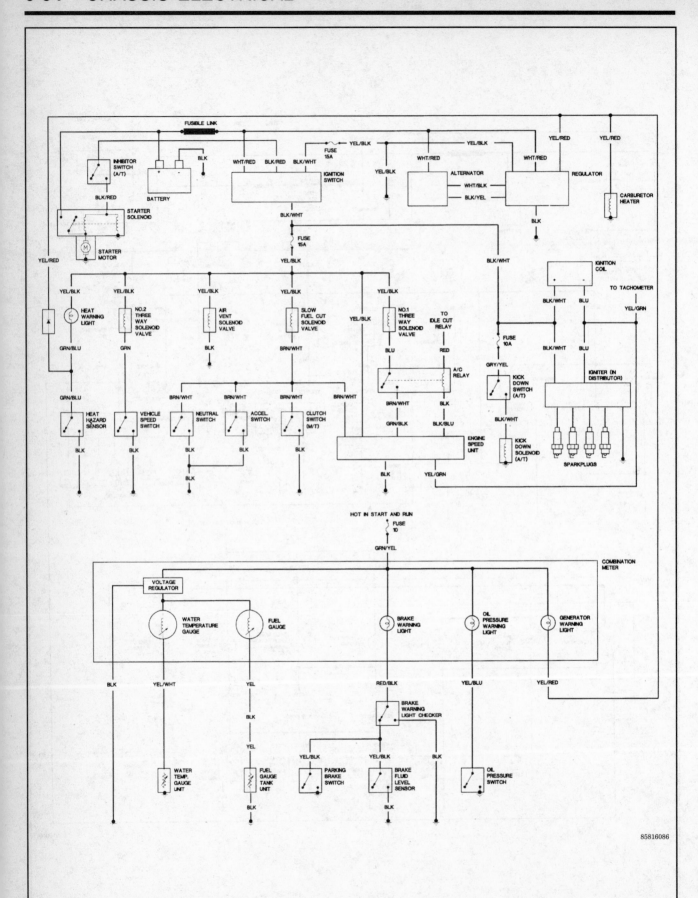

Fig. 74 Engine controls and gauges — 1981 GLC (rear wheel drive)

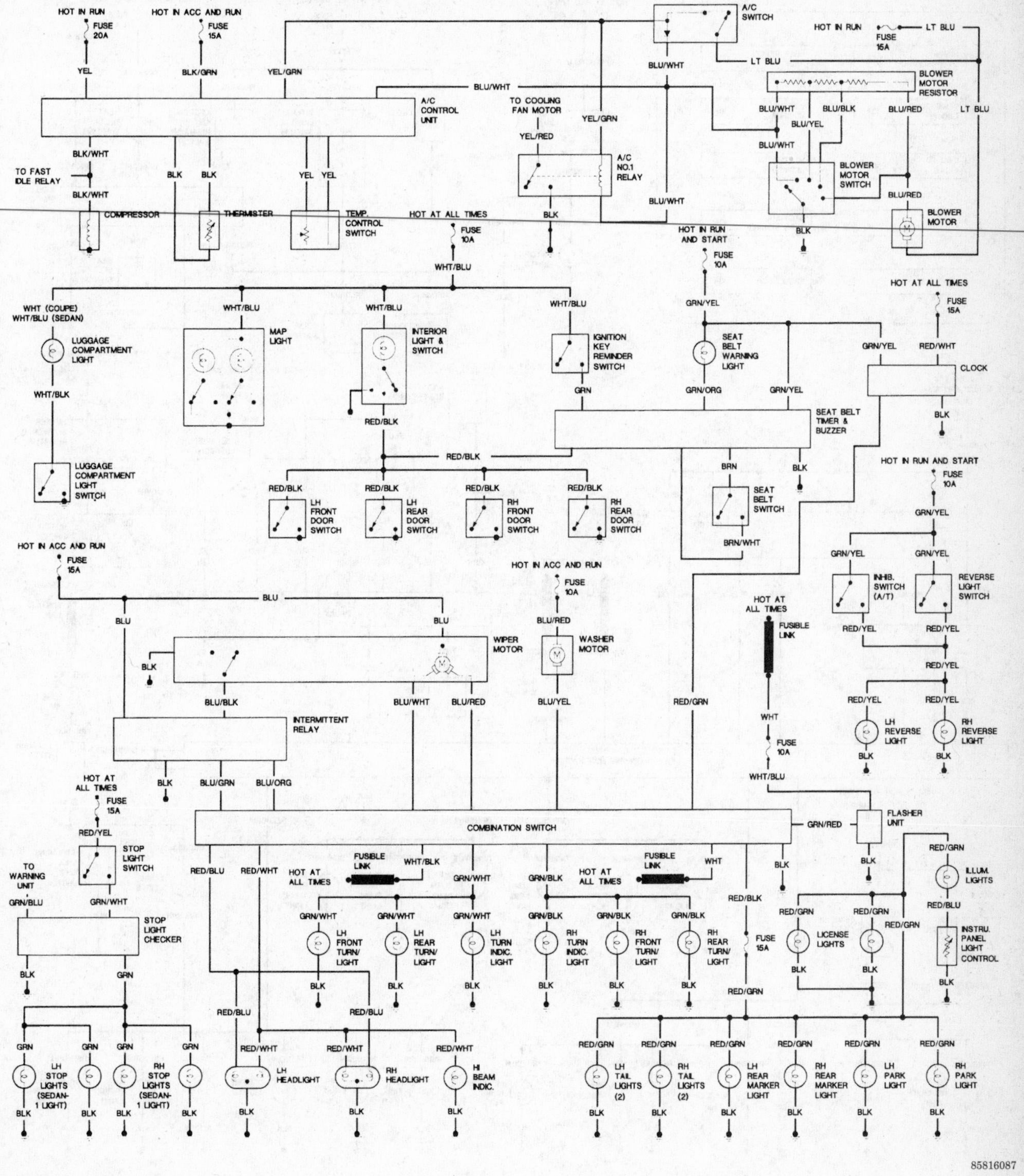

Fig. 75 Body wiring schematic — 1981 GLC (front wheel drive)

85816087

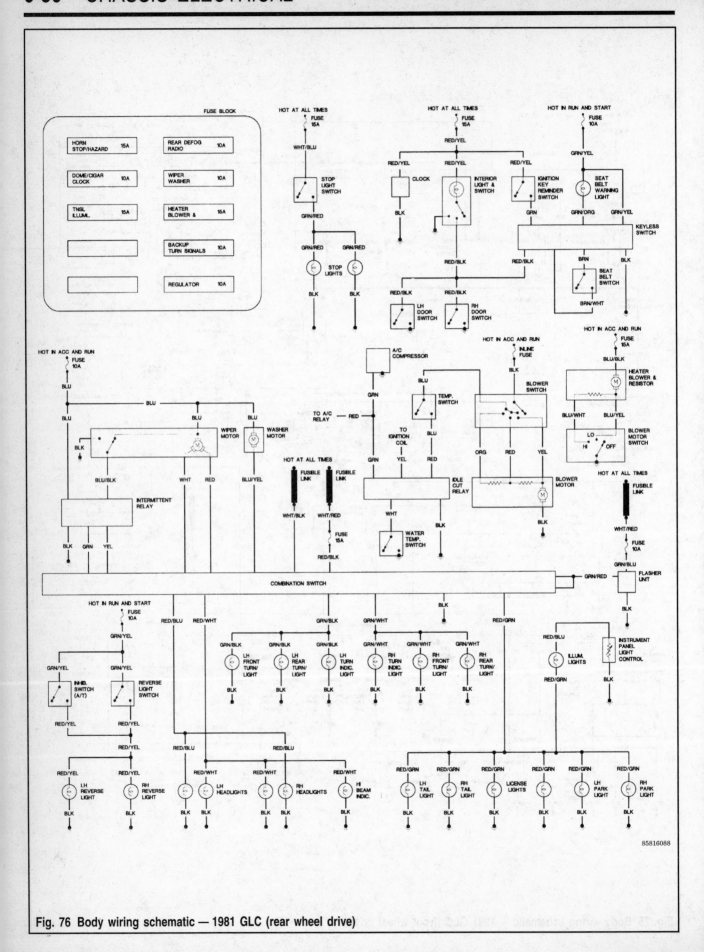

Fig. 76 Body wiring schematic — 1981 GLC (rear wheel drive)

85816088

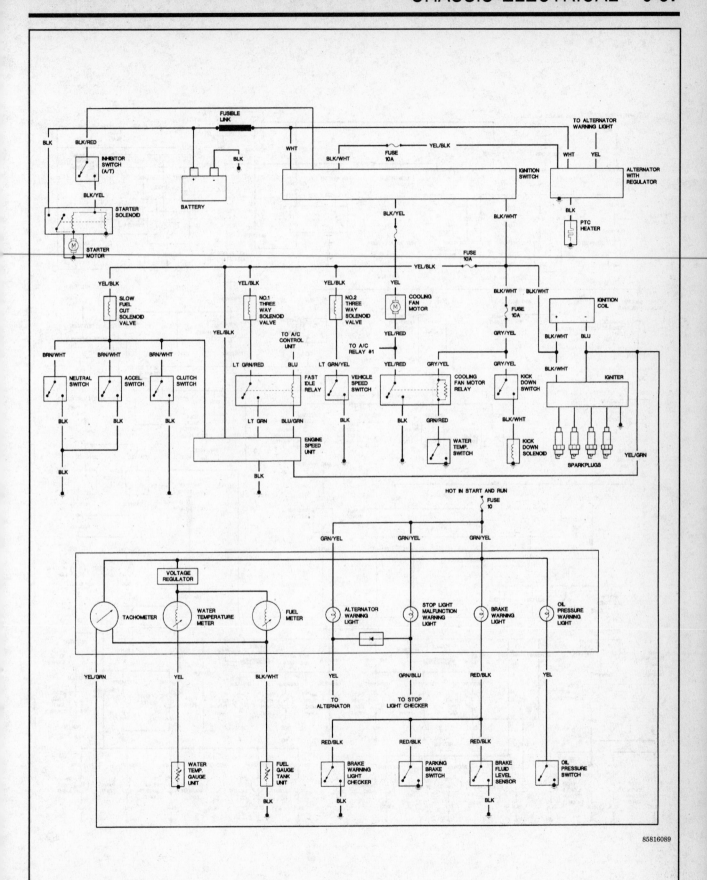

Fig. 77 Engine controls and gauges — 1982 GLC (front wheel drive)

85816089

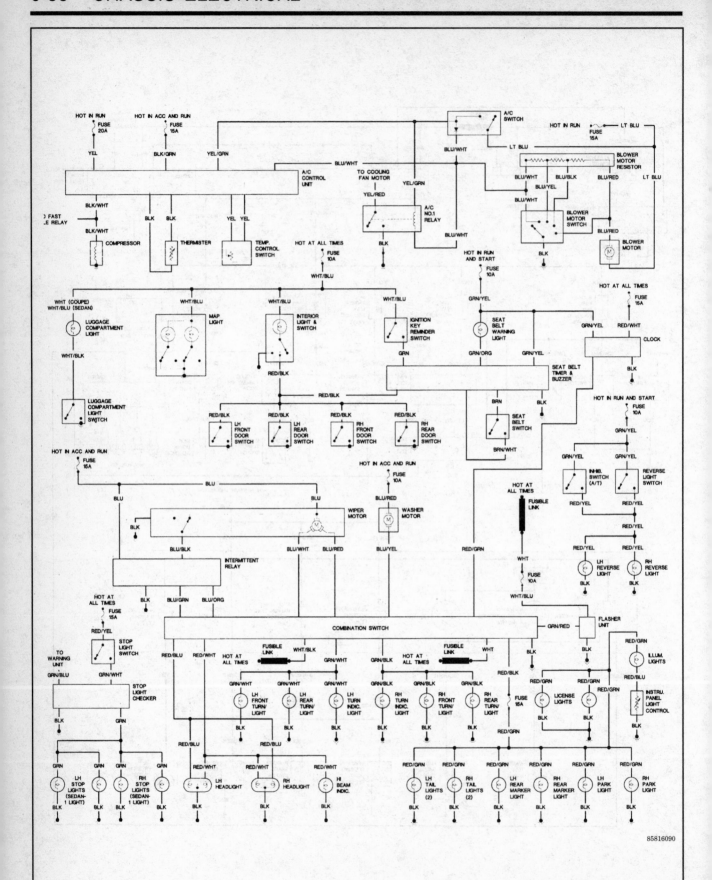

Fig. 78 Body wiring schematic — 1982 GLC (front wheel drive)

85816090

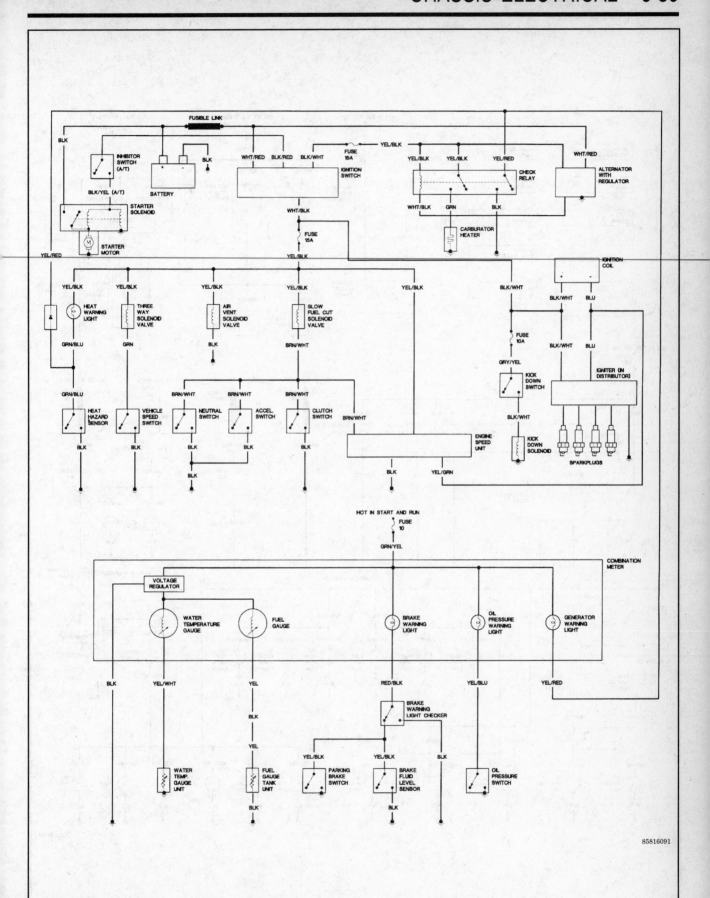

Fig. 79 Engine controls and gauges — 1982 GLC (rear wheel drive)

85816091

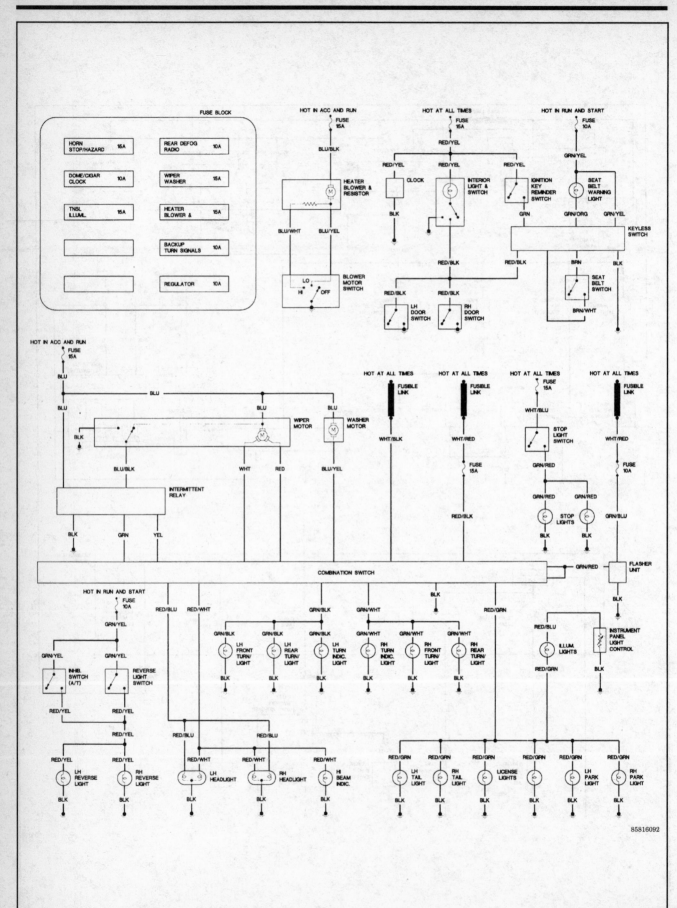

Fig. 80 Body wiring schematic — 1982 GLC (rear wheel drive)

85816092

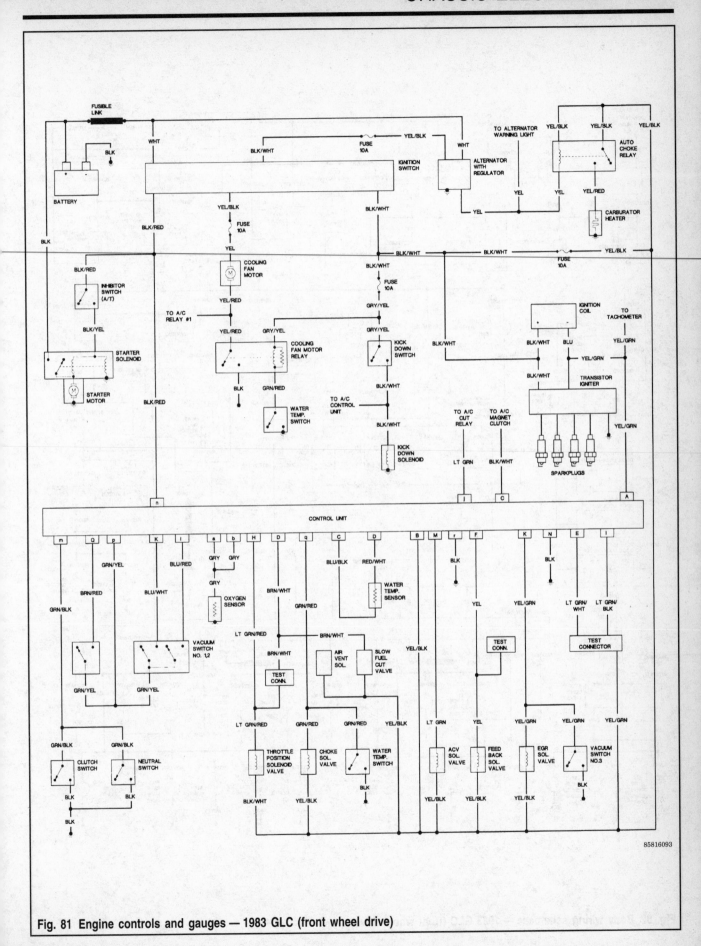

Fig. 81 Engine controls and gauges — 1983 GLC (front wheel drive)

85816093

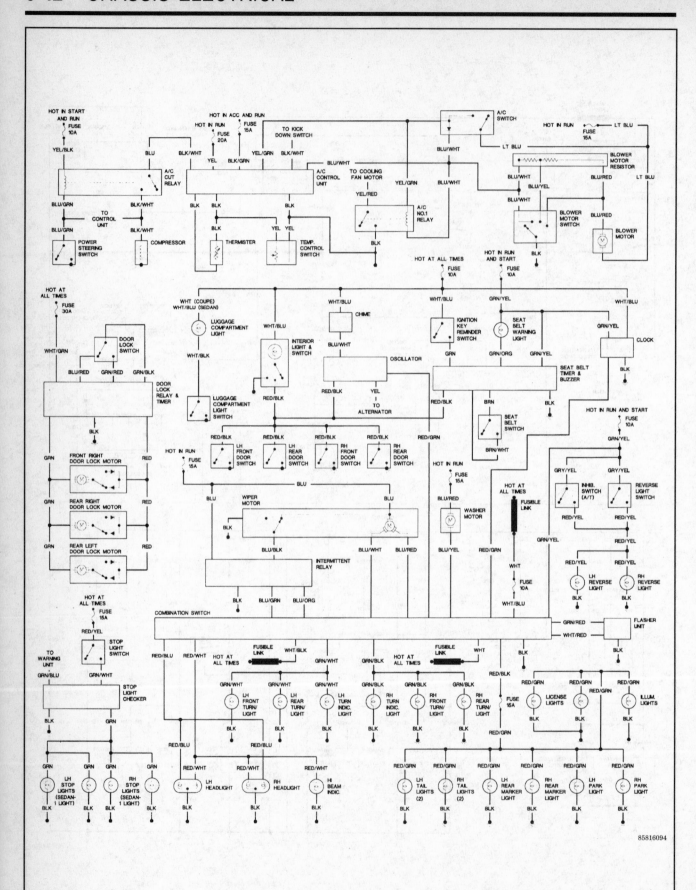

Fig. 82 Body wiring schematic — 1983 GLC (front wheel drive)

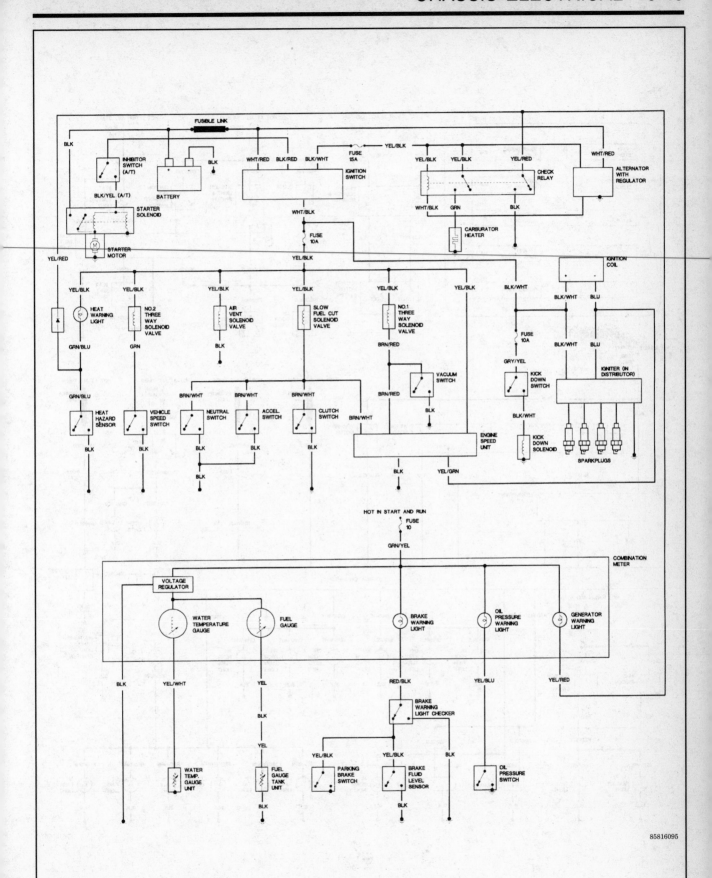

Fig. 83 Engine controls and gauges — 1983 GLC (rear wheel drive)

85816095

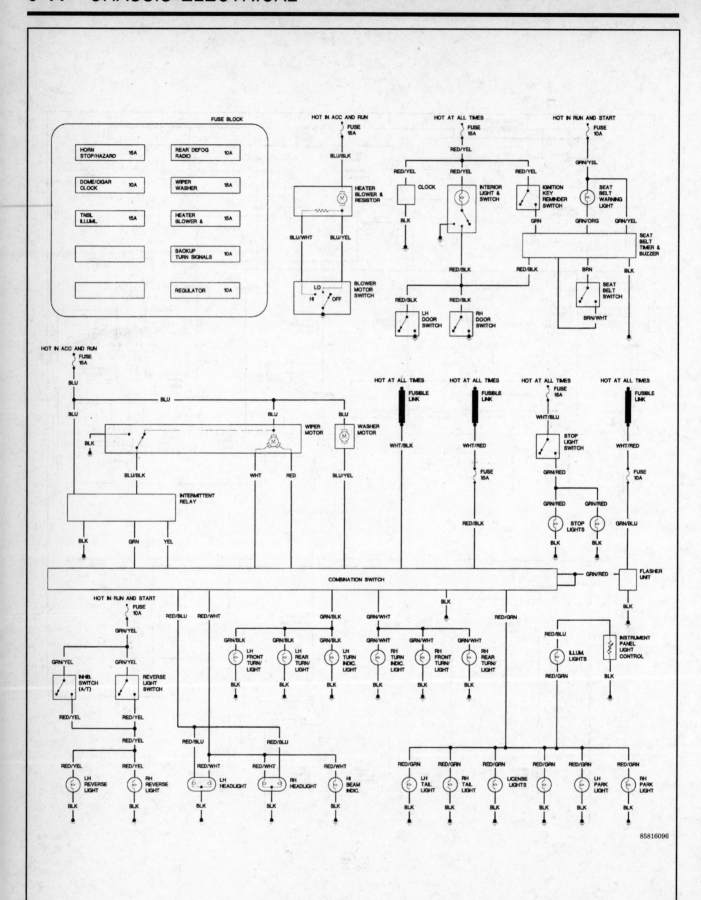

Fig. 84 Body wiring schematic — 1983 GLC (rear wheel drive)

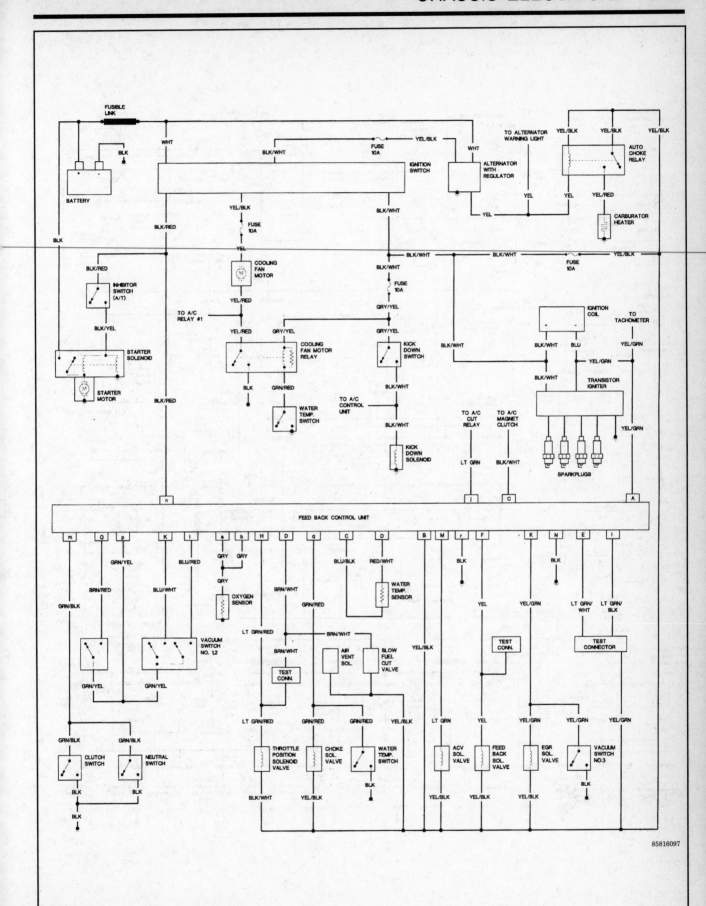

Fig. 85 Engine controls — 1984 GLC

85816097

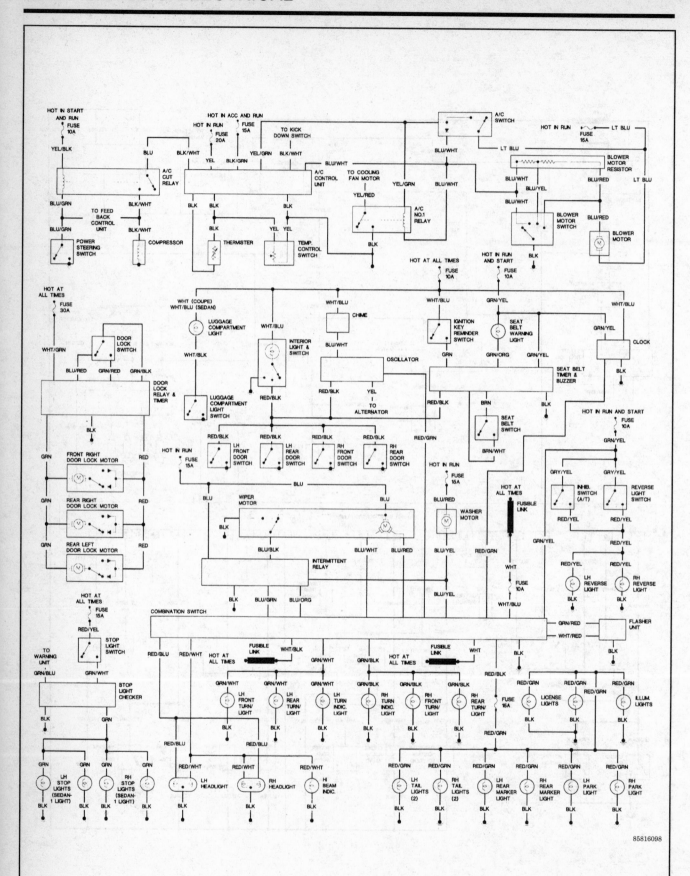

Fig. 86 Body wiring schematic — 1984 GLC

85816098

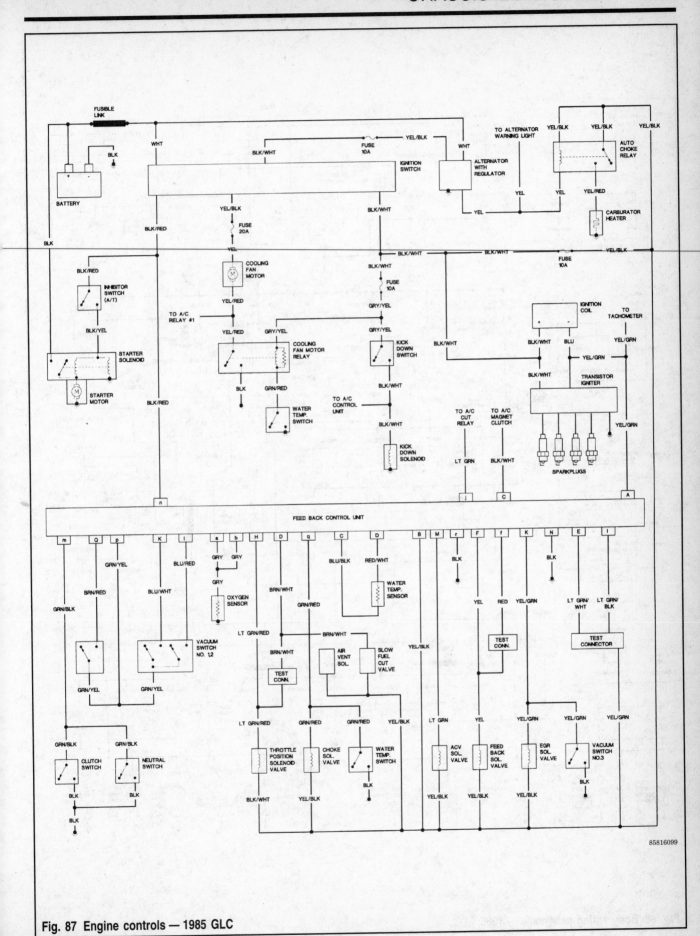

Fig. 87 Engine controls — 1985 GLC

85816099

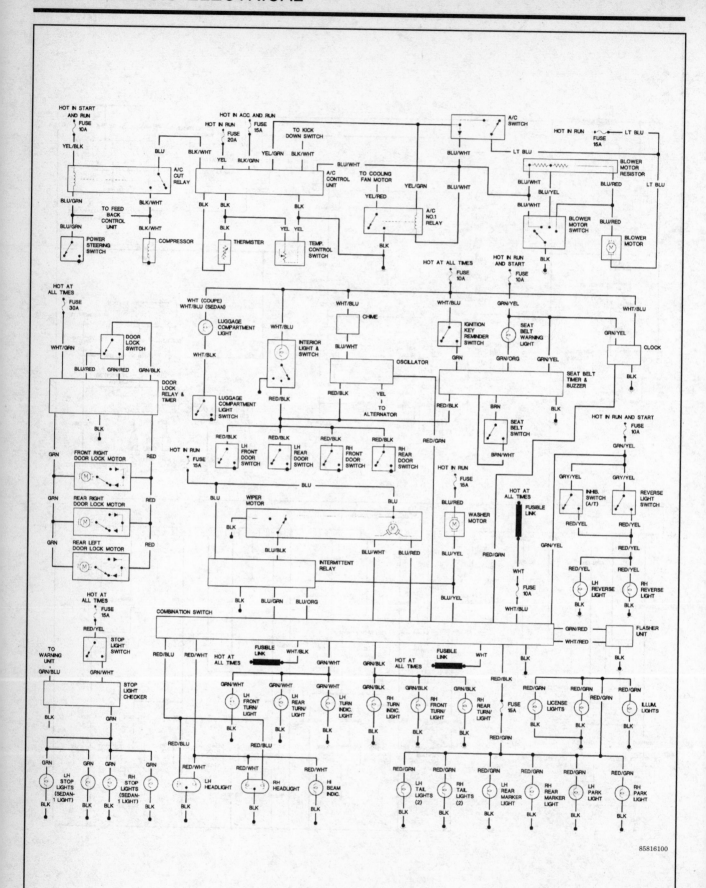

Fig. 88 Body wiring schematic — 1985 GLC

85816100

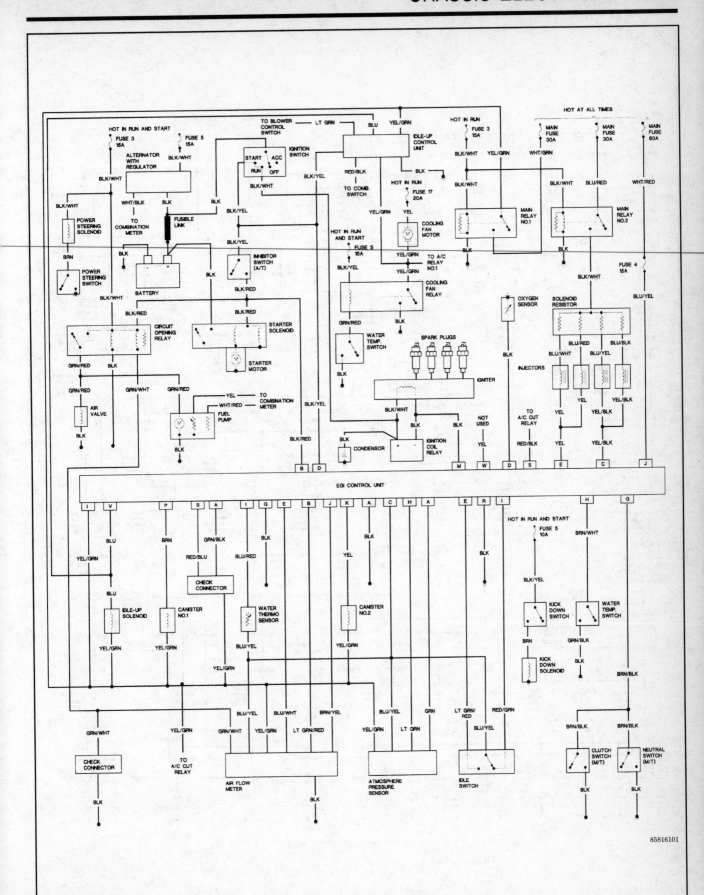

Fig. 89 Engine controls — 1986 323

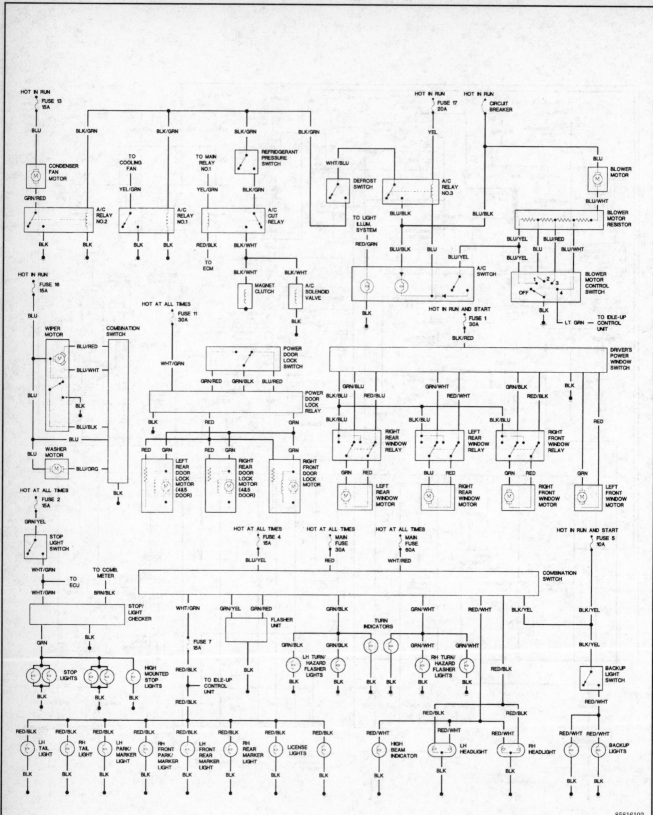

Fig. 90 Body wiring schematic — 1986 323

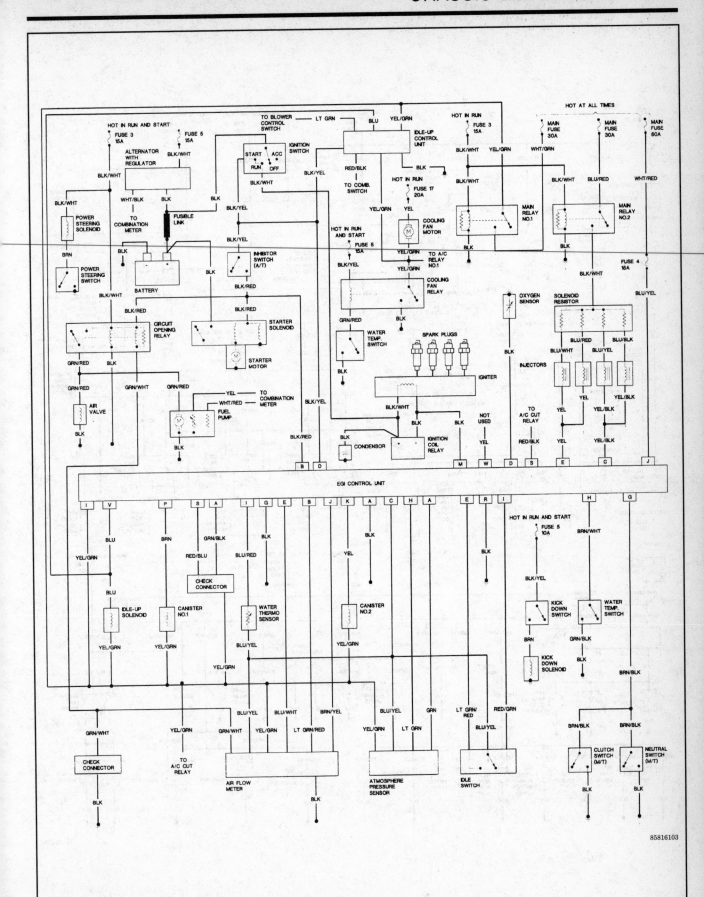

Fig. 91 Engine controls — 1987 323

85816103

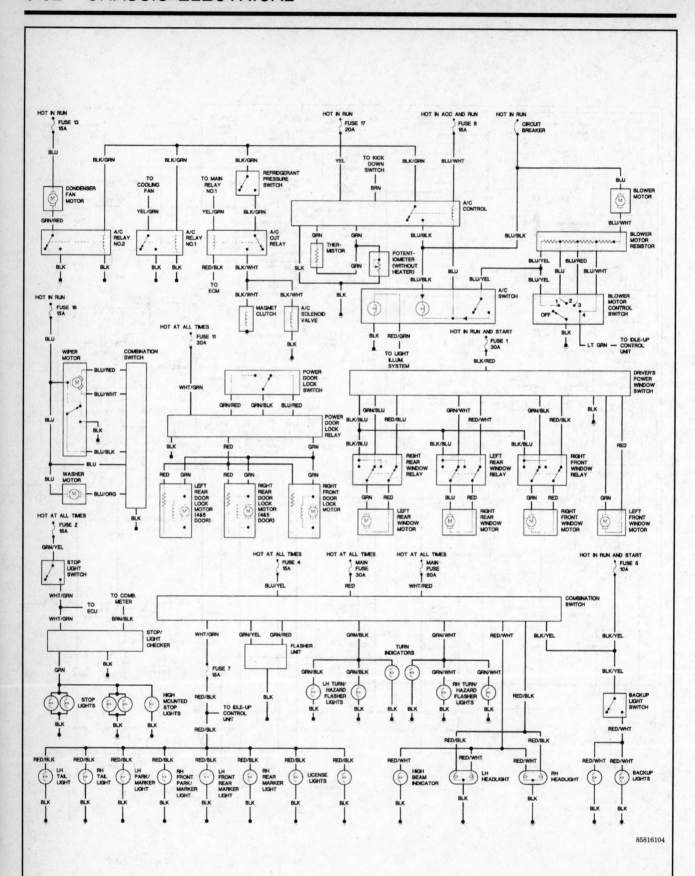

Fig. 92 Body wiring schematic — 1987 323

85816104

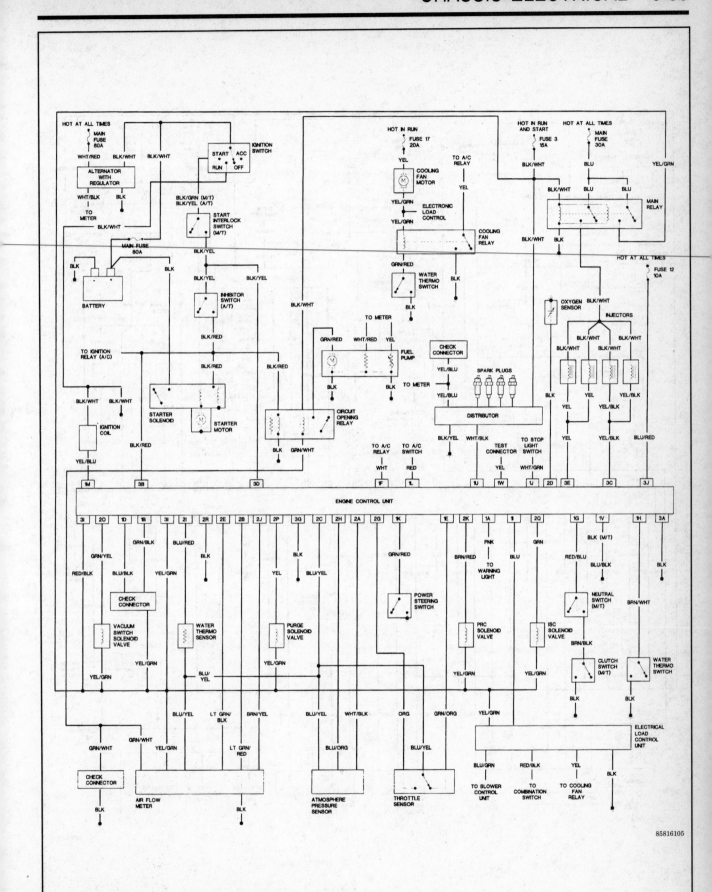

Fig. 93 Engine controls — 1988-89 323 (2wd non-turbo)

85816105

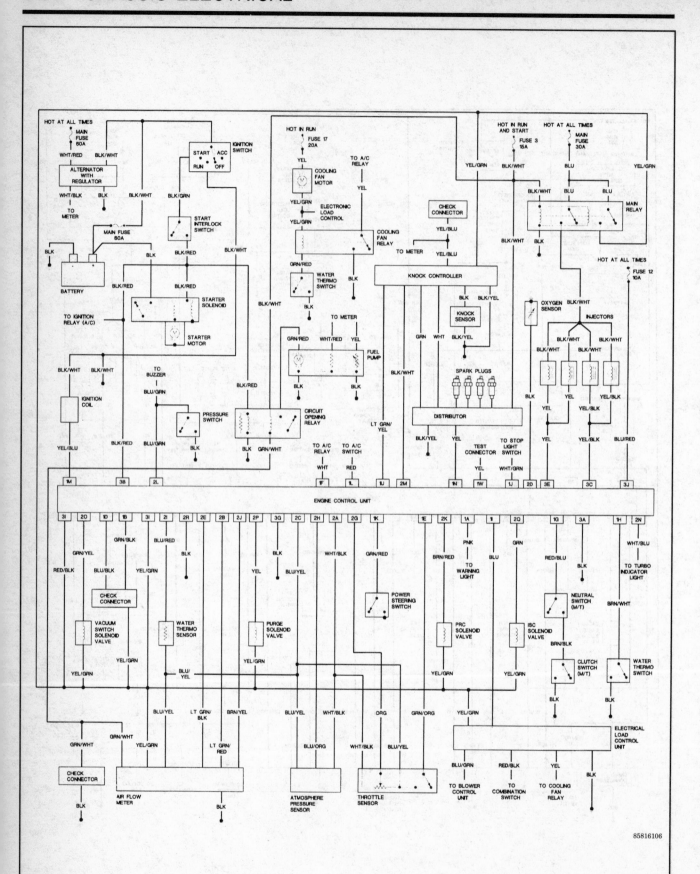

Fig. 94 Engine controls — 1988-89 323 (2wd turbo)

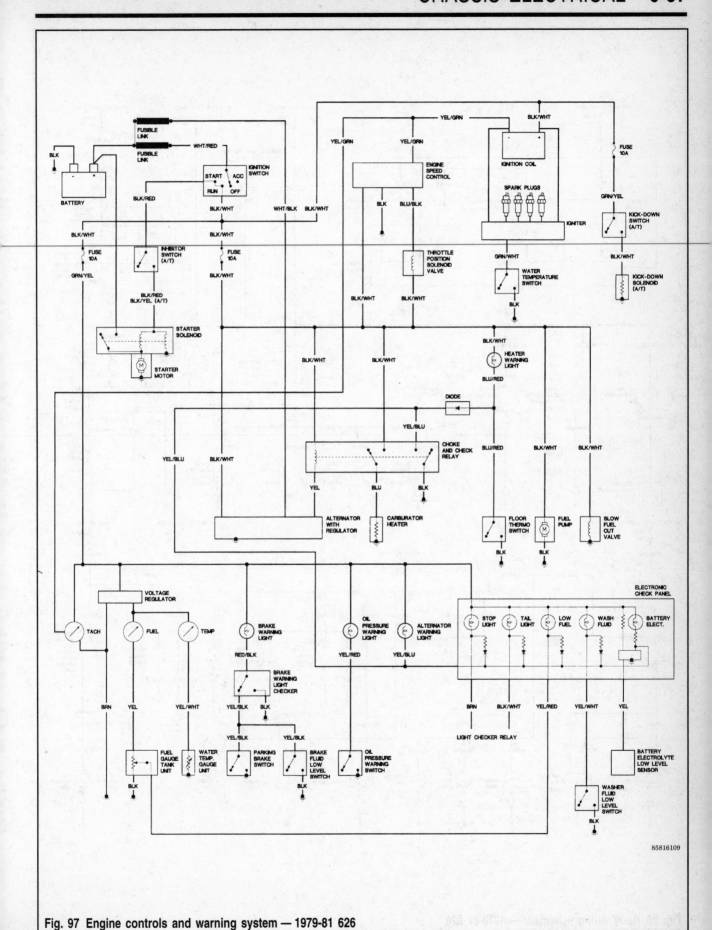

Fig. 97 Engine controls and warning system — 1979-81 626

85816109

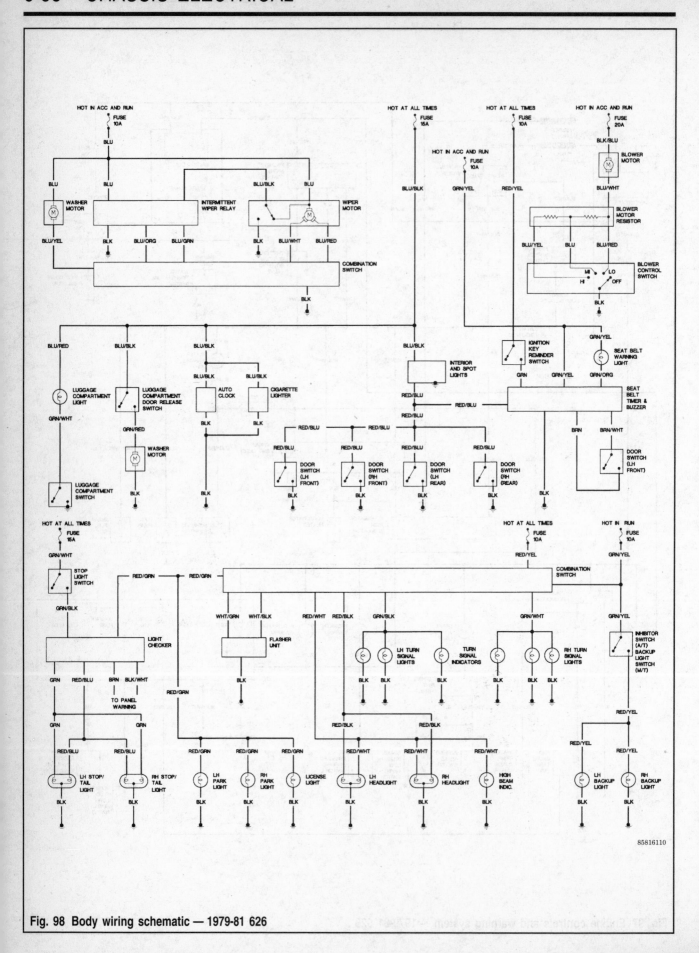

Fig. 98 Body wiring schematic — 1979-81 626

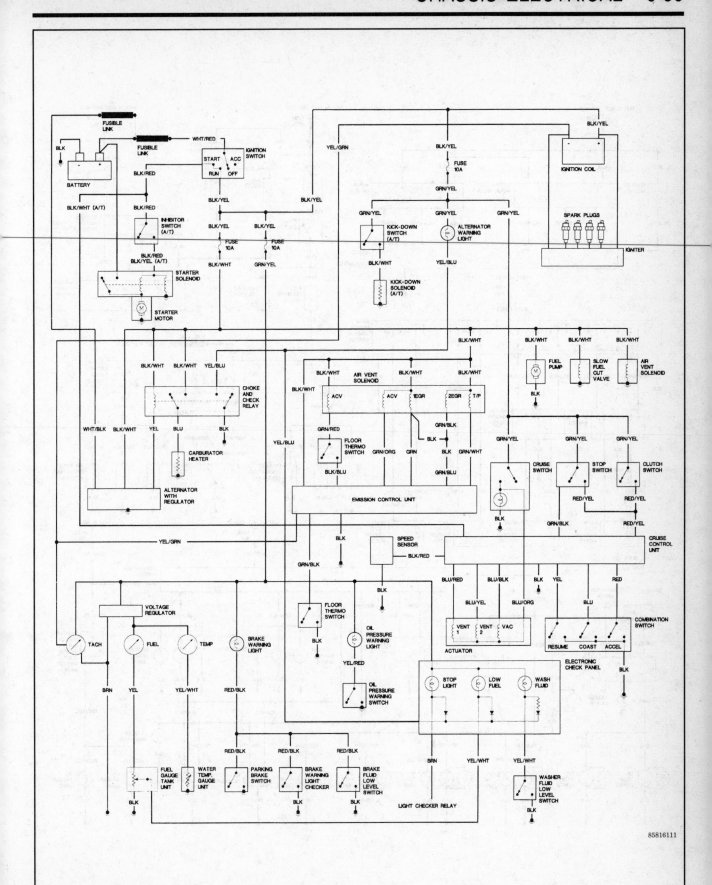

Fig. 99 Engine controls and warning system — 1982 626

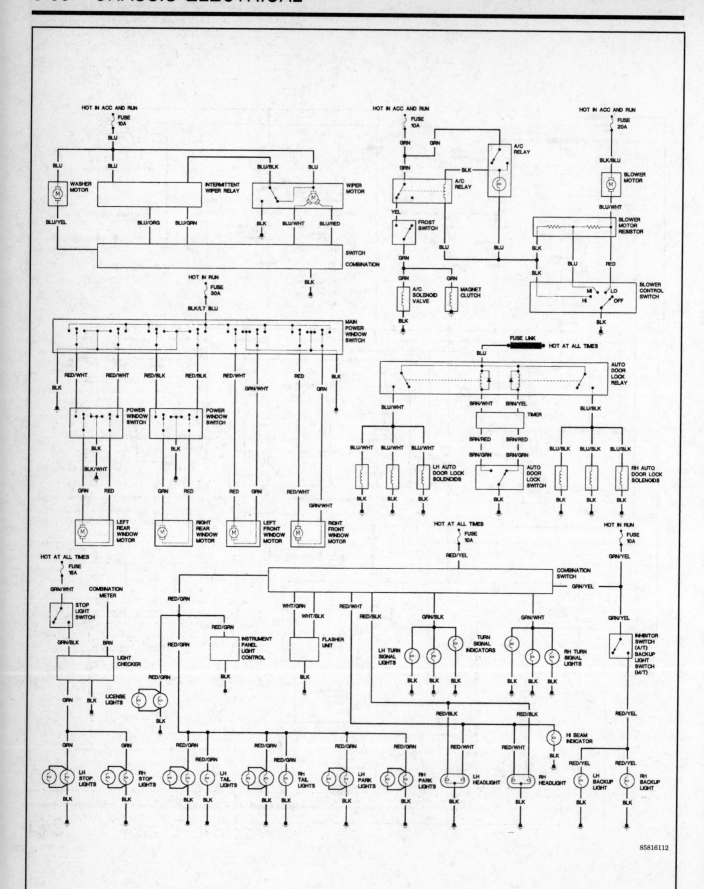

Fig. 100 Body wiring schematic — 1982 626

85816112

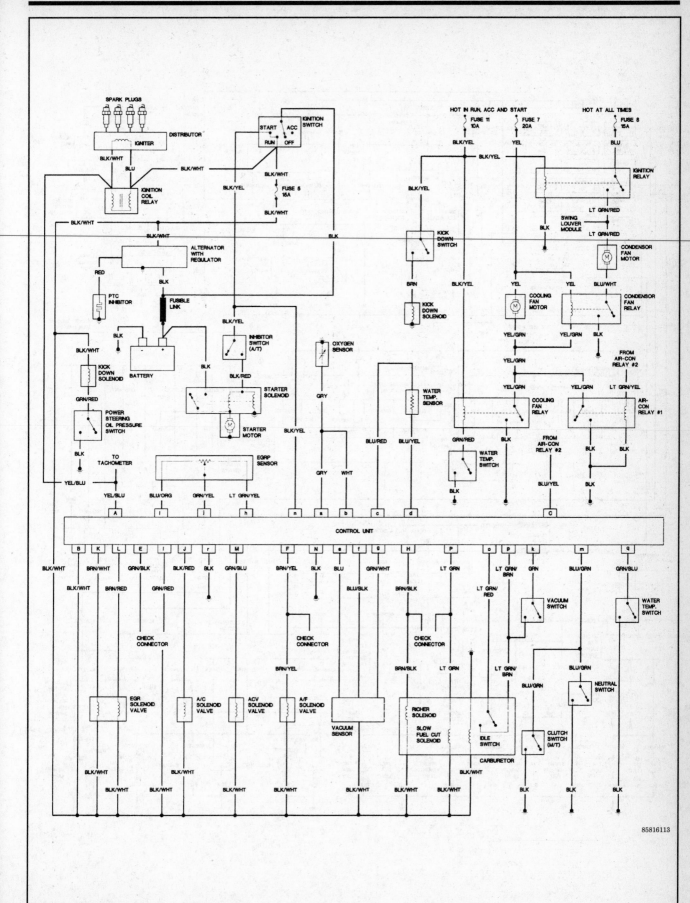

Fig. 101 Engine controls — 1983-84 626

85816113

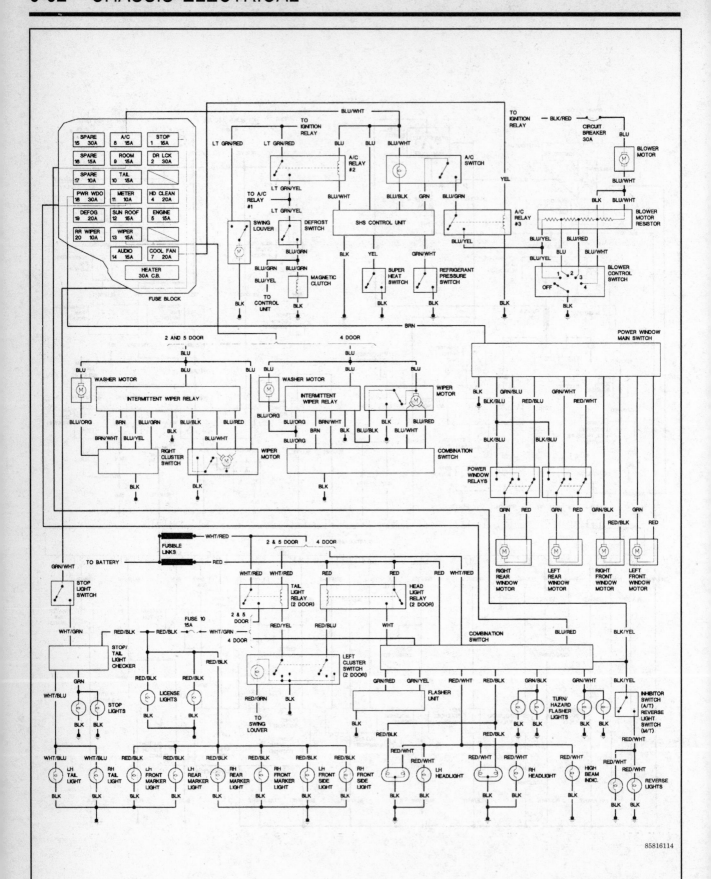

Fig. 102 Body wiring schematic — 1983-84 626

85816114

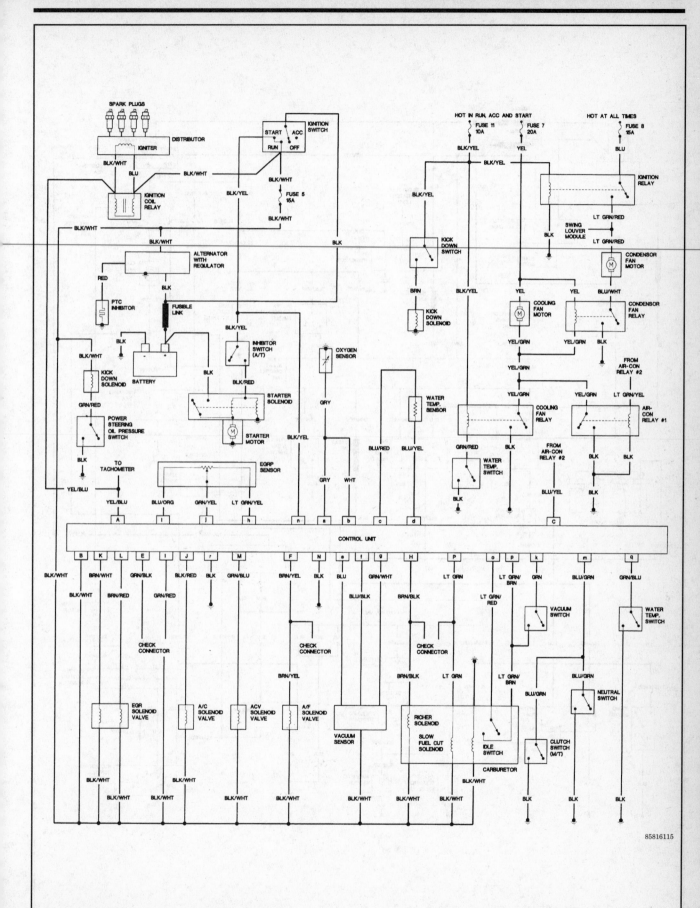

Fig. 103 Engine controls — 1985 626 (gasoline)

85816115

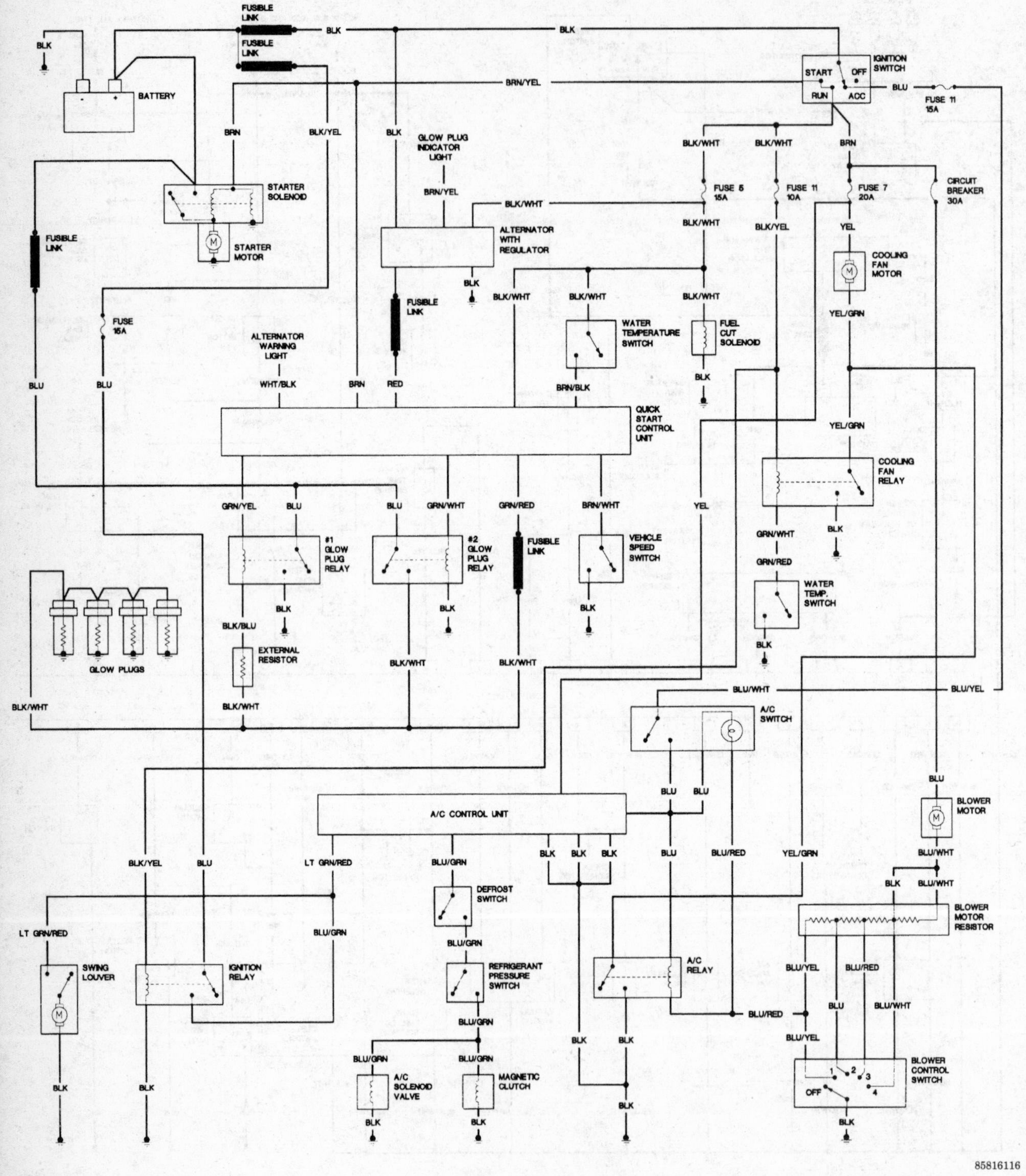

Fig. 104 Engine controls — 1985 626 diesel

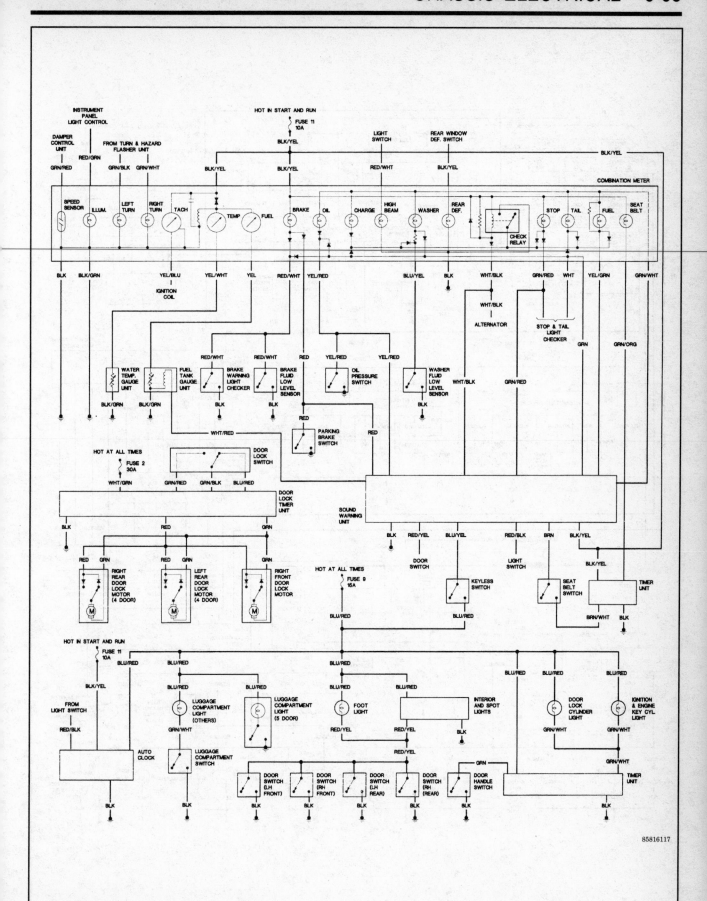

Fig. 105 Body wiring schematic — 1985 626

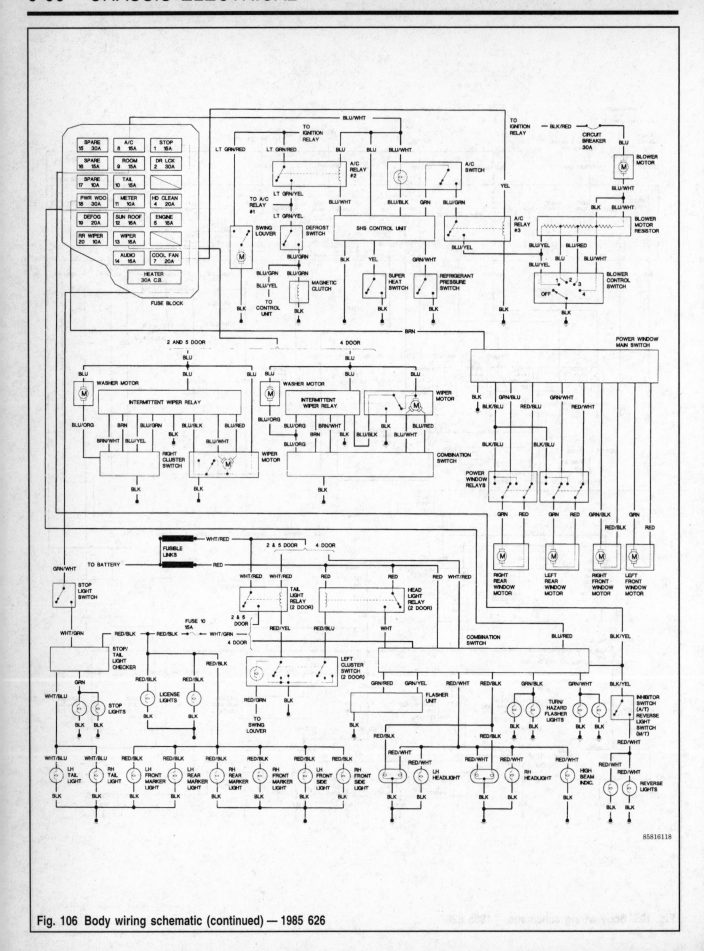

Fig. 106 Body wiring schematic (continued) — 1985 626

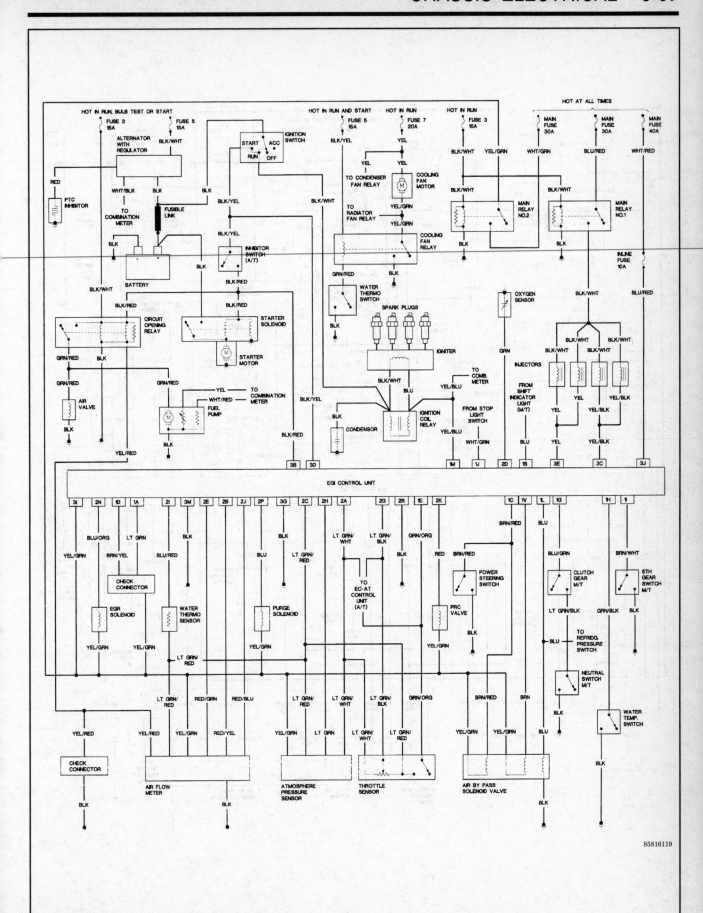

Fig. 107 Engine controls — 1986-87 626 (non-turbo)

85816119

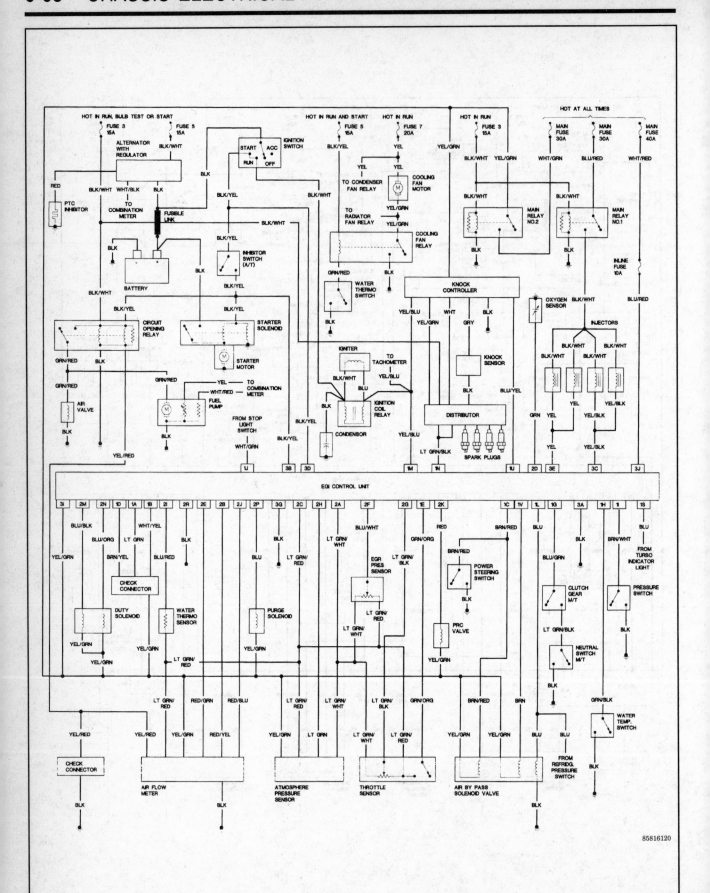

Fig. 108 Engine controls — 1986-87 626 (turbo)

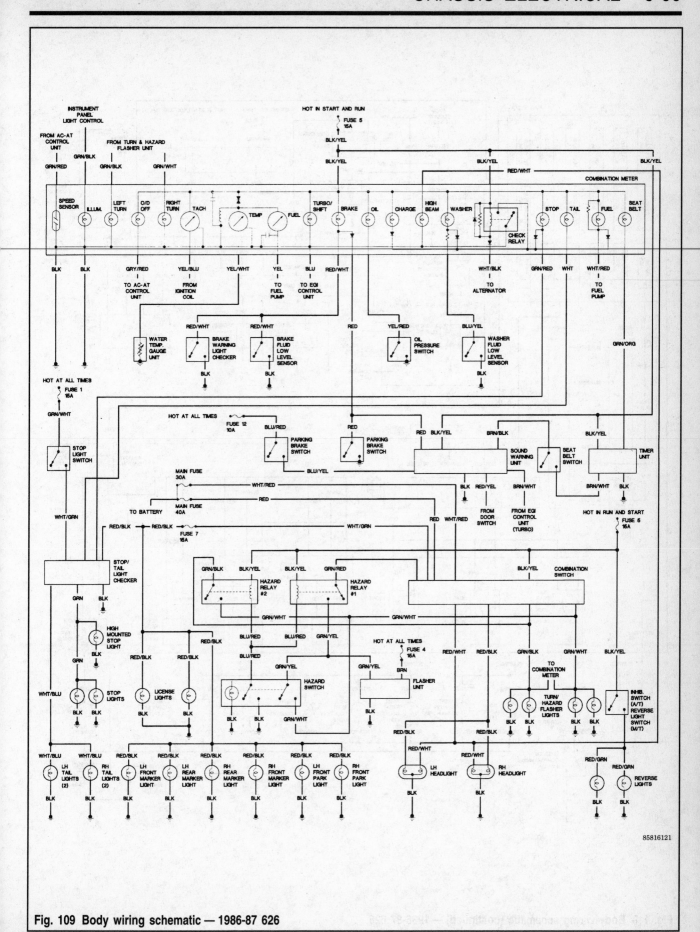

Fig. 109 Body wiring schematic — 1986-87 626

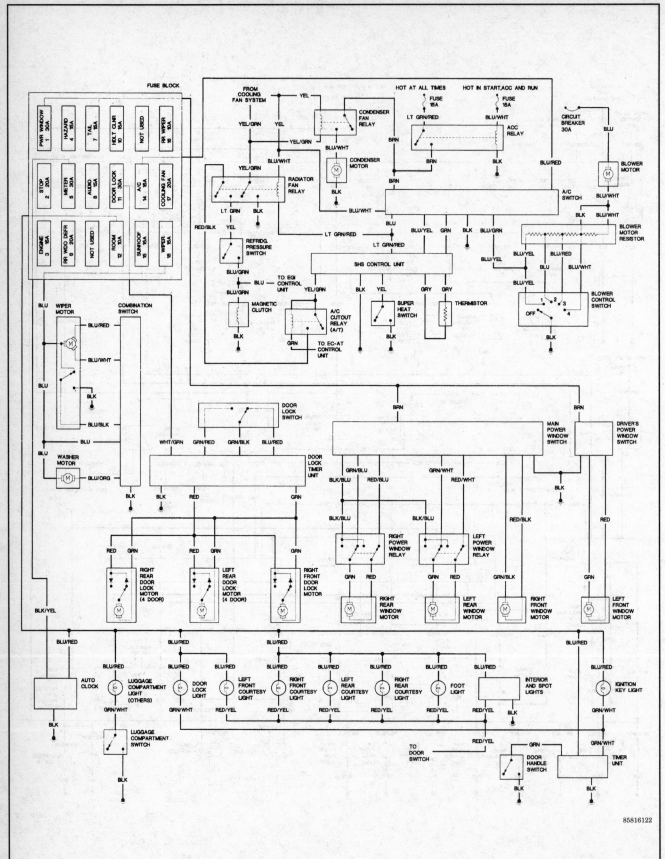

Fig. 110 Body wiring schematic (continued) — 1986-87 626

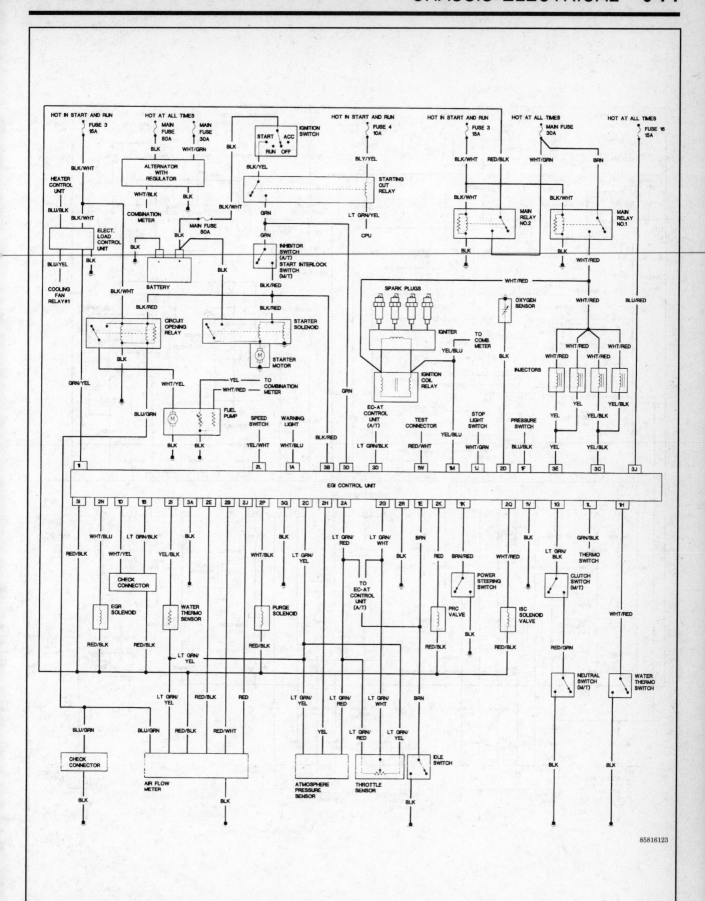

Fig. 111 Engine controls — 1988-89 626 (non-turbo)

85816123

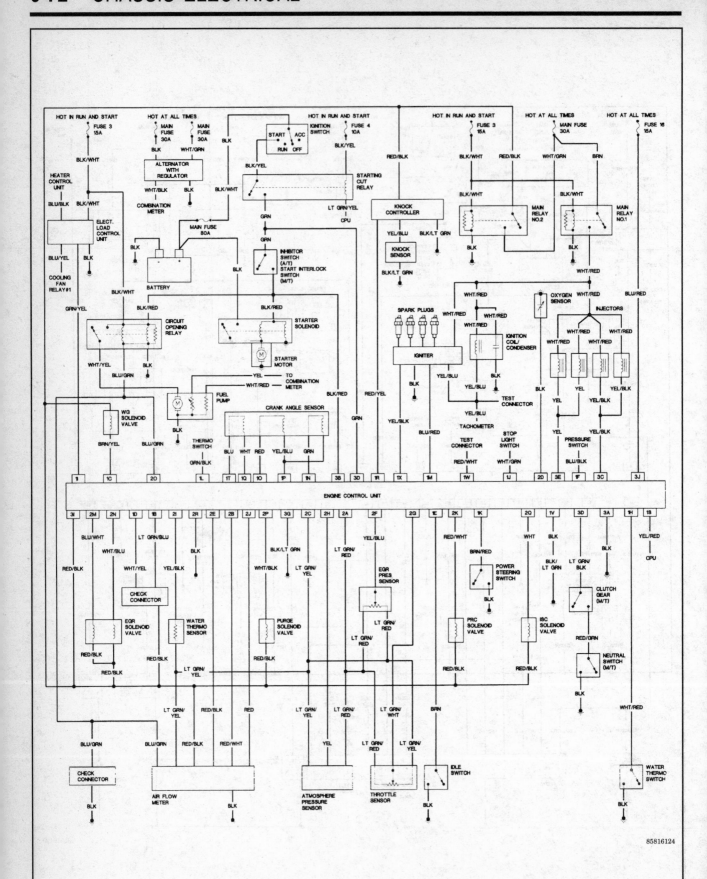

Fig. 112 Engine controls — 1988-89 626 (turbo)

85816124

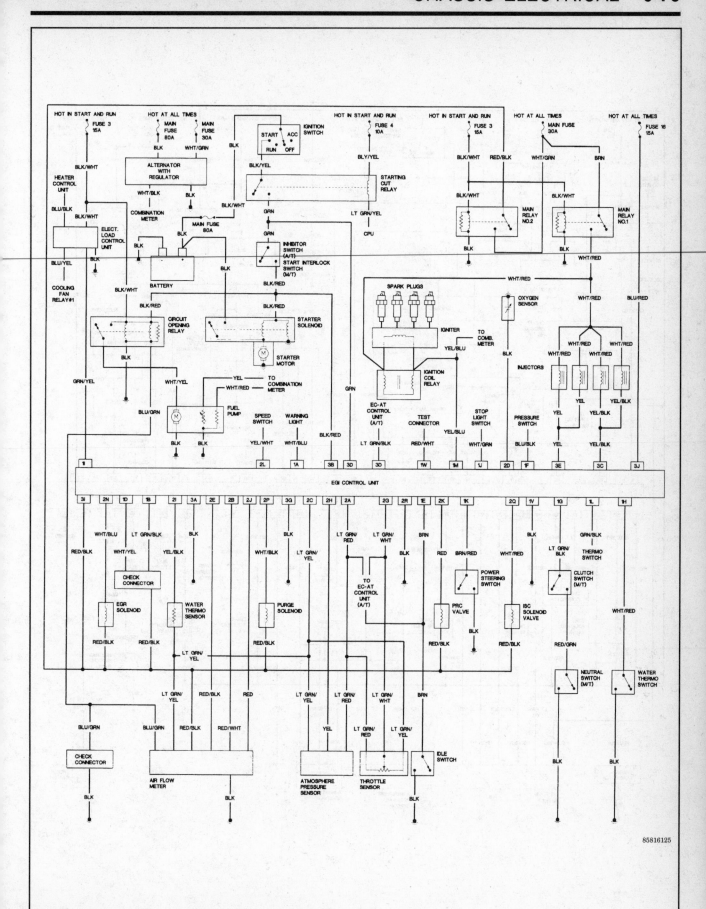

Fig. 113 Engine controls — 1988-89 MX-6 (non-turbo)

85816125

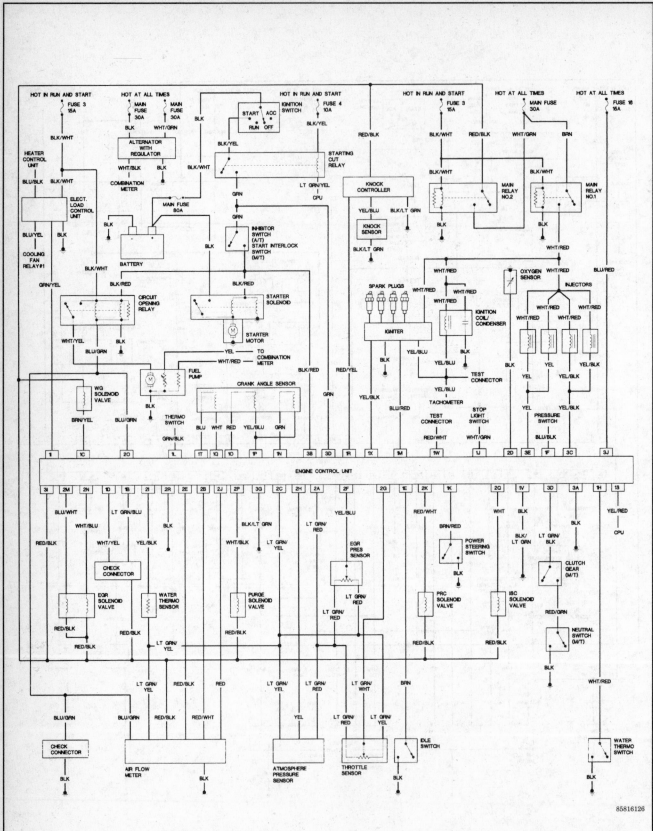

Fig. 114 Engine controls — 1988-89 MX-6 (turbo)

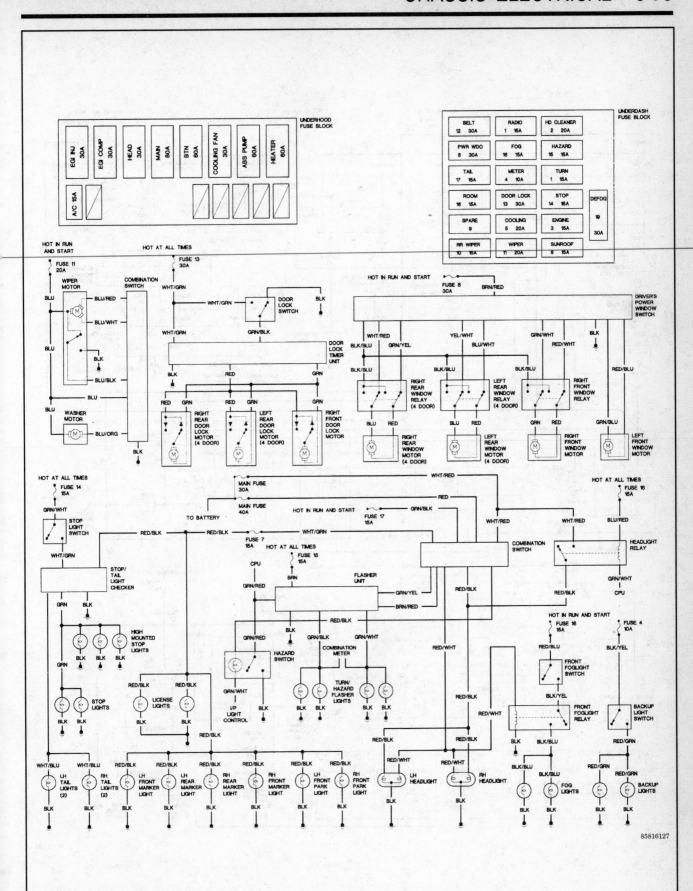

Fig. 115 Body wiring schematic — 1988-89 626

85816127

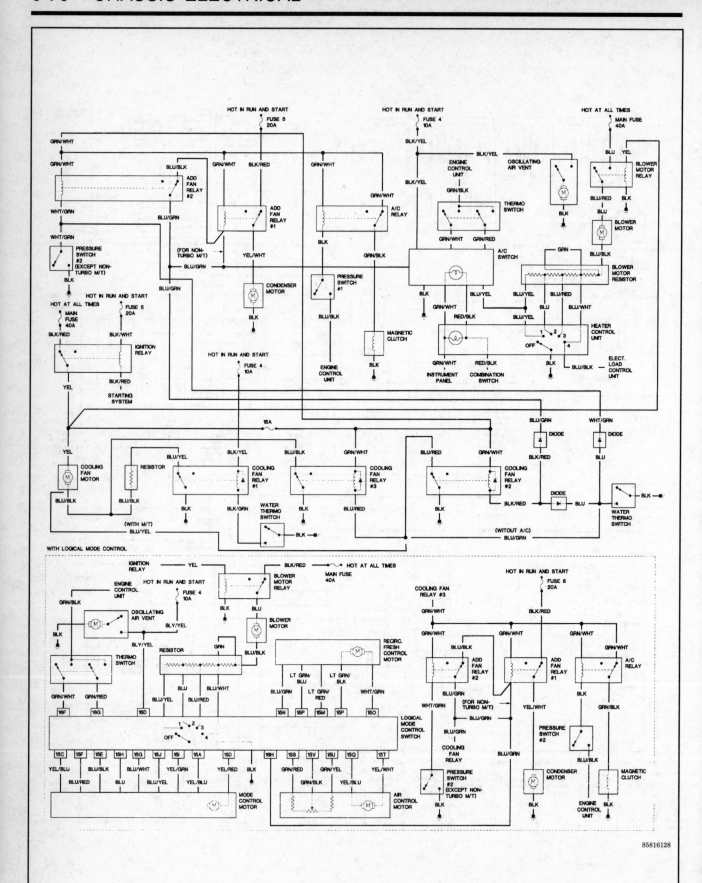

Fig. 116 Body wiring schematic (continued) — 1988-89 626

85816128

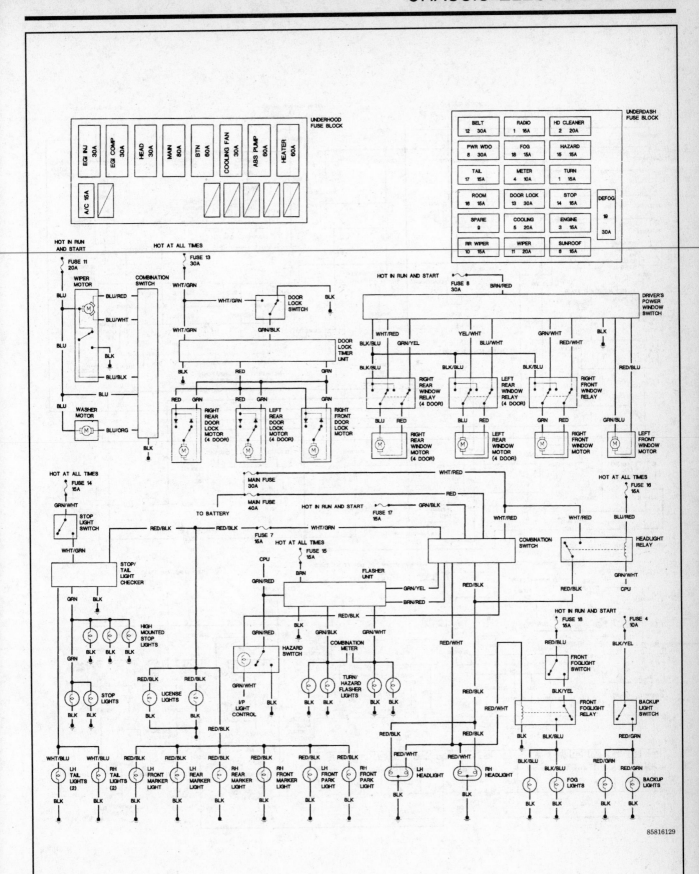

Fig. 117 Body wiring schematic — 1988-89 MX-6

85816129

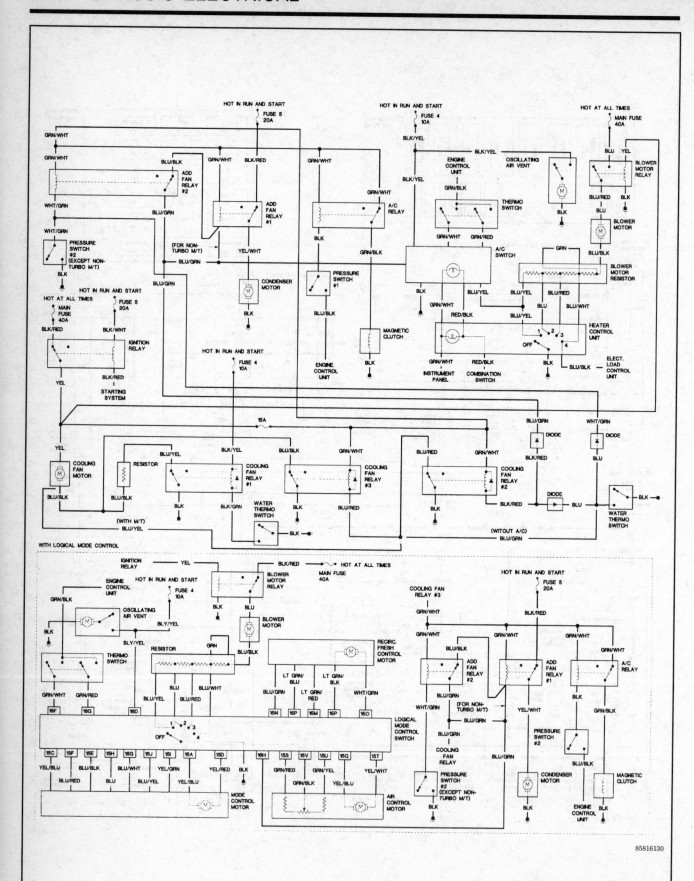

Fig. 118 Body wiring schematic (continued) — 1988-89 MX-6

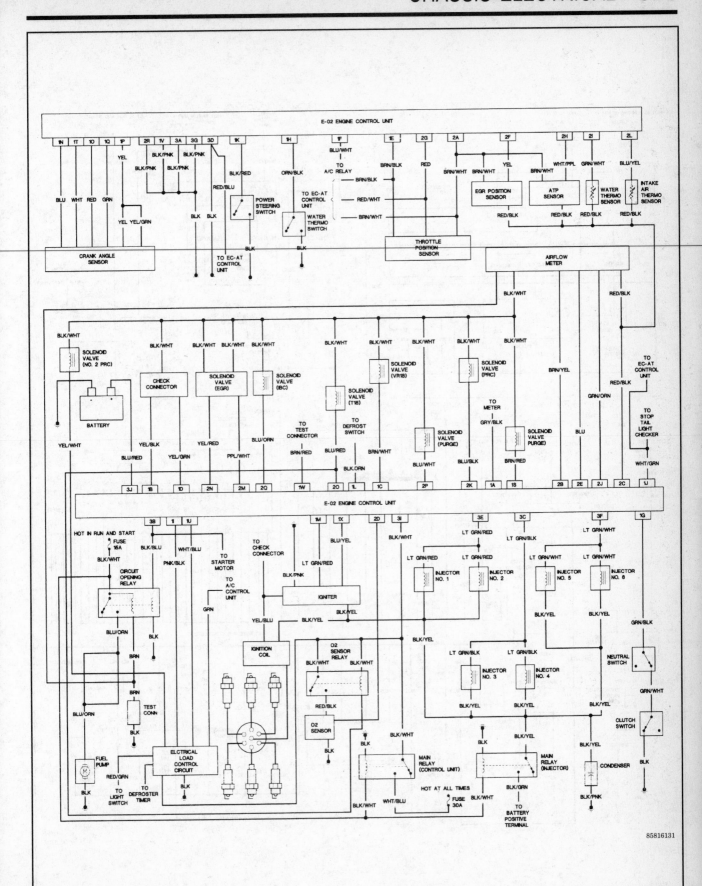

Fig. 119 Engine controls — 1988-89 929

85816131

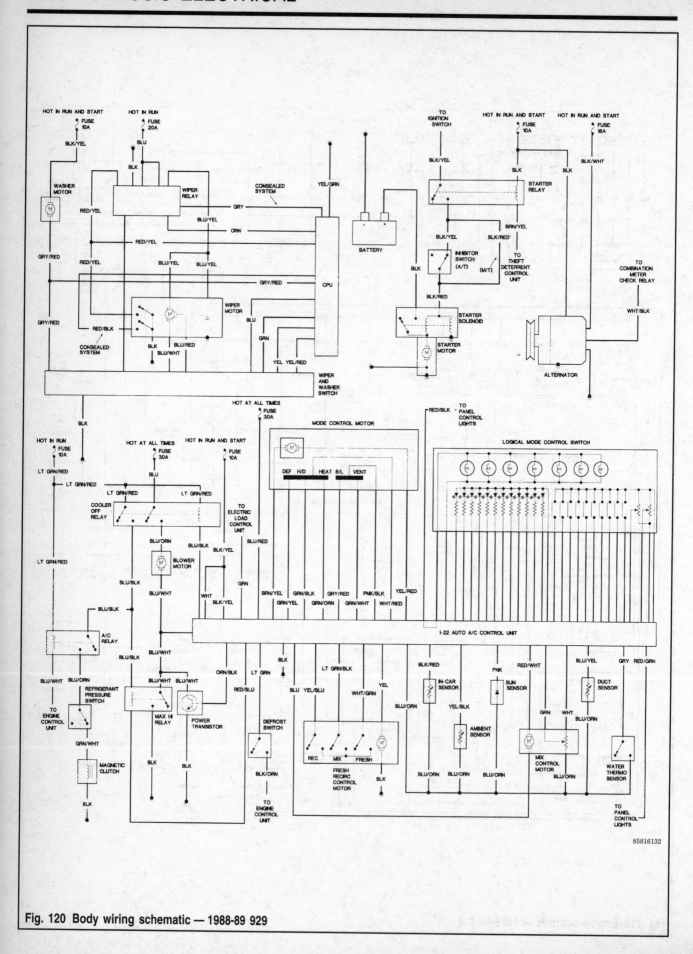

Fig. 120 Body wiring schematic — 1988-89 929

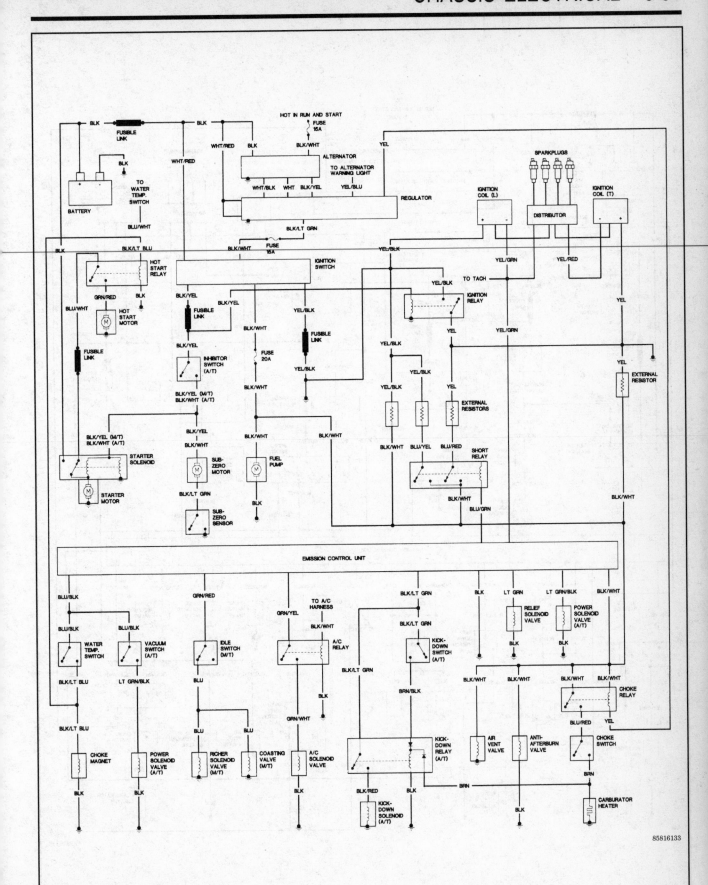

Fig. 121 Engine controls — 1979-80 RX-7 (except California)

85816133

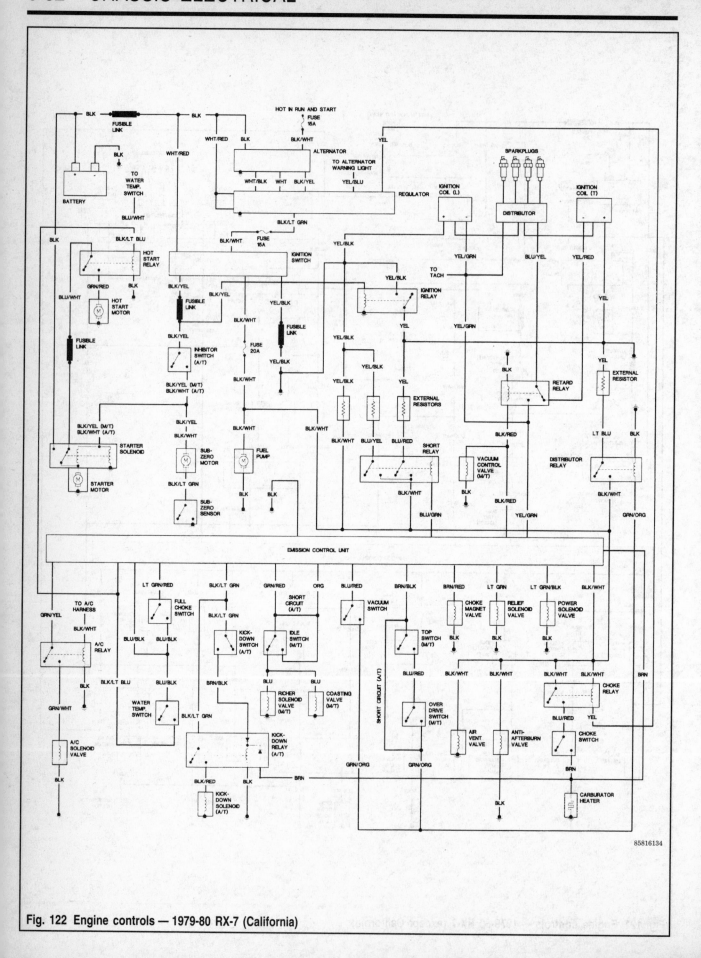

Fig. 122 Engine controls — 1979-80 RX-7 (California)

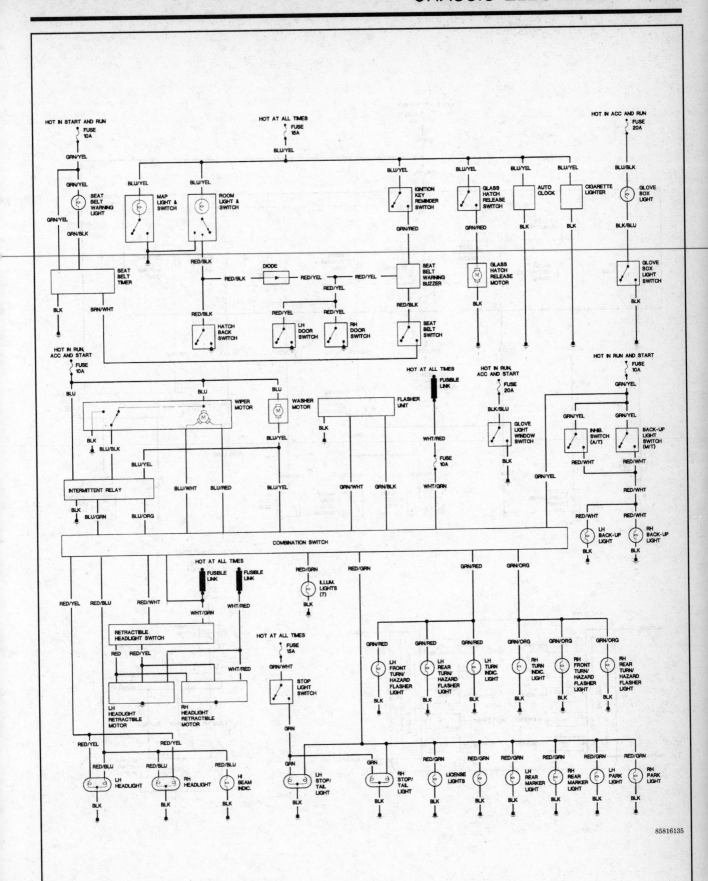

Fig. 123 Body wiring schematic — 1979-80 RX-7

85816135

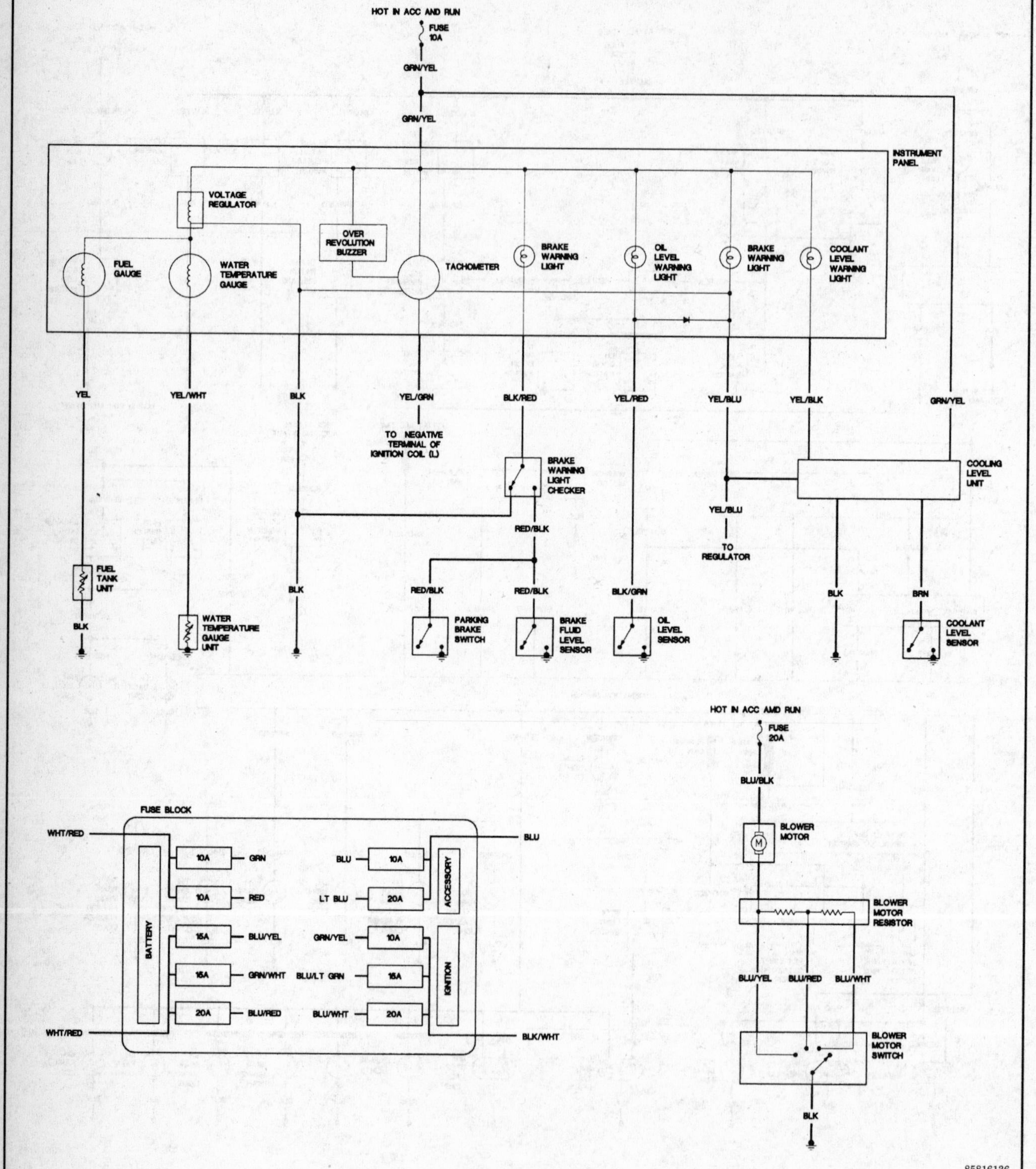

Fig. 124 Body wiring schematic (continued) — 1979-80 RX-7

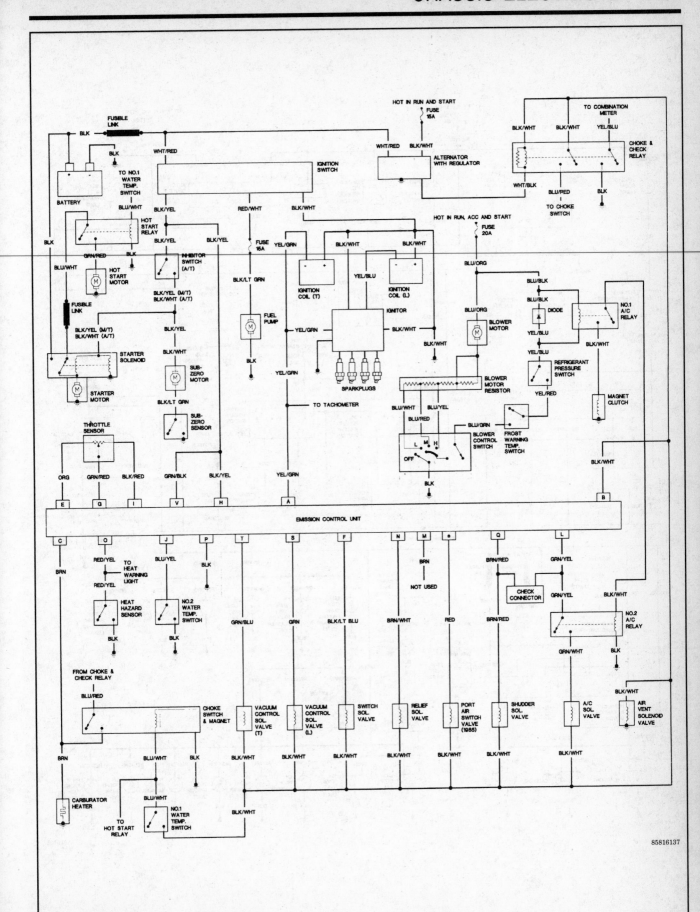

Fig. 125 Engine controls — 1981-83 RX-7

85816137

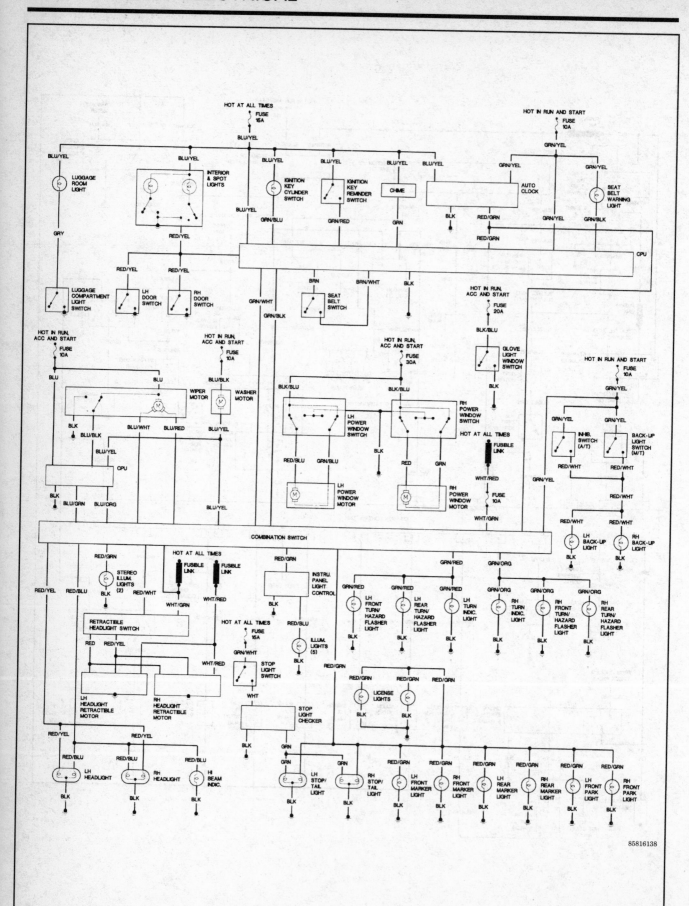

Fig. 126 Body wiring schematic — 1981-83 RX-7

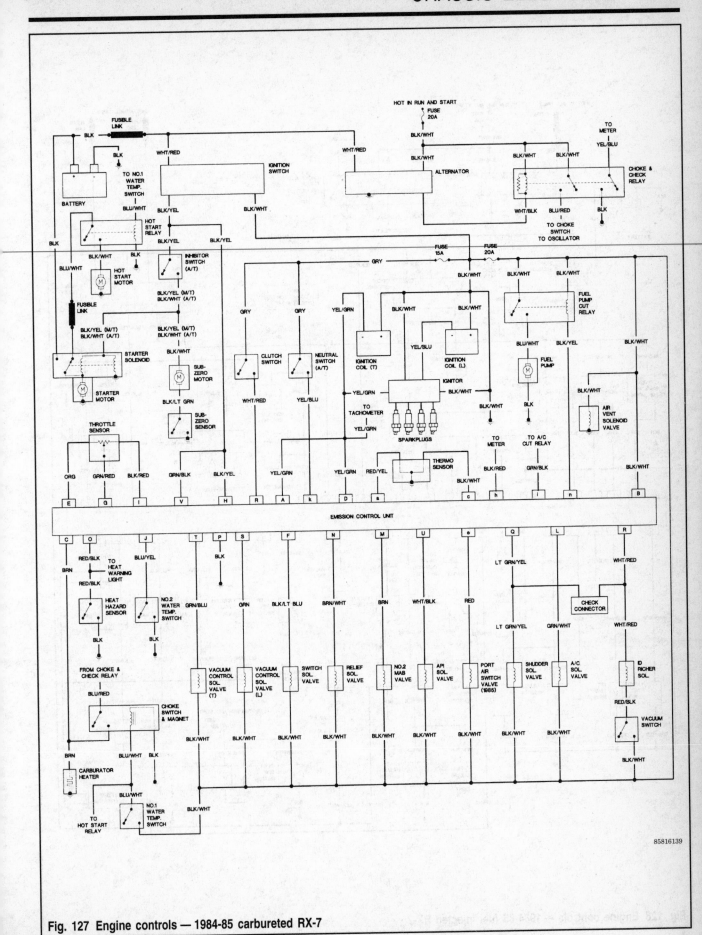

Fig. 127 Engine controls — 1984-85 carbureted RX-7

85816139

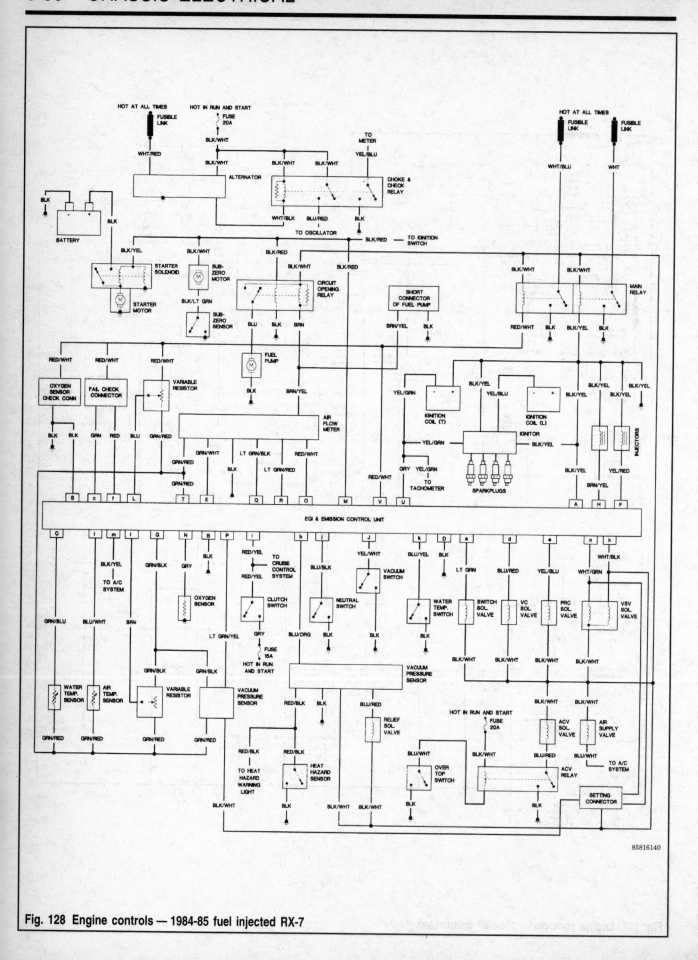

Fig. 128 Engine controls — 1984-85 fuel injected RX-7

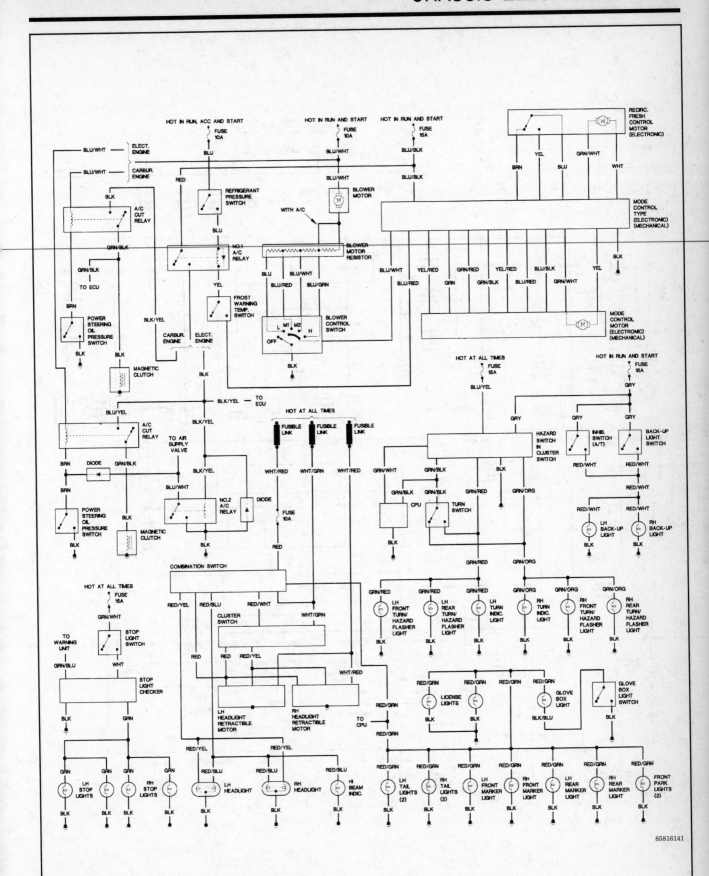

Fig. 129 Body wiring schematic — 1984-85 RX-7

85816141

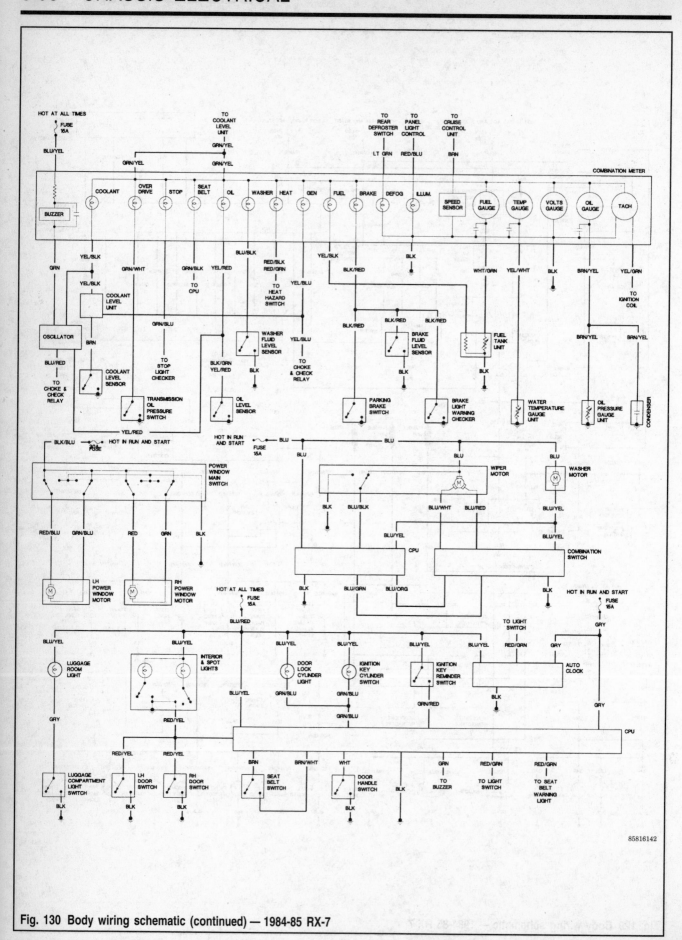

Fig. 130 Body wiring schematic (continued) — 1984-85 RX-7

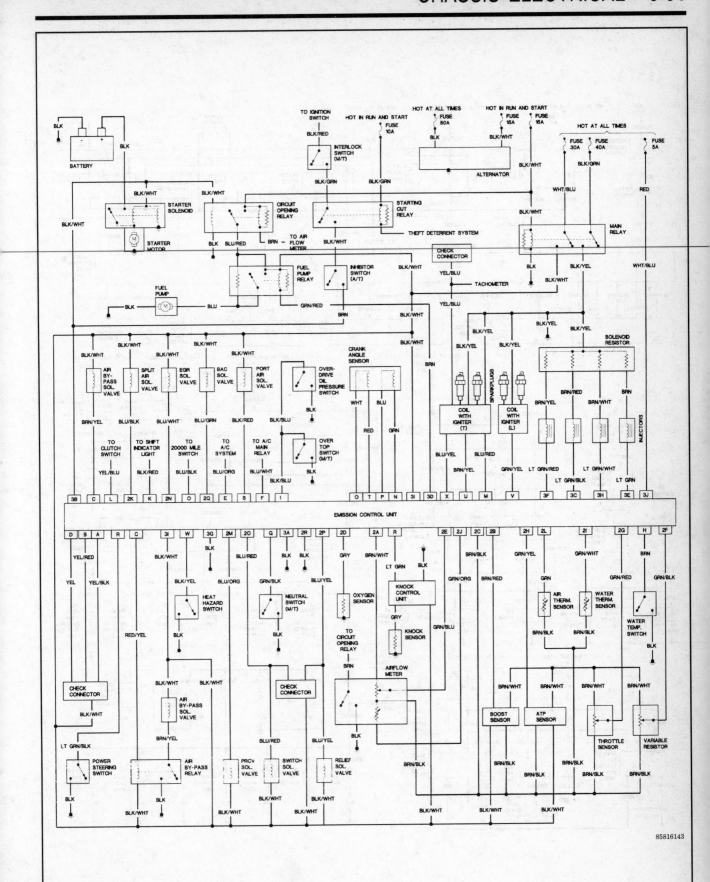

Fig. 131 Engine controls — 1986 RX-7

85816143

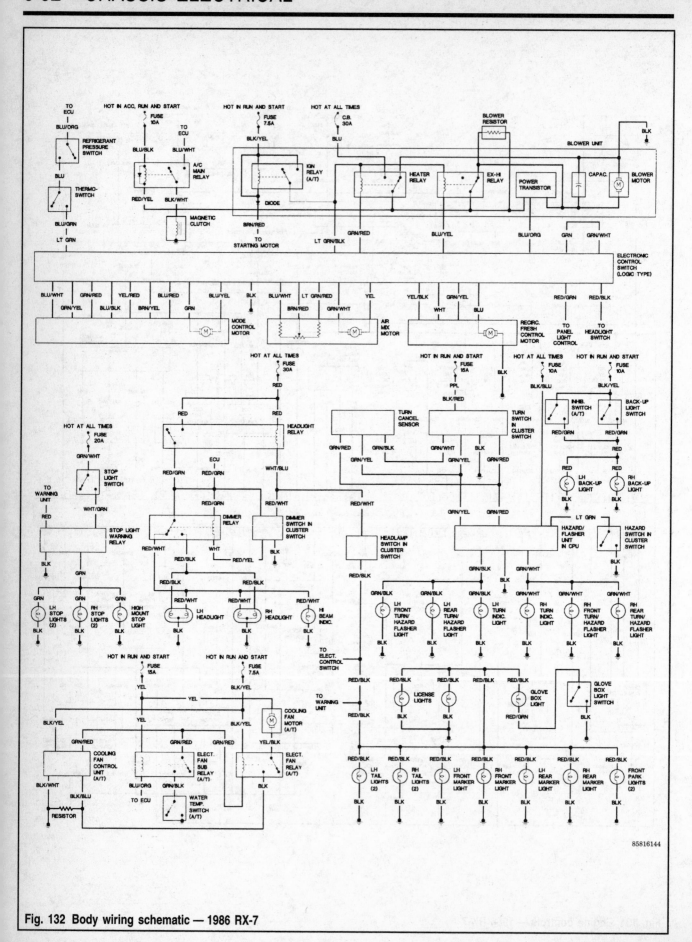

Fig. 132 Body wiring schematic — 1986 RX-7

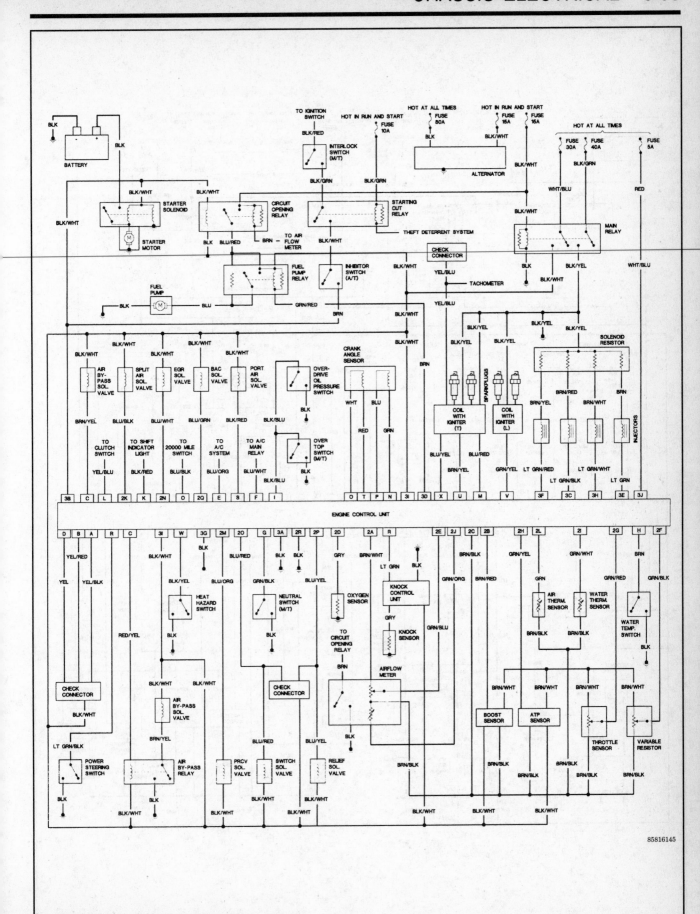

Fig. 133 Engine controls — 1987 RX-7 (non-turbo)

85816145

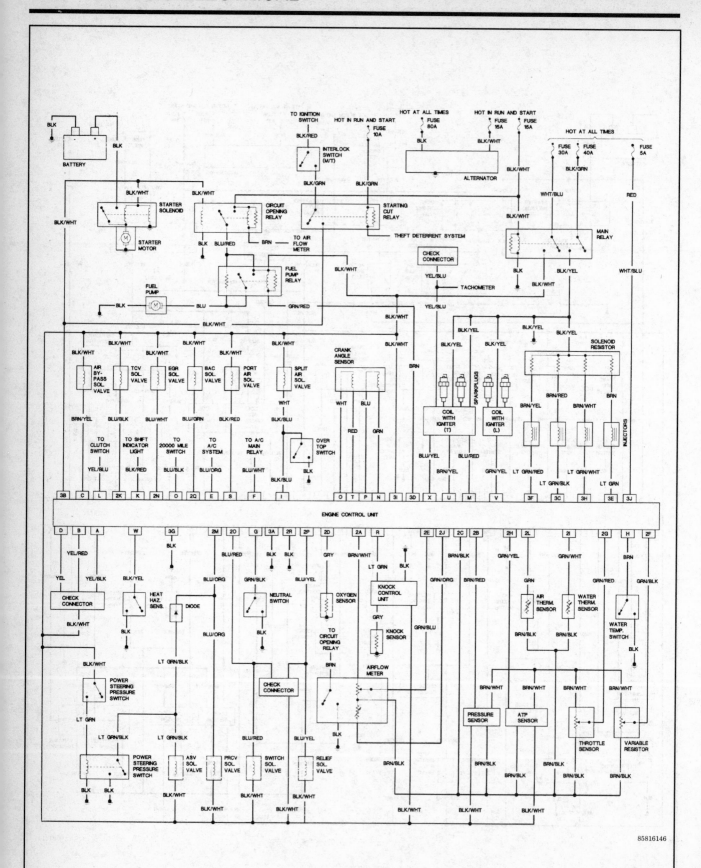

Fig. 134 Engine controls — 1987 RX-7 (turbo)

85816146

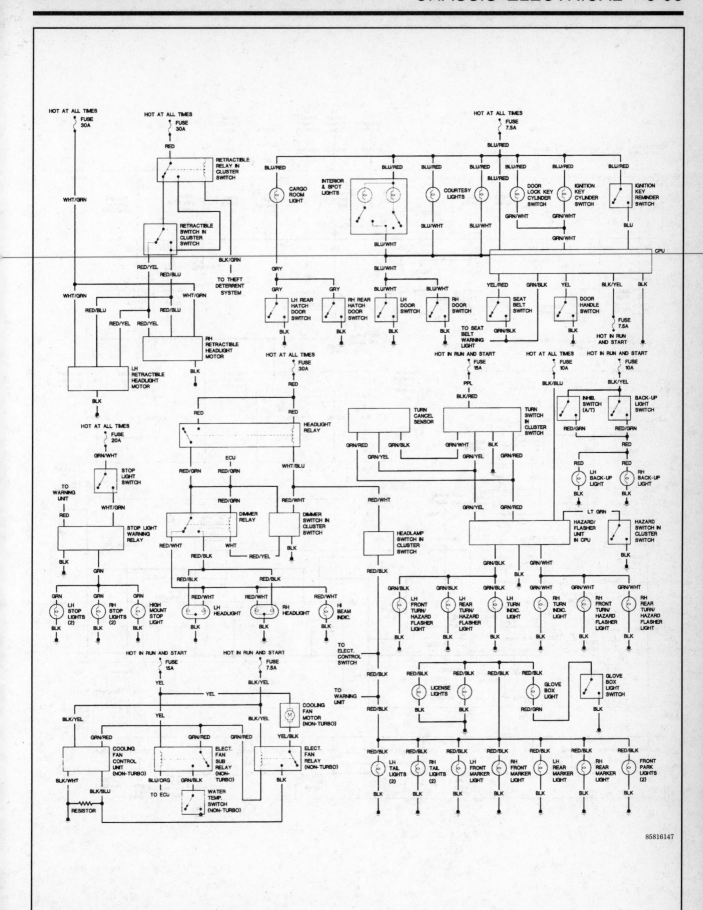

Fig. 135 Body wiring schematic — 1987 RX-7

85816147

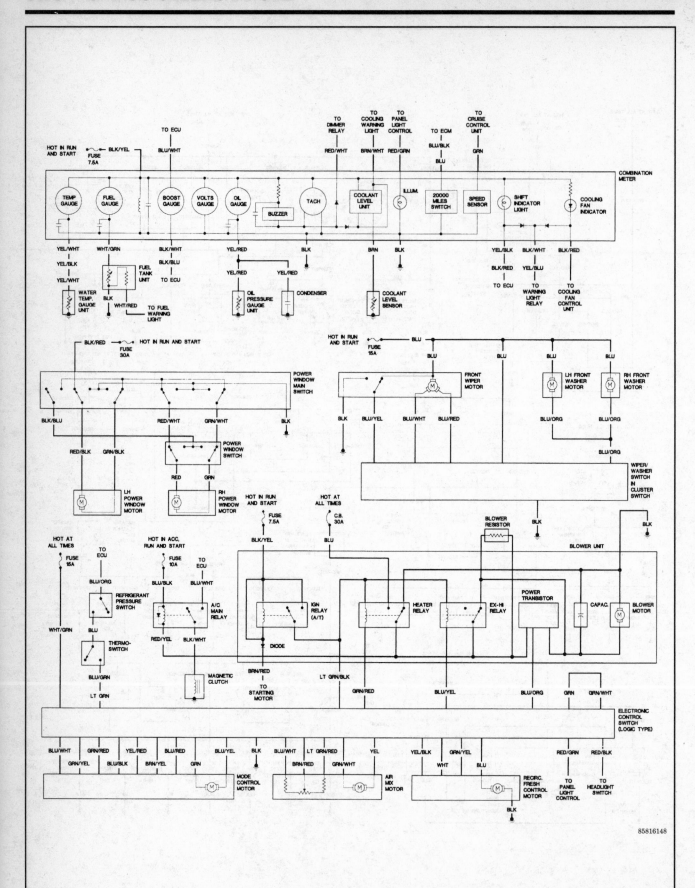

Fig. 136 Body wiring schematic (continued) — 1987 RX-7

85816148

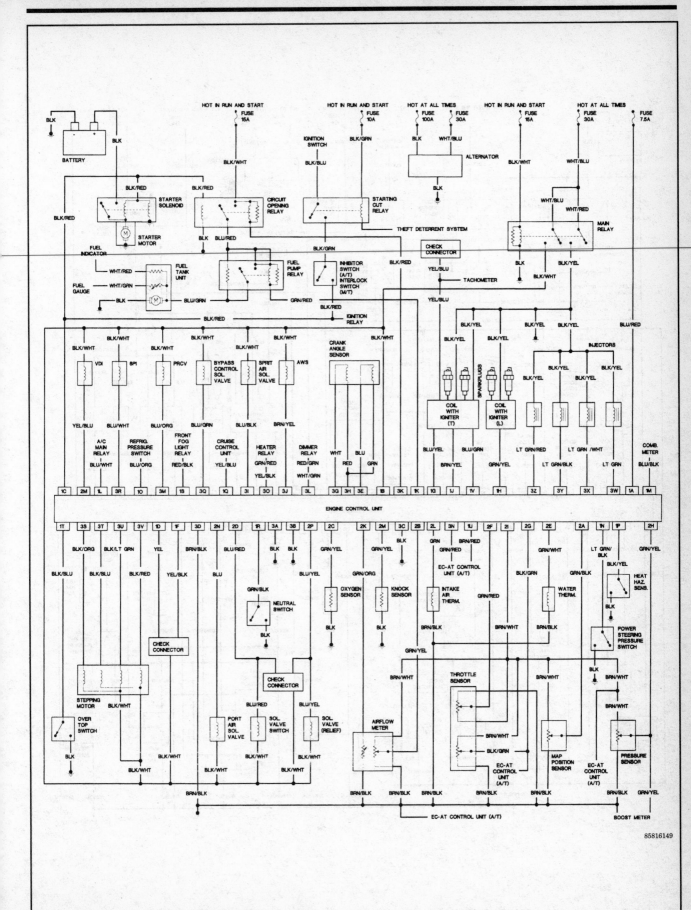

Fig. 137 Engine controls — 1988-89 RX-7 (non-turbo)

85816149

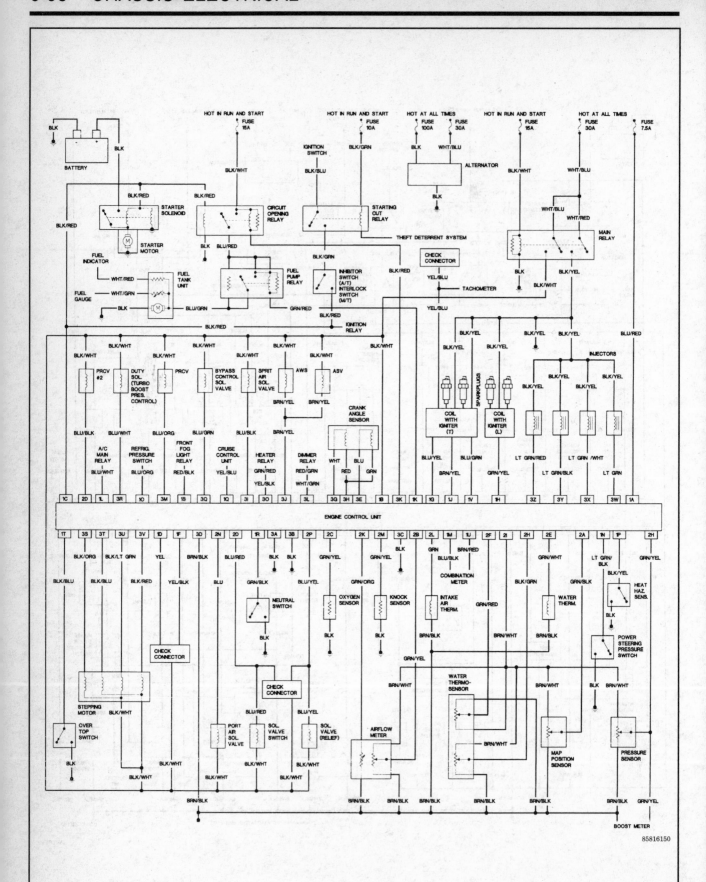

Fig. 138 Engine controls — 1988-89 RX-7 (turbo)

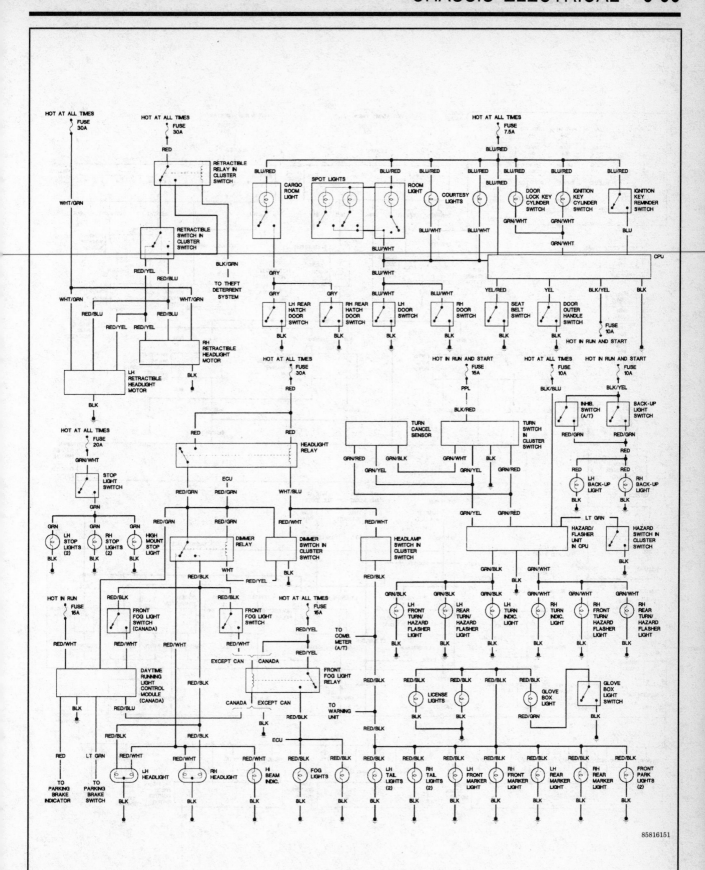

Fig. 139 Body wiring schematic — 1988-89 RX-7

85816151

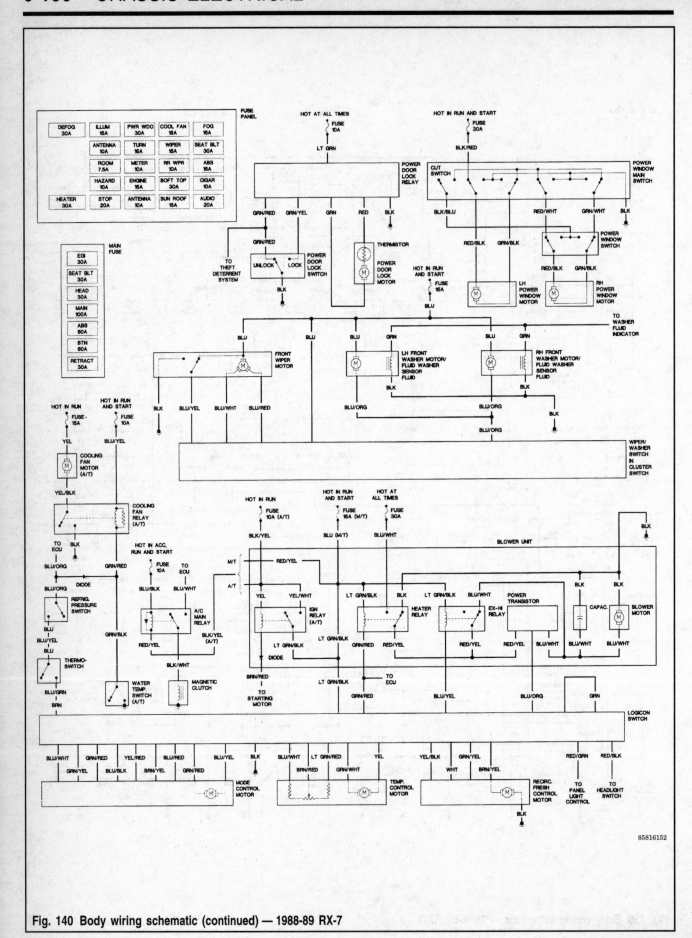

Fig. 140 Body wiring schematic (continued) — 1988-89 RX-7

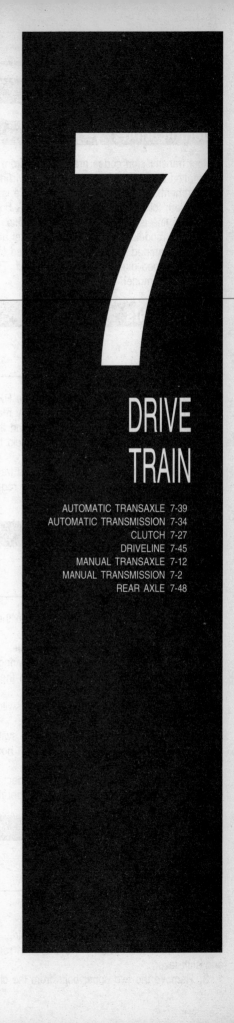

7

DRIVE
TRAIN

MANUAL TRANSMISSION

Identification

Most transmission codes are available from the vehicle information code plate located on the cowl (in the engine compartment). The first portion of the code is the transmission designation; following this, there is a blank box. At the right end of the line is the axle or final drive ratio.

On other models, the transmission model and serial number are either stamped on a plate that is bolted to the transmission case or stamped directly on the case itself. The location varies from model-to-model.

Adjustments

SHIFT LEVER

The shift lever on models other than the RX-7 may be adjusted during transmission installation by means of shims on the three bolts between the cover plate and the packing. The force required to move the shift knob should be 4.4-8.8 lbs. (2-4 kg).

On the RX-7, either a four or five-speed transmission is available. The shift linkage is internal and requires no adjustment.

Back-Up Light Switch

REMOVAL & INSTALLATION

The back-up light switch is threaded into the extension housing near the speedometer cable.

1. Disconnect the negative battery cable.
2. Label, then unfasten the electrical wiring connectors.
3. Loosen and remove the switch from the extension housing.
4. Remove the metal gasket from the switch.

To install:
5. Position a new metal gasket on the switch.
6. Thread the switch into the extension housing and tighten it just enough to crush the gasket.
7. Engage the switch wiring, then connect the negative battery cable and check that the switch operates properly.

Transmission

REMOVAL & INSTALLATION

GLC and GLC Wagon

1. Disconnect the negative battery cable.
2. Put the transmission in Neutral, then remove the console and shift lever.
3. Remove the two upper bolts from the clutch housing.

4. Raise the vehicle and support it securely on axle stands or a lift.
5. Drain the transmission oil and replace the plug.
6. Remove the driveshaft, and plug or cover the hole in the extension housing.
7. Disconnect the speedometer cable and back-up light switch wires.
8. Disconnect the exhaust pipe hanger from the bracket on the clutch housing.
9. Remove the exhaust pipe support bracket from the clutch housing. Disconnect the clutch cable at the release lever.
10. Remove the lower clutch housing cover.
11. Remove the starter electrical connections, then remove the bolts and starter from the engine.
12. Disconnect the exhaust pipe hanger at the extension housing.
13. Place a jack under the engine, using a block of wood to protect the oil pan. Make sure the jack can securely support the weight of the engine.
14. Disconnect the transmission support member at the transmission.
15. Remove clutch housing-to-engine attaching bolts.
16. Carefully slide the transmission rearward until the input shaft has cleared the clutch disc, and lower it out of the car.

To install:
17. Carefully raise the transmission into position and slide the unit forward to engage the input shaft and the clutch disc. Align the clutch plate with an arbor or an old input shaft.
18. Install the clutch housing-to-engine bolts, then snug them evenly and alternately to hold the transmission in place. Install the frame member-to-transmission support attaching nuts. Tighten all the nuts and bolts properly at this time.
19. Remove the transmission jack.
20. Connect the exhaust pipe hanger to the extension housing.
21. Engage the starter motor with the flywheel ring gear, then install the mounting bolts and nuts. Connect the starter wiring.
22. Install the lower clutch housing cover plate.
23. Connect the clutch cable to the release lever, then connect the exhaust pipe support bracket to the clutch housing.
24. Connect the back-up switch wires and the speedometer cable.
25. Make sure that the transmission drain plug is installed and tightened properly.
26. Connect the driveshaft and lower the vehicle.
27. Install and tighten the remaining two clutch housing bolts.
28. Install the console shift lever and connect the negative battery cable.
29. Adjust clutch and shift linkage. Refill the transmission with the proper grade of gear oil.

1. Remove the gearshift lever knob.
2. Remove the console box.
3. Remove the gearshift lever boot and the gearshift lever.

4. Disconnect the negative battery cable.

5. Raise the vehicle and safely support it with jackstands.

6. Drain the transmission lubricant.

7. Disconnect the driveshaft.

8. Disconnect the exhaust pipe hanger.

9. Remove the starter motor.

10. Disconnect the back-up switch wire.

11. Disconnect the speedometer cable.

12. Place a jack under the engine, protecting the oil pan with a block of wood.

13. Remove the transmission attaching bolts and remove the transmission.

To install:

14. Carefully raise the transmission into position and slide the unit forward to engage the input shaft and the clutch disc. Align the clutch plate with an arbor or an old input shaft.

15. Install the bell housing-to-engine bolts, then snug them evenly and alternately to hold the transmission in place. Install the frame member-to-transmission support attaching nuts. Tighten all the nuts and bolts properly at this time.

16. Remove the transmission jack.

17. Connect the speedometer cable. Connect the back-up light switch wiring. Engage the starter motor with the flywheel ring gear, then install the mounting bolts and nuts. Connect the starter wiring.

18. Connect the exhaust pipe hanger.

19. Connect the driveshaft and lower the vehicle.

20. Connect the negative battery cable.

21. Install the gearshift lever and boot.

22. Install the console box and screw the knob onto the gearshift lever.

23. Add lubricant until the level reaches the bottom of the filler plug hole. Adjust the clutch linkage.

929

1. Remove the gearshift lever knob.

2. Remove the console box.

3. Remove the gearshift lever boot and the gearshift lever.

4. Disconnect the negative battery cable.

5. Raise the vehicle and safely support it with jackstands.

6. Drain the transmission lubricant. Wipe off the plug threads and replace it.

7. Disconnect the driveshaft.

8. Disconnect the speedometer cable from the rear of the extension housing. Disengage the multi-connectors from the transmission labelling or noting their connections to assure proper installation.

9. Disconnect the exhaust pipe hanger bracket by removing the through-bolt and spacer.

10. Disconnect the exhaust pipe from the exhaust manifold.

11. Remove the heat insulator from the bottom of the vehicle.

12. Unscrew and remove the protector from the clutch release cylinder. Unbolt the clutch release cylinder from the transmission housing, but leave the hydraulic line connected. Tie the release cylinder and line off to the side and out of the way.

13. Disconnect the wiring and remove the starter.

14. Place a jack under the engine, using a block of wood to protect the oil pan. Make sure the jack can securely support the weight of the engine.

15. Disconnect the transmission support mounts at the frame.

16. Remove transmission-to-engine attaching bolts.

17. Carefully slide the transmission rearward until the input shaft has cleared the clutch disc, and lower it out of the car.

To install:

18. Carefully raise the transmission into position and slide the unit forward to engage the input shaft and the clutch disc. Align the clutch plate with an arbor or an old input shaft.

19. Install the bell housing-to-engine bolts, then snug them evenly and alternately to hold the transmission in place. Install the frame member-to-transmission support attaching bolts. Torque the frame member and engine-to-transmission bolts to 27-38 ft. lbs. (37-51 Nm).

20. Remove the transmission jack.

21. Engage the starter motor with the flywheel ring gear, then install the mounting bolts and nuts. Connect the starter wiring. The starter bolts are torqued to 23-34 ft. lbs. (31-46 Nm).

22. Attach the clutch release cylinder to the transmission housing and install the protector.

23. Install the heat insulator. Connect the exhaust pipe using a new gasket. Torque the exhaust pipe nuts to 23-34 ft. lbs. (31-46 Nm).

24. Connect the exhaust pipe hanger to the extension housing. Torque the through-bolt to 12-17 ft. lbs. (16-23 Nm).

25. Connect the electrical wiring and speedometer cable.

26. Connect the driveshaft and lower the vehicle.

27. Connect the negative battery cable.

28. Insert the gear shift lever into the extension housing with the boot. The shift lever retaining screws are torqued to 67-95 inch lbs. (8-11 Nm). Install the console box and screw the knob onto the gearshift lever.

29. Add lubricant until the level reaches the bottom of the filler plug hole. Adjust the clutch linkage.

RX-7

1. Disconnect the negative battery cable. Remove the clutch release cylinder and tie the clutch release cylinder up out of the way. Do not disconnect the hydraulic line from the clutch release cylinder.

2. Remove the air cleaner assembly, from carbureted engines only.

3. Remove the bolts attaching the transmission to the rear end of the engine. Unscrew and remove the gear shift lever knob. Remove the console box, if so equipped.

4. Remove the gear shift lever boot and boot plate. Remove the gear shift lever and retainer assembly.

5. Raise the vehicle and support it safely. Remove the front and rear engine under covers. Remove the converter under cover and disconnect the air pipe.

6. Remove the converter brackets. Remove the rear exhaust pipe and converter assembly. Remove the front exhaust pipe and monolith converter assembly.

7. Remove the floor under covers. Drain the transmission oil into a suitable drain pan. Remove the driveshaft.

8. Disconnect the wiring and remove the starter motor. On 1986-89 RX-7s, unbolt and remove the crossmember from the frame. Remove the bolts attaching the transmission to the rear end of the engine. Disconnect the couplers from the back-up lamp switch.

9. Place a transmission jack under the transmission. Disconnect the speedometer cable. Remove the nuts attaching the transmission support to the vehicle. Place a piece of wood approximately 1 in. in height between the oil pan and the center link. This will prevent the engine from interfering with the dash panel.

10. Slide the transmission rearward until the main shaft clears the clutch disc, then carefully remove the transmission from under the vehicle.

To install:

11. Carefully raise the transmission into position, then slide the unit forward to engage the input shaft and the clutch disc. Align the clutch plate with an arbor or an old input shaft.

12. Install the bell housing-to-engine bolts, then snug them evenly and alternately to hold the transmission in place. Install the frame member-to-transmission support attaching bolts. Tighten all bolts at this time.

13. Connect the back-up switch wiring. Install the starter and connect the wiring. On 1986-89 models, bolt the crossmember to the frame.

14. Connect the driveshaft. Install the floor covers.

15. Install the front exhaust, monolith converter, converter and rear exhaust pipe using new gaskets as required.

16. Connect the air pipe and install the converter under cover. Install the front and rear engine under covers. Lower the vehicle.

17. Insert the gear shift lever and retainer assembly into the transmission opening. Install the boot plate and boot.

18. Install the console box and screw the knob onto the shift lever. Install the remaining rear engine-to-transmission bolts.

19. On carbureted engines, install the air cleaner.

20. Attach the clutch release cylinder and connect the negative battery cable.

21. Adjust the clutch and shift linkage. Refill the transmission and road test the vehicle.

OVERHAUL

626 4 and 5-Speed Transmission
▶ **See Figures 1 and 2**

The 4 and 5-speed transmission are basically the same, with an additional housing located between the adapter plate and the rear extension housing, to support the 5th/reverse gears. Additional roller bearings are used in the housing to prevent shaft misalignment.

DISASSEMBLY

1. Remove the throw-out bearing return spring, throw-out bearing and the release fork.

2. Remove the bearing housing.

3. Remove the input shaft and countershaft snaprings.

4. Remove the floorshift lever retainer, complete with gasket.

5. Unfasten the cap bolt, then withdraw the spring, steel ball, select lock pin and spring from the retainer.

6. Remove the extension housing. Turn the control lever as far left as it will go and slide the extension housing off the output shaft.

7. Remove the spring seat and spring from the end of the shift control lever.

8. Loosen the spring cap, then withdraw the spring and plunger from their bores.

9. Remove the control rod and boss from the extension housing.

10. Remove the speedometer driven gear. Remove the back-up light switch.

11. Remove the speedometer drive gear.

12. Tap the front ends of the input shaft and countershaft with a plastic hammer, then remove the intermediate housing assembly from the transmission case.

13. Remove the three cap bolts; then withdraw the springs and lockballs.

14. Remove the reverse shift rod, reverse idler gear and shift lever.

15. Remove the setscrews from all the shift forks and push the shift rods rearward to remove them. Remove the shift forks.

16. Withdraw the reverse shift rod lockball, spring and interlock pins from the intermediate housing.

17. Remove reverse gear and key from the output shaft.

18. Remove the reverse countergear.

19. Remove the countershaft and output shaft from the intermediate housing.

20. Remove the bearings from the intermediate housing and transmission case.

21. Remove the snapring from the output shaft.

22. Slide the 3rd/4th clutch hub, sleeve, synchronizer ring and 3rd gear off the output shaft.

23. Remove the thrust washer, 1st gear, sleeve, synchronizer ring and 2nd gear from the rear of the output shaft.

ASSEMBLY

1. Install the 3rd/4th synchronizer clutch hub on the sleeve. Place the 3 synchronizer keys in the clutch hub key slots. Install the key springs with their open ends 120 degrees apart.

2. Install 3rd gear and the synchronizer ring on the front of the output shaft. Install the 3rd/4th clutch hub assembly on the output shaft. Be sure that the larger boss faces the front of the shaft.

3. Secure the gear and synchronizer with the snapring.

4. Repeat Step 1 for the 1st/2nd synchronizer assembly.

5. Position the synchronizer ring on 2nd gear. Slide 2nd gear on the output shaft so that the synchronizer ring faces the rear of the shaft.

6. Install the 1st/2nd clutch hub assembly on the output shaft so that its oil grooves face the front of the shaft. Engage the keys in the notches on the 2nd gear synchronizer ring.

7. Slide the 1st gear sleeve onto the output shaft. Position the synchronizer ring on 1st gear. Install the 1st gear on the output shaft so that the synchronizer ring faces forward. Rotate the 1st gear as required to engage the notches in the synchronizer ring with the keys in the clutch hub.

8. Slip the thrust washer on the rear of the output shaft. Install the needle bearing on the front of the output shaft.

9. Install the synchronizer ring on 4th gear and install the input shaft on the front of the output shaft.

10. Press the countershaft rear bearing and shim into the intermediate housing, then press the countershaft into the rear bearing.

11. Keep the thrust washer and 1st gear from falling off the output shaft by supporting the shaft. Install the output shaft on

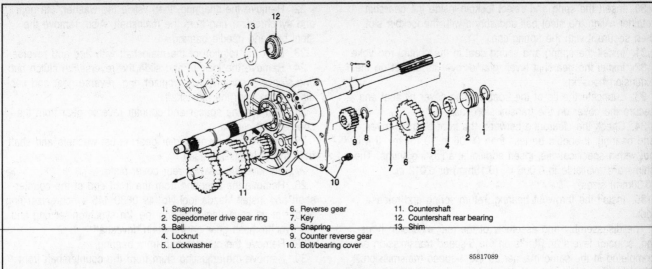

1. Snapring
2. Speedometer drive gear ring
3. Ball
4. Locknut
5. Lockwasher
6. Reverse gear
7. Key
8. Snapring
9. Counter reverse gear
10. Bolt/bearing cover
11. Countershaft
12. Countershaft rear bearing
13. Shim

85817089

Fig. 1 Gear train position in 4-speed transmission with intermediate housing

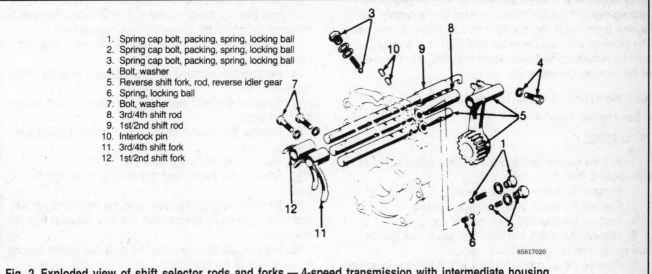

1. Spring cap bolt, packing, spring, locking ball
2. Spring cap bolt, packing, spring, locking ball
3. Spring cap bolt, packing, spring, locking ball
4. Bolt, washer
5. Reverse shift fork, rod, reverse idler gear
6. Spring, locking ball
7. Bolt, washer
8. 3rd/4th shift rod
9. 1st/2nd shift rod
10. Interlock pin
11. 3rd/4th shift fork
12. 1st/2nd shift fork

85817020

Fig. 2 Exploded view of shift selector rods and forks — 4-speed transmission with intermediate housing

the intermediate housing. Be sure that each output shaft gear engages with its opposite on the countershaft.

12. Tap the output shaft bearing and shim into the intermediate housing with a plastic hammer. Install the cover.

13. Install reverse gear on the output shaft and secure it with its key.

➡The chamfer on the teeth of both the reverse gear and the reverse countergear should face rearward.

14. Install the reverse countergear.

15. Install the lockball and spring into the bore in the intermediate housing. Depress the ball with a screwdriver.

16. Install the reverse shift rod, lever and idler gear at the same time. Place the reverse shift rod in the Neutral position.

17. Align the boxes and insert the shift interlock pin.

18. Install the 3rd/4th shift rod into the intermediate housing and shift bores. Place the shift rod in Neutral.

19. Install the next interlock pin in the bore.

20. Install the 1st/2nd shift rod.

21. Install the lockballs and springs in their bores. Install the cap bolt.

22. Install the speedometer drive gear and lockball on the output shaft, then install its snapring.

23. Apply sealer to the mating surfaces of the intermediate housing. Install the intermediate housing in the transmission case.

24. Install the input shaft and countershaft front bearings in the transmission case.

25. Secure the speedometer driven gear.

26. Install the control rod through the holes in the front of the extension housing.

27. Align the key with the keyway and install the yoke on the end of the control rod. Install the yoke lockbolt.

28. Fit the plunger and spring into the extension housing bore, then secure with the spring cap.

29. Turn the control rod all the way to the left and install the extension housing on the intermediate housing.

30. Insert the sprig and select lockpin inside the gearshift retainer. Align the steel ball and spring with the lockpin slot, then secure it with the spring cap.

31. Install the spring and spring seat in the control rod yoke.

32. Install the gearshift lever retainer over its gasket on the extension housing.

33. Lubricate the lip of the front bearing cover oil seal and secure the cover on the transmission case.

34. Check the clearance between the front bearing cover and bearing. It should be less than 0.006 in. (0.15mm). If it is not within specifications, insert additional adjusting shims. The shims are available in 0.006 in. (0.15mm) or 0.012 in. (0.30mm) sizes.

35. Install the throwout bearing, return spring and release fork.

The disassembly and assembly of the rear extension housing, selector levers and forks on the 5-speed transmission are completed in the same manner as the 4-speed transmission. After this has been done, the added housing can be removed by taking out the retaining bolts. The housing will have to be lightly tapped with a soft-faced hammer. The removal of the housing exposes the 5th/reverse synchronizer assembly, the reverse countergear, the countershaft and mainshaft bearings. The bearings are pulled from the shafts and the gears can then be removed. The transmission assembly is in the reverse of the disassembly procedure.

RX-7 (Non-Turbo) 5-Speed Transmission
◆ See Figures 3 and 4

DISASSEMBLY

1. Pull the release fork outward until the spring clip of the fork releases from the ballpivot.

2. Remove the fork and release bearing.

3. Remove the clutch busing shim and gasket.

4. Remove the gearshift lever retainer and gasket.

5. Remove the spring and steel ball, select lock spindle and spring from the gearshift lever retainer.

6. Remove the extension housing with the control lever end down to the left as far as it will go.

7. Remove the control lever end, key and control rod.

8. Remove the lock plate and speedometer gear.

9. Remove the back-up light switch and gasket.

10. Remove the snapring and slide the speedometer drive gear from the mainshaft.

11. Remove the bottom cover and gasket.

12. Remove the shift rod ends.

13. Remove the rear bearing housing.

14. Remove the snapring, then remove the mainshaft rear bearing, thrust washer and race, using Mazda puller No. 49 0839 425C or equivalent.

15. Remove the washer and countershaft rear bearing, using Mazda puller No. 49 0839 425C or equivalent.

16. Remove the counter 5th gear.

17. Remove the intermediate housing.

18. Remove the springs and shift locking balls.

19. Remove the two blind covers and gaskets from the case.

20. Remove the reverse/5th shift rod, fork and interlock pin.

21. Remove the 1st/2nd and 3rd/4th shift forks, rods and interlock pins.

22. Remove the snapring, then slide the washer, 5th gear and synchronizer ring from the mainshaft. Also, remove the steel ball and needle bearing.

23. Lock the rotation of the mainshaft with 2nd and reverse.

24. Remove the locknut and slide the reverse/5th clutch hub and sleeve assembly, synchronizer ring, reverse gear and needle bearing from the mainshaft.

25. Remove the spacer and counter reverse gear from the countershaft.

26. Remove the reverse idler gear, thrust washers and shaft from the transmission case.

27. Remove the bearing rear cover plate.

28. Remove the snapring from the front end of the countershaft and install Mazda tool No. 49 0839 445 synchronizer ring holder or its equivalent between the 4th synchronizer ring and the synchromesh gear on the main driveshaft.

29. Remove the countershaft front bearing.

30. Remove the adjusting shim from the countershaft front bearing bore.

31. Remove the countershaft center bearing outer race.

32. With a special puller and attachment, remove the mainshaft front bearing, thrust washer and inner race along with the adjusting shim from the mainshaft front bearing bore.

33. Remove the snapring and remove the main driveshaft bearing.

34. Remove the countershaft center bearing inner race with the puller.

35. Separate the input shaft from the mainshaft and remove the input shaft.

36. Remove the synchronizer ring and needle bearing from the input shaft.

37. Remove the mainshaft assembly.

38. Remove the 1st/2nd and 3rd/4th shift forks from the case.

39. Remove the snapring, then slide the 3rd/4th clutch hub and sleeve assembly, synchronizer ring and 3rd gear from the mainshaft.

40. Remove the thrust washer, 1st gear and needle bearing from the rear of the mainshaft.

41. Press out the needle bearing inner race, synchronizer ring, 1st and 2nd clutch hub, sleeve assembly, synchronizer ring and 2nd gear from the mainshaft.

ASSEMBLY

1. Install the 3rd/4th clutch hub into the sleeve, place the 3 keys into the clutch hub slots and install the springs onto the hub.

2. Assemble the 1st/2nd and reverse/5th clutch hub and sleeve as described in Step 1.

3. Install the needle bearing, 2nd gear, synchronizer ring and 1st/2nd clutch assembly on the rear section of the mainshaft.

4. Press on the 1st gear needle bearing inner race.

5. Install the 3rd gear and synchronizer ring onto the front section of the mainshaft.

6. Install the 3rd/4th clutch assembly onto the mainshaft.

7. Install the snapring on the mainshaft.

8. Install the needle bearing, synchronizer ring, 1st gear and thrust washer on the mainshaft.

9. Install the mainshaft assembly.

10. Install the needle bearing on the front end of the mainshaft.

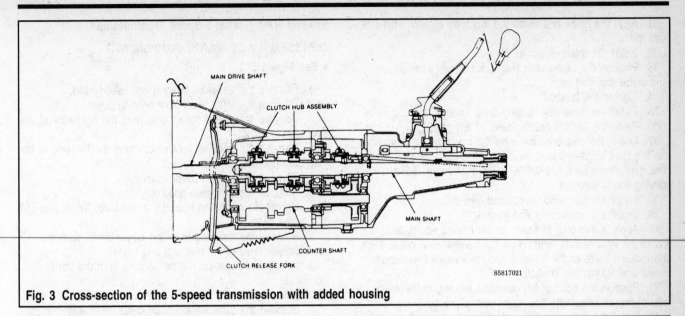

MAIN DRIVE SHAFT

CLUTCH HUB ASSEMBLY

MAIN SHAFT

COUNTER SHAFT

CLUTCH RELEASE FORK

85817021

Fig. 3 Cross-section of the 5-speed transmission with added housing

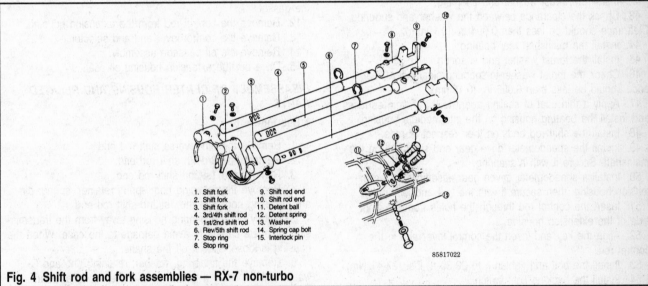

1. Shift fork
2. Shift fork
3. Shift fork
4. 3rd/4th shift rod
5. 1st/2nd shift rod
6. Rev/5th shift rod
7. Stop ring
8. Stop ring
9. Shift rod end
10. Shift rod end
11. Detent ball
12. Detent spring
13. Washer
14. Spring cap bolt
15. Interlock pin

85817022

Fig. 4 Shift rod and fork assemblies — RX-7 non-turbo

11. Install the 1st/2nd and 3rd/4th shift forks in their respective clutch sleeves.

12. Check the mainshaft bearing end-play. Check the depth of the mainshaft bearing bore in the case. Measure the mainshaft bearing height. The difference indicates the required adjusting shim to give a total end-play of less than 0.004 in. (0.1mm).

13. Install the synchronizer ring holder tool between the 4th synchronizer ring and the synchromesh gear on the input shaft.

14. Position the shims and mainshaft bearing in the bore and install with a press.

15. Install the input shaft bearing in the same way.

16. Check the countershaft front bearing end-play in the same way as the mainshaft bearing end-play.

17. Install the front bearing snapring.

18. Press the countershaft center bearing into position.

19. Install the bearing cover plate.

20. Install the reverse idler gearshaft, thrust washers and reverse idler gear.

21. Install the counter reverse gear and spacer on the rear end on the countershaft.

22. Install the thrust washer and press the needle bearing inner race of the reverse gear on the mainshaft.

23. Install the needle bearing, reverse gear, synchronizer ring, reverse/5th clutch assembly and new mainshaft locknut on the mainshaft.

24. Lock the mainshaft with the 2nd and reverse gears. Tighten the locknut to 95-152 ft. lbs. (129-206 Nm).

25. Install the needle bearing, synchronizer ring and 5th gear on the mainshaft.

26. Install the thrust washer, steel ball and snapring on the mainshaft.

27. Check the thrust washer-to-snapring clearance. It should be 0.004-0.012 (0.10-0.30mm).

28. Install the 1st/2nd shift rod through the holes in the case and fork.

29. Install the interlock pin with a special installer and guide.

30. Install the 3rd/4th shift rod through the holes in the case and fork.

31. Align the holes and install the lockbolts of each shift fork and rod.

32. Install the interlock pin as above.

33. Position the reverse/5th shift fork on the clutch sleeve and install the shift rod.

34. Tighten the lockbolt.

35. Install the three shift locking balls, springs and cap bolts.

36. Place the 3rd/4th clutch sleeve in 3rd gear.

37. Check the clearance between the synchronizer key and the exposed edge of the synchronizer ring with a feeler gauge. The gap should be 0.026-0.079 in. (0.65-2.00mm). Adjust by varying thrust washers.

38. Install the two blind covers and gaskets.

39. Install the undercover and gasket.

40. Apply a thin coat of sealer to the mating edges and install the intermediate housing on the transmission case. Align the lockbolt holes of the housing and reverse idler gearshaft, install and tighten the lockbolt.

41. Position the counter 5th gear and bearing to the rear end of the countershaft, then install with a press.

42. Install the thrust washer and snapring.

43. Check the clearance between the washer and snapring. Clearance should be less than 0.004 in. (0.10mm).

44. Install the mainshaft rear bearing.

45. Install the thrust washer and snapring.

46. Check the thrust washer-to-snapring clearance. Clearance should be less than 0.006 in. (0.15mm).

47. Apply a thin coat of sealing agent to the mating surfaces and install the bearing housing on the intermediate housing.

48. Install the shift rod ends on their respective rods.

49. Install the speedometer drive gear and steel ball on the mainshaft. Secure it with a snapring.

50. Install a speedometer driven gear assembly on the extension housing, then secure it with the bolt and lock plate.

51. Insert the control rod through the holes from the front side of the extension housing.

52. Align the key and insert the control lever end in the control rod.

53. Install the bolt and tighten it to 20-30 ft. lbs. (27-41 Nm).

54. Install the back-up light switch.

55. Place the gasket on the case, then install the extension housing with the control lever end down and as far to the left as it will go.

56. Insert the select lock spindle and spring from the underside of the shift lever retainer.

57. Install the steel ball and spring in alignment with the spindle groove, then install the spring cap bolt.

58. Install the gearshift lever retainer and gasket on the extension housing.

59. Check the bearing end-play. Measure the depth of the bearing bore in the housing. Measure the height of the bearing protrusion. The difference indicates the thickness of the shim needed. The end-play should be less than 0.004 in. (0.10mm).

60. Place the gasket on the front side of the case. Apply lubricant to the lip of the oil seal and install the clutch housing on the case.

61. Install the release bearing and fork on the clutch housing.

929 and RX-7 (Turbo) 5-Speed Transmission

DISASSEMBLY OF MAJOR COMPONENTS

▶ See Figure 5

1. Remove the throwout bearing and release fork.

2. Remove the input shaft front bearing cover.

3. Remove the speedometer gear from the right side of the extension housing.

4. Remove the back-up light switch from the left side of the extension housing.

5. Remove the control cover assembly.

6. Remove the shift gate assembly.

7. Unbolt the extension housing, rotate if clockwise and pull it from the case.

8. Remove the snapring from the output shaft, then the speedometer drive gear, snapring and key.

9. Unbolt and separate the bellhousing from the transmission case.

10. Drive the oil seal from the bellhousing.

11. Remove the transmission case lower cover and discard the gasket.

12. Remove the control rod from the extension housing.

13. Remove the control lever end and selector.

14. Remove the oil passage assembly.

15. Drive out the extension housing oil seal.

DISASSEMBLY OF CENTER HOUSING AND RELATED PARTS

▶ See Figure 6

1. Remove the 5th/reverse shift rod end.

2. Remove the 3rd/4th shift rod end.

3. Remove the 1st/2nd shift rod end.

4. Remove the retaining ring, spring retainer, spring, pin and retaining ring from the 1st/2nd shift rod end.

5. Gently pry the bearing housing away from the transmission case. Be careful to avoid damage to the case. When the housing is loose, slide it off the shafts.

6. Remove the snapring, washer, retaining ring and C-washers then, using a puller, remove the mainshaft rear bearing.

➡Tag the C-washers as to front and rear. They have different thicknesses.

7. Uncrimp the tabs on the countershaft rear bearing locknut, shift the clutch hub sleeves to 1st and reverse engagement, and, using holding fixture 49 S120 440, or equivalent, remove the locknut. When reassembling, a new locknut **must** be used.

8. Using a puller, remove the countershaft bearing.

9. Remove the counter 5th gear and spacer from the rear of the countershaft.

10. Remove the idler gear shaft retaining bolt from the center housing.

11. Remove the oil guide.

12. Separate the center housing from the case by tapping it loose with a plastic mallet.

REMOVAL OF 5TH/REVERSE GEAR AND RELATED PARTS

▶ See Figure 7

1. Remove the 3 shift rod spring bolts, then remove the balls and springs.

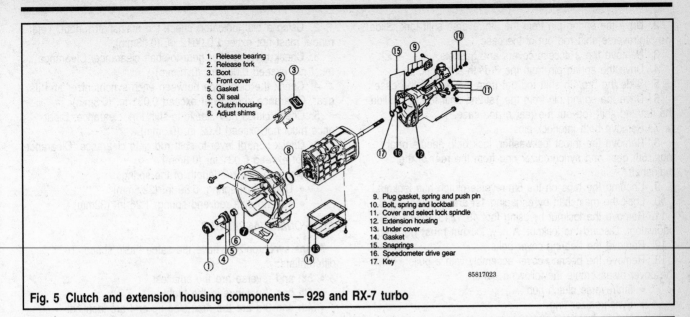

1. Release bearing
2. Release fork
3. Boot
4. Front cover
5. Gasket
6. Oil seal
7. Clutch housing
8. Adjust shims

9. Plug gasket, spring and push pin
10. Bolt, spring and lockball
11. Cover and select lock spindle
12. Extension housing
13. Under cover
14. Gasket
15. Snaprings
16. Speedometer drive gear
17. Key

85817023

Fig. 5 Clutch and extension housing components — 929 and RX-7 turbo

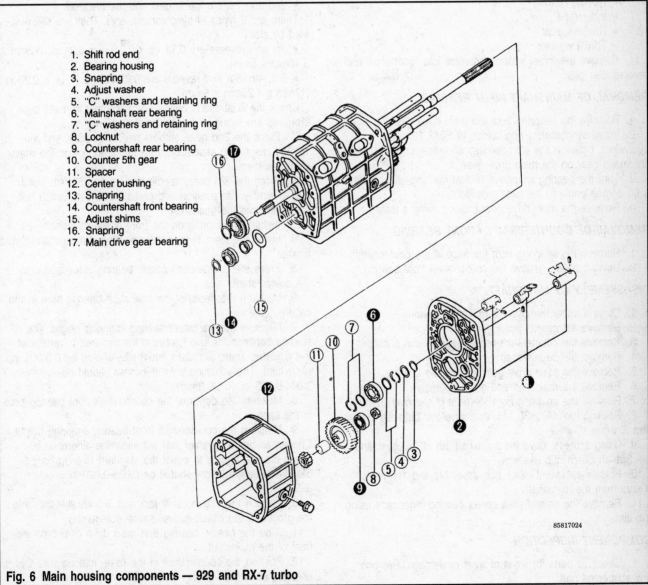

1. Shift rod end
2. Bearing housing
3. Snapring
4. Adjust washer
5. "C" washers and retaining ring
6. Mainshaft rear bearing
7. "C" washers and retaining ring
8. Locknut
9. Countershaft rear bearing
10. Counter 5th gear
11. Spacer
12. Center bushing
13. Snapring
14. Countershaft front bearing
15. Adjust shims
16. Snapring
17. Main drive gear bearing

85817024

Fig. 6 Main housing components — 929 and RX-7 turbo

2. Drive the spring pin from the 5th/reverse shift fork. Slide the 5th/reverse shift rod out of the case.

3. Remove the 2 access covers and gaskets.

4. Drive the spring pin from the 3rd/4th shift fork.

5. Slide the 3rd/4th shift rod out from the rear of the case.

6. Drive the spring pin from the 1st/2nd shift fork and slide the 1st/2nd shift rod out the rear of the case.

7. Remove both interlock pins.

8. Remove the thrust lockwasher, lock ball, needle bearings, 5th gear and synchronizer ring from the rear of the mainshaft.

9. Uncrimp the tabs on the 5th/reverse clutch hub locknut.

10. Lock the mainshaft by engaging 1st and reverse gears.

11. Remove the locknut by using tool 49 1243 465A, or equivalent. Discard the locknut. A new locknut **must** be used.

12. Remove the bearing cover bolts.

13. Remove the bearing cover assembly with a puller. From the cover disassemble the following parts:
- 5th/reverse clutch hub
- Synchronizer ring
- Needle bearing
- Inner race
- Reverse gear
- Thrust washer

14. Remove the thrust washers, reverse idler gear shaft and reverse idler gear.

REMOVAL OF MAINSHAFT INPUT BEARING

1. Remove the snapring from the main drive gear.

2. Install synchronizer ring holder 49 F017 101, or equivalent, between the 4th speed synchronizer ring and synchromesh gear on the main drive gear.

3. Turn the bearing snaprings so that the ring ends are at a 90 degree angle to the case grooves.

4. Remove the main drive gear bearing using a puller.

REMOVAL OF COUNTERSHAFT FRONT BEARING

1. Remove the snapring from the front of the countershaft.

2. Using a puller, remove the countershaft front bearing.

DISASSEMBLY OF MAINSHAFT

1. Using a puller, remove the mainshaft bearing.

2. Remove 1st gear.

3. Remove the countershaft center bearing with a puller.

4. Remove the countershaft.

5. Remove the main drive gear and needle bearing.

6. Remove the mainshaft and gear assembly.

7. Remove the snapring from the front of the mainshaft.

8. Position tool 49 0636 145, or equivalent, between 2nd and 3rd gears.

9. Using a press, drive the mainshaft out of 3rd gear and the 3rd/4th clutch hub assembly.

10. Press the 1st/2nd clutch hub assembly and 1st gear sleeve from the mainshaft.

11. Remove the countershaft center bearing inner race using a puller.

COMPONENT INSPECTION

1. Check all parts for signs of wear or damage. Replace any suspected part.

2. Using a dial indicator, check the mainshaft runout. Total runout must not exceed 0.0012 in. (0.03mm).

3. Check reverse idler gear-to-shaft clearance. Clearance must not exceed 0.006 in. (0.15mm).

4. Check the clearance between each synchronizer and its gear. Clearance should not exceed 0.031 in. (0.8mm).

5. Check clutch hub sleeve-to-shift fork clearance. Clearance must not exceed 0.02 in. (0.5mm).

6. Check control lever-to-shift rod gate clearance. Clearance must not exceed 0.031 in. (0.8mm).

7. Measure the free length of the springs.
- Detent ball spring: 0.89 in. (22.5mm)
- 1st/2nd shift rod end spring: 1.26 in. (32mm)

COMPONENT ASSEMBLY

All the synchronizers have the same basic shape. To differentiate:
- 5th and reverse are the smallest
- 5th has 2 notches in the teeth
- 4th and 3rd are the next size up and are identical
- 2nd and 1st are the largest and are identical

There are 2 types of synchronizer keys. They are differentiated by size.
- 1st and reverse are 0.71 in. x 0.21 in. x 0.24 in. (18mm x 5.45mm x 6mm)
- 3rd, 4th, 5th and reverse are 0.67 in. x 0.17 in. x 0.20 in. (17mm x 4.25mm x 5mm)

Check the illustrations before any assembly to make sure the parts are facing in the right direction

1. Place the 2nd gear, with its needle bearing, and the 1st/2nd clutch hub assembly, on a press and press the mainshaft into them.

2. Place the 3rd gear, needle bearing and 3rd/4th clutch hub assembly into position and press the 3rd/4th clutch hub assembly onto the mainshaft.

3. Install the snapring on the front of the mainshaft.

4. Install the inner race, needle bearing, 1st gear and thrust washer.

5. Press the countershaft center bearing inner race onto the countershaft.

6. Measure the depth of the mainshaft bearing bore in the case.

7. Measure the mainshaft bearing snapring height. The difference between the two figures is the required thickness of the adjusting shim. Standard thrust play should be 0-0.004 in. (0-0.1mm). The adjusting shim thickness should be 0.004-0.012 in. (0.1-0.3mm).

8. Measure the depth of the countershaft front bearing bore in the case.

9. Measure the countershaft front bearing snapring height. Choose an adjusting shim that will allow the difference between the two figures to equal the standard bearing height. Standard bearing height should be 0.035-0.039 in. (0.9-1.0mm).

10. Position the 1st/2nd shift fork and 3rd/4th shift fork into the groove of the clutch hub and sleeve assembly.

11. Slide the needle bearing and main drive gear onto the front of the mainshaft.

12. Position the countershaft in the case, making sure that it engages each gear on the mainshaft.

13. Using a suitable length of pipe, drive on the countershaft center bearing.

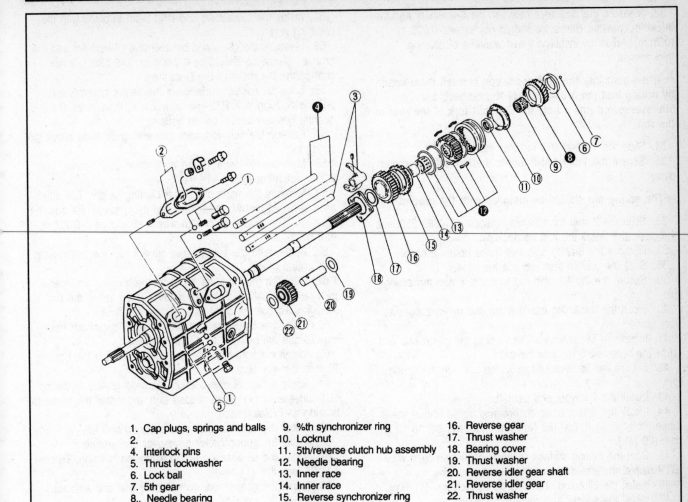

1. Cap plugs, springs and balls
2.
4. Interlock pins
5. Thrust lockwasher
6. Lock ball
7. 5th gear
8.. Needle bearing
9. %th synchronizer ring
10. Locknut
11. 5th/reverse clutch hub assembly
12. Needle bearing
13. Inner race
14. Inner race
15. Reverse synchronizer ring
16. Reverse gear
17. Thrust washer
18. Bearing cover
19. Thrust washer
20. Reverse idler gear shaft
21. Reverse idler gear
22. Thrust washer

85817025

Fig. 7 5th/reverse gear components — 929 and RX-7 turbo

14. Install the correctly predetermined shim on the mainshaft bearing.

15. Using a suitable length of pipe, drive on the mainshaft bearing.

16. Install the bearing cover and tighten the bolts to 20 ft. lbs. (27 Nm).

17. Install the synchronizer ring holder tool between the 4th synchronizer ring and the synchromesh gear on the main drive gear.

18. Using a driver, install in the main gear bearing.

19. Install the main gear bearing snapring.

20. Place the correctly predetermined shim in the countershaft front bearing.

21. Drive the countershaft front bearing on using a bearing driver.

22. Install the snapring.

➡**The countershaft bearing snapring is smaller than the mainshaft bearing snapring.**

23. Install the reverse idler gear and shaft with a spacer on each side of the gear.

24. Install the counter reverse gear and spacer, with the chamfer on the gear forward.

25. Install the thrust washer, reverse gear, inner race, needle bearing and clutch hub assembly.

26. Engage 1st and reverse gears to lock the mainshaft.

27. Install a new locknut on the mainshaft and torque it to 174 ft. lbs. (236 Nm) using tool 49 1243 465A, or equivalent.

28. Check the clearance between the synchronizer key and the exposed edge of the synchronizer ring. The clearance must not exceed 0.08 in. (2.0mm). If it does, adjust it by adding or deleting thrust washers at the mainshaft bearing front and rear.

➡**Total combined thickness of the front and rear thrust washers should not exceed 0.24 in. (6mm).**

29. Stake the locknut onto the shaft.

30. Install the synchronizer ring, 5th gear and needle bearing.

31. Install the 5th gear lock ball and thrust lockwasher.

32. Install the 5th gear 0.12 in. (3mm) thick C-washers and retaining ring.

33. Measure the clearance between the C-washers and the thrust lockwasher. Clearance should not exceed 0.008 in. (0.2mm). Adjust by installing thrust washers of differing thicknesses.

➡**When installing the shift rods, you can tell them apart by noting that the 3rd/4th rod is the longest; the 5th/reverse rod has a hole for the shift fork at the rear of the rod.**

34. Slide the 1st/2nd shift rod into the case.
35. Secure the 1st/2nd shift fork to the rod with the spring pin.

➡**The spring pin should be installed with the groove.**

36. Slide the 2 shift for assembly guides, 49 0862 350, into the case and install the first interlock pin.
37. Remove the 3rd/4th shift fork guide from the case.
38. Slide the 3rd/4th shift rod into the case.
39. Secure the 3rd/4th shift rod to the fork with the spring pin.
40. Insert the remaining interlock pin and remove the shift fork guide.
41. Install the 5th/reverse shift fork onto the clutch hub and slide the reverse/5th rod into the case.
42. Secure the 5th/reverse fork to the rod with the spring pin.
43. Install the 2 covers and gaskets.
44. Install the detent balls, springs and bolts. Torque the 2 upper bolts to 43 ft. lbs. (58 Nm) and the lower bolt to 19 ft. lbs. (26 Nm).
45. Coat the mating surface of the transmission case with RTV gasket material and install the center housing.
46. Install the oil guide. Torque it to 95 inch lbs. (11 Nm).
47. Install the spacer and counter 5th gear.
48. Align the reverse idler gear shaft boss with the holding bolt hole, then install the bolt and gasket. Torque the bolt to 122 inch lbs. (14 Nm).
49. Drive on the countershaft rear bearing using a bearing driver.
50. Install the mainshaft holder.
51. Engage 1st and reverse gears to lock the countershaft.
52. Install the countershaft locknut and torque the nut to 145 ft. lbs. (196 Nm). Stake the nut.
53. Drive on the mainshaft rear bearing.

54. Install the C-washers and hold them in place with the retaining ring.
55. Measure the clearance between the C-washers and the groove. Clearance should be 0-0.004 in. (0-0.1mm). If not, change the thickness of the C-washers.
56. Coat the contact surfaces of the center housing and bearing housing with RTV gasket material, then install the bearing housing on the center housing.
57. Engage the shift rod ends and shift rods, then install the spring pins.
58. Measure the depth of the main drive gear bearing bore in the clutch housing.
59. Measure the main drive gear bearing height. The difference between the two is the required thickness of the adjusting shim. The adjusting shim thickness should be 0-0.004 in. (0-0.1mm).
60. Apply oil to the seal lip and drive it into the bellhousing with a seal driver.
61. Coat the mating surfaces of the bellhousing and transmission case with RTV gasket material, then install the bellhousing. Torque the bolts to 34 ft. lbs. (46 Nm).
62. Install the input shaft bearing cover in the clutch housing. Torque the bolts to 19 ft. lbs. (26 Nm).
63. Install the bottom cover and gasket. Torque the bolts to 95 inch lbs. (11 Nm).
64. Apply a coat of molybdenum disulfide grease to the contact surfaces of the clutch release arm and install the throwout bearing and release arm.
65. Install the speedometer gear snapring and key.
66. Install the speedometer drive gear and snapring.
67. Install the oil passage in the extension housing. Torque it to 95 inch lbs. (11 Nm).
68. Install the control rod, control lever end and selector.
69. Install the roll pins.

➡**Make sure that the inner shift lever and shift rod end are aligned.**

70. Coat the contact surfaces of the extension housing and bearing housing with RTV gasket material.
71. Apply RTV sealant to the bolt threads and install the extension housing. Torque the bolts to 35 ft. lbs. (47 Nm).
72. Coat the mating surfaces of the shift control lever case and transfer case with RTV gasket material, then install the shift control case. Apply RTV to the bolts and tighten them to 22 ft. lbs. (30 Nm).

MANUAL TRANSAXLE

Identification

Most transaxle codes are available from the vehicle information code plate located on the cowl (in the engine compartment). The first portion of the code is the transmission designation; following this, there is a blank box. At the right end of the line is the axle or final drive ratio.

On other models the transaxle model and serial number are either stamped on a plate that is bolted to the transmission case or stamped directly on the case itself. The location varies from model-to-model.

Adjustments

SHIFT LEVER ADJUSTMENT

Front Wheel Drive

The shift lever on most models may be adjusted during transmission installation by means of adjusting shims on the three bolts between the cover plate and the packing. The force required to move the shift knob should be 4.4-8.8 lbs. (2-4 kg).

Four Wheel Drive

▶ See Figure 8

1. Set the transaxle shift lever (in the vehicle) to the Neutral position.

2. On the transaxle, make sure the shift and select levers are also in the Neutral position.

3. Remove the shift lever console.

4. Disconnect the shift and select cables from the control levers by removing the pins, flat washers and spring clips. The clips must be replaced.

5. Make sure the select cable end hole aligns with the select lever pin. If not aligned, loosen cable adjusting nut **A** and rotate the cable end until the holes are aligned.

6. Place the shift lever at the center of its front-to-rear stoke.

7. Make sure the select cable end hole aligns with the select lever pin. If not aligned, loosen cable adjusting nut **B** and rotate the cable end until the holes are aligned.

8. Connect the cables.

Back-Up Light Switch

REMOVAL & INSTALLATION

The back-up light switch is threaded into the transaxle case.

1. Disconnect the negative battery cable.

2. Remove the wire clamp from the transaxle case that secures the switch wire.

3. Disengage the electrical wiring multi-connector.

4. Loosen and remove the switch from the transaxle case.

To install:

5. Remove the metal gasket from the switch and install a new one.

6. Thread the switch into the transaxle case and tighten just enough to crush the gasket.

7. Connect the wiring and install the wire clamp.

8. Connect the negative battery cable and check for proper switch operation.

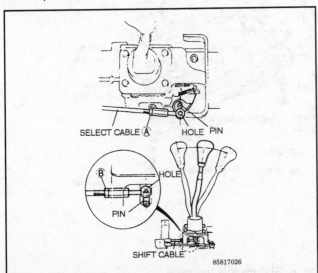

SELECT CABLE Ⓐ   HOLE PIN

B   HOLE

PIN

SHIFT CABLE

85817026

Fig. 8 Shift lever adjustment — 1988-89 323 with 4wd

Transaxle

REMOVAL & INSTALLATION

GLC

▶ See Figures 9, 10 and 11

1. Raise the vehicle and support it safely. Disconnect the negative battery cable.

2. Disengage all electrical wiring and connections. Mark these units to aid in reassembling. Drain the transaxle oil.

3. Remove the front wheels. Disconnect the lower ball joints from the steering knuckles. Pull the driveshafts from the differential gears.

➡ **A circlip is positioned on the driveshaft ends and engages in a groove, machined in the differential side gears. The driveshafts may have to be forced from the differential housing to release the clip from the groove. Do not apply a sharp impact. Do not allow the driveshaft's free end to drop, otherwise may occur to the ball and socket joints as well as to the rubber boots. Wire the shafts to the vehicle body when released from the differential.**

4. Support the engine with a jack or lift, and raise it slightly. Now, separate the shift control rod from the shift rod.

5. Remove the extension bar from the transaxle. Remove the crossmember.

6. Remove the rubber mount from the transaxle case. Remove the starter.

7. Support the transaxle securely with a jack. Then remove the transaxle mounting bolts, and remove it from the car.

To install:

8. Raise the transaxle into position with the jack, then install and tighten the mounting bolts.

9. Install the starter and connect the wiring. Install the rubber mount onto the transaxle case.

10. Bolt the crossmember to the frame and connect the extension bar to the transaxle.

11. Connect the shift rod to the control rod.

12. Insert the driveshafts into the differential gears. Connect the lower ball joints to the steering knuckles. Mount the front wheels.

13. Connect all electrical wiring and the negative battery cable.

14. Fill the transaxle to the proper level and adjust the clutch linkage.

1983-87 626

▶ See Figures 12, 13, 14, 15 and 16

1. Disconnect the negative battery cable.

2. Disconnect the speedometer cable at the transaxle.

3. Remove the clutch cable bracket mounting bolts. Disconnect the cable at the release lever, then remove the mounting bracket.

4. Remove the ground wire attaching bolt and the wiring harness clip from the transaxle. Remove the starter.

5. Support the engine via the hooks in a secure manner from above.

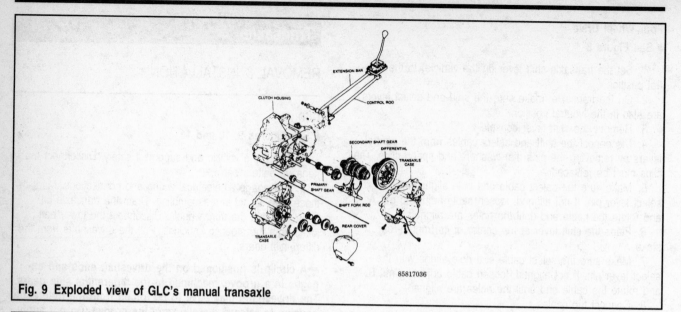

Fig. 9 Exploded view of GLC's manual transaxle

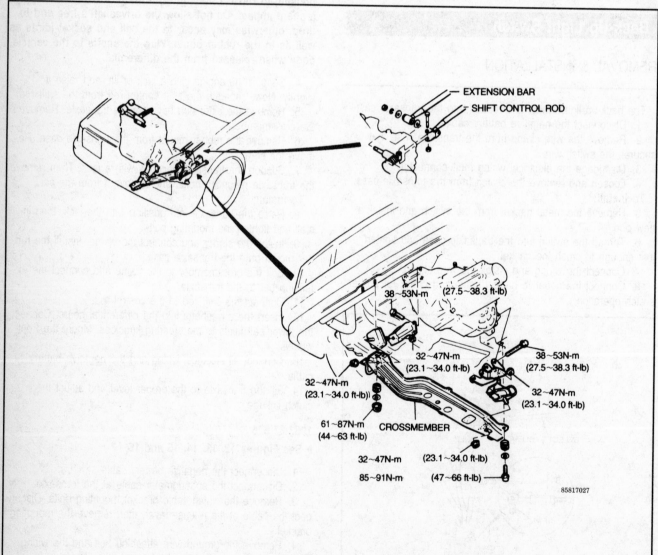

Fig. 10 Disconnecting shift linkage and removing the crossmember — GLC manual transaxle

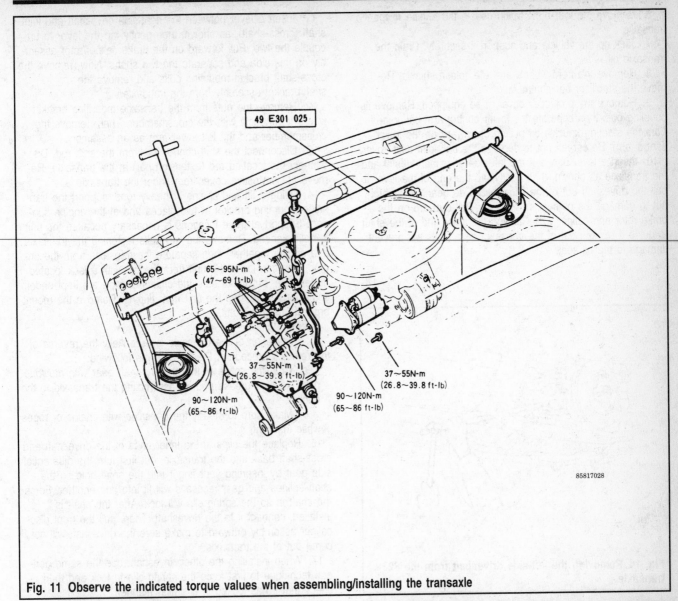

49 E301 025

65~95N·m
(47~69 ft-lb)

37~55N·m
(26.8~39.8 ft-lb)

90~120N·m
(65~86 ft-lb)

37~55N·m
(26.8~39.8 ft-lb)

90~120N·m
(65~86 ft-lb)

85817028

Fig. 11 Observe the indicated torque values when assembling/installing the transaxle

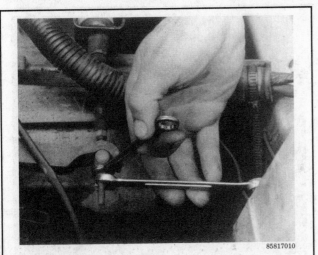

85817010

Fig. 12 Loosen the nuts which secure the clutch cable to the release lever . . .

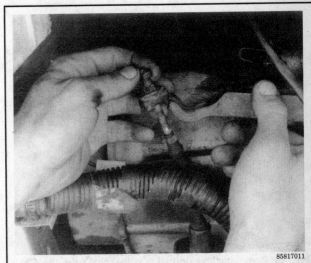

85817011

Fig. 13 . . . then disengage the cable from the lever

6. Remove the four bolts which couple the engine to the transaxle.

7. Jack up the vehicle and support it securely. Drain the transaxle oil.

8. Remove the front wheels and the splash shields. Remove the stabilizer bar control link.

9. Remove the protective cover, if so equipped. Remove its coupling bolt, then separate the lower control arm ball joint from the steering knuckle by pulling downward on the lower control arm. Be careful not to damage the ball joint dust cover.

10. Insert a lever between the left-side driveshaft U-joint and the transaxle as shown, then gently tap the end of the lever to pull the driveshaft out of the differential side gear. Be careful not to damage the oil seal in the case. Pull outward on the brake rotor and caliper while holding the inner end of the shaft to guide it straight out of the transaxle case. This will prevent damage to the oil seal.

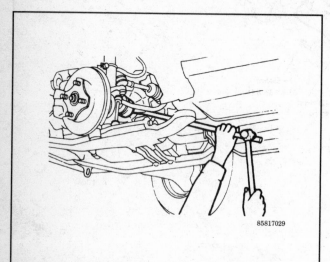

Fig. 14 Removing the left-side driveshaft from the 626 transaxle

Fig. 15 Removing the right-side driveshaft from the 626 transaxle

11. Insert a lever between the right-side driveshaft and joint shaft (cross-shaft), as shown, then gently tap the lever to uncouple the two. Pull forward on the brake caliper/rotor assembly on this side and separate the two shafts. Now, remove the cross-shaft bracket mounting bolts and remove the shaft/bracket assembly from the transaxle.

12. Remove the nuts from the transaxle mounting bracket where it connects with the crossmember. Then, remove the crossmember and the left lower arm as an assembly.

13. Disconnect the shift control rod from the shift rod. Disconnect the locating rod (extension bar) at the transaxle. Remove the protective cover from under the transaxle.

14. Using a lift and chains or heavy rope, support the transaxle mounting bracket at two places and at the engine support. Support at three locations is necessary because the unit is not balanced. Remove the two bolts fastening the transaxle and engine together, then separate the transaxle from the engine. You can lower the unit from the car with a jack located underneath, but make sure the chains or rope are kept under some tension to stop the unit from tipping. Remove the mount brackets from the unit.

To install:

15. Installation of the transaxle is essentially the reverse of the removal procedure. Please note the following:

a. Coat the spline of the primary shaft gear with molybdenum disulfide grease prior to assembling the transaxle to the engine.

b. Make sure to steady the transaxle with chains or ropes while installing it.

16. Replace the clips at the inner ends of the driveshaft and cross-shaft back into the transaxle, but first turn the differential side gear by inserting your finger into the shaft hole so the shaft splines and gear recesses will fit into one another. Force the shaft in so the spring clip will lock. After the shaft is installed, connect it to the driveshaft. Then, pull the front disc-caliper assembly outward to make sure the driveshaft will not come out of the transaxle.

17. When installing the other driveshaft, use the same general technique to first force the spring clip to lock and then check that it has locked in a similar manner.

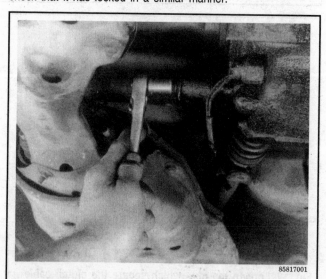

Fig. 16 Disconnect the locating rod at the transaxle

Observe the following torque figures:
- Transaxle mount-to-transaxle: 28-38 ft. lbs. (38-51 Nm)
- Transaxle-to-engine bolts: 66-85 ft. lbs. (89-115 Nm)
- Cross-shaft bracket mounting bolts: 32-45 ft. lbs. (43-61 Nm)
- Ball joint-to-steering knuckle: 32-40 ft. lbs. (43-54 Nm) — When torquing the nuts fastening the stabilizer bar to the control link, make sure that 1 in. (25mm) of bare thread is visible.
- Engine-to-transaxle bolts: 66-68 ft. lbs. (89-92 Nm)
- Engine mount installing nuts: 17-21 ft. lbs. (23-28 Nm)

1988-89 626 and MX-6

▶ See Figures 17 and 18

1. Remove the battery and battery carrier.
2. Disconnect the main fuse block, distributor lead and air flow meter connector. Remove the air cleaner assembly.
3. On turbocharged engines, disconnect the intercooler hoses. On non-turbocharged engines, remove the resonance chamber.
4. Disconnect the speedometer cable and the transaxle grounds.
5. Raise and support the vehicle safely, then remove the front wheels and splash shield. Drain the transaxle oil into a suitable waste container.
6. Remove the clutch release cylinder and disconnect the tie rod ends using the proper tool.
7. Remove the stabilizer control links. Remove the nuts and bolts from the lower control arm ball joints, then pull the lower control arms downward to separate them from the steering knuckles. Be careful not to damage the ball joint dust boots.
8. Insert a small pry bar between the left driveshaft and the transaxle case, then tap the end of the lever to uncouple the driveshaft from the differential side gear. Pull the front hub forward and separate the driveshaft from the transaxle. Remove the left joint shaft bracket. Separate the right driveshaft and joint shaft in the same manner as the left.

➡ Do not insert the lever too deeply between the shaft and the case or the oil seal lip could be damaged. To avoid damage to the oil seal, hold the CV-joint at the differential with one hand and pull the driveshaft straight out.

9. Once both drive and joint shafts are removed, install differential side gear holders 49-G030-455 (turbo), 49-G027-003 or their equivalents in the differential side gears to hold them in place and prevent misalignment.
10. Remove the gusset plates and under cover. Remove the extension bar and the control rod. Remove the surge tank bracket. Disconnect the wiring and remove the starter.
11. Suspend the engine from the engine hanger bracket with a suitable lifting device or engine support fixture.
12. Remove the No. 4 and No. 2 engine mounts and bracket. Disconnect the rubber hanger from the crossmember, then remove the crossmember and left-side lower control arm as an assembly.
13. Lean the engine towards the transaxle and support the transaxle with a jack. Remove the transaxle-to-engine mounting bolts and slide the transaxle from underneath the vehicle.

To install:

14. Attach a thick rope to two places on the transaxle. Place a board on the jack and lower the transaxle onto the board. Using the jack, lift the transaxle into position and throw the

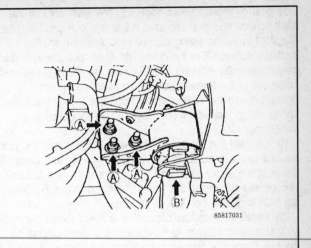

Fig. 17 No. 4 transaxle mount — 1988-89 626 and MX-6

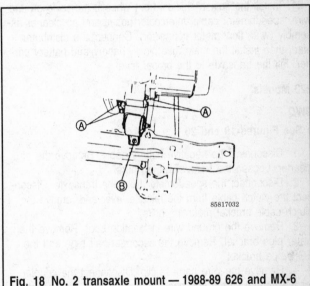

Fig. 18 No. 2 transaxle mount — 1988-89 626 and MX-6

end of the rope over the support fixture bar. Tension the rope to guide the transaxle onto its mounts while lifting the transaxle with the jack. Once the transaxle is in place, have an assistant install the transaxle-to-engine mounting bolts and torque them to 66-68 ft. lbs. (89-92 Nm). Install the No. 4 engine mount and torque nuts A to 47-66 ft. lbs. (64-89) and nuts B to 49-69 ft. lbs. (66-93 Nm). Install the No. 2 engine mount and torque nuts A on non-turbo engines to 27-38 ft. lbs. (37-51 Nm) and 49-69 ft. lbs. (66-93 Nm) on turbo engines. Torque nuts B to 55-69 ft. lbs. (75-93 Nm) on both engines.
15. Install the crossmember and left-side lower control arm assembly. Torque the bolts to 27-40 ft. lbs. (37-51 Nm) and the nuts to 55-69 ft. lbs. (75-93 Nm).
16. Remove the jack and rope. Remove the support fixture.
17. Install the starter and connect the wiring. Attach the surge tank bracket and gusset plate. Install the end plate, clutch release cylinder and remaining gusset plates. Torque the gusset plate bolts to 27-38 ft. lbs. (37-51 Nm).
18. Replace the clips at the inner ends of the driveshaft and cross-shaft back into the transaxle, but first turn the differential

side gear by inserting your finger into the shaft hole so the shaft splines and gear recesses will fit into one another. Force the shaft in so the spring clip will lock. After the shaft is installed, connect it to the driveshaft. Then, pull the front disc-caliper assembly outward to make sure the driveshaft will not come out of the transmission. When installing the other driveshaft, use the same general technique to first force the spring clip to lock and then check that it has locked in a similar manner.

19. Connect the lower arm ball joints to the steering knuckles and torque the nuts to 32-40 ft. lbs. (43-54 Nm). Clean the inside of the under cover and fill the notches with a suitable silicone sealant. Install the under cover and torque the retaining bolts to 67-95 inch lbs. (8-11 Nm).

20. Install the stabilizer bar control link and thread the nuts so that 0.79 in. (20mm) of the through-bolt protrudes above the bar. Once this dimension is obtained, hold the adjusting nuts and torque the locknuts to 12-17 ft. lbs. (16-23 Nm). Connect the tie rod ends using new cotter pins. Torque the tie rod end nuts to 22-33 ft. lbs. (30-45 Nm).

21. Install the splash shields, front wheels, transaxle ground wire, speedometer cable, intercooler hoses and air cleaner assembly (w/air flow meter connector). Connect the distributor lead, then install the main fuse block, battery and battery carrier. Fill the transaxle to the proper level.

323 Models

2WD

▶ **See Figures 19 and 20**

1. Disconnect the negative battery cable. Remove the air cleaner. Loosen the front wheel lug nuts.

2. Disconnect the speedometer from the transaxle. Disconnect the clutch cable from the release lever and remove the clutch cable bracket mounting bolts.

3. Remove the ground wire installation boot. Remove the water pipe bracket. Remove the secondary air pipe and the EGR pipe bracket.

4. Remove the wire harness clip. Disconnect the coupler for the neutral switch and back-up lamp switch. Disconnect the body ground connector.

5. Remove the two upper transaxle mounting bolts. Mount the engine support tool 49-ER301-025A or equivalent to the engine hanger.

6. Raise and support the vehicle safely. Drain the transaxle oil into a suitable container and remove the front wheels.

7. Remove the engine under cover and side covers. Remove the front stabilizer.

8. Remove the lower arm ball joints and the knuckle clinch bolts, then pull the lower arm downward and separate the lower arms from the knuckles.

9. Separate the driveshaft by pulling the front hub outward. Make sure not to use too much force at once, increase the force gradually. Be sure the driveshaft's ball joint is bent to its maximum extent. Do not allow the axle shafts to drop, otherwise damage may occur to the ball and socket joints as well as to the rubber boots. Wire the shafts to the vehicle body when released from the differential.

10. Remove the transaxle crossmember. Separate the change control rod from the transaxle. Remove the extension bar from the transaxle. Remove the wiring and the starter motor.

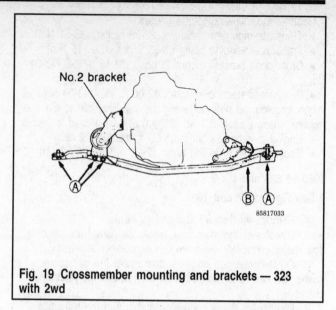

Fig. 19 Crossmember mounting and brackets — 323 with 2wd

11. Remove the end plates. Lean the engine toward the transaxle side to lower the transaxle by loosening the engine support hook bolt. Support the transaxle with a suitable transaxle jack.

12. Remove the necessary engine brackets. Remove the remaining transaxle mounting bolt and No. 2 engine bracket. Lower the jack and slide the transaxle out from under the vehicle.

To install:

13. Before installing the transaxle, coat the splines of the primary shaft gear with molybdenum disulfide grease.

14. Attach a thick rope to two places on the transaxle. Place a board on the jack and lower the transaxle onto the board. Using the jack, lift the transaxle into position and throw the end of the rope over the support fixture bar. Tension the rope to guide the transaxle onto its mounts while lifting the transaxle with the jack. Once the transaxle is in place, have an assistant install all the transaxle-to-engine mounting bolts. Torque the bolts to to 47-66 ft. lbs. (64-89 Nm).

15. Install the end plates and the starter motor. Install the extension bar and control rod. Torque the extension bar nuts to 23-34 ft. lbs. (31-46 Nm) and the change control rod nuts to 12-17 ft. lbs. (16-23 Nm).

16. Attach the No. 2 mounting bracket to the transaxle and torque the bracket bolts to 27-38 ft. lbs. (37-51 Nm). Install the crossmember and left-side lower control arm assembly. Torque bolts **A** to 47-66 ft. lbs. (64-89 Nm) and bolts **B** to 20-34 ft. lbs. (27-46 Nm).

17. Remove the jack and rope. Remove the support fixture.

18. Install the starter and connect the wiring. Attach the surge tank bracket and gusset plate. Install the end plate, clutch release cylinder and remaining gusset plates. Torque the gusset plate bolts to 27-38 ft. lbs. (37-51 Nm).

19. Replace the clips at the inner ends of the driveshaft and cross-shaft back into the transaxle, but first turn the differential side gear by inserting your finger into the shaft hole so the shaft splines and gear recesses will fit into one another. Force the shaft in so the spring clip will lock. After the shaft is installed, connect it to the driveshaft. Then, pull the front disc-caliper assembly outward to make sure the driveshaft will not come out of the transmission. When installing the other

driveshaft, use the same general technique to first force the spring clip to lock and then check that it has locked in a similar manner.

20. Connect the lower arm ball joints to the steering knuckles and torque the nuts to 32-40 ft. lbs. (43-54 Nm).

21. Install the stabilizer bar and adjust as follows: Tighten the locknuts and the adjusting nuts so that 0.43 in. (11mm) of the through-bolt threads protrude above the top of nut **B** in the illustration. This is dimension **C**. Once this dimension is obtained, tighten nut **B** to 23-33 ft. lbs. (31-45 Nm) and bolts **A** to 9-13 ft. lbs. (12-18 Nm). Connect the tie rod ends using new cotter pins.

22. Install the engine under and side covers. Install the front wheels and lower the vehicle. Connect the body ground wire, then engage the neutral and back-up switch coupler. Install the EGR pipe bracket, secondary air pipe and water pipe bracket. Attach the clutch cable mounting bracket and connect the clutch cable to the release lever.

23. Connect the speedometer cable, then install the air cleaner assembly. Connect the negative battery cable. Adjust clutch and shift linkage as required. Refill the transaxle with the proper grade of gear oil.

4WD

▶ **See Figures 20 and 21**

1. Remove the battery and the air cleaner assembly. Disconnect the speedometer cable in the center. Remove the clutch release cylinder retaining bolt and clip, then remove the clutch release cylinder. Raise and support the vehicle safely, then drain the transaxle *and* engine oil.

2. Disconnect the neutral safety switch, back-up lamp switch, differential lock sensor switch and differential lock motor electrical connectors. Disconnect the transaxle shift and select control cables from the transaxle by removing the pins and cable retaining clips. Route the cables off to the side and out of the way.

3. Mount the engine support fixture 49-8017-5A0 or equivalent to the engine strut mounting blocks. To mount the support fixture, first the nuts must be removed from the mounting blocks. Remove the No. 4 engine mount bracket and remove the front wheels.

4. Remove the side cover and under cover. Remove the driveshaft and crossmember. Remove the oil filter and differential lock assembly (the differential lock assembly is fastened with three bolts). Disconnect the starter wiring, then remove the starter and stabilizer bar.

5. Disconnect the tie rod end from the lower control arm. Insert a small pry bar between the driveshaft and the transaxle case, then tap the end of the lever to uncouple the driveshaft from the differential side gear. Remove the remaining driveshaft in the same manner. Insert differential side gear holder 49-B027-001 or equivalent to hold the side gears in place and prevent misalignment.

6. Remove the end plate bolts, then connect a suitable hoist and lifting strap to the transaxle. Lift the transaxle and transfer carrier assembly out of the engine.

To install:

7. Attach a thick rope to two places on the transaxle. Place a board on the jack and lower the transaxle onto the board. Using the jack, lift the transaxle into position and throw the end of the rope over the support fixture bar. Tension the rope to guide the transaxle onto its mounts while lifting the transaxle with the jack. Once the transaxle is in place, have an assistant install all the transaxle-to-engine and transfer mounting bolts. Torque the bolts to 66-86 ft. lbs. (89-117 Nm).

8. Install the end plates.

9. Replace the clips at the inner ends of the driveshaft and cross-shaft back into the transaxle, but first turn the differential side gear by inserting your finger into the shaft hole so the shaft splines and gear recesses will fit into one another. Force the shaft in so the spring clip will lock. After the shaft is installed, connect it to the driveshaft. Then, pull the front disc-caliper assembly outward to make sure the driveshaft will not come out of the transmission. When installing the other driveshaft, use the same general technique to first force the spring clip to lock and then check that it has locked in a similar manner. When installing the joint shaft, torque mounting bolts to 31-46 ft. lbs. (42-62 Nm).

10. Connect the tie rods to the lower arm and torque the pinch bolts to 32-40 ft. lbs. (43-54 Nm). Install and adjust the stabilizer bar as described in Step 21 of the 2wd 323's proce-

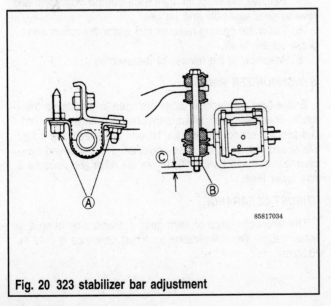

Fig. 20 323 stabilizer bar adjustment

85817034

Fig. 21 No. 4 mounting bracket — 323 with 4wd

85817035

dure. Dimension **C** for 4wd vehicles is 0.33 in. (8.5mm) and the torque specs are the same.

11. Install the starter, differential lock assembly, oil filter, driveshaft, side covers and under covers. Install the front wheels and lower the vehicle.

12. Install the No. 4 mounting bracket. Torque nuts **A** to 37-45 ft. lbs. (50-61 Nm) and nuts **B** to 14-19 ft. lbs. (19-26 Nm).

13. Remove the support fixture and replace the strut mounting block nuts. Torque the nuts to 17-22 ft. lbs. (23-30 Nm). Connect the shift and select control cables using new retaining clips. Connect all the electrical and sensor wiring.

14. Fill the transaxle to the proper level through the speedometer drive gear opening. Fill the crankcase. Adjust the shift and select control cables as previously described.

OVERHAUL

Disassembly and Assembly of Major Components

➡**The following procedures cover both the 4-speed and 5-speed transaxles on all applicable models. The 5-speed unit has a rear cover which easily distinguishes it from the other unit.**

5th GEAR

1. Remove the rear cover. Remove the roll pin that secures the 5th gear shift fork to the selector shaft. Shift the transaxle unit into either 1st or 2nd gear.

➡**Do not shift into 4th gear or you may cause damage to the gears.**

2. Move the 5th gear clutch sleeve, to engage 5th gear and double lock the transaxle.

3. Straighten the tab of the locknut on both the primary and secondary shafts. Remove the locknuts from the shafts.

4. Pull the 5th gear clutch hub assembly out along with the 5th fork.

➡**Remove the fork to gain access to the primary shaft locknut.**

5. Reinstall the 5th gear clutch hub and move the sleeve to the 5th gear position in order to lock the transaxle.

6. Remove the primary shaft locknut and remove the 5th gear from the transaxle case.

To assemble:

7. Install the 5th gear on the primary shaft. Be sure that the marked boss is facing toward the locknut. Install the bushing and the 5th gear on the secondary shaft.

8. Install the synchronizer ring, the clutch hub and the selector fork. Do not install the shift fork pin.

➡**The stop washer or plate for the clutch hub must be installed between the locknut and clutch hub to prevent overtravel of the clutch when shifting into reverse gear and to prevent the synchronizer keys from falling out.**

9. Install the locknuts on both shafts and tighten them slightly.

10. Shift into 1st or 2nd gear only, using the control rod. Shift into 5th gear to double lock the transaxle.

11. Tighten the primary shaft locknut and lock the hub.

➡**Do not tighten the secondary shaft locknut until the selector fork is installed. Remove the locknut and clutch hub from the secondary gear shaft, then reassemble it with the selector fork. Do not insert the drive pin at this time.**

12. Move the 5th gear selector clutch to engage the 5th gear in order to lock the transaxle.

13. Shift the unit into either 1st or 2nd gear.

14. Install the roll pin securing the 5th gear shift fork to the selector shaft. Install the cover.

PRIMARY SHAFT

The Mazda manual transaxle uses two types of primary shafts, one for the 4-speed transaxle and another for the 5-speed transaxle. Both shafts are made as a cluster with reverse, 1st, 2nd, 3rd and 4th gears integral. The 5th gear (when equipped) is splined into the end of the shaft.

SECONDARY SHAFT

The secondary shaft assembly consists of the secondary shaft, gears, clutch hub and sleeve assemblies, synchronizer rings and bearings. The secondary shaft is manufactured integrally with the final drive gear.

There are three different types of secondary shafts used in the 4-speed transaxle and 2 different types used in the 5-speed transaxle. All of these shafts vary by the number of gear teeth on the final drive gears.

➡**The combination of the final drive gear on the secondary shaft and ring gear are identified by the groove provided in the construction of each individual gear.**

SECONDARY GEARS

1. Install a suitable bearing puller in the grooves between the gear and the gear spline of 4th gear. Remove the bearing and the 4th gear from the assembly.

2. Remove the snapring on the 3rd and 4th clutch hub. Slide out the clutch hub and the sleeve assembly.

3. Remove the 3rd gear, the thrust washer and the 2nd gear.

4. Remove the snapring, then slide out the clutch hub and reverse gear assembly and 1st gear.

5. Install the bearing remover tool under the rollers and press out the shaft.

6. Assembly is the reverse of disassembly.

SYNCHRONIZER RINGS

Bridge-type synchronizer rings are used in the Mazda transaxle. There are three different synchronizer rings; 1 for 2nd, 3rd and 4th speed, another for 1st and 3rd speed and 1 for 5th speed, if the vehicle is so equipped. The 1st speed synchronizer ring can be identified from the other two because it has fewer teeth.

THRUST CLEARANCE

The thrust clearance of each gear is checked by using a feeler gauge. The specification for thrust clearance is 0.02 in. (0.5mm).

REVERSE IDLER SHAFT AND SHIFT ROD

▶ See Figure 22

The reverse idler shaft has an integral mounting post which is secured to the case with a bolt. When installing the idler shaft, align the holes of the shaft with the notch in the transaxle case. When installing reverse shift rod to the shift gate, be sure that the screw holes are aligned and that the hole of the shift rod is not 180 degrees out of phase.

BEARING PRELOAD ADJUSTMENT

▶ See Figures 23, 24 and 25

➡When the clutch housing, transaxle case, primary shaft, secondary shaft, bearings or differential case are replaced, the bearing preload should be checked and adjusted as necessary.

1. Remove the oil seal and the differential bearing outer race. Adjust the shim from the transaxle case.

2. Remove the bearing outer races from the primary and secondary shafts. Adjust the shims from the transaxle case and the clutch housing.

3. Reinstall the outer races to the transaxle case.

4. Install the outer races (removed in Step 2) to their respective selectors. Install the selectors, primary shaft assembly and secondary shaft assembly to the clutch housing.

5. Install the transaxle case, then place the ten collars between the transaxle case and the clutch housing.

6. To properly settle each bearing, using the tool, turn the selector in a direction where the gap is widened until it cannot be turned by hand. Then turn the selector in the opposite direction until the gap is eliminated. Manually turn the selector to a direction where the gap becomes wider until the selector cannot be turned.

➡Make sure that the shaft turns smoothly.

7. Measure the gap of the selector with a feeler gauge.

➡This measurement should be taken at 90 degree intervals along the circumference of the selector.

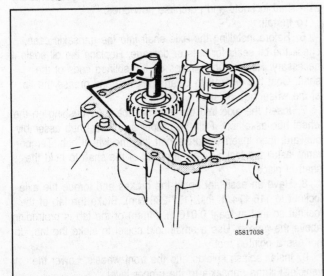

Fig. 22 Reverse idler shaft alignment

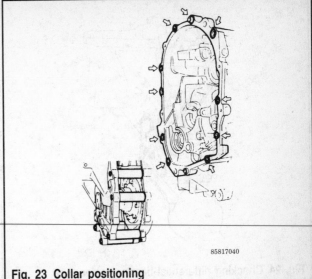

Fig. 23 Collar positioning

8. Take the maximum reading and determine the shim to be used as follows.

9. For the primary shaft bearing, first subtract 0.04 in./1mm (thickness of the diaphragm spring) from the gap (determined in Step 7).

Example: Gap measurement of 0.054 in. (1.39mm) minus 0.039 in. (1mm) equals 0.015 in. (0.39mm); select the next larger and closer shim, which would be 0.016 in. (0.40mm).

➡Do not use more than 2 shims.

10. For the secondary shaft bearing, select a shim which has a thickness that is larger and closer to the gap (determined in Step 7).

Example: For a gap measurement 0.017 in. (0.42mm), select the next larger and closer shim, which would be 0.018 in. (0.45mm).

➡Do not use more than 2 shims to accomplish this task.

11. For the differential bearing, set the preload adapters (tool 49-00180-510A and 49-FT01-515 or equivalents) to the pinion shaft through the hole for the driveshaft of the transaxle case. Hook a spring scale to the adapter and check the bearing preload.

➡While checking the preload, turn the selector until the reading of the spring scale becomes 1.1-1.5 lbs. (0.50-0.68 kg).

12. Measure the gap of the selector on the differential using a feeler gauge.

➡This measurement should be taken at 90 degree intervals along the circumference of the selector.

13. Select a shim that has a thickness larger and closer to the maximum reading that was taken in the previous step.

Example: For a gap measurement of 0.021 in. (0.54mm), select the next larger and closer shim, which would be 0.024 in. (0.60mm).

➡Do not use more than 3 shims to accomplish this task.

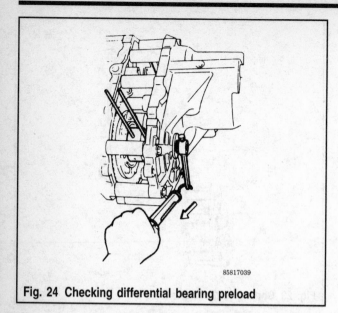

85817039

Fig. 24 Checking differential bearing preload

14. Remove the shim selectors and each bearing outer race. Install the shims selected in previous steps between the transaxle case and bearing outer race.

➡️**A diaphragm spring is used to keep the bearing preload as specified and also to maintain low level gear noise. When installing the diaphragm spring, be sure it is in the proper direction.**

15. When installing the oil funnel on the clutch housing, be sure that it is in the proper position.

16. After transaxle assembly, recheck the preloads of the differential bearing and the primary shaft bearing.

17. The differential bearing preload should be 0.3-6.6 inch lbs. 0.034-0.739 Nm) and the reading on the spring scale should be 0.07-1.7 lbs (0.03-0.77 kg).

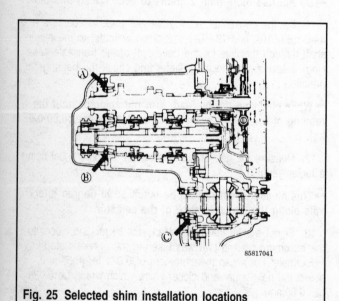

85817041

Fig. 25 Selected shim installation locations

18. The primary shaft preload should be 1.7-3.5 inch lbs. (0.2-0.4 Nm) and the reading on the spring scale should be 0.4-0.9 lbs. (0.18-0.41 kg).

DIFFERENTIAL

The final gear is helical cut with the same tooth design as that used in the transmission. No adjustments are required.

There are three different ring gears in numbers of gear teeth on the manual transaxle. They are indicated by the marks (grooves) provided on the gear outer surface.

The backlash between the differential side gear and pinion gear is adjusted by the thrust washer installed behind the side gear teeth. There are 3 different thicknesses of thrust washers available.

When checking the backlash, insert both driveshafts into the side gears.

Halfshafts

REMOVAL & INSTALLATION

GLC

1. Raise and support the vehicle safely. Remove both front wheels and splash shields. Drain the transaxle fluid.

2. Loosen the drive axle locknut at the center of the disc brake hub after raising the lock tab. Apply brake pressure while loosening.

3. Remove the lower ball joint from the steering knuckle by pulling down on the bar and disconnecting the ball joint.

4. Remove the axle shaft from the transaxle case by pulling the brake caliper outward with increasing force. While applying outward force, hit the driveaxle shaft with a brass hammer, if necessary, to help in removal. Beware, if the shaft is withdrawn too fast you may risk damaging the oil seal.

5. Remove the locknut and pull the axle shaft from the steering knuckle. Remove the axle shaft and plug the transaxle case with a clean rag to prevent dirt from entering. Discard the axle shaft locknuts and purchase new ones.

   To install:

6. Before installing the axle shaft into the transaxle case, check the oil seals for cuts or damage. Replace the oil seals if necessary. Replace the circlips on the splined ends of the shaft. Coat the oil lip with clean ATF fluid and grease the lip of the wheel hub oil seal.

7. Insert the axle into the transaxle case by pushing on the wheel hub assembly. Pull the caliper and wheel hub assembly outward, then insert the driveshaft into the wheel hub. Temporarily install the locknut onto the end of the shaft to hold the shaft in place.

8. Have an assistant apply the brakes and torque the axle locknut to 116-174 ft. lbs. (157-236 Nm). Stake the tab of the locknut so that at least 0.016 in. (4mm) of the tab is protruding above the groove. Use a small cold chisel to stake the tab, do not use a pointed tool.

9. Install splash shields and the front wheels. Lower the vehicle. Fill the transaxle to the proper level.

323, 626 and MX-6

▶ See Figures 26, 27 and 28

➡On 1988-89 626s and MX-6s, removal and installation of halfshafts is the same for manual and automatic transaxles. On 323s with 4wd, refer to the REAR AXLE portion of this section for rear halfshaft removal and installation.

1. Raise the vehicle and support it on axle stands. Drain the lubricant from the transaxle.

2. Remove the front wheels and splash pan. Raise the tab on the wheel hub locknut, and then have someone apply the brakes as you loosen the nut.

3. Remove the tow nuts, bushings, and washers, then disconnect the stabilizer bar from the steering knuckle.

4. Remove the clinch bolts and nuts, then pry the lower control arm downward in order to separate the steering knuckle and lower ball joint. Be careful not to damage the ball joint dust cover.

On the left side:

5. Insert a lever (for automatic transaxles, you'll have to use a chisel) between the driveshaft and transaxle case (don't go in too for, or you will damage the seal). Tap the end of the pry bar or chisel lightly to pull the shaft out of the case just until it unlocks.

6. Remove the driveshaft locknut from the center of the brake rotor. Pull the front hub outward and toward the rear. Disconnect the driveshaft from the wheel hub. If necessary, use a puller. Then, pull the driveshaft straight out of the transaxle, supporting the joint on the transaxle side to prevent damage to the seal. Seal the transaxle opening with a clean rag.

On the right side:

7. Insert a lever between the joint shaft and driveshaft, then gently tap on the outer end of the lever to separate the two shafts.

8. Remove the driveshaft locknut, then pull the front hub outward and toward the rear. Disconnect the driveshaft from the front hub. If necessary, use a puller. Then, disconnect the driveshaft from the cross-shaft completely.

9. If it is necessary to remove the cross-shaft, remove the cross-shaft mounting bracket bolts, then remove the shaft and

Fig. 26 Insert a lever between the left-side driveshaft and transaxle case

Fig. 27 Pull the front hub outward and separate the driveshaft from the transaxle

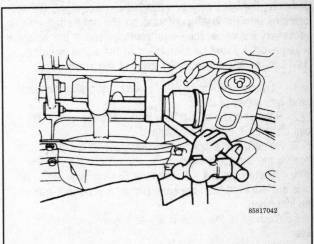

Fig. 28 Levering the joint shaft and right-side driveshaft apart on the 626

bracket as an assembly, being careful not to disturb the position of differential gears. Cover the opening in the differential case with a clean rag.

10. Installation is the reverse of removal, but note these points:

a. Check the transaxle oil seal for damage and replace it if necessary.

b. Replace the clips at the inner ends of the driveshaft or cross-shaft where they are locked into the differential gears in the transaxle.

c. Install the shafts into the transaxle carefully to avoid damage to the oil seal. Push the joint in on the differential side. Check the differential gears for alignment before attempting to install the shafts. If they are not aligned, turn them with your finger, as necessary.

d. After installation, pull the hub forward to make sure the driveshaft remains locked in the transaxle.

e. Install a new locknut onto the outer end of the driveshaft, adjusting wheel bearings as described in section

8. Crimp the tabs over after they are aligned with the groove in the driveshaft.

f. Tighten the stabilizer bar link nut until 1 in. (25mm) of thread is exposed.

g. Torque the lower control arm-to-ball joint nut and bolt to 32-40 ft. lbs. (43-54 Nm).

h. Torque the control link for the lower arm and stabilizer bar to 9-13 ft. lbs. (12-18 Nm); except for the 1988-89 626s and MX-6s on which it should be 12-17 ft. lbs. (16-23 Nm).

i. Refill the differential with fresh fluid meeting proper specifications.

CV-JOINT OVERHAUL

◗ See Figures 29, 30, 31, 32, 33, 34, 35, 36, 37, 38 and 39

GLC

➡The joint on the wheel side of the drive axle is non-rebuildable. If worn, the joint and axle must be replaced. However, the boot may be changed as necessary. Do not interfere with the balancer found on the right shaft unless necessary for wheel joint boot replacement. If the balancer is removed, it must be reinstalled in the same position (14.45 in. or 367mm from the front of the wheel joint).

1. Remove the boot band by raising the locking clip and band with a pair of pliers.

2. Remove the lock clip from the inner edge of the ball joint casting. Remove the casting.

3. Remove the snapring from the end of the splines, then remove the cage and bearings.

4. Carefully pry the balls from the bearing cage. After the balls are removed, turn the cage slightly and remove it from the inner ring.

5. Wash all of the parts in a safe solvent and inspect for wear.

➡CV-joint overhaul parts are available in kits for serviceable (inner) joints. Replacement boots should be available for all outer ends.

6. Install the replacement parts in the reverse order of disassembly. Always use the grease supplied with the kits. Tape the spline ends of the shaft when installing the rubber boots.

323, 626 and MX-6
◗ See Figure 40

1. Disassemble the driveshaft (halfshaft) as shown in the exploded view. The clip (2) should be removed with a small prytool, while the snapring (4) should be removed with snapring pliers or a similar tool.

2. Pull the ball bearings, inner ring and cage out of the shaft while still assembled. Insert an small prytool between the inner ring and cage to gently pry each ball out. Matchmark the cage and inner ring, then turn the cage 30 degrees and pull it off the inner ring.

3. Assemble in the reverse order, being careful to thoroughly repack bearings in the grease supplied with the kit.

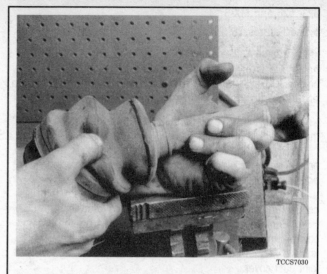
TCCS7030

Fig. 29 Check the CV-boot for wear or damage

TCCS7031

Fig. 30 Release (or cut) the outer band from the CV-boot

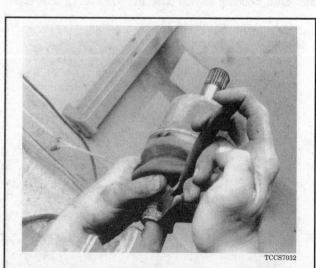
TCCS7032

Fig. 31 Use cutters to carefully release the inner band from the CV-boot

TCCS7033

Fig. 32 Remove the CV-boot from the joint housing

TCCS7037

Fig. 35 Thoroughly clean and inspect the CV-joint housing

TCCS7035

Fig. 33 Remove the CV-joint housing assembly to access the joint components

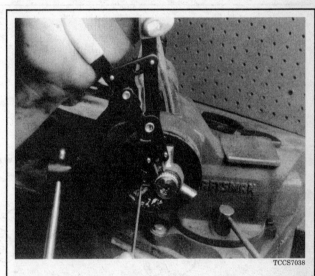

TCCS7038

Fig. 36 Remove the CV-joint outer snapring

TCCS7036

Fig. 34 Carefully remove the CV-joint components

TCCS7041

Fig. 37 Remove the CV-joint assembly

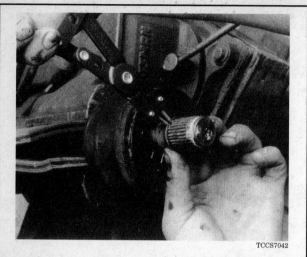

TCCS7042

Fig. 38 Use a pair of snapring pliers to remove the CV-joint inner snapring

TCCS7043

Fig. 39 Installing the CV-joint assembly

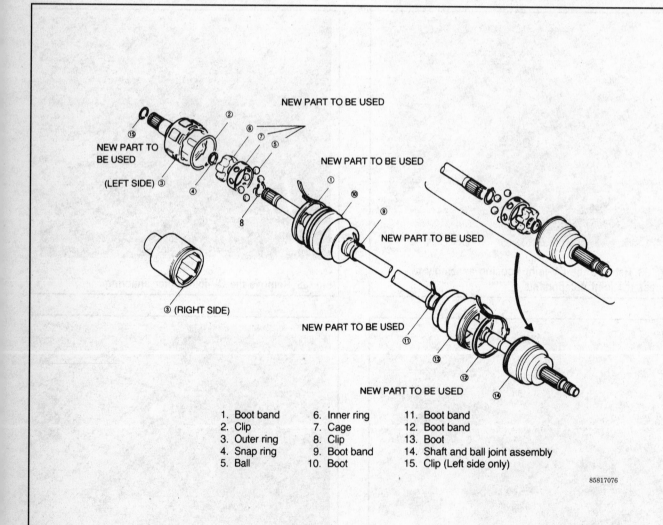

1. Boot band	6. Inner ring	11. Boot band
2. Clip	7. Cage	12. Boot band
3. Outer ring	8. Clip	13. Boot
4. Snap ring	9. Boot band	14. Shaft and ball joint assembly
5. Ball	10. Boot	15. Clip (Left side only)

85817076

Fig. 40 Exploded view of 626 driveshaft and CV-joint; 323 and MX-6 similar

CLUTCH

Adjustments

PEDAL HEIGHT

▶ **See Figures 41 and 42**

1. Remove the floor mat.
2. Loosen the locknut on the adjusting bolt, stopper bolt or clutch switch.
3. Turn the adjusting bolt until the clearance between the upper surface of the pedal pad and the firewall is within specification:
   - 1982-83 GLC: 7.28-7.68 in. (185-195mm)
   - 1984-85 GLC: 9.06-9.25 in. (230-235mm)
   - 1979-85 RX-7: 7.28-7.68 in. (185-195mm)
   - 1986-89 RX-7: 8.46-8.86 in. (215-225mm)
   - 1982-88 626: 8.46-8.66 in. (215-220mm)
   - 1988-89 626 and MX-6: 8.50-8.70 in. (216-221mm)
   - 1986-89 323 (cable type): 8.43-8.62 in. (214-219mm)
   - 1988-89 323 (hydraulic type): 9.02-9.21 in. (229-234mm)
   - 1988-89 929: 8.46-8.66 in. (215-220mm)
4. After adjustment, tighten the locknut.

FREE-PLAY

1979-82 626

The free-play of the clutch pedal before the pushrod contacts the piston in the master cylinder should be 0.02-0.12 in. (0.50-3.00mm).

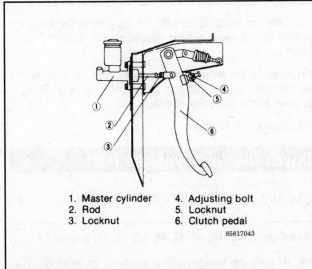

1. Master cylinder
2. Rod
3. Locknut
4. Adjusting bolt
5. Locknut
6. Clutch pedal

85817043

Fig. 41 Clutch pedal height adjustment — hydraulic type

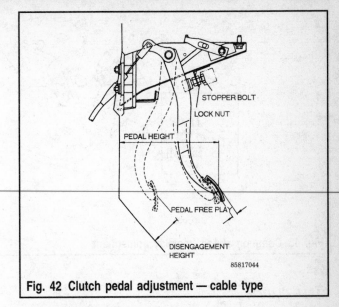

STOPPER BOLT
LOCK NUT
PEDAL HEIGHT
PEDAL FREE PLAY
DISENGAGEMENT HEIGHT
85817044

Fig. 42 Clutch pedal adjustment — cable type

To adjust free-play, loosen the locknut and turn the pushrod until the proper adjustment is obtained. Tighten the locknut after the adjustment is complete.

GLC, MX-6, 929, RX-7 and 1983-89 626

CABLE CLUTCH

▶ **See Figure 43**

1. First, depress the clutch pedal and measure the distance between the pedal's normal height and the point at which the clutch begins to disengage (effort increases) in order to determine the free-play. The play should be:
   - GLC: 0.43-0.67 in. (11-17mm)
   - 626: 0.43-0.67 in. (11-17mm) for non-turbocharged models
   - 626: 0.20-0.51 in. (5-13mm) for turbocharged models
2. If play is incorrect, loosen the locknut on the clutch cable. Pull the release fork backward so as to create a clearance between the adjusting nut roller and fork. The clearance should be about 0.06-0.09 in. (1.5-2.3mm) for rear wheel drive vehicles or 0.08-0.12 in. (2-3mm) for front wheel drive vehicles. Adjust the nut if necessary, then recheck the adjustment at the pedal. When the adjustment is correct, tighten the locknut.
3. If the adjustment is correct, the distance from the bottom of the pedal to the floor when the clutch is fully disengaged should be at least 3.19 in. (81mm).

HYDRAULIC CLUTCH

Loosen the locknut on the clutch master cylinder pushrod. Turn the pushrod to obtain free-play between the pedal and pushrod as specified below. Tighten the locknut on the pushrod when the adjustment is complete.
   - GLC: 0.08-0.12 in. (2-3mm)
   - 626/MX-6: 0.02-0.12 in. (0.6-3mm)
   - 929: 0.02-0.12 in. (0.5-3mm)
   - RX-7: 0.08-0.12 in. (2-3mm)

Fig. 43 Common clutch free-play adjustment

323

CABLE CLUTCH

Depress the pedal lightly and measure the free-play. Free-play should be 0.35-0.59 in. (9-15mm). If not within specification, adjust the free-play as follows:

1. On 1988-89 vehicles, depress the clutch pedal 7 times and straighten the clutch cable in the cable bracket.

2. Depress the release lever and pull the pin away from the lever. Then, adjust the clearance between the pin and the adjusting lever by turning the adjusting nut. On 1986-87 vehicles, the clearance should be between 0.06-0.10 in. (1.5-2.5mm). On 1988-89 vehicles, the clearance should be 0.08-0.12 in. (2-3mm).

3. After adjustment, ensure that when the clutch is disengaged, the distance between the floor and the upper center of the pedal is 3.3 in. (84mm).

4. Recheck the pedal height and adjust if necessary.

HYDRAULIC CLUTCH

Loosen the locknut on the clutch master cylinder pushrod. Turn the pushrod to obtain 0.2-0.5 in. (5-13mm) free-play between the pedal and the pushrod. Tighten the locknut on the pushrod when the adjustment is complete.

CLUTCH RELEASE CABLE

Rear Wheel Drive GLC

▶ See Figure 44

Loosen the locknut and put tension on the outer cable (pull, do not push) while turning the adjusting nut until the clearance shown in the illustration is 0.06-0.09 in. (1.5-2.3mm). Then, tighten the locknut.

Front Wheel Drive GLC

1. Loosen the locknut on the end of the clutch cable, near the release lever. (The release lever is mounted on top of the transaxle case.)

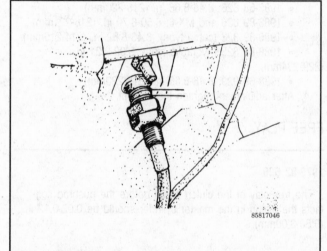

Fig. 44 Clutch release cable adjustment — GLC with rear wheel drive

2. Turn the adjusting nut until the gap (clearance) between the roller on the cable and the release lever is 0.08-0.12 in. (2-3mm).

➡In order to get an accurate measurement, be sure to pull the roller toward the end of the cable while pushing the lever in the opposite direction.

3. Tighten the locknut.

Driven Disc and Pressure Plate

REMOVAL & INSTALLATION

▶ See Figures 45, 46, 47, 48, 49, 50, 51, 52, 53 and 54

1. Remove the transmission or transaxle, as detailed earlier in this section.

2. Attach a braking device to the flywheel (to keep it from turning during clutch cover removal and installation).

3. Temporarily install a clutch arbor to prevent the clutch cover from falling.

➡**An old input shaft makes an excellent arbor.**

4. Unfasten the bolts which secure the clutch cover/pressure plate, one turn at a time in sequence, until the clutch spring tension is released. Do not remove the bolts on at a time.

5. Remove the clutch disc and arbor.

➡**Be careful not to get grease or oil on the surface of the clutch disc.**

6. Unhook the return spring from the throwout (release) bearing and remove the bearing.

7. Pull out the release fork until its retaining spring frees itself from the ball stud. Withdraw the fork from the housing.

To install:

8. Clean the flywheel and pressure plate surfaces with fine emery paper. Be sure that there is no oil or grease on them.

Fig. 47 Unfasten and remove its retaining bolts. . .

Fig. 45 Unfasten and remove the transaxle's clutch housing from the engine

Fig. 48 . . . then remove the clutch cover

Fig. 46 A clutch arbor will keep the clutch and pressure plate assembly aligned during removal or installation

Fig. 49 The clutch disc is positioned against the flywheel

Fig. 50 Remove the clutch disc from the flywheel

Fig. 51 The throwout bearing and release fork surround the input shaft in the clutch housing

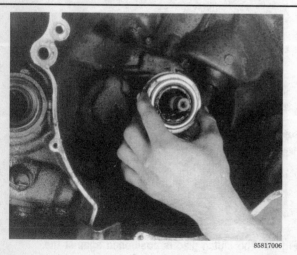

Fig. 52 Remove the throwout bearing from the release fork

9. Use an arbor to center the clutch disc during installation. Install the clutch disc with the long end of its hub facing the transmission/transaxle.

➡**Use an old input shaft to center the clutch disc, if an arbor is not available.**

10. Align the O-mark on the clutch cover with the reamed hole of the O-mark on the flywheel.

11. Tighten the clutch cover bolts, using 2-3 passes of a crisscross pattern, to 13-20 ft. lbs. (18-27 Nm). Remove the arbor/input shaft and flywheel braking device.

12. Grease the pivot pin. Insert the release fork through its boot so that its retaining spring contacts the pivot pin.

13. Lightly grease the face of the throwout bearing and its clutch housing retainer.

14. Install the throwout bearing and return spring. Check the operation of the release fork and throwout bearing for smoothness.

15. Install the transmission or transaxle.

Clutch Master Cylinder

REMOVAL & INSTALLATION

▶ **See Figures 55, 56 and 57**

1. On 1988-89 626 and MX-6 equipped with ABS, remove the ABS relay box located forward of the brake power booster on the driver's side. Unfasten the hydraulic line from the master cylinder outlet. On 1988-89 turbocharged 626/MX-6s and on all 929s, disconnect the line from the banjo fitting, leave the union fitting connected to the master cylinder.

2. Remove the nuts which secure the master cylinder assembly to the firewall. On some vehicles one or both of these nuts are accessible from the inside of the cabin.

3. Withdraw the master cylinder and gasket straight out; away from the firewall. Inspect the gasket. If it is still in good condition use it again, otherwise a new gasket must be used during installation.

To install:

4. Place the gasket and the master cylinder onto the firewall and attach with the nuts. Connect the line to the outlet connection. On 1988-89 626/MX-6s with ABS, install the ABS relay box.

5. Bleed the hydraulic system as detailed below.

OVERHAUL

▶ **See Figure 58**

1. Thoroughly clean the outside of the master cylinder.

2. Drain the hydraulic fluid from the cylinder. Unbolt the reservoir from the cylinder body. If equipped with banjo fittings, loosen the union bolt, then remove the fitting and gaskets from the body of the master cylinder. Discard the old gaskets.

3. Remove the boot from the cylinder.

4. Release the wire piston stop with a screwdriver and withdraw the stop washer.

5. Withdraw the piston, piston cups, and return spring from the cylinder bore.

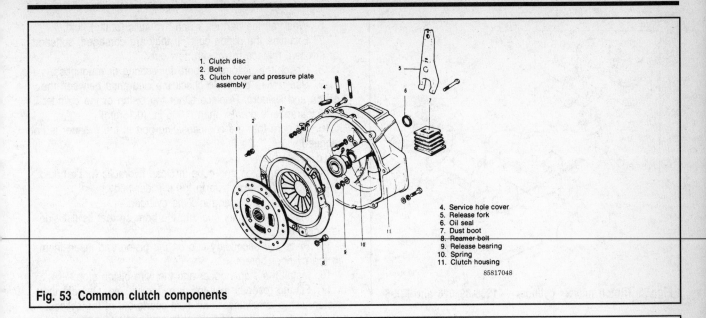

1. Clutch disc
2. Bolt
3. Clutch cover and pressure plate assembly

4. Service hole cover
5. Release fork
6. Oil seal
7. Dust boot
8. Reamer bolt
9. Release bearing
10. Spring
11. Clutch housing

85817048

Fig. 53 Common clutch components

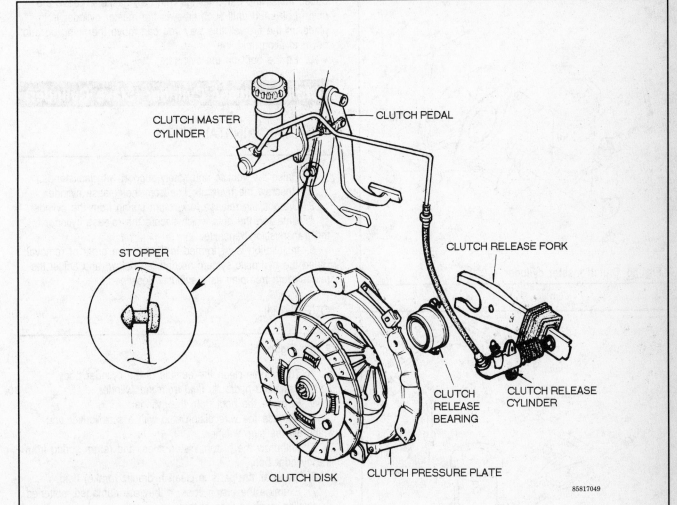

CLUTCH MASTER CYLINDER

CLUTCH PEDAL

STOPPER

CLUTCH RELEASE FORK

CLUTCH RELEASE BEARING

CLUTCH RELEASE CYLINDER

CLUTCH DISK

CLUTCH PRESSURE PLATE

85817049

Fig. 54 RX-7 clutch components; other hydraulic systems are similar

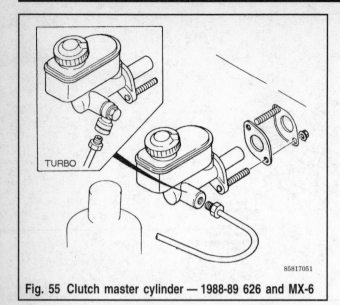

Fig. 55 Clutch master cylinder — 1988-89 626 and MX-6

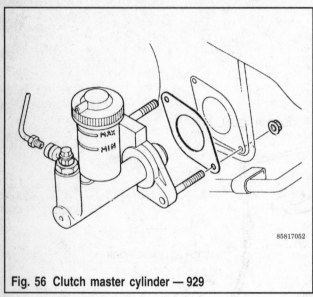

Fig. 56 Clutch master cylinder — 929

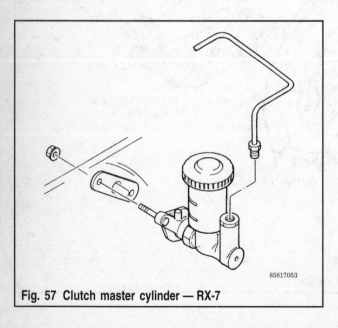

Fig. 57 Clutch master cylinder — RX-7

6. Wash all the parts in clean hydraulic (brake) fluid.

7. Examine the piston cups. If they are damaged, softened, or swollen, replace them with new ones.

8. Check the piston and bore for scoring or roughness.

9. Use a wire gauge to check the clearance between the piston and its bore. Replace either the piston or the cylinder if the clearance is greater than 0.006 in. (0.15mm).

10. Be sure that the compensating port in the cylinder is not clogged.

To assemble:

11. Dip the piston and cups in clean hydraulic (brake) fluid.

12. Bolt the reservoir up to the cylinder body.

13. Fit the return spring into the cylinder.

14. Insert the primary cup into the bore so that its flat side is facing the piston.

15. Place the secondary cup on the piston and insert them in the cylinder bore.

16. Install the stop washer and the wire piston stop.

17. Fill the reservoir half-full of hydraulic fluid. Operate the piston with a screwdriver until fluid spurts out of the cylinder outlet. Install the banjo fittings with new gaskets. Leave the union bolt snug until such time as the master cylinder is in place on the firewall this way you can move the fitting up and down to align fluid line.

18. Fit the boot on the cylinder.

Clutch Release Cylinder (Slave Cylinder)

REMOVAL & INSTALLATION

1. Raise the vehicle and safely support with jackstands.

2. Unscrew the hydraulic line from the release cylinder.

3. Unhook the release fork return spring from the cylinder.

4. Unfasten the nuts which secure the release cylinder to the transmission/transaxle.

5. Installation is performed in the reverse order of removal. Bleed the hydraulic system as detailed below, and adjust the release fork free-play as previously described.

OVERHAUL

▶ **See Figure 59**

1. Thoroughly clean the outside of the cylinder body.

2. Drain the hydraulic fluid from the cylinder.

3. Remove the boot from the cylinder.

4. Release the wire piston stop with a screwdriver and withdraw the stop washer.

5. Withdraw the piston, piston cups, and return spring from the cylinder bore.

6. Wash all the parts in clean hydraulic (brake) fluid.

7. Examine the piston cups. If they are damaged, softened, or swollen, replace them with new ones.

8. Check the piston and bore for scoring or roughness.

9. Use a wire gauge to check the clearance between the piston and its bore. Replace either the piston or the cylinder if the clearance is greater than 0.006 in. (0.15mm).

To assemble:

10. Dip the piston and cups in clean hydraulic (brake) fluid.

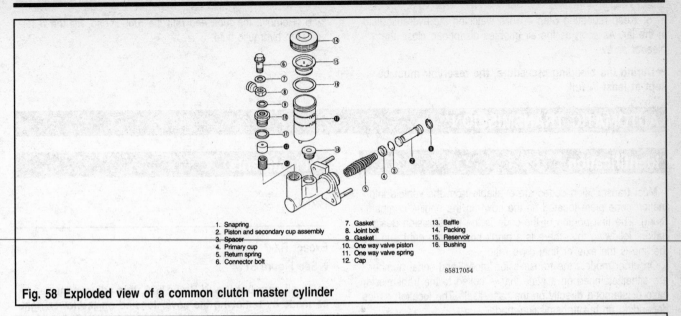

Fig. 58 Exploded view of a common clutch master cylinder

1. Snapring
2. Piston and secondary cup assembly
3. Spacer
4. Primary cup
5. Return spring
6. Connector bolt
7. Gasket
8. Joint bolt
9. Gasket
10. One way valve piston
11. One way valve spring
12. Cap
13. Baffle
14. Packing
15. Reservoir
16. Bushing

85817054

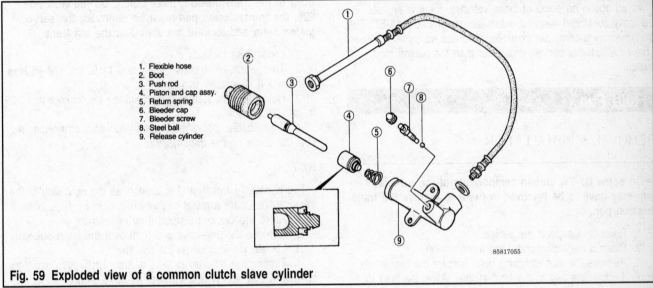

1. Flexible hose
2. Boot
3. Push rod
4. Piston and cap assy.
5. Return spring
6. Bleeder cap
7. Bleeder screw
8. Steel ball
9. Release cylinder

85817055

Fig. 59 Exploded view of a common clutch slave cylinder

11. Fit the return spring into the cylinder.

12. Insert the primary cup into the bore so that its flat side is facing the piston.

13. Place the secondary cup on the piston and insert them in the cylinder bore.

14. Install the stop washer and the wire piston stop.

15. Fit the boot on the cylinder.

HYDRAULIC SYSTEM BLEEDING

▶ **See Figure 60**

1. Remove the rubber cap from the bleeder screw on the release cylinder.

2. Place a bleeder tube over the end of the bleeder screw.

3. Submerge the other end of the tube in a jar half-filled with hydraulic (brake) fluid.

4. Depress the clutch pedal fully and allow it to return slowly.

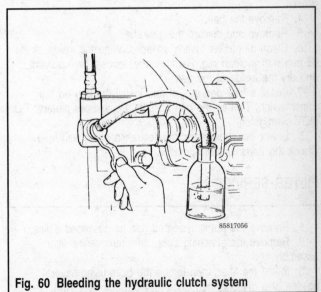

85817056

Fig. 60 Bleeding the hydraulic clutch system

5. Keep repeating Step 4 while watching the hydraulic fluid in the jar. As soon as the air bubbles disappear, close the bleeder screw.

➡ During the bleeding procedure, the reservoir must be kept at least ¾ full.

AUTOMATIC TRANSMISSION

Identification

Most transmission codes are available from the vehicle information code plate located on the cowl (in the engine compartment). The first portion of the code is the transmission designation; following this, there is a blank box. At the right end of the line is the axle or final drive ratio.

On other models the transmission model and serial number are either stamped on a plate that is bolted to the transmission case or stamped directly on the case itself. The location varies depending on the transmission model.

As an option on some of these vehicles, there is an electronically controlled 4-speed automatic designated R4A-EL. The transmission is computer controlled and has no owner-serviceable or adjustable components other than the neutral start switch.

Fluid Pan

REMOVAL & INSTALLATION

➡ On some RX-7s, certain components of the exhaust system may have to be removed in order to remove the transmission pan.

1. Raise and support the vehicle.
2. Place a drain pan under the transmission.
3. Remove the pan attaching bolts (except the two at the front). Loosen the two at the front slightly. Allow the fluid to drain.
4. Remove the pan.
5. Remove and discard the gasket.
6. Clean all gasket mating surfaces. Wipe the inside of the oil pan with a clean rag. Remove any deposits with solvent and dry the inside of the pan.
7. Install a new pan gasket and install the pan on the transmission. Tighten the pan bolts in a crisscross pattern. DO NOT overtighten.
8. Lower the vehicle and fill the transmission with fluid. Check the transmission operation.

FILTER SERVICE

1. Remove the transmission oil pan as described ealier.
2. Remove the attaching bolts, then remove the filter assembly.
3. Install the filter, then torque the bolts using several passes of a diagonal sequence to 4-5 ft. lbs. (5-7 Nm).

Adjustments

BAND

Except RX-7

♦ See Figure 61

➡ On all cars but the GLC and 626, this adjustment can be made by removing the cover located on the lower right front of the transmission (three bolts). On the GLC and 626, the transmission pan must be removed; the servo piston stem and locknut are visible at the left front.

1. Loosen the locknut.
2. Torque the servo piston stem to 9-11 ft. lbs. (12-15 Nm), then back it off exactly two turns.
3. Hold the stem stationary and tighten the locknut to 11-29 ft. lbs. (15-39 Nm).
4. If applicable, install the transmission pan; otherwise, install the cover on the transmission.

RX-7

The band adjustment stud is located on the right side of the transmission under a metal cap which is held by three bolts.
1. Raise the car and support it on jackstands.
2. Remove the protective cap from over the band adjuster.
3. Loosen the locknut on the adjuster.
4. Tighten the adjuster to 9-11 ft. lbs. (12-15 Nm) using the special Mazda socket (tool number 49-0378-345) or an equivalent tool.

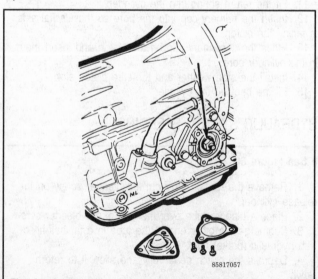

85817057

Fig. 61 Automatic transmission band adjustment

5. Back off the adjuster two full turns.

6. Hold the adjuster from moving and tighten the locknut to 11-29 ft. lbs. (15-39 Nm).

7. Install the protective cap.

SHIFT LINKAGE

1978-84 Except RX-7

▶ **See Figure 62**

1. Place the transmission selector lever in Neutral.

2. Disconnect the clevis from the lower end of the selector arm.

3. Move the manual lever to the N position.

➡**The N position is the third detent from the back.**

4. Loosen the two clevis retaining nuts and adjust the clevis so that it freely enters the lever hole.

5. Tighten the retaining nuts.

6. Connect the clevis to the lever and secure with the spring washer, flat washer and retaining clip.

1979-81 RX-7

▶ **See Figure 63**

1. Shift the selector lever into the Neutral position.

2. Raise the vehicle and support it on jackstands.

3. Disconnect the T-joint from the lower end of the selector lever operating arm.

4. Move the manual selector lever on the transmission into the Neutral position, which is the third detent position from the rear of the transmission. Adjust the T-joint so that it freely enters the hole in the selector lever operating arm.

5. Tighten the attaching nuts.

6. Connect the T-joint to the selector lever operating arm and secure.

7. Lower the vehicle and check the operation of the transmission in each selector lever position.

1982-85 RX-7

1. Remove the boot plate.

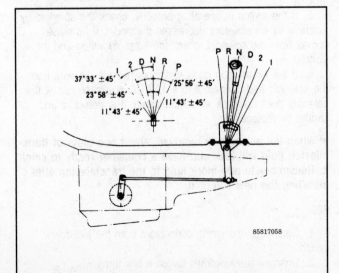

Fig. 62 Transmission shift linkage adjustment

2. Place the shifting lever in the Park position.

3. Loosen the selector lever plate setting bolt.

4. Raise and support the vehicle safely.

5. Place the selector rod at the Park position, the first detent position from the rear of the transmission.

6. Torque the selector lever plate setting bolt to 30 ft. lbs. (41 Nm). Check the operation after adjustment.

1986-89 RX-7

▶ **See Figure 64**

1. Remove the shifter cover.

2. Turn locknuts **A** and **B** to the proper adjusting position (see illustration).

3. Move the shifter level to the Park position.

4. Shift the transmission. Make sure the vehicle is supported safely when working underneath.

5. Turn locknut **A** by hand until it just touches the shifter lever, then back it off 1 full turn.

6. Torque locknut **B** to 8 ft. lbs. (11 Nm).

7. Move the shifter and make sure there is a click at each gear when shifting from Park through 1st. The positions of the selector lever and the indicator should be exact. The release button should return smoothly when used to shift the selector.

929

▶ **See Figure 65**

1. Remove the console shifter cover assembly. Position the transmission selector lever in the Park detent.

2. Loosen locknuts **A** and **B** (see illustration). Move the selector from the Park range by moving the manual shaft linkage on the transmission.

3. Using a feeler gauge, check the clearance between the first locknut, behind the shifter bracket. Adjust the shift lever and locknut to 0.04 in. (1mm).

4. Remove the feeler gauge and tighten locknut **B**.

5. On 1989 929s, measure the clearance between the guide plate and the guide pin in the Park position. There should be about 0.04 in. (1mm) clearance on the front side and about 0.02 in. (0.5mm) for the rear side.

6. Move the selector lever through the other gear ranges and check to be sure that there is clearance between the selector lever bracket and the guide pin.

7. If clearance does not exist, readjust both locknuts.

KICKDOWN SWITCH & DOWNSHIFT SOLENOID

Except 626

▶ **See Figure 66**

➡**The kickdown switch is located on the accelerator linkage above the pedal.**

1. Check the accelerator linkage for smooth operation.

2. Turn the ignition **ON**, but do not start the engine.

3. Depress the accelerator pedal fully to the floor. As the pedal nears the end of its travel, a light click should be heard from the downshift solenoid.

4. If the kickdown switch operates too soon/too late, loosen the locknut on the switch shaft. Adjust the shaft so that the accelerator linkage makes contact with it when the pedal is

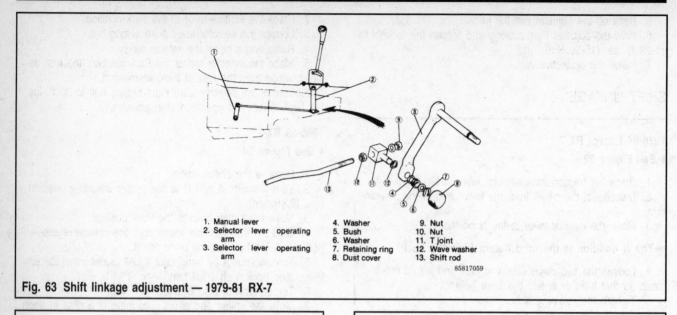

1. Manual lever
2. Selector lever operating arm
3. Selector lever operating arm
4. Washer
5. Bush
6. Washer
7. Retaining ring
8. Dust cover
9. Nut
10. Nut
11. T joint
12. Wave washer
13. Shift rod

85817059

Fig. 63 Shift linkage adjustment — 1979-81 RX-7

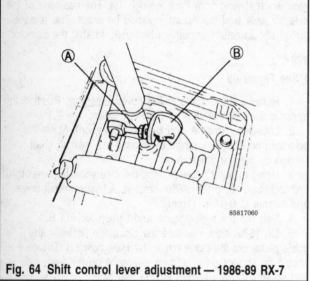

85817060

Fig. 64 Shift control lever adjustment — 1986-89 RX-7

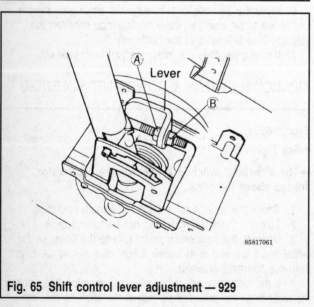

Lever

85817061

Fig. 65 Shift control lever adjustment — 929

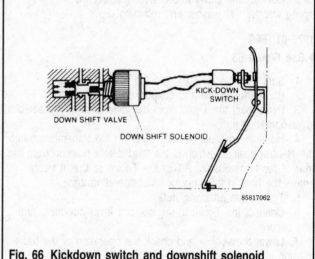

KICK-DOWN SWITCH

DOWN SHIFT VALVE

DOWN SHIFT SOLENOID

85817062

Fig. 66 Kickdown switch and downshift solenoid adjustment

depressed approximately ⅞ of the way to the floor. Tighten the locknut.

5. If the switch is operating properly, check the solenoid by listening as an assistant depressed the pedal. If no noise comes from the solenoid, check the solenoid wiring and the switch.

6. If the circuit is in good condition, remove the wire from the solenoid and connect it to a 12V DC power source. If the solenoid does not click when connected, it is defective and should be replaced.

➡️**When the solenoid is removed, about two pints of transmission fluid will leak out; have a container ready to catch it. Remember to add more fluid to the transmission after installing the new solenoid.**

626

1. Disengage the wiring connectors from the kickdown switch.
2. Unscrew the kickdown switch a few turns.

3. Fully depress the accelerator pedal.

4. Gradually thread in the kickdown switch until you hear a clicking sound then tighten it inward ½ turn more.

5. Tighten the locknut and attach the wiring connectors.

Neutral Safety (Inhibitor) Switch

REMOVAL & INSTALLATION

1. Disconnect the linkage from the gear selector lever on the switch.

2. Unbolt and remove the switch from the transmission.

3. Place the new switch onto the transmission and bolt it in place.

4. Connect the selector lever linkage and adjust the switch.

ADJUSTMENT

GLC

▶ See Figure 67

1. Adjust shift linkage as described earlier. Put the selector lever in the Neutral position (3rd detent from the rear).

2. Remove the transmission manual lever retaining nut and pull the lever off the switch.

3. Loosen (do not remove) the two switch retaining bolts and remove the alignment pin hole screw at the bottom of the switch.

4. Gently rotate the switch back and forth while attempting to insert a 0.08 in. (2mm) diameter pin into the alignment pin hole. When alignment is correct, the pin will slide through the hole in the internal rotor. Tighten the switch attaching bolts and remove the pin.

5. Reinstall the alignment pin hole screw. Position the manual lever back onto the switch shaft, then install the washer and nut.

6. Check switch operation. If the switch still does not work, i.e., the car starts in positions other than Park or Neutral, replace the switch. With the key in the **ON** (not **START**) position, shift the selector into Reverse; the backup lights should be on. If not, check the bulbs and wiring or replace the inhibitor switch.

626

1. Place the transmission selector lever in the Neutral position.

2. Loosen the neutral switch attaching screws.

3. Position the manual shift lever shaft in the Neutral position by adjusting the range select lever. The proper Neutral position is where the slot of the manual shaft is positioned vertically and the detent position in the shaft engages correctly with a click sound.

4. Move the neutral switch so that the identification marks on the switch body and the sliding plate are aligned.

5. Tighten the neutral switch adjusting screws.

6. Check the adjustment by trying to start the engine in all gears. It should only start in Park and Neutral.

929 and RX-7

▶ See Figure 68

1. Shift the selector lever to the Neutral position.

2. Raise and safely support the vehicle.

3. Loosen the inhibitor switch mounting bolts.

4. Unfasten the screw underneath the switch body.

5. Move the switch body so that the screw hole in the case aligns with the small hole inside the switch.

6. Check the alignment by inserting a 0.08 in. (2mm) diameter pin through the holes. Once the proper alignment is obtained, remove the pin and tighten the switch mounting bolts. Install and lightly tighten the screw.

7. Check the system for proper operation. If the switch still does not work (it still allows the car to start in positions other than Park or Neutral), replace the switch. With the key in the **ON** (not **START**) position, shift the selector into Reverse; the backup lights should be on. If not, check the bulbs and wiring or replace the inhibitor switch.

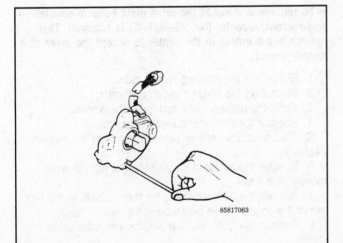

Fig. 67 Adjusting the GLC neutral safety switch

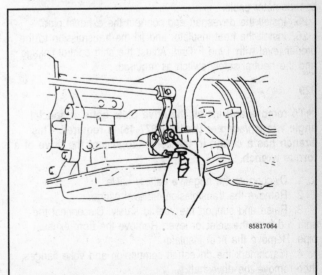

Fig. 68 Inhibitor switch adjustment — 929 and RX-7

Transmission

REMOVAL & INSTALLATION

GLC and 626

1. Disconnect the negative battery cable.
2. Drain the transmission.
3. Remove the heat insulator.
4. Disconnect the exhaust pipe.
5. Disconnect the driveshaft at the rear axle flange.
6. Remove the driveshaft.
7. Disconnect the speedometer cable.
8. Disconnect the shift rod.
9. Remove all vacuum hoses.
10. Disconnect all wiring.
11. Disconnect the oil cooler lines.
12. Remove the access cover from the lower end of the converter housing.
13. Matchmark the drive plate and torque converter for re-alignment, then remove the converter bolts.
14. Support the transmission with a jack and remove the crossmember.
15. Remove the converter housing-to-engine bolts.
16. Remove the filler tube.
17. Separate the flexplate and the converter.
18. Remove the transmission and converter as an assembly.

To install:

19. Raise the transmission into the vehicle, then align the matchmarks on the torque converter and the drive plate. Install the drive plate bolts and tighten them evenly.
20. Install the filler tube.
21. Install the converter-to-housing bolts and tighten them evenly.
22. Install the crossmember and remove the transmission jack.
23. Attach the access cover to the lower end of the converter housing.
24. Connect the oil cooler lines, vacuum hoses, shift rod and speedometer cable.
25. Install the driveshaft and connect the exhaust pipe.
26. Install the heat insulator and fill the transmission to the proper level with Type F fluid. Adjust the shift control linkage and the neutral safety switch as required.

929

➡To remove and install the drive plate bolts, a special angle wrench/adapter (No. 49-0877-45) is required. This wrench has a cutout in the center to accept the drive of a torque wrench.

1. Disconnect the negative battery cable.
2. Remove the transmission oil level gauge.
3. Raise and support the vehicle safely. Disconnect the shift rod from the selector lever. Remove the front exhaust pipe. Remove the heat insulator.
4. Matchmark the driveshaft companion and yoke flanges, then remove the driveshaft.
5. Unbolt and remove the starter. Disconnect the speedometer cable.

6. Label and disconnect the inhibitor switch connector, the turbine sensor connector, the lock-up solenoid connector and the solenoid valve connector from the wiring harness.
7. Remove the oil vacuum pipes, then plug the ends. Remove the undercover.
8. Support the transmission with a suitable jack and unbolt the crossmember.
9. Matchmark the drive plate and torque converter for re-alignment, then remove the converter bolts.
10. Using the special tool, remove the torque converter housing-to-engine bolts and separate the transmission from the drive plate. Push the wiring harness bracket off to the side. Remove the transmission from the vehicle.

To install:

11. Raise the transmission into the vehicle, then align the matchmarks on the torque converter and the drive plate. Install the torque converter housing-to-engine bolts and torque them down in an alternate pattern to 27-38 ft. lbs. (37-51 Nm). Attach the wiring harness to the transmission and torque the bracket bolt to 23-34 ft. lbs. (31-46 Nm). Install the drive plate bolts and snug them first. Using the special tool, finally tighten them evenly to 25-36 ft. lbs. (34-49 Nm).
12. Attach the crossmember to the frame and torque the bolts to 29-42 ft. lbs. (39-60 Nm). Remove the transmission jack and install the under cover.
13. Install the vacuum and oil pipes.
14. Engage all the wiring multi-connectors to the wiring harness.
15. Connect the speedometer cable and install the starter.
16. Align the driveshaft yoke and companion flanges, then connect the driveshaft. Torque the driveshaft bolts to 27-38 ft. lbs. (37-51 Nm).
17. Connect the exhaust pipe using a new gasket. Torque the through-bolt to 12-17 ft. lbs. (16-23 Nm) and the nuts to 23-34 ft. lbs. (31-46 Nm). Install the heat insulator.
18. Connect the shift rod to the selector lever using a new spring clip.
19. Fill the transmission to the proper level and replace the oil level gauge. Connect the negative battery cable.

1979-85 RX-7

➡To remove and install the drive plate bolts, a special angle wrench/adapter (No. 49-0877-45) is required. This wrench has a cutout in the center to accept the drive of a torque wrench.

1. Disconnect the negative battery cable.
2. Disconnect the inhibitor switch connector.
3. Apply the parking brake and block the wheels.
4. Remove the converter housing upper cover.
5. Disconnect the vacuum sensing tube from the vacuum diaphragm.
6. Remove the air cleaner assembly and the converter housing side cover.
7. Remove the bolts attaching the transmission to the rear end of the engine. Raise and support the vehicle safely.
8. Remove the front, the rear and the converter under covers.
9. Remove the air pipe and the converter brackets.
10. Remove the rear of the exhaust pipe and the pellet converter assembly.

11. Remove the front exhaust pipe and the monolith converter assembly.

12. Remove the floor under covers.

13. Remove the driveshaft, then install the turning holder tool 49-0259-440 into the rear of the extension housing, to prevent the fluid from leaking from the housing.

14. Disconnect the starter wiring connectors.

15. Remove the starter and the lower converter housing cover.

16. For reinstallation purposes, place an alignment mark on the drive plate and the torque converter.

17. Remove the bolts securing the torque converter to the drive plate.

18. Remove the bolts that attach the transmission to the rear of the engine.

19. Properly support both the engine and the transmission assemblies.

20. Disconnect the speedometer cable and the selector rod at the selector lever.

21. Remove the nuts that attach the transmission support to the body.

22. Using a transmission removal jack, lower the transmission slightly and remove the fluid coolant tubes.

23. Slide the transmission rearward, until the input shaft clears the eccentric shaft, then remove the transmission/torque converter assembly from under the vehicle.

To install:

24. Position the transmission under the vehicle and slide the unit forward until the input shaft engages the eccentric shaft. Make sure that the matchmarks on the torque converter and drive plate are aligned. Connect the fluid tubes to the transmission.

25. Install the transmission support-to-body nuts and tighten them evenly.

26. Connect the shift rod to the selector lever and connect the speedometer cable to the transmission.

27. Remove the transmission jack and install the converter-to-drive plate bolts. Torque the bolts to 25-36 ft. lbs. (34-49 Nm) using the special tool.

28. Install the lower converter housing cover and the starter.

29. Connect the driveshaft and install the floor under covers.

30. Connect the monolith converter and exhaust pipe assemblies using new gaskets.

31. Connect the pellet converter and rear exhaust pipe section using new gaskets. Install the converter brackets and the air pipe. Install the undercovers (front, rear and converter).

32. Lower the vehicle and install the transmission-to-rear engine bolts. Torque the bolts to 23-34 ft. lbs. (31-46 Nm).

33. Install the converter housing side cover and the air cleaner assembly.

34. Connect the vacuum sensing tube to the diaphragm. Install the converter housing upper cover.

35. Connect the inhibitor switch connector and the negative battery cable.

36. Fill the transmission to the proper level. Adjust the inhibitor switch and shift linkage as required.

1986-89 RX-7

➡**To remove and install the drive plate bolts, a special angle wrench/adapter (No. 49-0877-45) is required. This wrench has a cutout in the center to accept the drive of a torque wrench.**

1. Disconnect the negative battery cable. Raise and safely support the vehicle.

2. Remove the exhaust pipe with the heat insulator.

3. Matchmark and disconnect the driveshaft. Install the turning holder tool 49-0259-440 into the rear of the extension housing, to prevent the fluid from leaking from the housing.

4. Remove the vacuum and oil pipes, then plug the ends.

5. Remove the starter bracket and starter.

6. Disconnect the speedometer cable.

7. Disconnect the shift rod from the transmission.

8. Remove the oil level gauge and filler pipe.

9. Disengage the harness multi-connector.

10. Remove the service hole coupler.

11. Support the transmission with a jack and remove the transmission mounting bolts. Slide the transmission rearward, until the input shaft clears the eccentric shaft, then remove the transmission/torque converter assembly from under the vehicle.

To install:

12. Position the transmission under the vehicle and slide the unit forward until the input shaft engages the eccentric shaft. Make sure that the matchmarks on the torque converter and drive plate are aligned. Install the transmission-to-engine bolts and torque them to 23-34 ft. lbs. (31-46 Nm).

13. Install the service hole coupler and engage the harness multi-connector.

14. Install the filler pipe and oil level gauge.

15. Connect the shift rod to the control lever on the transmission.

16. Connect the speedometer cable.

17. Install the starter and starter bracket.

18. Connect the vacuum and oil pipes.

19. Remove the holding tool and connect the driveshaft flanges and torque the bolts to 36-43 ft. lbs. (49-58 Nm).

20. Install the exhaust pipe and heat insulator.

21. Connect the negative battery cable. Fill the transmission to the proper level. Adjust the inhibitor switch and shift linkage as required.

AUTOMATIC TRANSAXLE

Identification

On all models, the vehicle information code plate mounted on the cowl (in the engine compartment) lists the transmission or transaxle type. On the third line (labeled Transaxle), the transaxle model is listed, preceding a space. The serial number is stamped following the space.

Fluid Pan

REMOVAL & INSTALLATION

▶ **See Figure 69**

1. Raise and support the vehicle.

2. Place a drain pan under the transmission pan.

3. Remove the drain plug located at the lower part of the transaxle and drain the fluid. If the plug gasket is worn, replace it.

4. On 1988-89 626s and MX-6s, remove the left-side splash shield.

5. Loosen the oil pan retaining bolts and lower the oil pan and gasket to the ground. Remove the gasket and discard it.

6. Wipe the inside of the pan and the gasket sealing surfaces with a clean rag. If there are magnets on the bottom of the pan, note where they are attached. Remove them to clean the pan, but remember to put them back in their original positions.

7. Install the new gasket onto the pan and raise the pan onto the transaxle. Make sure the gasket mates evenly with the groove in the pan.

8. Install the retaining bolts and torque them in a crisscross pattern to 67-95 inch lbs. (8-11 Nm). DO NOT overtighten the bolts. It doesn't take much torque to compress the gasket and form a good seal. Check frequently to ensure the gasket is installed properly.

9. On 1988-89 626s and MX-6s, install the left-side splash shield.

10. Wipe off the threads of the plug and install the gasket. Install the drain plug and tighten it into the bottom of the transaxle.

11. Fill the transaxle to the proper level. Start the engine and check the fluid level (see Section 1). Check for fluid leaks around the pan sealing surface and the drain plug.

STRAINER SERVICE

1. Raise and safely support the vehicle.

2. Place a drain pan under the transmission pan.

3. Remove the drain plug located at the lower part of the transaxle and drain the transaxle fluid.

4. Remove the oil pan and gasket as described above.

5. Unbolt and remove the oil strainer from the valve body. If the strainer is clogged or deformed, replace it.

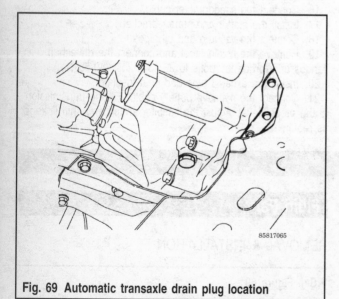

Fig. 69 Automatic transaxle drain plug location

6. Remove and discard the O-ring from the strainer outlet.

7. Coat the new O-ring with fresh transmission oil and install the O-ring into the stainer outlet.

8. Install the strainer onto the valve body and secure with the bolts. Torque the bolts to 67-95 inch lbs. (8-11 Nm).

9. Install the oil pan with a new gasket.

10. Install the drain plug and fill the transaxle to the proper level. Start the engine and check the fluid level (see Section 1). Check for fluid leaks around the pan sealing surface and the drain plug.

Adjustments

SHIFT LINKAGE & SELECTOR LEVER

1986-87 323 Sedan/Hatchback, 1988-89 323 Wagon and 1983-86 626

▶ **See Figure 70**

1. Engage the parking brake. Remove the shift lever boot. Loosen both locknuts on the cable.

2. Shift the lever to the Neutral position. Shift the selector on the side of the transaxle to the same position by counting detents.

3. Turn the lower locknut until it just touches the shifter collar. Then, torque the upper locknut to 67-95 inch lbs. (8-11 Nm).

4. Have someone watch the lever on the transaxle. Slowly push the lever toward Park until the lever on the transmission just begins to move, and note how far the shifter has moved. Return the lever to the Neutral position and repeat the procedure going toward the Drive position. If the distances are the same in both directions, the adjustment is correct. If not, adjust the shifter as follows:

• If the shift lever moves too far in the forward direction — tighten the LOWER locknut

• If the shift lever moves too far to the rear — tighten the UPPER locknut

1988-89 323 (Except Wagon), 1987-89 626 and MX-6

▶ **See Figure 71**

1. Remove the shifter cover and loosen locknuts **A** and **B** (see illustration).

2. On some models of the 626 and MX-6 a lockbolt will be threaded into the center of the shift adjust lever (between the locknuts). If present, the lockbolt must be loosened before adjustment.

3. Shift the selector lever to the Park position and make sure that a click is heard at each position from Park to 1st.

4. Shift the transaxle to the Park position by moving the manual shaft on the transaxle.

5. If present, tighten the lockbolt to 67-95 inch lbs. (8-11 Nm).

6. Turn locknut **A** until it just contacts the manual shaft lever.

7. Back off locknut **A** one full turn and tighten locknut **B** to 67-95 inch lbs. (8-11 Nm).

8. Repeat Step 2 in order to verify that a click is heard at each position.

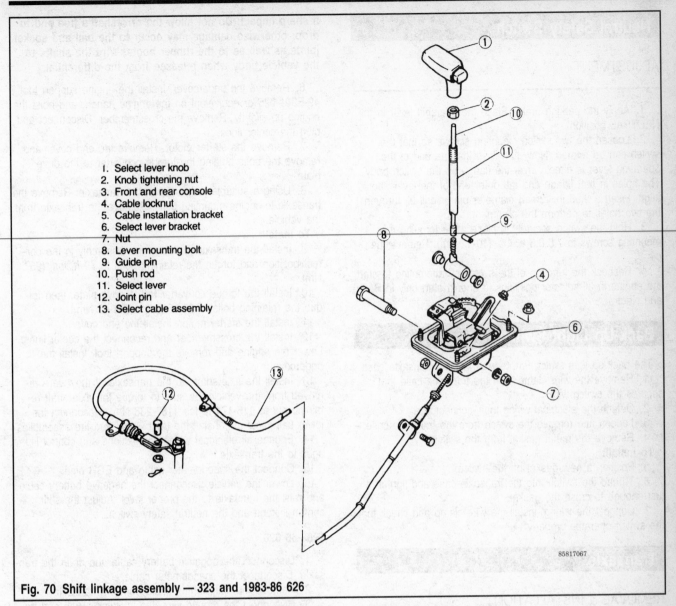

1. Select lever knob
2. Knob tightening nut
3. Front and rear console
4. Cable locknut
5. Cable installation bracket
6. Select lever bracket
7. Nut
8. Lever mounting bolt
9. Guide pin
10. Push rod
11. Select lever
12. Joint pin
13. Select cable assembly

Fig. 70 Shift linkage assembly — 323 and 1983-86 626

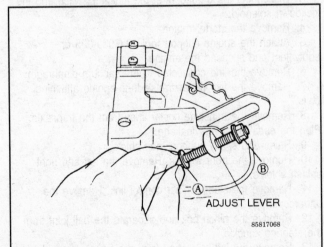

ADJUST LEVER

Fig. 71 Selector lever adjustment — 1988-89 323 (non-wagon), 1987-89 626 and MX-6

9. Make sure that the position of the selector lever matches the positions on the indicator plate. Make sure the shifter button operates smoothly when the shifter lever is moved.

KICKDOWN SWITCH & DOWNSHIFT SOLENOID

323, 626 and MX-6

1. Disconnect the wires from the kickdown solenoid (located above the accelerator pedal) and attach a continuity tester. Have someone slowly depress the accelerator pedal as you read the tester to check for continuity. It should begin when the accelerator pedal is depressed 7/8 of the way.

2. If the adjustment is incorrect, loosen the locknut and turn the switch clockwise for earlier engagement or counterclockwise for later engagement. Tighten the locknut and reconnect the wires.

Neutral Safety Switch

ADJUSTMENT

1. Apply the parking brake. Place the gearshift lever in the NEUTRAL position.

2. Loosen the two switch mounting screws so that the switch can be rotated. Now, turn it so that the end of the operating lever is directly over the flange on the switch body. The holes in that flange and the outer end of the lever should align. Insert a 0.08 in. (2mm) diameter pin or drill bit through the two holes to perform the alignment.

3. Hold the switch securely in place while torquing the mounting screws to 7.5-8.5 ft. lbs. (10-12 Nm). Remove the pin.

4. Recheck the function of the switch by attempting to start the engine in all selector positions. It should start only in Park and Neutral.

Back-Up Light Switch

The back-up light switch is threaded into the transaxle case.

1. Remove the wire clamp from the transaxle case that secures the switch wire.

2. Detach the electrical wiring multi-connector.

3. Loosen and remove the switch from the transaxle case.

4. Remove the metal gasket from the switch.

To install:

5. Position a new gasket on the switch.

6. Thread the switch into the transaxle case and tighten it just enough to crush the gasket.

7. Connect the wiring, install the wire clamp and check that the switch operates properly.

Transaxle

REMOVAL & INSTALLATION

GLC

1. Disconnect the negative battery cable. Raise and support the vehicle safely. Drain the transaxle fluid. Properly support the rear end of the engine.

2. Disconnect the speedometer cable and EGR pipe.

3. Disengage all electrical wiring connections and control linkages from the transaxle.

4. Remove the front tires. Disconnect the lower ball joints and pull the lower arm downward. Separate the lower arms from the knuckles.

5. Remove the axle shafts from the transaxle by prying with a suitable pry bar inserted between the shaft and the case. Be sure not to damage the oil seals.

➡**A circlip is positioned on the driveshaft ends and engages in a groove, machined in the differential side gears. The driveshafts may have to be forced from the differential housing to release the clip from the groove. Do not apply**

a sharp impact. **Do not allow the driveshaft's free end to drop; otherwise damage may occur to the ball and socket joints as well as to the rubber boots. Wire the shafts to the vehicle body when released from the differential.**

6. Remove the undercover. Install the engine support tool 49-E301-025 or equivalent on the engine hanger and hoist the engine up slightly. Remove the crossmember. Disconnect and plug the cooler lines.

7. Remove the starter motor. Remove the end cover and remove the bolts holding the torque converter to the drive plate.

8. Using a suitable jack, support the transaxle. Remove the transaxle-to-engine mounting bolts. Remove the transaxle from the vehicle.

To install:

9. Install the transaxle to the engine assembly in the correct position and torque the retaining bolts to 70 ft. lbs. (95 Nm).

10. Install the torque converter to the drive plate, then torque the retaining bolts to 25-36 ft. lbs. (34-49 Nm).

11. Install the starter motor. Install the end cover.

12. Install the crossmember and reconnect the cooler lines. Lower the engine and remove the support tool. Install the undercover.

13. Install the axle shafts to the transaxle. If they were removed from the vehicle, be sure to torque the axle shaft retaining nut to 116-174 ft. lbs. (157-236 Nm). Reconnect the lower ball joints and install the front wheel and tire assemblies.

14. Engage all electrical wiring connections and control linkages to the transaxle.

15. Connect the speedometer cable and EGR pipe.

16. Lower the vehicle. Reconnect the negative battery cable and refill the transaxle to the proper level. Adjust the shift control linkage and the neutral safety switch.

1983-86 626

1. Disconnect the negative battery cable and drain the transaxle. Disconnect the speedometer cable.

2. Remove the shift control cable from the transaxle.

3. Disconnect the ground wire, the inhibitor switch and the kickdown solenoid.

4. Remove the starter motor.

5. Attach the engine support tool 49-G030-025 or equivalent and suspend the engine.

6. Remove the line connected to the vacuum diaphragm.

7. Remove the five upper transaxle-to-engine attaching bolts.

8. Remove the transaxle cooler lines from the transaxle. Plug the ends to prevent leakage.

9. Raise and safely support the vehicle.

10. Remove the front wheels. Remove the left and right splash shields.

11. Remove the stabilizer bar control link. Remove the undercover.

12. Remove the pinch bolt and separate the ball joint from the steering knuckle.

13. Remove the left axle shaft from the transaxle by inserting a chisel between the axle shaft and the bearing housing. Tap the end of the chisel lightly in order to separate the axle shaft from the transaxle.

14. Pull the front hub outward and remove the axle shaft from the transaxle. Support the axle shaft during and after removal to avoid damaging the CV-joints and boots.

15. Pull the right axle shaft from the transaxle by inserting a prybar between the axle shaft and the joint shaft, then carefully force the axle shaft coupling open.

16. Pull the front hub out and remove the axle shaft from the joint shaft. Support the axle shaft during and after removal to avoid damaging the CV-joints and boots. Remove the joint shaft assembly from the transaxle.

17. Remove the transaxle undercover and torque converter-to-drive plate bolts. Support the transaxle assembly. Remove the crossmember and the left-side lower arm together as an assembly.

18. Attach a safety chain to the transaxle mounting brackets in two places and attach the rope over the engine support bar.

19. Remove the lower two transaxle-to-engine bolts. Lower the transaxle to the floor.

To install:

20. Install the transaxle mount bracket if removed. Install the transaxle to the engine assembly in the correct position and torque the upper retaining bolts to 66-86 ft. lbs. (89-117 Nm).

21. Install the crossmember and the transaxle mount nuts. Torque the mount nuts to 31-40 ft. lbs. (42-54 Nm).

22. Install the torque converter to the drive plate, then torque the retaining bolts to 25-36 ft. lbs. (34-49 Nm).

23. Install the under cover.

24. Install the axle shafts with new circlips (gap at the top of the groove) in the transaxle. After installing the axle shaft pull the front hub outward to make sure the axle shaft does not come out. Mount the joint shaft bracket if necessary.

25. Install the ball joints to the steering knuckle and torque to 32-40 ft. lbs. (43-54 Nm).

26. Install the stabilizer bar control link. Torque the stabilizer bar control link bolt so that 1 in. (25mm) of the bolt is exposed.

27. Install the splash shields and wheel/tire assemblies.

28. Lower the vehicle. Reconnect the transaxle cooler lines.

29. Install the lower transaxle retaining bolts and torque to 66-86 ft. lbs. (89-117 Nm).

30. Connect the vacuum diaphragm line.

31. Install the starter and electrical connections.

32. Reconnect the wiring to the inhibitor switch, kickdown solenoid and ground wire.

33. Reconnect the shift control and speedometer cables. Adjust the shift control linkage and the neutral safety switch. Refill the transaxle to the proper level.

1986-87 323

1. Disconnect the negative battery cable. Remove the air cleaner.

2. Disconnect the speedometer and throttle cable from the transaxle. Disconnect the shift control cable from the transaxle.

3. Remove the ground wire. Remove the water pipe bracket. Remove the secondary air pipe and the EGR pipe bracket.

4. Remove the wire harness clip. Disconnect the inhibitor switch, the kickdown solenoid and any other necessary solenoids or switches.

5. Remove the upper transaxle mounting bolts. Disconnect the neutral switch connector and the vacuum line from the

vacuum diaphragm. Disconnect and plug the transaxle oil cooler lines. Mount the engine support tool 49-ER301-025A or equivalent to the engine hanger.

6. Raise and support the vehicle safely. Drain the transaxle oil, then remove the front wheel and tire assemblies.

7. Remove the engine under cover and side covers.

8. Remove the lower arm ball joints and the knuckle clinch bolts, then pull the lower arm downward and separate the lower arms from the knuckles.

9. Separate the axle shafts from the transaxle by prying with a suitable pry bar inserted between the shaft and the case. Be sure not to damage the oil seals.

10. Support the transaxle assembly. Remove the transaxle crossmember. Remove the starter motor and electrical connection.

11. Remove the end plate. Lean the engine toward the transaxle side and lower the transaxle by loosening the engine support hook bolt. Support the transaxle with a suitable floor jack.

12. Remove the necessary engine brackets. Remove the remaining transaxle mounting bolt. Lower the jack and slide the transaxle out from under the vehicle.

To install:

13. Install the transaxle to the engine assembly in the correct position and torque the retaining bolts to 47-66 ft. lbs. (64-89 Nm).

14. Install the torque converter to the drive plate, then torque the retaining bolts to 25-36 ft. lbs. (34-49 Nm).

15. Install the starter motor. Install the end cover.

16. Install the crossmember and reconnect the cooler lines.

17. Install the axle shafts with new circlips (gap at the top of the groove) in the transaxle. After installing the axle shaft pull the front hub outward to make sure the axle shaft does not come out.

18. Install the lower ball joint to the steering knuckle.

19. Install the under and side covers. Install the wheel and tire assemblies.

20. Lower the vehicle. Engage all electrical wiring connections and control linkages to the transaxle.

21. Connect the speedometer cable, throttle cable, secondary air pipe, water pipe bracket and EGR pipe.

22. Install the air cleaner and engine ground wire.

23. Reconnect the negative battery cable. Adjust the shift control and neutral safety start switch.

1987-89 626 and MX-6

1. Remove the battery and battery carrier.

2. Disconnect the engine fuse block.

3. Disconnect the center distributor terminal.

4. Disconnect the airflow meter connector and remove the air cleaner assembly.

5. On turbocharged vehicles, remove the intercooler-to-throttle body hose and the air cleaner-to-turbocharger hose.

6. On non turbocharged vehicles remove the air cleaner hose, resonance chamber and chamber bracket.

7. Disconnect the speedometer cable.

8. Disconnect and label the transaxle control electrical connectors, inhibitor switch, solenoid valve, pulse generator (if so equipped), fluid temperature switch and all ground wires from the transaxle case.

9. Disconnect the selector and throttle cable.

10. Raise and safely support the vehicle. Drain the transaxle fluid and remove the front wheels.

11. Remove the splash shields. Disconnect and plug the transaxle cooler lines.

12. Disconnect the tie rod ends with a suitable tool. Remove the stabilizer bar control links.

13. Remove the left and right lower arm ball joint retaining bolts and nuts. Pull the lower arms downward to separate them from the steering knuckles.

14. Separate the left axle shaft from the transaxle by carefully prying with a tool inserted between the axle shaft and the transaxle case. Do not damage the transaxle oil seal.

15. Remove the right joint shaft bracket.

16. Remove the right axle shaft from the transaxle by carefully prying with a bar inserted between the axle shaft and transaxle case.

17. Install transaxle plugs 49-G030-455 or equivalent into the differential side gears.

➡**Failure to install the transaxle plugs may allow the differential side gears to become mispositioned.**

18. Remove the exhaust pipe hanger and gusset plates.

19. Remove the torque converter cover.

20. Remove the torque converter retaining nuts.

21. Remove the starter motor and access brackets.

22. Mount an engine support bar, 49-G017-5A0 or equivalent, and attach it to the engine hanger.

23. Remove the center transaxle mount and bracket.

24. Remove the left transaxle mount.

25. Remove the nut and bolt attaching the right transaxle mount to the frame.

26. Remove the crossmember and left lower arm as an assembly.

27. Position a transmission jack under the transaxle and secure the transaxle to the jack.

28. Remove the engine-to-transaxle bolts.

29. Before the transaxle can be lowered out of the vehicle, the torque converter studs must be clear of the flexplate. Insert a tool between the flexplate and converter and carefully disengage the studs.

30. Lower the transaxle out of the vehicle.

To install:

31. Place the transaxle on a transmission jack. Be sure the transaxle is secure.

32. Raise the transaxle to the proper height and mount the transaxle to the engine.

➡**Align the torque converter studs and flexplate holes.**

33. Install the engine-to-transaxle bolts and tighten to 66-86 ft. lbs. (89-117 Nm).

34. Install the center transaxle mount and bracket. Tighten the bolts to 27-40 ft. lbs. (37-51 Nm) and the nuts to 47-66 ft. lbs. (64-89 Nm).

35. Install the left transaxle mount. Tighten the transaxle-to-mount attaching nut to 63-86 ft. lbs. (85-117 Nm). Tighten the mount to bracket bolt and nut to 49-69 ft. lbs. (66-93 Nm).

36. Install the crossmember and left lower arm as an assembly. Tighten the bolts to 27-40 ft. lbs. (37-51 Nm) and the nuts to 55-69 ft. lbs. (75-93 Nm).

37. Install the right transaxle mount bolt and nut. Tighten to 63-86 ft. lbs. (85-117 Nm).

38. Install the starter motor and access brackets.

39. Install the torque converter nuts and tighten to 32-45 ft. lbs. (43-61 Nm).

40. Install the converter cover and tighten the bolts to 69-85 inch lbs. (8-10 Nm).

41. Install the gusset plate-to-transaxle bolts and tighten to 27-38 ft. lbs. (37-51 Nm).

42. Replace the circlip located on the end of each axle shaft.

43. Remove the transaxle plugs and install the axle shafts.

44. Attach the lower arm ball joints to the knuckles.

45. Install the tie rod ends and tighten the nuts to 22-33 ft. lbs. (30-45 Nm). Install new cotter pins.

46. Install the bolts and nuts to the lower arm ball joints. Tighten to 32-40 ft. lbs. (43-54 Nm).

47. Install the stabilizer link assemblies. Turn the nuts on each assembly until 25 bolt threads can be measured from the upper nut. When then length is reached, secure the upper nut and back off the lower nut until a torque of 12-17 ft. lbs. (16-23 Nm) is reached.

48. Connect the oil cooler outlet and inlet hoses.

49. Install the splash shields.

50. Install the front wheel and tire assemblies.

51. Reconnect the throttle cable.

52. Connect the range selector cable to the transaxle case and tighten the bolt to 22-29 ft. lbs. (30-39 Nm).

53. Connect the ground wires to the transaxle case and tighten to 69-95 inch lbs. (8-11 Nm).

54. Engage the transaxle control electrical connectors and attach the control harness to the transaxle clips. On turbocharged vehicles, install the intercooler-to-throttle body hose and the air cleaner-to-turbocharger hose.

55. Connect the speedometer cable.

56. Install the resonance chamber and bracket, then tighten to 69-95 inch lbs. (8-11 Nm).

57. Install the air cleaner assembly. Tighten the bolt to 23-30 ft. lbs. (31-41 Nm) and the nuts to 69-95 inch lbs. (8-11 Nm).

58. Connect the airflow meter connector.

59. Connect the center distributor terminal lead.

60. Connect the main fuse block and tighten to 69-95 inch lbs. (8-11 Nm). Install the battery carrier and battery, then tighten to 23-30 ft. lbs. (31-41 Nm).

61. Remove the engine support bracket.

62. Fill the transaxle to the proper level. Adjust the shift control linkage and the neutral safety switch.

1988-89 323

1. Disconnect the negative battery cable. Remove the air cleaner.

2. Disconnect the speedometer and throttle cable from the transaxle. Disconnect the shift control cable from the transaxle.

3. Remove all ground wires from the transaxle case.

4. Remove the wire harness clip. Disconnect the inhibitor switch, the overdrive release solenoid and any other necessary electrical connections.

5. Remove the upper transaxle mounting bolts. Disconnect and plug the transaxle oil cooler lines. Mount the engine support tool 49G0175A0 or equivalent to the engine hanger.

6. Raise and support the vehicle safely. Drain the transaxle oil, then remove the front wheel and tire assemblies.

7. Remove the engine under cover and side covers. Remove the torque converter to engine retaining bolts.

8. Remove the left and right lower arm ball joint knuckle clinch bolts. Remove the stabilizer bar control link assemblies. Pull the lower arm downward and separate the lower arms from the knuckles.

➡**Install transaxle plugs 49-B027-006 or equivalent into the differential side gears after axle shaft removal. Failure to install the transaxle plugs may allow the differential side gears to become mispositioned.**

9. Separate the axle shafts from the transaxle by prying with a suitable pry bar inserted between the shaft and the case. Be sure not to damage the oil seals.

10. Support the transaxle assembly. Remove the transaxle crossmember. Remove the starter motor and electrical connection.

11. Remove the end plate. Lean the engine toward the transaxle side and lower the transaxle. Support the transaxle with a suitable floor jack.

12. Remove the necessary engine brackets. Remove the remaining transaxle mounting bolts. Lower the jack and slide the transaxle out from under the vehicle.

To install:

13. Install the transaxle to the engine assembly and torque the retaining bolts to 41-59 ft. lbs. (56-80 Nm).

14. Install the torque converter to the drive plate, then torque the retaining bolts to 25-36 ft. lbs. (34-49 Nm).

15. Install the starter motor and bracket. Install the end cover.

16. Install the crossmember and reconnect the cooler lines.

17. Install the axle shafts with new circlips (gap at the top of the groove) in the transaxle. After installing the axle shaft pull the front hub outward to make sure the axle shaft does not come out.

18. Install the lower ball joint to the steering knuckle.

19. Install the stabilizer link assemblies. Turn the nuts on each assembly until 0.33 in. (8.5mm) of bolt thread can be measured from the upper nut. When then length is reached, secure the upper nut and back off the lower nut until a torque of 9-13 ft. lbs. (12-18 Nm) is reached.

20. Install the under and side cover. Reconnect the oil cooler hoses, then install the wheel and tire assemblies.

21. Lower the vehicle. Engage all electrical wiring connections and control linkage to the transaxle.

22. Reconnect the speedometer and throttle cable to the transaxle.

23. Install the air cleaner and all ground wires.

24. Reconnect the negative battery cable. Refill the transaxle with the proper amount and type fluid. Adjust the shift control linkage and the neutral safety switch.

Halfshafts

Halfshaft removal, installation and overhaul procedures for automatic transaxles are the same as for manual transaxles, which are described earlier in this section.

DRIVELINE

Driveshaft and U-Joints

REMOVAL & INSTALLATION

Rear Wheel Drive GLC

▸ **See Figures 72 and 73**

1. Raise the rear end of the car and support it using jackstands.

✳✳CAUTION

Be sure that the car is securely supported. Remember, you will be working underneath it.

2. Matchmark the flanges on the driveshaft and pinion so that they may be installed in their original position.

3. Remove the four bolts which secure the driveshaft to the pinion flange.

4. Lower the back end of the driveshaft and slide the front end out of the transmission.

5. Plug up the hole in the transmission to prevent it from leaking.

➡**Use an old U-joint yoke or, if none is available, place a plastic bag secured with rubber bands over the hole.**

6. To install, slide the front end of the driveshaft into the transmission and raise the rear end of the shaft onto the

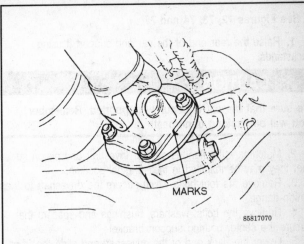

Fig. 72 Matchmark the driveshaft flanges before removing the driveshaft

pinion flange making sure that the matchmarks are aligned properly. Install the flange bolts and torque to 25-27 ft. lbs. (34-37 Nm).

7. Lower the vehicle.

1979-82 626

▸ **See Figures 72 and 73**

The driveshaft used on 626 models is removed in a manner similar to that outlined for GLC models. The only difference in

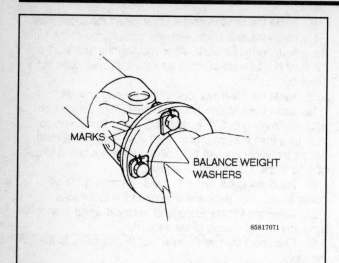

85817071

Fig. 73 If so equipped, be sure to also matchmark the balance washers

the removal procedure is that the center bearing must be unbolted prior to driveshaft removal. Remove the driveshaft and the center bearing as a single unit.

➡**Do not remove the oil seals and the center bearing from the support unless they are defective.**

Installation is performed in the reverse order of removal. Tighten the center bearing support bolts to 27-38 ft. lbs. (37-51 Nm) for the 626 and the driveshaft-to-pinion flange bolts to 25-27 ft. lbs. (34-37 Nm).

929

▶ **See Figures 72, 73, 74 and 75**

1. Raise the rear end of the car and support it using jackstands.

✳✳CAUTION

Be sure that the car is securely supported. Remember, you will be working underneath it.

2. Matchmark the flanges on the driveshaft and pinion so that they may be installed in their original position.
3. Remove the four bolts which secure the driveshaft to the pinion flange.
4. Remove the bolts, washers, bushings and spacers that secure the center bearing support bracket.
5. Lower the back end of the driveshaft and slide the front end out of the transmission.

➡**Transmission fluid may flow out of the rear of the transmission when the yoke is removed, so either use the turning holder (tool number 49 S120 440) or a used driveshaft yoke to plug the transmission.**

To install:

6. Slide the front end of the driveshaft into the transmission and raise the rear end of the shaft onto the pinion flange, making sure that the matchmarks are aligned properly.
7. Torque the flange bolts to 36-43 ft. lbs. (49-58 Nm).
8. Using the exploded view as a guide, assemble the washers, bushings and spacers onto the support bracket bolts,

then install the bracket onto center bearing. Torque the bracket bolts to 27-38 ft. lbs. (37-51 Nm).

9. Check the front and rear driveshafts for proper alignment (see illustration) after the center bearing support is in place and torqued down. If the shafts are not aligned as shown, adjust the height of the center bearing support bracket with shims and bolts which may be purchased at your local Mazda dealer.

RX-7

▶ **See Figures 72 and 73**

1. Raise the rear of the car and support it on jackstands.
2. Matchmark the position of the rear driveshaft, pinion yokes and balance washers so that the driveshaft will be installed in the same position and to avoid the possibility of vibration problems.
3. Remove the four attaching bolts at the rear of the driveshaft, and remove the driveshaft toward the rear of the vehicle, sliding it out of the back of the transmission.

➡**Transmission fluid may flow out of the rear of the transmission when the yoke is removed, so insert use the turning holder (tool number 49-0259-440) into the rear of the housing or a used driveshaft yoke to lug the transmission.**

4. Install the driveshaft in the reverse order of removal. Be careful not to damage the rear transmission seal when installing the driveshaft on the splined shaft in the transmission. Make sure you align the matchmarks made earlier on the driveshaft yokes and balance washers. The yokes on the driveshaft and the rear axle must be aligned as they were when removed or the driveshaft may be out of balance and cause vibration. Tighten the bolts to 25-27 ft. lbs. (34-37 Nm) on 1979-85 models and 36-43 ft. lbs. (49-58 Nm) on 1986-89 models.

If a new driveshaft was installed and the vehicle is experiencing vibration problems, the driveshaft may have to be balanced. Balancing is performed by placing weights on the flange bolts at different locations on the flange. The balance weights are available in 0.12 oz. (3.4 g) and 0.20 oz. (5.7 g) sizes from your local Mazda dealer.

U-JOINT OVERHAUL

▶ **See Figures 76 and 77**

Perform this procedure with the driveshaft removed from the car.

1. Matchmark both the yoke and the driveshaft so that they can be returned to their original balancing position during assembly.
2. Remove the bearing snaprings from the yoke.
3. Use a hammer and a brass drift to drive in one of the bearing cups. Remove the cup which is protruding from the other side of the yoke.
4. Remove the other bearing cups by pressing them from the spider. On the GLC and 626, bearings may be removed by tapping on the base of the yoke with a hammer.
5. Withdraw the spider from the yoke.
6. Examine the spider journals for rusting or wear. Check the bearing for smoothness or pitting.

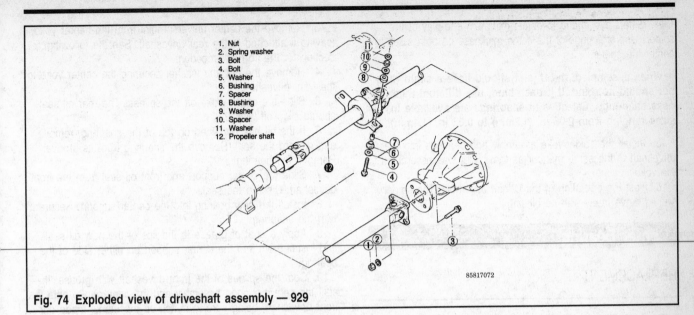

1. Nut
2. Spring washer
3. Bolt
4. Bolt
5. Washer
6. Bushing
7. Spacer
8. Bushing
9. Washer
10. Spacer
11. Washer
12. Propeller shaft

Fig. 74 Exploded view of driveshaft assembly — 929

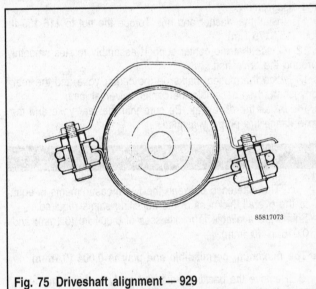

Fig. 75 Driveshaft alignment — 929

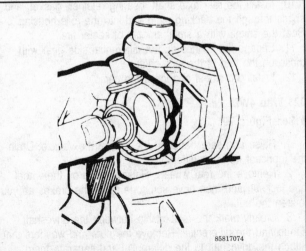

Fig. 76 Removing the U-joint spider. Note the protruded position of the bearing cup.

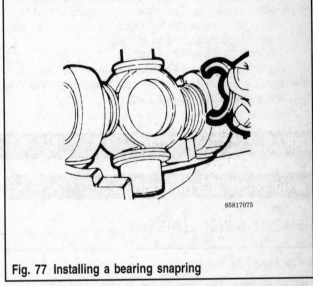

Fig. 77 Installing a bearing snapring

7. Measure the spider diameter. On the 626 the minimum diameter is 0.58 in. (14.7mm), and on the GLC it is 0.50 in. (12.7mm). If diameter is too small, replace the spider. Mazda does not provide spider diameter for the RX-7 and 929.

➡**The spider and bearing are replaced as a complete assembly only.**

8. Check the seals and rollers for wear or damage.
To assemble:
9. Pack the bearing cups with grease.
10. Fit the rollers into the cups and install the dust seals.
11. Place the spider in the yoke and them fit one of the bearing cups into its bore in the yoke.
12. Press the bearing cup home, while guiding the spider into it, so that a snapring can be installed.
13. Press-fit the other bearings into the yoke.

14. Select a snapring to obtain minimum end-play of the spider. Use snaprings of the same thickness on both sides to center the spider.

➡**When assembled, the U-joint should have a slight drag but should not bind. If it does bind, use different thickness snaprings. Selective fit snaprings are available in sizes ranging from 0.05 in. (1.2mm) to 0.06 in. (1.4mm).**

15. Install the spider/yoke assembly and bearings into the driveshaft in the same manner as the spider was assembled to the yoke.

16. Test the operation of the U-joint assembly. The spider should move freely with no binding.

Center Bearing

REPLACEMENT

The center support bearing is a sealed unit which requires no periodic maintenance. The following procedure should be used if it becomes necessary to replace the bearing. You will need a pair of snapring pliers for this job.

1. Remove the driveshaft assembly.
2. To maintain driveline balance, matchmark the rear driveshaft, the center yoke and the front driveshaft so that they may be installed in their original positions.

REAR AXLE

Axle Shaft, Bearing and Seal

REMOVAL & INSTALLATION

⯈ **See Figure 78**

Except 323 With 4WD, 929 and RX-7

➡**The left and the right rear axle shafts are not interchangeable, as the left shaft is shorter than the right. It is, therefore, not a good idea to remove them both at once.**

1. Remove the wheel cover and loosen the lug nuts.
2. Raise the rear of the car and support the axle housing on jackstands.
3. Unfasten the lug nuts and remove the wheel.
4. Remove the brake assembly. (See Section 9.)
5. Unfasten the nuts which secure the brake backing plate and the bearing retainer to the axle housing.
6. Withdraw the axle shaft with a puller.

To install:

7. Apply grease to the oil seal lips and then insert the oil seal into the axle housing.
8. On all models but GLC check the axle shaft end-play in the following manner:
   a. Temporarily install the brake backing plate on the axle shaft.
   b. Measure the depth of the bearing seal and then measure the width of the bearing outer race.

3. Remove the center universal joint from the center yoke, leaving it attached to the rear driveshaft. See the following section for the correct procedure.
4. Remove the nut and washer securing the center yoke to the front driveshaft.
5. Slide the center yoke off the splines. The rear oil seal should slide off with it.
6. If the oil has remained on top of the snapring, remove and discard the seal. Remove the snapring from its groove. Remove the bearing.
7. Slide the center support and front oil seal from the front driveshaft. Discard the seal.
8. Install the new bearing into the center support. Secure it with the snapring.
9. Apply a coat of grease to the lips of the new oil seals, and install them into the center support on either side of the bearing.
10. Coat the splines of the front driveshaft with grease. Install the center support assembly and the center yoke onto the front driveshaft, being sure to match up the marks made during disassembly.
11. Install the washer and nut. Torque the nut to 116-130 ft. lbs. (157-176 Nm).
12. Check that the center support assembly rotates smoothly around the driveshaft.
13. Align the mating marks on the center yoke and the rear driveshaft, then assemble the center universal joint.
14. Install the driveshaft. Be sure that the rear yoke and the axle flange are properly aligned.

   c. The difference between the two measurements is equal to the overall thickness of the adjusting shims required. Shims are available in thicknesses of 0.004 in. (0.1mm) and 0.016 in. (0.4mm).

➡**The maximum permissible end-play is 0.004 (0.1mm).**

9. Remove the backing plate and apply sealer to the rear axle surfaces which contact it. Install the backing plate again.
10. Install the rear axle shaft, bearing retainer, gasket, and shims through the backing plate and into the axle housing. Coat the shims with a small amount of sealer first.
11. Engage the splines on the differential side gear with those on the end of the axle shaft.
12. Install the wheel and lower the car.

323 With 4WD

⯈ **See Figure 79**

1. Raise and safely support the rear of the vehicle. Drain the lubricant from the differential.
2. Remove the rear wheels. Raise the tab on the wheel hub locknut, and then have someone apply the brakes as you loosen the nut.
3. Clearly mark the relationship between the driveshaft flange and the differential. Remove the nuts and washers that attach the driveshaft to the differential and separate them.
4. Disconnect the lateral link from the rear axle hub by removing the through-bolt and washer. Disconnect the trailing link in the same manner.

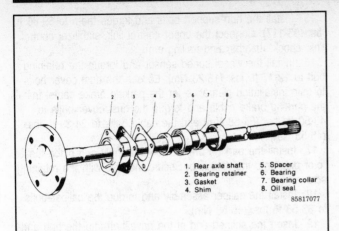

1. Rear axle shaft
2. Bearing retainer
3. Gasket
4. Shim
5. Spacer
6. Bearing
7. Bearing collar
8. Oil seal

85817077

Fig. 78 Components of the rear axle shaft assembly

Mark	Thickness mm (in)	Mark	Thickness mm (in)
1	6.29 (0.2476)	12	6.73 (0.2650)
2	6.33 (0.2492)	13	6.77 (0.2665)
3	6.37 (0.2508)	14	6.81 (0.2681)
4	6.41 (0.2524)	15	6.85 (0.2697)
5	6.45 (0.2539)	16	6.89 (0.2713)
6	6.49 (0.2555)	17	6.93 (0.2728)
7	6.53 (0.2571)	18	6.97 (0.2744)
8	6.57 (0.2587)	19	7.01 (0.2760)
9	6.61 (0.2602)	20	7.05 (0.2776)
10	6.65 (0.2618)	21	7.09 (0.2791)
11	6.69 (0.2634)		

85817079

Fig. 79 Spacer selection chart — 323 with 4wd

5. Lower the driveshaft flange from the differential and pull the splined end from the wheel hub. If the driveshaft is stuck in the hub, use special hub puller 49-0839-425C or equivalent to withdraw the hub so you can remove the driveshaft.

6. Unbolt and remove the rear axle assembly from the shock absorber support.

To replace the bearings and oil seals:

7. Press the wheel hub and disc plate from the knuckle using an arbor press and special attachments 49-B026-102, 49-G033-102 and 49-G030-727 or their equivalents. Support the wheel hub and disc plate to keep it from falling.

8. Matchmark the wheel hub and the disc plate, then remove wheel hub.

9. Support the wheel hub on V-blocks with the bolts facing down. Place special tool 49-0636-145 or equivalent between the oil seal and the hub. Press the outer bearing and oil seal from the hub. Save the spacer.

10. Pry the inner oil seal from the wheel hub with a small prytool, then drive the inner and outer bearing races out of the hub using a brass drift punch and a hammer.

11. Install the new inner and outer bearing races, then seat them in the knuckle by tapping alternately and evenly using the brass drift and hammer.

12. Install the inner bearing, original spacer and outer bearing, then place special preload adjustment tool 49-B001-727 or equivalent on top of the outer bearing. Torque the special tool to 17 inch lbs (2 Nm). Mount the knuckle in a protected jaw vise so that the jaws are clamped on the wheel hub shaft. Hook a spring scale to the knuckle and measure the preload. The correct preload is 1.74-6.94 inch lbs (0.2-0.8 Nm). If not as specified, adjust the preload by selecting the appropriate spacer from the accompanying chart. If the bearing preload is greater than the specified amount, select a thicker spacer. If the bearing preload is less than the specified amount, select a thinner spacer. If the preload is within the specified value, use the old spacer.

➡Although Mazda recommends packing the bearings after installation (with the seals driven into position), you may wish to pack them before installation to assure proper greasing. If you decide to grease the bearings before installation, just make sure that the preload measurements/adjustments have already been performed as the grease would adversely affect your measurements.

13. Install the inner bearing into the knuckle. Coat the lip of the inner oil seal with a good quality lithium based grease and install the seal using special seal installer tool 49-B001-795 or equivalent. A piece of pipe or socket that closely approximates the diameter of the seal may be substituted for this tool. Install the outer bearing and outer oil seal in the same manner as the inner. If not done already, pack the inner and outer bearings with lithium based grease.

14. Place the disc plate onto the wheel hub so that the matchmarks are aligned and install the wheel hub retaining bolts. Torque the bolts to 33-40 ft. lbs. (45-54 Nm).

15. Press the hub into the knuckle.

To install:

16. Attach the knuckle assembly to the shock absorber support and torque the retaining bolts to 58-86 ft. lbs. (79-117 Nm).

17. Insert the splined end of the driveshaft into the wheel hub, then connect the trailing and lateral links. Torque the trailing link bolt to 69-86 ft. lbs. (93-117) and the lateral link bolt to 46-55 ft. lbs. (62-75).

18. Attach the driveshaft flange to the differential by aligning the matchmarks. Torque the flange nuts to 36-43 ft. lbs. (49-58 Nm).

19. Install a new locknut and torque it to 116-174 ft. lbs. (157-236 Nm) Stake the locknut tab into the groove of the spindle using a small cold chisel.

20. Install the rear wheels and lower the vehicle.

929

▶ **See Figure 80**

1. Raise and safely support the rear of the vehicle.

2. Remove the rear wheels and uncrimp the tab on the rear axle nut with a small cold chisel. Have an assistant apply the brakes and loosen the rear axle nut and washer. Discard the nut and washer as they must be replaced with new ones.

3. Mark the relationship of the driveshaft flange to the differential and unbolt the driveshaft. Lower the driveshaft flange and withdraw the splined end from the axle.

4. Remove the caliper and support the assembly with a piece of rope or wire to relieve the stress on the brake line. Leave the brake line connected.

5. Remove the retaining screws and pull the rotor disc from the wheel hub.

6. Remove the parking brake shoe assembly (see Section 9) and disconnect the parking brake cable by loosening the dust cover bolts. If equipped with ABS, disconnect and remove the wheel speed sensor from the rear hub support. Position the sensor off to the side and out of the way.

7. Disconnect the trailing arm, shock absorber, stabilizer control link, upper control link and lower control links (front and rear).

8. Unfasten the bolts and remove the rear axle/hub support assembly.

To replace the oil seal and bearing:

9. Place the bearing support hub in special support fixture 49-HO26-108 or equivalent and press the axle flange from the hub. Look at the axle flange after it is freed from the hub. If the bearing inner race is still attached to the flange, use a grinding wheel to remove the race metal until only 0.02 in. (0.5mm) remains, then remove the rest with a cold chisel.

10. Remove the oil seal hub. With snapring pliers, remove the bearing retaining ring and press the bearing from the hub spindle. Purchase a new oil seal and bearing.

11. Press a new bearing into the hub and replace the snapring. Coat the lip of the new oil seal with multi-purpose grease and install the seal into the hub.

12. Press the axle flange into the hub using special installer tools 49-F026-102 and 49-H026-104 or equivalent.

To install:

13. Support the axle by hand and connect the rear lower link to the wheel side. Torque the fastener to 40-55 ft. lbs. (54-75 Nm). Connect and tighten the front lower link in the same manner. The body side bolts will be torqued later.

14. Connect the upper link (wheel side) to the hub support and torque the retaining bolt to 40-55 ft. lbs. (54-75 Nm). The body side bolts will be torqued later.

15. Install the hub support bolts and torque them to 69-86 ft. lbs. (93-117). Connect the upper control link, stabilizer control link, shock absorber and trailing arm.

16. Install the wheel speed sensor and torque the retaining bolt to 12-17 ft. lbs. (16-23 Nm). Loosen the dust cover bolts to gain installation clearance for the parking brake cable. Install the parking brake cable and torque the dust cover bolts to 40-50 ft. lbs. (54-68 Nm) and the cable bolts to 34-39 ft. lbs. (46-53 Nm).

17. Install the parking brake shoe assembly and place the rotor disc onto the axle hub. Secure the disc with the retaining screws.

18. Install the caliper assembly and torque the caliper bolts to 33-50 ft. lbs. (45-68 Nm).

19. Insert the splined end of the driveshaft into the hub and raise the driveshaft flange so that the matchmarks on the flange and differential are aligned. Install the flange bolts and torque them to 40-47 ft. lbs. (54-64 Nm).

20. Install the new washer and axle nut. Have an assistant apply the brakes and torque the nut to 174-231 ft. lbs. (236-313 Nm). Stake the tab of the locknut with a small cold chisel so that at least 0.16 in. (4mm) protrudes above the spindle groove.

21. Install the rear wheels and lower the vehicle. Bounce the rear of the vehicle several times to seat the suspension. Torque the body side lower link front bolts to 69-86 ft. lbs. (93-117) and the rear bolts to 54-86 ft. lbs. (73-117 Nm). Torque the body side upper link bolts to 69-86 ft. lbs. (93-117). Torque the stabilizer link bolts to 27-38 ft. lbs. (37-51 Nm). Torque the shock absorber bolts to 54-69 ft. lbs. (73-93 Nm).

22. Have the rear toe-in adjusted.

1979-85 RX-7

▶ See Figures 81, 82 and 83

1. Loosen, but do not remove, the rear wheel lug bolts.

2. Raise the vehicle and safely support it on jackstands. Remove the wheels.

3. Remove the brake drum and shoes or the disc brake caliper and disc as instructed in Section 9.

4. Disconnect the four bolts attaching the brake backing plate to the axle housing.

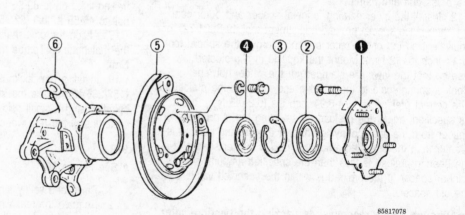

1. Axle flange
2. Oil seal
3. Retaining ring
4. Rear axle bearing
5. Dust cover
6. Rear hub support

85817078

Fig. 80 Exploded view of rear axle and hub assembly — 929

5. Disconnect the parking brake cable clip and remove the cable. Disconnect any interfering brake lines attached to the backing plate.

6. Remove the axle shaft/backing plate assembly by attaching a slide hammer to the axle shaft.

7. Remove the inner oil seal by prying it out.

➡Remove the inner oil seal only if it is defective, because the seal will probably be damaged when removed.

To replace the bearing:

8. The wheel bearing can be pressed off the axle shaft using bearing separator (tool number 49 8531 746 or equivalent) and its attachment (tool number 49 0259 747 or equivalent). Assemble the separator and attachment as shown in the illustration.

9. If the separator and its attachment are not available, or if the press does not generate enough force to press off both the bearing and its retaining collar, grind the bearing retaining

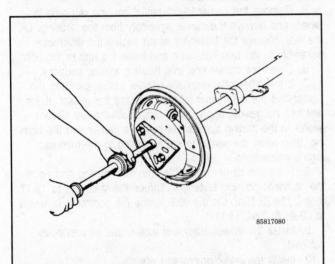

Fig. 81 Removing the axle shaft and brake backing plate with a slide hammer — 1979-85 RX-7

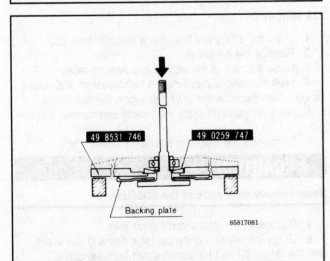

Fig. 82 Press the bearing from the axle shaft with separator and attachment tools

collar down, then cut it with a chisel to loosen its grip. Remove the collar.

10. Remove the bearing with a puller or a press. Remove the spacer and backing plate.

11. Install the backing plate and spacer on the axle shaft with the chamfer of the spacer toward the axle shaft flange.

12. Position the bearing on the axle shaft and press it until the spacer comes in contact with the shoulder on the shaft.

13. Clean off the new bearing retaining collar and its mounting space on the axles shaft, then press the bearing retaining collar on the shaft until it firmly contacts the bearing inner race.

➡Never lubricate the retaining collar when installing. Always use a new bearing retaining collar. If the bearing retaining collar can be press fit using less than 2.7 tons (5,900 lbs.) of pressure, replace the collar with a tighter fitting one.

To install:

14. If removed, lubricate and install the new oil seal in the axle shaft housing. Apply grease to the oil seal lip.

15. Install the axle shaft in the reverse order of removal, being careful not to damage the oil seal with the splined end of the shaft. Engage the splines on the shaft with the splines in the rear axle.

1986-89 RX-7

▶ **See Figure 84**

1. Loosen the rear wheel lug nuts. Raise and safely support the rear of the vehicle.

2. Remove the rear wheels. Raise the tab on the wheel hub locknut, and then have someone apply the brakes as you loosen the nut.

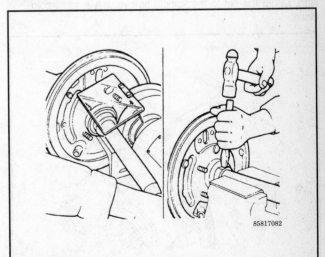

Fig. 83 If necessary, the collar can be removed with a hammer and chisel

3. Remove the caliper and support the assembly with a piece of rope or wire to relieve the stress on the brake line. Leave the brake line connected.

4. Remove the retaining screws and pull the rotor disc from the wheel hub. On vehicles equipped with ABS, remove the speed sensor probe from the knuckle. Move the probe off to the side and out of the way.

5. Unbolt and pull the rear knuckle assembly from the driveshaft.

To replace the bearing:

6. Remove the dust cover. The wheel hub can now be pressed from the toe control hub using bearing installer tool 49-F026-102 or equivalent and wheel hub puller 49-F026-103 or equivalent.

7. Install fan pulley boss puller 49-0636-145 or equivalent onto the hub and press the inner race from the hub using bearing installer tool 49-F026-102 or equivalent.

8. Remove the snapring from the bore of the toe control hub and press the bearing outer race from the hub using attachment 49-F027-007 or equivalent.

9. Press the new bearing and race assembly into the toe control hub using bearing installer tool 49-F026-102 or equivalent and bearing separator attachment 49-0259-748 or equivalent.

10. Install a new snapring and install the dust cover.

11. Press the hub onto the knuckle using the installer tool described in Step 9.

To install:

12. Mount the hub onto the driveshaft and the rear axle casing. Torque the knuckle bolts to 46-69 ft. lbs. (62-93 Nm) and the driveshaft bolts to 82-111 ft. lbs. (111-150 Nm).

13. Install the disc plate and caliper assemblies. If equipped with ABS, insert the speed sensor probe into the knuckle. The tip of the probe must be aligned with the edge of the rotor. Check the clearance between the sensor and the sensor rotor with a feeler gauge. The clearance should be 0.016-0.04 in. (0.4-1.0mm).

14. Install a new axle nut. Have an assistant depress the brake pedal and torque the nut to 174-231 ft. lbs. (236-313 Nm). Crimp the nut to the spindle groove with a small cold chisel.

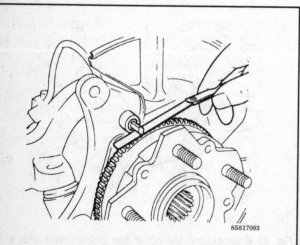

85817083

Fig. 84 Checking the clearance between the speed sensor and rotor — 1986-89 RX-7

15. Mount the rear wheels and lower the vehicle.

Differential Carrier

REMOVAL & INSTALLATION

Except 323 With 4WD and 1986-89 RX-7

▶ **See Figure 85**

1. Raise the vehicle and support it safely with jackstands.

2. Using wrench 49-0259-730 or equivalent, remove the differential drain plug and drain the lubricant from the differential. Install the plug after all of the fluid has drained. On the 929 this special tool is not required; use a socket to remove the drain plug.

3. Remove the axle shafts.

4. Remove the driveshaft.

5. Remove the carrier-to-differential housing retaining fasteners and remove the carrier assembly from the housing. On the 929, remove the fasteners which secure the differential assembly to the rear subframe and lower the unit to the floor.

6. Clean the carrier and axle housing mating surfaces.

7. If the differential originally used a gasket between the carrier and the differential housing, replace the gasket. If the unit had no gasket, apply a thin film of oil-resistant silicone sealer to the mating surfaces of both the carrier and the housing, then allow the sealer to set according to the manufacturer's instructions.

8. Place the carrier assembly onto the housing and install the carrier-to-housing fasteners. Torque the fasteners to 12-17 ft. lbs. (16-23 Nm). On the 929, torque the subframe fasteners to 69-86 ft. lbs. (93-117).

9. Install the driveshaft(s) and axle shafts as previously outlined.

10. Install the brake drums and wheels.

11. Fill the differential with the proper amount of SAE 80W-90 fluid (see the Capacities Chart in Section 1).

323 With 4WD

1. Drain the differential fluid into a suitable drain pan.

2. Remove the driveshaft.

3. Raise the rear of the vehicle and support safely.

4. Mark the relationship between the driveshaft and output flanges, then separate the driveshafts from the differential.

5. Have an assistant apply the brakes and remove the axle nut.

6. Disconnect the stabilizer from the crossmember.

✳✳CAUTION

Never remove both ends of the stabilizer.

7. Disconnect the lateral and trailing links.

8. Grasp the wheel hub by the rotor disc and pull it out until the driveshaft can be disconnected from the spline.

9. Support the differential with a jack and remove the mounting hardware from the front and rear attachment points. Lower the differential to the floor.

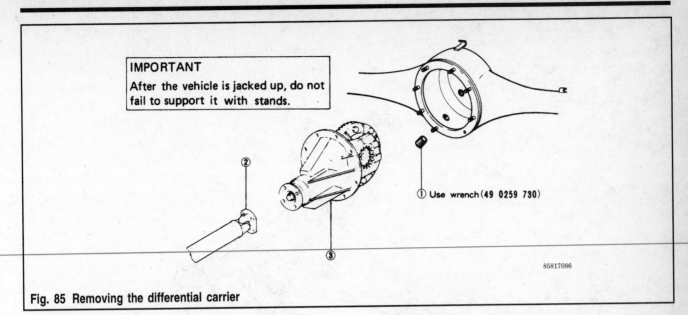

IMPORTANT

After the vehicle is jacked up, do not fail to support it with stands.

① Use wrench (49 0259 730)

85817086

Fig. 85 Removing the differential carrier

To install:

10. Raise the differential up into the frame, then install the front and rear fasteners. Torque the front fasteners to 33-50 ft. lbs. (45-68 Nm) and the rear fasteners to 80-97 ft. lbs. (108-131 Nm).

11. Insert the driveshaft spline into the wheel hub and align the matchmarks on the driveshaft with the output shaft. Install the flange fasteners and torque them to 36-43 ft. lbs. (49-58 Nm).

12. Connect the lateral link and torque the mounting bolt to 69-86 ft. lbs. (93-117). Connect the trailing link to the cross-member and torque the mounting bolt to 9-13 ft. lbs. (12-18 Nm).

13. Install the driveshaft and torque the flange bolts to 20-22 ft. lbs. (27-30 Nm).

14. Mount the wheels and lower the vehicle.

15. Fill the differential to the proper level (see Capacities Chart) and install the drain plug.

1986-89 RX-7

▶ **See Figure 86**

1. Raise and safely support the rear of the vehicle.
2. Remove all necessary exhaust system components needed to gain removal clearance.
3. Drain the fluid from the differential.
4. Matchmark the relationship between the driveshaft and output flanges (no. 1 in the illustration).
5. Unbolt and separate the driveshafts (halfshafts) from each side of the differential. Support the driveshafts from the frame with a piece of rope so they will not interfere with the removal of the differential.
6. Matchmark and remove the driveshaft (no. 2 in the illustration).
7. Remove the mounting nut located at the left side of the differential support member, and allow the member to hang down.
8. Remove the sub-link fasteners.
9. Support the differential with a jack, then remove the differential carrier, case and member fasteners. Lower the differential from the vehicle.

To install:

10. Raise the differential assembly into position with the jack. Install the member, carrier and case fasteners. Torque the carrier fasteners to 65-77 ft. lbs. (91-104 Nm) and the case fasteners to 54-69 ft. lbs. (73-93 Nm). Torque the left member nut and the sub-link fasteners to 54-69 ft. lbs. (73-93 Nm).

11. Install the driveshaft and torque the bolts to 36-43 ft. lbs. (49-58 Nm).

12. Install the driveshafts and torque the flange bolts to 40-47 ft. lbs. (54-64 Nm).

13. Fill the differential to the proper level. Install and tighten the drain plug to 29-40 ft. lbs. (39-54 Nm).

14. Install all removed exhaust system components.

15. Lower the vehicle.

Pinion Seal

REMOVAL & INSTALLATION

1. Raise and support the front end on jackstands.
2. Matchmark and remove the driveshaft.
3. Remove the wheels and brake calipers.
4. Using an inch lbs. torque wrench on the companion flange nut, measure and record the differential rotational torque.
5. Hold the companion flange and remove the locknut.
6. Using a puller, remove the companion flange.
7. Use a center punch to deform the seal, then pry it from the bore.
8. Coat the outer edge of the new seal with sealer and drive it into place with a seal driver.
9. Coat the seal lip with clean gear oil.
10. Lubricate (with chassis lube) and install the companion flange.
11. Install the nut and tighten it until the previously noted rotational torque is achieved. Torque on the nut should not exceed 130 ft. lbs. (176 Nm).
12. Install the driveshaft.

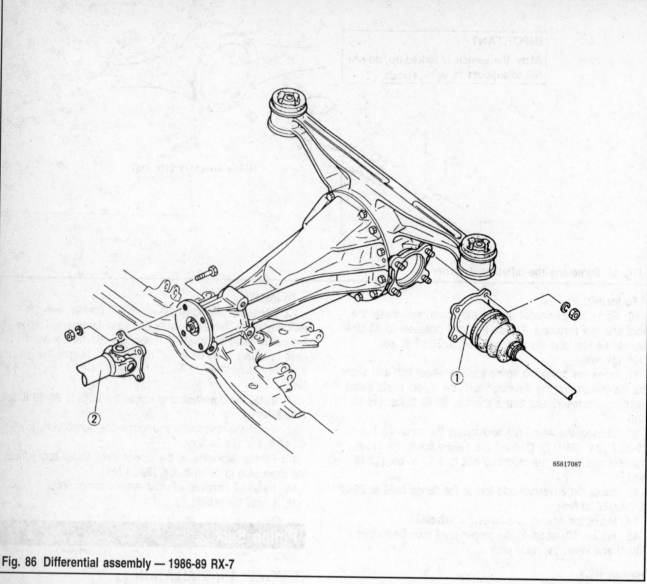

Fig. 86 Differential assembly — 1986-89 RX-7

13. Replace any lost gear oil.

Axle Housing

REMOVAL & INSTALLATION

1. Raise the vehicle on a hoist and support the axle assembly with a suitable lifting device. Drain the lubricant from the axle housing and remove the driveshaft.

2. Remove the wheel, drum and necessary brake components.

3. Disconnect the brake cable from the lever and bakcing plate.

4. Disconnect the hydraulic brake lines from the connectors.

5. Disconnect the shock absorbers from the axle brackets.

6. Remove the nuts and washers from the U-bolts.

7. Remove the U-bolts, spring plates and spacers from the axle assembly.

8. Lower the jack and remove the axle assembly.

To install:

9. Raise the axle housing into place, then install the spacers, spring plates and U-bolts.

10. Install the U-bolt nuts and washers. Remove the jack.

11. Connect the shock absorbers to the axle brackets.

12. Connect and tighten the brake lines.

13. Connect the parking brake cable to the lever on the brake flange lever plate.

14. Install the rear brakes, brake drum and rear wheels.

15. Connect the driveshaft and refill the axle housing.

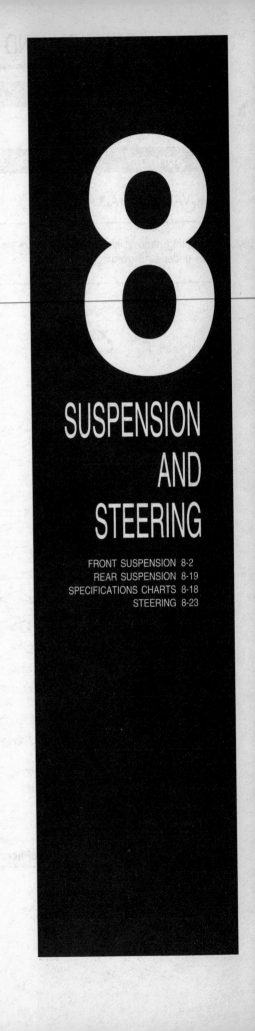

8

SUSPENSION AND STEERING

FRONT SUSPENSION

♦ See Figures 1, 2, 3, 4, 5 and 6

Coil Springs

REMOVAL & INSTALLATION

Coil spring removal and installation is covered later in this section under strut overhaul procedures.

Shock Absorbers

REMOVAL & INSTALLATION

Shock absorber removal and installation is covered later in this section under strut overhaul procedures. Two types of shock absorbs are used: the sealed cartridge and the open oil type.

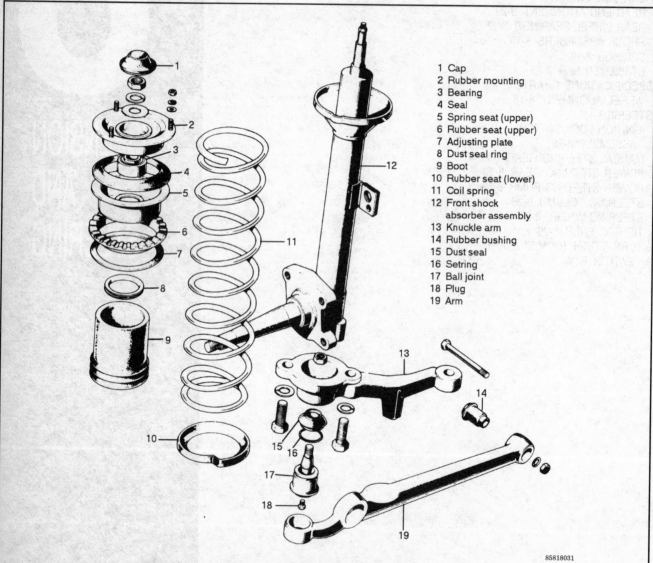

1 Cap
2 Rubber mounting
3 Bearing
4 Seal
5 Spring seat (upper)
6 Rubber seat (upper)
7 Adjusting plate
8 Dust seal ring
9 Boot
10 Rubber seat (lower)
11 Coil spring
12 Front shock absorber assembly
13 Knuckle arm
14 Rubber bushing
15 Dust seal
16 Setring
17 Ball joint
18 Plug
19 Arm

85818031

Fig. 1 Exploded view of common MacPherson strut on rear wheel drive vehicles

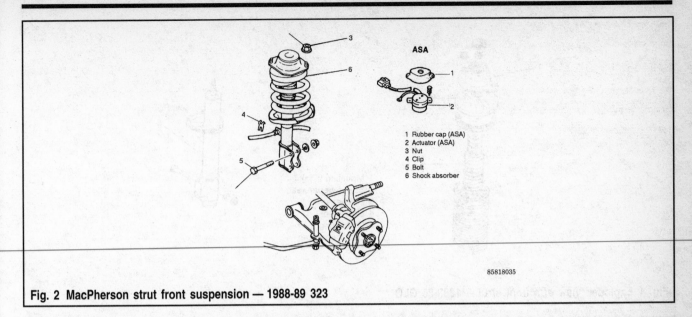

85818035

Fig. 2 MacPherson strut front suspension — 1988-89 323

ASA

1 Rubber cap (ASA)
2 Actuator (ASA)
3 Nut
4 Clip
5 Bolt
6 Shock absorber

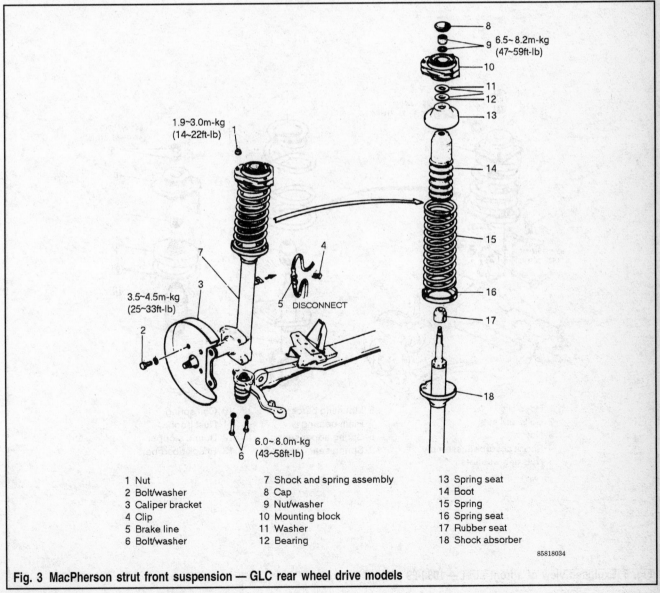

1.9~3.0m-kg
(14~22ft-lb)

3.5~4.5m-kg
(25~33ft-lb)

6.0~8.0m-kg
(43~58ft-lb)

5 DISCONNECT

6.5~8.2m-kg
(47~59ft-lb)

1 Nut	7 Shock and spring assembly	13 Spring seat
2 Bolt/washer	8 Cap	14 Boot
3 Caliper bracket	9 Nut/washer	15 Spring
4 Clip	10 Mounting block	16 Spring seat
5 Brake line	11 Washer	17 Rubber seat
6 Bolt/washer	12 Bearing	18 Shock absorber

85818034

Fig. 3 MacPherson strut front suspension — GLC rear wheel drive models

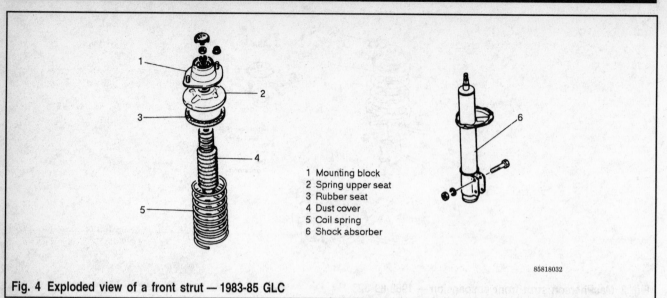

1 Mounting block
2 Spring upper seat
3 Rubber seat
4 Dust cover
5 Coil spring
6 Shock absorber

85818032

Fig. 4 Exploded view of a front strut — 1983-85 GLC

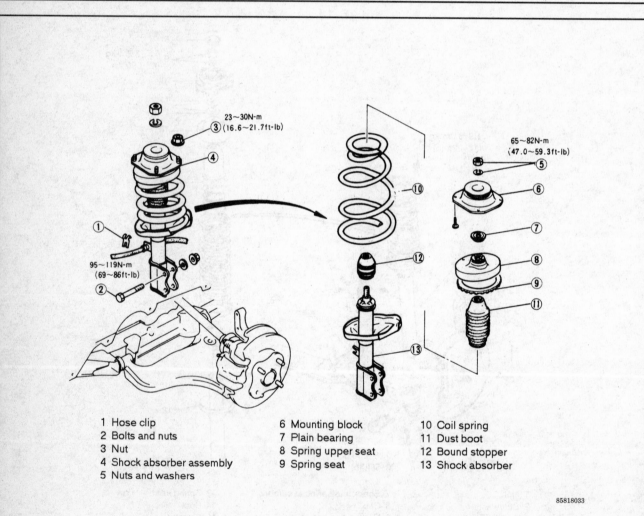

23~30N·m
(16.6~21.7ft-lb)

95~119N·m
(69~86ft-lb)

65~82N·m
(47.0~59.3ft-lb)

1 Hose clip	6 Mounting block	10 Coil spring
2 Bolts and nuts	7 Plain bearing	11 Dust boot
3 Nut	8 Spring upper seat	12 Bound stopper
4 Shock absorber assembly	9 Spring seat	13 Shock absorber
5 Nuts and washers		

85818033

Fig. 5 Exploded view of a front strut — 1983-89 626

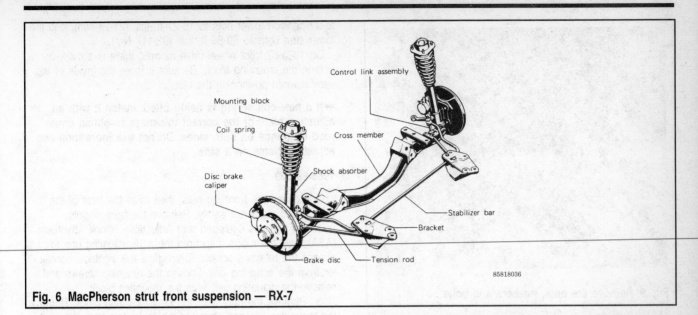

Fig. 6 MacPherson strut front suspension — RX-7

TESTING

This test can be done without removing the shock absorber from the vehicle.

Visually inspect the shock absorber for evidence of leakage. If an excessive amount of oil is found, the shock is defective and must be replaced.

If there is no sign of excessive leakage (a small amount of weeping is normal) bounce the car at one corner by pressing up and down on the fender or bumper. When you have the car bouncing as much as possible, step back and count how many times the car bounces by itself until it stops. It should stop bouncing after the first rebound. If it continues to bounce past the center point of its up-and-down motion more than once, the shock absorbers are worn and should be replaced.

MacPherson Struts

REMOVAL & INSTALLATION

Except RX-7, 929 and 1988-89 323, 626 and MX-6
▶ See Figures 7, 8, 9 and 10

1. Remove the wheel cover and loosen the lug nuts.
2. Raise the front of the vehicle and support it with jackstands. Do not jack it or support it by any of the front suspension members. Remove the wheel.
3. On rear wheel drive models, remove the caliper and disc as described in Section 9.
4. Support the strut from underneath, then unfasten the nuts which secure the upper shock mount to the top of the wheel arch. Disconnect the brake line from the strut.
5. Remove the two bolts that secure the lower end of the shock to the steering knuckle arm.
6. Remove the shock and coil spring as a complete assembly.
7. Mount the strut (shock/spring) assembly in a vise. Protect the shock tube by placing a piece of soft metal on either

Fig. 7 From inside the engine compartment, unfasten the nuts which secure the upper shock mount

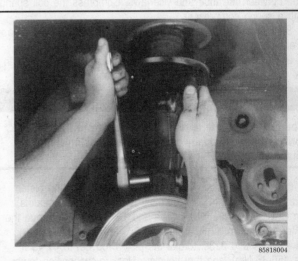

Fig. 8 Use two wrenches to loosen the bolts which secure the lower end of the shock absorber assembly

Fig. 9 Remove the nuts, washers and bolts . . .

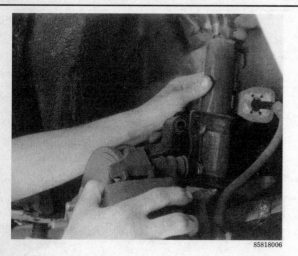

Fig. 10 . . . then separate the shock absorber from the steering knuckle arm

side between the tube and vice jaws. Compress the coil spring with a spring compressor.

8. Hold the upper end of the shock piston rod with a pipe wrench and unfasten the locknut.

9. Remove the parts from the top of the shock absorber in the order shown in the appropriate illustration.

❈❈CAUTION

When removing the spring compressor from the coil spring, do so gradually so that spring tension is not released all at once.

10. During installation, tighten the nut on top of the piston rod to 10 ft. lbs. (14 Nm) on most rear wheel drive models. On GLCs with front wheel drive and 1979-82 626s, torque the piston rod nut to 47-59 ft. lbs. (64-80 Nm). On front wheel drive GLCs and 323s, torque the piston rod nut to 41-49 ft. lbs. (56-66 Nm), and the mounting block-to-suspension tower to 17-21 ft. lbs. (23-28 Nm). On 1983-87 626s, torque the piston rod nut to 47-59 ft. lbs. (64-80 Nm), the mounting block-

to-suspension tower nuts to 16-21 ft. lbs. (21-28 Nm), and the lower strut bolts to 69-86 ft. lbs. (93-117 Nm).

On 1983-87 front wheel drive models, there is a mark or hole in the mounting block. Be sure it faces the inside of the vehicle when positioning the block.

➥**If a new coil spring is being fitted, match it with an adjusting plate of the correct thickness to obtain equal road clearance on both sides. Do not use more than two adjusting plates on a side.**

1988-89 323

1. Loosen the front lug nuts, then raise the front of the vehicle and support it safely. Remove the front wheels.

2. On vehicles equipped with Adjustable Shock Absorbers (ASA), peel the rubber cap from the ASA actuating unit to expose the retaining screws. Disengage the electrical connector from the actuating unit. Loosen the retaining screws and remove the actuating unit from the mounting block.

3. Remove the nuts from the strut mounting block. Remove the brake line clip and separate the brake line from the strut tower mounting tab. Position the brake line off to the side.

4. Remove the two bolts from the shock tower mounting bracket and remove the strut assembly.

5. To install, position the strut assembly onto the suspension tower so that the white dot on the mounting block faces toward the inside of the vehicle. Maneuver the shock tower mounting bracket onto the steering knuckle and insert the two bolts. Install the mounting block nuts and make them finger-tight. Torque the shock tower mounting bolts to 69-86 ft. lbs. (93-117 Nm). Place the brake line into the mounting tab on the shock tower and push the brake line clip to hold it in place. Torque the mounting block nuts to 22-27 ft. lbs. (30-37 Nm).

6. On ASA equipped vehicles, place the actuating unit onto the mounting block and install the retaining screws. Torque the retaining screws to 14-21 ft. lbs. (19-28 Nm). Fasten the electrical connector and install the rubber cap.

7. Install the front wheels and lower the vehicle.

1988-89 626 and MX-6

1. Loosen the front lug nuts, then raise the front of the vehicle and support it safely. Remove the front wheels.

2. Remove the brake line clip and separate the brake line from the strut tower mounting tab. Position the brake line off to the side.

3. On vehicles equipped with ABS, use a long extension to remove the ABS harness bracket bolt. Remove the harness and bracket, then position them off to the side and out the way. On vehicles equipped with Auto Adjusting Suspension (AAS), peel the rubber cap from the AAS actuating unit to expose the retaining screws. Disengage the electrical connector from the actuating unit. Loosen the retaining screws and remove the actuating unit from the mounting block.

4. Remove the two nuts and one bolt and remove the ignition coil bracket from the mounting block studs. Remove the lower clinch bolts and mounting block nuts. Remove the strut assembly from the vehicle. Remove the adjust plate from the mounting block.

To install:

5. Place the adjusting plate on the mounting block. Position the strut assembly onto the suspension tower so that the white dot on the mounting block faces the towards the inside of the

vehicle. Maneuver the shock tower mounting bracket onto the steering knuckle and insert the two bolts. Install the mounting block nuts and make them finger-tight. Torque the shock tower mounting bolts and the mounting block nuts to 69-86 ft. lbs. (93-117 Nm).

6. Connect the ignition coil bracket to the mounting block. On AAS equipped vehicles, place the actuating unit onto the mounting block and install the retaining screws. Torque the retaining screws to 14-21 ft. lbs. (19-28 Nm). Engage the electrical connector and install the rubber cap. On ABS equipped vehicles, connect the ABS harness and bracket to the shock tower, then torque the mounting bolt to 12-17 ft. lbs. (16-23 Nm).

7. Place the brake line into the mounting tab on the shock tower and push the brake line clip to hold it in place. Install the front wheels and lower the vehicle.

929

1. Loosen the front lug nuts, then raise the front of the vehicle and support it safely. Remove the front wheels.

2. Remove the brake line clip and separate the brake line from the strut tower mounting tab. Position the brake line off to the side.

3. On vehicles equipped with Auto Adjusting Suspension (AAS), remove the AAS harness bracket bolt. Remove the harness and bracket, then position them off to the side and out the way. Disengage the electrical connector from the AAS actuating unit. Peel the rubber cap from the AAS actuating unit.

4. Remove the lower clinch bolts and mounting block nuts. Remove the strut assembly from the vehicle.

5. To install, position the strut assembly onto the suspension tower so that the white dot on the mounting block faces the towards the inside of the vehicle. Maneuver the shock tower mounting bracket onto the steering knuckle and insert the two bolts. Install the mounting block nuts and make them finger-tight. Torque the shock tower mounting bolts to 69-86 ft. lbs. (93-117 Nm) and the mounting block nuts to 23-33 ft. lbs. (31-45 Nm).

6. On AAS equipped vehicles, engage the electrical connector and install the rubber cap. Connect the AAS harness and bracket to the shock tower, then torque the mounting bolt to 12-17 ft. lbs. (16-23 Nm).

7. Place the brake line into the mounting tab on the shock tower and push the brake line clip to hold it in place. Install the front wheels and lower the vehicle.

RX-7

▶ See Figure 11

The RX-7 uses a strut-type front suspension in which shock absorber and coil spring are mounted on a rotating strut. (This assembly takes the place of the conventional upper arm and ball joint.) The strut is fastened to the upper inside fender well and to the lower arm. The front suspension is equipped with both tension rods and a stabilizer bar.

1. Raise the front of the car and support it safely

2. Remove the front wheel, brake caliper and rotor assembly (see Section 9).

3. On 1979-85 models, remove the brake backing plate. Remove the brake fluid hose attaching clip on the strut and

remove the two bolts attaching the strut to the steering knuckle/lower arm assembly.

4. Open the engine compartment and note the position of a triangular mark on the top of the strut (it must be installed in the same location it is now facing). On 1986-89 models, there is white dot painted on the mounting block instead of a triangle. During installation, the dot must face towards the front inside of the engine.

5. On 1979-85 models, after installing the strut, measure the distance from the ground to the center of each headlight. If the distance on each side is not within 0.59 in. (15mm) of the other side, adjust the height with adjusting plates available from your local Mazda dealer. Do not use more than two adjusting plates on each side.

6. Tighten the upper strut attaching nuts to 17-22 ft. lbs. (23-30 Nm) and the knuckle arm to strut bolts to 43-51 ft. lbs. (58-69 Nm).

OVERHAUL

➡Strut overhaul includes removal and installation of both the coil spring and shock absorber.

1. Remove the strut from the vehicle, as previously described. Loosen but DO NOT remove the center attaching nut at the top of the strut.

2. Hold the strut in a protected jaw vise and compress the coil spring using a suitable spring compressor.

3. Remove the lock nut and washer from the top of the strut, then remove the mounting block and adjusting plate, the seat, thrust bearing and spring seat.

4. Remove the coil spring, the shock absorber dust boot and the rebound bumper.

5. To test the shock absorber, hold the strut in its upright position and work the piston rod up and down its full length of travel four or five times. If a strong resistance is felt, the shock absorber is functioning properly. If the resistance is not strong, or if there is a sudden lack of resistance, the shock absorber is defective and should be replaced. If the outside of the strut is covered with shock oil the absorber should be replaced.

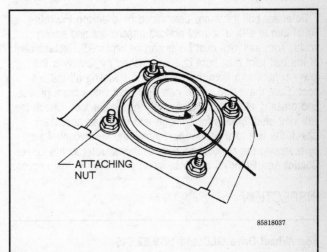

ATTACHING NUT

85818037

Fig. 11 Note the location of the triangular mark before removing the strut

6. Hold the strut body in a vise, then remove the cap nut cover and the cap nut. Mazda makes a special socket (tool number 49-0259-700A) to remove the cap nut.

7. Remove the O-ring on the piston rod guide.

8. Remove the inner shock absorber assembly from the strut tube.

9. Check all strut components for wear, and check the coil spring for cracks. Check the shock absorber seal for damage. Drain and clean the strut.

10. Assembly is essentially the reverse of disassembly. Observe the following.

➡**Cartridge shock absorbers are available as replacements for the open oil type.**

11. If open oil type shock absorbers are used:

a. Install the shock piston and fill the reservoir with 225cc of fresh shock absorber fluid.

b. Install the special pilot (tool number 49-0370-590) or some other protector over the threads of the shock absorber plunger rod (in order to protect the oil seal in the cap nut), grease the seal and install the cap nut carefully onto the strut.

c. Tighten the cap nut temporarily with the plunger rod extended as far as it will go. Make sure the rod is not binding.

d. Fully lower the piston rod and tighten the cap nut to 36-43 ft. lbs. (49-58 Nm) with nut wrench (tool number 49 0259 700A).

12. On cartridge type shock absorbers, tighten the cap nut to 58-108 ft. lbs. (79-146 Nm) with nut wrench tool number 49-0259-700A.

13. Apply rubber grease to the upper strut thrust bearing.

Ball Joints

▶ **See Figure 12**

➡**Ball joints are pressed into the lower control arms and cannot be removed. In the event of a defective ball joint, the lower control arm and ball joint must be replaced as an assembly.**

Defective ball joints are determined by checking the rotational torque with a special preload attachment and spring scale. Torn ball joint dust boots can be replaced. Replacement of the ball joint dust boot is accomplished by removing the lower control arm from the vehicle and chiseling off the old boot. Coat the inside of the new dust boot with lithium grease and press it into the ball joint using the proper tool. Check the ball joint stud threads for damage and repair as necessary. Check the ball joint preload and install the lower control arm by reversing the removal procedure. Please refer to the Lower Control Arm Removal and Installation procedure in this section.

INSPECTION

Rear Wheel Drive GLC and 1979-82 626

1. Check the dust boot for wear or cracks, and replace if necessary.

2. Raise the vehicle until the wheel is off the ground. Grab the tire at top and bottom, then alternately pull it toward you

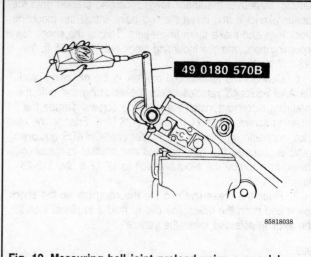

Fig. 12 Measuring ball joint preload using a special attachment and spring scale

and push it away to check for ball joint end-play. Wear limit is 0.04 in. (1mm). If necessary, replace ball joint and control arm assembly. See control arm removal and installation procedure above. When installing ball joint nut, torque to 43-51 ft. lbs. (58-69 Nm) on the GLC and 46-69 ft. lbs. (62-93 Nm) on the 626.

Front Wheel Drive GLC

1. Raise the vehicle and support it securely. Remove the front wheel.

2. Unbolt the ball joint where it connects to the lower arm. Put the hook of a spring scale in the outer bolt hole. Turn the ball joint back and forth several times and then measure the rotating torque on the spring scale. Turn the joint slowly and make sure the scale stays at 90 degrees to the joint lever. Rotating torque should be 6.3-10.9 lbs. Otherwise, replace the ball joint.

323, MX-6, 929 and RX-7; 1983-89 626

➡**This procedure is usually done with a preload attachment tool, such as Mazda No. 49-0180-510B or equivalent . Do not attempt to make this test without the proper tool.**

1. Raise and support the vehicle safely. Remove the wheel.

2. Remove the cotter pin and nut (which secure the tie-rod end) from the knuckle arm, then use a puller to separate the tie-rod from the knuckle.

3. Unbolt the lower end of the shock absorber.

4. Remove the nut, then withdraw the rubber bushing and washer which secure the stabilizer bar to the control arm.

5. Unfasten the nut and bolt which secure the control arm to the frame member.

6. Check the ball joint dust boot for cracks and tears. Replace as necessary.

7. Shake the ball joint stud a couple of times before measuring the preload. Check the amount of pressure required to turn the ball stud, by hooking a pull scale into the tie rod hole in the knuckle arm. Pull the spring scale until the arm just begins to turn, this should require 4.4-7.7 lbs. on the 626, MX6 and 1986-89 RX-7, 1-2.2 lbs. on the 1986-87 323, 4.0-6.8 lbs. on 1988-89 323 and 1.1-2.6 lbs. on the 929. If the reading is

lower than 1.2 lbs. on the 1979-85 RX7, replace the ball joint and the suspension arm as a unit.

REMOVAL & INSTALLATION

Rear Wheel Drive GLC and 1979-82 626

Refer to the Control Arm removal and installation procedure. When installing the ball joint nut, torque it to 43-51 ft. lbs. (58-69 Nm) on the GLC or 46-69 ft. lbs. (62-93 Nm) on the 626.

Front Wheel Drive GLC

1. Raise the vehicle and support it securely by the front crossmember. Remove the front wheel.
2. Remove the pinch bolt and nut from the bottom of the strut. Pull the ball stud out.
3. Remove the two bolts attaching the joint lever to the lower control arm, and remove the assembly.
4. Install in reverse order. Check and adjust front end alignment, if necessary.

323, MX-6, 929 and RX-7; 1983-89 626

See the following procedure for lower control arm removal and installation. If the ball joint is defective, the control arm and joint are replaced as an assembly.

Control Arm

REMOVAL & INSTALLATION

Rear Wheel Drive GLC and 626, 929 and RX-7
▶ See Figure 13

1. Loosen the front lug nuts, then raise the front of the vehicle and support it safely. Remove the front wheels.
2. Remove the brake line clip and separate the brake line from the strut tower mounting tab. Position the brake line off to the side.
3. Remove the cotter pin and nut (which secure the tie-rod end) from the knuckle arm, then use a puller to separate the tie-rod from the knuckle.
4. Unfasten the bolts which secure the lower end of the shock absorber to the knuckle arm.
5. Remove the nut then withdraw the rubber bushing and washer which secure the stabilizer bar to the control arm.
6. Unfasten the nut and bolt which secure the control arm to the frame member.
7. Push outward on the strut assembly while removing the end of the control arm from the frame member.
8. Remove the control arm and steering knuckle arm as an assembly.
9. Install the assembly in a vise. Remove its cotter pin and unfasten the ball joint nut; then separate the knuckle arm from the control arm with a puller.
10. Installation of the control arm is performed in the reverse order of its removal. Torque the control arm-to-crossmember nut and bolt to 29-40 ft. lbs. (39-54 Nm).

1981-82 Front Wheel Drive GLC

1. Loosen the wheel lugs, raise the car and safely support it on jackstands. Remove the front wheel.
2. Remove the through-bolt connecting the lower arm to the steering knuckle.
3. Remove the bolts and nuts mounting the control arm to the body (two inner and three outer).
4. Remove the lower control arm.
5. Installation is the reverse order of removal. Mounting Torque:
   - Ball Joint to Steering Knuckle: 32-40 ft. lbs. (43-54 Nm)
   - Outer Bolts: 43-54 ft. lbs. (58-73 Nm)
   - Inner Bolts: 69-86 ft. lbs. (93-117 Nm)

1983-85 Front Wheel Drive GLC

1. Support the vehicle front end via the crossmember on axle stands.
2. Remove the two bolts which fasten the ball joint to the lower arm.
3. Now, remove the two bolts attaching the rear of the lower arm to the body, and the three connecting the front of the lower arm to the body.
4. To install, reverse the removal procedure, torquing the front three bolts mounting the unit to the body to 69-86 ft. lbs. (93-117 Nm), and rear body bracket bolts to 43-54 ft. lbs. (58-73 Nm), and the knuckle to arm bolts to 32-40 ft. lbs. (43-54 Nm).

1983-89 626 and MX-6

1. Support the front of the vehicle via the crossmember on safety stands. Remove the splash shield from the side on which you'll be working.
2. Remove the two locknuts, washers, bushings, bolt and spacer that link the stabilizer bar to the lower arm. Keep the parts in order.
3. Remove the pinch bolt and nut, then remove the stem of the ball joint from the strut.
4. Remove the nuts, washers, and bolts which fasten the inner two hinge joints of the arm to the body, then remove the arm.
5. For installation, reverse the above procedures, but wait for final tightening of the two hinge bolts linking the arm to the body until all parts are assembled, the other parts are torqued, and the weight of the car can rest on the wheel. Torque the hinge bolts fastening the arm to the body to 69-93 ft. lbs. at this point. Torque the pinch bolt for the ball joint to 32-39 ft.lb (1983-87) and 27-40 ft. lbs. (1988-89).

1986-89 323

1. Jack up the front of the vehicle and support it with jackstands.
2. Remove the wheel and splash shield. Remove the nut, bolt, bushings and retainers that secure the stabilizer bar to the lower control arm.
3. Remove the pinch bolt and nut, then separate the ball joint from the steering knuckle.
4. Remove the nuts, washers, and bolts which fasten the inner two hinge joints of the arm to the body, then remove the arm.

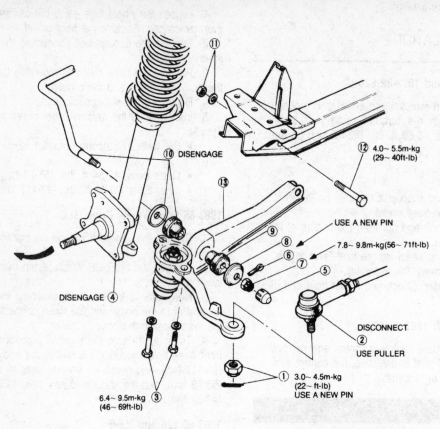

1 Nut/cotter pin
2 Tie rod
3 Bolt/washer
4 Shock absorber
5 Stop

6 Cotter pin
7 Nut
8 Washer
9 Rubber bush
10 Stabilizer bar/washer/rubber bush

11 Nut/washer
12 Bolt
13 Control arm and steering
   knuckle arm

85818039

Fig. 13 Exploded view of the control arm mounting — GLC rear wheel drive models

5. Installation is the reverse of the removal procedure. Torque the lower arm mounting bolt to 66-86 ft. lbs. (89-117 Nm).

929

1. Loosen the front wheel lug nuts. Raise the front of the vehicle and support safely. Remove the front wheels.

2. Remove the nut, retainer and rubber bushing from the lower control arm through-bolt and lift the stabilizer bar from the bolt. Remove the bolt spacer and remove the bolt from the lower control arm with the remaining bushings and retainers. Keep all parts in order.

3. Remove the cotter pin and pinch bolt and nut, then separate the tie rod end from the compression rod.

4. Disconnect and remove the compression rod from the lower control arm by removing the three nuts and bolts.

5. Remove the pinch bolt and nut, then separate the ball joint from the knuckle arm. Remove the lower control arm. Service the ball joint dust boot at this time. Press the old

rubber bushing from the arm and press a new bushing in using special tools 49-HO34-202 and 49-HO34-201.

To install:

6. Maneuver the lower control arm into position, then install the retaining bolt through the bushing and install the nut. Torque the bolt to 54-69 ft. lbs. (73-93 Nm).

7. Connect the knuckle arm to the ball joint and the steering knuckle. Torque the ball joint pinch bolt to 69-91 ft. lbs.

8. Connect the compression rod to the lower control arm with the three nuts and bolts. Connect the tie rod end to the compression rod and secure with pinch nut. Torque the tie rod pinch nut to 69-91 ft. lbs.

9. From underneath the control arm insert the through-bolt with spacer, rubber bushings and retainers in the proper order. Connect the stabilizer bar to the end of the bolt and install the remaining rubber bushings and retainers. Install and tighten the stabilizer bar nut.

10. Install the front wheels and lower the vehicle. Tighten the front wheel lug nuts.

1979-85 RX-7

The lower control arm and ball joint are replaced as an assembly.

1. Jack the front of the vehicle and support it. Remove the front wheels.
2. Remove the two lower strut to steering knuckle bolts.
3. Disconnect the tie-rod end at the steering knuckle by removing its cotter pin and castle nut, then breaking it free with either a puller or a ball joint removal tool.
4. Disconnect the stabilizer bar and the tension rod from the control arm.
5. Remove the nut attaching the steering knuckle arm to the lower control arm and disconnect the knuckle arm using a suitable puller.
6. Remove the control arm-to-crossmember attaching bolt and remove the control arm.
7. Check the control arm and steering knuckle arm for deformities and cracks, check the control arm bushings for damage. New bushings can be pressed into the control arm.
8. If the ball joint dust covers are ripped, but the ball joint itself is still good, remove the dust boot retaining ring with a drift and remove the dust boot. Fill the new dust boot with lithium grease and install it on the ball joint. Press the retaining ring into place using a large socket and a vise.
9. Install the control arm in the reverse order of removal, noting the following: when installing the control arm to crossmember attaching bolt, tighten it finger-tight until the whole assembly is installed, then lower the car and jounce it a few times to settle the bushing, then tighten the bolt to 29-40 ft. lbs. (39-54 Nm). Tighten the ball joint-to-knuckle arm nut to 43-51 ft. lbs. (58-69 Nm), tighten the knuckle arm to strut bolts to 43-51 ft. lbs. (58-69 Nm) and tighten the tension rod to control arm fastener to 40-50 ft. lbs.

1986-89 RX-7

1. Jack the front of the vehicle and support it safely. Remove the front wheels.
2. Disconnect the stabilizer bar from the control link by removing the nut and bolt.
3. Remove the bolt that attaches the control link to the control arm. Disconnect the control link from the control arm.
4. Remove the control arm-to-steering knuckle bolt. Remove the bolts that attach the control arm to the frame. Remove the control bushing through-bolt.
5. Remove the lower control arm. Service the ball joint dust boot at this time. If the ball joint is defective, replace the lower control arm.
6. To install, maneuver the lower control arm into position, then insert the control bushing through-bolt and make the nut hand-tight. Install the frame, steering knuckle and control link attaching bolts. Tighten all the bolts and nuts properly.
7. Connect the stabilizer bar to the control link and tighten the bolt.
8. Install the front wheels and lower the vehicle.

Tension Rod and Stabilizer Bar

REMOVAL & INSTALLATION

1979-82 626

1. Raise the vehicle and support it safely.
2. Remove the tension rod attaching nuts from the suspension arm.
3. Remove the nuts, washers and rubber bushings holding the tension rod to the bracket, then remove the tension rod.
4. Remove the control rod assembly.
5. Remove the stabilizer bar support plate and bushings.
6. Install the stabilizer bar bushings and support plate. When installing the stabilizer bushing with the support plate, place the open end of the bushing toward the front.
7. Install the control rod assembly.
8. Install the tension rod and bracket with bushings and washers.
9. Install the tension rod attaching nuts to the suspension arm.
10. Lower the vehicle.

1983-85 GLC

1. Raise the vehicle and support it securely on axle stands. On both sides, unlock the two locknuts and remove the washers, bushings, spacer and bolt that fastens the sway bar to the front suspension. Keep all parts in order.
2. Now, on either side, remove the two machine screws which fasten the sway bar bushing to the body via a U-shaped clip, and remove the clip. The bar will now be released and can be removed.
3. To install, the removal procedure should be reversed. Torque the nuts linking the bar to the suspension arm until 0.24 in. (6mm) of bare thread is exposed.

1983-89 626, MX-6 and 929
▶ See Figure 14

1. Raise the vehicle and support it securely on axle stands.
2. Remove the engine under cover on 929.
3. On both sides, unlock the two locknuts and remove the washers, bushings, spacer and bolt that fastens the sway bar to the front suspension. Keep all parts in order.
4. Now, on either side, remove the two machine screws which fasten the sway bar bushing to the body via a U-shaped clip, and remove the clip. The bar will now be released and can be removed.
5. Installation is the reverse of removal. Tighten the nuts linking the bar to the suspension arm until 0.24 in. (6mm) of bare thread is exposed. Torque the machine screws which fasten the U-shaped clip and bushing to the body to 32-39 ft. lbs. for 1983-87 626s, 27-40 ft. lbs. for 1988-89 626/MX-6s and 37-45 ft. lbs. for 929s. Also, when assembling the U-shaped rubber bushings to the bar, align the bushing with the line on the bar and install it so the slit faces the rear of the car. On 929s, this line is yellow. Tighten the locknuts on top of the bolt linking the sway bar to the steering knuckle until 0.98 in. (25mm) of bare thread is exposed for 1983-87 626s,

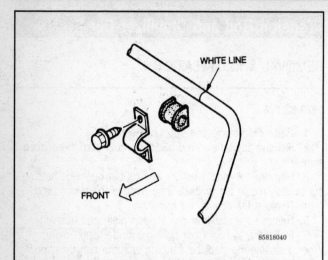

Fig. 14 Align the bushing with the line on the bar, so slit faces rearward — 626/MX-6 shown; 929 similar

0.71-0.91 in. (18-23mm) for 1988-89 626/MX-6s and 0.59 (15mm) for 929s.

1986-89 323

1. Raise the vehicle and support it safely. On 1988-89 323s, remove the engine under cover.

2. Remove the two locknuts, washers, bushings, bolt and spacer that link the stabilizer bar to the lower arm. Keep the parts in order.

3. Remove the nuts, washers, rubber bushings and bracket holding the stabilizer bar to frame and remove the stabilizer bar.

4. Inspect the stabilizer bar for damage such as bends, cracks, or metal deterioration. Inspect the bushings for signs of wear or deterioration and replace as necessary.

5. To install, mount the bushings so that the seam faces the rear of the chassis.

6. Mount the bracket side of the stabilizer first and temporarily tighten it. After mounting the control link side, tighten to the specified torque with the vehicle in the unloaded condition.

7. Tighten the stabilizer bar bushing and bracket bolts to 23-34 ft. lbs. (31-46 Nm).

8. On 1986-87 323s, tighten the bushing to control arm nut so that there is 0.43 in. (11mm) of thread exposed at the top of the control link. On 1988-89 models, the control link stud has two sets of nuts on each side. Torque each top nut to 9-13 ft. lbs.

1979-85 RX-7

▶ See Figures 15 and 16

1. Raise the front of the vehicle and support it on jackstands.

2. Remove the engine gravel shield.

3. Unfasten the tension rod attaching nuts and remove the tension rod.

4. Disconnect both ends of the stabilizer bar from the control links.

5. Remove the stabilizer bar support plates and rubber bushings.

6. Remove the right and left brackets which mount tension rods and stabilizer bar to the body, then remove the stabilizer.

7. Install the stabilizer bar brackets (with the stabilizer bar in them) to the body and tighten the attaching nuts.

8. Install both ends of the stabilizer bar to the control links and tighten the nuts so that 0.51 in. (13mm) of the bolt threads protrude from above the nut as shown in the illustration.

9. Install the stabilizer bar rubber bushings and support plates so that the open end of the bushing is positioned toward the front of the car. Tighten the support plate attaching bolts temporarily.

10. Install the front ends of the tension rods to the brackets and tighten nut **A** in the illustration so that 0.28 in. (7mm) of threads protrude above the nut. Then tighten nut **B** to 80-108 ft. lbs. Make sure you install the rubber bushings as shown in the illustration.

11. Install the rear of the tension rods to the control arms and tighten the nuts to 40-50 ft. lbs.

12. Lower the vehicle and jounce it a few times, then tighten the support plates of the stabilizer bar.

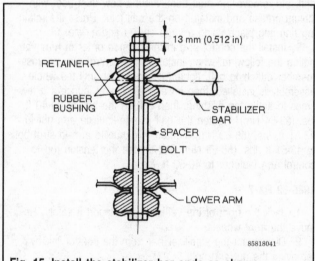

Fig. 15 Install the stabilizer bar ends as shown — 1979-85 RX-7

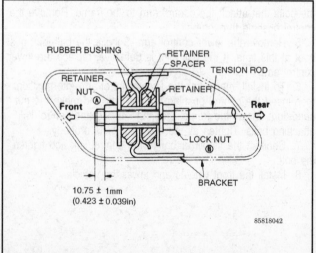

Fig. 16 Install the tension rod ends as shown — 1979-85 RX-7

1986-89 RX-7

▶ See Figure 17

➡This procedure covers removal and installation of the control link also.

1. Raise the front of the vehicle and support it safely.
2. Remove the stabilizer U-bracket bolts, then remove the bracket and the rubber bushings.
3. Disconnect the stabilizer bar from the control link by removing the bolt, nut and washer. Remove the stabilizer bar.
4. Remove the bolt that attaches the control link to the control arm. Disconnect the control link from the control arm and remove it.
5. Inspect the stabilizer bar and control link for damage such as bends, cracks, or metal deterioration. Inspect the bushings for signs of wear or deterioration and replace as necessary.
6. Assemble the U-brackets and bushings onto the stabilizer bar so the bushing seams face the front. Slide the bushings on the bar so that the edges are aligned with the white lines as shown. Install the stabilizer bar and temporarily tighten the bracket bolts. Install the control link to the stabilizer bar and temporarily tighten the bolt.
7. Lower the vehicle and tighten the bracket bolts to 13-20 ft. lbs. and the control link bolt to 27-37 ft. lbs.

Front Wheel Bearings

For front wheel bearing service on rear wheel drive vehicles, see Section 1 of this manual.

Front Hub and Bearing

➡The following procedures apply only to FWD vehicles.

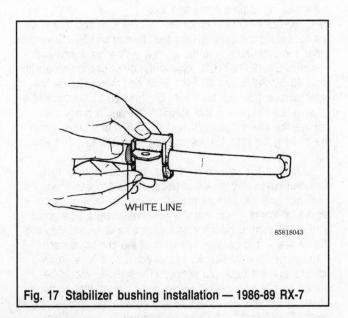

WHITE LINE

85818043

Fig. 17 Stabilizer bushing installation — 1986-89 RX-7

REPLACEMENT

1981-85 GLC (Except Wagon)

▶ See Figure 18

➡This procedure requires many special tools. Check on the availability of these before starting. It may be cheaper for you to have some aspects of the work done professionally than to buy certain tools.

1. Follow the necessary steps of the disc brake rotor removal & installation procedure, as described in Section 9 of this manual, in order to remove the rotor from the hub.
2. Arrange the bearing remover (Mazda tool No. 49-F401-365 or equivalent) and attachment B (49-F401-368 or equivalent) as shown and, with a press, remove the outer bearing's inner race. Make sure the hub does not fall and get damaged.
3. Use a brass drift and a hammer to strike the edge of the outer race and remove it. Tap all around the race, forcing it out in small increments.
4. Wash parts in solvent before inspecting. Inspect the knuckle for damage, rust in the bearing bore, or a bad dust cover or seal.
5. If the dust cover must be replaced, tap it in place with a hammer and a pipe of 3.19 in. (81mm) in diameter. Make sure the dust cover is properly positioned.
6. Fit the bearing outer race into the knuckle with a brass rod and hammer. Make sure it seats in the knuckle.
7. Check the bearing preload by installing a spacer selector (Mazda tool No. 49-B001-727 or equivalent) in a vise and assembling to it the steering knuckle along with the original spacer. Bearing preload (the torque required to start it turning) should be 1.7-6.9 inch lbs (0.2-0.8 Nm). This is equivalent to 0.5-1.9 lbs. measured by a spring scale at the caliper mounting hole of the knuckle. The tool must be tightened to 145 ft. lbs. in 36 ft. lb. increments. As each increment is completed, rotate the bearing to seat it properly, make sure it turns smoothly, then repeat the tightening operation until 145 ft. lbs. is reached. Make sure you again turn the bearing to seat it before reading the preload.
8. If the preload is outside specifications, increase the thickness of the spacer to decrease it if it is too high; decrease the thickness of the spacer to increase the preload if it is too low. There is a mark stamped on the outer periphery of the spacer that represents its thickness (see the table). A change in thickness of one number changes the preload 1.7-3.5 inch lbs. (0.2-0.4 Nm).
9. Substitute a new spacer, and repeat the preload measuring procedure until the preload meets specification.
10. Apply grease to the lip of a new outer oil seal and gently tap it in with a plastic hammer. Make sure the surface is flush with the knuckle when it's installed.
11. In the same way, but using an appropriate installer (Mazda tool No. is 49 B001 795) install a new inner seal.
12. Fill these areas with lithium grease meeting NGLI No. 2 specification: the spaces between the bearing rollers; the space between the inner and outer bearings; the space between each bearing and the adjacent seal.

13. Using the spacer selector described above and a press, install the wheel hub into the knuckle. This requires as much as 6,613 lbs. pressure.

14. Install the knuckle to the suspension system in reverse of the removal procedure, using a new driveshaft locknut, and observing the following torque figures:

- Rotor-to-hub bolts: 33-39 ft. lbs.
- Knuckle-to-strut bolts: 58-86 ft. lbs.
- Knuckle-to-ball joint: 33-39 ft. lbs.
- Lower arm-to-ball joint: 69-96 ft. lbs.
- Knuckle and brake caliper: 41-48 ft. lbs.
- Driveshaft locknut: 116-174 ft. lbs.
- Knuckle-to-tie rod end: 28-32 ft. lbs.

Make sure to stake over the driveshaft locknut with a dull punch until it is indented into the groove in the shaft at least 0.16 in. (4mm). Use a new cotter pin for the tie rod end nut.

Stamped mark	Thickness
1	6.285 mm (0.2474 in)
2	6.325 mm (0.2490 in)
3	6.365 mm (0.2506 in)
4	6.405 mm (0.2522 in)
5	6.445 mm (0.2538 in)
6	6.485 mm (0.2554 in)
7	6.525 mm (0.2569 in)
8	6.565 mm (0.2585 in)
9	6.605 mm (0.2600 in)
10	6.645 mm (0.2616 in)
11	6.685 mm (0.2631 in)
12	6.725 mm (0.2648 in)
13	6.765 mm (0.2663 in)
14	6.805 mm (0.2679 in)
15	6.845 mm (0.2695 in)
16	6.885 mm (0.2711 in)
17	6.925 mm (0.2726 in)
18	6.965 mm (0.2742 in)
19	7.005 mm (0.2758 in)
20	7.045 mm (0.2774 in)
21	7.085 mm (0.2789 in)

85818044

Fig. 18 Spacer thickness selection chart — GLC and 1986-87 323

323, MX-6, and 1983-89 626

▶ See Figures 18, 19, 20, 21, 22 and 23

➡This procedure requires many special tools. Read the procedure over first, and determine availability of the special tools before you start work. In some cases, it may be less expensive to have certain operations performed by a local repair shop than to purchase the appropriate tools.

1. Loosen the lug nuts. Raise the vehicle and support it safely. Remove the tire and wheel.

2. Raise the staked tab from the hub center nut, remove the nut from the axle. Apply the brake to help hold the rotor while loosening the nut.

3. Using ball joint puller tool 49-0118-850C or equivalent, separate the tie rod end from the steering knuckle. Disconnect the horseshoe clip that retains the brake line to the strut. On the 626 and MX6, remove the stabilizer bar control link from the control arm as described previously in this section.

4. Remove the mounting bolts that hold the caliper assembly to the knuckle. Do not allow the caliper to be supported by the brake hose; support it with wire.

5. Remove the through-bolt and nut that retains the lower ball joint to the steering knuckle and disconnect the ball joint.

6. Remove the two bolts and nuts retaining the strut to the steering knuckle. Separate the steering knuckle and hub from the strut and axle shaft. On 626 and MX-6 with ABS, remove the speed sensor from the strut bracket.

7. The hub is pressed through the wheel bearings into the knuckle. Removal/replacement of the hub requires wheel hub puller tool No. 49-G030-725/49-G030-727 (or equivalent) for the 1983-87 626 and 323, or Nos. G49-G033-102, 104 and 105 (or equivalent) for 1988-89 626 and MX-6.

➡On 1988-89 626 and MX-6, if there is an inner race on the front wheel hub, grind or machine a section of the bearing inner race to approximately 0.02 in. (0.5mm) and remove it with a small cold chisel.

8. Remove the inner oil seal and bearing. Remove the outer bearing using a press and tool 49-G030-725/49-G030-728 for the 1983-87 626 and 323 in order to remove the bearing from the steering knuckle. Drive the outer and inner race from the knuckle with a brass drift and hammer. On 1988-89 323, remove the outer bearing race with tools 49-B092-372 and 49-F401-366A and then withdraw the outer oil seal from the front hub. On 1988-89 323, remove the bearing outer race with tool 49-FT01-361 and a press and remove the wheel bearing. On 1988-89 626 and MX-6, press the bearing from the hub using tools, 49-G033-102, 104 and 106.

9. Inspect the knuckle for cracks, heat damage, or rust. The dust cover may be left in place unless it is damaged. If it must be replaced, note its position before removal or scribe alignment marks. Then, install a new one using a pipe about 3.19 in. (81mm) in diameter and a hammer or press. Replace the oil seal if it is damaged or worn at the contact surface.

10. Inspect the oil seal for proper position. If it has moved upward, press it back into position. The knuckle should be placed so it is securely supported by its center, that is, the center of the knuckle should be aligned with the spindle of the press. Then, press in the new bearing with a piece of pipe

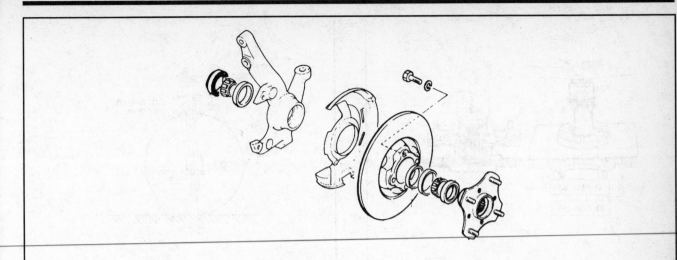

85818050

Fig. 19 Front hub, knuckle and bearing assembly — 323

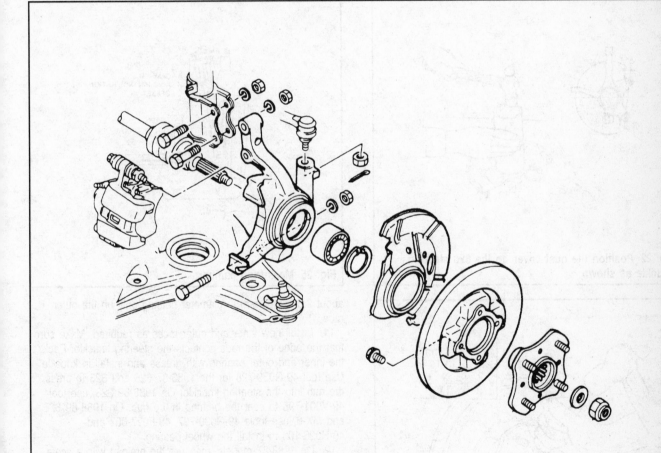

85818051

Fig. 20 Front hub, knuckle and bearing assembly — 626

85818045

Fig. 21 Removing the outer front wheel bearing's inner race — 1983-87 626

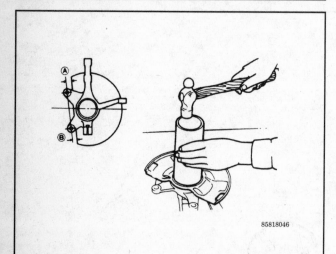

85818046

Fig. 22 Position the dust cover on the 626 steering knuckle as shown

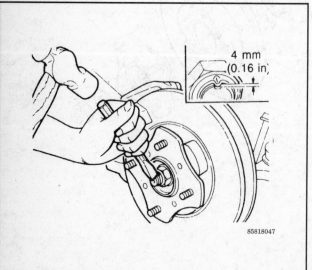

85818047

Fig. 23 Staking the front hub locknut

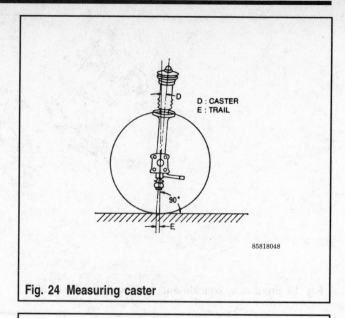

85818048

Fig. 24 Measuring caster

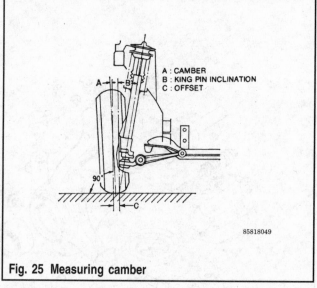

85818049

Fig. 25 Measuring camber

about 2.6 in. (66mm) in diameter bearing only on the outer race.

11. Install new inner and outer races as required. Make sure that the edge of the race contacts the steering knuckle. Pack the inner and outer bearing with grease and install in knuckle. Use tool 49-G030-728 for the 1983-87 626 and 323 to press the hub into the steering knuckle. On 1988-89 323, use tool 49-V001-795 to seat the bearing in the hub. On 1988-89 626 and MX-6, use tools 49-G030-797, 49-F027-007 and 49-H026-103 to install the wheel bearing.

12. On 1983-87 models, measure the preload with a scale connected to the caliper mounting hole on the knuckle. Various spacers are available to increase or decrease the preload. Preload should be 1.7-6.9 ft. lbs.

13. On 1988-89 323, measure/adjust the preload as follows:

a. Insert the bearing and spacer into the steering knuckle and install tool 49-B001-727. Tighten the tool to 145 ft. lbs.

b. Connect a spring scale to caliper mounting bolt hole on the dust cover and pull on the scale to measure the bearing preload (starting rotation torque). This preload should be

0.53-2.55 lbs. for 13 in. wheels and 0.48-2.35 lbs. for 14 in. wheels. When tightening the preload tool, torque in 36 ft. lb. increments.

c. If the preload is not within specification, spacers are available in a variety of thicknesses to adjust it. Increase the spacer thickness when the preload is too high and decrease the thickness when preload is too low.

14. Install the inner and outer grease seals. Press fit the hub through the bearings into the knuckle.

15. Installation of the knuckle and hub is in the reverse order of removal. Always use a new axle locknut and cotter pin. On 323s, torque the axle shaft locknut to 116-174 ft. lbs. On the 626 and MX6 torque the locknut to 116-124 ft. lbs. Stake the locknut after tightening. Use a small cold chisel to stake the locknut tab. After the tab is staked, make sure that at least 0.16 in. (4mm) of the tab is in the groove.

Front End Alignment

CASTER AND CAMBER

▶ **See Figures 24 and 25**

Caster is the forward or rearward tilt of the upper end of the kingpin, or the upper ball joint, which results in a slight tilt of the steering axis forward or backward. Rearward tilt is referred to as a positive caster, while forward tilt is referred to as negative caster.

Camber is the inward or outward tilt from the vertical, measured in degrees, of the front wheels at the top. An outward tilt gives the wheel positive camber. Proper camber is critical to assure even tire wear.

Caster and camber are preset by the manufacturer. They require adjustment only if the suspension and/or steering linkage components are damaged; with the exception of RX-7s and rear wheel drive 626s, caster and camber changes can only be made by replacing damaged parts.

On 1979-82 626s, caster and camber may be changed by rotating the shock absorber support. If they cannot be brought within specifications, replace or repair suspension parts as necessary.

On RX-7s, caster and camber are adjusted by changing the position of the upper strut mounting block.

➡ **Front end alignment is not a procedure for the do-it-yourselfer. Since caster and camber are best checked with an alignment machine, figures in the accompanying chart** are only intended for reference. Measurement and adjustment procedures are only given here for toe-in setting, which is adjustable on all vehicles.

TOE-IN

▶ **See Figure 26**

Toe-in is the difference in the distance between the front wheels, as measured at both the front and rear of the front tires.

1. Raise the front of the car so that its front wheels are just clear of the ground.

2. Use a scribing block to mark a line at the center of each tire tread while rotating the wheels by hand.

3. Measure the distance between the marked lines at both their front and rear.

➡ **Take both measurements at equal distances from the ground.**

4. Toe-in is equal to the difference between the front and rear measurements (front figure is smaller).

5. To adjust the toe-in, loosen the tie rod locknuts and turn both tie rods an equal amount until the proper measurement is obtained.

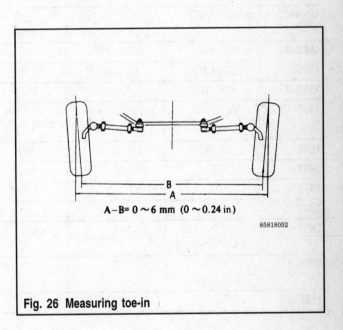

A−B= 0 ~ 6 mm (0 ~ 0.24 in)

85818052

Fig. 26 Measuring toe-in

WHEEL ALIGNMENT

Year	Model	Caster (deg.) Range	Caster (deg.) Preferred	Camber (deg.) Range	Camber (deg.) Preferred	Toe-in (in.)	Kingpin (deg.)
1978	GLC RWD CPE	5/8P to 2 1/3P	1 29/60P	1/3P to 1P	2/3P	0–0.24	8.5
1979–80	GLC RWD CPE	1/4P to 2 2/5P	1 1/3P	1/4P to 1 1/4P	3/4P	0–0.24	8.75
1979–82	GLC StaWgn	1P to 2 1/2P	1 3/4P	1/2P to 1 1/2P	1P	0–0.24	8.75
1983	GLC StaWgn	5/6P to 2 1/3P	1 3/5P	1/4P to 1 1/4P	3/4P	0–0.24	8.72
1981–82	GLC FWD	1 1/6P to 2 2/3P	1 11/12P	5/12P to 1 5/12P	11/12P	0.12 out to 0.12 in	12.17
1983–84	GLC FWD	1 1/6P to 1 2/3P	1 1/4P	2/5P to 1 2/5P	9/10P	0.12 out to 0.12 in	12.17
1985	GLC FWD	1 3/16P to 2 11/16P	1 15/16P	7/16P to 1 7/16P	15/16P	0–0.25	12.19
1986–87	323	13/16P to 2 5/16P	1 9/16P	1/16P to 1 1/2P	13/16P	0.03–0.25	12.38
1988–89	323 2WD	1 3/16P to 2 5/16P	1 9/16P	5/16P to 1 5/16P	1 3/16P	0.05 out to 0.20 in	12.38
1988	323 4WD	1 3/16P to 2 9/16P	1 13/16P	9/16P to 1 9/16P	1 1/6P	0.09 out to 0.40 in	12.00
1989	323 4WD	1 1/16P to 2 9/16P	1 13/16P	17/32P to 1 17/32P	1 1/16P	0.09 out to 0.40 in	12.00
1979–82	626 RWD	R 2 31/32P to 4 2/5P L 2 2/5P to 3 31/32P	3 3/4P 3 1/6P	3/4P to 1 3/4P	1 1/4P	0–0.24	10.66
1983–84	626 FWD	5/6P to 2 2/5P	1 2/3P	1/6N to 1 5/6P	1/3P	0–0.24	8.72
1985	626 FWD	15/16P to 2 7/16P	1 11/16P	3/16N to 13/16P	5/16P	0–0.24	12.94
1986–87	626 FWD	15/16P to 2 7/16P	1 11/16P	①	②	0–0.24	12.94
1988–89	626 FWD	7/16P to 1 15/16P	1 3/16P	7/16N to 1 1/16P	5/16P	0–0.24	12.19
	MX-6	7/16P to 1 15/16P	1 3/16P	7/16N to 1 1/16P	5/16P	0–0.24	12.19
1988	929	3 3/4P to 5 1/4P	4 1/2P	1/4P to 1 3/4P	1P	0–0.24	12.69
1989	929	4 3/16P to 5 11/16P	4 15/16P	1/4P to 1 3/4P	1P	0.03–0.28	12.69
1979	RX-7	15/16P to 2 7/16P	1 11/16P	11/16P to 13/16P	3/4P	0–0.24	10.75
1980	RX-7	③	④	11/16P to 13/16P	3/4P	0–0.24	10.75
1981–85	RX-7 13 in. wheels	⑤	⑥	1/2P to 1 1/2P	1P	0–0.24	10.75
1981–85	RX-7 14 in. wheels	⑤	⑥	1/16P to 1 1/16P	9/16P	0–0.24	10.75
1986–89	RX-7	3 15/16P to 5 7/16P	4 5/32P	3/16N to 13/16P	5/16P	0–0.24	13.75

① Sedan: 5/6P to 2 1/3P
Coupe: 1P to 2 1/2P
Wagon: 1P to 2 1/3P

② Sedan: 1 1/2P
Coupe: 1 5/6P
Wagon: 1 2/3P

③ Right: 4P to 5P
Left: 3 1/2P to 4 1/2P

④ Right: 4 1/2P
Left: 4P

⑤ Right: 3 11/16P to 4 11/16P
Left: 3 3/16P to 4 3/16P

⑥ Right: 4 13/16P
Left: 3 11/16P

858180C1

REAR SUSPENSION

Springs

REMOVAL & INSTALLATION

GLC Wagon

1. Remove the wheel cover and loosen the lug nuts.
2. Raise the back end of the car and support it with jackstands.
3. Remove the lug nuts and the wheel.
4. Support the rear axle housing with jackstands.
5. Disconnect the lower part of the shock from the spring clamp. Unfasten the nuts which secure the U-bolt. Withdraw the U-bolt seat, rubber pad, plate, and the U-bolt itself.
6. Unfasten the two bolts and the nut that secure the spring pin to the front end of the rear spring.
7. Pry the spring pin out with a large, flat pry bar inserted between the spring pin and its body bracket.
8. Remove the nuts and the bolts which attach the rear shackle to the car's body.
9. Withdraw the rear spring assembly, complete with its shackle.
10. Remove the shackle assembly from the end of the spring.
11. Pull the rubber bushings out from both ends of the spring.
12. When installing the rubber bushings, do not lubricate them. Tighten the U-bolt securing nuts to 30 ft. lbs., and both the spring pin and the shackle pin to 14 ft. lbs.

GLC and 1983-89 626

Rear coil spring removal is performed as part of the shock absorber removal operation. See the appropriate following section for the combined procedure.

1979-82 626

1. Raise the rear end of the vehicle and support it with jackstands. Place the jackstands under the bracket on the front sides of the lower arms.
2. Remove the rear wheel.
3. Place a jack under the rear axle housing to support it.
4. Remove the shock absorber lower attaching nut and disengage the shock absorber form the rear axle housing.
5. Remove the lateral rod from the right side of the axle housing.
6. Remove the upper link attaching nut from the rear of the axle housing.
7. Remove the lower arm attaching nut from the rear axle housing.
8. Remove the control rod attaching nut and remove the bushings, spacer and washers. Disengage the rear stabilizer bar from the control rod if so equipped.
9. Slowly lower the jack to relieve the spring pressure on the lower arm, then remove the spring.
10. During installation of the coil spring, make sure the open end of the spring faces the rear axle housing. Tighten all bolts temporarily then after the vehicle is lowered to the ground

torque to specifications. Upper link and lower arm to axle housing, 66 ft. lbs., Lateral rod to axle housing, 66 ft. lbs.

1979-85 RX-7

▶ See Figures 27 and 28

➡Rear coil spring removal on 1986-89 RX-7 is performed as part of the shock absorber removal operation. See the appropriate following section for the combined procedure.

1. Raise the rear of the vehicle and support it on jackstands. Remove the rear wheel. Support the rear axle under the differential housing with a floor jack.

➡Do not place the jackstands under the rear axle assembly. See the end of Section 1 for proper placement.

2. Disconnect the lower shock absorber mounting bolt. Disconnect the upper link and the lower link where they attach to the rear axle assembly.
3. Disconnect the stabilizer bar front ends (if equipped with a stabilizer bar).
4. Disconnect the right and left watt links at the rear axle housing.
5. Carefully lower the rear axle housing on the floor jack just enough to remove the coil springs.
6. Install the coil spring with the painted mark on the coils positioned closer to the rear axle casing than to the upper spring mount.
7. Connect the ends of the stabilizer bar and tighten the nuts until 0.17 in. (4.3mm) of the bolt threads protrude from the nut.
8. When installing the shock absorber on the left-hand side, install the lower side attaching bolts with the bolt heads facing toward the inside. Install the rear bolt for each upper link with the bolt heads facing toward the inside of the car.
9. When installing all components, temporarily tighten all fasteners, lower the car and tighten all fasteners fully. Observe the following torques:
   - Upper and lower links to bracket: 56-76 ft. lbs.
   - Watt link-to-rear axle: 47-59 ft. lbs. (64-80 Nm)
   - Rear shock absorber lower mount: 47-59 ft. lbs. (64-80 Nm)

Shock Absorbers

REMOVAL & INSTALLATION

Rear Wheel Drive GLC

1. Raise the rear of the vehicle and support securely via the frame side rails. Remove the wheels.
2. Remove the upper shock absorber bolt from inside the fender well.
3. Remove the lower shock bolt and nut, then remove the shock.
4. To remove the rear spring, support the lower control arm with a jack. Remove the pivot bolt which connects the lower control arm and rear axle.

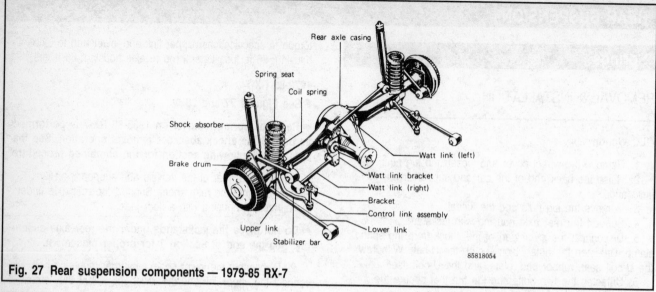

Fig. 27 Rear suspension components — 1979-85 RX-7

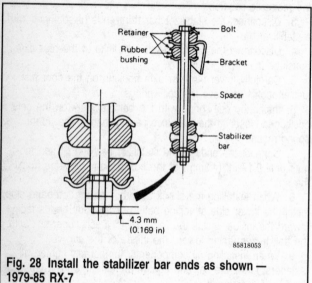

Fig. 28 Install the stabilizer bar ends as shown — 1979-85 RX-7

5. Very slowly lower the jack until the spring pressure has been relieved, and remove the spring.

6. Install the spring in reverse order of removal, but do not fully tighten the pivot bolt. Then, lower the vehicle until it is at normal ride height and torque the bolt to 47-59 ft. lbs. (64-80 Nm).

Front Wheel Drive GLC

1. Remove the side trim panels form inside the trunk. Loosen and remove the top mounting nuts from the shock absorber assembly.

2. Loosen the rear wheel lugs, raise the car and safely support it on jackstands.

3. Remove the rear wheels. Disconnect the flexible brake hose from the strut.

4. Disconnect the trailing arm from the lower side of the strut. Separate the lateral link and strut by removing the bolt assembly.

5. Remove the strut from the lower unit by removing the two through nuts and bolts.

6. Remove the strut, and brake assembly. Clamp the strut assembly in a vise and loosen the nut at the top of the shock absorber.

✳✳CAUTION

Do not remove the nut at this time.

7. Compress the coil spring with a compressor tool. Remove the top nut and bracket. Remove the coil spring.

8. After mounting the strut assembly, lower the car to the ground and torque the mountings; Piston rod and mounting block: 41-60 ft. lbs. Mounting block and tower mount: 16-20 ft. lbs. Lower mounts: 40-50 ft. lbs.

1979-82 626

1. Raise the rear end of the vehicle and place jackstands under the bracket on the front side of the lower arms.

2. Remove the rear wheel.

3. Remove the bracket attaching nuts from the upper end of the shock absorber.

4. Remove the lower shock absorber retaining nut and remove the shock absorber.

✳✳CAUTION

Do not disassemble the gas sealed type shock absorber as it contains highly compressed gas. Defective shocks should be replaced.

5. During installation, torque the upper bracket bolts to 28 ft. lbs., the lower bracket bolts to 32 ft. lbs., and the shock absorber attaching nuts to 53 ft. lbs.

1983-87 626

▶ See Figures 29 and 30

1. Jack up the rear of the vehicle and support the crossmember with safety stands.

2. Remove the bolts and nuts attaching the lower end of the strut to the knuckle spindle, then carefully lower the sus-

pension arm. Remove the brake hose clip from the lower end of the strut. Support the strut from underneath.

3. Remove the rear seat and trim. Remove the attaching nut and washer on either side the strut tower. Now, remove the support and remove the strut from the car.

4. Clamp the shock gently in a vise, using soft metal plates on either side to protect the shock tube from distortion. Keep the piston rod of the shock from turning while using a box wrench to carefully loosen the nut on the piston rod only enough for it to reach the top of the threads. The nut must remain securely fastened because the spring pressure is still dangerous.

5. Use two clamps designed for this purpose to compress the spring, one on either side. When the spring is securely compressed so there is no tension on the spring seat, remove the nut, washer, and mounting block and spring seat. Also remove the dust boot, spring, and stop. You can now replace the shock or have it rebuilt.

6. If you're replacing the spring, make sure to release the clamps carefully and gradually before attempting to remove

Fig. 29 Use two wrenches to unfasten the lower end of the strut (shock absorber) from the knuckle spindle

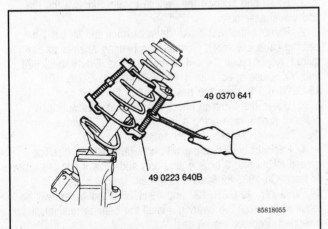

Fig. 30 Compressing the rear spring on a front wheel drive 626. Although Mazda part numbers are shown, an equivalent tool may be used, but it must be designed specifically for this job

them. Also, be sure to clamp the new spring adequately for it to be installed safely. Make sure the spring is properly seated top and bottom and that the seat, block, washer, and nut are secure before releasing spring tension.

7. Once the spring tension is held by the nut at the top of the unit, torque it to 47-59 ft. lbs. (64-80 Nm). Torque the mounting block installation nuts located behind the rear seat to 17-21 ft. lbs. (23-28 Nm), and the bolts fastening the lower end of the strut to the knuckle spindle to 69-86 ft. lbs. (93-117 Nm).

1988-89 626 and MX-6
▶ **See Figure 30**

1. Jack up the rear of the vehicle and support the cross-member with safety stands.

2. Remove the rear wheels. Release the U-shaped clip from the lower shock absorber mounting bracket and move the brake line out of the way. On vehicles equipped with ABS, disconnect the ABS wiring harness and mounting bracket from the lower portion of the shock absorber.

3. Release the trunk side trim fasteners and carefully pull the trim forward to reveal the upper portion of the shock absorber.

4. On vehicles equipped with AAS, disconnect the connector from the AAS actuating unit on top of the spring. Loosen the screws and remove the actuating unit.

5. On vehicles equipped with 4WS, disconnect the strut bar from the forked strut bar bracket by removing the bolt and lockwasher. Unfasten the nuts and remove the bracket from the spring mounting block.

6. Remove the nuts from the mounting block. Remove the lower shock mounting bolts and remove the shock absorber assembly from the vehicle.

7. Disassembly of the rear shock absorber is basically the same as described in Steps 4-6 of the 1983-87 626 procedure. The only step that you will have to add is if your vehicle is equipped with AAS. After the coil spring is removed, use needle nose pliers to check the rotation of the AAS actuating rod. The rod should turn freely. During installation, torque the upper shock absorber nuts to 34-36 ft. lbs. and lower mounting bolts to 69-86 ft. lbs. (93-117 Nm). If equipped with AAS, torque the actuating unit retaining screws to 22-31 inch lbs. (2.5-3.5 Nm).

323

1. Jack up the rear of the vehicle and support it with safety stands. On 1988-89 vehicles equipped with AAS, peel the rubber cover from the actuating unit and disengage the electrical connector. Unbolt the actuating unit from the mounting block.

2. On 1986-87 323s, compress the coil spring by using the coil spring holders 49 0223 640B and 49 0370 641, then remove the nut at the upper end of the piston rod.

3. Remove the bolts and nuts attaching the lower end of the strut to the rear suspension arm, and carefully lower the arm. Remove the brake hose clip from the lower end of the strut and move the brake hose out of the way. Support the strut from underneath.

4. Remove the nuts from the top of the spring mounting block, then remove the shock absorber assembly.

5. Remove the nut and washer that secure the shock absorber to the mounting block, then remove the mounting block,

spring seat and dust boot. Then remove the bound stopper and the coil spring.

6. When installing the spring, check that the spring is well seated in the upper and lower seats. When installing the mounting block on the vehicle, make sure that the white point is to the inside of the vehicle. Torque the upper mounting nuts to 17-22 ft. lbs. (23-30 Nm) and the lower mounting bolts to 45-50 ft. lbs (2WD) and 58-86 ft. lbs. (4WD). If equipped with ASA, torque the actuating unit retaining bolts to 14-21 ft. lbs. (19-28 Nm).

929

1. Jack up the rear of the vehicle and support it with safety stands. Remove the rear wheels.
2. On vehicles equipped with AAS, remove the seal plate from the actuating unit and disengage the electrical connector.
3. Remove the upper mounting nuts and remove the lower mounting bolt and lockwasher.
4. Install the shock with the lower mounting bolt and upper mounting nuts. Torque the lower bolt to 54-69 ft. lbs. (73-93 Nm) and the upper nuts to 17-22 ft. lbs. (23-30 Nm).
5. Connect the AAS actuating unit connector and install the seal plate.
6. Install the rear wheels and lower the vehicle.

1979-85 RX-7

▶ See Figure 31

➡Coil spring removal and installation for 1979-85 models is addressed separately in the preceding "Coil Spring" section. On 1986-89 RX-7s, the coil and shock absorber are one assembly.

1. Raise the rear of the car and support it on jackstands.
2. Remove the rear wheel(s).
3. Open the luggage compartment hatch and remove the side trim from over the upper shock absorber mounts.
4. Disconnect the upper shock absorber mounts.
5. Remove the bolts holding the shock absorber lower ends and remove the shock absorbers.
6. Maneuver the right shock into position and tighten the lower shock mounting bolt to 47-59 ft. lbs. (64-80 Nm).
7. Tighten the upper mounts on the shock absorbers so that 0.32 in. (8.2mm) of thread protrudes from the nut as illustrated.
8. When installing the left side shock absorber, install the lower mounting bolt with its head toward the inside.
9. Install the rear wheels and lower the vehicle.

1986-89 RX-7

Removal and installation of the rear shock absorber is the same as for previous RX-7s, except that on 1986-89 models, the coil and shock absorber are combined as one unit.

BOUNCE TEST

Each shock absorber can be tested by bouncing the corner of the vehicle until maximum up and down movement is obtained. Release the car; it should stop bouncing after one or

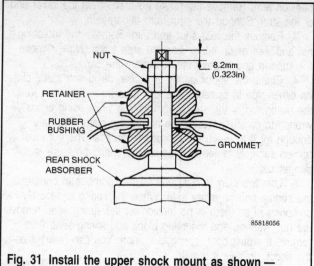

Fig. 31 Install the upper shock mount as shown — 1979-85 RX-7

two bounces. Compare both front corners or both rear corners, but do not compare the front to the rear. If one corner bounces longer than the other, it should be inspected for damage; replace the shock if necessary.

Rear Wheel Bearings

➡The procedures described here apply only to front wheel drive vehicles. For rear wheel bearing replacement on rear wheel drive vehicles, please refer to the rear axle portion of Section 7.

REPLACEMENT

➡On 1988-89 626 and MX-6, a number of special tools are required to remove the rear wheel bearing. Determine the availability of these tools before attempting to service the rear wheel bearings.

1. Raise and support the vehicle safely. Remove the tire and wheel assembly.
2. Remove the rear brake drum or rotor and lift out the bearing cage assembly. Remove the bearing retainer as required. Never reuse the old wheel bearings. On 1988-89 626 and MX-6, use special tools 49-G033-102, 49-G026, 101, 49-G026-103 to drive the bearing out of the rotor disc.
3. Use a blunt drift to knock the bearing race out, then press in a new race using a bench press and suitable mandrel. Tap until the race is fully seated in the hub.
4. Pack the new bearing with a suitable lithium disulfide grease (NGLI No. 2 or is equivalent) and drive it into the drum or rotor. On 1988-89 626s and MX-6s, special tools 49-G030-797, 49-G026-102 and 49-H026 or equivalent will be required to install the bearing. Install the bearing retainer, if so equipped. Replace the oil seal.
5. Complete the installation of the brake drum or rotor in the reverse of the removal procedure. Adjust the bearing preload.

Stabilizer Bar

REMOVAL & INSTALLATION

▶ **See Figure 32**

1. Raise and support the rear end on jackstands.
2. Remove the bolts (along with the bushings, retainers and spacers) which fasten the stabilizer bar to the lateral links.
3. Unfasten and remove the retaining bushings and brackets.
4. Remove the stabilizer bar.
5. Inspect all parts for wear or damage and replace any suspect parts.
6. Installation is the reverse of removal. Install all fasteners hand-tight, then lower the vehicle to the ground. With the weight of the vehicle on the wheels, tighten the retaining bushing bracket fasteners to 38 ft. lbs. (51 Nm). Tighten the lateral link bolts until 0.59 (15mm) of thread is visible above the nut.

85818007

Fig. 32 Each end of the stabilizer bar is fastened to a front lateral link — 1984 626 shown

Rear End Alignment

Due to the complex nature of rear alignment procedures and the equipment needed to perform them, it is best that such an adjustment be referred to an alignment specialist.

STEERING

Steering Wheel

REMOVAL & INSTALLATION

Except RX-7

▶ **See Figures 33, 34, 35, 36, 37 and 38**

1. Remove the screws which secure the ornament or crash pad/horn button assembly to the steering wheel. If there are no mounting screws, pry the pad off, starting at the top. Remove the assembly.
2. Make matchmarks on the steering wheel and steering shaft.
3. Unfasten the steering wheel hub nut. Attach a suitable puller and remove the steering wheel by tightening the puller's center bolt.

✳✳CAUTION

The steering column is collapsible; pounding on it or applying excessive pressure to it may cause it to deform, in which case the entire column will have to be replaced.

4. Installation of the steering wheel is performed in the reverse order of removal. Tighten the steering wheel nut to 25-36 ft. lbs. (34-49 Nm).

RX-7

1. Disconnect the negative battery cable.

85818012

Fig. 33 Common Mazda steering wheel

2. Remove the horn cap and make matchmarks on the steering column shaft and the steering wheel to insure that the wheel is installed in the correct position.
3. Pull the steering wheel off with a puller.

✳✳CAUTION

The steering column is collapsible; pounding on it or applying excessive pressure to it may cause it to deform, in which case the entire column will have to be replaced.

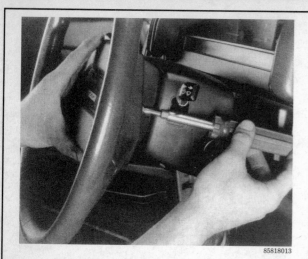

Fig. 34 If applicable, unfasten the screws which retain the cover ornament . . .

Fig. 35 . . . and remove the ornament from the wheel

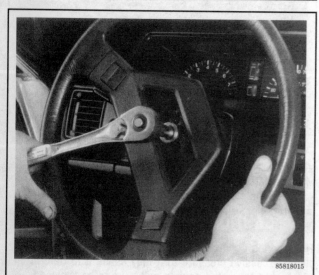

Fig. 36 Unfasten the steering wheel hub nut

Fig. 37 Install a suitable puller and tighten the center bolt to disengage the steering wheel

Fig. 38 When the wheel comes free of the column, remove the puller and then the wheel

4. Install the steering wheel in the reverse order of removal, being sure to align the matchmarks made during removal. Tighten the steering wheel nut to 22-29 ft. lbs. (30-39 Nm).

Turn Signal (Combination) Switch

REMOVAL & INSTALLATION

GLC, 323, 626, MX-6 and 929
▶ See Figures 39 and 40

1. Disconnect the negative battery cable.
2. Remove the horn cap/ornament.
3. Unfasten the steering wheel attaching nut, and remove the wheel with a puller.
4. Unfasten the attaching screws, and remove the upper and lower (or right and left) steering column covers.

85818018

Fig. 39 Separate the two column covers to expose the combination switch

5. Detach the connector for the combination switch or, if the ignition switch is being replaced, detach the connectors for both the ignition and combination switches.

6. Remove the retaining ring from the steering column (not required on 1983-89 626).

7. Unfasten the retaining screw, then remove the combination switch.

To install:

8. Install the combination switch and secure with the retaining screw.

9. Install the steering column retaining ring (if so equipped).

10. Connect all combination or ignition switch connectors.

11. Install the steering column covers with their retaining screws. On 1988-89 626, MX-6 and 929, once the combination switch is in place and the covers are installed, set the front wheels straight, then align the combination switch and steering angle sensor marks as shown.

12. Install the steering wheel and horn cap/ornament.

13. Connect the negative battery cable and check all the functions of the combination switch for proper operation.

Ignition Lock/Switch Assembly

REMOVAL & INSTALLATION

Except RX-7
▶ **See Figure 41**

1. Remove the combination switch as described earlier in this section. Using a small cold chisel and hammer, make a groove in each ignition lock retaining screw wide enough to accept a flat blade screwdriver. Remove the retaining screws, then withdraw the ignition switch assembly.

2. Install the switch with new screws. Break their heads off to make the switch difficult for a thief to remove.

3. Reverse the remaining steps of the removal procedure to install the combination switch. While tightening the steering lock mounting screws, insert the ignition key and check the lock for proper operation.

RX-7

1. Disconnect the negative battery cable.

2. Remove the steering wheel. See above for procedures.

3. Remove the steering column covers and the air duct.

4. Disengage the electrical connections of the switch. Mark them for reassembly.

5. Remove the stop ring cancel cam and spring from the column shaft, then remove the combination switch.

6. Wedge a length of wood or pipe under the switch to protect the steering shaft from the shock of the hammer blows. Using a chisel and hammer, break the bolts that attach the steering lock body to the column jacket. Remove the ignition switch from the column jacket.

7. Use new break-away head bolts to attach the switch body and tighten them until the heads shear off.

8. Install the combination switch, air duct, steering column covers, steering wheel by reversing the removal procedure.

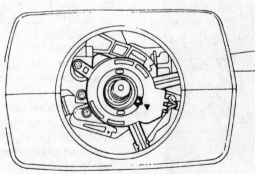

85818058

Fig. 40 Combination switch and steering angle sensor — 1988-89 626, MX-6 and 929

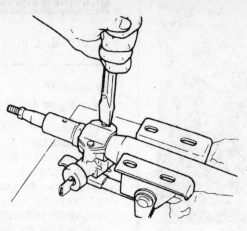

85818059

Fig. 41 Create slots which permit a screwdriver to remove the ignition lock retaining screws

Steering Column

REMOVAL & INSTALLATION

▶ See Figure 42

1. Disconnect the negative battery cable.
2. Remove the steering wheel.
3. Remove the column covers.
4. Remove the lower instrument panel section.
5. Remove the heater duct from under the column.
6. Remove the combination switch.
7. Remove the column bracket-to-instrument panel bolts.
8. Remove the bolt at the steering shaft-to-intermediate shaft coupling bolt and pull the column up and out of the vehicle.

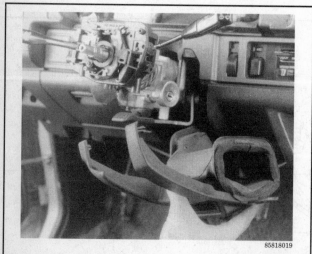

85818019

Fig. 42 The lower instrument panel section may include a blower duct

9. Installation is the reverse of removal. Observe the following torque values:
- Coupling bolt: 87 inch lbs. (10 Nm)
- Column bracket: 17 ft. lbs. (23 Nm)
- Steering wheel nut: 36 ft. lbs. (49 Nm)

Tie Rod Ends

REMOVAL & INSTALLATION

▶ See Figures 43, 44, 45, 46, 47, 48, 49, 50 and 51

1. If an alignment machine is not available, measure the length of the tie rod you'll be working on. Remove the cotter pin(s) and castellated nut(s) from one or both ends of the rod, depending on whether one or both ends require replacement.

➡Mark the relationship between the flats of the tie rod end nut and the tie rod before loosening the nut.

2. Place a wrench on the flat portion of the tie rod end to hold it stationary and loosen the locknut with a second wrench.
3. Use a tie rod end puller to free either or both ends from the steering knuckle or center link. Mazda sells a puller (tool no. 49-0118-850C) designed specifically for this purpose.
4. Unscrew the end from the tie rod.
To install:
5. Loosen the tie rod locknuts, then insert the rod ends through the holes in the steering knuckle and/or center link. If only one end is being replaced, screw the end onto the tie rod, then position the ballstud through the steering knuckle (or center link). Install the castellated nut(s) and torque them to 22-33 ft. lbs. (30-45 Nm), then install new cotter pin(s).
6. If an alignment machine is available, adjust the toe-in, then torque the tie rod locknuts to 51-58 ft. lbs. (69-79 Nm). If the car must be taken to a shop for alignment, turn the tie rod so that the length is the same as it was before the part(s) were replaced, torque both locknuts and have the toe-in checked as soon as possible.

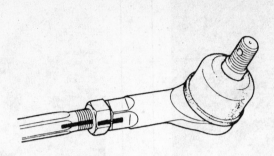

85818060

Fig. 43 Make tie rod end alignment marks before loosening the components

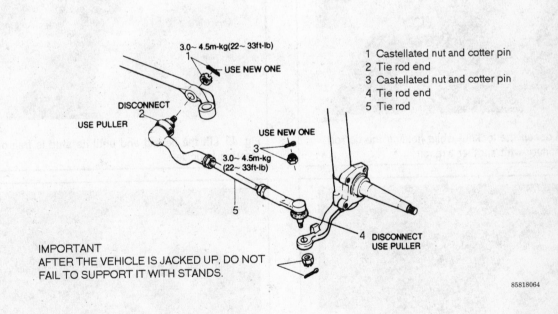

3.0~ 4.5m-kg(22~ 33ft-lb)

1 — USE NEW ONE

DISCONNECT
2
USE PULLER

USE NEW ONE

3

3.0~ 4.5m-kg
(22~ 33ft-lb)

5

1 Castellated nut and cotter pin
2 Tie rod end
3 Castellated nut and cotter pin
4 Tie rod end
5 Tie rod

4 DISCONNECT
USE PULLER

IMPORTANT
AFTER THE VEHICLE IS JACKED UP, DO NOT
FAIL TO SUPPORT IT WITH STANDS.

85818064

Fig. 44 Replacing rear wheel drive GLC tie rod ends

Fig. 45 Remove the cotter pin which passes through the castellated nut and tie rod end

Fig. 46 Loosen the locknut while holding the tie rod end stationary with another wrench

Fig. 47 Remove the castellated nut with a socket wrench

Fig. 48 Separate the tie rod end from the steering knuckle (or center link) with a specialized puller

Fig. 49 Lift the tie rod end until its stud is free of the steering knuckle

Fig. 50 Unscrew and remove the tie rod end

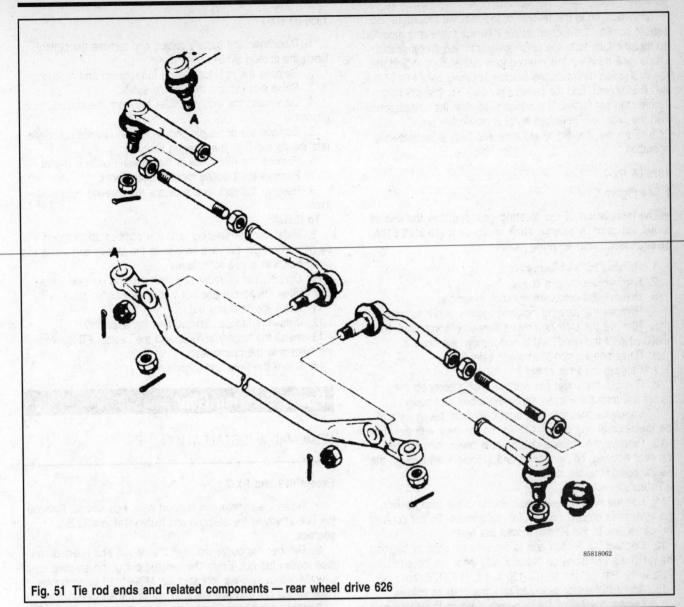

Fig. 51 Tie rod ends and related components — rear wheel drive 626

Manual Steering Gear

REMOVAL & INSTALLATION

Except RX-7

▶ See Figure 52

1. Raise the vehicle's front end and support it on axle stands. Remove the bolt which secures the universal joint in the steering shaft to the gearbox.

2. Remove the cotter pin from the tie rod end ballstud and loosen the nut. Press the ballstud out of the steering knuckle with a vice-like tool such as MB991113 or equivalent, then remove the nut. Do the same on the other side.

3. Cut the band off the steering joint rubber boot.

4. Remove the left and right tie-rods from the gearbox housing, Remove the bolts that secure the mounting bracket and rubber mountings, and pull the gearbox out of the vehicle. Work slowly to keep the unit from being damaged.

Fig. 52 Remove the boot band, then slide the rubber boot off the tie rod

5. Installation is the reverse of the removal procedure. Be sure to position the rubber sleeve in which the unit is mounted so that the tabs fit in the notch away from the crossmember. Use a new band for the steering joint rubber boot. Adjust the toe-in. Tighten the mounting bracket attaching bolts to 43-58 ft. lbs. (58-79 Nm), and the ballstud nut to 17 ft. lbs. (23 Nm). Tighten the nut further, if necessary, to align the castellations with the cotter pin hole and install a new cotter pin.

6. Turn the steering wheel back and forth to test steering operation.

1979-85 RX-7

▶ See Figure 53

➡The installation of the steering gear requires the use of a dial indicator, a column shaft attachment (49-0180-510A or equivalent) and a spring scale.

1. Remove the steering wheel.
2. Remove the column covers.
3. Remove the combination switch assembly.
4. Remove the steering lock and ignition switch assembly.
5. Remove the steering column support bracket. Mark the relationship of the hood hinges and remove the hood.
6. Raise and support the vehicle safely.
7. Remove the front wheel.
8. Remove the cotter pin and nut, then disconnect the center link from the Pitman arm using a ball joint puller.
9. Unbolt the steering gear from the frame, taking note of the presence of any shim for realigning the gear with the shaft.
10. Remove the steering column dust cover, then remove the gear housing, column jacket and aligning shim through the engine compartment.

To install:

11. Bolt the steering gear assembly in place, then position the shim in its original position for realignment. Do not connect the center link to the Pitman arm at this time.
12. Connect the Pitman arm to the selector shaft by aligning the matching serrations on the arm with those on the shaft. Torque the Pitman arm to 108-130 ft. lbs. (146-176 Nm).
13. Adjust the sector gear and rack backlash as follows:
   a. Grasp the sector shaft and move it side-to-side several times to make sure that it turns freely without binding. Then, move the Pitman arm to the center (neutral) position of its travel.
   b. Mount a dial indicator to the Pitman arm end and adjust the backlash of the Pitman arm by turning the adjusting screw in or out until the reading on the dial indicator is 0 (no backlash).
   c. Once the backlash is set, tighten the adjusting screw locknut to retain the adjustment.
14. Install the steering lock and combination switch assembly.
15. Fit attachment 49-0180-510A or its equivalent to the end of the column shaft and connect a spring scale to the attachment. Pull on the spring scale to measure the worm shaft preload. The preload should be 1.32-2.65 lbs. Connect the Pitman arm to the center link.
16. Install the steering column covers and the steering wheel. Fill the steering gear housing with A.P.I GL4, SAE 90 lubricant, if the old fluid was drained. Check the front end alignment.

1986-89 RX-7

1. Disconnect the battery cables and remove the battery. Drain the cooling system.
2. Remove the radiator cooling fan, shroud and radiator.
3. Raise and support the vehicle safely.
4. Disconnect the front stabilizer bar from the steering rack assembly.
5. Remove the cotter pin and tie rod end castle nut. Separate the tie rod from the steering knuckle.
6. Remove the pinch bolt at the steering column U-joint.
7. Remove the steering rack mounting bolts.
8. Remove the rack and separate the steering column U-joint.

To install:

9. Maneuver the steering rack into position and support it by hand. Connect the rack linkage to the U-joint and install the pinch bolt with a new lockwasher.
10. Connect the tie rod end to the steering knuckle. Install and tighten the tie rod end nut with a new cotter pin.
11. Install the stabilizer bar.
12. Install the radiator, shroud and fan assembly.
13. Install the battery and connect the cables. Fill the cooling system to the proper level.
14. Check the front end alignment.

Power Steering Gear

REMOVAL & INSTALLATION

Except 929 and RX-7

1. Raise the vehicle and support it on axle stands. Remove the bolt attaching the steering shaft universal joint to the gearbox.
2. Remove the cotter pin from the tie rod end ballstud and then loosen the nut. Press the ballstud out of the steering knuckle with a vice-like tool such as MB991113 or equivalent. Remove the nut and pull the stud out of the knuckle.
3. Place a drain pan under the gearbox and the disconnect the pressure and return hose connectors with a flare nut wrench, and allow the fluid to drain.
4. Unbolt and remove the two bolts in each gearbox mounting clamp with a ratchet and long extension, working from the engine compartment side.
5. Pull the gearbox out the right side of the vehicle, working carefully to keep the unit from being damaged.
6. Install in reverse order, noting the following points: Make sure the rubber mounting sleeve is positioned so the flat side faces the crossmember and apply adhesive to the rounded side so the slit will not open up when the unit is clamped in place. Torque the gearbox mounting bolts to 43-58 ft. lbs. (58-79 Nm) and the ballstud nut to 17 ft. lbs. (23 Nm), then turn farther to align castellations with the cotter pin hole and install a new cotter pin.
7. Have someone keep the power steering reservoir filled with Dexron®II automatic transmission fluid as you perform this procedure. Disconnect the high tension wire and use the starter to spin the engine while you turn the steering wheel from stop-to-stop several times. Lower the vehicle, reconnect the ignition wire and start the engine, letting it idle. Have

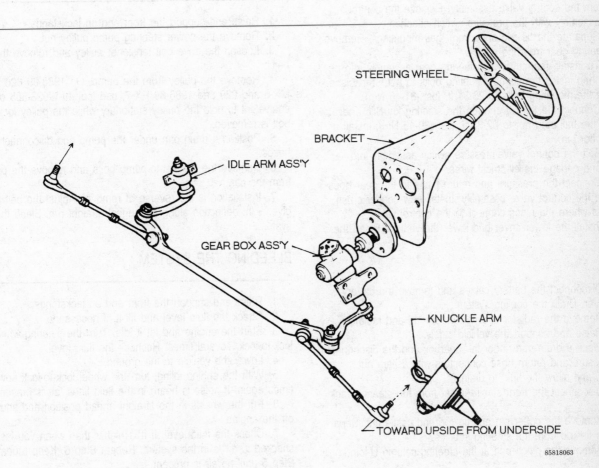

STEERING WHEEL

BRACKET

IDLE ARM ASS'Y

GEAR BOX ASS'Y

KNUCKLE ARM

TOWARD UPSIDE FROM UNDERSIDE

85818063

Fig. 53 Manual steering gear and linkage assembly — 1979-85 RX-7

someone continue to turn the steering wheel from lock-to-lock continuously until there are no more bubbles in the power steering fluid reservoir and the level remains constant as the wheel is turned back and forth. Stop the procedure. Make sure the fluid reservoir is full. Check for leaks. Adjust the toe-in.

929

1. Disconnect the negative battery cable. Raise and support the vehicle safely. Remove the wheel and tire assemblies.

2. Remove the lower steering gear assembly cover. Remove the steering damper.

3. Place a drain pan under the gearbox and the disconnect the pressure and return hose connectors with a flare nut wrench, and allow the fluid to drain. Disengage the electrical wire from the control valve assembly. Remove the control valve assembly with the pressure switch attached.

4. Separate the tie rod ends from their mountings. Remove the steering gear from the vehicle.

5. To install, maneuver the steering gear assembly into position, then install the clamp mounting bolts to hold it in place. Torque the mounting bolts to 23-34 ft. lbs. (31-46 Nm).

6. Connect the tie rod ends to the steering knuckle and torque the ball stud nut to 22-33 ft. lbs. (30-45 Nm). Install a new cotter pin.

7. Bolt the control valve/pressure switch assembly into place and engage the electrical wires.

8. Connect the pressure and return pipes to the gear housing and the control valve assembly. Install new copper crush washers where the pipes connect to the control valve.

9. Install the lower cover and lower the vehicle. Bleed the system.

RX-7

1. Disconnect the battery cables and remove the battery and cover. Drain the cooling system.

2. Remove the radiator cooling fan, shroud and radiator.

3. Raise and support the vehicle safely.

4. Place a drain pan under the gearbox and the disconnect the pressure and return hose connectors with a flare nut wrench, and allow the fluid to drain.

5. Disconnect the front stabilizer bar from the steering rack assembly.

6. Remove the cotter pin and tie rod end castle nut. Separate the tie rod from the steering knuckle.

7. Remove the pinch bolt at the steering column U-joint.

8. Remove the steering rack mounting bolts and power steering hoses.

9. Remove the rack and separate the steering column U-joint.

10. Installation is the same as described for 1986-89 RX-7s with manual steering gear. Bleed the system as described in the following portion of this section. Check the front end alignment.

Power Steering Pump

REMOVAL & INSTALLATION

1. Raise and support the front end on jackstands.

2. Remove the power steering pump pulley nut.

3. Loosen the drive belt tensioner pulley and remove the belt.

4. Remove the pulley from the pump. On 1988-89 626, MX-6 and 929 and 1986-89 RX-7, use tool 49-W023-585 or equivalent to hold the pulley stationary while the pulley lock bolt is removed.

5. Position a drain pan under the pump and disconnect the hoses.

6. Remove the bracket-to-pump bolts and remove the pump from the car.

7. Installation is the reverse of removal. Adjust the belt to give ½ in. deflection along its longest straight run. Bleed the system.

BLEEDING THE SYSTEM

1. Raise and support the front end on jackstands.

2. Check the fluid level and fill it, if necessary.

3. Start the engine and let it idle. Turn the steering wheel lock-to-lock, several times. Recheck the fluid level.

4. Lower the vehicle to the ground.

5. With the engine idling, turn the wheel lock-to-lock several times again. If noise is heard in the fluid lines, air is present.

6. Put the wheels in the straight ahead position and shut off the engine.

7. Check the fluid level. If it is higher than when you last checked it, air is in the system. Repeat Step 5. Keep repeating Step 5 until no air is present.

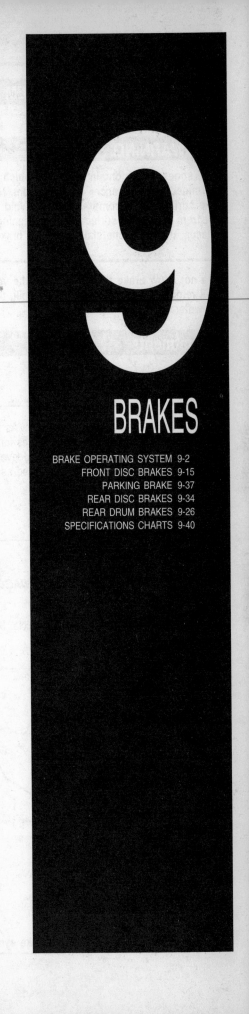

9

BRAKES

BRAKE OPERATING SYSTEM

▶ See Figure 1

✳✳WARNING

Brake shoes often contain asbestos, which has been determined to be a cancer causing agent. Never clean the brake surfaces with compressed air! Avoid inhaling any dust from any brake surface! When cleaning brake surfaces, use a commercially available brake cleaning fluid.

➡Do not allow brake fluid to spill on the vehicle's finish; it will remove the paint. In case of a spill, flush the area with water.

Adjustments

DISC BRAKES

Disc brakes are self-adjusting by design. As the brake pads and discs wear, fluid pressure compensates for the amount of wear. Because this action causes the fluid level to go down, its level should be checked and replenished as often as is necessary.

DRUM BRAKES

Rear Wheel Drive Vehicles

ALL 1978-80 MODELS AND 1981 GLC WAGON

▶ See Figure 2

1. Raise and securely support the vehicle. Make sure the parking brake is fully released.

2. Loosen the anchor pin locknut, then hold the locknut and turn the anchor pin in the indicated direction until the wheel locks.

➡The anchor pins on each wheel are turned in opposite directions. On the right side, the forward pin turns clockwise, and the rear pin counterclockwise. On the left side, the forward pin turns counterclockwise, and the rear pin clockwise.

3. Turn the anchor pin back just until the wheel turns freely. Hold the adjustment and tighten the locknut.

4. Repeat for the other brake shoe on the same wheel, then adjust both shoes on the other rear wheel.

MOST 1981 AND LATER MODELS

▶ See Figure 3

➡These rear drum brakes are self-adjusting and normally only require a manual adjustment after the brake shoes have been replaced, or when the length of the adjusting rod has otherwise been altered.

1. Block the front wheels, raise the car, and safely support it with jackstands.
2. Release the parking brake completely.
3. Remove the adjusting hole plugs from the backing plate.
4. Insert a screwdriver into hole **A**. Engage the star wheel with a screwdriver, then turn it in the direction of the arrow stamped on the backing plate until the brake shoes are fully expanded and the wheel will not turn.
5. Insert a screwdriver into hole **B**. Push the pawl lever of the self-adjuster to turn the adjusting wheel in the reverse direction of the arrow.
6. Back off the star wheel about 3-4 notches. The wheel should rotate freely, without dragging. If it does not, turn the adjuster an additional notch.
7. Fit the plugs into the adjusting hole, then repeat the adjusting procedure for the other side rear brake shoes.

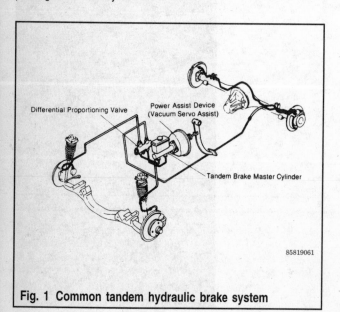

Fig. 1 Common tandem hydraulic brake system

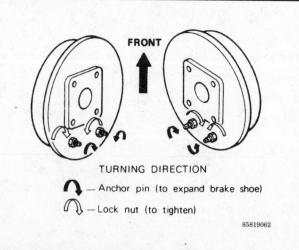

TURNING DIRECTION

↻ —Anchor pin (to expand brake shoe)

⊔ —Lock nut (to tighten)

85819062

Fig. 2 Adjusting the rear drum brakes — 1978-80 models

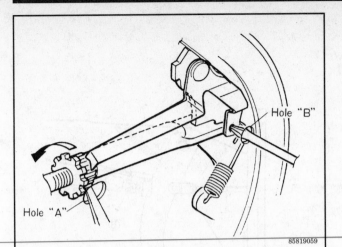

Fig. 3 Drum brake adjustment is made through holes A and B of the backing plate — 1981-85 RWD models

Front Wheel Drive Vehicles

Front wheel drive models are equipped with self-adjusting drum brakes for which no external adjustment is required.

BRAKE PEDAL

1978-82 GLC and 1979-82 626

▶ See Figure 4

1. Detach the wiring from the brake light switch terminals.
2. Loosen the locknut on the switch.
3. Turn the switch until the distance between the pedal and the floor is:
   • GLC with rear wheel drive and manual transmission: 7.50 in. (190mm)
   • GLC with rear wheel drive and automatic transmission: 7.67 in. (195mm)
   • GLC with front wheel drive: 8.50 in. (215mm)
   • 626: 8.67 in. (220mm)
4. Tighten the locknut on the switch, then attach the wiring.
5. Loosen the locknut located on the pushrod.
6. Rotate the pushrod until 0.28-0.35 in. (7-9mm) of pedal free travel is obtained.
7. Tighten the pushrod locknut.

1983-87 626

1. Remove the blower duct. Measure the pedal height (distance from the center of the brake pedal's upper surface to the firewall, behind the insulation). It should be 8.43-8.62 in. (214-219mm).
2. If adjustment is necessary, detach the brake lamp switch electrical connector, then loosen the switch locknut. Turn the switch so that it does not contact the pedal.
3. Loosen the locknut, then turn the operating rod until the pedal height is correct.
4. Depress the brake pedal several times, in order to eliminate vacuum in the line.
5. Gently depress the pedal by hand and check the free-play. If necessary, turn the operating rod until the pedal free-

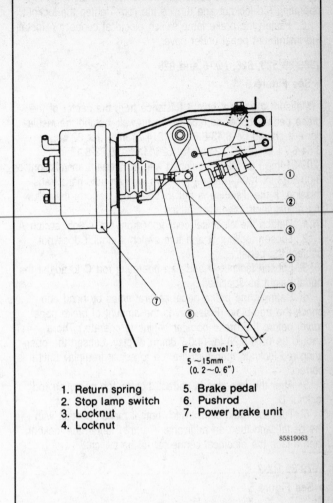

Free travel:
5~15mm
(0.2~0.6")

1. Return spring
2. Stop lamp switch
3. Locknut
4. Locknut
5. Brake pedal
6. Pushrod
7. Power brake unit

Fig. 4 Brake pedal and related components — 1978-82 GLC and 626

play is 0.28-0.35 in. (7-9mm). Tighten the operating rod locknut.
6. Turn the brake lamp switch until it contacts the pedal, and then an additional ½ turn. Tighten the locknut, then attach the electrical connector. Install the blower duct.

1983-85 GLC and 1986-87 323

1. Remove the under cover from the instrument panel. Detach the brake lamp switch electrical connector.
2. Loosen the brake lamp switch locknut, then turn the switch outward until the pedal does not touch it.
3. Loosen the operating rod locknut, then turn the rod to adjust the pedal height to 8.46-8.66 in. (215-220mm) on the GLC, or 8.62-8.82 in. (219-224mm) on the 323. Measure from the center of the brake pedal's upper surface to the firewall (behind the insulation). Fasten the position of the operating rod with the locknut.
4. Screw the brake lamp switch inward until it just touches the pedal, and then an additional ½ turn.
5. Check the free-play in the brake pedal. It should be 0.28-0.35 in. (7-9mm) on the GLC, or 0.16-0.28 in. (4-7mm) on

the 323. If necessary, adjust the free-play by loosening the operating rod locknut and turning the rod. Tighten the locknut.

6. Fasten the brake lamp switch electrical connector. Install the instrument panel under cover.

1988-89 323, 626, MX-6 and 929

▶ See Figure 5

Measure the pedal height (distance from the center of the brake pedal's upper surface to the firewall, behind the insulation). It should be 8.43-8.62 in. (214-219mm) for 323s, 8.54-8.74 in. (217-222mm) for 626/MX-6s, 8.23-8.43 in. (209-214mm) for 929s equipped with a manual transmission, or 8.03-8.23 in. (204-209mm) for 929s with an automatic transmission. If the distance is not as specified, perform the following adjustments (see illustration):

1. Detach the electrical connector from brake light switch **A**.
2. Loosen locknut **B** and turn switch **A** until it does not contact the pedal.
3. Loosen locknut **D** and turn operating rod **C** to adjust the pedal height as specified.
4. Depress the brake pedal several times by hand and check the free-play. (Free-play is the amount of brake pedal travel before the brake booster begins to operate.) There should be 0.16-0.28 in. (4.0-7.0mm) of play. Loosen the operating rod locknut, then turn the rod to adjust free-play until it is correct.
5. After the free-play is correct, tighten the operating rod locknut **D**.
6. Turn the brake light switch until it makes contact with the pedal, and then an additional ½ turn. Tighten the locknut, then attach the electrical connector to the switch.

1979-89 RX-7

▶ See Figure 5

Measure the pedal height (distance from the center of the brake pedal's upper surface to the firewall, behind the insulation). It should be 7.48-7.68 in. (190-195mm) for 1979-85 models, or 8.07-8.27 in. (205-210mm) for 1986-89 models. If the distance is not as specified, perform the following adjustments (see illustration):

1. Detach the connector from brake light switch **A**.
2. Loosen locknut **B** and turn switch **A** until it does not contact the pedal.
3. Loosen locknut **D** and turn operating rod **C** to adjust pedal height as specified.
4. Depress the brake pedal several times by hand and check the free-play. There should be 0.28-0.35 in. (7.0-9.0mm) for 1979-85 models, or 0.16-0.28 in. (4.0-7.0mm) of play for 1986-89 models. Loosen the operating rod locknut and turn the rod to adjust the pedal play until it is correct.
5. After the free-play is within specifications, tighten operating rod locknut **D**.
6. Turn the brake light switch until it makes contact with the pedal, then tighten the locknut. Attach the electrical connector to the switch.

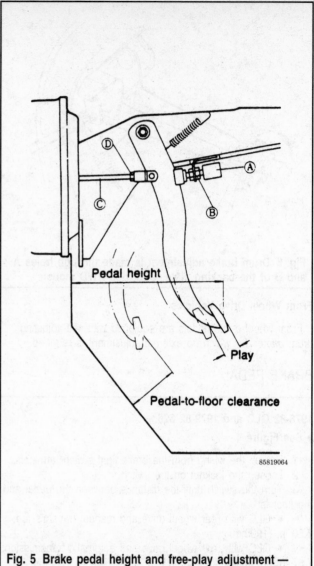

Fig. 5 Brake pedal height and free-play adjustment — 1988-89 323, 626, MX-6 and 929; 1979-89 RX-7

Brake Light Switch

REMOVAL & INSTALLATION

▶ See Figure 6

1. Detach the electrical connector from the switch.
2. Loosen the locknut and adjusting nut, then remove the switch from the mounting bracket above the brake pedal.

To install:

3. Position the switch into the mounting bracket and secure with the attaching nuts.
4. Turn the brake light switch until it makes contact with the pedal, and then an additional ½ turn. Tighten the locknut.
5. Connect the electrical wiring and check the operation of the switch.

Fig. 6 The brake light switch is usually fastened to its bracket with two nuts

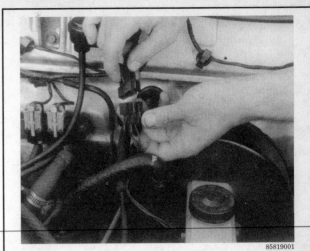

Fig. 7 Disconnect the wire which runs to the fluid level sensor in the master cylinder

Master Cylinder

REMOVAL & INSTALLATION

▶ **See Figures 7, 8, 9, 10 and 11**

1. Remove the air cleaner for clearance if necessary.

2. Detach the fluid level sensor connector and/or the pressure switch connector (bottom of the master cylinder on RX-7s).

3. Place a rag under the hydraulic lines and loosen their fittings at the master cylinder. (If equipped with ABS, loosen, then disconnect the union fittings and washers. Discard the washers as they must be replaced with ones.) Position a container to collect any escaping brake fluid, then detach the hydraulic lines from the master cylinder.

➡**On older 626 models which have a fluid reservoir located separately from the master cylinder, disconnect the lines which run between the two and plug them to prevent leakage.**

4. Unfasten the nuts which secure the master cylinder to the power brake unit.

5. Withdraw the master cylinder assembly from the power brake unit. (If so equipped, remove the old gasket from the power brake unit.) On 1988-89 626s and MX-6s equipped with either a manual transaxle or ABS, and on all 929s, remove the clutch pipe mounting bracket from the power brake unit.

➡**Be careful not to spill brake fluid on the painted surfaces of the car, as it makes an excellent paint remover.**

To install:

6. On 1988-89 626s, MX-6s and 929s, install the clutch pipe mounting bracket if so equipped. If applicable, place a new gasket onto the brake power unit mounting studs. Position the master cylinder onto the mounting studs, then install and tighten the nuts.

7. Connect the hydraulic brake lines to the master cylinder. On ABS equipped vehicles, install new washers and torque the fitting union bolts to 16-20 ft. lbs. (22-27 Nm).

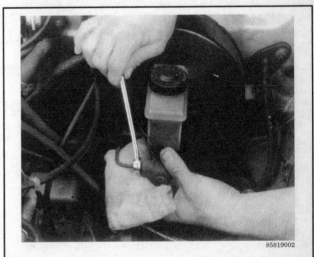

Fig. 8 Loosen the hydraulic lines at the master cylinder while holding a rag beneath them

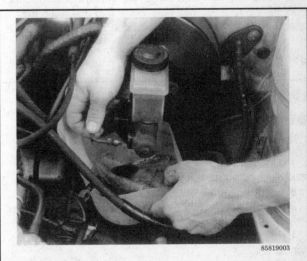

Fig. 9 Disconnect the hydraulic lines and collect the brake fluid as it drains

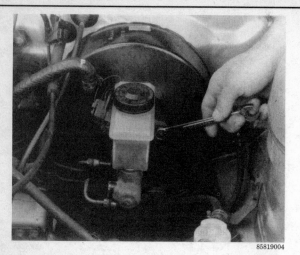

Fig. 10 Unfasten the nuts which secure the master cylinder to the power brake booster

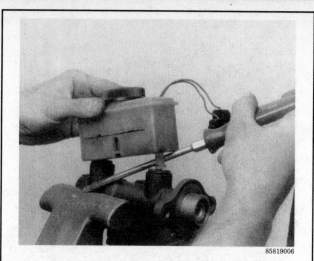

Fig. 12 Use a small prytool to separate the reservoir from the master cylinder body

Fig. 11 Separate the master cylinder from the power brake booster

8. Fasten the fluid level sensor and/or harness connectors.

9. Fill the reservoir with clean brake fluid and bleed the system, as described later in this section.

OVERHAUL

▶ See Figures 12, 13, 14, 15, 16, 17, 18, 19, 20 and 21

Rear Wheel Drive GLC

▶ See Figure 22

1. Clean the outside of the master cylinder and drain any brake fluid remaining in it.

2. Position the master cylinder in a vice.

3. Carefully separate the reservoir from the master cylinder body.

4. Remove the two bushings from the top of the master cylinder body.

5. Remove the pipe fitting(s), packing, check valve(s) and spring(s) from the bottom of the master cylinder.

6. Remove the piston stop wire and stop washer.

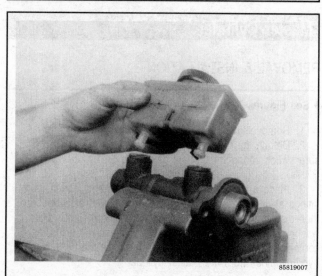

Fig. 13 Lift the reservoir off the cylinder body

Fig. 14 Pull the bushings from the cylinder body

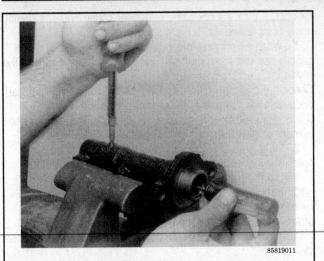

Fig. 15 The stop screw and O-ring are located on the underside of the cylinder body

Fig. 16 Compress and remove the snapring while depressing the primary piston assembly

Fig. 17 Withdraw the primary piston assembly from the cylinder bore . . .

Fig. 18 . . . followed by the secondary piston assembly

7. Withdraw the primary piston assembly.

8. Push the secondary piston in with the screwdriver, then remove the stop bolt.

9. Gradually withdraw the screwdriver, then allow the secondary piston, cups and return spring to come out of the cylinder. If they will not come out under spring pressure, gently apply compressed air to the outlet hole.

10. Wash all components in clean brake fluid. NEVER use gasoline or kerosene, as it dissolves rubber parts. Examine the piston cups and replace any that are worn, torn, or swelled. Check the cylinder bore for roughness or scoring. Check clearance between the piston and cylinder bore; the wear limit is 0.006 in. (0.15mm). If clearance exceeds the limit, replace the cylinder or piston(s).

11. Dip the pistons and cups in clean brake fluid.

12. Insert the secondary piston assembly into the master cylinder. Push the piston in as far as it will go with a screwdriver, then install the stop bolt and washer. Remove the screwdriver.

13. Insert the primary piston assembly, then install the piston stop washer and stop wire.

14. Install the spring(s), check valve(s), packing and pipe fitting(s) to the bottom of the cylinder.

15. Make sure the piston cups do not cover the compensating ports, then install new bushings and attach the reservoir.

16. Depress the primary piston and withdraw the snapring from the rear of the cylinder bore.

17. Withdraw the washers, piston, cups, spacer, seat, and return spring from the cylinder bore.

1979-82 626

1. Clean the outside of the master cylinder and drain any brake fluid remaining in it.

2. Position the master cylinder in a vice.

3. Remove the bleeder screw, the check valve and spring, and the piston stop ring.

4. Withdraw the primary piston assembly.

5. Push the secondary piston in with the screwdriver, then loosen the stop bolt.

6. Gradually withdraw the screwdriver, then allow the secondary piston, cups and return spring to come out of the

Fig. 19 Exploded view of common master cylinder components

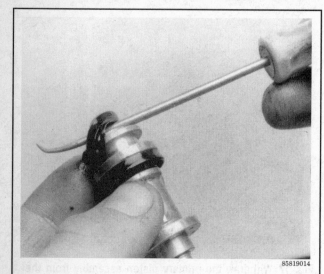

Fig. 20 Removing a piston cup

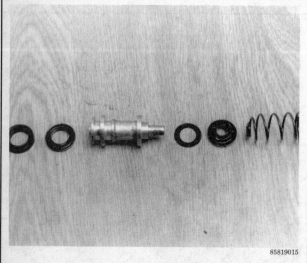

Fig. 21 Secondary piston components

cylinder. If they will not come out under spring pressure, gently apply compressed air to the outlet hole.

7. Wash all components in clean brake fluid. NEVER use gasoline or kerosene, as it dissolves rubber parts. Examine the piston cups and replace any that are worn, torn, or swelled. Check the cylinder bore for roughness or scoring. Check clearance between the piston and cylinder bore; the wear limit is 0.006 in. (0.15mm). If clearance exceeds the limit, replace the cylinder or piston(s).

8. Make sure the compensating ports in the cylinder are open.

9. Dip the pistons and cups in clean brake fluid.

10. Insert the secondary piston assembly into the master cylinder. Push the piston in as far as it will go with a screwdriver, then tighten the stop bolt. Remove the screwdriver.

11. Insert the primary piston assembly, then install the piston stop ring.

12. Install the check valve and spring, as well as the bleeder screw.

Front Wheel Drive GLC, 1983-87 626 and 1986-89 323

◗ **See Figures 23 and 24**

1. Clean the outside of the master cylinder and drain any brake fluid remaining in it.

2. Position the master cylinder in a vice.

3. Carefully separate the reservoir from the master cylinder body.

4. Remove the two bushings from the top of the master cylinder body.

5. Remove the stop screw and the O-ring from the bottom of the master cylinder.

6. Remove the secondary piston assembly from the bore.

➡**Blow out the assembly with compressed air, if necessary.**

7. Wash all of the components in clean brake fluid.

❋❋WARNING

Never use kerosene or gasoline to clean the master cylinder components.

8. Examine all of the piston cups and replace any that are worn, damaged, or swollen.

9. Check the cylinder bore for roughness or scoring. Check the clearance between the piston and cylinder bore with a feeler gauge. Replace either the piston or the cylinder, if the clearance exceeds 0.006 in. (0.15mm).

10. Blow any dirt and remaining brake fluid out of the cylinder with compressed air.

To assemble:

11. Dip all of the components, except for the cylinder, in clean brake fluid.

12. Insert the return spring and the valve components into the cylinder bore.

13. Fit the secondary cup(s) and the primary cup over the secondary piston. The flat side of the cups should face the piston.

14. Place the secondary piston components into the cylinder bore.

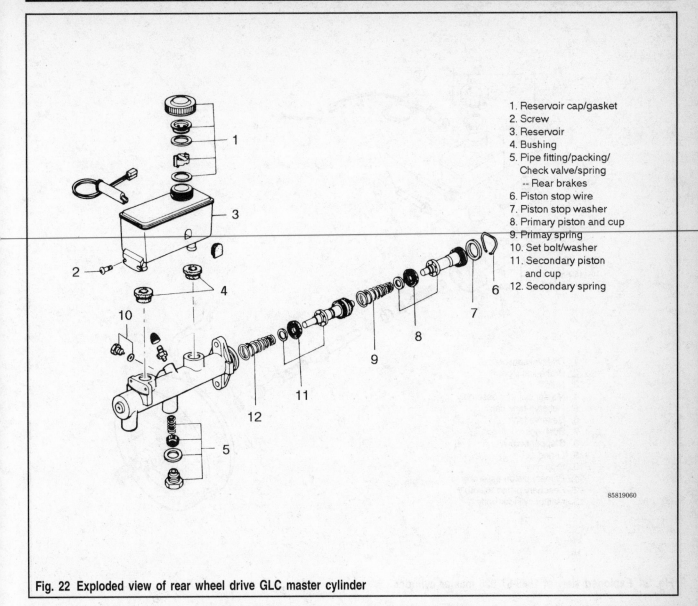

1. Reservoir cap/gasket
2. Screw
3. Reservoir
4. Bushing
5. Pipe fitting/packing/
   Check valve/spring
   -- Rear brakes
6. Piston stop wire
7. Piston stop washer
8. Primary piston and cup
9. Primay spring
10. Set bolt/washer
11. Secondary piston
    and cup
12. Secondary spring

85819060

Fig. 22 Exploded view of rear wheel drive GLC master cylinder

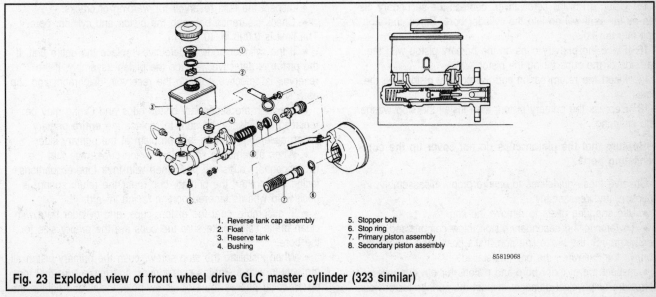

1. Reverse tank cap assembly
2. Float
3. Reserve tank
4. Bushing
5. Stopper bolt
6. Stop ring
7. Primary piston assembly
8. Secondary piston assembly

85819068

Fig. 23 Exploded view of front wheel drive GLC master cylinder (323 similar)

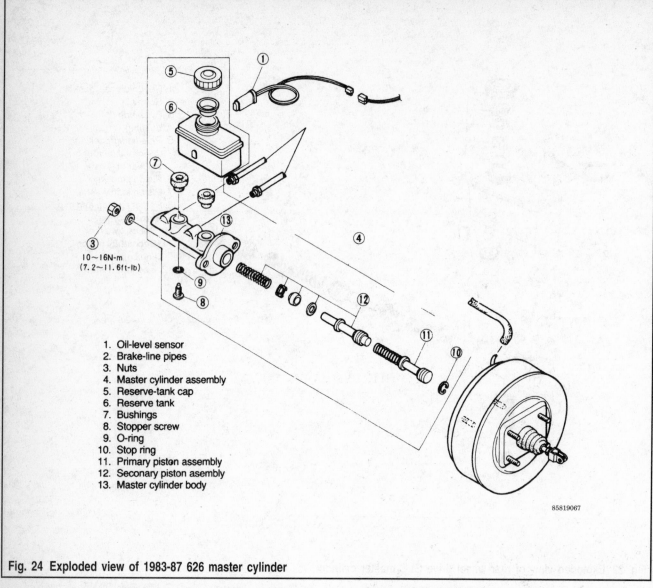

1. Oil-level sensor
2. Brake-line pipes
3. Nuts
4. Master cylinder assembly
5. Reserve-tank cap
6. Reserve tank
7. Bushings
8. Stopper screw
9. O-ring
10. Stop ring
11. Primary piston assembly
12. Seconary piston asembly
13. Master cylinder body

10~16N-m
(7.2~11.6ft-lb)

85819067

Fig. 24 Exploded view of 1983-87 626 master cylinder

15. Using a Phillips screwdriver, depress the secondary piston as far as it will go into the cylinder bore. Screw the stop bolt into the hole.

16. Place the primary cups on the primary piston with the flat side of the cups facing the piston.

17. Insert the return spring and the primary piston into the bore.

18. Depress the primary piston, then install the stop washer and snapring.

➡**Be sure that the piston cups do not cover up the compensating ports.**

Observe these guidelines to ensure proper disassembly, inspection, and reassembly:

• Use snapring pliers to remove the ring.

• To remove the secondary piston, blow compressed air gently through the brake line port that's positioned toward the front of the car when the unit is installed.

• Inspect the cylinder bore and pistons for obvious wear, corrosion, or physical damage. Inspect the springs for obvious damage or weakness.

• Inspect the fluid reservoir for warping or cracks.

• Check clearance between the piston and cylinder bore. The limit is 0.006 in. (0.15mm).

• If the cylinder body is defective, replace the entire unit. If the piston is defective, replace the piston assembly. If the reservoir is defective, replace the reservoir, diaphragm and cap as a set.

• Although the secondary piston cups and O-ring may be replaced individually, be sure to replace the **entire** primary piston assembly, if there is a problem at the primary side.

• When assembling secondary piston cups, note that the two secondary cups are positioned with their tapered portions facing each other; the primary cup (near the return spring) is positioned with its tapered portion facing inward.

• In assembly, coat the piston, cups, and cylinder bore with clean brake fluid. Make sure the cups are the proper size for the bore.

• When installing the stop screw, push the primary piston all the way in with a Phillips screwdriver, and make sure that the piston collar passes the stop screw hole. Install and tighten the screw with the piston held in position. Then, test the position of the piston by repeatedly forcing it in and releasing it with the screwdriver. It should remain properly positioned inside the master cylinder.

➡The GLC master cylinder has no stop screw, and its bore size is only ¹³⁄₁₆ in. (20.64mm). Check the outer surface of the piston cups and outer cylinder surface for appropriate markings.

• Adjust the power brake unit pushrod clearance as described later in this section.

1988-89 626, MX-6 and 929

▸ See Figures 25 and 26

1. Clean the outside of the master cylinder and drain any brake fluid remaining in it.
2. Position the master cylinder in a vice.
3. If equipped with ABS, loosen, then remove the union fittings and washers. Discard the washers as they must be replaced with new ones.
4. Carefully remove the reservoir from the master cylinder body. If equipped with ABS, remove the filter screen and check it for clogging. Moderate accumulations of debris may be removed with compressed air. If the filter screen is unfit for service, replace it.
5. Remove the two bushings from the top of the master cylinder.
6. Use a Phillips head screwdriver to remove the stop screw and the O-ring from the bottom of the master cylinder. Replace the O-ring.
7. Depress the primary piston, then withdraw the snapring from the rear of the cylinder bore with snapring pliers.
8. Withdraw the washers, piston, cups, spacer, seat, and return spring from the cylinder bore.
9. Remove the secondary piston assembly from the bore.

➡Blow out the assembly with compressed air, if necessary, and use a rag to catch the piston.

10. Wash all of the components in clean brake fluid.

✳✳WARNING

Never use kerosene or gasoline to clean the master cylinder components.

11. Examine all of the piston cups and replace any that are worn, damaged, or swollen.
12. Check the cylinder bore for roughness or scoring. Measure the diameter of each cylinder bore; it should be 0.875 in. (22.22mm). If the diameter is not as specified, replace the master cylinder body.
13. Blow the dirt and the remaining brake fluid out of the cylinder with compressed air.

To assemble:

14. Dip all of the components, except for the cylinder, in clean brake fluid.
15. Insert the return spring and the valve components into the cylinder bore.
16. Fit the secondary cup and the primary cup over the secondary piston. The flat side of the cups should face the piston.
17. Place the secondary piston components into the cylinder bore.
18. Using a Phillips head screwdriver, depress the secondary piston as far as it will go into the cylinder bore. Screw the stop bolt (with new O-ring) into the hole. The stopper screw requires only 17-22 inch lbs. (2-2.5 Nm) of torque.
19. Place the primary cups on the primary piston with the flat side of the cups facing the piston.
20. Insert the return spring and the primary piston into the bore.
21. Depress the primary piston, then install the stop washer and snapring.

➡Be sure that the piston cups do not cover up the compensating ports.

Observe these guidelines to ensure proper disassembly, inspection, and reassembly:
• Use snapring pliers to remove the ring.
• To remove the secondary piston, blow compressed air gently through the brake line port that's positioned toward the front of the car when the unit is installed.
• Inspect the cylinder bore and pistons for obvious wear, corrosion, or physical damage. Inspect the springs for obvious damage or for weakness.
• Inspect the fluid reservoir for warping or cracks.
• If the cylinder body is defective, replace the entire unit (see disassembly step 12). If the piston is defective, replace the piston assembly. If the reservoir is defective, replace the reservoir, diaphragm and cap as a set.
• Although the secondary piston cups and O-ring may be replaced individually, be sure to replace the **entire** primary piston assembly, if there is a problem at the primary side.
• When assembling the secondary piston, note that the cups are positioned with their tapered portions facing each other. Make sure the cups are the proper size for the bore.
• In assembly, coat the piston, cups, and cylinder bore with clean brake fluid.
• When installing the stop screw, push the primary piston all the way in with a Phillips screwdriver, and make sure the

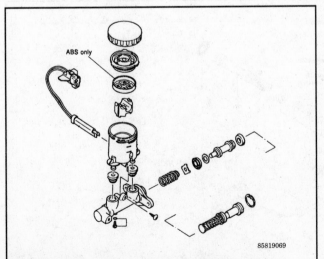

ABS only

85819069

Fig. 25 Exploded view of 1988-89 626/MX-6 master cylinder

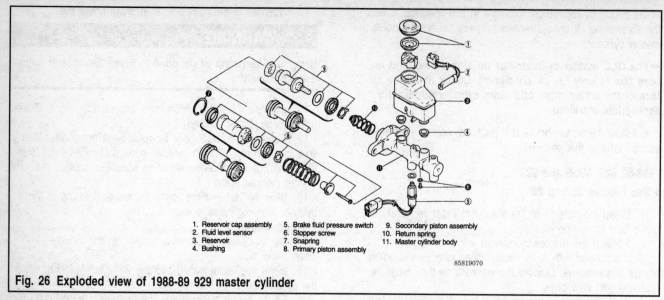

1. Reservoir cap assembly
2. Fluid level sensor
3. Reservoir
4. Bushing
5. Brake fluid pressure switch
6. Stopper screw
7. Snapring
8. Primary piston assembly
9. Secondary piston assembly
10. Return spring
11. Master cylinder body

85819070

Fig. 26 Exploded view of 1988-89 929 master cylinder

piston passes the stop screw hole. Install and tighten the screw with the piston held in position. Then test the position of the piston by repeatedly forcing it in and releasing it with the screwdriver. It should remain properly positioned inside the master cylinder.

• Adjust the power brake unit pushrod clearance as described later in this section.

1979-89 RX-7
♦ See Figure 27

1. Clean the outside of the master cylinder and drain any brake fluid remaining in it.
2. Position the master cylinder in a vice.
3. Carefully remove the reservoir from the master cylinder body.
4. Remove the two reservoir mounting bushings.
5. Remove the stop ring, then withdraw the primary piston assembly and spring.
6. To remove the secondary piston, push in the piston using a screwdriver and remove the stop bolt. Do not allow the

piston to come forward yet. On 1979-85 models, insert a guide pin into the stop bolt hole to prevent the rubber secondary cup of the secondary piston from cutting itself when it moves past the hole.

➡**If you are replacing the secondary cup, the guide pin need not be used.**

7. If so, equipped, remove the joint bolt (not used on all 1981 disc brake models), check valve and spring. On 1986-89 models, unscrew the brake fluid pressure switch from the bottom of the master cylinder. Clean all parts in fresh brake fluid, then check them for damage. Do not use gasoline or kerosene. Blow parts dry with compressed air. Check the piston cups and replace any that are damaged, worn, softened or swelled. Examine the cylinder bore and pistons for wear, roughness or scoring. Measure the clearance between the cylinder bore and the pistons with a flat bladed feeler gauge. If clearance is more than 0.006 in. (0.15mm), replace either the piston, cylinder or both.

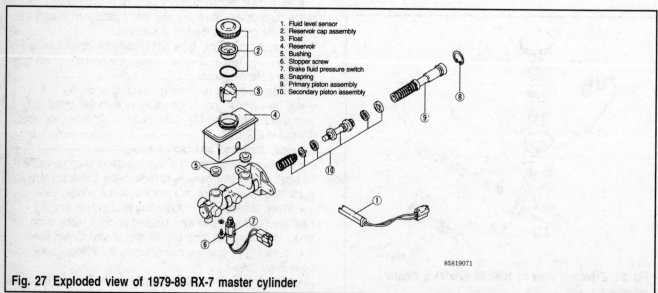

1. Fluid level sensor
2. Reservoir cap assembly
3. Float
4. Reservoir
5. Bushing
6. Stopper screw
7. Brake fluid pressure switch
8. Snapring
9. Primary piston assembly
10. Secondary piston assembly

85819071

Fig. 27 Exploded view of 1979-89 RX-7 master cylinder

To assemble:

8. Dip the cups and pistons in clean brake fluid, then assemble the primary and secondary pistons with the tapered ends of the cups facing inward.

9. On 1979-85 models, fit the guide pin into the stopper bolt hole before installing the secondary piston, to prevent the piston cup from catching and tearing on the edge of the hole. When installing the stop screw on 1986-89 models, push the primary piston all the way in with a Phillips screwdriver, and make sure the piston passes the stop screw hole. Install and tighten the screw with the piston held in position. Test the position of the piston by repeatedly forcing it in and releasing it with the screwdriver. It should remain properly positioned inside the master cylinder.

10. Install the secondary piston. After pushing it back behind the stopper bolt hole, remove the guide pin, then install the stopper bolt and washer.

11. If applicable, install the joint bolt, check valve and spring. Tighten the joint bolt to 43-51 ft. lbs. (58-69 Nm).

12. If applicable, install the brake fluid pressure switch.

13. Before installing the reservoir, make sure the compensating ports are not covered by the primary and secondary piston cups.

Power Brake Booster

REMOVAL & INSTALLATION

➡The booster can be rebuilt, although several special tools are necessary. Refer rebuilding to an outside repair facility.

1. Remove the master cylinder as described earlier in this section.

2. Disconnect the vacuum hose from the booster. On most late model cars, there is a check valve pressed into the vacuum hose that you will not be able to see. (On 626s and MX-6s with electronically controlled transaxles, and on 929s, the check valve is visible.) Before disconnecting the vacuum hose, note the direction of the arrow on the hose or on the valve. It should always be pointing toward the engine.

3. From inside the car, disconnect the push rod fork from the brake pedal by removing the clevis pin. Unfasten the attaching nuts, then remove the booster and gasket.

4. Install the brake booster with a new gasket and tighten the attaching nuts.

5. Connect the brake pedal linkage to the push rod fork. Grease the clevis pin.

6. Connect the vacuum hose in the proper direction and install the master cylinder. Bleed the system as described later in this section.

ADJUSTMENTS

Pushrod Clearance

This procedure is required after rebuilding the master cylinders on 1983-89 models. It requires the use of a special tool since the clearance between the power brake unit pushrod and master cylinder piston cannot be measured when the two are assembled. For 1983-85 models, use Mazda tool no. 49-B002-765 or equivalent, and for 1986-89 models, use Mazda tool no. 49-F043-001 or equivalent. Since this is a simple adjustment, you might find that, if the tool is expensive, it would actually be cheaper to take the brake unit and rebuilt master cylinder to a qualified mechanic to have it performed. On 1986-89 models, you will also need a vacuum pump in addition to the special tool.

1983-85 MODELS
▶ **See Figure 28**

1. Set the unit on the end of the master cylinder with the head of the adjusting bolt upward. Make sure both legs rest on the master cylinder mounting flange, then turn the bolt downward until it just touches the bottom of the pushrod recess in the piston.

2. Turn the unit upside down and rest the other ends of the legs on the mounting flange on the power brake unit. There should be no vacuum in the unit. If there is any gap between the power brake unit pushrod, loosen the pushrod locknut and turn the pushrod until it just touches the head of the bolt. Tighten the locknut. This will ensure a pushrod-to-piston clearance of 0.016-0.024 in. (0.4-0.6mm) on the 626, 0.004-0.020 in. (0.1-0.5mm) on the GLC, and 0.004-0.012 in. (0.1-0.3mm) on the RX-7.

1986-89 MODELS

1. Set the special tool on the end of the master cylinder with the head of the adjusting bolt upward. Make sure both legs rest on the master cylinder mounting flange, then then turn the bolt downward until it just touches the bottom of the pushrod recess in the piston.

2. Disconnect the vacuum hose from the power brake unit and connect a vacuum source to the end of the hose. Apply 19.7 in. Hg (66.5 kPa) of vacuum to the power brake unit.

3. Turn the unit upside down and rest the other ends of the legs on the mounting flange on the power brake unit. Check the clearance between the end of the gauge and the pushrod of the power brake unit. There must be no clearance. Loosen the pushrod locknut and turn the pushrod until all the clearance is removed.

Proportioning Valve

REMOVAL & INSTALLATION

▶ **See Figure 29**

The proportioning valve regulates the pressure to the rear brakes, reducing it under hard braking, to minimize lockup of the rear wheels. The valve can be removed after detaching the connections, and unfastening the mounting bolts. The use of a line wrench is highly recommended, especially when there are a number of connections (such as on the 1988-89 626 and MX-6). When installing, use the inlet and outlet arrows on the body of the valve to make connections properly from the master cylinder and to the wheels. Be sure to note the **F** marking, indicating the port leading to the front brakes. Bleed the system after completing the installation.

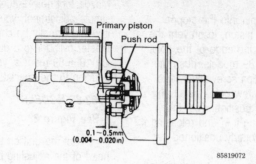

Fig. 28 Install the power brake unit with clearance between the pushrod and primary piston (GLC shown, others similar)

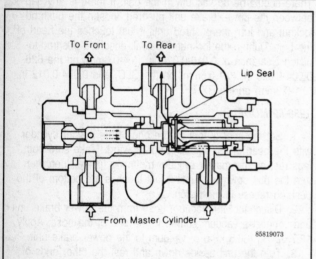

Fig. 29 Cutaway view of a common brake proportioning valve

CENTERING THE BRAKE FAILURE WARNING VALVE

After a partial failure of the brake system, this valve will go off-center and will activate the warning light. Simply bleed the system after repairs are complete, make sure the master cylinder reservoir has plenty of fluid in it, and depress the brake pedal several times until the light goes out.

Brake Hoses

REMOVAL & INSTALLATION

➡The use of Mazda special brake line wrench 49-0259-770B will make the disconnecting and connecting of the brake line fittings an easy task.

1. Loosen the brake line flare nut using the proper tool and remove the brake hose. If you are disconnecting a flexible hose, use a back-up wrench to prevent the hose from twisting. Drain the brake fluid into a small waste container and keep the fluid away from painted surfaces. Brake fluid makes fantastic paint remover!

2. Inspect the brake hose for cracks, swelling and signs of leakage (weeping) or deterioration. Replace the hose if is no longer fit for service. Check the flare nut and threaded connections for damage.

3. Connect the brake hose and tighten the flare fittings properly. Make the hose is connected so that it is not allowed to contact any moving parts.

4. Bleed the system as described below and run the tip of your finger all the way around the connection to ensure a tight fit.

Bleeding Brake System

DISC BRAKES

▶ See Figure 30

1. Remove the bleeder screw cap from the caliper which is furthest from the master cylinder.

➡Keep the master cylinder reservoir at least ¾ full during the bleeding operation.

2. Install a vinyl tube over the bleeder screw. Submerge the other end of the clear vinyl tube in a jar half full of clean brake fluid.

3. Open the bleeder valve. Have an assistant fully depress the brake pedal and allow it to return slowly.

4. Repeat this operation until air bubbles cease flowing into the jar.

5. Close the valve, remove the tube, and install the cap on the bleeder valve. Replenish the reservoir to the proper level and repeat the procedure for the other side.

Fig. 30 Bleeding the front disc brakes. Note that the wheel need not be removed

FRONT DISC BRAKES

Disc Brake Pads

INSPECTION

▶ **See Figure 31**

Most models provide an inspection slot in the top of the caliper for checking the pad thickness after the front wheels are removed. However, if the thickness seems marginal, the pads should be removed from the caliper and checked. Models not having an inspection slot will require pad removal to check the thickness of the friction material.

The front disc brake pads are equipped with wear indicators that ride above the surface of the rotor. When the brake wears to its minimum thickness, the wear indicator is allowed to contact the rotor's surface, making a squealing or chirping noise while driving.

REMOVAL & INSTALLATION

Rear Wheel Drive GLC

▶ **See Figure 32**

These models use a single piston caliper that slides on a mounting bracket attached to the steering knuckle.

➡ **Although it is advisable to disassemble only one side at a time, be sure to replace brake pads on both sides of the vehicle.**

1. Loosen the wheel lugs, then raise the front of the car and safely support it on jackstands. Remove the front wheels.

DRUM BRAKES

1. Remove the bleeder screw cap from the wheel cylinder which is furthest from the master cylinder.

➡**Keep the master cylinder reservoir at least ¾ full during the bleeding operation.**

2. Install a vinyl tube over the bleeder screw. Submerge the other end of the clear vinyl tube in a jar half full of clean brake fluid.
3. Depress the brake pedal rapidly several times.
4. Keep the brake pedal depressed and open the bleeder valve. Close the valve without releasing the pedal.
5. Repeat this operation until bubbles cease to appear in the jar.
6. Remove the tube and install the cap on the bleeder valve.

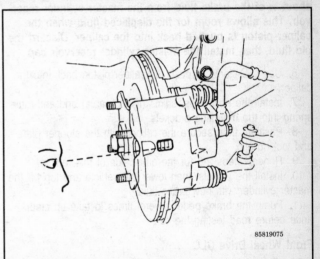

Fig. 31 Inspect front pad thickness through the hole in the caliper

2. Remove the locking clip and stopper plate which secure the caliper.
3. Lift the caliper from the mounting bracket, then support the caliper with a piece of wire so it is not hanging by the brake hose.

➡**Variations in pad retainers, anti-rattle and retaining springs occur from year to year. Work on one side at a time, and note the position of each spring, etc. for correct installation.**

4. Remove the anti-rattle spring.
5. Slide the outboard and inboard pads from the mounting bracket. Note their location, then remove any shims, if so equipped.

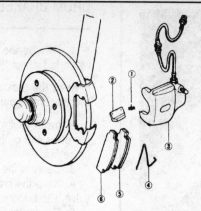

1. Locking clip
2. Stopper plate
3. Caliper
4. Anti-rattle spring
5. Brake shoe
6. Brake shoe

85819076

Fig. 32 Front disc brake components — RWD GLC

To install:

➡Prior to the installation of new brake pads, remove about ⅓ of the brake fluid from the master cylinder reservoir. This allows room for the displaced fluid when the caliper piston is pushed back into the caliper. Discard the old fluid, then install the master cylinder reservoir cap.

6. Use a C-clamp to push the caliper piston back into the caliper.

7. Install the new pads, shims (if applicable) and anti-rattle spring into the mounting brackets.

8. Position, then secure the caliper with the stopper plate and locking clip.

9. Repeat Steps 2-8 for the other side of the vehicle.

10. Install the wheels, then lower the vehicle and top off the master cylinder with new brake fluid.

11. Pump the brake pedal several times to take up clearance before road testing the car.

Front Wheel Drive GLC

◗ See Figure 33

➡Although it is advisable to disassemble only one side at a time, be sure to replace brake pads on both sides of the vehicle.

1. Raise the front of the vehicle, support it with safety stands, and remove the front wheels.

2. Unclip the brake hose at the shock absorber by pressing the lower clip outward with a screwdriver and then forcing the clip downward.

3. Use a screwdriver to release the spring clip at the top of the caliper by forcing it inward and then forward.

4. Pull out the lower slide pin, then pivot the caliper upward and wire it to the strut to hold it in this position.

➡Do not disconnect the brake line from the caliper or you will have to bleed the brakes.

5. Turn the wheel hub until one of the four indentations lines up with the pads. Remove the pad, shim and spring on either side. Remove the springs from the pads.

To install:

➡Prior to the installation of new brake pads, remove about ⅓ of the brake fluid from the master cylinder reservoir. This allows room for the displaced fluid when the caliper piston is pushed back into the caliper. Discard the old fluid, then install the master cylinder reservoir cap.

6. Clean the exposed piston surface, then use a C-clamp to depress the caliper piston back into the caliper. This will permit the new, thicker pad to be installed.

7. Install the parts in reverse order of their removal, making sure to transfer the shim and spring to the new pad. If either is warped or fatigued, replace it. Be sure to apply grease sparingly to the contact surface between the pad mounting support and the caliper assembly, as well as to both surfaces of the outer/inner shims, slide pin and bushing.

8. Repeat Steps 2-7 for the other side of the vehicle.

9. Install the wheels, then lower the vehicle and top off the master cylinder with new brake fluid.

10. Pump the brake pedal several times to take up clearance before road testing the car.

1979-82 626

These models use a caliper that floats on guide pins and bushings that are threaded into a mounting bracket.

➡Although it is advisable to disassemble only one side at a time, be sure to replace brake pads on both sides of the vehicle.

1. Loosen the wheel lugs, then raise the front of the car and safely support it on jackstands. Remove the front wheels.

2. Disconnect the horseshoe clip retaining the brake hose to the front strut. Remove the caliper guide pins and anti-rattle springs or clips.

➡Variations in pad retainers, anti-rattle and retaining springs occur from year to year. Work on one side at a time, and note the position of each spring, etc. for correct installation.

3. On 1979-81 models, remove the mounting pins, then lift the caliper up and away from the disc rotor. (On 1982 models,

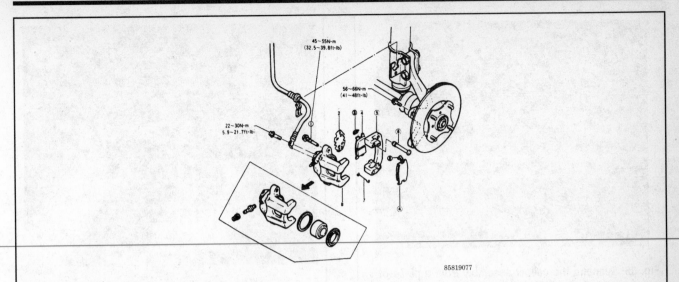

Fig. 33 Front disc brake components — FWD GLC

remove the lower pin bolt which retains the caliper to the mount, then pivot the caliper upward.) Support the caliper with wire; do not permit it to hang by the brake hose.

➡**Do not disconnect the brake line from the caliper or you will have to bleed the brakes.**

4. Remove the anti-rattle spring, then slide the outboard pad from the mounting bracket. Remove the inboard pad from the caliper or mounting bracket. Note the location of any shims for reinstallation.

➡**Prior to the installation of new brake pads, remove about ⅓ of the brake fluid from the master cylinder reservoir. This allows room for the displaced fluid when the caliper piston is pushed back into the caliper. Discard the old fluid, then install the master cylinder reservoir cap.**

5. Use a C-clamp to push the caliper piston back into the caliper.

6. Pad installation for all models is the reverse of removal. Apply grease sparingly to the contact surface between the pad mounting support and the caliper assembly, as well as to both surfaces of the outer/inner shims, the slide pin and bushing.

7. Repeat Steps 2-6 for the other side of the vehicle.

8. Install the wheels, then lower the vehicle and top off the master cylinder with new brake fluid.

9. Pump the brake pedal several times to take up clearance before road testing the car.

323, MX-6 and 1983-89 626

▶ **See Figures 34, 35, 36, 37, 38, 39, 40, 41 and 42**

➡**Although it is advisable to disassemble only one side at a time, be sure to replace brake pads on both sides of the vehicle.**

1. Raise the vehicle and safely support it on axle stands. Remove the front wheels.

2. Remove the two caliper installation bolts, then pull the caliper off the disc. Suspend the caliper by a piece of wire or twine to prevent putting tension on the brake hose.

➡**Do not disconnect the brake line from the caliper or you will have to bleed the brakes.**

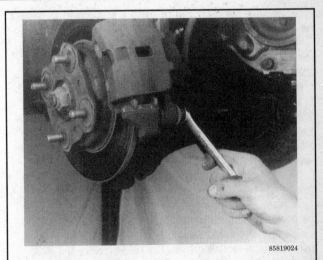

Fig. 34 Use a socket wrench to loosen and remove the caliper mounting bolts

Fig. 35 Remove the caliper (with the pads attached) from the rotor

Fig. 36 Suspend the caliper assembly from a piece of wire or twine to avoid stretching the brake hose

3. Remove the outer pad by using a screwdriver to release the clip. Then, remove the inner pad.

4. Remove about one-third the brake fluid from the reservoir in the master cylinder. Use a large C-clamp or Mazda's special tool to force the piston back into the caliper.

To install:

5. If either or both pads shows excessive wear, replace both pads. Before reattaching the caliper, push the sleeve toward the outside of the caliper, so the sleeve boot does not get pinned between the caliper and steering knuckle and possibly tear.

6. Lightly coat the new pad shims with brake grease and install them on the pads.

7. Make sure that the piston is pushed inward, then install the new pads and shims onto the mounting support.

8. Lower the caliper assembly onto the mounting support, then install the mounting bolts. On 1983-87 626s and 323s, torque the upper installation bolt to 12-18 ft. lbs. (16-24 Nm) and the lower installation bolt to 15-21 ft. lbs. (20-28 Nm). On 1988-89 323s, torque the upper and lower caliper bolts to

Fig. 37 Remove the outer brake pad from the caliper

Fig. 38 Remove the inner brake pad from the caliper

Fig. 39 Use a large C-clamp to retract the piston into its bore, so that the new thicker pads will fit

29-36 ft. lbs (39-49 Nm). On 1988-89 626s and MX-6s, torque the upper and lower caliper bolts to 23-30 ft. lbs. (31-41 Nm) .

9. Repeat Steps 2-8 for the other side of the vehicle.

10. Install the wheels, then lower the vehicle and top off the master cylinder with new brake fluid.

11. Pump the brake pedal several times to take up clearance before road testing the car.

929

▶ See Figure 43

➡Although it is advisable to disassemble only one side at a time, be sure to replace brake pads on both sides of the vehicle.

1. Raise and safely support the front end on jackstands.
2. Remove the wheels.
3. Remove the lower lock pin bolt from the caliper.

➡Do not disconnect the brake line from the caliper or you will have to bleed the brakes.

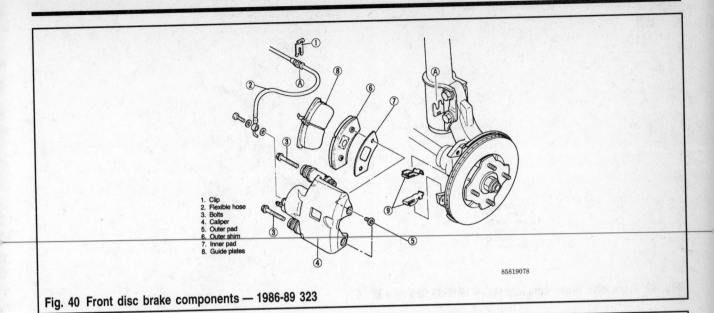

1. Clip
2. Flexible hose
3. Bolts
4. Caliper
5. Outer pad
6. Outer shim
7. Inner pad
8. Guide plates

85819078

Fig. 40 Front disc brake components — 1986-89 323

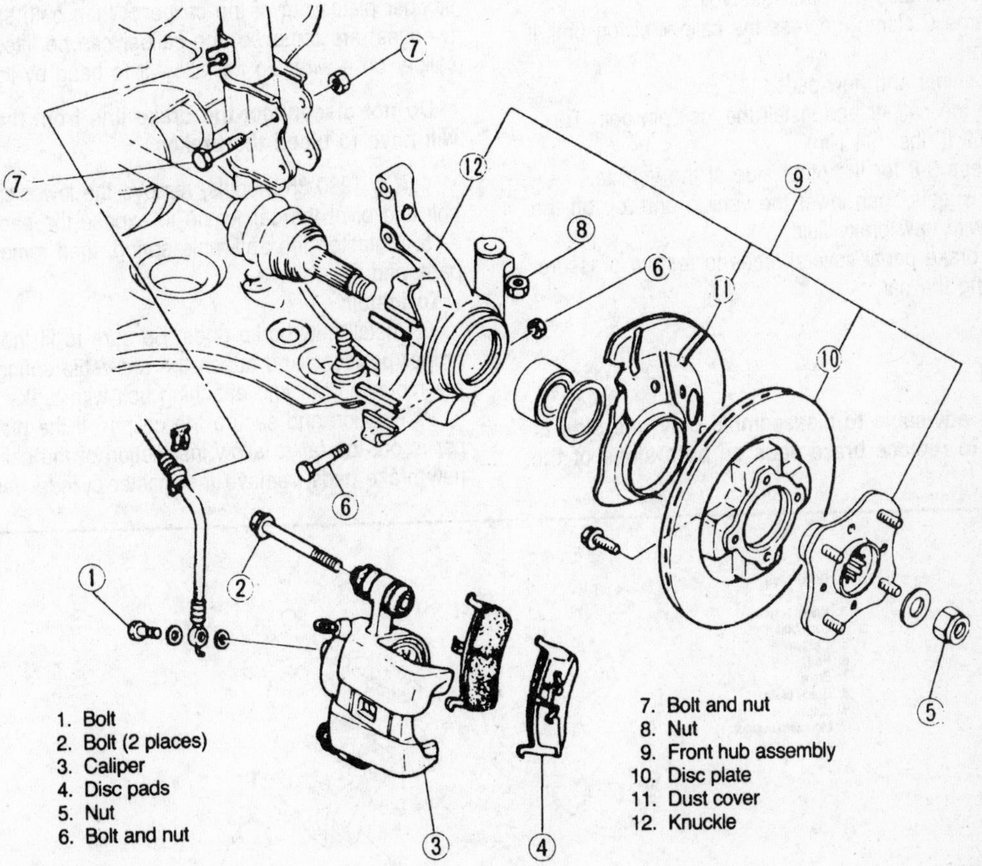

1. Bolt
2. Bolt (2 places)
3. Caliper
4. Disc pads
5. Nut
6. Bolt and nut
7. Bolt and nut
8. Nut
9. Front hub assembly
10. Disc plate
11. Dust cover
12. Knuckle

85819079

Fig. 41 Front disc brake components — 1983-87 626

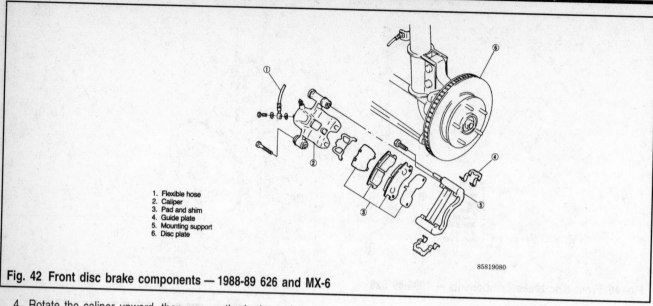

1. Flexible hose
2. Caliper
3. Pad and shim
4. Guide plate
5. Mounting support
6. Disc plate

85819080

Fig. 42 Front disc brake components — 1988-89 626 and MX-6

4. Rotate the caliper upward, then remove the brake pads and shims.

To install:

5. Open the master cylinder reservoir cap and remove about one-third of the fluid from the reservoir.

6. Using a large C-clamp, depress the caliper piston until it bottoms in its bore.

7. Install the shims and new pads.

8. Reposition the caliper and install the lock pin bolt. Torque the bolt to 69 ft. lbs. (94 Nm).

9. Repeat Steps 3-8 for the other side of the vehicle.

10. Install the wheels, then lower the vehicle and top off the master cylinder with new brake fluid.

11. Pump the brake pedal several times to restore pressure before road testing the car.

1979-85 RX-7

♦ See Figure 44

➡Although it is advisable to disassemble only one side at a time, be sure to replace brake pads on both sides of the vehicle.

1. Raise the front of the car and safely support it on jackstands.

2. Remove the front wheels.

3. On 1979 models, remove the locking clips and pull the stopper plates out of the caliper. When both stopper plates (wedges) are removed, the caliper can be lifted off. Hang the caliper on a wire; do not allow it to hang by its brake line.

➡**Do not disconnect the brake line from the caliper or you will have to bleed the brakes.**

4. On 1980-85 models, remove the lower caliper attaching bolt and pivot the caliper up to expose the pads.

5. Unfasten the anti-rattle spring, then remove the brake pads and their shims.

To install:

6. Install new brake pads. Be sure to fit the shims in the proper positions and attach the anti-rattle spring. Coat the caliper mounting pin and attaching bolt with brake grease.

7. Position and secure the caliper. If the piston in the caliper is out too far to allow installation of the caliper with the new brake pads, remove the master cylinder reservoir cap and

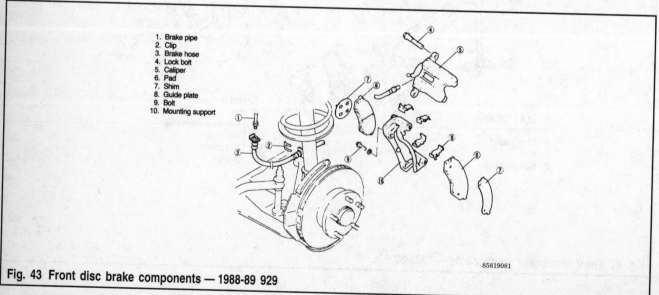

1. Brake pipe
2. Clip
3. Brake hose
4. Lock bolt
5. Caliper
6. Pad
7. Shim
8. Guide plate
9. Bolt
10. Mounting support

85819081

Fig. 43 Front disc brake components — 1988-89 929

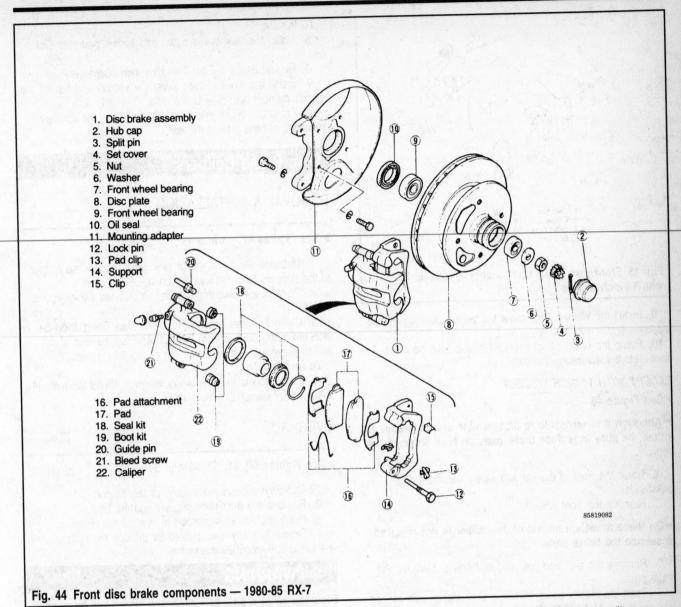

1. Disc brake assembly
2. Hub cap
3. Split pin
4. Set cover
5. Nut
6. Washer
7. Front wheel bearing
8. Disc plate
9. Front wheel bearing
10. Oil seal
11. Mounting adapter
12. Lock pin
13. Pad clip
14. Support
15. Clip

16. Pad attachment
17. Pad
18. Seal kit
19. Boot kit
20. Guide pin
21. Bleed screw
22. Caliper

85819082

Fig. 44 Front disc brake components — 1980-85 RX-7

remove about one-third of the brake fluid from the reservoir, then press in the piston. If the piston will not press in, bleed the caliper as follows: submerge one end of a piece of hose in a container of brake fluid and attach the other end to the caliper bleeder valve, then open the valve and push in the piston. When the piston is in far enough, close the valve.

8. Repeat Steps 3-7 for the other side of the vehicle.

9. Install the wheels, then lower the vehicle and top off the master cylinder with new brake fluid.

10. Pump the brake pedal several times to take up clearance before road testing the car.

1986-89 RX-7

WITH 14-INCH WHEELS

▶ **See Figure 45**

➡**Although it is advisable to disassemble only one side at a time, be sure to replace brake pads on both sides of the vehicle.**

1. Raise the front of the car and safely support it on jackstands.

2. Remove the front wheels.

3. Remove the lower caliper attaching bolt and pivot the caliper up to expose the pads. Remove the anti-rattle spring. Hang the caliper on a wire; do not allow it to hang by its brake line.

➡**Do not disconnect the brake line from the caliper or you will have to bleed the brakes.**

4. Unfasten the anti-rattle spring, then remove the brake pads and their shims.

5. Push the caliper piston in with a C-clamp, or with Mazda expansion tool 49-0221-600C or equivalent.

To install:

6. Install the new pads onto the mounting support, then attach the anti-rattle spring.

7. Lower the caliper onto the mounting support and install the attaching bolt. Torque the bolt to 23-30 ft. lbs. (31-41 Nm).

8. Repeat Steps 3-7 for the other side of the vehicle.

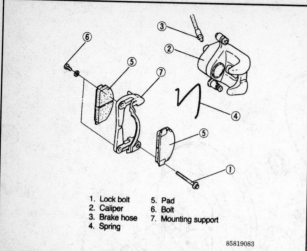

1. Lock bolt
2. Caliper
3. Brake hose
4. Spring
5. Pad
6. Bolt
7. Mounting support

85819083

Fig. 45 Front disc brake components — 1986-89 RX-7 with 14-inch wheels

9. Install the wheels, then lower the vehicle and top off the master cylinder with new brake fluid.
10. Pump the brake pedal several times to take up clearance before road testing the car.

EXCEPT WITH 14-INCH WHEELS

▶ See Figure 46

➡Although it is advisable to disassemble only one side at a time, be sure to replace brake pads on both sides of the vehicle.

1. Raise the front of the car and safely support it on jackstands.
2. Remove the front wheels.

➡On these models, removal of the caliper is not required to service the brake pads.

3. Remove the clip, pad pins and pad spring. Remove the brake pads.
4. Push the caliper piston in with a C-clamp, or with Mazda expansion tool 49-0221-600C or equivalent.

To install:
5. Install the new brake pads, pad spring, pad pins and clip.
6. Repeat Steps 3-5 for the other side of the vehicle.
7. Install the wheels, then lower the vehicle and top off the master cylinder with new brake fluid.
8. Pump the brake pedal several times to take up clearance before road testing the car.

Disc Brake Calipers

REMOVAL & INSTALLATION

▶ See Figures 47, 48 and 49

1. Unfasten the bolts and/or pins which secure the caliper to the support, then remove the caliper.
2. Remove the disc brake pads, as detailed earlier in this section.
3. Clean the area around the brake hose fitting, then detach the hydraulic line from the caliper. Plug the end of the line to prevent the entrance of dirt or the loss of fluid.

To install:
4. Installation is the reverse of removal. Bleed the hydraulic system after completing installation.

OVERHAUL

▶ See Figures 50, 51, 52, 53 and 54

1. Thoroughly clean the outside of the caliper.
2. Remove the dust boot retainer and the boot.
3. Place a piece of hardwood in front of the piston.
4. Gradually apply compressed air through the hydraulic line fitting and withdraw the piston.

✳✳WARNING

Blow the air in a little at a time; the piston will be pushed out forcefully if air is blown in too suddenly.

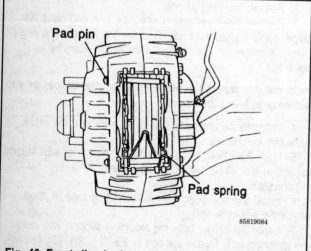

Pad pin

Pad spring

85819084

Fig. 46 Front disc brake components — 1986-89 RX-7 except with 14-inch wheels

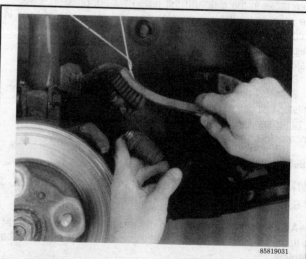

85819031

Fig. 47 Brush away any dirt before disconnecting the brake hose from the caliper

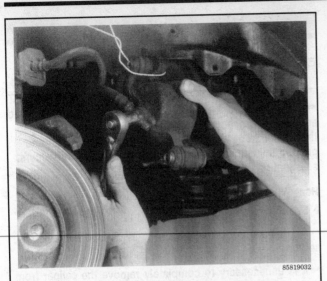

Fig. 48 Use a socket wrench to loosen the fitting . . .

Fig. 49 . . . then disconnect the brake hose from the caliper

Fig. 50 With a piece of hardwood over the bore, gradually apply compressed air through the hydraulic line fitting to dislodge the piston

Fig. 51 Remove the piston from the caliper

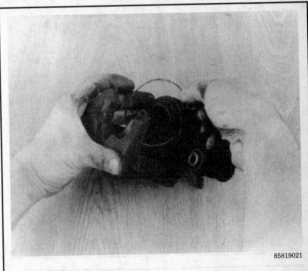

Fig. 52 Remove the retainer from the piston

➡️If the piston is frozen and cannot be removed from the caliper, tap lightly around it, while air pressure is being applied.

5. Withdraw the piston and dust seal from the caliper bore. Remove the retaining ring and dust seal.

6. If necessary, remove the bleeder screw.

7. Wash all of the parts in clean brake fluid. Dry them off with compressed air.

✳️✳️CAUTION

Do not wash the parts in kerosene or gasoline.

8. Examine the caliper bore and piston for scores, scratches, or rust. Replace either part, as required. Minor scratches or scoring can be corrected by dressing with crocus cloth. On late model GLCs, remove the caliper bushing with a slide pin and inspect it for excess wear or cracks.

9. Remove the piston seal from the caliper. Discard the old dust seal and piston seal, then replace them with new ones. Apply clean brake fluid to the piston and bore.

10. Assemble the caliper in the reverse order of disassembly. On late model GLCs, apply grease to the dust boot and piston seal according to the directions in the kit. Install the dust boot onto the piston, then install the assembly into the caliper. Apply grease to the slide pin and bushing.

11. On late model 626 and all MX-6, 929 and RX-7 vehicles, install the dust seal onto the piston, then install the assembly into the caliper. Apply the red grease packed in the seal kit to the piston seal. Apply the orange grease to the dust seal. Also apply the orange grease to the pin's outer circumference, the inner surface of the bushing, and the dust boot.

85819022

Fig. 53 Remove the dust seal from the piston

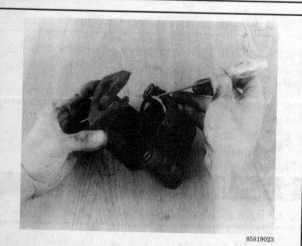

85819023

Fig. 54 Reach in and remove the piston seal from the caliper bore, but be VERY CAREFUL not to score or damage the caliper

Brake Disc (Rotor)

REMOVAL & INSTALLATION

➡️For front wheel bearing removal, installation and preload adjustment procedures on rear wheel drive cars, see Section 1. For front wheel bearing removal, installation and preload adjustment procedures on front wheel drive cars, see Section 8.

Rear Wheel Drive GLC and 1979-82 626

▶ See Figure 55

1. Remove the caliper assembly, as detailed earlier in this section.

➡️It is unnecessary to completely remove the caliper from the car. Leave the hydraulic line connected to it and wire the caliper to the underbody of the car so that it is out of the way.

2. Check the disc run-out, as detailed later in this section, before removing it from the car.

3. Withdraw the cotter pin, nut lock, adjusting nut, and washer from the spindle.

4. Remove the thrust washer and outer bearing from the hub.

5. Pull the brake disc/wheel hub assembly off of the spindle.

6. Unbolt and separate the brake disc from the hub, after matchmarking them for proper installation.

✳✳CAUTION

Do not drive the disc off of the hub.

To install:

7. Installation of the disc and hub is performed in the reverse order of removal. Adjust the bearing preload.

Front Wheel Drive GLC

1981-82 MODELS

1. Loosen the lug nuts, raise the front of the car and safely support it on jackstands. Remove the tire and wheel. Check the disc run-out, as detailed later in this section, before removing it from the car.

2. Raise the staked tab from the hub center nut, remove the nut from the axle. Apply the brake to help hold the rotor while loosening the nut.

3. Remove the brake caliper and support it properly off to the side.

4. Pull the rotor from the hub.

5. Install the rotor onto the hub. Install the caliper assembly.

6. Always use a new axle locknut and tighten it to 116-174 ft. lbs. (157-236 Nm). Stake the locknut after tightening.

7. Install the front wheels and lower the vehicle.

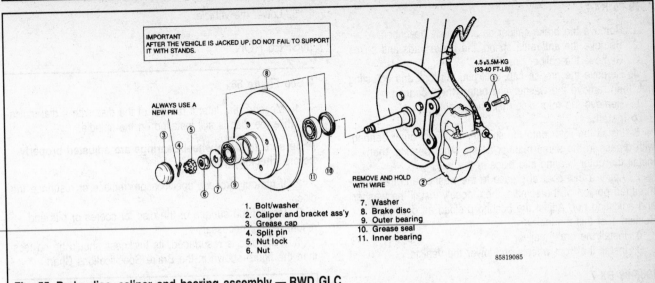

IMPORTANT
AFTER THE VEHICLE IS JACKED UP, DO NOT FAIL TO SUPPORT IT WITH STANDS.

ALWAYS USE A NEW PIN

4.5 ₅5.5M-KG (33-40 FT-LB)

REMOVE AND HOLD WITH WIRE

1. Bolt/washer
2. Caliper and bracket ass'y
3. Grease cap
4. Split pin
5. Nut lock
6. Nut
7. Washer
8. Brake disc
9. Outer bearing
10. Grease seal
11. Inner bearing

85819085

Fig. 55 Brake disc, caliper and bearing assembly — RWD GLC

1983-85 MODELS

1. Raise the vehicle and support it via the crossmember, using safety stands. Inspect the rotor as described below. Check for wheel bearing play be grasping the tires at the top and bottom, then attempting to rock them. There should be not noticeable play. Make sure you don't confuse normal play in the ball joint at the bottom of the strut with wheel bearing play. Also, spin the tire; make sure it turns smoothly and that there is no bearing noise. If there is looseness, the hub/knuckle should be disassembled and the bearing preload adjusted, as described in Section 8.

2. Remove the wheel and tire.

3. Raise the claw of the clip fastening the brake line to the strut and separate the line from the strut.

4. Remove the caliper from the strut (see the appropriate procedure above) and hang it up out of the way. The hydraulic line need not be disconnected.

5. Pull the rotor from the hub with by rocking it back and forth.

To install:

6. Install the rotor onto the hub.

7. Install the caliper assembly and torque the caliper bolts to 41-48 ft. lbs. (56-65 Nm).

8. Install a new driveshaft locknut, torque it to 116-174 ft. lbs. (157-236 Nm) and then stake it onto the groove in the end of the driveshaft with a dull punch or similar device. Use a new cotter pin on the tie rod end locknut.

9. Install the front wheels and lower the vehicle.

323, MX-6 and 1983-89 626

1. Raise the vehicle and support it securely by the center crossmember using axle stands. Inspect the disc brake rotor as described below. If the disc requires replacement or machining, inspect the wheel bearing and then remove it.

2. Spin the tire to check for roughness in the bearing or unusual noise. Then, remove the wheel and unfasten the brake caliper, as described above. Hang the caliper out of the way without disconnecting the hydraulic line.

3. Pull the rotor from the hub.

To install:

4. Install the rotor onto the hub.

5. Install the brake caliper and torque the upper bolt to 12-18 ft. lbs. (16-24 Nm) and the lower bolt to 14-22 ft. lbs. (19-30 Nm) on 1986-87 323s and 1983-87 626s. On 1988-89 323s, torque both caliper bolts to 29-36 ft. lbs. (39-49 Nm), and on 1988-89 626s and MX-6s, torque both caliper bolts to 58-72 ft. lbs. (79-98 Nm).

6. Install a new driveshaft locknut and torque it to 116-174 ft. lbs. (157-236 Nm) on 323s and 1983-87 626s, or 174-235 ft. lbs. (236-318 Nm) on 1988-89 626s and MX-6s. Crimp the nut into the groove in the axle with a dull tool until at least a 0.06 in. (1.5mm) indentation is produced.

7. Install the wheel, then lower the vehicle.

929

1. Raise the front of the car and support it on jack stands.

2. Remove the front wheel. Check the disc run-out, as detailed later in this section, before removing it from the car.

3. Remove the brake caliper and its bracket. Do not disconnect the brake line from the caliper, instead, hang the caliper, brake line still attached, out of the way on a piece of wire.

➡Never allow the caliper to hang by the brake line.

4. Gently pry the grease cap from the rotor disc. Be careful not to bend the cap.

5. Using a small cold chisel, unstake the tab on the bearing locknut. Loosen the locknut and remove it from the spindle shaft along with the washer. Discard the locknut, as a new one must be used on assembly. Set the washer aside.

6. Pull the rotor disc from the spindle shaft with a back and forth rocking motion.

To install:

7. Install the disc plate with the washer and the new locknut. Adjust the bearing preload.

8. Stake the locknut tab with a small cold chisel. The tab should have a 0.16 in. (4mm) clearance from the shaft groove.

9. Install the caliper assembly and torque the retaining bolts to 65-87 ft. lbs. (88-118 Nm).

10. Install the wheels and torque the lug nuts to 65-87 ft. lbs. (88-118 Nm).

11. Lower the vehicle.

1979-85 RX-7

1. Remove the brake caliper as previously described.
2. Remove the anti-rattle spring, the brake pads and shims.
3. Remove the caliper bracket.
4. Remove the grease cap, split pin, nut lock and adjusting nut, then remove the washer and outer wheel bearing.
5. Remove the rotor disc from the spindle.

To install:

6. Install the rotor onto the spindle. Pack the outer bearing with grease in the same manner as the inner bearing, then install the outer bearing into place in the hub.
7. Apply a thin coat of grease to the washer and the threaded portion of the spindle, then loosely install the washer and adjusting nut. Adjust the bearing preload as described in Section 1 of this manual.
8. Install the brake caliper.
9. Install the front wheels and lower the vehicle.

1986-89 RX-7

1. Raise the front of the car and support it on jack stands.
2. Remove the front wheel.
3. Remove the brake caliper and its bracket. Do not disconnect the brake line from the caliper, instead, hang the caliper, brake line still attached, out of the way on a piece of wire.

➡**Never allow the caliper to hang by the brake line.**

4. Remove the grease hub cap, cotter pin, the set cover and the locknut.
5. Remove the wheel hub and the rotor disc carefully from the wheel spindle. Remove the washer and the outer bearing.

To install:

6. Install the wheel hub and rotor disc.
7. Adjust the bearing preload as described in Section 1 of this manual.
8. Install the caliper and torque the retaining bolts to 58-72 ft. lbs. (79-98 Nm).

9. Lower the vehicle.

INSPECTION

▶**See Figure 56**

1. Measure the lateral run-out of the disc with a dial indicator while the disc is still installed on the spindle.

➡**Be sure that the wheel bearings are adjusted properly before checking run-out.**

2. If run-out exceeds specification, replace or resurface the disc.
3. Inspect the surface of the disc for scores or pits and resurface it, if necessary.
4. If the disc is resurfaced, its thickness should be no less than the figure shown in the Brake Specifications Chart.

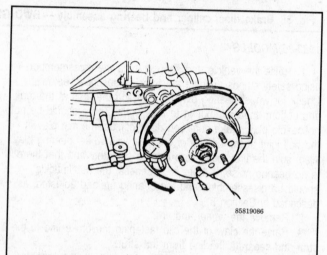

85819086

Fig. 56 Checking lateral run-out of the brake disc with a dial indicator

REAR DRUM BRAKES

Brake Drums

✳✳CAUTION

Brake shoes may contain asbestos, which has been determined to be a cancer causing agent. Wear an approved filter mask or respirator whenever working around brakes, to avoid inhaling dust from any brake surface. Never clean brake components with compressed air! Instead, use a commercially available brake cleaning fluid.

REMOVAL & INSTALLATION

Rear Wheel Drive Vehicles

1. Remove the wheel disc and loosen the lug nuts.

2. Raise the rear of the car and support it with jackstands.
3. Remove the lug nuts and the rear wheel.
4. Be sure that the parking brake is fully released.
5. Remove the bolts or screws which secure the drum to the rear axle shaft flange or center locknut.

➡**If the drum will not come off easily, screw the drum securing bolts into the two tapped holes in the drum. Tighten the bolts evenly in order to force the drum away from the flange.**

6. Adjust the shoes after installation is completed or prior to installation on GLC.

Front Wheel Drive GLC, 323, 626 and MX-6

▶ **See Figures 57, 58, 59, 60, 61, 62 and 63**

1. Loosen the rear wheel lugnuts. Raise the vehicle and support it securely. Remove the lugnuts and wheel.
2. If equipped, carefully pry off the hub (grease) cap.

85819034

Fig. 57 Remove the grease cap to expose the hub retainer

85819035

Fig. 58 Use a hammer and chisel to carefully unstake the locknut

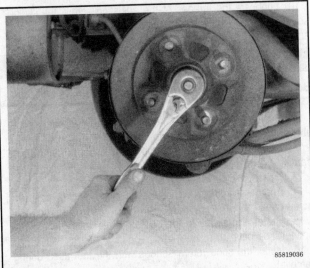

85819036

Fig. 59 Use a socket wrench to loosen . . .

85819037

Fig. 60 . . . then remove the locknut

85819038

Fig. 61 The hub washer seats against the outer bearing

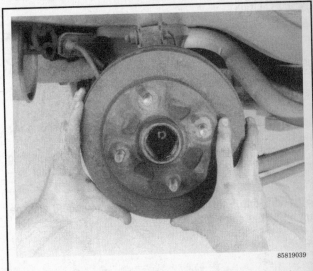

85819039

Fig. 62 Grasp the brake drum by its edges . .

85819040

Fig. 63 . . . and pull it away from the vehicle

3. Unstake the locknut and remove it. Pull off the drum, being careful to catch the washer and bearings if they fall out of the center of the drum. If it is difficult to remove the drum:

- On GLC, remove the lever stop from the backing plate to increase the brake shoe clearance.
- On 323, 626 and MX-6, remove the backing plate plug to increase the shoe clearance. If this does not make it easy to remove the drum, loosen the parking brake lever adjustment nut or the operating stop lever at the backing plate.

To install:

4. Install the brake drum with the washer and bearing. Install a new locknut and adjust the preload as described in Section 8. On 1988-89 626s and MX-6s, torque the locknut to 72-130 ft. lbs. (98-176 Nm).

➡**Be sure to stake the new locknut when the preload adjustment is complete.**

5. If equipped, install the grease cap.
6. Install the rear wheels and lower the vehicle.

INSPECTION

1. Examine the drum for cracks or overheating spots. Replace the drum if either of these are present.
2. Check the drum for scoring. Light scoring can be corrected with sandpaper.
3. Check the drum with a dial indicator for out-of-roundness; turn the drum if it is beyond the specifications shown in the Brake Specifications Chart.
4. If the drum must be turned because of excessive scoring or out-of-roundness, the drum's inside diameter should not exceed the specifications shown in the chart.

➡**If one drum is turned, the opposite drum should also be turned to the same size.**

Brake Shoes

REMOVAL & INSTALLATION

Rear Wheel Drive Models
➤ See Figures 64 and 65

✱✱CAUTION

Brake shoes may contain asbestos, which has been determined to be a cancer causing agent. Wear an approved filter mask or respirator whenever working around brakes, to avoid inhaling dust from any brake surface. Never clean brake components with compressed air! Instead, use a commercially available brake cleaning fluid.

➡**When removing and installing brake shoes, work on one side at a time so that, if necessary, you can refer to the undisturbed assembly on the other side for reference.**

1. Perform the brake drum removal procedure, as previously detailed. Make sure that the parking brake is fully released.
2. Clean the dirt from the brake components with an aerosol brake cleaner.
3. Remove the return springs from the upper side of the shoe using a brake spring removal tool.
4. Remove the return springs from the lower side of the shoes in the same manner as Step 3.
5. Remove the shoe retaining spring by compressing the retaining spring while turning the pin 90 degrees.
6. Withdraw the primary shoe and the parking brake link.
7. Disengage the parking brake lever from the secondary shoe by unfastening its retaining clip.
8. Remove the secondary shoe.
9. Inspect the linings and replace them if they are worn, badly burned or saturated with oil or grease. See the Brake Specifications chart in this section.

To install:

10. Lubricate the threads of the adjusting screw, the sliding surfaces of the shoes, and the backing plate flanges with a small quantity of grease.

✱✱WARNING

Be careful not to get oil or grease on the lining surfaces.

11. Position the parking brake lever on the secondary shoe and secure with its retaining clip.
12. Install the eye of the parking brake cable through the parking brake lever.
13. Fit the link between the shoes.
14. Engage the shoes with the slots in the anchor (adjusting screw) and the wheel cylinder.
15. Fasten the shoes to the backing plate with the retaining springs and pins.
16. Install the shoe return springs with the tool used during removal.

➡**If a slight amount of grease has gotten on the shoes during installation, it may be removed by light sanding.**

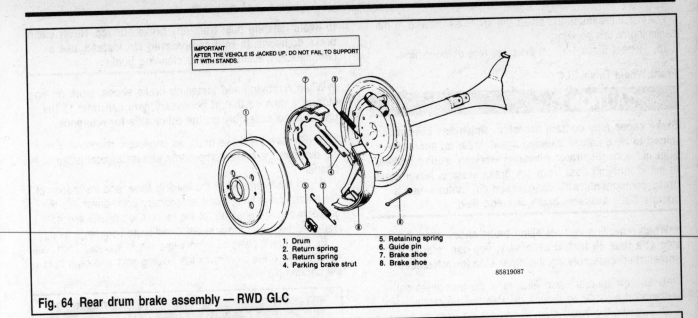

IMPORTANT
AFTER THE VEHICLE IS JACKED UP, DO NOT FAIL TO SUPPORT
IT WITH STANDS.

1. Drum
2. Return spring
3. Return spring
4. Parking brake strut
5. Retaining spring
6. Guide pin
7. Brake shoe
8. Brake shoe

85819087

Fig. 64 Rear drum brake assembly — RWD GLC

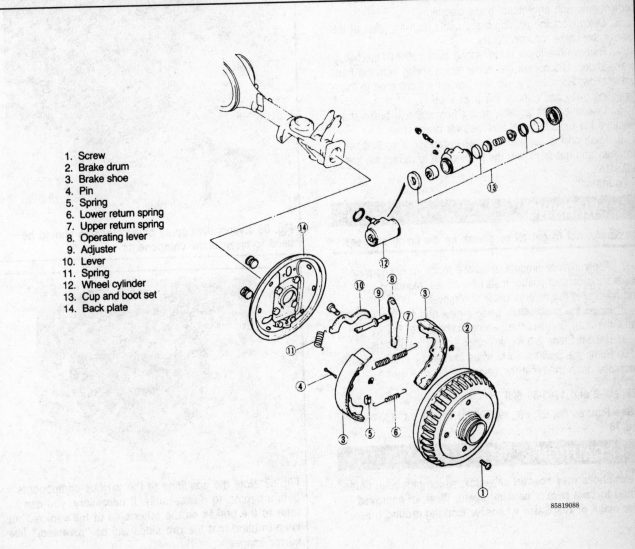

1. Screw
2. Brake drum
3. Brake shoe
4. Pin
5. Spring
6. Lower return spring
7. Upper return spring
8. Operating lever
9. Adjuster
10. Lever
11. Spring
12. Wheel cylinder
13. Cup and boot set
14. Back plate

85819088

Fig. 65 Rear drum brake components — RX-7

17. Install the drum and adjust the shoes as detailed at the beginning of this section.

18. Repeat Steps 1-17 on the other side of the vehicle.

Front Wheel Drive GLC

❋❋CAUTION

Brake shoes may contain asbestos, which has been determined to be a cancer causing agent. Wear an approved filter mask or respirator whenever working around brakes, to avoid inhaling dust from any brake surface. Never clean brake components with compressed air! Instead, use a commercially available brake cleaning fluid.

➡When removing and installing brake shoes, work on one side at a time so that, if necessary, you can refer to the undisturbed assembly on the other side for reference.

1. Loosen the rear wheel lugs, raise the rear of the car and support it safely on jackstands. Remove the rear wheels.

2. Remove the brake drum. Clean the dirt from the brake components with an aerosol brake cleaner.

3. Disconnect the parking brake cable from the lever at the rear of the brake mounting plate.

4. Remove the lower return spring from between the two brake shoes. Disconnect the upper return spring from the front brake shoe. Remove the clip that holds the front shoe to the mounting plate and remove the front shoe.

5. Disconnect the adjuster spring from the rear brake shoe. Remove the mounting clip and the rear brake shoe.

6. Push on the adjuster lever while rotating a screwdriver between and quadrant and the knurled pin to retract the self-adjuster.

To install:

❋❋WARNING

Be careful not to get oil or grease on the lining surfaces.

7. Apply a small amount of grease to the mounting plate brake shoe contact points. Install the shoes, mounting clips and springs in the reverse order of removal.

8. Install the brake drum using a new hub nut (be sure to stake the nut). Connect the parking brake cable.

9. Repeat Steps 2-8 for the other side of the vehicle.

10. Pump the pedal several times to adjust the drum-to-shoe clearance, then road test the vehicle.

323, MX-6 and 1983-89 626

▶ See Figures 66, 67, 68, 69, 70, 71, 72, 73, 74, 75, 76, 77 and 78

❋❋CAUTION

Brake shoes may contain asbestos, which has been determined to be a cancer causing agent. Wear an approved filter mask or respirator whenever working around brakes, to avoid inhaling dust from any brake surface. Never clean brake components with compressed air! Instead, use a commercially available brake cleaning fluid.

➡When removing and installing brake shoes, work on one side at a time so that, if necessary, you can refer to the undisturbed assembly on the other side for reference.

1. Remove the brake drum, as previously described. Clean the dirt from the brake components with an aerosol brake cleaner.

2. To ease removal of the leading shoe, and installation of the return spring later, insert an ordinary screwdriver into the gap between the quadrant of the automatic adjuster mechanism and twist it in the arrowed direction to release tension.

3. Use brake pliers to remove the return springs. Then, use needle nose pliers to remove the holding pins and clips from the backing plate.

Fig. 66 Evaporative spray brake cleaners should be used to clean brake components

Fig. 67 Note the positions of the various components before beginning disassembly. If necessary, you can refer to the brakes on the other side of the vehicle, but keep in mind that the two sides will be "reversed," like mirror images

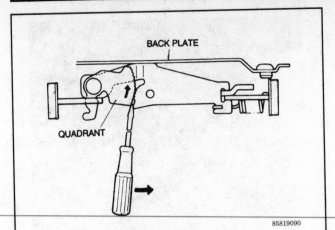

BACK PLATE

QUADRANT

85819090

Fig. 68 Release tension on the self-adjuster mechanism by inserting a screwdriver and moving the quadrant in the arrowed direction

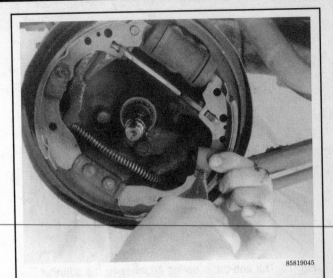

85819045

Fig. 71 Use needlenose pliers to twist . . .

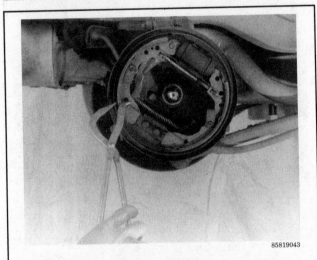

85819043

Fig. 69 Remove the upper and lower return springs which bridge the leading and trailing shoes

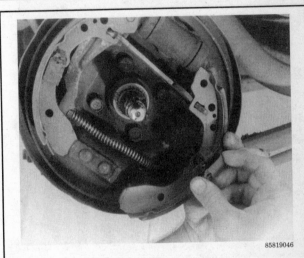

85819046

Fig. 72 . . . then disengage the clips and pins which secure the shoes to the backing plate

85819044

Fig. 70 Brake pliers are specially designed for this task

4. Push the bottoms of the shoes outward in order to release them from the anchors and then unhook them at the wheel cylinder. Remove the leading shoe first.

➤ Although the leading and trailing brake shoes can be removed separately, it may be easier to remove them as an assembly, with the self-adjuster and anti-rattle spring. In any event, they must be replaced in sets.

5. Remove the anti-rattle spring and adjuster, if new shoes are to be installed. Unless the replacement trailing shoe comes with another operating lever, also remove the retainer which fastens the lever to the shoe, then separate the operating lever.

6. The linings must be at least 0.04 in. (1mm) thick or conform to inspection standards in your state. Replace them regardless of the thickness if there are any signs of peeling or

Fig. 73 The anti-rattle spring attaches to the adjuster and the trailing shoe

Fig. 74 The adjuster can be removed with the leading shoe

Fig. 75 Separate the operating lever (connected to the parking brake cable) from the trailing shoe

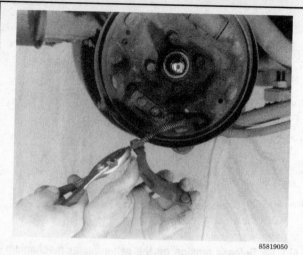

Fig. 76 If necessary, disengage the end of the parking brake cable from the operating lever

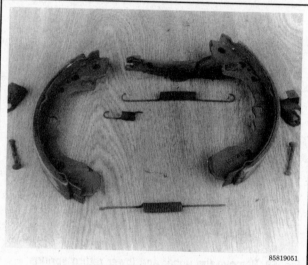

Fig. 77 Disassembled brake shoes and related hardware

cracks. The brake drum should be turned if there is grooving or cracking. The limit on inner diameter is 7.9 in. (201mm).

➡Brake shoes should be replaced as a set on each wheel. Both rear wheels should be serviced if either side shows excessive wear.

To install:

7. Apply grease to the areas shown in the accompanying illustration by both types of arrows.

8. If applicable, insert the operating lever pivot pin through the trailing shoe and secure with a new horseshoe clip.

9. Connect the upper return spring to the trailing shoe assembly.

✳✳WARNING

Be careful not to get oil or grease on the lining surfaces.

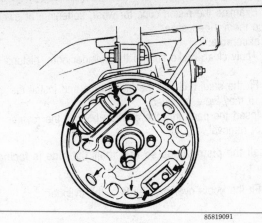

Fig. 78 Grease the wheel cylinder and anchor pin (at the spots indicated by the thicker arrows), and the backing plate (at the spots indicated by the thinner arrows)

10. Position the trailing brake shoe against the wheel cylinder and anchor plate. Retain the trailing shoe with the holding pins and clips.

11. Install the adjuster and anti-rattle spring to the trailing shoe.

12. Connect the lower return spring to the trailing and leading brake shoes.

13. Install the leading brake shoe onto the adjuster, then to the wheel cylinder and anchor plate.

14. Install the remaining upper return spring.

15. Repeat Steps 1-13 for the other side of the vehicle.

16. Be sure to apply the brakes several times before the vehicle is driven; the shoe clearance will be adjusted automatically.

Wheel Cylinders

REMOVAL & INSTALLATION

▶ See Figures 79 and 80

1. Remove the brake drums and shoes as detailed previously.

2. Disconnect the hydraulic line from the wheel cylinder by unfastening the flare nut on the rear of the backing plate. Use a flare nut wrench.

3. Plug the line to prevent dirt from entering the system or brake fluid from leaking out.

4. Unfasten the nuts which secure the wheel cylinder to the backing plate and remove the cylinder.

To install:

5. Attach the wheel cylinder to the backing plate and install the attaching nuts.

6. Unplug the fluid lines and connect them to their respective connections on the rear of the backing plate.

7. Install the brake drums. Bleed the hydraulic system and adjust the brake shoes after installation is completed.

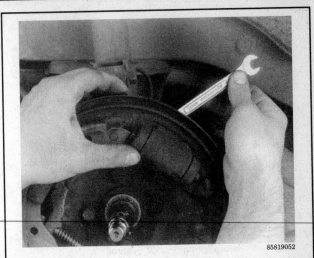

Fig. 79 Disconnect the flexible brake line from the wheel cylinder

OVERHAUL

▶ See Figure 81

1. Remove the boots at either end of the wheel cylinder.

2. Withdraw the pistons, piston cups, pushrods, filling blocks (GLC, 323, 626 and MX-6 only), and return spring.

3. Wash all of the components in clean brake fluid.

❋❋CAUTION

Never use kerosene or gasoline to clean wheel cylinder components.

4. Check the cylinder bore and piston for roughness or scoring. Use a wheel cylinder hone, if necessary.

5. Measure the clearance between the cylinder and the piston with a feeler gauge. If the clearance if greater than 0.006 in. (0.15mm), replace either the piston or the cylinder.

Fig. 80 Unfasten and remove the wheel cylinder from the backing plate

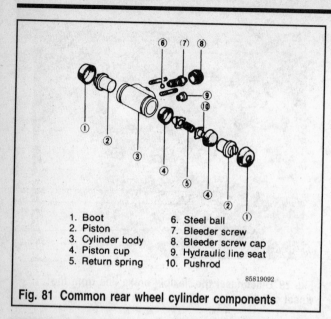

1. Boot
2. Piston
3. Cylinder body
4. Piston cup
5. Return spring
6. Steel ball
7. Bleeder screw
8. Bleeder screw cap
9. Hydraulic line seat
10. Pushrod

85819092

Fig. 81 Common rear wheel cylinder components

6. Examine the piston cups for wear, softening, or swelling; replace them if necessary.

To assemble:

7. Apply clean brake fluid to the cylinder bore, pistons, and cups.

8. Fit the steel ball into the bleed hole and install the screw, if they were removed.

9. Insert the parts into the cylinder bore in the reverse order of removal.

➡**Install the piston cups so that their flat side is facing outward.**

10. Fit the boots over both ends of the cylinder.

REAR DISC BRAKES

Rear disc brakes are found on some models of the 323, 626/MX-6, 929 and RX-7. The basic design of the caliper and pads is identical to that of the front disc brakes on the same vehicle; therefore, for pad removal and installation, caliper removal and installation, and caliper overhaul, see the applicable procedures for front disc brakes **with the exception of those vehicles detailed below.**

Brake Pads

REMOVAL & INSTALLATION

1988-89 323, 626 and MX-6
▶ **See Figures 82, 83 and 84**

➡**To install the brake pads, Mazda brake piston wrench 49-FA18-602 or equivalent is required to turn the piston into the caliper to allow for the thicker new pads.**

1. Loosen the rear wheel lug nuts and release the parking brake. Raise the rear of the vehicle and support safely. Remove the rear wheels.

➡**When removing and installing brake pads, work on one side at a time so that, if necessary, you can refer to the undisturbed assembly on the other side for reference.**

2. Reach behind the caliper with a box end wrench and disconnect the parking brake cable from the cable mounting bracket, then from the operating lever.

3. On 323s, remove the lower caliper mounting bolt and swing the caliper upward to where the V-spring is accessible. Remove the V-spring, pads and shims. On 626s and MX-6s, the V spring, pads and shims are removed in the same manner except that the upper caliper bolt is removed and the caliper is moved downward to expose the V spring. Support the caliper assembly with a piece of rope or wire from the strut to prevent straining the brake hose.

To install:

4. Coat the new pad shims with brake grease and attach them to the new pads.

5. Using the special tool, turn the piston fully into the caliper bore until the groove in the piston is aligned with the inner pad alignment pin (see illustration).

6. Once the piston is aligned, install the new pads and pad shims onto the mounting support. Install the pad clips.

7. Lift or lower the caliper onto the mounting support and install the attaching bolt. Torque the bolt to 12-17 ft. lbs. (16-23 Nm).

8. Connect the end of the parking brake cable to the operating lever, then tighten the locknut so that there is no clearance between the cable end and the lever.

9. Repeat Steps 2-8 for the other side of the vehicle.

10. Install the rear wheels. Apply the brakes a few times, then rotate the wheels to make sure that there is no excessive brake drag while the wheels are turning.

11. Lower and road test the vehicle.

929

➡**To install the brake pads, Mazda brake piston wrench 49-0221-600C or equivalent is required to seat the piston into the caliper to allow for the thicker new pads.**

1. Loosen the rear wheel lug nuts and release the parking brake. Raise the rear of the vehicle and support safely. Remove the rear wheels.

➡**When removing and installing brake pads, work on one side at a time so that, if necessary, you can refer to the undisturbed assembly on the other side for reference.**

2. Remove the lower lock pin from the caliper, then lift the caliper up and tie it off to the strut to relive the strain on the brake hose.

3. Remove the guide clips from the mounting support.

4. Remove the pads and shims from the mounting support.

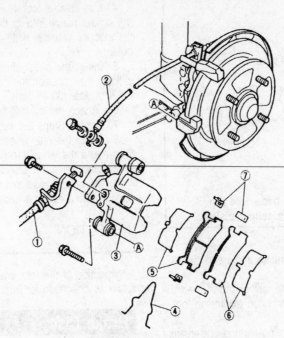

1. Parking brake cable and bracket
2. Flexible hose
3. Caliper
4. V-spring
5. Inner pad and outer shim
6. Outer pad and shim
7. Guide plate

85819093

Fig. 82 Rear disc brake components — 1988-89 323

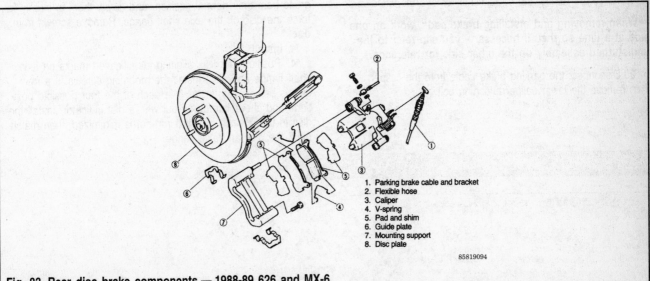

1. Parking brake cable and bracket
2. Flexible hose
3. Caliper
4. V-spring
5. Pad and shim
6. Guide plate
7. Mounting support
8. Disc plate

85819094

Fig. 83 Rear disc brake components — 1988-89 626 and MX-6

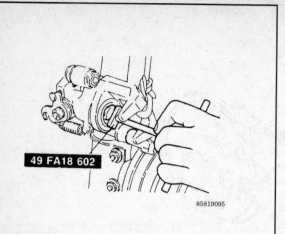

49 FA18 602

85819095

Fig. 84 Before installing new brake pads, use the special tool to push in and align the caliper piston

To install:

5. Coat the new shims with brake grease and install the shims and pads onto the mounting support.

6. Install the guide clips and push the caliper piston inward using a small C-clamp or Mazda special piston expansion tool 49-0221-600C or equivalent.

7. Position the caliper onto the mounting support and install the lower lock pin bolt. Torque the bolt to 12-17 ft. lbs. (16-23 Nm).

8. Repeat Steps 2-7 for the other side of the vehicle.

9. Install the rear wheels. Apply the brakes a few times, then rotate the wheels to make sure that there is no excessive brake drag while the wheels are turning.

10. Lower and road test the vehicle.

1979-89 RX-7

➡To install the brake pads, Mazda brake piston wrench **49-FA18-602 or equivalent is required to seat the piston into the caliper to allow for the thicker new pads.**

1. Raise the rear of the vehicle and remove the wheels.

➡When removing and installing brake pads, work on one side at a time so that, if necessary, you can refer to the undisturbed assembly on the other side for reference.

2. Disconnect the parking brake cable from the caliper, then remove the lower caliper attaching bolt.

3. Lift up the lower side of the caliper and remove the anti-rattle springs, pads, and shims. Support the caliper with a piece of rope or wire to relieve the stain on the brake hose.
To install:

4. Use special tool 49-FA18-602 or equivalent to fully screw the caliper piston into its bore. Turn the piston so that one of the stopper grooves in it is pointing toward the pad inspection hole.

5. Install the pads, shims and anti-rattle springs into the caliper, then position the caliper. Tighten the caliper bolt to 22-30 ft. lbs. (30-41 Nm).

6. Attach the parking brake cable.

7. Repeat Steps 2-6 for the other side of the vehicle.

8. Install the rear wheels. Apply the brakes a few times, then rotate the wheels to make sure that there is no excessive brake drag while the wheels are turning.

9. Lower and road test the vehicle. Adjust the play in the parking brake cable, if necessary.

INSPECTION

Inspection of the rear brake pads is performed exactly the same as described for front disc brake pads.

Brake Disc

REMOVAL & INSTALLATION

1. Properly support the vehicle on stands and remove the rear wheels. Check the lateral run-out of the disc with a dial indicator. Refer to the Brake Specifications chart at the end of this section for run-out limits.

2. Remove the bolts attaching the caliper bracket, and remove the caliper and bracket as an assembly, and wire it to the rear spring or strut.

3. Fully release the parking brake. Remove the disc attaching screws, install them into the tapped holes about 90 degrees from their normal position, and screw them in evenly to force the disc off the axle shaft flange. Remove screws from disc.
To install:

4. Position the disc, aligning identification marks on axle shaft flange and disc. Install the mounting screws. If a new disc is being used, install it in each of the four possible positions and check lateral run-out with a dial indicator. Install the disc in the position in which run-out is minimized, then match-mark the disc and axle flange.

PARKING BRAKE

Cables

REMOVAL & INSTALLATION

▶ **See Figures 85 and 86**

1. Remove the brake lever covers (or console if applicable).
2. Remove the adjusting screw from the cable at the parking brake lever.
3. Raise the car and support it safely.
4. Working underneath the car, unhook the tension spring at the front of the cable.
5. Remove the cotter pins and remove the link pins attaching the rear ends of the cable to the rear brake half cables.
6. Remove the cable.

To install:

7. Route and attach the new cable(s). Install the link pins with new cotter pins.
8. Fasten the tension spring at the front of the cable.

➡ **Turn the adjusting nuts so that the equalizer is at a 90 degree angle to the front parking brake cable.**

9. Lower the vehicle, then install the cable adjusting screw at the brake lever.
10. Adjust the brake lever stroke as described below, then install the lever covers or console.

Brake Lever

ADJUSTMENT

▶ **See Figures 87, 88, 89 and 90**

1. Adjust the rear brake shoes.
2. Unfasten the screw(s) and remove the brake lever covers or console.

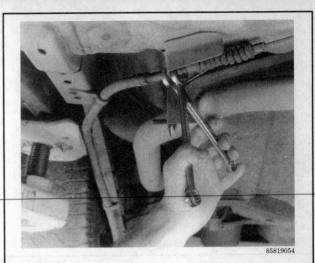

Fig. 86 Use a pair of wrenches to turn the cable adjusting nuts

3. Adjust the front cable with the nut or screw located at the rear of the parking brake handle. Use the following list to determine how many notches are required to engage the parking brake.

- GLC rear wheel drive: 3-7
- GLC front wheel drive: 5-9
- 323 1986: rear disc 9-15; rear drum 7-11
- 323 1987: 7-11
- 323 1988: 5-7
- 323 1989: rear disc 5-7; rear drum 6-8
- 626 1979-82: 5-7
- 626 1983-87: 7-9
- 626/MX-6 1988-89: 5-7
- 929: 6-8
- RX-7 1979-83: 3-7
- RX-7 1984-85: 6-8
- RX-7 1986-89: 4-5

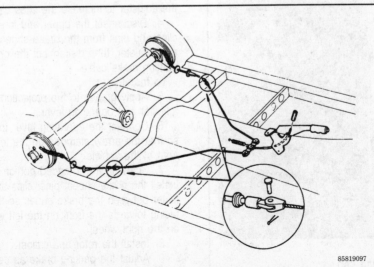

Fig. 85 Common parking brake cable configuration — RX-7 shown, others similar

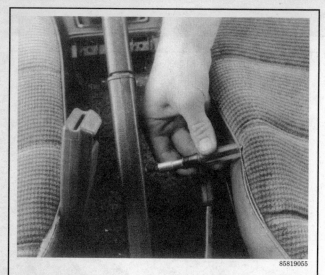

Fig. 87 Unfasten the screw(s) . . .

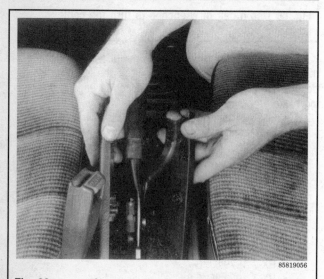

Fig. 88 . . . and remove the parking brake lever covers

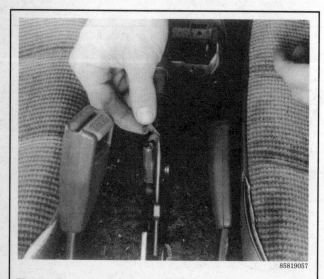

Fig. 89 Remove the retaining clip . . .

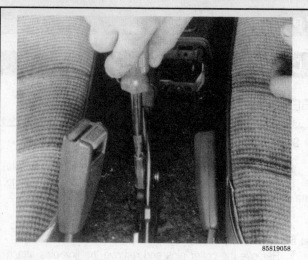

Fig. 90 . . . then use a screwdriver to turn the adjustment nut

4. Operate the parking brake several times; check to see that the rear wheels do not drag when it is fully released. Also, make sure that the brake warning light illuminates when the lever is pulled up one notch, but goes out when it is fully released.

5. Install the brake lever covers or console.

Brake Shoes

REMOVAL & INSTALLATION

929
▶ See Figure 91

1. Loosen the rear wheel lug nuts. Raise the vehicle and support safely. Remove the rear wheels.

2. Remove the disc brake caliper and support it with a piece of rope or wire to avoid straining the brake hose.

3. Remove the rotor disc from the wheel hub. If the disc is stubborn, remove the cap from the adjusting screw and turn the adjuster to increase the shoe clearance.

4. Disconnect the upper and lower return springs, anchor clips and pins from the brake shoes. Remove the brake shoes and adjuster, then disconnect the operating lever from the parking brake cable.

To install:

5. Apply grease to the projections on the backing plate, adjuster and operating lever.

6. Connect the operating lever to the parking brake cable so that the arrow stamped on the lever is pointing towards the front of the vehicle.

7. Screw in the threaded portion of the adjuster completely. Install the brake shoes, pins, clips and springs. Place the adjuster between the brake shoes so that the threaded part is facing towards the front on the left wheel and towards the rear on the right wheel.

8. Install the rotor and caliper.

9. Adjust the parking brake as described below. Mount the rear wheels and lower the vehicle.

ADJUSTMENT

929

▶ **See Figure 92**

1. Remove the disc brake service hole cap.

2. Insert a flat blade screwdriver through the hole and turn the adjuster down until the rotor locks.

3. When the rotor locks, push the adjuster up 3-5 notches in the opposite direction to set.

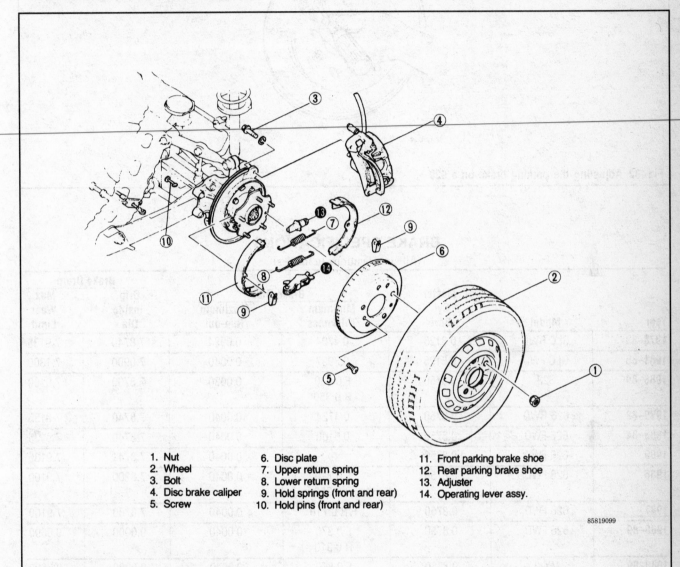

1. Nut	6. Disc plate	11. Front parking brake shoe
2. Wheel	7. Upper return spring	12. Rear parking brake shoe
3. Bolt	8. Lower return spring	13. Adjuster
4. Disc brake caliper	9. Hold springs (front and rear)	14. Operating lever assy.
5. Screw	10. Hold pins (front and rear)	

85819099

Fig. 91 Parking brake components — 929

85819098

Fig. 92 Adjusting the parking brake on a 929

BRAKE SPECIFICATIONS
(All specifications in inches)

Year	Model	Master Cyl. Bore	Brake Disc Minimum Thickness	Brake Disc Maximum Run-out	Brake Drum Orig. Inside Dia.	Brake Drum Max. Wear Limit
1978–83	GLC RWD	0.8125	0.4724	0.0024	7.8740	7.9135
1981–85	GLC FWD	0.8125	0.3937	0.0040	7.0900	7.1300
1986–89	323	0.8750	F 0.630 R 0.350	0.0030	7.8700	7.9100
1979–82	626 RWD	0.8750	0.4724	0.0040	7.8740	7.9135
1983–84	626 FWD	0.8750	0.5100	0.0040	7.8740	7.9135
1985	626 FWD	0.8750	①	0.0040	7.8741	7.9135
1986	626 FWD	0.8750	F 0.710 R 0.350	0.0040	7.8700	7.9100
1987	626 FWD	0.8750	F/R 0.710	0.0040	7.8700	7.9100
1988–89	626 FWD	0.8750	F 0.870 R 0.310	0.0040	9.0000	9.0600
1988–89	MX-6	0.8750	F 0.870 R 0.310	0.0040	9.0000	9.0600
1988–89	929	0.8750	F 0.870 R 0.310	0.0040	—	—
1979–85	RX-7	0.8125	F 0.6693 R 0.3543	0.0040	7.8741	7.9135
1986–89	RX-7	0.8750	F 0.790 R②	0.0040	—	—

① Gasoline engine: 0.550
  Diesel engine: 0.710
② With 13 inch wheels: 0.710
  With 14 inch wheels: 0.310

858190C1

EXTERIOR

INTERIOR

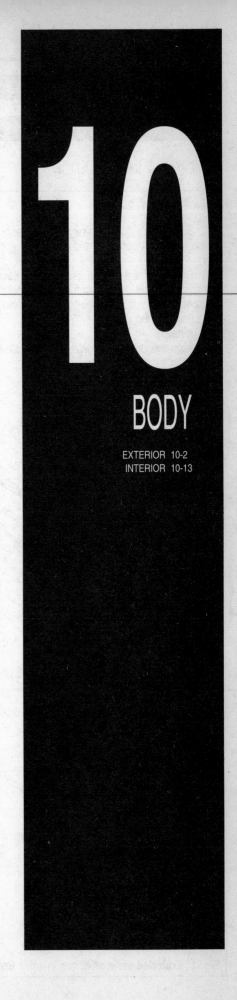

10

BODY

EXTERIOR

Doors

REMOVAL & INSTALLATION

▶ **See Figures 1, 2 and 3**

1. Support the door securely. Then, using a wax pencil or crayon, make an outline of the hinge where it attaches to the door.

2. Remove the door trim panel, and unfasten the electrical connectors for the power windows, door locks etc. (if equipped). Remove the hinge-to-door attaching bolts.

3. Remove the door.

To install:

4. Align the door hinge with the mark previously made on the door.

5. Install the hinge-to-door attaching bolts.

6. Attach the electrical connections.

7. Tighten the bolts securely. Check the door for proper movement and, if applicable, operation of power accessories.

ADJUSTMENT

Door Latch Striker

▶ **See Figure 4**

➡**The door latch striker can be adjusted laterally and vertically as well as fore and aft. The striker should not be adjusted to correct door sag.**

1. Loosen the attaching screws and move the door latch striker as required.

2. Tighten the attaching screws and check the door for fit. Repeat the procedure if necessary.

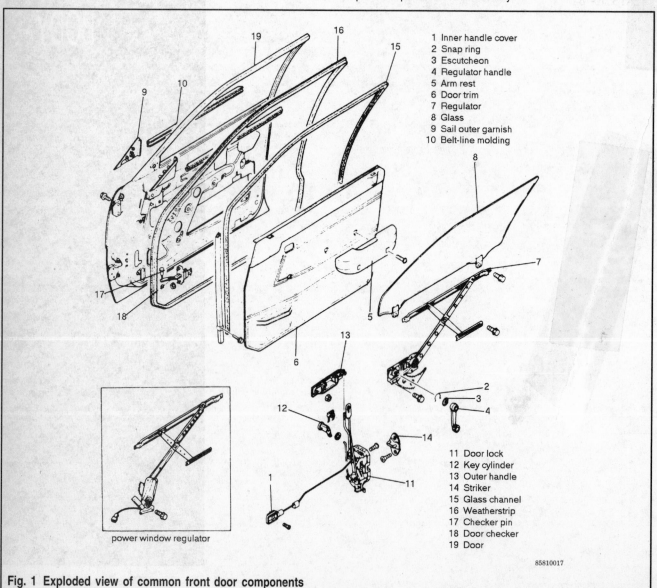

1 Inner handle cover
2 Snap ring
3 Escutcheon
4 Regulator handle
5 Arm rest
6 Door trim
7 Regulator
8 Glass
9 Sail outer garnish
10 Belt-line molding

11 Door lock
12 Key cylinder
13 Outer handle
14 Striker
15 Glass channel
16 Weatherstrip
17 Checker pin
18 Door checker
19 Door

power window regulator

85810017

Fig. 1 Exploded view of common front door components

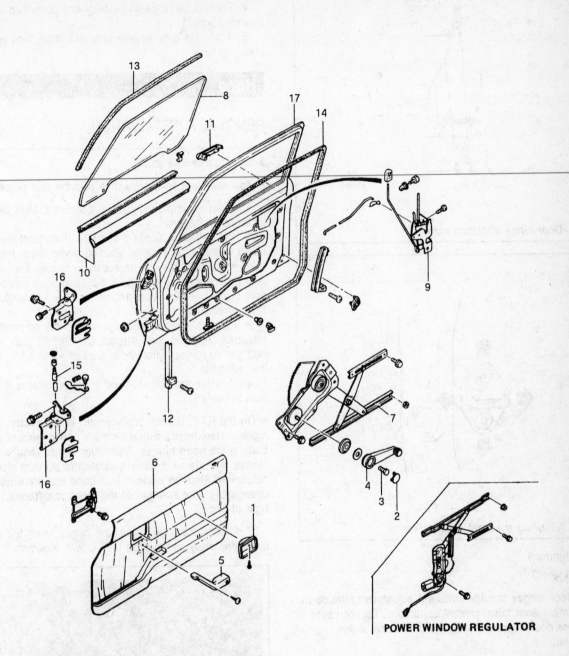

POWER WINDOW REGULATOR

1 Inner handle cover	7 Regulator	12 Glass guide
2 Regulator handle cap	8 Glass	13 Glass channel
3 Bolt	9 Door lock	14 Weatherstrip
4 Regulator handle	10 Outer and inner weatherstrip	15 Checker pin
5 Arm rest	11 Outer handle	16 Door checker
6 Door trim		17 Door

85810020

Fig. 2 Front door components — 1979-85 RX-7

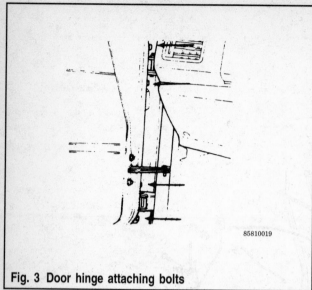

Fig. 3 Door hinge attaching bolts

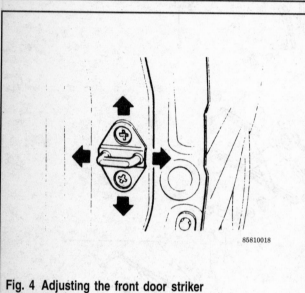

Fig. 4 Adjusting the front door striker

Door Alignment

▶ **See Figure 3**

➡The door hinges provide sufficient adjustment latitude to correct most door misalignment conditions. Do not cover up a poor door alignment with the door latch striker adjustment.

1. Loosen the hinge attaching bolts and move the hinge as required.
2. Tighten the attaching bolts and check the door for fit. Repeat the procedure if necessary.

Door Hinge

REMOVAL & INSTALLATION

▶ **See Figure 3**

1. Have an assistant support the door.

2. Remove the hinge-to-body attaching bolts.
3. Remove the hinge-to-door attaching bolts and remove the hinge.
4. Position the hinge to the body and door, then install the attaching bolts.
5. Adjust the door as previously described, then tighten the attaching bolts.

Hood

REMOVAL & INSTALLATION

▶ **See Figures 5, 6 and 7**

➡**You will need an assistant to perform this procedure.**

1. Open the hood and support it securely. Mark the hinge locations on the hood.
2. On 1988-89 626, MX-6 and 929, disconnect the windshield washer hose from its retaining clamp. If the hood is being replaced, it may be necessary to remove the hood insulator fasteners (using the proper tool) and hood insulator, the front seal rubber insulators and seal rubber for transfer to the replacement hood.
3. Have an assistant hold the hood in the up position. If equipped, lower the hood support. On 1988-89 929s, disconnect the stay damper from both sides of the hood by removing the ball studs.
4. Unfasten the hinge-to-hood bolts and remove the hood from the vehicle.

➡**On the RX-7, if hood replacement is necessary, do not replace steel hoods with aluminum hoods without also replacing the hood hinges. Aluminum hoods require special hinges that are electrically insulated to prevent electrolytic corrosion. Also, be advised that hood locks are not interchangeable. The strength of the locks is different for each type of hood.**

5. Position the hood against the hinges, using the marks made previously on the hood to help with alignment.

Fig. 5 Mark the hinge locations on the hood

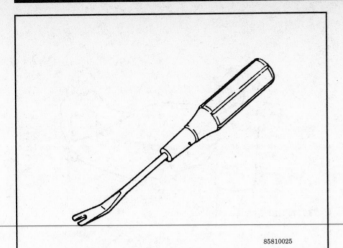

Fig. 6 Hood insulator fastener removal tool

Fig. 7 Use a socket wrench to unfasten the hood retaining bolts

6. Have an assistant hold the hood in position. Install the hinge-to-hood bolts, then raise the hood support, if so equipped. On 1988-89 929, connect the stay dampers to the hood and torque the ball studs to 14-19 ft. lbs. (19-26 Nm). In 1988-89 626, MX-6 and 929, connect the windshield washer hose. If applicable, also install the front seal rubber, seal rubber insulators, hood insulator and fasteners.

7. Tighten all bolts securely and check the hood for proper alignment.

ALIGNMENT

The hood is provided with to-and-fro, up-and-down or side-to-side adjustments.

To make the to-and-fro or side-to-side adjustments:

1. Loosen the hood attaching bolts and move the hood to the proper position, then tighten the attaching bolts.

2. Repeat the procedure if necessary.

To make the up-and-down adjustment (at the rear of the hood):

3. Loosen the hood stop bolts.

4. Using a screwdriver, turn the hood stop screws clockwise to lower the hood and counterclockwise to raise the hood. Hood is at the proper height when it is flush with the fenders.

5. Tighten the hood stop bolts.

6. Repeat the procedure if necessary.

LATCH ADJUSTMENT

▶ See Figure 8

1. Make sure that the hood is properly aligned.

2. Loosen the hood latch attaching bolts. Move the latch as necessary to align with the latch dowel, then tighten the attaching bolts.

3. Loosen the locknut on the hood latch dowel. Turn the dowel clockwise to pull the hood tighter or counterclockwise to loosen it. The proper height is when the top of the hood is flush with the fenders.

4. Tighten the dowel locknut after the proper adjustment has been obtained.

Hatch (Back Door)

REMOVAL & INSTALLATION

Except RX-7 With Glass Hatch and 1988-89 626/MX-6
▶ See Figures 9 and 10

1. Open the hatch fully and disconnect the negative battery cable.

2. Carefully remove the trim fasteners with a flat screwdriver, then remove the trim.

3. Disconnect the wiring couplings and the ground wire.

4. Pull out the wiring harness from the hatch, and route it off to the side and out of the way.

5. If equipped, disconnect the washer hose at the nozzle located on the hatch and pull it out.

6. Support the hatch with a suitable bar. Unfasten the ball studs from both the upper and lower ends of the stay dampers, then remove the stay dampers.

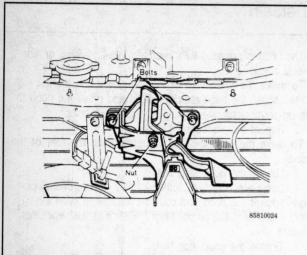

Fig. 8 Loosen the attaching bolts to reposition the hood latch, if necessary

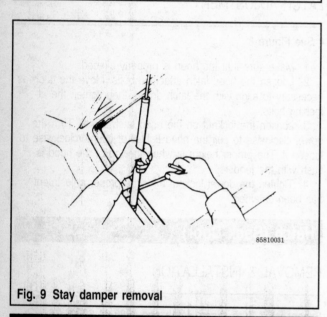

Fig. 9 Stay damper removal

❄❄CAUTION

Never disassemble the stay damper, as the cylinder is filled with gas. Do not apply oil or paint to the piston rod. Be careful not to damage the piston rod. Do not turn the piston rod and the cylinder when the piston rod is extended. When discarding the stay damper, drill a 0.08-0.12 in. (2-3mm) hole in the bottom of the damper to release the gas. Make sure to protect yourself against any metal particles that may be spewen into the air by the compressed gas during drilling.

7. Unfasten the hatch-to-hinge attaching bolts and remove the hatch.

8. Installation is the reverse of the removal procedure. Open and close the hatch several times to ensure proper operation.

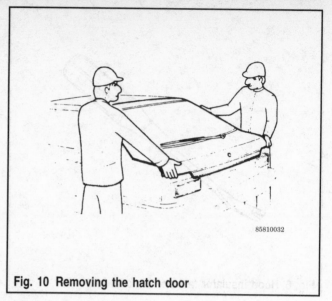

Fig. 10 Removing the hatch door

1988-89 626 and MX-6
▶ See Figures 9, 10 and 11

1. Disconnect the negative battery cable and remove the trim that surrounds the rear hatch.

2. Detach the connector from the luggage compartment light and unscrew the light from its socket.

3. Remove the rear hatch screen. Be careful not to rip or tear the screen when removing it.

4. Locate and unfasten the rear defroster and wiper motor electrical connectors. Pull the wiring through the rear hatch.

5. Disconnect the wiper arm from the wiper motor shaft, then unbolt and remove the wiper motor.

6. Remove the push button release rod and rear hatch opener.

7. Release the retainer from the key cylinder by pushing it with a small flat blade screwdriver and withdraw the key cylinder.

8. Remove the stay damper mounting bolts and disconnect the rear washer hose.

❄❄CAUTION

Never disassemble the stay damper as the cylinder is filled with gas. Do not apply oil or paint to the piston rod. Be careful not to damage the piston rod. Do not turn the piston rod and the cylinder when the piston rod is extended. When discarding the stay damper, drill a 0.08-0.12 in. (2-3mm) hole in the bottom of the damper to release the gas. Make sure to protect yourself against any metal particles that may be spewen into the air by the compressed gas during drilling.

9. Remove the wiring harness and route it off to the side.

10. Have an assistant grasp and support the rear hatch and remove the rear hatch-to-hinge mounting bolts. Remove the hatch.

11. Installation is basically the reverse of the removal procedure. If the hatch screen was damaged, purchase a new one. Check the hatch alignment and adjust the rear hatch hinge. Close and open the hatch several times to ensure that it

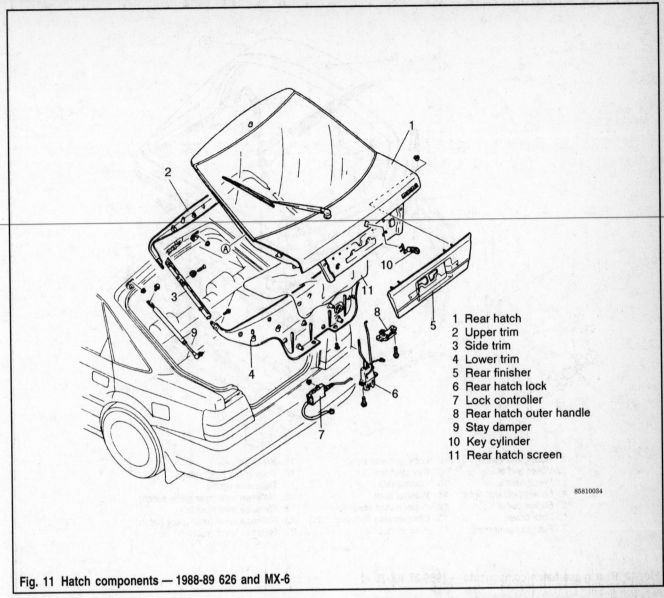

1 Rear hatch
2 Upper trim
3 Side trim
4 Lower trim
5 Rear finisher
6 Rear hatch lock
7 Lock controller
8 Rear hatch outer handle
9 Stay damper
10 Key cylinder
11 Rear hatch screen

85810034

Fig. 11 Hatch components — 1988-89 626 and MX-6

operates properly. Check the operation of the rear windshield wipers.

RX-7 With Rear Glass Hatch

▶ See Figure 12

1. Disconnect the negative battery cable and open the rear glass hatch.

2. Support the hatch with a section of broomstick or equivalent.

3. On 1986-87 models, detach the electrical connector from the rear wiper motor.

4. On 1979-85 models, detach the defroster connector from the rear pillar. On 1986-87 models, disconnect and remove the rear defroster wiring from the right and left sides of the glass hatch.

5. On 1979-85 models, remove the rear side pillar trim. Disconnect the right and left damper stays on all models. Close the hatch and remove the rear top garnish and top ceiling. Be careful not to damage the filament on the rear of the hatch.

6. On 1986-87 models, disconnect the rear washer hose.

7. Remove the four rear glass hatch hinge nuts. Release the hatch lock and remove the glass hatch with the hinges attached. Remove the damper stays, hinges and lock striker as required.

✻✻CAUTION

Never disassemble the stay damper as the cylinder is filled with gas. Do not apply oil or paint to the piston rod. Be careful not to damage the piston rod. Do not turn the piston rod and the cylinder when the piston rod is extended. When discarding the stay damper, drill a 0.08-0.12 in. (2-3mm) hole in the bottom of the damper to release the gas. Make sure to protect yourself against any metal particles that may be spewen into the air by the compressed gas during drilling.

To install:

8. Position the rear glass hatch onto the mounting hinges and have an assistant install the four mounting nuts. Tighten the nuts.

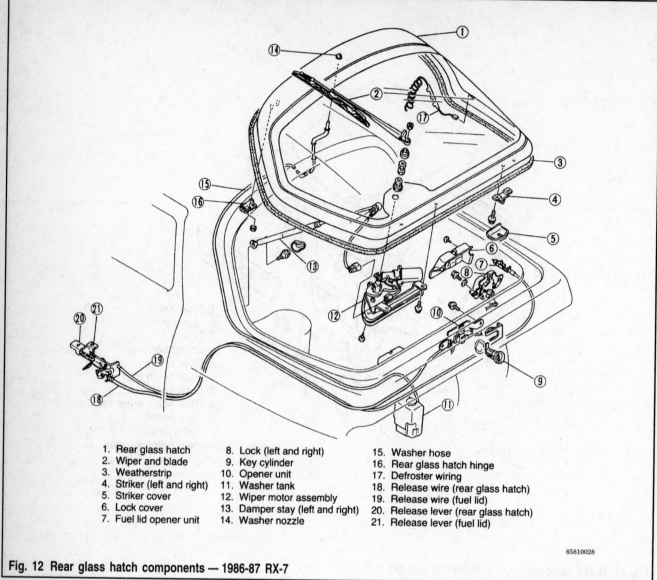

1. Rear glass hatch
2. Wiper and blade
3. Weatherstrip
4. Striker (left and right)
5. Striker cover
6. Lock cover
7. Fuel lid opener unit
8. Lock (left and right)
9. Key cylinder
10. Opener unit
11. Washer tank
12. Wiper motor assembly
13. Damper stay (left and right)
14. Washer nozzle
15. Washer hose
16. Rear glass hatch hinge
17. Defroster wiring
18. Release wire (rear glass hatch)
19. Release wire (fuel lid)
20. Release lever (rear glass hatch)
21. Release lever (fuel lid)

85810028

Fig. 12 Rear glass hatch components — 1986-87 RX-7

9. Connect the rear washer hose (1986-87) and install the the rear top garnish and top ceiling. Open the hatch and connect the damper stays. On 1979-85 models, install the rear side pillar trim.

10. Connect the rear defroster wiring to the right and left sides of the glass. Connect the rear wiper motor connector on 1986-87 models.

11. Adjust the rear glass hatch and check for proper opening and closing.

ALIGNMENT

Except RX-7 With Rear Glass Hatch
▶ See Figures 13 and 14

1. To align the to-and-fro position of the hatch, loosen the hinge attaching bolts on both the hatch and the body.

2. To adjust the hatch's up-and-down position, loosen the hinge attaching bolts on the hatch, as well as the lock and striker attaching bolts.

3. To adjust the hatch for closing, move the lock and striker.

4. Make all necessary adjustments by moving the hatch in the appropriate directions for the desired adjustments and tighten the attaching bolts. Open and close the hatch several times to ensure proper operation.

RX-7 With Rear Glass Hatch

1. Open the rear glass hatch and remove the upper portion of the weather strip.

2. Remove the rear end of the top ceiling and the rear header pads.

3. Close the rear hatch and loosen the hinge attaching nuts from the inside of the vehicle. Move the hatch as required until it is evenly aligned with the with the body lines. Once alignment is achieved, tighten the nuts.

4. Install the remaining components in reverse of the removal procedure. Open and close the hatch several times to ensure proper operation.

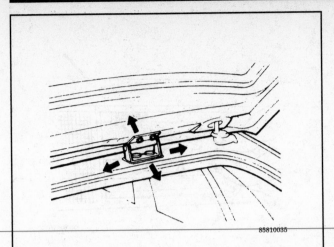

Fig. 13 Adjusting the hatch door hinge

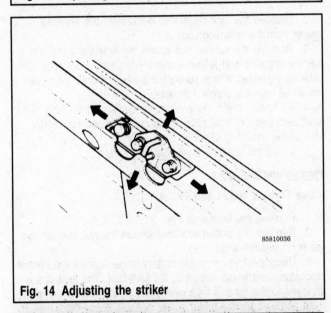

Fig. 14 Adjusting the striker

Trunk Lid

REMOVAL & INSTALLATION

▶ See Figure 15

➡Trunk lid removal/installation is more easily performed with the help of an assistant.

1. Open and support the trunk lid securely.
2. Mark the position of each trunk lid hinge in relation to the trunk lid. Disconnect the trunk lid stay from its mounting bracket, if so equipped.
3. Remove the fasteners (usually 2) attaching each hinge to the trunk lid.
4. Remove the trunk lid from the vehicle.

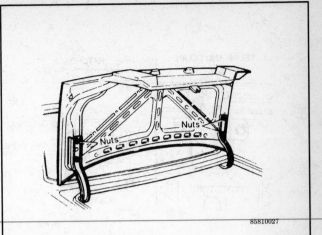

Fig. 15 Common trunk lid mounting

To install:
5. Align the marks on the trunk lid with the hinges.
6. Install the hinge-to-trunk lid nuts or bolts.
7. Tighten the trunk lid fasteners and adjust if necessary.

ADJUSTMENT

▶ See Figures 16 and 17

➡On the 1986-89 RX-7, the trunk lid striker is stamped with an F mark indicating the front of the vehicle. If the striker was removed, make sure that the directional mark is facing towards the front of the vehicle before attempting any adjustment.

1. Loosen the striker attaching bolts, and move the striker as required.
2. Tighten the attaching bolts.
3. To make the to-and-fro or side-to-side adjustment, loosen the trunk lid attaching bolts and move the trunk lid as necessary. Tighten the trunk lid attaching bolts.
4. To make the up-and-down adjustment, loosen the hinge-to-hinge support attaching bolts and raise or lower the hinge as necessary. The trunk lid is at the correct height when it is flush with the trunk deck.

Grille

REMOVAL & INSTALLATION

323

1. Remove the single screw from the center of the radiator.
2. Open the tabs of the three radiator fasteners using a small flat blade screwdriver and remove the radiator grille.
3. To install, position the grille and align the fastener holes with the holes in the body. Once they are aligned, press the fasteners into place and install the center installation screw.

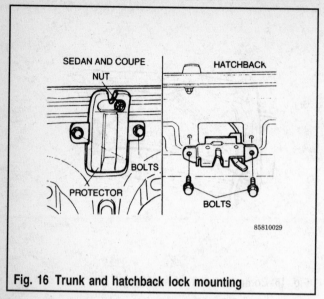

Fig. 16 Trunk and hatchback lock mounting

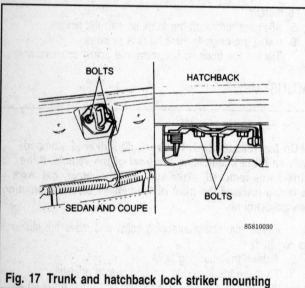

Fig. 17 Trunk and hatchback lock striker mounting

626 and MX-6

▶ **See Figure 18**

1. Using the tip of a small flat bladed screwdriver, open the tabs of the fasteners and remove the radiator grille. The number of fasteners will vary depending on the model year.

2. To install, position the grille and align the fastener holes with the holes in the body. Once they are aligned, press the fasteners into place.

Antenna

REPLACEMENT

323

▶ **See Figure 19**

1. Remove the instrument panel as described later in this section.

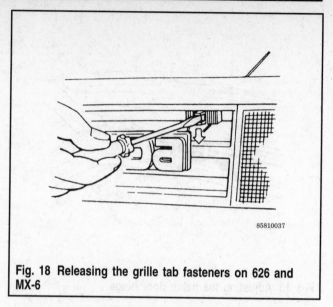

Fig. 18 Releasing the grille tab fasteners on 626 and MX-6

2. Remove the kick panel and disconnect the antenna feeder from the retaining clips.

3. Remove the screws that attach the antenna base and pull the antenna and feeder assembly from the front pillar. On vehicles equipped with a sunroof, the sunroof drain pipe with come out with the antenna assembly.

4. To install, insert the antenna feeder and drain pipe (if so equipped) into the front pillar opening and attach the feeder wire to the mounting clips.

5. Install the antenna base retaining screws.

1988-89 626 and MX-6

▶ **See Figures 20, 21 and 22**

1. Remove the front side trim.

2. Remove the undercover and loosen the nut and remove the hood release knob.

3. Disconnect the negative battery cable. Locate the central processing unit which is part of the joint box. The joint box is attached to the driver's side wheel well in the engine compartment across from the brake power booster. Disconnect the

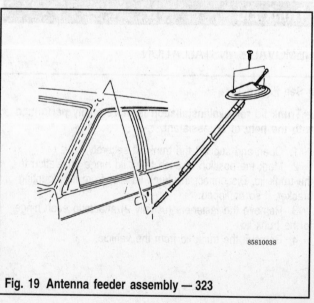

Fig. 19 Antenna feeder assembly — 323

connectors from the CPU. Release the locking clip using moderate finger pressure pull the unit from the joint box.

4. Disconnect the harness connectors from the joint box. Remove the joint box mounting bracket nut. Release the lock at the back of the joint box and remove the joint box.

5. Below the steering column and air duct, you will find the antenna feeder connector. Disconnect the feeder wire from the plug. Disconnect the connector from the antenna motor.

6. Remove the motor mounting bracket bolt and screws, and remove the antenna motor with the antenna mast. Slide the joint sleeve upward to disengage the motor from the mast.

7. Connect a 12-volt battery and a ground wire to the **R** and **W** terminals of the motor service connector to operate the motor. (Connect the negative cable to the **W** terminal and the positive cable to the **R** terminal.) Carefully pull the cable from the motor housing with the motor running.

➡**Even if the mast is broken or missing, make sure that all the cable is fed from the motor.**

8. Remove the antenna base mounting screws and withdraw the antenna from the front pillar.

9. A temporary protective cover is attached with tape to each new mast kit. The cover is there to protect the plastic rack cable and to make the installation easier. Before beginning the installation, extend the mast fully.

10. Take the plastic protective cover and install it over the base of the mast to protect the plastic cable. Use the tape provided in the kit to hold the tube in place.

11. Tape the antenna plug to the tip of the protector tube so that it will not be damaged or catch on body during installation.

12. Insert the antenna mast into the roof opening and carefully and slowly feed it down at the same angle as the windshield pillar. When the mast is fully inserted into the windshield pillar, remove the plastic tube and pull the antenna lead inside the passenger compartment. Carefully feed the plastic rack cable into the motor housing. The serrated side of the cable must face toward the motor as shown in the illustration.

13. Using the 12-volt battery, connect the positive lead to the **W** terminal and the negative lead to the **R** terminal on the antenna motor service connector. Operate the motor until all of the new cable is reeled into the motor housing.

14. Push the mast base into the motor housing joint. When the mast is locked properly, a faint click will be heard. Jiggle the mast base back and forth a few times to verify that the base is locked properly.

15. Check the operation of the antenna mast. The cable slack can be self adjusted by operating the motor a few times until the mast is fully extended. Complete the installation of the remaining components by reversing the removal procedure.

RX-7

♦ **See Figure 23**

1. On 1979-85 models, remove the right rear trunk side trim. On 1986-89 models, remove the left rear trunk side trim.

2. Disconnect the antenna feeder and connector.

3. Remove the power motor bracket attaching nuts and remove the antenna assembly from the vehicle.

4. To install, position the motor onto it mounting and install the attaching nuts.

5. Connect the wiring and install the trunk side trim. Check the antenna for proper operation.

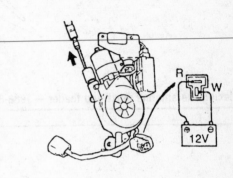

85810039

Fig. 20 Apply a 12-volt power source to the antenna motor, in order to remove the plastic cable

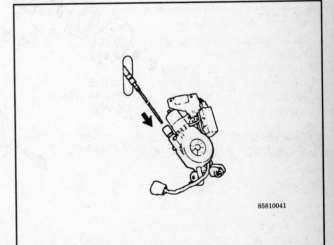

85810041

Fig. 21 The serrated part of the plastic cable must face the motor housing

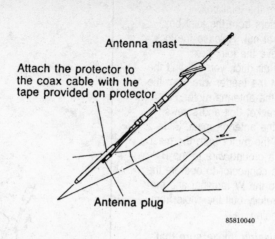

Antenna mast

Attach the protector to
the coax cable with the
tape provided on protector

Antenna plug

85810040

Fig. 22 Installing the antenna mast and feeder — 1988-89 626 and MX-6

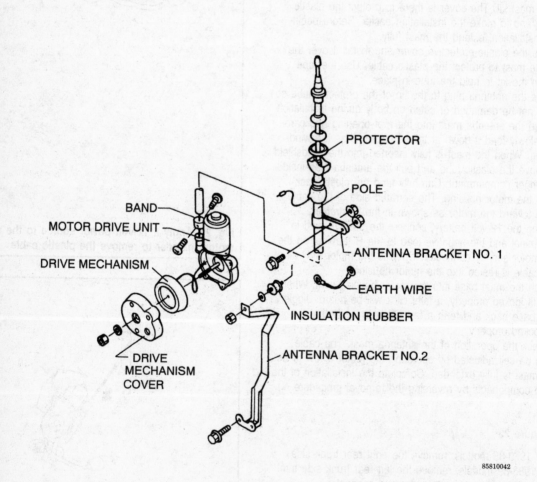

PROTECTOR

POLE

ANTENNA BRACKET NO. 1

BAND

MOTOR DRIVE UNIT

DRIVE MECHANISM

EARTH WIRE

INSULATION RUBBER

ANTENNA BRACKET NO.2

DRIVE
MECHANISM
COVER

85810042

Fig. 23 Power antenna components — 1979-85 RX-7

INTERIOR

Instrument Panel and Pad

REMOVAL & INSTALLATION

▶ See Figures 24, 25, 26, 27, 28, 29, 30 and 31

1. Disconnect the negative battery cable.
2. If so equipped, unfasten the inside hood release handle.
3. Remove the steering wheel and the lower steering column cover.
4. Remove the glove box, switch panel and console.
5. Remove the meter (gauge) hood, heater control panel mounting screws and separate the heater controls from the instrument panel frame. Remove the combination meter.
6. Remove the air duct(s) and the steering shaft mounting bracket bolts. Allow the column to lower.

Fig. 24 Loosen the retaining nut to unfasten the inside hood release handle

Fig. 25 If necessary, remove the dash mounted speaker covers to access hidden instrument panel bolts

Fig. 26 Due to space limitations, some bolts are best removed with an open end or box wrench

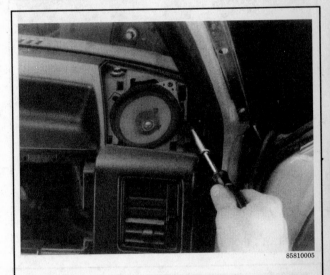

Fig. 27 Other bolts are easily removed with a socket

7. Disconnect and label the meter wiring. Unfasten the mounting bolts and remove the crash pad and instrument panel.

To install:

8. Position and fasten the crash pad and instrument panel, being careful to route the wiring correctly. Attach the meter wiring to its appropriate connections.
9. Raise the steering column to its normal operating position and install the steering shaft mounting bracket bolts. Connect the air ducts.
10. Install the combination meter. Install the heater controls into the instrument panel frame with the mounting screws. Attach the meter hood.
11. Install the console, switch panel and glove box.
12. Install the steering wheel column cover and steering wheel.
13. If applicable, attach the inside hood release handle.

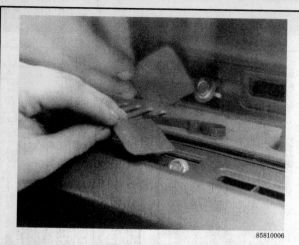

Fig. 28 Some of the instrument panel attaching bolts are hidden behind removable trim covers or plugs. Carefully pry off the cover . . .

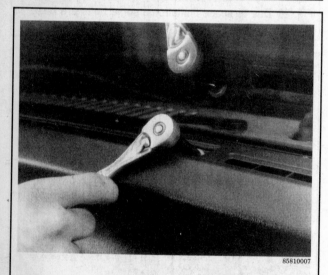

Fig. 29 . . . then remove the bolts with a socket

Fig. 30 The glove box must be removed to unfasten some of the instrument panel retaining bolts

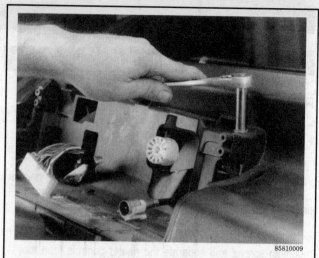

Fig. 31 Other retaining bolts are accessible with the meter hood and combination meter removed

14. Connect the negative battery cable.

Console

REMOVAL & INSTALLATION

▶ See Figures 32, 33 and 34

1. Disconnect the negative battery cable.
2. Remove the shift lever knob.
3. Unfasten and remove the parking brake lever covers.
4. Remove the rear seat ashtray.
5. Unfasten and remove the rear console.
6. Unfasten and remove the front console.
7. Installation is the reverse of the removal procedure.

Fig. 32 Lift out the rear seat ashtray to access a retaining screw

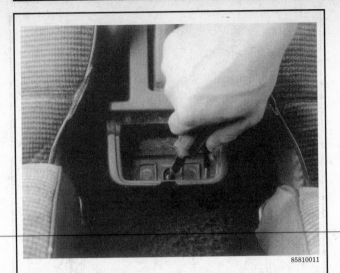

Fig. 33 Unfasten the rear console from the floor

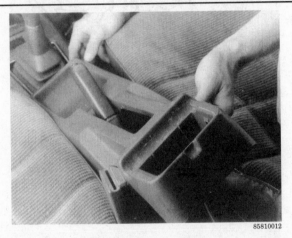

Fig. 34 After removing the screws which fasten the two consoles together, lift the rear console up and slide it over the parking brake lever

Door Panels

REMOVAL & INSTALLATION

▶ See Figure 35

1. Remove the window regulator handle, on non-power window equipped vehicles.
2. Remove the arm rest as required.
3. Remove the door lock knob.
4. Remove the inner door handle cover.
5. Using a flat screwdriver with the blade wrapped in tape, gently separate the door trim panel clips from the door.
6. Remove the door trim panel.
7. Place the door trim panel into position on the door.

8. Apply pressure to the trim panel in the areas where the trim panel clips attach to the door.
9. Install the inner door handle cover, door lock knob and the arm rest.

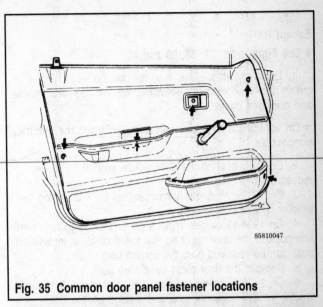

Fig. 35 Common door panel fastener locations

Door Lock Cylinder

REMOVAL & INSTALLATION

1. Remove the regulator handle, arm rest etc.
2. Remove the trim panel and watershield.
3. Remove the bolts attaching the inner handle and remove the inner handle.
4. Raise the glass fully and disconnect the remote control rod from the lock cylinder.
5. Remove the door lock attaching screw(s) and remove the door lock.
6. Remove the retainer that secures the door lock cylinder to the door inner panel and remove the lock cylinder.
7. Installation is the reverse of the removal procedure.

Hatch/Rear Door Lock

REMOVAL & INSTALLATION

1. Using a flat screwdriver, gently dislodge the trim fasteners and remove the door trim.
2. Disconnect the rod for the push button release.
3. Remove the push button securing clip, then remove the push button.
4. Unfasten the door lock attaching bolts and remove the door lock.
5. Installation is the reverse of the removal procedure.
6. Adjust the door as described previously in this section.

Door Glass and Regulator

REMOVAL & INSTALLATION

Except RX-7

▶ See Figures 36, 37, 38, 39 and 40

1. Lower the door glass, then remove the inner handle cover, door lock knob (if necessary), window regulator handle and door trim panel.

➡ On vehicles with power windows, unfasten the electrical connectors.

2. Carefully peel off the door screen so that it can be reused.

3. On 1978-83 models remove the six bolts attaching the window regulator to the door.

4. On 1984-89 models replace the window regulator handle and position the door glass so that the door glass installation bolts can be removed from the service hole.

5. Remove the door glass installation bolts.

6. On 1978-83 models, remove the door glass, then take out the window regulator through the large access hole.

7. On 1983-89 models, remove the door glass. Unfasten the window regulator installation bolts, then remove the regulator through the service access hole. Remove the window motor mounting bolts and separate the motor from the regulator.

8. Installation is the reverse of the removal procedure. If the the vehicle is equipped with power windows, connect the leads of the motor to a battery and run the regulator to the down position before installing the motor. Cycle the window several times to make sure that everything is in good working order.

1979-85 RX-7

1. Remove the regulator handle and the inner handle cover.

2. Remove the attaching screws and remove the arm rest.

3. Remove the trim panel and the inner handle assembly.

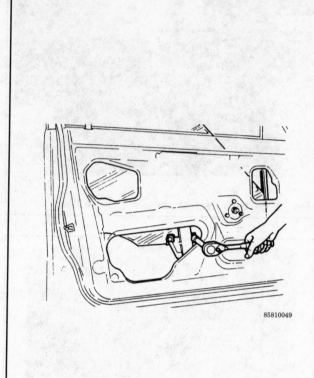

Fig. 37 Removing the door glass installation bolts

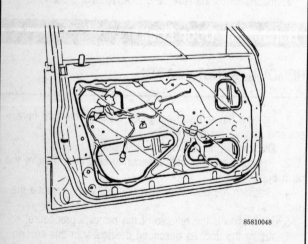

Fig. 36 The door screen is accessible after the door trim panel has been removed

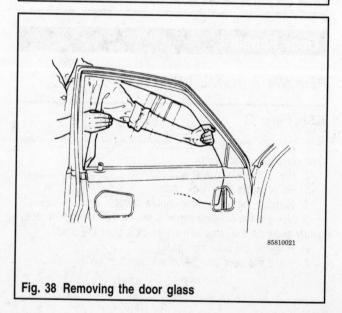

Fig. 38 Removing the door glass

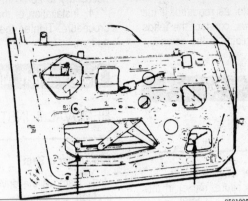

Fig. 39 Window regulator attaching bolts

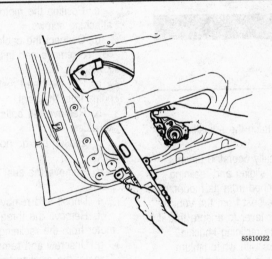

Fig. 40 Removing the window regulator

4. Remove the watershield. Remove the screws and screw grommets that attach the glass and regulator. Remove the glass.

5. Remove the regulator attaching bolts and pull the regulator out through the access hole. On vehicles equipped with power windows, remove the power window mounting bolts and separate the motor from the regulator.

❋❋CAUTION

Exercise extreme caution when removing the power window motor. Once free, the assembly will release the actuating spring and allow the regulator gear to return to the up position.

6. During installation, adjust the regulator as required. If the vehicle is equipped with power windows, connect the leads of the motor to a battery and run the regulator to the down position before installing the motor.

1986-89 RX-7

1. Remove the sail inner garnish located opposite the rear view mirror.

2. Remove the inner handle cover by removing the attaching screws. Remove the door trim.

3. Disconnect the courtesy light electrical connectors. Operate the power window switch to raise the glass 9.06 in. (230mm) from the fully open position. Disconnect the negative battery cable and power window switch connector.

4. Remove the inner handle.

5. Disconnect the speaker wire and remove the speaker.

6. Remove the upper stopper by removing the attaching nuts.

7. Remove the weather strip.

8. Using a suitable length extension, remove the door glass attaching bolts through the bolt access holes. Remove the door glass by pulling upward and out of the guide.

9. Remove the regulator attaching bolts and pull the regulator out through the access hole. On vehicles equipped with

power windows, remove the power window mounting bolts and remove the motor from the regulator.

10. During installation, adjust the regulator as required. If the the vehicle is equipped with power windows, connect the leads of the motor to a battery and run the regulator to the down position before installing the motor.

Electric Window Motor

REMOVAL & INSTALLATION

For removal and installation of the power window motor, refer to the Door Glass and Regulator procedure, earlier in this section.caution>Some power window regulators are held under extreme spring pressure. Be sure to pin or otherwise lock such assemblies in position to prevent sudden, uncontrolled release of the spring tension as the component is unbolted and removed.

Seats

REMOVAL & INSTALLATION

▶ **See Figures 41, 42 and 43**

1. Remove the bolts and nuts that attach the adjusting rails to the mounting brackets.
2. On vehicles equipped with electrically operated driver's seats, unfasten the front and rear lifting, sliding and reclining motor connectors. After the seat is detached from its mounting, carefully determine how to maneuver the seat from the vehicle.
3. Manually operate the seat adjuster lever to ensure that it moves smoothly and do the same for the reclining knuckle. Lightly coat the adjusting lever and tracks with white lithium grease or silicone and work the lubricant in by manually operating the adjusting lever. Wipe all the excess lubricant from the adjuster mechanism. Check the adjustment lever for excessive wear and replace as required. Check the seat-to-adjuster

mounting bolts and all screws for looseness and tighten as necessary to 28-38 ft. lbs. (38-51 Nm).

4. Installation of the seat is the reverse of the removal procedure. Tighten the mounting bolts in an even and alternate pattern.

Power Seat Motor

REMOVAL & INSTALLATION

929 Driver's Seat

1. Remove the driver's seat from the vehicle and set it on a clean, flat surface.
2. To remove and install the sliding and reclining motor, perform the following:
    a. Unscrew the cable from the motor using pliers.
    b. Remove the retaining screws and remove the motor from its mounting.
    c. Position the motor onto the mounting and install the attaching screws.
    d. Connect the cable to the motor and tighten it properly.
3. To remove and install the reclining motor, perform the following:
    a. Pull the head rest and the two headrest mounting poles from the seat.
    b. Remove the bolts from the front part of the reclining knuckles.
    c. Loosen but do not remove the rear reclining knuckle bolts.
    d. Remove the seat back cushion from the seat back frame.
    e. Unbolt and remove the reclining knuckle (3 bolts).
    f. Remove the three attaching screws and remove the motor from the reclining knuckle.
    g. Unscrew and remove the bracket from the motor. Transfer the existing bracket to the new motor.
    h. Complete the installation in reverse of the removal procedure.
4. Install the driver's seat and make sure that all the motors are functioning properly.

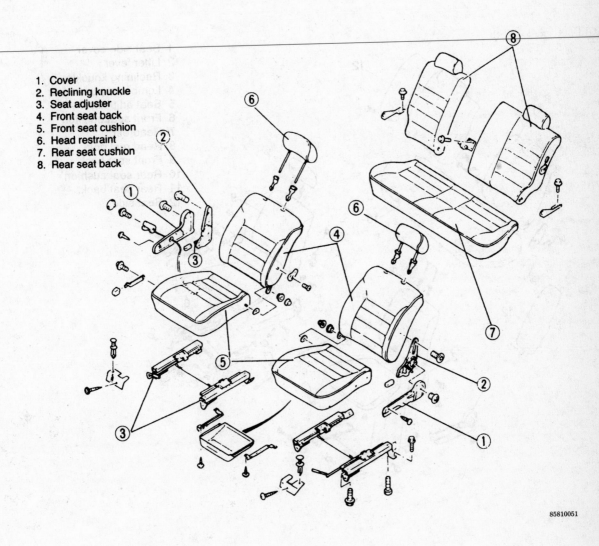

1. Cover
2. Reclining knuckle
3. Seat adjuster
4. Front seat back
5. Front seat cushion
6. Head restraint
7. Rear seat cushion
8. Rear seat back

85810051

Fig. 41 Front and rear seat components — 323

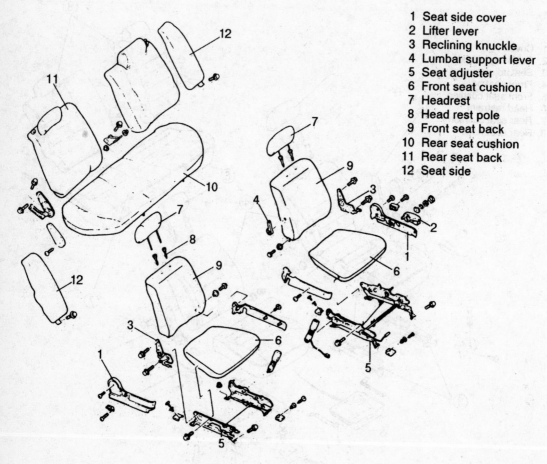

1 Seat side cover
2 Lifter lever
3 Reclining knuckle
4 Lumbar support lever
5 Seat adjuster
6 Front seat cushion
7 Headrest
8 Head rest pole
9 Front seat back
10 Rear seat cushion
11 Rear seat back
12 Seat side

85810053

Fig. 42 Front and rear seat components — 626 and MX-6

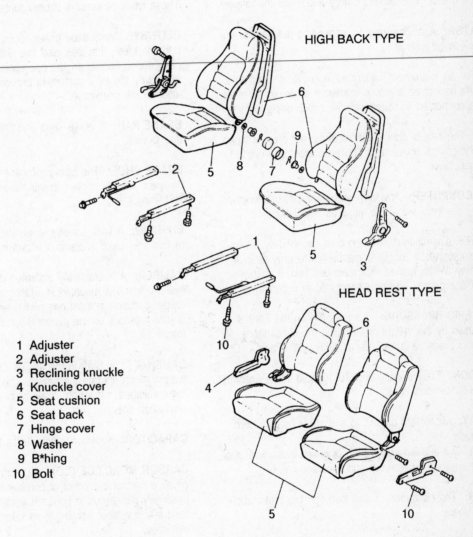

HIGH BACK TYPE

HEAD REST TYPE

1 Adjuster
2 Adjuster
3 Reclining knuckle
4 Knuckle cover
5 Seat cushion
6 Seat back
7 Hinge cover
8 Washer
9 B*hing
10 Bolt

85810052

Fig. 43 Seat components — early model RX-7

GLOSSARY

AIR/FUEL RATIO: The ratio of air-to-gasoline by weight in the fuel mixture drawn into the engine.

AIR INJECTION: One method of reducing harmful exhaust emissions by injecting air into each of the exhaust ports of an engine. The fresh air entering the hot exhaust manifold causes any remaining fuel to be burned before it can exit the tailpipe.

ALTERNATOR: A device used for converting mechanical energy into electrical energy.

AMMETER: An instrument, calibrated in amperes, used to measure the flow of an electrical current in a circuit. Ammeters are always connected in series with the circuit being tested.

AMPERE: The rate of flow of electrical current present when one volt of electrical pressure is applied against one ohm of electrical resistance.

ANALOG COMPUTER: Any microprocessor that uses similar (analogous) electrical signals to make its calculations.

ARMATURE: A laminated, soft iron core wrapped by a wire that converts electrical energy to mechanical energy as in a motor or relay. When rotated in a magnetic field, it changes mechanical energy into electrical energy as in a generator.

ATMOSPHERIC PRESSURE: The pressure on the Earth's surface caused by the weight of the air in the atmosphere. At sea level, this pressure is 14.7 psi at 32°F (101 kPa at 0°C).

ATOMIZATION: The breaking down of a liquid into a fine mist that can be suspended in air.

AXIAL PLAY: Movement parallel to a shaft or bearing bore.

BACKFIRE: The sudden combustion of gases in the intake or exhaust system that results in a loud explosion.

BACKLASH: The clearance or play between two parts, such as meshed gears.

BACKPRESSURE: Restrictions in the exhaust system that slow the exit of exhaust gases from the combustion chamber.

BAKELITE: A heat resistant, plastic insulator material commonly used in printed circuit boards and transistorized components.

BALL BEARING: A bearing made up of hardened inner and outer races between which hardened steel balls roll.

BALLAST RESISTOR: A resistor in the primary ignition circuit that lowers voltage after the engine is started to reduce wear on ignition components.

BEARING: A friction reducing, supportive device usually located between a stationary part and a moving part.

BIMETAL TEMPERATURE SENSOR: Any sensor or switch made of two dissimilar types of metal that bend when heated or cooled due to the different expansion rates of the alloys. These types of sensors usually function as an on/off switch.

BLOWBY: Combustion gases, composed of water vapor and unburned fuel, that leak past the piston rings into the crankcase during normal engine operation. These gases are removed by the PCV system to prevent the buildup of harmful acids in the crankcase.

BRAKE PAD: A brake shoe and lining assembly used with disc brakes.

BRAKE SHOE: The backing for the brake lining. The term is, however, usually applied to the assembly of the brake backing and lining.

BUSHING: A liner, usually removable, for a bearing; an anti-friction liner used in place of a bearing.

CALIPER: A hydraulically activated device in a disc brake system, which is mounted straddling the brake rotor (disc). The caliper contains at least one piston and two brake pads. Hydraulic pressure on the piston(s) forces the pads against the rotor.

CAMSHAFT: A shaft in the engine on which are the lobes (cams) which operate the valves. The camshaft is driven by the crankshaft, via a belt, chain or gears, at one half the crankshaft speed.

CAPACITOR: A device which stores an electrical charge.

CARBON MONOXIDE (CO): A colorless, odorless gas given off as a normal byproduct of combustion. It is poisonous and extremely dangerous in confined areas, building up slowly to toxic levels without warning if adequate ventilation is not available.

CARBURETOR: A device, usually mounted on the intake manifold of an engine, which mixes the air and fuel in the proper proportion to allow even combustion.

CATALYTIC CONVERTER: A device installed in the exhaust system, like a muffler, that converts harmful byproducts of combustion into carbon dioxide and water vapor by means of a heat-producing chemical reaction.

CENTRIFUGAL ADVANCE: A mechanical method of advancing the spark timing by using flyweights in the distributor that react to centrifugal force generated by the distributor shaft rotation.

CHECK VALVE: Any one-way valve installed to permit the flow of air, fuel or vacuum in one direction only.

CHOKE: A device, usually a moveable valve, placed in the intake path of a carburetor to restrict the flow of air.

CIRCUIT: Any unbroken path through which an electrical current can flow. Also used to describe fuel flow in some instances.

CIRCUIT BREAKER: A switch which protects an electrical circuit from overload by opening the circuit when the current flow exceeds a predetermined level. Some circuit breakers must be reset manually, while most reset automatically.

COIL (IGNITION): A transformer in the ignition circuit which steps up the voltage provided to the spark plugs.

COMBINATION MANIFOLD: An assembly which includes both the intake and exhaust manifolds in one casting.

COMBINATION VALVE: A device used in some fuel systems that routes fuel vapors to a charcoal storage canister instead of venting them into the atmosphere. The valve relieves fuel tank pressure and allows fresh air into the tank as the fuel level drops to prevent a vapor lock situation.

COMPRESSION RATIO: The comparison of the total volume of the cylinder and combustion chamber with the piston at BDC and the piston at TDC.

CONDENSER: 1. An electrical device which acts to store an electrical charge, preventing voltage surges. 2. A radiator-like device in the air conditioning system in which refrigerant gas condenses into a liquid, giving off heat.

CONDUCTOR: Any material through which an electrical current can be transmitted easily.

CONTINUITY: Continuous or complete circuit. Can be checked with an ohmmeter.

COUNTERSHAFT: An intermediate shaft which is rotated by a mainshaft and transmits, in turn, that rotation to a working part.

CRANKCASE: The lower part of an engine in which the crankshaft and related parts operate.

CRANKSHAFT: The main driving shaft of an engine which receives reciprocating motion from the pistons and converts it to rotary motion.

CYLINDER: In an engine, the round hole in the engine block in which the piston(s) ride.

CYLINDER BLOCK: The main structural member of an engine in which is found the cylinders, crankshaft and other principal parts.

CYLINDER HEAD: The detachable portion of the engine, usually fastened to the top of the cylinder block and containing all or most of the combustion chambers. On overhead valve engines, it contains the valves and their operating parts. On overhead cam engines, it contains the camshaft as well.

DEAD CENTER: The extreme top or bottom of the piston stroke.

DETONATION: An unwanted explosion of the air/fuel mixture in the combustion chamber caused by excess heat and compression, advanced timing, or an overly lean mixture. Also referred to as "ping".

DIAPHRAGM: A thin, flexible wall separating two cavities, such as in a vacuum advance unit.

DIESELING: A condition in which hot spots in the combustion chamber cause the engine to run on after the key is turned off.

DIFFERENTIAL: A geared assembly which allows the transmission of motion between drive axles, giving one axle the ability to turn faster than the other.

DIODE: An electrical device that will allow current to flow in one direction only.

DISC BRAKE: A hydraulic braking assembly consisting of a brake disc, or rotor, mounted on an axle, and a caliper assembly containing, usually two brake pads which are activated by hydraulic pressure. The pads are forced against the sides of the disc, creating friction which slows the vehicle.

DISTRIBUTOR: A mechanically driven device on an engine which is responsible for electrically firing the spark plug at a predetermined point of the piston stroke.

DOWEL PIN: A pin, inserted in mating holes in two different parts allowing those parts to maintain a fixed relationship.

DRUM BRAKE: A braking system which consists of two brake shoes and one or two wheel cylinders, mounted on a fixed backing plate, and a brake drum, mounted on an axle, which revolves around the assembly.

DWELL: The rate, measured in degrees of shaft rotation, at which an electrical circuit cycles on and off.

ELECTRONIC CONTROL UNIT (ECU): Ignition module, module, amplifier or igniter. See Module for definition.

ELECTRONIC IGNITION: A system in which the timing and firing of the spark plugs is controlled by an electronic control unit, usually called a module. These systems have no points or condenser.

END-PLAY: The measured amount of axial movement in a shaft.

ENGINE: A device that converts heat into mechanical energy.

EXHAUST MANIFOLD: A set of cast passages or pipes which conduct exhaust gases from the engine.

FEELER GAUGE: A blade, usually metal, of precisely predetermined thickness, used to measure the clearance between two parts.

FIRING ORDER: The order in which combustion occurs in the cylinders of an engine. Also the order in which spark is distributed to the plugs by the distributor.

FLOODING: The presence of too much fuel in the intake manifold and combustion chamber which prevents the air/fuel mixture from firing, thereby causing a no-start situation.

FLYWHEEL: A disc shaped part bolted to the rear end of the crankshaft. Around the outer perimeter is affixed the ring gear. The starter drive engages the ring gear, turning the flywheel, which rotates the crankshaft, imparting the initial starting motion to the engine.

FOOT POUND (ft. lbs. or sometimes, ft.lb.): The amount of energy or work needed to raise an item weighing one pound, a distance of one foot.

FUSE: A protective device in a circuit which prevents circuit overload by breaking the circuit when a specific amperage is present. The device is constructed around a strip or wire of a lower amperage rating than the circuit it is designed to protect. When an amperage higher than that stamped on the fuse is present in the circuit, the strip or wire melts, opening the circuit.

GEAR RATIO: The ratio between the number of teeth on meshing gears.

GENERATOR: A device which converts mechanical energy into electrical energy.

HEAT RANGE: The measure of a spark plug's ability to dissipate heat from its firing end. The higher the heat range, the hotter the plug fires.

HUB: The center part of a wheel or gear.

HYDROCARBON (HC): Any chemical compound made up of hydrogen and carbon. A major pollutant formed by the engine as a byproduct of combustion.

HYDROMETER: An instrument used to measure the specific gravity of a solution.

INCH POUND (inch lbs.; sometimes in.lb. or in. lbs.): One twelfth of a foot pound.

INDUCTION: A means of transferring electrical energy in the form of a magnetic field. Principle used in the ignition coil to increase voltage.

INJECTOR: A device which receives metered fuel under relatively low pressure and is activated to inject the fuel into the engine under relatively high pressure at a predetermined time.

INPUT SHAFT: The shaft to which torque is applied, usually carrying the driving gear or gears.

INTAKE MANIFOLD: A casting of passages or pipes used to conduct air or a fuel/air mixture to the cylinders.

JOURNAL: The bearing surface within which a shaft operates.

KEY: A small block usually fitted in a notch between a shaft and a hub to prevent slippage of the two parts.

MANIFOLD: A casting of passages or set of pipes which connect the cylinders to an inlet or outlet source.

MANIFOLD VACUUM: Low pressure in an engine intake manifold formed just below the throttle plates. Manifold vacuum is highest at idle and drops under acceleration.

MASTER CYLINDER: The primary fluid pressurizing device in a hydraulic system. In automotive use, it is found in brake and hydraulic clutch systems and is pedal activated, either directly or, in a power brake system, through the power booster.

MODULE: Electronic control unit, amplifier or igniter of solid state or integrated design which controls the current flow in the ignition primary circuit based on input from the pick-up coil. When the module opens the primary circuit, high secondary voltage is induced in the coil.

NEEDLE BEARING: A bearing which consists of a number (usually a large number) of long, thin rollers.

OHM:(Ω) The unit used to measure the resistance of conductor-to-electrical flow. One ohm is the amount of resistance that limits current flow to one ampere in a circuit with one volt of pressure.

OHMMETER: An instrument used for measuring the resistance, in ohms, in an electrical circuit.

OUTPUT SHAFT: The shaft which transmits torque from a device, such as a transmission.

OVERDRIVE: A gear assembly which produces more shaft revolutions than that transmitted to it.

OVERHEAD CAMSHAFT (OHC): An engine configuration in which the camshaft is mounted on top of the cylinder head and operates the valve either directly or by means of rocker arms.

OVERHEAD VALVE (OHV): An engine configuration in which all of the valves are located in the cylinder head and the camshaft is located in the cylinder block. The camshaft operates the valves via lifters and pushrods.

OXIDES OF NITROGEN (NOx): Chemical compounds of nitrogen produced as a byproduct of combustion. They combine with hydrocarbons to produce smog.

OXYGEN SENSOR: Used with the feedback system to sense the presence of oxygen in the exhaust gas and signal the computer which can reference the voltage signal to an air/fuel ratio.

PINION: The smaller of two meshing gears.

PISTON RING: An open-ended ring which fits into a groove on the outer diameter of the piston. Its chief function is to form a seal between the piston and cylinder wall. Most automotive pistons have three rings: two for compression sealing; one for oil sealing.

PRELOAD: A predetermined load placed on a bearing during assembly or by adjustment.

PRIMARY CIRCUIT: The low voltage side of the ignition system which consists of the ignition switch, ballast resistor or resistance wire, bypass, coil, electronic control unit and pick-up coil as well as the connecting wires and harnesses.

PRESS FIT: The mating of two parts under pressure, due to the inner diameter of one being smaller than the outer diameter of the other, or vice versa; an interference fit.

RACE: The surface on the inner or outer ring of a bearing on which the balls, needles or rollers move.

REGULATOR: A device which maintains the amperage and/or voltage levels of a circuit at predetermined values.

RELAY: A switch which automatically opens and/or closes a circuit.

RESISTANCE: The opposition to the flow of current through a circuit or electrical device, and is measured in ohms. Resistance is equal to the voltage divided by the amperage.

RESISTOR: A device, usually made of wire, which offers a preset amount of resistance in an electrical circuit.

RING GEAR: The name given to a ring-shaped gear attached to a differential case, or affixed to a flywheel or as part of a planetary gear set.

ROLLER BEARING: A bearing made up of hardened inner and outer races between which hardened steel rollers move.

ROTOR: 1. The disc-shaped part of a disc brake assembly, upon which the brake pads bear; also called, brake disc. 2. The device mounted atop the distributor shaft, which passes current to the distributor cap tower contacts.

SECONDARY CIRCUIT: The high voltage side of the ignition system, usually above 20,000 volts. The secondary includes the ignition coil, coil wire, distributor cap and rotor, spark plug wires and spark plugs.

SENDING UNIT: A mechanical, electrical, hydraulic or electro-magnetic device which transmits information to a gauge.

SENSOR: Any device designed to measure engine operating conditions or ambient pressures and temperatures. Usually electronic in nature and designed to send a voltage signal to an on-board computer, some sensors may operate as a simple on/off switch or they may provide a variable voltage signal (like a potentiometer) as conditions or measured parameters change.

SHIM: Spacers of precise, predetermined thickness used between parts to establish a proper working relationship.

SLAVE CYLINDER: In automotive use, a device in the hydraulic clutch system which is activated by hydraulic force, disengaging the clutch.

SOLENOID: A coil used to produce a magnetic field, the effect of which is to produce work.

SPARK PLUG: A device screwed into the combustion chamber of a spark ignition engine. The basic construction is a conductive core inside of a ceramic insulator, mounted in an outer conductive base. An electrical charge from the spark plug wire travels along the conductive core and jumps a preset air gap to a grounding point or points at the end of the conductive base. The resultant spark ignites the fuel/air mixture in the combustion chamber.

SPLINES: Ridges machined or cast onto the outer diameter of a shaft or inner diameter of a bore to enable parts to mate without rotation.

TACHOMETER: A device used to measure the rotary speed of an engine, shaft, gear, etc., usually in rotations per minute.

THERMOSTAT: A valve, located in the cooling system of an engine, which is closed when cold and opens gradually in response to engine heating, controlling the temperature of the coolant and rate of coolant flow.

TOP DEAD CENTER (TDC): The point at which the piston reaches the top of its travel on the compression stroke.

TORQUE: The twisting force applied to an object.

TORQUE CONVERTER: A turbine used to transmit power from a driving member to a driven member via hydraulic action, providing changes in drive ratio and torque. In automotive use, it links the driveplate at the rear of the engine to the automatic transmission.

TRANSDUCER: A device used to change a force into an electrical signal.

TRANSISTOR: A semi-conductor component which can be actuated by a small voltage to perform an electrical switching function.

TUNE-UP: A regular maintenance function, usually associated with the replacement and adjustment of parts and components in the electrical and fuel systems of a vehicle for the purpose of attaining optimum performance.

TURBOCHARGER: An exhaust driven pump which compresses intake air and forces it into the combustion chambers at higher than atmospheric pressures. The increased air pressure allows more fuel to be burned and results in increased horsepower being produced.

VACUUM ADVANCE: A device which advances the ignition timing in response to increased engine vacuum.

VACUUM GAUGE: An instrument used to measure the presence of vacuum in a chamber.

VALVE: A device which control the pressure, direction of flow or rate of flow of a liquid or gas.

VALVE CLEARANCE: The measured gap between the end of the valve stem and the rocker arm, cam lobe or follower that activates the valve.

VISCOSITY: The rating of a liquid's internal resistance to flow.

VOLTMETER: An instrument used for measuring electrical force in units called volts. Voltmeters are always connected parallel with the circuit being tested.

WHEEL CYLINDER: Found in the automotive drum brake assembly, it is a device, actuated by hydraulic pressure, which, through internal pistons, pushes the brake shoes outward against the drums.

MASTER
INDEX